Antique Trader®
Antiques &
Collectibles
2006 Price Guide

Edited by
Kyle Husfloen

©2005 by KP Books

Published by

kp books
An Imprint of F+W Publications

700 East State Street • Iola, WI 54990-0001
715-445-2214 • 888-457-2873

Our toll-free number to place an order or obtain
a free catalog is (800) 258-0929.

Library of Congress Catalog Number: 2005906857

ISBN: 0-87349-989-1

Designed by Wendy Wendt

Edited by Kyle Husfloen

Printed in United States

We keep getting better

2006 annual offers more color photos, builds on tradition

Another year has flown by and, after months of preparation, I'm happy to present to you the newest edition of the *Antique Trader Antiques & Collectibles Price Guide 2006.* With the tremendous reception we received for our 2005 edition, our first in ALL-COLOR, I'm again excited to have this all-new guide to share with you. As with each annual guide, we have included a comprehensive overview of the world of collecting, this year highlighted by over 5,800 full-color illustrations!

This monumental book had fairly humble beginnings back in 1970 when it began as a quarterly paperback magazine. Due to its popularity it was soon expanded to a bi-monthly publication, followed in 1984 but our first large annual edition. With 35 years of price gathering experience behind us we have built on this tradition in order to present this detailed and up-to-date reference, an invaluable addition to the reference libraries of all collectors, dealers and appraisers.

Over the decades there have been many trends in collecting and we have carefully monitored these so that our listings reflect not only long-established categories but also include information on popular new collectibles. To ensure that we offer the best reference possible, we have always taken pride in preparing detailed and accurate listings. Rather than a simple one-line description, we strive to give you important details such as material, construction, color, pattern, maker, date of production and size. Those factors are important for a true understanding of the significance of an object and makes the Antique Trader Antiques & Collectibles Price Guide an important learning tool, not just a listing of prices. As always, we have worked diligently to make sure our information is accurate and our descriptions, prices and illustrations have been carefully proofed and double-checked. However, the editors, publisher nor contributors can assume responsibility for any losses that might be incurred as a result of consulting this guide, or of typographical or other errors.

Each year my staff and I gather new material from a wide spectrum of sources, including leading auction houses, dealers, collectors and specialized experts. We then work diligently to edit, arrange, enter and proof this huge volume of information into a book that is both handy and easy to use but also attractive to read. We want this book to be a real pleasure to refer to and study. As with all such guides, however, please keep in mind that the prices listed here should serve only as a guide to current retail replacement values. Many factors, including quality, rarity, condition and regional demand, will effect what a particular item may sell for in a specific market.

We have arranged our nearly 12,500 listings into dozens of categories and sub-categories. Most of these are arranged in alphabetical order and many begin with a brief introductory note about the topic. In the Ceramics and Glass sections, we often also provide a copy of the factory or maker's mark or marks for your edification. Rather than mixing in listings for our three largest sections, Ceramics, Furniture and Glass, we have arranged them into their own sections in this guide. Within these sections the specific sub-categories are then arranged alphabetically. The actual listings in nearly all our categories are also arranged alphabetically by the name of the object. For example, listings in "Advertising Items" could go from "Ashtray" to "Calendar" to "Door push" and so forth. Likewise, in Glass and Ceramics categories items could start with "Bowl" and continue with "Candy dish," "Decanter" through "Vase" or "Wall pocket."

To provide you with an easy-to-use shortcut to specific topics the back of our guide concludes with a comprehensive cross-referenced Index.

In our effort to keep abreast of new and evolving collecting fields we also strive to include a number of new categories each year. This year we're pleased to offer new listings for the Chase Brass & Copper Company, and Whiting & Davis purses in our "Purses & Bags" category. In the Glass section we have included for the first time Higgins Glass and in our Lamps & Lighting Devices section you will find a great listing of Moss Lamps. If Toys are your favorite field, check out our special section on Educational & Scientific Toys.

The above new categories, as well as many others that appear regularly, are provided to us by various experts, and we must offer them our special thanks. Their dedication and efforts help insure that we can offer you the most accurate and timely price guide on the market. For further details on these people please review the following SPECIAL CONTRIBUTORS listing.

There are many other companies and individuals I must also thank. Among the photographers who have contributed to this edition are: Stanley L. Baker, Minneapolis, Minn.; Susan N. Cox, El Cajon, Calif., Susan Eberman, Bedford, Ind.; Pat McPherson, Ramona, Calif.a; John Petzold and Dr. Leslie Pina.

For other photographs, artwork, data or permission to photograph in their shops, we sincerely express appreciation to the following auctioneers, galleries, individuals and shops: Alderfers, Hatfield, Pa.; Frank H. Boos Gallery, Bloomfield Hills, Mich.; Brookside Antiques, New Bedford, Massachusetts; Robert S. Brunk Auction Services, Asheville, N.C.; Canes Through The Ages, Richmond, Ill.; Charlton Hall Galleries, Columbia, S.C.; Christie's, New York, N.Y.; Cincinnati Art Galleries, Cincinnati, Ohio; Copake Country Auction, Copake, N.Y.; William Doyle Galleries, New York, N.Y.; Early American History Auctions, Inc., La Jolla, Calif.; Dr. Robert Elsner, Boynton Beach, Fla.; Garth's Auctions, Delaware, Ohio; Glass-Works Auctions, East Greenville, Pa.; Green Valley Auctions, Mt. Crawford, Va. and Guyette and Schmidt, West Farmington, Maine.

Also to Norman Heckler & Company, Woodstock Valley, Conn.; Heritage-Slaters Americana, Dallas, Texas; Jackson's International Auctioneers, Cedar Falls, Iowa; Mary Ann Johnston, New Cumberland, W.Va.; James D. Julia, Fairfield, Maine; Henry Kurtz, Ltd., New York, N.Y.; McMasters Harris Auctions, Cambridge, Ohio; Dr. James Measell, Marietta, Ohio; Gary Metz's Muddy River Trading Company, Salem, Va.; Mom's Antique Mall, Oronoco, Minn.; Neal Auction Company, New Orleans, La.; New Orleans Auction Galleries, New Orleans, La.; Richard Opfer Auctioneering, Inc., Timonium, Md.; Pacific Glass Auctions, Sacramento, Calif.; Past Tyme Pleasures, Los Altos, Calif.; Rich Penn, Waterloo, Iowa; Dave Rago Arts & Crafts, Lambertville, N. J.; Skinner, Inc., Bolton, Mass.; Sloan's Miami, Miami, Fla.; Swann Auction Galleries, New York, N.Y.; Temples Antiques, Eden Prairie, Minn.; R. and K. Townsend, Rochester, Minn.; Tradewinds Antiques, Manchester-by-the-Sea, Mass.;' Treadway Gallery, Cincinnati, Ohio; C. Williams, Rochester, Minn.; and York Town Auctions, York, Pa.

For everyone who consults our *Antique Trader Antiques & Collectibles Price Guide 2006,* I hope it will prove a delightful experience and that our new volume will be the cornerstone of your collecting reference library. Detailed, colorful and comprehensive, it offers something for everyone!

My staff and I welcome all letters from readers, especially those of constructive critique, and will make every effort to respond. Meanwhile, here's hoping your ongoing treasure hunt brings you nothing but joy.

Kyle Husfloen, editor

SPECIAL CONTRIBUTORS
Index by subject

Shelley China: Mannie Banner, David Chartier, Bryan Goodlad, Edwin E. Kellogg, Gene Loveland and Curt Leiser
Stoneware: Bruce and Vicki Waasdorp
Torquay Pottery: Lee and Marlene, Graham
Vernon Kilns: Pam Green
Warwick: John Rader, Sr.
Zeisel (Eva) Designs: Pat Moore
Zsolnay: Federico Santi

GLASS
Amberina: Louis O. St. Aubin Jr.
Animals: Helen and Bob Jones
Cambridge: Helen and Bob Jones
Carnival Glass: Jim and Jan Seeck
Central Glass Works: Helen and Bob Jones
Custard Glass: Dr. James Measell
Cut Glass: House of Brilliant Glass
Depression Glass: Debbie and Randy Coe

Duncan & Miller: Helen and Bob Jones
Fenton: Helen and Bob Jones
Fostoria: Helen and Bob Jones
Fry: Helen and Bob Jones
Heisey: Helen and Bob Jones
Higgins Glass: Donald-Brian Johnson
Imperial: Helen and Bob Jones
McKee: Helen and Bob Jones
Morgantown: Helen and Bob Jones
New Martinsville: Helen and Bob Jones
Paden City: Helen and Bob Jones
Pattern Glass: Randall McKee; Nancy Smith, Lamplight & Old Glass
Wall Pockets: Bobbie Zucker Bryson
Westmoreland: Helen and Bob Jones, Frank Chiarenza

Contributor directory

Dale Abrams
960 Bryden, Rd.
Columbus, OH 43205
(614) 258-5258

Jo Allers
2500 Greywolf
Hiawatha, IA 52233

Andre Ammelounx
P.O. Box 136
Palatine, IL 60078
(847) 991-5927

Mannie Banner
126 S.W. 15th St.
Pembroke Pines, FL 33027

Ellen Bercovici
5118 Hampden Lane
Bathesda, MD 20814
(301) 652-1140
eb625@verizon.net

Johanna Billings
P.O. Box 244
Danielsville, PA 18038-0244

Sandra Bondhus
P.O. Box 100
Unionville, CT 06085
nbondhus@pol.net

James R. and Carol S. Boshears
375 W. Pecos Rd., #1033
Chandler, AZ 85225-7405
(480) 899-9757

Bobbie Zucker Bryson
1 St. Eleanoras Lane
Tuckahoe, NY 10707
(914) 779-1405
Napkindoll@aol.com

Dana Cain
5061 S. Stuart Ct.
Littleton, CO 80123
dana.cain@att.net

Charles W. Casad
801 Tyler Ct.
Monticello, IL 61856-2246

David Chartier
1171 Waterside
Brighton, MI 48114

Frank Chiarenza
The Frank Chiarenza Museum of Glass
39 W. Main St.
Meriden, CT 06451-4110
(203) 639-9778
chiarenzaglassmuseum@snet.net

The Clocksmith
806 El Camino Real
San Carlos, CA 94070
www.theclocksmith.com

Debbie and Randy Coe
1240 S.E. 40th Ave.
Hillsboro, OR 97123
coeran@aol.com

Les and Irene Cohen
P.O. Box 17001
Pittsburgh, PA 15235
am4ah@yahoo.com

Amphora Collectors International
10159 Nancy Dr.
Meadville, PA 16335
(814) 333-3125
www.amphoracollectors.org

Marion Cohen
14 Croyden Ct.
Albertson, NY 11507
(516) 294-0055

Neva Colbert
69565 Crescent Rd.
St. Clairsville, OH 43950
(740) 695-2355
georgestreet@1st.net

CAS Collectors
206 Grove St.
Rockton, IL 61072
www.cascollectors.com

Caroline Torem-Craig
New York, New York

Robert N. Culver
3081 Sand Pebble Cove
Pinckney, MI 48169
rculver107@aol.com

Kerra Davis
925 Bud St.
Blackshear, GA 31516
kbb@gate.net

Leonard Davis
New York, New York

Bev Dieringer
P.O. Box 536
Redding Ridge, CT 06876
dieringer1@aol.com

Del E. Domke
16142 N.E. 15th St.
Bellevue, WA 98008-2711
(425) 643-3359
delyicious@aol.com

Debbie DuBay
Limoges Antiques Shop
20 Post Office Ave.
Andover, MA 01810
(978) 470-8773

James Elliot-Bishop
500 S. Farrell Dr., S-114
Palm Springs, CA 92264
gmcb@ix.netcom.com

Joe Fex
5061 S. Stuart St.
Littleton, CO 80123
joefex@att.net

Bryan Goodlad
44 Long Meadows
Bramhope
Leeds LS1 69DS
ENGLAND

Joan M. George
67 Stevens Ave.
Oldbridge, NJ 08856
drjgeorge@nac.net

Roselyn Gerson
12 Alnwick Rd.
Malverne, NY 11565
(516) 593-8746
compactldy@aol.com

Lee and Marlene Graham
214 N. Rondu Rd.
McHenry, IL 60050

Pam Green
You Must Remember This
P.O. Box 822
Hollis, NH 03049
ymrt@aol.com
www.ymrt.com

Jeannie Greenfield
310 Parker Rd.
Stoneboro, PA 16153
(724) 376-2584
dlg3684@yahoo.com

Linda Guffey
2004 Fiat Court
El Cajoon, CA 92019-4234
Gufantique@aol.com

Burdell Hall
201 W. Sassafras Dr.
Morton, IL 61550
(309) 263-2988
bnbhall@mtco.com

Carl Heck
Box 8416
Aspen, CO 81612
(970) 925-8011
www.carlheck.com

Ellen R. Hill
P.O. Box 56
Bennington, NH 03442
(603) 588-4099
MSMULB@aol.com

Alma Hillman
362 E. Main St.
Searsport, ME 04974
oldivory@acadia.net

K. Robert and Bonne L. Hohl
47 Fawn Dr.
Reading, PA 19607

Tim Holthaus
CAS Collectors Association
P.O. Box 46
Madison, WI 53701-0046

House of Brilliant Glass
www.brilliantglass.com

Joan Hull
1376 Nevada S.W.
Huron, SD 57350

Hull Pottery Association
11023 Tunnel Hill N.E.
New Lexington, OH 43764

Helen and Bob Jones
Berkeley Springs, WV
BGlances@aol.com

Donald-Brian Johnson
3329 South 56th St., #611
Omaha, NE 68106
donaldbrian@webtv.net

Dorothy Kamm
P.O. Box 7460
Port St. Lucie, FL 34985-7460
(772) 465-4008
dorothykamm@adelphia.let

Edwin E. Kellogg
4951 N.W. 65th Ave.
Lauderhill, FL 33319

Gary Kirsner
Glentiques, Ltd.
1940 Augusta Terrace
P.O. Box 8807
Coral Springs, FL 33071
gkirsner@myacc.net

Vivian Kromer
11 800 Shanklin St.
Bakersfield, CA 93312
(661) 588-7768

Curt Leiser
National Shelley China Club
12010 38th Ave. NE
Seattle, WA 98125
(206) 362-7135
curtispleiser@cs.com

Elyce Litts
P.O. Box 394
Morris Plains, NJ 07950
(908) 964-5055
happymemories@worldnet.att.net

Gene Loveland
11303 S. Alley Jackson Rd.
Grain Valley, MO 64029

Mary McCaslin
6887 Black Oak Ct. E.
Avon, IN 46123
(317) 272-7776
maryjack@indy.rr.com

Randall McKee
(262) 657-6958

Susan N. Cox and Pat McPherson
Country Town Antiques
738 Main St.
Ramona, CA 92065

Dr. James Measell
c/o Fenton Art Glass Co.
700 Elizabeth St.
Williamstown, WV 26187
(304) 375-6122
www.fentonartglass.com

David G. Miller
1971 Blue Fox Dr.
Lansdale, PA 19446-5505
(610) 584-6127

Florence Ceramics Collectors Society
FlorenceCeramics@aol.com

Miniature Lamp Collectors Club
www.nightlightclub.org

Pat Moore
695 Monterey Blvd., Apt. 203
San Francisco, CA 94124
ezcclub@pacbell.net

Mark Moran
5887 Meadow Dr. S.E.
Rochester, MN 55904
(507) 288-8006

Reg G. Morris
7360 Martingale
Chesterland, OH 44026
min@modex.com

Rhona Nabi
The Silver Lady Antiques
P.O. Box 27
Foxboro, MA 02035
(781) 784-9184
silant@aol.com

Joan C. Oates
1107 Deerfield Lane
Marshall, MI 49068
koates120@earthlink.net

Gail Peck
Country Crock Antiques
2121 Pearl St.
Fremont, NE 68025
(420) 721-5721

Beth Pulsipher
Prairie Home Antiques
240 N. Grand
Schoolcraft, MI 49087

Arlene Rabin
P.O. Box 243
Fogelsville, PA 18051
jwhelden@enter.net

John Rader, Sr.
Vice President, National Assn. of
Warwick China & Pottery Collectors
(Betty June Wymer, 28 Bachmann Dr.,
Wheeling, WV 26003, 304-232-3031);
editor, "The IOGA" Club Quarterly
Newsletter; author, *Warwick China*
(Schiffer Publishing, 2000)
780 S. Village Dr., Apt. 203
St. Petersburg, FL 33716
(727) 570-9906

Jim and Jamie Saloff
P.O. Box 339
Edinboro, PA 16412
tim.saloff@verizon.net

Louis St. Aubin Jr.
Brookside Antiques
New Bedford, MA
Brooksideartglass@aol.com

Federico Santi
The Drawing Room Antiques
152 Spring St.
Newport, RI 02840
(401) 841-5060
www.drawrm.com

R.O. Schmitt Fine Arts
P.O. Box 1941
Salem, NH 03079
(603) 893-5915

Peggy Sebek
3255 Glencairn Rd.
Shaker Heights, OH 44122
pegsebek@earthlink.net

Jim and Jan Seeck
Seeck Auctions
P.O. Box 377
Mason City, IA 50402
(641) 424-1116
jimjan@seeckauction.com

Jeff Siptak
4013 Russellwood Dr.
Nashville, TN 37204

Nancy Smith
Lamplight and Old Glass
P.O. Box 6192
Grand Rapids, MI 49506

Steve Stone
12795 W. Alameda Pkwy.
Lakewood, CO 80225
Sylvanlvr@aol.com

Michael G. Strawser Auctions
P.O. Box 332
Wolcottville, IN 46795
(260) 854-2859
www.majolicaauctions.com

Phillip Sullivan
P.O. Box 69
South Orleans, MA 0266
(508) 255-8495

Tea Leaf Club International Membership
P.O. Box 377
Belton, MO 64012
www.tealeafclub.com

Tim Trapani
7543 Northport Dr.
Boynton Beach, FL 33437

Jim Trautman
R.R. 1
Orton, Ontario, Canada LON 7N0
trautman@sentex.net

Nora Travis
13337 E. South St.
Cerritos, CA 90701
(714) 521-9283
Travishrs@aol.com

Bruce and Vicki Waasdorp
P.O. Box 434
Clarence, NY 14031
(716) 759-2361
www.antiques-stoneware.com

Elaine Westover
210 Knox Hwy. 5
Abingdon, IL 61410-9332

Kathryn Wiese
Retrospective Modern Design
P.O. Box 1138
Kamuela, HI 97643
retrodesign@earthlink.net

Dannie Woodard
1310 S. Bowie Dr.
Weatherford, TX 76080
al1310@aol.com

Judy Wucherer
Transitions of Wales, Ltd.
P.O. Box 1441
Brookfield, WI 53045

North American Torquay Society
214 N. Ronda Rd.
McHenry, IL 60050
(815) 385-2040

ABC PLATES

Ceramic

These children's plates were popular in the late 19th and early 20th centuries. An alphabet border was incorporated with nursery rhymes, maxims, scenes or figures in an apparent attempt to "spoon feed" a bit of knowledge at mealtime. An important reference book in this field is A Collector's Guide to ABC Plates, Mugs and Things *by Mildred L. and Joseph P. Chalala (Pridemark Press, Lancaster, Pennsylvania, 1980)*

"Base Ball Striker and Catcher" Plate

Base Ball Striker and Catcher," 7 1/8" d., from the "American Sports" series, green transfer of a batter ("striker") & catcher (ILLUS.).. **$600**

Bird, 7 1/4" d., brown transfer of titmouse in branches & print alphabet, marked "England"... **175**

"Diamond" Series ABC Plate

Diamond, 7 5/8" d., from "Diamond" series, center diamond shows man & horse, four sepia pictures surrounding center diamond illustrate the rest of the story, also known as a comic book of the 1800s (ILLUS.).. **175**

"Exhibition Prize Rabbits" ABC Plate

"Exhibition Prize Rabbits," black transfer of long-eared rabbits, writing under picture hard to decipher (ILLUS.) **275**

"Federal Generals" ABC Plate

"Federal Generals," 6" d., black transfer showing four Civil War generals on horseback (ILLUS.)...................................... **400**

"The Finding of Moses" ABC Plate

"Finding of Moses (The)" from the "Bible Pictures" series, multicolor scene of two women finding Moses in the bulrushes, letters & floral decorations in space not taken up by center scene (ILLUS.) **250**

Children Sledding ABC Plate

Sledding, 7 3/8" d., center illustration of children & toy bears sledding, circled by printed letters of the alphabet in addition to the embossed letters on the rim (ILLUS.)............ **250**

"The Sponge Bath" ABC Plate

"Sponge Bath (The)," 7 7/8" d., black & white, image of young boy bathing in large tub, laughing as he pulls fully clothed child into the water, large printed letters on rim (ILLUS.)................................. **175**

"Turk" ABC Plate

"Turk," 7 1/4" d., from the "Nations of the World" series, Brownhills Pottery Company, transfer w/polychrome highlights depicts woman in costume, letters to the side rather than in circle on rim of plate (ILLUS.).. **225**

Girls Holding Umbrella ABC Plate

Umbrella, 7" d., black transfer w/color added of two girls under an umbrella, an old woman & other children watching from a doorway (ILLUS.)... **250**

"Whom Are You For" ABC Plate

"Whom are you for," 5 1/8" d., center picture of a field sentry w/bayonet stopping two solders, colors added (ILLUS.).............. **250**

ADVERTISING ITEMS

Thousands of objects made in various materials, some intended as gifts with purchases, others used for display or given away for publicity, are now being collected. Also see various other categories and Antique Trader Advertising Price Guide.

Boot jack, cast iron, "Use Musselman's Plug Tobacco," flat flaring top w/U-form end, raised on short peg feet, ca. 1900, 9 1/2" l.. **$69**

1891 Simmons Hardware Calendar

Calendar, 1891, "Simmons Hardware Co., " rectangular, cardboard w/paper pad, wood frame, portrait of young woman w/"Simmons Hardware Co. - St. Louis, Mo. - J.I.C. Horse Nails - Finished and Pointed and Made From Best Norway Fillets," 13 x 16 1/2" (ILLUS.) **250-350**

Bemis Bros. Bag Co. Calendar

Calendar, 1903, "Bemis Bros. Bag Co.," rectangular, lithographed cloth, red w/white & yellow lettering, center w/white circle depicting head of a buffalo in black & white & surrounded by a circle of white dots, flanked by torches above bags & marked above "Animals that Are Hunted," Bemis Bros. Bag Co., St. Louis, Missouri, each page features different animal & colors, ca. 1903, 11 x 16" (ILLUS.) **450-650**

Calendar, 1905, "Metropolitan Life Insurance," lithograph, long rectangular shape, colorful floral illustration w/faces of four pretty young girls in the centers of blooming roses, 12 separate calendar panels below, "Metropolitan Life Insurance Co. - 1905" at top, 8 x 25" **99**

Long 1907 Life Insurance Calendar

Calendar, 1907, "Metropolitan Life Insurance Co.," long narrow roll-down paperstyle, four round color reserves showing the stages in a woman's life, flowers & small calendar blocks joining the images, excellent condition, 12 x 33" (ILLUS.) **345**

Osborne Harvesting Machines 1909 Calendar

Calendar, 1909. "Osborne Harvesting Machines," full color illustration of cowboy on galloping horse aiming rifle at antelope in distance, "Osborne - Harvesting Machines - and - Farm Implements" in upper right, w/full calendar pad for 1909 & band at top, 13 1/2 x 20" (ILLUS.) **935**

Rare Figural Cigar Advertising Clock

Unusual Insurance Company Clock

three-quarters figure of an elegant gentleman w/advertising on his chest at one end & another figure of a man holding an open cigar box w/advertising at the other end, an inset round clock dial w/Roman numerals & framed by leaves in the center, bronzed finish, ca. 1890s, keys present, clock not running, 16" l., 11 1/4" h. (ILLUS., top of page) **1,854**

Clock, "Old Guardian Coal," wooden case, square, white face w/black Arabic numerals, center color illustration of St. Bernard dog standing guard over fair-haired tot playing w/ball beneath "Old Guardian - Our Best Coal," ca. 1940 .... **198**

OshKosh B'gosh Neon Wall Clock

Clock, "OshKosh B'gosh Work Clothes," electric wall neon-type, octagonal case w/a green reverse-painted outer border over the neon, orange wording on dial, sweep seconds hand, ca. 1938, apparently not working, 19" w. (ILLUS.)............... **316**

Clock, "Fireman's Insurance Co. - Newark, NJ," cast gilt-metal, an upright ornate scroll-cast case w/advertising below the round inset dial w/Arabic numerals, the top cast w/the figure of a standing fireman holding a fire horn & leaning on a fire hydrant, 1905, clock not working, 9 1/4" h. (ILLUS.) **651**

Clock, "L.O. Grothe & Co. - Montreal - the Boston Cigar - The Peg-Top Cigar," cast gilt-metal, long oblong base w/a cast

Alma Polish Counter Display Box

Counter display box, "Alma Polish," square wood w/hinged lift top w/color printed label inside in black, white & red, further advertising on the sides & front, all-original, early 20th c., 15 1/2" w., 7" h. (ILLUS.)... **115**

Counter display box, "D.M. Ferry & Co.," oak, rectangular, inside of hinged lid decorated w/color litho by Calvert of children in wide-brimmed hats working in flower garden & "Choice Flower Seeds - from D.M. Ferry & Co. -Detroit, Mich.," 7 x 11", 4" h.. **165**

Nice Early Fairy Soap Display Box

Counter display box, "Fairbanks Fairy Soap," square wood w/each side printed in black & gold w/advertising, original color-printed label inside the lid decorated

w/red roses, early 20th c., 17" w., 8" h. (ILLUS.)... **489**

Gilt Edge Dressing Shoes Display Box

Counter display box, "Gilt Edge Dressing Ladies Shoes," rectangular wood w/lift top printed inside w/black advertising, printed ads on each end, early 20th c., 11 3/4 x 18" (ILLUS.) **81**

Octagonal Hardware Cabinet

Counter display cabinet, ash & soft maple, octagonal revolving-type, 72 pie-shaped drawers w/wood pulls, The American Bolt & Screw Case, Dayton, Ohio, Pat. Apr. 27 '80-May 12 '03, 21 1/2" x 33" (ILLUS.)... **2,500-3,500**

Early Winchester Tools Counter Sign

Counter display sign, "Winchester Tools - 1866-1920," rectangular cardboard w/easel back, printer in red, blue, black & gold, additional wording "Bargain counter tools go to the junk heap too quick. Buy Winchester Tools for long service," early 20th c., crease in upper corner, minor edge scuffs, 8 1/2 x 10 1/2" (ILLUS.) **468**

Wheatlet Display Card

Display card, "Wheatlet," cardboard easel-back display w/full-color illustration of Uncle Sam standing on globe of world, holding hat in one hand & gesturing toward box of Wheatlet & bowl of cereal sitting atop it, bowing to crowd of men looking up at him, "Eaten and Enjoyed by all Na-

tions" in red below figure, "Made only by - The Franklin Mills Co. - Lockport, N.Y. U.S.A." at bottom of display, 1899, 3 1/2 x 6 1/4" (ILLUS.) **121**

Display case, canes or walking sticks, cylindrical, wood frame w/four curved glass panels, one panel decorated w/color illustration of sailing ship, insert w/holes for holding canes upright, 22" d., 42" h. **2,860**

Display figure, "National Tailoring Co.," composition figure on oak base reading "National Tailoring Co." on front, figure in black tux & top hat, white shirt, tie & gloves, 32" h. **1,045**

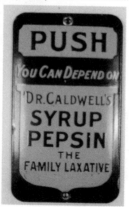

Baltimore Enamel Novelty Door Push

Door push, "Baltimore Enamel & Novelty Co.," rectangular, porcelain on metal, green w/black & white letters reading "Please Close Door - The Baltimore Enamel & Novelty Co.," ca. 1910, 2 3/4 x 4" (ILLUS.) **175-250**

Dr. Caldwell's Door Push

Door push, "Dr. Caldwell's Syrup Pepsin," rectangular, porcelain on metal, black & yellow, reads "Push - You Can Depend on Dr. Caldwell's Syrup Pepsin - The Family Laxative," ca. 1920s, 3 3/4 x 6 3/8" (ILLUS.) **200-250**

Fan Promoting The Adirondacks

Hand fan, "Merkel & Gelman," cardboard, color illustration of lake scene w/mountains in the distance, the handle decorated w/floral decoration in bright yellow, red & green, the back reading "Nature's Mirror - The Adirondacks - Fashion's Mirror - Merkel & Gelman - Glens Falls - Lake George," early 1900s, 11" l. (ILLUS.) **45**

Singer Mfg. Company Fan

Hand fan, "Singer Manufacturing Co.," paper w/wooden handle, color illustration of four birds on flowering branch above "Compliments of The Singer Manufacturing Co. - Fifty-First Season," back w/illustration of woman sitting at sewing machine entwined in a giant red "S" w/"Singer * Sewing * Machines" in white, the rest filled w/product information, 1900, 15" l. (ILLUS.) **50**

Hand mirror, "See yourself in Buster Brown Shoes," flat round handled printed composition back w/an image of Buster Brown & Tige & wording in black, pink rose border, light surface soil, mirror surface very worn, early 20th c., 4 1/4" l. (ILLUS., top next column) **55**

Early Buster Brown Hand Mirror

Early Illinois Watch Lincoln Print

Lithograph, "The Lincoln Watch," color lithograph on canvas bust portrait of Abraham Lincoln, promotional piece for the Illinois Watch Company, in original wide gold shadowbox frame, minor losses, ca. 1910, 11 x 14" (ILLUS.) **138**

B.P.O.E. Match Safe

Match safe, "B.P.O.E." (Benevolent & Protective Order of Elks), brass w/silver plate, rectangular, embossed fraternal symbols & marked "Cervus Alles," ca. 1910, 1 1/2 x 2 3/4" (ILLUS.) **150-200**

Scarce Early Auto Pinback Button

Pinback button, "Van Brunt Vehicles," celluloid, color-printed image of Lady Liberty at one side holding a wreath above the image of a small early open automobile sitting atop a globe, produced by an early, short-lived auto manufacturer, ca. 1900, 2 1/4" d. (ILLUS.) **481**

Unusual Majolica Advertising Plate

Plate, "Chew Rose Leaf Fine Cut [tobacco]," majolica w/a white pebbled ground, large applied pink roses & green leaves along one side, Avalon Line mark of David Haynes, Baltimore, Maryland, ca. 1880s, minor loss to petals, 8 3/4" d. (ILLUS.) **77**

Angelus Marshmallows Pocket Mirror

Pocket mirror, "Angelus Marshmallows," oval, celluloid, cupid standing on square base marked "Angelus Marshmallows" playing horn & holding box also marked

"Angelus Marshmallows," Rueckheim Bros. & Eckstein, Chicago, Illinois, ca. 1900, 1 3/4 x 2 3/4" (ILLUS.) **125-175**

Kern Barber Supply Co. Pocket Mirror

Pocket mirror, "August Kern Barber Supply Company," round, celluloid, center w/image of barber chair marked "America" & border w/"August Kern Barber Supply Co. - Saint Louis, MO.," ca. 1910, 2" d. (ILLUS.)... **125-175**

Cascarets Pocket Mirror

Pocket mirror, "Cascarets," round, celluloid, image of cupid on chamber pot above "Cascarets - Did It - They Work While You Sleep" & "All Going Out - Nothing Coming In," Sterling Remedy Company, Chicago, Illinois, ca. 1910, 2" d. (ILLUS.)....................................... **100-150**

Checkers Popcorn Pocket Mirror

Pocket mirror, "Checkers Popcorn," round, celluloid, an image of a red & white checkered box marked "Checkers" w/"Eat - Eat - Eat" above & "A Nice Prize in Each Package - Shotwell Mfg. Co. Chicago" below, ca. 1910, 2 1/4" d. (ILLUS.) **150-200**

Early Coffee Pine Shipping Crate

Shipping crate, "Washburn Halligan Coffee - Davenport, IA," long low rectangular pine box, flat hinged lid w/two braces, printed black advertising on sides, printed paper label inside lid, early 20th c., 12 1/4 x 26", 9 1/2" h. (ILLUS.) **138**

Snow White Bakery Store Box

Store box, "Iten's Product - Snow White Bakery - Clinton, IA," deep rectangular pine box w/a flat hinged lid & metal bail handles on the ends, early 20th c., 13 3/4 x 22", 12 1/4" h. (ILLUS.) **104**

Red Goose Shoes Neon Store Display

Store display, "Red Goose Shoes," porcelain neon figural goose, red outlined in white when lit, on black base, reads "Red Goose Shoes" on breast, 2 x 3" section cut out of rear cover, 6 x 12", 24" h. (ILLUS.) **1,955**

Store display, "Rit Dye," metal, rectangular w/peaked top, front w/colorful litho illustration of woman in blue dress holding pink garment above "Cake or Flake - 10¢," top reads "Never say 'dye' - say RIT," 14" w., 17" h. **275**

Store display, Santa, h.p. papier-mâché w/composition head, standing figure holds long list, electrified movements include nodding head & raising hand holding quill pen, 52" h. **1,150**

Store display, "The Brown Bilt Shoe," die-cut metal, sign on base reading "The Brown Bilt Shoe," the top w/room for display of one pair of shoes, 12" h. **165**

Store Display for Wilson Rugs

Store display, "Wilson Rugs," miniature wooden loom w/6 x 8" rug still on the loom & connected to its balls of yarn in grey, white, red, black, cream & pink, "WILSON" spelled out in black letters on cream panel at top of rug, 1930s-40s, 11 x 14 1/2" (ILLUS.) **125**

Store display, "Wrigley's Chewing Gum," die-cut tin, black arrow man w/round moon face holding four original boxes of gum, ca. 1920 .... **1,265**

Store display figure, "Eskimo Pie," electric animated figure of Eskimo child stands on base behind green sign reading "Eskimo Pie 10¢," arm moves up & down, 32" h. **468**

Store display/dispenser, "Wrigley's Chewing Gum," metal, revolving-type, four sided frame on circular base **176**

5/A Horse Blankets Thermometer

Thermometer, "5/A Horse Blankets," round, yellow metal w/paper face, black numbers & black diamond shape in center marked "We've Got 'Em - You Want 'Em - 5/A Horse Blankets," & marked along bottom near frame "Standard Thermometer and Electric Company, Peabody, Massachusetts, Pat. May 8, 1888," 9 1/4" d. (ILLUS.) **200-250**

Barrel Remodeling Co. Thermometer

Thermometer, "Barrel Remodeling Company," round, metal w/paper face, black numbers, image of barrel in center over "Barrel Remodeling Co. - Barrels Bought

and Sold - Kansas City, Mo.," litho by The American Art Works, Coshocton, Ohio, ca. 1900, 9 1/4" d. (ILLUS.) **175-225**

Boschee's Syrup Thermometer

Thermometer, "Boschee's August Flower German Syrup," round, yellow metal w/paper face, black numbers, center w/yellow lettering outlined in black reading "August Flower for Liver, Indigestion, Constipation - for Coughs, Colds, Bronchitis, etc. - Use Boschee's German Syrup," ca. 1900, 9 1/2" d. (ILLUS.) **200-250**

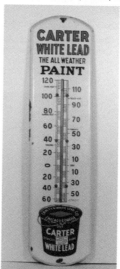

Carter White Lead Paint Thermometer

Thermometer, "Carter White Lead Paint," porcelain on metal, white, red & black, "Carter White Lead - The All Weather Paint" at the top, paint bucket at bottom marked "Carter White Lead Co. - Chicago & Omaha - Carter - Strictly Pure - White Lead," dated March 16, 1915, 7 x 27" (ILLUS.) **250-350**

Rare Early Moxie Thermometer

Thermometer, "Moxie," die-cut tin, long hanging-type w/the half-length figure of the Moxie man at the top, advertising in orange, white, yellow & black, scattered surface scuffs, scrapes & blemishes, missing thermometer tube, needs cleaning, early 20th c., rare, 12" w., 18" h. (ILLUS.).. **1,898**

NR & Tums Thermometer

Thermometer, "NR (Nature's Remedy) Laxative & Tums," rectangular, porcelain on metal, top marked "NR - All Vegetable Laxative - Come In - If You Get It Here It's Good" & marked at the bottom "Tums - Quick Relief for Acid Indigestion," black & red w/white lettering, ca. 1920, 7 x 27" (ILLUS.)... **250-350**

OshKosh Overalls Thermometer

Thermometer, "OshKosh Overalls," rectangular, metal, red & yellow w/"OshKosh B'gosh - Work Wear" at the top & "The World's Best Overall - Union Made" at the bottom, ca. 1920, 10 x 25 1/2" (ILLUS.)
.... **475-600**

Thermometer, "Pepsi-Cola," color-printed tin, tall rectangular form w/rounded ends, dark blue panels at the top & bottom, top w/"Buy Pepsi-Cola - Big, Big Bottle" in white & red, the large thermometer down the center white panel, bottom panel w/Pepsi-Cola logo & further advertising, ca. 1940s, somewhat ambered, only minor marks, small dent at top mounting hole, 27" h. (ILLUS. right with other Pepsi-Cola thermometer)................... **330**

Two Tall Pepsi-Cola Thermometers

Thermometer, "Pepsi-Cola," color-printed tin, tall rectangular form w/rounded ends, a color portrait of a pretty woman at the top sipping from a long straw that goes down beside the thermometer to a color picture of a bottle at the bottom, white ground printed w/"Weather Cold or Weather Hot - Pepsi-Cola Hits the Spot," red & white logo banner at the bottom, 1940s, few short scratches, slight bit of touch-up, few nicks & dents around mounting holes, 27" h. (ILLUS. left with other Pepsi-Cola thermometer, bottom previous page) **578**

Large Rare Red Crown Thermometer

Thermometer, "Red Crown Gasoline - for Power Mileage," porcelain, hanging-type, long narrow rectangular type printed in white, black & orange, produced for Polarine, early 20th c., couple of large chips on lower left & top center, redwood frame appears original, 20" w., 73" h. (ILLUS.) **1,140**

Thermometer, "The Emporium Department Store," rectangular wood w/rounded top & slightly curved edges, painted white w/blue lettering reading "The Emporium Department Store - Dyersville's Leading Merchants Over 40 Years - Complete Head to Foot Outfitters for Men - Women - and - Children," ca. 1920, 9 x 21" (ILLUS., top next column) **150-200**

Department Store Thermometer

ARCHITECTURAL ITEMS

In recent years the growing interest in and support for historic preservation has spawned a greater appreciation of the fine architectural elements that were an integral part of early building, both public and private. Where, in decades past, structures might be razed and doors, fireplace mantels, windows, etc., hauled to the dump, today all interior and exterior details from unrestorable buildings are salvaged to be offered to home restorers, museums and even builders who want to include a bit of history in a new construction project.

Carved Lion Head Building Ornament

Building ornament, carved & painted wood, squared model of a lion's head, half-round w/detailed mane, snout & whiskers, possibly by John H. Bellamy, Kittery Point, Maine, late 19th c., 7 x 8" (ILLUS.) **$8,963**

Very Elegant Wrought-iron Entrance Gates

Gold-trimmed Gothic Arch Doors

Church doors, painted & parcel-gilt wood, the pair forming a large Gothic arch, decorated w/conforming panels w/applied molding in the form of a panoply of Gothic quatrefoils, second half 19th c., each 20" w., 7' 4" h., pr. (ILLUS.)......................... **748**

Cupola top, patinated copper, octagonal paneled dome w/a sphere on baluster finial & octagonal square-form base, old verdigris surface, America, 19th c., 35 1/2" w., 4' 1 1/2" h. **3,408**

Entrance gates, wrought iron, each w/an arched toprail w/spearhead decoration over a body of square column design decorated w/scrolling floral overlays, ending w/a rectangular panel, decorated w/highlights of gold w/mounting bars, Europe, 19th c., 12' 2" w., overall 99" h., pr. (ILLUS., top of page)................................. **2,300**

Entryway, painted pine, Classical style, a five-raised-panel door w/fan carving above, flanked by paneled columns w/weathered green & white paint, New

England, first half 19th c., 60 1/2" w., 8' 3 1/2" h... **3,173**

Fanlight, painted pine, Federal style, the arched frame painted white, green painted louvers, ca. 1800, 86" l., 22" h. (minor wear)... **1,410**

![Elaborate Carved Fireplace Surround]

Elaborate Carved Fireplace Surround

Fireplace surround, carved wood, a molded egg-and-dart valance supporting carved paterae over pairs of carved & fluted columns resting on plinth bases & flanking three concave shell carvings above a rectangular mirror above a serpentine mantelpiece, on a carved corbel bisecting a floral-carved surround, trimmed w/egg-and-dart molding, Europe, ca. 1900, molding at left side of valance broken, 12 1/2 x 60", 7' 9" h. (ILLUS.) **1,380**

Three Early Painted & Stenciled Window Cornices

Window cornices, painted & gilt-trimmed wood, each long piece w/blocked recessed end panels filled w/gilt pineapple-filled compotes, a long narrow cross panel stenciled w/a band of flowers below the scroll-cut & arched crestrail centered by a stenciled basket of fruit, America, mid-19th c., 42 1/4" l., 6 7/8" h., set of 3 (ILLUS., top of page) **4,183**

ART DECO

Interest in Art Deco, a name given an art movement stemming from the Paris International Exhibition of 1925, continues to grow today. This style flowered in the 1930s and actually continued into the 1940s. A mood of flippancy is found in its varied characteristics - zigzag lines resembling the lightning bolt, sometimes steps, often the use of sharply contrasting colors such as black and white and others. Look for prices for the best examples of Art Deco design to continue to rise. Also see JEWELRY, MODERN.

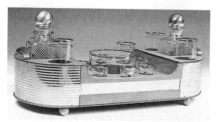

Art Deco Portable Bar in Wood & Metal

Bar, portable, wood & metal, a long narrow oval form in wood trimmed around each end w/curved line-incised metal panels, raised on small metal ball feet, fitted w/square glass decanters, sets of glasses & an ice bucket, one glass missing, ca. 1950, 24" l. (ILLUS.) **$184**

Brown Bakelite Portable Bar

Bar, portable-type, brown Bakelite, the narrow long oval base w/chrome side rail handles & cream Bakelite tab end handles, each end w/an opening to hold a square liquor bottle w/a taller center compartment to hold six gilt-edged glasses, ca. 1950, 24" l. (ILLUS., bottom previouis page) **259**

Centerpiece bowl, glass, Macassar ebony & chrome, a wide shallow paneled pressed translucent frosted celery green glass bowl w/a Chinese Lantern plant decoration, shaped & upswept ebony

French Art Deco Centerpiece Bowl in Glass, Ebony & Chrome

side handles, resting on a ringed chrome foot, glass embossed at edge "Ezan - France," ca. 1930, 17 1/2" l., 6 1/4" h. (ILLUS., top of page) **345**

Unusual Egyptian Revival Dresser Box

Dresser box, cov., wood & copper, figural, Egyptian Revival style, model of an ancient Egyptian sarcophagus, bentwood form overlaid in embossed copper w/Egyptian designs & blue opaque glass scarabs, the sides trimmed in tooled leather, dark rich patina w/verdigris oxidation, silk-lined, ca. 1925, 12" l. (ILLUS.) **460**

French Art Deco Table Lamp

Lamp, table model, 11" d. domical shade in pink stained glass w/graduated rings topped by a molded stylized rose blossom, raised on a squared nickel-plated brass stem & hexagonal foot embossed w/geometric designs, shade marked "Vlieghe - France - 1137," ca. 1925, minor flakes on shade, overall 19" h. (ILLUS.) **518**

Lamp, table model, figural, bronzed metal, glass & marble veneer, a rectangular thin marble-veneered base fitted at one end w/a large bronzed metal model of a polar bear w/one paw raised, a frosted glass iceberg-shaped shade in the center & two bronzed metal penguins at the other end, unsigned, France, ca. 1930, 31" l., 12" h. **1,495**

Two of Five Iron Art Deco Panels

Art Deco Mirror with Tennis Players

Mirror, table model, a long rectangular arched beveled mirror plate framed along the sides & base w/a silvered bronze frame depicting a pair of stylized tennis players, probably France, ca. 1920s, some minor loss to mirror silvering, 16 x 24" (ILLUS.).. **345**

Panels, cast & wrought iron, each tall rectangular piece composed of vertical bars accented w/angular bars & an applied wrought foliate pendant at the top & scrolling bars near the base, Europe, ca. 1920s, three panels 43 1/2 x 70 1/4", two panels 37 1/2 x 70 1/4", set of five (ILLUS. of part, top of page) **2,760**

Tile, gilt plaster, molded in relief w/a stylized image of a nude Josephine Baker in a dancing pose, the background w/half-circles, squares & rays, possibly from one of the inner halls of the Folies Bergere in Paris, France, overall gilt finish, in a stepped walnut frame, tile 19 x 19 1/2" (ILLUS., next column) **6,900**

Art Deco Josephine Baker Gilt Tile

ART NOUVEAU

Art Nouveau's primary thrust was between 1890 and 1905, but commercial Art Nouveau productions continued until about World War I. This style was a rebellion against historic tradition in art. Using natural forms as inspiration, it is primarily characterized by undulating or wavelike lines and whiplashes. Many objects were made in materials ranging from glass to metals. Figural pieces with seductive maidens with long, flowing hair are especially popular in this style. Interest in Art Nouveau remains high, with the best pieces by well known designers bringing strong prices. Also see JEWELRY, ANTIQUE.

Lovely Art Nouveau Portrait Plaque with Swan & Iris Border

Art Nouveau Bust of Pretty Maiden

Bust of a young woman, cast bronzed metal, the maiden wearing a fancy ruffled & flared bonnet & a wrapped gown w/wide ruffled sleeves, embossed mark "H. Jacobs - copyright 1904 by Napoleon Alliot," 18" h. (ILLUS.) **$100-200**

Charger, porcelain, large round form h.p. w/a large colorful bust portrait of a partially veiled maiden w/red poppies in her black hair, against a stippled gilt ground w/stylized scattered light green flowers, the wide border decorated w/alternating swimming white swans & yellow iris w/green leaves within a dark blue outer band, artist-signed in the lower left w/a date of 1900, unmarked by maker, iron armature for hanging, 20" d. (ILLUS., top of page) **1,006**

Fine Art Nouveau Lamp with Daum Shade

Lamp, table model, bronze & glass, the figural base modeled as an exotic Art Nouveau maiden standing on a sunburst-style base, her arms raised above her head holding a floral wreath that supports a ribbed half-round inverted glass shade signed "Daum Nancy - France," base signed "E. Soleau-Paris - A. Fery," France, early 20th c., overall 16" h. (ILLUS., bottom previous page) **2,990**

Cast Bronze Art Nouveau Paper Knife

Art Nouveau Lamp with Steuben Shade

Lamp, table model, the bronze base w/a high arched stem cast w/a whiplash design & suspending a signed Steuben glass shade w/an iridescent golden brown exterior & Calcite interior, unsigned base probably by Majorelle, France, ca. 1900, overall 18 1/2" h. (ILLUS.)..................................... **633**

Paper knife, cast bronze, a long flat tapering blade w/rounded tip, the flaring handle cast w/ivy leaves & vines, signed "Hirsch," France, ca. 1900, 11 1/4" l. (ILLUS., top of page)...................... **92**

Pretty Rorstrand Art Nouveau Vase

Vase, porcelain, footed bulbous body in white molded w/large light green oak leaves up the sides below the wide rounded pale green shoulder & a wide neck composed of light purple molded poppy blossoms, crowned mark of the Rorstrand Porcelain Factory w/painted numbers & monograms, ca. 1910, 5 3/4" h. (ILLUS.) **359**

AUDUBON PRINTS

John James Audubon, American ornithologist and artist, is considered the finest nature artist in history. In about 1820 he conceived the idea of publishing a full color book portraying every known species of American bird in its natural habitat. He spent years in the wilderness capturing their beauty in vivid color only to have great difficulty finding a publisher. In 1826 he visited England, received immediate acclaim, and selected Robert Havell as his engraver. "Birds of America," when completed, consisted of four volumes of 435 individual plates, double-elephant folio size, a combination of aquatint, etching and line engraving. W.H. Lizars of Edinburgh engraved the first ten plates of this four-volume series. These were later retouched by Havell, who produced the complete set between 1827 and early 1839. In the 1840s, another definitive work, "Viviparous Quadrupeds of North America," containing 150 plates, was published in America. Prices for Audubon's original double-elephant folio size prints are very high and beyond the means of the average collector. Subsequent editions of "Birds of America," especially the chromolithographs done by Julius Bien in New York (1859-60) and the smaller octavo (7 x 10 1/2") edition of prints done by J.T. Bowen of Philadelphia in the 1840s, are those that are most frequently offered for sale.

Anyone interested in Audubon prints needs to be aware that many photographically produced copies of the prints have been issued during this century for use on calendars or as decorative accessories, so it is best to check with a print expert before spending a large sum on an Audubon purported to be from an early edition.

American Cross Fox by Audubon

American Cross Fox - Plate VI - hand-colored lithograph by J.T. Bowen, Philadelphia, ca. 1845, pale old mat staining, some foxing & creases, some edge losses, minor soiling, 21 3/16 x 27 1/2" (ILLUS., bottom previous page) **1,315**

American Goldfinch by Audubon

American Goldfinch - Plate 33, hand-colored etching, engraving & aquatint by Robert Havell, London, 1827-38, framed, scattered foxing, time staining & soiling, few small edge tears, 25 1/8 x 39" (ILLUS.) **5,736**

Rare American White Pelican Print

American White Pelican - Plate CCCXI - hand-colored etching, engraving & aqua-

tint by Robert Havell, Jr., London, 1827-38, framed, only minor scuffs & stains, one tear, mounted on mat, 28 1/8 x 38 3/16" (ILLUS.) **65,725**

The Bird of Washington Print

Bird of Washington (The) - Plate 11, hand-colored etching, engraving & aquatint by Robert Havell, Jr., London, 1827-38, framed, few pale foxmarks, minor scuffing, some margin loss, small tears & losses in margin, 25 7/8 x 39 1/8" (ILLUS.) **8,365**

Black-bellied Darter - Plate CCCXVI, hand-colored engraving by Robert Havell, Jr., London, 1827-38, framed, 25 5/8 x 38 1/2" (minor staining, partially restored tears & tiny losses to margins, binding holes at left, hinged to the mat) .. **16,730**

Blue Crane - Plate 372, hand-colored lithography by J. Bien, New York, ca. 1859-1860, framed, 26 1/2 x 39 1/2" (foxing & small losses & tears in margins, mat & time staining, surface soiling & hanging creases) **4,183**

Little Auk - Plate CCCXXXIX, hand-colored etching, engraving & aquatint by Robert Havell, London, 1827-38, framed, 21 1/2 x 28 3/4" (pale staining & soiling, soft crease in upper right corner of margin) **1,793**

Piping Plover - Plate CCXX, hand-colored etching, engraving & aquatint by Robert Havell, London, 1827-38, framed, 21 1/4 x 27 1/2" (staining, occasional foxmark, sheet laid down on Masonite board) **2,032**

Rose-breasted Grosbeak - Plate CXXVII, hand-colored etching, engraving & aquatint by Robert Havell, Jr., London, 1827-38, framed, 25 1/8 x 31" (minor soiling, occasional foxmark, mat staining, few small losses & tears at margin edges) **5,019**

Victorian Bamboo Pram-style Baby Carriage

BABY MEMENTOES

Everyone dotes on the new baby, and through many generations some exquisite and unique gifts have been carefully selected with a special infant in mind. Collectors now seek items from a varied assortment of baby mementos, once tokens of affection to the newborn babe. Also see CHILDREN'S BOOKS.

Carriage, bamboo twin pram-style, the bamboo frame fitted w/two seats, flat side panels painted w/scenes, long curved push handles out the back, metal-rimmed large wheels w/wire spokes, some cracking, late 19th c., 24 x 64", 34" h. (ILLUS., top of page) **$316**

Elaborate Victorian Wicker Carriage

Carriage, wicker, very elaborately woven design w/the platform area composed of ornate tight scrolls w/the back forming a continuous arch into the scroll-trimmed top, wooden framework & upright curved push handles, the large wooden wheels w/delicate scrolls between the spokes, some paint loss, late 19th c., 54" l., 47" h. (ILLUS.) **403**

Czech Pottery Baby Feeding Plate

Feeding plate, pottery, round w/low flat sides & a wide flattened rim, printed on the inside bottom w/a color scene of children, the top rim printed in color w/flowers & the word "Baby," Czechoslovakia, ca. 1920s, 5 1/2" d. (ILLUS.) **69**

BANKS

Original early mechanical and cast-iron still banks are in great demand with collectors. Their scarcity has caused numerous reproductions of both types and the novice collector is urged to exercise caution. The early mechanical banks are especially scarce and some versions are seldom offered for sale but, rather, are traded with fellow collectors attempting to upgrade an existing collection. Numbers after the bank name in mechanical banks refer to those in John Meyer's Handbook of Old Mechanical Banks. However, another book Penny Lane—A History of Antique Mechanical Toy Banks, by Al Davidson, provides updated information and the number from this new volume is indicated in parenthesis at the end of each mechanical bank listing.

In past years, our standard reference for cast-iron still banks was Hubert B. Whiting's book Old Iron Still Banks, but because this work is out of print and a well illustrated book, The Penny Lane Bank Book—Collecting Still Banks by Andy and Susan Moore pictures and describes numerous additional banks, we will use the Moore numbers as a reference after the name of each listing. Other newer books on still banks include Iron Safe Banks by Bob and Shirley Peirce (SBCCA publication), The Bank Book by Bill Norman (N), Coin Banks by Banthrico by James Redwine (R), and Monumental Miniatures by Madua & Weingarten (MM). We will indicate the Whiting or other book reference number, with the abbreviation noted above, in parenthesis at the end.

The still banks listed are old and in good original condition with good paint and no repair unless otherwise noted. An asterisk (*) indicates this bank has been reproduced at some time.

Mechanical

Cash register - tin, semi-mechanical, model of a stylized cash register w/single central pull lever, decorated w/overall gold & black scrolls & red trim, "Thrift Bank" in red on lower front, American Can Co., early 20th c., 5 1/2" h. (some wear) **$115**

Chief Big Moon - 42 - Indian seated in front of teepee holding fish w/flipping frog and pond, J. & E. Stevens, 1899, PL 108 .... **2,243**

Clown on Globe - 49 - w/turning & flipping mechanism, red & orange outfit, blue sphere & tan base, J. &. E. Stevens, 1890, coin trap missing (PL 127) **4,025**

Darktown Battery - 56 - three black baseball figures - pitcher, catcher, & batter - multicolored, known in rarer white player version, J. & E. Stevens, ca. 1888, probable repaint of pitcher, 9 3/4", PL 146 .... **1,840**

Indian Shooting Bear - 129 - Indian kneeling w/rifle shooting coin into bear, ca. 1883, 10 1/2" l., PL 257 (minor paint wear) **1,380**

Teddy and the Bear - 226 - Teddy Roosevelt shoots the bull's-eye, raises his head & the bear pops out of the brown tree, green base, J. & E. Stevens, ca. 1907, PL 459... **1,265**

Toad on Stump - 103 - (PL 475) **575**

Uncle Sam w/Satchel & Umbrella - 231 - coin is dropped into open satchel, w/moving hand & mouth, red, white, blue & gold, Shepard Hardware, PL 493.............. **1,955**

Pottery

Rare Redware Sgraffito Bank

Bulbous-form, redware w/sgraffito decoration, wide squatty rounded shape topped by a ringed knob finial, brown & pale amber glaze, the front incised overall w/flowering leafy vines, large birds, a flowerpot & the profile bust of a man wearing a hat, a coin slot on the shoulder above the inscription "William Mountjoy is a very good boy mad (sic) the 29 May 1839," Pennsylvania, professional repair, 5 3/4" h. (ILLUS.)... **4,888**

Green-glazed Spaniel Dog Bank

Model of a dog, seated spaniel facing viewer, overall dark green glaze, probably from Ohio & early 20th c., excellent condition, 5" h. (ILLUS.)..................................... **358**

Model of a frog, seated frog w/head high up, dark green alkaline glaze, probably early 20th c., excellent condition, 4" h. **88**

Still

Bear with Honey Pot Still Bank

*Bear - Bear with Honey Pot - 717 - cast iron, Hubley Mfg. Co., 1936, original gold paint, 6 1/2" h., W. 327 (ILLUS.) **187**

*Bear - Begging Bear - 715 - cast iron, A.C. Williams Co., original black paint, ca. 1910, Arcade Mfg. Co., 1910-25, 5 3/8" h. **144**

Black Boy - Two-Faced Black Boy (Negro Toy Bank) - 84 - cast iron, black, gold & silver, A.C. Williams Co., 1901-19, 3 1/8" h. (W. 44) **218**

Black Boy - Young Negro - 172 - cast iron, bust of black boy w/wide closed mouth, white collar, blue bow tie & red shirt, England, early 20th c., 4 1/2" h. **173**

Black Boy - Young Negro - 170 - cast iron, bust, embossed "The Young Nigger Bank" on back, England, 4 1/2" h. (W. 42) **345**

Black Man - Darkey (Sharecropper) - 173 - cast iron, w/toes visible on one foot, "Give Me A Penny" across his front, no paint, A.C. Williams Co., 1901, 5 1/2" h. (W. 18) **150**

*Boy Scout (Soldier Boy) - 45 - cast iron, original gold paint, A.C. Williams Co., 1910-34, 5 7/8" h. (W. 14) **150**

*Building - Colonial House (House with Porch) - 992 - cast iron, A.C. Williams Co., 1910-34, original silver & red paint, 2 3/4 x 3 7/8 x 4" h., W. 404 .... **201**

Buster Brown & Tige Still Bank

Buster Brown & Tige - 241 - cast iron w/gold finish, Tige sitting at Buster's feet, 5" h. (ILLUS.) **115**

*Cow - 553 - cast iron, standing animal, worn original gold paint, A.C. Williams Co., ca. 1920, 5 1/4" l., 3 3/8" h. (W. 200) **173**

Early Domed "Crystal Bank"

"Crystal Bank" - 926 - clear glass cylinder w/cast iron base & domed open rib top, Arcade Mfg. Co., 1910-25, 2 11/16" d., 3 7/8" h., W. 243 (ILLUS.) **144**

*Elephant - Elephant with Howdah (large) - 474 - cast iron, worn original paint, A.C.

Williams Co., 1910-30s, 6 3/8" l., 4 7/8" h. (W. 63) **69**

Foxy Grandpa (Grandpa Bank) - 320 - cast iron, w/screw, worn original gold paint, Wing Mfg. Co. 1900 & Hubley Mfg. Co. 1920s, 5 1/2" h. (W. 23) **196**

Globe - Globe Bank - 781 - cast iron, w/eagle on top, worn original red paint, Enterprise Mfg. Co., 1875, 5 3/4" h. **460**

Lincoln Hat Still Bank

Hat - Lincoln High Hat - 1380 - cast iron, "Pass Around the Hat," American-made, ca. 1882, 3" d., 2 3/8" h., W. 259 (ILLUS.) **201**

Humpty Dumpty (Seated) - cast iron, figure seated on stone wall, original polychrome paint, Shepard Hardware Co., early 20th c., similar to No. 337, 5 1/2" h. **546**

Pig - "Decker's Iowana" - 603 - cast iron, worn original gold paint, American-made, 4 3/8" l., 2 5/16" h. (W. 182) **104**

Pig - "I Made Chicago Famous" (small) - 629 - cast iron, J.M. Harper Co., original black paint, 1902, 4 1/8" l., 2 1/8" h. (W. 177) **184**

Pig - Republic Pig - 330 - cast iron, pig standing on hind legs & dressed in suit & tie, "Bank on Republic Pig Iron," Wilton Products, 1970, 7" h. **69**

Pig - "The Wise Pig" - 609 - painted cast iron, seated on haunches w/plaque w/writing across stomach, Hubley Mfg. Co., ca. 1930-36, 2 7/8" l., 6 5/8" h. (W. 175) **81**

*Rabbit - Begging Rabbit - 566 - cast iron, original gold body paint & red eyes, A.C. Williams Co., 1908-20s, 5 1/8" h. (W. 98) **92**

Rabbit - Bugs Bunny at Tree Trunk - 278 - white metal, Metal Moss Mfg. Co., late 1930s, original worn paint, 5 3/4" l., 5 1/2" h. **127**

Safe - "Junior Safe Deposit" - 897 - cast iron, combination lock, American-made, early 20th c., 2 1/8 x 3 3/8 x 4 5/8" h. **69**

BARBERIANA

A wide variety of antiques related to the tonsorial arts have been highly collectible for many years, especially 19th- and early-20th-century shaving mugs and barber bottles and, more recently, razors. We are now combining these closely related categories under one heading for easier reference. A selection of other varied pieces relating to barbering will also be found below.

Barber Bottles

Barber Bottle with White Mill Scene

Amethyst, footed bulbous base tapering to a ringed lady's leg neck, the side h.p. in white enamel w/a large scene of a water mill w/"Bay Rum" written above it, rolled lip, pontiled base, unusual scene, ca. 1900, 7 3/4" h. (ILLUS.) **$364**

Blue with Gold Art Nouveau Bottle

Cobalt blue, ovoid optic-ribbed body tapering to a lady's leg neck w/rolled lip, the sides h.p. in an Art Nouveau style decorated w/gold bands & stripes highlighted by stylized white & green blossoms, pontiled base, ca. 1900, 8 3/8" h. (ILLUS.) **392**

Blue Bottle with Fine Stag Decoration

Cobalt blue, footed optic-ribbed tapering conical shape, large oval reserve on the front w/a color transfer print of a large stag based on the Monarch of the Glen painting, gold scroll border & white enameled lily-of-the-valley trim, tooled lip, pontiled base, ca. 1900, 8" h. (ILLUS.) **392**

Cased Cranberry Hobnail Barber Bottle

Cranberry cased in clear, Hobnail patt., bulbous body tapering to a three-ringed cylindrical neck w/a tooled mouth, one hob w/small tip chip, ca. 1900, 7" h. (ILLUS.) **123**

Pretty Cologne Bottle with Swallows

Milk glass, slightly tapering cylindrical body w/a tall cylindrical neck w/rolled lip, a large arched central h.p. scene of a flock of flying blue swallows above pink rose vines, "Cologne" written across the top, pontiled base, ca. 1900, 8 3/4" h. (ILLUS.) **364**

Turquoise Blue Decorated Barber Bottle

Turquoise blue, optic ribbed w/footed spherical body & a tall double-ringed cylindrical neck w/tooled mouth, the sides enameled in color w/stripes of stylized tiny flowers & leaves, pontiled base, ca. 1900, 7 5/8" h. (ILLUS.) **112**

Mugs

Fraternal

Ancient Order of United Workmen Mug

Ancient Order of United Workmen, a large American shield on anchor logo flanked by leafy swags above the name in gold above the gold base band, "Elite - France" mark on the base, ca. 1900, 3 5/8" h. (ILLUS.) **90**

Unusual Fraternal Order Shaving Mug

P.C.R. - A.O.F. (above elk's head) - U.B.C., a gold emblem medal in the center front below the name in gold, possibly double-type for the Ancient Order of Foresters & the United Brotherhood of Carpenters, ca. 1900, 3 5/8" h. (ILLUS.)...... **134**

Occupational

Blacksmith Occupational Shaving Mug

Blacksmith, rectangular panel on the front w/a colored scene of a blacksmith shoeing a horse, floral sprigs at the sides & worn gold name above, base marked "Vienna, Austria," ca. 1900, 3 5/8" h. (ILLUS., two views) **115**

Electric trolley driver, a large h.p. colorful scene of a red open-sided trolley full of passengers, name in worn gold at top, gold bands below, "J. & C. - Bavaria" mark on base, ca. 1900, 3 7/8" h. (ILLUS.) **476**

Early Grocer's Shaving Mug

Rare Coal Wagon Driver Shaving Mug

Coal wagon driver, large h.p. color scene of a man driving a green coal wagon w/red wheels pulled by white horses, name in gold above & gold base band, ca. 1900, 3 5/8" h. (ILLUS.) **504**

Grocer, h.p. color scene of a grocery store front below the large gold name at the top framed w/delicate gold vining scrolls, gold band trim, ca. 1900, 3 1/2" h. (ILLUS.) **336**

Unusual Plumber Mug

Electric Trolley Driver Shaving Mug

Plumber, h.p. large color scene of a plumber working on a boiler w/a pedestal sink in the background, name in gold above & gold trim bands, "Germany" impressed in the base, ca. 1900, 3 3/4" h. (ILLUS.).......... **532**

Sportsman Shaving Mug

Sportsman, h.p. color scene of a hunter pointing his rifle w/his dog on point, lake & mountains in the background, name in gold at top, gold base bands, barber supply company name on base, 4" h. (ILLUS.) **308**

General Items

Early Koken White Porcelain Chair

Barber chair, white porcelain & brown leather, Koken hydraulic model, early 20th c., 46" h. (ILLUS.)................................ **863**

Green Barber Waste Bowl

Barber waste bowl, medium green glass, deep half-round optic-ribbed design enameled w/stylized florals & trimmed w/gold bands, smooth base, polished rim, ca. 1900, 2 3/4" h. (ILLUS.).................. **168**

Stars & Stripes Opalescent Waste Vase

Barber waste vase, cylindrical, opalescent blue in the Stars & Stripes patt., smooth base, tooled & polished rim, ca. 1900, 3 3/4" h. (ILLUS.) **112**

Mary Gregory Shaving Paper Vase

Shaving paper vase, cylindrical, cobalt blue w/Mary Gregory-style decoration in white enamel w/a Victorian girl & boy hitting a tennis ball over a net, smooth base, polished rim, unusual scene, ca. 1900, 7 1/4" h. (ILLUS.) **728**

Rare Blue Art Nouveau Paper Vase

Shaving paper vase, cylindrical frosted cobalt blue w/optic ribbing, smooth base,
polished rim, Art Nouveau decoration
w/gold bands & stripes highlighted w/styl-
ized large white & green florals, ca. 1900,
7 1/8" h. (ILLUS.) **952**

wreath w/pink blossoms & small orange &
blue leafy sprigs, pale yellow w/gold trim
around base, smooth base, polished rim,
late 19th - early 20th c., 8" h. (ILLUS.) **960**

BARBIE DOLLS & COLLECTIBLES

*At the time of her introduction in 1959, no one
could have guessed that this statuesque doll
would become a national phenomenon and eventually the most famous girl's plaything produced.*

*Over the years, Barbie and her growing range
of family and friends have evolved with the times,
serving as an excellent mirror of the fashion and
social changes taking place in American society.
Today, after more than 40 years of continuous
production, Barbie's popularity remains
unabated among both young girls and older collectors. Early and rare Barbies can sell for
remarkable prices, and it is every Barbie collector's hope to find mint condition "#1 Barbie."*

Dolls

Rare #1 Ponytail Barbie with Box

Barbie, "#1 Ponytail Barbie," display doll,
blonde hair in braid, pale red lips, cheek
blush, hoop earrings, finger & toe paint,
wearing #876 Sweater Girl outfit w/or-
ange knit shell & cardigan sweater, grey
flannel sheath skirt, black #1 open-toed
shoes, w/black pedestal stand & metal
prongs, near mint in box, box very good
condition (ILLUS.) **$9,000**

Green Cut to Clear Shaving Paper Vase

Shaving paper vase, cylindrical w/molded
rim, cut-overlay w/grass green cut to
clear w/a horizontal almond-shaped
bands, one w/cane cutting, punties & vertical almonds around the middle & a panel-cut base band, star-cut bottom, pol-
ished rim, ca. 1900, 8 1/8" h. (ILLUS.) **224**

Cherub-decorated Shaving Paper Vase

Shaving paper vase, milk glass, wide baluster form w/ringed base & flaring wide
mouth, a central color transfer of frolicking
cherubs surrounded by a h.p. green

#3 Ponytail Barbie as Registered Nurse

Barbie, "#3 Ponytail Barbie," straight-leg,
brunette hair, red lips, earring holes, finger & toe paint, wearing "Registered Nurse" outfit, doll in good condition w/some fading, rubbing & discoloration, outfit in very good condition, water bottle end torn off, glasses missing (ILLUS.) **550**

#4 Ponytail Barbie with Original Box

Barbie, "#4 Ponytail Barbie," straight-leg, blonde hair, red lips, nostril paint, cheek blush, earring holes, finger & toe paint, wearing black & white striped swimsuit, pearl earrings, glasses, booklet, wire & pedestal stand, partial box insert w/original box, new mint doll, box very good (ILLUS.) **550**

#3 Ponytail Barbie in Swimsuit

Barbie, "#3 Ponytail Barbie," straight-leg, brunette hair, red lips, nostril paint, earring holes, finger & toe paint, wearing black & white striped swimsuit, hair slightly fuzzy, bottom rubberband replaced, slight fading & discoloration (ILLUS.) **400**

#4 Ponytail Barbie as Candy Striper

Barbie, "#4 Ponytail Barbie," straight-leg, brunette hair, red lips, earring holes, nostril, finger & toe paint, wearing "Candy Striper" outfit, doll in fair condition w/stiff & fuzzy ponytail, some fading, discoloration & repainting, outfit w/blouse, pinafore & cap only age discolored, frayed & yellowed (ILLUS.) **225**

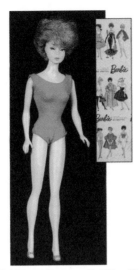

Bubblecut Barbie with Titian Hair

Barbie, "Bubblecut Barbie," straight-leg, titian hair, finger & toe paint, earring holes, wearing red nylon swimsuit, red open-toed shoes, pearl earrings, gold wire stand, very good condition w/some fading & discoloration, box in good condition, no box insert (ILLUS.) **130**

Barbie, "Japanese Side-part Barbie," straight-leg, ash blonde hair w/turquoise ribbon, red lips, cheek blush, nostril paint, wearing original multi-colored striped swimsuit, very good condition, eyelashes repainted, slight fading **875**

Swirl Ponytail Barbie in Original Case

Barbie, "Swirl Ponytail Barbie" in case, straight-leg, brunette hair in original set

w/yellow hair ribbon & metal hairpin, beige lips w/tint of orange, nostril, finger & toe paint, wearing original gold & white-striped swimsuit, in case w/white open-toed shows & Fashion Booklet & in cellophane bag, new mint (ILLUS.) **675**

Swirl Ponytail Blonde Barbie

Barbie, "Swirl Ponytail Barbie," straight-leg, platinum blonde hair, white lips, earring holes, finger & toe paint, wearing red nylon swimsuit & white open-toed shoes, hair slightly fuzzy, ends of ponytail straight, face slightly dark, very good condition (ILLUS.) **285**

Brunette Twist 'n Turn Barbie in Box

Near Mint Barbie & Ken Complete Gift Set

Barbie, "Twist 'n Turn Barbie," bent-leg, brunette hair w/plastic cover, pink lips, cheek blush, original colorful swimsuit, wrist tag, clear plastic stand & booklet, apparently never removed from box (ILLUS., bottom previous page)... **345**

Barbie & Ken Gift Set, includes a straight-legged Ken w/flocked brunette hair w/clear plastic bag cover, beige lips, wearing red knit swim trunks, striped jacket, wrist tag, in white cardboard box w/cardboard neck insert & black wire stand, also a #6 Ponytail Barbie, straight-legged w/titian hair in original set, light pink lips, finger & toe paint, wearing red nylon one-piece swimsuit, pearl earrings, wrist tag, booklet & red open-toed shoes, in white cardboard box w/cardboard foot & neck inserts & black wire stand, complete in original large box w/various outfits, never removed from box, near mint (ILLUS., top of page)................................ **1,700**

Bild Lilli, original German-made doll that inspired Barbie, blonde hair w/black velvet ribbon, red lips, nostril paint, black earrings, painted black shoes, wearing yellow print flannel skirt, black knit top & white knit shorts, w/a grey poodle & two Bild newspaper sections w/"Lilli" cartoon inside, very good condition, head & shoes repainted, hair slightly fuzzy, some body discoloration, newspapers discolored & w/cut-outs (ILLUS., next column) **2,500**

Rare Original German Bild Lilli Doll

Black Francie with Titian Hair

Francie, "Twist 'n Turn Francie," black complexion w/dark titian hair, bright pink lips, wearing original swimsuit, wrist tag, good condition w/some darkening & green toning, swimsuit age discolored, lightly soiled & w/hole in mesh at front (ILLUS.)..... **600**

"Mod Hair Ken" in Original Box

Ken, "Mod Hair Ken," No. 4224, never removed from box, 1972 (ILLUS.).................... **65**

Black Twist-'n-Turn Francie

Francie, Twist-'n-Turn model, black skin w/brunette hair w/original plastic cover, bright pink lips, original wrist tag, near mint (ILLUS.)... **1,000**

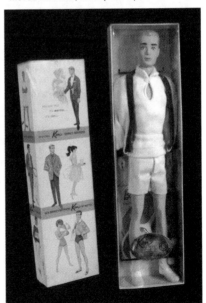

Straight-leg Ken in Original Box

Ken, straight-leg model, painted blonde hair, beige lips, wearing "Time For Tennis" outfit, apparently never removed from box, 1960s (ILLUS.)............................. **325**

Skooter Cut 'n Button Costumes Set in Original Box

Skooter Cut 'n Button Costumes Gift Set, straight-leg doll w/brunette hair w/original hair ribbon ties, beige lips w/tint of pink color, in box w/cardboard box insert, gold wire stand, booklet, instruction booklet, two-piece red & white swimsuit, red flat shoes, white plastic comb & brush, Sew-Free clothing well assembled, near mint (ILLUS.) **375**

Clothing & Accessories

Skipper's Irwin Roadster in Original Box

Automobile, Skipper's Irwin Roadster, green plastic w/orange plastic interior, white steering wheel, clear plastic windshield, grey wheel inserts, grey-painted accessories, cardboard Skipper form in seat, in box w/original cellophane cover, dated 1964, mint in box (ILLUS.) **550**

Barbie & Midge traveling case, blue vinyl w/pictures of Barbie & Midge on the front, includes accessories & two ca. 1960s Japanese Barbies & about 15 1960s & 1970s outfits, couple of splits in case, 13 1/2 x 17 1/2", the group (ILLUS., next column) **240**

Barbie & Midge Case & Accessories

Barbie Lamé Sheath Clothing Set

Clothing set, "Lamé Sheath," gold & navy blue w/navy blue open-toed shoes, gold clutch purse w/button accent, booklet, on card w/hanger in original Barbie Pak w/paper label & cellophane cover, never removed from package (ILLUS.) **195**

Original Barbie Metal Compact

Compact, round hinged goldtone metal w/"B" initial, very good condition, inner mirror scratched, indentation on bottom (ILLUS. of several views) **350**

Pillow, round, lavender w/yellow, black, pink & white illustrations of Barbie in various costumes & poses, "Barbie and Ken" in script in center, 1961, 11 1/2" d. **240**

BASEBALL MEMORABILIA

Baseball was reputedly invented by Abner Doubleday as he laid out a diamond-shaped field with four bases at Cooperstown, New York. A popular game from its inception, by 1869 it was able to support its first all-professional team, the Cincinnati Red Stockings. The National League was organized in 1876, and though the American League was first formed in 1900, it was not officially recognized until 1903. Today, the "national pastime" has millions of fans, and collecting baseball memorabilia has become a major hobby with enthusiastic collectors seeking out items associated with players such as Babe Ruth, Lou Gehrig, and others who became legends in their own lifetimes. Although baseball cards, issued as advertising premiums for bubble gum and other products, seem to dominate the field, there are numerous other items available.

Early Reach Sporting Goods Display

Advertising display, "'Reach' Sporting Goods," color-printed cardboard, large red lettering outlined in gold printed over the large standing image of an early pitcher atop a baseball w/the company logo, good color, fragile, early 20th c., 10 1/2 x 19" (ILLUS.) **$1,180**

1948 Ted Williams Nabisco Promotional Ring & Advertisement

Advertising promotional toy, Nabisco Ted Williams ring, a 1948 mail-in item, a gilt-metal ring stamped at the sides w/crossed bats & a baseball & topped by a spring-loaded figure of Ted Williams that actually swings the bat, w/an original printed advertisement w/some damage on the right end, ring in excellent condition (ILLUS. of two views & the ad, top of page) **369**

Album-scorecard, printed on stiff paper, from the 1910 World Series, white cover printed in black & white w/images of a walking bear cub approaching a rearing elephant, reads "Players in the World's Series - Baseball Championship- 1910 - Issued by The Chicago Daily News," 48 pp., 3 3/4 x 6 1/4" (ILLUS., next column) **513**

Bank, plastic, modeled as a conical red bat rack holding ten creamy yellow snap-on bats, sold via mail-order by Hillerich & Bradsby w/a red & blue cardboard tag & original cardboard shipping box w/company logo, 1960s, rack 6" h. (ILLUS. of bank & box, top next page) **327**

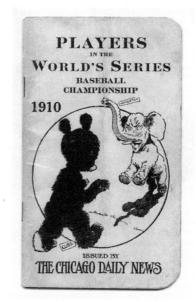

1910 World Series Album/Scorecard

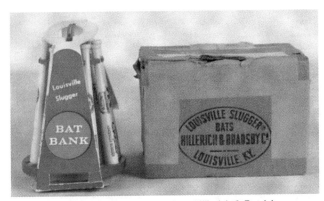

Baseball Bat Plastic Bank from Hillerich & Bradsby

1927 St. Louis Browns Signed Baseball

Baseball, 1927 St. Louis Browns team-signed ball, features 20 signatures including Wingard, Stewart, Bennett, Nevers & many more, shellacked (ILLUS.) **493**

Baseball, 1937 St. Louis Cardinals team-signed ball, twenty-five team members including Mize, Frisch, Martin, Durocher, Dean & Don Padgett, unofficial model, signed in blue fountain pen, well-toned (ILLUS. of two views, bottom of page) **658**

1989 Oakland Athletics Signed Ball

Baseball, 1989 Oakland Athletics team-signed ball, includes 24 team members from the World Champion team (ILLUS.)..... **598**

1937 St. Louis Cardinals Team-signed Baseball

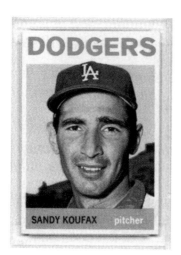

1964 Topps Sandy Koufax Card

Baseball card, Sandy Koufax, Topps, 1964, graded NM-MT 8, cased (ILLUS.).. **237**

Early Ty Cobb Piedmont Baseball Card

Baseball card, Ty Cobb, Detroit, Piedmont Cigarette series, advertising on the reverse, bright colors, early 20th c., rare, mounted in plastic block, card 1 1/2 x 2 1/2" (ILLUS.)................................. **720**

Ty Cobb "Bat on Shoulder" Card

Baseball card, Ty Cobb, T206, "bat on shoulder" pose, graded EX-MT 6, cased (ILLUS.).. **3,215**

Early Walter Johnson Baseball Card

Baseball card, Walter Johnson, T206, printed in color, graded EX-MT 6, in plastic case (ILLUS.) **2,381**

Part of the 1951 Topps Red Back Set

Baseball card set, 1951 Topps "Red Back" set, includes Kiner, Feller, Snider, Berra, Wynn, Hodges & more, grades EX/MT to VG, complete set of 52 (ILLUS. of part)....... **754**

1950s "Batter Rou Baseball Game"

Game, "Batter Rou Baseball Game," board-type, endorsed by Dizzy Dean, made by Memphis Plastic Enterprises, 1955, complete & near mint, box 9 x 19" (ILLUS. of complete game, top of page) **160**

Early "'Inside' Baseball" Board Game

Game, "'Inside' Baseball," board-type, square board w/rounded corners in lithographed tin showing a baseball diamond in green w/yellow & orange details, large metal spinner, w/all 20 of its player disks, featuring a 1913 World Series game between the Athletics & the Giants, w/original instructions, produced by Popular Games Co., overall excellent condition, board 17 1/2" sq. (ILLUS.) **506**

Gloves, souvenir-type, heavy white cloth w/thin black stripes, printed "Go Go - Sox," probably made for fans of the Chicago White Sox to wear during cold weather at games, handwritten illegible date on the wrist "1959," palms mildly soiled, pr. (ILLUS.) **244**

Lapel Pin with Photo of Johnny Evers

Lapel pin, oval celluloid center w/a photograph & name of Johnny Evers, ornate stamped scrolling brass frame, ca. 1915, minor damage but overall very good condition (ILLUS.) **332**

Letter, handwritten in blue ink on paper, written to "Shoeless" Joe Jackson by Bill Justus, requesting help in finding employment, postmarked April 16, 1937, w/envelope, 8 1/2 x 11" **127**

Chicago White Sox Souvenir Gloves

Early Commemorative Baseball Mug

1945 Chicago Cubs Pennant

1960 New York Yankees Pennant

Mug, stoneware, commemorative-type, yellow exterior printed in dark blue "Globe Base Ball Association - Warwick Club - Sept. 15, 1907," central caricature figure of the league-sponsoring Globe newspaper, excellent condition, 4 3/8" h. (ILLUS., bottom previous page) **562**

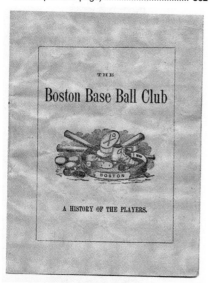

Early Boston Base Ball Club Pamphlet

Pamphlet, "The Boston Base Ball Club - A History of the Players," published in 1873 to promote the credibility of baseball in general, biographical sketches of players, yellow paper covers, 16 pp., overall excellent condition, 4 1/4 x 5 1/2" (ILLUS.) **1,558**

Pennant, printed felt, Chicago Cubs, dark green w/white animal mascots & wording, reads "World Series - Chicago Cubs - 1945," small hole through reinforcing felt, overall excellent condition, 25" l. (ILLUS., top of page) **543**

Pennant, printed felt, New York Yankees, blue w/white wording & pink & red top hat logo, reads "American League Champions - New York Yankees - 1960," roster list of players at wide end, fine condition (ILLUS., second from top)........................... **150**

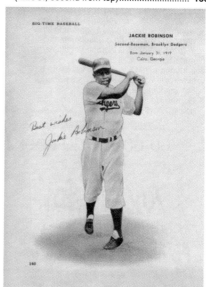

Jackie Robinson Autographed Photo

Photograph, full-length printed photo pose of Jackie Robinson swinging a bat, boldly signed by him, the reverse of this page w/a photo of Pee Wee Reese & also signed by him, from Big-Time Baseball, near mint, 8 x 10 1/2" (ILLUS., bottom previous page) **991**

Babe Ruth-inscribed 1930s Photograph

Photograph, sepia-toned photo of Babe Ruth in a batting pose, inscribed to a teammate, Jimmie Reese, and dated 1931, overall excellent condition, 3 x 4" (ILLUS.)...................................... **1,454**

Roberto Clemente-signed Photograph

Photograph, team-issued color portrait of Roberto (Bob) Clemente, printed signature & actual blue ink autograph on the photo, ca. late 1960s, near mint (ILLUS.) **1,072**

Pinback button, advertising-type, "Morton's Buster Brown Bread," yellow ground printed w/a picture of Buster Brown in red, blue & white along w/the small figure of a tiger leaning on a baseball bat, a large circle w/a black & white photo image of a smiling Ty Cobb, produced around 1908-1910 to

Rare Buster Brown Pin with Ty Cobb Photo

appeal to fans of the Detroit Tigers baseball team, overall excellent condition, 1 1/4" d. (ILLUS.)...................................... **1,475**

Scarce Federal League Booster Pin

Pinback button, souvenir-type, celluloid printed in red & white to resemble a baseball w/crossed bats in the lower section, red & white wording reads "Booster - Federals - 1914," from the short-lived Federal League, near mint condition, 7/8" d. (ILLUS.)... **185**

Early Babe Ruth Souvenir Pinback

Pinback button, souvenir-type, large celluloid w/black & white half-length photo of Babe Ruth at bat, sold by vendors at Yankee Stadium, ca. 1920s-30s, excellent condition, 1 3/4" d. (ILLUS., bottom previous page) **591**

(BACK)

(FRONT)

Rare World Series Ticket Stub Signed by Ruth & Gehrig

Ticket stub, 1926 game four of the World Series, autographed across the back by Babe Ruth & Lou Gehrig in black fountain pen, the front w/printed seat information & an owner-penned inscription "Babe Ruth hit 3 home-runs - Oct. 6th 1926 - New York vs St Louis," actual game date was October 7th, rare, 2 x 4 1/4" (ILLUS. of front & back, top of page)... **3,335**

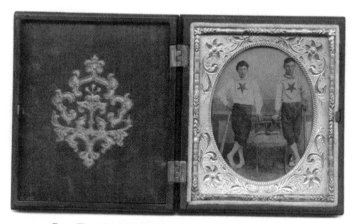

Rare Tintype of Candy Cummings & Another Ballplayer

Tintype, 1/6th plate, rare cased image of ballplayer Candy Cummings, inventor of the curveball, posed on the left w/an unknown player, one of only four known images of Cummings, mid-19th c., closed 3 1/4 x 3 3/4" (ILLUS. open)... **407**

Rare Early Tobacco Silk Premium Featuring Baseball Players

Rare Tintype of an Early Baseball Team

Tintype, framed & matted image of eight members of the Norway Lake, Maine, baseball team in full uniform & w/equipment, fine bright image, excellent condition, second half 19th c., image 2 1/4 x 3 1/2" (ILLUS.).............................. **1,180**

Tobacco silk, No. S110, a large white square printed in color w/five images of period baseball players in action, a baseball diamond & equipment around the center, early 20th c., overall excellent condition, framed, 27 x 28" (ILLUS., top of page).. **3,557**

BASKETS

The American Indians were the first basket weavers on this continent and, of necessity, the early Colonial settlers and their descendants pursued this artistic handicraft to provide essential containers for berries, eggs and endless other items to be carried or stored. Rye straw, split willow and reeds are but a few of the wide variety of materials used. Nantucket baskets, plainly and sturdily constructed, along with those made by specialized groups, would seem to draw the greatest attention to this area of collecting.

Miniature "Buttocks" Basket

"**Buttocks**" **basket,** miniature, woven splint, 16-rib construction, flat bentwood handle, varnished, very good color, 6 1/2" l., 4" h. plus handle (ILLUS., bottom previous page) **$104**

Blue-painted "Buttocks" Basket

"**Buttocks**" **basket,** woven splint, 24-rib construction, bentwood handle, original blue paint, 12 1/2" l., 6 1/2" h. (ILLUS.)........ **460**

Red-painted Gathering Basket

Gathering basket, woven splint, round w/deep sides & wrapped rim, arched carved bail handle, shaded red paint w/blue & white lashing & white free-hand decoration on the handle, America, 19th c., wear, one break on the lashing, 14 1/2" d., 11 1/4" h. (ILLUS.) **411**

Green-painted Gathering Basket

Gathering basket, woven splint, round w/deep sides, wrapped rim & bentwood swing handle, kicked-up base, old green paint, broken splints w/some missing around the rim, America, 19th c., 16" d., 17 1/2" h. (ILLUS.) **460**

Large Splint "Melon" Basket

"**Melon**" **basket,** woven splint, 34-rib construction, oblong w/bentwood handle, tightly woven w/good patina, minor splint break on bottom, America, 19th c., 18" l., 16" h. (ILLUS.) **201**

Fine Quality Nantucket Basket

Nantucket basket, finely woven splint, deep round sides w/wrapped rim & carved swing handle, turned wooden base w/two incised lines, America, late 19th - early 20th c., 5 3/8" d., overall 7" h. (ILLUS.)... **3,819**

Nantucket basket, finely woven splint, oval w/wrapped rim, carved wood swing handle secured w/brass ears, turned oval wood bottom, probably late 19th - early 20th c., 11 1/4" d., 7" h. (a few breaks & losses on side & rim lashing) **294**

Nantucket basket, finely woven splint, deep round sides w/wrapped rim & carved wood swing handle, turned wood bottom, America, late 19th c., 8 1/4" d. height overall 9 3/4" h. **588**

Nantucket basket, finely woven splint, slightly tapering round shape w/wrapped rim & carved bentwood swing handle secured w/brass ears, turned wood base, probably 20th c., 9" d., height w/handle 11"... **441**

Deep Rounded Shaker Basket

Shaker basket, woven splint, deep round sides w/wrapped rim & high arched carved handle w/letters "OLS" pyrographically pricked into both ends, Mount Lebanon, New York, late 19th c., some losses, 11 1/4" d., 14 1/4" h. (ILLUS.).......... **206**

BIRDCAGES

Large Victorian Building-form Birdcage

Ornate Bronze Birdcage

Bronze, in the Chinese Chippendale taste, the long rectangular wire-sided cage surmounted by three stepped pagoda-form structures, raised on cluster square legs, the whole accented w/gilt & patination & mounted w/floral bosses & fret piercings, Europe, 19th c., 21 x 60 1/2", 7' h. (ILLUS.)... **$10,350**

Gilt-metal & wood, model of an elaborte palazzo-style house w/Gothic arch windows & arcade, the rectangular deep base carved to resemble stone blocks w/a large flight of stairs at the front, late 19th c., 15 x 24", 19" h. .... **1,000 - 1,500**

Wire & wicker, tall octagonal form w/wire sides & laced wicker between the shaped roof supports, wire pagoda-style roof w/turned wood center finial, stepped base w/removable floor, painted pale green, Victorian, 18" w., 29" h....................... **220**

Wire & wood, building-shaped, multi-tiered w/three peaked roof sections, removable bottom tray slides out from front, three trapeze bars & four doors, Victorian, 21 1/2 x 37 1/2", 28" h. (ILLUS., next column).. **460**

BLACK AMERICANA

Over the past decade or so, this field of collecting has rapidly grown. Today almost anything that relates to Black culture or illustrates Black Americana is considered a desirable collectible. Although many representations of African-Americans, especially on 19th- and early-20th-century advertising pieces and housewares, were cruel stereotypes, even these are collected as poignant reminders of how far American society has come since the dawning of the Civil Rights movement, and how far we still have to go. Other pieces related to this category will be found from time to time in such categories as Advertising Items, Banks, Character Collectibles, Kitchenwares, Signs and Signboards, Toys and several others. For a complete overview of this subject see Antique Trader Black Americana Price Guide, 2nd Edition.

Candy box, cardboard, "Bamboo Coons - National Candy Co. Detroit," rectangular, the lid in black & white w/border of bamboo sticks framing scene of a chubby African native child perched on a vine, the sides of the box decorated w/heads of other children, late 19th - early 20th c., unlisted, rare, light overall soiling, 6 1/2 x 9", 2 1/4" h. (ILLUS. of two views, bottom of page)... **$754**

Rare "Bamboo Coons" Candy Box

Black Fireman Head Containers

Dog & Black Newsboy Clock

Clock, bronzed cast-metal, figural, the cast in the form of a large shaggy walking dog w/African-American newsboy on his back, the dial of clock in the side of the dog, dial marked "Regent Mfg. Co., Chicago," works stamped "Patented...Jan. 13, 1891," not working, 7" l. (ILLUS.) **288**

Wolfe Studio "Aunt Jemima" Jar

Cookie jar, "Aunt Jemima," ceramic, polka dot dress, plaid kerchief & striped apron w/wording, artist-made, Wolfe Studio, Michigan, modern (ILLUS.) **225**

Rare Elongated Body Butler Jar

Cookie jar, Basket Handle Butler figure, elongated body, herringbone trousers, mate to Mammy w/elongated body, Japan, 8 1/2" h. (ILLUS.) **3,000**
Cookie jar, Black Fireman, smiling head w/mustache & red helmet complete w/badge, wire bail handle, Japan (ILLUS. second from right w/other Black Fireman pieces, top of page) **500-700**

Polka Dot Mammy Creamer, Sugar & Teapot

"Objective Save Hip Hop" Astronaut Dolls

Creamer, Polka Dot Mammy, ceramic, figural Polka Dot Mammy w/plaid apron, loop handles (ILLUS. front right with Polka Dot Mammy sugar bowl & teapot, top of page) **800**

Doll, De La Soul doll, jointed vinyl, figures of Pos, Dave & Maseo dressed as astronauts, box marked "De La Soul - Objective Save Hip Hop," by Maru & Daisy Age, Inc., made in China, 2003, each (ILLUS. of three, second from top) **75**

Doll, Knickerbocker cloth "Beloved Belindy," round paper hang-tag marked "Raggedy Ann's Beloved Belindy - A Character Created by Johnny Gruelle - © Bobbs-Merrill Co., Inc., 1965 - Joy of a Toy™ - Knickerbocker - Knickerbocker Toy Company Inc., New York, U.S.A. - Exclusive Manufacturer," dress tag reads "Beloved Belindy - © Bobbs-Merrill Co., Inc. 1965 - CAL-T-5 All New Material," brown body, black plastic disk eyes w/white circles, single stroke brows, red triangle nose, body w/molded & painted socks & shoes, wearing original red & white dress w/stars, brown plaid shawl & bandanna & white lace-trimmed apron, holding un-jointed bisque white baby w/molded bonnet in long lace-trimmed dress, overall excellent condition, 7 1/2" (ILLUS.)............. **600**

Beloved Belindy Doll in Original Box

closed smiling mouth surrounded by white area, jointed at shoulders, elbows, hips & knees, red & white striped legs w/red feet, wearing original red kerchief, dress w/red & white polka dot bodice & yellow & white skirt w/white apron, pantaloons, unplayed-with in original box, 15" (ILLUS.).. **925**

Finely Detailed Black Stockinette Doll

Doll, stockinette black lady, black stockinette head sewn on black cloth body, exaggerated needle sculptured features, black shoe button eyes w/white backgrounds, black embroidered brows, red embroidered nostril accents, red embroidered mouth, needle sculptured ears, short black wool curls, cloth body w/upper arms, lower arms, upper legs & lower legs made separately & sewn together, mitten hands w/stitched thumb, front of foot made separately, bias tape down back seam, wearing probably original red print dress, white apron & pants, overall excellent condition, late 19th - early 20th c., 20" (ILLUS.) **1,025**

Doll, stockinette WPA Little Black Sambo, stamped on lower back "WPA - Handi-craft - Project #860 - Milwaukee, Wisconsin - Sponsored by Milwaukee County and Milwaukee State Teachers College," also marked on jacket & shoes "Designed by Helen Clark," the stockinette head painted brown w/brown eyes, closed mouth, curly black cotton string hair, brown cloth body tab-jointed at shoulders & hips, stitched fingers & separate thumb, hard soles on round feet w/no toes, wearing original red double-breasted jacket, blue short pants & purple & red shoes, slight fading & wear, 1930s, 22" (ILLUS., top next page)........... **1,850**

Kuhnlenz Black Mammy & Baby Dolls

Doll, Kuhnlenz (Gebruder) bisque socket head black Mammy & baby, marked "34.17," black head w/set dark pupiless eyes, open mouth w/four upper teeth, yarn or string wig, five-piece composition

Scarce WPA Little Black Sambo Doll

Terri Lee "Patti Jo" Girl Doll

Doll, Terri Lee "Patti Jo," marked "Terri Lee" on head, "Terri Lee - Pat. Pending" on back, Terri Lee tag on the coat, brown hard plastic head, painted brown eyes, accented nostrils, closed red mouth, original black synthetic wig, five-piece hard plastic body, wearing blue & white gingham dress w/white pleated trim, matching panties, replaced socks & vinyl shoes, navy blue coat w/red trim, black

snood on hair, some flaking on body & slight color wear, 1950s, 16" (ILLUS.) **525**

Discontinued Tupac Shakur Doll

Doll, Tupac Shakur, jointed vinyl, from All Entertainment, Inc., China, 2002, produced without proper permission & discontinued (ILLUS.) **250**

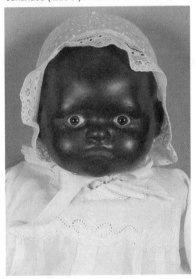

Black Wax Dream Baby Doll

Doll, wax Dream Baby, marked "A.M. - 341 - Germany," poured black wax head, set brown glass eyes, closed mouth, cloth body w/black wax over composition hands, wearing a white baby dress made w/early fabric, old slip & flannel diaper, antique bonnet, only light flaking, shoulder seams restitched, 17" (ILLUS.) **468**

Two Views of a Wavine Hair Dressing Jar

Hair dressing jar, "Wavine Hair Dressing," cylindrical glass jar w/twist-off metal lid, wrap-around paper label w/sketched portrait of pretty black girl w/long wavy hair, Boyd Mfg. Co., Birmingham, Alabama, ca. 1930s (ILLUS. of two views, top of page)...... **150**

of woman on front, Newbro Mfg. Co., Atlanta, Georgia, early 20th c., some wear (ILLUS.)... **75**

Queen Hair Dressing Tin

Hair dressing tin, "Queen Hair Dressing," printed metal w/snap-on lid, small picture

"Joe Louis Hair Pomade" Tin

Hair pomade tin, "Joe Louis Hair Pomade," low round printed metal tin, photo of Joe Louis on cover, Joe Louis Products Co., Chicago, ca. 1950s (ILLUS.)........................ **200**

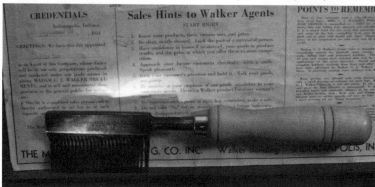

Madam C.J. Walker Hair Pressing Comb

Hair pressing comb, turned wood handle, steel comb, Madam C.J. Walker name marked on the comb, early 20th c.(ILLUS.) **350**

Hattie McDaniel Signed Photograph

Photograph, black & white portrait of actress Hattie McDaniel shown wearing long mink coat & standing by fireplace of her Beverly Hills home, personally inscribed & dated 1944, minor border tear (ILLUS.) **759**

Early Gold Dust Pinback Button

Pinback button, celluloid, "Gold Dust Washing Powder," color design of large crossed American flags against white background above black & gold logo w/Gold Dust twins, red & blue wording reads "The Best Flag - The Best Cleaner. - You Can't Beat Them!," ca. 1898, 1 1/4" d. (ILLUS.) **193**

Pitcher, cov., Black Mammy, water-type, ceramic, Weller lookalike Mammy figure w/her white kerchiefed head forming the cover, wearing white & blue plaid dress w/large blue-dotted white apron, Maruhon Ware, Japan (ILLUS. back row far left with other Maruhon Ware pieces) **1,000**

Poster for "Black Patti Troubadours"

Poster, "Black Patti Troubadours," printed in dark blue on white, a large round cover photo of a smiling May Lang, The Louisiana Lassie, ca. 1890, 21 x 28" (ILLUS.) **230**

Rare Josephine Baker 1930s Poster

Poster, "Josephine Baker," large stylized Art Deco bust portrait of Baker by Jean Chassaing, Paris, 1931, large size, rare (ILLUS.) **16,100**

African Woman Head Salt & Peppers

Salt & pepper shakers, Black Fireman, smiling head w/mustache & red helmet complete w/badge, wire bail handle, Japan, pr. (ILLUS. far left w/other Black Fireman pieces, top of page 54) **150**

Salt & pepper shakers, ceramic, figural, exaggerated head of African woman w/red lips, Japan, ca. 1940, pr. (ILLUS., top of page) **125**

Black Rag Doll with Embroidery

Rag doll, black cloth w/unjointed neck, facial features embroidered w/tan floss, hair indicated w/black floss embroidery, body stitch-jointed at shoulders, elbows, hips & knees, no detail of fingers or toes on hands & feet, wearing plaid dress w/smocked bodice, large white collar & cuffs, matching pants, white apron w/eyelet trim, light wear, spots of soil on upper left leg, early 20th c., 22" (ILLUS.) **400**

"Cuban Giants Schottische" Sheet Music

Sheet music, "Cuban Giants Schottische," by T.E. Townsend, refers to a championship Black baseball team, black wording on white, 1888 (ILLUS.) **311**

Fine Venetian Carved Blackamoors

Stands, carved, ebonized & gilded wood, the base carved as full-figure kneeling blackamoor boy wearing short breeches carved to simulate woven grass & fitted w/painted mother-of-pearl eyes, each figure supporting a round top w/gilded chain border, figure on carved tasseled cushion, Venice, Italy, 19th c., 11 1/4" d., 21" h., pr. (ILLUS., top of page) **6,900**

Sugar bowl, Polka Dot Mammy, ceramic, figural Polka Dot Mammy w/plaid apron, loop handle (ILLUS. front left with Polka Dot Mammy creamer & teapot) **1,000**

Sugar bowl (or jam jar), cov., Black Mammy, ceramic, Weller lookalike Mammy figure w/her white kerchiefed head forming the cover, wearing white & blue plaid dress w/large blue-dotted white apron, Maruhon Ware, Japan **800**

Syrup pitcher (or creamer), cov., Black Mammy, ceramic, Weller lookalike Mammy figure w/her red kerchiefed head forming the cover, wearing white & red plaid dress w/large red-dotted white apron, Maruhon Ware, Japan **800**

Teapot, Black Fireman, smiling head w/mustache & red helmet complete w/badge, wire bail handle, Japan (ILLUS. third from left w/other Black Fireman pieces)... **450**

Teapot, Black Mammy, ceramic, figural, modeled as black Mammy w/the base formed by her wide green skirt & apron, holding a long red wedge of watermelon at front, yellow blouse & white striped kerchief, bottom marked "USA," overall crazing, 8" l., 8" h. (ILLUS., next column) **94**

Teapot, Black Mammy, ceramic, Weller lookalike Mammy figure w/her red kerchiefed head forming the cover, wearing white & red plaid dress w/large red-dotted white apron, Maruhon Ware, Japan **1,200**

Colorful Black Mammy Teapot

Teapot, Polka Dot Mammy, ceramic, figural Polka Dot Mammy w/plaid apron, loop handle (ILLUS. back center with Polka Dot Mammy creamer & sugar bowl) **2,000**

Rare Polka Dot Mammy Teapot

Teapot, Polka Dot Mammy, ceramic, head of Polka Dot Mammy, Japan, ca. 1940s (ILLUS.)... **1,000**

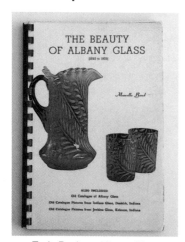

Walking Stick with Finely Carved Head

Walking stick, carved ebony, the handle finely carved w/the head of grinning black man wearing a link silver chain necklace, an elephant ivory ring collar separating the top from the lower ebony shaft ending in an ivory tip, found in England, ca. 1890, overall 35 1/2" l. (ILLUS. of part)........ **784**

BOOKS

Antiques-Related

Early Book on Albany Glass

Bond, Marcelle, "The Beauty of Albany Glass, 1893-1902," copyright 1972, Pub-

lishers Printing House, Berne, Indiana (ILLUS.).. **$16**

Buxton Roseville Pottery Book

Buxton, Virginia, "Roseville Pottery - For Love or Money," 1977, color & black & white, hard cover, 320 pp., original dust jacket w/tear in the back, 7 1/4 x 10" (ILLUS.) **196**

Book on Pincushion Dolls

Marion, Frieda, "China Half-figures Called Pincushion Dolls," Collector Books, 1977 reprint (ILLUS.) **30**

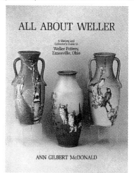

McDonald "All About Weller" Book

McDonald, Ann Gilbert, "All About Weller - A History and Collector's Guide to Weller Pottery, Zanesville, Ohio," 1989, color & black & white, soft covers, 220 pp., 8 3/8 x 11" (ILLUS., bottom previous page) **81**

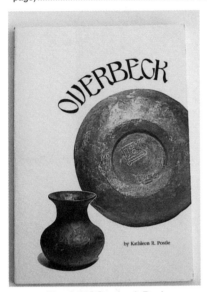

Reprint of Overbeck Book

Postle, Kathleen R., "Overbeck," copyright 1978 by The Indiana Historical Society, 1998 reprint by Western Wayne Heritage shown (ILLUS.) **15**

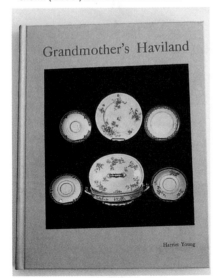

"Grandmother's Haviland" Book

Young, Harriet, "Grandmother's Haviland," 1970, Wallace-Homestead Book Co. (ILLUS.) **31**

BOTTLES

Bitters

(Numbers with some listings below refer to those used in Carlyn Ring's For Bitters Only.)

Brown's Bitters in Unusual Coloring

Brown's Celebrated Indian Herb Bitters - Patented Feb. 11, 1868, figural Indian queen, inward rolled mouth, smooth base, unusual coloring w/arms & upper body in yellow w/a hint of green, head-dress & lower portion in yellowish amber, highlighted by old red & yellow paint, 12 1/8" h. (ILLUS.) **$1,792**

Rare Cannon's Dyspeptic Bitters Bottle

Cannon's Dyspeptic Bitters, square w/beveled corners & sloped shoulder, a stack of six cannon barrels embossed on three of the sides, additional decoration on the shoulders & top portion of the labeled panel, applied sloping collared mouth, smooth base, golden amber, small flat flake from side of mouth, tiny flake off one of the cannonballs at the base of one corner, some stain on mouth, 1860-80, 9 5/8" h. (ILLUS.) **5,040**

DeAndries Sarsaparilla Bitters Bottle

DeAndries (Dr.) - Sarsaparilla Bitters - E.M. Rusha New Orleans, rectangular w/paneled sides, columnar corners, applied sloping collar mouth, smooth base, root beer amber, some exterior highpoint wear & scratches, 10" h. (ILLUS.) **1,349**

Apricot Strawberry Puce Drake's Bitters

Drake's (S T) - 1860 - Plantation - X - Bitters - Patented - 1862, cabin-shaped, six-log, applied sloping collared mouth, smooth base, brilliant medium apricot strawberry puce, 10" h., D-105 (ILLUS.) **420**

Drake's (S T) - 1860 - Plantation - X - Bitters - Patented - 1862, cabin-shaped, six-log, brilliant apricot puce, 10" h., D-105 (ILLUS., top of next column) **1,344**

Apricot Puce Drake's Plantation Bitters

S.T. Drake's Plantation Bitters in Yellow

Drake's (S T) - 1860 - Plantation - X - Bitters - Patented - 1862, cabin-shaped, four-log, applied sloping collar mouth, ca. 1862-70, yellowish w/a hint of green, 10" h., D-110 (ILLUS.) **1,904**

Another Greeley's Bourbon Bitters

Greeley's Bourbon Bitters, barrel-shaped, ten rings above & below center band, applied mouth, smooth base, ca. 1855-70, medium puce w/grey tone, 9" h. (ILLUS., bottom previous page) **728**

Herkules Bitters Bottle with Label

Herkules Bitter - AC (monogram) - 1 Quart, ball-shaped, tooled mouth w/ring, two flattened side panels, one panel w/full original paper label, emerald green, 1870-90, 7 1/2" h. (ILLUS. of bottle & label) **2,016**

Greeley's Bourbon Bitters in Grey Puce

Greeley's Bourbon Bitters, barrel-shaped, ten rings above & below center band, applied mouth, smooth base, ca. 1855-70, light to medium grey puce, 9 1/4" h. (ILLUS.) **1,344**

Greeley's Bitters in Unusual Puce Color

Greeley's Bourbon Bitters, barrel-shaped, ten rings above & below center band, applied square collared mouth, smooth base, ca. 1860-80, bright medium greyish puce, 9" h. (ILLUS.) **532**

Holtzermann's Stomach Bitters Bottle

Holtzermann's - Patent - Stomach - Bitters, cabin-shaped, four-roof, applied sloping collared mouth, smooth base, ca. 1860-80, golden amber w/red tone, 9 1/4" h. (ILLUS.) **2,128**

Nice National Bitters Figural Bitters

National Bitters, figural ear of corn, "Patent 1867" on base, applied sloping collared mouth w/ring, smooth base, yellowish amber, ca. 1870, 12 1/2" h. (ILLUS.) **672**

Fine Romaine's Crimean Bitters Bottle

Romaine's Crimean Bitters - W. Chilton & Co., square modified cabin form w/paneled sides, columnar corners & angled paneled shoulder, "Romaine's Crimean Bitters - Patend 1863" around base band, applied sloping collared mouth, smooth base, yellowish amber, gouge on neck just below collar, ca. 1860-80, 10 1/8" h. (ILLUS.).. **784**

Seward & Bentley - Buffalo. N.Y. - Constitution - Bitters, rectangular w/paneled sides, applied sloping collared mouth, smooth base, brilliant golden amber w/reddish tone, 1860-70, 9 3/8" h. (ILLUS., top next column) **1,792**

Seward & Bentley Constitution Bitters

Tippecanoe Bitters in Rare Color

Tippecanoe (birch bark & canoe design), H.H. Warner & Co., cylindrical, "Patent Nov. 20. 83 - Rochester - N.Y. - 2" on smooth base, applied disc mouth, yellow olive, 9" h. (ILLUS.)................................... **3,920**

Rare Travellers Bitters Bottle

Travellers Bitters, rectangular w/rounded side panels, cabin-like shoulder, front panel embossed w/a figure of a man walking w/a cane (Robert E. Lee), applied sloping collared mouth, smooth base, golden amber, 1860-80, small flat chip on base, pinpoint bruise to right of figure, minor exterior wear & scratches, rare, 10 1/2" h. (ILLUS.) **5,320**

Figurals

Early Russian Bear Bottle

Bear, sitting up w/collar suspending a shield-shaped medallion on its chest, medallion lettered "BABOAB - WPP-MTEPA," a cylindrical neck w/bulbed base at the top, on a molded rectangular base, dense yellow olive, probably Russia, 1860-70, some separation of glass near left foot & base, chip & bruise w/line below right foot, early Kummel bear, 10 1/4" h. (ILLUS.) **308**

Fine Cobalt Blue Figural Clam Bottle

Clam, ground lip, smooth base, threaded neck for metal cap, ca. 1885-95, cobalt blue, no metal cap, 5" h. (ILLUS.) **1,064**

Flasks

Flasks are listed according to the numbers provided in American Bottles & Flasks and Their Ancestry *by Helen McKearin and Kenneth M. Wilson.*

Green Washington-Eagle Flask

GI-14 - Washington bust below "General Washington" - American eagle w/shield w/seven bars on breast, head turned to right, "E Pluribus Unum" in semicircle above, vertically ribbed edges, w/"Adams & Jefferson July 4. A.D. 1776" & "Kensington Glassworks Philadelphia," pontil scarred base, sheared & tooled lip, bright medium green, chip on edge of pontil, pt. (ILLUS.) **$6,160**

Fine Washington - Frigate Flask

GI-28 - Washington bust below "Albany Glass Works," "Albany NY" below bust - full-rigged ship sailing to right, applied sloping collared mouth, pontil scar, vertically ribbed edges, strongly embossed, bright aqua, pt. (ILLUS.) **672**

Deep Amethyst Washington - Taylor Flask

Gl-38 - Washington bust below "The Father of His Country" - Taylor bust below "Gen. Taylor Never Surrenders" & "Dyottville Glass Works Philada.," smooth base, sheared mouth, medium to deep grey amethyst, tiny shallow mouth flake, pt. (ILLUS.) **5,040**

Rare Blue Washington - Taylor Flask

Gl-40b - Washington bust below "The Father of His Country" - Taylor bust below "Genl Taylor Never Surrenders," four buttons on his coat, smooth edges, applied double collared lip, pontil scar, midnight blue, pt. (ILLUS.) **7,840**

Cobalt Blue Washington - Taylor Flask

Gl-40b - Washington bust below "The Father of His Country" - Taylor bust below "Genl Taylor Never Surrenders," four buttons on his coat, smooth edges, sheared mouth, pontil scar, shape slightly elongated, cobalt blue, pt. (ILLUS.) **4,480**

Washington Flask in Cobalt Blue

Gl-42 - Washington bust below "The Father of His Country" - Taylor bust, "A Little More Grape Captain Bragg," pontil scarred base, sheared mouth, deep cobalt blue, heavy scratching & high point wear, qt. (ILLUS.) **7,840**

Orangish Amber Washington - Taylor Flask

Washington/Taylor Flask

GI-54 - Washington bust without queue, bust of Taylor in uniform, smooth base, applied mouth, deep olive yellow, qt. (ILLUS.)........ **4,480**

Yellow Washington - Taylor Flask

GI-55 - Washington bust w/short queue & plain toga - Taylor bust w/collar decoration missing, smooth edges, sheared mouth, pontil scar, yellow w/a topaz tone, pt. (ILLUS.).. **3,360**

Emerald Green Washington-Taylor Flask

GI-54 - Washington bust without queue - Taylor bust in uniform, open pontil, applied sloping double collar mouth, medium to deep emerald green, qt. (ILLUS.)....... **952**

GI-55 - Washington bust w/short queue & plain toga - Taylor bust w/collar decoration missing, smooth edges, sheared mouth, pontil scar, orangish amber, shallow small flake on top of mouth, pt. (ILLUS., top next column)... **840**

Washington Flask in Scarce Color

GI-55 - Washington & Taylor busts, open pontil, sheared lip, many air bubbles, medium amber, pt. (ILLUS., bottom previous page) **3,640**

Yellowish Lafayette - Clinton Flask

GI-80 - "Lafayette" above bust & "T. S." & bar below - "De Witt Clinton" above bust & "Coventry C-T" below, corrugated edges, sheared mouth, pontil, bright yellowish olive w/a lot of yellow, pt. (ILLUS.) **1,904**

Pure Green Lafayette/Clinton Flask

GI-81a - Lafayette bust w/"Lafayette" & "S & C - De Witt Clinton" above/Clinton bust facing right above "C-T," corrugated edges, scarred base, sheared & tooled lip, a true medium olive green without any trace of amber, surface flake off inside edge of lip, 1/2 pt. (ILLUS.) **4,760**

Lafayette - Masonic Arch Flask

GI-84 - "Lafayette" above bust & "T. S." & bar below - Masonic arch, pillar & pavement w/Masonic emblem inside arch, horizontal corrugated edges, horizontal rib at base, sheared mouth, pontil, yellow olive, roughness & chipping to lower portion of side seam during making, 1/2 pt. (ILLUS. of flask & close-up on side seam) **4,480**

Lafayette-Liberty Cap Flask

GI-85 - "Lafayette" above bust & "Covetry [sic] - C-T" below - French liberty cap on pole & semicircle of eleven five-pointed stars above, "S & S" below, fine vertical ribbing, two horizontal ribs at base, sheared lip, pontil scar, yellow olive, some exterior highpoint wear, slight impression on Lafayette side, pt. (ILLUS.) **952**

Topaz Yellow Kossuth Calabash

GI-113 - "Kossuth" above bust - tall tree in
foliage, calabash-style, smooth edges,
applied sloping collared mouth w/ring,
pontil scar, topaz yellow w/a hint of olive,
qt. (ILLUS.).. **960**

Quart Eagle Flask in Orange Amber

Fine Columbia - American Eagle Flask

GI-117 - bust of Columbia with Liberty cap
w/"Kensington" inscribed below - American eagle w/"Union Co." inscribed below,
single broad vertical rib, inward rolled
sheared mouth, pontil scar, bright aqua
(ILLUS.).. **1,064**
GII-26 - American eagle w/banner in beak
above stellar motif obverse & reverse,
horizontally corrugated edges, sheared &
tooled lip, pontil scarred base, orange
amber, tiny flake off medial rib at base, qt.
(ILLUS., top next column) **4,480**
GII-31 variant - Vertical ribbing & a large
plain oval panel on each side, no eagle in
panels, sheared mouth, pontil scar, probably Louisville Glassworks, Louisville,
Kentucky, 1850-55, yellowish green, pt.
(ILLUS., second next column)...................... **960**

Variant Ribbed & Paneled Flask

Amber "Ravenna" Flask

Pale Cornucopia Flasks

GII-37 - "Ravenna" over anchor over "Glass Company," iron pontil scarred base, applied ringed lip, amber, pt. (ILLUS., bottom previous page) **784**

aqua, 1/2 pt. (ILLUS. center w/other pale cornucopia flasks, top of page) **264**

GII-44 - American eagle w/head turned right, holding arrows in right foot, olive branch in left, scattered sunrays around head - Cornucopia w/Produce, vertically ribbed edges, plain lip & pontil, pale green aqua w/some olive around mouth, 1/2 pt. (ILLUS. right w/other pale cornucopia flasks, top of page) **253**

Rare Eagle - Dyottville Historic Flask

GII-38 - American eagle w/shield & banner in its beak w/wording "E Pluribus Unum," on a rocky formation - "Dyottville Glass Works - Philada" on reverse, sheared mouth, smooth base, light to medium puce, professionally cleaned, pt. (ILLUS.) **9,600**

GII-43 - American eagle w/head turned right, holding arrows in right foot, olive branch in left, scattered sunrays around head - Cornucopia w/Produce, vertically ribbed edges inscribed "E Pluribus Unum - One of Many - Kensington Glassworks Philadelphia," sheared lip & pontil,

Eagle - Willington Flask in Red Amber

GII-61 - American eagle below "Liberty" - inscribed in four lines "Willington - Glass Co - West Willington - Conn," smooth edges, applied sloping collar mouth, smooth base, brilliant red amber shading to yellow at shoulders, qt. (ILLUS.) **2,128**

Cornucopia Flasks

GII-72 - American eagle w/head turned right & standing on rocks - Cornucopia w/Produce, vertically ribbed edges, plain neck, yellowish amber, pt. (ILLUS. right w/other cornucopia flasks, top of page) **165**

GII-73 - American eagle w/head turned right & standing on rocks - Cornucopia w/Produce & "X" on left, vertically ribbed edges, sheared lip w/pontil, amber w/some olive, pt. (ILLUS. center w/other cornucopia flasks, top of page) **275**

w/fruit of large size w/tail curled to left, sheared mouth, pontil scar, olive amber, pt. (ILLUS.) **6,720**

Rare Pantaloon Eagle - Cornucopia Flask

GII-75 - American eagle of large size facing right w/large shield w/three vertical bars, full-front view of the legs that appear to be wearing pantaloons - Cornucopia

"Pittsburgh, Pa." Flask in Rare Color

GII-104 - American eagle above oval enclosing "Pittsburgh, Pa.," smooth base, applied ring lip, deep yellowish olive green, qt. (ILLUS.) **896**

Eagle Flask in Scarce Yellow Olive

GII-106 - American eagle facing left above oval panel obverse & reverse, w/"Pittsburgh PA" in oval on obverse, narrow vertical rib on edges, smooth base, applied mouth, yellow olive, pt. (ILLUS.).......... **448**

Double Eagle Flask in Sapphire Blue

GII-108 - American eagle w/head to left above oval obverse & reverse, w/"Pittsburgh, PA" in oval obverse & plain oval on reverse, narrow vertical side rib, applied collared mouth w/ring, smooth base, deep sapphire blue, pt. (ILLUS.) **4,200**

GIII-2 - Cornucopia w/produce obverse & reverse, vertically ribbed edges, sheared

tooled lip & pontil, aqua, 1/2 pt. (ILLUS. left with two other pale cornucopia flasks) **132**

GIII-7 - Cornucopia w/produce - Urn w/produce, vertically ribbed edges, sheared lip w/pontil, light to medium olive green, 1/2 pt. (ILLUS. left with other cornucopia flasks)... **132**

Cornucopia & Urn New York Flask

GIII-16 - Cornucopia with Produce & curled to right - Urn with Produce & w/"Lancaster. Glass.Works N.Y.," vertically ribbed edges, sheared mouth, iron pontil, light bluish green, pt. (ILLUS.) **728**

Rare Masonic - American Eagle Flask

GIV-1 - Masonic emblems - American eagle w/ribbon reading "E Pluribus Unum" above & "I-P" (old-fashioned J) below in oval frame, sheared lip, open pontil, medium to dark purple, pt. (ILLUS.)............. **35,840**

Strawberry Puce Baltimore Monument Flask

GVI-2 - Baltimore Monument above "Balto." - Sloop sailing to the right w/"Fells" above & "Point" below, vertically ribbed edges, sheared lip, pontil, medium to deep strawberry puce, pinpoint shallow mouth flake, some exterior haze, 1/2 pt. (ILLUS.) **4,480**

Yellowish Olive Sunburst Flask

GVIII-3 - Sunburst w/twenty-four rounded rays obverse & reverse, horizontal corrugated edges, smooth rounded shoulder to sheared mouth, pontil scar, yellowish olive, minor exterior highpoint wear, pt. (ILLUS.)... **1,456**

Rare Corn - Baltimore Monument Flask

GVI-4 - "Baltimore" below monument - "Corn For The World" in semicircle above ear of corn, smooth edges, applied lip band, open pontil, brilliant bubbly topaz, pinpoint flake on side of mouth, qt. (ILLUS.) **3,360**

Keen - P&W Sunburst Flask

GVIII-8 - Sunburst w/twenty-eight triangular sectioned rays obverse & reverse, center raised oval w/"KEEN" reading from top to bottom on obverse & "P & W" on reverse, sheared lip, open pontil, ribbed sides, light yellowish amber w/olive tone, small in-the-making burst bubble near base of one panel, pt. (ILLUS.)................................. **728**

Reddish Amber Summer Tree Flask

Summer Tree - Winter Tree Flask

GX-18 - Spring Tree (leaves & buds) - Summer Tree, smooth edges, applied sloping double collar mouth, light bluish green, pontil scar w/in-the-making small chip, qt. (ILLUS.)... **616**

Very Rare Flag - New Granite Flask

GX-28 - American flag (large) to right - "New Granite Glass Works" in arc over "Stoddard - N.H.," sheared mouth, pontil scar, yellowish olive, minor mouth & neck blemishes, 1/2 pint (ILLUS.).................... **28,000**

Spring Tree - Summer Tree Topaz Flask

GX-18 - Spring Tree (leaves & buds) - Summer Tree, smooth edges, applied sloping double collar mouth, pontil scar, yellowish topaz w/citron tone, qt. (ILLUS.) **4,200**

GX-19 - Summer tree - Winter tree, smooth base, double collar mouth, dense reddish amber, very minor exterior wear, qt. (ILLUS., top next column)............................ **2,128**

Rare Yellow Clasped Hands - Eagle Flask

GXII-18 - Clasped hands above oval, all inside shield - American eagle w/plain shield above oval frame, base w/"L & W" inside disc-shaped frame, applied mouth w/ring, smooth base, yellow w/hint of olive amber, pt. (ILLUS., bottom previous page) **1,120**

Sailor/Banjo Player Flask

GXIII-8 - Sailor dancing a hornpipe on an eight-board hatch cover, above a long rectangular bar - Banjo player sitting on a long bench, smooth edges, smooth base, applied double collar mouth, yellow w/amber tone, 1/2 pt. (ILLUS.) **560**

Sailor/Banjo Player Flask in Rare Color

GXIII-8 - Sailor dancing a hornpipe on an eight-board hatch cover, above a long rectangular bar - Banjo player sitting on a long bench, smooth edges, smooth base,

applied double collar mouth, brilliant light to medium olive yellow, 1/2 pt. (ILLUS.) **1,456**

Olive Green Dancer/Soldier Flask

GXIII-13 - Soldier wearing a spiked helmet - Rectangular frame enclosing "Balt. Md." below, dancer w/"Chapman," smooth edges, smooth base, applied ring mouth, olive green, pt. (ILLUS.) **3,640**

Horseman/Hound Flask in Olive Yellow

GXIII-16 - Horseman, hound on reverse, pontil scarred base, applied ring mouth, olive yellow, qt. (ILLUS.) **1,232**

Granite Glass Co. - Stoddard Flask

Traveler's Companion - Star Flask

GXIV-7 - "Traveler's Companion" arched above & below stylized duck - eight-pointed star, smooth sides, sheared mouth, iron pontil, reddish amber, 1/2 pt. (ILLUS.).. **784**

Union Glass Works Aqua Flask

Golden Amber Granite Glass Flask

GXV-7 - "Granite - Glass - Co." inscribed in three lines - "Stoddard - NH" inscribed in two lines, smooth edges, applied double collared roughly tooled mouth, smooth base, deep golden amber, pt. (ILLUS.)........ **728**

GXV-7 - "Granite - Glass - Co." inscribed in three lines - "Stoddard - NH" inscribed in two lines, smooth edges, sheared mouth, tubular pontil, medium yellowish olive, pt. (ILLUS., top next column) **2,016**

GXV-23 - "Union Glass Works - New London CT" - plain reverse, applied double collared mouth, smooth base, aqua, pt. (ILLUS., second next column)..................... **616**

German Pattern Molded Flask

Pattern molded, flattened oblong form w/tiny flared & tooled mouth, twenty-four vertical ribs, brilliant sapphire blue, probably Germany, 1775-1825, 4 7/8" w., 7 1/2" h. (ILLUS.)... **1,232**

New England Yellow Olive Pitkin Flask

Pitkin, thirty-six ribs tightly swirled to the right, yellowish olive, sheared mouth, tubular pontil scar, New England, ca. 1780-1830, 4 3/4" h. (ILLUS.) **1,456**

Green Midwestern Pitkin Flask

Pitkin, twenty-four ribs swirled to the right, sheared mouth, pontil scar, Midwest America, 1800-30, brilliant medium green w/an olive tone, 5 3/4" h. (ILLUS.) **1,008**

Inks

Signed Domical Greenish Aqua Ink

Domical w/central neck, greenish aqua, embossed around sides "Wood's - Black. Ink - Portland," inward rolled mouth, tubular pontil, 1840-60, in-the-making fissure in neck, 2 1/2" h. (ILLUS.) **504**

Early Farleys Ink Bottle in Olive

Octagonal w/angled shoulder to short wide cylindrical neck, yellowish olive, embossed around the sides "Farleys - Ink," sheared mouth, pontil scar, probably a Stoddard glasshouse, Stoddard, New Hampshire, 1845-60, weak embossing, 1 7/8" h. (ILLUS.) **840**

Rare Twelve-sided Master Ink in Olive

Twelve-sided cylindrical, master size, light to medium yellowish olive, heavily ribbed shoulder, cylindrical neck w/applied collared mouth w/pouring spout, open pontil scar, ca. 1830-60, 5 3/4" h. (ILLUS.) **5,040**

Olive Yellow Umbrella-type Ink Bottle

Umbrella-type (8-panel cone shape), brilliant light olive yellow, inward-rolled mouth, pontil scar, professionally cleaned, 1840-80, 2 3/8" h. (ILLUS., bottom previous page) **1,140**

Rare Cobalt Blue Umbrella Ink

Umbrella-type (8-panel cone shape), cobalt blue, inward rolled mouth, pontil scar, 1840-60, 2 1/2" h. (ILLUS.) **2,464**

Rare Larger Cobalt Blue Umbrella Ink

Umbrella-type (8-panel cone shape), cobalt blue, inward rolled mouth, tubular pontil, minor exterior high point wear, some internal ink residue, ca. 1830-60, 2 7/8" h. (ILLUS.) **5,320**

Dark Yellowish Green Ink Bottle

Umbrella-type (8-panel cone shape), dark yellowish green w/olive tone, inward rolled mouth, pontil scar, 1840-60, pinhead-sized flake on one base corner, 2 1/4" h. (ILLUS.) **672**

Green Marked Umbrella-type Ink

Umbrella-type (8-panel cone shape), light to medium green, embossed in panel "M & P - New York," inward rolled mouth, tubular pontil, 1840-60, 2 3/4" h. (ILLUS.) **728**

Medicines

Rare ABL Myers Rock Rose Bottle

ABL Myers AM - Rock Rose - New Haven, rectangular w/paneled sides & beveled corners, applied heavy collared mouth, iron pontil scar, ca. 1845-60, brilliant bluish green, 9 1/2" h. (ILLUS.) **5,600**

Carters Spanish Mixture with Label

Carter's **Spanish Mixture,** cylindrical, applied sloping double collar mouth, ring-open original pontil, 99 percent original paper label, ca. 1845-55, forest green, 8" h. (ILLUS., bottom previous page) **1,456**

Rare Dr. Guysott's Compound Bottle

Guysott's (Dr.) - Compound - Extract of - Yellow Dock & - Sarsaparilla, square w/beveled corners, applied sloping collared mouth, crude iron pontil scar, ca. 1840-60, light to medium bright bluish green, 8 7/8" h. (ILLUS.) **2,016**

Dr. Guysott's Compound Bottle

Guysott's (Dr.) - Compound - Extract of - Yellow Dock & - Sarsaparilla, square w/beveled corners, applied sloping collared mouth, pontil scar, ca. 1840-60, aqua w/ 90 percent original stained paper label, 9 1/8" h. (ILLUS.) **1,232**

Howard's - Vegetable - Cancer and - Canker Syrup, rectangular w/beveled corners, rounded shoulders & applied square collared mouth, pontil scar, a Stoddard, New Hampshire glasshouse, ca. 1846-60, yellowish olive, interior bubble burst w/some residue, 7 3/8" h. (ILLUS., top next column) **14,560**

Extremely Rare Howard's Bottle

Scarce Early Medicine Bottle

Liquid - Opodeldoc, cylindrical, thin flared lip, pontil, yellowish olive, probably Keene Marlboro Street Glassworks, Keene, New Hampshire, 1820-40, mouth repair, 4 3/8" h. (ILLUS.) **1,792**

Myers Rock Rose Medicine Bottle

Myers - Rock Rose - New Haven, rectangular w/beveled corners, applied sloping collared mouth, tubular pontil, aqua, ca. 1840-60, 9" h. (ILLUS., bottom previous page) **532**

Old Dr. J. Townsend's Sarsaparilla

Old Dr. - J. Townsend's - Sarsaparilla - New York, square w/beveled corners, applied sloping collar mouth, iron pontil, bluish green, ca. 1845-60, some light interior haze, 9 3/4" h. (ILLUS.) **616**

Very Rare Rushton & Aspinwall Bottle

Rushton & Aspinwall New-York - Compound Chlorine Tooth Wash, rectangular w/beveled corners, wide flattened flared lip, tubular pontil, yellowish amber w/faint olive tone, ca. 1840-60, some faint exterior haze, 5 7/8" h. (ILLUS.) **15,680**

Scott & Stewart - United States - Syrup - New York, rectangular w/beveled corners, applied sloping collared mouth, iron pontil, light bluish green, ca. 1845-60, 9 1/2" h. (ILLUS., top next column) **3,360**

Townsend's (Dr.) - Sarsaparilla - Albany - NY, square w/beveled corners, applied sloping collared mouth, iron pontil, yellowish olive, small flat flake on side of mouth, ca. 1845-60, 9 1/4" h. (ILLUS., second next column) **448**

Rare Scott & Steward Syrup Medicine

Townsend's Sarsaparilla in Yellow Olive

Townsend's Sarsaparilla Medicine Bottle

Townsend's (Dr.) - Sarsaparilla - Albany - NY, square w/beveled corners, applied sloping collared mouth, iron pontil, bright green, variant w/small lettering, ca. 1845-60, 9 3/8" h. (ILLUS., bottom previous page) **616**

Olive U.S.A. Hosp. Dept. Bottle

U.S.A. - Hosp. Dept., cylindrical w/rounded shoulder, applied double collared mouth, smooth base, olive w/slight bit of yellow, possibly Baltimore Glass Works, Baltimore, Maryland, ca. 1860-70, small very shallow burst bubble on shoulder, 9 1/8" h. (ILLUS.) **672**

Mineral Waters, Sodas & Sarsaparillas

Soda Water Bottle with Paper Label

Bigelow & Co - Springfield Mass., cylindrical w/applied sloping collar mouth, original metal closure, smooth base, brass collar stamped "Allenders Patent July 24, 1858 - New London, CT," also paper label on reverse for "Witch Hazel - Geo. H. Thomas - Granville, Mass.," medium green, rare, 1/2 pt. (ILLUS.) **420**

Yellowish Amber Caladonia Spring Bottle

Caladonia Spring - Wheelock VT, cylindrical w/applied sloping collared mouth w/ring, smooth base, possibly Stoddard, New Hampshire, yellowish amber, strong embossing, qt. (ILLUS.) **728**

Yellowish Olive Caladonia Spring Bottle

Caladonia Spring - Wheelock VT, cylindrical w/applied sloping collared mouth w/ring, smooth base, possibly Stoddard, New Hampshire, yellowish olive, qt. (ILLUS.) **728**

Rare Caladonia Spring Mineral Water

Caladonia Spring - Wheelock VT, cylindrical w/applied sloping collared mouth w/ring, smooth base, possibly Stoddard, New Hampshire, olive amber, qt. (ILLUS., bottom previous page)............... **1,008**

Yellow Olive Congress Water Bottle

Green John Clarke Mineral Water

Clarke (John) around shoulder, cylindrical w/rounded shoulder & tall neck w/applied sloping collared mouth w/ring, smooth base, forest green, ca. 1860-70, rare, qt. (ILLUS.)... **560**

Haddock & Sons Ten Pin Soda Water

Haddock & Sons, modified ten pin-form soda water, crudely applied collared mouth, pontil scar, attributed to the Coventry Glassworks, Coventry, Connecticut, 1830-48, light yellowish olive, 1/2 pt., 7" h. (ILLUS.) **1,792**

Rare Coldbrook Medicinal Spring Water

Coldbrook Medicinal - Spring Water, cylindrical w/tall tapering neck & applied sloping collared mouth w/ring, smooth base, ca. 1860-80, yellow amber w/olive tone, dug example, two cracks in neck, some staining, very rare bottle, qt. (ILLUS.) **560**

Congress Water (on shoulder), cylindrical w/applied sloping double collar mouth w/ring, smooth base, ca. 1850-60, deep yellowish olive, qt. (ILLUS., top next column)... **448**

Blue J.W. Harris Soda Water Bottle

Harris (J.W.) Soda New Haven, Conn., octagonal w/slender neck & heavy applied collared mouth, iron pontil, sapphire blue, ca. 1845-60, professionally cleaned, some small chips & small burst bubble on one plain panel, 1/2 pt. (ILLUS., bottom previous page) **364**

Teal Blue Highrock Congress Spring Bottle

Highrock Congress Spring (design of a rock), C. & W. Saratoga N.Y., cylindrical w/applied sloping double collared mouth w/ring, smooth base, ca. 1865-75, teal blue, strong embossing, pt. (ILLUS.) **1,064**

Rare Iodine Spring Water Bottle

Iodine Spring Water - L - South Hero. VT, cylindrical w/tall cylindrical neck w/applied sloping collared mouth w/ring, smooth base, golden amber w/slight olive tone, ca. 1860-80, qt. (ILLUS.) **2,352**

Tassie & Co. - Brooklyn, octagonal w/long sloping shoulder, applied sloping collared mouth, iron pontil, bluish green, ca. 1845-60, rare New York soda, pt., 7 3/8" h. (ILLUS., top next column) **1,456**

Rare Tassie & Co. Soda Water Bottle

Ted Williams Root Beer Bottle

Ted's Delicious Creamy Root Beer, clear w/crown top, half-length color pyro image of Ted Williams at bat, yellow & white wording, unopened, 1950s, 7 oz. (ILLUS.) **25-50**

Pickle Bottles & Jars

Yarnall Bros. Cathedral Pickle Jar

Aqua, six-sided cathedral-type w/fancy Gothic windows, one panel embossed "Yarnall Bros.," applied collared mouth, smooth base, ca. 1860-80, 13 1/4" h. (ILLUS., bottom previous page) **364**

Six-sided Gothic Arch Pickle Jar

Bright green, six-sided cathedral-type w/Gothic windows, outward rolled mouth, iron pontil, ca. 1845-60, 13 1/4" h. (ILLUS.)..................................... **532**

Rare Figural Pickle Jar

Citron, figural, model of a lighthouse, embossed ring trademark reading "Skilton Foote & Co.'s - Bunker Hill Pickle," tooled sloping collared mouth, smooth base, 1870-90, minor interior stain spots, 11" h. (ILLUS.).. **3,080**

Deep greenish aqua, cylindrical w/diamond design band near base, embossed band around shoulder reads "Wells Miller & Provost," fluted shoulder & neck w/rolled mouth, open pontil scar, ca. 1840-60, 4 1/2" h. (ILLUS., top next column) **960**

Marked Cylindrical Pickle Jar

Six-sided Cathedral Pickle Jar

Honey amber, six-sided cathedral-type w/simple Gothic windows, cylindrical ringed neck w/outward rolled mouth, smooth base, ca. 1860-80, rare color, 13 1/8" h. (ILLUS.) **960**

Tall Marked Underwood Pickle Jar

Light bluish green, cylindrical w/seven large rounded vertical panels up the body & sixteen flutes on the shoulder, ringed neck w/outward rolled mouth, iron pontil, embossed mark "Wm. Underwood - & Co. - Boston," ca. 1845-60, 11 1/2" h. (ILLUS., bottom previous page) **1,456**

Bluish Green Cathedral Pickle Jar

Light bluish green, four-sided cathedral-type w/Gothic windows, outward rolled mouth, iron pontil, ca. 1845-60, 11 1/2" h. (ILLUS.) **1,008**

Large Green Cathedral Pickle Jar

Light to medium bright green, four-sided cathedral-type w/Gothic windows on three sides, cylindrical ringed neck w/outward rolled mouth, pontil scar, Willington Glass Works, West Willington, Connecticut, ca. 1840-60, some very minor haze spots, 11 1/4" h. (ILLUS.) **1,792**

Light to medium bright green, four-sided cathedral-type w/Gothic windows, outward rolled mouth, smooth base, Willington Glass Works, West Willington, Connecticut, 1860-70, 11 3/4" h. (ILLUS., top next column) **2,240**

Rare Connecticut Cathedral Pickle Jar

Bright Green Four-sided Cathedral Pickle

Light to medium bright green, four-sided cathedral-type w/three fancy Gothic windows, outward rolled mouth, smooth base, ca. 1860-70, shallow tiny flake on top of mouth, 11 3/4" h. (ILLUS.) **1,120**

Rare Early Yellowish Green Pickle Jar

Light yellowish green, squared upright cloverleaf-form, outward rolled mouth, pontil scar, probably a Stoddard, New Hampshire glasshouse, ca. 1840-60, 7 3/4" h. (ILLUS.) **1,008**

Lobed Dark Olive Amber Pickle Jar

Yellowish olive amber, octofoil upright lobed sides tapering to an outward rolled mouth, smooth base, Stoddard, New Hampshire, ca. 1860-70, 8" h. (ILLUS.)
.... **1,064**

Whiskey & Other Spirits

Rare Bininger & Co. Gin Bottle

Gin, "Bininger (A.M.) & Co. - N.Y.," square w/beveled corners & applied flared mouth, iron pontil, medium bluish green, 9 3/8" h. (ILLUS.) **2,352**

Gin, free-blown large straight-sided square form w/crude outward rolled mouth, tubular pontil, deep yellowish olive, possibly America, 1780-1820, some exterior wear & scratches, 14 7/8" h. (ILLUS., top next column) **1,680**

Olive Giant-sized Blown Gin Bottle

Crude Early Blown Gin Bottle

Gin, free-blown paddled square form w/rounded shoulders to a heavy applied sloping collared mouth, pontil scar, dense olive amber, early & crude, possibly American, 1780-1820, 17 1/2" h. (ILLUS.).......... **2,576**

Rare Handled Flask with Elephant

Whiskey, elephant figure molded on one side, "Pint" embossed on the other, flattened chestnut form w/solid applied strap handle, applied mouth w/ring, large rectangular iron pontil, bright bubbly deep golden amber, ca. 1845-60, small potstone w/iridescent bruise in pinhead-sized mouth flake, 6" h. (ILLUS., bottom previous page) **1,792**

Cannon-shaped Gayen Whiskey Bottle

Whiskey, "Gayen (J.T.) - Altona," figural cannon, large round collared mouth, smooth base, deep reddish amber, ca. 1860-80, 1/2 pt. (ILLUS.)................................ **960**

Early Griffith Hyatt & Co. Whiskey Jug

Whiskey, "Griffith Hyatt & Co. - Baltimore," arched panel on front, bulbous ovoid shape tapering to neck w/applied mouth

& applied handle, open pontil, probably Baltimore Glassworks, Baltimore, Maryland, 1840-60, yellowish amber, 7" h. (ILLUS.) **1,008**

Early Mold-blown Whiskey Jug

Whiskey, "J.F.T. & Co. - Philad." embossed in circular seal on the shoulder, mold-blown pear shape w/twenty-six vertical ribs, applied double collared mouth & applied handle w/fancy rigaree at base, pontil scar, light yellowish amber, American, 1840-60, 7" h. (ILLUS.) **2,016**

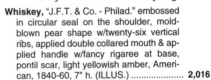

Clear Flask-shaped Whiskey Bottle

Whiskey, "Martin (Eugene) - Opera House Bar - Austin, Tex.," clear strap-sided flask shaped w/double collared applied mouth, smooth base, nearly complete paper label reading "AJL. Schneider is the leader in good whiskey, wines and cigars - Fresh beer on tap," ca. 1880-1900, some minor interior residue (ILLUS.)..................... **960**

Rare Early Cobalt Blue Sealed Whiskey

Whiskey, "Neal's Ambrosia - Whiskey - Philada" in applied shoulder seal, cylindrical tapering to a tall neck w/an applied sloping collared mouth w/ring, smooth base, cobalt blue, America, ca. 1860-70, some very minor interior haze & wear, 9 1/4" h. (ILLUS.) **3,080**

Weeks & Gilson Whiskey Bottle

Whiskey, "Weeks & Gilson. So. Stoddard N.H.," embossed around base, cylindrical w/applied sloping collared mouth w/ring, smooth base, light olive amber, shallow open bubble on neck, ca. 1860-70, 12" h. (ILLUS.)... **1,008**

Wine, "Brooks (P.C.) - 1820" embossed in applied shoulder seal, cylindrical tapering to a tall neck w/applied sloping collared mouth w/ring, pontil scar, dense olive amber, England, ca. 1820, 9 1/2" h. (ILLUS., top next column) **1,792**

Early English Sealed Wine Bottle

BOXES

Bentwood box, single piece of thin poplar bent into an oval shape w/a bentwood band at the bottom & cover rim, no overlapping seam in the body, square-headed nails attaching the cover & baseboard, old reddish brown sponged decoration w/dark green & yellow swags, first half 19th c., 12 1/2" l., 7 1/2" h. (splits in the body, minor edge damage).................... **$1,495**

Fine Early Painted Hanging Candle Box

Candle box, painted & decorated pine, long rectangular form w/square nail construction, a sloping hinged lid & a high arched backplate w/a hanging hole, original darkened salmon paint w/a simple painted star & basket of flowers design in white & yellow, probably Pennsylvania, early 19th c., some wear, 5 x 12 1/4", 7 5/8" h. (ILLUS.) **5,980**

Early Inlaid & Curly Maple Boxes

Federal era box, inlaid mahogany veneer & cherry, rectangular w/flat hinged cover, raised on front French feet joined by a serpentine apron, banded border inlay & a shield-shape inlaid keyhole escutcheon, the interior divided into three compartments, early 19th c., age split in bottom, 5 3/8 x 10", 5 1/4" h. (ILLUS. bottom with curly maple box) **2,415**

Rose-decorated Hanging Box

Hanging box, painted & decorated poplar & pine, a deep rectangular dovetailed case w/a sloped hinged cover opening to a deep well w/divided interior above a narrow lower drawer w/small brass knob & divided interior, the tall narrow waisted backboard w/a heart-form lobed top around a large hanging hole, overall old dark olive green background paint w/narrow dark blue border, the center of the cover & top front panel painted w/a large red white-trimmed rose w/shaded green

leaves, the drawer front w/a matching leaf sprig, old heavy varnish w/touch-ups on sides w/cover pegs broken out, some wear & damage, attributed to the Pennsylvania Amish, first-half 19th c., 7 x 10 1/2", overall 15 1/2" h. (ILLUS.)...... **4,370**

Knife boxes, Federal style, inlaid mahogany, each w/a shaped sloping hinged top opening to a fitted interior above a conforming shaped case, on a molded base, American or English, 1790-1810, 14" h., pr. **4,780**

Finely Painted Student School Box

School box, curly maple, rectangular dovetailed form w/flat hinged cover, delicately painted designs, mainly in green, red & tan including foliage borders, agricultural tools & sheaves of wheat around the sides w/a finely done scene on the top of a dove, basket of roses, quiver of arrows & caduceus, all intertwined w/ribbons & vining flowers, brass ball feet, divided interior lined w/pink paper w/penciled notes, alligatoring to the heavy varnish, New England, early 19th c., 6 1/4 x 10 1/4", 3 5/8" h. (ILLUS.) **6,613**

Storage box, curly maple, deep rectangular form w/flat hinged cover, iron strap hinges & spring latch, good patina, early 19th c., worm holes in bottom, 4 1/2 x 7 1/2", 3 3/4" h. (ILLUS. top with inlaid Federal era box) **690**

Rare Early Decorated Pennsylvania Box

Storage box, painted & decorated pine, rectangular w/a hinged domed top, each side & cover w/a reddish ground bordered by pale yellow, the sides w/large stylized red & white tulips & carnations w/green leaves, the top painted w/a large lattice urn filled w/flowers, tin & wire staple hinges & hasp, penciled note on inside top reads "Made in 1802," attributed to Heinrich Bucher, Berks County, Pennsylvania, some wear, minor edge damage, 6 1/8 x 9 1/4", 4 3/4" h. (ILLUS.) **12,938**

CANDLESTICKS & CANDLEHOLDERS

Louis XVI-Style Bouquet Candelabra

Candelabra, gilt- and patinated-bronze, six-light, Louis XVI taste bouquet-style, a lobed scroll-footed base modeled as a short column trimmed w/floral swags supporting a seated putti holding aloft a large gilt-bronze bouquet fitted w/six up-turned candlesockets, not electrified, France, third quarter 19th c., 28" h., pr. (ILLUS.).. **$2,530**

Gilt-bronze & Marble Candelabra

Candelabra, gilt-bronze & marble, four-light, a carved grey marble plinth base on tiny gilt-bronze paw feet supporting a bulbous urn-form pedestal w/a slender leaf-trimmed shaft issuing four scroll-trimmed upturned candlearms all centered by slender shaft w/upright scrolling finial, France, late 19th c., 22 1/2" h., pr. (ILLUS.) **518**

French Gilt-Bronze Candelabra

Candelabra, gilt-bronze, seven-light, a round foot w/a domed acanthus leaf-cast top supporting a reeded standard below a fancy disk below the spiral-reeded top socket supporting six upturned spiraling & leaf-trimmed candlearms surrounding a central upright holder w/matching leaf decoration & a removable flame cap in the socket, French Empire style, France, ca. 1860, 29" h., pr. (ILLUS.) **1,610**

Candelabra with Oriental Figures

Candelabra, gilt-bronze, three-light, Orien-tal taste, a square foot supporting a heavy dark patinated reeded column be-low the figure of an Oriental man on one & an Oriental woman on the other, each of them w/leafy scrolls w/tiny bells issuing from their heads below a leaf-cast blos-som supporting three leaf-trimmed up-turned & outswept candlearms ending in bird heads topped by leaf-cast inverted bell sockets, objects missing from hand of one figure, France, late 19th c., 20 1/2" h., pr. (ILLUS.) **1,610**

Unusual Figural Gilt-bronze Candelabrum

Early Capstan-style Candlestick

Candlestick, brass, capstan-style, a wide low cylindrical ring-trimmed base centered by a single short knobbed socket w/large extractor holes in the sides, minor damage, socket w/soldered repair, early, 5 1/4" d., 4 1/2" h. (ILLUS.) **633**

Sterling Georg Jensen Candelabrum

Candelabrum, sterling silver, five-light, Art Deco style, a paneled domed & stepped base tapering to a paneled standard topped by leafy scrolls & petals centered by a pine cone finial & issuing five slender reeded upturned arms ending in simple paneled candlesockets, designed by Johan Rohde for Georg Jensen Silversmithy, Denmark, ca. 1930, 17" h. (ILLUS.) **11,353**

Gothic-style Gilt-brass Candlestick

Candlestick, gilt-brass, "Fonthill" style in the Gothic Revival taste, a triangular scroll-footed base composed of Gothic arch panels surrounding the ornate standard composed of Gothic designs in a knopped & stepped form topped by a pricket-type socket surrounded by a scalloped Gothic-style gallery, England, late 19th c., electrified, 44 1/2" h. (ILLUS.) **2,070**

Early English Sterling Taperstick Holders

Taperstick holders, sterling silver, a molded squared base w/chamfered shell-form corners & w/an engraved crest, a knopped- and ring-turned baluster stem supporting a ringed campana-form socket, William Grundy, London, England, 1748, 5" h., pr. (ILLUS.) **3,910**

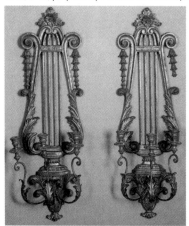

Lyre-form Regency-Style Wall Sconces

Wall sconces, giltwood, a flat-backed leaf-carved urn-form base issuing three leafy scroll arms ending in candlesockets, the upper section designed as a tall narrow openwork lyre design trimmed w/leafy scrolls & husk pendants, Regency-Style, England, ca. 1900, 44 1/2" h., pr. (ILLUS.) **2,300**

CANES & WALKING STICKS

Ash walking stick, carved in a folk art style w/a carved head finial above assorted figures carved in relief on the sides including men, women & a child, frogs, a spiraling snake, an anchor, heart, hand, a mug & various fowl, iron tip, probably America, 19th c., 35 7/8" l. (ILLUS. right with whalebone walking stick, top next column) **$1,528**

Carved Ash & Whalebone Walking Sticks

Bamboo & silver cane, the curved bamboo shaft mounted w/a silver lion's head fitted w/glass eyes, probably Italy, late 19th - early 20th c., 32 1/4" l. (ILLUS. second from right w/three walking sticks, top next page) **470**

Blowpipe gun walking stick, a flattened brass-finished metal knop opening to the mouthpiece, a floating firing pin & breech opening w/straight pull for loading, mahogany-finished bamboo shaft, France, ca. 1870, 36" l. (ILLUS. second from left with a cane & two other walking sticks, top next page) **2,115**

Chick & Egg-Handled Cane

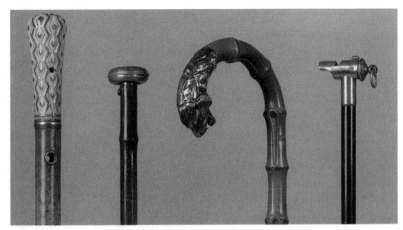

A Cane & Three Unusual Walking Sticks

Ebonized wood, ivory & horn cane, the ebonized wood shaft joined by a silver ferrule to the figural handle composed of a carved horn chick w/tiny glass eyes emerging from a carved elephant ivory egg, probably England, ca. 1900, overall 35 1/4" l. (ILLUS. of part, bottom previous page) **1,008**

Ebony & Ivory Napoleon Shadow Cane

Ebony & ivory cane, the ebony shaft w/a horn ferrule joining it to the turned elephant ivory handle, the handle, when held to light to cast a shadow, showing a shadow portrait of the Emperor Napoleon I, carried by followers of the exiled emperor, France, ca. 1825, overall 36 1/4" l. (ILLUS. of handle & shadow) **2,016**

English Cane with Figural Handle

Ebony, silver & synthetic ivory cane, the ebony shaft joined by a bronze ferrule to a figural handle w/a carved synthetic ivory head of a Victorian coachman wearing a silver cap & collar, England, second half 19th c., overall 36" l. (ILLUS. of part) **952**

Enameled wood & ivory cane, the black enameled shaft w/a horn ferrule & giltmetal collar joining it to the figural carved elephant ivory handle, the handle carved as a realistic cat head w/an articulated mouth opening to reveal a red tongue, pushing neck bow activates mouth, inset w/clear glass eyes, probably England, ca. 1890, overall 36 1/2" l. (ILLUS. of handle, top next page) **1,680**

Unusual Carved Cat Head Cane

Cane with Finely Enameled Silver Handle

Fruitwood & enameled silver, the fruitwood shaft joined by a brass & iron ferrule to the round sterling quality silver
handle, the handle decorated around the
sides w/colorful enameled scrolls & flowers in the champleve manner, the top w/a
fancy initial in the design, silver hallmarks
are probably Swedish, ca. 1910, overall
34 1/4" l. (ILLUS. of part) **1,120**

Glass cane, clear blown body applied
w/thin red & yellow threads, the square
section handle w/a twisted neck, the
squared shaft ending in a further twist,
America, early 20th c., 32" l. (ILLUS. right
with two other glass canes, top next col-
umn) **176**

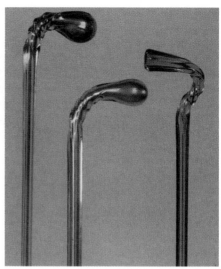

Three Old Blown Glass Canes

Glass cane, copper-cored clear blown type
w/a globular grip & an alternating twisted
& squared shaft, America, early 20th c.,
32" l. (ILLUS. center with two other glass
canes, top of column) **206**

Glass cane, gold-cored clear blown-type,
globular grip & an alternating twisted &
squared shaft, America, early 20th c.,
37" l. (ILLUS. left with two other glass
canes, top of column) **206**

Gold metal wire & metal walking stick,
"Le Diabolique" defense-type, the pommel w/a woven gold metal wire & gold
metal end cap, on a faux bamboo shaft
w/the top section of grained wood & the
body in faux-painted metal, razor blades
emerging from areas along the metal
shaft when the pommel is pulled, France,
19th c., 34 1/4" l. (ILLUS. far left with
three other walking sticks, top of next
page) **5,288**

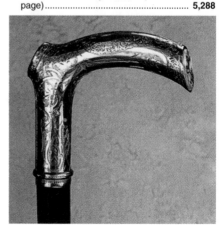

Fine American Victorian Cane

Four Walking Sticks with Varied Handles

Gold, quartz & tropical wood cane, the rich dark tropical wood shaft w/a white metal & iron ferrule connecting to the tau-shaped handle of gold, the presentation-type handle finely engraved overall w/leafy scrolls & inset w/double gold quartz inlays, handle at least 18k gold, America, ca. 1870, overall 36 1/4" l. (ILLUS. of part, bottom previous page) **6,160**

Gold-washed silver & ebonized hardwood walking stick, the figural handle in the form of a rabbit head set w/glass eyes, on an ebonized hardwood shaft w/horn ferrule, the silver head hallmarked for London, 1898, retailed by Briggs, England, 36" l. (ILLUS. second from left with three other walking sticks, top of page) **588**

Gutta percha cane, figural, the smooth gutta percha shaft w/a white metal ferrule & silver collar joined to a figural gutta percha L-shaped handle molded as a lady's leg, finely detailed w/a high-buttoned boot, textured stocking w/garter & ruffled lace knickers, America, ca. 1890, overall 33 1/4" l. (ILLUS. of handle, bottom of page) **476**

Ivory & hardwood walking stick, the ivory handle carved w/a realistic bust of Voltaire, on an ebonized hardwood shaft, late 19th c., 32 3/8" l. (ILLUS. right with ivory tusk-handled cane, next page) **1,880**

Unusual Gutta Percha Lady-leg Cane

Ivory piqué & malacca walking stick, the tall round ivory handle decorated w/vertical zigzag lines of metal piqué offset w/zigzag incising, the tip w/a stylized flowerhead-shaped piqué & incising, a hole drilled through the handle, a malacca wood shaft w/brass eyelet holes, England, probably late 17th c., 38 1/8" l. (ILLUS. far left with a cane & two other walking sticks, top page 95) **5,170**

Rare Early English Dated Cane

Ivory & Wood Cane & Walking Stick

Ivory & rosewood cane, the curved ivory tusk handle incised & stained w/the owner's name, a rosewood shaft carved to conform w/the size of the ivory, England, early 20th c., 35 1/4" l. (ILLUS. right with carved ivory walking stick) **411**

Jasper ware, gilt-metal & hardwood walking stick, the pommel handle composed of blue & white jasper ware, the top w/a charioteer design & the sides w/flat leaves, atop a three-tiered gilt-metal collar w/the top tiers engine-turned, on a hardwood shaft w/a lead-tipped brass ferrule, England, late 19th c., 36 1/4" l. (ILLUS. far right with three other walking sticks, top previous page) **441**

Malacca & ivory cane, honey-toned malacca shaft w/a brass & iron ferrule & silver collar joining it to the rare "pique" decorated rounded elephant ivory handle, the handle finely inlaid overall w/scrolls & crosses made of metal eyelets, also inlaid w/"A.R. 69," England, rare very early example, 1669, overall 36" l. (ILLUS. of head, top next column).......................... **11,760**

Narwhal & Whale's Tooth Canes

Narwhal ivory & silver walking stick, the narwhal ivory shaft topped w/a floral-chased & embossed sterling silver monogrammed grip, rubbed hallmarks on the silver, England, 19th c., 32 3/8" l. (ILLUS. left with whale's tooth & mahogany cane)
.... **3,408**

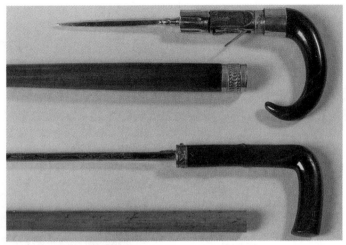

Rare Pepper Box Gun & Sword Canes

Pepper box gun cane, the mahoganized hardwood crook handle forming the handle of the six-barreled revolver, set to center w/a 5" stiletto blade, the whole fitted in a hardwood shaft, Germany, ca. 1880, 35" l. (ILLUS. top with sword cane, top of page) **5,875**

Silver overlay & partridgewood walking stick, the metal handle formed as chain links, the top w/an open loop, the collar marked by the Gorham Mfg. Co., Providence, Rhode Island, on a partridgewood shaft w/an iron-tipped brass ferrule, America, early 20th c., 33 3/4" l. (ILLUS. second from right with three other walking sticks, top page 97) **940**

the sterling silver cylindrical handle ornately cast overall w/rose blossoms, handle w/the mark of the Unger Brothers, ca. 1900, overall 36 1/4" l. (ILLUS. of handle) **560**

Sword cane, a wood pommel & shaft, the shaft enclosing a double-edged blade signed "Thomas Aiala," Spain, blade 16th c., overall 33 3/4" l. (ILLUS., top of next page) **1,880**

Sword cane, the L-shaped horn handle w/a gilt-metal collar set w/a push button that releases a steel blade w/incised scrolls & traces of bluing, set into a malacca wood shaft, America, late 19th - early 20th c., 34 1/2" l. (ILLUS. bottom with pepper box gun cane, top of page) **1,410**

Cane with Unger Bros. Silver Handle

Sterling silver & ebony cane, the ebony shaft joined by a replaced brass ferrule to

Fine Tortoiseshell Jeweled Cane

Sword Cane with Early Marked Blade

Tortoiseshell veneer, gold & silver cane, the entire cylindrical shaft covered w/tortoiseshell veneer & a solid tortoiseshell ferrule, the ornate top in a Renaissance-style design in silver & gold w/four identical arched gateways each framing a gold standing armored knight or his wife, the top modeled w/a round shield w/chased floral & leaf designs centering a large faceted amethyst, Europe, early 19th c., overall 35" l. (ILLUS. of part, bottom previous page)... **3,360**

Whale's tooth ivory & mahogany cane, the L-shaped ivory handle ending in three carved faces of men w/different expressions, a beaded sterling silver monogrammed collar to the mahogany shaft w/horn ferrule, America, late 19th c., 38" l. (ILLUS. right with narwhal walking stick, page 98)... **1,880**

Whalebone & baleen walking stick, carved & turned w/the shaft composed of sections of turned whalebone joined w/baleen pegs, a mother-of-pearl button top & baleen tip, America, 19th c., several age cracks, 34 1/2" l. (ILLUS. left with carved ash walking stick, page 98) **1,293**

Whistle-handled walking stick, the handle formed w/a white-metal whistle attached to a slender ebony shaft, horn ferrule, early 20th c., 36 1/4" l. (ILLUS. far right with a cane & two other walking sticks, page 95).. **470**

CANS & CONTAINERS

Wonder Mist Auto Cleanser Tin

Auto cleanser & polisher, "Wonder Mist," large upright rectangular can w/a pry-off spout at one side of the flat top, a yellow paper label printed w/black wording centering the picture of an early 20th c. sedan, overall staining & some rust (ILLUS.)............ **$46**

Early Korff's Cacao Square Tin

Cacao, "Korff's Cacao," large upright square tin w/fitted flat cover, colorful paper labels centered by round reserves w/portraits of pretty women, Dutch, late 19th - early 20th c., 8" h. (ILLUS.)................. **81**

Large Bunte Fine Confections Can

Candy, "Bunte Fine Confections," large upright cylindrical can w/a pry-off cover, green background w/a wide center band printed w/a scene of the factory in black & flanked by fancy gold bands, late 19th - early 20th c., some paint loss & rust, 10" d., 14" h. (ILLUS.) **35**

Edward Sharp English Toffee Tin

Candy, "Edward Sharp and Sons, Ltd. of Maidstone, Kent - The Toffee Specialists," rectangular low tin w/a color street scene of Canterbury, England on the cover, coats-of-arms printed around the size, ca. 1940s, some wear, 5 3/4 x 7", 2" h. (ILLUS.) **12**

Colorful Early Sunset Trail Cigar Tin

Cigar, "Sunset Trail," oval upright tin w/flat hinged lid, dark blue background, printed on the side w/a large oval color scene of a cowboy & cowgirl riding on horseback at sunset, large orange panels w/wording at the ends, fine condition, early 20th c., 6" l., 5 1/2" h. (ILLUS.) **575**

Cigars, "Possum Cigars - 3 for 5¢ - 'Am Good and Sweet,'" large cylindrical size w/flat fitted lid, red background w/dark gold w/brown reserves w/white & yellow wording around a color image of a white possum, slight wear, 5 1/4 d., 5 1/4" h. (ILLUS., top next column) **403**

Possum Cigars Tin with Gold Ground

Colorful Reichard's Cadet Cigar Tin

Cigars, "Reichard's Cadet," short cylindrical tin w/fitted cover, pale blue background w/an oblong red banner w/brown, gold & green decorations framing a color bust portrait of a young military cadet in uniform, some overall wear, late 19th - early 20th c., 5" h. (ILLUS.)..................................... **69**

Tungsten Cigar Tin with Exotic Maiden

Cigars, "Tungsten Cigars," cylindrical tin w/a flat fitted cover, color paper label depicting a lovely maiden in a diaphanous gown dotted w/stars arching back above a picture of the earth, a lighted electric bulb raised in one of her hands, worn cover & light wear & soiling on the label, late 19th - early 20th c., 5" h. (ILLUS., bottom previous page) **127**

Boston Coach & Axle Oil Can

Coach & axle oil, "Boston Coach & Axle Oil," upright rectangular can w/a screw-off cap on the flat top, dark yellow label w/black & white wording, a product of the Standard Oil Company, late 19th - early 20th c. (ILLUS.) **46**

Early Black Boy Coffee Can

Coffee, "Black Boy Pure Coffee," 1/2 lb. can, cylindrical w/fitted metal lid, paper label in dark orange w/black wording & image of a black boy wearing a turban, ca. 1920s-30s, 3 1/4" d., 4 1/4" h. (ILLUS.) **116**

Coffee, "Bluhill Coffee," 5 lb. cylindrical lunch pail-style w/domed shoulder, short cylindrical neck w/pry-off cover & a wire bail handle w/turned wood grip, dark blue sides w/white bands & a rectangular panel w/black wording & a black & white picture of a cup of coffee, early 20th c., 7" d., 10" h. (ILLUS., top next column) **330**

Bluhill Coffee Lunch Pail 5 lb. Can

Ten Pound ButterNut Coffee Pail

Coffee, "ButterNut Coffee," 10 lb. pail, tall cylindrical can w/flat fitted cover & wire bail handle w/turned wood grip, large color paper label on the front w/coffee trees & beans flanking the red, white & black wording, late 19th - early 20th c., 13 1/2" h. (ILLUS.) **46**

Holland House I lb. Coffee Can

English Cookie Tin with Detailed Village Scene

Coffee, "Holland House Coffee," 1 lb. round tin, key-wind lid, brown background printed w/coffee beans, yellow wording around the silvery white image of a silver coffee service, early 20th c., 5" d., 3 3/4" h. (ILLUS., bottom previous page) **66**

My Favorite Coffee 3 lb. Can

Coffee, "My Favorite High Grade Coffee," 3 lb. cylindrical can w/fitted cover, original paper label w/a dark green ground w/white, red & black wording & a scene on the back of an older man & his granddaughter saucering coffee, early 20th c., 9 1/2" h. (ILLUS.) **81**

Cookies, decorative low rectangular metal tin w/rounded corners, the top printed in brown on cream w/a detailed scene of an early English village, titled "An Old Fashioned Lancashire Holiday - A Preston Guild in the 17th Century - The Solemnization Ceremony in the Market Place," England, ca. 1940s, 5 1/2 x 7 1/2", 3 1/4" h. (ILLUS., top of page) **10**

Heinrich Haeberlin Cookie Can

Cookies, "Heinrich Haeberlin," cylindrical can w/flat pry-off cover, golden background w/a band of writing around the rim, oval reserves around the sides showing an early German village & a knight slaying a dragon, Germany, early 20th c. (ILLUS.) **125**

1940s Marshall Field Cookie Tin

Cookies, "Marshall Field & Company - Christmas Cookies," low round cylindrical tin w/a pry-off cover, black background printed w/red, white & black stylized Christmas trees & red & white wording, ca. 1940s, 9 3/4" d. (ILLUS., bottom previous page) **15**

Early Hazard Kentucky Rifle Powder Tin

Gunpowder, "Hazard Powder Co. - Kentucky Rifle Gunpowder," flattened 1 lb. tin w/a very small pry-off cap, red background w/a large yellow center circle printed in black w/a scene of an early hunter shooting his rifle, his dog at his side, some wear & alligatored finish, late 19th - early 20th c., 1 1/2 x 4", 5 1/2" h. (ILLUS.)...................................... **134**

Towle's Log Cabin Syrup 2 lb. tin

Syrup, "Towle's Log Cabin Syrup," 2 lb. size tin, rectangular cabin shape printed in color as a log cabin w/children playing inside & outside & woman cooking at open fireplace, 1950s, minor dings & scratches, 2 3/4 x 5", 4 1/2" h. (ILLUS.)..................... **55**

Tobacco, "Dixie Kid Cut Plug," lunch box, rectangular, yellow ground decorated at the front center w/a picture of a black baby, flat top w/wire bail handle, early 20th c., 5 x 8", 4" h. (minor paint loss) **184**

Early Edgeworth Pipe Tobacco Tin

Tobacco, "Edgeworth Extra High Grade Sliced Pipe Tobacco," small flat rectangular tin, printed in dark & light blue w/a large background diamond & decorative scrolls, early 20th c. (ILLUS.)......................... **25**

Tobacco, "Game Fine Cut Tobacco," rectangular store bin w/thin fitted cover, color scene of grouse in a field on both sides, 7 1/4 x 8 x 11 1/2" (ILLUS., top next page).. **575**

Half and Half Tobacco Pocket Tin

Tobacco, "Half and Half," vertical pocket tin w/flip-up top, dark green & black background w/a wide white diagonal band w/black wording, a red circle in the upper left w/label of Burley and Bright Tobacco Co., ca. 1930s, 4 1/4" h. (ILLUS.) **10**

Mayo's Satisfied Customer Roly Poly

Game Fine Cut Tobacco Store Bin

Tobacco, "Mayo's," Roly Poly Satisfied Customer tin, a few scratches on top of head, otherwise very good condition, 7" h. (ILLUS., bottom previous page) **518**

Mayo's Roly Poly Singing Waiter Tin

Tobacco, "Mayo's," Roly Poly Singing Waiter (ILLUS.) **403**

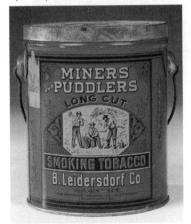

Miners and Puddlers Tobacco Pail

Tobacco, "Miners and Puddlers Long Cut Smoking Tobacco," cylindrical pail w/flat fitted lid & wire bail handle, red background printed in black & creamy white w/a central black & white reserve showing a group of miners, late 19th - early 20th c., very good condition, 5 1/4" d., 6 1/2" h. (ILLUS.) **230**

Old Virginia Smoking Tobacco Tin

Tobacco, "Old Virginia Smoking Tobacco," round tin w/grey twist-off cover, red sides w/white wording & a small central black oval w/brown tobacco leaves, ca. 1940s, light wear (ILLUS.) **15**

Tobacco, "Pastime Plug Tobacco - John Finzer & Bros.," 18 lb. large low rectangular box, printed in red & shades of black w/a large scene of an early hunter firing at birds w/his hunting dog beside him, inside lid w/a fine lithograph of a horse & rider jumping a hedge, some paint wear & scratching, late 19th c., 9 1/2 x 12 1/2" (ILLUS., top next page) **259**

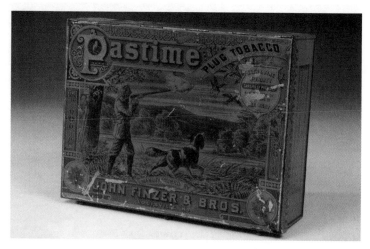

Large Pastime Plug Tobacco 18 lb. Box

Squadron Leader Pocket Tin

Tobacco, "Squadron Leader Mixture Tobacco," flat rectangular pocket tin w/rounded corners, colorful lid w/thin red border band around blue sky & color image of World War I biplane in battle, wording in white, red & black, Samuel Gawith & Co., early 20th c., 3 1/4 x 4 1/4" (ILLUS.).. **134**

Tobacco, "Sure Shot," rectangular store bin w/a long flat lid, the long sides lithographed in yellow, black, red & green w/a scene of a Native American w/bow & arrow & marked "Sure Shot - Chewing Tobacco - It Touches The Spot," some denting to lid, overall light rust spots & wear, 10 1/4 x 15 1/2", 7" h. (ILLUS., bottom of page)... **259**

Sure Shot Chewing Tobacco Store Bin

CAT COLLECTIBLES

Kitten Paint-by-Number Set

Paint by number set, kitten in boat & kitten at vanity, 16 x 12", ca. 1970 (ILLUS.) **$10-15**

Pencil holder, plastic, mod orange, ca. 1960, 3 1/2" (ILLUS.) **5-10**

Mod Orange Plastic Pencil Holder

Tom Pez Dispenser

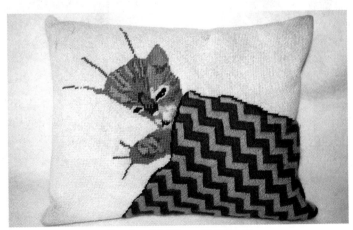

Needlepoint Pillow with Chessie

Marbled Green Plastic Sewing Box

Pez dispensers, Tom (of Tom and Jerry), MGM, Japan only, ca. 1980 (ILLUS., previous page).. **10-15**

Pillow, needlepoint throw-type pillow, Chessie, C&O Railroad mascot, ca. 1960 (ILLUS., bottom previous page) **25-35**

Puzzle, Top Cat, frame tray-type, Top Cat sips milk from straw, Whitman, ca. 1960... **15-25**

Record LP, "Linus the Lionhearted," General Foods/Premier Albums, ca. 1964 .... **15-30**

Record LP, Pink Panther, film score, Henry Mancini, RCA Victor Dynagroove, 1963...... **5-10**

Salt & Pepper Shakers Black Cats

Cat with Paw Raised Salt Shaker

Salt shaker, ceramic cat, w/paw raised (other shaker is bird cage), made in Japan, 2 1/4" (ILLUS. of one) **4-6**

Salt & pepper shakers, ceramic, black cats w/gold & red accents, 3" h., Japan, pr. (ILLUS., next column) **8-12**

Sewing box, marbled green plastic, kittens embossed on clear plastic lid, 9 1/2", ca. 1940-50 (ILLUS., top of page).................. **15-25**

Cat's Paw Rubber Heels Boxes

Shoe heels, Cat's Paw Rubber Heels, various box art from different years, 4 h." box, Canada, each (ILLUS.) **4-8**

Panther on Rock Cliff TV Lamp

Figural Cat Tin Litho Penny Whistle

Toy, whistle, figural cat tin litho penny whistle, Japan, 1930 (ILLUS.) **25-45**

Black & Gold Tiger TV Lamp

TV Lamp, ceramic, black & gold tiger w/original shade, 18" ca. 1950 (ILLUS.).... **35-65**
TV Lamp, ceramic, black panther on gray rock cliff, 5 x 12", ca. 1950 (ILLUS., top of page) **35-50**

Figural Items

Kitten with Ball Wind-up Toy

Toy, wind-up tin, kitten on it's back w/ball, Japan, ca. 1950 (ILLUS.) **30-50**

Figural Whimsical Tabby

Figurine, ceramic, grey tabby kitten w/big eyes, paw up, whimsical, ca. 1960, 3 1/4" h. (ILLUS., bottom previous page).... **8-12**

Fluffy White Kitten Figurine

Figurine, ceramic, kitten, fluffy & white, ca. 1960, 2 1/2" h. (ILLUS.) **15-20**

Grey Tabby Standing Figurine

Figurine, ceramic, kitten, grey tabby w/green eyes, standing up, "CK 45B," 2 3/4" h. (ILLUS.) **8-12**

Kitten on Boot Figurine

Figurine, ceramic, kitten on boot, Phil Papel Imports, Japan, 2 x 3 1/2" h. (ILLUS.) **20-30**

Kitten with Hat Figurine

Figurine, ceramic, kitten w/hat, 3" h. (ILLUS.) **5-10**

Ceramic Leopard by Wade

Figurine, ceramic, miniature leopard, by Wade, England, 2" l. (ILLUS.) **3-5**

Mr. Jinks Figurine

Figurine, ceramic, Mr. Jinks (misspelled "Jinx"), Ideas Inc., early 1960s, 5 1/2" h. (ILLUS.) **75-125**

CERAMICS

Abingdon

From about 1934 until 1950, Abingdon Pottery Company, Abingdon, Illinois, manufactured decorative pottery, mainly cookie jars, flowerpots and vases. Decorated with various glazes, these items are becoming popular with collectors who are especially attracted to Abingdon's novelty cookie jars.

Also see Antique Trader Pottery & Porcelain Ceramics Price Guide, 4th Edition. *Also see* Antique Trader Stoneware and Blue & White Pottery Price Guide *and* Antique Trader Teapots Price Guide.

Abingdon Round Ashtray

Abingdon Mark

Abingdon Octagonal Ashtray

Ashtray, octagonal, turquoise, No. 551, 1941-46, 7 x 7" (ILLUS.) **$25**
Ashtray, round, turquoise, No. 555, 1941-46, 8" d. (ILLUS., top next column) **25**
Book ends, model of Scottie dog, No. 650, 7 1/2" h., pr **200**

Abingdon Humpty Dumpty Cookie Jar

Cookie jar, Humpty Dumpty, red chimney base, h.p. details on figural cover, Model 707, 11" h. (ILLUS.) **259**

Abingdon Display Sign

Display sign, marked "Abingdon" (ILLUS.) **300**

Abingdon Flower Boat & Fruit Boat

Two Abingdon Mantel Pieces

Flower boat, Fern Leaf, oblong ribbed leaf shape, pink, No. 426, 1937-38, 13 x 4" (ILLUS. left w/fruit boat, bottom previous page) **100**

Fruit boat, Fern Leaf, oblong ribbed leaf shape, white, No. 432, 1938-39, 6 1/2 x 15" (ILLUS. right w/flower boat, bottom of previous page) **100**

Mantel pieces, cov., handled, bird & floral decoration on white ground, No. KR22, rare, each (ILLUS. of two, top of page) **65**

Abingdon Pottery Daisy Pattern Teapot

Teapot, cov., Daisy patt., white body w/blue daisy-shaped cover, also found w/a yellow daisy cover, each (ILLUS. of teapot with blue cover) **65**

Abingdon Gamma Vase

Vase, 8" h., Gamma, short bulbous base connected to tall slightly flaring lobed neck by applied side handles, turquoise, No. 107, 1938-39 (ILLUS.) **40**

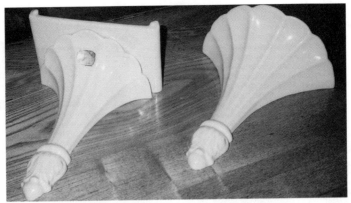

Abingdon Acanthus Wall Bracket & Wall Pocket

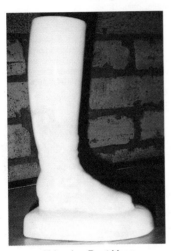

Abingdon Boot Vase

The number of collectors in this category is growing while availability of better or rarer pieces is shrinking. Consequently, prices for all pieces are appreciating, while those for better and/or rarer pieces, including restored rare pieces, are soaring.

The price ranges presented here are retail. They presume mint or near mint condition or, in the case of very rare damaged pieces, proper restoration. They reflect such variables as rarity, design, quality of glaze, size and the intangible "in-vogue factor." They are the prices that knowledgeable sellers will charge and knowledgeable collectors will pay.

Amphora-Teplitz Marks

Vase, 8" h., model of a boot, white, No. 584, 1947 (ILLUS.).. **45**

Vase, 8" h., Wreath, circular on ribbed ogee base, leaf garland, bow & star decoration, pink, No. 467, 1938-39 (ILLUS., top next column)... **95**

Wall bracket, Acanthus, pink, No. 589, 1947, 7" h. (ILLUS. left w/wall pocket, top of page).. **65**

Wall pocket, Acanthus, pink, No. 648, 1948, 8 3/4" h. (ILLUS. right w/wall bracket, top of page) **65**

Amphora-Teplitz

In the late 19th and early 20th centuries numerous potteries operated in the vicinity of Teplitz in the Bohemian region of what was Austria but is now the Czech Republic. They included Amphora, RStK, Stellmacher, Ernst Wahliss, Paul Dachsel, Imperial and lesser-known potteries such as Johanne Maresh, Julius Dressler, Bernard Bloch and Heliosine.

Amphora Russian Folk Art Teapot

Teapot, cov., Russian Folk Art Series, tall ovoid form w/flared foot & flat rim, arched C-form handle from rim to shoulder, short angled shoulder spout w/an arched brace to the rim, decorated on center front w/a large stylized bust portrait of a Russian cleric w/black beard & brown & blue hat, the portrait enclosed by a ring of blue stars & blue dots w/other bands of dots & teardrops about the top & base, all against a tan ground, the reverse w/a design of multiple triangles enclosed w/a ring of stars, impressed "Austria - Amphora" in ovals & "11892,47 - G" plus a crown, ca. 1907-08, 8 1/4" h. (ILLUS.) **$295**

Amphora Teapot with Mackintosh Rose

Teapot, cov., bulbous nearly spherical body tapering to a low angled neck, a short angled shoulder spout & a triple-loop handle down the side, the side centered by a large almond-shaped reserve in dark blue decorated w/the Mackintosh Rose design flanked by a wide dark blue medial band w/small pink blossoms on stems, the upper & lower band in white w/mottled blue & scattered small yellow flowerheads, the band & scattered flowerheads continuing around the sides, impressed "Austria - Amphora" in ovals w/a crown, impressed "3964,44," also w/a decorator's mark, ca. 1900-15, 6 1/4" h. (ILLUS.) **450**

Boldly Striped Amphora Teapot

Teapot, cov., bulbous ovoid body tapering to a small angled rim, short shoulder spout & triple loop side handle, boldly painted w/alternating stripes of graduating overlapping blue circles & white stripes w/bands of brown scrolls centered by small dark blue diamonds, black rim, spout & handle, impressed "Austria - Amphora" in ovals w/crown & "Imperial Am-

phora" in a circle, impressed numbers "3975,46 - G," 1900-15, 6" h. (ILLUS.) **250**

Colorful Amphora Florina Series Teapot

Teapot, cov., Florina Series, spherical body w/a short shoulder spout & simple C-form handle, painted w/a bold design of geometric stylized flowers & leaves w/lenticular frits on both the front & back, in shades of dark rose pink, dark blue & black on a mottled mustard yellow ground, impressed on base "Imperial Amphora" in a circle & "Austria - Amphora" in ovals w/crown & impressed numbers "122212,64," 1900-15, 5 1/2" h. (ILLUS.) **695**

Amphora King Tut Series Teapot

Teapot, cov., King Tut Series, a footed tall ovoid body tapering to a flat mouth, an arched handle from rim of mouth to shoulder & short angled shoulder spout w/an arched strap to the rim, the sides in lavender blue molded & decorated in the center w/a large winged globe in cobalt blue, green & yellow enclosed by two undulating long blue snakes, other Egyptian symbols scattered around the sides & in rim & base bands, the back further decorated w/a portrait of a bearded Egyptian w/a braided tail at the top of his head & more symbols, marked on base "Made in Czecho-Slovakia - Amphora" in double ovals, impressed numbers "12203," a Roman numeral "I" & an "M" in underglaze black & a "J" in underglaze blue, ca. 1918-1939, 8 1/2" h. (ILLUS.) **195**

Fine Wahliss Secessionist Vase

Vase, 9 5/8" h., Secessionist Style, heavy ovoid body molded around the sides w/a band of large stylized lotus pads in deep red & green w/gold trim, four short arched openwork stem handles in gold from the neck to the edge of the pads, against a mottled dark brown & white ground w/gold stripes at the lower body, mark of Ernst Wahliss, early 20th c. (ILLUS.) **3,220**

Amphora Vase with Scattered Cabochons

Vase, 10" h., slightly flaring cylindrical form w/molded in-body rib to the wide shoulder centering a wide low mouth, the mottled gold & brown ground molded overall

w/a design of small rings highlighted by inset marbleized glazed cabochons around the sides, Amphora - Austria mark, ca. 1900 (ILLUS.) **489**

Teplitz Flower-decorated Vase

Vase, 11" h., dome-footed widely tapering ovoid body w/a ringed neck below the high petaled & rolled rim, ornate looped openwork gold shoulder handles, the foot in dark gold, the body in cream decorated overall w/pale lavender blossoms below the green neck & rim, marked "Turn - Teplitz," ca. 1900 (ILLUS.) **288**

Unusual Poppy & Maiden Vase

Vase, 11 3/8" h., figural, modeled as a large poppy w/the shaded blue & gold trimmed blossom at the top above the green stem & serrated leaves, also entwined w/the arching figure of a half-nude Art Nouveau maiden, raised on a cross-form dark blue & gold foot, vine professionally restored, mark of Riessner, Stellmacher & Kessel (ILLUS.).. **1,150**

Amphora Vase with Figural Pheasant

Vase, 16 1/4" h., figural, a footed wide squatty base mounted w/the model of a long-tailed realistic exotic pheasant beside a tall swelled cylindrical neck molded w/gilt veins up to the widely fanned compressed mouth, shaded green, blue & yellow w/heavy gold trim, Amphora mark, Model 4272 - 52, ca. 1904 (ILLUS.) **1,434**

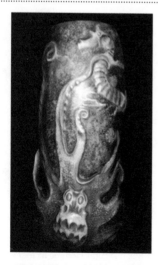

Rare Amphora Octopus Vase

Vase, 16 1/2" h., a massive fantasy piece w/a large golden iridescent octopus around the bottom, its tentacles extend-ing around the sides & up to the top where they grab a large swimming sea horse, a particularly rare style of octopus w/only one known at present, impressed "Amphora" & "Austria" in ovals, a crown & "4597 - 50" (ILLUS.) **8,000-8,500**

Vase, 16 1/2" h., fine Paul Dachsel creation in an undulating freeform design consisting of several abstract trees extending from the bottom to the top where a branch wraps around the top & then down dividing into other branches w/a series of red-glazed leaves, numerous white "jewels" suggesting seeds & seed pods attached to the branches & trunks, red leaves w/gold-tinged ends, very rare form, stamped over the glaze w/intertwined "PD - Turn - Teplitz," impressed "1115" **4,500-5,500**

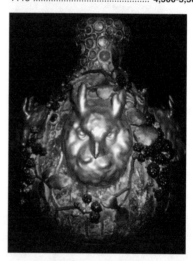

Rare Owl Head Vase

Vase, 17" h., massive bulbous bottle-form w/four finely detailed gold-finished owl heads projecting from the sides surrounded by brambles, leaves & many clusters of berries & numerous "jewels" of various sizes & colors interspersed among the brambles, unusual & complicated design, some similar pieces w/other animal heads exist but few survive intact, rare, impressed "Amphora" in oval, a crown & "8160" (ILLUS.) **8,500-9,500**

Vase, 18 1/4" h., 15 1/4" d., figural, the very wide low cushion base in deep red molded w/large stylized purple blossoms each centered by a jewel, centered by a wide swelled cylindrical neck in shaded gold also molded w/matching purple blossoms, a kneeling nude gold Art Nouveau maiden at one side of the base reaching up to the rim, after a model by Riessner, Amphora, Austria, ca. 1900 (ILLUS., top next page) **20,315**

Very Ornate & Rare Figural Amphora Vase

Tall Amphora Portrait Vase **87095**

Vase, 21 1/2" h., portrait-type, a very large profiled Sarah Bernhardt portrait inspired by Gustav Klimt featuring a majestic bird headdress w/eleven "jewels" of various sizes & colors, the figure w/long flowing hair streaming from under the headdress to her shoulders, below her neck is a jeweled butterfly, on one side a golden sun rises from the ocean emitting numerous golden rays, bluish green metallic background w/heavy gold detail, impressed

"Amphora" & "Austria" in a lozenge, a crown & "02047 - 28" (ILLUS.) **15,000-16,000**

Banko Ware

These collectible Japanese pottery wares were produced for domestic use and also exported in the late 19th and early 20th century. Pieces are finely detailed and composed of very thin clays in various colors including white, marbleized, grey, brown and tapestry. Traditional as well as whimsical pieces were produced, especially teapots. Banko Ware pieces generally have impressed markings on the base or handle. Decorative details could be painted, incised or applied in low or high relief.

Banko Ware Figural Bird Teapot

Teapot, cov., figural, model of a peacock, the cover in the top of the back, brightly enameled, beige clay, impressed "Made in Japan" mark, ca. 1920, 6 1/2" l., 4 1/2" h. (ILLUS.) **$200**

Colorful Elephant & Rider Banko Teapot

Teapot, cov., figural, model of an elephant w/a seated rider atop the cover, grey clay w/brightly enameled blanket on the back, unmarked, Japan, pictured in a dated 1916 Vantine's catalog, 6" l., 6" h. (ILLUS., top of page) **200**

Rare Banko Cottage-shaped Teapot

Teapot, cov., figural, modeled as a thatched roof cottage, top of roof forming the cover, applied in relief w/flowers, trimmed w/bright enamels on the grey clay ground, fine woven brass wire bail handle, two impressed signatures on the base, Japan, ca. 1900, 5 1/2" l., 3 1/2" h. (ILLUS.)... **400**

Teapot, cov., grayware, squatty bulbous body applied w/brightly enameled "1000 Treasures" design in high relief, twisted brown & grey clay rope w/bows applied around the rim & flaring crimped neck, inset cover w/knob finial, includes Banko tea infuser inside, marked w/impressed

Banko "1000 Treasures" Teapot

round Banko signature, Japan, ca. 1900, 4 1/2" l., 4" h. (ILLUS.) **135**

Banko Teapot with Cranes & Flowers

Teapot, cov., grayware, squatty bulbous body enameled w/flying cranes & flowers, twisted brown & grey clay applied handle & rope around the crimped flaring neck, inset cover w/knob finial, unsigned, Japan, ca. 1900, 4 1/2" l., 3" h. (ILLUS.)........ **50**

Belleek

Belleek china has been made in Ireland's County Fermanagh for many years. It is exceedingly thin porcelain. Several marks were used, including a hound and harp (1865-1880), and a hound, harp and castle (1863-1891). A printed hound, harp and castle with the words "Co. Fermanagh Ireland" constitutes the mark from 1891. Belleek-type china also was made in the United States last century by several firms, including Ceramic Art Company, Colombian Art Pottery, Lenox Inc., Ott & Brewer and Willets Manufacturing Co.

American Belleek
Marks:

American Art China Works - R&E, 1891-95

AAC (superimposed), 1891-95

American Belleek Company - Company name, banner & globe

Ceramic Art Company - CAC palette, 1889-1906

Colombian Art Pottery - CAP, 1893-1902

Cook Pottery - Three feathers w/"CHC," 1894-1904

Coxon Belleek Pottery - "Coxon Belleek" in a shield, 1926-1930

Gordon Belleek - "Gordon Belleek," 1920-28

Knowles, Taylor & Knowles - "Lotusware" in a circle w/a crown, 1891-96

Lenox China - Palette mark, 1906-1924

Ott & Brewer - crown & shield, 1883-1893

Perlee - "P" in a wreath, 1925-1930

Willets Manufacturing Company - Serpent mark, 1880-1909

Cook Pottery - Three feathers w/"CHC

Candlesticks and Lamps
Lenox, candlesticks, black w/Art Deco-style enameled flowers accented w/raised gold, palette mark, 8 1/4" h., pr. **$225**

Jars, Boxes and Miscellaneous
Lenox, condiment jar & cover, tapering hexagonal form w/domed cover, white ground w/blue jewel beading w/gold paste swags, sterling finial, palette mark, 4 1/2" w., 5 1/2" h. **325**

Lenox, ice bucket, h.p. w/Deco-style basket of flowers, palette mark, 5 1/2" h., 6 1/4" w. **225.00**

Lenox Belleek Jar with Falcons

Lenox Belleek, cylindrical jar w/wide flattened shoulder to a thin rolled rim & inset domed cover w/small pointed knob finial, h.p. around the sides w/five repeating panels, each w/a fierce green falcon below a green geometric band, outlined in black on a tan ground, inkstamp mark, repair to the rim, 9 5/8" h. (ILLUS.) **374**

Geisha Dresser Jar

Ott and Brewer, dresser jar, cov., cylindrical form, h.p. w/illustration of geisha, gold accents on lid, sword & crown mark, 5 1/2" h., 3 1/2" d. (ILLUS.) **425**

Mugs

Mug with Rose Swags & Gilding

Willets, tall cylindrical form w/slightly flaring base, applied handle, h.p. rose swags on cream ground, heavy gilding on rim, handle & raised leaf design around base, serpent mark, 5 1/2" h. (ILLUS.) **260**

Willets Mug with Peaches

Willets, tall, slightly ovoid form w/h.p. decoration of peaches & foliage on deep orange ground, serpent mark, 5 3/4" h. (ILLUS.) **160**

Pitchers, Creamers and Ewers

Willets, pitcher, 10 1/2" h., tankard-type, h.p. fruit decoration all over, artist-signed, serpent mark **750**

Willets, pitcher, 11 1/4" h., tankard-type, h.p. grapes, leaves & vines on light green matte ground, artist-signed "Fisher," serpent mark.......................... **625**

Willets, pitcher, 15" h., tankard-type, h.p. w/berries all around...................... **825**

Salt Dips

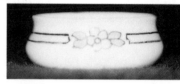

Artist-signed Lenox Salt Dip

Lenox, h.p. w/a stylized band & blossom design, signed by E. Sweeny, palette mark, 1 1/2" d. (ILLUS.) **55**

Willets Salt with Lustre Exterior 89375

Willets, pink lustre exterior, cream-colored interior, serpent mark, 2" d. (ILLUS.) **56**

Sets

Lenox, coffee set: pedestal-based cov. coffeepot, cov. sugar & creamer; h.p. flowers in gold shields w/heavy gold accents, artist-signed "Kaufman," palette mark, the set **1,450**

Creamer & Sugar in Sterling Holders

Lenox, creamer & open sugar, cream color porcelain inserts w/flaring rims in sterling silver reticulated footed holders, palette mark, 3 1/2" h. creamer, 2 1/2" h. sugar, pr. (ILLUS., bottom previous page) **275**

Lenox, salt & pepper shakers, h.p. w/small sprays of flowers, palette mark, 2 1/2" h., pr. **120**

Vases

Delicate Ceramic Art Company Vase

Ceramic Art Company, 9 1/4" h., ovoid egg-shaped body in creamy white decorated w/a raised gold body band & h.p. delicate gold flowering vines around the sides, a tall cylindrical gold neck flanked by large gold reticulated loop handles (ILLUS.) **403**

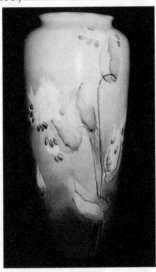

Lenox Vase with Blossom Seeds

Lenox, 10 1/4" h., tapering cylindrical body w/a short wide flared neck, h.p. w/open seed pods w/white & brown seeds & green leaves, shaded brown to cream ground, palette mark (ILLUS.)...................... **700**

Lenox, 11 1/2" h., 5 1/2" d., impressionistic h.p. decoration w/gold trim, palette mark **500**

Lenox, 12 1/2" h., ovoid body tapering to a short flared neck, h.p. w/large chrysanthemums w/soft gold highlights, palette mark.. **895**

Lenox, 15 1/2" h., cylindrical, h.p. Oriental women, trees & foliage, palette mark.......... **350**

Rose-decorated Willets Vase

Willets, 11" h., wide ovoid body w/the shoulder centered by a small cylindrical neck, h.p. w/very large white & pink roses & green leaves on a pale blue ground (ILLUS.)... **184**

Willets, 11" h., 6 1/2" d., bulbous shape w/a short, small neck w/fluted rim, h.p. w/flowers & heavy gold paste accents, serpent mark... **900**

Willets, 11 1/2" h., cylindrical, h.p. w/large roses of different shades of pink w/green leaves & gold trim, serpent mark **625**

Willets, 12" h., tapering from a small top to a flared bottom, h.p. clusters of roses, artist-signed "M.A. Minor - 1902," serpent mark **1,400**

Willets, 13" h., 6" d., bulbous form w/a short flared neck, h.p. overall w/pink, red & white roses w/soft gold highlights, serpent mark... **1,800**

Willets, 13" h., 9" d., bulbous shape w/a short pinched neck w/fluted rim, h.p. overall w/pink, red & white roses, serpent mark.. **1,850**

Willets, 13 3/4" h., 8" d., undecorated, urn-shaped w/curved applied handles, serpent mark.. **125**

Willets, 15 1/2" h., waisted cylindrical form, h.p. overall w/hyacinths w/gold accents, artist-signed "E. Miler," serpent mark.. **1,050**

Miscellaneous

Fine Lotus Ware Porcelain Teapot

Knowles, Taylor & Knowles, teapot, Lotus Ware, Valenciennes shape, Fish Net patt., East Liverpool, Ohio, 1890s (ILLUS., top of page) **350**

Lenox, ice bucket, h.p. w/Deco-style basket of flowers, palette mark, 5 1/2" h., 6 1/4" w. **225**

Rare Ott & Brewer Figural Tray

Ott & Brewer, tray, long narrow shell form molded on top w/a reclining figure of Venus wearing a diaphanous gown, fired-on gold trim, 3 1/4 x 11" (ILLUS.) **2,415**

Floral-decorated Willets Belleek Teapot

Willets, teapot, cov., squatty bulbous body w/inset cover w/arched gold handle, C-scroll handle & serpentine spout, white ground h.p. w/a wide center band of stylized pink, white & lavender blossoms & green leaves w/narrow matching bands

around the rim & edge of cover, the lower body & shoulder decorated w/bands of black-outlined white panels, artist-signed, crack in handle into body, late 19th - early 20th c. (ILLUS.) **104**

Irish Belleek

Basket Ware

Two Forget-Me-Not Trinket Boxes

Trinket boxes, cov., Forget-Me-Not patt., D111-III, each (ILLUS. of two) **$1,000**

Comports & Centerpieces

Boudoir Candlestick with Flowers

Candlestick, Boudoir patt. w/applied flowers, D1506-I, 3" h. (ILLUS.) **1,600**

Tri-Dolphin & Shell Pedestal Comport

Comport, Tri-Dolphin & Shell Pedestal
patt., D1149-I (ILLUS.) **4,200**

Rare Globe Amphora Lamp Unlit

Lamp, table model, Globe Amphora patt.,
colored & gilt trim, clear glass globe
shade, double wick, D1529-I, 22 1/2" h.
(ILLUS. unlit) **6,000**

Earthenware

Earthenware Trivet with Flowers

Trivet, round, hand-painted lily-of-the-val-
ley, D1057-I (ILLUS.) **800**

Figurines

Inkstand, Mermaid patt., oblong serpentine
shape w/reclining mermaid molded along
one side, D274-II, 9 1/2" l. (ILLUS., bot-
tom of page).. **4,600**
Trinket box, cov., Jack on Shore patt., D24-
II (ILLUS., top next page)......................... **3,200**

Rare Bird Nest Wall Bracket

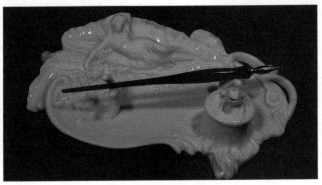

Rare Mermaid Inkstand

Jack on Shore Figural Trinket Box

Wall bracket, Bird Nest model, elongated nest composed of twigs w/a bird perched on the rim, D1801-I, 12" h. (ILLUS., previous page).. **3,600**

Wall brackets, Irish Squirrel, model of squirrel among leafy branches, D1803-I, pr. **6,600**

Museum Display Patterns (Artichoke, Chinese, Finner, Five O'Clock, Lace, Ring Handle Ivory, Set #36 & Victoria)

Bone china bread plate, heavy pink ground & gilt trim, D844-I (ILLUS. left with teacup & saucer, bottom of page) **680**

Bone china teacup & saucer, heavy pink ground & gilt trim, D848-I (ILLUS. right with bread plate, botto of page) **620**

Chinese tea urn, figural cover, ornate winged dragon spout, twisted rope-form overhead handle, large winged dragon support on round base w/paw feet, decorated (D482-I) **15,000**

Chinese tray, round, decorated (D487-I) ... **3,200**

Lace plate, 6" d., decorated (D806-I) **600**

Lace teacup & saucer, decorated (D799-I)
.... **1,600**

Ring Handle bread plate, Limoges decoration (D824-I) **1,400**

Ring Handle creamer & open sugar bowl, Limoges decoration (D826-I & D826-I), pr. **1,200**

Ring Handle egg cup, Limoges decoration (D830-I) **440**

Ring Handle teacup & saucer, Crane (Bittern) decoration (D819-I) **840**

Bone China Bread Plate & Teacup and Saucer

Religious Items & Lithophanes

Belleek Cherub Head Water Font

Holy water font, Cherub head w/spread
wings, D1110-VI.. **100**
Holy water font, Coral & Shell (D1111-V) **100**
Holy water font, Sacred Heart font, #8
(D1114-II) **320**
Lithophane, Madonna, Child & Angel
(D1544-VII)... **600**

Teawares

It is hard to believe that Belleek produced such a wide range of tea sets, which included teapots. Depending on where one draws a line, there are some 38 known distinctive shapes and, when colors and sizes are taken into account, the variations exceed 100.

The patterns can be divided into four main design groups, with two misfits (Chinese and Mask do not fit into any group): Marine (Echinus, Neptune, etc.), Geometric (fan, scroll, etc.), Floral (Shamrock, Lily, Grass, etc.), and Celtic. The make-up of the individual sets differs enormously. The smaller sets consist of the basic necessities for serving a cup of tea on a tray: tray, cup and saucer, small teapot (enough for one cup) cream and sugar. Other sets have a much wider range of pieces.

Many of these sets also included either a teakettle or coffeepot. Belleek distinguished its teakettle by a handle over the top of the base, as opposed to the side handle like the teapot. Coffeepots, like teapots, had their handles on the side, but were taller in design.

Most of these sets, including the teapot, were introduced in the late 1st period early 2nd period. Some of these teapots have been reproduced within the last five years at the Pottery without much change in the design, which goes to prove what great designs were made at the beginning.

Other teapots have been slightly modified. For example, the Lace, Limpet and Shell teapots lost their feet in later designs. These modifications were mostly implemented to help with the production, making it speedier and, therefore, saving costs. The spout on other teapots including the Tridacna pattern was shortened, again to prevent damage whilst being shipped.

It is worth the collector's while to study the teapots because the more rare examples are highly sought after and worth a great deal, whereas the more common teapots, although still highly collectible, are not so looked for.- Lady Marion LanghamUnless otherwise noted, all the following are "teapots." Teakettles are identified by the handle formed "over the top" as opposed to being attached to the side.

The "bracketed" range of prices given is based on period (of manufacture), size and decoration.

All pricing given here is for the earlier Black Mark periods, i.e., 1st Period (ca. 1863-1890), 2nd Period (ca. 1891-1926) and 3rd Period (ca. 1926-1946)

Belleek produced many of its teapots, but not all, in three sizes, these identified, of course, as small, medium and large.

Known tints are Pink, Green, Blue and Orange. Decoration may be a "heavy" application of a mixture of the tints (refer to example of Footed Echinus) or more elaborate such as hand painted flowers or scenes. Eugene Sheerin, Belleek's most famous artist, once painted an entire breakfast set utilizing the Ring Handled Ivory Pattern, with each piece of the set displaying a different Irish scene.

All photos courtesy of Lady Marion Langham.

Undecorated Erne Pattern Tea Set

Belleek Aberdeen Pattern Breakfast Tea Set

Unnamed Belleek Pattern with Celtic Design & Green Trim

Tea set: cov. teapot, creamer & cup & saucer; Erne patt., undecorated, 2nd period, creamer $220-260; cup & saucer, $260-320; teapot only (ILLUS. of group, bottom previous page) **$700-800**

Tea set: cov. teapot, creamer, open sugar & cups & saucers; Aberdeen breakfast set, no tray, D494-II (ILLUS., top of page) **2,200**

Tea set: cov. teapot, creamer & two cups & saucers; unnamed pattern w/Celtic design trimmed in green, 2nd period, creamer, $300-400; each cup & saucer, $300-400; teapot only (ILLUS. of group, second from top of page) **600-800**

Victoria Pattern Teapot with Gold Trim

Teapot, Victoria patt., gold trim, 2nd period
(ILLUS., top of page)......................... **800-1,200**

Vases & Spills
Dolphin and Shell Vase, green tint, D137-II . **1,400**
Fish Spill, tall fish standing in its tail, D184-I **880**
Nile Vase, large size (D84-III) **520**
Onion Spill, large size (D156-I) **680**
Pierced Shamrock Vase, tall tapering
ovoid form w/pierced rim, D1217-II **480**
Prince Arthur Vase, flowered (D1218-II)......... **920**
Specimen Holder, large size, D185-I **2,000**
Straw Basket, model of a long basket w/ap-
plied flowers, D79-II **600**

Miscellaneous
*Items produced, but with NO matching tea set
pieces.*

Cleary salt dip, oblong, pink tint & gilt trim
(D295-II).. **100**
Flask, ovoid form, gilt Harp, Hound & Castle
logo at the center in gold, D1523-I............. **2,000**
Heart plate, scalloped edges, Size 2, h.p.
flowers, D635-III **120**

Irish Armorial Pot

Irish Pot, armorial souvenir decoration,
D1503-I (ILUS.).. **320**
Irish Pot, Size 2, D207-II **160**
Irish Pot, Size 2, D207-III **120**
Irish Pot creamer & open sugar bowl,
Size 2, D232-II, pr. **240**

Lifford Creamer

Lifford creamer, double spout, D301-III
(ILLUS.)... **140**

Model of Irish Harp

Model of Irish Harp, small size, D77-II
(ILLUS.) **400**
Ring Handle plate, 6" d., Limoges Decora-
tion, D822-I **600**

Shell & Coral salt spoon, 3 1/2" l. (D2107-
II).. 100
Shell plateau, bowl-shaped, medium size,
D792-I 380
Shell sugar bowl, open, large size, D602-I..... 600
Toy creamer & open sugar bowl, Cleary
patt. (D249-III), pr............................... 160
Toy creamer & open sugar bowl, Sham-
rock patt. (D234-II), pr......................... 220

Two Irish Belleek Ribbed Tumblers

Tumbler, cylindrical w/ribbing around the
lower half, Size 2, D281-I (ILLUS. left)........ 200
Tumbler, cylindrical w/ribbing around the
lower half, Size 6, D285-III (ILLUS. right)....... 80

Bennington

*Bennington wares, which ranged from stone-
ware to parian and porcelain, were made in Bennington, Vermont, primarily in two potteries, one
in which Captain John Norton and his descendants were principals, and the other in which
Christopher Webber Fenton (also once associated
with the Nortons) was a principal. Various marks
are found on the wares made in the two major
potteries, including J. & E. Norton, E. & L. P.
Norton, L. Norton & Co., Norton & Fenton,
Edward Norton, Lyman Fenton & Co., Fenton's
Works, United States Pottery Co., U.S.P. and others.*

*The popular pottery with the mottled brown on
yellowware glaze was also produced in Bennington, but such wares should be referred to as
"Rockingham" or "Bennington-type" unless they
can be specifically attributed to a Bennington,
Vermont factory.*

Flask, in shape of book, flint enamel glaze
in light brown & teal green, impressed
"Departed Spirits," 7 3/4" h...................... $1,265
Flask, in shape of book, running flint enamel
glaze, impressed "Departed Spirits G,"
5 5/8" h... 935
Picture frame, oval w/wide ringed rounded
sides, overall mottled Rockingham glaze,
few underside flakes, mid-19th c.,
8 3/4 x 9 3/4" (ILLUS., top of next col-
umn)... 489
Pitcher, 9 1/4" h., parian, Waterfall patt.,
molded in relief as a cylindrical waterfall
w/rocks showing through, United States
Pottery, 1852-58... 518

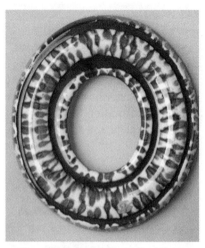

Bennington Rockingham Oval Frame

Pitcher, 9 3/8" h., parian, Cascade patt., cylindrical form molded w/an overall waterfall on rocky cliff design, tree branch handle, glazed interior, Bennington relief
lozenge mark 550
Pitcher, 9 1/2" h., parian, bulbous paneled
& deeply waisted form w/a flat rim & wide
arched spout, molded overall w/flowering
vines w/a vine-wrapped handle, United
States Pottery, ca. 1850-58 518

Berlin (KPM)

*The mark KPM was used at Meissen from 1724
to 1725, and was later adopted by the Royal Factory, Konigliche Porzellan Manufaktur, in Berlin.
At various periods it has been incorporated with
the Brandenburg scepter, the Prussian eagle or
the crowned globe. The same letters were also
adopted by other factories in Germany in the late
19th and early 20th centuries. With the end of the
German monarchy in 1918, the name of the firm
was changed to Staatliche Porzellan Manufaktur
and though production was halted during World
War II, the factory was rebuilt and is still in business. The exquisite paintings on porcelain were
produced at the close of the 19th century and are
eagerly sought by collectors today.*

Centerpiece, in the Vienna style, a deep
oval bowl w/serpentine sides pierced at
the rim & flanked by large gold scrolling
loop handles, the front finely painted w/a
Classical view representing the Arts in a
garden setting & the reverse depicting
Neptune as a child riding a dolphin
w/other putti, a gold bead band around
the base of the bowl & raised on a deep
maroon pedestal w/gilt scroll decoration
& an oblong gold foot w/block feet alternating w/dolphin mask feet between
gold knobs, titled in German on the bottom, blue sceptre mark, late 19th c.,
15" l. (ILLUS., top next page)................ $4,183

Outstanding Ornate Berlin Centerpiece

Very Rare Berlin Pate-Sur-Pate Charger

Berlin Charger with Lovely Portrait

Charger, pate-sur-pate, round w/a wide dished rim band in white decorated w/ornate gold Art Nouveau floral looping panels w/small forget-me-nots & roses, the wide center w/a celadon green ground painted & hand-tooled in white slip w/a scene of a diaphanously clad Bacchante pouring a vessel of wine into Pan's lips as he kneels beside a tree stump, blue sceptre & iron-red orb marks, ca. 1895, 13 3/4" d. (ILLUS.) **5,378**

Charger, round, the wide border band w/a cobalt blue ground very ornately painted in gold w/alternating panels of a wreath & crown & scrolls in pointed arcs, the center painted in color w/a bust portrait of a 16th c. lady w/a fancy headdress, signed by Wagner, in a deep square giltwood shadowbox frame lined in red velvet, late 19th c., 16" d. (ILLUS., top next column) **2,185**

Berlin Model of a Red Squirrel

Model of a squirrel, seated animal in dark brick red holding a brown acorn, on a green & brown stump molded w/acorns & oak leaves, some gold wear, second half 19th c., 10" h. (ILLUS., previous page) **1,150**

KPM Plaque of "The Sistine Madonna"

Plaque, oval, decorated w/a color copy of "The Sistine Madonna" after Raphael, mounted in an elaborate rectangular giltwood pierce-carved frame composed of scrolling acanthus leaves w/a red velvet liner, fitted in a glazed rectangular shadowbox frame, impressed sceptre & KPM marks, late 19th c., plaque 13 1/2 x 17" (ILLUS.) **4,025**

Plaque with Exotic Woman Musician

Plaque, rectangular, finely painted w/the portrait of an exotic raven-haired beauty playing a lyre carved as the head of an Egyptian pharaoh, a brazier at her feet, impressed monogram & sceptre mark, titled on the back, late 19th - early 20th c.,

mounted in giltwood frame, 6 1/4 x 9 3/8" (ILLUS.) **4,183**

Charming KPM Plaque with Family

Plaque, rectangular, painted w/a winter scene of an elderly grandfather just outside a cottage door & standing holding a small baby w/his little granddaughter nearby, titled "The First Snowfall," impressed sceptre & KPM marks, artist-signed, in a fancy acanthus leaf-carved wooden frame, late 19th c., plaque 7 1/2 x 10" (ILLUS.) **4,370**

Berlin KPM Plaque in Ornate Gilt Frame

Plaque, rectangular, scene of two young women w/long flowing hair & wearing diaphanous gowns holding floral garland above their heads, reverse impressed "KPM" w/scepter, in very ornate gilt wood frame of pierced scroll decoration, 19th c., 7 1/2 x 10" (ILLUS.) **4,830**

Extraordinary Berlin Plaque with an Elaborate Classical Scene

Plaque, rectangular, a long classical scene depicting the goddess Aurora & her attendants, after a painting by Guido Reni, inscribed & titled on the back along w/a label reading "Painted for Mermood and Jaccurd Jewelry Co., St. Louis," impressed KPM & other marks, artist-signed, mounted in an elaborate reticulated giltwood framed, plaque 8 x 13" (ILLUS., top of page) **10,638**

Bisque

Bisque is biscuit china, fired a single time but not glazed. Some bisque is decorated with colors. Most abundant from the Victorian era are figures and groups, but other pieces, from busts to vases, were made by numerous potteries in the United States and abroad. Reproductions have been produced for many years, so care must be taken when seeking antique originals.

Large Berlin KPM Bolted Urn

Urn, octagonal stepped base below ringed pedestal supporting baluster-form body w/trumpet neck, two gilt coiled snake-form handles, front w/h.p. decoration of winged cherub among floral bouquet, reverse w/butterflies & florals, marked w/red orb & blue underglaze circle, late 19th c., 18 3/4" h. (ILLUS.)........................ **3,680**

Lovely Bisque Family Group

Figure group, a family group all wearing 18th c. costume, a young man standing close behind & a pretty young woman looking down, a young boy in front reaching up to them, finely painted ornate costumes in shades of blue, pink & gold &

fine facial features, on a rounded rockwork base, printed anchor mark, late 19th c., some very minor professional repairs, 26" h. (ILLUS.) **$1,955**

Charming Victorian Girl by a Fountain

Figure of a Victorian girl, the young blonde-haired girl walking down rocky steps & leaning on a low wall w/a lion head fountain issuing blue water, wearing a short ruffled blue dress, large blue bonnet & blue shoes, carrying a brown basket on her arm, nice coloring, "R" in diamond mark, perhaps Royal Rudolstadt, Germany, ca. 1900, 10" h. (ILLUS.) **80-100**

Charming Bisque Group of Woman & Goat

Figure of a woman & goat, the woman standing wearing an 18th c. peasant costume in white, blue & pink w/overall tiny painted flowers, holding a sheaf of grain & looking down at a small goat jumping up to nibble on the flowers gathered in her skirt, on a round socle base decorated w/blue & gold bands & delicate blue & yellow ribbon band, late 19th c., minor repair, 18" h. (ILLUS.) **374**

Bisque Figures of Boy & Girl

Figures of boy & girl, the girl wearing yellow skirt w/red bows & white ruffled hem, white blouse, pale blue bodice & overskirt w/white lacy trim, orange shoes, tam-like hat, holding white & orange fan in one hand, the boy in short yellow pants w/white ruffled cuffs, matching yellow jacket, pale blue stockings & shirt, yellow & orange boots, & white hat w/orange trim, standing w/one hand on hip, the other at hat, unmarked, Germany, ca. 1900, 14" h., pr. (ILLUS.) **201**

Bisque Children Blowing Soap Bubbles

Figures of children blowing bubbles, girl wearing a cream dress w/pink floral decoration & gold trim at collar & hem, boy w/pink flower-decorated knee breeches & cream shirt w/dotted ruffled neck & cuffs, each holding a bubble pipe to mouth & each sitting on bench that also holds bowl for soapy water, h.p. features, unmarked, Heubach, Germany, ca. 1900, 13" h., pr. (ILLUS.) **978**

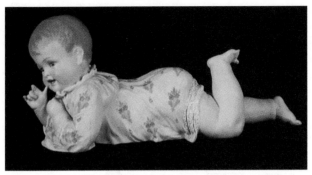

Charming Reclining Piano Baby

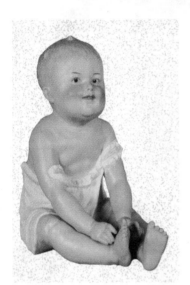

Marked Heubach Seated Piano Baby

Piano baby, seated unjointed figure w/blue intaglio eyes, open-closed mouth w/two upper teeth, molded & painted blonde hair, molded baby dress w/ruffle & green ribbon trim unfastened on right shoulder & falling off left shoulder, reaching for his right foot, overall excellent condition, marked on lower back by the Gebruder Heubach factory, Germany, ca. 1900, 8" h. (ILLUS.) **413**

Piano baby, unjointed figure of a baby lying on its stomach w/one hand near its mouth & one leg bent up, h.p. blue eyes, open-closed mouth w/two lower teeth, molded & painted brown hair, molded blue dress w/blue flowers & lace edging at the neck, sleeves & hem, minor firing line at back of neck, some paint missing from repair, 17" l. (ILLUS., top of page) **270**

Blanc De Chine

This ware is a fine white Chinese porcelain with a rich clear glaze. It became popular in France in the early 18th century and remained popular in Europe and America through the 19th century. Fine figural pieces are most often found, with the earlier examples bringing the highest prices.

Guanyin Figures Mounted as Lamps

Figures of Guanyin, each standing gracefully w/flowing gown & one hand out, the other holding a lotus stem, raised on a lotus-trimmed pedestal base, China, 19th c., now mounted as lamps, overall 15" h., 1 pr. (ILLUS., pr.) **$382**

Blanc de Chine Mythological Horses

Model of mythological horses, facing pair of standing animals w/mascaron heads & antlers looking back over their shoulders & their razor-like backs & raised tails, raised on fitted carved wood bases, China, 19th c., one w/broken & repaired leg, each 10" l., 13 1/4" h., pr. (ILLUS., top of page) **1,150**

Early Chinese Blanc-de-Chine Vases

Vases, 5 1/8" h., footed squatty bulbous lower body molded w/wide lappets & tapering to a tall cylindrical neck flanked by elephant head handles suspending rings, China, 18th c., pr. (ILLUS.) **311**

Blue & White Pottery

The category of blue and white or blue and grey pottery includes a wide variety of pottery, earthenware and stoneware items widely produced in this country in the late 19th century right through the 1930s. Originally marketed as inexpensive wares, most pieces featured a white or grey body molded with a fruit, flower or geometric design and then trimmed with bands or splashes of blue to highlight the molded pattern. Pitchers, butter crocks and salt boxes are among the numerous items produced, but other kitchenwares and chamber sets are also found. Values vary depending on the rarity of the embossed pattern

and the depth of color of the blue trim; the darker the blue, the better. Some entries refer to several different books on Blue and White Pottery. These books are: Blue & White Stoneware, Pottery & Crockery *by Edith Harbin (1977, Collector Books, Paducah, KY);* Stoneware in the Blue and White *by M.H. Alexander (1993 reprint, Image Graphics, Inc., Paducah, KY); and* Blue & White Stoneware *by Kathryn McNerney (1995, Collector Books, Paducah, KY).*

Apple cider cooler, cov., w/spigot, 13" d., 15" h. **$425**

Miniature Blue & White Bank

Bank, miniature, jug-form, stenciled rectangle w/"Money Bank" (ILLUS.) **650**
Basin, embossed Apple Blossom patt., Burley-Winter Pottery Co., 9" d. **185**
Batter jar, cov., stenciled Wildflower patt., Brush-McCoy Pottery Co., small, 6" d., 5 3/4" h. (ILLUS. right with Wildflower batter pail, top next page) **350**
Batter pail, bail handle, stenciled Wildflower patt., Brush-McCoy Pottery Co., 4 7/8" h. (ILLUS. left with batter jar, top next page) **375**

Wildflower Batter Jar & Pail

Advertising Beater Jar

Beater jar, advertising-type, "Stop And Shop at Wagner's Cash Grocery, Kingsley, Iowa," 4 3/4" h. (ILLUS.) **325**

Bowl, 4" d., 2" h., berry, embossed Flying Bird patt., w/advertising, A.E. Hull Pottery Co. **450**

Bowl, 4" d., 2" h., berry/cereal, plain w/pale blue rim band **55**

Bowl, 7" d., embossed Beaded Rose patt., A.E. Hull Pottery Co. **150**

Reverse Pyramids-Picket Fence Bowl

Bowl, 7 1/2" d., 5" h., embossed Reverse Pyramids w/Reverse Picket Fence patt., Ruckles Pottery (ILLUS.) **90-100**

Bowl, stenciled Nautilus patt., rim handles, A.E. Hull Pottery Co. **325**

Bowl, 7" d., 2 1/2" h., embossed Venetian patt., same as Reverse Pyramids w/Reverse Picket Fence but w/honeycomb at bottom, Roseville Pottery (ILLUS., bottom of page) **50**

Embossed Venetian Pattern Bowl

Bowls, nesting-type, embossed Cosmos patt., A.E. Hull Pottery Co., depending on size, each **165-275**

Stenciled Wildflower Bowl

Bowls, nesting-type, stenciled Wildflower patt., Brush-McCoy Pottery Co., 4" to 14" d., depending on size (ILLUS. of 10" d. size) **150-450**

Brush vase, embossed Bow Tie (Our Lucile) patt., w/rose decal, Brush-McCoy Pottery Co., 5 1/2" h. **115**

Willow Pattern Brush Vase

Brush vase, embossed Willow (Basketweave & Morning Glory) patt., Brush-McCoy Pottery Co., small, 4 3/4" h. (ILLUS.) **325**

Butter crock, cov., embossed Butterfly patt., Nelson McCoy Sanitary Stoneware Co., 10 lb. size, 9 1/2" d., 6" h. **275**

Cows & Columns Butter Crock

Butter crock, cov., embossed Cows and Columns patt., found in five sizes from 2 lbs. to 10 lbs., Brush-McCoy Pottery Co., ranges (ILLUS.) .... **425-650+**

Butter crock, cov., embossed Eagle patt., A.E. Hull Pottery Co., 6" d., 6" h. (ILLUS. right, top next page) **700**

Butter crock, cov., embossed Grape and Leaves Low patt., Robinson Clay Products, 6 1/2" d., 3" h. **250**

Butter crock, cov., embossed Indian Good Luck Sign (Swastika) patt., produced by Nelson McCoy Sanitary Stoneware Co., Robinson-Ransbottom Pottery Co. & The Crooksville Pottery Co., 6 1/4" d., 5 1/4" h. **175**

Butter crock, cov., embossed Jersey Cow patt., 4" h. **1,000**

Butter crock, cov., embossed Leaf Flemish patt., 8" d., 7" h. **200**

Butter crock, cov., stenciled Dutch Scene patt., Brush-McCoy Pottery Co., 6 3/4" d., 5" h. **325**

Canister, cov., embossed Willow (Basketweave & Morning Glory) patt., "Barley," Brush-McCoy Pottery Co., average 6 1/2 to 7" h., each. **1,000**

Stenciled Floral Pattern Canister

Canister, cov., stenciled Floral patt., "Coffee," probably A.E. Hull Pottery Co., 5 7/8" h. (ILLUS.) **275**

Embossed GrapeWare Canister

Eagle Butter and Salt Crocks

Canister, embossed GrapeWare patt., "Pepper," no cover, 3 3/8" h. (ILLUS., page 235) **400**

Canister, cov., stenciled Wildflower patt., blank, Brush-McCoy Pottery Co., 2 gal. **425**

Casserole, cov., embossed GrapeWare patt., Brush-McCoy Pottery Co. (ILLUS. with extra cover, bottom of page) **425**

Chamber pot, cov., embossed Apple Blossom patt., Burley-Winter Pottery Co., 11" d., 6" h. (ILLUS., top next column) **375**

Chamber pot, cov., embossed Open Rose and Spearpoint Panels patt., A.E. Hull Pottery Co., 9 1/2" d., 6" h. **300**

Cooking or preserving kettle, cov., bail handle, embossed Peacock patt., Brush-McCoy Pottery Co., 5 qt. **1,100**

Apple Blossom Chamber Pot

Embossed GrapeWare Casserole

Lovebird Pattern Milk Crock

Embossed Cattail Advertising Mug

Cosmos Jardiniere & Pedestal

Jardiniere & pedestal, embossed Cosmos patt., possibly Weller or Burley-Winter Pottery Co., jardiniere 6" h., pedestal 5 1/2" h. (ILLUS.) **2,000**

Match holder, model of a duck, 5 1/2" d., 5" h. **250**

Milk crock, embossed Apricot patt., A.E. Hull Pottery Co., 10" d., 5" h. **225**

Milk crock, embossed Lovebird patt., w/bail handle, A.E. Hull Pottery Co., 9" d., 5 1/2" h. (ILLUS., top of page) **500**

Mug, embossed Cattail patt., w/advertising, Western Stoneware Co., 3" d., 4" h. (ILLUS., top next column) **275**

Mug, embossed Grape Cluster in Shield patt., 12 oz. **195**

Bluebird Decal Hall Boy Pitcher

Pitcher, 9" h., 7" d., Bluebird decal, hall boy-style, Brush-McCoy Pottery Co. (ILLUS.).. **425**

Pitcher, Diffused Blue, plain smooth shape, found in 1/4-, 1/2-, 5/8- & 1-gallon size, smallest is rarest, depending on the size **150-225**

Blue Stupid Pattern Pitcher

Pitcher, 8" h., 6" d., Stupid patt., Diffused Blue bands (ILLUS.) **450**

Ramekin or nappy, embossed Peacock patt., Brush-McCoy Pottery Co., 4" d. **300**

Roaster, cov., stenciled Wildflower patt., Brush-McCoy Pottery Co., 12" d., 8 1/2" h. **450**

Advertising Hanging Salt Box

Salt box, cov., Diffused Blue patt., Western Stoneware advertising-type, "You Need Salt, We Need You - The Hodgin Store, Whittier, Iowa," 4 1/4" h. (ILLUS.) **600**

Salt box, cov., embossed Apple Blossom patt., Burley-Winter Pottery Co., 6" d., 4" h. **400**

Salt box, cov., embossed Daisy on Snowflake patt. (ILLUS., top next column) **250-275**

Salt box, cov., embossed Good Luck Sign (Swastika) patt., Nelson McCoy Sanitary Stoneware Co., Robinson-Ransbottom Pottery Co. & The Crooksville Pottery Co., 6" d., 4" h. **250**

Embossed Daisy on Snowflake Salt Box

Salt box, cov., embossed Grape and Basketweave patt., 6" d., 4" h. **250**

Salt box, cov., embossed Raspberry patt., Brush-McCoy Pottery Co., 5 1/2" d., 5 1/2" h. **250**

Salt box, cov., hanging-type, embossed Eagle patt., A.E. Hull Pottery Co., 6" d., 4" h. (ILLUS. left w/Eagle butter crock) **600**

Sand jar, embossed Polar Bear patt., Uhl Pottery Co., 12 1/4" d., 14 1/2" h. **1,250**

Embossed Apple Blossom Slop Jar

Slop jar, cov., embossed Apple Blossom patt., Burley-Winter Pottery Co., 10" h. (ILLUS.) **350**

Slop jar, cov., embossed Rose & Fishscale patt., A.E. Hull Pottery Co., 10" h. **325**

Apple Blossom Water Cooler

Lighter Grey Catbird with Hyacinths

Water cooler, cov., embossed Apple Blossom patt., w/spigot, 13" h. (ILLUS.) **1,000**
Water cooler, cov., embossed Cupid patt.,
w/spigot, Western Stoneware, 5 gal............. **725**
Water cooler, cov., embossed Polar Bear
patt., w/ spigot, Uhl Pottery Co., 4 gal......... **725**

Boehm Porcelains

*Although not antique, Boehm porcelain sculp-
tures have attracted much interest as Edward
Marshall Boehm excelled in hard porcelain sculptures. His finest creations, inspired by the beauties of nature, are in the forms of birds and
flowers. Since his death in 1969, his work has
been carried on by his wife at the Boehm Studios
in Trenton, New Jersey. In 1971, an additional
studio was opened in Malvern, England, where
bone porcelain sculptures are produced. We list
both limited and non-limited editions of Boehm.*

Bobcat with Cubs, the mother cat on a
large tree stump holding one cub in her
mouth, the other climbing up to her, rockwork base, marked & numbered under
base, 14" l., 9" h. (ILLUS., top next page)
.... **$863**
Catbird with Hyacinths, a light grey bird
w/wings down, perched in front of large
white & lavender hyacinth blossoms,
marked & numbered on base 483,
14 1/2" h. (ILLUS., top next column) **748**

Dark Catbird with Hyacinths

Catbird with Hyacinths, large dark grey
bird w/one wing open, beside tall white &
lavender hyacinth blossoms, marked &
numbered on base 483, 14" h. (ILLUS.) **690**

Bobcat Mother & Cubs

Flamingo on Nest with Chick

Flamingo, nesting bird w/head curved down to feed a chick peeking out from under wing, Audubon Society edition, marked & numbered on base 40316-98, 14 1/2" l., 13 1/4" h. (ILLUS., above).......................... **2,875**

Green Jays, each perched on a rustic branch w/orange berries, marked & numbered on the base 486, one 12" w. x 19" h., the other 10" w. x 14 1/2" h., pr. (ILLUS., next column) **1,955**

Boehm Green Jays on Berried Branches

Wood Thrushes on Flowering Branches

Boehm Red-Winged Blackbirds

A Varied Bunting on Large Flower

Red-Winged Blackbirds, a male & female each modeled on cattails, marked & numbered on base #426, very good condition, 15 1/2" h., the pair (ILLUS.) **2,530**

Varied Bunting, small bird perched at the base of a tall stem of orange bell-shaped blossoms, marked & numbered on the base 481, three flower buds detached, 23 1/2" h. (ILLUS., top next column) **2,185**

Wood Thrushes, a male & female perched on white-flowered branches, the female feeding a nest of chicks, the male w/head up singing, ca. 1965, marked & numbered on the bases 485, each 15" h., pr. (ILLUS., top of page) **3,680**

Whooping Crane in flight, large black & white bird, Audubon Society edition, marked & numbered 40254 on base, 18 1/2" h. (ILLUS., bottom next column) ... **1,380**

Boehm Whooping Crane in Flight

Buffalo Pottery

Incorporated in 1901 as a wholly owned subsidiary of the Larkin Soap Company, founded by John D. Larkin of Buffalo, New York, in 1875, the Buffalo Pottery was a manufactory built to produce premium wares to be included with purchases of Larkin's chief product, soap.

In October 1903, the first kiln was fired and Buffalo Pottery became the only pottery in the world run entirely by electricity. In 1904 Larkin offered its first premium produced by the pottery. This concept of using premiums caused sales to skyrocket and, in 1905, the first Blue Willow pattern pottery made in the United States was introduced as a premium.

The Buffalo Pottery administrative building, built in 1904 to house 1,800 clerical workers, was the creation of a 32-year-old architect, Frank Lloyd Wright. The building was demolished in 1953, but many critics considered it to be Wright's masterpiece.

By 1910 annual soap production peaked and the number of premiums offered in the catalogs exceeded 600. By 1915 this number had grown to 1,500. The first catalog of premiums was issued in 1893 and continued to appear through the late 1930s.

John D. Larkin died in 1926, and during the Great Depression the firm suffered severe losses, going into bankruptcy in 1940. After World War II the pottery resumed production under new management, but its vitreous wares were generally limited to mass-produced china for the institutional market.

Among the pottery lines produced during Buffalo's heyday were Gaudy Willow, Deldare, Abino Ware, historical and commemorative plates, and unique handpainted jugs and pitchers. In the 1920s and 1930s the firm concentrated on personalized wares for commercial clients including hotels, clubs, railroads, and restaurants.

In 1983 Oneida Silversmiths bought the pottery, an ironic twist since, years before, Oneida silver had been featured in Larkin catalogs. The pottery has now ceased all domestic production of ceramics. - Phillip M. Sullivan.

Buffalo Pottery Mark

Deldare Ware (1908-1909, 1923-1925)

Note: "Fallowfield Hunt" and "Ye Olden Days" scenes are similarly priced for the equivalent pieces in this line.

Calling card tray, round w/tab handles, "Ye Lion Inn" scene, 7 3/4" d. (ILLUS. center row far left with other Deldare pieces, bottom of page) **$250-350**

Charger, "An Evening at Ye Lion Inn," decorated by W. Forster, 1908, some superficial scratches, 13 1/2" d. (ILLUS., next page) **403**

Chocolate set: tall tapering hexagonal covered chocolate pot w/serpentine handle decorated w/"Ye Village Street" scene & two tapering conical chocolate cups, artist-signed, 1909, small rim repairs on cups, chocolate pot 10 1/2" h., the set (ILLUS. center with Deldare chop plate & tankard pitcher, top of next page) **1,500-3,000**

Chop plate, large round form w/dished center, "An Evening At Ye Lion Inn" scene, pierced in back w/hanging holes, artist-signed, 1909, 13 1/2" d. (ILLUS. right with Deldare chocolate set & tankard pitcher, top of next page) **500-1,000**

Dresser tray, rectangular, "Dancing Ye Minuet" scene, 9 x 12" (ILLUS. back row, left with other Deldare pieces, bottom of page) **650-750**

Large Grouping of Buffalo Deldare Pieces

Buffalo Deldare Chocolate Set, Chop Plate & Tankard Pitcher

Deldare Ye Lion Inn Charger

Fruit bowl, 9" d., 3 3/4" h.,"Ye Village Tavern" scene, 1909 (ILLUS. back row, right with other Deldare pieces, bottom of page 143) **400-600**

Mug, miniature, "The Fallowfield Hunt" scene, artist-signed, 1909, 2 1/4" h. (ILLUS. front row, second from left with large group of Deldare pieces, bottom of page 143 .... **288**

Pin tray, long rectangular form w/rounded corners, "Ye Olden Days" scene, artist-signed, 1909, 3 1/2 x 6 1/4" (ILLUS. front row, far left with various other Deldare pieces, bottom of page 143).................. **200-300**

Pitcher, 12 1/2" h. tankard-type, double-decorated w/"The Great Controversy" scene on one side & "All You Have To Do To Teach a Dutchman English" scene on the other side, artist-signed, 1908 (ILLUS. left with Deldare chocolate set & chop plate, top of page) **600-1,000**

Powder jar, cov., round w/domed cover, "Ye Village Street" scene, artist-signed, 1908, 4 1/4" d. (ILLUS. center row, left with other Deldare pieces, bottom of page 143) **300-500**

Tea tile, round w/reticulated metal frame, "Traveling In Ye Olden Days" scene, artist-signed, 1908, 9" d. (ILLUS. front row, second from right with various other Deldare pieces, bottom of page 143) **400-600**

Teacup & saucer, large cylindrical cup w/tapering base & angled handle, "Ye Olden Days" scene, artist-signed, 1909, saucer 6" d., the set (ILLUS. front row third from left with various other Deldare pieces, bottom of page 143) .... **300+**

Vase, 9" h., tall waisted cylindrical form, "Ye Olden Days" scene, 1909 (ILLUS. front row, far right with various other Deldare pieces, bottom of page 143) **1,400**

Miscellaneous Pieces

Buffalo Pottery Buffalo Hunt Platter

Platter, 11 x 14", rectangular w/rounded corners & gently scalloped edges, dark teal blue-green wide border around a transfer-printed central scene of a Native American buffalo hunt, ca. 1910 (ILLUS.) **288**

Teapot, cov., tea ball-type w/built-in tea ball, Argyle patt., blue & white, 1914 .... **300**

Teapot, cov., Blue Willow patt. (1905-1916), square, 2 pts., 5 1/2 oz. **350**

Ceramic Arts Studio of Madison

Founded in Madison, Wisconsin, in 1941 by two young men, Lawrence Rabbitt and Reuben Sand, this company began as a "studio" pottery. In early 1942 they met an amateur clay sculptor, Betty Harrington and, recognizing her talent for modeling in clay, they eventually hired her as their chief designer. Over the next few years Betty designed over 460 different pieces for their production. Charming figurines of children and animals were a main focus of their output in addition to models of adults in varied costumes and poses, wall plaques, vases and figural salt and pepper shakers.

Business boomed during the years of World War II when foreign imports were cut off and, at its peak, the company employed some 100 people to produce the carefully hand-decorated pieces.

After World War II many poor-quality copies of Ceramic Arts Studio figurines appeared and when, in the early 1950s, foreign imported figurines began flooding the market, the company found they could no longer compete. They finally closed their doors in 1955.

Since not all Ceramic Arts Studio pieces are marked, it takes careful study to determine which items are from their production.

Ceramic Arts Studio Marks

Accordion Lady, 8 1/2" h. **$500-600**
Adam & Eve (one-piece), 12" h. ... **Too rare-price**
Adonis & Aphrodite, 7" h. & 9" h., pr. **500-650**
African Man vase, stylized mask on ringed base, dark brown, 8" h. (ILLUS., top next column) **125-150**
African Man wall pocket, 7 3/4" h. **150-175**
African Woman vase, 8" h. **125-150**
African Woman wall pocket, 7 3/4" h. **150-175**
Alice & White Rabbit, 4 1/2" h. & 6" h., pr. **350-450**

Ancient Cat, 4 1/2" h. **80-100**
Ancient Kitten, 2 1/2" h. **70-90**
Archibald the Dragon, 8" h. **175-200**

African Man Mask Vase

Attitude & Arabesque wall plaques, 9 1/4" h., pr. **70-100**
Autumn Andy, Four Seasons group, 5" h. **160-190**
Baby Girl Skunk, Dinky, 2" h. **30-40**
Baby Mermaid, diving, 2 1/2" h. **150-175**
Baby Mermaid, sitting, 3" h. **175-200**
Balinese Dancers, Man & Woman, 9 1/2" h., pr. **200-250**
Ballerina ewer, 4 1/4" h. **60-75**
Ballet dancer, man & woman, shelf-sitters, 6 1/4" & 6 1/2", pr. **120-150**
Banjo girl, shelf-sitter, 4" h. **140-160**
Barbershop Quartet mug (1949), 3 1/2" h. **650-750**
Barbie, head vase, 7" h. **125-150**
Bashful Girl, dark hair, 4 1/2" h. **100-125**
Becky, head vase, 5 1/4" h. **100-125**
Bedtime Boy, 4 3/4" h. **75-95**

Daisy Donkey & Elsie Elephant

Rare Egyptian Woman Figure

Gay 90s Man & Woman #2

Gay 90s Man & Woman #2, 6 3/4" h. &
    6 1/2" h., pr. (ILLUS.) **110-150**
Gingham Dog & Calico Cat salt & pepper
    shakers, 2 3/4", 3", pr. **80-100**
Girl with Kitten, shelf-sitter, 4 1/4" h. **75-100**
Gleeful Imp, sitting, 3 1/2" h. **500-550**
Grace wall plaque, 9" h. **25-35**
Greg wall plaque, 9 1/2" h. **25-35**
Gremlin, sitting, 2" h. **250-300**
Gremlin, standing, 4" h. **250-300**

Daisy Donkey, 4 3/4" h. (ILLUS. left with
    Elsie Elephant, top of page) **85-100**
Egyptian Woman, 9 1/2" h. (ILLUS.) **700-750**
Elephant & Sabu salt & pepper shakers,
    5" h. & 2 3/4" h., pr. **170-210**
Elsie Elephant, 5" h. (ILLUS. right w/Don-
    key, top of page) **85-110**
English Setter, Kirby, 2" l. **150-175**
Farmer Boy & Girl, shelf-sitters, 4 3/4" h.,
    pr. **70-90**
Fawn, Indian group, 4 1/4" h. **85-100**
Fighting Cocks salt & pepper shakers,
    3 1/4" h. & 3 3/4" h., pr. **80-100**
Fighting Leopards, 3 1/2" h., 6 1/4" l. **180-250**
Fire Man & Fire Woman, dark red,
    11 1/4" h., pr. **400-450**
Flute Girl, 4 1/2" h. **140-160**
Flute Lady, 8 1/2" h. **500-600**
Fox & Goose, 3 1/4" h., 2 1/4" h., pr. **300-350**
French Horn Man, 6 1/2" h. **500-600**
Frog & toadstool salt & pepper shakers,
    figural, 2" & 3" h. pr. **100-130**
Gay 90s Couple #1, Harry & Lillibeth,
    6 1/2" h. & 6" h., pr. **90-110**

Rare Guitar Man Figure

Hamlet & Ophelia Wall Plaques

Guitar Man, stylized seated figure, grey glaze, 6 1/2" h. (ILLUS., previous page)
.... **500-600**

Gypsy Man & Woman, 6 1/2" h. & 7" h., pr.
.... **80-90**

Hamlet wall plaque, 8" h. (ILLUS. right with Ophelia plaque, top of page)................. **180-220**

Hans & Katrinka, Chubby Dutch, 6 1/2" h., 6 1/4" l., pr... **100-140**

Happy Imp, lying, 3 1/2" h......................... **500-550**

Harem Girl, kneeling, 4 1/2" h.................. **100-125**

Harem Girl, reclining, 6" l.......................... **100-125**

Harlequin Boy with Mask, 8 3/4" h......... **900-950**

Harlequin Girl with Mask, 8 1/2" h........... **900-950**

Honey or Sonny Spaniel bank, 5 3/4" h., each **300-350**

Honey Pot with bee, 4" h. **150-175**

Horse head up & down salt & pepper shakers, figural, 3 1/4" h., pr. **40-80**

House Mouse, 3" l. **90-110**

Hunter, Al, 7 1/2" h.................................. **125-200**

Jack Be Nimble Wall Plaque

Jack Be Nimble wall plaque, 5" h. (ILLUS.)
.... **400-450**

Jack in Beanstalk wall plaque, 6 1/2" h. (ILLUS., top next page)........................ **360-400**

Jack & Jill, shelf-sitters, 4 3/4" h., 5" h. **90-120**

Hear No Evil Candleholder

Hear No Evil candleholder, 5" h. (ILLUS.)
.... **80-100**

Hiawatha, Indian Group, 4 1/2" h. **220-250**

Hippo ashtray, 3 1/2" h............................. **100-120**

Lion & Lioness Figures

Jack in Beanstalk Wall Plaque

Lion, 7 1/4" l. (ILLUS. left w/lioness, top of
    page) **170-190**
Lion King, 4" h. **350-400**
Lioness, 5 1/2" l. (ILLUS. right with lion, top
    of page) **170-190**
Little Bo Peep, 5 1/2" h. **30-40**
Little Boy Blue, reclining, 4 1/2" l. **30-40**
Little Lamb, 3 5/8" h. **30**

Lorelei on Shell Planter

Lorelei on Shell planter, 6" h. (ILLUS.) ... **250-300**
Lotus & Manchu, head vases, 7 1/2" h., pr.
    .... **150-200**
Lovebirds, 2 3/4" h. **34-45**
Lover Boy, 5" h. **100-125**

Rare Kabuki Man & Woman

Kabuki Dancers, man & woman, 8 1/2" h.
    & 6" h., rare, pr. (ILLUS.) **1,600-2,000**
Kangaroo Mother & Joey, 4 3/4" h.,
    2 1/2" l. **130-170**
King's Jester Flutist Man, 11 1/2" h. **100-200**
King's Jester Lutist Woman, 12" h. **100-200**
Lady Rowena, on charger, 8 1/4" h. **145-175**
Lightning Stallion, 5 3/4" h. **150-175**
Lillibelle bell, 6 1/2" h. **75-85**

Man & Woman Dance Pair

Macabre Dance Man & Woman, 9" h.,
    7 3/4" h., pr. (ILLUS.) **1,800-2,000**

Madonna with Bible, 9 1/2" h.................. **325-350**
Madonna with Child, 6" h........................ **200-220**

Madonna with Halo Figure

Madonna with Halo, 9 1/2" h. (ILLUS.) **300-700**
Mary Contrary wall plaque, 5" h. (ILLUS.,
  top next column).................................... **160-180**
Mary & her lamb, 6 1/4" h., 3 3/4" h., pr. **85-105**
Maurice & Michelle, shelf-sitters, 7" h., pr.
  .... **130-150**

Mermaid on Rock, 4" h. **150-175**
Mermaid wall plaque, 6" h. (ILLUS. top left,
  w/Neptune & Sprites, bottom of page) .. **350-400**
Minnehaha, Indian group, 6 1/2" h........... **260-290**

Mary Contrary Wall Plaque

Modern Colt, 7 1/2" h. **225-250**
Modern Doe, reclining, 3 3/4" h. **100-125**
Modern Fawn, 2" h. **75-100**
Mop-Pi & Smi-Li, 6" h., pr........................... **50-80**
Mother & Baby Monkey snugglers, 4" h. &
  2" h., pr... **40-60**
Mother & Baby Spaniel, 2 1/4" h. &
  1 1/2" h., pr.. **50-60**
Mother Bear & Baby Bear snugglers,
  4 1/4" h., 2 1/4" h., white glaze, pr. **40-60**

Mermaid, Neptune & Sprites

Mother Black Bear & Cub, Realistic,
3 1/4" h., 2 1/4" h. **320-380**
Mother Cow & Calf snugglers, 5 1/4" h. &
2 1/2" h., pr.. **100-300**
Mother Seal on Rock, 5" h....................... **500-600**
Mother & Young Donkey, 3 1/4" h. & 3" h.,
pr. **320-380**
Mouse & Cheese salt & pepper shakers,
2" h. & 3" l., pr. **20-30**

Mr. Blankety Blank Bank

Mr. Blankety Blank bank, 4 1/2" h.
(ILLUS.)... **120-140**
Mr. & Mrs. Monkey, 4" h., 3 1/2" h., pr. **180-250**
**Mr. & Mrs. Penguin salt & pepper shak-
ers,** 3 3/4" h., pr. **100-150**
Mr. Skunk, 3" h. **45-60**
Mr. Toby mug, seated, holding mug,
3 1/4" h. **75-95**

Mrs. Blankety Blank Bank

Mrs. Blankety Blank bank, 4 1/2" h.
(ILLUS.)... **120-140**

Neptune wall plaque, 6" h. (ILLUS. bottom
left with Mermaid)................................... **350-400**

Nineteenth Century Couple

Nineteenth (19th) Century Man, 6 3/4" h.
(ILLUS. left w/woman).......................... **250-300**
Nineteenth (19th) Century Woman,
6 1/2" h. (ILLUS. right w/man).............. **250-300**
Nip & Tuck, shelf-sitters, 4 1/4" h., 2" l., pr. ... **50-70**
**Oakie on Spring Leaf salt & pepper shak-
ers,** figural, 1 1/2" h., 2" l., pr. **120-140**
Ophelia wall plaque, 8" h. (ILLUS. left with
Hamlet wall plaque) **180-220**
**Ox & covered wagon salt & pepper shak-
ers,** 3" l., pr. **100-135**

Paisley Pig Bank

Paisley Pig bank, 5 1/2" l., 3" h. (ILLUS.)
.... **325-375**
Palomino Colt, 5 3/4" h. **150-175**
Panda with hat, 2 3/4" h. **200-225**
Pansy, Ballet Group, standing, 6" h. **300-320**
Panther, 6 1/2" l. **200-250**
**Paul Bunyan & evergreen tree salt & pep-
per shakers,** 4 1/2" h., 2 1/2" h., pr. **200-250**
**Peek & Boo Siamese Cat & Kitten salt &
pepper shakers,** 4 1/4" h. & 3 1/4" h., pr.
.... **60-75**
Pensive, 6" h.. **150-175**
Persian Mother, shelf-sitter, 4 1/4" h. **50-60**
Pete & Polly Parrot, shelf-sitters, mauve,
7 1/2" h., pr.. **170-250**
Sprite wall plaque, fish down, 4 1/4" h.
(ILLUS. bottom right with Mermaid) **300-350**
Sprite wall plaque, fish up, 4 1/4" h.
(ILLUS. top right with Mermaid) **300-350**

Triad Girls

Triad Girl center, 5" h. (ILLUS. center of
three Triad girls) **90-120**
Triad Girl left, 7" h. (ILLUS. left of the three
girls) **80-110**
Triad Girl right, 7" h. (ILLUS. right of the
three girls) **80-110**
Vase, Comedy & Tragedy, snuggler for En-
core man or lady (double sided), 1 pc... **125-150**
Violet, Ballet Group, sitting, 3 1/2" h. **220-240**
Violin Lady, 8 1/2" h. **500-600**
Water Man & Water Woman, chartreuse,
11 1/2" h., pr. **250-400**
Wee Chinese Boy & Girl, 3" h., pr. **30-40**
Wee Dutch Boy & Girl, 3" h., pr. **30-40**
**Wee Elephant Boy & Girl salt & pepper
shakers,** figural, bisque, pink, 3 1/2" h.,
3 1/4" h., pr.. **50-80**
Wee Indian Boy, Indian Group, 3" h. **20-25**
Wee Indian Girl, Indian Group, 3 1/4" h. **20-25**
**Wee Piggy Boy & Girl salt & pepper shak-
ers,** 3 1/4" h. & 3 1/2" h., pr...................... **50-70**
**Wee Scotch Boy & Girl salt & pepper
shakers,** figural, 3 1/4" h., 3" h., pr. **70-80**
Wee Swedes salt & pepper shakers, figur-
al, 3 1/4" h., 3" h., pr............................... **100-130**
White Wally, ball up, 4 1/2" h. **220-250**
White Willy, ball down, 4 1/2" h. **220-250**
White Winney, sleeping, 5 1/2" l............... **220-250**
White Woody, 3 1/4" h.............................. **220-250**
Willing Girl, blonde, 5" h........................... **100-125**
Winter Willie, Four Seasons group, 4" h. ... **90-120**
Young Love Couple, shelf-sitters,
4 1/2" h., pr.. **80-100**
Zebra, 5" h.. **350-450**
Zor & Zorina wall plaques, 9" h., pr. **120-220**
Zorina lamp, table model, original tags, by
Moss Mfg... **175-200**
Zulu Man & Woman #1, 5 1/2" h. & 7" h.,
pr... **1,100-1,400**

Chinese Export

*Large quantities of porcelain have been made
in China for export to America from the 1780s,
much of it shipped from the ports of Canton and
Nanking. A major source of this porcelain was
Ching-te-Chen in the Kiangsi province, but the
wares were also made elsewhere. The largest
quantities were blue and white. Prices fluctuate
considerably depending on age, condition, decoration, etc.*

*CANTON and ROSE MEDALLION export
wares are listed separately.*

Chinese Export Helmet-shape Creamer

Creamer, helmet-shaped, armorial-type,
blue band decoration & h.p. blue, red &
gold crest below the spout, ca. 1790,
6 3/4" l., 5 1/2" h. (ILLUS.) **$500**
Dish, squared shape w/lobed corners, dec-
orated w/a h.p. central scene depicting a
master w/concubines & servants, floral &
butterfly border band, late 18th - early
19th c., 9" w. (ILLUS. right with models of
hawks, top next page)................................. **863**

One of a Pair of Armorial Dishes

Dishes, round, armorial-type, decorated
w/two dark blue overglazed bands centering the colorful arms of Oliphant impal-
ing Browne, minor decoration wear, ca.
1790, 6 1/8" d., 1 1/4" h., pr. (ILLUS. of
one).. **920**
Models of hawks, colorful perched birds in
a muted famille rose palette, late 18th -
early 19th c., 10" h., pr. (ILLUS. left with
squared dish with scene) **489**

Chinese Export Dish & Models of Hawks

Early Armorial Plate & Pots de Creme

Plate, 8 3/4" d., armorial-type, wide fancy floral-decorated rim in underglaze-blue, the center painted w/a the large arms of Godfrey w/a Latin motto, hairline in bottom, ca. 1725 (ILLUS. right with pots de creme, second from top) **1,093**

rose honeycomb background, centering a scene of a tall vase, table & flowering branch, roughness to glaze on half the rim, minor rim flakes & two small hairlines, ca. 1750 (ILLUS.) **403**

Famille Rose Chinese Export Plate

Plate, 9" d., famille rose palette, wide rim painted w/sepia cartouches on a pale

One of a Pair of Fitzhugh Pattern Plates

Plates, 10" d., green Fitzhugh patt., ca. 1800, pr. (ILLUS. of one) **1,150**

Tea set: tall tapering cov. teapot, short oval cov. teapot, helmet-shaped creamer, cov. sugar bowl, upright rectangular cov. tea caddy, cake plate & two handleless cups & saucers; each piece h.p. w/a sepia & orange spread-winged eagle & shield, gilt trim, late 18th c., tall teapot 10" h., the set **8,338**

Tea set: tall tapering cylindrical cov. teapot, short oval cov. teapot & undertray, upright rectangular cov. tea caddy, serving plate, two large handleless tea cups, one smaller tea cup & saucer; each piece h.p. w/an orange & black spread-winged eagle w/an oval medallion decorated w/the initials "SSD," made for the American market, late 18th - early 19th c., tall teapot 9 1/2" h., the set **5,000**

Small Chinese Teapot with Piercing

Teapot, a footed spherical double-walled style w/the outer layer pierced overall w/a delicate green vine w/orange blossoms, a light blue shoulder band & the matched domed & pierced cover w/a button finial, a C-form handle & a straight angled silver spout, unmarked, late 18th - early 19th c., chips & repairs on cover, small chip on base rim, 6" h. (ILLUS.)................................ **230**

Colorfully Decorated Chinese Teapot

Teapot, a round foot below a low flaring base below a wide slightly concave body band below a wide slightly rounded shoulder centering a short gold neck, a serpentine spout & C-scroll handle, the high domed cover w/a gold ball finial above a scene of a woman & a cartouche of a man above a band of flowers & birds, the wide shoulder painted overall w/colorful birds, flowers & butterflies, the body band decorated w/continuous scenes of Chinese ladies, ca. 1840, restoration to rim & spout, chip at pot mouth, wear to cover gilt, 9" h. (ILLUS.)............................... **690**

Colorful Rose Medallion Teapot

Teapot, cov., Rose Medallion patt., a round flaring foot supporting a wide urn-form body w/a serpentine spout & C-scroll handle, the high domed cover w/a gold ball finial, the cover, shoulder & body all decorated w/h.p. cartouches featuring birds, flowers & butterflies or Chinese figures, gold trim, ca. 1860, 11" l., 10 1/2" h. (ILLUS.)... **920**

Small Famille Rose Teapot

Teapot, Famille rose palette, footed squatty spherical body w/straight spout & C-form handle, domed flanged cover w/pointed knob finial, h.p. w/Chinese figures in a landscape, 19th c., 5 1/2" h. (ILLUS.)........... **288**

Teapot, tall tapering cylindrical body w/a straight angled spout & twisted strap handle, the flanged domed cover w/a knob finial, decorated for the American market w/a rusty orange design of an American eagle w/floral-decorated shield, similar to a design used by the Nichols Family of Salem, Massachusetts, late 18th - early 19th c., two small hairlines w/dings, overall 10" h. (ILLUS., next page)...................... **920**

Very Colorful Famille Rose Armorial Tureen

American-market Chinese Teapot

Tureen, cov., armorial-type, famille rose palette, footed squatty bulbous oval body w/gilt twisted branch end handles, domed cover w/gilt artichoke finial, decorated w/continuous scenes of Chinese figures in a landscape on the cover, the base painted w/the arms of Grant w/family mottoes, a rim band decorated w/flowers, butterflies & birds, the sides w/a continuous scene of Chinese figures on balconies & in gardens, portions of interior cover rim restored, gilt wear, glaze flaws, ca. 1810, 13 1/2" l., 9" h. (ILLUS., top of page) **4,140**

Urn, cov., wide baluster-form body w/foo dog head & ring shoulder handles, domed cover w/figural foo lion finial, famille rose palette, the sides painted w/large reserves w/festival scenes & crowds of Chinese figures, floral background & wide geometric base band, cover finial w/broken tail, second half 19th c., 21" h. (ILLUS., top next column) **403**

Vase, 9 1/2" h., moon flask-form, short cylindrical neck flanked by figural red dragon handles above the flattened round sides w/a blue ground ornately decorated w/white floral scrolls, one side w/a large round reserve painted w/a color scene of mounted warriors, the other sides w/a reserve of birds among flowering branches, upright base w/a pink & green geometric

design, worn gilt on mouth rim, ca. 1880 (ILLUS., bottom of column) **374**

Colorful Large Chinese Export Urn

Chinese Export Moon Flask Vase

Clifton Pottery

William A. Long, founder of the Lonhuda Pottery, joined Fred Tschirner, a chemist, to found the Clifton Art Pottery in Newark, New Jersey, in 1905. Crystal Patina was its first art pottery line and featured a subdued pale green crystalline glaze later also made in shades of yellow and tan. In 1906 its Indian Ware line, based on the pottery made by American Indians, was introduced. Other lines the Pottery produced include Tirrube and Robin's-egg Blue. Floor and wall tiles became the focus of production after 1911, and by 1914 the firm's name had changed to Clifton Porcelain Tile Company, which better reflected its production.

Clifton Crystal Patina Vase

Vase, 6 1/8" h., Crystal Patina line, footed squatty bulbous lower body tapering to a wide cylindrical neck w/a flaring rim, shaped light brown to pale green glaze w/long dark green streaks, incised company logo, dated 1906 (ILLUS.) **$288**

Clifton Vase in the Tirruba Line

Vase, 8 1/2" h., 5 1/4" d., Tirruba Line, footed bottle-form w/a wide squatty lower body tapering sharply to a flaring neck, matte red ground h.p. w/a white nastur-

tium blossom & pale green leaves up the side, stamped "Clifton - 140" (ILLUS.) **374**

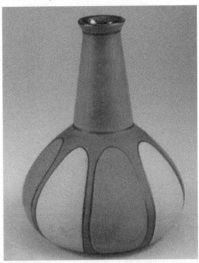

Clifton Indian Ware Gourd-form Vase

Vase, 11 1/2" h., Indian Ware, bulbous gourd-form body w/a tall tapering cylindrical neck, dark brown ground decorated around the bottom w/alternating ovals of tan & medium brown, marked "Middle Mississippi Valley - 231" (ILLUS.) **690**

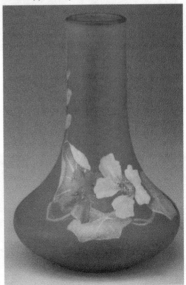

Clifton Vase with Nasturtium Blossoms

Vase, 12" h., 8 1/4" d., Tirruba Line, wide squatty bulbous base tapering sharply to a tall cylindrical neck, painted w/a large yellow & red nasturtium blossom & green leafy vine, marked "Clifton - Tirruba -254" (ILLUS.)... **805**

Copeland & Spode

W.T. Copeland & Sons, Ltd., has operated the Spode Works at Stoke, England, from 1847 to the present. The name Spode was used on some of its productions. Its predecessor, Spode, was founded by Josiah Spode about 1784 and became Copeland & Garrett in 1843, continuing under that name until 1847. Listings dated prior to 1843 should be attributed to Spode.

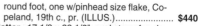

Copeland & Spode Mark

Copeland Imari Pattern Compotes

Compotes, open, 9 1/4" d., Imari patt., the shallow round bowls w/three floral panels alternating w/cobalt blue & gold bands, pedestal base w/decorated panels on the round foot, one w/pinhead size flake, Copeland, 19th c., pr. (ILLUS.)...................... **$440**

Platter, 17 1/2 x 22 1/2" oval, transfer design of flowers including chrysanthemums in blue, impressed Spode mark, first half 19th c.. **523**

Charming Colorful Copeland Salt Dip

Salt dip, triple, three deep rounded dishes joined across the top w/an arched three-part handle in white w/gold wrapped ribbon decor, each bowl decorated on the exterior in color w/a shell surrounded by entwined rose & cornflower garlands, each interior w/a berried laurel wreath, dated 1895, printed gold crowned Copeland mark, mark of retailer T. Goode & Son, London, 4" w. (ILLUS.) **1,673**

Tea set: cov. teapot, cov. sugar bowl, creamer, eight 9" d. plates & eight cups & saucers; Classical Revival style, serving pieces of squatty bulbous oblong boat shape w/angled collars & inset domed covers w/button finials, pointed C-scroll handles, each piece decorated w/a dark cinnamon brown band painted w/gilt roses, marked "Spode - Copelands China - England - Tiffany & Co. - New York," ca. 1890s, one plate w/small flake, gilt wear to rims, teapot 5" h., the set (ILLUS., bottom of page) **715**

Copeland-Spode China Tea Set

Copeland-Spode Buttercup Teapot

ribbed spout & C-form handle, England, early 20th c. (ILLUS., top of page) **85**

Early Spode Porcelain Teawares

Sevres-style Copeland Teacup & Saucer

Tea set: cov. teapot & seven handled cups & saucers; the oval pot w/upright sides & a flat shoulder centered by a domed cover w/oval knob finial, serpentine spout & C-form handle, each piece decorated w/a wide orange-painted band trimmed w/stylized white flowerheads & bands of gilt leaves, Spode, Pattern No. 878, England, ca. 1820, some gilt wear, two saucers w/hairlines, the set (ILLUS. of part) **405**

Teacup & saucer, footed deep rounded teacup decorated in the Sevres-style w/a cobalt blue ground centering a large oval reserve of colorful fruits framed by fancy gilt scrolling, matching saucer, printed green Copeland monogram marks, ca. 1870, saucer 5 1/2" d., set (ILLUS., top next column) **538**

Teapot, cov., Buttercup patt., squatty ribbed body w/concave ribbed shoulder & low domed cover w/blossom finial, straight

Lovely Copeland Portrait Vases

Vases, cov., 11" h., a square foot & tapering pedestal in white w/heavy gold trim, the large ovoid body tapering to a short flaring neck w/domed cover & pointed knob finial, long low C-scroll handles from the shoulder to the vase, each painted on the front w/a large oval reserve portrait of an 18th c. beauty surrounded by a gold background painted overall w/meandering pink & green rose vines, neck & cover w/gold decoration matching the foot, printed green Copeland marks, ca. 1900, artist-signed, pr. (ILLUS.) **1,793**

Cowan

R. Guy Cowan opened his first pottery studio in 1912 in Lakewood, Ohio. The pottery operated almost continuously, with the exception of a break during the First World War, at various locations in the Cleveland area until it was forced to close in 1931 due to financial difficulties.

Many of this century's finest artists began with Cowan and its associate, the Cleveland School of Art. This fine art pottery, particularly the designer pieces, are highly sought after by collectors.

Many people are unaware that it was due to R. Guy Cowan's perseverance and tireless work that art pottery is today considered an art form and found in many art museums.

Cowan Marks

Simple Modernistic Cowan Bowl

Bowl, 9 5/8" d., 4 1/2" h., a flat-bottomed simple widely flaring trumpet-form body w/a flattened rim, luminous light lavender Wisteria glaze, inkstamp mark "RGC" (ILLUS.) **$100-150**

Bust of a man, "Antinea," a stylized head w/a long neck, raised on a tall block base, overall black glaze, designed by A. Drexler Jacobson, one of a limited edition of 100, unmarked (ILLUS., top next column)
.... **3,220**

Black Bust of Antinea

"Polo" Charger in Russet Brown Glaze

Charger, "Polo" patt., round, decorated w/a raised design of stylized polo players on horseback, overall Russet Brown glaze, part of a sporting-related series designed by Viktor Schreckengost, artist initials, impressed company name & logo, ca. 1930, 11 1/8" d. (ILLUS.) **345**

Fine Cowan "Polo" Charger

Charger, "Polo" patt., round, decorated w/a raised design of stylized polo players on a brown or blue horse, hand-painted trim, part of a sporting-related series designed by Viktor Schreckengost, artist initials, impressed company name & logo, ca. 1930, 11 1/8" d. (ILLUS., previous page).. **1,380**

Cowan Art Deco Floral Charger

Charger, round, a wide outer band molded in relief w/Art Deco style flowers & vines w/a cluster of smaller florals in the center circle, overall Oriental Red glaze, impressed name & logo, 13" d. (ILLUS.) **259**

Oriental Red Cowan Console Set

Console set: 11" d. bowl & pair of low candleholders; the flat-bottomed rounded bowl w/widely flaring sides, the oblong candleholders w/low scrolled handles from the edge to the central socket, all marked, Oriental Red glaze, candlesticks, 5" l., 1 3/4" h., bowl 11" d., 3" h., the set (ILLUS.) **200-300**

Figurine, "Margarita," a tall stylized figure of a standing woman wearing a long robe w/flowing hood, slightly crouching as if crying, on an oblong wedge-form base, glossy celadon green Claire de Lune glaze, one of no more than 50 produced, designed by Waylande Gregory, impressed company name & logo, firing line on the bottom, 16" h. (ILLUS., top next column) **5,290**

Figurine, "Woodland Nymph," a slender, long-legged young woman seated on a tall tree stump, Special Ivory glaze, designed by Waylande Gregory in 1930, made in a limited edition, professional restoration to left arm, a bit of dark crazing, 13 7/8" h. (ILLUS., middle next column) **575**

Rare Figure of "Margarita"

Tall Cowan Woodland Nymph Figurine

Lobed Oriental Red Cowan Humidor

Humidor, cov., wide flaring cylindrical melon-ribbed base w/a rounded rim, domed & stepped lobed cover w/large button finial, overall Oriental Red glaze, Shape X-7, marked, 5 3/4" h................................ **200-300**

Egyptian Blue Cowan Jar & Cover

Jar, cov., bulbous nearly spherical body w/a fitted domed cover, overall Egyptian Blue body glaze, matte black cover, impressed company mark & R.G. Cowan logo, 7" h. (ILLUS.)...................................... **259**

Cowan Aztec-Style Lamp Base

Lamp base, Aztec-style, an oblong shaped & scroll-trimmed foot below the tall tapering ovoid body incised w/large tiered chevron & sawtooth devices, tan glaze highlighted w/black & a milky overglaze, impressed mark, 11 3/8" h. (ILLUS.)............ **288**

Cowan Lakeware Line Blue Urn

Urn, Lakeware Line, footed classical campana-form w/upturned C-scroll handles on the gadrooned lower body, Peacock blue glaze, Shape V-101, 8" h. (ILLUS.) **115**

Hexagonal Oriental Red Cowan Vase

Vase, 6 1/8" h., footed hexagonal body w/a narrow shoulder & short flaring neck, overall mottled Oriental Red glaze, impressed company name & R.G. Cowan logo (ILLUS.)... **161**

Cowan "Gypsy Moth" Blue Vase

Vase, 12 3/4" h., "Gypsy Moth" patt., tall baluster-form body w/a short flaring neck, a model of an open-winged moth on each shoulder, overall glossy striated Delphinium blue glaze (ILLUS.) **403**

Dorothy Doughty Birds

These magnificent porcelain birds were created by the talented artist Dorothy Doughty for the Royal Worcester Porcelain Factory in Worcester, England, beginning in 1935. They are life-sized, beautifully colored and crafted with the greatest artistry.

Blue Tits, "Blue Tit, Parvs Caer Olevs and Pussy Willow," signed & w/Royal Worcester mark, ca. 1964, pr. (ILLUS., top next page).. **$2,415**

Cactus Wrens, "Cactus Wren Heleodyles Brunneicapillus Coues: & Prickly Pear," on stands, signed & w/Royal Worcester mark, ca. 1965, 11" h., pr. (ILLUS., middle next page) **2,358**

Dorothy Doughty Blue Tits & Pussy Willow

Cactus Wrens & Prickly Pear Cactus

Extinct Carolina Paroquet

Carolina Paroquet, "Extinct Carolina Paroquet, Con Ucop sis Carolinensis," signed & w/Royal Worcester mark, 18" l., 6 1/2" h. (ILLUS.) **1,380**

Cerulean Warblers, "Cerulean Warbler, Dendroica Cerulia and Maple," signed & w/Royal Worcester mark, in original fitted case, ca. 1965, 8 1/4" h., pr. (ILLUS. of one, below with Little Downy Woodpecker, next page).. **1,725**

King Fisher, "King Fisher, Alcedo Ispida and Autumn Beech," Model No. 3395, signed & w/Royal Worcester mark, in original fitted case, ca. 1964, 12 1/2" w., 12" h. (ILLUS., next page) **1,610**

Little Downy Woodpeckers, "Little Downy Woodpecker, Dendrocopus Pubescens and Pecan," signed & w/Royal Worcester mark, in original fitted case, ca. 1967, 11 1/4" h., pr. (ILLUS. of one, above with Cerulean Warbler, next page).................. **3,220**

Mockingbird, "Mocking-Bird, Mimus Polyglottis," signed & w/Royal Worcester mark, ca. 1964, 11" h. (ILLUS. left with Myrtle Warbler, top of next page).............. **3,220**

Mockingbird & Myrtle Warbler Doughty Figurines

Cerulean Warbler & Little Downy Woodpecker

King Fisher & Autumn Beech

Myrtle Warbler, "Myrtle Warbler, Dendrocia Coronata Coronata," signed & w/Royal

Worcester mark, ca. 1958, one blossom reattached, 10" h. (ILLUS. right with Mockingbird, top of page) **1,150**

Red Cardinals, "Red Cardinal, Richmondena Cardinalis," signed & w/Royal Worcester mark, male w/two leaves detached, female w/three leaves detached, 12" h., pr. (ILLUS., top next column)........ **2,760**

Male & Female Red Cardinals

Doulton & Royal Doulton

Doulton & Co., Ltd., was founded in Lambeth, London, in about 1858. It was operated there until 1956 and often incorporated the words "Doulton" and "Lambeth" in its marks. Pinder, Bourne & Co., Burslem was purchased by the Doultons in 1878 and in 1882 became Doulton & Co., Ltd. It added porcelain to its earthenware production in 1884. The "Royal Doulton" mark has been used since 1902 by this factory, which is still in operation. Character jugs and figurines are commanding great attention from collectors at the present time.

John Doulton, the founder, was born in 1793. He became an apprentice at the age of 12 to a pot-

ter in south London. Five years later he was employed in another small pottery near Lambeth. His two sons, John and Henry, subsequently joined their father in 1830 in a partnership he had formed with the name of Doulton & Watts. Watts retired in 1864 and the partnership was dissolved. Henry formed a new company that traded as Doulton & Co.

In the early 1870s the proprietor of the Pinder Bourne Co., located in Burslem, Staffordshire, offered Henry a partnership. The Pinder Bourne Co. was purchased by Henry in 1878 and became part of Doulton & Co. in 1882.

With the passage of time the demand for the Lambeth industrial and decorative stoneware declined whereas demand for the Burslem manufactured and decorated bone china wares increased.

Doulton & Co. was incorporated as a limited liability company in 1899. In 1901 the company was allowed to use the word "Royal" on its trademarks by Royal Charter. The well known "lion on crown" logo came into use in 1902. In 2000 the logo was changed on the company's advertising literature to one showing a more stylized lion's head in profile.

Today Royal Doulton is one of the world's leading manufacturers and distributors of premium grade ceramic tabletop wares and collectibles. The Doulton Group comprises Minton, Royal Albert, Caithness Glass, Holland Studio Craft and Royal Doulton. Royal Crown Derby was part of the group from 1971 until 2000 when it became an independent company. These companies market collectibles using their own brand names.

Royal Doulton Marks

Animals & Birds

Cat, seated animal, red "Flambé" glaze, 1977-96, 11" h.. **$248**

Cat, Siamese, seated, glossy cream & black, DA 129, 4" h. (ILLUS., top of column) **30**

Cat, Siamese Cat, standing, cream & black, HN 2660, 1960-85, 5" h. **125**

Dog, Airedale Terrier, K 5, 1931-55, 1 1/4 x 2 1/4" **275**

Dog, American Great Dane, light brown, HN 2602, 1941-60, 6 1/2" h.............................. **650**

Dog, Bulldog, HN 1047, standing, brown & white, 1931-38, 3 1/4" **215**

Dog, Bulldog, HN 1074, standing, white & brown, 1932-85, 3 1/4"................................. **195**

Dog, Bulldog, K 1, seated, tan w/brown patches, 1931-77, 2 1/2" **95**

Siamese Cat

Dog, Cocker Spaniel, golden w/dark brown patches, HN 1187, 1937-69, 5"................... **125**

Dog, Cocker Spaniel, liver & white, 1931-60, HN 1002, 6 1/2" h. **575**

Dog, Cocker Spaniel, "Lucky Star of Ware," black coat w/grey markings, HN 1020, 1981-85, 5" **175**

Dog, Cocker Spaniel, seated, K9A, golden brown w/black highlights, 1931-77, 2 1/2" h... **95**

Dog, Cocker Spaniel w/pheasant, seated, white coat w/dark brown markings, red & brown pheasant, HN 1029, 1931-68, 3 1/2" h... **215**

Dog, Cocker Spaniel w/Pheasant, seated, white coat w/dark brown markings, red, brown & green pheasant, HN 1062, 1931-68, 3 1/2" **215**

Dog, Cocker Spaniel, white w/black markings, HN 1078, 1932-68, 3" h...................... **175**

Dog, Cocker Spaniel, white w/black markings, HN 1109, 1937-85, 5".......................... **140**

Dog, Cocker Spaniel, white w/light brown patches, HN 1037, 1931-68, 3 1/2"............. **175**

Dog, Collie, dark & light brown coat, white chest, shoulders & feet, HN 1059, 1931-85, 3 1/2"... **195**

Dog, Collie, dark & light brown coat, white chest, shoulders & feet, medium, HN 1058, 1931-85, 5" h............................... **185**

Dog, Dalmatian, "Goworth Victor," white w/black spots, black ears, HN 1114, 1937-68, 4 1/4" **375**

Dog, English Setter, "Maesydd Mustard," off-white coat w/black highlights, HN 1050, 1931-85, 5 1/4" h. **135**

Dog, English Setter w/pheasant, grey w/black markings, reddish brown bird, yellowish brown leaves on base, HN 2529, 1939-85, 8" h. **515**

Dog, Greyhound, white w/dark brown patches, HN 1077, 1932-55, 4 1/2" **575**

Dog, Irish Setter, Ch. "Pat O'Moy," reddish brown, HN 1054, 1931-60, 7 1/2" h. **725**

Dog, Irish Setter, "Pat O'Moy," reddish brown, HN 1055, 1931-85, 5" **175**

Dog, Labrador, standing, black, DA 145,
1990-present, 5" h.. **55**
Dog, Scottish Terrier, Ch. "Albourne Arthur,"
black, HN 1016, 1931-85, 3 1/2" **175**
Dog, Scottish Terrier, seated, black & white,
K 18, 1940-77, 2 1/4 x 2 3/4" **125**
Dogs, Cocker Spaniels sleeping, white dog
w/brown markings & golden brown dog,
HN 2590, 1941-69, 1 3/4" h. **105**
Duck, Drake, standing, white, HN 806,
1923-68, 2 1/2" h... **105**
Kitten, looking up, tan & white, HN 2584,
1941-85, 2"... **75**
Tiger on a Rock, brown, grey rock, HN
2639, 1952-92, 10 1/4 x 12" **1,150**

Beatrix Potter

The John Beswick factory in Longton, Stoke on Trent, celebrated its 100th anniversary in 1994. Originally, it produced earthenware household items and decorative ornaments. With the passage of time, the product line became more diverse and the decorations more ornate and attractive. Moreover, small domestic, farmyard and wild animal figurines were added to the product lines. Beswick was a family-owned and family-run pottery. As the owners neared retirement, they realized there were no next of kin to carry on the business. They sold the company to Royal Doulton in 1969.

Beatrix Potter is known the world over. Generations of children since the early 1900s have been fascinated by the antics of her coterie of small animals in her series of illustrated children's "Tales of Peter Rabbit and Friends." These storybook characters have been produced as small china figurines since the 1920s, but it was not until 1947 that Beswick gained copyright approval from the Frederick Warne Co., the Peter Rabbit book publisher, to manufacture and market them. Upon acquisition of the manufacturing rights, Royal Doulton continued to promote and sell the Beatrix Potter figures using the Beswick trademark until 1989, when it switched to a "Royal Albert" underprint. Royal Albert was another of its famous product lines and had greater brand recognition in the United States. The backstamp change was not well received by the global collector community. Within a decade, the Beswick backstamp was reintroduced and used on the Beatrix Potter figurines until the end of 2002, when the Warne license expired. The old Beswick factory was closed.

All the Beatrix Potter figurines were assigned a "P" or production model number. Although these "P" numbers do not appear on the figures themselves, they are used extensively by collectors to uniquely identify a particular figure.

Many varieties of backstamp exist. They indicate a period of manufacture and influence secondary market values. The basic types of backstamp are shown. If collectible subtypes exist, a range of market values is given for the basic type. Many special backstamps were used in the 1990s to promote sales. These details are outside the scope of this compendium.

Basic Beatrix Potter Backstamps

And This Pig Had None, P3319, Beswick
Made in England backstamp, 1992-98
(ILLUS.)... **$50**

And This Pig Had None Figure

And This Pig Had None, P3319, crown
backstamp, 1992-98 (ILLUS.) **60**
Appley Dappley, P2333, bottle in, Beswick
Made in England backstamp, 1975-2002 ....

Appley Dappley

Appley Dappley, P2333, bottle in, brown
line backstamp, 1975-2002 (ILLUS.) **70**
Appley Dappley, P2333, bottle in, crown
backstamp, 1975-2002 .... **35**
Aunt Pettitoes, P2276, brown line backs-
tamp, 1970-93... **75**

Fierce Bad Rabbit Figure

Fierce Bad Rabbit, P2586, feet in, light brown rabbit, crown backstamp, 1980-97 (ILLUS.)... **50**

Fierce Bad Rabbit, P2586, feet in, light brown rabbit, John Beswick script backstamp, 1980-97 .... **150**

Flopsy, Mopsy & Cottontail, P1274, brown line backstamp, 1954-97 .... **95**

Flopsy, Mopsy & Cottontail, P1274, crown backstamp, 1954-97 .... **40**

Flopsy, Mopsy & Cottontail, P1274, gold circle/oval backstamp, 1954-97 .... **350**

Flopsy, Mopsy & Cottontail

Flopsy, Mopsy & Cottontail, P1274, John Beswick script backstamp, 1954-97 (ILLUS.)... **150**

Foxy Whiskered Gentleman, P1277, Beswick Made in England backstamp, 1954-2002 .... **35**

Foxy Whiskered Gentleman, P1277, brown line backstamp, 1954-2002 .... **90**

Foxy Whiskered Gentleman

Foxy Whiskered Gentleman, P1277, crown backstamp, 1954-2002 (ILLUS.) **50**

Foxy Whiskered Gentleman, P1277, gold circle/oval backstamp, 1954-2002 .... **350**

Foxy Whiskered Gentleman, P1277, John Beswick script backstamp, 1954-2002 .... **165**

Gentleman Mouse Made a Bow

Gentleman Mouse Made a Bow, P3200, crown backstamp, 1990-96 (ILLUS.) **78**

Goody & Timmy Tiptoes

Goody & Timmy Tiptoes, P2957, brown line backstamp, 1986-96 (ILLUS.) **300**

Jeremy Fisher Catches a Fish

Jeremy Fisher Catches a Fish, P3919, Beswick Made in England backstamp, 1999-2002 (ILLUS.)....................................... **65**

John Joiner Figure

John Joiner, P2965, crown backstamp, 1990-97 (ILLUS.).. **55**
Lady Mouse, P1183, Beswick Made in England backstamp, 1950-2000 .... **35**
Lady Mouse, P1183, brown line backstamp, 1950-2000.. **85**

Lady Mouse Figure

Lady Mouse, P1183, crown backstamp, 1950-2000 (ILLUS.) **55**
Lady Mouse, P1183, gold circle/oval backstamp, 1950-2000 .... **200-350**

Lady Mouse Made a Curtsey

Lady Mouse Made a Curtsy, P3220, crown backstamp, 1990-97 (ILLUS.)....................... **45**
Little Pig Robinson Spying, P3031, brown line backstamp, 1987-93 .... **250**

Little Pig Robinson Spying

Little Pig Robinson Spying, P3031, crown backstamp, 1987-93 (ILLUS.)..................... **125**
Miss Dormouse, P3251, crown backstamp, 1991-95 (ILLUS., top next page)................... **90**
Mr. Benjamin Bunny, P1940, pipe in, lilac jacket, Beswick Made in Endland backstamp, 1975-2000 .... **35**

Miss Dormouse Figure

Mr. Jeremy Fisher

Mr. Jeremy Fisher, P1157, large spots on head, striped legs, crown backstamp, 1950-2002 (ILLUS.) **35**

Mr. Jeremy Fisher, P1157, large spots on head, striped legs, gold circle/oval backstamp, 1950-2002 .... **425**

Mr. Todd, P3091, crown backstamp, 1988-93 .... **125**

Mr. Todd Figure

Mr. Todd, P3091, John Beswick script backstamp, 1988-93 (ILLUS.) **275**

Mrs. Rabbit, P1200, umbrella in, Beswick Made in England backstamp, 1975-2002 ...... **35**

Mrs. Rabbit, P1200, umbrella in, brown line backstamp, 1975-2002 .... **70**

Mr. Benjamin Bunny

Mr. Benjamin Bunny, P1940, pipe in, lilac jacket, brown line backstamp, 1975-2000 (ILLUS.) **75**

Mr. Benjamin Bunny, P1940, pipe in, lilac jacket, crown backstamp, 1975-2000 .... **40**

Mr. Benjamin Bunny, P1940, pipe in, lilac jacket, John Beswick script backstamp, 1975-2000 .... **125**

Mr. Jeremy Fisher, P1157, large spots on head, striped legs, Beswick Made in England backstamp, 1950-2002 .... **35**

Mr. Jeremy Fisher, P1157, large spots on head, striped legs, brown line backstamp, 1950-2002 .... **70**

Peter with Postbag

Peter with Postbag, P3591, crown backstamp, 1996-2002 (ILLUS.)............................. **40**
Pickles, P2324, brown line backstamp, 1971-82 .... **425**

Black-colored Pig-Wig

Pig-Wig, P2381, black pig, brown line backstamp, 1972-98 (ILLUS.)............................. **550**
Pig-Wig, P2381, grey pig, gold circle/oval backstamp, 1972-98 .... **very rare**
Pigling Bland, P1365, lilac jacket, Beswick Made in England backstamp, 1975-98 .... **55**

Pickles Figure

Pickles, P2324, gold circle/oval backstamp, 1971-82 (ILLUS.).. **650**

Pigling Bland

Pigling Bland, P1365, lilac jacket, brown line backstamp, 1975-98 (ILLUS.) **70**
Pigling Bland, P1365, lilac jacket, crown backstamp, 1975-98 .... **55**

Tabitha Twitchit & Miss Moppet

Tabitha Twitchit & Miss Moppet, P2544, crown backstamp, 1976-93 (ILLUS.)............ **125**
Tabitha Twitchit & Miss Moppet, P2544, John Beswick script backstamp, 1976-93 .... **300**
Timmy Tiptoes, P1101, brown line backstamp, 1948-80 .... **125**

Timmy Tiptoes

Timmy Tiptoes, P1101, gold circle/oval backstamp, 1948-80 (ILLUS.) **265**

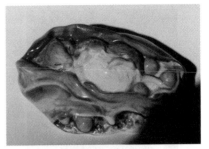

Timmy Willie Sleeping

Timmy Willie Sleeping, P2996, brown line backstamp, 1986-96 (ILLUS.)...................... **225**
Timmy Willie Sleeping, P2996, crown backstamp, 1986-96 .... **65**
Tom Kitten, P1100, light blue suit, Beswick Made in England backstamp, 1980-99 .... **35**
Tom Kitten, P1100, light blue suit, brown line backstamp, 1980-99 .... **90**

Tom Kitten Figure

Tom Kitten, P1100, light blue suit, crown backstamp, 1980-99 (ILLUS.)........................ **35**
Tom Kitten, P1100, light blue suit, John Beswick script backstamp, 1980-99 .... **120**

Tommy Brock Figure

Tommy Brock, P1348, large eye patch, spade handle in, Beswick Made in England backstamp, 1975-2002 (ILLUS.) 35

Tommy Brock, P1348, large eye patch, spade handle in, brown line backstamp, 1975-2002 65

Tommy Brock, P1348, large eye patch, spade handle in, crown backstamp, 1975-2002 40

Tommy Brock, P1348, large eye patch, spade handle in, John Beswick script backstamp, 1975-2002 120

Bunnykins Figurines

Airman, DB 199, limited edition of 5000, 1999 75

Angel, DB 196, white & yellow, 1999 to present 45

Aussie, DB 58, gold & green, 1988................. 750

Banjo Player, DB 182, white & red striped blazer, black trousers, yellow straw hat, 1999, limited edition of 2,500 150

Bathtime, DB 148, white bathrobe w/grey trim, yellow towel & duck, 1994-97................ 50

Be Prepared, DB 56, dark green & grey, 1987-96....................... 60

Bedtime, DB 79, third variation, light blue & white, 1988..................... 850

Billie and Buntie Bunnykins Sleigh Ride, DB 4, blue, maroon & yellow, 1972-97.......... 45

Bowler, DB 145, white, beige & black, 1994, limited edition of 1,000 265

Bridesmaid, DB 173, yellow dress, dark yellow flowers, 1997-99................................. 40

Brownie, DB 61, brown uniform, yellow tie, 1987-93...................... 75

Captain Cook, DB 251, dark blue & yellow, 2002, limited edition of 2,500 150

Carol Singer Bunnykins

Carol Singer, DB 104, dark green, red, yellow & white, 1991, USA Backstamp, limited edition of 300 (ILLUS.) 400

Cavalier, DB 179, red tunic, white collar, black trousers & hat, yellow cape, light brown boots, 1998, limited edition of 2,500............................ 265

Bunnykins Christmas Surprise

Christmas Surprise, DB 146, cream & red, 1994-2000 (ILLUS.) 50

Clarinet Player, DB 184, blue & white striped jacket, grey trousers, yellow straw hat, 1999, limited edition of 2,500 150

Clown, DB 129, white costume w/red stars & black pompons, black ruff around neck, 1992, limited edition of 250 1,500

Easter Greetings Bunnykins

Father Christmas Limited Edition

Bunnykins Footballer

Bunnykins Nurse with Green Cross

Nurse, DB 74B, dark & light blue & white, green cross, 1994-2000 (ILLUS.).................. **40**

Olympic, DB 28A, white & blue, 1984-88 .... **195**

On Line, DB 238, pink & blue, 2001, limited edition of 2,500... **135**

Oompah Band, DB 23, 24, 25, 26B, 27, red, 1990, the set **650**

Out for a Duck, DB 150, white, beige & green, 1995, limited edition of 1,250 .... **315**

Paperboy, DB 77, green, yellow, red & white, 1989-93.. **105**

Pilgrim, DB 212, tableau, brown & green, 1999, limited edition of 2,500 .... **125**

Policeman, DB 64, dark blue uniform, 1988-2000.. **45**

Bunnykins Postman

Postman, DB 76, dark blue & red, 1989-93 (ILLUS.)... **120**

Prince Frederick, DB 94, red, blue & yellow, Royal family series, 1990, limited edition of 250 .... **465**

Princess Beatrice, DB 47, pale green, Royal Family series, 1986-90............................ **105**

Queen Sophie, DB 46, blue & red, Royal Family series, 1986-90................................. **145**

Rise and Shine, DB 11, maroon, yellow & blue, 1973-88... **125**

Robin Hood resin stand, for Robin Hood Collection, brown & green, 2001.................... **60**

Runners, DB 205, 1999, limited edition of 2,500, the set (sold only in set of 5)............. **625**

Sandcastle Money Box, DB 228, 2002, to mark the 30th anniversary of Bunnykins figures **225**

Santa Music Box

Santa, Music Box, DB 34, red, white, brown, 1988-91 (ILLUS.).............................. **215**

Saxophone Player, DB 186, navy & white striped shirt, blue vest, black trousers, 1999, limited edition of 2,500 .... **180**

Schoolboy, DB 66, blue, white & grey, 1988-91.. **155**

Sheriff of Nottingham, DB 265, red cross on white apron, blue cloak, 2002 .... **65**

Sightseer, DB 215, pink dress, 2000................ **50**

Sleighride, DB 4, 1972-91 .... **45**

Sousaphone, DB 105, dark green, red & yellow, Oompah Band series, 1991, limited edition of 200 .... **500**

Sousaphone, DB 86, blue uniform & yellow sousaphone, Oompha Band series, 1990, limited edition of 250 .... **500**

Sundial, DB 213, red, blue & white, produced only in 2000....................................... **50**

Susan as Queen of the May

Susan Bunnykins as Queen of the May, DB 83, white polka dot dress w/blue, brown chair, 1990-91 (ILLUS.) **165**

Swimmers, DB 206, 1999, limited edition of 2,500, the set (sold only in set of 5) **625**

Tally Ho!, DB 12, burgundy, yellow, blue, white & green, 1973-88 .... **105**

Tally Ho!, Music Box, DB 33A, maroon coat, yellow jumper, 1984-93 .... **255**

Tennis, DB 277, tableau, issued in a pair w/Strawberries, 2003, limited edition of 3,000, pr. **150**

Touchdown, DB 100 (University of Indiana), white & red, 1990, limited edition of 200 .... **625**

Touchdown, DB 29B (Boston College), maroon & gold, 1985, limited edition of 50..... **2,000**

Touchdown, DB 97 (University of Michigan), yellow & blue, 1990, limited edition of 200 .... **625**

Touchdown, DB 99 (Notre Dame), green & yellow, 1990, limited edition of 200 .... **625**

Town Crier, DB 259, black, red & yellow, 2002, limited edition of 2,500 .... **175**

Trumpet Player, DB 210, green striped coat, 2000, limited edition of 2,500 .... **175**

Trumpeter, DB 24, red, blue & yellow, Oompah Band series, 1984-90 .... **105**

Uncle Sam, DB 50, blue, red & white, 1986 to present **45**

Welsh Lady, DB 172, light pink & yellow dress, black hat, 1997, limited edition of 2,500 .... **225**

Will Scarlet, DB 264, green & orange, 2002 ...... **60**

With Love, DB 269, tinged yellow, w/engraveable nameplate, 2002 .... **65**

Character Jugs

Anne of Cleves

Anne of Cleves, large, D 6653, 7 1/4" h. (ILLUS.).. **$240**

Aramis

Aramis, large, D 6441, 7 1/4" h. (ILLUS.,
  previous page) **90**
'Arriet, tiny, D 6256, 1 1/4" h............................ **150**
'Arry, large, D 6207, 6 1/2" h. **185**
Auld Mac, miniature, D 6253, 2 1/4" h. **40**
Auld Mac "A," large, D 5823, 6 1/4" h.............. **60**
Bacchus, miniature, D 6521, 2 1/2" h. **35**
Beefeater, small, D 6233, 3 1/4" h. **35**

Blacksmith

Blacksmith, D 6571, large, 7" h. (ILLUS.) **90**
Busker (The), large, D 6775, 6 1/2" h. **85**
Cap'n Cuttle, mid, D 5842, 5 1/2" h. **75**
Capt. Ahab, small, D 6506, 4" h. **65**
Capt Henry Morgan, miniature, 2 1/4" h. **40**
Capt. Hook, small, D 660, 4" h. **350**
Cardinal (The), tiny, D 6258, 1 1/2" h. **165**

Catherine of Aragon

Catherine of Aragon, large, D 6643, 7" h.
  (ILLUS.)... **85**
Cavalier (The), large, D 6114, 7" h. **105**
City Gent, large, D 6815, 7" h. **140**
Cliff Cornell, large, variation No. 1, light
  brown suit, brown & cream striped tie,
  9" h. (ILLUS. left, top next column) **450**
Cliff Cornell, large, variation No. 3, dark
  brown suit, green, black & blue designed
  tie, 9" h. (ILLUS. right, top next column) **750**

Cliff Cornell Toby Jugs

Cliff Cornell, small, variation No. 1, light
  brown suit, brown & cream striped tie,
  5" h.. **1,500**
Cliff Cornell, small, variation No. 2, blue
  suit, 5" h. **3,500**
Cliff Cornell, small, variation No. 3, dark
  brown suit, 5" h. **250**
Dick Turpin, horse handle, large, D 6528,
  7" h.. **80**
Dick Turpin, horse handle, miniature, D
  6542, 2 1/4" h... **35**
Dick Turpin, miniature, D 6128, 2 1/4" h. **35**
Dick Turpin "A," pistol handle, D 5485,
  6 1/2" h. **125**
Drake, small, D 6174, 3 1/4" h. **55**
Falconer (The), miniature, D 6547, 2 3/4" h. **35**
Farmer John, large, D 5788, 6 1/2" h. **125**
Farmer John, small, D 5789, 3 1/4" h. **65**
Fat Boy, mid, D 5840, 5" h. **125**
Fat Boy, miniature, D 6139, 2 1/2" h.................. **45**
Fortune Teller (The), small, D 6503,
  3 3/4" h.. **250**
General Gordon, large, D 6869, 7 1/4" h. **225**

George Washington

George Washington and George III, large,
  D 6749, 7 1/4" h. (ILLUS. of Washington
  side) **125**

Lawyer (The), small, D 6504, 4" h. **40**
Little Mester Museum Piece, large, D
6819, 6 3/4" h. **115**
Lobster Man, large, D 6617, 7 1/2" h. **65**
London 'Bobby' (The), large, D 6744, 7" h. **100**
Long John Silver, miniature, D 6512,
2 1/2" h. **40**

Lord Nelson

Lord Nelson, large, D 6336, 7" h. (ILLUS.) **315**
Macbeth, large, D 6667, 7 1/4" h. **90**
Mephistopheles, large, w/verse, D 5757,
7" h. **2,250**
Mephistopheles "A," small, two-faced,
w/verse, D 5758, 3 3/4" h. **850**
Merlin, small, D 6536, 3 3/4" h. **40**
Mine Host, miniature, D 6513, 2 1/2" h. **40**
Mr. Micawber, mid, D 5843, 5 1/2" h. **130**

Mr. Pickwick

Mr. Pickwick, large, D 6060, 5 1/2" h.
(ILLUS.) **105**
Mr. Pickwick, tiny, D 6260, 1 1/4" h. **110**
Mr. Quaker, large, D 6738, 7 1/2" h. **650**
Neptune, small, D 6552, 3 3/4" h. **40**
Old Charley, large, D 5420, 5 1/2" h. **65**
Old King Cole, large, D 6036, 5 3/4" h.
(ILLUS., top next column) **230**

Old King Cole

Paddy

Paddy, large, D 5753, 6" h. (ILLUS.) **120**
Paddy, tiny, D 6145, 1 1/4" h. **45**

Parson Brown

Parson Brown "A," large, D 5486, 6 1/2" h.
(ILLUS., previous page) 125
Pearly King, large, D 6760, 6 3/4" h. 125
Pearly Queen, large, D 6759, 7" h. 115
Poacher (The), variation 2, large, D 6429,
7" h. 80
Red Queen (The), large, D 6777, 7 1/4" h. 125
Robinson Crusoe, miniature, D 6546,
2 3/4" h. 40
Romeo, large, D 6670, 7 1/2" h. 75
Ronald Reagan, large, D 6718, 7 3/4" h. 750

Sairey Gamp

Sairey Gamp, large, No. 5451, 6 1/4" h.
(ILLUS.) 65
Sairey Gamp, tiny, D 6146, 1 1/4" h. 60
Sam Johnson, large, D 6289, 6 1/4" h. 245

Sam Weller, large, D 6064, 6 1/2" h.
(ILLUS.) 80
Sam Weller, tiny, D 6147, 1 1/4" h. 40
Sancho Pança, large, D 6456, 6 1/2" h. 85
Santa Claus, plain handle, large, D 6704,
7 1/2" h. 125
Scaramouche, large, first version, D 6558,
7" h. (ILLUS., below) 825
Simon the Cellarer, large, D 5504, 6 1/2" h.
.... 110
Simon the Cellarer, small, D 5616,
3 1/2" h. 40

Scaramouche

Sam Weller

Simple Simon

Simple Simon, large, D 6374, 7" h. (ILLUS., previous page) **475**
Sir Francis Drake, large, D 6805, 7" h. **105**

Sir Thomas More

Sir Thomas More, large, D 6792, 6 3/4" h. (ILLUS.) **210**

The Sleuth

Sleuth (The), large, D 6631, 7" h. (ILLUS.) **65**
Tam O'Shanter, miniature, D 6640, 2 1/2" h. **40**
Toby Philpots, large, D 5736, 6 1/4" h. **105**
Tony Weller, large, D 5531, 6 1/2" h. (ILLUS., top next column) **105**
Touchstone, large, D 5613, 7" h. **245**
Ugly Duchess, large, D 6599, 6 3/4" h. (ILLUS., middle next column) **625**
Uncle Tom Cobbleigh, large, D 6337, 7" h. **275**

Tony Weller

Ugly Duchess

Veteran Motorist

Veteran Motorist, large, D 6633, 7 1/2" h. (ILLUS.) **85**

The Walrus & Carpenter

Walrus & Carpenter (The), large, D 6600,
7 1/4" h. (ILLUS.) **165**

Figurines

Ace (The), HN 3398, white, 1991-95............. **$195**
Adele, HN 2480, flowered white dress,
1987-92.. **175**
Affection, HN 2236, purple, 1962-94.............. **115**
Ajax, HN 2908, red, green & gold, 1980, lim-
ited edition of 950...................................... **475**
Alexandra, HN 2398, patterned green
dress, yellow cape, 1970-76 .... **215**
Alison, HN 2336, blue & white, 1966-92.......... **175**
Amy, HN 3316, blue & rose, Figure of the
Year series, 1991 .... **950**
An Old King, HN 2134, purple, red, green &
brown, 1954-92 .... **450**
April, HN 2708, white dress w/flowers,
Flower of the Month series, 1987................ **225**
Aragorn, HN 2916, tan, 1981-84 .... **140**
As Good As New, HN 2971, blue, green
and tan, 1982-85....................................... **150**
August, HN 3165, white & blue dress
w/poppies, Flower of the Month Series,
1987 .... **275**
Autumn Breezes, HN 1911, green & pink,
1939-76.. **325**
Autumn Breezes, HN 1913, green dress,
blue jacket, 1939-71.................................. **275**
Autumn Breezes, HN 1934, red, 1940-97
(ILLUS.)... **375**
Autumn Breezes, HN 2131, orange, yellow
& black, 1990-94 (ILLUS., top next col-
umn)... **250**
Autumn Breezes, HN 2147, black & white,
1955-71 .... **350**
Autumntime, HN 3231, golden brown,
R.D.I.C.C. Four Seasons Series (Style
Four), 1989... **175**
Ballad Seller, HN 2266, pink, 1968-73 .... **250**
Balloon Man (The), HN 1954, black & grey,
1940 to present **240**
Beat You To It, HN 2871, pink, gold & blue,
1980-87 .... **475**

Autumn Breezes

Bedtime

Bedtime, HN 1978, white w/black base,
1945-97 (ILLUS.) **80**
Bedtime Story, HN 2059, pink, white, yel-
low & blue, 1950-98................................... **330**
Belle, HN 2340, green dress, 1968-88.............. **70**
Belle O' the Ball, HN 1997, red & white,
1947-79 .... **350**
Bernice, HN 2071, pink & red, 1951-53........ **1,050**
Bess, HN 2003, purple cloak, 1947-50 .... **850**
Biddy, HN 1513, red dress, blue shawl,
1932-51.. **180**
Biddy Penny Farthing, HN 1843, green &
lavender, 1938 to present **300**
Bill Sykes, M 54, black & brown, 1932-81......... **65**
Blithe Morning, HN 2021, mauve & pink
dress, 1949-71.. **295**
Blithe Morning, HN 2065, blue & pink
dress, 1949-71.. **325**

Blithe Morning, HN 2065, red dress, 1950-73 .... **225**

Boatman (The), HN 2417, yellow, 1971-87 ..... **250**

Bonnie Lassie, HN 1626, red dress, 1934-53 .... **575**

Boy from Williamsburg, HN 2183, blue & pink, 1969-83 .... **215**

Bride (The), HN 2873, white w/gold trim, 1980-89 .... **175**

Bride (The), HN 3284, style 4, white, 1990-97 .... **175**

Bridesmaid, M 30, pink & lavender, 1932-45 .... **450**

Bridesmaid (The Little), HN 2196, white dress, pink trim, 1960-76 .... **105**

Bridget, HN 2070, green, brown & lavender, 1951-73 .... **280**

Bunny, HN 2214, turquoise, 1960-75 .... **200**

Buttercup, HN 2309, green dress w/yellow sleeves, 1964-97 .... **185**

Buz Fuz, M 53, black & red, 1932-83 .... **65**

Camellia, HN 2222, pink, 1960-71 .... **225**

Captain Cuttle, M 77, yellow & black, 1939-82 .... **65**

Captain (The), HN 2260, black & white, 1965-82 .... **225**

Carol, HN 2961, white, 1982-95 .... **180**

Carolyn, HN 2112, white & green flowered dress, 1953-65 .... **300**

Carpet Seller (The), HN 1464A, (hand closed), green & orange, 1931-69 .... **225**

Carpet Seller (The), HN 2776, Flambé, 1990 to present **400**

Catherine, HN 3044, white, 1985-96 .... **75**

Catherine of Aragon, HN 3233, green, blue & white dress, 1990, limited edition of 9,500 .... **695**

Charlotte

Charlotte, HN 3813, brown figure, ivory dress, 1996-97 (ILLUS.) **225**

Child from Williamsburg, HN 2154, blue dress, 1964-83 .... **150**

Chloe, HN 1765, blue, 1936-50 .... **450**

Christine, HN 2792, flowered blue & white dress, 1978-98 .... **255**

Christmas Time, HN 2110, red w/white frills, 1953-67 .... **545**

Cissie

Cissie, HN 1809, pink dress, 1937-93 (ILLUS.) **100**

Claire, HN 3209, red, 1990-92 .... **175**

Claribel, HN 1951, red dress, 1940-49 .... **400**

Clarinda, HN 2724, blue & white dress, 1975-81 .... **175**

Clarissa, HN 2345, green dress, 1968-81 .... **185**

Clown (The), HN 2890, gold & grey, 1979-88 .... **425**

Cookie, HN 2218, pink & white,1958-75 .... **125**

Coralie, HN 2307, yellow dress, 1964-88 .... **95**

Cup O' Tea, HN 2322, dark blue & grey, 1964-83 .... **175**

Dainty May, M 67, pink skirt, blue overdress, 1935-49 .... **625**

Daisy

Daisy, HN 3805, ivory & gold, Charleston series, 1996-97 (ILLUS.) **250**

Darling, HN 1319, white w/black base, 1929-59 .... **175**

Rare Four O'Clock Doulton Figurine

Four O'Clock, HN 1760, modeled by Leslie Harradine, 1936-49 (ILLUS.)..................... **2,000**

Giselle, The Forest Glade, HN 2140, white & blue, 1954-65.......................... **425**

Good Morning, HN 2671, blue, pink & brown matte, 1974-76 .... **175**

Goody Two Shoes, M 80, blue skirt, red overdress, 1939-49 .... **115**

Grand Manner, HN 2723, lavender-yellow, 1975-81... **245**

Granny's Shawl, HN 1647, red cape, 1934-49 .... **625**

Harmony

Harmony, HN 2824, grey dress, 1978-84 (ILLUS.)... **225**

Hazel, HN 1797, orange & green dress, 1936-49... **550**

He Loves Me, HN 2046, flowered pink dress, 1949-62....................................... **250**

Her Ladyship, HN 1977, red & cream, 1945-59... **425**

Hilary, HN 2335, blue dress, 1967-81............. **195**

Home Again, HN 2167, red & white, 1956-95 .... **175**

Homecoming (The), HN 3295, blue, pink & green, 1990, limited edition of 9,500, Children of the Blitz series **325**

Honey, HN 1909, pink, 1939-49...................... **525**

Hornpipe (The), HN 2161, blue jacket, blue & white striped trousers, 1955-62 .... **750**

HRH Prince Phillip, Duke of Edinburgh, HN 2386, black & gold, 1981, limited edition of 1,500 .... **463**

HRH the Prince of Wales, HN 2883, purple, white & black, limited edition of 1,500, 1981 .... **450**

Innocence, HN 2842, red, 1979-83 .... **205**

Invitation, HN 2170, pink, 1956-75.................. **215**

Irene, HN 1621, pale yellow dress, 1934-51 .... **525**

Isadora, HN 2938, lavender, 1986-92 .... **350**

Ivy, HN 1768, pink hat, lavender dress, 1936-79... **105**

Jack, HN 2060, green, white & black, 1950-71 .... **175**

Jacqueline, HN 2001, pink dress, 1947-51 .... **800**

Jane, HN 2806, yellow dress, 1983-86 .... **300**

Jane, HN 3260, green, blue & yellow, 1990-95 .... **275**

Janet, HN 1537, red dress, 1932-95............... **125**

Janet, M 69, pale green skirt, green overdress, 1936-49... **425**

Janet, HN 1916, pink & blue, 1939-49............. **350**

Janice, HN 2022, green dress, 1949-55.......... **715**

Janine, HN 2461, turquoise & white, 1971-95 .... **275**

Jennifer, HN 2392, blue dress, 1981-92......... **295**

Jill, HN 2061, pink & white, 1950-71................ **175**

Joan, HN 2023, blue, 1949-59 .... **225**

Judge (The), HN 2443A, gloss, red & white, 1976-92... **260**

Judith, HN 2089, red & blue, 1952-59............. **405**

Judith, HN 2278, yellow, 1986-89 .... **225**

Julia, HN 2705, gold, 1975-90 .... **265**

June, HN 2991, lavender & red, 1988-94 .... **235**

Karen, HN 1994, red dress, 1947-55............... **450**

Karen, HN 2388, style two, red & white, 1982 to present... **350**

Kate, HN 2789, white dress, 1978-87 .... **150**

Kathleen, HN 3100, purple, cream & pink, 1986... **275**

Katrina, HN 2327, red, 1967-69...................... **275**

Kelly, HN 2478, white w/blue flowers, 1985-92 .... **220**

Kirsty, HN 3213, red, 1988-97........................ **175**

Ko-Ko, HN 2898, yellow & blue, 1980-85 .... **650**

L'Ambitieuse, HN 3359, rose & pale blue, 1991, RDICC, limited edition of 5,000.......... **350**

Lady April, HN 1958, red dress, 1940-49........ **425**

Penelope, HN 1901, red dress, 1939-75 .... **375**
Penny, HN 2338, green & white dress, 1968-95 .... **75**
Pensive, HN 3109, white w/yellow flowers on skirt, 1986-88 .... **175**
Piper (The), HN 2907, green, 1980-92 .... **350**
Polly, HN 3178, green & lavender, 1988-91 .... **215**
Polly Peachum, HN 550, red dress, 1922-49 .... **750**
Polly Peachum, M 21, red gown, 1932-45 ...... **600**
Premiere, HN 2343, hand holds cloak, green dress, 1969-79 .... **195**

Pride & Joy

Pride & Joy, HN 2945, brown, gold & green, RDICC, 1984 (ILLUS.) **275**
Priscilla, M 24, red, 1932-45............................ **600**
Promenade, HN 2076, blue & orange, 1951-53... **2,250**
Prue, HN 1996, red, white & black, 1947-55 .... **550**
Queen of the Ice, HN 2435, cream, Enchantment Series, 1983-86 .... **195**
Rachel, HN 2919, gold & green, 1981-84 .... **215**
Rebecca, HN 2805, pale blue & lavender, 1980-96.. **450**
Regal Lady, HN 2709, turquoise & cream, 1975-83.. **195**
Rosabell, HN 1620, red & green, 1934-38.... **1,400**
Rosamund, M 32, yellow dress tinged w/blue, 1932-45.. **950**
Rosemary, HN 3698, mauve & yellow, 1995-97 (ILLUS., top next column) **315**
Rowena, HN 2077, red, 1951-55 .... **750**
Sabbath Morn, HN 1982, red, 1945-1959 ...... **295**
Sairey Gamp, HN 2100, white dress, green cape, 1952-67 .... **475**
Sam Weller, M 48, yellow & brown, 1932-81 ...... **65**
Samwise, HN 2925, black & brown, Middle Earth Series, 1982-84 .... **725**
Sandra, HN 2275, gold, 1969-97 .... **225**
Sara, HN 2265, red & white, 1981-97.............. **275**
Secret Thoughts, HN 2382, green 1971-88 .... **195**
Sharon, HN 3047, white, 1984-95.................... **90**
Shore Leave, HN 2254, 1965-79 .... **295**
Silks and Ribbons, HN 2017, green, red & white dress, 1949 to present **225**
Simone, HN 2378, green dress, 1971-81 .... **135**

Rosemary

Sleepyhead, HN 2114, 1953-55 .... **2,250**
Soiree, HN 2312, white dress, green overskirt, 1967-84 .... **175**
Solitude, HN 2810, cream, blue & orange, 1977-1983.. **325**
Sophie, HN 3257, blue & red, 1990-92........... **225**
Spring, HN 2085, 1952-59.............................. **395**
Spring Flower, HN 1807, green skirt, greyblue overskirt, 1937-59 .... **525**
Spring Morning, HN 1922, green coat, 1940-73.. **225**
Spring Morning, HN 1922, pink & blue, 1940-73.. **225**

Spring Walk

Spring Walk, HN 3120, blue, 1990-92 (ILLUS.).. **305**
St. George, HN 2067, purple, red & orange blanket, 1950-76 .... **2,250**
Stiggins, M 50, black suit, 1932-1982 .... **65**
Summer, HN 2086, red gown, 1952-59 .... **450**
Summer's Day, HN 2181, 1957-62 .... **275**

Miscellaneous

Shylock Baby Feeding Plate

Baby feeding plate, Dickens Ware, pale yellow rim & interior color scene of "Shylock," brown printed backstamp, early 20th c., 8 1/2" d. (ILLUS.)...................... **$75-100**

Tony Weller Dickens Ware Charger

Charger, Dickens Ware, round, color scene of Tony Weller, early 20th c., 13 1/2" d. (ILLUS.).. **200-300**

Fine Small Doulton Sung Ware Compote

Compote, cov., 2 3/4" h., Sung Ware, flaring octagonal low pedestal base supporting the wide rounded octagonal bowl w/a

conforming fitted domed cover, a mottled Flambé glaze in shades of dark & light blue & deep red, Flambé & Sung marks, decorated by Noke & Moore, early 20th c. (ILLUS.).. **690**

Yellow Ginger Jar with Bird & Flowers

Ginger jar, cov., bulbous nearly spherical body w/a domed cover, bright yellow ground painted in colorful enamels w/a long-tailed bird-of-paradise flying among stylized pendent flowers & fruiting branches, Model No. 1256C, date code for December 1925, 10 3/4" h. (ILLUS.) **1,315**

Royal Doulton Humidor with Landscape

Humidor, cov., thin footing on slightly swelled cylindrical body w/wide flat rim, inset metal-fitted patented cover, h.p. w/a continuous stylized landscape scene, impressed mark, early 20th c., 5 3/4" h. (ILLUS.).. **207**

Scarce Silicon Ware Doulton Owl Jar

Jar, cov., Silicon Ware, stylized model of a bulbous owl, the domed head forming the cover, the head w/finely incised & enameled light blue & white feathers around the dark blue-ringed white eyes, the body w/stylized blossom-like designs across the breast in dark & light blue, white & cream, further blue & white scaled feathers across the back, a dark buff ground, Doulton Lambeth - Silicon logo, some very minor nicks, 7 5/8" h. (ILLUS.) **1,093**

Classical Doulton-Lambeth Jardiniere

Jardiniere & pedestal, heavy pottery, large hexagonal urn-form jardiniere w/the side panels molded in relief w/classical designs of white putti playing musical instruments among leafy scrolls against a blue ground, dark brown borders & pale yellow rim, the conforming paneled pedestal w/matching decoration, top of jardiniere stamped "Doulton - Lambeth," restoration around rim of jardiniere, few small chips on pedestal, late 19th c., jardiniere 18 1/4" w., 15 1/2" h., pedestal 13" w., 20 1/2" h., 2 pcs. (ILLUS.) **2,530**

Large Rouge Flambé Leaping Salmon

Model of a salmon, Rouge Flambé, the leaping fish glazed in dark red shading to black, Model No. 666, early 20th c., 12 1/2" h. (ILLUS.) **638**

Dutch Series Party Set

Party set: rectangular plate & squared cup; Series Wares, Dutch Series, scenes of Dutch people at the waterfront around the sides, ca. 1920, the set (ILLUS.) **200**

Series Ware Pitcher with Old Bob Scene

Unusual Cockerel Royal Doulton Tea Set

Pitcher, 7 3/4" h., Series Ware, Old English Coaching Scenes, yellow ground w/figure of elderly man in long overcoat, stagecoach design rim band, inside of rim printed in black "Old Bob Ye Guard," ca. 1953-67 (ILLUS.)...................... **173**

"The Cup That Cheers" Series Ware Plate

Plate, 9" d., Series Ware, Sayings Ware Series, "The Cup That Cheers," center bust portrait of an elderly woman drinking tea,

band of teacups around the rim, ca. 1907 (ILLUS.)... **300**

Welsh Ladies Series Sugar Bowl

Sugar bowl, cov., Series Ware, Welsh Ladies Series, long straight-sided oval body w/angled end handles & flattened shoulder centering a flat covers w/peaked finial, scenes of Welsh ladies around the sides, introduced in 1906 (ILLUS.)............... **300**

Tea set: cov. teapot, open sugar & creamer; Cockerel patt., the teapot modeled as a rooster, the sugar bowl as a hen & the creamer as a chick, introduced ca. 1935, the set (ILLUS., top of page).................... **2,500**

Doulton-Lambeth Hunting Ware Tea Set

Under the Greenwood Tree Tea Tile

Tea set: large cov. teapot, small cov. teapot, cov. sugar bowl & creamer; Hunting Ware line, dark brown shaded to tan ground decorated w/applied relief-molded English hunting scenes, Doulton-Lambeth marks, ca. 1905, the set (ILLUS., bottom previous page) **600**

Tea tile, oval, Series Ware, Under the Greenwood Tree Series, color scene of Robin Hood seated under a tree watching archers in the distance, "Lincoln The Forest of Sherwood" around the rim, introduced in 1914 (ILLUS., top of page) **250**

Rare Royal Doulton Bone China Teapot

Teapot, cov., bone china, hand-painted w/images of exotic birds & heavy gilt scroll trim, painted by Joseph Birbeck, ca. 1910 (ILLUS.) **2,000**

Teapot, cov., Bunnykins Series, model of a large rabbit, designed by Charles Noke, introduced in 1939 (ILLUS., top next page) **3,000**

Beswick Figural Panda Teapot

Teapot, cov., Beswick Ware, figural Panda, introduced in 1989 (ILLUS.) **300**

Royal Doulton Cadogan Teapot

Teapot, cov., Cadogan-style pot, decorated in the Crows patt., ca. 1907 (ILLUS.) **2,000**

Doulton Titanian Ware Bird of Paradise Teapot

Teapot, cov., Titanian Ware, Bird of Paradise patt., introduced in 1919 (ILLUS.)......... **800**

Miniature Doulton Titanian Ware Vase

Vase, miniature, 3 3/8" h., Titanian Ware, flat-bottomed wide bulbous ovoid body tapering to a wide flat mouth, overall shaded glossy green to dark blue glaze, Titanian backstamp (ILLUS.)........................ **173**

Small Doulton Titanian Ware Vase

Vase, 3 1/2" h., 4" d., Titanian Ware, footed bulbous slightly tapering body w/a flattened shoulder centering a short flaring neck, soft celadon green ground decorated w/a small brown & white bird on a flowering branch, decorated by H. Allen, marked "Royal Doulton Flambé - Titanian - Young White-Throat" (ILLUS.)................... **489**

Vase, 6 3/4" h., wide shoulder tapering toward the base, extended neck, decorated w/white daffodils w/blue centers outlined w/white slip on a mottled light olive green ground, impressed mark "t - 1898" & inscribed "MW".. 150

Vase, 7" h., Flambé Ware, footed wide bulbous body w/wide shoulder tapering to short cylindrical neck w/molded rim, rich red glaze w/swirling mottled grey, black, blue & cream, artist-signed, Charles Noke, ink stamp & Doulton paster on bottom 350

Vase, 8" h., baluster-form w/a flaring domed foot tapering to a slender ovoid body w/a slender cylindrical neck w/a widely flaring rolled rim, dark green neck & foot, the body decorated overall w/a molded floral design on beige w/green, gold & turquoise blue highlights, "Slater's Patent" mark, ca. 1883 125

Vase, 8 1/8" h., Rouge Flambé, slender ovoid body w/a tiny flaring neck, red flambé glaze w/a landscape in black 150

Spherical Doulton Rouge Flambé Vase

Vase, 9" h., Rouge Flambé, nearly spherical body w/a short cylindrical neck, red w/black swirls & gold flecks, marked on the bottom "Royal Doulton Flambé - Veined - 1618," early 20th c. (ILLUS.) .. **200-300**

Vase, 9" h., Welsh Ladies decoration **225**

Hannah & Lucy Barlow Silicon Ware Vase

Vase, 9 1/4" h., Silicon ware, design of grazing horses, initialled Hannah & Lucy Barlow, 1884 (ILLUS.) **1,750**

Vase, 9 1/2" h., handled, flow blue, Babes in the Woods series **800**

Fine Doulton Sung Ware Scenic Vase

Vase, 8 5/8" h., Sung Ware, simple swelled cylindrical body tapering to a flat mouth, decorated by Charles Noke w/an elaborate scene of an Arab potter at his wheel, working under a grape arbor loaded w/grapes, background mottled Flambé glaze in shades of deep purple, deep red, gold & blue, Flambé logo on the base w/"Sung Noke No. 915," crazing w/several long craze lines, early 20th c. (ILLUS.)....... **2,990**

Vase, 8 7/8" h., dome footed w/wide cylindrical body, the narrow shoulder tapering to wide waisted cylindrical neck decorated w/sprays of prunus & flanked by bronzed elephant head handles, flat rim, decorated in the style of Japanese lacquerwork w/wading birds among reeds between printed gilt borders of mons & ruyi-head forms in gold, platinum & red on brown ground, impressed & gilt-printed "DOULTON, BURSLEM - 863 - AP," ca. 1882 (tiny chip to underside rim of foot) **2,750**

Rouge Flambé Vase with Landscape

Vase, 9 1/2" h., Rouge Flambé, a large nearly spherical body w/a short cylindrical neck, the deep red ground decorated w/a black rural landscape scene w/a cottage & trees in the center ground & cows in a barnyard, marked (ILLUS.)..................... **431**

Pair of Babes in the Wood Vases

Vases, 9 1/2" h., bulbous form w/flaring neck, Babes in the Wood series, one w/design of girl looking into woman's basket, the oehter w/girl holding the hem of woman's cloak, pr. (ILLUS.) **2,500**

Doulton Aubrey Pattern Wash Set

Washbowl & pitcher set, Aubrey patt., the deep wide rounded bowl & tall tapering cylindrical tankard pitcher w/a swelled rim & short rounded rim spout, long angled handle, a light blue Art Nouveau design composed of stylized rounded blossoms & long undulating stems & leaves, geometric border bands, ca. 1910, very minor wear & tiny glaze nicks on rim of bowl, pitcher 12 3/4" h., the set (ILLUS.) **460**

Whiskey jug w/stopper, stoneware, advertising-type, bulbous ovoid body w/a wide shoulder centered by a small cylindrical neck w/tiny knobbed stopper, small loop shoulder handle, brown neck & handle shaded to tan below, the front w/applied ship & label reading "Special Highland Whiskey" in olive green & cream, stopper w/"Dewar's Whiskey," 7 1/8" h. **115**

Florence Ceramics

Some of the finest figurines and artwares were produced between 1940 and 1962 by the Florence Ceramics Company of Pasadena, California. Flo-

rence Ward began working with ceramics following the death of her son, Jack, in 1939.

Mrs. Ward had not worked with clay before her involvement with classes at the Pasadena Hobby School. After study and firsthand experience, she began production in her garage, using a kiln located outside the garage to conform with city regulations. The years 1942-44 were considered her "garage" period.

In 1944 Florence Ceramics moved to a small plant in Pasadena, employing fifty-four employees and receiving orders of $250,000 per year. In 1948 it was again necessary to move to a larger facility in the area with the most up-to-date equipment. The number of employees increased to more than 100. Within five years Florence Ceramics was considered one of the finest producers of semi-porcelain figurines and artwares.

Florence created a wide range of items including figurines, lamps, picture frames, planters and models of animals and birds. It was her extensive line of women in beautiful gowns and gentlemen in fine clothes that gave her the most pleasure and was the foundation of her business. Two of her most popular lines of figurines were inspired by the famous 1860 Godey's Ladies' Book and by famous artists from the Old Master group. In the mid-1950s two bird lines were produced for several years. One of the bird lines was designed by Don Winton and the other was a line of contemporary sculpted bird and animal figures designed by the well-known sculptor Betty Davenport Ford.

There were several unsuccessful contemporary artware lines produced for a short time. The Driftware line consisted of modern freeform bowls and accessories. The Floraline is a rococo line with overglazed decoration. The Gourmet Pottery, a division of Florence Ceramics Company, produced accessory serving pieces under the name of Scandia and Sierra.

Florence products were manufactured in the traditional porcelain process with a second firing at a higher temperature after the glaze had been applied. Many pieces had overglaze paint decoration and clay ruffles, roses and lace dipped in slip prior to the third firing.

Florence Marks

Figures

"Annabel," Godey lady, standing w/right arm bent & carrying a basket of flowers, left arm in outward position, long full jacket w/gold trim, large hat, articulated fingers, 8 " h. **$400-450**

"Camille," woman standing & wearing white dress trimmed in gold, shawl over both arms made entirely of hand-dipped lace, brown hair, white triangular hat w/applied pink rose, ribbon tied to right side of neck, two hands, 8 1/2" h. **300-350**

"Carol," girl standing wearing a high-front bonnet & jacket w/tiered shoulders above a widely flaring dress over tiered pantaloons, 7 3/4" h. **200-250**

"Caroline," brocade fabric dress, 15" h. **3,500-4,500**

"Catherine," seated on an open-backed settee, no hat variation, 7 3/4" l., 6 3/4" h. **650-700**

"The Christening" Figure Group

"Christening (The)," woman w/dress trimmed in lace at neck, sleeves & front of dress holding an infant in a long white christening dress, articulated fingers, 10" h. (ILLUS.) **2,000-2,500**

"Cindy," young woman standing in long flaring gown, arms bent & away from the body, 8" h. **225-300**

"Clarissa," woman in full-sleeved jacket & long swirled & pleated skirt, bonnet & holding a muff in right hand, left hand on her shoulder, articulated hand, 7 3/4" h. **175-200**

"Claudia," ruffled dress w/lace trim, lace shawl on shoulders, large hat, articulated hands, 8 1/4" h. **250-275**

"Diane," woman in Victorian costume wearing a high rounded bonnet w/feather & a high-collared long coat opening over a ruffled dress, one arm down at side holding a muff, articulated hands, 8" h. **225-275**

Rare Dora Lee Figure

"Dora Lee," woman wearing a long widely flaring & swirling royal red gown, a small round hat on her head w/a ribbon, arms away from the body, 9 1/2" h. (ILLUS.) .... **750 TO 900**

"Edward," man in late Victorian costume sitting in an armchair, holding his bowler hat on one knee, 7" h. **200-250**

Florence "Her Majesty" Figure

"Her Majesty," woman in 18th c.-style long dress w/long sleeves, fitted bodice w/standup collar, white w/gold trim, 7" h. (ILLUS., previous page) **175-200**

"Jeannette," Godey lady, rose colored full-skirted dress w/peplum, white collar, flower at neck, left hand holding hat w/bow, right hand holding parasol, 7 3/4" h. **125-150**

"John Alden," man dressed in dark grey kneebritches, light grey coat, shoes & large brim hat & holding a gun, 9 1/4" h. **175-200**

"Joyce," woman wearing full off-the-shoulder gown w/shoulder ruffles, a wide-brimmed picture hat, arms away at the front, 8 1/2" h. **325-350**

Florence "Love Letter" Figurine

Rare "Little Princess" Figure

"Little Princess," girl standing in a long-sleeved very wide 17th c. farthingale gown, her hair in long curls, arms outstretched to edges of gown, 8 1/2" h. (ILLUS.) **1,000-1,250**

"Love Letter," woman standing reading a small letter, her hair piled on her head, wearing an off-the-shoulder long gown w/lace bands, 12" h. (ILLUS., top next column) **1,500-1,750**

"Melanie," Godey lady, wearing a close-fitting bonnet & long-sleeved long coat over a wide dress, arms at her sides, 7 1/2" h. **100-125**

"Mikado," very tall Japanese man wearing small round cap, floor-length long-sleeved jacket above draped lower garment on round base, 15" h. **300-350**

"Our Lady of Grace," Madonna figure wearing long cloak w/gathered arms over long gown, on rounded domed base, 10 3/4" h. **175-200**

"Pamela" with Bonnet & Basket

"Pamela," girl standing wearing a flower-trimmed bonnet & long swirling short-sleeved dress, a basket of flowers in one hand, 7 1/2" h. (ILLUS.) **450-475**

"Peter," man standing wearing Victorian frock coat over lacy cravat, one leg to side & leaning on a scroll pedestal w/a hand holding his top hat, 9 1/4" h......... **225-250**

"Prima Donna," woman in ornate 18th c. costume, her hair piled high & trimmed w/flowers, wearing a wide gown w/upright lacy collar, long ruffle-edged sleeves, the front of the gown formed by wide drapes opening over a tiered lacy underskirt, arms away from front, 10" h. **550-625**

"Victor," man w/head tilted wearing a Victorian outfit, holding top hat in right hand, frock coat over long pants, swirling long cape, 9 1/4" h. **175-225**

"Victoria," woman in Victorian dress seated on serpentine-back tufted Victorian settee, variation w/no bonnet, rose red gown w/ruffle-trimmed panels at waist, ruffled hem trim, arms away, 8 1/4" l., 7" h. **325-350**

Flow Blue

Flow Blue ironstone and semi-porcelain was manufactured mainly in England during the second half of the 19th century. The early ironstone was produced by many of the well known English potters and was either transfer-printed or hand-painted (brush stroke). The bulk of the ware was exported to the United States or Canada.

The "flow" or running quality of the cobalt blue designs was the result of introducing certain chemicals into the kiln during the final firing. Some patterns are so "flown" that it is difficult to ascertain the design. The transfers were of several types: Asian, Scenic, Marble or Floral.

The earliest Flow Blue ironstone patterns were produced during the period between about 1840 and 1860. After the Civil War Flow Blue went out of style for some years but was again manufactured and exported to the United States beginning about the 1880s and continuing through the turn of the century. These later Flow Blue designs are on a semi-porcelain body rather than heavier ironstone and the designs are mainly florals. Also see Antique Trader Pottery & Porcelain Ceramics Price Guide, *3rd Edition.*

ALBION (W. & E. Corn, ca. 1900)
Butter pat, 3 1/4" d. **$45**

ALDINE (W.H. Grindley & Company, ca. 1891)
Plate, dinner, 10" d... **100**
Vegetable dish, cov., footed, 12" l. from handle to handle, 8" h. **300**

AMOY (Davenport)
Teapot, cov., Amoy patt., Squat Sixteen Panel Fluted body shape, ca. 1850 (ILLUS., bottom of page)............................ **950**

Amoy Squatty Paneled Shape Teapot by Davenport

Amoy Octagon Shape Flow Blue Teapot

Teapot, cov., Octagon body shape, ca.
   1850 (ILLUS.).. **650**

**ANCIENT RUINS (G.L. Ashworth Bros.,
ca. 1891 - made first by Mason Potteries)**
Pitcher, 6" h. **375**

**ANEMONE (Cumberlidge, Humphreys &
Hele, ca. 1889-93)**
Biscuit jar, cov., 6 1/2" h. (ILLUS., top next
   column) **175**

ARABESQUE (T. J. & J. Mayer)
Teapot, cov., Long Octagon body
   shape, ca. 1845 (ILLUS., bottom of page) **650**

Anemone Covered Biscuit Jar

ARCADIA (Arthur J. Wilkinson, ca. 1907)
Tea cup & saucer, cup, 3 1/4" d., 2 1/4" h.,
   saucer, 5 1/2" d.. **115**

ARGYLE (Myott, Son & Co., ca. 1898)
Teapot, cov., , 6" h. **300**

ARGYLE (W.H. Grindley & Co., ca. 1896)
Butter pat, 3 1/2" d. **45**
Demitasse   cup   &   saucer,   cup
   3" d. x 3 1/2" h., saucer 4 1/2" d. **165**
Oyster bowl, 6" d. x 3" h.................................. **175**

Arabesque Pattern Teapot with Long Octagon Body Shape

Bouquet Vegetable Dish

BOMBAY JAPAN (Minton & Co., ca. 1852)
Fruit compote, 9" d., 3" h. 225

BOUQUET (Henry Alcock & Co., ca. 1895)
Vegetable dish, cov., footed, 12" l. (ILLUS.,
top of page) 300

BRAZIL (W.H. Grindley & Company, ca. 1891)
Creamer, 3 1/2" h. 175
Cup & saucer 115
Platter, 14" l. 200

Brazil Sugar Bowl

Sugar bowl, cov., 5" h. (ILLUS.) 250

BRITISH SCENERY (Davenport & Co., ca. 1856)
Charger, 13" d. 350

British Scenery Platter

Platter, 19" l. (ILLUS.) 750
Vegetable bowl, oval, 10" l., 3 1/2" h. 400

BURMESE (Thomas Rathbone & Co., ca. 1912)
Serving dish, rectangular, pierced, two-
handled, 13 1/2" l., 9" w. (ILLUS., top
next page) 375

CALICO (Warwick China Co., American, ca. 1887-1910, aka Daisy Chain)

Calico Tankard-type Pitcher

Pitcher, 7 1/2" h., 9" w. (ILLUS.) 275

CAMBRIDGE (Alfred Meakin, ca. 1891)
Bone dish, crescent shape, 7" l. 75
Butter dish, cov., no insert, 7 1/2" w. under-
plate, ... 250
Pitcher, milk 325
Pitcher, 5 1/2" h. 200
Plate, luncheon, 9" d. (ILLUS. next page) 85
Platter, 14" l. 325
Relish dish, oval, 8 1/2" l. 145
Soup plate 92
Vegetable dish, cov., 9" l. 275

Burmese Serving Dish

Cambridge Luncheon Plate

Sugar Canister

CANDIA (Cauldon Ltd., ca. 1910) (This pattern looks like "Roseville" by John Maddock)
Syrup, cov., w/pewter lid, 6 1/2" h.................... 300

CANNISTER (maker unknown, marked "Germany," ca. 1891) - Miscellaneous (These cannisters, spice jars & kitchen items were made for export. They arrived without the name of the intended contents i.e. "Tea" or "Sugar." Machines were used to print the name after arrival. They were also in different shapes & languages.)
Box for pickled herring, very unusual, 6 x 14", 6" h. (ILLUS., top next page).......... 575
Canister, cov., marked "Sugar," 6" d., 8" h. (ILLUS., top next column) 225
Salt box, hanging type, 5 x 7", 8 1/2" h. (ILLUS., bottom next column) 275
Spice jar, cov., 5" h. 75

Hanging Salt Box

Long Box for Pickled Herring

CANTON (James Edwards, ca. 1845)
Chamber pot, cov., 9" d., 7" h. **450**

CARLTON (Samuel Alcock & Co., ca. 1850)

Carlton Pattern Sauce Tureen

Sauce tureen, cov., rosebud finial, 7 1/2" handle to handle, 8 1/2" d. underplate (ILLUS.).. **575**
Vegetable dish, cov., rosebud finial **625**

CARNATION (Furnivals, Ltd., ca. 1890)
Plate, dinner, 10" d... **90**

CASHMERE (Francis Morley, ca. 1850)
Teapot, cov., Broad Shoulder body shape, ca. 1850, each (ILLUS. of two size variations, bottom of page).................. **950**
Teapot, cov., Classic Gothic body shape, ca. 1850, each (ILLUS. of two size variations, top next page) **950**

Cashmere Pattern Morley Teapots in Two Sizes

Classic Gothic Cashmere Pattern Flow Blue Teapots

Split Primary Body Shape Cashmere Teapots

Two Views of the Rare Cashmere Syrup Pitcher with Side Handle

Teapot, cov., Split Panel Primary body
shape, ca. 1850, each (ILLUS. of two
size variations, middle of previous page).. **1,200**
Teapot, cov., Straight Line Primary
shape, ca. 1850.. **1,200**
Syrup pitcher, side handle, wide squatty
base w/sharply tapering paneled sides,
rare & unusual, 4 1/2" h. (ILLUS., bottom
previous page) **1,800**

CECIL (Thomas Till & Son, ca. 1891)
Bone dish, crescent-shaped.............................. **65**
Cup & saucer **80**
Plate, bread, 6" d... **50**

CHAPOO (John Wedge Wood - aka Wedg.wood, ca. 1850)

Chapoo Teapot in Variant Body Shape

Teapot, cov., Double Line Primary body
shape, ca. 1850 (ILLUS.) **550**

Tall Chapoo Pattern Flow Blue Teapot

Teapot, cov., Tall No Line Primary body
shape (ILLUS.)... **1,200**

CHEN-SI (John Meir, ca. 1835)

Chen-Si Flow Blue Teapot by Meir

Teapot, cov., Eight Sided Primary Belted
body shape (ILLUS.).................................... **650**

CHINESE (Thomas Dimmock & Co., ca. 1845)

Drainer, 10 x 14" (ILLUS., top next page)........ **575**
Pitcher, water, 8 1/2" h. **425**
Tea set: cov. teapot, oversized cov. sugar &
creamer; Primary body shape, teapot
9" h., the set **2,800**

1840s Chinese Pattern Teapot

Teapot, cov. (ILLUS.)....................................... **800**

CLARENCE (W.H. Grindley & Co., ca. 1900)

Clarence Platter

Platter, 16" l. (ILLUS., top of page) **450**

CLAYTON (Johnson Bros., ca. 1902)
Chamber set: pitcher & bowl, chamber pot, toothbrush holder & shaving mug; the set . **2,000**
Platter, 16" l. **450**

Clayton Soup Plate

Soup plate w/flanged rim, luncheon, 9" d. (ILLUS.).. **95**
Vegetable dish, open, oval, 9" l...................... **165**

CLEOPATRA (Edward Walley, ca. 1845)
Teapot, cov., 9" h. **725**

CLOVER (W.H. Grindley & Co., ca. 1910)
Platter, 16" l. **275**

CLYTIE (Wedgwood & Co., ca. 1908)
Plate, dinner, 10" d., w/turkey design.............. **175**
Platter, 19" l., w/turkey design **1,000**

COLONIAL (J. & G. Meakin, ca. 1891)
Butter pat, 3 1/2" d. **45**
Vegetable bowl, open, oval, 9" l...................... **125**

CONWAY (New Wharf Pottery & Co., ca. 1891)
Platter, 14" l. **225**

Conway Vegetable Bowl

Vegetable bowl, open, round, 9 1/2" d. (ILLUS.).. **195**

CRACKED ICE (International Pottery Company, American, ca. 1860-1920)
Cake plate, 10 1/2" d. **125**

CRAWFORD RANGES (Sampson Bridgwood & Son, ca. 1885) (These were pieces made for American export to advertise the Crawford Cooking Ranges. They were given away with the purchase of a range.)
Pitcher, 8" h. **250**
Plate, 10" d... **125**

CRUMLIN (Myott, Son & Co., ca. 1900)
Creamer, 4 1/2" h... **125**

Meakin Devon Pattern Flow Blue Dinner Service

Pitcher, 8" h. 275
Plate, 10" d., w/scalloped rim 95

CYPRUS (Wm. Davenport, ca. 1850)
Platter, 16" l. 425

DAISY (Burgess & Leigh, ca. 1897)

Daisy Soup Plate

Soup plate w/flanged rim, 9" d. (ILLUS.) 95

DELAMERE (Henry Alcock & Co., ca. 1900)

Delamere Soup Bowl

Bowl, soup, franged edge rim, 10" d.
  (ILLUS.)... 115

DELFT (Minton, ca. 1893)
Creamer, 5" h... 125
Plate, dinner, 10" d... 100

DEVON (Alfred Meakin, ca. 1907)
Dinner service: thirteen 9 3/4" d. dinner
  plates, twelve 7 1/2" d. soup plates,
  twelve bread & butter plates, eleven dessert plates, twelve dessert bowls, seventeen saucers-underplates, eight coffee
  cups & four saucers, eight teacups & four
  saucers, one gravy boat, open sugar
  bowl, creamer, 8 1/2" d. vegetable dish,
  small oval relish dish, two open oval vegetable dishes, one two-handled cov. vegetable tureen, oval chop platter & matching 16" l. roasted meats platter & cov.
  butter dish, the set (ILLUS., top of page)
  3,220

DOROTHY (Johnson Bros., ca. 1900)
Butter pat, 3 1/2" d. 45
Pitcher, 6 1/2" h. 175
Vegetable bowl, cov....................................... 275

EBOR (Ridgways, ca. 1910)

Ebor 10" Dinner Plate

Plate, 10" d. (ILLUS.) 115

GOTHIC (Jacob Furnival & Co., ca. 1850)

Pitcher & Bowl Set in Gothic Pattern

Pitcher & bowl set, 13 1/2" h. pitcher,
14" d. bowl, the set (ILLUS.) **1,800**

GRACE (W. H. Grindley & Co., ca. 1897)
Bone dish, crescent shape, 7" l. 75
Creamer, 5" h. 175
Gravy boat w/underplate 175
Platter, 12" l. 150
Sugar, cov., 5" h., 7" handle to handle 250

GRAPE (unknown maker, ca. 1840)

Gaudy Grape Flow Blue Teapot

Teapot, cov., free-hand Gaudy Ironstone,
Ten Panel Primary shape (ILLUS.) **650**

GRAPES (Unknown, ca. 1850s, brush-stroke painted)
Plate, 9" d., scalloped, reticulated (ILLUS.,
top next column) **175**

Reticulated Plate in Grapes Pattern

GRENADA (Henry Alcock & Co., ca. 1891)
Pitcher, 7" h. 200

Grenada 10" Plate

Plate, 10" d. (ILLUS.) **100**

HEATH'S FLOWER (Thomas Heath, ca. 1850)

Heath's Flower Flow Blue Teapot

Teapot, cov., free-hand, Full Panel Gothic body shape (ILLUS.) **650**

Gothic Decagon Heath's Flower Teapot

Teapot, cov., free-hand, Gothic Decagon body shape (ILLUS.) **650**

Heath's Flower Six Sided Gothic Teapot

Teapot, cov., free-hand, Six Sided Gothic (Lantern) body shape (ILLUS.) **650**

HINDOSTAN (Wood & Brownfield, ca. 1845)
Platter with meat well, 20" l. tree platter........ **650**

HOLLAND (Johnson Bros., ca. 1891)
Bone dish, crescent shape, 7" w. **75**
Butter dish, cov. **300**
Cake plate, tab handles, 9" w. **175**
Platter, 12" l. **125**

HONG KONG (Charles Meigh, ca. 1840)
Relish dish, shell mitten **250**
Teapot, cov., Long Octagon body shape (ILLUS., bottom of page)............................ **850**

Meigh Hong Kong Pattern Teapot in the Long Octagon Shape

Fluted Hong Kong Pattern Teapot by Meigh

Hong Kong Flow Blue Teapot by Meigh

Teapot, cov., Ridged Square body shape
(ILLUS.).. **750**

Teapot, cov., Twelve Panel Fluted body
shape (ILLUS., top of page) **950**

*Hong Kong Teapot in Vertical Panel Gothic
Shape*

Teapot, cov., Vertical Panel Gothic body
shape (ILLUS.).. **750**

**HUMPHREY'S CLOCK (Ridgways, ca.
1900)**
Tea set, child's, 36 pcs................................. **2,000**

INDIA (Villeroy & Boch, German, ca. 1845)
Plate, 8" d., pierced.. **150**
Teapot, cov., 8" h. **600**

Leon 16" Platter

LEAF & BERRY (Unknown, ca. 1860s, brush-stroke painted)

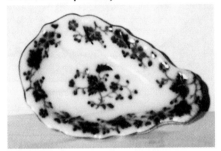

Leaf & Berry Relish Mitten

Relish mitten, marked w/impressed "Real Ironstone," a mark that G.L. Ashworth & Bros. impressed on their pieces ca. 1862, 8 1/2" w. (ILLUS.) **275**

LEAF & SWAG (Unknown, probably 1850s, brush-stroke painted)

Leaf & Swag 8 1/2" Plate

Plate, 8 1/2" d. (ILLUS.) **150**

LEON (J. & G. Meakin, ca. 1890)
Gravy boat **150**
Platter, 16" l. (ILLUS., top of page) **400**

LESBURY (Armstrong & Co., marked "Cetemware," ca. 1906)

Lesbury Covered Sauce Tureen

Sauce tureen, cov. (ILLUS.) **175**

LILY (Thomas Dimmock & Co., ca. 1844)

Lily Pitcher by Thomas Dimmock & Co.

Pitcher, 8" h. (ILLUS., previous page) **325**

LOIS (New Wharf Pottery & Co., ca. 1891)

Lois Soup Bowl

Soup bowl, flanged edge, 10" d. (ILLUS.) **95**

LONSDALE (Ridgways, ca. 1910)
Demitasse cup & saucer, 2 1/2" h. **125**

Lonsdale Platter by Ridgways

Platter, 14 x 17" (ILLUS.) **500**

LORNE (W.H. Grindley & Co., ca. 1900)
Pitcher, 7" h. **300**
Vegetable bowl, cov. **275**

LUGANO (Ridgways, ca. 1890)
Creamer, 4 1/2" h. **200**
Gravy boat **125**

MADRAS (Doulton & Co., ca. 1900)
Tea set: teapot, cov. sugar & creamer; the
set **750**

MANDARIN (John Maddock, ca. 1850)
Pitcher, 6" h. **225**

MANHATTAN (Henry Alcock, ca. 1900)
Teapot, cov., footed deeply waisted ruffled
unnamed body shape (ILLUS., top next
column) **450**

Manhattan Pattern Teapot by Alcock

Manhattan Flow Blue Teapot

Teapot, cov., unnamed body shape (ILLUS.) **450**

MANILLA (Podmore, Walker & Co., ca. 1834-1859)
Shell mitten relish, 8" w. **275**

MARBLE (Warwick China Co., American, ca. 1893)
Ferner, 8" d. **275**
Syrup pitcher, 6" h. **325**

MARCHEIL NEIL (W.H. Grindley & Co., ca. 1895)
Oyster bowl, 5 1/2" d., 3" h. **175**

Marcheil Neil Flow Blue Teapot

Teapot, cov., deeply waisted & lobed unnamed body shape (ILLUS.) **450**

Marguerite 18" Platter

Plate, 10" d. 95
Platter, 14" l. 200
Vegetable dish, individual size, 5 1/2" 90

MARGUERITE (W.H. Grindley & Co., ca. 1891)
Creamer 175
Platter, 18" l. (ILLUS., top of page) 525
Sugar, cov. 250
Teapot, 6 1/2" h. 500

MARIE (W. H. Grindley & Co., ca. 1891)
Butter pat, 3 1/2" d. 40
Plate, 8" d., dessert 75
Relish dish, oval, 8" l 95
Sugar, cov. 225

MARQUIS, THE (Also See Marquis II) (W. H. Grindley & Co., ca. 1906)
Tea cup & saucer (ILLUS., bottom previous
   column) 95

MARTHA WASHINGTON (Unknown, ca. 1900 aka "Chain of States")
Tea cup & saucer 115

MEISSEN (Brown-Westhead, Moore & Co., ca. 1895)

Meissen Tab-handled Cake Plate

Cake plate, tab handles, 10" d. (ILLUS.) 175

MELBOURNE (W.H. Grindley & Co., ca. 1891)
Comport, on pedestal, 9 1/2" d., 4 3/4" h. 350

Tea Cup & Saucer in The Marquis Pattern

Non Pareil Flow Blue Teapot

MOREA (J. Goodwin, ca. 1878)

Morea Plate

Plate, 8 1/2" d. (ILLUS.) 100

MORNING GLORY (John Ridgway, ca. 1845)
Pitcher, 7" h. 525

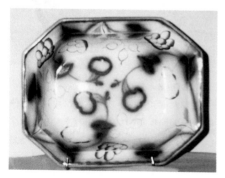

Morning Glory Vegetable Dish

MORNING GLORY (Unknown, ca. 1850s, brush-stroke, gaudy)
Coffeepot, cock's comb handle 1,100
Sugar, cov., cock's comb handles 600
Vegetable dish, open, 7 x 8 1/2" (ILLUS.)....... 200

MURIEL (Upper Hanley Pottery, ca. 1895)
Plate, 10" d... 95

NANKIN (F. & R. Pratt, ca. 1840)
Shaving mug 175

NING PO (R. Hall & Co., ca. 1845)
Platter, 15" l. 400

NON PAREIL (Burgess & Leigh - Middle-port Potteries, ca. 1891)
Creamer, 4 1/2" h... 175
Egg cup 150
Pitcher, 6" h. 200
Teapot, cov., oblong boat-shaped body
 (ILLUS., top of page).................................. 650
Teapot 575

Open Vegetable Bowl in Non Pareil Pattern
Vegetable dish, open, oval, 10" d. (ILLUS.) 175

NORMANDY (Johnson Bros., ca. 1900)
Vegetable dish, open, tab handles, 9 1/2" l. 175

Meakin Ovando Pattern Flow Blue Dinner Service

OLYMPIA (Johnson Bros., ca. 1890)

Olympia Pitcher

Pitcher, 7" h. (ILLUS.) 200

OLYMPIA (W. H. Grindley & Co., ca. 1894)

Olympia Covered Soup Tureen

Soup tureen, cov., round (ILLUS.) 300

OREGON (T.J. & J. Mayer, ca. 1845)
Cup & saucer, no handles 175

Early Mayer Oregon Pattern Teapot

Teapot, cov., Classic Gothic body shape
(ILLUS.) 650

ORIENTAL (Ridgways, ca. 1891)

Oriental Fruit Compote by Ridgways

Fruit compote, footed, two handles, 10" d.,
6" h. (ILLUS.) 750
Sauce tureen w/underplate 275

ORIENTAL (Samuel Alcock & Co., ca. 1840)
Plate, 13" d., two open tab handles 450
Relish dish, shell mitten 275

Two Pelew Pattern Teapots in the Grape Octagon Shape

Tea cup & saucer, gilded, ring-handled, rare in that most cups were made without handles & very little gilding was done, 4" d., 3 1/4" h. cup, 6" d. saucer **175**

OSAKA (James Kent, Old Foley Pottery, ca. 1905)
Biscuit barrel **200**

OSBORNE (Ridgways, ca.1905)
Teapot, 7 1/2" h., 10" w. from spout to handle **400**

OVANDO (Alfred Meakin, ca. 1891)
Dinner service: nine 9" d. dessert plates, nine 6" d. saucers, seven bread & butter plates, six soup plates, six dessert bowls, one 8 1/2" l. oval relish dish, 9 3/4" l. oval vegetable dish, sauceboat, 12 1/2" l. oval meat platter, 16" l. oval meat platter, two-handled oval cov. vegetable dish, two-handled round cov. vegetable dish, handled sugar bowl w/no cover & handles repaired, the set (ILLUS., top of previous page) **1,840**

OXFORD (Johnson Bros., ca. 1900)
Mustard jar, cov., 4 1/2" h. **275**
Plate, 9" d. **85**

OYAMA (Doulton & Co., ca. 1902)
Teapot **275**

PASTORAL (J. & T. Furnival, ca. 1843)

Teapot, cov., Tall Primary Single Line body shape (ILLUS., top next column).............. **1,200**

PEKIN (Arthur J. Wilkinson, ca. 1909) (Royal Staffordshire)
Tea cup & saucer **100**

PEKING (unknown maker, ca. 1845)
Teapot, cov., Six Sided Primary Belted body shape (ILLUS., bottom next column).. **600**

Tall Pastoral Pattern Flow Blue Teapot

Early Peking Pattern Flow Blue Teapot

PELEW (E. Challinor, ca. 1840)

Pelew Pattern Teapot in Long Decagon Body Shape

Teapot, cov., Grape Octagon body shape, each (ILLUS. in two size variations, top of previous page) 650

Teapot, cov., Long Decagon body shape (ILLUS., top of page) **1,400**

PENANG (Wm. Ridgway, ca. 1840)

Mitten relish 275

Teapot, cov., Twelve Panel Fluted shape (ILLUS., bottom of page) **750**

Early Penang Flow Blue Pattern Teapot

Savoy 18" Platter

ROYSTON (Johnson Bros., ca. 1891)

Royston Platter

Platter, 14" l. (ILLUS.) **175**

SAVOY (Johnson Bros., ca. 1900)
Platter, 18" l. (ILLUS., top of page) **300**

SCINDE (J. & G. Alcock, ca. 1840)
Teapot, cov., child's size, Double Line Primary body shape (ILLUS. left with adult size teapot, top next page)...................... **1,200**

Scinde Pumpkin-shape Teapot

Teapot, cov., Eight Panel Pumpkin shape body (ILLUS.)... **650**
Teapot, Double Line Primary body shape (ILLUS. right with child's teapot, top next page)... **600**

SEAWEED (Wm. Ridgway, ca. 1856)

Dinner Rim Soup Bowl in Seaweed

Rim soup bowl, flanged edge, 10" d. (ILLUS.) **100**

SEVILLE (New Wharf Pottery & Co., ca. 1891)
Creamer, 5" h... **165**
Plate, 9" d... **85**

SHANGHAE (Jacob Furnival & Co., ca. 1860)

9" Shanghae Plate

Plate, 9" d., 14-sided (ILLUS.) **150**
Platter, 18" l. **900**

Scinde Regular & Child's Size Flow Blue Teapots

Squatty Shanghai Pattern Flow Blue Teapot

Two Sizes of Flow Blue Snowflake Pattern Teapots

SHANGHAI (W.H. Grindley & Co., ca. 1898)

Charger, 11" d... 300
Compote, w/pedestal 325
Pitcher, 8" h... 325
Plate, 10" d.. 100
Platter, 14" d. 225
Teapot, cov., footed wide squat body
  (ILLUS., prevoius page) 450

Shanghai Flow Blue Demitasse Teapot

Teapot, cov., tall ovoid demitasse pot
  (ILLUS.)... 450
Vegetable dish, cov., oval 250

SHELL (Wood & Challinor, ca. 1840; E. Challinor, ca. 1860)
Teapot 675

SHUSAN (F. & R. Pratt & Co., ca. 1855)
Teapot (ILLUS., top next column) 525

SIMLA (Elsmore & Forster, ca. 1860)
Platter, 14" l. 250

Teapot in Shusan Pattern

SINGA (Cork, Edge & Malkin, ca. 1865)

Singa Loving Cup

Loving cup/tyg, two-handled, 5" h.,
4 3/4" d., 8 1/4" w. from handle to handle
  (ILLUS.)... 350

SNOWFLAKE (unknown maker, ca. 1840)
Teapot, cov., Plain Round body shape, also
  found in purple or a combination of blue
  & purple, each (ILLUS. of two sizes, top
  of page).. 750

Very Large Doulton Turkey Platter

TURKEY (Doulton & Co., ca. 1900) (Doulton produced more than one design with a turkey)
Platter, 24" l. (ILLUS.) 1,200

WALDORF (New Wharf Pottery & Co., ca. 1892)
Bowl, 5" d., berry... 38
Creamer, 5 1/2" h... 150
Plate, 10" d.. 95
Platter, 12" l. 175
Vegetable bowl, open, 9" l. oval...................... 125

WARWICK PANSY (Warwick China Co., American, ca. 1900)
Cake plate, w/tab handles, 10 1/2" l. 200
Candy dish, flutes (scalloped), 5" d. 125
Celery dish, 4 x 9" oblong 225
Pitcher, 7" h. 275
Syrup pitcher w/undertray, 8" h..................... 375

WATTEAU (Doulton & Co., ca. 1891)
Egg cup 175
Mustard jar w/attached tray, 3 1/2" h............. 250

WATTEAU (Doulton & Co., ca. 1891)

Watteau Oil Lamp

Oil lamp, converted to electric, 26" h.
(ILLUS.)... 2,200

Watteau Dinner Plate

Plate, 10 1/2" d. (ILLUS.) 150

WATTEAU (Doulton & Co., ca. 1891)
Platter, 14" l. 275
Teapot, 6" h. 375

WEST POINT (Rowland & Marsellus Importers, ca. 1893-1933)
Souvenir plate, 10" d. 125

WHAMPOA (Mellor, Venables & Co., ca. 1840)
Ginger jar, cov., 6" h..................................... 375

WILD ROSE (Warwick China Co., American, ca. 1898-1910)
Cake plate, w/tab handles, 12" d. 250
Chocolate set: 8" h. pot & six cups; the set .. 2,000
Pitcher, 7" h. 250
Spittoon, 5" h. x 8" d...................................... 650
Syrup pitcher, 6 1/2" h. 275

WILLOW (Doulton & Co., ca. 1891)
Chamber pot, 10" d. x 6" h. 300

WILLOW (Keeling & Co., ca. 1886)

Keeling & Co. Willow Pattern Teapot

Teapot, cov., oval tankard shape (ILLUS.)....... **450**

WREATH JAPAN (Minton & Co., ca. 1852)
Plate, 10 1/2" d... **125**

YEDDO (Arthur J. Wilkinson, ca. 1907)
Berry bowl drainer w/undertray **475**

YORK (Cauldon, Ltd., ca. 1905)
Tea cup & saucer **100**
Waste bowl, 5" d... **125**

Fulper Pottery

The Fulper Pottery was founded in Flemington, New Jersey, in 1805 and operated until 1935, although operations were curtailed in 1929 when its main plant was destroyed by fire. The name was changed in 1929 to Stangl Pottery, which continued in operation until July of 1978, when Pfaltzgraff, a division of Susquehanna Broadcasting Company of York, Pennsylvania, purchased the assets of the Stangl Pottery, including the name.

Fulper Marks

Flower frog, figural, model of a large oval scarab beetle, nice matte green glaze, unmarked, 3 1/4" l., 1 1/2" h. (ILLUS., top next column)... **$150**

Fulper Scarab Beetle Flower Frog

Squatty Copper Dust Fulper Vase

Vase, 4 3/4" h., 5 3/4" d., wide low squatty lower body w/a wide tapering shoulder to the wide flat mouth flanked by squared scroll handles, Copper Dust Crystalline glaze, incised racetrack mark (ILLUS.)........ **575**

Bulbous Fulper Copper Dust Vase

Vase, 5 1/2" h., 5" d., bulbous ovoid body tapering to a low wide molded mouth, Copper Dust Crystalline glaze, raised racetrack mark (ILLUS.) **1,035**

Bulbous Cafe-au-Lait Fulper Vase

Vase, 7" h., 9 1/2" d., wide squatty bulbous tapering form w/a flat closed rim flanked by square buttressed handles, cafe-au-lait glaze, rectangular ink mark (ILLUS.)...... **748**

Cucumber Glaze Squatty Fulper Vase

Vase, 6" h., 8 1/2" d., footed wide squatty bulbous body w/a short wide cylindrical neck surrounded by three short loop handles, Cucumber Crystalline glaze, raised racetrack mark (ILLUS.) **1,150**

Fulper Vase with Blue-Amber Glaze

Vase, 7 1/2" h., 6" d., bulbous ovoid gourd-form body w/a slightly tapering cylindrical neck flanked by curved handles to the shoulder, blue & amber Crystalline glaze, incised racetrack mark (ILLUS.).................. **546**

Elegant Ivory Flambé & Yellow Fulper Vase

Vase, 10 1/2" h., 4 1/2" d., simple tall baluster-form body, Ivory Flambé glaze drip-
ping over a mustard yellow matte ground,
ink racetrack mark (ILLUS.) **805**

Rare Fulper Cattail Flambé-glazed Vase

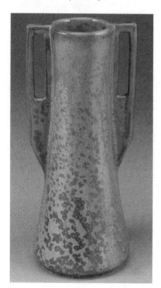

Leopard Skin Glazed Fulper Vase

Vase, 11" h., 4 3/4" d., tall gently tapering
cylindrical body w/a flat mouth flanked by
long squared buttressed handles, fine
Leopard Skin Crystalline glaze, rectangu-
lar ink mark (ILLUS.) **1,093**
Vase, 13" h., 4 3/4" d., tall slightly tapering
cylindrical body molded in relief overall in
cattails, glossy bluish grey & Moss Flambé glaze, rectangular ink mark (ILLUS.,
top next column).. **4,313**

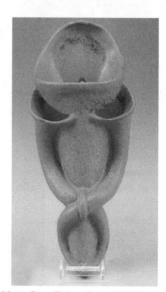

Matte Blue Fulper Triple Wall Pocket

Wall pocket, triple, a central tapering cone
w/a high upturned back rim flanked
down the sides w/smaller entwined
open-topped cones, matte blue glaze,
remnant of rectangular ink mark,
11 1/2" h. (ILLUS.)....................................... **374**

Geisha Girl Wares

Geisha Girl Porcelain features scenes of Japanese women in colorful kimonos along with the flora and architecture of turn-of-the-century Japan. Although bearing an Oriental motif, the wares were produced for Western use in dinnerware and household accessory forms favored during the late 1800s through the early 1940s. There was minimal production during the Occupied Japan period. Less ornate wares were distributed through gift shops and catalogs during the 1960s-70s; some of these are believed to have been manufactured in Hong Kong. Beware overly ornate items with fake Nippon marks that are in current production today, imported from China. More than a hundred porcelain manufacturers and decorating houses were involved with production of these wares during their heyday.

Prices cited here are for excellent to mint condition items. Enamel wear, flaking, hairlines or missing parts all serve to lower the value of an item. Prices in your area may vary.

More than 275 Geisha Girl Porcelain patterns and pattern variations have been catalogued; others are still coming to light.

The most common patterns include:

Bamboo Tree

Battledore

Child Reaching for Butterfly

Fan series

Garden Bench series

Geisha in Sampan series

Meeting series

Parasol series

Pointing series

The rarest patterns include:

... And They're Off

Bellflower

Bicycle Race

Capricious

Elegance in Motion

Fishing series

Foreign Garden

In Flight

Steamboat

The most popular patterns include:

Boat Festival

Butterfly Dancers

By Land and By Sea

Cloud series

Courtesan Processional

Dragonboat

Small Sounds of Summer

So Big

Temple A

A complete listing of patterns and their descriptions can be found in The Collector's Encyclopedia of Geisha Girl Porcelain. Additional patterns discovered since publication of the book are documented in The Geisha Girl Porcelain Newsletter.

References: Litts, E., Collector's Encyclopedia of Geisha Girl Porcelain, Collector Books, 1988; Geisha Girl Porcelain Newsletter, P.O. Box 3394, Morris Plains, NJ 07950.

Teapot, cov., Bow B patt. in reserve on floral backdrop, cobalt blue border w/gold striping, gold upper edge & spout rim................ **$45**

Toy Size Geisha Girl Porcelain Teapot

Teapot, cov., child's size, spherical body w/wide flat rim, short angled spout & C-form handle, low domed cover w/knob finial, Bow B stenciled patt., scalloped cobalt blue border, gold lacing, these were sometimes packaged w/candy, first quarter 20th c., overall 5 1/2" l., 3 1/2" h. (ILLUS.).. **25**

Individual Size Geisha Girl Teapot

Teapot, cov., individual size, bulbous melon-lobed body w/serpentine spout & ornate scroll handle, lobed domed cover w/loop handle, Garden Bench C stenciled patt., cobalt blue & red border, marked "Japan," overall 7" l., 4 1/2" h. (ILLUS.).. **35**

Miniature Geisha Girl Porcelain Teapot

Teapot, cov., miniature premium-type, squatty bulbous body w/straight spout, C-form handle, inset cover w/knob finial, Geisha in Cards patt., scalloped blue border, base stamped w/advertising "Café Martin New York," first quarter 20th c., 2" h. (ILLUS.) **35**

Painted Miniature Geisha Girl Teapot

Teapot, cov., miniature, squatty bulbous lobed form w/tiny spout & handle, Court Lady hand-painted patt., red border, first quarter 20th c., overall 3 1/2" l., 2" h. (ILLUS.).. **15**

Geisha Girl One-Cup Teapot

Teapot, cov., one-cup size, nearly spherical body w/a serpentine spout & C-form handle, tapering to a flat cover w/pointed knob finial, Cloud B patt., red border w/cherry blossoms, unusual steam hole in center of finial instead of on the lid itself, first quarter 20th c., 4" h. (ILLUS.)......... **25**

Ikebana in Rickshaw Geisha Girl Teapot

Teapot, cov., squatty bulbous body w/a short spout & upswept scroll handle, domed cover w/knob finial, Ikebana in Rickshaw patt., scalloped cobalt blue border, gold lacing, first quarter 20th c., overall 8" l., 4" h. (ILLUS.)............................... **38**

Bamboo-handled Geisha Girl Teapot

Teapot, cov., squatty bulbous body w/serpentine spout, inset domed cover & bamboo swing bail handle, Footbridge A patt., red border, red background stencil of vine & flowers w/a pale red wash, marked on base in Japanese "Nihon" w/Mt. Fuji logo, first quarter 20th c., overall 8" l., 5 1/2" h. (ILLUS.) **40**

Fancy Ribbed Geisha Girl Porcelain Teapot

Teapot, cov., squatty bulbous melon-ribbed body, shaped spout & ornate ring handle, low domed cover w/knob finial, Fan Silhouette of Hoo Bird patt., bluish green border, gold lacing, marked in Japanese on the base "Dai Nihon Tashiro tsukuru," first quarter 20th c. (ILLUS.)........................... **55**

Geisha Girl Teapot with Unusual Design

Teapot, cov., standard size, spherical body w/low domed cover, serpentine spout, C-form handle, unusual That Way, Mon stenciled patt., brown edging w/h.p. cranes around the rim, base marked in Japanese "Dai Nihon Tashiro tsukuru," first quarter 20th c., overall 7 1/4" l., 5" h. (ILLUS.)... **55**

Garden Bench Q Geisha Girl Teapot

Teapot, cov., standard size, squatty bulbous body w/serpentine spout & loop handle, Garden Bench Q h.p. patt., red, pine green, mint green & gold border, base marked w/"T" in a cherry blossom & "Japan," first quarter 20th c., overall 8" l., 4 1/2" h. (ILLUS.) **35**

Tall Geisha Girl Pointing D Pattern Teapot

Teapot, cov., tall ribbed body flaring at the base, serpentine spout & ornate C-scroll handle, domed cover w/arched scroll handle, Pointing D patt., red border, gold lacing, overall 6 1/4" l., 6" h. (ILLUS.) **45**

Gonder

Lawton Gonder founded Gonder Ceramic Arts in Zanesville, Ohio, in 1941 and it continued in operation until 1957.

The firm produced a higher priced and better quality of commercial art potteries than many firms of the time and employed Jamie Matchet and Chester Kirk, both of whom were outstanding ceramic designers. Several special glazes were developed during the company's history and Gonder even duplicated some museum pieces of Chinese ceramic. In 1955 the firm converted to the production of tile due to increased foreign competition. By 1957 its years of finest production were over.

Increase price ranges as indicated for the following glaze colors: red flambé - 50 percent, antique gold crackle - 70 percent, turquoise Chinese crackle - 40 per cent, white Chinese crackle - 30 per cent.

Lamp, model of Foo dog, 8" h................. **$125-150**
Lamp, cookie jar shape, Mold No. P-24, 8 1/2" h.. **20-40**

Planter, rectangular, Mold No. 701,
5 3/4 x 7 1/2" **15-30**
Planter, square flared form, Mold No. 733,
2 1/2 x 6 1/2" **15-30**
Planter bottom, Mold No. 724, for African
Violet planter No. 738, 4 x 5" **5-10**
Planter set: top & bottom; Mold No. 738, African Violet, 2 3/4" h., 4 1/4" w., the set **15-25**
Planter top, No. 1000, for African Violet
planter No. 738, 4 x 4", 5 1/4" h. **25-40**

Gonder La Gonda Pattern Teapot

Teapot, cov., upright rectangular form, La Gonda patt., creamy yellow glaze, Mold
914 (ILLUS.) **50-75**
Teapot, cov., Mold No. P-31, 6 1/2" h. **15-25**
Vase, 6 1/2" h., bulbous base w/scalloped
trumpet-form neck, Mold E-49 .... **10-25**
Vase, 7 1/4 x 8", cuspidor top, Mold No. 559
.... **200-250**
Vase, 8" h., flared bulb to square top, Oriental design, Mold No. 537 or 718 .... **100-125**
Vase, 8" h., flaring form w/relief-molded
swans at base, Mold No. H-47 .... **20-30**
Vase, 8" h., flat, Lotus design, Mold No. 402
.... **25-40**
Vase, 9" h., lyre shape, Mold No. J-57 .... **75-100**
Vase, 9" h., shell form, three dolphins at
base, Mold No. H-85 .... **50-65**
Vase, 9" h., squatty bulbous base, tapering
cylindrical neck, twisted handles, Mold
No. H-5 .... **25-35**

Gouda

While tin-enameled earthenware has been made in Gouda, Holland since the early 1600s, the productions of modern factories are attracting increasing collector attention. The art pottery of Gouda is easily recognized by its brightly colored peasant-style decoration, with some types having achieved a cloisonné effect. Pottery workshops located in or near Gouda include Regina, Zenith, Plazuid, Schoonhoven, Arnhem and others. Their wide range of production included utilitarian wares as well as vases, miniatures and large outdoor garden ornaments.

Gouda Pottery Marks

Colorful Gouda Astra Vase

Vase, 7 1/4" h., bulbous ovoid body tapering to a tall slender flaring trumpet neck, decorated in a bold colorful stylized design reminiscent of an Oriental carpet in shades of brick red, yellow, white, dark blue & turquoise blue, marked "Gouda - Holland - Astra" (ILLUS.) **$138**

Gouda Vase with Stylized Flowers

Vase, 7 5/8" h., bulbous ovoid body tapering to a small bulbed neck w/flat rim, bold simple stylized floral design on a ground consisting of alternating orange & green triangles separated by blue, marked "Archipel Holland" w/other marks (ILLUS.) **127**

Gouda Vase with Tall Flowering Stems

Vase, 7 7/8" h., footed squatty compressed lower body tapering to a tall gently flaring neck, tall swirling leafy stems w/blue bellflowers up the neck, cobalt blue lower body, marked "Gouda Holland 617/2/278," restored base chip (ILLUS.).................... **100-150**

Tall Stylized Floral Gouda Vase

Vase, 12 1/2" h., flaring foot below the sharply flaring body w/a wide rounded shoulder centering a trumpet-form neck, decorated w/bold stylized florals in shades of orange, dark blue & green, marked "Anemoon Holland 23.E - 21," minor glaze bubbling (ILLUS.)...................... **184**

Grueby

Some fine art pottery was produced by the Grueby Faience and Tile Company, established in Boston in 1891. Choice pieces were created with molded designs on a semi-porcelain body. The ware is marked and often bears the initials of the decorators. The pottery closed in 1907.

GRUEBY

Grueby Pottery Mark

Small Cylindrical Grueby Bowl

Bowl, 3" d., 4 1/4" h., a small footring supporting the deep vertical & slightly uneven sides, wide flat rim, dappled green matte glaze, impressed mark, two pinhead-sized glaze pops (ILLUS.)................. **$805**

Wide Shallow Blue Grueby Bowl

Bowl, 5 3/8" d., 1 7/8" h., wide low rounded sides & a wide flat molded rim, overall medium-dark blue matte glaze, impressed mark (ILLUS.)................................ **345**

Yellow & Brown Grueby Candlestick

Candlestick, a wide flat dished base w/low vertical sides, centered by a tapering ringed shaft w/an ovoid socket w/a flattened flared rim, mottled yellow & brown matte glaze, circular tulip-style insignia, No. 227, glazed-over chip at top rim, 5 3/8" h. (ILLUS.) **460**

Plaque, rectangular, architectural-type, carved & modeled w/a family of elephants in black against a bluish grey ground, mounted in a black box frame, two firing lines in body, restoration to one, small chip to one corner, stamped mark, 14 x 23" (ILLUS., top next page).............. **9,775**

Grueby Tile with White Rabbit & Shrub

Large Grueby Plaque with Elephant Family

Tile, square, a large white rabbit crouched behind a small stylized leafy shrub in white, both outlined in dark blue against a pale blue ground, impressed tulip-style mark, burst glaze bubbles, some small edge nicks, 3 7/8" w. (ILLUS., previous page) **690**

Grueby Vase with Broad Green Leaves

Vase, 5 1/2" h., 4 1/2" d., bulbous ovoid body w/a wide rolled rim, crisply tooled w/broad leaves up the sides, covered in a leathery dark green glaze, some high-point nicks, circular mark (ILLUS.) **2,875**

Vase, 6 1/4" h., squatty bulbous form w/a wide flat mouth, molded around the shoulder w/seven flower buds alternating w/seven wide leaves down the sides, mottled matte yellow glaze, unmarked, restoration to center of base, ca. 1908 (ILLUS., top next column) **5,288**

Yellow Grueby Vase with Buds & Leaves

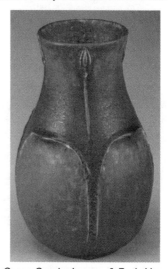

Green Grueby Leaves & Buds Vase

Vase, 7 1/2" h., 4 1/2" d., ovoid body tapering to a wide gently flaring neck, tooled

& applied w/rounded leaves around the lower half w/four buds up the sides, medium matte green glaze, small nick to one leaf edge, mark obscured by glaze (ILLUS.) **2,875**

Rare Large Grueby Vase with Leaves

Vase, 12 1/2" h., 8 1/4" d., rare large form w/bulbous body centered by a flaring cylindrical neck, tooled & applied w/large wide pointed overlapping leaves, fine organic matte green glaze, couple of very minor edge nicks, by Marie Seaman, stamped round mark (ILLUS.) **11,500**

Hall China

Founded in 1903 in East Liverpool, Ohio, this still-operating company at first produced mostly utilitarian wares. It was in 1911 that Robert T. Hall, son of the company founder, developed a special single-fire, lead-free glaze that proved to

be strong, hard and nonporous. In the 1920s the firm became well known for its extensive line of teapots (still a major product), and in 1932 it introduced kitchenwares, followed by dinnerwares in 1936 and refrigerator wares in 1938.

The imaginative designs and wide range of glaze colors and decal decorations have led to the growing appeal of Hall wares with collectors, especially people who like Art Deco and Art Moderne design. One of the firm's most famous patterns was the "Autumn Leaf" line, produced as premiums for the Jewel Tea Company. For listings of this ware see "Jewel Tea Autumn Leaf."

Helpful books on Hall include The Collector's Guide to Hall China *by Margaret & Kenn Whitmyer, and* Superior Quality Hall China - A Guide for Collectors *by Harvey Duke (An ELO Book, 1977).*

HALL CHINA

Hall Marks

Salt & pepper shakers, Radiance shape, canister-style, Chinese Red, pr. $120
Salt & pepper shakers, Rose White patt., holes form letters "S" & "P," pr. 35
Salt & pepper shakers, Sani-Grid (Pert) shape, Rose Parade patt., pr. 35
Soup tureen, cov., Clover style, Crocus patt. 350
Stack set, Medallion line, lettuce green 95
Sugar bowl, cov., Art Deco, Crocus patt. 35
Sugar bowl, cov., Modern, Red Poppy patt. 40
Tea tile, octagonal, art-glaze blue & white 65
Teapot, c0v., Aladdin shape, oval opening, w/infuser, Cobalt Blue w/gold trim 110
Teapot, cov., Airflow shape, Chinese Red 130
Teapot, cov., Aladdin shape, Cobalt Blue w/gold trim, 6-cup 125

Hall Gold Swag Aladdin Shape Teapot

Aladdin Shape Teapot with Serenade Pattern

Teapot, cov., Aladdin shape, round opening
for cover & insert, Gold Swag decoration
(ILLUS., bottom previous page) **70-75**

Hall Aladdin Marine Blue Teapot

Teapot, cov., Aladdin shape, round opening
w/insert, Marine Blue (ILLUS.) **65-75**

Hall Aladdin Maroon Teapot

Teapot, cov., Aladdin shape, round opening
w/insert, Maroon (ILLUS.) **65-75**
Teapot, cov., Aladdin shape, w/infuser, Serenade patt. (ILLUS., top of page)................. **350**

Hall Aladdin Shape Wildfire Pattern Teapot

Teapot, cov., Aladdin shape, Wildfire patt.,
w/oval infuser, 1950s (ILLUS.)...................... **75**
Teapot, cov., Albany shape, Emerald Green
w/"Gold Special" decoration.......................... **60**

Reissued Hall Automobile Teapot

Teapot, cov., Automobile shape, Autumn
Leaf patt., reissue for China Specialties
w/commemorative stamp on the bottom,
1993 (ILLUS.)... **175**

Hook Cover Chinese Red Teapot

Teapot, cov., Hook Cover shape, Chinese
   Red (ILLUS., top of page) **250**
Teapot, cov., Illinois shape, Canary Yellow **200**

Illinois Teapot with Maroon & Gold Decoration

Teapot, cov., Illinois shape, Maroon w/gold
   decoration (ILLUS.) **225**
Teapot, cov., Illinois shape, Stock Brown
   w/gold decoration **140**
Teapot, cov., Indiana shape, Warm Yellow
   w/gold decoration, 6-cup **450**

Teapot, cov., Jewel Tea Autumn Leaf patt.,
   Aladdin shape, round opening for domed
   cover (ILLUS., bottom of page) **75-85**
Teapot, cov., Kansas shape, Ivory w/gold
   decoration **400**
Teapot, cov., Lipton Tea shape, Light Yel-
   low **60**
Teapot, cov., Lipton Tea shape, Maroon **45**

Mustard Yellow Lipton Tea Shape Teapot

Teapot, cov., Lipton Tea shape, Mustard
   Yellow (ILLUS.) **40**

Hall Jewel Tea Autumn Leaf Aladdin Teapot

Star Shape Teapot with Gold Stars

Teapot, cov., Star shape, Cobalt Blue
   w/Standard Gold decoration........................ **125**
Teapot, cov., Star shape, Turquoise w/gold
   decoration (ILLUS., top of page)........... **100-125**

Hall Sundial - Blue Blossom Teapot

Teapot, cov., Sundial shape, Blue Blossom
   patt. (ILLUS.)... **300**
Teapot, cov., Sundial shape, Canary Yellow
   w/gold decoration, 6-cup............................... **85**
Teapot, cov., Surfside shape, Emerald
   Green w/gold decoration, 6-cup................... **200**
Teapot, cov., T-Ball Bacharach shape,
   Black w/gold label on base, 6-cup............... **195**
Teapot, cov., Tea-for-Four shape, Stock
   Green... **125**
Teapot, cov., Tea-for-Two shape, Pink
   w/gold decoration (ILLUS., top next col-
   umn)... **150**
Teapot, cov., Tea-for-Two shape, Stock
   Brown w/gold decoration.............................. **100**
Teapot, cov., Thorley series, Apple shape,
   Black w/gold decoration................................. **95**

Tea-for-Two Teapot in Pink & Gold

Teapot, cov., Thorley series, Grape shape,
   Ivory w/Special Gold & rhinestone deco-
   ration.. **295**
Teapot, cov., Thorley series, Starlight
   shape, Pink w/gold & rhinestone decora-
   tion.. **125**
Teapot, cov., Thorley series, Windcrest
   shape, Lemon Yellow w/gold decoration....... **95**
Teapot, cov., Tip-Pot Twinspout shape,
   Forman Family, Inc., Emerald Green............. **95**

New Hall Special Order Teapot

Teapot, cov., white squatty bulbous body
   w/a molded band of squared chain

around the middle decorated w/green sprigs, made for Longaberger Baskets, modern (ILLUS.).. **75**

Teapot, cov., Windshield shape, Ivory Gold Label line... **50**

Hampshire Pottery

Hampshire Pottery was made in Keene, New Hampshire, where several potteries operated as far back as the late 18th century. The pottery now known as Hampshire Pottery was established by J.S. Taft shortly after 1870. Various types of wares, including Art Pottery, were produced through the years. Taft's brother-in-law, Cadmon Robertson, joined the firm in 1904 and was responsible for developing more than 900 glaze formulas while in charge of all manufacturing. His death in 1914 created problems for the firm, and Taft sold out to George Morton in 1916. Closed during part of World War I, the pottery was later reopened by Morton for a short time and manufactured white hotel china. From 1919 to 1921, mosaic floor tiles became the main production. All production ceased in 1923.

Hampshire Marks

Low Squatty Hampshire Bowl

Bowl, 2 1/4" h., wide flattened cushion-form body w/slightly raised flat mouth, molded around the top w/alternating knobs & swastikas under a mottled dark green glaze, short, tight rim line, impressed mark (ILLUS.).. **$207**

Hampshire Vase with Streaky Glaze

Vase, 7 1/4" h., very slightly swelling cylindrical body w/a low wide ringed neck, overall mottled & streaky dark blue & pink matte drip glaze, designed by Cadmon Robertson, company logo, Shape No. 106, some grinding chips around the base (ILLUS.).. **690**

Peacock-glazed Hampshire Vase

Vase, 7 1/2" h., very slightly swelling cylindrical body w/a lightly molded wave-like band just below the low wide ringed neck, overall two-tone "peacock" glaze, designed by Cadmon Robertson, company logo, Shape No. 105 (ILLUS.)...................... **690**

Harker Pottery

The Harker Pottery was established in East Liverpool, Ohio, in 1840 by Benjamin Harker, Sr. In 1890 the pottery was incorporated as the Harker Pottery Company. By 1911 the company had acquired the former plant of the National China Company and in 1931 Harker purchased the closed pottery of Edwin M. Knowles in Chester, West Virginia.

Harker's earliest products were yellowware and Rockingham-glazed wares produced from local clay. After 1900 whiteware was made from imported materials. Perhaps their best-known line is Cameoware, decorated on solid glazes with white "cameos" in a silhouette fashion.

There were many other patterns and shapes created by Harker over the years. In 1972 the pottery was closed after it was purchased by the Jeanette Glass Company.

Harker Pottery Marks

Teapots - Miscellaneous

Aladdin Pattern Teapot in Teal Green

Teapot, cov., Aladdin patt., short squatty bulbous shape w/short neck, loop handle, squatty serpentine spout, short foot, domed lid w/disk handle, in deep teal green w/cream highlights on finial & rim, ca. 1950 (ILLUS.) **$20**

Harker Anna Pattern Teapot

Teapot, cov., Anna patt., bulbous Art Deco footed body shape, angled handle, short serpentine spout, line decoration around rim & lid, floral decoration on body in shades of blue, violet & rose w/green leaves, no backstamp, 1930s (ILLUS.) **20**

Blue Dainty Flower Teapot by Harker

Teapot, cov., Blue Dainty Flower patt., Zephyr shape, cylindrical body tapering in at shoulder, angled handle, serpentine spout, stepped base, light blue w/cream-colored stylized floral design on body, cream finial on lid & line decoration on rim, part of Cameoware line, ca. 1935 (ILLUS.) **35**

Buckeye Pattern Teapot by Harker

Teapot, cov., Buckeye patt., Zephyr shape, cylindrical body tapering in at shoulder, angled handle, serpentine spout, stepped base, white body decorated w/silver line decoration on rim, lid & finial & image of large red flower amid smaller red, green & white flowers & green leaves, originally called English Ivy, ca. 1939 (ILLUS.) **25**

Emmy Pattern Teapot by Harker

Teapot, cov., Emmy patt., Zephyr shape, footed squatty ovoid body w/tapering shoulder, angled handle, short spout, the body w/vertical embossed chevron lines, line decoration on lid & finial, the body decorated w/flowers in deep orange/red, purple/blue & yellow w/delicate green leaves, part of the G.C. line, ca. 1940 (ILLUS.) **15**

Harker Gadroon Shape Teapot

Teapot, cov., Gadroon shape, 1940s
(ILLUS., top of page) **50**

Harker Honeymoon Cottage Teapot

Teapot, cov., Honeymoon Cottage patt.,
footed cylindrical body w/slightly tapering
shoulder, C-form handle, slightly serpentine spout, the body & lid decorated w/a
cottage at the end of a lane bordered
w/flowers, all in bright primary colors on
white ground, red line decoration on rim,
lid & finial, ca. 1930 (ILLUS.) **50**

Rare Lisa Teapot in Gargoyle Shape

Teapot, cov., Lisa patt., Gargoyle or Regal
shape, tall rectangular body tapering out
to shoulder, then in to rim, long serpentine spout, C-form handle, all ribbed, the
handle w/applied thumbrest, the slightly
domed lid w/cut-out applied finial, upper
body decorated w/flowers in vibrant blue
& violet w/green leaves, teapot rare in
this shape, ca. 1930 (ILLUS.) **65**

Teapot, cov., Mallow patt., BakeRite, HotO-
ven ware **45**
Teapot, cov., Modern Age/Modern Tulip
patt., BakeRite, HotOven ware **20-30**

Harker Pottery Modern Tulip Teapot

Teapot, cov., Modern Tulip patt., Zephyr
shape, cylindrical ovoid shape tapering in
at shoulder, angled handle, slightly serpentine spout, stepped base, gold line
decoration on rim, lid & finial, body decorated w/stylized tulip in autumn shades,
similar to Jewel Tea Autumn Leaf, ca.
1940 (ILLUS.) **30**

Petit Point Pattern Teapot by Harker

Teapot, cov., Petit Point patt., Zephyr
shape, cylindrical body tapering in at
shoulder, angled handle, serpentine
spout, stepped base, horizontal band of
decoration just below shoulder filled
w/petit point-like rendering of flowers in
soft shades of pink, blue, yellow & green,
line decoration on rim, lid & spout, ca.
1940 (ILLUS.) **50**

Vintage Pattern Teapot on Zephyr Shape

Teapot, cov., Vintage patt., Zephyr shape, cylindrical body tapering in at shoulder, stepped base, angled handle, slightly serpentine spout, the body decorated w/horizontal band of entwined grapevines w/purple fruit, the rim & finial accented w/green line decoration, ca. 1935 (ILLUS.).. **40**

White Rose Pattern Teapot by Harker

Teapot, cov., White Rose patt., cylindrical body tapering in at shoulder, angled handle, serpentine spout, stepped base, blue w/cream-colored stylized floral design on body, cream finial & line decoration on rim, part of Cameoware line made for Montgomery Ward, ca. 1935 (ILLUS.) **45**

Harker Woodsong Pattern Teapot

Teapot, cov., Woodsong patt., squatty bulbous body w/short spout, branch handle & domed cover w/twig finial, overall greenish yellow ground decorated w/an overall shadow design of scattered delicate maple leaves, Chester, West Virginia, ca. 1960 (ILLUS.)............................ **45**

Haviland

Haviland porcelain was originated by Americans in Limoges, France, shortly before the mid-19th century and continues in production. Some Haviland was made by Theodore Haviland in the United States during the last World War. Numerous other factories also made china in Limoges. Also see LIMOGES.

Haviland Marks

Chocolate set: tall tapering pot & six tall cups & saucers; Albany patt., white w/narrow floral rim bands & gold trim, late 19th - early 20th c., the set (ILLUS., bottom of page).. **$288**

Haviland Albany Pattern Chocolate Set

Haviland Dinner Service in the Albany Pattern

Haviland Dinnerware in Blank No. 5

Dinner service: service for eight w/five-piece place settings & additional bowls, pitcher, gravy boat & other pieces; mostly Blank No. 5 w/delicate pink floral decoration, late 19th - early 20th c., 54 pcs. (ILLUS. of part) **748**

Dinner service: twelve 8-piece place settings w/additional open & cov. vegetable dishes & oval platter; Albany patt., white w/narrow floral rim bands & gold trim, late 19th - early 20th c., the set (ILLUS., top of page) **661**

Haviland Scenic Dish

Dish, shell-shaped, incurved rim opposite pointed rim, h.p. scene of artist's waterside studio, decorated by Theodore Davis, front initialed "D," back w/presidential seal & artist's signature, part of Hayes presidential service, 8 x 9 1/2" (ILLUS.) **1,925**

Dresser tray, h.p. floral decoration, 1892 mark **95**

Haviland Mayonnaise

Mayonnaise bowl w/attached underplate, decorated w/pink wild roses touched w/yellow, Schleiger 141D, 5" d. (ILLUS.) **145**

Mayonnaise bowl w/underplate, cov., leaf-shaped, Blank No. 271A **166**

Muffin server, No. 31 patt., Blank No. 24 .... **225**

Mustache cup & saucer, No. 270A patt., Blank No. 16 .... **220**

Mustard pot w/attached underplate, cov., CFH/GDM, copper color w/gold floral design overall, cov. w/spoon slot, 2 1/2 x 4" **225**

Olive dish, No. 257 patt. **99**

Haviland Oyster Plate

Oyster plate, six clam-shaped sections w/round center section for sauce, white, 8" d. (ILLUS.) **175**

Pitcher, 8 5/8" h., Art Deco stylized figural "Farewell" cat in yellow & white, base in-

Squatty Haviland Porcelain Teapot

scribed "Theodore Haviland Limoges/France Copyright Depose" & "E.M. Sandoz sc" **895**

Gold-decorated Lemonade Pitcher

Pitcher, 9" h., tankard-shaped lemonade-type, Ranson blank, delicate floral band around the upper body trimmed in gold, gold handle & trim bands, factory-decorated, Haviland & Co. mark (ILLUS.)............ **225**

Pitcher, 9 1/2" h., No. 279 patt., Blank No. 643 .... **225**

Plate, dinner, No. 72.. **40**

Plate, 7 1/2 x 8 1/2", heart-shaped, Baltimore Rose patt. **275**

Plate, 9 1/2" d., scalloped edge, cobalt & gold w/floral center...................................... **225**

Plate, dinner, 9 1/2" d., Dammouse antique rose w/gold medallion & flowers.................. **180**

Plate, dinner, 9 1/2" d., Feu de Four, Poppy & Seeds... **125**

Plate, dinner, 9 1/2" d., Schleiger 19, Silver Anniversary **35**

Teapot, cov., wide squatty bulbous tapering sides w/a flat rim, low domed cover w/arched finial, upright serpentine spout & C-scroll handle, white w/gold trim & thin yellow leaftip bands around the rim & cover, double Haviland mark, ca. 1900 (ILLUS., top of page)...................................... **75**

Hull

In 1905 Addis E. Hull purchased the Acme Pottery Company in Crooksville, Ohio. In 1917 the A.E. Hull Pottery Company began to make a line of art pottery for florists and gift shops. The company also made novelties, kitchenware and stoneware.

Hull's Little Red Riding Hood kitchenware was manufactured between 1943 and 1957 and is a favorite of collectors, as are the beautiful matte glaze vases it produced.

In 1950 the factory was destroyed by a flood and fire, but by 1952 it was back in production. Hull added its newer glossy glazed pottery plus pieces sold in flower shops under the names Regal and Floraline. Hull's brown dinnerware lines achieved great popularity and were the main lines being produced prior to the plant's closing in 1986.

References on Hull Pottery include: Hull, The Heavenly Pottery, 7th Edition, 2001 and Hull, The Heavenly Pottery Shirt Pocket Price Guide, 4th Edition, 1999, by Joan Hull. Also The Dinnerwares Lines *by Barbara Loveless Click-Burke (Collector Books 1993) and* Robert's Ultimate Encyclopedia of Hull Pottery *by Brenda Roberts (Walsworth Publishing Co., 1992). -- Joan Hull, Advisor.*

Hull Marks

Basket, Wildflower patt., No. 79, 10 1/4" h.
.... **$2,000**
Basket, Magnolia Gloss patt., No. H-14,
10 1/2" h.. **300**
Basket, Poppy patt., No. 601, 12" h............. **1,300**
Basket, Ebb Tide patt., model of a large
shell w/long fish handle, No. E-11,
16 1/2" l. **300**

Sun Glow Pattern Casserole

Casserole, cov., Sun Glow patt., No. 51-
7 1/2", 7 1/2" d. (ILLUS.) **50**
Coaster/spoon rest, Gingerbread Boy
patt., 5" l. **50**
Console bowl, Butterfly patt., wide-shoul-
dered disk-form w/closed rim, raised on
long curved tab feet, pebbled white
ground, No. B21, 10" d............................ **195**
Cornucopia-vase, Woodland Gloss patt.,
No. W10-11", 11" h. **65**
Cornucopia-vase, Woodland Matte patt.,
pink ground, No. W10-11", 11" h.................. **198**
Cornucopia-vase, Dogwood patt., No. 511,
11 1/2" h. **275**
Cornucopia-vase, double, Magnolia Gloss
patt., No. H-15, 12" h. **125**
Cornucopia-vase, double, Magnolia Matte
patt., No. 6, 12" h. **175**
Cornucopia-vase, double, Water Lily patt.,
No. L-27-12", 12" h................................... **250**
Cornucopia-vase, double, Bow-Knot patt.,
No. B13, 13 1/2" h. **295**

Ewer, Wild Flower patt., pink & blue, No. W-
11-8 1/2", 8 1/2" h. **163**
Ewer, Calla Lily patt., No. 506, 10" h. **350**
Ewer, Mardi Gras/Granada patt., No. 31,
10" h.. **135**
Jardiniere, Poppy patt., No. 603, 4 3/4" h. **175**
Jardiniere, Water Lily patt., No. 23-5 1/2",
5 1/2".. **125**
Jardiniere, Woodland Matte patt., pink &
yellow, No. W7-5 1/2", 5 1/2" h. **145**
Jardiniere, Orchid patt., No. 310, 6" h............ **225**
Jardiniere, Sueno Tulip patt., No. 115-33-
9", 9" h. **350**
Planter, bust of the Madonna, yellow, No.
24, 7" h.. **35**
Planter, model of a pheasant, No. 61, 6 x 8" **50**
Planter, model of swan, yellow glossy
glaze, Imperial line, No. 69,
8 1/2 x 10 1/2", 8 1/2" h. **50**
Planter, Blossom Flite patt., No. T12,
10 1/2" l.. **95**
Teapot, cov., Bow-Knot patt., turquoise &
blue, B-20-6", 6" h................................ **450-650**
Teapot, cov., Little Red Riding Hood patt. **400**

Hull Magnolia Gloss Teapot

Teapot, cov., Magnolia Gloss patt., H-20-
6 1/2", 1947-48 (ILLUS.) **65**
Teapot, cov., Parchment & Pine patt., S-11
(ILLUS., bottom of page)............................ **105**

Hull Parchment & Pine Teapot

Teapot, cov., Water Lily patt., No. L18-6" . 250-300
Teapot, cov., Dogwood patt., No. 507,
5 1/2" h... 280
Teapot, cov., House 'N Garden line, Mirror
Brown, 6" h.. 25-35
Teapot, cov., Parchment & Pine patt., No.
S-11, 6" h.. 80
Vase, 6" h., Wild Flower patt., No. W-3-6",
two handles, embossed flower spray,
background shading pink at top, cream
center, blue at base, matte finish 55
Vase, 6 1/2" h., Rosella patt., No. R-6-6 1/2" 40

Hull Royal Woodland Vase

Vase, 6 1/2" h., Royal Woodland patt., pale
turquoise w/white overall splotching,
darker handles & rim, marked "Hull W4-
6 1/2 U.S.A." (ILLUS.) 38

Hull Thistle Pattern Vase

Vase, 6 1/2" h., Thistle patt., blue ground,
No. 55 (ILLUS.)... 150
Vase, 7" h., Butterfly patt., No. B10-7" 55
Vase, bud, 7" h., Ebb Tide patt., No. E1 75
Vase, 7 1/2" h., Royal Woodland patt., No.
W8.. 40
Vase, 8 1/2" h., double-bud, Woodland
patt., No. W15-8 1/2", glossy 65
Vase, 8 1/2" h., Magnolia Matte patt., pink &
blue, No. 1-8 1/2"... 125
Vase, 8 1/2" h., Open Rose (Camellia) patt.,
No. 126 325
Vase, 10 1/2" h., Butterfly patt., No. B14-
10 1/2"... 100
Vase, 10 1/2" h., Poppy patt., No. 605............. 450
Vase, 10 1/2" h., Water Lily patt., pink &
green, No. L-12-10 1/2" 300
Vase, 12" h., handled, Tokay patt., No. 12-
12".. 125
Vase, 12 1/2" h., Magnolia patt., No. 22-
12 1/2"... 325
Wall pocket, model of an iron, Sun Glow
patt., unmarked, 6" h...................................... 65
Wall pocket, Rosella patt., No. R-10,
6 1/2" h... 85

Hummel Figurines & Collectibles

The Goebel Company of Oeslau, Germany, first produced these porcelain figurines in 1934, having obtained the rights to adapt the beautiful pastel sketches of children by Sister Maria Innocentia (Berta) Hummel. Every design by the Goebel artisans was approved by the nun until her death in 1946. Although not antique, these figurines with the "M.I. Hummel" signature, especially those bearing the Goebel Company factory mark used from 1934 and into the early 1940s, are being sought by collectors, although interest may have peaked some years ago. A good reference is Luckey's Hummel Figurines & Plates, Identification and Value Guide *by Carl F. Luckey (Krause Publications).Trademarks:TMK 1 - Crown - 1934-1950TMK 2 - Full Bee - 1940-1959TMK 3 - Stylized Bee - 1958-1972TMK 4 - Three Line Mark - 1964-1972TMK 5 - Last Bee - 1970-1980TMK 6 - Missing Bee - 1979-1991TMK 7 - Hummel Mark - 1991-1999TMK 8 - Goebel Bee - 2000-*

Hummel Marks

A Fair Measure, #345, 4 3/4" h., new style,
Trademark 5.. $350-450
Adoration, #23/I, 6 1/4" h., Trademark 6......... 430
Advent Boy with Horse candleholder,
#117, 3 1/2" h., Trademark 4 100-125
Advent Girl with Fir Tree candlestick,
#116, 3 1/2" h., Trademark 2 150-200

Adventure Bound, #347, 7 1/4 x 8", Trademark 5 .... **5,000-6,000**
Angel Cloud font, #206, 2 1/4 x 4 3/4", Trademark 2 .... **250-350**
Angel Duet font, #146, 2 x 4 3/4", Trademark 3 .... **250-275**
Angel Lights candleholder, #241, 8 1/3 x 10 1/3", Trademark 5 .... **400-500**
Angel with Accordion, #238/B, 2 1/2" h., Trademark 4 .... **125**
Angel with Trumpet, #238/C, 2 1/2" h., Trademark 4 .... **125**
Angelic Song, #144, 4" h., Trademark 1 .... **550**
Apple Tree Boy, #142/I, 6" h., Trademark 5 .... **400-450**
Apple Tree Boy & Apple Tree Girl book ends, 5 1/4" h., Trademark 3, pr. **425**
Apple Tree Boy table lamp, #230, 7 1/2" h., Trademark 3 .... **375-400**
Artist (The), #304, 5 1/2" h., Trademark 3 .... **2,000-3,000**
Autumn Harvest, #355, 4 3/4" h., Trademark 6 .... **250**
Ba-Bee Rings plaques, #30A & #30B, boy & girl, 5" d., Trademark 2, pr. **250-350**
Bashful, #377, 4 3/4" h., Trademark 5 ..... **400-600**
Be Patient, #197/I, 6 1/4" h., Trademark 2 .... **550-650**
Big Housecleaning, #363, 4" h., Trademark 4 .... **1,500-2,500**
Bird Duet, #169, 4" h., Trademark 4 .... **225-250**
Birthday Serenade, #218/2/0, reverse mold, 4 1/4" h., Trademark 3 .... **400-450**
Blessed Child (Infant of Krumbad), #78/III, 5 1/4" h., Trademark 3 .... **75-100**
Book Worm, #3/I, 5 1/2" h., Trademark 3 .... **600-700**
Boy with Toothache, #217, 5 1/2" h., Trademark 2 .... **400-600**
Chick Girl candy dish, #57/III, old style, 5 1/4" h., Trademark 3 .... **300-350**
Chicken Licken, #385, 4 3/4" h., Trademark 5 .... **350-400**
Child in Bed plaque, #137/B, 2 3/4" d., Trademark 2 .... **250-350**
Cinderella, #337, new style, eyes closed, 5 1/2" h., Trademark 5 .... **250-300**
Confidentially, #314, 5 1/2" h., Trademark 3 .... **1,000-1,500**
Congratulations, #17/0, early version, no socks, 6" h., Trademark 2 .... **450-550**
Congratulations, #17/0, newer version, w/socks, 6 1/4" h., Trademark 3 .... **250-300**
Cow (Ox), #214/K, Nativity set piece, 6 1/2" l., Trademark 2 .... **160**
Culprits, #56A, 6 1/4" h., Trademark 2 .... **375-425**
Dealer display plaque, #187 (Moon Top), 4 x 5 1/2", Trademark 4 .... **375-475**
Doll Mother, #67, 4 3/4" h., Trademark 2 .... **600-700**
Duet, #130, 5 1/4" h., Trademark 3 .... **450-475**
Eventide, #99, 4 3/4" h., Trademark 5 ..... **400-500**
Farewell, #65/I, 4 3/4" h., Trademark 3 .... **350-450**
Farm Boy, #66, 5 1/4" h., Trademark 3 .... **300-325**
Feathered Friends, #344, 4 3/4" h., Trademark 5 .... **350-400**
Festival Harmony, #172/II, angel w/mandolin, 11" h., Trademark 3 .... **700-800**

Flower Madonna Hummel in Color

Flower Madonna, #10/I, color, 8 1/4" h., Trademark 3 (ILLUS.) **575-675**
Follow the Leader, #369, 7" h., Trademark 4 .... **1,350-1,400**
For Father, #87, 5 1/2" h., Trademark 4 ... **325-350**
For Mother, #257, 5 1/4" h., Trademark 3 **700-800**
Friends, #136/V, 10 3/4" h., Trademark 2 .... **2,000-3,000**
Girl with Doll, #239B, 3 1/2" h., Trademark 4 .... **100-200**
Globe Trotter, #79, 5" h., Trademark 2 .... **350-450**
Going to Grandma's, #52/I, 6" h., Trademark 2 .... **550-650**
Good Friends, 4" h., Trademark 4 .... **350-400**
Good Friends table lamp, #228, 7 1/2" h., Trademark 3 .... **550-650**
Good Hunting, #307, 5 1/4" h., Trademark 6 .... **300-325**
Good Shepherd, #42/0, 6 1/4" h., Trademark 2 .... **500-550**
Goose Girl, #47/3/0, 4" h., Trademark 3 .. **250-350**
Goose Girl, #47/II, 7 12/" h., Trademark 5 .... **450-500**
Happiness, #86, 4 3/4" h., Trademark 1 ... **400-500**
Happy Birthday, #176, 5 1/3" h., Trademark 1 .... **1,150**
Happy Days, #150/0, 5 1/4" h., Trademark 5 .... **325-350**
Happy Pastime, #69, 3 1/2" h., Trademark 3 .... **350-450**
Hear Ye, Hear Ye, #15/I, 6" h., Trademark 1 **1,600-1,700**
Heavenly Lullaby, #262, 3 1/2 x 5", Trademark 4 .... **600-700**
Heavenly Protection, #88/II, 9 1/4" h., Trademark 3 .... **1,000-1,200**
Home From Market, #198/I, 5 3/4" h., Trademark 4 .... **375-400**
Joyful candy box, #III/53, 6 1/4" h., Trademark 2 .... **475-500**

Joyous News, #27/3, 4 1/4 x 4 3/4", Trademark 1 .... **2,000**

Just Resting, #112/I, 5" h., Trademark 2
.... **400-600**

Kiss Me, w/socks, 6" h., Trademark 4 ...... **400-450**

Knitting Lesson, #256, 7 1/2" h., Trademark 5 .... **550-650**

Let's Sing ashtray, #114, 3 1/2 x 6 3/4", Trademark 4 .... **250-350**

Little Bookkeeper, #306, 4 3/4" h., Trademark 3 .... **1,000+**

Little Gabriel, #32/0, 5" h., Trademark 3 .. **250-300**

Little Hiker, #16/2/0, 4 1/4" h., Trademark 2
.... **250-350**

Little Sweeper, #171, 4 1/2" h., Trademark 5 .... **200-250**

Lost Sheep, #68/0, 5 1/2" h., Trademark 2
.... **325-350**

Merry   Wanderer   plaque,   #92, 4 3/4 x 5 1/8", Trademark 3 .... **250-350**

Mountaineer, #315, 5 1/4" h., Trademark 4
.... **400-450**

Playmates, #58/I, 4 1/2" h., Trademark 3
.... **400-500**

Prayer Before Battle, #20, 4 1/4" h., Trademark 1 .... **650**

Retreat to Safety plaque, #126, 4 3/4 x 5", Trademark 3... **250-350**

Ride Into Christmas Hummel Figurine

Ride into Christmas, #396, 5 3/4" h., Trademark 6 (ILLUS.) **525**

Ring Around the Rosie, #348, 6 3/4" h., Trademark 5.. **3,200**

School Boy, #82/2/0, 4" h., Trademark 2
.... **400-500**

School Boy, #82/II, 7 1/2" h., Trademark 5
.... **550-650**

School Girl, #81/0, 5 1/4" h., Trademark 5
.... **300-400**

Sensitive Hunter, #6/0, 4 3/4" h., Trademark 3 .... **350-450**

Shepherd's Boy, #64, 5 1/2" h., Trademark 2 .... **450-550**

Signs of Spring, #203/2/0, 4" h., Trademark 4 .... **425-525**

Silent Night candleholder, #54, 5 1/2" l., 4 3/4" h., Trademark 1 .... **1,100**

Singing Lesson, #63, 2 3/4" h., Trademark 3... **200-300**

Skier, #59, 5 1/4" h., Trademark 3 .... **400-500**

Smart Little Sister, #436, 4 3/4" h., Trademark 4 .... **400-500**

Soldier Boy, #332, red cap, 6" h., Trademark 4 .... **650**

Spring Cheer, #72, 5" h., Trademark 5 ..... **250-300**

St. George, #55, 6 3/4" h., Trademark 5... **400-450**

Standing Boy plaque, #168, 4 1/8 x 5 1/2", Trademark 2... **800-900**

Trademark 3 Stormy Weather Hummel

Stormy Weather, 71, 6 1/4" h., Trademark 3 (ILLUS.)... **900-1,000**

Strolling Along, #5, 4 3/4" h., Trademark 2
.... **750-950**

Surprise, #94/I, 5 1/2" h., Trademark 3 .... **450-550**

Trumpet Boy, #97, 4 3/4" h., Trademark 2
.... **300-400**

Tuneful   Goodnight   plaque,   #180, 4 3/4 x 5", Trademark 3 .... **300-400**

Umbrella Boy, #152/0 A, 5" h., Trademark 3... **1,000-1,200**

Village Boy, #51/I, 7 1/4" h., Trademark 3
.... **550-650**

Watchful Angel, #194, 6 1/2" h., Trademark 3.. **600-700**

Wayside Devotion, #28/II, 7 1/2" h., Trademark 1 .... **1,500**

Wayside Harmony, #111/3/0, 3 3/4" h., Trademark 3.. **200-300**

Weary Wanderer, #204, 6" h., Trademark 4
.... **400-500**

Worship, #84/V, 13" h., Trademark 4
.... **1,250-1,350**

Imari

This is a multicolor ware that originated in Japan, was copied by the Chinese, and imitated by English and European potteries. It was decorated in overglaze enamel and underglaze-blue. Made in Hizen Province and Arita, much of it was exported through the port of Imari in Japan. Imari often has brocade patterns.

Large Colorful Imari Covered Jar

Jar, cov., large bulbous ovoid body w/a short cylindrical neck fitted w/a high domed cover w/large knob finial, the cover w/scenes of birds & flowers, the sides decorated w/cartouches showing birds in flight above flowering branches in garden fences, worn gilt, restoration to finial, chip on inner cover rim, small chips on inner jar mouth, ca. 1870, 16 1/2" h. (ILLUS.)..... **$500**

Umbrella stand, tall cylindrical form, bands of stylized leaves & blossoms around the top & base, the center decorated overall w/traditional stylized flowers & birds in a garden setting, Japan, late 19th c., 23 1/4" h. **1,610**

Elaborately Mounted Imari Vase

Vase & clock, 20 1/2" h., the large ovoid covered jar w/bold designs in rust red &

cobalt blue on white fitted at the front w/an French clock within a bronze dore fruit & leaf mount, the vase fitted into an ornate scroll-cast bronze dore base & large high scrolled handles, the vase & cover rims w/bronze dore mounts & a pineapple finial, clock marked "Rue Caummet, No. 42, Paris," France, ca. 1870 (ILLUS.)....................................... **850-950**

Ironstone

The first successful ironstone was patented in 1813 by C.J. Mason in England. The body contains iron slag incorporated with the clay. Other potters imitated Mason's ware, and today much hard, thick ware is lumped under the term ironstone. Earlier it was called by various names, including graniteware. Both plain white and decorated wares were made throughout the 19th century. Tea Leaf Lustre ironstone was made by several firms.

General

Cake plate, round w/molded scroll rim handles, Moss Rose patt., Dale & Davis, Trenton, New Jersey, ca. 1880s, 10" d. (gold trim faded)... **$90**

Compote, large shallow grape leaf-shaped bowl atop a flaring pedestal base, Moss Rose patt., unmarked, ca. 1880s (some underglaze spots & four tiny rim flakes)....... **140**

Dinner service: 12 plates, open oval two-handled tureen & undertray; each piece w/a broad transfer-printed border band w/a black background decorated w/a bold garland of stylized large white, yellow green & iron-red flowers & leaves, trimmed w/gilt leaf sprigs, Pattern No. B.4540, Ashworth Bros., England, ca. 1880, undertray 14 1/2" l., the set (ILLUS., top next page) **3,346**

Mustache cup & saucer, Moss Rose patt., Coxon & Company, Trenton, New Jersey, ca. 1880s, pr. (gold trim faded) **120**

English Imari-style Paneled Pitcher

Pitcher, 8 1/2" h., paneled bulbous baluster-form body w/a shaped rim & wide rim spout & high arched ornate S-scroll han-

Ashworth Ironstone Partial Dinner Service

dle, bold Imari-style h.p. decoration in the Gaudy Welsh taste, glaze flaws at rim, England, mid-19th c. (ILLUS.)............... **100-200**

Mason's Ironstone Paneled Pitcher

Pitcher, 11 3/8" h., a squatty bulbous paneled & angled lower body tapering to a wide gently flaring paneled neck & C-scroll handle, transfer-printed design of a Chinese landscape w/flying birds & larger flowers hand-tinted in shades of red, brown & green, Mason's, England, mid-19th c. (ILLUS.).. **288**

Soup tureens, cov., oval scalloped low pedestal base supporting the large squatty bulbous oblong body w/a flaring rim & large angled end handles, a stepped domed cover w/a large flower finial, transfer-printed w/a design of large stylized flowers & leaves in shades of rust red, pink, green & cobalt blue, cobalt blue handles & finial, England, second half 19th c., 8 x 13 1/4", 10 1/2" h., pr. (ILLUS., bottom of page)........................... **2,185**

Pair of Large Colorful English Ironstone Soup Tureens

White Ironstone Napier Shape Tea Set

American Ironstone Syrup Pitcher

Syrup pitcher w/hinged metal cover, slightly swelled cylindrical body w/embossed wild roses & leaves around the sides decorated in pink & shades of green, embossed neck band, angled loop handle, base marked "Bennett's Pat. 1873," American, 1870s, 7 3/4" h. (ILLUS.) **92**

Tea set: cov. teapot, cov. sugar bowl & creamer; all-white, Napier shape, by Bridgewood & Son, England, ca. 1860s, the set (ILLUS., top of page)....................... **600**

Tea set: cov. teapot, cov. sugar bowl, creamer, two cups & saucers & rectangular tray; serving pieces w/a flattened moon flask body, stepped rectangular covers w/blossom finials, each piece w/a white ground decorated w/a bold molded cobalt blue-painted stylized flower & leaf branch, the teapot & creamer w/molded figural blue monkey-shaped handles, George Jones, England, late 19th c., chip on one cup, very minor nicks, the set (ILLUS., bottom of page)... **896**

Rare George Jones Blue & White Ironstone Tea Set

Ceres Shape White Ironstone Teapot

Teapot, cov., all-white, Ceres shape, by
Elsmore & Forster, England, ca. 1857
(ILLUS.).. **250-350**

Early Gothic White Ironstone Teapot

Grape Octagon Teapots in Two Sizes

Teapot, cov., all-white, Grape Octagon
shape, child's size, various makers, ca.
1850s (ILLUS. left with full-sized teapot)
.... **175-225**

Early Full Panel Gothic Shape Teapot

Teapot, cov., all-white, Full Panel Gothic
shape, by Jacob Furnival, England, ca.
1840s (ILLUS.) **325-350**
Teapot, cov., all-white, Gothic shape, by T.
& R. Boote, England, ca. 1847 (ILLUS.,
top next column).................................... **300-325**
Teapot, cov., all-white, Grape Octagon
shape, adult size, various makers, ca.
1850s (ILLUS. right with child's teapot)
.... **150-200**

Hyacinth Pattern Teapot by W. & E. Corn

Teapot, cov., all-white, Hyacinth patt., W. &
E. Corn, England, ca. 1870 (ILLUS.) **135**

Portland Shape Ironstone China Teapot

Teapot, cov., all-white, Portland shape, by
Elsmore & Forster, England, ca. 1860s
(ILLUS.).. **240-260**
Teapot, cov., all-white, Prairie shape (aka
New Grenade shape), adult size, by T. &
R. Boote, England, ca. 1850s **200-225**

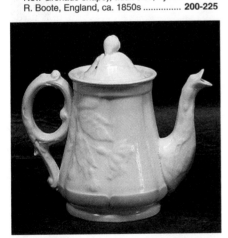

Prairie Shape Ironstone Child's Teapot

Teapot, cov., all-white, Prairie shape (aka
New Grenade shape), child's size, by T.
& R. Boote, England, ca. 1850s (ILLUS.)
.... **175-200**
Teapot, cov., all-white, Prize Bloom shape,
by T. J. & J. Mayer, England, ca. 1853
(ILLUS., top next column) **250-300**
Teapot, cov., all-white, Rib & Chain shape,
by J.W. Pankhurst, England, ca. 1860s
(ILLUS., middle next column) **225-250**
Teapot, cov., all-white, Single Line Primary
shape, by E. Challinor, T. J. & J. Mayer &
others, England, ca. 1845 (ILLUS., bot-
tom next column).................................. **225-250**

Prize Bloom White Ironstone Teapot

Rib & Chain Shape Ironstone Teapot

Ironstone Single Line Primary Teapot

Potter's Co-Operative "Perfect" Teapot

Teapot, cov., footed body w/wide squatty base tapering up the ribbed sides to a flat rim, domed cover w/scroll finial, tall serpentine spout, fancy C-scroll handle, delicate printed floral decoration, Potter's Co-Operative, East Liverpool, Ohio, base stamped "Perfect" in a rust-colored cartouche, ca. 1900 (ILLUS.) **60**

Cartwright Teapot with Pansies

Teapot, cov., footed bulbous nearly spherical body w/molded rim w/shoulder rings for wire bail handle w/wooden grip, domed cover w/button final, upright spout, decorated w/large pansies & leaves, Cartwright Brothers, East Liverpool, Ohio, late 19th - early 20th c. (ILLUS.) **45**

Teapot, cov., footed bulbous ovoid body w/a wide flat rim, domed cover w/arched finial, long serpentine spout & C-scroll handle, molded details, Potter's Co-Operative, East Liverpool, Ohio, ca. 1880s (ILLUS., top next column) **70**

Potter's Co-Operative Ovoid Teapot

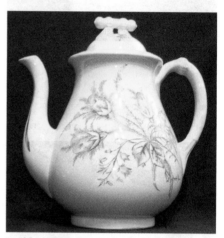

Moss Rose Teapot by Cartwright Bros.

Teapot, cov., Moss Rose patt., footed ovoid body w/domed cover & bar finial, Cartwright Brothers, East Liverpool, Ohio, late 19th c. (ILLUS.) **30**

American Moss Rose Pattern Teapot

Teapot, cov., Moss Rose patt., footed ovoid body w/molded ribbing around the base, flared neck & domed cover w/pointed button finial, tall spout & angled molded handle, Operative Pottery, unlisted maker, probably East Liverpool, Ohio, ca. 1890s (ILLUS., previous page) **50**

American Moss Rose Pattern Teapot

Teapot, cov., Moss Rose patt., spherical body w/C-scroll handle, serpentine spout & ringed & domed metal cover, produced by Knowles, Taylor, Knowles Pottery, East Liverpool, Ohio, late 19th - early 20th c. (ILLUS.) **100-125**

Etruria Pottery Moss Rose Teapot

Teapot, cov., Moss Rose patt., squatty bulbous lightly ribbed tapering ironstone body w/serpentine spout & pointed C-scroll handle, domed cover w/arched finial, Etruria Pottery Co. (Ott & Brewer), Trenton, New Jersey, ca. 1880s (ILLUS.) **65**

Early Trenton Pottery Teapot

Teapot, cov., ovoid body tapering to a flaring rim, domed cover w/bar finial, printed leafy sprig decoration, Trenton Pottery, Trenton, New Jersey, ca. 1870 (ILLUS.)........ **60**

Floral-decorated American Ironstone Teapot

Teapot, cov., tall ovoid body w/serpentine spout, C-form handle & domed cover w/arched finial, decorated w/delicate printed florals, Wm. Brunt & Son, East Liverpool, Ohio, 1878-92 (ILLUS.) **65**

Early Steubenville Pottery Teapot

Teapot, cov., tall squared body w/a long squared spout & squared handle, squared domed cover w/squared loop finial, white w/gold band around the body & cover, Steubenville Pottery, Steubenville, Ohio, late 19th c. (ILLUS.) **35**

American Dresden Pottery Works Teapot

Teapot, cov., tapering cylindrical body w/ribbed panels, long spout, double-C-scroll handle, domed cover w/loop finial, printed w/delicate floral vines & gold trim, Dresden Pottery Works (Potter's Co-Operative), East Liverpool, Ohio, ca. 1900 (ILLUS., previous page) **45**

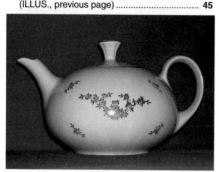

Pioneer Pottery Pearl China Teapot

Teapot, cov., wide squatty bulbous body w/a small cover & flaring finial, angled spout & C-form handle, decorated w/a fine sprig design, stamped "Pearl China," Pioneer Pottery, East Liverpool, Ohio, ca. 1930s (ILLUS.)............................... **35**

One of Two Early Ironstone Vases

Vases, cov., wide hexagonal cylindrical body w/a wide rounded shoulder centered by a short flaring & flattened neck, large gold dolphin-shaped shoulder handles, paneled domed cover w/large paneled & pointed gold finial, h.p. in the Chinese famille rose palette including cobalt blue, brick red, dark pink, brown & green, the front & back w/a chrysanthemum issuing from a vase & flowering peonies on leafy branches, England, ca. 1815, 20" h., pr. (ILLUS. of one) **15,535**

Tea Leaf Ironstone

Bowl, oval, 10" l., Lily of the Valley patt., Anthony Shaw **250**
Brush box, cov., Lily of the Valley patt., Anthony Shaw (tiny glaze flake, underglaze chip on base) **775**
Brush vase, Bullet patt., Anthony Shaw (stilt mark on base) **160**
Brush vase, Fish Hook patt., Alfred Meakin **170**
Brush vase, footed cylindrical shape, Wedgwood & Co. **175**

Meakin Cylindrical Brush Vase

Brush vase, gently waisted cylindrical form w/scalloped rim, Alfred Meakin (ILLUS.)...... **375**
Brush vase & underplate, tapering cylindrical form, Davenport, 2 pcs. (small base chip) **1,250**
Butter dish, cover & insert, Cable patt., Anthony Shaw, 3 pcs. (slight crazing, discoloration on cover rim & insert) **450**
Butter dish, cover & insert, Iona patt., gold Tea Leaf, Powell & Bishop, the set................ **40**
Butter dish, cover & insert, Lily of the Valley patt., Anthony Shaw (small base chip, plain liner) **280**
Cake plate, Daisy patt., Anthony Shaw **80**
Cake plate, Victory (Dolphin) patt., John Edwards... **180**

Shaw Fig Cousin Small Chamber Pot

Chamber pot, Fig Cousin patt., Anthony Shaw, small size, some rim lustre wear, 7 3/4" d., 5" h. (ILLUS.) 450

Chamberpot, cov., Lily of the Valley patt., Anthony Shaw (mild crazing & discoloration) 325

Coffeepot, cov., Chinese patt., Anthony Shaw 250

Wilkinson Scalloped Open Compote

Compote, open, 11" d., 7 1/4" h., scalloped bowl on pedestal base, Arthur Wilkinson, Ltd., mild crazing (ILLUS.) 400

Creamer, Brocade patt., Alfred Meakin 175

Creamer, Gentle Square patt., J. Furnival, 5 1/4" h. (small base chip) 225

Niagara Fan Creamer & Sugar Bowl

Creamer, Niagara Fan patt., Anthony Shaw, 5" h. (ILLUS. right with Niagara Fan sugar bowl) 325

Creamer, Square Ridged patt., Henry Burgess, 5 1/2" h. (tiny potting marks) 350

Creamer, Square Ridged patt., Wedgwood & Co., 5 1/2" h. 100

Creamer & cov. sugar bowl, Empress patt., Micratex by Adams, ca. 1960s, pr....... 110

Creamer & open sugar, individual size, Empress patt., Micratex by Adams, ca. 1960s, pr. 240

Gravy boat, Brocade patt., Alfred Meakin 60

Gravy boat, Chelsea patt., Alfred Meakin (underglaze potting specks) 55

Gravy boat, Square Ridged patt., Mellor, Taylor 40

Ladle, soup-type, Alfred Meakin (rim glaze spot) 475

Mush bowl, Alfred Meakin 55

Mustache cup & saucer, Anthony Shaw, pr. (moderate crazing) 475

Pitcher, 7" h., Gentle Square patt., Furnival (some glaze wear) 260

Pitcher, hot water-type, footed spherical body & wide cylindrical neck w/rim spout, heavy squared handle, Mayer China Co., Beaver Falls, Pennsylvania, ca. 1890......... 475

Pitcher, 7" h., Peerless patt., Edwards 375

Pitcher, 8" h., Fish Hook patt., Alfred Meakin 175

Pitcher, 8" h., Scroll patt., Alfred Meakin 210

Potato bowl, Chelsea patt., Wedgwood & Co., 10 1/2" w. (slight utensil marks) 110

Relish dish, Lily of the Valley patt., mitten-shaped, Anthony Shaw 400

Shaving mug, Favorite patt., W.H. Grindley & Co. 900

Shaving mug, Iona patt., Powell & Bishop, gold Tea Leaf 80

Lily of the Valley Shaving Mug

Shaving mug, Lily of the Valley patt., Anthony Shaw (ILLUS.) 270

Shaw Cable Three-piece Soup Tureen

Soup tureen, cover & undertray, Cable patt., Anthony Shaw, minor inner lid rim roughness, the set (ILLUS.) **350**
Sugar bowl, cov., Niagara Fan patt., Anthony Shaw (ILLUS. left with Niagara Fan creamer) **600**

Bamboo Shape Tea Leaf Teapot

Teapot, cov., Bamboo shape, Alfred Meakin, England, 1870s, one of the most common body styles (ILLUS.) **125-165**
Teapot, cov., Bordered Fuchsia patt., Anthony Shaw (finial repair) **700**
Teapot, cov., Empress patt., Micratex by Adams, ca. 1960s **130**

Huron Shape Tea Leaf Teapot

Teapot, cov., Huron shape, Wm. Adams, England, ca. 1858, early & elusive body style (ILLUS.) **500-650**

Rare Jumbo Shape Tea Leaf Teapot

Teapot, cov., Jumbo shape, Henry Alcock, England, ca. 1880s, rare & unusual example, w/elephant heads in finial & on the handle (ILLUS.) **500-650**
Teapot, cov., Niagara Fan patt., Anthony Show, 9 1/2" h. (very minor base rim flake) **500**
Tray, rectangular w/rounded corners & scrolled loop end handles, Henry Burgess, 18-20" l. **150**
Vegetable dish, cov., oval, Lily-of-the-Valley patt., Anthony Shaw **425**
Vegetable dish, cov., oval, Plain Round patt., Henry Burgess, 12 1/2" l. **160**
Vegetable dish, cov., Square Ridged patt., Henry Burgess **70**
Washbowl & pitcher, Hexagon patt., Anthony Shaw, 2 pcs. (mild crazing, spider crack in bowl base) **275**

Rare Burgess Chrysanthemum Waste Jar

Waste jar, cov., Chrysanthemum patt., handled, Henry Burgess, gold Tea Leaf w/slight wear (ILLUS.) 900

Shaw Hexagonal Master Waste Jar

Waste jar, cov., Hexagon patt., Anthony Shaw, some crazing, professional repair to one side panel (ILLUS.) 600

Meakin Brocade Waste Jar & Insert

Waste jar & insert, Brocade patt., Alfred Meakin, hairline in one handle, chip on insert (ILLUS.) 2,000

Tea Leaf Variants

Baker, oval, Ceres shape, copper lustre border trim, Elsmore & Forster, 7 1/4" l. (slight crazing) 100

Butter pat, deep round, Teaberry patt., unmarked 130

Butter pat, Teaberry patt., square, J. Clementson (slight discoloration) 140

Cake plate, Teaberry patt., Augusta shape, J. Clementson, 10 1/4" d. 575

Coffeepot, cov., Ceres shape, copper lustre trim, Elsmore & Forster (small old inside rim chip) 275

Coffeepot, cov., Pomegranate patt., Panelled shape, Edward Walley (minor rim wear) 200

Rare Lustre Band Gothic Foot Bath

Foot bath, Gothic shape, lustre band decoration, deep rectangular form w/angled corners, angled loop end handles, Livesley & Powell, minor wear, two flakes below one handle, one handle repaired, hairline repairs (ILLUS.) 900

Gravy boat, Teaberry patt., New York shape, J. Clementson (faint foot stain) 525

Tobacco Leaf Child's Mug

Mug, child's, Tobacco Leaf patt., Elsmore & Forster, some crazing (ILLUS.) 425

Nappy, Teaberry patt., Heavy Square shape, Clementson Bros., 4 1/4" w. (lustre wear) 100

Pitcher, 7 1/2" h., Tulip shape, cobalt blue plume decoration, Elsmore & Forster (slight crazing inside bottom) 375

Plate, 7" d., Morning Glory patt., Portland shape, Elsmore & Forster 45

Relish dish, Gothic shape, elongated shellstyle, lustre band trim, Edward Walley (minute rim flakes) 260

Fancy George Adam Soup Tureen

Soup tureen, cover, ladle & undertray, ornate rounded & fluted shape decorated w/blue scrolls around the rims & gold lustre trim, George Adam, slight lustre wear, crazing on undertray, chip under tray handle, 4 pcs. (ILLUS., previous page) **200**

Rare Prairie Teapot with Coral Decor

Teapot, cov., Coral patt., Prairie shape, J. Clementson, England, ca. 1860s, rare motif (ILLUS.) **650-850**

Draped Leaf Teapot with Morning Glory

Teapot, cov., Morning Glory patt., Draped Leaf shape, 1870s-80s (ILLUS.) **300-400**
Teapot, cov., New York shape, copper lustre & cobalt blue trim, J. Clementson **425**
Teapot, cov., Panelled Grape shape, copper lustre & cobalt blue band decoration, J. Furnival, spout flake (ILLUS., top next column) **225**
Teapot, cov., Pomegranate patt., Niagara shape, Edward Walley, crack in cover finial (ILLUS., middle next column) **160**
Teapot, cov., Ring o' Hearts shape, lustre band trim, Livesley & Powell **275**

Panelled Grape Teapot with Blue & Lustre

Pomegranate Pattern Niagara Teapot

Teapot, cov., Teaberry patt., Balanced Vine shape, J. Clementson **375**

New York Shape with Teaberry Design

Quartered Rose and Ring 'O Hearts Blue-trimmed Teapots

Teapot, cov., Teaberry patt., New York shape, J. Clementson, England, ca. 1858 (ILLUS., previous page) **400-500**

Teapot, Quartered Rose body shape w/blue sprigs, copper lustre bands & red & blue pinstripes, J. Furnival, England, ca. 1853 (ILLUS. left with Ring 'O Hearts teapot, top of page).. **350**

Teapot, Ring 'O Hearts body shape w/blue sprigs, copper lustre bands & red & blue pinstripes, Livesley & Powell, England, ca. 1857 (ILLUS. right with Quartered Rose teapot, top of page) **350**

Vegetable dish, cov., Ring o' Hearts shape, lustre band decor & heavy trim, Livesley Powell & Co... **250**

Vegetable dish, cov., Teaberry patt., Heavy Square shape, Clementson Bros. (minor corner wear, two inside base rim chips)....... **625**

Vegetable dish, cov., Teaberry patt., Quartered Rose shape, unmarked, 14" l. (flake on handle) **625**

Morning Glory Covered Vegetable Dish

Vegetable dish, open, oval, Morning Glory patt., Portland shape, Elsmore & Forster, small cover rim flake, 16" l. (ILLUS.)............ **325**

Waste bowl, Teaberry patt., 14-panel shape, unmarked (some crazing, tiny base flake) **230**

Kutani

This is a Japanese ware from the area of Kutani, a name meaning "nine valleys" where porcelain was made as early as about 1675. The early wares are referred to as "Ko-Kutani" and "Ao-Ko Kutani."

Fancy Kutani Covered Bowl

Bowl, cov., 14" l., 9 1/2" h., squatty bulbous base w/a short wide rolled rim supporting a domed cover w/figural foo lion finial, crouching lion shoulder handles, white panels on the sides of the base & cover delicately painted w/flowers & birds in flight in pale greens & earth tones, fancy deep red ground w/ornate gilt trim, signed under base, small cracks at rim, normal wear, ca. 1880 (ILLUS.) **$863**

Fine Bronze-mounted Kutani Bowl

Centerpiece, a wide shallow ceramic bowl h.p. w/round panels depicting figures, birds & fowl, fitted w/a pierced bronze rim band w/ring handles & supported on a round gilt-bronze base w/figural elephant head feet, late 19th c., 14 1/2" d., 6" h. (ILLUS., top of page) **1,380**

Fancy Japanese Dragon Teapot

Teapot, cov., ovoid white body w/fancy moriage decoration w/an undulating dragon body continuing up onto the domed cover to form the dragon head finial, the dragon body handle continuing into the body & ending in a painted dragon head, a tall dragon head spout, in shades of red, brown & white, marked "Kutani China - Japan," ca. 1920s (ILLUS.) **85**

Teapot, cov., pedestal base supporting the wide squatty body w/a short wide neck, serpentine spout & C-scroll handle, low domed cover w/pointed finial, Fan Dance A & Flower Gathering A patterns in reserves, unusual pink background, gold border, signed "Kutani," Japan, first quarter 20th c., 5" h. (ILLUS., bottom of page) **95**

Geisha Girl Teapot with Unusual Pink Background

Decorative Japanese Kutani Teapot

Teapot, cov., round scalloped foot below the wide ovoid body tapering to a short neck w/high domed cover w/figural butterfly finial, serpentine spout, ornate C-scroll handle, completely hand-painted w/Japanese Geisha, red & gold borders, signed "Watayasu Sei," Japan, late 19th - early 20th c., 6" h. (ILLUS.) **75**

Footed Kutani Teapot in So Big Pattern

Teapot, cov., three-footed squatty bulbous body w/serpentine spout & C-form handle, low domed cover w/knob finial, hand-painted So Big patt., geometric pine green & red border w/gold trim, signed "Kutani," Japan, late 19th - early 20th c., overall 8" l., 5" h. (ILLUS.) **60**

Kutani Bottle-form Vase

Vase, 9 1/2" h., bottle-form, bulbous spherical base w/a tall stick neck, decorated w/stylized colorful butterflies & gold scrolls on a deep red ground, marked on the base, late 19th c. (ILLUS.) **240**

Lefton

The Lefton China Company was the creation of Mr. George Zoltan Lefton who migrated to the United States from Hungary in 1939. In 1941 he embarked on a new career and began shaping a business that sprang from his passion for collecting fine china and porcelains. Though his funds were very limited, his vision was to develop a source from which to obtain fine porcelains by reviving the postwar Japanese ceramic industry, which dated back to antiquity. As a trailblazer, George Zoltan Lefton soon earned the reputation as "The China King".

Counted among the most desirable and sought after collectibles of today, Lefton items such as Bluebirds, Miss Priss, Angels, all types of dinnerware and tea-related items are eagerly acquired by collectors. As is true with any antique or collectible, prices may vary, depending on location, condition and availability.

For additional information on the history of Lefton China, its factories, marks, products and values, readers should consult Collector's Encyclopedia of Lefton China, Books I and II *and The Lefton Price Guide by Loretta DeLozier.*

Lefton China Elegant Rose Three-piece Tea Set

Lefton China Violets Pattern Tea Set Pieces

Tea set: cov. teapot, cov. sugar bowl & creamer; Elegant Rose patt., oval upright cylindrical ribbed bodies, decorated w/clusters of large red roses & green leaves on a white ground, sponged gold trim, ca. 1955-65 (ILLUS., bottom previous page) **$200-250**

Tea set: cup & saucer; Violets patt., funnel-shaped cup, No. 2300 (ILLUS. front with Lefton teapots, above) **35-40**

Tea set: teapot, short, round w/swirled rib design, Violets patt., No. 20610 (ILLUS. left with other Lefton pieces, top of page) **75-95**

Tea set: teapot, tall w/gently lobed pear-shaped body w/scroll handle, Violets patt., No. 092 (ILLUS. right with other Lefton Violets pieces, top of page)............ **75-95**

Tea set: 9" d. plate, Violets patt., No. 2910 (ILLUS. back with Lefton teapots, top of page)... **30-35**

Teapot, cov., Dresden shape, Elegant Rose patt., No. 2032... **55-65**

Teapot, cov., figural Dutch Girl, blonde hair, wide white apron & dark blue dress, No. 2699 (ILLUS.)....................................... **225-250**

Teapot, cov., figural Miss Priss, No. 1516 .... **150-200**

Lefton Rose Chintz Teapot

Teapot, cov., footed squatty bulbous lobed body w/serpentine spout, ring handle & cover finial, Rose Chintz patt., ca. 1970s (ILLUS.)... **35**

Small Lefton China Teapot

Teapot, cov., individual size, Rose Chintz patt., ca. 1960s (ILLUS.)................................ **20**

Lefton Dutch Girl Teapot

Lenox

The Ceramic Art Company was established at Trenton, New Jersey, in 1889 by Jonathan Coxon and Walter Scott Lenox. In addition to true porcelain, it also made a Belleek-type ware. Renamed Lenox Company in 1906, it is still in operation today.

Lenox China Mark

Fine Lenox Painted Tankard Pitcher

Pitcher, 13" h., tankard-type, footed tall gently tapering cylindrical sides w/a scalloped rim & large arched rim spout, fancy C-scroll handle, h.p. w/large red cherry on a leafy branch, pale yellow to brick-red handle, artist-signed, early 20th c. (ILLUS.) **$196**

Fine CAC-Lenox Cabinet Plate

Plate, 10 3/8" d., cabinet-type, a wide maroon rim band decorated w/ornate gilt floral swags & scrolls, the center h.p. w/a bust portrait of a lovely maiden w/long

brown hair holding a cluster of pink roses, Ceramic Art Company monogram & Lenox wreath mark, artist-signed, ca. 1903-07 (ILLUS.) **1,434**

Sunday Brunch Lenox China Teapot

Teapot, cov., Butler's Pantry Series, Sunday Brunch design, tapering cylindrical ruffled form, undecorated, modern (ILLUS.) **45**

Lenox Teapot in Butler's Pantry Series

Teapot, cov., Butler's Pantry Series, tapering cylindrical form w/molded V-shaped panels, undecorated, modern (ILLUS.).......... **45**

Modern Lenox Christmas Tree Teapot

Teapot, cov., Christmas Tree patt., figural decorated tree, modern (ILLUS., previous page) **75**

Newer Lenox Garden Party Teapot

Teapot, cov., Garden Party patt., Butler's Pantry series, modern (ILLUS.)...................... **45**

New Lenox China Pumpkin Teapot

Teapot, cov., pumpkin-shaped, molded scrolling leaf panels alternating w/plain panels, vine finial, produced in 2004 (ILLUS.) **75**

Teapot, cov., Summer Enchantment patt., footed squatty spherical body w/serpentine spout, C-form handle & domed cover w/figural butterfly finial, colorful butterfly & vine decoration, modern (ILLUS.)............... **75**

Lenox Summer Enchantment Teapot

Limoges

Limoges is the generic name for hard paste porcelain that was produced in one of the Limoges factories in the Limoges region of France during the 19th and 20th centuries. There are more than 400 different factory identification marks, the Haviland factory marks being some of the most familiar. Dinnerware was commonly decorated by the transfer method and then exported to the United States.

Decorative pieces were hand painted by a factory artist or were imported to the United States as blank pieces of porcelain. At the turn of the 20th century, thousands of undecorated Limoges blanks poured into the United States, where any of the more than 25,000 American porcelain painters decorated them. Today hand-painted decorative pieces are considered fine art. Limoges is not to be confused with American Limoges. (The series on collecting Limoges by Debby DeBay, Living With Limoges, Antique Limoges at Home and Collecting Limoges Boxes to Vases are excellent reference books.)

Charger, h.p. w/dark flowers on light ground, underglaze factory mark in green "AK [over] D France," (Klingenberg), 15" d. **$1,000**
Chocolate set: 12 1/5" pot, 5 cups & saucers, 14" oval tray; h.p., underglaze factory mark in green "J.P.L. France," (Jean Pouyat-Limoges) the set **3,000**
Fish set: 24 1/2" l. oval platter & twelve 9 1/2" d. plates; each h.p. w/a naturalistic game fish in a lake scene, heavy gold border band, artist-signed, late 19th c., the set (ILLUS., below) **2,300**

Large Limoges Fish Service

Tea Set & Tray Decorated with Clusters of Roses

Jardiniere, footed, side handles at top, underglaze factory mark in green "T&V France," (Tressemann & Vogt) very rare blank, 11 1/2" h. **2,000**

Jardiniere, on original base, no handles, underglaze factory mark in green "D&Co.," (R. Delinieres) 11 x 12" **2,500**

Jardiniere, original base, elephant head handles, raised gold paste trim, underglaze factory mark in green "J.P.L.," 11 1/5" h. **3,000**

Planter or jardiniere, blank attributed to the d'Albis & Romanet Factory, swan handles, overglaze factory decorating mark in red "Elite Works," (Bawo & Dstter) 8 x 10" **1,500**

Plaque, h.p. & trimmed in heavy gold, underglaze factory mark "Limoges" in star (Coiffe), 13 1/4" h. **1,200**

Punch set: bowl, base, tray, cups; h.p. at White's Art Co., Chicago, underglaze factory mark in green "D&Co.," rare, the set .. **5,500**

Punch set: bowl w/original base, tray, cups; h.p. by unknown artist w/dark grapes & heavy gilt, underglaze factory mark in green "T&V Limoges France," the set **3,500**

All-Gold Limoges Tea Set

Tea set: cov. tall teapot, cov. sugar, creamer & four cups & saucers; tall urn-shaped bodies w/angular handles, overall gold decoration, signed on the base "Healy Gold 1891," factory mark in green "Limoges CMC France," the set (ILLUS.) **800**

Limoges Tea Set with Roses on a Yellow Background

Tea set: cov. teapot, cov. sugar bowl, creamer & oblong tray; round bulbous bodies, gold handles & ring finials, h.p. w/clusters of pink & red roses & green leaves, heavy gold trim, factory mark of A. Klingenberg, Limoges, France, ca. 1890s-1910, the set (ILLUS., top of previous page) **900**

Tea set: cov. teapot, cov. sugar bowl, creamer & rectangular tray; squatty bulbous bodies tapering to ruffled bases, rolled slightly ruffled rim, domed covers w/gold loop finials, ornate gold scroll handles, each piece w/a pale yellow background h.p. w/pink roses & green foliage, tiny single-cup teapot, factory mark of Jean Pouyat, Limoges, ca. 1891-1932, the set (ILLUS.,bottom of previous page) **800**

Limoges Tea Set with Images of Cherubs

Tea set: cov. teapot, cov. sugar bowl & creamer; squatty bulbous bodies, each piece h.p. w/a scene of cherubs, artist-signed "MY" & dated "1904," blank marked by Jean Pouyat, Limoges, France, the set (ILLUS.)............................ **1,500**

Pouyat Tea Set Painted with Violets

Tea set: cov. teapot, cov. sugar bowl & creamer; squatty bulbous bodies w/gold C-scroll handles, gold serpentine spout & gold loop finials, each piece h.p. w/purple violets & green leaves, factory mark of Jean Pouyat, Limoges, France, ca. 1891-1932, the set (ILLUS.)......................... **800**

Tea set: cov. teapot, cov. sugar bowl, creamer, tea strainer & round tray; squatty bulbous bodies w/domed covers, finely h.p. w/roses, heavy gold trim, artist-signed, factory mark "Venice - T&V - France," Tressemann & Vogt, ca. 1892-1907, the set **1,900**

Tea set: cov. teapot, cov. sugar bowl, creamer & two cups & saucers; footed squatty bulbous bodies w/gold loop handles & finials, h.p. w/popular violets decoration, factory mark of Tressemann & Vogt, Limoges, France, ca. 1892-1907, the set **600**

Floral-decorated Limoges Set on Tray

Tea set: cov. teapot, cov. sugar, creamer & round tray; each piece in an oblong upright tapering shape w/oval covers, gold C-scroll handles, h.p. w/colorful florals, factory mark of Delinieres & Co., Limoges, France, ca. 1894-1900, the set (ILLUS.) **1,500**

Tea set: cov. teapot, cov. sugar, creamer & round tray; each piece w/a tall tapering waisted body, decorated w/alternating narrow mottled green stripes & stripes w/gold S-scroll bands, ornate gold C-scroll handles, artist-signed, factory mark of Tressemann & Vogt, Limoges, France, ca. 1892-1907, teapot 7" h., the set **1,900**

Limoges Set Retailed by Tiffany & Co.

Tea set: cov. teapot, cov. sugar, creamer & tray; squatty hexagonal bodies raised on a paneled pedestal base, a wide shoulder tapering to a flared rim, domed covers w/knob finials, white w/gold band decoration, made in Limoges to be retailed by Tiffany & Company, New York, ca. 1900, the set (ILLUS.)............... **1,500**

Tea set: cov. teapot, cov. sugar, tall coffeepot & creamer; teapot, sugar & creamer w/footed squatty bulbous shapes & flared scalloped rims, all pieces decorated w/gold wedding band decoration, Haviland & Co. factory mark, ca. 1876-89, the set **350**

Limoges Elite - France Porcelain Teapot

Teapot, cov., footed squatty bulbous body tapering to a domed cover w/arched finial, serpentine spout, C-scroll handle, marked w/Bawo & Dotter "Elite - France" mark, ca. 1900 (ILLUS.) **30**

Miniature Rose-decorated Teapot

Teapot, cov., miniature, ribbed & slightly tapering cylindrical body w/a scalloped rim, domed cover w/gold knob finial, short spout & C-scroll handle, h.p. w/pretty roses, initials of artist on the base, factory mark of Bernardaud & Co., Limoges, France, ca. 1914-30s (ILLUS.) **400**

Small Rose-decorated Limoges Teapot

Teapot, cov., single-cup size, squared bulbous body w/a short flared & scalloped rim, domed cover w/squared loop finial, angular scroll handle & beaded serpentine spout, h.p. w/large roses, factory mark of Tressemann & Vogt, Limoges, France, ca. 1892-1907 (ILLUS.) **300**

Studio-decorated Limoges Gold Teapot

Teapot, cov., slightly tapering cylindrical body w/flat cover w/arched loop finial, C-form handle & long serpentine spout, overall gold-etched decoration, signed by American decorating studio artist "Osborne," blank marked by Jean Pouyat Company, Limoges, France, 1891-1932, small size (ILLUS.) **300**

Limoges-style Rose-painted Teapot

Teapot, cov., squatty bulbous body w/a flaring scalloped rim, domed cover w/gold loop finial, short spout, C-scroll handle, h.p. w/large roses, unmarked, Limoges-style, late 19th - early 20th c. (ILLUS.) **200**

Fine Factory-decorated Limoges Teapot

Teapot, cov., squatty bulbous body w/low domed cover w/gold loop finial, gold serpentine spout & fancy C-form gold handle, factory-decorated w/large roses, underglaze factory mark for Mavaleix, P.M., ca. 1908-14, overglaze decorating mark "Coronet - George Borgfeldt," ca. 1906-20, 4" h. (ILLUS.) **600**

Fancy Roses & Gold Limoges Teapot

Teapot, cov., wide squatty bulbous body tapering to a small domed cover w/twisted loop finial, serpentine spout, twisted loop handle, unusual decoration of h.p. roses framed by heavy gold & w/gold on the interior, gold cover, spout & handle, artist-signed on the bottom "KLR - 1890," Limoges factory "AK" mark (Landenberg Mark 3), France, ca. 1880s-90 (ILLUS.).............. **800**

Tall Rose-decorated Limoges Vase

Vase, 13" h., tall swelled ovoid body w/a flat gilt rim, h.p. overall w/large pink, white, red & yellow roses & leafy stems, artist-signed, La Porcelaine Limousine, Limoges mark (ILLUS.)... **489**

Vase, 13 1/8" h., in Royal Vienna-style, bulbous ovoid lower body tapering to a tall cylindrical neck w/a molded gold rim, gold scroll handles from the shoulder to center of the neck, deep iridescent ruby ground decorated on the lower body w/a portrait of a lovely young woman kneeling & praying, titled "Devotion," gold border w/ornate leafy scrolls, narrow neck bands w/a wider top Greek key design band, R. Délinières, late 19th - early 20th c. (ILLUS., top next column) **2,868**

Very Fine Délinières Limoges Vase

Vase, 14" h., unique lion head handles, h.p. by "Mrs CW Lamson, Erie, PA," dated March 16, 1901, underglaze factory mark in green "D&Co." **2,500**

Liverpool

Liverpool is most often used as a generic term for fine earthenware products, usually of creamware or pearlware, produced at numerous potteries in this English city during the late 18th and early 19th centuries. Many examples, especially pitchers, were decorated with transfer-printed patriotic designs aimed specifically at the American buying public.

Liverpool Pitcher with American Ship

Pitcher, 8 1/2" h., jug-type, decorated w/black transfer-printed scenes w/some hand-tinting & gilt trim, one side w/a sailing ship under full sail & flying an American flag, the other side w/a circular medallion enclosing a Latin inscription, all surrounded by circles w/the names of the first 13 states, tight crow's-foot in the base, early 19th c. (ILLUS.) **$1,725**

Rare Boston Fusiliers Liverpool Pitcher

Pitcher, 9 1/2" h., jug-type, decorated w/black transfer-printed scenes w/some hand-tinting & gilt trim, the front w/a large oval wreath medallion topped by Masonic devices & enclosing a full-length portrait of an officer in full uniform & holding the Massachusetts state flag, the border band inscribed "Aut Vincere Aut Mori - Success to the Independent Boston Fusiliers, Incorporated July 4th, 18787 - America Fore Ever...," the reverse w/an oval design w/the allegorical figures of Liberty, Justice & Peace above the inscription "United We Stand - Divided We Fall," a wreath above the figures includes 16 stars surmounted by an American flag, a floral design below the spout, base chip, very minor discoloration & enamel loss, rare design (ILLUS.) **11,163**

Pitcher, 10 1/4" h., jug-type, decorated w/black transfer-printed scenes, the front w/a large oval memorial scene w/weeping willows flanking a monument to George Washington w/a mourning fig-

Washington Memorial Liverpool Pitcher

ure below, a ribbon across the top inscribed "Washington In Glory" & a bottom ribbon w/"America In Tears," the back w/a scene of an American ship under full sail, a spread-winged American eagle below the spout, imperfections, early 19th c. (ILLUS.) **1,293**

Pitcher, 11" h., jug-type, decorated w/black transfer-printed scenes w/some hand-tinting & gilt trim, one side w/a large grouping of Masonic symbols between pillars, the other side w/a ship under full sail flying an American flag & titled "Nancy of Boston," decorated under the spout w/the figure of a standing woman leaning on a large anchor below a wreath w/the inscription "Edward and Nancy Staples," accompanied by a letter giving the history of the ship, ca. 1806, wear, base hairline & repaired spout (ILLUS., bottom of page).. **3,450**

Two Views of an Early Liverpool Pitcher with the Ship Nancy of Boston

Lladro

Spain's famed Lladro porcelain manufactory creates both limited- and non-limited-edition figurines as well as other porcelains. The classic simple beauty of the figures and their subdued coloring make them readily recognizable and they have an enthusiastic following.

Lady Swinging Golf Club Lladro Figure

Lady Swinging Golf Club, No. 6689, 14 1/2" h. (ILLUS.) **$115**

Lladro Mother & Child Figurine

Mother & child, tall slender mother looking down at her child wearing a blue nightgown, 14" h. (ILLUS.).................................... **316**

Tall Mother & Infant Lladro Figurine

Mother & infant, matte finish, a young mother wearing a long mottled blue robe & holding her infant close to her face, No. 2429, 18 1/4" h. (ILLUS.) **259**

Majolica

Majolica, a tin-enameled glazed pottery, has been produced for centuries. It originally took its name from the island of Majorca, a source of figuline (potter's clay). Subsequently it was widely produced in England, Europe and the United States. Etruscan majolica, now avidly sought, was made by Griffen, Smith & Hill, Phoenixville, Pa., in the last quarter of the 19th century. Most majolica advertised today is 19th or 20th century. Once scorned by most collectors, interest in this colorful ware so popular during the Victorian era has now revived and prices have risen dramatically in the past few years.

Etruscan

Bread tray, Oak Leaf patt., pink edge, 12" l. (ILLUS. bottom row, right, with other Etruscan plates & trays) **$358**

Grouping of Etruscan Plates & More

Plate, 9" d., Cauliflower patt. (ILLUS. top row, left, with other Etruscan plates & trays) **150-225**

Plate, 9" d., Classical line, Dog patt., green center w/pink border band (ILLUS. center row, right, with other Etruscan plates & trays) **110**

Plate, 9" d., Maple Leaf on Basketweave pat., large green leaf on pale yellow & pink ground (ILLUS. center row, left, with other Etruscan plates & trays) **193**

Plate, 9" d., Maple Leaves patt., on pink background, rim nick (ILLUS. top row, center, with other Etruscan plates & trays) **138**

Plate, 9" d., Overlapping Begonia Leaf patt. (ILLUS. center row, middle, with other Etruscan plates & trays) **110**

Plate, 9" d., Strawberry & Apple patt., white ground (ILLUS. top row, right, with other Etruscan plates & trays) **110**

Shell & Seaweed Plates & Platter

Plates, 7" d., Shell & Seaweed patt., set of 3 (ILLUS. of one, bottom row right with other Shell & Seaweed pieces) **440**

Plates, 8" d., Shell & Seaweed patt., nick to one, set of 4 (ILLUS. of one, bottom row left with other Shell & Seaweed pieces) **715**

Platter, 14" l., Shell & Seaweed patt. (ILLUS. top row with Shell & Seaweed plates) **495**

Scarce Etruscan Sardine Box

Sardine box, cov., Water Lily patt., rectangular base w/molded white water lilies & green leaves on a pink ground w/a brown ropetwist border band, the rectangular flat-topped cover w/matching decor & a

figural swan finial, professional restorations, 2 pcs. (ILLUS.) **825**

Etruscan Cauliflower Pattern Teapot

Teapot, cov., Cauliflower patt., the body molded as a head of cauliflower in creamy white & dark green, green spout & handle, marked on bottom, Griffin, Smith & Hill, Phoenixville, Pennsylvania, late 19th c., minor roughness on interior rim, interior rim chip on cover, 5 1/2" h. (ILLUS.).. **374**

American Shell & Seaweed Teapot

Teapot, cov., Shell & Seaweed patt., spherical body molded as large shells trimmed w/seaweed, mottled green coral-form handle & spout, mottled pink, brown & green cover w/shell finial, Griffin, Smith & Hill, Phoenixville, Pennsylvania, late 19th c., 10" l., 6 1/2" h. (ILLUS.) **525-575**

Tray, Geranium patt., white flowers & green leaves on a light yellow ground, brown branch handles, 10 x 12 1/2" (ILLUS. bottom row, left, with other Etruscan plates & trays) **238**

Tray, oval, Grape patt., grape clusters & leaves on tan ground, entwined vine brown border band (ILLUS. bottom row, center, with other Etruscan plates & trays) **220**

General

Bread tray, oval, New England Aster patt., dark pink blossoms & green leaves on a cream ground, green border embossed "Eat To Live Not Live To Eat"....................... **330**

Bread tray, oval, Wheat patt., brown center, green leaves & yellow wheat, brown border band embossed "Eat Thy Bread With Thankfulness," 13" l. **303**

Bust of a young boy, the realistically modeled and colored bust show the smiling youth wearing a brown cockade hat w/purple bow, a shirt w/a large ruffled white collar, blue inner jacket & lavender outer jacket trimmed along the edge w/ball-shaped tassels, Brothers Urbach,

Germany, 19th c., minor glaze loss, 19" h. (ILLUS., below) **748**

Lovely Majolica Bust of a Young Boy

Cake stand, on three knob feet, Pond Lily patt., 9" d. **165**

French Fern Pattern Cheese Keeper

Cheese keeper, cov., Fern patt., tall cylindrical cover w/a flat top, the sides molded w/large green fern leaves on a brown ground, the cover w/water lily pads & a blossom finial, base w/green ferns on the flanged rim, France, late 19th c., minor nicks to cover finial, rim chip on cover, 11 1/2" h. (ILLUS.) **880**

George Jones Pansy Pattern Cheese Dish

Cheese keeper, cov., Pansy patt., wide cylindrical cover w/flat top, pink blossoms on green leafy vines around the sides against a cobalt blue ground, George Jones, England, late 19th c., professional repair to cover handle, base 10 1/4" d., overall 7 1/2" h. (ILLUS.) **3,850**

Victoria Pottery Majolica Compote

Compote, open, 9" d., 5" h., Basketweave & Maple Leaf patt., wide gently fluted shallow bowl w/a turquoise basketweave design & large brown & green leaves, turquoise basketweave pedestal w/green leaves & white blossoms, Victoria Pottery Co. (ILLUS.) **605**

Compote, open, 9 1/2" d., Begonia Leaf patt., unmarked **132**

Condiment server, four shell-shaped lobes in alternating pink & pale green centered by a shell handle, 9" l. **358**

Unusual Minton Majolica Creambowls

Creambowls, figural, a large naturalistic nautilus shell bowl supported on a pedestal composed of entwined dolphins & green seaweed, on a round disk-form gadrooned green oval foot, Minton, England, Model No. 902, date code for 1862, overall 9" h., pr. (ILLUS.)................. **3,824**

Cup & saucer, Pineapple patt., nice color **275**

Brownfield Blackberry Egg Basket

Egg basket, the oval basket w/vertical sides molded in relief w/blackberries on leafy blossoming vines against a yellow basketweave ground, cobalt blue upper border, double bamboo-form arched handle from side to side, the interior fitted w/six holes to support eggs, Brownfield, England, late 19th c., 11 1/2" l., 6 1/2" h. (ILLUS.).. **990**

Holdcroft Blackamoor Garden Seat

Garden seat, figural, Blackamoor patt., three mottled green & brown bun feet supporting a base w/a cobalt blue border band supporting a brown mound issuing the figural pedestal composed of a full-figure Blackamoor youth seated among green & brown cattails, the top composed of a flattened cobalt blue cushion-form seat w/yellow ropetwist border, profes-

sional restoration to the seat, Holdcroft, England, late 19th c., overall 17 1/2" h. (ILLUS.).. **6,050**

Rare Stork Jardiniere-Stand

Jardiniere-stand, figural, a model of a very tall stork in grey, black, white & gold standing holding a fish in its beak, a flaring cylindrical container behind it formed as a cluster of cattails & leaves, Hugo Lonitz, late 19th c., repairs to stork body & beak & tips of cattails, fine detail (ILLUS.)............. **8,800**

Unusual Majolica Marmalade Pot

Marmalade pot, cov., Apple Blossom patt., the high domed top w/spoon opening molded w/a brown branch handle & pink blossoms & green leaves on a turquoise ground, the base w/a turquoise ground banded w/brown wicker design & a flanged rim w/further blossoms & leaves, George Jones, England, late 19th c., interior rim chips on rim of cover, 5" h. (ILLUS.)... **2,475**

Pitcher, 7" h., Eagle with Rabbit patt., footed w/flat round sides, cobalt blue ground **165**

Fine George Jones Basketweave & Floral Tea Set

Pitcher, 7 1/4" h., Wheat patt., cylindrical sides molded w/long green leaves & yellow green on a pink ground, ribbon-wrapped brown handle, George Jones, England **4,400**

Pitcher, 9" h., figural, white swan forms the top of the body w/the neck curving down to form handle, lower ovoid body in cobalt blue w/green leaves, John Bevington, England, late 19th c. **1,100**

Pitcher, 10" h., figural, model of mother monkey holding her baby, French, late 19th c. **275**

Pitcher, 10 1/2" h., figural, model of standing pig dressed as waiter, Frie Onnaing, France, late 19th c. **605**

Pitcher, 12" h., Chrysanthemum patt., Avalon Faience mark of the Chesapeake Pottery, Baltimore, Maryland, late 19th c. **66**

Plate, 9" d., Summer Sun patt., sun face molded in the center surrounded by a bird, butterfly & grapes, in golden yellows & brown **275**

Plate, 9 1/2" d., Fern & Floral patt., cobalt blue ground & pink Greek key border band **248**

Plates, 8 1/2" d., Overlapping Begonia Leaf patt., dark green w/dark pink borders, set of 4 .... **605**

Platter, 11" l., oblong w/scalloped rim, Dog & Doghouse patt., dark brown, green & cream **275**

Syrup pitcher w/hinged pewter cover, molded floral design, Edwin Bennett Pottery, Baltimore, Maryland, late 19th c. **154**

Tea set: Bamboo & Fern patt., cov. teapot, cov. sugar bowl & creamer; each body molded as a cluster of yellow bamboo w/long green fern leaves wrapping around the lower body, Wardle & Co., England, late 19th c., minor nicks on teapot, mismatched sugar cover, the set (ILLUS. right with Daisy pattern set) **308**

Tea set: Basketweave & Floral patt., cov. teapot, cov. sugar bowl, creamer, two cups & saucers & oblong handled tray; serving pieces w/tapering ovoid bodies molded around the bottom w/bands of tan basketweave below a cobalt blue upper body molded w/branches of pink blossoms & green leaves, domed covers w/arched twig handles, brown branch handles & spout, George Jones, England, late 19th c., professional repair to sugar cover rim, one cup & saucer repaired, teapot cover not perfect fit, tray 19 1/2" l., teapot 7" h., the set (ILLUS., top of page)... **3,640**

Tea set: Basketweave & Floral patt., cov. teapot, cov. sugar bowl & creamer; wide squatty bulbous molded pale blue basketweave bodies decorated w/branches of pink blossoms & green leaves, brown branch handles, flattened covers w/white blossom finials, probably England, late 19th c., rim chip on creamer, the set (ILLUS. right with Floral Branch pattern tea set, center of page 266) **196**

Bird & Fan and Cranes Pattern Tea Sets

Cauliflower & Bird and Fan Majolica Tea Sets

Tea set: Bird & Fan patt., cov. teapot, cov. sugar bowl & creamer; spherical bodies molded w/colorful fans, each w/a flying bird against a pebbled pale yellow background, brown branch handles & spout, probably England, late 19th c., minor spout chip on teapot, the set (ILLUS. left with Cranes pattern tea set, bottom previous page) **308**

Tea set: Bird & Fan patt., cov. teapot, cov. sugar bowl & creamer; spherical body molded w/an open white fan w/flying blue, red & yellow bird, flanked by pink blossoms, all on a pale blue ground, branch spout & handles, Fielding, England, late 19th c., chip on sugar cover, the set (ILLUS. right with Wedgwood Cauliflower tea set, top of page) **392**

Tea set: Blackberry & Basketweave patt., cov. teapot, cov. sugar bowl & creamer; each piece w/a spherical body molded on the lower half w/a band of tan basketweave, the upper half in cobalt blue molded w/blackberry vines in pink & green, brown branch handles & spout, mottled basketweave covers w/ring finials, probably England, late 19th c., the set (ILLUS. right with Oriental pattern tea set, bottom next page) **364**

Tea set: Cauliflower patt., cov. teapot, cov. sugar bowl & creamer; each piece modeled as a white head of cauliflower w/wide green leaves, Josiah Wedgwood, England, late 19th c., minor spout nicks on teapot, teapot 6" h., the set (ILLUS. left with Bird & Fan tea set w/pale blue ground, top of page)..................................... **924**

Tea set: Cranes patt., cov. teapot, cov. sugar bowl & creamer; spherical bodies molded around the lower half w/a yellow basketweave design, the wide upper band w/a pale blue ground molded w/bands of brown flying cranes, brown twig handles & spout, probably England, late 19th c., minor glaze nicks, the set (ILLUS. right with Bird & Fan pattern tea set with yellow ground, bottom previous page) **168**

Tea set: Daisy patt., cov. teapot, cov. sugar bowl & creamer; each piece w/a hexagonal body in dark brown, the panels molded w/large white & yellow daisy blossoms & green leaves, angled green branch handles & spout, figural flower finials, mark of the Victoria Pottery Company, late 19th c., professional spout repair on creamer, the set (ILLUS. left with Bamboo & Fern pattern set, bottom of page)... **784**

Daisy Pattern & Bamboo & Fern Pattern Majolica Tea Sets

Extremely Rare George Jones Drum Pattern Tea Set

Floral Branch Pattern & Basketweave & Floral Pattern Sets

Oriental Pattern & Blackberry & Basketweave Pattern Tea Sets

Tea set: Drum patt., cov. teapot, cov. sugar bowl & creamer; each piece w/a spherical body designed as a round drum w/wide cobalt blue bands separated by narrow brown bands joined by interwoven rope bands w/buckles, strap & buckle handles & a drum stick spout, very rare design, George Jones, England, late 19th c., teapot 6" h., the set (ILLUS., top of previous page) **12,320**

Tea set: Floral Branch patt., cov. teapot, cov. sugar bowl & creamer; wide cylindrical bodies w/narrow shoulder bands, pale blue background molded w/a large branch w/green leaves & a stylized pink & white blossom, brown branch handles, covers w/flower bud finials, probably England, late 19th c., hairline in creamer, the set (ILLUS. left with Basketweave & Floral tea set, middle of previous page) **364**

Tea set: Oriental patt., cov. teapot, cov. sugar & creamer; each piece w/an upright square body w/swelled panels on the sides, each corner w/a pale yellow molded band, cobalt blue ground w/shaded pale green & white swelled panels molded w/an Oriental slender tree w/green leaves & pink blossoms & a perched brown bird, squared pale yellow bamboo handles & a bamboo spout, the low domed covers w/a seated Oriental man forming the finial, probably England, late 19th c., repair to teapot cover finial, teapot 7" h., the set (ILLUS. left with Blackberry & Basketweave tea set, left at bottom of previous page) **364**

Teapot, cov., Bird & Bird's Nest patt., figural, England, late 19th c., professional spout tip repair, 9" l. **1,176**

Teapot, cov., Chinaman patt., figural, model of a large brown melon w/green stem spout & handle, the figure of a Chinese

Holdcroft Figural Chinaman Teapot

man climbing on the side, wearing a dark blue robe, cream-colored pants & black shoes, Holdcroft, England, third quarter 19th c., 9 1/2" l., 7" h. (ILLUS.) **4,400**

Teapot, cov., Chinaman patt., modeled as a rotund seated Chinese man holding a large brown dramatic mask to one side, the mask issuing a green & yellow spout, a rope handle at his other side, his head forming the cover, shown wearing a pale blue jacket w/small red, green & white blossoms & dark green pants & brown shoes, Model No. 1838, Mintons, England, date code for 1874, 8 1/4" h. (ILLUS. far right with two other majolica teapots, page 269) **4,465**

Teapot, cov., Fan & Scroll with Insect patt., pebbled background, Fielding & Co., England, late 19th c., minor spout nick, 7" l. **252**

Teapot, cov., figural Chinaman patt., produced by Minton, based on Victorian original, limited edition of 2,500, introduced in 2000 (ILLUS.) **650**

Reissued Minton Chinaman Figural Teapot

Minton Reissue of Monkey Teapot

Teapot, cov., figural Monkey model & coconut patt., made by Minton, reissue of Victorian original, limited edition of 1,793, introduced in 1993 (ILLUS.) **850**

Teapot, cov., Flowering Branch patt., flat-sided moon-shaped body w/concave base, the sides in cobalt blue molded w/a large brown branch w/green leaves & white & pink blossoms, rectangular domed cover w/blossom finial, brown branch spout & handle, probably England, late 19th c., 7" h. (ILLUS. bottom left with three other teapots, page 270) **812**

Teapot, cov., Gondolier patt., the body modeled as an elongated Chinese gondola-style sailing ship w/tall upturned stern & bow, the bow forming the spout, the body of the pot composed of the molded brown cargo, white sail & triangular panels of light blue sky between the rigging ropes, a rigging rope connecting the top of the sail w/the top of the stern, the figure of a bent-over Chinese man forming the finial on the cover, Model No. 3520/30, George Jones, England, diamond registry date of 1876, 12 1/2" h. (ILLUS. center top with two other majolica teapots, next page) **32,900**

English Japonisme Majolica Teapot

Teapot, cov., Japonisme style, a flattened demi-lune form in turquoise blue, the flat cover w/a small squared finial, straight angled spout & simple C-form handle, the shoulder molded w/a stylized fret design, the sides molded w/an Oriental figure preparing tea in a garden & a large stylized blossom on a leafy stem, England, possibly by Joseph Holdcroft or Samuel Lear, ca. 1880, 9 3/4" l. (ILLUS.) **2,271**

Figural Lemon Mintons Teapot

Teapot, cov., Lemon patt., model of a large yellow lemon w/molded green leaves around the sides & forming the base, green stem spout & handle, cover modeled as an inverted mushroom, Mintons, England, date code for 1873, Shape No. 643, 7" l., 4 1/2" h. (ILLUS.) **8,800**

Teapot, cov., Mintons Fish patt., figural, limited edition produced by Royal Doulton, 20th c. **616**

Teapot, cov., Monkey & Coconut patt., body modeled as a large mustard yellow coconut w/the figure of a seated brown monkey at one end grasping the nut, wearing a black jacket w/dark red blossoms & green leaves, the grey head w/pale green knob finial forming the cover, molded green leaves below the curved brown bamboo-form spout, the tail of the monkey forming the handle, Mintons, England, third quarter 19th c., minor hairline in spout, 8 1/2" l., 6" h. (ILLUS., top next page) **6,440**

Teapot, cov., Monkey & Coconut patt., the bulbous body modeled as a seated grey monkey wearing a dark blue outfit w/large pink polka dots, its arms & legs wrapped around a large mustard yellow coconut w/green leaves, the stem forming the spout, the monkey's head & shoulders forming the cover w/a blue knob finial, Model No. 1844, Mintons, England, date letter for 1874, 9" h. (ILLUS. far left with two other majolica teapots, bottom next page) **8,225**

Mintons Monkey & Coconut Figural Teapot

Three Rare Victorian Figural Majolica Teapots

George Jones Figural Rooster Majolica Teapot

Four Nice Majolica Teapots

Teapot, cov., Ribbon, Bow, Daisy & Wheat patt., fine details, Fielding & Co., England, late 19th c., 6" h. **392**

Teapot, cov., Rooster patt., model of a large, colorful, realistic rooster in shades of brown, yellow & green, red comb & wattle, oval base, George Jones, England, third quarter 19th c., 11" l. (ILLUS., top of page) **7,700**

Teapot, cov., Shell, Seaweed & Waves tea-kettle-style, wide squatty angled body molded w/pink & green seashells & seaweed on a cobalt blue ground, low domed cover w/shell finial, dark blue spout, overhead green ropetwist handle, England, late 19th c., professional rim re-pair on cover, 8" h. (ILLUS. top left with three other teapots, middle of page) **1,344**

Teapot, cov., Stork & Water Lily patt., upright rectangular body, molded brown corner & edge bands framing cobalt blue panels, all on small brown tab feet, each side w/a grey stork among green water lilies, stepped rectangular cover w/band of green leaves & a brown twig finial, long angled brown branch spout & squared branch handle, probably England, late 19th c., professional repair to spout & cover finial, 6 1/2" h. (ILLUS. bottom right with three other teapots, middle of page) **280**

Extraordinary Mintons Majolica Teapot

Teapot, cov., Vulture & Snake patt., an elaborately modeled design w/a large standing vulture w/a yellow & black body & pink neck & head grasping the head & body of a large writhing green snake, both on a rockwork base, Model No. 1851, designed by H.H. Crealock, Mintons, England, dated ca. 1872, 8 3/8" h. (ILLUS.)... **89,625**

Teapot, cov., Wild Rose & Trellis patt., spherical body composed of alternating cobalt blue bands & yellow bands of basketweave w/wild rose leafy vine, blue spout w/molded leafy vine, angled brown twig handle, domed cover w/basketweave & leaves w/arched twig finial, probably England, late 19th c., crazing, hairline, 7" h. (ILLUS. top right with three other teapots, page 270) **448**

Tray, oval, Butterfly & Orchid patt., large white, pink & green blossoms & green leaves & large black & brown butterflies against a dark brown ground, George Jones, England, late 19th c., 11" l. **2,420**

Holdcroft Banana Plant Umbrella Stand

Umbrella stand, Banana Plant design, tall upright triangular form, the front sides molded in bold relief w/a cluster of tall wide green & yellow leaves & leafy branches w/molded bulbous brown fruit, turquoise blue background & a bark-textured pale greenish brown band at the rim & base, Joseph Holdcroft, England, ca. 1880, overall 21 1/4" h. (ILLUS.)............... **3,346**

Minton Vase with Daisy-like Flowers

Vase, 6 3/4" h., footed wide bulbous ovoid body tapering to a short flaring cylindrical neck w/a gold rim band flanked by loop handles, molded w/clusters of white & yellow daisy-like flowers on the sides above a yellow basketweave band around the base, Minton, England, No. 1316, second half 19th c., minor nicks on flowers (ILLUS.) **770**

Wall pocket, a long cartouche-form backplate in brown molded w/red & green Christmas holly, a long yellow wicker basket holder at the center, T.C. Brown, Westhead, Moore & Co., England, late 19th c., 10 1/2" l. **660**

Marblehead

This pottery was organized in 1904 by Dr. Herbert J. Hall as a therapeutic aid to patients in a sanitarium he ran in Marblehead, Massachusetts. It was later separated from the sanitarium and directed by Arthur E. Baggs, a fine artist and designer, who bought out the factory in 1916 and operated it until its closing in 1936. Most wares were hand-thrown and decorated and carry the company mark of a stylized sailing vessel flanked by the letters "M" and "P."

Marblehead Mark

Pitcher, 8 3/4" h., 5 1/2" d., tankard-type, tall corseted body w/a flat mouth & small rim spout, angled side handle, incised panels down the sides incorporating stylized flower blossoms in brown, green & indigo on a speckled matte green ground, stamped ship mark & initials of artist Hannah Tutt (ILLUS., top next page)............. **$5,750**

Marblehead Tankard Pitcher with Flowers

Marblehead Mini Vase with Grapes

Vase, miniature, 3 1/2" h., 3" d., bulbous squatty ovoid body w/a wide flat mouth, decorated around the rim w/dark blue grapes & leaves against a speckled grey ground, impressed ship mark (ILLUS.) **2,300**

Floral-decorated Marblehead Vase

Vase, 4 1/8" h., small tapering ovoid body w/a wide flat mouth, decorated w/six stylized flowers in green & rust up around the sides against an oatmeal yellow ground, by Hannah Tutt, impressed logo (ILLUS.)
.... **2,415**

Marblehead Vase with Carved Geese

Vase, 6" h., 5 1/2" d., wide squatty gourd-form tapering to a wide flat mouth, carved in relief around the top w/a continuous band of stylized flying geese in black against a dark green matte ground, unmarked (ILLUS.).. **2,875**

Extremely Rare Marblehead Vase

Vase, 7 1/4" h., swelled cylindrical body tapering to a wide flat mouth, the sides w/tall narrow vertical panels divided by narrow black stripes, each panel topped by a stylized brown flowerhead w/yellow center, against a matte green ground, decorated by Hanna Tutt, ca. 1908 (ILLUS.) **50,190**

Simple Dark Blue Marblehead Vase

Vase, 7 3/4" h., gently tapering cylindrical body w/a thin flared mouth, red clay covered in a mottled blue matte glaze, impressed mark (ILLUS.) **403**

McCoy

Collectors are now seeking the art wares of two McCoy potteries. One was founded in Roseville, Ohio, in the late 19th century as the J.W. McCoy Pottery, subsequently becoming Brush-McCoy Pottery Co., later Brush Pottery. The other was also founded in Roseville in 1910 as Nelson McCoy Sanitary Stoneware Co., later becoming Nelson McCoy Pottery. In 1967 the pottery was sold to D.T. Chase of the Mount Clemens Pottery Co., who sold his interest to the Lancaster Colony Corp. in 1974. The pottery shop closed in 1985. Cookie jars are especially collectible today.

A helpful reference book is The Collector's Encyclopedia of McCoy Pottery, *by the Huxfords (Collector Books), and* McCoy Cookie Jars From the First to the Latest, *by Harold Nichols (Nichols Publishing, 1987).*

McCoy Mark

McCoy Indian Head Cookie Jar

Cookie jar, Indian Head, ca. 1954 (ILLUS.)... **$633**
Jardiniere, Loy-Nel-Art line, wide bulbous shape w/a wide molded flat rim, painted w/large orange tulips & green leaves on a shaded dark brown ground, unmarked, ca. 1905, 6 1/2" h. **173**

McCoy Quilted Pattern Jardiniere

Jardiniere, Quilted patt., glossy glaze, deep aqua, marked, 1954, 10 1/2" d., 7 1/2" h. (ILLUS.)... **144**

McCoy Pottery Shaded Brown Teapot

Teapot, cov., spherical body w/molded rings around the bottom, short spout, squared handle, low domed cover w/pointed loop finial, shaded brown glaze, ca. 1948 (ILLUS.) **25**

McCoy Strawberry Country Teapot

Teapot, cov., Strawberry Country patt., heavy cylindrical white body w/short spout & C-form handle, printed w/a cluster of strawberries, blossoms & leaves, flat green cover w/knob finial, 1970s (ILLUS.) **25**

Meissen

Meissen Blue Onion Pattern Dinner Service

The secret of true hard paste porcelain, known long before to the Chinese, was "discovered" accidentally in Meissen, Germany by J.F. Bottger, an alchemist working with E.W. Tschirnhausen. The first European true porcelain was made in the Meissen Porcelain Works, organized about 1709. Meissen marks have been widely copied by other factories. Some pieces listed here are recent.

Meissen Mark

Elaborate Meissen Victorian Centerpiece

Centerpiece, allegorical, the flaring reticulated oblong top base w/open end handles decorated overall w/encrusted color-

ful flowers & green leaves among gilt-trimmed scrolls, raised on an ornate flower-encrusted pedestal w/a flower-painted scrolled cartouche above a group of children representing the Four Seasons around the scrolled base, blue crossed-swords mark, modeled by Leuteritz, ca. 1880, overall 17 3/8" h. (ILLUS.)............. **$7,768**

Dinner service: ten 10" d. dinner plates, nine cups & saucers, eight cream soup bowls & eight underplates; Blue Onion patt., all marked w/the blue crossed swords, 19th c., the set (ILLUS. of part, top of page)... **1,725**

Mother & Children Figure Group

Figure group, a young mother in 18th c. costume seated holding her bare-bottomed toddler across her lap w/a switch to spank it in her other hand, her young daughter pulling at her arm to dissuade her, on a round molded & gilt-trimmed base, blue crossed-swords mark, late 19th c., 10 1/4" h. (ILLUS.) **3,585**

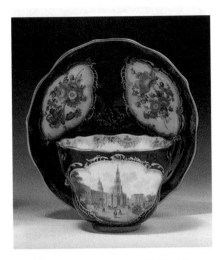

Meissen Cup & Saucer with City View

Teacup & saucer, the cup w/a cobalt blue
ground painted on the side w/a large oblong reserve w/a color scene of a church
in Dresden, bordered in gold scrolls, the
matching cup w/three oblong reserves
painted w/colorful floral bouquets outlined w/gold scrolls, scene titled "Kathol
Kirche zu Dresden," blue crossed-swords
mark, ca. 1850 (ILLUS.) **1,076**

Small Early Meissen Porcelain Teapot

Teapot, cov., nearly spherical slightly tapering body decorated w/a robin's-egg blue
ground, the flat cover w/a gold knob finial,
short curved shoulder spout & pointed
arch handle, each side centered by a h.p.
color scene of merchants haggling at
quayside within a gold border, the cover
w/two smaller views, "indianische Blu-
men" design under spout & on handle,
blue crossed-swords mark, 1735-40,
overall 4 1/4" l., 4 1/4" h. (ILLUS.) **4,780**
Urn, a flaring gadrooned foot joined by a
white-beaded disk to the large ovoid urn-
form body w/gold gadrooning around the
lower portion below the wide white central band h.p. w/a large bouquet of colorful flowers, the tapering neck in deep pink

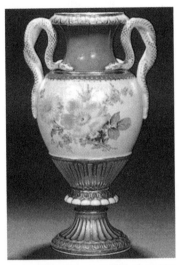

Fancy Floral-decorated Meissen Urn

below the heavy gold rolled & gadrooned
rim, white & gold entwined serpent handles at each side, blue crossed-swords
mark, late 19th c., 11" h. (ILLUS.) **518**

Cobalt Blue Meissen Vase with Putti

Vase, 6 5/8" h., footed bottle-form body tapering to a ringed neck w/a widely flaring
rim, cobalt blue ground enameled in
white in the Limoges style w/a pair of am-
orous putti sitting on a leafy branch, one
extending a floral wreath to a third in flight
releasing a dove, gold banding at the
foot, neck ring & rim, blue crossed-
swords mark, probably designed by E.A.
Leuteritz, ca. 1880 (ILLUS.) **2,868**

Mettlach

Ceramics with the name Mettlach were produced by Villeroy & Boch and other potteries in the Mettlach area of Germany. Villeroy and Boch's finest years of production are thought to be from about 1890 to 1910. Also see STEINS.

Mettlach Mark

Drinking set: tall tapering cylindrical tankard pitcher w/hinged pewter cover & twelve cylindrical beakers; paint-underglaze decoration, the pitcher decorated w/tan bands at the top & base, a large black Prussian eagle at the front w/bands featuring the crests of various German cities above & below, each beaker decorated w/a different German city crest below a border band naming the city, pitcher No. 2893-1200 & beakers No. 2327-1200, beakers 1/4 L , pitcher 3 1/4 L, the set (ILLUS., bottom of page) **$1,811**

Jardiniere, Aesthetic Movement-style, the round disk foot w/a molded leaftip band supporting the wide compressed rounded lower body decorated w/oblong panels w/stylized flowers below wide slightly tapering sides below the low rounded leaftip rim, leafy C-scroll handles at the lower body each mounted by a figure of a putto playing a mandolin, the sides decorated w/a continuous frieze of Renaissance era beauties in a garden among fruiting trees all painted in shades of blue & brown, No. 1355, ca. 1880, signed by Warth, 16 3/8" d., 23" h. (ILLUS., top next column)... **4,183**

Lovely Mettlach Aesthetic Jardiniere

Mettlach Phanolith Jardiniere

Jardiniere, Phanolith type, a wide disk foot supporting the wide cylindrical body w/a flared rim, dark blue ground decorated w/applied white relief mythological figures & pale green florals around the sides, incised mark, 8" h. (ILLUS.).............. **690**

Large Mettlach Drinking Set Decorated with German City Crests

Pilsner Beaker with the Munich Child

Pilsner beaker, a flaring foot supporting a tall gently flaring bowl, the sides decorated in color w/a scene of the Munich Child framed by brick red & deep yellow bands on a creamy ground, No. 2775-1014, 1/2 L (ILLUS.) **432**

Art Nouveau-style Mettlach Pitcher

Pitcher, 5 1/2" h., bulbous octagonal lower body tapering to tall cylindrical sides w/a wide long angled spout & angled handle, stylized Art Nouveau decorated in deep gold & dark blue w/stylized fruiting trees up the sides & geometric panels around the lower body, marked "Mettlach Reg. US Pat. Off. - Made in Germany," ca. 1920s (ILLUS.) **115**

Art Nouveau Floral Mettlach Planter

Planter, Art Nouveau-style, oblong scrolling base band below the squatty bulbous body tapering to a scalloped gadrooned rim w/six C-scroll handles curving down from the rim to the shoulder, the body in dark blue etched & decorated overall w/stylized six-petaled dark & light blue flowers w/brown centers, the border bands in pale green & dark brown, No. 2417, 10 x 16 1/2", 8" h. (ILLUS.) **1,150**

Mettlach Snow White & Dwarfs Plaque

Plaque, an etched color scene of Snow White & the Seven Dwarfs against a dark blue ground, decorated by H. Schlitt, minor gold wear, No. 2148, 17" d. (ILLUS.).. **1,116**
Plaques, each etched w/a colorful scene of figures from Germanic folklore, one showing Siegfried & Gertrude, the other Lohengrin's Ankunst, No. 3163 & No. 3165, 17" d., each (ILLUS. of both, bottom of page) **1,840**

Two Mettlach Folklore Plaques

Mettlach Punch Bowl Set

Punch bowl, cover & underplate, a footed bulbous squatty bowl w/a short wide cylindrical neck & low domed cover w/leaf loop finial, large loop shoulder handles w/satyr mask terminals, red foot, body & neck bands, the body band decorated w/a continuous white relief scene of dancing peasants, the background body in a putty color, No. 2087, 8 L, the set (ILLUS.) **1,208**

Mettlach Vase with Germanic Maidens

Vase, 12 3/4" h., a tapering foot below the wide squatty compressed lower body tapering to the tall ringed & flaring cylindrical upper body, the lower body & foot w/etched stylized bands in shades of brown, tan, white & green, the upper body a dark brown ground decorated on each side w/an etched keyhole-shaped panel featuring a full-length color portrait of a Germanic maiden, decorated by Gorig, No. 1749 (ILLUS.)......................... **284**

One of Two Red Mettlach Vases

Vases, 13 1/2" h., tall ovoid body w/long elephant head figural handles, etched & glazed to resemble Oriental cloisonné, the bright red ground decorated w/zigzag bands & stylized flowers & leafy scrolls in shades of blue, white, green & purple, No. 1870 (ILLUS. of one)............................. **575**

Mocha

Mocha decoration is found on basically utilitarian creamware or yellowware articles and is achieved by a simple chemical reaction. A color pigment of brown, blue, green or black is given an acid nature by infusion of tobacco or hops. When this acid nature colorant is applied in blobs to an alkaline ground color, it reacts by spreading in feathery seaweed designs. This type of decoration is usually accompanied by horizontal bands of light color slip. Produced in numerous Staffordshire potteries from the late 18th until the late 19th centuries, its name is derived from the similar markings found on mocha quartz. In addition to the seaweed decoration, mocha wares are also seen with Earthworm and Cat's Eye patterns or a marbleized effect.

Bowl, 6" d., 3 1/4" h., footed deep rounded shape w/a flat rim, an upper wide salmon red band outlined in black & decorated w/black seaweed design, England, mid-19th c. (one minor footring chip, hairline) **$353**

Mocha Canister, Mug & Pitcher

Canister, cov., wide cylindrical body w/incised lines near the top, domed cover w/disk finial, yellowware decorated around the middle w/thin dark brown bands flanking a wide white band w/blue seaweed designs, matching design on the cover, professional restoration to chipping & glaze flaking in the cover, tight full-length line through body, 19th c., 8" h. (ILLUS. center with mocha mug & pitcher, bottom previous page) **220**

Mocha Chamber Pot with Earthworm Pattern

Chamber pot, pearlware, footed squatty bulbous form w/a flared flattened rim, C-form handle, dark brown upper & lower bands decorated in the Cat's-eye patt., the wider central grey band decorated w/Earthworm patt. in blue, ochre & white, one rim chip, faint spider crack in base, ca. 1830, 11 3/8" d., 5 3/4" h. (ILLUS.) **1,410**

Flowerpot & undertray, slightly tapering cylindrical body w/narrow flanged rim, conforming undertray, the pot & tray each w/bands of mottled green & brown encrusting below bands of blue & brown slip w/black slip-inlaid beading, probably Yorkshire, England, ca. 1800, 6 3/4" h., 2 pcs. (one area of glaze & slip loss on pot, numerous glaze flakes on interior & base, hairlines).. **940**

Jar, cov., small footed baluster-form w/a domed cover & knob finial, the base w/a dark reddish brown band above a wide light brown band decorated w/black seaweed design, England, early 19th c., 3 1/4" h. (cracks) **1,116**

Mocha Jar with Seaweed Decoration

Jar, cov., yellowware, cylindrical w/thin incised rings around the lower body, a white & brown central band decorated w/black seaweed decoration, domed cover w/button finial decorated w/another brown seaweed-decorated band, ca.

1850, tight hairline, minor flake under cover, 4 1/2" h. (ILLUS.) **242**

Mixing bowl, small foot below the deep rounded sides w/a wide rolled rim, yellowware decorated under the rim w/a wide white band flanked by thin blue bands & decorated w/dark navy blue seaweed design, late 19th - early 20th c., 12" d., 5 3/4" h. (overall very tight age lines) **330**

Rare Mocha Earthworm Child's Mug

Mug, child's, yellow-glazed earthenware, cylindrical w/C-scroll handle, green ground decorated w/a bold black & white Earthworm patt., thin white & black rim & base bands, partial impressed mark on base, chips to base edge, glaze wear on rim, early 19th c., 2 5/8" h. (ILLUS.).......... **2,938**

Mug, cylindrical w/applied strap handle, dark yellow base & rim bands outlined in black & flanking the wide center band decorated w/bands of black inlaid rouletting & engine turning in a block checked design, England, ca. 1790, 6" h. (stress cracks at rim) **881**

Mug, cylindrical w/applied strap handle, pale yellow base & rim bands outlined in black, the main body decorated overall w/random splashes of slip in bluish grey, white & black on a deep rust red background, England, ca. 1790, 5 7/8" h. (minor rim chip restoration) **2,115**

Mug, cylindrical w/applied strap handle, upper & lower bands in dark olive green & brown flanking central bands of S-curved engine turning, half-pint, England, ca. 1800, 3 3/4" h. (minor lines in base) **470**

Mug, cylindrical w/molded base band & C-form handle, yellowware w/thin brown bands flanking a wide white band decorated w/blue seaweed designs, professional restoration to the replaced handle, glaze age crazing, 19th c., 3 3/4" h. (ILLUS. left with mocha canister & pitcher) **358**

Mug, porter-type, short cylindrical shape w/flared base, applied strap handle w/foliate terminals, dark brown rim & base bands, the putty-colored body decorated w/a painted random design of brown, white & black short slip trailings or dashes, England, ca. 1830, 3 1/8" h. (one hairline) **999**

Scarce Mocha Seaweed Mustard Jar

Mustard jar, cov., pearlware, footed bulbous ovoid body tapering to a flat rim, domed cover w/spoon notch & knob finial, C-form handle, dark brown body & cover bands each decorated in the black seaweed decoration, finial repair, small rim & base chips, early 19th c., 3 1/2" h. (ILLUS.).. **1,645**

Pitcher, 7" h., wide cylindrical lower body tapering to a cylindrical neck w/pinched rim spout, C-form handle, yellowware decorated w/pair of thin brown bands flanking a wide white band decorated w/blue seaweed design, surface roughness at spout under the glaze, 19th c. (ILLUS. right with mocha mug & canister)... **495**

Mocha Seaweed Decor Salt Dip

Salt dip, pearlware, footed wide squatty bulbous form w/a slightly flared rim, dark brown body band decorated in the black seaweed decoration, white foot, thin black & green rim bands, cracked, rim chip, early 19th c., 2 3/4" d. (ILLUS.) **558**

Tea caddy, wide cylindrical body w/an angled shoulder to a short cylindrical neck, green reeded bands around the shoulder & base, the shoulder & body decorated in marbleized slip in white, brown & ochre, England, late 18th - early 19th c., 4 1/2" h. (repair to rim) **1,645**

Waste bowl, footed w/flaring flat sides, blue background w/blue Earthworm patt. band, early 19th c., 5" d., 2 1/2" h. (hairlines in bottom)... **330**

Moorcroft

William Moorcroft became a designer for James Macintyre & Co. in 1897 and was put in charge of the art pottery production there. Moorcroft developed a number of popular designs, including Florian Ware, while with Macintyre and continued with that firm until 1913, when it discontinued the production of art pottery.

After leaving Macintyre in 1913, Moorcroft set up his own pottery in Burslem, where he continued producing the art wares he had designed earlier, introducing new patterns as well. After William's death in 1945, the pottery was operated by his son, Walter.

MOORCROFT

Moorcroft Marks

Moorcroft Claremont Pattern Bowl

Bowl, 8 1/4" d., 3 3/4" h., Claremont patt., wide shallow form, the interior decorated w/large mushrooms in shades of maroon & light green against a shaded midnight blue & dark green ground, Moorcroft-Burslem mark & William Moorcroft signature, professionally repaired (ILLUS.) **$345**

Fine Moorcroft Dawn Pattern Box

Box, cov., Dawn patt., footed wide squatty bulbous body topped by a low-domed inset cover w/button finial, decorated around the body w/a stylized hilly landscape w/trees below a border band of small overlapping scales, similar scene around the cover, a slightly crystalline glaze in shades of dark & light blue, green, white & rose, impressed "Moorcroft - Made in England" on base & painted initials of William Moorcroft, faint overall crazing, 6 1/4" d., 4" h. (ILLUS.)........... **2,300**

Extremely Rare Silver-mounted Claremont Coffee Service

Coffee service: tall ovoid cov. coffeepot, cov. sugar bowl & creamer; Claremont patt., each piece decorated w/large mushrooms in shades of blues, greens & deep maroon against a shaded blue ground, each silver-mounted around the rim & base w/a band of sterling silver blossoms, made for Shreve & Co., San Francisco & so marked, silver stamped "Shreve & Co. - Sterling," ca. 1905, coffeepot 9 3/4" h., the set (ILLUS., top of page) **16,800**

Moorcroft Pomegranate Cracker Jar

Cracker jar, cov., Pomegranate patt., barrel-shaped body w/a silver plate rim, cover & swing bail handle, in shades of cobalt blue, deep red, mustard yellow & green, marked "Moorcroft - Burslem -

102" w/Moorcroft signature, restoration around base, ca. 1916, 5 1/4" d., 9 1/2" h. (ILLUS.) **489**

Lamp, baluster-form body decorated in the Springtime Flowers patt. on a cream to cobalt blue ground, fitted on a round brass foot & w/a pierced cap & electric fitting, body 10" h. **990**

Moorcroft Anemones Table Lamp

Lamp, table model, Anemones patt., footed ovoid body tapering to a wide flat mouth w/electrical fittings, the foot in dark blue, the body in a shaded pale yellow decorated w/large blue, white & pink blossoms & green leaves, stamped mark & original paper label, early 20th c., base 10" h., overall 19" h. (ILLUS.)................................. **523**

Moorcroft Blackberry Pattern Vase

Vase, 7" h., Blackberry patt., baluster-form body w/a short, wide rolled neck, large mottled deep red & green leaves & clusters of large dark purple berries around the shoulder against a mottled brown & dark blue & green ground, impressed mark & facsimile signature, faint crazing (ILLUS.).. **575**

Vase, 10" h., ovoid base w/long neck & flaring rim, decorated w/band of anemones on cobalt blue & green ground, facsimile signature & impressed factory mark, W.M. script (ILLUS., top next column) **805**

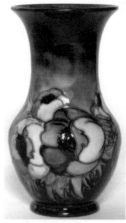

Moorcroft Vase with Anemones

Morton Potteries

Cliftwood Art Potteries, Inc. (1920-1940)

Tea set: cov. teapot, cov. sugar bowl, creamer, cups & saucer & 8" d. plate; the serving pieces w/urn-shaped paneled bodies w/ringed tapering shoulders, each w/a Matte Old Rose glaze, Cliftwood Art Potteries, Morton, Illinois, 1920-40, the set (ILLUS., bottom of page)............... **$135-180**

Cliftwood Art Potteries Old Rose Glazed Tea Set

Cliftwood Art Potteries Pink Teapot

Teapot, cov., footed urn-shaped fluted body w/a tapering ringed neck & flattened cover w/large disk finial, serpentine spout, C-scroll handle, Matte Old Rose glaze, Cliftwood Art Potteries, Morton, Illinois, 1920-40, 8-cup size (ILLUS.) **40-50**

Cliftwood Art Potteries Green Teapot

Teapot, cov., footed urn-shaped fluted body w/a tapering ringed neck & flattened cover w/large disk finial, serpentine spout, C-scroll handle, yellowware w/glossy thin Apple Green glaze, Cliftwood Art Potteries, Morton, Illinois, 1920-40, 8-cup size (ILLUS.).. **40-50**

Cliftwood Teapot and Trivet

Teapot, cov., nearly spherical teapot w/inset cover w/arched handle, serpentine spout, C-form handle, overall dark bluish mulberry drip glaze, on a matching round three-toed trivet, Cliftwood Art Potteries, Morton, Illinois, 1920-40, 8-cup size, 2 pcs. (ILLUS.) **80-100**

Morton Pottery Company (1922-1976)

Salt & pepper shakers, models of tiny white teapots w/h.p. red & blue florals & blue trim, Morton Pottery Company, Morton, Illinois, 1922-76, 2 1/4" h., pr. (ILLUS. right with Morton toy miniature teapot, top page 284) **18-24**

Morton Pottery Advertising Teapot

Teapot, cov., globe-shaped w/serpentine spout, C-form handle, low domed cover w/knob finial, the side impressed w/a rectangular panel advertising "Krug's Market - Meats & Groceries," overall mottled brown & green Woodland glaze on a yellowware body, Morton Pottery Company, Morton, Illinois, ca. 1930s (ILLUS.) **95-125**

Morton Teapot with Woodland Glaze

Teapot, cov., spherical body w/serpentine spout, C-form handle, low domed cover w/knob finial, yellowware w/overall dark brown & green sponged Woodland glaze, Morton Pottery Company, Morton, Illinois, early 20th c. (ILLUS.) **75-100**

Small "Tea Time" Morton Teapot

Teapot, cov., squatty bulbous body embossed w/a clock face under "Tea Time" on each side, short spout, C-form handle, disk cover w/button finial, forest green glaze, 4-cup size, Morton Pottery Company, Morton, Illinois, 4 3/4" h. (ILLUS.) **30-40**

Morton Pottery Miniature Toy Teapot & Salt & Pepper Shakers

Pilgrim Blue Morton Twin Tea Set

Teapot, cov., twin tea set, an upright rectangular cov. hot water & cov. teapot w/curved front & back edges & angled handle, on a fitted conforming tray base, dark Pilgrim Blue glaze in blue & green sponging, each pot 2-cup size, Morton Pottery Company, Morton, Illinois, early 20th c., the set (ILLUS.) **150-175**

Toy, miniature dollhouse-size, ribbed body & angled handle, burgundy glaze, Morton Pottery Company, Morton, Illinois, 1922-76, 2 1/4" h. (ILLUS. left with salt & pepper shakers, top of page) **8-12**

Morton Pottery Teapot Wall Pocket

Wall pocket, model of a ribbed teapot w/oblong opening at top, white w/h.p. red cherries & green leaves, Morton Pottery Company, Morton, Illinois, 1922-76, 6 1/2 x 8" (ILLUS.)..................................... **25-35**

Rapp Brothers Brick & Tile Company & Morton Pottery Works (1877-1915) - Morton Earthenware Company (1915-1917)

Ovoid Morton Rockingham Teapot

Teapot, cov., bulbous ovoid pineapple-shaped body tapering to a small mouth, tall serpentine spout, C-scroll handle, small domed cover w/button finial, overall dark brown Rockingham glaze, Morton Pottery Works (Rapp Bros.), Morton, Illinois, 1877-1917, 8-cup size (ILLUS.) **80-90**

10   Rockingham Ware

EMMET TEA POTS. Per Doz.
36s.............................$2.65
30s............................. 3.00
24s............................. 3.50

PINEAPPLE TEA POTS.
42s 2   pints...........$2.40
36s............ 2½ pints............ 2.65
30s............3¼ pints............ 3.00
24s............4   pints 3.50
18s............5¼ pints............ 4.25
12s............7   pints............ 5.50

Emmet and Pineapple Shape Morton Pottery Works Teapots in Catalog

Teapot, cov., Emmet patt. teapot, footed spherical body, brown Rockingham glaze, Model 36s, Morton Pottery Works (Rapp Bros.), Morton, Illinois, 1877-1917, 5-cup size (ILLUS. at top in catalog page, previous page) **45-50**

Teapot, cov., Emmet patt. teapot, footed spherical body, brown Rockingham glaze, Model 30s, Morton Pottery Works (Rapp Bros.), Morton, Illinois, 1877-1917, 7-cup size (ILLUS. at top in catalog page, previous page) **55-60**

Teapot, cov., Emmet patt. teapot, footed spherical body, brown Rockingham glaze, Model 24s, Morton Pottery Works (Rapp Bros.), Morton, Illinois, 1877-1917, 8-cup size (ILLUS. at top in catalog page, previous page) **65-75**

Morton Pottery Works Pear-shaped Pot

Teapot, cov., individual size, pear-shaped body w/upright spout & C-scroll handle, small domed cover w/large knob finial, overall medium brown Rockingham glaze, Morton Pottery Works (Rapp Bros.), Morton, Illinois, 1877-1917, 1 1/2 cup size (ILLUS.)...................................... **40-50**

Acorn-shaped Morton Pottery Teapot

Teapot, cov., inverted acorn shape, serpentine spout, branch handle, small domed cover w/knob finial, overall dark brown Rockingham glaze, Morton Pottery Works (Rapp Bros.), 1877-1917, 3 3/4 cup size (ILLUS.)...................................... **80-90**

Morton Pottery Works Miniature Pot

Teapot, cov., miniature, squatty flat-bottomed shape w/flared neck & fitted cover w/knob finial, paneled spout & angled handle, overall brown Rockingham

glaze, Morton Pottery Works (Rapp Bros.), Morton, Illinois, 1877-1917, 1 3/4 oz. (ILLUS.) **75-100**

Ovoid Pineapple-shaped Morton Teapot

Teapot, cov., pineapple patt., light brown Rockingham glaze, Model 42s, Morton Pottery Works (Rapp Bros.), Morton, Illinois, 1877-1917, 2-cup size (ILLUS.) **80-90**

Teapot, cov., Pineapple patt. teapot, footed ovoid body, brown Rockingham glaze, Model 42s, Morton Pottery Works (Rapp Bros.), Morton, Illinois, 1877-1917, 4-cup size (ILLUS. at bottom on catalog page, previous page) **30-40**

Teapot, cov., Pineapple patt. teapot, footed ovoid body, brown Rockingham glaze, Model 36s, Morton Pottery Works (Rapp Bros.), Morton, Illinois, 1877-1917, 5-cup size (ILLUS. at bottom on catalog page, previous page) **40-50**

Teapot, cov., Pineapple patt. teapot, footed ovoid body, brown Rockingham glaze, Model 30s, Morton Pottery Works (Rapp Bros.), Morton, Illinois, 1877-1917, 7-cup size (ILLUS. at bottom on catalog page, previous page) **50-60**

Teapot, cov., Pineapple patt. teapot, footed ovoid body, brown Rockingham glaze, Model 24s, Morton Pottery Works (Rapp Bros.), Morton, Illinois, 1877-1917, 8-cup size (ILLUS. at bottom on catalog page, previous page) **60-70**

Teapot, cov., Pineapple patt. teapot, footed ovoid body, brown Rockingham glaze, Model 18s, Morton Pottery Works (Rapp Bros.), Morton, Illinois, 1877-1917, 10-cup size (ILLUS. at bottom on catalog page, previous page) **70-80**

Teapot, cov., Pineapple patt. teapot, footed ovoid body, brown Rockingham glaze, Model 12s, Morton Pottery Works (Rapp Bros.), Morton, Illinois, 1877-1917, 14-cup size (ILLUS. at bottom on catalog page, previous page) **80-90**

Squatty Morton Pottery Works Teapot

Teapot, cov., squatty bulbous body w/a low cylindrical neck, low domed cover w/button finial, serpentine spout, C-scroll han-

Morton Rebecca at the Well Teapots

dle, overall dark brown Rockingham glaze, Morton Pottery Works (Rapp Bros.), Morton, Illinois, 1877-1917, 6-cup size (ILLUS.) **50-60**

Teapot, cov., Rebecca at the Well patt., tapering cylindrical body w/domed cover, serpentine spout, C-scroll handle, dark brown Rockingham glaze, Morton Pottery Works (Rapp Bros.), Morton, Illinois, 1877-1917, 7 pt. size (ILLUS. left with other Rebecca at the Well teapot, top of page).. **175-200**

Teapot, cov., Rebecca at the Well patt., tapering cylindrical body w/domed cover, serpentine spout, C-scroll handle, light brown Rockingham glaze, Morton Pottery Works (Rapp Bros.), Morton, Illinois, 1877-1917, 8 1/2 pt. size (ILLUS. right with other Rebecca at the Well teapot, top of page) **150-175**

Mulberry

Mulberry or Flow Mulberry ironstone wares were produced in the Staffordshire district of England in the period between 1840 and 1870 at many of the same factories that produced its close "cousin," Flow Blue china. In fact, some of the early Flow Blue patterns were also decorated with the dark blackish or brownish purple mulberry coloration and feature the same heavy smearing or "flown" effect. Produced on sturdy ironstone bodies, the designs were either transfer-printed or hand-painted (Brushstroke) with an Asian, Scenic, Floral or Marble design. Some patterns were also decorated with additional colors over or under the glaze; these are designated in the following listings as "w/polychrome."

Quite a bit of this ware is still to be found and is becoming increasingly sought-after by collectors, although presently its values lag somewhat behind similar Flow Blue pieces. The standard references to Mulberry wares is Petra Williams' book, Flow Blue China and Mulberry Ware, Similarity and Value Guide and Mulberry Ironstone - Flow Blue's Best Kept Little Secret, by Ellen R. Hill.

ATHENS (C. Meigh, ca. 1845)

Athens Mulberry Teapot by Meigh

Teapot, cov., Vertical-Paneled Gothic shape (ILLUS.)... **$450**

ATHENS (Wm. Adams & Son, ca. 1849)
Teapot, cov., Full-Paneled Gothic shape......... **300**

BLUEBELL & LEAF (unknown maker, England, ca. 1850)

Bluebell & Leaf Brush Stroke Teapot

Teapot, cov., brush stroke-type, Full-Paneled Gothic shape (ILLUS.).......................... **550**

BOCHARA (James Edwards, ca. 1850)

Bochara Flow Mulberry Teapot

Large Mulberry Corean Pattern Dinner Service

Teapot, cov., Pedestaled Gothic shape
(ILLUS., top of page)................................... **325**

COREAN (Podmore, Walker & Co., ca. 1850)

Dinner service: fourteen 7 3/4" plates, three dessert plates, one bread & butter plate, 4" w. butter pat, one dinner plate, two handleless cups & saucers, waste bowl, cov. handled octagonal sauce tureen, cov. sugar bowl, footed 10" h. cov. teapot, 9 3/4" d. open vegetable dish, large round open fruit bowl, one 10 3/4" l. octagonal bacon platter & one octagonal meat platter, the set (ILLUS., middle of page).. **1,265**

Corean Teapot with Cockscomb Handle
Teapot, cov., Cockscomb handle (ILLUS.) **695**

Corean Pattern Gothic Teapot
Teapot, cov., Full-Paneled Gothic shape
(ILLUS.).. **350**

DORA (E. Challinor, ca. 1850)

Dora Baltic Shape Teapot
Teapot, cov., Baltic shape (ILLUS.) **500**

FLORA (T. Walker, ca. 1847)

Flora Pattern Gothic Shape Teapot
Teapot, cov., Classic Gothic shape (ILLUS.) **325**

FLOWER VASE (T.J. & J. Mayer, ca. 1850)
Teapot, cov., w/polychrome, Prize Bloom
shape **560**

LADY PEEL (F. Morley, ca. 1850)

Lady Peel Mulberry Teapot
Teapot, cov., Primary shape (ILLUS.)............. **450**

LAHORE (Podmore, Walker & C., ca. 1840)

Graduated Set of Lahore Pattern Mulberry Pitchers

Pitchers, Gothic shape, graduated set of four, the set (ILLUS., top of page)............... **920**

LASSO (W. Bourne, ca. 1850)

Lasso Pattern Mulberry Teapot

Teapot, cov., Full-Paneled Gothic shape (ILLUS.).. **450**

MARBLE (Mellor Venables, ca. 1845)
Teapot, cov., child's, Vertical Paneled Gothic shape.. **350**

Marble Pattern Gothic Shape Teapot

Teapot, cov., Vertical Paneled Gothic shape (ILLUS.) **350-400**

PELEW (Edward Challinor, ca. 1850)

Pelew Pumpkin-shaped Teapot

Teapot, cov., pumpkin shape (ILLUS.) **350**

PERUVIAN (John Wedge Wood, ca. 1850)
Teapot, cov., 16-Paneled shape **400**

PHANTASIA (J. Furnival, ca. 1850)
Teapot, cov., w/polychrome, cockscomb handle **700**

SCINDE (T. Walker, ca. 1847)

Primary Shape Scinde Teapot

Teapot, cov., Primary shape (ILLUS.).............. **450**

Washington Vase Teapots in Two Similar Sizes

SHAPOO (T. & R. Boote, ca. 1850)
Teapot, cov., Primary shape 450

WASHINGTON VASE (Podmore, Walker, & Co., ca. 1850)
Teapot, cov., Classic Gothic shape, each (ILLUS. of two sizes, top of page) **350-450**

Newcomb College

This pottery was established in the art department of Newcomb College, New Orleans, Louisiana, in 1897. Each piece was hand-thrown and bore the potter's mark & decorator's monogram on the base. It was always a studio business and never operated as a factory. Its pieces are, therefore, scarce, with the early wares being eagerly sought. The pottery closed in 1940.

Newcomb College Pottery Mark

Small Squatty Newcomb College Bowl

Bowl, 2 1/2" h., wide squatty flat-bottomed form tapering to a wide flat rim, dark blue ground molded w/a band of light blue spaced blossoms around the shoulder,

decorated by Sadie Irvine, potted by Joseph Meyer, 1926 (ILLUS.) **$1,610**

Newcomb Bowl with Pink Blossoms

Bowl, 5 1/4" d., 2 7/8" h., footed wide low compressed lower body below a wide steeply tapering shoulder to the wide flat mouth, the shoulder decorated w/clusters of pale pink blossoms below leafy green stems against a dark blue ground, the lower body in medium blue, decorated by Henrietta Bailey, potted by Joseph Meyer, dated 1920 (ILLUS.) **1,840**

Bulbous Newcomb Jar with Trees

Rare Set of Newcomb College Mugs with Blossoms

Jar, cov., wide bulbous ovoid body tapering to a flat mouth flanked by large thick loop shoulder handles in dark blue, flattened inside cover w/a dark blue knob finial, decorated around the sides w/groups of tall slender trees in dark blue w/a leafy canopy at the top, impressed logo, date code for 1910, unobtrusive overall crazing, tiny nick on lower edge of cover, 4 7/8" h. (ILLUS.) **3,680**

Scarce Newcomb Jar with Live Oaks

Jar, cov., wide bulbous ovoid body tapering to a flat rim w/a low domed cover w/disk finial, carved decoration of live oaks & Spanish moss in dark blue & pale green on a denim blue ground, matte glaze, decorated by A.F. Simpson, 1929, original paper label, 4 1/2" d., 5" h. (ILLUS.).... **8,625**

Mugs, tankard-type, tapering cylindrical form w/thick angled handle in dark blue, painted w/large stylized saracena blossoms & undulating leaves in brushed light blue over white against a dark blue ground, incised base rings, decorated by Marie de Hoa LeBlanc, potted by Joseph Meyer, glossy glaze, 1901, 5 1/4" h., set of 4 (ILLUS., top of page).......................... **9,488**

Newcomb Tankard Pitcher with Flowers

Pitcher, 7 1/2" h., 5 1/2" d., tankard-type, tapering cylindrical body w/a rim spout & long angled dark blue handle, decorated w/large open medium blue tulip blossoms on tall green leafy stems, dark blue top band, panels of tiny dark blue horizontal striping between each set of leaves, glossy glaze, painted by Elizabeth Rogers, potted by Joseph Meyer, ca. 1900 (ILLUS.)... **5,750**

Rare High-glaze Newcomb College Teapot

Teapot, cov., "Solitaire," wide squatty bulbous body w/a short angled spout, low slightly tapering cover w/knob finial, C-form handle, rare early high-glaze shaded green, potted by Joseph Fortune Meyer, decorated by Irene Borden Keep, fully signed & numbered, 1901, 4" h. (ILLUS., previous page) **2,300**

Newcomb Tyg with Motto Band

Tyg (three-handled mug), motto-type, wide tapering cylindrical body flanked by three long C-form handles, each panel modeled w/grape clusters & vines in shaded blue, a continuous band around the base w/phrase "Till Love and Life Are One - Live and Love," glossy glaze, decorated by Sadie Irvine, potted by Joseph Meyer, dated 1909, 6" d., 4 3/4" h. (ILLUS.) **5,865**

Miniature Glossy Newcomb College Vase

Vase, miniature, 3 1/4" h., glossy glaze, bulbous nearly spherical body w/the creamy yellow sides incised w/vertical stripes, the shoulder incised w/overlapping cobalt blue scales outlined in pale green, a short wide cobalt blue rim, decorated by Sadie Irvine, potted by Kenneth Smith, dated 1933 (ILLUS.)... **2,070**

Vase, miniature, 3 7/8" h., flat-bottomed wide ovoid body w/a wide short cylindrical neck, a very dark blue & green Spanish moss in oak trees design against a pink ground, decorated by Sadie Irvine, potted by Jonathan Hunt, dated 1929 (ILLUS., top next column) **2,300**

Dark Blue & Pink Spanish Moss Vase

Small Moss, Oaks & Moon Newcomb Vase

Vase, 4" h., wide flat-bottomed bulbous ovoid form tapering to a wide low molded rim, dark blue Spanish moss in oaks decoration against a pale blue sky w/a pale yellow full moon, decorated by Sadie Irvine, potted by Kenneth Smith, dated 1933 (ILLUS.).. **2,875**

Small Squatty Floral Band Newcomb Vase

Vase, 4 3/4" h., footed wide squatty bulbous body tapering to a short tapering cylindrical neck, incised around the wide shoulder w/a continuous band of large white blossoms & green leaves against the mottled dark blue matte ground, decorated by Anna Frances Simpson, dated 1916 (ILLUS.)... **2,645**

Nippon

"Nippon" is a term used to describe a wide range of porcelain wares produced in Japan from the late 19th century until about 1921. It was in 1891 that the United States implemented the McKinley Tariff Act, which required that all wares exported to the United States carry a marking indicating their country of origin. The Japanese chose to use "Nippon," their name for Japan. In 1921 the import laws were revised and the words "Made in" had to be added to the markings. Japan was also required to replace the "Nippon" with the English name "Japan" on all wares sent to the United States.

Many Japanese factories produced Nippon porcelain, much of it hand-painted with ornate floral or landscape decoration and heavy gold decoration, applied beading and slip-trailed designs referred to as "moriage." We indicate the specific marking used on a piece, when known, at the end of each listing. Be aware that a number of Nippon markings have been reproduced and used on new porcelain wares.

Rose-decorated Nippon Chocolate Set

Chocolate set: cov. tall ovoid pot & 12 cups & saucers; each piece h.p. w/large yellow, red & lavender roses & green leaves on a shaded brown to cream ground, marked, pot 7 3/4" h., the set (ILLUS.)....... **$173**

Swan & Lake Scene Nippon Chocolate Set

Chocolate set: tall tankard cov. pot w/ornate loop handle & five tall cups & saucers; each piece h.p. w/a lakeside scene of swimming swans w/trees in the foreground, Nippon mark, pot 8" h., the set (ILLUS.).. **173**

Humidor, cov., cylindrical body w/a flared rim, wide domed cover w/large knob finial, decorated w/a large relief-molded owl in brown, black & white perched on a leafy oak tree branch, on shaded yellow to orange & brown ground, tiny flakes inside rim & cover, green "M" in Wreath mark, 7" h. (ILLUS., top next column)......... **748**

Rare Noritake Molded Owl Humidor

Nippon Humidor with Landscape Scene

Humidor, cov., hexagonal barrel-shaped body & conforming domed cover w/a large squared knob finial, the sides h.p. w/a continuous rural landscape w/large trees in the foreground, a paneled geometric rim band, the cover w/a similar landscape, green "M" in Wreath Nippon mark, 6 1/2" h. (ILLUS.).............................. **230**

Muffineer, a tapering paneled body w/molded & slightly swirled ribbing to a rounded shoulder & flat top pierced w/small holes, a C-form handle, the white ground decorated around the base w/a gold band & fine gold scrolls against thin blue panels, the upper half h.p. w/large gilt scrolls w/tiny pink blossoms & blue panels, blue "Maple Leaf" mark, 4 3/4" h. (ILLUS. bottom row, far right, with other Nippon pieces, top next page)... **69**

Powder box, cov., three small peg feet supporting the wide squatty bulbous body & fitted domed cover, white ground decorated around the base w/very ornate delicate gilt floral scrolls, matching gold decor on the cover centered by red roses, green "Maple Leaf" mark, 6" d. (ILLUS. bottom row, second from right with various other Nippon pieces, top next page)..... **138**

Floral-decorated Nippon Tea Set

A Large Grouping of Fine Varied Nippon Pieces

Tea set: cov. teapot, cov. sugar bowl, creamer & six cups & saucers; bulbous bodies on the serving pieces, each h.p. w/stylized pink & yellow floral border bands w/green leaves & gilt trim, unmarked, early 20th c., the set (ILLUS., previous page) **150**

Nippon Teapot with Birds in a Tree

Teapot, cov., bulbous ovoid body w/a serpentine spout, C-scroll handle & low domed cover w/gold loop finial, decorated w/colorful birds in a blossoming tree, "M" in Wreath mark, ca. 1911 (ILLUS.) **40**

Noritake-Nippon Porcelain Teapot

Teapot, cov., footed wide squatty bulbous body w/a high domed cover w/button fin-

ial, short spout & C-form handle, decorated around the top & cover w/ornate gold scrolls & delicate roses, early Noritake-Nippon mark, ca. 1910-20 (ILLUS.) **50**

Vase, 7" h., a tapering cylindrical lower body flaring into a large bulbous upper body centered by a short gold-decorated neck w/pointed sides & integral high arched gold handles down to the shoulder, the pastel lavender to cream ground ornately decorated overall w/large Coralene clusters of pink & deep rose blossoms & green leaves outlined in gold, 1909 patent mark (ILLUS. bottom row, second from left with various Nippon pieces, top of page).. **460**

Brown Nippon Vase with Castle Scene

Vase, 8" h., footed wide cylindrical body w/a wide shoulder tapering to a short neck w/rolled rim, pointed scroll shoulder handles, dark brown ground decorated on the front w/a stylized landscape showing a castle above a forest of trees in shades of brown, green, pale yellow & blue, a brown & white slip Greek key band near the base & around the base of the decorated neck, blue "Maple Leaf" mark (ILLUS.).................. **127**

Blue & Gold Nippon Vase with Roses

Vase, 9 3/4" h., raised disk foot below the wide gently tapering cylindrical body topped by a deep rounded cupped neck flanked by angled gold handles, a medium blue ground decorated on the body w/a pair of gold leafy bands also enclosing a large oval reserve, the reserve & space between the bands h.p. w/a continuous lakeside landscape featuring large red roses in the foreground, a white band just below the neck trimmed w/gilt florals & further gilt florals on the blue neck, green "M" in Wreath mark (ILLUS.) **230**

Nippon Vase with Bands of Large Roses

Vase, 10" h., a tall ovoid body tapering to a small trumpet neck flanked by arched gold shoulder handles, the shaded grey to white ground h.p. around the base & shoulder w/large clusters of yellow & pink roses & pale green leaves w/gold highlights, blue "Maple Leaf" mark (ILLUS.) **316**

Nippon Vase with Delicate Gold & Florals

Vase, 10 3/4" h., a low four-lobed gold foot below the tall cylindrical body w/a swelled shoulder ring & low rounded shoulder centering a short ringed neck, four upright scroll handles around the top of the shoulder, the sides w/a white ground decorated w/delicate gold pendants, jewels & swags surrounding a large shield-shaped reserve bordered in gold & salmon pink & enclosing a cluster of salmon pink peony blossoms & green leaves, green "M" in Wreath mark (ILLUS.)............. **196**

Wall plaque, round, pierced to hang, h.p. w/an expansive landscape w/groves of trees in meadows sloping down to a river, mountains in the distance, in shades of dark & light green, purple, lavender, pink & white, blue "M" in Wreath mark, 10" d. (ILLUS. front row, far left with various other Nippon pieces, top previous page) ... **100-200**

Wall plaque, pierced to hang, round, molded in relief w/a lion & lioness in a rocky landscape, natural coloration, green "M" in wreath mark, 10 1/2" d. (ILLUS. back row, far right with various other Nippon pieces, top previous page)................... **475-575**

Wall plaque, pierced to hang, round, a relief-molded bellowing bull elk in the foreground w/a painted lakeside landscape in the background, green "M" in Wreath mark, 11" d. (ILLUS. back row, second from right with various Nippon pieces, top previous page) **400-600**

Wine jugs w/original bulbous stoppers, a bulbous ovoid body tapering to a short flared neck & arched brown handle, fitted w/a bulbous stopper, each h.p. around the base & shoulder w/a black band highlighted by black & white shields flanked by pairs of small seated green lions, a similar band around each stopper, the wide body band decorated w/a continuous panoramic landscape scene w/a flowering tree in the foreground and a pathway w/cottage & clumps of trees behind, a lake & mountains in the background, all in shades of green, pale blue, white & black, blue "Maple Leaf" mark, 9 1/2" h., matched pair, each (ILLUS. top row, far left with various other Nippon pieces, top of previous page)................... **1,610**

North Dakota School of Mines

All pottery produced at the University of North Dakota School of Mines was made from North Dakota clay. In 1910, the University hired Margaret Kelly Cable to teach pottery making, and she remained at the school until her retirement. Julia Mattson and Margaret Pachl also served as instructors between 1923 and 1970. Designs and glazes varied through the years ranging from the Art Nouveau to modern styles. Pieces were marked "University of North Dakota - Grand Forks, N.D. - Made at School of Mines, N.D." within a circle and also signed by the students until 1963. Since that time, the pieces bear only the students' signatures. Items signed "Huck" are by the artist Flora Huckfield and were made between 1923 and 1949.

North Dakota School of Mines Mark

North Dakota Covered Wagon Bowl-Vase

Bowl-vase, wide squatty spherical form w/low molded flat mouth, "Covered Wagon" patt., a wide incised band of oxendrawn wagons around the shoulder, matte dark brown glaze w/darker brown highlights, by Margaret Cable, ink mark, signed, titled & numbered "186," 7 1/4" d., 6 1/2" h. (ILLUS.) **$1,093**

Pink-striped North Dakota Vase

Vase, 4 3/8" h., wide flat-bottomed short bulbous body w/a wide rounded shoulder tapering to the flat mouth, a dark blue ground decorated w/a repeating design of pink stripes w/a ring at each end alter-

nating w/pink stripes w/the two rings at the center, short medium blue bars alternating w/pink stripes at the rim & base, decorated by Beverly Bushaw, 1937, ink stamp mark, light crazing (ILLUS.)............ **1,725**

North Dakota School of Mines Vase

Vase, 5 5/8" h., bulbous ovoid body tapering to a wide flat mouth, carved jack-in-the-pulpit blossoms around the sides in brown highlighted w/black slip, stamped mark on the base & incised "Flower-Jack-in-the-Pulpit - Huck 74 A," short tight line at rim professionally repaired (ILLUS.) **863**

North Dakota Vase with Bentonite Glaze

Vase, 7 3/8" h., flat-bottomed swelled cylindrical body w/a wide flat molded mouth, Bentonite glaze, a brown ground decorated w/a large very dark brown stylized flowering cactus, dark brown rim band, decorated by J. Mattson, No. 1023 (ILLUS.)...... **2,760**

North Dakota Floral-striped Vase

Vase, 11 1/8" h., gently swelled cylindrical body w/a narrow rounded shoulder to the low flaring neck, decorated around the sides w/stripes composed of large mustard yellow blossoms & dark green leaves against a pale yellow ground, decorated by L. Thorne & Huckfield, Shape No. 576, chip & areas of fired-on red glaze (ILLUS.) **575**

Ohr (George) Pottery

George Ohr, the eccentric potter of Biloxi, Mississippi, worked from about 1883 to 1906. Some think him to be one of the most expert throwers the craft will ever see. The majority of his works were hand-thrown, exceedingly thin-walled items, some of which have a crushed or folded appearance. He considered himself the foremost potter in the world and declined to sell much of his production, instead accumulating a great horde to leave as a legacy to his children. In 1972 this collection was purchased for resale by an antiques dealer.

Ohr Pottery Marks

Ohr Bisque Clay Bowl-Vase

Bowl-vase, footed squatty body w/deeply indented & folded sides below a flattened rounded shoulder, bisque red clay, script signature, 5" d., 3 3/4" h. (ILLUS.) **$2,875**

Small Pinched Black Ohr Pitcher

Pitcher, 2 1/2" h., 4 1/4" l., a round foot below the body pulled & pinched into a large spout opposite a thin, pointed finform handle, rolled rim, speckled gunmetal glaze, repairs to handle & rim edge, stamped "G.E. OHR - Biloxi, Miss." (ILLUS.) **5,463**

Double-bulb Black Ohr Pitcher

Pitcher, 5 1/2" h., 3 3/4" d., footed spherical lower body w/a small waist below the deep cupped upper body w/a flaring rim & wide folded rim spout, arched loop handle, mirror black & eggplant glazed, stamped "G.E. OHR - Biloxi, Miss." (ILLUS.) **6,325**

Small George Ohr Pottery Teapot

Teapot, cov., a cylindrical slightly waisted body w/a flattened shoulder centering a short cylindrical neck, serpentine spout & long C-form handle, small inset cover w/large mushroom knop, covered overall in a green speckled glossy glaze, stamped "GEO. E. OHR/BILOXI, MISS.," minor restoration to spout, rim & cover, 6 1/2" l., 4 1/4" h. (ILLUS.) **5,581**

Teapot, cov., a large size pot w/a footring supporting the wide squatty bulbous body tapering to a cupped neck w/inset flat cover, long serpentine spout & simple C-form handle, covered in a spectacular white, red & pink glaze sponged on an amber ground, stamped "G.E. OHR/ Biloxi, Miss.," late 19th - early 20th c., 12 1/2" l., 5 1/2" h. (ILLUS., top of next page) **55,813**

Extremely Rare George Ohr Pottery Teapot

Miniature Ohr Vase in Raspberry & Amber

Vase, 3 1/4" h., 3" d., wide domed base w/medial ring below the trumpet-form neck w/pinched & twisted rim, overall raspberry & amber glossy glaze, stamped "GEO. E. OHR," tight line in the base (ILLUS.) **1,955**

Footed Shaker-style Ohr Vase

Vase, 4 3/4" h., 2 1/4" d., footed shaker-style body tapering to a tiny flared mouth, overall mottled forest green glossy glaze, stamped "G.E. OHR - BILOXI," touch-up to rim, minor base abrasion (ILLUS.) **3,105**

Squatty Twisted-neck Ohr Vase

Vase, 4 3/4" h., 3 3/4" d., wide squatty bulbous lower body centered by a cylindrical deeply twisted neck w/a bulbed top w/a flaring crimped rim, gunmetal black glaze, stamped "GEO. E. OHR - Biloxi, Miss.," minute rim nick & small kiln kiss (ILLUS.) .. **5,463**

Small Bisque Twisted Ohr Vase

Vase, 3 3/4" h., 4" d., bulbous squatty form w/a deep in-body twist around the center, bisque red clay fired to a dark brown sheen, stamped "GEO. OHR" (ILLUS.)..... **2,760**

Ohr Vase with Rare Volcanic Glaze

Vase, 6" h., 2 3/4" d., bulbous ovoid lower body tapering to a waisted neck w/cylindrical top, overall unusual raspberry & white volcanic glaze on a glossy blue ground, stamped "G.E. OHR - Biloxi, Miss.," underglaze firing line inside neck (ILLUS.) **14,950**

Owens

Owens pottery was the product of the J.B. Owens Pottery Company, which operated in Ohio from 1890 to 1929. In 1891 it located in Zanesville and produced art pottery from 1896, introducing "Utopian" wares as its first art pottery. The company switched to tile after 1907. Efforts to rebuild after the factory burned in 1928 failed, and the company closed in 1929.

Owens Pottery Mark

Owens Utopian Jug with Ear of Corn

Jug, Utopian Line, bulbous body w/an integral arched loop handle across the top to the upright cylindrical neck w/a tiny spout, decorated w/a large yellow ear of corn w/green leaves against a dark brown ground, painted by Tot Steele, impressed mark, Shape No. 1266, 7 1/2" h. (ILLUS.) **$259**

Rare Owens Utopian Kerosene Lamp

Lamp, kerosene-type, Utopian Ware, the base composed of a tall baluster-form vase h.p. w/a profile bust portrait of a Native American woman titled "Gentle Bird - Flatheads," in dark brown, black & dark green on a shaded dark brown to green ground, fitted into a scroll-cast & footed cast metal base, a copper band supporting the font fitted into the top, w/early burner & cased amber ball shade & clear chimney, painted by Mae Timberlake, bottom of lamp w/Utopian mark, 13 7/8" h. (ILLUS.)... **4,025**

Tall Owens Mug with Indian Portrait

Mug, Lightweight Line, flaring ringed base & tall slightly tapering cylindrical sides, large angled handle, h.p. large bust portrait of a Native American Chief by Albert Haubrich, Shape No. 830, completely oversprayed, indicating some restoration, 7 5/8" h. (ILLUS.) **431**

Utopian Vase with Nasturtiums

Vase, 10 1/4" h., Utopian Ware, cylindrical body w/a wide flattened shoulder centered by a tiny neck, decorated w/dark orange nasturtium blossoms & long green leafy stems against a dark to medium brown ground, impressed "Owens 1010" (ILLUS.).. **259**

Fine Utopian Portrait Vase

Vase, 10 1/2" h., 5 1/2" d., Utopian Line, tall swelled cylindrical form w/a flat mouth, h.p. w/a half-length bust portrait of a Native American titled "Sanches Apache," dark brown, reddish brown,

cream & black on a shaded brown to tan ground, by artist A.F. Best, some glaze lifting, early 20th c. (ILLUS.)..................... **2,530**

Tall Owens Utopian Vase with Roses

Vase, 11" h., simple footed tall ovoid body w/a tiny neck, h.p. w/large yellowish orange roses & green leafy stems against a shaded dark brown to green ground, Owens Utopian logo, artist-signed (ILLUS.).. **460**

Vase, 11 3/4" h., footed large bulbous ovoid body tapering to a tiny cylindrical neck, pierced w/rectangles on the shoulder, rectangular relief panels w/stylized swans on the sides, matte green glaze, impressed "Owens 1025"......................... **1,495**

Tall Slender Owens Lotus Ware Vase

Vase, 14" h., Lotus Ware, a tall slender baluster-form body, h.p. w/pale white & blue pansies around the middle against a blue shaded to white ground, Owens mark, Shape No. 016 (ILLUS.)............................... **460**

Paris & Old Paris

China known by the generic name of "Paris" and "Old Paris" was made by several Parisian factories from the 18th through the 19th century; some of it is marked and some is not. Much of it was handsomely decorated.

Delicate Old Paris Cachepot & Drain Plate

Cachepot & drain plate, in the Louis XVI style, the round disk-form gold-banded drain plate supporting the trumpet-form pot w/a white ground finely decorated w/delicate gold florals & swags & deep red & blue scrolls, blue underglaze "A" mark under plate, late 18th c., 7 3/4" d., overall 8 1/4" h., the set (ILLUS.) **$1,380**

Old Paris Cup & Saucer with Children

Cup & saucer, the cylindrical cup in white w/a grisaille scene of children in 18th c. attire holding a rooster, gold edge banding & handle, matching saucer w/a scene of a seated girl, workshop of Le Petit Carousel, last quarter 18th c., restoration to handle, saucer 6" d., cup 4" h., the set (ILLUS.) **575**

Paris Porcelain Incense Burners

Incense burners, figural, one modeled as a seated knight wearing a maroon outfit trimmed in gold, the other as a Medievel lady wearing a long maroooon gowm & long green robe, each on a rectangular platform base w/black marbleizing about the gilt-trimmed white scroll base, Franed, second quarter 19th c., 6 x 7", 10 1/4" h., pr. (ILLUS.) **575**

Old Paris Figural Inkstand with Cupid

Inkstand, figural, four gold paw feet supporting a gold-banded oval base mounted by the white figure of Cupid holding a garland of flowers & seated on rockwork next to the inkwell formed by a deep flaring basket w/a short oval basket beside it, a gold cylindrical quill holder behind him, the edge of the stand inscribed in gold script w/a couplet by Voltaire, perhaps Dagoty, ca. 1810, 6" h. (ILLUS.) **1,016**

Potpourri jars, cov., a cubical form fitted w/a square tapering cover w/block finial, gold dentil bands around the top & base w/gold corner bands ending in figural swan feet, each side panel w/a dark blue ground h.p. w/a large oval reserve decorated w/a colorful bouquet of flowers outlined in delicate gilt floral borders, possibly Jacob Petite, 19th c., some damage to gallery, one w/a body crack, 5" sq., 7" h., pr. (ILLUS., top next page) **575**

Gold & White Paris Porcelain Tea Set

Very Ornate Paris Potpourri Jars

Pair of Fine Paris Porcelain Vases

Large Elaborate Old Paris Vases

Rare 18th Century Old Paris Wine Glass Cooler

Tea set: cov. teapot, cov. sugar bowl, creamer & two handled cups & saucers; each w/a squatty bulbous body w/alternating narrow stripes of gold & white, teapot & sugar w/flanged & scalloped rims molded w/shells & inset covers w/acorn finial, the other pieces w/the same design, France, first half 19th c., teapot 6 1/2" h., the set (ILLUS., bottom page 301) **2,760**

Vases, 6 1/2" h., rhyton-form terminating in a figural eagle head, raised on an oblong scroll-molded platform base, the cornucopia-form body in celeste blue w/a gilt-bordered white reserve h.p. w/colorful flowers, the rim & eagle trimmed in gold, the base in pink w/gold trim, France, late 19th c., pr. (ILLUS., middle previous page) **633**

Vases, 17 1/4" h., footed tall ovoid body tapering to a trumpet neck, the shoulders mounted w/large figural white goat-head handles, the sides & shoulders ornately trimmed w/applied blue flowers & green leaves all trimmed in gold, the front white panel h.p. w/a colorful bouquet of flowers, late 19th c., restoration & repairs to rim & handles, pr. (ILLUS., bottom previous page) **748**

Wine glass cooler, oval squatty rounded form w/a deeply scalloped rim forming rests for the feet of the wine glasses, gold-trimmed cattail end handles, the sides h.p. w/a continuous band of delicate vining flowers between gold borders, the lower body w/scattered tiny flowers, gold rim & foot band, two variant iron-red stenciled crowned "M" marks for Monsieur's Factory, ca. 1790, 13 1/4" l. (ILLUS., top of page)................................. **7,768**

Paul Revere Pottery

This pottery was established in Boston, Massachusetts, in 1906, by a group of philanthropists seeking to establish better conditions for underprivileged young girls of the area. Edith Brown served as supervisor of the small "Saturday Evening Girls Club" pottery operation, which was moved, in 1912, to a house close to the Old North Church where Paul Revere's signal lanterns had been placed. The wares were mostly hand decorated in mineral colors, and both sgraffito and molded decorations were employed. Although it became popular, it was never a profitable operation and always depended on financial contributions to operate. After the death of Edith Brown in 1932, the pottery foundered and finally closed in 1942.

Paul Revere Marks

Paul Reverse Bowl with Greek Key Rim

Bowl, 6" d., 3" h., deep rounded sides w/a wide flat rim, brown semi-matte ground decorated around the rim w/a cuerda seca band of Greek key in taupe & ivory on white, signed "SEG - 10.12 - FL" (ILLUS.) **$1,116**

Paul Revere Child's Breakfast Set

Breakfast set: child's, 7 1/2" d. plate & 3 5/8" h. mug; each h.p. w/a circle enclosing a picture of a white rabbit lying on a green grassy mound, white & blue outer bands, initialed by the artist, early 20th c., the set (ILLUS.) **1,116**

Paul Revere Jardiniere with Lotus Band

Jardiniere, wide bulbous squatty body w/a closed rim, yellow ground w/a wide rim band in cuerda seca w/black-outlined white lotus blossoms trimmed w/yellow, stamped mark, firing lines around rim & base, two restored rim chips, 9" d., 7" h. (ILLUS.) **1,495**

Plate, 7 5/8" d., decorated w/incised geese in mottled green on a speckled blue ground, painted mark "S.E.G. 6-13," & artist's initials "I.G.," ca. 1913 .... **489**

Paul Reverse Dinner Plate with Lotus

Plate, dinner, 10" d., dark greyish blue ground decorated around the rim in cuerda seca w/a band of stylized white lotus blossoms, signed "SEG - AM - 11-14," rim bruise, small chips to footring (ILLUS.) **646**

Vase, 6 1/4" h., 3 3/4" d., simple ovoid body w/a wide flat rim, dark bluish grey lower body, a wide shoulder band in cuerda seca decorated w/a band of stylized oak leaves & acorns in green, brown & pale blue, inkstamped "SEG - AM - 12-17," 1917 (ILLUS., top next column) **4,025**

Fine Paul Reverse Vase with Oak Leaves

Pewabic

Mary Chase Perry (Stratton) and Horace J. Caulkins were partners in this Detroit, Michigan, pottery. Established in 1903, Pewabic Pottery evolved from their Revelation Pottery, "Pewabic" meaning "clay with copper color" in the language of Michigan's Chippewa Indians. Caulkins attended to the clay formulas and Mary Perry Stratton was artistic creator of forms & glaze formulas, eventually developing a wide range of colors for her finely textured glazes. The pottery's reputation for fine wares and architectural tiles enabled it to survive the Depression years of the 1930s. After Caulkins died in 1923, Mrs. Stratton continued to be active in the pottery until her death, at age 94, in 1961. Her contributions to the art pottery field are numerous.

Pewabic Pottery Mark

Small Blue Pewabic Bowl

Bowl, 3" d., small round foot supporting the deep wide bell-formed bowl, a medium blue glaze applied over an iridescent yellowish green glossy glaze, round logo, some areas of thin glaze near the rim (ILLUS., previous page) **$374**

Pewabic Commemorative Paperweight

Paperweight, round disk-type, presentation-type, the center carved w/a city skyline along a lake incised "Detroit" in shades of dark iridescent bluish green & brown, the outer brown border band incised "GFWC - 1935," 3" d. (ILLUS.) **173**

Pewabic Paperweight with Fish

Paperweight, square tile-form, incised w/a large light brown fish against a mottled blue & green ground, circular seal mark, 2 3/4" w. (ILLUS.)... **58**

Plate, dinner, 9 1/4" d., a crackle ivory ground decorated in squeezebag w/a border band w/pairs of facing white rabbits alternating w/a green tree or shrub, outlined in black, stamped company name, few minor glaze nicks (ILLUS., top next column)... **2,875**

Vase, experimental-type, a crimped uneven foot below the wide squatty disk-form body tapering sharply to a wide short cylindrical neck, a mottled white neck band above the dark rusty brown drippy glaze covering the sides, oak leaf mark & round

paper label, some burst air bubbles & a base chip (ILLUS., middle this column) **431**

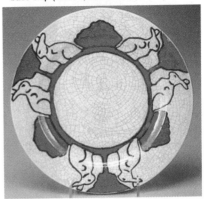

Rare Pewabic Plate with Rabbits

Squatty Experimental Pewabic Vase

Pewabic Stacked Pots-style Vase

Vase, stacked pots-style, composed of three small sharply tapering ovoid pots w/small mouths clustered together & topped in the center by a single matching pot, overall glossy grey glaze, unmarked (ILLUS.).. **138**

Pewabic Vase with Stylized Flowers

Vase, 7" h., wide cylindrical body w/a tapering rounded shoulder to the wide short
cylindrical mouth, glossy glaze h.p. w/a
repeating design of clusters of round
brick-red stylized flowers on slender leafy
stems against a mustard yellow ground,
dark bands at the neck & base, round
company sticker (ILLUS.).......................... **1,150**

Spherical Dark Blue Pewabic Vase

Vase, 7 1/8" h., footed spherical body w/a
short flaring neck, overall dark blue matte
glaze w/silvery iridescent patches, im-
pressed twice w/logo (ILLUS.) **690**

Phoenix Bird & Flying Turkey Porcelain

*The phoenix bird, a symbol of immortality and
spiritual rebirth, has been handed down through
Egyptian mythology as a bird that consumed itself
by fire after 500 years and then rose again,
renewed, from its ashes. This bird has been used to
decorate Japanese porcelain designed for export for
more than 100 years. The pattern incorporates a
blue design of the bird, variously known as the
"Flying Phoenix," the "Flying Turkey" or the "Ho-
o," stamped on a white ground. It became popular
with collectors because of the abundant supply
resulting from the long period of time the ware was
produced. Pieces can be found marked with Japanese characters, with a "Nippon" mark, a "Made in
Japan" mark or an "Occupied Japan" mark.
Although there are several variations to the pattern and border, we have grouped them together
since values seem to be quite comparable. A word*

*of caution to collectors: Phoenix Bird pattern is
still being produced. The standard reference for
this category is Phoenix Bird Chinaware by Joan
Collett Oates.*

Large Flying Turkey Pattern Teapot

Teapot, cov., Flying Turkey (extra-large)
patt., footed spherical body w/serpentine
spout & ring handle, flattened cover
w/knob finial, marked w/six Japanese
characters, ca. 1920s-30s, 9" l., 5 3/4" h.
(ILLUS.).. **$65**

Melon-lobed Flying Turkey Teapot

Teapot, cov., Flying Turkey patt., squatty
bulbous melon-lobed body on tab feet,
short spout, D-form handle, domed cover w/knob finial, marked w/six Japanese
characters, ca. 1920s-30s, 8" l., 5" h.
(ILLUS.) **85**

Flying Turkey (Style A) Pattern Teapot

Teapot, cov., Flying Turkey patt. (Style A,
fatter bird), footed squatty bulbous body
w/shaped spout & C-form handle, low
domed cover w/knob finial, marked
"Made in Japan," ca. 1920s-30s, 7" l.,
3 3/4" h. (ILLUS.) **35**

Flying Turkey, Style B Teapot

Teapot, cov., Flying Turkey patt., Style B, skinny bird, footed squatty wide bulbous body w/C-form handle & serpentine spout, low domed cover w/knob finial, marked "Japan" w/three Japanese characters, ca. 1920s, 6 5/8" l., 4 1/2" h. (ILLUS.)... **35**

Flying Turkey (Style B) Pattern Teapot

Teapot, cov., Flying Turkey (Style B) patt., scalloped flaring foot, bulbous ovoid body w/a flared scalloped rim, serpentine spout & fancy C-scroll handle, domed cover w/ring finial, marked w/six Japanese characters, ca. 1920s-30s, 6 5/8" l., 5 3/8" h. (ILLUS.) **65**

Japanese Howo Pattern Small Teapot

Teapot, cov., Howo patt., tea-for-two size, bulbous tapering body w/short spout & squared handle, low domed cover w/button finial, marked "Sometuke - Nippon," Japan, early 20th c., 6 1/4" l., 4 1/4" h. (ILLUS.)... **35**

Extra Large Modern Phoenix Teapot

Teapot, cov., Modern Phoenix (T-Bird) patt., extra large upright squared body w/curved shoulders to a squared domed cover w/ovoid finial, angular spout & squared loop handle, original sticker but unmarked, made by Takahashi of Japan, post-1970, 9" l., 7 1/4" h. (ILLUS.) **25-35**

Unusual Modern Phoenix Pattern Teapot

Teapot, cov., Modern Phoenix (T-Bird) patt., square body w/angled shoulders, square cover w/ovoid finial, angled upright handle, tall upright square porcelain handle, unmarked but by Takahashi of Japan, post-1970, 6 1/4" l., 8" h. (ILLUS.) **45**

Modern Phoenix Rectangular Teapot

Teapot, cov., Modern Phoenix (T-Bird) patt., upright rectangular body w/short angled spout, C-scroll handle, low domed cover w/flower bud finial, unmarked but produced by Takahashi of Japan, post-1970, 8 1/2" l., 5" h. (ILLUS.) **35**

Two Phoenix Bird Individual-sized Teapots

Heavy Phoenix Bird Pattern Teapot

Teapot, cov., Phoenix Bird patt., heavy-weight footed bulbous body w/a wide shoulder tapering to a flat rim, serpentine spout, D-form handle w/thumbrest, flat cover w/button finial, not original cover, marked "Made in Japan" in three lines, ca. 1920s-30s, 9" l., 4 1/2" h. (ILLUS.) **65**

Teapot, cov., Phoenix Bird patt., individual-size, bulbous body w/a wide flat mouth, short angled spout, D-form handle, domed cover w/knob finial, originally came w/a round-bottomed strainer, marked "Made in Japan," ca. 1920s-30s, 5 1/4" l., 4" h. (ILLUS. left with other individual teapot, top of page) **25**

Teapot, cov., Phoenix Bird patt., individual-size, bulbous body w/a wide flat mouth, short angled spout, D-form handle, domed cover w/knob finial, originally came w/a round-bottomed strainer, marked "Made in Japan," ca. 1920s-30s, 5 1/4" l., 3 5/8" h. (ILLUS. right with other individual teapot, top of page) **25**

Phoenix Bird - Morimura Bros. Teapot

Teapot, cov., Phoenix Bird patt., large bulbous body w/long upright serpentine spout & wide D-form handle, low domed cover w/knob finial, Morimura Brothers mark & "Japan," ca. 1922, largest of four sizes, overall 10" l., body 6" d., 5 3/4" h. (ILLUS.) **35-40**

Squatty Phoenix Bird Pattern Teapot

Teapot, cov., Phoenix Bird patt., low foot & wide squatty bulbous body, short serpentine spout, large ring handle, low domed cover w/angled ring handle, blue band around foot, unmarked but matches pieces w/the "T" inside flower & "Japan" mark, ca. 1920s-30s, 7 1/2" l., 4 1/4" h. (ILLUS.) **45**

Small HO-O Border Phoenix Bird Pot

Teapot, cov., Phoenix Bird patt., nearly spherical body w/flattened cover & knob finial, C-form handle, short serpentine spout, unusual steam hole in cover finial, HO-O heart-like border variant, unmarked, 5 1/2" l., 4" h. (ILLUS.) **35-40**

Japanese Twin Phoenix Pattern Teapot

Teapot, cov., Twin Phoenix patt., squatty ovoid body w/serpentine spout & C-form handle, low domed cover w/arched handle, band of decoration around top & cover, marked "Sometuke, Nippon," Japan, early 20th c., 7 3/4" l., 4 1/2" h. (ILLUS.) **45**

Twin Turkey Teapot on Tiny Figure Feet

Teapot, cov., Twin Turkey patt., squatty bulbous body raised on five tiny figural Buddha-like feet, serpentine spout, long C-form handle, cover w/knob finial, unmarked, ca. 1920s-30s, 8" l., 5" h. (ILLUS.) **110-125**

Quimper

This French earthenware pottery has been made in France since the end of the 17th century and is still in production today. Because the colorful decoration on this ware, predominantly of Breton peasant figures, is all hand-painted and each piece is unique, it has become increasingly popular with collectors in recent years. Most pieces offered today date from about the mid-19th century to the present. Modern potteries continue to operate today, with contemporary examples available in gift shops.

The standard reference in this field is Quimper Pottery A French Folk Art Faience *by Sandra V. Bondhus (privately printed, 1981).*

Quimper Marks

Fine HB Quimper Tea Set with Rouen-inspired Pattern

Tea set: cov. tall teapot, cov. sugar bowl & creamer; Rouen-inspired patt., each piece w/blue-trimmed angular handles, domed covers w/pointed finials, each painted w/the figure of a male Breton musician in a landscape, elaborate upper borders of stylized florals in cobalt blue, yellow & red, mark of HB Quimper, only slight glaze wear under sugar cover, France, early 20th c., the set (ILLUS.) **$575**

Quimper Modern Movement Pattern Teapot & Creamer

Fine Decor Riche Decorated Teapot

Teapot, cov., Decor Riche patt., a swirled & waisted Rococo Louis XV-style body w/a low domed cover w/dark blue ring finial, a long serpentine spout & an ornate dark blue C-scroll handle, w/large scene of dancing peasants in a landscape & dark blue & mustard yellow trim, marked "HenRiot Quimper 126," mint, 9 1/4" h. (ILLUS.) **350**

Detailed HB Quimper Pattern Teapot

Teapot, cov., HB Quimper patt., simple ovoid body w/a squared angled spout & squared angled handle, low domed cover w/a pointed finial, decorated w/a colorful scene of a French peasant in a landscape, naive flowers, leaves, ermine tails & lattice around the top, signed only "HB 7/4" on the bottom, mint, 9" h. (ILLUS.) **350**

Unusual Quimper Drip-type Teapot

Teapot, cov., two-part drip-type, colorful Rouen-inspired decoration, the cylindrical top section w/angled handle & low domed cover w/button finial & a sieve bottom painted w/a scene of a Breton peasant playing a musical instrument in a landscape, a fancy border in dark blue w/gold & green scrolls, florals & leaves, this section for holding the loose tea to which hot water is added, the lower squatty bulbous pot w/a long serpentine spout & C-form handle decorated around the upper half w/a matching band of dark blue, gold & green, marked "HB Quimper 8/274," mint, overall 9 1/2" h. (ILLUS.) **425**

"Fruits de la Mer" Pattern Teapot

Teapot, cov., "Fruits de la Mer" patt., black glaze ground w/conch shells & seaweed decoration, by Guy Trevoux, Henriot Quimper, 9 1/2" h., mint (ILLUS.)................ **250**

Teapot & matching creamer, Modern Movement patt., the tall tapering paneled teapot w/a long upright spout, angled handle, the domed paneled cover w/a tall ovoid finial, creamer in a similar shape, each h.p. w/bold shades of orange, dark blue, black & green on a white ground, panels w/figures, lattice or stylized flower burst designs, mark of HB, Quimper, France, near mint, teapot 9 3/4" h., 2 pcs. (ILLUS., top of previouis page) **275**

R.S. Prussia & Related Wares

Ornately decorated china marked "R.S. Prussia" and "R.S. Germany" continues to grow in popularity. According to the Third Series of Mary Frank Gaston's Encyclopedia of R.S. Prussia (Collector Books, Paducah, Kentucky), these marks were used by the Reinhold Schlegelmilch porcelain factories located in Suhl in the Germanic regions known as "Prussia" prior to World War I, and in Tillowitz, Silesia, which became part of Poland after World War II. Other marks sought by collectors include "R.S. Suhl," "R.S." steeple or church marks, and "R.S. Poland."

The Suhl factory was founded by Reinhold Schlegelmilch in 1869 and closed in 1917. The Tillowitz factory was established in 1895 by Erhard Schlegelmilch, Reinhold's son. This china customarily bears the phrase "R.S. Germany" and "R.S. Tillowitz." The Tillowitz factory closed in 1945, but it was reopened for a few years under Polish administration.

Prices are high and collectors should beware of the forgeries that sometimes find their way onto the market. Mold names and numbers are taken from Mary Frank Gaston's books on R.S. Prussia.

The "Prussia" and "R.S. Suhl" marks have been reproduced, so buy with care. Later copies of these marks are well done, but quality of porcelain is inferior to the production in the 1890-1920 era.

Collectors are also interested in the porcelain products made by the Erdmann Schlegelmilch factory. This factory was founded by three brothers in Suhl in 1861. They named the factory in honor of their father, Erdmann Schlegelmilch. A variety of marks incorporating the "E.S." initials were used. The factory closed circa 1935. The Erdmann Schlegelmilch factory was an earlier and entirely separate business from the Reinhold Schlegelmilch factory. The two were not related to each other.

R.S. Prussia & Related Marks

R.S. Germany

R.S. Germany Berry Set with Roses

Berry set: 10" d. master bowl & six sauce bowls; each decorated w/a border band of pale pink & white roses on a shaded pink to white ground, gold border band, two sauces w/chips, the set (ILLUS.)......... **$161**

R.S. Prussia

Lily Mold R.S. Prussia Bowl with Roses

Bowl, 10" d., Lily mold (Mold 29), large pale blue rim blossoms alternating w/clusters of small pink roses, a large cluster of pink roses against a teal blue ground in the center, unmarked (ILLUS.)........................... **173**

R.S. Prussia Bowl with Roses

Bowl, 10 1/2" d., Grape mold (Mold No. 2), decorated w/a large red & white rose w/green leaves inside, the sides & border in shaded dark blue, green & yellow w/a touch of red, minute under-rim flake (ILLUS.) **184**

Bowl, 10 1/2" d., Mold 211, heavy gold trim on the outer scalloped rim, the interior lobes decorated w/clusters of pink roses w/a larger central cluster (ILLUS., top next page).. **288**

Mold 211 R.S. Prussia Bowl with Roses

Mold 79 R.S. Prussia Bowl with Roses

Bowl, 10 1/2" d., Mold 79, five shaded deep teal reserves alternating w/creamy fanned devices, the center decorated w/yellow, white & pink roses (ILLUS.) **184**

Mold 80 Floral Bowl Trimmed in Green

Bowl, 10 1/2" d., Mold 80, shaded green border arches alternating w/white double scrolls, five shaded green interior panels outlining a white five-petal design filled w/a large bouquet of red, pink & yellow roses & green leaves (ILLUS.) **207**

R.S. Prussia Mold 97 Floral Bowl

Bowl, 10 1/2" d., Mold 97, red-tipped white fanned border panels alternating w/pale peach arched panels highlighted w/small pink floral cluster, a large cluster of pink & red roses in the center (ILLUS.) **196**

Mold 182 Bowl with White Lilies

Bowl, 11" d., Mold 182, the small scalloped border decorated w/cream on green lily blossoms or a small cluster of white blossoms, the center a large cluster of white lilies & blossoms amid green leaves (ILLUS.).. **150**

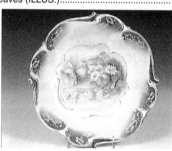

R.S. Prussia Scroll-bordered Bowl

Bowl, 11" d., molded double C-scrolls around the border enclosing deep teal panels, the center decorated w/reflected red roses & white daisies (ILLUS.).............. **184**

Mold 642 Chocolate Pot with Florals

R.S. Prussia Tea Set with Alternating Decorative Panels

Chocolate pot, cov., Mold 642, gold sprig & scroll trim at the top & base, the sides decorated w/various scattered blossoms in pink, white & lavender on a white ground, satin finish, 10" h. (ILLUS., previous page) **374**

R.S. Prussia Carnation Mold Cracker Jar

Cracker jar, cov., Carnation mold, long oval form w/scalloped base & embossed floral rim, ornate pointed double loop handle, the rim blossoms in pale blue against a green ground, pink & blue florals around the body w/a stenciled band of scrolling florals around the base, minor flakes, unmarked, 9" l. (ILLUS.).................................. **230**

Mold 510 Rose-decorated Cracker Jar

Cracker jar, cov., Mold 510, squatty bulbous form w/flaring scalloped rim & rolled side loop handles, gold rim & base band, the sides decorated w/a large bouquet of pink roses & green leaves on a shaded green to white ground, 6" h. (ILLUS.) **184**

Mold 627 Cracker Jar with Large Florals

Cracker jar, cov., Mold 627, gilt-trimmed leafy scroll handles & gilt-trimmed panels flanking wide panels w/bouquet of pink & white flowers & green leaves, gold-trimmed tab feet, minor roughness, 7" h. (ILLUS.)... **259**

Tea set: cov. teapot, cov. sugar bowl, creamer & cup & saucer; lobed waisted bodies w/ruffled rims, decorated w/alternating panels of gold floral decoration on cream ground bordered w/green leafy vines & cream flowers on pale blue/grey ground, gold trim over all, the set (ILLUS., top of page) **350-400**

Tea set: cov. teapot, cov. sugar bowl, creamer, cup & saucer; Mold 704, slender paneled tapering bodies, angled handles, ruffled rims, short feet, decorated w/delicate pink flowers, green vining leaves & Cupids, gold trim, early 20th c., the set (ILLUS., top next page)............. **300-350**

R.S. Prussia Mold 704 Tea Set

Two Unmarked R.S. Prussia Teapots

Teapot, cov., egg-shaped body on a round pedestal foot, decorated w/dainty white flowers & green leaves on pastel green, pink, beige & white ground, unmarked, 7" d., 6 1/4" h. (ILLUS. left, above)........ **135-150**

R.S. Prussia Medallion Teapot

Teapot, cov., Medallion mold (Mold 631), waisted paneled body w/ruffled scalloped rim, four short feet, angled handle, serpentine spout, lid w/cut-out finial, cobalt blue base w/gold vining decoration, body w/scene of sailing vessel on water w/cliffs rising on either side, gold beading at rim & finial, gold line decoration on handle & spout (ILLUS.)...................................... **350-450**

Teapot, cov., Mold 474, Laurel Wreath patt., exotic form w/squatty bulbous bottom tapering to a tall narrow trumpet neck w/scalloped rim, tall shoulder spout, angular openwork handle, domed cover w/pointed finial, 8 3/4" h. (ILLUS., next page)... **800-1,400**

R.S. Prussia Mold 616 Teapot

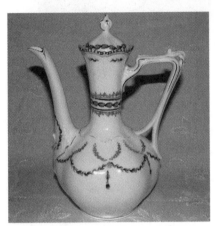

Unusual R.S. Prussia Mold 474 Teapot

Teapot, cov., Mold 616, tall inverted pear-shaped body on a ribbed & paneled pedestal base, ornate C-scroll handle, long spout, domed cover w/pointed finial, decorated w/a large bouquet of pink roses, gold trim, 7 1/4" h. (ILLUS., top of page)
.... **800-1,400**

R.S. Prussia Young Lovers Teapot

Teapot, cov., spherical body w/flaring ruffled rim & short foot, C-scroll handle, slightly serpentine spout, peaked inset lid, decorated w/gold filigree & line decoration & central scene of lovers holding hands in pastoral landscape, a large deep pink rose above them & leafy garlands cascading on either side (ILLUS.)
.... **200-250**

Teapot, cov., squatty bulbous body w/wide shoulder raised on a square pedestal foot, decorated w/pink roses & green leaves on a pastel green ground, unmarked, 7 1/2" d., 5 3/4" h. (ILLUS. right w/unmarked egg-shaped teapot, middle previoius page) **135-150**

R.S. Prussia Sweet Gum Ball Teapot

Teapot, cov., Sweet Gum Ball mold, lobed bulbous body on short feet, tapering in at shoulder to flaring cut-out ruffled neck, cut-out angled handle, slightly curved spout, domed inset lid w/finial, decorated w/shadow leaves in shades of green & blue/green & embellished w/embossing & line decoration, rare mold (ILLUS.)........... **475**

Other Marks

Bowl, 10" d., Mold 468, a large central color scene of a courting couple in 18th c. costume, the fancy border composed of pointed arched panels in dark green trimmed in gold & an outer deep red border panel w/fancy gilt & decorated w/six small floral reserves, green E.S. Saxe mark (ILLUS., next page)............................ **150**

R.S. Poland Tea Set

Fancy E.S. Saxe Bowl with Color Scene

Tea set: cov. teapot, cov. sugar bowl & creamer; Mold 601, each w/ovoid body, scrolled loop handle, domed lid w/finial, disk foot, decorated w/draping band of shadow leaves in pale blue/green shades & gold trim, R.S. Poland, early 20th c., the set (ILLUS., top of page) **450-500**

R.S. Poland Teapot with Oak Branches

Teapot, cov., squatty bulbous shape tapering to rim, short foot, angled handle, slightly serpentine spout, peaked cut-out lid, double-marked "RS Poland," decorated w/oak branch w/leaves & acorns & shadow leaves, line decoration on spout, handle, foot, rim & lid, R.S. Poland (ILLUS.).. **375**

Red Wing

Various potteries operated in Red Wing, Minnesota, from 1868, the most successful being the Red Wing Stoneware Co., organized in 1878. Merged with other local potteries through the years, it became known as Red Wing Union Stoneware Co. in 1894, and was one of the largest producers of utilitarian stoneware items in the United States. After a decline in the popularity of stoneware products, an art pottery line was introduced to compensate for the loss. This was reflected in a new name for the company, Red Wing Potteries, Inc., in 1930. Stoneware production ceased entirely in 1947, but vases, planters, cookie jars and dinnerwares of art pottery quality continued in production until 1967, when the pottery ceased operation altogether.

Red Wing Marks

Art Pottery

Modernistic Red Wing Bowl

Bowl, 7 5/8" d., 5" h., deep rounded sides, white exterior & black interior, on a black rectangular plinth base, impressed "Red Wing U.S.A. 1333" (ILLUS., previous page) **$259**

Gondola-shaped Red Wing Bowl

Bowl, 8 3/8" l., 5 1/2" h., stylized gondola-shaped body tapering to arched rolled ends, white exterior & black interior, on a rectangular black plinth, impressed "1370" (ILLUS.) **150**

Red Wing Pottery Cookie Jar

Cookie jar, cov., barrel-shaped w/molded rim & wide cover w/disk finial, molded in relief w/cattails & the word "Cookies" against a stippled ground, dark brown bands at the rim & base w/tan center (ILLUS.)............ **250-300**

Red Wing Nokomis Line Cruet

Cruet w/original stopper, Nokomis Line, footed ovoid body w/an integral upright slender long spout joined w/a flat brace to the cylindrical ringed neck, curved handle from neck to shoulder, original cap-form stopper, overall mottled & drippy glaze in shades of green & brown, blue ink label, 8 3/4" h. (ILLUS.) **633**

Red Wing Nokomis Line Jug

Jug, Nokomis Line, bulbous ovoid body tapering to a cylindrical neck w/flared rim, small angled handle from rim to shoulder, overall mottled & drippy glaze in shades of green & brown, Shape No. 204, blue company ink stamp mark, 9 1/2" h. (ILLUS.) **460**

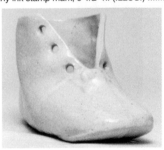

Model of a Miniature Baby Shoe

Model of a baby shoe, miniature, overall white glaze (ILLUS.)............................. **450-550**

Miniature Red Wing Spaniel Dog

Model of a dog, miniature, Staffordshire-style seated spaniel, white glaze w/blue eyes, 3" h. (ILLUS., previous page) **250-300**

Modern Style Red Wing Planter

Planter, modernistic upright flattened domed shape w/a recessed arching panel, dark brown glaze, No. B1418 (ILLUS.) **41**

Rare Red Wing Florist-style Vase

Vase, advertising florist-type, cylindrical w/flared base & molded flat rim, white glaze trimmed w/blue bands & blue rectangle enclosing "Alpha Floral Co.," early 20th c. (ILLUS.) **1,000-1,200**

Red Wing Nokomis Line Ovoid Vase

Vase, 7 1/4" h., Nokomis Line, simple ovoid body tapering to a small flat mouth, over-

all mottled streaky brown, green & blue glaze, Shape No. 206, round inkstamp mark, various tiny pinprick depressions in the glaze (ILLUS.) **230**

Tall Red Wing Nokomis Line Vase

Vase, 10 1/8" h., Nokomis Line, footed squatty cushion-form base tapering to a tall cylindrical neck w/a flaring rim, overall mottled & drippy glaze in shades of green & brown, Shape No. 196, Red Wing blue stamp mark (ILLUS.) **345**

Red Wing Nokomis Line Vase

Vase, 10 1/4" h., Nokomis Line, simple ovoid body w/a short wide cylindrical neck, overall mottled & drippy glaze in shades of green & brown, Shape No. 203 (ILLUS.) **690**

Red Wing Nokomis Vase with Tall Neck

Vase, 10 3/8" h., Nokomis Line, swelled cylindrical body w/a narrow shoulder & wide

More Common Red Wing Ashtray

tapering neck w/a flat mouth, overall mottled & drippy glaze in shades of green & brown, blue Red Wing ink mark, Shape 208 (ILLUS.) **575**

Brushed & Glazed Wares

Red Wing Brushed Ware Lion Vase

Vase, 7 1/2" h., Lion patt., bulbous ovoid body w/a wide round shoulder to the short wide flaring neck, lightly molded around the sides w/walking lions, overall mottled drippy glossy ochre-green & brown glaze above a matte lower body,

No. 164S, ca. 1931, couple of tiny base chips (ILLUS.) **127**

Dinnerwares & Novelties

Ashtray, earthenware, model of a wing w/a deep red glaze, bottom marked earthenware, "Red Wing Potteries" (ILLUS., top of page) **50-60**

Red Wing Pottery Bob White Teapot

Teapot, cov., Bob White patt., cream ground h.p. w/stylized quails, ca. 1956, 7 1/2" h. (ILLUS.) **125**

Teapot, cov., Village Green patt. **22**

Teapot, cover & stand, Bob White patt., the set **140**

Stoneware & Utility Wares

Two Views of a Maroon Baking Dish with Interior Advertising

Two Cylindrical Red Wing Beater Jars

Baking dish, advertising-type, wide flat bottom w/deep sides w/molded graduating bands, overall glossy maroon glaze, dark blue printed advertising on inside bottom (ILLUS. of two views, bottom previous page) **375-425**

Beater jar, advertising-type, cylindrical w/molded flat rim, white-glazed w/blue bands & blue advertising reading "Red Wing Beater Jar - Eggs - Cream - Salad Dressing" (ILLUS. left with similar advertising beater jar, top of page) **125-150**

Beater jar, advertising-type, cylindrical w/molded flat rim, white-glazed w/blue bands & blue South Dakota advertising (ILLUS. right with similar Red Wing Beater Jar, top of page) **275-325**

Red Wing Saffron Ware Ribbed & Banded Bowl

Bowl, nappie-style, Saffron ware, ribbed sides below the wide flat rim decorated w/a white band flanked by thin brown bands (ILLUS.) **250-300**

Rare Small Paneled & Sponged Bowl

Bowl, 5" d., deep rounded paneled sides & a wide molded rim, overall red & blue sponging on white (ILLUS.) **550-650**

Large Paneled & Sponged Bowl

Bowl, 11" d., deep rounded paneled sides & a wide molded rim, overall red & blue sponging on white (ILLUS., top of page) **325-350**

Miniature Commemorative Butter Churn

Butter churn, cov., miniature, advertising- and commemorative-type, swelled cylindrical body w/a flared rim, eared handles & original cover w/wooden dasher, white-glazed w/blue script number above a pair of printed birch leaves above a printed oval w/advertising, also marked "Iowa Chapter Red Wing Collectors Society 2nd Annual Conf. 1994," 4" h. (ILLUS.) **127**

Small 2-Gallon Red Wing Butter Churn

Butter churn, cov., tapering cylindrical body w/molded rim & inset cover, white-glazed w/a large blue printed size number above a 4" red wing mark & the blue oval Red Wing Union Stoneware mark, 2 gal. (ILLUS.).. **475-525**

Very Rare Red Wing 4-Gallon Churn

Butter churn, tall slightly tapering cylindrical salt-glazed body w/thick molded rim & eared handles, cobalt blue slip-quilled "4" above a large leaf, impressed Red Wing Stoneware mark on the side, 4 gal. (ILLUS.) **3,000-3,500**

Very Large Red Wing Butter Crock

Butter crock, wide cylindrical body w/molded rim, white-glazed, printed w/a large dark blue rectangle w/"20 lbs." above a 4" red wing mark, 20 lb. (ILLUS.) **1,000-1,200**

Half-Gallon Advertising Honey Crock

Crock, advertising-type, cylindrical w/molded rim, white glaze printed in black w/an oval enclosing Wisconsin honey advertising, 1/2 gal. (ILLUS.)................. **200-250**

1-Gallon Crock with Large Wing Mark

Crock, cylindrical w/molded rim, white glaze printed w/the large 4" red wing logo, 1 gal. (ILLUS.) **500-600**

2-Gallon Nebraska Advertising Crock

Crock, advertising-type, cylindrical w/molded rim, white glaze printed in black w/a script "2" above an oval enclosing Nebraska advertising, 2 gal. (ILLUS.) **2,000-2,500**

Minnesota Stoneware 2-Gallon Crock

Crock, cylindrical w/molded rim, white glaze printed in black w/a script "2" above two elephant ear leaves & an oval Minnesota Stoneware Company mark, 2 gal. (ILLUS.) **125-150**

Red Wing Crock with Wing & Oval Marks

Crock, cylindrical w/molded rim, white glaze printed w/a large blue size number, large red wing logo & the oval mark of the Red Wing Union Stoneware Company, 5 gal. (ILLUS.).. **175-200**

Crock, cylindrical w/molded rim & eared handle, white glaze w/fancy printed blue marking "Fresh Oysters," 6 gal. (ILLUS., next page) **2,000-2,500**

Two Views of Rare Labeled Minnesota Stoneware Miniature Jug

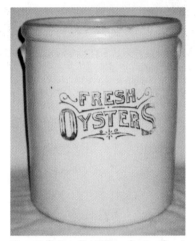

Rare 6-Gallon Red Wing Oyster Crock

Advertising Beehive Jug with Birch Leaves

Jug, beehive-shaped, advertising-type, white glaze, printed blue birch leaves mark & an oval panel w/Kansas advertising (ILLUS.)...................................... **2,500-3,000**

Jug, miniature, beehive-shaped, overall dark brown glaze, original yellow paper label for the Minnesota Stoneware Company on the base, 1/8 pt. (ILLUS. of side & bottom, top of page) **1,000-1,200**

Very Rare Gallon Red Wing Fruit Jar

Fruit (or canning) jar, dome-top style, twist-on metal lid, printed blue shield logo of the Red Wing Union Stoneware Company, 1 gal. (ILLUS.) **4,500-5,500**

Minnesota-Michigan Miniature Jug

Jug, miniature, fancy-style, white base & brown shoulder, printed in blue "Minnesota - Michigan," 1/8 pt. (ILLUS.).......... **275-325**

Unique Cherry Band Advertising Pitcher

Pitcher, 9 1/4" h., embossed Cherry Band patt., advertising-type, white glaze w/large blue rectangle w/unique printed image of a two-story store above advertising dated 1914 (ILLUS.) **3,000-3,500**

Very Rare Red Wing Sponged Hall Boy

Pitcher, 9 1/4" h., tall cylindrical hall-boy style w/molded rings, overall red & blue sponging (ILLUS.) **3,500-4,000**

Red Wing Advertising Refrigerator Jar

Refrigerator jar, advertising-type, short cylindrical stacking-type w/molded rim, white glaze decorated w/blue band & printed w/advertising for a Nebraska merchant, early 20th c. (ILLUS.) **500-600**

Very Rare Red Wing Stoneware Spittoon

Spittoon, deep cylindrical salt-glazed form w/top opening & oval side drain opening, double-stamped on the side "Red Wing Stoneware Company" (ILLUS.) **3,000-3,500**

Rare Sponged Red Wing Umbrella Stand

Umbrella stand, cylindrical w/flaring molded base & banded rim, overall red & blue sponging, 18" h. (ILLUS.) **2,000-2,500**

Water cooler, cov., hand-thrown ovoid wide body w/molded rim, white glazed w/blue bands, large 4" red wing mark & oval Red Wing Union Stoneware mark, "Water Cooler" in blue, "2" on inside bottom, 2 gal., no spigot, rare (ILLUS., top next page) **5,000-6,000**

Rare Hand-thrown Red Wing Cooler

Very Rare Red Wing Stoneware Cooler

Water cooler, slightly tapering cylindrical salt-glazed body w/molded rim & eared handle, molded hexagonal spigot hole at bottom front, blue slip-quilled "8" above a stylized daisy, side stamped "Red Wing Stoneware Co.," 8 gal. (ILLUS.).... **8,000-10,000**

Redware

Red earthenware pottery was made in the American colonies from the late 1600s. Bowls, crocks and all types of utilitarian wares were turned out in great abundance to supplement the pewter and handmade treenware. The ready availability of the clay, the same used in making bricks and roof tiles, accounted for the vast production. The lead-glazed redware retained its reddish color, although a variety of colors could be obtained by adding various metals to the glaze. Interesting effects occurred accidentally through unsuspected impurities in the clay or uneven temperatures in the firing kiln, which sometimes resulted in streaks or mottled splotches.

Redware pottery was seldom marked by the maker.

Apple butter jar, bulbous ovoid body w/a wide flat thin molded rim, fine mottled brownish green alkaline glaze, probably New York state origin, excellent condition, ca. 1830, 6" h. **$275**

Scarce Redware Butter Churn

Butter churn, ovoid form w/two sides handles, partial brown glaze, incised decoration of star punch, swag & waves in eight horizontal rows, possibly Maine, 19th c., chips, cracks & missing pieces, overall 14 1/2" h... **2,588**

Rare Signed Redware Crock

Crock, wide ovoid body w/a wide flat rim, interior brown glaze, exterior w/incised line at shoulder above stamped mark of Benjamin Dodge, Portland, Maine, 19th c., one small rim chip, 7 1/4" d., 8 1/4" h. (ILLUS.) **1,898**

Dish, shallow round form, reddish brown interior glaze, probably made in Pennsylvania, 19th c., 8" d., 1 3/4" h. (minor surface wear) 55

Flowerpot, tapering cylindrical form w/flat molded rim, unglazed, impressed mark of A. Wilcox, West Bloomfield, New York, ca. 1850, 6 1/4" h. (dime-sized chip at rim) 110

Food mold, Turk's turban form, mottled red & brown alkaline glaze, ca. 1850, 9 1/2" d., 3" h. (couple of surface chips on exterior) 44

Food mold, Turk's turban form, brown peppered alkaline glaze, attributed to the Wilcox factory, West Bloomfield, New York, early 19th c., 10 1/2" d., 3 3/4" h. (minor surface wear at bottom) 44

Jar, footed bulbous ovoid body tapering to a wide flat flared neck, applied eared handles, incised linear bands on neck & shoulder, dark brown splotches on a dark orangish red ground, eastern United States, early 19th c., 10 1/4" h. (glaze wear on rim & handle edges, few base chips) 470

Redware Milk Bowl with Sponging

Milk bowl, deep flat angled sides w/molded flat rim, dark brown sponged bands up the exterior & around the rim, leadglazed, 19th c., 11" d. (ILLUS.) 288

Mug, very tall slender cylindrical form w/C-form handle, overall brick red alkaline glaze, unsigned but attributed to the redware factory in Bergholtz, New York, ca. 1860, 10" h. (minor chipping at base & rim) 99

Preserve jar, cov., flat-bottomed cylindrical form curving up to a wide flat cupped mouth w/an inset flat cover w/button finial, fine burnt orange peppered glaze, attributed to the Wilcox factory, Bloomfield or Morganville, New York, ca. 1840, 8" h. (surface wear on rim chip, few surface chips at base, rim chipping on cover) 165

Early Redware Salt Dip

Salt dip, round foot & short wide stem supporting a deep rounded bowl w/flat rim, mottled brown alkaline glaze, ca. 1850, excellent condition, 2 1/4" h. (ILLUS.)........... 66

Redware Teapot Glazed in Drippy Blue

Teapot, cov., wide slightly waisted cylindrical body w/a thin shoulder & low flat neck, serpentine spout & C-scroll handle, inset cover w/button finial, ivory-colored base clay covered in a mottled runny dark blue, the base & interior glazed in dark reddish brown, 19th c., minor glaze flakes on spout, 5 1/2" h. (ILLUS.) 138

Rockingham Wares

The Marquis of Rockingham first established an earthenware pottery in the Yorkshire district of England around 1745, and it was occupied afterwards by various potters. The well-known mottled brown Rockingham glaze was introduced about 1788 by the Brameld Brothers and became immediately popular. It was during the 1820s that the production of true porcelain began at the factory, and it continued to be made until the firm closed in 1842. Since that time the so-called Rockingham glaze has been used by various potters in England and the United States, including some famous wares produced in Bennington, Vermont. Very similar glazes were also used by potteries in other areas of the United States including Ohio and Indiana, but only wares specifically attributed to Bennington should use that name. The following listings will include mainly wares featuring the dark brown mottled glaze produced at various sites here and abroad.

Bowl, 10 1/2" d., 3" h., flat bottomed w/deep canted sides, yellowware w/overall dark mottled brown glaze, molded ribbing on exterior bottom, late 19th - early 20th c., excellent condition **$66**

Bowl, 11" d., 5" h., small footring below the wide deep rounded sides w/a thick molded & rolled rim, the exterior molded w/a repeating design of columns, yellowware w/overall dark brown mottled glaze, late 19th - early 20th c. (minor surface wear, small shallow stone ping on interior)............. 99

Bowl, 11 1/2" d., 3 3/4" h., footring below the wide rounded bowl w/a flaring rolled rim, yellowware w/overall dark mottled brown glaze, molded pattern of columns around the sides, late 19th c. (short hairline at rim extending from worn small chip) 44

Coffeepot, cov., miniature, tapering cylindrical body w/a large rim spout & angled handle, inset cover w/knob finial, yellow-

Rockingham Creamer & Hound-handled Pitcher

ware w/overall dark brown mottled glaze, uncommon form, late 19th c., 4 1/2" h. **358**

Creamer, footring below the bulbous ovoid body tapering to a curved rim w/broad upright spout & C-scroll handle, each side molded in relief w/a fancy scrolled oval frame enclosing the bust profile of a man, yellowware w/very dark brown mottled glaze, late 19th c., 4 1/2" h. **121**

Creamer, tapering ovoid body w/an undulating rim & wide arched spout, C-scroll handle, yellowware w/overall mottled dark brown Rockingham glaze, 19th c., 5 1/2" h. (ILLUS. left with hound-handled pitcher, top of page) **44**

man snorting snuff on each side, overall dark mottled brown Rockingham glaze, possibly Bennington, Vermont, or East Liverpool, Ohio, excellent condition, first half 19th c., 7 1/2" h. (ILLUS.) **248**

Early Rockingham Ware Foot Warmer

Foot warmer, wide flattened half-round form w/two molded indentations on the top for feet, a small spout at the top end, overall mottled brown glaze, American-made, ca. 1860, underside crazing, small flakes in the glaze, 7" w., 10" h. (ILLUS.) **230**

Mug, waisted cylindrical form w/molded base band, C-form strap handle, yellowware w/finely mottled dark brown glaze, excellent condition, late 19th c., 3 1/2" h. **77**

Mug, cylindrical w/molded base band, C-form handle, yellowware w/boldly spotted overall mottled brown glaze, excellent condition, late 19th c., 3 3/4" h. **358**

Pie plate, round flat-bottomed form w/canted sides, yellowware w/overall light mottled brown glaze, late 19th c., 9 1/2" d. (minor glaze crazing on bottom, rim chip) **33**

Pie plate, round flat-bottomed form w/canted sides, yellowware w/overall finely speckled dark mottled brown glaze, late 19th c., 9 1/2" d. (tight clay separation line down from rim from firing) **66**

Early Flask with Scene of Man Taking Snuff

Flask, flattened ovoid body w/small neck, yellowware molded in relief w/an oval reserve enclosing a half-length portrait of a

Pie plate, round flat-bottomed form w/canted sides, yellowware w/overall bold dark mottled brown glaze, late 19th c., 9 3/4" d. (surface wear at bottom edge, minor glaze wear on interior)........................... **44**

Pie plate, round flat-bottomed form w/canted sides, yellowware w/overall dark mottled brown glaze, late 19th c., 9 3/4" d. (minor glaze wear on bottom) **66**

Pie plate, round flat-bottomed form w/canted sides, yellowware w/overall boldly spotted dark mottled brown glaze, late 19th c., 10 1/4" d. (minor surface wear on bottom, tight hairline from rim into bottom)................... **55**

Pie plate, round flat-bottomed form w/canted sides, yellowware w/overall bold dark mottled brown glaze, late 19th c., 10 3/4" d. (very tight hairline down from rim to center bottom) **22**

Hound-handled Molded Rockingham Pitcher

Pitcher, 6 1/2" h., hound-handled, flat-bottomed swelled cylindrical body w/a flattened shoulder to the neck w/a wide arched spout, the body molded in relief w/a continuous hound & deer hunting scene, molded vine band around the neck, yellowware w/overall dark brown Rockingham glaze, possibly West Troy Factory, Troy, New York, ca. 1860, excellent condition (ILLUS.)............................ **275**

Rockingham Pitcher with Hunting Scene

Pitcher, 6 1/2" h., hound-handled, wide bulbous body w/a flattened shoulder to the wide flared neck & wide arched spout, relief-molded w/stag hunting scene, overall very dark brown glaze, possibly Bennington, Vermont, ca. 1850 (ILLUS.) **144**

Pitcher, 8" h., footed paneled body w/large pointed petals at the bottom of each side panel, shaped rim w/wide arched spout, C-scroll handle, yellowware w/overall dark mottled brown glaze, 19th c. (very minor chip at rim)... **66**

Pitcher, 8 1/4" h., cylindrical w/a molded design of a peacock & palm trees on each side, yellowware w/overall dark brown mottled glaze, excellent condition, late 19th c. **88**

Pitcher, 8 1/2" h., hound-handled, footed baluster-form body w/a wide arched spout, the body deeply molded w/a design of hanging dead game including ducks, rabbits & a fox, yellowware w/overall dark brown mottled Rockingham glaze, few minor glaze wear spots, rare design, mid-19th c. (ILLUS. right with creamer, top previous page)................ **248**

Hound-handled Rockingham Pitcher

Pitcher, 9 1/2" h., yellowware w/overall mottled dark brown glaze, molded hound handle, wide baluster form shape molded in relief w/eight panels of hanging game & fowl, a molded eagle under the wide spout, minor hairline in bottom, minor glaze wear, ca. 1850 (ILLUS.) **121**

Platter, 9 1/2 x 12 1/2", wide rectangular form w/canted corners & shallow angled sides, yellowware w/overall finely mottled dark brown glaze, 19th c. (some glaze wear & surface scratching from use) **176**

Rockingham Rebecca at the Well Teapot

Teapot, cov., footed ovoid body w/swan's-neck spout & C-form handle, domed cover w/bud-form finial, mottled brown glaze w/relief-molded scene of Rebecca at the well, early 20th c., Ohio, 8 1/2" h. (ILLUS.) **200**

Rockingham Gothic Arch Tobacco Jar

Tobacco jar, cov., wide molded base below the paneled body w/a large Gothic arch in each panel, wide rolled rim & inset cover w/knob handle, molded leaf scroll side handles, overall dark brown mottled glaze, attributed to Bennington, Vermont, ca. 1847-58, some nicks on top rim, cover replaced, 8" w., 8 1/2" h. (ILLUS.) **288**

Unusual Rockingham Washboard

Washboard, rectangular wooden frame enclosing a yellowware washboard w/a mottled brown glaze, minor glaze wear, overall wear to frame, ca. 1880, 25" h. (ILLUS.).. **550**

Rookwood

Considered America's foremost art pottery, the Rookwood Pottery Company was established in Cincinnati, Ohio, in 1880 by Mrs. Maria Nichols Longworth Storer. To accurately record its development, each piece carried the Rookwood insignia or mark, was dated, and, if individually decorated, was usually signed by the artist. The pot-

tery remained in Cincinnati until 1959, when it was sold to Herschede Hall Clock Company and moved to Starkville, Mississippi, where it continued in operation until 1967.

A private company is now producing a limited variety of pieces using original Rookwood molds.

Rookwood Mark

Early Silver-overlaid Rookwood Basket

Basket, squatty rounded shape w/the sides folded up and the ends pulled out, a broad peaked handle from side to side, Standard glaze decorated w/yellow flowers & buds & large green leaves against a shaded dark to light brown ground, decorated w/silver overlay in a leafy scroll design around the ends, rim & handle, silver marked by the Gorham Mfg. Co., breaks & losses to silver, 1893, Harriet Wilcox, 7 x 10 1/2" (ILLUS.).................... **$2,185**

Rookwood Standard Glaze Humidor

Humidor, cov., wide gently tapering cylindrical body w/a low flaring serpentine rim & inside flat cover w/knob finial, Standard glaze, decorated w/a scene of two Native American dancers against a dark brown to brownish green ground, 1893, Harriet Wilcox, 6 1/2" d., 6 1/2" h. (ILLUS.) **1,115**

Tall Rookwood Mug with Portrait

Mug, tankard-type, base band & tall tapering cylindrical sides w/an angled handle, Standard glaze, decorated w/a three-quarters length portrait of a Native American, Chief Mountain (Big Brave) - Blackfeet, against a dark green to golden yellow ground, 1899, Grace Young, 6 1/2" d., 7 1/2" h. (ILLUS.) **4,600**

Paperweight, model of a seated squirrel on a half-round log, bluish green matte glaze, No. 6025, 1928, 4 1/4" h. **303**

Tall Rookwood Silver-overlaid Pitcher

Pitcher, 10" h., 5" d., tankard-type, a base band below the tall tapering slender body w/a small rim spout & squared handle, Standard glaze decorated w/a school of green fish against a shaded yellow to orange ground, further decorated w/silver overlay pierced scrolls around the base & a grapevine around the rim, a silver-clad handle, silver marked by the Gorham Mfg. Co., 1894, Matthew Daly (ILLUS.) **3,335**

Lovely Rookwood Porcelain Landscape Plaque

Plaque, long horizontal rectangular form, decorated w/a misty lakeside landscape w/trees in the foreground, in shades of dark & light green, blue, grey & lavender, in a wide flat oak frame, 1922, E. Timothy Hurley, glaze miss, plaque 4 x 8" (ILLUS.) **4,313**

Extraordinary Rookwood Portrait Vase

Very Rare Rookwood Sea Green Vase

Vase, 12 7/8" h., slender tapering cylindrical form w/a flaring rim, Sea Green glaze, decorated w/a large fish swimming among sea grass, in shades of green against a pale yellow ground, 1899, Albert Valentien (ILLUS.)............................ **17,925**

Vase, 16" h., 15" w., pillow-type, wide flattened & rounded form w/a narrow pinched-in rim, Standard glaze, decorated w/a large bust portrait of the Native American Chief Hollow Horn Bear - Sioux, against a shaded dark brown to orange & green ground, 1900, Matthew Daley (ILLUS., top of page).................... **74,750**

Vase, 23 1/2" h., 11" d., broad ovoid body tapering to a wide cylindrical neck w/a flared rim, Limoges-style, the body decorated w/a continuous Japanese-inspired

Very Early Rookwood Vase

scene of birds perched on blossoming branches against a tan ground highlighted w/brown & white, the neck in dark green w/a gold rim, 1883, Albert Valentien (ILLUS.)... **5,750**

Rose Medallion & Rose Canton

The lovely Chinese ware known as Rose Medallion was made through the past century and into the present one. It features alternating panels of people and flowers or insects, with most pieces having four medallions with a central rose or peony medallion. The ware is called Rose Canton if florals and birds or insects fill all the panels. Unless otherwise noted, our listing is for Rose Medallion ware.

Rose Medallion Pitcher & Covered Vegetable Dishes

Pitcher, 6 3/4" h., flat-bottomed bulbous ovoid body tapering to a wide arched spout & arched loop handle, alternating panels of figures & birds among flowers, some gilt wear, late 19th c. (ILLUS. left with pair of vegetable dishes, top of page) **805**

Fine Rose Medallion Punch Bowl

Punch bowl, deep rounded sides, decorated around the exterior & interior w/alternating panels featuring domestic scenes or birds in gardens, border band of alternating floral panels, w/a carved wood stand, ca. 1800, 15 1/4" d., 6 1/4" h. (ILLUS.) **1,265**

Tall Rose Medallion Vase

Vase, 25" h., traditional form w/swelled cylindrical body tapering to a tall cylindrical neck w/a wide flattened rim, gilt figural foo dogs & salamanders at the shoulder, decorated w/large alternating figural & flower & butterfly panels, chip on bottom of base, late 19th c. (ILLUS.) **920**

Rose Medallion Vegetable Dish

Vegetable dish, cov., rectangular notched corners, the domed cover w/a large figural fruit finial & alternating panels of Chinese figures on parquet floors & bird, butterflies & flowers, interior of bottom w/matching design centering a bird perched on flowering branches w/a butterfly against a conforming ground w/a wide gold rim, the sides of the base w/four red & green floral sprays, heavy gilt wear, small chips to interior & base rim, ca. 1880, 10 x 10 3/4", 6 3/4" h. (ILLUS.) **920**
Vegetable dishes, cov., low oval form w/a wide flattened flanged rim w/serpentine edge, low domed cover w/pine cone finial, decorated w/floral panels, 8 1/2 x 11", 4" h., pr. (ILLUS. right with pitcher) **690**

Roseville

Roseville Pottery Company operated in Zanesville, Ohio, from 1898 to 1954, having been in business for six years prior to that in Muskingum County, Ohio. Art wares similar to those of Owens and Weller Potteries were produced. Items listed here are by patterns or lines.

Roseville

Roseville Mark

Apple Blossom (1948)
White apple blossoms in relief on blue, green or pink ground; brown tree branch handles.

Blue Fanned Apple Blossom Basket

Basket, flattened fan-shaped body w/widely flaring arched rim, high round overhead branch handle, blue ground, No. 309-8", 8" h. (ILLUS.) **$175-275**

Green Fanned Apple Blossom Basket

Basket, flattened fan-shaped body w/widely flaring arched rim, high round overhead branch handle, green ground, No. 309-8", 8" h. (ILLUS.) **150**

Long Green Apple Blossom Basket

Basket, footed, long narrow body, low overhead branch handle, green ground, No. 310-10", 11 1/2" l., 10" h. (ILLUS.) **316**

Apple Blossom Round Candlesticks

Candlesticks, footed, spherical form w/small branch handles, green ground, No. 351-2", 2" h., pr. (ILLUS.) **92**

Tall Green Apple Blossom Ewer

Ewer, tall, footed, slender ovoid body w/a tall arched spout & branch handle, green ground, No. 318-15", 15" h. (ILLUS.) **374**
Jardiniere & pedestal base, green ground, jardiniere, No. 302-8", 8" h., pedestal, No. 305-8", 24 1/2" h., 2 pcs. (minor flake on foot of jardiniere) **690**
Teapot, cov., blue ground, No. 371-P **300**
Teapot, cov., pink ground, No. 371-P **250**

Spherical Green Apple Blossom Vase

Vase, 6" h., spherical body w/asymmetrical rim & handles, green ground, chips under base, No. 342-6" (ILLUS.) **173**

Baneda (1933)

Band of embossed pods, blossoms and leaves on green or raspberry pink ground.

Fine Footed Green Baneda Jardiniere

Jardiniere, footed, wide bulbous body w/wide flat mouth, two-handled, green ground, No. 626-5", 5" h. (ILLUS.) **690**

Footed Bulbous Pink Baneda Vase

Vase, 6" h., bulbous body w/slightly flaring rim, small loop shoulder handles, raspberry pink ground, gold Roseville sticker, glaze bruise inside one handle, minor glaze bursts, No. 591-6" (ILLUS.) **316**

Footed Bulbous Green Baneda Vase

Vase, 6" h., bulbous body w/slightly flaring rim, small loop shoulder handles, green ground, No. 591-6" (ILLUS.) **500**

Small Footed Bulbous Baneda Vase

Vase, 6 1/4" h., footed bulbous body w/short slightly flaring rim, small loop shoulder handles, raspberry pink ground, light glaze crazing, No. 591-6" (ILLUS.) **489**

Fine Raspberry Pink Baneda Vase

Vase, 7" h., footed wide cylindrical body tapering to short wide cylindrical neck, small loop handles, raspberry pink ground, No. 592-7" (ILLUS.) **575**

Cylindrical Pink Baneda Vase

Vase, 7 1/4" h., footed, swelled cylindrical body tapering to a short, wide, cylindrical neck flanked by small down-curved loop handles, raspberry pink ground, minor glaze skips, No. 590-7" (ILLUS., previous page) **350-450**

Raspberry Pink Bulbous Baneda Vase

Vase, 8" h., footed, globular w/shoulder handles, raspberry pink ground, small gold foil sticker, repair at base, No. 595-8" (ILLUS.) **431**

Large Green Baneda Vase

Vase, 9" h., cylindrical w/short collared neck, handles rising from shoulder to beneath rim, green ground, No. 594-9" (ILLUS.)...... **1,610**

Bushberry (1948)
Berries and leaves on blue, green or russet bark-textured ground; brown or green branch handles.

Green Bushberry Hanging Basket

Basket, hanging type w/original chains, green ground, pin nick on body, No. 465-5", 7" d. (ILLUS.) **173**

Bushberry Basket with Branch Handle

Basket, footed bulbous body w/wide uneven rim, long angular overhead branch handle, green ground, No. 370-8", 8" h. (ILLUS.).. **196**

Green Bushberry Book Ends

Book ends, green ground, No. 9, pr. (ILLUS.)... **200-300**

Bushberry Console Bowl & Flower Frog

Console bowl & flower frog, long, narrow boat-shaped bowl raised on a low forked branch pedestal forming pointed end handles & raised on an oval foot, No. 45 flower frog w/round low pedestal base, topped by a leaf & high curved & pointed open branch handle, green ground, bowl No. 1-10", 10" l., 2 pcs. (ILLUS.).................. **259**

Blue Bushberry Jardiniere

Jardiniere, 3" h., small side handles, globular, blue ground, No. 657-3" (ILLUS.)........... **138**
Teapot, cov., blue ground, No. 2............... **250-350**
Teapot, cov., russet ground, No. 2............ **150-250**

Tall Bushberry Blue Floor Vase

Vase, 18" h., floor type, footed baluster-form body w/angled branch shoulder handles, blue ground, two small chips to outer rim edge, No. 41-18" (ILLUS.)............................ **403**

Cherry Blossom (1933)

Sprigs of cherry blossoms, green leaves and twigs with pink fence against a combed blue-green ground or creamy ivory fence against a terra cotta ground shading to dark brown.

Terra Cotta Cherry Blossom Bowl-Vase

Bowl-vase, wide, squatty, bulbous body tapering to a wide, flat, molded mouth flanked by small loop handles, terra cotta ground, partial triangular sticker, No. 350-5", 5" h. (ILLUS.)................................... **259**

Pink & Blue Cherry Blossom Bowl-Vase

Bowl-vase, wide, squatty, bulbous body tapering to a wide, flat, molded mouth flanked by small loop handles, pink & blue ground, blisters in the flowers, No. 350-5", 5" h. (ILLUS.)................................... **288**

Bulbous Cherry Blossom Jardiniere

Jardiniere, squatty bulbous body w/a wide molded rim flanked by small loop handles, terra cotta ground, No. 627-5", 5" h. (ILLUS.)... **316**

Small Squatty Cherry Blossom Vase

Vase, 4" h., compressed squatty bulbous body w/a short, slightly flared neck flanked by small loop handles, pink & blue ground, some peppering in glaze, No. 617-3 1/2" (ILLUS.) **316**

Pink-Blue Ovoid Cherry Blossom Vase

Vase, 7" h., ovoid body w/tiny shoulder handles, pink & blue ground, No. 623-7" (ILLUS.) **403**

Ovoid Cherry Blossom Vase

Vase, 7" h., ovoid body w/tiny shoulder handles, terra cotta ground, unmarked, No. 623-7" (ILLUS.) **374**

Cylindrical Cherry Blossom Vase

Vase, 7 1/2" h., footed cylindrical body w/small loop handles near the rim, pink & blue ground, No. 620-7" (ILLUS.) **403**

Tall Cherry Blossom Vase

Vase, 10" h., slender ovoid body w/wide cylindrical neck, loop handles from shoulder to middle of neck, terra cotta ground, small glaze miss on rim, No. 626-10" (ILLUS.) **500**

Chloron (1907)

Molded in high relief in the manner of early Roman and Greek artifacts. Solid matte green glaze, sometimes combined with ivory. Very similar in form to Egypto.

Rare Chloron Fish-form Candleholder

Candleholder, chamberstick-type, oblong shallow fish-form base w/flat upright fishtail handle at one end, the shaft molded as upright folded green leaves around a bud-form candlesocket, No. 341-7", 7" h. (ILLUS.) **1,093**

Unusual Bubbled Chloron Vase

Vase, 8" h., wide squatty bulbous lower body w/overall large bubble-like raised design tapering to a ribbed neck flaring to a lobed, cupped rim w/low ruffled rim, uncommon & intricate Chloron inkstamp mark, bruise & nick at rim, No. 23-8" (ILLUS., previous page) **489**

Clematis (1944)

Clematis blossoms and heart-shaped green leaves against a vertically textured ground, white blossoms on blue, rose-pink blossoms on green and ivory blossoms on golden brown.

Blue Clematis Hanging Basket

Basket, hanging type, blue ground, no chains, No. 470-5", 5" h. (ILLUS.) **100-150**

Brown Clematis Basket with High Handle

Basket, waisted cylindrical body w/a high rounded arch overhead handle w/forked ends at each side, brown ground, No. 387-7" (ILLUS.) **173**

Green Clematis Long Console Bowl

Console bowl, long, low, narrow oblong form w/upright tiered sides & rim, pointed end handles, green ground w/pink blossoms, No. 458-10", 10" l. (ILLUS.) **100-150**

Brown Clematis Cookie Jar

Cookie jar, cov., brown ground, tiny glazed pit in body, No. 3-8", 8" h. (ILLUS.) **250-300**

Blue Clematis Cornucopia-Vase

Cornucopia-vase, flattened fanned & tiered sides w/angular handle at the front, resting on a rectangular base, blue ground, No. 193-6", 6" h. (ILLUS.) **75-85**

Cornucopia-vase, flattened fanned & tiered sides w/angular handle at the front, resting on a rectangular base, green ground w/pink blossom, No. 193-6", 6" h. **65-75**

Clematis Brown Creamer & Sugar

Creamer & open sugar bowl, brown ground, Nos. 5-C & 5-S, pr. (ILLUS.) **69**

Tall Blue Clematis Ewer

Ewer, footed squatty bulbous lower body tapering sharply to a tall forked neck w/a very tall arched spout, long pointed handle from rim to shoulder, blue ground, No. 17-10", 10 1/2" h. (ILLUS.) **125-175**

Brown Clematis Ewer

Ewer, footed squatty bulbous lower body tapering sharply to a tall forked neck w/a very tall arched spout, long pointed handle from rim to shoulder, brown ground w/creamy yellow flowers, No. 17-10", 10 1/2" h. (ILLUS.) **150-200**

Pale Green Clematis Ewer

Ewer, footed squatty bulbous lower body tapering sharply to a tall forked neck w/a very tall arched spout, long pointed han-

dle from rim to shoulder, shaded pale green ground w/white flowers, No. 17-10", 10 1/2" h. (ILLUS.) **104**
Teapot, cov., brown ground, No. 5, 7" h. .. **150-200**
Teapot, cov., green ground, No. 5 .... **150-200**

Green & Pink Clematis Vase

Vase, 8" h., footed bulbous ovoid body tapering to a short cylindrical neck flanked by pointed shoulder handles, green ground w/pink blossoms, No. 107-8" (ILLUS.) **161**

Tall Green & Pink Clematis Vase

Vase, 10 1/4" h., footed tall ovoid body w/a wide flat mouth flanked by small pointed loop handles, green ground w/pink flowers, No. 111-10" (ILLUS.) **138**

White & Blue Clematis Vase

Vase, 12 1/2" h., tall gently swelled cylindrical body w/a flat mouth, open angled handles near the rim, blue ground, No. 112-12" (ILLUS., previous page)........... **150-200**

Corinthian (1923)
Deeply fluted ivory and green body below a continuous band of molded grapevine, fruit, foliage and florals in naturalistic colors, narrow ivory and green molded border at the rim.

Footed 7" Corinthian Vase

Vase, 7" h., footed, swelled cylindrical sides w/molded neck band & flaring rim band, old gift shop sticker, slight firing line at base, No. 216-7" (ILLUS.)............................ **150**

Cosmos (1940)
Embossed blossoms against a wavy horizontal ridged band on a textured ground, ivory band with yellow and orchid blossoms on blue, blue band with white, and orchid blossoms on green or tan.

Small Green Cosmos Jardiniere

Jardiniere, two-handled, green ground, No. 649-3" (ILLUS.) **104**

Flared Rectangular Blue Cosmos Vase

Vase, 8 1/2" h., rectangular foot below the wide waisted rectangular body w/a flaring crenelated rim, low arch handles down the sides, blue ground, No. 950-8" (ILLUS.) **230**

Dahlrose (1924-28)
Band of ivory daisy-like blossoms and green leaves against a mottled tan ground.

Small Dahlrose Candleholders

Candleholders, angular handles rising from low slightly domed base, No. 1069-3", 3" h., pr. (ILLUS.) **150-250**

Oval Dahlrose Center Bowl

Center bowl, 11" l., footed oval squatty bulbous body tapering to a wide flared rim, angular end handles from rim to shoulder, No. 180-8" (ILLUS.) **260-290**

Footed Ovoid Dahlrose Vase

Vase, 8" h., small conical foot supporting the bulbous ovoid body w/a wide molded mouth flanked by tiny pointed shoulder handles, No. 365-8" (ILLUS.) **230**

Bulbous Dahlrose Vase

Vase, 8" h., footed, bulbous lower body w/a slightly tapering upper half below the molded incurved mouth, angled handles from the rim to the shoulder, No. 367-8" (ILLUS.) **150-200**

Dogwood I - Smooth (1916-19)
White dogwood blossoms and brown branches against a smooth green ground.

Bulbous Dogwood I Jardiniere

Jardiniere, bulbous cylindrical form w/wide flat closed rim, No. 590-9", 9 1/2" h. (ILLUS.) **173**
Planter tub, oval w/upright undulating rounded sides, 11 1/4" l., 6" h. **350-400**

Large Dogwood I Vase

Vase, 14 1/2" h., tall ovoid form tapering to a flat mouth, openwork branches just below the rim, a bruise on one side, some minor glaze pits, No. 140-15" (ILLUS.) **431**

Dogwood II - Textured (1926)
Vase, 7 1/4" h., footed bulbous ovoid body tapering to a low wide rolled mouth, No. 301-7" **200-275**

Donatello (1915)
Deeply fluted ivory and green body with wide tan band embossed with cherubs at various pursuits in pastoral settings.

Wide, Low Donatello Bowl

Bowl, 8 1/2" d., 3 1/2" h., wide, low, cylindrical form, No. 238-7" (ILLUS.)............... **125-150**

Large Squatty Donatello Jardiniere

Jardiniere, wide bulbous squatty form w/a wide flaring short neck, No. 579-12", 12" h. (ILLUS.) **374**

Large Donatello Jardiniere & Pedestal

Jardiniere & pedestal base, 12" h. jardiniere, No. 579-12", overall 34" h., 2 pcs. (ILLUS.)... **1,000-1,200**

Donatello 10" Wall Pocket

Wall pocket, bullet-shaped w/arched backplate, No. 1202-10", 10" h. (ILLUS.) **184**

Falline (1933)

Curving panels topped by a semi-scallop separated by vertical pea pod decorations; blended backgrounds of tan shading to green and blue or tan shading to darker brown.

Rare Nearly Spherical Falline Vase

Vase, 6 1/4" h., nearly spherical body w/a rounded shoulder band below the slightly flaring cylindrical neck flanked by C-scroll handles, brown shaded to pale yellow & green, unmarked, No. 644-6" (ILLUS.) **1,610**

Globular Falline Vase in Tan & Brown

Vase, 7" h., globular body tapering to stepped shoulder & wide cylindrical neck w/shoulder loop handles, shaded tan to brown ground, gold sticker on bottom, repair to top of one handle, small nick on other, No. 648-7" (ILLUS., previous page) **374**

Trumpet-form Falline Vase

Vase, 8 1/4" h., 6" d., footed trumpet form w/a widely flaring rim, low arched handles from under the rim to mid-body, tan shading to green & blue, No. 646-8" (ILLUS.) **1,495**

Falline Trumpet Vase in Tan & Brown

Vase, 8 1/4" h., 6" d., footed trumpet form w/a widely flaring rim, low arched handles from under the rim to mid-body, tan shading to brown, small gold sticker, No. 646-8" (ILLUS.) **690**

Ribbed Falline Vase

Vase, 9" h., two large handles rising from midsection to neck, horizontally ribbed lower section, shaded brown, small body nick, edge of one handle professionally repaired, No. 652-9" (ILLUS.) **460**

Tall Falline Vase in Shaded Brown

Vase, 14" h., tall cylindrical body w/a flat mouth flanked by small loop handles, dark brown shading to tan w/pale green pods, small bruise on footring, unobtrusive firing separation under footring, No. 654-13 1/2" (ILLUS.) **1,725**

Freesia (1945)

Trumpet-shaped blossoms and long slender green leaves against wavy impressed lines, white and lavender blossoms on blended green, white and yellow blossoms on shaded blue, or terra cotta and brown.

Freesia Basket with High Arched Handle

Basket, footed, flattened & flaring ovoid body w/a divided rim, long arched overhead handle, terra cotta ground, No. 390-7", 7" h. (ILLUS.) **138**

Blue Freesia Console Set

Console Set: 10" d. footed squatty rounded bowl w/small angled side handles & a pair of short domed candleholders; blue ground, bowl No. 7-10", candleholders No. 1160-2", the set (ILLUS.) **150**

Short Terra Cotta Freesia Ewer

Ewer, footed, squatty body w/a wide shoulder tapering to a short split neck w/high arched spout, loop handle from rim to shoulder, terra cotta ground, No. 19-6", 6" h. (ILLUS.) **104**

Squatty Blue Freesia Ewer

Ewer, footed, squatty body w/a wide shoulder tapering to a short split neck w/high arched spout, loop handle from rim to shoulder, blue ground, No. 19-6", 6" h. (ILLUS.) **115**
Jardiniere, footed nearly spherical body w/a very wide flat mouth flanked by tiny rim handles, terra cotta ground, No. 669-6", 6" **175-250**
Teapot, cov., blue ground, No. 6 .... **200-250**
Teapot, cov., green ground, No. 6 .... **150-250**
Teapot, cov., terra cotta ground, No. 6 ..... **150-250**

Bulbous Terra Cotta Freesia Urn-Vase

Urn-vase, footed, bulbous body w/a wide sloping shoulder to a wide flat mouth, angled loop handles at edges of shoulder, terra cotta ground, No. 463-5", 5" h. (ILLUS.) **69**

Terra Cotta Freesia Urn-Vase

Urn-vase, two-handled, bulbous body tapering to wide cylindrical neck, terra cotta ground, No. 196-8", 8 1/2" h. (ILLUS.).. **140-160**

Blue Freesia Wall Pocket

Wall pocket, waisted long body w/small angled side handles, blue ground, small glazed-over chip, No. 1296-8", 8 1/2" h. (ILLUS.).. **138**

8" Freesia Terra Cotta Wall Pocket

Wall pocket, waisted long body w/small angled side handles, terra cotta ground, No. 1296-8", 8 1/2" h. (ILLUS.) **161**

Fudji (1904)
Same technique as Rozane Woodland. Sometimes trimmed w/dots & studs & wavy lines. Matte-finished ground. Detailed decorations are in high gloss.Kovel-See Rozane Woodland--when the dots were omitted, it was called Fujiyama or Rozane Fudji.

Fine Early Roseville Fudji Vase

Vase, 6 1/2" h., upright squared & twisted form tapering to a small low flared mouth, decorated w/a dark brown chrysanthemum on a tall green leafy stem against a dark brown to pale green ground, marked, minor expert repair at rim (ILLUS.)................ **863**

Futura (1928)
Varied line with shapes ranging from Art Deco geometrics to futuristic. Matte glaze is typical although an occasional piece may be high gloss.

Small Mug-style Futura Vase

Vase, 6" h., 3 1/2" d., cylindrical body swelling to wider bands at the top & base, long pierced angled handles down the sides, tan w/dark blue bands & handles, No. 381-6" (ILLUS.) **460**

Spherical Futura Footed Vase

Vase, 7" h., spherical top w/large pointed dark blue & green leaves curving up the sides, resting on a gently sloped rectangular foot, shaded blue & green blue ground, No. 387-7" (ILLUS.) **1,093**
Vase, 8" h., square, slightly tapering body twisting toward the rim, pink ground, No. 425-8" (ILLUS., top next page) **431**

Futura Pink Twist 8" Vase

Futura Ovoid Thistle Vase

Vase, 8" h., semi-ovoid, flaring foot, flat closed handles from midsection to neck, molded trailing thistles on side, purple & mauve, No. 427-8" (ILLUS.) **805**

Cone-shaped Roseville Futura Vase

Vase, 8 1/4" h., 5" d., conical body on flat disk base, buttressed sides, orange w/green buttresses & blue base, No. 401-8" (ILLUS.) **690**

Gardenia (1940s)
Large white gardenia blossoms and green leaves over a textured impressed band on a shaded green, grey or tan ground.

Small Gardenia Candleholders

Candleholders, small domed shape, green ground, No. 651-2", 2" h., pr. (ILLUS.) **81**
Vase, 8" h., handles rising from base to mid-section, cylindrical body, tan ground, No. 683-8" **173**

Imperial II (1924)
Much variation within the line. There is no common characteristic, although many pieces are heavily glazed, and colors tend to run and blend.

Small Bulbous Imperial II Vase

Vase, 6" h., bulbous ovoid tapering body w/wide banding, thin flat rolled rim, mottled purple & yellow glaze, marked w/a gold foil label, No. 469-6" (ILLUS.) **316**

Globular Deep Rose Imperial II Vase

Vase, 7" h., globular body tapering to a wide tapering neck w/horizontal ribbing, mottled dark rose glaze, No. 471-7" (ILLUS.) **690**

Wide Squatty Blue Imperial II Vase

Vase, 7" h., wide squatty hemispherical turquoise blue body w/a wide gently sloping shoulder centering a cylindrical neck w/a band of molded inverted-comma designs in mottled yellow & white, No. 474-7" (ILLUS.) **288**

Wide Handled Imperial II Vase

Vase, 8 1/8" h., two handles at shoulder, expanding cylinder w/light horizontal ribbing around lower quarter of body, slightly crystalline rust over caramel matte glaze, No. 478-8" (ILLUS.)...................................... **431**

Handsome Dark Blue Imperial II Vase

Vase, 9 1/2" h., baluster form w/short wide cylindrical neck w/wave-like band, cobalt blue ground, No. 477-9 1/2" (ILLUS.)........ **1,265**

Rare Mottled Imperial II Wall Pocket

Wall pocket, canted sides w/rounded bottom, horizontal wide ribbing at base & narrow ribbing at midsection, green & pale lavender mottled glaze, No. 1263, 6 1/2" h. (ILLUS.) **920**

Ixia (1930s)
Embossed spray of tiny bell-shaped flowers and slender leaves, white blossoms on pink ground, lavender blossoms on green or yellow ground.

Long Ixia Centerpiece with Candleholders

Centerpiece, one-piece console set w/six candleholders attached to center bowl, yellow shaded to brown ground, minor firing separation at base end, No. 328-11 1/2", 13" l. (ILLUS.) **518**

Jonquil (1931)
White jonquil blossoms and green leaves in relief against textured tan ground, green lining.

Vase, 3" h., wide, low, squatty, tapering, cylindrical body w/wide flat mouth, inverted D-form loop handles from rim to edge of base, No. 523-3" **175-275**

Small Tapering Jonquil Vase

Vase, 4 1/2 h., footed, wide, tapering cylindrical body w/a flat rim flanked by small loop handles, No. 539-4" (ILLUS., previous page) **150**

Small Bulbous Jonquil Vase

Vase, 6" h., footed, bulbous body w/a short wide cylindrical neck flanked by small loop handles, No. 538-6" (ILLUS.) **316**

Jonquil Vase No. 526-6 1/2"

Vase, 6 1/2" h., bulbous base w/wide, slightly tapering sides to a wide flat mouth, curved handles from rim to midsection, No. 526-61/2" (ILLUS.)................................. **374**

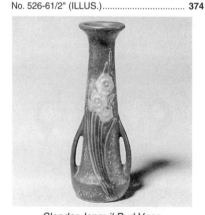

Slender Jonquil Bud Vase

Vase, bud, 7" h., swelled base & a tall slender tapering body w/a widely flaring trum-

pet mouth, low arched handles from edge of base to part way up the sides, No. 102-7" (ILLUS.) **546**

Juvenile (1916 on)
Transfer-printed and painted on creamware with nursery rhyme characters, cute animals and other motifs appealing to children.

Two-handled Juvenile Line Mug

Mug, two-handled, Sunbonnet Girl design, 2 7/8" h. (ILLUS.) **173**

Luffa (1934)
Relief-molded ivy leaves and blossoms on shaded brown or green wavy horizontal ridges.

Rare Tall Luffa Jardiniere & Pedestal

Jardiniere & pedestal, large bulbous jardiniere w/small angled rim handles, pedestal w/widely flaring base tapering to a cylindrical column w/raised platform top, green ground, No. 631-10", overall 28" h. (ILLUS.).. **1,725**

Luffa Lamp Base with No Fittings

Lamp base, footed bulbous body w/a narrow rounded shoulder centered by a flattened closed top flanked by small angled shoulder handles, brown ground, lamp No. 7005, no electric fittings, 9 3/4" h. (ILLUS.) **345**

Small Spherical Luffa Vase

Vase, 6" h., nearly spherical body tapering slightly to a wide, flat mouth flanked by tiny pointed rim handles, green ground, small gold sticker, No. 255-6" (ILLUS.) **345**

Brown Luffa Vase No. 684-6"

Vase, 6 1/4" h., swelled cylindrical body tapering slightly to a flat mouth flanked by pointed rim handles, brown ground, No. 684-6" (ILLUS.) **230**

Green Luffa Vase No. 684-6"

Vase, 6 1/4" h., swelled cylindrical body tapering slightly to a flat mouth flanked by pointed rim handles, green ground, No. 684-6" (ILLUS.) **259**

Very Tall Luffa Vase

Vase, 14 1/2" h., footed, tall, swelled, cylindrical body w/a wide flaring mouth flanked by small pointed rim handles, green ground, No. 692-14" (ILLUS.) **690**

Magnolia (1943)

Large white blossoms with rose centers and black stems in relief against a blue, green or tan textured ground.

Basket, large fan-shaped body w/a wide, low & pointed overhead handle, tan ground, No. 385-10", 10" h. **230**
Basket, large fan-shaped body w/a wide, low & pointed overhead handle, blue ground, No. 385-10", 10" h. **250-300**

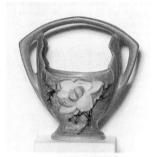

Blue Magnolia Basket

Basket w/ornate overhead handle, blue
ground, No. 383-7" (ILLUS.) **230**
Console set: low, narrow, long bowl
w/painted end handles & a pair of low
candleholders w/curved pointed handles;
green ground, bowl No. 450-10", candle-
holders No. 1156-2", the set **225-250**

Tan Magnolia Cookie Jar

Cookie jar, cov., shoulder handles, tan
ground, No. 2-8, overall 10" h. (ILLUS.)
.... **200-300**

Green Magnolia Cookie Jar

Cookie jar, cov., shoulder handles, green
ground, No. 2-8, overall 10" h. (ILLUS.) **207**

Blue Magnolia Cornucopia-Vase

Cornucopia-vase, blue ground, No. 184-6",
6" h. (ILLUS.) **81**

Very Tall Magnolia Ewer

Ewer, wide, squatty base tapering sharply
to a slender neck w/a divided rim w/a
high, long, arched spout, angled shoulder
handle, tan ground, No. 15-15", 15" h.
(ILLUS.).. **345**
Jardiniere & pedestal, blue ground, No.
665-10", jardiniere 10" h., 30 1/4" h., 2
pcs. **1,000-1,500**

Ball-shaped Blue Magnolia Pitcher

Pitcher, cider, 7" h., ball-shaped w/pointed arch handle, blue ground, No. 1327 (ILLUS., previous page) **259**

Long Magnolia Planter in Tan

Planter, long rectangular shape, two-handled, tan ground, No. 389-8", 8" l. (ILLUS.) **90-115**
Teapot, cov., green ground, No. 4 .... **350-400**
Teapot, cov., tan ground, No. 4................. **250-350**

Large Blue Magnolia Vase

Vase, 9" h., footed wide ovoid body w/a wide flat shoulder & flat mouth, long angled shoulder handles down the sides, blue ground, glaze chip on shoulder, No. 94-9" (ILLUS.) **150**

Unusual Tan Magnolia Vase

Vase, 9 1/4" h., footed, wide, half-round lower body w/a wide, flat shoulder centered by a large trumpet neck, large pointed angular handles from top of base to center of neck, tan ground, No. 93-9" (ILLUS.).. **104**

Magnolia Vase with Unusual Shape

Vase, 9 1/4" h., footed, wide, half-round lower body w/a wide, flat shoulder centered by a large trumpet neck, large pointed angular handles from top of base to center of neck, blue ground, chips under the base, No. 93-9" (ILLUS.) **138**

Unusual Green Magnolia Vase

Vase, 9 1/4" h., footed, wide, half-round lower body w/a wide, flat shoulder centered by a large trumpet neck, large pointed angular handles from top of base to center of neck, green ground, No. 93-9" (ILLUS.) **138**

Large Green Magnolia Floor Vase

Vase, floor type, 18 1/2" h., footed, large ovoid body w/a thin flared mouth & pointed shoulder handles, green ground, No. 100-18" (ILLUS., previous page)................. **500**

Matt Green (before 1916)

Matte green glaze on smoking set, jardinieres, fern dishes, hanging baskets, planters, some smooth with no pattern, some embossed with leaves or children's faces spaced evenly around the top.

Wide Squatty Matt Green Bowl

Bowl, 13" d., 8 1/2" h., footed, wide, squatty, rounded body w/a wide thick rolled rim flanked by loop shoulder handles, original paper label, No. 456-9" (ILLUS.) **230**

Matt Green Gate-form Double Bud Vase

Vase, double bud, 5" h., 8" w., fluted columns joined by a gate, No. 7 (ILLUS.) **115**

Paneled 10" Matt Green Wall Pocket

Wall pocket, tapering half-round three-paneled body below the high stepped & arched backplate w/hanging hole, No. 1211-10", 10" l. (ILLUS.) **345**

Paneled & Impressed Wall Pocket

Wall pocket, tapering half-round three-paneled body w/impressed dotted triangles at the top of each panel below the high stepped & arched backplate w/another impressed triangle & a long hanging hole, 10 1/4 l. (ILLUS.).. **316**

Floral-embossed Matt Green Wall Pocket

Wall pocket, long, round trumpet-form body lightly embossed w/blossoms on stems, the high arched backplate pierced w/oblong openings & a hanging hole, 4 3/4" w., 11 1/4" l. (ILLUS.)........................ **403**

Moderne (1930s)

Art Deco-style rounded and angular shapes trimmed with an embossed panel of vertical lines and modified swirls and circles, white trimmed with terra cotta, medium blue with white, and turquoise with a burnished antique gold.

Moderne Pattern Turquoise Compote

Compote, 5" h., open stem, turquoise, No.
295-6 (ILLUS., previous page) **196**

Morning Glory (1935)
*Delicately colored blossoms and twining vines
in white or green with blue.*

Flaring Morning Glory Vase

Vase, 5 1/4" h., footed, flaring sides w/small
angled handles at midsection, white
ground, No. 723-5" (ILLUS.) **300-400**

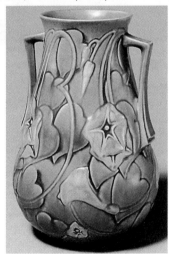

Tall Tapering Morning Glory Vase

Vase, 10 1/2" h., bulbous base tapering to
wide molded rim, two-handled, white
ground, No. 730-10" (ILLUS.) **1,495**

Mostique (1915)
*Indian designs of stylized flowers and arrow-
head leaves, slip decorated on bisque, glazed interiors. Occasional bowl glazed on outside as well.*

Vase, 6" h., gently tapering cylindrical body
w/a flared flat mouth, heavy dark green
bands around the base & rim w/a pair of
light green leaves flanking a white four-
petal diamond-shaped blossom on two
sides, tan ground, some small base
chips, No. 3-6" (ILLUS., top next column) **230**

Mostique Vase with Tall Leaves & Flower

Mostique 8" Vase with White Blossom

Vase, 8" h., gently swelled cylindrical form
w/flat closed rim, a white four-petal diamond-form blossom above three angular
green leaves around the sides, No. 10-8"
(ILLUS.).. **374**

Geometric Green Mostique Vase

Vase, 8" h., swelled base below tall cylindrical sides w/a wide flat mouth, narrow
dark green incised bands around the
base & top, two sides of the top incised
w/a dark green & red fanned diamond design above dark green angular panels all
on a pale green ground, small rim chip,
No. 8-8" (ILLUS.) **259**

Flaring Mostique Vase in Grey & Blue

Vase, 8 1/4" h., waisted cylinder w/wide flaring mouth, large handles rising from above base to midsection, geometric design, dark blue, brick red & white on a grey ground, No. 532-8" (ILLUS.) **230**

Cylindrical Mostique Vase with Leaves

Vase, 10" h., cylindrical w/wide closed mouth, dark green incised rings around the base & light green matching rings around the top, decorated w/a dark green square enclosing a square white blossom & suspending a pale green sprig of incised leaves, light tan ground, N0. 15-10" (ILLUS.) **460**

Baluster Mostique Vase with Flowers

Vase, 10" h., baluster-form body w/thin incised dark green rings around the base & the neck, the sides incised w/large stylized pairs of green leaves centering a dark green & deep red blossom bud, light tan ground, No. 18-10" (ILLUS.) **316**

Simple Waisted Cylindrical Mostique Vase

Vase, 10 1/4" h., tall waisted cylindrical body w/widely flaring rim, band of yellow spearpoint on green shafts up around the sides alternating w/small blue triangles on a grey ground, No. 164-10" (ILLUS.) **161**

Unusual Mostique Window Box

Window box, long narrow upright rectangular shape, the long sides w/dark green incised bands along the top rim & down the sides, the top center w/two squared four-petal blossoms in pink & white above three dark green triangular leaves, pale green ground, 5 1/2 x 11", 6" h. (ILLUS.)..... **805**

Panel (Rosecraft Panel 1920)
Background colors are dark green or dark brown; decorations embossed within the recessed panels are of natural or stylized floral arrangements or female nudes.

Rare Rosecraft Panel Vase with Nudes

Vase, 11" h., footed conical form w/long low
angular handles from rim down sides,
nude in panel, dark brown ground, No.
298-11" (ILLUS., previous page).............. **1,380**

Panel Wall Pocket with Nude

Wall pocket, conical form w/ruffled rim
flanked by cut-out panels, nude decoration in orange, dark brown ground, repair
to lip, 7" h. (ILLUS.)...................................... **316**

Rosecraft Panel Wall Pocket with Leaves

Wall pocket, wide conical shape w/rounded
end, leaves in panel, brown ground, 9" h.
(ILLUS.).. **431**

Peony (1942)

*Floral arrangement of white or dark yellow
blossoms with green leaves on textured, shaded
backgrounds in yellow with mixed green and
brown, pink with blue, and solid green.*

Console bowl, long, narrow, oblong form
w/arched sides & stepped flaring end
above tiny pointed handles, gold ground,
No. 432-12", 12" l.................................. **200-225**
Cornucopia-vase, pink & green ground,
No. 171-8", 8" h... **104**
Model of a conch shell, gold ground, No.
436, 9 1/2" w. **175-200**
Teapot, cov., gold ground, No. 3.............. **200-250**
Teapot, cov., green ground, No. 3 .... **150-225**

Peony Shaded Pink to Green 8" Vase

Vase, 8" h., footed, large ovoid body tapering to a low flared mouth, pointed shoulder handles, deep pink shaded to green
ground w/yellow flowers, No. 63-8"
(ILLUS.).. **115**

Gold Peony Tall Vase

Vase, 12 1/2" h., footed tall ovoid body tapering to a short flared neck flanked by
pointed loop handles, gold ground, No.
67-12" (ILLUS.)... **288**

Pink to Green Peony Floor Vase

Vase, 18" h., floor type, round domed foot & tall ovoid body w/a wide flared rim, pointed angular shoulder handles, pink shaded to green ground w/yellow flowers, No. 70-18" (ILLUS., previous page)................... **460**

Green Peony 18" Floor Vase

Vase, 18" h., floor type, round domed foot & tall, ovoid body w/a wide, flared rim, pointed angular shoulder handles, green ground, No. 70-18" (ILLUS.) **500**

Pine Cone (1935 & 1953)
Realistic embossed brown pine cones and green pine needles on shaded blue, brown or green ground. (Pink is extremely rare.)

Almond-shaped Pine Cone Ashtray

Ashtray, almond-shaped w/long pine needles curving around one end, green ground, No. 499, 4 1/2" l. (ILLUS.)................. **81**
Basket, w/overhead branch handle, asymmetrical fanned & pleated body, brown ground, No. 408-6", 6 1/2" h. (ILLUS., top next column).. **489**
Bowl, 4" d., bulbous spherical body w/incurved rim, green ground, No. 278-4"......... **207**

Fanned & Pleated Pine Cone Basket

Squatty Bulbous Pine Cone Bowl

Bowl, 4" d., squatty bulbous spherical body w/closed rim, blue ground, No. 278-4" (ILLUS.).. **288**
Bowl, 6" d., wide low form w/incurved sides & small angled twig handles, green shaded to cream, No. 425-6"............................... **276**

Single Blue Pink Cone Candleholder

Candleholder, flat disc base supporting candle nozzle in the form of a pine cone flanked by needles on one side & branch handle on the other, blue ground, No. 112-3", 3" h. (ILLUS.)................................... **161**

Pine Cone Triple Candleholder

Candleholder, triple, domed round base w/an open high arched pine needle & branch supporting three graduated cup-form sockets, green ground, No. 1106-5 1/2", 5 1/2" h. (ILLUS.) **173**

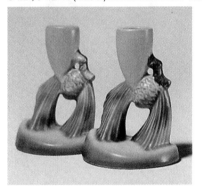

Pine Cone Pine Sprig Candleholders

Candleholders, oblong base supporting two thick pine needle clusters & a pine cone w/small branch supporting the egg-shaped candle socket, green ground, No. 451-4", 4" h., pr. (ILLUS.)............................. **230**

Simple Brown Pine Cone Candlesticks

Candlesticks, wide round foot tapering to a tall cylindrical socket w/slightly flared rim, brown ground, No. 1099-4 1/2", 4 1/2" h., pr. (ILLUS.).. **288**

Blue Pine Cone Cornucopia-Vase

Cornucopia-vase, blue ground, couple of very minor glaze pits, No. 126-6", 6" h. (ILLUS.).. **196**

Brown Pine Cone Cornucopia-Vase

Cornucopia-vase, brown ground, some minor glaze peppering, No. 126-6", 6" h. (ILLUS.).. **184**

Small Spherical Pine Cone Jardiniere

Jardiniere, spherical w/two twig handles, brown ground, No. 632-3", 3" h. (ILLUS.) **173**

Brown Pine Cone Pillow-type Vase

Vase, 8 1/2" h., pillow-type, wide flattened bulbous body w/asymmetrical branch handles, brown ground, gold foil label, No. 114-8" (ILLUS.).. **374**

Large Footed Cylindrical Pine Cone Vase

Vase, 10" h., foot w/flaring ringed short pedestal supporting a wide cylindrical body w/a nearly flat wide rim, long angular handles down the sides, brown ground, No. 910-10" (ILLUS.) **633**

Horn-shaped Blue Pine Cone Vase

Vase, 8 1/2" h., horn-shaped w/fanned & pleated rim, pine needles & cone-form handle from base of oval foot to midsection, blue ground, No. 490-8" (ILLUS.)......... **431**

Fine Blue Pine Cone Footed Vase

Vase, 10 1/2" h., footed expanding cylinder w/wide flat mouth flanked by small twig handles, blue ground, No. 709-10" (ILLUS.) **748**

Pine Cone Vase with Unusual Rim

Vase, 10" h., footed, two-handled bulbous body tapering to wide tall cylindrical neck w/irregular cut-out rim, brown ground, tiny nick on cut-out rim, No. 848-10" (ILLUS.)...... **403**

Tall Tapering Blue Pine Cone Vase

Vase, 12" h., tall tapering corseted form w/asymmetric branch handles, blue ground, No. 712-12" (ILLUS.) **748**

Green Double Pine Cone Wall Pocket

Wall pocket, double, two flaring conical containers joined by an arched pine cone & needle top handle, green ground, silver Roseville paper label, No. 1273-8", 8 1/2" h. (ILLUS.) **460**

Poppy (1930s)
Shaded backgrounds of blue or pink with decoration of poppy flower and green leaves.

Large Pink Roseville Poppy Basket

Basket, wide trumpet-form w/high & wide arched handle, pink ground, glaze skip on the handle, No. 347-10", 10" h. (ILLUS.) **316**

Rare Tall Poppy Ewer

Ewer, very tall slender ovoid body w/a split neck & high arched spout, C-scroll handle, pink ground, foil label, No. 880-18", 18" h. (ILLUS.) **550-650**

Small Pink Poppy Jardiniere

Jardiniere, footed, squatty, spherical body w/a wide, flat mouth flanked by tiny handles at rim, pink ground, No. 642-3", 3 1/2" h. (ILLUS.) **104**

Grey to Yellow Poppy Jardiniere

Jardiniere, footed, wide, bulbous, ovoid body w/a very wide flat mouth flanked by tiny C-scroll handles, grey shaded to yellow ground, No. 642-6", 6" h. (ILLUS.)......... **161**

Green to Pink Poppy Jardiniere

Jardiniere, footed, wide, bulbous, ovoid body w/a very wide, flat mouth flanked by tiny C-scroll handles, green shaded to pink ground, No. 642-6", 6" h. (ILLUS.) **184**

Pink Poppy Tall Floor Vase

Vase, 18 1/4" h., floor type, footed, tall, ovoid body w/a closed mouth & C-scroll shoulder handles, pink ground, No. 879-18" (ILLUS.) **1,200-1,400**

Rozane (1900)
Dark blended backgrounds; slip decorated underglaze artware.

Tall Rozane Tankard Pitcher with Grapes

Pitcher, 14" h., tankard-type, flaring base & tall slightly tapering sides w/a pinched rim spout & long, low C-form handle, decorated w/a dark bluish black grape cluster & dark green leaves down from the rim on a dark green shaded to gold to brown ground, Royal Rozane mark, nominal overall glaze crazing, decorated by Walter Myers (ILLUS.).................................. **259**

Small Rozane Vase with Clover

Vase, 4" h., wide bulbous baluster-form body tapering to a tiny rolled neck, decorated w/orange clover blossoms & green leaves on a dark shaded brown ground, artist-initials, glaze inclusion, few minor glaze pits (ILLUS.) **104**

Exceptional Large Rozane Royal Vase

Vase, 23 3/8" h., tall ovoid body w/a narrow rounded shoulder & a wide low flat neck, decorated w/life-sized yellow irises, buds & dark green leaves on a shaded dark brown ground, Rozane Royal mark, signed by Walter Myers (ILLUS.)............ **10,063**

Silhouette (1950)
Recessed area silhouettes nature study or female nudes. Colors are rose, turquoise, tan and white with turquoise.

Unusual Silhouette Basket

Basket, rectangular wedge-shaped foot supporting a squared football-form body w/curved rim, overhead asymmetrical handle, florals, brown ground, No. 710-10", 10" h. (ILLUS.) **104**

Basket w/asymmetrical rim & overhead handle, florals, tan, No. 709-8", 8" h........... **127**

Brown Silhouette Console Set

Console set: long, narrow, footed, rectangular console bowl & a pair of short tapering candleholders; brown ground, florals, candleholders No. 751-3", bowl No. 730-10", bowl 10" l., the set (ILLUS.) **115**

Ewer, rectangular foot supporting sharply tapering slender squared sides ending in an upright rolled spout, pointed long handle, florals, brown ground, No. 717-10", 10" h. **200-300**

Footed Urn-form Silhouette Vase

Vase, 8" h., urn-form tapering ovoid body raised on four angled feet on a round disc base, wide, slightly flaring mouth, female nude, brown ground, No. 763-8" (ILLUS.) **460**

Turquoise Blue Silhouette Vase with Nude

Vase, 10" h., small open handles between square base & waisted cylindrical body, shaped rim, female nudes, turquoise ground, No. 787-10" (ILLUS.) **750-850**

Snowberry (1946)
Brown branch with small white berries and green leaves embossed over spider-web design in various background colors (blue, green and rose).

Blue Fan-shaped Snowberry Basket

Basket, footed, fan-shaped body w/wide looped & pointed handle, shaded blue ground, No. 1BK-7", 7" h. (ILLUS.) **150-175**

Shaded Rose Snowberry Basket

Basket, round foot below the wide, flattened ovoid body w/a downswept rim, asymmetrical overhead handle, shaded rose ground, No. 1BK-8", 8" h. (ILLUS.) **250-275**

10" Green Snowberry Basket

Basket, wide, round foot tapering to a flaring, cylindrical body w/a steeply angled rim, curved overhead handle, shaded green ground, No. 1BK-10", 10" h. (ILLUS.)............ **161**

Shaded Green Snowberry Console Bowl

Console bowl, boat-shaped, pointed end handles, shaded green ground, No. 1BL2-12", 12" l. (ILLUS.)................................ **92**

Shaded Rose Snowberry Console Bowl

Console bowl, boat-shaped, pointed end handles, shaded rose ground, No. 1BL2-12", 15" l. (ILLUS.) **100-150**

Bulbous Blue Snowberry Jardiniere

Jardiniere, wide bulbous body w/a wide flat mouth flanked by small angled shoulder handles, shaded blue ground, No. 1J-6", 6" h. (ILLUS.) **200-300**

6" Bulbous Rose Snowberry Jardiniere

Jardiniere, wide, bulbous body w/a wide, flat mouth flanked by small angled shoulder handles, shaded rose ground, No. 1J-6", 6" h. (ILLUS.)..................................... **104**

Green Snowberry Rose Bowl

Rose bowl, bulbous body tapering to a four-notch mouth flanked by small pointed shoulder handles, shaded green ground, No. 1RB-5", 5" h. (ILLUS.) **100-130**
Teapot, cov., shaded green ground, No. 1TP **200-250**

Crescent-shaped Snowberry Pillow Vase

Vase, 6 1/2" h., pillow type w/crescent-shaped body w/wedge-form foot, asymmetrical side handles, shaded green ground, No. 1FH-6" (ILLUS.) **115**

Pink Snowberry Wall Pocket

Wall pocket, wide, half-round form tapering to a pointed base, low angled handles along the lower sides, shaded rose ground, No. 1WP-8", 8" w., 5 1/2" h. (ILLUS.).. **200-300**

Green Snowberry Window Box

Window box, long, rectangular form w/pointed end handles, shaded green ground, No. 1WX-8", 8" l. (ILLUS.)........ **150-200**

Sunflower (1930)
Tall stems support yellow sunflowers whose blooms form a repetitive band. Textured background shades from tan to dark green at base.

Very Large Sunflower Jardiniere

Jardiniere, large, bulbous form w/a ringed rim around the wide, flat mouth, No. 619-12", 12" h. (ILLUS.) **3,000-4,000**
Jardiniere & pedestal, jardiniere No. 619-10", 10" h., overall 29" h., 2 pcs. (ILLUS., top next column).. **4,140**
Urn-vase, nearly spherical w/short wide neck, No. 489-7", 7" h. (ILLUS., middle next column).. **978**

Fine Sunflower Jardiniere & Pedestal

Spherical Sunflower Urn-Vase

Small Spherical Sunflower Vase

Vase, 4" h., spherical body tapering to a wide, low, flared rim flanked by rounded loop shoulder handles, original foil sticker, No. 566-4" (ILLUS.) **450-550**

Teasel (1936)

Embossed decorations of long stems gracefully curving with delicate spider-like pods. Colors and glaze treatments vary from monochrome matte to crystalline. Colors are beige to tan, medium blue highlighted with gold, pale blue, and deep rose (possibly others).

Footed Squatty Teasel Bowl

Bowl, 4" d., low pedestal foot below the wide, squatty, bulbous body w/a closed rim, tiny pointed side handles, pale blue ground, No. 342-4" (ILLUS.) **175-200**

Vase, 8" h., closed handles at shoulder, low foot, beige shading to tan, No. 884-8".......... **259**

Deep Rose Teasel Vase

Vase, 9" h., closed handles at base, flaring mouth, deep rose, No. 886-9" (ILLUS.). **100-150**

Thorn Apple (1930s)

White trumpet flower with leaves reverses to thorny pod with leaves. Colors are shaded blue, brown and pink.

Low Rounded Blue Thorn Apple Bowl

Bowl, 5" d., wide, squatty, rounded form w/wide, flat rim flanked by tiny angled rim

handles, shaded blue ground, No. 306-5" (ILLUS.)....................................... **104**

Thorn Apple Blue Bowl-Vase

Bowl-vase, footed, spherical form w/three openings & buttressed handles, shaded blue ground, No. 305-6", 10" w., 6 1/4" h. (ILLUS.)....................................... **173**

Thorn Apple Brown Centerpiece

Centerpiece, long, narrow, rectangular foot supporting short, slender trumpet-form candle sockets at each end centered by a half-round spherical bowl resting on a large leaf cluster, shaded brown ground, No. 313, 11" l., 4 1/2" h. (ILLUS.).......... **325-400**

Upright Flattened Thorn Apple Vase

Vase, 6" h., round disk foot supporting a wide, flattened, vertical body w/stepped sides & rim, angled handles at the base, shaded brown ground, No. 812-6" (ILLUS.) **150-175**

Thorn Apple Triple Wall Pocket

Wall pocket, triple, white blossom & green leaf across top, shaded pink ground w/large green leaf, repair to lower portion, No. 1280-8", 8" h. **345**

Tourmaline (1933)
Although the semi-gloss medium blue, highlighted around the rim with lighter high gloss and gold effect seems to be accepted as the standard Tourmaline glaze, the catalogue definitely shows this and two other types as well. One is a mottled overall turquoise, the other a mottled salmon that appears to be lined in the high gloss but with no overrun to the outside.

Blue Tourmaline Urn-Vase

Urn-vase, round pedestal foot below the bulbous ribbed lower body below wide, slightly flaring cylindrical sides flanked by long angled handles, mottled blue ground, unnumbered, 6 1/4" h. (ILLUS.) **104**
Vase, 7" h., footed, swelled, cylindrical body tapering to a short, wide neck w/flared rim, drippy mottled turquoise, No. A-308-7" (ILLUS., top next column) **104**

Drippy Turquoise Tourmaline Vase

Turquoise to Pink Tourmaline Vase

Vase, 7" h., footed, swelled, cylindrical body tapering to a short, wide neck w/flared rim, turquoise shading to mottled pink, No. A-308-7" (ILLUS.) **104**

Mottled Blue Roseville Tourmaline Vase

Vase, 8 1/4" h., base handles, bulbous tapering to flared rim, mottled blue, No. A-332-8" (ILLUS.) **127**

Vista (1920s)

Embossed green coconut palm trees & lavender blue pool against grey ground.

Undulating Cylindrical Vista Basket

Basket, undulating cylindrical form w/flaring rim, pointed overhead handle, unmarked, some touched-up rim chips, 10" h. (ILLUS.) **403**

Ovoid Vista Basket with Arched Handle

Basket, footed, slender, ovoid body, unmarked, high arched overhead handle, rim chip, tiny base chips, 12" h. (ILLUS.) **403**

28" Vista Jardiniere & Pedestal

Jardiniere & pedestal, 9 1/2" h. jardiniere on a flaring pedestal base, jardiniere No.

589-9", chip on top of pedestal, overall 28" h., 2 pcs. (ILLUS.) **1,610**

Vista Vase with Flaring Foot

Vase, 9 3/4" h., cylindrical body tapering to flared base, flattened shoulder w/flat molded mouth, unmarked, No. 127-10" (ILLUS.) **633**

Rare Vista Wall Pocket

Wall pocket, ovoid bullet shape w/a high arched backplate, glaze chip on back, 9 1/2" h. (ILLUS.) **690**

Water Lily (1943)

Water lily and pad in various color combinations: tan to brown with yellow lily, blue with white lily, pink to green with pink lily.

Light Blue Water Lily Basket

Basket, cylindrical, w/widely flaring rim, pointed overhead handle, pale blue ground, No. 380-8", 8" h. (ILLUS., previous page) **150**

Unusual Brown Water Lily Basket

Basket, round foot supporting a wide, flattened, ovoid body w/the serpentine rim pulled up into a tall, curved three-tier section at one end, asymmetrical overhead handle, tan shaded to brown ground, No. 382-12", 12" h. (ILLUS.) **250-350**

Water Lily Blue Cornucopia-Vase

Cornucopia-vase, large water lily blossom applied at base, pale blue ground, No. 177-6", 6" h. (ILLUS.) **100-150**

Tan to Brown Water Lily Ewer

Ewer, squatty, flared bottom tapering to a tall split neck w/high arched spout & high pointed loop handle, tan to brown ground, No. 10-6", 6" h. (ILLUS.) **100-125**

Blue Water Lily Pattern Ewer

Ewer, squatty flared bottom tapering to a tall split neck w/high arched spout & high pointed loop handle, blended blue ground, No. 10-6", 6" h. (ILLUS.) **92**

Tall Water Lily Ewer

Ewer, disk foot below a bulbous, ovoid body tapering to a divided rim w/a long upright arched spout, large angular shoulder handle, light blue ground, No. 12-15", 15" h. (ILLUS.) **400-500**

Small Blue Water Lily Jardiniere

Jardiniere, squatty, bulbous lower body w/low, wide, cylindrical sides to an incurved rim, small angled handles from rim to lower body, pale blue ground, No. 663-4", 4" h. (ILLUS.) **100-150**

Brown Water Lily 15 1/2" Floor Vase

Vase, 15 1/2" h., round, stepped foot below the tall, ovoid body w/a closed mouth flanked by angular shoulder handles, tan shading to brown ground, No. 83-15" (ILLUS.).. **350-450**

Tall Brown Water Lily Floor Vase

Vase, 16 1/4" h., floor type, footed, tall, ovoid body w/swelled shoulder & short, wide neck, angled handles from shoulder to mid-body, shaded tan to brown ground, No. 84-16" (ILLUS.) **250-350**

White Rose (1940s)
White roses and green leaves against a vertically combed ground of blended blue, brown shading to green, or pink shading to green.

Water Lily 15 1/2" Floor Vase

Vase, 15 1/2" h., round stepped foot below the tall ovoid body w/a closed mouth flanked by angular shoulder handles, pale blue ground, glaze nick on a petal, firing separations & blistering on flower centers, No. 83-15" (ILLUS.)........................ **460**

Large Blue White Rose Basket

Basket, footed, widely flaring fanned body w/downswept rim, sweeping handle rising from base to rim at opposite side, blended blue ground, No. 364-12", 12 1/2" h. (ILLUS.) **275-325**

White Rose Pink to Green Candleholders

Candleholders, two-handled, low, pink shading to green ground, No. 1141-2", 2" h., pr. (ILLUS.) **104**

Brown & Green White Rose Vase

Vase, 8 1/2" h., small footring below a squatty bulbous base & tall, wide, cylindrical body w/notched flat rim, long loop handles from rim to edge of base, brown shading to green ground, No. 985-8" (ILLUS.).. **127**

White Rose Brown & Green 9" Vase

Vase, 9" h., footed, wide, tapering, cylindrical body w/large handles from foot to shoulder, notched rim, brown shading to green ground, No. 986-9" (ILLUS.) **150-250**
Vase, 12 1/2" h., tall, ovoid body tapering to a notched rim flanked by angled shoulder handles, pink shading to green ground, No. 991-12" (ILLUS., top next column) **250-350**
Vase, 18 1/2" h., floor type, tall ovoid body tapering to a low notched rim, large looped shoulder handles, brown shaded to green ground, No. 994-18" (ILLUS., middle next column) **403**

Tall Ovoid Pink & Green White Rose Vase

White Rose 18 1/2" Floor Vase

Wincraft (1948)

Revived shapes from older lines such as Pine Cone, Bushberry, Cremona, Primrose and others. Vases with animal motifs, contemporary shapes in high gloss of blue, tan, lime and green.

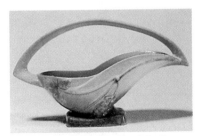

Long, Low Tan Wincraft Basket

Basket, rectangular foot supporting very long, narrow, arched boat-shaped body, long, low overhead handle, berries & foliage in relief on glossy brown shading to tan ground, No. 209-12", 12" h. (ILLUS.) **150-200**

Large Blue Wincraft Basket

Basket, rectangular concave foot supporting fanned body w/divided arched rim, high overhead handle forming two loop handles to one side, glossy blue ground, No. 210-12", 12" h. (ILLUS.) **200-250**

Low Oblong Wincraft Bowl

Bowl, 8" l., low foot supporting the low, oblong, two-lobed bowl w/pointed end tab handles, glossy green ground, No. 226-8" (ILLUS.) **100-150**

Blue Domed Wincraft Creamer & Sugar

Creamer & open sugar bowl, flat-bottomed domed shape w/cylindrical neck, small angled loop handles, glossy blue ground, No. 250C & 250S, 2 1/2" & 3 1/2" h., pr. (ILLUS.) **100-150**

Blue Wincraft Bell-form Ewer

Ewer, bell-form body below a tall neck w/upright tall spout & angled shoulder handle, glossy blue ground, No. 216-8", 8" h. (ILLUS.) **104**

Green & Brown Wincraft Flowerpot

Flowerpot, thin disk foot & widely flaring flat sides, glossy green to brown ground, No. 256-5", 5" h. (ILLUS.) **92**

Glossy Blue Wincraft Flowerpot

Flowerpot, thin disk foot & widely flaring flat sides, glossy green to brown ground, glossy blue ground, No. 256-5", 5" h. (ILLUS.) **80**
Teapot, cov., brown & yellow ground, No. 271-P **100-150**

Wincraft Football-form Vase

Vase, 6" h., a square foot supporting a nearly horizontal football form w/integral fin-like handles at each end, glossy brown to tan ground, No. 241-6" (ILLUS.) **100-150**

Cylindrical Wincraft Green Vase

Vase, 10" h., cylindrical w/flat disk base, relief arrowroot leaf & blossom decoration on glossy green ground, No. 285-10" (ILLUS.)... **175-200**

Box-like Wincraft Wall Pocket

Wall pocket, rectangular box-like holder w/horizontal ribbing & ivy leaves as rim handle, glossy light green to brown ground, No. 266-4", 8 1/2" h. (ILLUS.) **173**

Windsor (1931)

Brown or blue mottled glaze, some with leaves, vines and ferns, some with a repetitive band arrangement of small squares and rectangles in yellow and green.

Lamp, tall baluster-form base w/shaded reddish brown to brown Windsor glaze, fitted on a round cast-metal openwork base w/a shell & scroll design & a matching top fitting rim, pottery section 8 7/8" h. (ILLUS., top next column) **633**

Elegant Lamp with Windsor Glaze

Spherical Windsor Vase with Ferns

Vase, 7 1/8" h., large spherical body tapering to a wide short flaring neck w/slender curved handles from rim to shoulder, stylized ferns against mottled blue ground, No. 551-7", chip on back edge of one handle (ILLUS.).. **633**

Scarce Windsor Vase with Blossoms

Vase, 8 1/2" h., two-handled cylindrical body w/low flat rim, decorated w/thin straight green stems suspending a long leaf & small yellow blossoms around the shoulder on a mottled blue ground, w/a small black Roseville sticker, No. 552-8" (ILLUS.).. **978**

Wisteria (1933)

Lavender wisteria blossoms and green vines against a roughly textured brown shading to deep blue ground or brown shading to yellow and green; rarely found in only brown.

Low Squatty Wisteria Bowl

Bowl, 6 1/2" d., 2 1/2" h., wide, low, flaring, squatty form w/a wide, closed rim, brown shaded to yellow & green ground, unmarked (ILLUS.).................................... **150-200**

Small Wisteria Bowl-Vase

Bowl-vase, squatty, bulbous form tapering sharply to a flat mouth flanked by small loop handles, brown & blue ground, No. 242-4", 4" h. (ILLUS.).................................... **431**

4" Spherical Wisteria Bowl-Vase

Bowl-vase, bulbous, spherical form tapering to a small, flat mouth flanked by tiny rounded shoulder handles, brown shading to yellow & green ground, No. 632-4", 4" h. (ILLUS.) **316**

Small Wisteria Bowl-Vase

Bowl-vase, bulbous spherical form tapering to a small flat mouth flanked by tiny shoulder handles, brown shaded to yellow & green ground, No. 632-5", 5" h. (ILLUS.).. **450-550**

Bulbous Spherical Wisteria Bowl-Vase

Bowl-vase, bulbous, spherical form tapering to a small, flat mouth flanked by tiny shoulder handles, brown shading to yellow & green ground, No. 632-5", 5" h. (ILLUS.).. **450-500**

9 1/2" Wisteria Console Bowl

Console bowl, narrow, oblong form w/upright sides & small pointed end handles, brown ground, No. 243-5 x 9", 9 1/2" l. (ILLUS., previous page) **345**

Squatty Tapering Wisteria Vase

Vase, 4" h., squatty, w/angular handles on sharply canted shoulder, blue ground, gold triangular sticker, No. 629-4" (ILLUS.) **500-700**

Tapering Ovoid Small Wisteria Vase

Vase, 6" h., ovoid body tapering to short, cylindrical neck flanked by small loop handles, blue ground, No. 631-6" (ILLUS.) **546**

Rare Ovoid 6 1/2" Wisteria Vase

Vase, 6 1/2" h., 4" d., bulbous, ovoid body w/a wide shoulder tapering up to a small

mouth, small angled shoulder handles, mottled blue & yellow ground, No. 630-6" (ILLUS.).. **748**

Globular 6 1/2" Wisteria Vase

Vase, 6 1/2" h., globular w/small, flat mouth & tiny angular shoulder handles, brown shaded to green & yellow ground, No. 637-6 1/2" (ILLUS.) **575**

Bulbous Waisted Wisteria Vase

Vase, 7" h., bulbous waisted ovoid body w/small pointed shoulder handles, brown ground, No. 634-7" (ILLUS.) **633**

8" Brown Shaded to Yellow Wisteria Vase

Vase, 8" h., 6 1/2" d., wide, tapering, cylindrical body w/small angled handles flanking the flat rim, brown shaded to yellow & green ground, No. 633-8" (ILLUS.) **575**

Fine Flaring Wisteria Vase

Vase, 10 1/4" h., bulbous lower body tapering sharply to a tall trumpet neck, angled handles from center of neck to lower body, brown ground, No. 682-10" (ILLUS.) **1,035**

Zephyr Lily (1946)
Tall lilies and slender leaves adorn swirl-textured backgrounds of Bermuda Blue, Evergreen and Sienna Tan.

Green Zephyr Lily Basket

Basket, footed, cylindrical body flaring slightly to an ornate cut rim w/low, wide overhead handle, green ground, No. 395-10", 10" h. (ILLUS.) **161**

Green Zephyr Lily Book Ends

Book ends, green ground, No. 16, 5 1/2" h., pr. (ILLUS.)... **173**

Blue Zephyr Lily Cookie Jar

Cookie jar, cov., blue ground, No. 5-8", 10" h. (ILLUS.) **288**

Green & Brown Zephyr Lily Cornucopia

Cornucopia-vase, green shaded to brown ground, No. 204-8" 8 1/2" h. (ILLUS.)
.... **100-150**

Zephyr Lily Creamer & Open Sugar Set

Creamer & open sugar bowl, brown shaded to green ground, Nos. 7C & 7S, pr. (ILLUS.)... **125-150**
Ewer, footed baluster-form w/a tall neck w/tall forked rim & upright spout, handle from rim to shoulder, terra cotta ground, No. 24-15", 15" h.. **460**
Jardiniere, terra cotta ground, No. 671-8", 8" h. (minor touch-up on foot rim) **259**

Blue Zephyr Lily Tea Set

Tea set: cov. teapot, creamer & open sugar bowl; No. 7T, 7C & 7S, blue ground, 3 pcs. (ILLUS.) **550-600**
Teapot, cov., blue ground, No. 7T............. **250-350**
Teapot, cov., green ground, No. 7T **100-200**
Teapot, cov., terra cotta ground, No. 7T ... **200-250**

Zephyr Lily Urn-Vase in Green

Urn-vase, two-handled, green ground, No. 202-8", 8 1/2" h. (ILLUS.) **173**

Trumpet-form Zephyr Lily 9" Vase

Vase, 9" h., round, flaring foot tapering to a tall trumpet-form body, short angled handles at base, green ground, No. 136-9" (ILLUS.).. **161**
Vase, 12 1/2" h., handles rising from shoulder of compressed globular base to middle of slender neck w/flaring mouth, green ground, No. 140-12" (ILLUS., top next column).. **200-25**

Tall Green Zephyr Lily Vase

Vase, 12 1/2" h., handles rising from shoulder of compressed globular base to middle of slender neck w/flaring mouth, terra cotta & green ground, No. 140-12" **276**

Royal Bayreuth

Good china in numerous patterns and designs has been made at the Royal Bayreuth factory in Tettau, Germany since 1794. Listings below are by the company's lines, plus miscellaneous pieces. Interest in this china remains at a peak and prices continue to rise. Pieces listed carry the company's blue mark except where noted otherwise.

Among the important reference books in this field are Royal Bayreuth - A Collectors' Guide and Royal Bayreuth - A Collectors' Guide - Book II by Mary McCaslin (see Special Contributors list).

Royal Bayreuth Mark

Devil & Cards

Devil & Cards Candy Dish

Candy dish, shallow paneled dish composed of playing cards w/a figural seated devil handle, 6 1/2" w. (ILLUS.) **$288**

Mother-of-Pearl

Figural Spiky Shell Creamer

Creamer, figural Spiky Shell patt., pale lavender & pink highlights (ILLUS.) **81**

Rose Tapestry

Two-piece Rose Tapestry Dresser Set

Dresser set: 10" rectangular tray & cov. hair receiver; three-color roses decoration, blue marks, the set (ILLUS.) **460**

Tomato Items

Tomato Creamer & Sugar Bowl

Tomato creamer & cov. sugar bowl, creamer 3" d., 3" h., sugar bowl 3 1/2" d., 4" h., pr. (ILLUS.) **115**

Miscellaneous

Royal Bayreuth Musicians Berry Set

Berry set: 9 3/4" d. bowl & five 5" d. sauce dishes; Peasant Musicians decoration, 6 pcs. (ILLUS.) **250-300**

Royal Bayreuth Bowl with Roses

Bowl, 10 1/2" d., scalloped rim & molded interior lobes, decorated w/scattered pink roses & green leaves w/a satin finish, blue mark (ILLUS.) **115**

Royal Bayreuth Charger with Grapes

Charger, round w/lightly scalloped rim stenciled w/gilt sprigs, decorated w/large clusters of deep red & green grapes on a shaded pale green to white ground, blue mark, 13" d. (ILLUS.) **92**

Squatty Royal Bayreuth Ewer with Cows

Ewer, squatty bulbous form w/a flat cylindrical body band & wide flattened shoulder centered by a short cylindrical neck w/angled handle, green shoulder & lower body, side band decorated w/a continuous scene of cows in a landscape in shades of rust, green, brown & black, blue mark, 5" h. (ILLUS.) **104**

Royal Bayreuth Child's Tea Set

Royal Bayreuth Figural Apple Pitcher

Pitcher, water, 6" h., figural apple (ILLUS.)
.... **600-700**

Royal Bayreuth Elk Water Pitcher

Pitcher, water, 7" h., figural elk (ILLUS.)... **300-400**
Tea set: child's, cov. teapot, cov. sugar, creamer, two plates, & two cups & saucers; ovoid bodies, each piece decorated w/a scene of children playing, the set (ILLUS., top of page)............................ **750-850**

Royal Bayreuth "Tapestry" Tea Set

Tea set: cov. teapot, cov. sugar bowl & creamer; each w/a squatty bulbous body & gold handles, "Tapestry" decoration of white mums & purple violets on a pale blue ground, blue mark, Germany, early 20th c., teapot 7" l., the set (ILLUS.).... **460**
Tea set: cov. teapot, cov. sugar bowl & creamer; ovoid bodies, the sugar & creamer w/C-scroll handles, the teapot w/overhead fixed handle & serpentine spout, each piece decorated w/a colorful fairy tale scene, the set (ILLUS., top next page)... **350-400**

Small Royal Bayreuth Vase with Cows

Royal Bayreuth Fairy Tale Tea Set

Vase, 4 1/2" h., footed ovoid body tapering to a short flaring neck, decoration of cows watering w/mountains in the distance, in shades of purple, lavender, green, orange, brown & black, blue mark (ILLUS., previous page) **92**

gilt floral stencils around the lower body, a pale blue ground & shaded brown foot, blue mark (ILLUS.) **92**

Vase, 9" h., tall waisted cylindrical shape w/a flaring ruffled rim, three angular green scrolled branch handles around the sides, the main body in dark green, a color top band in the Toasting Cavalier design, blue mark (ILLUS., top next column) **184**

Royal Bayreuth Skiff with Sail Vase

Vase, 7" h., footed cylindrical form w/trumpet-form rim, central color band w/Skiff with Sail decoration, gold band borders trimmed w/delicate gilt stencil bands &

Tall Royal Bayreuth Cavaliers Vase

Royal Worcester

This porcelain has been made by the Royal Worcester Porcelain Co. at Worcester, England, from 1862 to the present. Royal Worcester is distinguished from wares made at Worcester between 1751 and 1862, which are referred to only as Worcester by collectors.

Royal Worcester Marks

Floral-decorated Royal Worcester Ewer

Ewer, tapering bulbous body w/a wide upright spout, an unusual gold figural ram's head & scroll handle, the creamy ground h.p. w/a tall bouquet of mums in shades of orange, pink, blue & green trimmed in gold, gold base & rim bands, magenta mark, Shape No. 1255, 9" h. (ILLUS.)... **$288**

Game set: twelve 9" d. scallop-edged plates, 13 x 17 1/2" oval platter w/molded bird head & wings end handles, 7 1/2" h. cov. sauce tureen w/molded bird head & wings end handles, two 5 x 7" oval dishes w/molded bird head & wings end handles, 5 x 8" scallop-handled serving dish; each piece h.p. in color w/a different game bird, very ornate delicate floral border band, each piece marked & dated 1889, the set (ILLUS., bottom of page)..... **4,600**

Outstanding Royal Worcester Flask

Pilgrim flask, an oblong flaring oval foot below the large flattened round body topped by a short conical reticulated neck, four gold square pegs around the outer edge alternating w/panels of turquoise strapwork, the double-walled sides decorated in the Persian taste w/a central rosette & radiating pierced concentric bands, the peripheral band enriched w/a ribbon enameled w/turquoise & white "jewels," magenta mark, by George Owen, ca. 1890, 6" h. (ILLUS.) **14,340**

Truly Extraordinary Royal Worcester Game Set

Rare Royal Worcester Aesthetic Movement Figural Teapot

Teapot, cov., Aesthetic Movement figural design, molded on one side as a late Victorian Aesthetic dandy wearing a large sunflower, one arm & bent wrist forming the spout, his other arm the handle, the reverse modeled as his female counterpart wearing a large lily, each wearing a dark green shirt w/white collar & a dark pink hat in the spirit of Oscar Wilde, inscribed on the bottom "Fearful consequences, through the laws of natural selection and evolution of living up to one's teapot," signed "Budge," marked & w/date code for 1882, 6" h. (ILLUS. of both sides, top of page)........................... **11,163**

Rare Reticulated Royal Worcester Pot

Teapot, cov., spherical white body w/an elaborate overall reticulated outer layer composed of fine honeycomb, diamonds & rings, the low domed cover, C-form handle & shaped spout all w/further reticulation, the cover w/a spire finial & applied pale turquoise beaded chain trim also used on the handle & spout, crafted by George Owen, impressed factory mark, ca. 1890 (ILLUS.)........................... **4,780**

Fine Royal Worcester Dragon Teapot

Teapot, cov., Oriental design w/squared block-style body in turquoise blue molded on the sides w/a flying bird in green, yellow, tan & pink w/pink & green floral bands, the flattened shoulders w/an impressed Greek key design, flat square cover w/pyramidal finial, squared curved corner spout w/the end opening formed by the head of a black dragon whose slender body arches across the top to form the handle, late 19th c., minor professional repair to spout, 7 1/2" h. (ILLUS.).. **3,360**

Fine Royal Worcester Ovoid Vase

Vase, 7 1/8" h., footed ovoid body w/reticulated small panels & motifs on the shoulder below the slender trumpet-form neck w/reticulated scrolls at the base, pointed angled shoulder handles, the foot in gold w/white beading, the lower body w/gilt-bordered gadrooning on the ivory body h.p. w/swags of deep pink & yellow roses suspended from ornately gilt scroll panels, gilt lattice panels on the upper shoulder & up the neck, the reticulated section trimmed in pale blue, magenta mark, Shape No. 1575, probably by George Owen & Henry Chair, retailer mark of Tiffany & Co., New York, dated 1897 (ILLUS., previous page) **6,573**

Ornate Bottle-form Royal Worcester Vase

Vase, cov., 14 1/2" h., bottle-form, a flaring foot in dark brown decorated w/a band of delicate gold arches, the bulbous creamy body decorated w/white pate-sur-pate blossoms & long gold leaves, a tall cylindrical reticulated brown neck w/molded gold arches below a spiral band, the flared rim supporting the reticulated domed brown cover w/a pointed finial & fancy gold trim, grotesque scrolled dragon gold shoulder handles, professional cover repair, magenta mark, Shape No. 1168, late 19th c. (ILLUS.) **748**

Russel Wright Designs

The innovative dinnerware designed by Russel Wright and produced by various companies beginning in the late 1930s was an immediate success with a society that was turning to a more casual and informal lifestyle. His designs, with their flowing lines and unconventional shapes, were produced in many different colors, which allowed a hostess to arrange creative tables.

Although not antique, these designs, which we list here by line and manufacturer, are highly collectible. In addition to dinnerwares, Wright was also known as a trendsetter in the design of furniture, glassware, lamps, fabric and a multitude of other household goods.

Russel Wright Marks

American Modern (Steubenville Pottery Co.)

Black Chutney After Dinner Coffeepot

Coffeepot, cov., after dinner, black chutney w/chartreuse cover (ILLUS.) **$100-135**

After Dinner Coffeepot & Dinner Plate

Coffeepot, cov., after dinner, granite grey (ILLUS. front with blue dinner plate) **85-105**

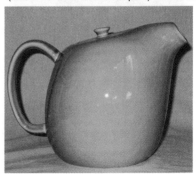

American Modern Chartreuse Coffeepot

Coffeepot, cov., chartreuse (ILLUS.) .... **225+**

Rare Cantaloupe Casual Restyled Teapot and Ripe Apricot Water Pitcher

Plate, dinner, 10" d., seafoam blue (ILLUS.
back with grey granite after dinner coffee-
pot, previous page) **20**

American Modern White Teapot

Teapot, cov., white (ILLUS.)...................... **110-135**

Casual China (Iroquois China Co.)

Three Casual China Carafes

Carafe, oyster, rare color (ILLUS. right with
other carafes)... **1,200+**
Carafe, parsley (ILLUS. left with other Ca-
sual China carafes) **550-650**
Carafe, sugar white (ILLUS. center with other Casual China carafes) **200-300**
Coffeepot, cov., after dinner, avocado yel-
low **135**

Casual China Redesigned Pitcher

Pitcher, redesigned, mustard gold (ILLUS.)
.... **400-500**
Pitcher, cov., ripe apricot, 1 1/2 qt., (ILLUS.
left with canteloupe teapot, top of page)
.... **125-135**
Teapot, cov., redesigned, cantaloupe, mid-
1950s (ILLUS., top of page)................. **600-750**

Mustard Gold Casual Restyled Teapot

Teapot, cov., redesigned, mustard gold,
mid-1950s (ILLUS.)............................... **250-350**

Ripe Apricot Casual Restyled Teapot

Teapot, cov., redesigned, ripe apricot, mid-1950s (ILLUS.) **150-175**

Sèvres & Sèvres-Style

Some of the most desirable porcelain ever produced was made at the Sèvres factory, originally established at Vincennes, France, and transferred, through permission of Madame de Pompadour, to Sèvres as the Royal Manufactory about the middle of the 18th century. King Louis XV took sole responsibility for the works in 1759, when production of hard paste wares began. Between 1850 and 1900, many biscuit and soft-paste pieces were made again. Fine early pieces are scarce and high-priced. Many of those available today are late productions. The various Sèvres marks have been copied, and pieces listed as "Sèvres-Style" are similar to actual Sèvres wares but not necessarily from that factory. Three of the many Sèvres marks are illustrated here.

Sèvres marks

Box, cov., casket-form, the low rectangular serpentine sides supported on ornate gold scrolled corner legs, the dark blue sides h.p. w/oval reserves w/colorful florals framed by ornate gilt scrolls, the hinged & low domed cover also in dark blue w/a large white reserve w/floral clusters & vines framing a central panel decorated w/a couple in 18th c. costume,

Fine Casket-form Sèvres-style Box

pseudo-Sèvres marks, late 19th c., 6 1/2" h. (ILLUS.) **$3,220**

Ornate Sèvres-style Bowl in Gilt-bronze Frame

Center bowl, Sèvres-style, gilt-bronze mounted, the long oval shallow bowl w/a dark blue exterior centering a large oval reserve w/a color scene of 18th c. lovers in a landscape, framed by ornate gold leafy vines, the white interiors decorated w/floral designs, a beaded gilt-brown rim band & slender inward-scrolled end handles connecting to the pedestal base w/scrolls raised on an oblong platform w/scroll feet, late 19th c., overall 20" l. (ILLUS.)... **2,875**

Bronze-mounted Sèvres-style Jardiniere

Very Fine Blue Sèvres-style Bronze-mounted Jardinieres

Jardiniere, Sèvres-style, gilt bronze-mounted, a wide low squatty bowl decorated w/upper & lower dark blue bands w/gilt stripes & floral clusters, a white central band h.p. w/playful putti alternating w/lion face masks, metal rim band joining arched scroll handles continuing down to the ornate scrolled metal platform raised on claw feet, ca. 1870, 11 1/2 x 26 1/2", 13 1/2" h. (ILLUS., previous page)........... **1,725**

Jardinieres, Sèvres-style, gilt bronze-mounted, a footed wide cylindrical body w/a dark blue ground, one side h.p. w/a large rectangular reserve of 18th c. figures in a woodland, the other side w/a large floral reserve, gold borders & lacy scrolls, metal rim band joined to lion mask & ring side handles continuing to the round base on ornate scrolled feet, blue interlaced "L"s mark, late 19th c., 10 1/2" d., 10 1/2" h., pr. (ILLUS., top of page)... **5,060**

Bleu Nouveau Gilt-decorated Sevres Tea Set

Tea set: cov. teapot, cov. sugar bowl, creamer & one cup & saucer; dark Bleu Nouveau ground, the serving pieces w/bulbous ovoid bodies, each piece decorated w/gilt leaf band around the base & a band of stylized blossoms & leaves around the shoulder, further leaf band & gilt line decoration on each piece, various decorator & potter marks, France, mid-19th c., teapot 6 1/4" h., the set (ILLUS.) **2,271**

Sevres-Style Decorated Teapot

Teapot, cov., cylindrical body w/flat shoulder centering a short neck & low domed cover w/pointed knob finial, curved rim spout & C-scroll handle, turquoise blue ground decorated on one side w/a vignette in color of a barefoot boy playing the flute w/a dog at his feet, the other side w/a colorful bouquet of flowers within a gilt scroll border, teapot 18th c., the decoration added later, spurious blue Sevres interlaced Ls mark, 5" h. (ILLUS.) **598**

Very Elaborate Classical-style Urn

Urn, cov., Sèvres-style, gilt bronze-mounted, a gilt-bronze notch-cornered foot below the cobalt blue ringed pedestal w/ornate gilt scrolls below the tall urn-form body supported on gilt-bronze leaves, the main body h.p. w/a continuous color scene of a semi-nude maiden frolicking w/putti in a garden setting, the shoulder cast w/a narrow metal band w/one side featuring frolicking putti, the other side w/a putto drawing a sword, the tapering cobalt blue neck & domed cover w/ornate gilt scrolling, upright gilt-bronze scroll shoulder handles & a gilt-bronze flame finial on the cover, late 19th c., overall 25 1/4" h. (ILLUS.) **3,346**

Vases, 13 1/8" h., simple ovoid body tapering to a tall trumpet neck, decorated in the Japanese taste to resemble cloisonné, the dark blue ground h.p. w/large purple peonies & rust-colored leafy stems, delicate white blossoms & stems around the neck, Sèvres factory marks, ca. 1875-80, pr. (ILLUS. of one, top next column) **4,780**

One of Two Sèvres Japanese Taste Vases

Shawnee

The Shawnee Pottery Company of Zanesville, Ohio, opened its doors for operation in 1936 and, sadly, closed in 1961. The pottery was inexpensive for its quality and was readily purchased at dime stores as well as department stores. Sears, Roebuck and Co., Butler Bros., Woolworth's and S. Kresge were just a few of the companies that were longtime retailers of this fine pottery.

Shawnee Pottery Company had a wide array of merchandise to offer, from knickknacks to dinnerware, although Shawnee is quite often associated with colorful pig cookie jars and the dazzling "Corn King" line of dinnerware. Planters, miniatures, cookie jars and Corn King pieces are much in demand by today's avid collectors. Factory seconds were purchased by outside decorators and trimmed with gold, decals and unusual hand painting, which makes those pieces extremely desirable in today's market and enhances the value considerably.

Shawnee Pottery has become the most sought-after pottery in today's collectible market.

Reference books available are Mark E. Supnick's book Collecting Shawnee Pottery, The Collector's Guide to Shawnee Pottery *by Duane and Janice Vanderbilt or* Shawnee Pottery - An Identification & Value Guide *by Jim and Bev Mangus.*

Shawnee
U.S.A.

Shawnee Mark

Bellflower Blue-glazed Shawnee Teapot

Clover Blossom Shawnee Teapot

Teapot, cov., Bellflower patt., light blue glaze, marked "U.S.A.," 6 3/4" h. (ILLUS., top of page)................................. **30-35**

Teapot, cov., Clover Blossom patt., embossed decoration, gold trim, marked "U.S.A.," 6-cup, 6 1/2" h. **425-575**

Teapot, cov., Clover Blossom patt., embossed decoration, marked "U.S.A.," 6-cup, 6 1/2" h. (ILLUS., second from top) **125-150**

Teapot, cov., Conventional patt., h.p. dark red blossom on leafy stem, marked "U.S.A.," 6 1/4" h. (ILLUS., bottom next column) **25-30**

Teapot, cov., Cornware, either "Corn King" or "Corn Queen" line, gold trimmed, marked "Shawnee 75," 30 oz., either **275-375**

Conventional Floral Shawnee Teapot

White Corn Gold-trimmed Shawnee Teapot

Teapot, cov., Cornware, either "Corn King" or "Corn Queen" line, marked "Shawnee 75," 30 oz., either **75-95**

Shawnee King Corn Teapot

Teapot, cov., Cornware line, King Corn patt., 30 oz. (ILLUS.) **85**
Teapot, cov., Cornware line, White Corn patt., gold-trimmed, 30 oz. (ILLUS., top of page) **275-375**

Shawnee Crisscross Pattern Teapot

Teapot, cov., Crisscross patt., marked "U.S.A.," 6" h. (ILLUS.).............................. **25-30**
Teapot, cov., Decorative Ribbed patt., marked "U.S.A.," 5" h. **25-30**
Teapot, cov., Elite patt., marked "U.S.A.," 6 3/4" h.. **45-50**

Teapot, cov., Elite patt., w/gold trim & decals, marked "U.S.A.," 6 3/4" h. **75-85**
Teapot, cov., Embossed Rose patt., marked "U.S.A.," 6 1/4" h........................ **45-55**
Teapot, cov., Embossed Rose patt., w/gold trim, marked "U.S.A.," 6 1/4" h. **65-75**
Teapot, cov., Fern or Wheat patt., individual size, yellow glaze, 2-cup **45-50**
Teapot, cov., Fern or Wheat patt., yellow glaze, 6" h. **30-35**

Gold-trimmed Fern Pattern Teapot

Teapot, cov., Fern or Wheat patt., yellow glaze, gold trim & decal, 6" h. (ILLUS.)..... **75-95**

Shawnee Figural Cottage Teapot

Teapot, cov., figural Cottage, marked "U.S.A. 7," 5 1/2" h. (ILLUS., previous page)... **375-450**

Two Granny Ann Teapots with Gold & Floral Decals

Teapot, cov., figural Granny Ann, green apron & shawl w/burgundy & yellow trim, w/gold decal shawl & trim, marked "Patented Granny Ann U.S.A." (ILLUS. right with other Granny Ann teapot, bottom previous page) **375-450**

Teapot, cov., figural Granny Ann, green apron & shawl w/burgundy & yellow trim, no gold decal shawl & trim, marked "Patented Granny Ann U.S.A." (ILLUS. left with other Granny Ann teapot, bottom previous page) **150-200**

Teapot, cov., figural Granny Ann, in peach w/blue trim or purple w/blue trim, marked "Patented Granny Ann U.S.A.," either..... **95-125**

Teapot, cov., figural Granny Ann, lavender apron w/gold trim & floral decals or peach apron w/blue & red trim w/gold trim & floral decals, marked "Patented Granny Ann U.S.A.," each (ILLUS. of both designs, top of page)................................. **225-275**

Teapot, cov., figural Tom the Piper's Son, airbrushed blues & reds w/gold trim, marked "Tom the Piper's Son Patented U.S.A. 44"... **150-175**

Rare Version of Tom the Piper's Son Teapot

Teapot, cov., figural Tom the Piper's Son, airbrushed matte reddish orange & greenish yellow w/gold trim, marked "Tom the Piper's Son Patented U.S.A. 44" (ILLUS.) **325-375**

Two Versions of the Tom the Piper's Sons Teapot

Teapot, cov., figural Tom the Piper's Son, white body w/h.p. trim or airbrushed in blues & reds, marked "Tom the Piper's Son patented U.S.A. 44," 7" h., each (ILLUS. of both designs) **85-125**

Shawnee Valencia Pattern Teapot

Teapot, cov., Valencia patt., dark bluish green glaze, 7 1/2" h. (ILLUS., top of page) **75-100**

Shelley China

Members of the Shelley family were in the pottery business in England as early as the 18th century. In 1872 Joseph Shelley formed a partnership with James Wileman of Wileman & Co. who operated the Foley China Works. The Wileman & Co. name was used for the firm for the next fifty years, and between 1890 and 1910 the words "The Foley" appeared above conjoined "WC" initials.

Beginning in 1910 the Shelley family name in a shield appeared on wares, although the firm's official name was still Wileman & Co. The company's name was finally changed to Shelley in 1925 and then Shelley China Ltd. after 1965. The firm changed hands in the 1960s and became part of the Doulton Group in 1971.

At first only average quality earthenwares were produced, but in the late 1890s new shapes and better quality decorations were used.

Bone china was introduced at Shelley before World War I, and these fine dinnerwares became very popular in the United States and are increasingly popular today with collectors. Thin "eggshell china" teawares, miniatures and souvenir items were widely marketed during the 1920s and 1930s and are sought-after today.

Shelley Mark

Hot water pot, cov., Regent Shape, Blackberry patt., 1933-1966 (ILLUS. right with Regent teapot) **$600-900**

Wileman Tall Hot Water Pot

Hot water pot, cov., tall, lobed cylindrical body, Wileman & Co., patt. No. 7447 (ILLUS.) **100-250**

Rare Attwell Child's Three-piece Rabbit Set

Attwell Boo-Boo Pattern Mushroom Tea Set

Tea set: child's, cov. teapot, open sugar & creamer; Rabbit Set, teapot in the shape of a duck, the creamer in the shape of a rabbit & the sugar in the shape of a chick, designed by Mabel Lucie Attwell, introduced in 1930, the set (ILLUS., top of page).. **1,700-1,800**

Tea set: cov. teapot, open sugar & creamer; Mushroom Set, Boo-Boo decoration, mushroom-shaped teapot & sugar bowl, figural Boo-Boo creamer, designed by Mabel Lucie Attwell, introduced in 1926, the set (ILLUS., second from top) **1,700-1800**

Colorful Alexandra Shape Teapot

Teapot, cov., Alexandra Shape, Wileman & Co., patt. No. 3737, introduced in 1887 (ILLUS.).. **600-900**

Attwell Boo-Boo Teapot in Mushroom Shape

Teapot, cov., Attwell Pixie patt., from Boo-Boo tea set, Mushroom shape w/scene of Boo-Boo on side, 1930 (ILLUS.) **550-850**

Teapot, cov., Auto Teapot Shape, lithographed Chintz Jacobean patt. No. 7850, from the Best Ware group, 1913 (ILLUS., next page)... **130-230**

Shelley Chamberlain Character Teapot

Shelley Chintz Jacobean Teapot

Shelley Old Sevres Teapot in Bute Shape

Teapot, cov., Bute Shape, Birds - Old Sevres patt., decorated in color w/images of exotic birds below a scrolling border band enclosing florals, 1890-1935 & 1949-1963 (ILLUS.).............................. **250-350**

Rataud's Orchid Teapot

Teapot, cov., Carlisle Shape, Floral Rataud's Orchid patt. No. 2408, from the Best Ware group, 1960 (ILLUS.)........... **100-200**

Teapot, cov., Character Shape, Lord Chamberlain patt. No. 3356, from the Intarsio group, 1898 (ILLUS., top of page) **600-1,000**

Shelley Child's Teapot with Florals

Teapot, cov., child's size, spherical body w/domed cover, C-form handle, serpentine spout, brown floral decoration, overall 5 7/8" l., 4 3/8" h. (ILLUS.)................ **150-250**

Cowham Beach Tent Teapot

Teapot, cov., children's line, Beach Tent Shape, part of the Beach set by Hilda Cowham, introduced in 1927 (ILLUS.)...... **1,700**

Rare Dainty Floral Shelley Teapot with Molded Blossoms & Trim

Dainty Floral Pink Panels Teapot

Teapot, cov., Dainty Floral Alternate Shape, Pink Panels patt. No. 11993, from the Best Ware group, 1919 (ILLUS.)........ **800-1,000**

Dainty Floral Chintz Maytime Teapot

Teapot, cov., Dainty Floral Shape, Chintz Maytime patt. No. 0105, from the Seconds group, 1943 (ILLUS.).............. **1,500-2,000**

Teapot, cov., Dainty Floral Shape, not usually seen w/the printed flowers on the brown & green panels, 7 1/2" l., 4 5/8" h. (ILLUS., top of page)......................... **700-1,100**

Dainty Pink Teapot in Dainty Garland Shape

Teapot, cov., Dainty Garland Shape, Dainty Pink patt. No. 051/P, from the Ideal group, 1938 (ILLUS.)....................................... **350-450**

Shelley Dainty Orange Teapot in Dainty Garlands Shape

Teapot, cov., Dainty Garlands Shape, Dainty Orange patt. No. 051/8, from the Ideal group, 1932 (ILLUS.) **350-450**

Shelley Draped Rosebud Teapot & Other Pieces in Ely Shape

Versailles Teapot & Other Pieces in Early Gainsborough Shape

Teapot, cov., Draped Rosebud patt. No. 13510, Repeat litho style, Ely shape from the Best Ware group, 1944, teapot only (ILLUS. w/other pieces, top of page) **150-250**

Teapot, cov., Early Gainsborough Shape, Versailles patt. No. 11426, Birds style, from the Best Ware group, 1925, teapot only (ILLUS. w/other pieces, middle of page).. **250-350**

Teapot, cov., Ely Shape, Rose Pansy-For-get-Me-Not Chintz gold banding, rare, ca. 1935-1965 (ILLUS., next column).. **600-900**

Rare Ely Shape Shelley Teapot

Wileman Empire Shape Teapot with Leafy Pattern 6531

Empire Shape Pot with Pattern 5044

Teapot, cov., Empire Shape, Wileman & Co., patt. No. 5044, 1893-1912, overall 9 1/4" l., 5" h. (ILLUS.) **300-600**

Teapot, cov., Empire Shape, Wileman & Co., patt. No. 6531, introduced in 1893 (ILLUS., top of page)............................ **400-800**

Art Deco Eve Teapot with Laburnum Pattern

Teapot, cov., Eve Shape, Art Deco design, Laburnum patt., 1933-1944 (ILLUS.) **600-900**

Art Deco Eve Bellflower and Leaves Teapot

Teapot, cov., Eve Shape, Bellflower and Leaves patt. No. 12559, from the Best Ware group, 1936 (ILLUS.).................. **300-400**

Teapot, cov., Eve Shape, hot water pot, Loganberry, Green patt. No. 12435, Fruit style, Best Ware group, 1935 (ILLUS. left with Eve Loganberry teapot & tea tile, top next page) **350-450**

Shelley Loganberry Teapot & Hot Water Jug in Eve Shape

Teapot, cov., Eve Shape, Loganberry Green patt. No. 12435, Fruit style, from the Best Ware group, 1935, add at least $100 for stand, teapot only (ILLUS. right w/stand & hot water jug, top of page).... **350-450**

Colorful Foley Shape Teapot

Teapot, cov., Foley Shape, Wileman & Co., patt. No. 7019, introduced in 1894 (ILLUS.)... **600-900**

Shelley Yachts Teapot in Foley Shape

Teapot, cov., Foley Shape, Yachts patt., Faience style, from the Best Ware group, 1905 (ILLUS.).. **200-300**

Queen Anne Teapot with Pattern No. 11495

Teapot, cov., Queen Anne Shape, Pattern No. 11495, stylized florals in panels, introduced in 1926 (ILLUS.)
.... **250-450**

Shelley Woodland Bluebells Scenic Teapot in Queen Anne Shape

Teapot, cov., Queen Anne Shape, Woodland Bluebells patt. No. 12155, Scenic style, from the Best Ware group, 1933 (ILLUS.)... **200-300**

Regent Shape Hot Water & Teapot in the Blackberry Pattern

Teapot, cov., Regent Shape, Blackberry patt., hard to find, 1933-1966 (ILLUS. left with hot water pot)
.... **600-900**

Shelley Floral Phlox Teapot in Regent Shape

Teapot, cov., Regent Shape, Phlox patt. No. 12190, orange, Floral style, from the Best Ware group, 1933 (ILLUS., top of page) **100-200**

Wileman Semi-Porcelain Teapot

Tall Wileman Pot in Shamrock Pattern

Teapot, cov., semi-porcelain, tall slightly tapering cylindrical form w/tall serpentine spout, C-form handle & domed cover w/large pointed finial, overall floral spring patt., Wileman & Co., 8" h. (ILLUS.)
.... **300-450**

Teapot, cov., semi-porcelain, wide half-round body w/wide shoulder to flat mouth, serpentine spout, angled handle, Wileman & Co., Shamrock patt. No. 8064, 7 3/8" l., 4 1/8" h. (ILLUS., top next column) **200-400**

Specially Made Pot with Tea Tile

Teapot, cov., Shamrock patt., wide waisted cylindrical shape w/rim spout, angled handle, concave flat cover w/button finial, overall floral sprig decoration, made for Letheby & Christopher, caterers, pot w/ca. 1925 Shelley mark, matching tea tile w/the Late Foley mark, teapot 6 3/8" w., 4 3/4" h., the set (ILLUS.)...... **200-300**

Shelley Chinese Peony Chintz Teapot with Blue Background

Teapot, cov., Tulip Shape, Chinese Peony Chintz patt., dark blue background, very rare (ILLUS., top next page) .... **900+**

Grouping of Shelley & Wileman Teapots in the Shamrock (No. 8064) Pattern

Teapot, cov., Victoria Shape, Kilkenny Commemorative decoration, pink floral vine on one side, Kilkenny crest on the other side, Wileman & Co., 1885-1925, overall 5 7/8" l., 3 7/8" h. **75-125**

Teapots, cov., grouping of Shelley & Wileman & Co. teapots in patt. No. 8064, each (ILLUS. left to right: Shelley New York Shape, Shelley tapered teapot on tea tile; Wileman smaller semi-porcelain teapot with pewter-repaired spout; tall Wileman semi-porcelain teapot; larger Wileman semi-porcelain teapot, middle of page) **200-450**

Slipware

This term refers to ceramics, primarily red-ware, decorated by the application of slip (semi-liquid paste made of clay). Such wares were made for decades in England and Germany and elsewhere on the Continent, and in the Pennsylvania Dutch country and elsewhere in the United States. Today, contemporary copies of early Slip-ware items are featured in numerous decorator magazines and offered for sale in gift catalogs.

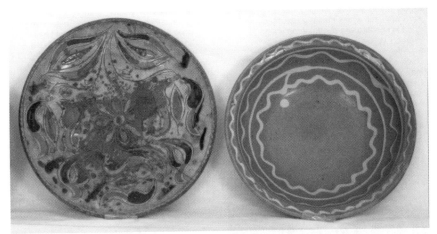

Yellow Slip-decorated Bowl & Sgraffito Charger

Slipware Star Flower Bowl & Line-decorated Dish

Bowl, 11" d., 3" h., wide shallow rounded form, redware w/applied light brown interior glaze decorated w/several yellow slip wavy bands around the interior sides, unglazed exterior, found in Pennsylvania, excellent condition, ca. 1870 (ILLUS. right with sgraffito charger, top of page).. **$1,073**

Bowl, 13" d., 4 3/4" h., flat bottom w/steeply angled sides & molded flat rim, the interior slip-decorated in yellow w/a large eight-point star flower surrounded by tiny blossoms in the bottom, the sides w/a row of tiny blossoms below a bold beaded swag band below an upper band of large seven-point star flowers alternating w/tiny dotted blossoms, small nick, flakes to rim & base, 19th c. (ILLUS. right with slipware dish, middle of page)..................... **431**

Charger, large shallow round form w/wide flanged rim, redware decorated w/concentric bands of squiggle slip decoration & a central long stylized leafy branch, Pennsylvania, 19th c., 11 5/8" d................ **1,195**

Rare Early Slipware Sgraffito Charger

Charger, round w/wide flanged rim, redware w/overall white interior glaze decorated in sgraffito w/a central large image in green, yellow & brown slip of Benjamin Franklin seated in a ladder-back armchair, surrounded by an incised verse in the Pennsylvania Dutch dialect that roughly translates "Work hard when you are a youth and after you are grown keep it up regardless of how hard the work is," wide flange decorated w/stylized flowers & leaves in yellow, green & brown, ca. 1779, early repair to a glued crack, 12" d. (ILLUS., previous page) **2,530**

Dated Slipware Charger with Bird

Charger, round w/wide gently sloped sides, the bottom interior w/a large slip-quilled black outlined bird w/cream dashes below the date "1822," thin cream border bands flanking a dark green squiggle band, Pennsylvania, 12 1/4" d. (ILLUS.) ... **3,107**

Charger, wide round shallow form, redware w/sgraffito decoration of tulips, leaves & a central flowerhead in the applied interi-

or glazes of yellow, orange, brown & green, Pennsylvania origin, extensive wear & chipping to surface, very old hairline at rim, ca. 1800, 12" d. (ILLUS. left with slipware bowl) **3,740**

Charger, wide shallow round form, tooled coggled rim, yellow slip loop bands above the script name "Jackson," probably a commemorative for President Andrew Jackson, typical Connecticut form, ca. 1830, 14" d. (some staining & surface chipping around rim) **3,850**

Dish, round shallow form w/a coggled rim, the interior slip-decorated in yellow w/triple short S-scroll bands flanking straight bands, each composed of four lines, all centered by a long wavy four-line band, Pennsylvania, 19th c., rim chips, 11 1/2" d. (ILLUS. left with star flower bowl) **805**

Spatterware

This ceramic ware takes its name from the "spattered" decoration, in various colors, generally used to trim pieces handpainted with rustic center designs of flowers, birds, houses, etc. Popular in the early 19th century, most was imported from England.

Related wares, called "stick spatter," had freehand designs applied with pieces of cut sponge attached to sticks, hence the name. Examples date from the 19th and early 20th century and were produced in England, Europe and America.

Some early spatter-decorated wares were marked by the manufacturers, but not many. Twentieth century reproductions are also sometimes marked, including those produced by Boleslaw Cybis.

Cup, handleless, Tree Trunk patt. in black w/green spatter leaves, purple spatter background, first half 19th c. (minor stains, crow's foot) **$303**

Spatterware Miniature Cup & Various Plates

Early Spatterware Plates & Teapots

Cup, miniature, handleless, footed w/flat flaring sides, Beehive patt., a yellow beehive surrounded by green spatter below a red spatter rim band, hairlines (ILLUS. front row, center w/spatter plates & platter, bottom of previous page) **2,530**

Cup plate, paneled edge, the center w/a small transfer-printed spread-winged eagle atop a flower urn w/some hand-coloring, a two-tone blue spatter border band, impressed on the back "Warranted," early 19th c., 3 3/4" w. (ILLUS. front row center w/spatterware teapots & plates, top of page) **300-600**

Cup & saucer, handleless, Four Petal Flower patt. in red & green, heavily sponged red & blue spatter background, first half 19th c. (minor stains in cup) **468**

Plate, 7 1/2" d., paneled rim, Fort patt. in grey, green, black & red, blue spatter background, first half 19th c. (minor knife scratches, flake on table ring) **303**

Plate, 8 1/4" d., Rainbow spatter in a bold four-color pinwheel design, yellow, green, red & dark brown w/green center, edge w/faint feather molding, first half 19th c. (hairlines, overall stains & flakes).. **9,900**

Plate, 8 1/4" d., round, Rainbow patt., a central bull's-eye design w/bands of dark brown & lavender, the border band w/alternating stripes of dark brown & lavender (ILLUS. front row, right, with miniature spatter cup & other plates) **1,840**

Plate, 9 1/2" d., Peafowl patt. in red, green & blue, blue spatter border, first half 19th c. (stains, mostly on back, flake & rim repair) **303**

Platter, 12 x 15 1/2", octagonal, Peafowl patt., a large central bird in deep red, blue, green & black, overall red spatter background, impressed "Adams" mark on the back, a few faint knife scratches (ILLUS. back row left, with miniature cup & other spatterware plates) **3,680**

Sauce dish, round w/flanged rim, Thistle patt., a red blossom & green leaves within a blue spatter background, 5 1/8" d. (ILLUS. front row left with miniature spatter cup & other plates) **259**

Soup plate, paneled flanged rim, Tulip patt. h.p. in red, blue, green & black, a wide red spatter border, impressed number on the back, 10 1/2" w. (ILLUS. back row right, with other spatterware plates & teapots) **2,185**

Soup plate, round w/flanged rim, Peafowl patt., a central bird in deep red, blue, yellow & black, overall light green spatter background, short hairline, 10" d. (ILLUS. back row right with miniature cup & other spatterware plates) **633**

Sugar bowl, cov., footed bulbous body w/a low-domed fitted cover w/knob finial, vertical rim strap handles, Rose patt. in red & green, brown spatter background, first half 19th c., 4 1/4" d. (interior stains) **468**

Sugar bowl, cov., footed squatty bulbous form w/rolled rim & inset cover w/knob finial, Rainbow spatter in alternating blue & green stripes up the sides, first half 19th c., 4 3/4" d., 4 1/2" h. (repairs to base & rim).. **330**

Tea set: child's, cov. teapot, cov. sugar bowl, two handleless cups & saucers; Fort patt., the teapot & sugar w/footed squatty bulbous bodies w/wide tapering paneled shoulders supporting domed covers w/button finials, teapot w/serpentine spout & C-scroll handle, sugar w/rolled tab handles, each piece w/a blue spatter ground centered by a painted fort building in black & brown w/green trees, England, ca. 1830, spout & rim flake on teapot, hairline on base of sugar, one cup w/repaired rim, teapot 4 3/8" h., the set (ILLUS., top next page)................................. **825**

Early Child's Spatterware Tea Set

Child's Green Spatterware Tea Set

Tea set: child's size, two cov. teapots, two cov. sugar bowls, two creamers, four handleless cups & one saucer; Peafowl patt., teapots & sugars w/footed squatty bulbous bodies w/flaring necks & inset domed covers w/pointed knob finials, each piece decorated w/a green spatter center band decorated w/a yellow, red & blue peafowl, similar designs w/slightly varying colors, England, ca. 1830, some damage & repair, teapots 4 1/4" h., the set (ILLUS. of part) **1,610**

Teapot, cov., footed squatty bulbous body w/serpentine spout & C-scroll handle, Peafowl patt., a long slender bird in dark yellow, blue & red against a banded green spatter ground, small flake on inner rim flange, 6" h. (ILLUS. bottom row, left, with other spatter teapot & plates) **1,840**

Teapot, cov., miniature, Peafowl patt., a large bird on the side in red, dark blue, green & black against a greenish blue spatter background, early 19th c., 3 5/8" h. (ILLUS. front row, right, with other spatterware teapot & plates) **748**

Teapot, cov., Peafowl patt., footed squatty bulbous body tapering to a flaring rolled neck, long shaped spout & C-scroll handle, low domed cover w/button finial, a light green spatter band around the shoulder above a large h.p. blue, yellow, red & black peafowl, England, ca. 1830, 6" h. (lid slightly undersized & different green, small flake on inner flange) **1,840**

Teapot, cov., Rainbow patt., flat-bottomed slightly tapering bulbous body w/an incurved shoulder tapering to a flat rim, long shaped spout & C-scroll handle, low domed cover w/button finial, decorated w/green spatter around the shoulder & vertical alternating stripes of red & green spatter around the body, England, ca. 1830, 7" h. (repaired spout & cover, additional flaking on cover) **633**

Rare Yellow Spatterware Teapot

Teapot, cov., Thistle patt., a flared base tapering to a wide bulbous ovoid body tapering to a cylindrical neck w/flat rim, serpentine spout & C-form handle, low domed cover w/button finial, bright yellow spatter ground centered by a large red & green thistle design, end of spout damaged, English-made, ca. 1830, 7" h. (ILLUS.) **4,140**

Chamber Set in Cream with Blue Sponging

Teapot, cov., Thumbprint patt., footed wide paneled body w/a squatty bulbous lower section below sides tapering to a flared rim, shaped spout & pointed scroll handle, domed cover w/pagoda finial, dark blue spatter background w/large black spatter overall thumbprints, England, ca. 1825-30, 7 1/2" h. (light overall stains w/a repaired spout & cover)................................. **690**

Toddy plate, round, Schoolhouse patt., a dark blue building in the center surrounded by green & brown spatter, a red spatter border band, 5 7/8" d. (ILLUS. back row, left, with other spatterware plates & teapots) **2,645**

Spongeware

Spongeware's designs were spattered, sponged or daubed on in colors, sometimes with a piece of cloth. Blue on white was the most common type, but mottled tans, browns and greens on yellowware were also popular. Spongeware generally has an overall pattern with a coarser look than Spatterware, to which it is loosely related. These wares were extensively produced in England and America well into the 20th century.

White-banded Blue Spongeware Bowl

Bowl, 8 3/4" d., 3 1/2" h., three bands of blue on white sponging alternating w/two narrow white bands, minor surface wear, late 19th - early 20th c. (ILLUS.)................. **$88**

Blue-sponged Butter Crock

Butter crock, wide flat-bottomed cylindrical form, overall dark blue sponging on white w/the printed word "Butter," excellent condition, 6 1/2" d., 4 1/4" h. (ILLUS.).......... **143**

Chamber set: washbowl & pitcher, round soap dish, shaving mug & master waste jar w/cover; cream background w/overall coarse blue sponging, minor losses to pitcher, late 19th - early 20th c., pitcher 10" h., the set (ILLUS., top of page) **546**

Dark Blue Sponged Charger

Charger, round dished form w/overall dark blue sponging on white, minor wear, late 19th c., 10 1/8" d. (ILLUS.) **173**

Creamer, footed bulbous ovoid body w/a rim spout & C-form handle, overall light blue sponging on white, 3 3/4" h. (some very minor spout roughness)........................ **220**

Rare Blue Spongeware Harvest Jug

Harvest jug, beehive-shaped w/high arched handle across the top above the short angled shoulder spout & round raised back shoulder opening, overall heavy blue sponging on white w/the incised & blue-tinted name "A. Noland," long U-shaped glued crack on the back, rare, ca. 1860, 13" h. (ILLUS.) **688**

Mug, bulbous ovoid body w/small C-form handle, bands of dark blue sponging on white around the rim & base, a relief-molded geometric design around the center of the body, 3" h. (one minor glaze flake on rim) **165**

Pitcher, 8 3/4" h., cylindrical body w/a flat rim & small pointed spout, large C-form handle, overall dense dark blue sponging on white, surface chip at side of base

(ILLUS. far right with three other sponged pitchers) **132**

Pitcher, 9" h., cylindrical body w/a flat rim & large pointed spout, small C-form handle, overall medium blue dense sponging on white w/a blue accent band at the rim, faint hairline from rim at left side of spout, couple of interior glaze flakes (ILLUS. far left with three other sponged pitchers)........ **176**

Pitcher, 9" h., cylindrical body w/flat rim & large pointed spout, large C-form handle, overall medium blue repeating leaf-like sponged rows on white, very minor glaze flake on right side of spout (ILLUS. second from right with three other sponged pitchers) **209**

Pitcher with Medium Blue Sponging

Pitcher, 9" h., cylindrical body w/flat rim & pointed spout, squared loop handle, overall fine medium blue sponging on white, flake on base, early 20th c. (ILLUS.) **288**

Pitcher, 9" h., cylindrical w/a flat rim & pinched spout, C-form handle, dark blue overall coarse sponging on white, late 19th - early 20th c. (tight hairline down from rim, minor flake at end of spout, minor use staining) **176**

Pitcher, 9" h., cylindrical w/a flat rim & pinched spout, C-form handle, medium blue finely mottled overall sponging on white, late 19th - early 20th c. (professional restoration to spout chip).................. **132**

Group of Four Spongeware Pitchers

Pitcher, 9" h., paneled cylindrical form w/rim spout & C-form handle, all over scattered large blue dot sponging on white, professional restoration to a large chip at spout & a couple of interior glaze flakes at rim, overall glaze crazing, late 19th - early 20th c. (ILLUS. second from left with three larger sponged pitchers, bottom previous page) **143**

Wavy Navy Blue Spongeware Pitcher

Pitcher, 9" h., slightly tapering cylindrical body w/pointed rim spout & small C-form handle, dark overall navy blue on white wavy design, hairline from rim near handle, late 19th - early 20th c. (ILLUS.) **176**

Boldly Sponged Blue & White Pitcher

Pitcher, 9" h., tall slightly tapering cylindrical body w/a molded rim w/pointed spout, C-form long handle, overall bold blue sponging on white, minor crazing in glaze, late 19th - early 20th c. (ILLUS.) **303**

Nice Uhl Pottery Spongeware Pitcher

Pitcher, 9 1/2" h., bulbous ovoid body tapering to a cylindrical neck, pinched spout & long C-form handle, overall medium blue sponging on white, marked on the base by the Uhl Pottery Co., Huntingburg, Indiana, early 20th c., excellent condition (ILLUS.) **303**

Platter, oblong shape, overall fine dark blue sponging on white, late 19th c., 10 1/4 x 13 3/4" **173**

Spittoon, footed bulbous rounded body tapering to a widely flaring rim, grey ground w/molded overall basketweave design decorated w/scattered bold dark blue sponging, few glaze flakes, small tight hairline at rim, 8" d., 5" h. (ILLUS. right with spongeware teapot & washbowl, bottom of page)... **66**

Teapot or pipkin, cov., wide bulbous slightly tapering cylindrical body w/a low flared rim w/spout, small C-form handle, white w/overall light blue "chicken wire" design sponging on white, minor glaze crazing, glaze flake at spout, unusual form, late 19th c., 5 3/4" h. (ILLUS. left with spongeware spittoon & washbowl, bottom of page)... **1,265**

Spongeware Spittoon, Teapot & Washbowl

Vegetable or loaf dish, shallow oblong form w/arched ends & flaring sides, overall very dense dark blue sponging on white, late 19th c., 9 1/4" l., 2" h. (minor glaze fleck imperfection on exterior) **99**

Washbowl, footed deep rounded flaring sides w/rolled rim, white ground decorated w/dark blue sponging around the top & base, the center w/two plain white bands flanking a dark blue band, full-length tight glued crack, late 19th - early 20th c., 14" d., 4 1/2" h. (ILLUS. center with spongeware teapot & spittoon)............. **121**

Blue Spongeware Pig Whimsey Figure

Whimsey, model of a standing pig, white Bristol glaze w/scattered blue spots, some surface chipping, ca. 1990, 5" l. (ILLUS.)... **303**

Staffordshire Figures

Small figures and groups made of pottery were produced by the majority of the Staffordshire, England potters in the 19th century and were used as mantel decorations or "chimney ornaments," as they were sometimes called. Pairs of dogs were favorites and were turned out by the carload, and 19th-century pieces are still available. Well-painted reproductions also abound, and collectors are urged to exercise caution before investing.

Staffordshire Spaniels & an Equestrian Group

Dogs, Spaniels, seated position looking at viewer, white w/large rust red spots, yellow chain collars & black face details, hairlines & minor flaking, 7 5/8" h., pr. (ILLUS. left & right w/sportsman equestrian group) **$316**

Equestrian group, a sportsman wearing a brown jacket & black boots mounted on a tan horse, green & brown mounted background base, hairlines, 7" h. (ILLUS. center with pair of spotted Spaniels)................. **345**

Figure group, a young woman standing & holding a jug at her side, wearing a feathered hat, pink blouse & dotted white dress, a spotted white lamb lying at her feet, applied coleslaw trim, oblong gilt-lined base, 1 3/4 x 3", 6 1/2" h. (ILLUS. center with figures of children on goats, bottom of page)... **132**

Figure groups, one w/a boy wearing a white outfit seated on a large white goat, the other w/a matching girl, oval gilt-lined bases, girl w/chip on back base, 3 1/4 x 7", 12 1/2" h., facing pr. (ILLUS. left & right with small figure group of standing girl, bottom of page) **1,760**

Three Staffordshire Figure Groups

Staffordshire Leaping Deer Spill Vases

Spill vases, figural, a leaping red & white stag above a spotted hound, all mounted on a green & brown stump-form base w/a central stump vase, 9" l., 11" h., opposing pr. (ILLUS.)... **316**

Staffordshire Transfer Wares

The process of transfer-printing designs on earthenwares developed in England in the late 18th century, and by the mid-19th century most common ceramic wares were decorated in this manner, most often with romantic European or Oriental landscape scenes, animals or flowers. The earliest such wares were printed in dark blue, but a little later light blue, pink, purple, red, black, green and brown were used. A majority of these wares were produced at various English potteries right up until the turn of the 20th century, but French and other European firms also made similar pieces and all are quite collectible. The best reference on this area is Petra Williams' book Staffordshire Romantic Transfer Patterns - Cup Plates and Early Victorian China (Fountain House East, 1978).

Platter, 12 x 15" oval, Bologna patt. by Adams, blue, ca. 1830s (knife marks w/light staining).. **$330**

Platter, 15 3/4" l., long octagonal shape, the center w/a romantic European landscape, the border design of flowering vines, dark mulberry grey, Rhone patt., Thomas, John & Joseph Mayer, ca. 1843-55 (ILLUS. right with Japan Flowers platter)... **259**

Platter, 17" l., oval w/gently scalloped rim, the center w/a large urn of flowers in the foreground & an exotic garden in the background, four small scenic panels around the rim alternating w/long scroll &

floral panels, deep rose on white, Japan Flowers patt., Ridgway, Morley, Wear & Company, ca. 1836-42 (ILLUS. left with Rhone pattern platter, bottom of page)........ **259**

Large Mulberry Vdina Platter

Platter, 17 1/2" l., octagonal, the center w/a large exotic mountainous landscape, the border band w/scroll-bordered panels of large roses, dark greyish mulberry on white, Vdina patt., Joseph Clementson, ca. 1845-64 (ILLUS.)............... **460**

Early Dark Blue Stubbs Platter

Platter, 15 1/4 x 18 1/4" oval, the oval center decorated w/a large cluster of fruit, the wide body band decorated w/large clusters of flowers alternating w/scrolled panels, early deep blue, back marked "Stubbs #18," first quarter 19th c. (ILLUS.).............. **1,150**

Platter, 16 x 19 1/2" oval, Parisian Chateau patt. by R. Hall, brown, ca. 1840s (rim wear).. **605**

Two Early Staffordshire Transfer-printed Platters

English Victorian Staffordshire Tea Set

Aesthetic Movement Style Soup Plates

Soup plates, round, Aesthetic Movement style, a Japonesque design w/a large fan w/ribbons in the center, the border band w/arched panels of Oriental motifs, dark blue on white, Browne-Westhead, Moore & Co., England, ca. 1875, 10" d., set of 9 (ILLUS.).. **230**

Sugar bowl, cov., deep bulbous boat-form w/small tab handle & flaring collar, high domed cover w/floral finial, dark blue scene of a man pulled on a low sled by two galloping horses, deer & woods in the backgrounde, thistle design on the cover, England, ca. 1830, 6 1/2" h. **770**

Tea set: cov. teapot, cov. sugar bowl, creamer, two handled cups & saucers & a large undertray; each serving piece of upright diamond shape, each wide side panel decorated w/overall small salmon-colored flowers separated by a narrow panel decorated w/stylized black cranes, blue & black floral neck border, mark of Powell & Bishop, England, second half 19th c., minor gilt wear, small flake on teapot spout, tray 14 x 21 1/2", teapot 5" h., the set (ILLUS., top of page)............... **330**

Stoneware

Stoneware is essentially a vitreous pottery, impervious to water even in its unglazed state, that has been produced by potteries all over the world for centuries. Utilitarian wares such as crocks, jugs, churns and the like were the most common productions in the numerous potteries that sprang into existence in the United States during the 19th century. These items were often enhanced by the application of a cobalt blue oxide decoration. In addition to the coarse, primarily salt-glazed stonewares, there are other categories of stoneware known by such special names as basalt, jasper and others.

Rare Early Stoneware Anchovy Jar

Anchovy jar, wide cylindrical body w/angled shoulder to a wide molded mouth, blue-trimmed impressed swimming fish & balloon design all around the shoulder, attributed to Old Bridge, New Jersey potter, in-the-making dark clay color, rare, ca. 1810, 1 qt., 6 1/2" h. (ILLUS.) **$743**

Bank, figural, reclining cat w/head raised & back leg lifted & scratching its side, realistic molded fur & details, overall mottled brown Rockingham glaze, probably 20th c., 6" h. **44**

Cowden & Wilcox Early Batter Jug

Batter jug, wide ovoid body tapering to a short, wide cylindrical neck, short angled shoulder spout, shoulder loops for holding the wire bail handle w/turned wood grip, cobalt blue brushed drooping flower below the impressed mark of Cowden & Wilcox, Harrisburg, Pennsylvania, on the back, brushed plume accents at spout & shoulder loops, design fry on blue, large, long stack mark in the back design, surface wear at base & bail handle, use staining, ca. 1850, 1 gal., 9" h. (ILLUS.) **880**

Bottle, figural, model of a recumbent pig, decorated w/cobalt blue spots & accents on the face, unsigned, two flakes, wear on ears & snout, late 19th - early 20th c., 6 1/8" l. **978**

Small Churn with Clover Decoration

Butter churn, swelled cylindrical body tapering to a thick molded mouth flanked by eared handles, cobalt blue slip-quilled large three-leaf clover design below the blue-tinted impressed mark of S. L. Pewtress & Co., Fairhaven, Connecticut & a size number, design fry, uncommon small size, ca. 1880, 2 gal., 12" h. (ILLUS.) **358**

Rare Early Iowa Stoneware Butter Churn

Butter churn, tall slightly tapering cylindrical body w/a flared molded rim & eared handles, cobalt blue brushed long stylized floral design at the top below the impressed mark "Cedar Falls, Iowa - 6," probably by Martin White, ca. 1865, crack on reverse w/minor losses, 6 gal., 17 1/4" h. (ILLUS.) **2,875**

Butter Churn with Large Stylized Flower

Butter churn, tall slightly ovoid body w/molded rim & eared handles, cobalt blue large slip-quilled bull's-eye flower design, impressed mark of New York Stoneware Co., Fort Edward, New York, ca. 1880, 5 gal., 17 1/2" h. (ILLUS.)... **330**

Nice Covered Cake Crock with Flowers

Cake crock, cov., eared handles, large cobalt blue brushed flower & leaves band around the sides, flat cover w/brushed blue leaves, unsigned, couple of rim chips, extensive knob chipping on cover, ca. 1850, 2 gal., 11" d., 7" h. (ILLUS.) **688**

Early Cream Pot with Script Name

Cream pot, ovoid body w/a wide cylindrical neck & flat rim flanked by eared handles, double stamped "2" above a cobalt blue script "Butter" on one side & "Dolly" on the other side, probably New York state, ca. 1840, professional restoration to a hairline, 2 gal., 10 1/2" h. (ILLUS.) **798**

Unsigned Flower-decorated Small Crock

Crock, flat-bottomed wide ovoid body tapering to a flattened molded wide mouth, light cobalt blue large brushed tulip above leaves design, unsigned but probably Pennsylvania origin, minor glaze burn or cinnamon clay color occurred in the making, minor surface wear & use staining on the back, ca. 1850, 1 pt., 5 1/4" h. (ILLUS.) **688**

Crock, bulbous ovoid body w/a wide slightly flared mouth flanked by eared handles, large brushed cobalt blue tulip design below the impressed mark of C. Hart & Co., Ogdensburg, New York, & impressed number, some glaze spider cracks & crazing on back, ca. 1855, 2 gal., 10" h. (ILLUS. right with two other New York state crocks, bottom of page) **220**

Crock, bulbous ovoid body w/a wide slightly flared mouth flanked by eared handles, cobalt blue slip-quilled antler design below a number, impressed mark of John B. Caire & Co., Pokeepsie (sic), New York, very tight hairline behind one handle, X-shaped body spider crack by other, heavy wear to interior brown Albany slip glaze, fairly uncommon maker, ca. 1850, 3 gal., 10" h. (ILLUS. left with two other New York state crocks, bottom of page) **220**

Three Early Crocks from New York State

Crock, cylindrical w/thick molded rim & eared handles, cobalt blue slip-quilled design of a flying bird chasing a butterfly, unsigned, probably New York state origin, surface chipping on inner & outer rim, two hairlines extending from rim at front & back of left handle, ca. 1880, 3 gal., 10 1/2" h. **495**

Crock, bulbous ovoid body w/a wide slightly flared mouth flanked by eared handles, cobalt blue large brushed stylized flower & stem below the blue-trimmed impressed mark "Manufactured for and Sold by Chapman & Thorp, Oxford, NY," rare mark, probably Albany area, cinnamon-colored glaze, stack marks, 3 gal., 12 1/2" h. (ILLUS. center with two other New York state crocks, bottom previous page) **743**

Fat Bird & Leaf Decor on Three-gallon Crock

Crock, cylindrical w/molded rim & eared handles, cobalt blue slip-quilled fat bird w/head up perched on a small leafy sprig, impressed mark "Ottman Bros. & Co. - Fort Edward, NY - 3," professional restoration to full-length hairline on front, ca. 1870, 3 gal., 10" h. (ILLUS.) **209**

Bennington Crock with Slender Bird

Crock, cylindrical w/molded rim & eared handle, dark cobalt blue slip-quilled slender bird w/crest perched on a leafy sprig design below the impressed mark "E. & L. P. Norton - Bennington, VT - 3," small stone ping in the design w/minor stain, stabilized long hairline from rim on the back, ca. 1880, 3 gal., 10 1/2" h. (ILLUS.) **633**

Cortland, New York Jug with Starburst Design

Jug, cylindrical body w/rounded shoulder tapering to a molded mouth, applied strap handle, unusual bold slip-quilled cobalt blue four-petal starburst w/arrows & dots design, impressed mark of Cortland, New York, minor glaze wear, surface chip on back base, ca. 1860, 1 gal., 11" h. (ILLUS.) **578**

Advertising Jug Made in Lyons, New York

Jug, flat-bottomed beehive shape w/small mouth & strap handle, advertising-type w/brushed cobalt blue inscription reading "R.H. Gilgallon - Scranton - Pa" & "2," made by Co-operative Pottery Co., Lyons, New York, cinnamon clay color in the making & some staining from use, ca. 1890, 2 gal., 12 1/2" h. (ILLUS.).................. **275**

F.B. Norton Jug with Parrot Design

Jug, cylindrical body tapering to a small molded mouth & strap handle, cobalt blue slip-quilled long parrot perched on a vertical leafy sprig below the impressed mark "F.B. Norton and Co. - Worcester, Mass. - 2," excellent condition, ca. 1870, 2 gal., 13 1/2" h. (ILLUS.)......................... **1,485**

Stoneware Milk Pan with Plume Decor

Milk pan, deep slightly flaring cylindrical sides w/a molded rim & pinched spout, decorated w/five small brushed cobalt blue plumes around the sides & three dashes under the spout, unsigned, size designation tooled just below the spout, X-shaped hairline at the base w/a grease stain, ca. 1850, 1 1/2 gal., 11 1/2" d., 6" h. (ILLUS.) **330**

Model of a dog, seated begging spaniel in cream w/dark bluish green applied accents under the Bristol glaze, probably

from Ohio, possibly early 20th c., minor surface wear, 5 1/2" h. (ILLUS., below) **495**

Small Stoneware Begging Spaniel Figure

Brown-glazed Stoneware Pitcher

Pitcher, 8 1/2" h., footed bulbous body tapering to a tall neck w/molded rim & deeply molded spout, strap handle, unsigned, overall dark brown alkaline glaze, some very minor surface chipping at the back rim, ca. 1870, 1/2 gal. (ILLUS.) **303**

Unusual Decorative Stoneware Water Cooler

Water cooler, wide disk foot supporting a wide tapering bulbous urn-form body w/loop shoulder handles, incised large addorsed perched birds trimmed in cobalt blue, brushed cobalt decoration of dots, lines & sprig bands around the neck & shoulder, the back w/a brushed cobalt blue double flower in a pot, mark of the Somerset Potters Works, Massachusetts, kiln burn on front, glued crack on front, in-the-making chip out of bung hole frame, ca. 1870, 3 gal., 15" h. (ILLUS.)..... **3,960**

Teco Pottery

Teco Pottery was actually the line of art pottery introduced by the American Terra Cotta and Ceramic Company of Terra Cotta (Crystal Lake), Illinois, in 1902. Founded by William D. Gates in 1881, American Terra Cotta originally produced only bricks and drain tile. Because of superior facilities for experimentation, including a chemical laboratory, the company was able to develop an art pottery line, favoring a matte green glaze in the earlier years but eventually achieving a wide range of colors including a metallic lustre glaze and a crystalline glaze. Although some hand-thrown pottery was made, Gates favored a molded ware because it was less expensive to produce. By 1923, Teco Pottery was no longer being made, and in 1930 American Terra Cotta and Ceramic Company was sold. A book on the topic is Teco: Art Pottery of the Prairie School, by Sharon S. Darling (Erie Art Museum, 1990).

Teco Mark

Vase, 5 1/4" h., 3" w., ovoid body framed by low integral buttress handles up the sides & joining the short cylindrical neck, smooth matte green glaze, stamped mark **$1,410**

Squatty Teco Vase with Loop Handles

Vase, 5 1/2" h., 8 1/2" l., squatty bulbous oblong form w/the sides pulled up to form integral loop handles flowing into the widely flaring rim of the short flaring neck, overall smooth matte green glaze, stamped mark (ILLUS., previous page) **1,998**

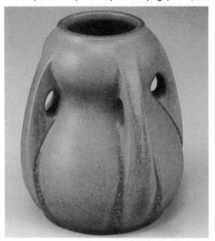

Teco Double Gourd Handled Vase

Vase, 6 3/4" h., 5 1/2" d., bulbous double-gourd body w/four heavy curved & squared handles from the base to the wide flat mouth, designed by W.B. Mundie, charcoal matte green glaze, stamped mark (ILLUS.) **4,313**

Unusual Glossy Crystalline Teco Vase

Vase, 11 1/4" h., footed bulbous bottle-form body w/tall gently flaring neck, glossy crystalline glaze in swirled deep reds & black, unmarked, tiny stilt pull on base (ILLUS.).. **748**

Vase, 22 5/8" h., rare design reminiscent of Van Briggle's "Lorelei" vase, the top mounted by a finely modeled nude wrapping backward around the small opening, the tall slender slightly swelled cylindrical body also molded w/a leafy vine down around the sides, all w/a mottled green glaze, stamped mark & No. 228, figure &

Extremely Rare Figural Teco Vase

one large leaf at top broken off & professionally restored (ILLUS.) **24,150**

Tiles

Tiles have been made by potteries in the United States and abroad for many years. Apart from small tea tiles used on tables, there are also decorative tiles for fireplaces, floors and walls. This is where present collector interest lies, especially in the late 19th century American-made art pottery tiles.

American Encaustic Tile Tableau

American Encaustic Tiling Co., Los An-
geles, California, branch, a vertical
rectangular tableau composed of twenty-
four 4" tiles depicting white water lily blossoms w/purple & green leaves floating on
mottled pale blue & brown water, factory
closed in 1929, mounted on plywood,
17 x 25" (ILLUS., previous page) **$978**

Cambridge Art Pottery Portrait Tile

Cambridge Art Pottery, Cambridge, Ohio,
square, molded in low-relief w/a realistic
bust profile of a pretty young Victorian
lady w/sausage curls, signed on back,
very minor back edge nicks, 6" sq.
(ILLUS.) **138**

**Cook Pottery Co., Trenton, New Jersey
(attributed),** rectangular, a detailed incised & glazed seascape w/two large galleons under full sail in the foreground,
smaller ships in the distance, a crystalline
glaze in shades of brown, mustard yellow, brick red, black, pale blue & green,
black slip mark on the back "Delft," minor
edge chips, early 20th c., overall
4 1/8 x 8 3/8" (ILLUS., bottom of page) **690**

Rare Arketex Corp. Tile

Arketex Corp., Brazil, Indiana, square
boldly molded in high-relief w/a stylized
grotesque face of a cougar, mottled gold
w/blue highlights & cobalt blue border
(ILLUS.) **995**

Long Tile with Galleons at Sea

Large Framed Owens Seascape Tile

Hartford Faience Portrait Tile

Hartford Faience Company, Hartford, Connecticut, rectangular, entitled "Eventide," showing a half-length portrait of a pretty young woman holding a cluster of flowers, golden hair & dark blue cloak, brown & green rockwork background & blue sky, molded grout lines, cement covering on the back, right upper corner broken & repaired, framed, 8 x 13" (ILLUS.).. **5,290**

Pair of International Tile Co. Tiles

International Tile and Trim Co., Brooklyn, New York, square, a facing pair, one w/a low-relief bust profile portrait of a beaded cavalier, the other w/a bust portrait of a young woman wearing a simple bonnet, overall glossy golden glaze, impressed marks on back, few small chips to one, firing line in rear on other, 6" w., pr. (ILLUS.) **230**

Arts & Crafts Landscape Tile by Mosaic

Mosaic Tile Co., Zanesville, Ohio, square, Arts & Crafts landscape of leafy trees w/a cottage in the distance, in pastel colors of turquoise blue, lavender, deep purple, pink & creamy yellow, impressed mark, in old frame & mounting, unobtrusive nicks on back edge, 6" w. (ILLUS.) **575**

Owens (J.B.) Pottery, Zanesville, Ohio, large rectangular plaque-type, raised line seascape showing two galleons sailing on churning sea composed of various shades of green, billowing white & lavender clouds in the blue sky, impressed marks on back, in a new wide flat black wood frame, small edge chips covered by

Harris Strong Sailboats Tile Tableau

frame, couple of nearly invisible pinpoint nicks to raised lines, early 20th c., 11 7/8 x 17 1/2" (ILLUS., top of previoius page) **4,830**

Strong (Harris G.), long rectangular tableau composed of 12 square tiles, forming a Modernistic stylized seascape w/racing sailboats on choppy water in shades of moss green, lavender, deep purple, light blue, white & dark brown, original wooden frame, overall 12 x 35 1/2" (ILLUS., top of page) **345**

w/twelve tiles, showing a scene of water buffalo lying outside a thatched hut, labels read "High Fired Hand Painted Ceramic Tiles by Harris G. Strong," framed, each 18 x 24", pr. (ILLUS.) **1,035**

One of Two Trent Tile Scenic Sets

Trent Tile Co., Trenton, New Jersey, rectangular, sets of three square tiles forming a scene, one showing three Classical maidens reclining in a woodland, the other showing a Classical maiden reaching up to pick cherries, overall shaded mulberry glossy glaze, each in a new wide black wood frame, impressed marks, some minor chips on high points & edges, each tile 6" sq., two sets (ILLUS. of one set) **863**

Torquay Pottery

In the second half of the 19th century several art potteries were established in the South Devon region of England to take advantage of a belt of fine red clay there. The coastal town of Torquay gives its name to this range of wares, which often featured incised sgraffito decoration or colorful country-style decoration with mottos.

The most notable potteries operating in the Torquay area were the Watcombe Pottery, The Torquay Terra-cotta Company and the Aller Vale Art Pottery, which merged with Watcombe Pottery

Framed Harris Strong Tile Tableaux

Strong (Harris G.), two matching tableaux, the first comprised of twelve tiles forming a scene of natives in colorful outfits seated beneath umbrellas, the second, also

in 1901 and continued production until 1962. Other firms whose wares are collectible include Longpark Pottery and The Devonmoor Art Pottery.

Early wares feature unglazed terra cotta items in the Victorian taste including classical busts, statuary and vases and some painted and glazed wares including examples with a celeste blue interior or highlights. In addition to sgraffito designs, other decorations included flowers, Barbotine glazes, Devon pixies framed in leafy scrolls and grotesque figures of cats, dogs and other fanciful animals, produced in the 1890s.

The dozen or so potteries flourishing in the region at the turn of the 20th century introduced their most popular product, Motto Wares, which became the bread and butter line of the local industry. The most popular patterns in this line included Cottage, Black and Colored Cockerels and Scandy, based on Scandinavian rosemaling designs. Most of the mottoes were written in English, with a few in Welsh. On early examples the sayings were often in Devonian dialect. These Motto Wares were sold for years at area seaside resorts and other tourist areas, with some pieces exported to Australia, Canada and, to a lesser extent, the United States. In addition to standard size teawares and novelties, some miniatures and even oversized pieces were offered.

Production at the potteries stopped during World War II, and some of the plants were destroyed in enemy raids. The Watcombe Pottery became Royal Watcombe after the war, and Longpark also started up again but produced simpler patterns. The Dartmouth Pottery, started in 1947, produced cottages similar to those made at Watcombe and also developed a line of figural animals, banks and novelty jugs. The Babbacombe Pottery (1950-59) and St. Marychurch Pottery (ca. 1962-69) were the last two firms to turn out Motto Wares, but these later designs were painted on and the pieces were lighter in color, with less detailing.

Many books on the various potteries are available, and information can be obtained from the products manager of the North American Torquay Society.

ToRQUAY
POTTERY

HELE CROSS
POTTERY
TORQUAY

WATCOMBE
TORQUAY

Torquay Pottery Marks

Smaller "Lakes" Teapot by Watcombe

Teapot, cov., faience "Lakes" decoration, very wide sharply tapering cylindrical body w/small inset cover w/knob finial, a very popular pattern in England but seldom offered in the U.S., Watcombe Pottery, 6" l., 4" h. (ILLUS.) **$165**

Watcombe Faience "Lakes" Teapot

Teapot, cov., faience "Lakes" decoration, wide tapering cylindrical body w/small inset cover w/knob finial, a very popular pattern in England but seldom offered in the U.S., Watcombe Pottery, 7" l., 4" h. (ILLUS.).. **195**

Royal Torquay Rosy Sunset Ships Teapot

Teapot, cov., faience Rosy Sunset Ships patt., flat-bottomed wide tapering cylindrical body w/angled shoulder & conical cover w/knob finial, decorated w/a scene of sailing ships at sunset, Royal Torquay Pottery, 4 7/8" l., 3 1/2" h. (ILLUS.)............... **95**

Rare Large Longpark Motto Ware Teapot with the Colored Cockerel Pattern

Teapot, cov., Motto Ware, Colored Cockerel patt., very large & rare design, wide low tapering cylindrical body w/an angled shoulder decorated w/a band of dots, conical cover w/button finial, short spout & large C-scroll handle, long motto reads "May we all in travelling thro this so called vale of tears - Find ever true and constant friends to share the cup that cheers," some professional restoration, Longpark Pottery, 9" l., 5" h. (ILLUS. of both sides, top of page) **350**

Rare Watcombe Colored Cockerel Teapot

Teapot, cov., Motto Ware, Colored Cockerel w/mottled blue wing patt., reads "Cum me artiez an 'ave a cup o tay," Watcombe Pottery, rare, 7 1/2" l., 5" h. (ILLUS.)............ **250**

Toy Size Cottage Pattern Teapot

Teapot, cov., Motto Ware, Cottage patt., toy size, footed spherical body w/an angled spout, C-form handle & small cover w/knob finial, reads "For my dolly," Roy-

al Watcombe Pottery, 4 7/8" l., 3 1/4" h. (ILLUS.) **175-200**

Motto Ware Gray Cockerel Teapot

Teapot, cov., Motto Ware, Gray Cockerel patt., footed spherical body w/a serpentine spout, C-form handle & small cover w/knob finial, reads "Good morning," Watcombe Pottery, 7 7/8" l., 4 3/4" h. (ILLUS.) **275**

Watcombe Faience Cock Fight Teapot

Teapot, cov., Motto Ware, Old English Cock Fight patt., faience decoration, wide slightly tapering cylindrical body w/serpentine spout & long C-form handle, small inset cover w/knob finial, rim reads "The English Cock," Watcombe Pottery, 6 1/2" l., 4 1/4" h. (ILLUS.) **250-300**
Teapot, cov., Motto Ware, scene of Lindisfarne Castle, miniature, faience decoration, spherical body w/angled spout, C-form handle, small cover w/knob finial, reads "Lindisfarne Castle - Holy Island," Royal Watcombe Pottery, 4 3/4" l., 3" h. (ILLUS., next page)............................... **180-200**

Watcombe Green Motto Ware Teapot

Watcombe Lindisfarne Castle Teapot

Teapot, cov., Motto Ware, wide flat-bottomed tapering cylindrical shape w/angled shoulder to a flat mouth w/a tapering cover w/double-knob finial, straight spout, C-form handle, reads "Du'ee drink a cup ov tay," green glaze, Watcombe Pottery, 6 1/2" w., 3 1/2" h. (ILLUS., top of page) **125-150**

Small Souvenir Sea Gull Pattern Teapot

Teapot, cov., souvenir ware, Sea Gull patt., miniature, spherical body w/a serpentine spout, C-form handle & small cover w/knob finial, reads "Lands End," Royal Watcombe Pottery, 4 7/8" l., 3" h. (ILLUS.) **180-200**

Rare Tiny Mini Aller Vale Teapot

Teapot, cov., tiny miniature size, early Forget-Me-Not h.p. decoration, white clay, Aller Vale Pottery, ca. 1890s, rare (ILLUS.).. **200**

Van Briggle

The Van Briggle Pottery was established by Artus Van Briggle, who formerly worked for Rookwood Pottery, in Colorado Springs, Colorado, at the turn of the century. He died in 1904, but the pottery was carried on by his widow and others. From 1900 until 1920, the pieces were dated. It remains in production today, specializing in Art Pottery.

Early Van Briggle Pottery Mark

Book ends, figural, a plump seated puppy on a rectangular block base, deep mulberry matte glaze w/dark blue on the puppy, marked, pr. (ILLUS., top next page)..... **$345**

Van Briggle Puppy Book Ends

Modern Van Briggle Native American Bust

Bust of Native American Chief, finely detailed, wearing a large feathered headdress, dark turquoise blue matte glaze, company logo on base w/"Van Briggle Colo. Springs Co. - Chief Two Moons - Cheyenne - Limited Edition No. 186 - 1979," 11 1/2" h. (ILLUS.) **196**

Early Brown Van Briggle Candlestick

Candlestick, a round foot tapering to a tall slender cylindrical shaft supporting a wide cupped socket, overall mottled dark brown matte glaze, dated 1914, small grinding chips off the base, 8 5/8" h. (ILLUS.).. **546**

Lady of the Lake Console Bowl & Flower Frog

Console bowl & flower frog, "Lady of the Lake" design, a low undulating oblong bowl w/incurved sides, one end w/an angled rockwork ledge mounted w/the kneeling figure of a maiden looking down into the bowl, a round flower frog inside mounted w/the model of a turtle, shaded blue & turquoise blue matte glaze, each piece marked, some interior staining, bowl 9 7/8 x 14 3/4", 2 pcs. (ILLUS.) **690**

Siren of the Sea Console Bowl & Frog

Console bowl & flower frog, "Siren of the Sea" design, turquoise blue matte glaze, a low footed & rounded shell-shaped bowl w/a full-length figure of a mermaid wrapping around the sides, a shell-form flower frog inside, frog 6" d., 2 3/4" h., bowl 8 x 13", 2 pcs. (ILLUS.) **460**

Damsel of Damascus Van Briggle Lamp

Lamp, table-type, "Damsel of Damascus" design, a kneeling peasant woman holding an urn on one shoulder, urn holding electric fittings, on a domed rockwork base, overall black matte glaze, signed on base, w/newer shade not shown, base 10 5/8" h. (ILLUS., previous page) **196**

Small Van Briggle Vase with Leaves

Vase, 4 1/4" h., squatty bulbous lower body tapering to a wide cylindrical neck w/a flat mouth, molded around the bottom w/large rounded leaves w/swirled stems up the sides, Mountain Craig Brown glaze w/green leaves (ILLUS.) **104**

Corseted Blue & Mulberry Van Briggle Vase

Vase, 6" h., ovoid corseted form w/a small flat mouth, lightly molded around the top w/stylized three-petaled flowers in undulating panels, dark blue flowers against a dark mulberry matte ground, marked (ILLUS.) **173**

Vase, 9 1/4" h., 4" d., "Lorelei," swelled cylindrical form w/a figure of a maiden draped around the rim, cobalt blue over a dark mulberry matte glaze, 1920-25, marked, overall crazing (ILLUS., top next column) **978**

Lorelei Vase in Dark Blue & Mulberry

Very Plain Mulberry Van Briggle Vase

Vase, 9 5/8" h., flat-bottomed completely smooth ovoid body tapering to a slender tall trumpet neck, overall deep mulberry matte glaze (ILLUS.) **115**

Tall Slender Van Briggle Floral Vase

Vase, 10 3/4" h., a tall very slender tapering cylindrical form, molded around the base w/scrolling leaves, slender stems up the sides w/tiny blossoms at the rim, shaded dark blue to pale green matte glaze, dated 1914, fine overall crazing (ILLUS.) **690**

Warwick

Numerous collectors have turned their attention to the productions of the Warwick China Manufacturing Company that operated in Wheeling, West Virginia, from 1887 until 1951. Prime interest seems to lie in items produced before 1911 that were decorated with decal portraits of beautiful women, monks and Native Americans. Fraternal Order items, as well as floral and fruit decorated items, are also popular with collectors.

Warwick Mark

Shaving Mug with Cardinal

Shaving mug, brown w/portrait of Cardinal, marked w/IOGA knight's helmet in green & "Warwick China" in black, decor code A-36 in red, ca. 1903, 3 1/2" d., 3 1/2" h. (ILLUS.).. **$75**

Warwick Portrait Teapot

Teapot, cov., h.p. portrait, "Gibson Girl" decor, turquoise & pink, matte finish, signed "H. Richard Boehm," marked w/IOGA knight's helmet in green, decor code M5, rare in this color, ca. 1910, 7 1/2" h. (ILLUS.).. **425**

Warwick Tudor Rose Pattern Teapot

Teapot, cov., Tudor Rose patt., Banquet Weight Ware, Wheeling, West Virginia, 1912-35 (ILLUS.) **50**
Vase, 6 1/2" h., Clytie shape, overall red ground w/poinsettia decoration, No. E-2...... **210**
Vase, 6 1/2" h., Clytie shape, tan shaded to brown ground w/beechnut decoration, matte finish, No. M-2.................................... **250**

Clytie Portrait Vase in Red Glaze

Vase, 6 1/2" h., Clytie style portrait vase, portrait of Madame Lebrun, red glaze, marked w/IOGA knight's helmet in grey, decor code I14 in red, rare, ca. 1908 (ILLUS.).. **325**
Vase, 6 1/2" h., Den shape, brown shaded to brown ground, pine cone decoration, No. A-64.. **290**
Vase, 8" h., Chicago shape, brown shaded to brown ground w/red & green floral decoration, No. A-40... **250**
Vase, 8" h., Duchess shape, brown shading to brown ground, color floral decoration, A-27 .... **155**
Vase, 8" h., Duchess shape, overall white ground w/color bird decoration, D-1............. **185**
Vase, 8" h., Grecian shape, brown shading to brown ground, color floral decoration, A-6 .... **190**
Vase, 8" h., Rose shape, overall red ground w/color portrait of Madame Recamier, No. E-1... **230**

Vase, 10" h., Roberta shape, brown shaded to brown ground, portrait of a monk, No. A-36.. 260

Vase with Gypsy Girl

Vase, 10 1/4" h., Bouquet #2 style, white w/gold trim & portrait of Gypsy girl, marked w/IOGA knight's helmet in green, ca. 1908 (ILLUS.)............................. 190

Vase, 10 1/2" h., Clematis shape, tan shaded to tan ground w/nut decoration, matte finish, No. M-64 290

Vase, 10 1/2" h., Magnolia shape, green shaded to green ground, color floral decoration, No. B-30 225

Vase, 11" h., Royal #1 shape, brown shaded to brown ground w/colored floral decoration, No. A-40 225

Vase, 11 1/2" h., Chrysanthemum #3 shape, brown shaded to brown ground, color floral decoration, No. A-6 160

Hibiscus Vase with Dogs

Vase, 11 1/2" h., Hibiscus shape, brown shaded to brown ground, large color

scene of red & black & white setter dogs hunting, No. A-50 (ILLUS.)........................... 375

Vase, 11 1/2" h., Regency shape, brown shading to brown ground, color floral decoration, A-40 240

Verona Shape Vase with Bird

Vase, 11 3/4" h., Verona shape, overall white ground, color bird decoration, D-1 (ILLUS.).. 185

Vase, 12" h., Bouquet #1 style, tall cylindrical form w/twig handles, colored transfer of a woman holding long-stemmed yellow roses, shaded ground 225

Vase, 13 1/2" h., Chrysanthemum #2 shape, overall charcoal ground decorated w/colored florals, No. C-6...................... 145

Vase, 13 1/2" h., Senator #2 shape, tan shading to brown ground, color portrait of a gypsy wearing scarf, matte finish, M-1...... 190

Vase, 15" h., A Beauty shape, brown shaded to brown ground w/red rose (American Beauty) decoration, No. A-20...................... 300

Vase, 15" h., A Beauty shape, white ground w/red rose (American Beauty) decoration, No. D-2.. 325

Vase, 15" h., Princess shape, brown shading to brown ground, color floral decoration, A-27.. 350

Commercial China

Warwick "Sumter Hospital" Creamer

Various Warwick Restaurant Mugs

Creamer, white w/two green bands & "Sumter Hospital" logo, 2 1/2" h. (ILLUS., previous page) 22

Cup & saucer, white w/"St. Gregory's" logo 22

Cup & saucer, white w/Crestwood pattern 25

Cup & saucer, white w/Dakota pattern 20

Mug, various decorations, marked w/Warwick knight's helmet in green, ca. 1940s, 3" d., 3 1/4" h., each (ILLUS. of five, top of page) 9

Mug, white w/green drape & emblem, "The Security Benefit Assoc.," 3 1/2" h. 15

Plate, 10" d., white w/gold band, "Souvenir of Pleasanton" decal 25

Plate, 10 1/4" d., white w/"The Washington Duke" logo 35

Platter, 15" l., white w/Wentworth Military Academy crest, maroon band inside rim, marked "Warwick China" in green, ca. 1930s 26

Syrup pitcher, cov., white w/"Johnny's" logo 40

Wedgwood

Reference here is to the famous pottery established by Josiah Wedgwood in 1759 in England. Numerous types of wares have been produced through the years to the present.

WEDGWOOD

Early Wedgwood Mark

Basalt Ware

Potpourri jar, cov., footed bulbous nearly spherical body w/angled loop shoulder handles, fitted low domed cover pierced overall w/small holes & centered by a striped spherical knob, the black ground of the body ornately decorated w/enamel & gilt designs of exotic birds among flowering vines, floral sprigs on the cover, impressed mark, finial possibly reglued, inner disk lid missing, ca. 1820, 13" h. (ILLUS. right with Basalt vase & Rosso Antico potpourri) **$3,055**

Wedgwood Basalt & Rosso Antico Pieces

Wedgwood Decorated Basalt Teapot

Teapot, cov., baluster-form body tapering to a flat rim w/low domed cover & button knob, serpentine spout & C-form handle, the black ground h.p. overall w/large blossoms & leaves in shades of brick red, white & green, Josiah Wedgwood, late 18th - early 19th c., 6 3/4" h. (ILLUS.)....... **1,495**

Teapot, cov., wide baluster-form body w/flat rim & low domed cover w/knob finial, shaped spout & C-scroll handle, black ground applied w/tall deep red Rosso Antico acanthus leaves & bellflowers around the sides, radiating applied leaves around the cover, impressed mark of Josiah Wedgwood, England, early 19th c., 7 1/4" h. (rim nick) **743**

Vase, 15 1/4" h., exaggerated antique bottle-form shape, footed bulbous body tapering to a very slender neck supporting a very wide dished & stepped rim, a round loop shoulder handle, the black ground decorated w/iron-red Grecian figures & stylized decorative banding, impressed mark, early 19th c. (ILLUS. center with Basalt & Rosso Antico potpourri jars) **14,100**

Caneware

Teapot, cov., footed wide squatty body w/a low domed cover w/button finial, short gently arched spout & arched C-scroll handle, smear-glazed & applied around the middle w/a wide band of tight scrolls & leaftips in green, radiating spearpoints applied around cover, impressed mark of Josiah Wedgwood, England, 19th c., 4" h. (faint spider crack in base................ **2,432**

Jasper Ware

Bowl, cov., 5 1/8" d., footed wide cylindrical form w/a flattened cover & disk finial, crimson ground decorated w/panels of white relief classical figures w/foliate vertical bars, impressed mark, ca. 1920 (ILLUS. bottom row, second from left, with large group of yellow & crimson Jasper Ware pieces, bottom of page).. **1,880**

Candlesticks, flaring foot below the cylindrical shaft & wide cupped socket rim, yellow ground applied w/black relief classical figures & palm trees, an arabesque floral foot band & leaftip top band, stain to one socket rim, impressed marks, ca. 1930, 7 3/4" h., pr. (ILLUS. top row, far left with large grouping of crimson & yellow Jasper Ware, bottom of page)........... **1,058**

Large Group of Crimson & Yellow Jasper Ware Pieces

Unusual Jasper Ware Doorknobs & Metal Fittings

Doorknob & escutcheon sets: two oval blue Jasper knobs each decorated w/a white relief figure of a Grecian woman within a white relief leaftip border band, w/pairs of fancy cast gilt-metal knob backplates & keyhole escutcheons, one handle cracked, 19th c., handle 1 5/8 x 2 1/2", 2 1/4" h., the set (ILLUS., top of page) **288**

Match box, cov., flared base & cylindrical sides w/a domed cover, crimson ground decorated w/applied white relief classical figures & a leaftip foot band, slight relief loss, impressed mark, ca. 1920, 2 3/4" h. (ILLUS. bottom row, second from right w/large grouping of crimson & yellow Jasper Ware pieces, top of page) **1,880**

Early Jasper Portrait Medallion

Medallion, portrait-type, oval, blue ground w/a bold white relief bust portrait of War-

ren Hastings, Governor-General of India, the name & title impressed below the bust, modeled by John Flaxman Jr., impressed mark, mounted in an ebonized wood frame, ca. 1787, medallion 3 1/2 x 4 3/8" (ILLUS.) **1,880**

Mustard pot on attached undertray, cov., the flaring dished undertray holding the wide short cylindrical pot w/a fitted domed silver plate cover, yellow ground applied w/black relief fruiting grapevine swags around the sides joined by small lion masks & rings, impressed mark, ca. 1930, rim chip on pot, interior stain, undertray rim restored, 4" h. (ILLUS. top row, second from right with the large grouping of crimson & yellow Jasper Ware pieces) **323**

Pitcher, miniature, 3 7/8" h., ovoid body w/pinched rim spout & long C-form handle, crimson ground decorated in white relief w/classical figures alternating w/vertical scroll bands, ca. 1920 (ILLUS. bottom row, fourth from right with large group of crimson & yellow Jasper Ware pieces) **1,528**

Pitcher, 4 3/4" h., jug-type, wide ovoid body w/a wide short cylindrical neck & arched spout, C-scroll handle, crimson ground decorated w/a band of white relief classical figures, the neck w/applied white swagging, ca. 1920, impressed mark, some relief loss (ILLUS. bottom row, third from left with large grouping of crimson & yellow Jasper Ware pieces) **499**

Pitcher, 5 3/4" h., jug-type, wide ovoid body w/a short cylindrical neck & rim spout, C-scroll handle, yellow ground decorated w/black relief classical figures around the body, black relief swags around the neck, impressed mark, ca. 1930 (ILLUS. top row, third from right with large grouping of crimson & yellow Jasper Ware pieces, bottom of page 659) **588**

Pitcher, 6 1/2" h., jug-type, wide ovoid body w/a short wide cylindrical neck & rim spout, C-scroll handles, crimson ground decorated w/a white relief band of classical figures, white relief swags around the neck, impressed mark, ca. 1920, shallow chip at side of spout (ILLUS. bottom row far left with large grouping of various crimson & yellow Jasper Ware pieces, bottom of page 659) **940**

Blue Jasper Ware Pitcher with Metal Lid

Pitcher, cov., 6 1/2" h., 3 3/4" d., slightly tapering cylindrical body w/loop handle & attached hinged metal lid, dark blue ground w/white relief Grecian figures around the bottom & a grapevine around the rim, marked "Wedgwood - England," late 19th - early 20th c. (ILLUS.) **185-200**

Portland vase, classic design w/a wide ovoid body tapering to a trumpet-form neck flanked by arched handles, yellow ground decorated w/white relief classical scenes, impressed mark, ca. 1900, footrim & rim chip, areas of relief repair, 7" h. (ILLUS. top row, second from left with various other pieces of crimson & yellow Jasper Ware, bottom of page 659) **2,115**

Wedgwood Jasper Diceware Tea Set

Tea set: cov. teapot, cov. sugar bowl & creamer; Diceware patt., each piece w/a black ground w/applied white vinework framing engine-turned dicing w/yellow quatrefoils, Josiah Wedgwood, first half 19th c., footrim chip on teapot ground out, sugar bowl 4" h., teapot 3 7/8" h., the set (ILLUS.) **1,081**

Tea set: miniature, cov. teapot, cov. sugar, creamer & oval tray; blue Jasper Ware, baluster-shaped pot & squatty bulbous sugar & creamer, all w/white relief Classical figures, modern, the set (ILLUS., bottom of page) **50**

Miniature Wedgwood Jasper Ware Tea Set

Josiah Wedgwood Jasper Ware Teapot

Teapot, cov., squatty bulbous form in green w/white relief Classical figures, regular size (ILLUS.) **65**

Vase, 5 1/2" h., round flaring foot below the flaring trumpet-form body, yellow ground decorated around the body w/blue relief classical figures highlighted by thin white bands, a band of blue relief palmette leaves around the foot, a blue relief narrow upper band w/a thin blue band near the rim, impressed mark, missing inner disk lid, restored chips below the base, 19th c. (ILLUS. top row, far right with the large group of crimson & yellow Jasper Ware pieces) **940**

Vase, cov., 11" h., Classical urn-form, a wide round foot & short pedestal base supporting a short swelled lower body issuing large upturned loop handles, the wide gently flaring cylindrical sides w/a wide rolled rim, inset domed cover w/a pointed knob finial, crimson ground, the body decorated w/a continuous scene of white relief classical figures, the foot & lower body w/white relief pointed & fanned leaf & a lappet band, the rolled rim w/another lappet band & the cover w/long white relief acanthus leaves, impressed mark, hairlines in the cover, finial restoration at join, ca. 1920 (ILLUS. bottom row, far right with large group of various crimson & yellow Jasper Ware pieces) **3,525**

Queensware

1940s Wedgwood Queens Ware Pot

Teapot, cov., footed squatty bulbous body in creamy white w/a short angled spout, upright squared handle & tapering domed cover w/knob finial, applied light blue grapevine band around shoulder & cover, marked "Wedgwood Embossed Queens Ware of Etruria & Barlaston," Josiah Wedgwood & Sons, England, ca. 1940, 8 3/4" l., 5" h. (ILLUS.) **70**

Rosso Antico

Potpourri jar, cov., footed bulbous nearly spherical body w/angled loop shoulder handles, fitted low domed cover pierced overall w/small holes & centered by a striped spherical knob, the matte terra cotta body enameled w/scattered large colorful flowers & leaves, impressed mark, restored rim chip on cover, early 19th c., 12 1/2" h. (ILLUS. left with Basalt potpourri jar & vase, page 425) **1,528**

Teapot, cov., squatty rounded shape w/nearly straight spout, flaring flanged front top rim & high angled handle, dark red ground applied w/Oriental-style white prunus blossoms & branches in relief, impressed mark of Josiah Wedgwood, England, early 19th c., 8 5/8" l. (nick to edge of spout) **1,175**

Teapot, cov., squatty rounded shape w/short slightly curved spout & high squared handle, dark red ground applied w/black bands of stylized Egyptian motifs & hieroglyphs, the slightly domed cover w/radiating fluting & a figural crocodile finial, impressed mark for Josiah Wedgwood, England, early 19th c., 4 1/2" h. (nicks to cover rim, restoration to finial, spout lip & handle, cover slightly misfit) **881**

Miscellaneous

Bowl, 7 1/8" w., octagonal, Dragon Lustre, the exterior w/a mottled blue ground under the large entwined dragon, a light mother-of-pearl interior, No. Z4829, printed mark, ca. 1920, slight glaze scratches (ILLUS. second from left with other Lustre ware pieces, top of next page) **470**

Box, cov., Dragon Lustre, wide squatty bulbous base w/domed cover & knob finial, orangish red ground decorated w/an entwined gold dragon, mottled purple interior, printed mark, ca. 1920, 5" h. (ILLUS. second from right with other Lustre pieces, top of next page) **1,116**

Punch bowl, Butterfly Lustre, a wide flaring round foot below the wide rounded bowl, deep ruby luster on the exterior w/butterflies & insects, a mother-of-pearl interior w/butterflies, No. Z4827, printed mark, ca. 1920, very slight interior gilt wear, 11" d. (ILLUS. third from right with other pieces of Lustre ware, top of next page) **2,820**

Grouping of Wedgwood Lustre Pieces

Modern Josiah Wedgwood Teapot

Teapot, cov., Mandarin patt., Queen's shape, Barleston, England, mid-20th c. (ILLUS.)... **35**

Early Wedgwood Pearlware Tureen

Tureen, cov., pearlware, a long lightly fluted oval pedestal base w/gadrooned band below the deep oval body w/light fluting around the sides & upswept scrolled ends above the ropetwist end handles, the steeply domed fluted cover topped by a nude figure seated atop a recumbent horse, dark blue banded highlights, impressed mark, early 19th c., overall 16 1/2" l. (ILLUS.).................................... **1,554**

Vase, 8 1/2" h., Hummingbird Lustre, simple baluster shape w/a short flaring neck, mottled blue exterior ground decorated w/large hummingbirds, orangish red mottled interior, No. Z5294, printed mark, ca. 1920 (ILLUS. far right with other Lustre pieces) **1,175**

Vase, 8 1/2" h., lustre-type in the "Daventry" patt., footed slender cylindrical body w/a narrow shoulder tapering to the trumpet-form neck, a plum-colored ground w/green-0utlined bands around the foot, center, shoulder & neck, the main background decorated w/stylized landscapes & florals trimmed in gold, No. Z5418, printed mark, ca. 1920 (ILLUS. far left with other Lustre pieces)........................... **3,290**

Nicely Hand Painted Wedgwood Vase

Vase, 12 3/4" h., china, footed slender ovoid body tapering to a widely flaring trumpet neck, a deep maroon lower body band trimmed overall w/delicate gilt flower sprigs, the wide white body band h.p. w/large leaf vines w/deep red, blue & yellow flowers, a gilt-trimmed maroon neck band below the white floral-decorated upper neck, marked (ILLUS.)........................... **196**

Weller

This pottery was made from 1872 to 1945 at a pottery established originally by Samuel A.

Weller at Fultonham, Ohio, and moved in 1882 to Zanesville. Numerous lines were produced, and listings below are by pattern or line.

Reference books on Weller include The Collectors Encyclopedia of Weller Pottery by Sharon & Bob Huxford (Collector Books, 1979) and All About Weller by Ann Gilbert McDonald (Antique Publications, 1989).

WELLER Weller Pottery

Weller Marks

Ardsley (1928)
Various shapes molded as cattails among rushes with water lilies at the bottom. Matte glaze.

Bulb bowl, lobed blossom form base w/leaf-form openwork top, pale green leaves on white, 4 7/8" h. **$69**

Vase, 9 1/2" h., bud-type, triple, four tall curved green leaves forming three small openings beside a tall molded blue iris blossom, molded green rockwork base........ **431**

Aurelian (1898-1910)
Similar to Louwelsa line but with brighter colors and a glossy glaze. Features bright yellow/orange brush-applied background along with brown and yellow transparent glaze.

Aurelian Ewer with Yellow Roses

Ewer, a thin widely flaring disk-form base tapering sharply to a tall slender neck w/a tri-lobed flaring mouth, long S-scroll handle from the top rim to the base, shaded dark to light brown ground h.p. w/large yellow roses & green leaves around the lower body, decorated by Marie Rauchfuss, Aurelian-Weller mark, 9" h. (ILLUS.).. **374**

Jug, footed squatty bulbous body w/a short small rolled neck & C-form shoulder handle, h.p. golden grapes & dark green leaves on a shaded gold to black ground,

impressed mark, initials of artist Helen Windle, 5" h. (ILLUS., below)...................... **345**

Aurelian Jug with Golden Grapes

Tall Aurelian Mug with Orange Fruits

Mug, flared ringed base below the tall slightly tapering sides, large C-form handle, h.p. large deep orange fruits & green leaves against a mottled gold & dark green & brown ground, decorated by Charles Chilcote, 6 1/2" h. (ILLUS.) **173**

Small Squatty Aurelian Vase

Vase, 4 1/4" h., three flared knob feet supporting the squatty bulbous body tapering to a low three-lobed rolled rim, h.p. yellow carnations & green leaves on a dark blackish brown ground, Aurelian mark, some dry crazing (ILLUS.) **184**

Aurelian Whiskey Jug with Grapes

Whiskey jug, footed nearly spherical body w/a short round shoulder spout & large arched handle across the top, h.p. w/large dark purple grapes & green leaves on a mottled yellow, dark brown & black ground, initialed by artist Frank Ferrell, 6 1/8" h. (ILLUS.).................................. **259**

Baldin (about 1915-20)
Rustic designs with relief-molded apples and leaves on branches wrapped around each piece.

Bowl, 7" d., wide squatty bulbous form w/wide short flared rim, molded w/large pink & white apples, green leaves & brown branches on a dark blue ground........ **201**

Blossom (mid-late 1930s)
Pale pink flowers & green leaves on a blue or green matte ground.

Jardiniere, footed bulbous body w/a wide rolled rim flanked by small loop shoulder handles, blue ground...................................... **81**

Blue & Decorated Hudson (1919)
Handpainted lifelike sprays of fruit blossoms and flowers in shades of pink and blue on a rich dark blue ground.

Vase, 7 1/2" h., octagonal slightly flaring body tapering slightly at the top to a flat mouth, decorated w/a dark pink band & pink blossoms around the top, dark blue ground, impressed mark **201**

Blue Louwelsa (ca. 1905)
A high-gloss line shading from medium blue to cobalt blue with underglaze slip decorations of fruits & florals and sometimes portraits. Decorated in shades of white, cobalt and light blue slip. Since few pieces were made, they are rare and sought after today.

Cylindrical Blue Louwelsa Vase

Vase, 5 1/8" h., simple cylindrical form, a dark blue ground h.p. w/large pansy-like blossoms in lavender, dark blue & black, impressed mark, glaze inclusion on back (ILLUS.).. **431**

Tall Floral Blue Louwelsa Vase

Vase, 11 1/2" h., tall slender ovoid form tapering to a small molded flat mouth, dark blue shaded to lighter blue ground h.p. w/large stylized black, dark blue & light blue blossoms up the sides, repair to the rim (ILLUS.)... **690**

Blue Ware (before 1920)

Classical relief-molded white or cream figures on a dark blue ground.

Vase, 12" h., cylindrical body w/closed-in rim, decorated w/a repeating scene of dancing maidens, trees & birds, narrow floral band below the rim 288

Vase, 12" h., slightly flaring cylindrical body w/a flared foot & flaring rim, decorated w/a repeating design of a tall cream-colored Grecian-style dancing woman holding aloft a cluster of grapes, shorter green trees & shrubs in the background, a band of rose cluster swags around the rim & a band of pink rose blossoms around the base 230

Bonito (1927-33)

Hand-painted florals and foliage in soft tones on cream ground. Quality of artwork greatly affects price.

Vase, 5" h., double-gourd form w/wide flat mouth, cream ground h.p. w/a large pink daisy-like flower & green leafy stem, impressed mark 143

Burnt Wood (1910)

Molded designs on an unglazed light tan ground with dark brown trim. Similar to Claywood but no vertical bands.

Unusual Tall Burnt Wood Vase

Vase, 15 1/2" h., a sharply tapering conical body below a wide shallow squared cupped rim supported on a winged scarab design, the body design showing the Three Wise Men on camelback following the Christmas star, some glaze misses inside the rim & some background unevenness (ILLUS.) 805

Coppertone (late 1920s)

Various shapes with an overall mottled bright green glaze on a "copper" glaze base. Some pieces with figural frog or fish handles. Models of frogs also included.

Cigarette or match holder, model of a lily pad bloom w/seated frog, 5 1/2" w., 4 1/2" h. 201

Console bowl & flower frog, shallow flaring & lobed bowl, molded, the rim at one end w/a model of a seated frog next to a water lily bud, a separate domed rockwork flower frog, flower frog 2 1/2" h., oval 10 1/2" l., 2" h., 2 pcs. 550-750

Model of a turtle, brown w/heavy green splotching, 6 1/2" l. 460

Rare Coppertone Bud Vase with Frog

Vase, bud, 9" h., 3 1/4" d., slender body w/flaring irregular rim, frog crawling up the side, mottled green & brown glaze (ILLUS.) 920

Dickensware 2nd Line (early 1900s)

Various incised "sgraffito" designs, usually with a matte glaze. Quality of the artwork greatly affects price.

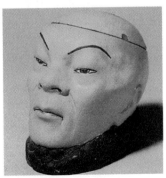

Dickensware II Chinaman Humidor

Humidor, cov., figural, model of a Chinese man's head, realistic coloring, two chips on edge of cover, 5 1/2" h. (ILLUS., previous page).. **431**

Vase, 7" h., triangular baluster-form body flaring at the base, the flat molded mouth w/three tiny loop handles, streaky dark blue ground incised w/pink & dark blue fish, impressed mark.................................... **311**

Dickensware 2nd Line Vase with Monk

Vase, 10 1/8" h., cylindrical w/a narrow angled shoulder to the flat low rounded rim, incised & colored portrait of a monk playing a flute, decorated by Anna Best, minor surface rubs (ILLUS.)............................ **288**

Vase, 11" h., tall ovoid body tapering slightly to a molded mouth, incised decoration of a shepherd & his sheep walking toward a group of trees, shaded green to brown ground, matte glaze, impressed mark......... **633**

Dresden (ca. 1907)
Simple forms with a blue or green matte ground slip-painted with dark blue Dutch scenes of windmills, sailboats or people, sometimes with a seascape in the distance.

Fine Dresden Vase with Windmill Scene

Vase, 10" h., simple cylindrical form, decorated w/a landscape with a Dutch windmill against a mottled blue over dark green ground, decorated by Levi Bur-

gess, barely visible glaze line down from rim (ILLUS.)... **575**

Eocean and Eocean Rose (1898-1925)
Early art line with various handpainted flowers on shaded grounds, usually with a clear glossy glaze. Quality of artwork varies greatly.

Fine Eocean Lamp Base with Birds

Lamp base, tall baluster form w/a cushion base, h.p. w/a pale tan crabapple bough w/pink & white blossoms descending from the rim & supporting two bluebirds against a shaded black body band, cast hole in base, Arthur Powell mark on base, slight overall crazing w/small glaze skip near base & rim, great color & composition, 15 1/4" h. (ILLUS.)..................... **1,610**

Dark Green Eocean Pitcher with Cherries

Pitcher, 6 1/4" h., a footed low wide cylindrical lower section w/a deep indented band joining it to the wide slightly tapering cylindrical upper body w/a wide rim spout & squared inverted D-form heavy handle from the side of the top to the side of the base, very dark green shaded to lighter green ground painted on the upper body w/dark red cherries & green leaves, marked, minor firing separations (ILLUS.) **230**

Eocean Vase with Large Yellow Rose

Vase, 7 1/8" h., flaring cylindrical body w/a wide rounded shoulder tapering to a short molded neck, h.p. w/a large pale yellow rose & green leaves atop long thorny stems down the sides, on a dark greyish blue to pale blue ground, initialed by the artist (ILLUS.) 345

Eocean Vase with Yellow Irises

Vase, 7 7/8" h., a cushion foot tapering to a tall ovoid body w/a wide low flared mouth, a black shaded down to grey ground painted w/a tall cluster of yellow irises accented w/pink & green leaves, unmarked (ILLUS.).. 259

Unusual Eocean Wine Carafe

Wine carafe, footed wide cylindrical body w/a narrow shoulder tapering to a wide cylindrical neck surrounded by six short integrated arched handles from the rim to the shoulder, dark green shaded to pale green ground, h.p. w/a large bunch of purple & green grapes w/leafy stems, decorated by Frank Ferrell, marked on base, missing the cover, 11 1/2" h. (ILLUS.) 575

Etched Floral (ca. 1905)

Various simple shapes decorated with incised flowers or berries outlined in black and usually against solid backgrounds in green, orange, yellow, beige, or pink.

Rare Etched Floral Jardiniere & Pedestal

Jardiniere & pedestal, the wide bulbous ovoid body w/a wide flat closed mouth, decorated w/a wide incised rim band of half-round sunflowers & large green leaves above the pale yellow body, the matching tall waisted pedestal w/a flaring base w/a leaf-molded ruffled foot, a matching sunflower band above the foot, signed by Frank Ferrell, small chip on inside of jardiniere & some interior staining, overall 31 1/4" h., 2 pcs. (ILLUS.) 2,070

Etna (1906)

Colors similar to Early Eocean line, but designs are molded in low relief and colored.

Mug, tall tapering cylindrical form w/angled loop handle, dark blue to grey shaded background decorated w/large pink & deep pink mum blossoms on pale green stems, impressed marks, 5 1/4" h.................. 92

Etna Vase with Dark Red Wild Roses

Vase, 5 1/2" h., a wide low squatty round base tapering sharply to a flaring neck, very dark green shaded to pale green ground painted w/dark maroon wild roses & dark green leaves, impressed Weller & Etna marks (ILLUS.).................................... **150**

Vase, 6" h., wide squatty bulbous lower body centered by tapering sides to a flat mouth, shaded dark blue to grey ground painted w/large pink & purple blossoms on slender stems, impressed marks **218**

Weller Etna Vase with Pink Blossoms

Vase, 9 3/4" h., slightly tapering cylindrical body flaring at the top, a black top shading down to dark grey & pale grey, painted w/large pink blossoms at the top & base joined by a slender green stem, Weller & Etna marks (ILLUS.)...................... **219**

Etna Vase Painted with Large Pink Poppy

Vase, 10" h., a slightly tapering cylindrical body w/a bulbous top centered by a short rolled neck, dark green shaded to pale green ground painted w/a large pink poppy blossom at the top w/green stems & leaves down the sides, marked, few underglaze color spots (ILLUS.) **219**

Flemish (mid-teens to 1928)

Clusters of pink roses and green leaves, often against a molded light brown basketweave ground. Some pieces molded with fruit or small figural birds. Matte glaze.

Rare Flemish Towel Bar with Birds

Towel bar, narrow oblong back plate molded in relief w/a pair of bluebirds at the top center w/pale green vines around the edges & a cluster of deep red blossoms at the lower edge, a long round curve-ended bar from end to end, tiny handle nick, 12" l., 6" h. (ILLUS.)......................... **1,610**

Floretta (ca. 1904)

An early line with various forms molded with clusters of various fruits or flowers against a dark brown, shaded brown or sometimes a dark grey to cream ground. Usually found with a glossy glaze but sometimes with a matte glaze.

Vase, 8" h., flat-bottomed ovoid form tapering sharply to a tiny flared neck, dark brown w/a central wide band of tan molded w/a large cluster of green grapes suspended below the neck, glossy glaze, impressed marks **81**

Vase, 8" h., a wide flattened ovoid body tapering sharply to a tiny flared neck, dark brown glossy ground molded down from the neck w/a large cluster of dark purple grapes, impressed mark **81**

Forest (mid-teens to 1928)

Realistically molded and painted forest scene.

Cylindrical Weller Forest Pitcher

Pitcher, 5 1/2" h., cylindrical w/small rim spout & branch handle, overall molded forest scene in color, chip at top of handle, marked on base (ILLUS., previous page) **173**

Tall Weller Forest Pattern Vase

Vase, 12" h., tall gently flaring waisted shape, woodland path through trees scene, some old glaze chips at rim (ILLUS.)....................... **230**

Weller Forest Wall Pocket with Owl

Wall pocket, conical w/owl peering out of tree trunk, die-stamped twice "Weller," chips on back edge of top & back edge of hanging hole, some glaze skips, 5 1/2 x 11" (ILLUS.)...................................... **207**

Fudzi (ca. 1905)

An early art line developed by Japanese artist Gazo Fudji. While the clay was still moist Fudji incised flowers and leaves with further dots of ornamentation and then colored the designs in rich orange, green or brown enamels. The background was left matte in softly shaded tones contrasting with the incised design.

Vase, 11 3/4" h., gently swelled cylindrical body tapering gently at the shoulder to a flat mouth, a tan shaded to pale blue ground incised w/large maroon & pale green poppy blossoms up the sides w/green leaves & buds near the base, unmarked (ILLUS., below) **2,185**

Large Scarce Fudzi Vase with Poppies

Garden Wares & Related Items

Between 1904 and 1948 the Weller Pottery Company manufactured a wide variety of garden items and related pieces such as planters. An especially wide selection of urns, birdbaths, figurines, fountains, sundials, toadstool seats and oil jars appeared in the 1920s and 1930s. The unique and whimsical human and animal figurals are among the desirable pieces on the market today.

Garden-style Hanging Basket with Birds

Basket, hanging-type, a wide rounded bowl form w/a narrow angled rim fitted w/hanging chains, all molded to resemble glossy green rockwork, four round holes spaced around the sides w/a model of a yellow & black goldfinch applied below each, tail repair to each bird, stress lines at each round hole, 9 1/2" d., 4 3/4" h. (ILLUS.)....... **460**

Glendale (early to late 1920s)

Various relief-molded birds in their natural habitats, lifelike coloring.

Vase, 4 1/2" h., bulbous body, wooded scene of white wren in nest, unmarked........ **201**

Wall pocket, cornucopia-form w/curved tall, arched & scalloped backplate pierced w/a hanging hole, the base molded w/a wren & its young on a flowering cherry blossom branch, unmarked, 6 1/2 x 12 1/2" **374**

Greenbriar (early 1930s)

Hand-made shapes with green underglaze covered with flowing pink overglaze marbleized with maroon striping.

Gourd-shaped Greenbriar Vase

Vase, 8" h., double-lobed gourd-form graduated body w/a short wide gently flaring neck, some short firing separations at base (ILLUS.) **104**

Greora (early 1930s)

Various shapes with a bicolor orange shaded to green glaze splashed overall with brighter green. Semigloss glaze.

Vases, 5" h., bulbous wide twisted body tapering slightly to a wide flat mouth, impressed mark, pr. **173**

Wall pockets, arrowhead shape w/pointed overhead handle, marked, 10 3/8" h., pr. **374**

Hudson (1917-34)

Underglaze slip-painted decoration, "parchment-vellum" transparent glaze.

Pale Hudson Bowl-vase with Roses

Bowl-vase, 3 5/8" h., wide squatty bulbous body tapering to a wide flat mouth, a pale green to yellow ground decorated w/large

yellow & white rose blossoms & green leaves, marked (ILLUS.) **173**

Vase, 5 1/2" h., bulbous ovoid body w/a wide shoulder & short cylindrical neck, white shaded to green ground decorated w/large white daisies on pale green leafy stems, artist-signed, impressed mark **230**

Vase, 5 1/2" h., wide bulbous body topped by a short cylindrical neck, creamy white shaded to pale green ground decorated w/large pale pink poppy-like blossoms on green leafy stems, artist-signed, impressed mark **316**

Hudson Vase with Colorful Flowers

Vase, 7" h., narrow flared foot supporting the swelled cylindrical body w/a widely flaring rim, dark blue shaded to lighter blue ground h.p. w/a cluster of five-petal white, pink, purple & blue blossoms on slender green stems, Weller mark & mark of artist Ruth Axline, small glaze miss at base (ILLUS.) **374**

Hudson Vase with Prunus Branches

Vase, 7 3/4" h., footed bulbous ovoid body tapering to a cylindrical neck w/molded rim flanked by small angular shoulder handles, a deep tan shading to pale yellow ground decorated around the neck & shoulder w/black prunus branches w/white blossoms, decorated by Mae Timberlake, Weller mark (ILLUS.) **431**

Weller Hudson Water Lily Vase

Vase, 7 3/4" h., footed ovoid body tapering to a wide short cylindrical neck w/molded rim flanked by angled handles from rim to shoulder, dark blue to pale yellow ground decorated w/a large white & green water lily w/a golden center & large lily pad leaves, signed by Mae Timberlake on side, some roughness at base (ILLUS.)....... **690**

Hudson Vase with Morning Glories

Vase, 8" h., simple swelled cylindrical form tapering to a wide flat mouth, shaded dark blue to dark grey ground decorated w/large blue & white morning glories on green leafy vines, decorated by Hester Pillsbury, marked on base (ILLUS.) **1,150**

Vase, 9 1/2" h., cylindrical body w/a narrow rounded shoulder to a wide flat mouth, light moss green shaded to cream ground painted w/a repeating design of yellow & white daffodils on tall pale green leafy stems, impressed mark **288**

Vase, 12" h., simple ovoid body tapering to a low widely flared neck, light blue shaded to pale pink ground h.p. w/a large cluster of pale pink, white & blue poppy-like blossoms on leafy stems, signed by Hester Pillsbury, drill hole in base removed part of the mark, few minor glaze inclusions (ILLUS., top next column)............ **920**

Hudson Vase with Large Flower Cluster

Hunter (before 1910)
Brown or green ground with under-the-glaze slip decoration of ducks, butterflies and probably other outdoor subjects. Signed only "HUNTER." High gloss glaze. Usually incised decoration.

Hunter Mug with Swimming Duck

Mug, wide ringed base below the tall slightly tapering cylindrical sides w/a flat mouth & large C-form handle, decorated w/a swimming brown & white duck against a mottled light green & brown shading to dark green ground, Hunter mark, roughness to rim, 6" h. (ILLUS.)............................ **259**

Rare Disk-form Hunter Vase with Fish

Vase, 1 1/4" h., 5" d., very low wide disk-form body w/a low molded central mouth, mottled green & yellow ground decorated w/a dark green & brown swimming fish, decorated by Edwin L. Pickens, Hunter mark on base, minor glaze inclusion & several pinpoint glaze pimples (ILLUS.)....... **748**

Hunter Pillow Vase with Flying Duck

Vase, 5 1/4" h., pillow-type, a flattened bulbous oblong body tapering to a narrow flared oval mouth, decorated w/a large soaring duck in brown & white below a band of dark green stripes around the top, a shaded dark golden yellow to mottled green background, Hunter mark, some very minor glaze rubs on back (ILLUS.) **518**

Jap Birdimal (1904)
Stylized Japanese-inspired figural bird or animal designs on various solid colored grounds.

Fine Jap Birdimal Umbrella Stand

Umbrella stand, gently swelled cylindrical form w/a swelling band below the wide low flaring neck, decorated w/slip-quilled landscape of tall dark blue trees in the foreground & smaller trees in the dis-

tance, all on a shaded medium to light blue ground w/a pale yellow moon, marked (ILLUS.)... **920**

Juneau (ca. 1933)
Simple forms decorated with a glossy mottled drip glaze in red, yellow, blue or green with the drips forming pointed arrow-like designs.

Juneau Vase with Drippy Red Glaze

Vase, 10 1/4" h., footed bulbous ovoid body tapering to a wide cylindrical neck flanked by angled handles from the top rim to the shoulder, mottled deep red, pink & maroon drip glaze, marked, few tiny glaze indentations (ILLUS.) **207**

Kenova (1920)
Simple shapes with a dark green or tan leather-like ground molded with raised designs, usually of roses or daisies but sometimes cameos of birds or women.

Rare Kenova Vase with Rose on Vine

Vase, 8" h., simple wide ovoid shape w/a wide flat mouth, molded w/a large red rose on a leafy green vine wrapping around the sides, Weller mark, museum label on the base, very rare (ILLUS.) **1,150**

L'Art Nouveau (1903-04)
Various figural and floral-embossed Art Nouveau designs.

Vase, 11 1/2" h., tall four-sided slightly tapering body w/molded bands around the base & up each corner, flared four-lobed rim w/a large pansy-like blossom molded in each lobe, pale green matte ground & pink blossoms, impressed mark................... **230**

Unusual Tall L'Art Nouveau Poppy Vase

Vase, 13 3/4" h., a compressed bulbous lower body w/tapering cylindrical sides up to a band of molded high-relief pink poppy blossoms below a small top band, shaded pale green background, impressed Weller mark, minor surface rubs (ILLUS.) **690**

Lorbeek (mid-1920s - 28)
Modernistic forms, usually geometric fan shapes, with a creamy white matte or glossy lavender pink glaze.

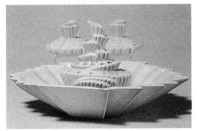

White Lorbeek Four-piece Console Set

Console set: 13 3/4" w. console bowl, 5" w. flower frog & a pair of low 2 1/2" h. candleholders; all w/a white glaze, some minor chips on bowl, the set (ILLUS.) **259**

Louwelsa (1896-1924)
Handpainted underglaze slip decoration on dark brown shading to yellow ground; glossy yellow glaze.

Clock, abstract design case w/a large ruffled rounded crest above large C-scrolls flanking the round dial w/Arabic numerals, painted small berry decoration on the dark shaded brown ground, impressed "Louwelsa Weller 639," 6 1/2" h. (minute edge flake touch-up, non-working).............. **219**

Ewer, footed bulbous ovoid body tapering to a tall slender neck w/a tri-form rim & wide spout, long S-scroll handle, shaded brown ground painted w/a yellow daffodil & long green leaves, 11" h. **259**

Jug, footed large spherical body w/a small short spout on one shoulder & an arched loop handle across the top, painted w/cherries & green & yellow leaves on a shaded dark brown to dark gold ground, decorated by William Hall, impressed mark, 7 1/2" h.. **288**

Louwelsa Tall Mug with Cherries

Mug, tall slightly tapering cylindrical body w/a thick D-form handle, decorated w/dark red cherries & green leaves against a dark background, Louwelsa Weller logo & number 562, several glaze scratches, 5 3/4" h. (ILLUS.) **127**

Small Squatty Louwelsa Pitcher

Pitcher, 5" d., three-footed wide squatty low body tapering to a short neck w/a wide arched spout & round loop handle, h.p. pink & deep red wild roses & green leaves on a shaded dark green ground, Louwelsa mark, some areas of dry glazing (ILLUS., previous page) **161**

Unusual Weller Louwelsa Pitcher-Jug

Pitcher, 10" h., jug-type, footed bulbous ovoid body tapering to a wide curved stove pipe-style cylindrical neck w/a second small cylindrical spout at the back of the neck above the C-form strap handle, decorated w/yellow cherries & green leaves w/some goldtone effect on a dark ground, Weller Louwelsa mark & "3 8," some minor in-the-making glaze flaws (ILLUS.).. **230**

Louwelsa Tankard with Indian Portrait

Pitcher, 16 3/4" h., tankard-type, stepped ringed foot below the tall slightly tapering cylindrical body w/small rim spout & large C-form handle, h.p. bust portrait of a Native American warrior against a black to gold ground, decorated by Marie Rauchfuss, subject identified on the base as High Bear, Sioux Chief w/Weller Louwelsa marks, some restoration to sides, ca. 1905 (ILLUS.).. **920**

Small Louwelsa Vase with Wild Roses

Vase, 4" h., footed wide low squatty lower body tapering sharply to a tall widely flaring trumpet neck, decorated w/red & yellow wild roses & dark green leaves on a dark background, numbered "239-1" & artist-initialed for Lillie Mitchell, tiny base nick (ILLUS.) **127**

Vase, bud, 9" h., widely flaring base tapering sharply to a tall slender trumpet neck w/flared rim, painted w/an orangish red wild rose blossom & green leaves on a dark brown ground, impressed "Weller Louwelsa F" (glaze flakes on rim)............... **127**

Tall Louwelsa Vase with Orange Flowers

Vase, 13 1/2" h., tall slender swelled cylindrical body tapering to a short cylindrical neck, dark blackish brown shaded to green ground, h.p. w/large orange trumpet vine flowers on leafy stems, decorated by Amelia Brown Sprague, Weller Louwelsa mark on base, some small glaze bubbles (ILLUS.) **460**

Tall Cylindrical Louwelsa Vase

Vase, 14 1/8" h., tall cylindrical body w/a thin shoulder & low rolled mouth, dark brown shaded to tan & pale green ground, h.p. w/large green & orange clematis-like blossoms on leafy vines, decorated by Anna Fulton Best, impressed marks, tight hairline at the rim, some dry crazing (ILLUS.) **230**

Manhattan (early 1930s-'34)
Simple modern shapes embossed with stylized leaves or leaves and blossoms and glazed in shades of green or brown. ....

Marengo (1926)
Wall pocket, long conical shape in deep orange lustre decorated w/tall stylized trees & distant hills in dark reddish brown outlined w/white, 8 3/4" l. **374**

Matt Green (ca. 1904)
Various shapes with slightly shaded dark green matte glaze and molded with leaves and other natural forms.

Matt Green Vase with Stylized Florals

Vase, 10 1/4" h., slightly waisted cylindrical body w/a flat rim, a repeating band of stylized looped scrolls around the top, the sides w/overall molded swirling stylized

Art Nouveau florals, impressed mark (ILLUS.) **316**

Muskota (1915 - late 1920s)
Figural pieces with human figures, birds, animals or frogs. Matte glaze.

Figure, woman kneeling on a raised rock platform looking over the edge, decorated in pale green & brown, 8" h. (chip repair) **230**

Scarce Muskota Kingfisher Fish Bowl Base

Fish bowl base, figural, a low oblong woodgrained base w/two short stumps rising from one end, one stump w/a white & blue Kingfisher perched on it, impressed Weller mark, repairs to beak & tail, 13 1/2" l., 11" h. (ILLUS.) **500**

Flower frog, figural, a rounded pale green base w/block feet topped by two figures, a white standing boy nude except for a cloth around his waist that he holds out, the second nude boy kneeling & peering over the edge of the base, catalog model No. 109, 7" h. (near mint except for a firing line) **518**

Muskota Figural Turtle Flower Frog

Flower frog, model of a green turtle w/a lily pad & white blossom on its back, impressed mark, small chip on side of lily pad, 9 1/2" l., 4 1/4" h. (ILLUS.) **330**

Flower frog, model of a woodpecker in brown w/a blue head & black beak perched on a domed brown twisted root base w/two small stump openings, glossy glaze, 5 1/2" h. **144**

Muskota Flower Frog with Two Ducks

Flower frog, model of two white ducks, one standing on the rim, the other below it swimming, pale green base, few minor glaze flakes, 5 1/2" h. (ILLUS.) **288**

Paragon (1934)

A late Art Deco line composed of bowls, vases and candlesticks molded with stylized rounded blossoms hidden among a dense design of long pointed angular leaves. Glazed in magenta, gold, blue and a semi-gloss white.

Magenta Paragon Bowl

Bowl, 4 1/2" h., bulbous nearly spherical form w/a wide flat mouth, dark magenta glaze, Weller script mark (ILLUS.) **127**

Perfecto (early 1900s)

Also known as "Matt Louwelsa." Predominantly sea green, blending into a delicate pink matte finish, unglazed painted decoration.

Vase, 4" h., small bulbous ovoid form tapering to a flat rim, shaded dark yellow lower body shading to creamy white & decorated around the middle w/a continuous band of thin branches w/light blue blossoms, impressed mark **288**

Vase, 5 1/2" h., simple ovoid form tapering to a small slightly flared rim, pale purple ground painted w/small stylized pink blossoms on green stems, artist-signed **288**

Weller Perfecto Vase with Irises

Vase, 7 1/4" h., gently swelled cylindrical body w/a narrow shoulder to the wide flat mouth, the pale blue ground decorated w/a tall cluster of dark blue & lavender irises & tall pale green leaves, painted by Dorothy England, impressed Weller mark, chip-bruise on rim (ILLUS.) **345**

Roma (1912-late '20s)

Cream-colored ground decorated with embossed floral swags, bands or fruit clusters...

Vase, 6 1/4" h., upright rectangular fan-shaped sides w/an openwork rim joined by crossbars, pair of red blossoms & blue berry cluster on each side, pale green border bands... **52**

Wall pocket, conical, incised vertical lines & decorated w/roses & grape cluster near top, green leaves w/yellow center at base, cream ground, 8 1/4" h......................... **92**

Scandia

A little known line composed of low bowls and vases with simple forms, each decorated with a creamy white vertical picket fence-like design against a black ground. Ca. 1915

A Pair of Weller Scandia Vases

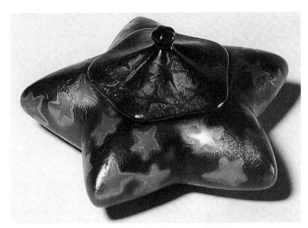

Unusual Sicardo Star-shaped Box

Vases, 7 5/8" h., gently swelled cylindrical body w/flat rim, tight hairline from rim of one, pr. (ILLUS.).. **138**

Sicardo (1902-07)

Various shapes with iridescent glaze of metallic shadings in greens, blues, crimson, purple or coppertone decorated with vines, flowers, stars or freeform geometric lines.

Box, cov., shaped as a five-pointed star w/a conforming cover w/knob finial, overall iridescent design of small stars, unmarked, cover restoration, some grinding chips on base, 2 1/2" w. (ILLUS., top of page)... **403**

Unusual Lobed Sicardo Vase

Vase, 6 3/4" h., squatty tapering four-part melon-lobed lower body below the wide squatty lobed top, small pointed loop handles from upper lobes to lower sides, overall iridescent sunflowers & leaves design in shades of red, blue & green, impressed Weller mark & signed on the side (ILLUS.) **2,645**

Sicardo Vase with Nasturtiums

Vase, 9 5/8" h., cylindrical w/a narrow rounded shoulder to the low flared mouth, overall design of stylized nasturtium blossoms & leaves in tones of gold, green, red & blue, some open pinpoint glaze bubbles in one area, signed on the side (ILLUS.)... **1,265**

Sicardo Vase with Spider Mum Design

Vase, 9 3/4" h., cylindrical w/a narrow rounded shoulder to the low flared mouth, overall design of stylized spider mums in tones of gold, green, red & blue, signed on the side (ILLUS.)....................... **1,840**

Very Rare Molded Sicardo Vase

Vase, 11" h., tall cylindrical lower body w/a bulbous shoulder centered by a small, short cylindrical neck, large relief-molded nasturtium blossoms & leaves around the shoulder w/stems & buds down the sides, colorful iridescent glaze, signed on the side, rare form (ILLUS.).......................... **10,350**

Silvertone (1928)

Various flowers, fruits or butterflies molded on a pale purple-blue matte pebbled ground.

Vase, 6 1/2" h., tapering form w/small loop handles near the rim, molded w/decorated daisies & leaves, marked........................ **259**

Vase, 8" h., ovoid body tapering to a wide flat mouth flanked by small loop branch handles, molded w/yellow & maroon tulip blossoms & green leaves, marked.............. **283**

Vase, 10" h., footed bulbous lower body tapering to a tall cylindrical neck w/molded rim, long angled handles from the edge of the rim to the shoulder, molded large daisy-like flowers in white & pale pink on green leafy stems, lavender pebbled ground, stamped mark................................. **288**

Souevo (1907-10)

Unglazed redware bodies with glossy black interiors. The exterior decorated with black & white American Indian geometric designs.

Bulbous Weller Souevo Vase

Vase, 5 3/8" h., flat-bottomed wide bulbous ovoid body w/a rounded shoulder to the low molded rim band, black rim above a thin scalloped band, the body decorated w/a wide white band painted w/large black Native American-style geometric designs, some staining (ILLUS.).................. **150**

Velvetone (late 1920s)

Blended colors of green, pink, yellow, brown, green, matte glaze.

Pink to Green Velvetone Vase

Vase, 4 3/4" h., bulbous ovoid body tapering to a widely flaring ruffled rim, pale pink shaded to light green, incised mark (ILLUS., previous page) **69**

White & Decorated Hudson (1917-34)
A version of the Hudson line usually with dark colored floral designs against a creamy white ground.

White & Decorated Vase with Branches

Vase, 8 7/8" h., simple tall ovoid body w/a low rolled mouth, creamy ground h.p. w/continuous curving black branches w/small purple blossoms & pale green leaves, impressed mark, pinpoint rim nick (ILLUS.).. **316**

Woodcraft (1917)
Rustic designs simulating the appearance of stumps, logs and tree trunks. Some pieces are adorned with owls, squirrels, dogs and other animals. Matte finish.

Mug, cylindrical tree trunk form w/three small molded foxes peeking out of trunk opening, double loop branch handle, large loop above smaller loop, 6" h. **431**

Low Cylindrical Planter with Foxes

Planter, wide low cylindrical log form w/three small embossed foxes peeking out on front, flat rim, short tight hairline at rim, 7 1/2" d., 4 1/4" h. (ILLUS.) **250**

Vase, bud, 10" h., cylindrical tree trunk form w/top opening & two short relief-molded

branch openings down the sides, apple & leaves down the front............................ **80 - 100**

Wall pocket, conical flattened form modeled as a tree trunk in green & brown w/entwined rose vine w/red flowers, an applied figural squirrel at the base, 9 1/2" h.. **345**

Wall pocket, long flattened trumpet form molded as a tree trunk w/molded leaves near the base & a round opening showing the head of an owl near the top, 11" l. **374**

Willow Wares

This pseudo-Chinese pattern has been used by numerous firms throughout the years. The original design is attributed to Thomas Minton about 1780, and Thomas Turner is believed to have first produced the ware during his tenure at the Caughley works. The blue underglaze transfer print pattern has never been out of production since that time. An Oriental landscape incorporating a bridge, pagoda, trees, figures and birds supposedly tells the story of lovers fleeing a cruel father who wished to prevent their marriage. The gods, having pity on them, changed them into birds, enabling them to fly away and seek their happiness together.

Blue

Large Blue Willow Ironstone Platter

Platter, 14 1/2 x 18", oval w/lightly shaped flanged rim, marked on the back "Ironstone China," England, 19th c. (ILLUS.) **$345**

Chinoiserie Teapot with Swan Finial

Teapot, cov., Chinoiserie style, diamond shaped body w/beveled corners on molded base, tapering slightly to scalloped neck, slightly domed cover tapering slightly to figural swan finial, C-form handle w/thumbrest, straight spout, unmarked, England, ca. 1800 (ILLUS.)..... **350-375**

Unmarked Chinoiserie Teapot

Teapot, cov., Chinoiserie style, ovoid body w/overall narrow ribbing, a short neck & domed ribbed cover tapering to the flat top w/pointed finial, C-scroll handle, slightly serpentine spout, embellished w/gold decoration on rim, spout & finial, unmarked, England, ca. 1800 (ILLUS.) **250-275**

Wedgwood & Co. Blue Willow Teapot

Teapot, cov., footed Gothic Panel Octagon shape, flared neck w/inset domed cover w/pointed finial, C-scroll handle, serpentine spout, Wedgwood & Co., England, ca. 1908+ (ILLUS.)................. **175-200**

Buffalo Pottery Blue Willow Teapot

Teapot, cov., individual size, spherical body on short foot, short cylindrical neck w/inset slightly domed cover w/button finial,

C-form handle, serpentine spout, Buffalo Pottery, Buffalo, New York, 1911 (ILLUS.).. **150-175**

Mason's Ironstone Blue Willow Teapot

Teapot, cov., John Turner Willow patt., footed rectangular shape w/incurved corners, tapering shoulder, rectangular beveled cover w/open loop finial, overhead stationary handle, angled spout, Mason's Ironstone, England, ca. 1890+ (ILLUS.) **200-225**

Unmarked Blue Willow Teapot

Teapot, cov., low ribbed cylindrical body on short foot, tapering shoulder, short cylindrical neck w/scalloped edge, ribbed, slightly domed cover w/flower-form finial, D-form handle, serpentine spout, unmarked, England, ca. 1820 (ILLUS.)..... **250-275**

Grafton China Blue Willow Teapot

Teapot, cov., ovoid body tapering to flaring neck, angled handle, serpentine spout, domed cover w/knob finial, embellished w/silver line decoration, marked "Grafton China," A.B. Jones & Sons, England, ca. 1930s (ILLUS.)...................................... **125-150**

Blue Willow Teapot with "Barber Pole" Decoration

Teapot, cov., squatty ovoid body w/short waisted neck, C-scroll handle & serpentine spout, peaked cover w/disk finial, neck w/band of gold vining decoration on dark blue ground, spout & handle w/blue & white "barber pole" stripes, gold line decoration at base, handle, spout, neck, cover & finial, marked "Pattern" on base, England, 19th c. (ILLUS.)...................... **250-275**

Miniature Blue Willow Teapot

Teapot, cov., miniature, lobed ovoid body, domed inset cover w/finial, C-scroll handle, serpentine spout, gold line decoration on handle, spout, rim & finial, Windsor China, England, 3 3/4" h. (ILLUS.)...... **15-20**

Blue Willow Teapot & Trivet

Teapot, cov., spherical body on short tapering foot, short neck w/inset cover w/but-

ton finial, C-scroll handle, serpentine spout, on matching round trivet, Grimwades, England, early 20th c., teapot 6" h., 2 pcs. (ILLUS.)............................ **250-275**

Blue Willow Teapot with Bamboo Look

Teapot, cov., tapering cylindrical shape slanting in at base, cover w/finial in the form of a curved bamboo shoot, the C-form handle & straight spout decorated in gold to resemble bamboo, gold highlights, marked on base "Semi China," England, early 20th c., 6" h. (ILLUS.)........ **250-275**

Other Colors

Gaudy Willow Teapot by Buffalo Pottery

Teapot, cov., Gaudy Willow patt., ovoid body on short foot, C-form handle, serpentine spout, slightly domed cover w/flat top & knob finial, rust, green & dark blue design, dark blue handle, spout & finial, gold highlights, marked "First Willow Ware Made in America," Buffalo Pottery, Buffalo, New York, 1905 (ILLUS.) **450-500**

Red Willow Mandarin Pattern Teapot

Teapot, cov., Red Willow, Mandarin patt., ribbed cylindrical body on short foot, tapering in at shoulder to slightly domed cover w/petaled finial, straight ribbed spout, overhead metal kettle handles w/porcelain grip, impressed "Copeland," England, 1880 (ILLUS.) **250-300**

Yellowware

Yellowware is a form of utilitarian pottery produced in the United States and England from the early 19th century onward. Its body texture is less dense and vitreous (impervious to water) than stoneware. Most, but not all, yellowware is unmarked and its color varies from deep yellow to pale buff. In the late 19th and early 20th centuries bowls in graduated sizes were widely advertised. Still in production, yellowware is plentiful and still reasonably priced.

Simple Deep Yellowware Bowl

Bowl, 8 1/2" d., 4" h., small footring & deep bulbous rounded sides w/rolled rim, minor age crazing to glaze, probably early 20th c. (ILLUS.) **$33**
Candlesticks, a stepped rectangular foot below the round stem & deep cylindrical

socket w/cupped rim, decorated overall w/a mottled yellow & dark green alkaline glaze, late 19th c., 6" h., pr. (minor age crazing) **853**
Food mold, miniature, round domed shape w/the interior molded w/vertical wide ribs & a swirled design at the top, late 19th - early 20th c., 4 3/4" d., 2 3/4" h. (very minor staining) **77**

Yellowware Mug with Molded Flowers

Mug, cylindrical w/molded base below two thin molded bands, relief-molded wide band of flowers & leaves around the body below a thin beaded rim band, C-form strap handle, tan band of glaze around the rim, stained from use, 19th c., 3" h. (ILLUS.) **77**

Zeisel (Eva) Designs

Hall China Company - Kitchenware

Tri-tone Teapot

Teapot, cov., 6-cup, Tri-tone, ca. 1954 (ILLUS.) **$85**

E. Zeisel Tri-Tone Side-handle Teapot

Teapot, cov., Tri-Tone side-handle model (ILLUS.) **95**

Klein Reed

New Eva Zeisel Design by Klein Reed

Teapot, cov., wide squatty bulbous body on
small base, woven wicker bail handle,
2002 (ILLUS.)... **200**

Monmouth Dinnerware

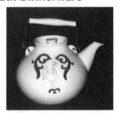

Lacey Wings Teapot with Bird Decoration

Teapot, cov., Lacey Wings patt., wire handle w/ceramic grip, Prairie Hen, w/bird
decoration, ca. 1952 (ILLUS.) **150**

Riverside

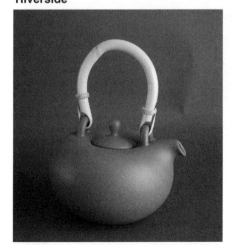

Reissue of the Riverside Design Teapot

Teapot, cov., design reissue, distributed by
The Orange Chicken, made by World of
Ceramics, 2002 (ILLUS.).............................. **200**

Schmid Dinnerware

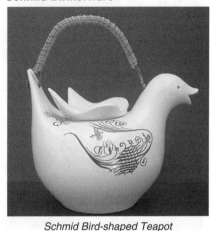

Schmid Bird-shaped Teapot

Teapot, cov., bird-shaped, rattan handle,
Lacey Wings, 1950s (ILLUS.) **50**

Lyric Pattern Teapot by Schmid

Teapot, cov., bird-shaped w/woven wicker
bail handle, Lyric patt., 1965 (ILLUS.).......... **225**

Schramberg

Early Zeisel Teapot by Schramberg

Reissue of early Schramberg Zeisel-designed Teapot

Zeisel Town & Country Teapot in Blue

Teapot, cov., footed tapering bulbous body decorated w/colorful polka dots, No. 3356, Pattern 3369, Germany, ca. 1930 (ILLUS., top of page)................................ **1,200**

Gobelin 13 Teapot

Teapot, cov., Gobelin 13 patt., Germany, 1930s (ILLUS.)... **900**

Teapot, cov., wide low cylindrical shape w/polka dot decoration, reissue of a 1929 design, Pattern 3366, produced for the Metropolitan Museum of Art, 2000 (ILLUS., top of page).................................... **125**

Town and Country Dinnerware - for Red Wing Potteries
Teapot, cov., ca. 1947, blue (ILLUS., second from top).. **200-225**

Watt Pottery
Teapot, cov., rattan handle, Animal Farm patt., ca. 1954 .... **600**

CHARACTER COLLECTIBLES

Numerous objects made in the likeness of or named after comic strip and comic book personalities or characters abounded from the 1920s to the present. Scores of these are now being eagerly collected and prices still vary widely. Also see DISNEY COLLECTIBLES and TOYS and "ANTIQUE TRADER TOY PRICE GUIDE."

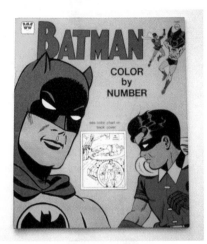

Batman Color by Number Book

Batman Color by Number book, large color images of Batman & Robin on the cover, full-page color guide chart on the back, Whitman Publishing Co., Racine, Wisconsin, 1966, large format, 11 1/2 x 13 1/2" (ILLUS.).............................. **$90**

Rare Early Jointed Betty Boop Doll

Betty Boop doll, jointed composition, w/original red heart label on her green dress, overall restoration to the composition, 1930s, 12" h. (ILLUS.).......................... **546**

Views of an Early Buster Brown Brush

Buster Brown hair brush, child's, silver plate handle & frame w/the oval top inset w/a porcelain plaque transfer-printed in color w/a scene of Buster & his dog, Tige, early 20th c., 5 1/2" l. (ILLUS. of both sides) **86**

1970s Captain Marvel Coloring Book

Captain Marvel coloring book, "Shazam! - Double Trouble Giant Comics to Color," blue background w/a large color image of Captain Marvel in red, yellow, white & black, Whitman Publishing Co., Racine, Wisconsin, 1975, 10 3/4 x 15" (ILLUS.) **20**

Early Charlie Chaplin Comic Book

Charlie Chaplin comic book, "Charlie Chaplin's Funny Stunts - In Full Color," by J. Keeley, 1917, eight pages in color, 12 x 16" (ILLUS.)... **35**

Scarce Early Foxy Grandpa Soap Figure

Foxy Grandpa soap statuette, eyes tinted a dark brown, name impressed in square base, minor wear on base, early 20th c. (ILLUS.).. **95**

Rare Early Happy Hooligan Clock

Happy Hooligan clock, molded composition, a standing figure of Happy Hooligan wearing a black suit, his hands in his pockets, a clock dial w/Arabic numerals in his stomach, clock marked by the New Haven Clock Company, only minor wear, clock not working, early 20th c., 10 1/4" h. (ILLUS.) **818**

Rare Early Shirley Temple Standee

Shirley Temple standee, a life-sized plywood cut-out w/a printed color portrait of Shirley Temple w/her facsimile signature, mid-1930s, 13" w., 48" h. (ILLUS.)............ **2,390**

Original Snoopy Cartoon Drawing

Snoopy cartoon drawing, original colored ink pen on paper showing Snoopy as the

World War I pilot, caption reading "Greetings To All - The Poor Blighters - At Solid Anchor!," signed in the lower right w/the artist's last name, w/original mailing envelope postmarked in 1971, sent to a serviceman serving in Viet Nam at a base called Solid Anchor, 11 x 14" (ILLUS.)...... **1,673**

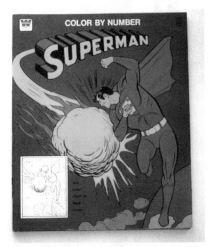

1960s Superman Color by Number Book

Superman Color by Number book, color cover art of Superman ready to smash a meteor, back cover w/a color guide chart, Whitman Publishing Co., Racine, Wisconsin, 1966 (ILLUS.) 90

1970 Tom & Jerry Colouring Book

Tom & Jerry Colouring Book, color cover picture of Tom playing a large tuba w/Jerry in the horn, Merrigold Press - Western Publishing Co., Racine, Wisconsin, 1970, 8 x 10 3/4" (ILLUS.)... 15

Wizard of Oz book, The Road to Oz, by L. Frank Baum, ca. 1909, hard covers, good condition.. 40

1969 Wonder Woman Coloring Book

Wonder Woman coloring book, titled "Homecoming High Jinks," colorful cover picture of Wonder Woman rescuing a man from a huge fire, back cover w/a Wonder Woman cut-out doll & outfits, Whitman Publishing Co., Racine, Wisconsin, 1969, 8 x 10 3/4" (ILLUS.) 40

CHASE BRASS & COPPER COMPANY

From 1930 until 1942, the Chase Brass & Copper Co. of Waterbury, Connecticut, produced an acclaimed line of Art Deco-inspired metal houseware items. These Chase "Specialties" encompassed six general categories, each designed to meet a particular household need: table electrics, buffet service articles, decorative items, drinking accessories, smokers' articles, and miscellaneous housewares. An additional Chase division operating during the same period produced lamps and lighting fixtures.Primary finishes for Chase Specialties included brass, copper, and the company's signature "Chase Chrome."

The company contracted with prominent industrial designers of the time, and among those credited with Chase pieces are Walter Von Nessen, Ruth and William Gerth, Lurelle Guild, Russel Wright, Rockwell Kent, Dr. Albert Reimann, and Harry Laylon.

Chase metal giftwares proved particularly popular during the Depression era of the 1930s, since they conveyed the look of elegance at an economical price, and were easy to maintain. Chase also popularized the vogue for at-home entertaining with its buffet service line, enlisting the promotional efforts of etiquette expert Emily Post. At the height of the firm's popularity in the mid-1930s, Chase wares were displayed in the lavishly decorated showrooms of New York City's Chase Tower.

Chase Pitchers & Mug

With the onset of World War II, Chase closed its Specialty division, devoting efforts to wartime production. The company now specializes in the production of brass rods for industrial use. Although the 12-year "Specialty" period was only a brief interlude in the history of Chase (the firm was established in 1876), more than 500 Specialty items were released, as were an equal number of lamps and lighting fixtures. Most are readily identifiable by the presence of the Chase logo: the engraved figure of a centaur and the words "CHASE U.S.A." Today's collectors prize Chase pieces for the same qualities that initially attracted buyers: eye-catching Deco-inspired designs, easy care, and good value for the investment.

References on the Chase Brass & Copper Co. include a four-volume series by Donald-Brian Johnson and Leslie Pina, released by Schiffer Publishing: Chase Complete (1999); 1930s Lighting: Deco & Traditional by Chase (2000); The Chase Catalogs: 1934 & 1935 (1998), and The Chase Era (2001). Photos for this category are by Dr. Pina.

Walter Von Nessen Coffee Set

Buffet Service Articles

Arcadia water pitcher, No. 90123, Walter Von Nessen design, 7 1/4" h. (ILLUS. right with other pieces, top of page) **$55-65**

Canape plate, No. 27001, Lurelle Guild design, 6 1/4" d. **15-20**

Cocktail ball, No. 90071, Russel Wright design, 3 3/8" d. **25-30**

Diplomat coffee set: 8" h. cov. coffeepot, 2 3/4" h. creamer & 4" h. sugar bowl; No. 17029, Walter Von Nessen design, set (ILLUS., top next column) **280-300**

Napkin clips, No. 90105 Elephant; No. 90106 Duck; No. 90107 Squirrel; No. 90108 Bunny, Harry Laylon design, each . **65-75**

Pancake & corn set: 5 1/4" h. pitcher, 6" d. tray, & salt & pepper shakers; No. 28003, Russel Wright design, set **200-250**

Pretzelman, No. 90038, Lurelle Guild design (ILLUS., bottom next column)........ **100-120**

Salem water pitcher, No. 90004, Ruth & William Gerth design, 9 3/4" h. (ILLUS. second from left with other pieces, top of page) **130-150**

Pretzelman No. 90038

Silent butler, No. 17111, Harry Laylon de-
sign, 11 3/8" l. **45-55**
Valentine serving set: 3 5/8" d. No. 90094
server & 10" d. No. 09019 tray; the set **65-75**

Decorative Items

Architex adjustable centerpiece, seven-
part, Lurelle Guild design **550-600**
Athena candelabra, No. 27030, Lurelle
Guild design, 13 1/2" h. **250-275**
Clipper bowl, No. 15006, Harry Laylon de-
sign, 11 3/8" d. **70-80**

Curl Candlesticks

Curl candlesticks, No. 21007, Albert Re-
imann design, 9" h., pr. (ILLUS.) **800-1,000**
Exquisite vase, N NS-285, Walter Von
Nessen design **300-350**
Four-tube bud holder, No. 11230, Ruth
and William Gerth design, 8 1/4" h. **25-50**
Horse book ends, No. 17044, Walter Von
Nessen design, 6 1/4" h., pr. **600-650**
Jumbo book ends, No. 17113, Walter Von
Nessen design, 4 3/4" h., pr. **400-450**
Puritan candle snuffer, No. 90151, Harry
Laylon design, 15 1/2" l. **75-90**
Ring vase, No. 17039, Walter Von Nessen
design, 9 1/2" h. **45-55**

Sentinel Book Ends

Sentinel book ends, No. 17109, 7 1/4" h.,
pr. (ILLUS.) **425-450**
Tarpon fish bowl, No. 90125, Helen Bishop
Dennis design, 7 7/8" d. **75-85**
Taurex candlestick, No. 24003 - Even,
7 1/8" h., or No. 24004 - Uneven,
9 3/4" h., Walter Von Nessen design,
each **75-80**

Drinking Accessories

Bacchus goblets, No. 90032, Ruth and
William Gerth design, 6" h., each **25-35**
Bacchus pitcher, No. 90036, Ruth and Wil-
liam Gerth design, 10 1/4" h. **150-160**
Bar caddy, No. 90141, Harry Laylon design
.... **10-15**

Blue Moon Cocktail Set

Blue Moon cocktail set: 12 1/4" h. shaker,
12" d. tray & 3 1/2" h. cups; No. 90077,
Howard Reichenbach & Harry Laylon de-
sign, set (ILLUS.) **280-320**
Cheshire mug, No. 90031, 4" h. (ILLUS.
third from left with other pieces) **30-40**
Gaiety cocktail shaker, No. 90034,
Howard Reichenbach design, 11 1/2" h. **40-45**
Ice bowl & tongs, No. 28008, Russel
Wright design, 7" d. **65-75**
Squeezit bottle opener, No. 90086, Harry
Laylon & Theodore H. Low design,
4 1/2" l. **40-50**
Tavern pitcher, No. 17026, Walter Von
Nessen design, 10 1/4" h. (ILLUS. left
with other pieces) **230-250**
Wine cooler, No. 27015, Rockwell Kent de-
sign, 8 1/2" d. **550-600**

Lamps

Binnacle Light (Wired) & Sconce Light

Binnacle light, No. 25002, Adolph Recker design, World's Fair logo, electrified, 5 1/2" h. (ILLUS. left and right w/sconce light, top of page) **100-120**
Sconce light, No. 16004, battery-operated, 7 7/8" h. (ILLUS. center w/binnacle light).. **40-50**

Miscellaneous

Barrel bank, No. 405005, 2 1/4" h. **80-90**
Bomb flashlight, No. 22001, August Mitchell design, 3 1/2" d.................................... **45-65**

Cat Doorstop No. 90034

Cat doorstop, No. 90034, Walter Von Nessen design, 8 1/2" h. (ILLUS.) **200-230**
Light-up vanity box, No. 01013, Sarah Lieberman design, 4 7/8" l. **100-125**
Newspaper rack, No. 27027, Lurelle Guild design, 11 3/8" h. **40-45**
Niagara watering can, No. 05004, Ruth & William Gerth design, 8 3/8" h. (ILLUS. third from left, bottom of page)................. **65-75**
Rain-Beau watering can, No. 05002, Ruth & William Gerth design, 6 1/4" h. (ILLUS. right with other watering cans, next column)... **50-60**
Sunshine watering can, No. 05003, Ruth & William Gerth design, 5" h. (ILLUS. second from left with other watering cans, next column)... **30-40**

Chase Watering Cans

Watering can, No. 11173, Ruth & William Gerth design (ILLUS. left with other watering cans, above) **65-75**

Smoker's Articles

Antelope ash receiver, No. 881, etched glass base, 4 1/2" d. **110-120**
Assembly smoke set: automatic lighter, four coasters, server, & 8 1/4" d. incidental tray; No. 850, Jay Ackerman design....... **120-130**
Drum smoke set: No. 893 Ashtray & No. 894 cigarette server; based on a Helen Bishop Dennis lamp design, set........... **150-160**
Hi-Lo smoker's stand, No. 836, Howard Reichenbach design, telescoping size 16 1/2" to 25 1/2" **120-130**
Lazy Boy smoker's stand, No. 17031, Walter Von Nessen design, 22" h. **400-500**
Pelican ash receiver, No. 17050, Walter Von Nessen design, 5 1/8" h. **140-150**

Rockwell Kent Cigarette Box

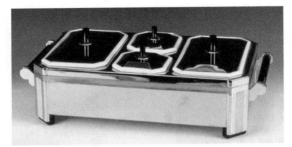

Lurelle Guild Buffet Server

Rockwell Kent cigarette box, No. 847, Rockwell Kent design, 6 1/2" l. (ILLUS., previous page) **1,000-1,200**

Rollaround Cigarette Box

Rollaround cigarette box, No. 841, Ruth & William Gerth design, 7" l. (ILLUS.) **90-130**
Snuffer ashtray, No. 845, George Burton design.. **60-70**

Table Electrics

Buffet server, No. 27011, Lurelle Guild design, 18" l. (ILLUS., top of page) **150-175**
Buffet warming oven, No. 90096, Charles Arcularius design, 10 1/4" l. **90-100**
Coronet coffee urn, No. 17088, Walter Von Nessen design, 12" h. **275-300**
Snack server, No. 90093, Howard Reichenbach design, 13" d. **75-85**

CHILDREN'S BOOKS

The most collectible children's books today tend to be those printed after the 1850s. While age is not completely irrelevant, illustrations play a far more important role in determining value. While first editions are highly esteemed, it is the beautiful illustrated books that most collectors seek. The following books, all in good to fine conditions, are listed alphabetically. Also see: BIG LITTLE BOOKS, and DISNEY COLLECTIBLES

A Visit to the Hospital, Wonder Books, 1958, written under the supervision of Lester L. Coleman, M.D., illustrated by Ken Rossi (ILLUS., top next column) **$15**

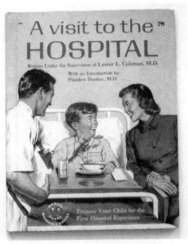

A Visit to the Hospital Wonder Book

Annette - Mystery at Moonstone Bay

Annette and the Mystery at Moonstone Bay, a Walt Disney title, by Doris Schroeder, illustrations by Adam Szwejkowski, Whitman Publishing, Racine, Wisconsin, 1962, hard cover (ILLUS.) **9**

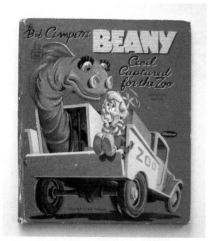

Beany - Cecil Captured for the Zoo Book

Beany - Cecil Captured for the Zoo, story & illustrations by Bob Clampett, Tell-A-Tale Book, Whitman Publishing, Racine, Wisconsin, hard cover, 1954, 5 1/2 x 6 1/4" (ILLUS.).................................... **20**

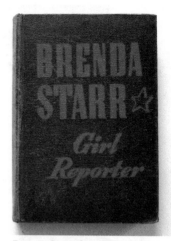

Brenda Starr, Girl Reporter Book

Brenda Starr - Girl Reporter, based on comic strip by Dale Mussick, Whitman Publishing, Racine, Wisconsin, hard cover, 1941 (ILLUS.) **12**

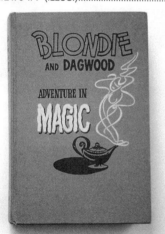

Blondie and Dagwood Adventure in Magic

Blondie and Dagwood - Adventure in Magic, by Chic Young, green cloth cover w/a magic lantern & genie, Whitman Publishing Co., Racine, Wisconsin, 1944 (ILLUS.)... **20**

Combat! - The Counterattack Book

Combat! - The Counterattack, by Franklin M. Davis Jr., illustrated by Arnie Kohn, based on 1960s TV series, Whitman Publishing, Racine, Wisconsin, hard cover, 1964 (ILLUS.) **25**

Early Automobiles Golden Library Book

Early Automobiles, Golden Library of Knowledge, subtitled "The Story of Horseless Carriages from the Clock Spring Car of 1649 to Henry Ford's Model T," Golden Press, New York, New York, w/dust jacket, 1961, 7 x 9 1/2" (ILLUS.)... **12**

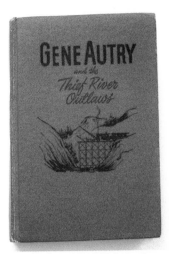

Gene Autry - The Thief River Outlaws

Gene Autry and the Thief River Outlaws, by Bob Hamilton, illustrations by Dan Muller, orange hard cloth cover w/railroad train illustration, Whitman Publishing, Racine, Wisconsin, 1944 (ILLUS.) **22**

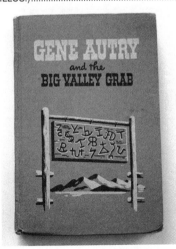

Gene Autry - The Big Valley Grab

Gene Autry and the Big Valley Grab, by W.H. Hutchinson, illustrations by Randy Steffen, Whitman Publishing, Racine, Wisconsin, hard cover, 1952 (ILLUS.) **22**

Great Men of Medicine

Great Men of Medicine, by Ruth Fox Hume, illustrations by Robert Frankenberg, World Landmark Book, published by Random House, New York, New York, w/color dust jacket, 1947 (ILLUS.)................. **12**

Hopalong Cassidy Takes Cards

Hopalong Cassidy Takes Cards, by Clarence E. Mulford, Garden City Publishing, New York, New York, 1937, worn binding (ILLUS.)... **15**

Invisible Scarlet O'Neil Book

Invisible Scarlet O'Neil, by Russell Stamn, based on a comic strip, Whitman Publishing, Racine, Wisconsin, 1943 (ILLUS.)......... **12**

I Decided Ding Dong School Book

I Decided, by Miss Frances, A Ding Dong School Book, Rand McNally & Co., Chicago, based on the children's TV show, worn binding, 1953 (ILLUS.) **50**

Lassie - Forbidden Valley Book

Lassie - Forbidden Valley, by Harry M. Timmons, based on TV series, color photo of Timmy & Lassie on the cover, Whitman Publishing, Racine, Wisconsin, hard cover, 1959 (ILLUS.)..................................... **12**

Roy Rogers & The Gopher Creek Gunman

Roy Rogers and The Gopher Creek Gunman, by Don Middleton, illustrated by Erwin L. Hess, blue & red cloth covers, Whitman Publishing, Racine, Wisconsin, 1945 (ILLUS.)... **22**

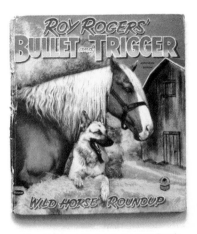

Roy Rogers' Bullet & Trigger Book

Roy Rogers' Bullet and Trigger - The Wild Horse Roundup, by Elizabeth Beecher & August Lenox, a Cozy Corner Book by Whitman Publishing, Racine, Wisconsin, color hard cover w/photo of Trigger & Bullet, 1953, 7 1/2 x 8 1/4" (ILLUS.) **15**

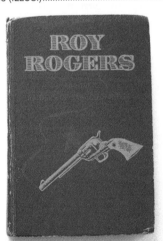

Roy Rogers - Raiders of the Sawtooth Ridge

Roy Rogers and the Raiders of the Sawtooth Ridge, by Snowden Miller, illustrated by Henry E. Valley, red hard cover w/yellow title & pistol, Whitman Publishing, Racine, Wisconsin, some binding wear, 1946 (ILLUS.) **22**

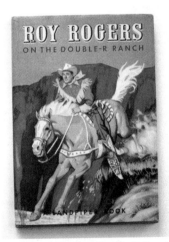

Roy Rogers on The Double-R Ranch

Roy Rogers on The Double-R Ranch, by Elizabeth Beecher, illustrations by Ernest Nordli, colorful hard cover, A Sandpiper Book by Simon & Schuster, New York, New York, 1951 (ILLUS.).............................. **45**

The Lone Ranger Rides Again Book

The Lone Ranger Rides Again, by Fran Striker, creator of the radio series, colorful dust jacket w/some damage, Grosset and Dunlap, New York, New York, back cover of dust jacket lists Hardy Boys Mystery Series titles, 1943 (ILLUS.).............. **35**

The Rebel - Based on the TV Show

The Rebel, by H.A. DeRosso, illustrated by Adam Szwejkowski, hard cover w/color image of Nick Adams as the TV show character Johnny Yuma, Whitman Publishing, Racine, Wisconsin, 1961 (ILLUS.).. **18**

The Real McCoys & Danger at the Ranch

The Real McCoys and Danger at the Ranch, by Cole Fannin, illustrated by Warren Tufts, based on the TV show, Whitman Publishing, Racine, Wisconsin, 1961 (ILLUS.).. **15**

The Son of The Phantom Book

The Son of The Phantom, by Lee Faulk & Ray Moore, based on the comic strip, blue & red hard cover, Whitman Publishing, Racine, Wisconsin, 1944 (ILLUS.) **15**

They Flew To Fame Book

They Flew To Fame, by Robert Sidney Bowen, illustrated by Geoffrey Briggs & Nel Clairmonte, true-life stories of aviation pioneers & heroes, colorful hard cover scene of a World War II pilot, Whitman Publishing, Racine, Wisconsin, 1963 (ILLUS.).. **15**

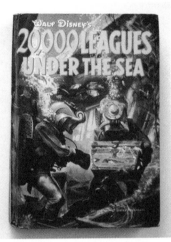

20,000 Leagues Under the Sea

Twenty Thousand (20,000) Leagues Under The Sea, by Jules Verne, Walt Disney edition, illustrated by John Steel & Hugh Huemer, colorful hard cover, Whitman Publishing, Racine, Wisconsin, 1955 (ILLUS.).. **22**

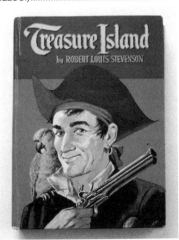

Whitman Edition of Treasure Island

Treasure Island, by Robert Louis Stevenson, illustrated by Paul Frame w/colorful hard cover picture of Long John Silver, Whitman Classic, Whitman Publishing, Racine, Wisconsin, 1955 (ILLUS.) **28**

Wells Fargo and Danger Station

Wells Fargo and Danger Station, by Sam Allison, illustrated by Robert L. Jenney, based on the 1950s TV show, hard cover, Whitman Publishing, Racine, Wisconsin, 1958 (ILLUS.)... **20**

Wiggletail Story Book

Wiggletail, story & illustrations by Charlie, Top Top Tales series, color hard cover picture, Whitman Publishing, Racine, Wisconsin, 1944 (ILLUS.) 10

A Book of Zane Grey Stories

Zane Grey, a compilation of his stories including "The Shortstop," "To All the Girls and All the Boys Who Love the Grand Old American Game," Grosset and Dunlop, New York, New York, red hard cover, 1937, 5 x 7 1/2" (ILLUS.)............................... 35

Little Golden Books

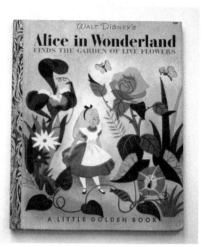

Alice in Wonderland - Garden of Live Flowers

"Alice in Wonderland Finds the Garden of Live Flowers (Walt Disney's)," No. D20, 1951, by Jane Werner, illustrated by Campbell Grant, 28 pp. (ILLUS.) **$17**

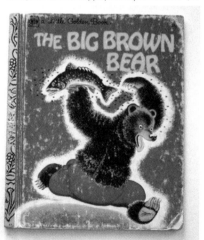

The Big Brown Bear Book

"Big Brown Bear (The)," No. 89, 1947, illustrations by Gustaf Tenggren, written by Georges Duplaix, 42 pp., some cover scuffing & wear (ILLUS.).................................. 6

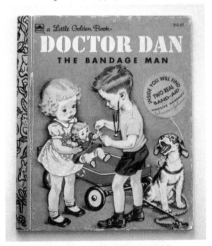

Walt Disney's Cinderella Book

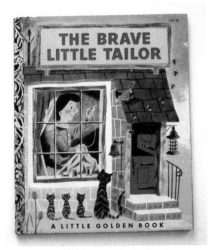

The Brave Little Tailor Book

"Brave Little Tailor (The)," No. 178, 1953, illustrated by J.P. Miller, 28 pp. (ILLUS.)........ **10**

"Cinderella (Walt Disney's)," No. D13, 1950, illustrated by Campbell Grant, dark blue background, 28 pp. (ILLUS.)................. **15**

Reissue of The Christmas Story

"Christmas Story (The)," No. 456-15, 1952 (1992 reissue), story by Jane Werner, illustrated by Eloise Wilkins (ILLUS.) **2-4**

Doctor Dan - The Bandage Man

"Doctor Dan - The Bandage Man," No. 312-27, 1950, by Helen Gaspard, illustrated by Corrine Malvern, two Johnson & Johnson Band-Aids inside (ILLUS.).............. **90**

Four Puppies Little Golden Book

"Four Puppies," No. 303-52, 1960, by Anne Heathers, illustrated by Lilian Obligado, some wear & cover tape stain (ILLUS.)... **5**

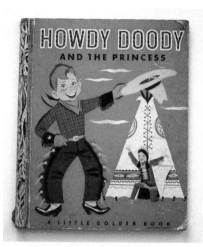

Howdy Doody And The Princess

"Howdy Doody And The Princess," No. 135, 1952, copyright by Kagran Corp., illustrations by Art Seiden, written by Edward Kean, 28 pp. (ILLUS.) **25**

Hopalong Cassidy - The Bar 20 Cowboys

"Hopalong Cassidy And The Bar 20 Cowboys," No. 147, 1952, copyright by Doubleday & Co., Inc., illustrations by Sahula-Dycke, written by E.M. Mulford, 28 pp., some cover wear (ILLUS.) **15**

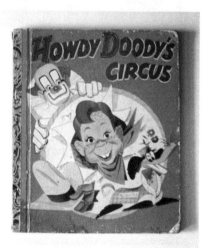

Howdy Doody's Circus

"Howdy Doody's Circus," No. 99, 1950, copyright by Robert E. Smith, illustrations by Liz Dauber, written by Don Gormley, 28 pp., some cover wear (ILLUS.) **15**

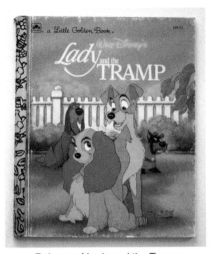

Reissue of Lady and the Tramp

"Lady and the Tramp (Walt Disney's)," No. 105-72, 1954 (1991 reissue), by Teddy Slater, illustrated by Bill Langley & Ron Dias (ILLUS.) **2-4**

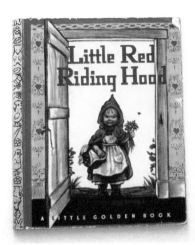

1948 Little Red Riding Hood Book

"Little Red Riding Hood," No. 42, 1948, story & illustrations by Elizabeth Orton Jones, 42 pp., slight cover damage (ILLUS.).. **25**

Little Golden ABC Reissue Book

"Little Golden ABC (The)," No. 200-31, 1951 (1979 reissue), illustrated by Cornelius DeWitt, 24 pp., slight cover wear (ILLUS.)....................................... **2-4**

The Lone Ranger & the Talking Pony

"Lone Ranger (The) and the Talking Pony," No. 310, 1958, by Emily Broun, illustrated by Frank Boole, based on the TV show, 24 pp. (ILLUS.) **15-20**

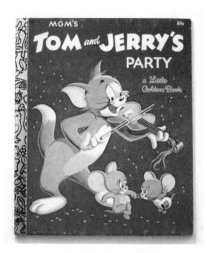

Tom And Jerry's Merry Party

"Tom And Jerry's Merry Party," No. 235, 1955 (1973 reissue), by Steffi Fletcher, illustrated by Harvey Eisenberg, 28 pp. (ILLUS.)... **4**

Early Winky Dink Little Golden Book

"Winky Dink," No. 266, 1956, by Ann McGovern, illustrated by Richard Scarry, based on the TV show, 24 pp., some cover wear (ILLUS.).. **15-20**

"Woody Woodpecker Takes A Trip (Walter Lantz)," No. 111-42, 1961, by Ann McGovern, illustrated by Al White & Ben DeNunez (ILLUS.,) **2-5**

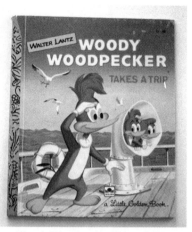

Woody Woodpecker Takes A Trip

CHRISTMAS COLLECTIBLES

Starting in the mid-19th century, more and more items began to be manufactured to decorate the home, office or commercial business to celebrate the Christmas season.

In the 20th century the trend increased. Companies such as Coca-Cola, Sears and others began producing special Christmas items. The inexpensive glass, then plastic Christmas tree decorations began to appear in almost every home. With the end of World War II the toy market moved into the picture with annual Santa Claus parades and the children's visits to Santa.

In the 21st century this trend continues, and material from earlier Christmas seasons continues to climb in value.

Bead ornament, spearpoint design w/small colored beads strung along a long wire, used in floral arrangements & other holiday displays, 1920s, each strand (ILLUS. of various colors, top next column) **$5**

Tiny Conical Paper Shade Holder Pin

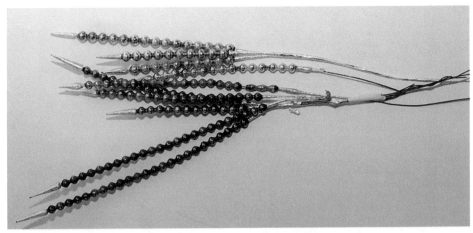

Early Bead on Wire Ornaments

Bubble light holder pin, tiny paper cone w/wire, held paper shades on the bubble light, rare (ILLUS.) **100**

Early Bubble Light Paper Shade

Bubble light shade, conical paper decorated w/dancing children & trees in red, green & black, also found in other designs, designed to fit onto tree bubble lights, made by the Sail-Me Company, Chicago, ca. 1930s, each (ILLUS.) **30-45**

Bubble Light Shade with Three Wise Men

Bubble light shade, conical paper decorated w/the Three Wise Men against a dark blue ground, also found in other designs, designed to fit onto tree bubble lights, made by the Sail-Me Company, Chicago, ca. 1930s, each (ILLUS.) **30-45**

Rare Father Christmas Candy Container

Candy container, bendable figure of Father Christmas wearing a red & white crepe paper outfit & w/a bisque mask face produced by Heubach, holding a sack & bundle of twigs & seated on a simulated wood log that forms the container, Germany, early 20th c., overall 9" h. (ILLUS.) **1,035**

Long Silvered Paper Door Swag

Seated Father Christmas Candy Container

John Wright Father Christmas Doll

Candy container, large figure of Father Christmas wearing a red crepe paper coat, cotton batting beard, hair & other trim, molded papier-mache painted face, blue crepe paper hands & black crepe paper boots, seated on a large cylindrical felt-covered base forming the container, Germany, early 20th c., some damage to boots & outfit, overall 18" h. (ILLUS.) **978**

Doll, Father Christmas, made by John Wright, red felt outfit w/white underclothing, molded mask face, carrying a cross staff & basket, original wrist tag, 18" h. (ILLUS., top next column) **1,553**

Door swag, silvered paper, composed of a small top wreath surrounding a tiny paper snowman & silver leaves w/a red bowl, long strands of tiny gold glass beads suspending silvered bells, Japan, ca. 1930s, 18" l. (ILLUS., top of page)............................. **35**

Early Pear Ornament with Leaves

Ornament, a molded realistic pear in yellow w/a touch of red covered w/clear beading, large attached green fabric leaves, Germany, ca. 1910 (ILLUS.) **200-250**

Chain of Colorful Glass Beads

Tree decoration, chain of small various colored glass beads, ca. 1920s, per foot
(ILLUS.).. **3-5**

Small Glass Fiber & Paper Ornament

Tree ornament, a small paper angel head
glued to a round white spun glass fiber
background, small hanging string, ca.
1920s, 2 1/4" d. (ILLUS.)................................ **35**

Rare Patriotic Glass Tree Ornament

Tree ornament, blown glass, a gilt top ball
w/a patriotic spread-winged American
eagle above a large red bell, Germany,
early 20th c., 4 1/4" h. (ILLUS.).................... **130**

Green Grape Cluster Ornament

Tree ornament, blown glass, grape cluster
w/interior green paint, ca. 1930s, 2 1/4" l.
(ILLUS.).. **25**

Clip-on Parrot Ornament with Feather Tail

Tree ornament, blown glass, parrot, clip-on
type, painted in pink, silver & blue, feath-
er tail, 1920s, 3 1/4" l. (ILLUS.).................... **110**

American Silver Pine Cone Ornament

Tree ornament, blown glass, pine cone in silver, ca. 1930s, American-made, 3 1/2" l. (ILLUS., previous page) **25**

Red Snow-covered Pine Cone Ornament

Tree ornament, blown glass, pine cone, red w/sprayed-on white snow, Germany, ca. 1920s-30s, 2 1/2" l. (ILLUS.) **35**

German Gold Pine Cone Ornament

Tree ornament, blown glass, pine gold painted gold, Germany, late 1920s, 4" l. (ILLUS.) **50**

Stern Santa Claus Tree Ornament

Tree ornament, blown glass, Santa Claus w/stern look holding a small green Christmas tree, Germany, ca. 1920s, 4 1/2" h. (ILLUS.) **95**

Silver Berry & Leaves Tree Ornament

Tree ornament, blown glass, silver berry w/leaves at the top, ca. 1930s, 3 1/2" l. (ILLUS.) **40**

Small Red Blown Glass Horn Ornament

Tree ornament, blown glass, small red horn, Germany, ca. 1920s, 2 1/2" l. (ILLUS.) **30**

Blown Glass Bird with Spun Glass Tail

Tree ornament, blown glass, songbird, clip-on style, blue body & black beak, spun glass tail intact, ca. 1920s, 5" l. (ILLUS.) **50**

Clip-on Bird Ornament Missing Tail

Tree ornament, blown glass, songbird, clip-
on style, red body & black beak, spun
glass tail missing, ca. 1920s (ILLUS.)............ **15**

Clip-on Bird Ornament Missing Tail

Tree ornament, blown glass, songbird in
silver & blue, clip-on style, originally had
a spun glass tail, found in many variations & more valuable w/tail intact, made
in Germany & Austria, ca. 1920s, each
(ILLUS. of one without tail)........................ **15-50**

Rare Early Swan Boat Blown Ornament

Tree ornament, blown glass, swan boat
w/silvered body & green neck, gold tinsel
cord from tail to neck for hanging, ca.
1918, 5" l. (ILLUS.)...................................... **150**

Tree ornament, blown glass & tinsel, a
large oblong red blown glass central ornament w/painted white stripes enclosed
by twisted gold tinsel, Germany, ca.
1910, 5" l. (ILLUS., top next column) **100**

Tree ornament, molded round peach in yellow covered w/tiny clear beads, gold tinsel around top & stem, Germany, ca.
1910, 2 1/2" l. (ILLUS., middle of next
column) **80**

Red Ball & Gold Tinsel Tree Ornament

Early Peach & Tinsel Tree Ornament

Tinsel Star & Red Balls Ornament

Tree ornament, six-point star composed of
tinsel-covered wire, a small red ball on
each arm & a larger red glass ball in the
center, wire hanger, 1920s, 4 1/4" w.
(ILLUS.)... **30**

Three Tiny Felt Tree Ornaments

Tree ornament, twisted felt yarn, various designs, 1920s, 1 1/2" h., each (ILLUS. of green ball w/red plume, Santa holding tiny green tree & red & white candy cane) **35**

Early Celluloid Angel Tree Topper

Tree topper, figural, a celluloid angel doll w/blonde hair & silvered paper wings & ribbon headband, light pink paper dress, ca. 1930s (ILLUS.) **95**

Small Wreath with Silver Heart

Wreath, a round thick sheared red fiber wreath trimmed w/white snow & enclosing a silver blown glass heart, ca. 1920s, 4" d. (ILLUS.) **50**

CIRCUS COLLECTIBLES

The romance of the "Big Top," stirred by memories of sawdust, spangles, thrills and chills, has captured the imagination of the American public for more than 100 years. Although the heyday of the traveling circus is now past, dedicated collectors and fans of all ages eagerly seek out choice memorabilia from the late 19th and early 20th centuries, the "golden age" of circuses.

Colorful Early Circus Poster with Scene

Poster, "Christy Bros. 5 Ring Wild Animal Show," large rectangular color print showing an overhead scene of a large crowd viewing thirty-five circus wagons filled w/various animals, very good colors, edge tears, minor stains, modern frame, produced by the Riverside Print Co., Chicago, Illinois, early 20th c., 30 x 44 1/4" (ILLUS.) **$978**

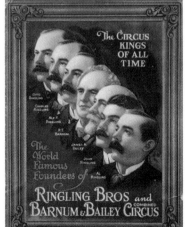

Great Ringling/Barnum & Bailey Sign

Sign, "Ringling Bros. and Barnum & Bailey Circus - The Circus Kings of All Time," heavy cardboard, color bust portraits of

Barnum, Bailey & the Ringling Brothers, self-framed, slight aging, early 20th c., 12 x 16" (ILLUS.).. **443**

Cole Bros. - Clyde Beatty Circus Sign

Window card, "Cole Bros. Circus - N.Y. Hippodrome - Starting Mar. 18," printed in full color w/a dramatic scene of Clyde Beatty, the lion trainer, in the ring, minor loss at corners & top border, creases repaired w/masking tape, ca. 1920s, 14 x 19 1/2" (ILLUS.).................................... **110**

CLOCKS

Le Coultre Anniversary Clock

Anniversary clock, Le Coultre, upright rectangular gilt-bronze footed frame w/glass sides, a large white dial w/Arabic numerals w/the works visible behind, France, ca. 1955, 9 3/4" h. (ILLUS.) **$518**

Banjo clock, Grant (William) attribution, Boston, Massachusetts, a round bell mounted at the very top above the round painted dial w/Roman numerals enclosed by a brass bezel & convex glass cover, dial signed by the maker, a tall tapering throat, reverse-painted stylized leaves & scrolls on a white ground & flanked by tall narrow openwork brass brackets above the rectangular pendulum box w/a reverse-painted panel decorated in color w/a rural landscape, eight-day weight-driven   alarm   movement, imperfections, ca. 1820, 32" h. (ILLUS. second from right with other banjo clocks & the mirror clock, top next page) **2,468**

Banjo clock, unmarked, Federal-style, the top w/a small cast-brass eagle on ball finial above the round painted iron dial w/Roman numerals within a molded brass bezel & convex glass cover, the mahogany case w/a tall narrow throat fitted w/a reverse-painted glass panel w/a wreath, swag & trophies on a white ground, the rectangular pendulum box also w/a reverse-painted glass panel decorated w/geometric designs on a white ground, brass eight-day weight-driven movement, Massachusetts, ca. 1820, imperfections, overall 33 3/4" h. (ILLUS. second from left with other banjo clocks and the mirror clock, top next page)... **2,115**

Banjo clock, Willard (Aaron, Jr.), Boston, Massachusetts, a round molded brass bezel enclosing the painted zinc dial w/Roman numerals above the tall narrow throat w/a simple reverse-painted panel above the pendulum box decorated w/another simple reverse-painted glass panel, brass eight-day weight-driven movement w/Willard mark, ca. 1820, imperfections, 28 1/2" h. (ILLUS. third from left with other banjo clocks and the mirror clock, top next page)................................. **1,645**

Banjo clock, Willard (Aaron, Jr.), Boston, Massachusetts, lyre-form carved mahogany case, a turned wood urn-form finial above the wooden bezel opening to the painted metal dial w/Roman numerals signed by the maker, the tall throat formed by a pair of tall carved leafy scrolls flanking a reverse-painted panel w/a red & gold stripe above the wood-framed pendulum box w/a reverse-painted red & gold glass panel, a tapering squared base drop, eight-day weight-driven movement, old refinish & replaced tablets, ca. 1825, 40 1/2" h. (ILLUS. far right with other banjo clocks and the mirror clock, top next page) **10,575**

Art Deco Quartz & Onyx Bedside Clock

Bedside clock, Caldwell (J.E.) & Co., Philadelphia, Art Deco style, an upright square pink quartz block w/beveled edges inset w/a square glass-covered dial w/Arabic numerals & an eight-day Swiss movement, a rectangular black onyx base w/molded edges, key-wound base, running, 3 x 3" (ILLUS.) **748**

Group of Early Banjo Clocks & a Mirror Clock

Early 20th Century Grandfather Clock

Fine Ansonia Crystal Regulator Clock

Crystal regulator, Ansonia Clock Company, New York, New York, ornate upright gilt-bronze case w/the domed top centered by a swag-draped urn above the floral-cast rounded scroll corners, ornate leafy scroll frame enclosing glass sides & front panel below the round dial w/Roman numerals & an open escapement surrounded by a brass bezel, a squared flaring scroll-cast base w/projecting scroll feet, late 19th c., 16 1/2" h. (ILLUS.)......... **1,380**

Grandfather, Herschede Clock Co. (attributed), Cincinnati, Ohio, the dark mahogany case w/an arched & molded cornice & frieze panel above the tall arched door, the upper arched glass panel over the ornate dial w/silvered metal chapter ring on the gilt face w/Arabic numerals & a h.p. moon dial w/ship scene, the long lower glass door panel showing the nine tube chimes & cylindrical weights & pendulum, the door flanked by round columns, glass sides, flat molded base, ca. 1910, 88" h. (ILLUS.)... **2,300**

Extraordinary English Grandfather Clock

Grandfather, Phillips & Sons (James), Bristol, England, ornately carved Chippendale Revival mahogany case, the inlaid broken-scroll pediment topped w/ball spiked finials above an arched molded cornice above an arched leaf-carved glazed door flanked by heavy carved corner scrolls, opening to the ornate silvered metal dial w/Arabic numerals & enhanced w/chased & engraved pierced gilt-bronze surround, a molded flaring molding above the tall waist section w/a tall glazed door w/delicate scrolling & lattice-carved wood overlay & flanked by heavy carved corner scrolls, the door showing the large pendulum & chime tubes, another flaring molding above the bottom section centered by a shell-and-scroll carved raised panel enclosing an inlaid leafy scroll panel surrounding a basket of flowers, carved scrolls at the corners, all resting on a heavy molded base w/stepped flattened block feet, the movement playing bow bells, St. Michael, Westminster & Withington chimes, ca. 1892, 18 1/2 x 29", 111" h. (ILLUS.) **37,950**

Rare Maryland Federal Grandfather Clock

Grandfather, Reynolds (John), Hagerstown, Maryland, Federal-style inlaid mahogany case, a broken-scroll pediment w/inlaid rosettes & an inlaid paterae centered by an urn-form finial above a shell-inlaid frieze panel above the arched top door flanked by colonettes & opening to a painted dial w/Roman numerals & a moon phase dial, the body of the case fitted w/a tall narrow door w/small leaf inlays at each corner & a central shell inlay, the stepped-out lower base w/an inlaid square band w/inlaid leaf corners & an oval reserve inlaid w/a spread-winged American eagle, a serpentine apron & short French feet, 1797-1814, restorations to feet & tympanum, 104 1/2" h. (ILLUS.)............................... **23,900**

Mirror clock, Classical style, the front of the case w/a giltwood frame w/half-round balusters w/rosette-carved corner blocks forming a long door, the top glass panel w/ornate reverse-painted decorations of gold & cream leafy scrolls on a black ground, a center round opening exposing the painted tin dial w/Roman numerals, the lower rectangular panel set w/a mirror, eight-day brass rack & snail movement, probably New Hampshire, ca. 1825, imperfections including replaced tablet, 4 1/4 x 13", 29 1/2" h. (ILLUS. far left with the group of banjo clocks)............ **1,763**

Attractive Art Deco Veneered Clock

Ansonia Oak Gingerbread-style Clock

Shelf or mantel, Ansonia Clock Co., New York, New York, gingerbread-style kitchen shelf clock, the stamped oak case w/a high arched & scroll-cut crest molded w/overall ornate scrolling leaf & shell-like design above the arched panel w/tall glazed door opening to a metal dial w/Roman numerals, the lower door decorated w/gilt-stenciled swag design, smaller tapering scroll-stamped wings flanking the lower door, molded flat flaring base, late 19th c., 22" h. (ILLUS.)................................ **184**

Shelf or mantel, Art Deco-style, walnut & rosewood veneer, the long gently arched case w/fine veneered designs centering a domed glass round door w/brass bezel opening to a yellow chapter ring w/silvered Arabic numerals, ca. 1920s, 18 1/2" l. (ILLUS., top of page)....................... **81**

Shelf or mantel, Atkins Clock Mfg., Bristol, Connecticut, upright stepped rosewood veneer case, a flat top w/blocked front corners above an upper case w/canted corner panels flanking a glazed door over the painted dial w/Roman numerals & gilt-stenciled on black border, a mid-molding w/canted corners stepped out slightly above canted paneled front corners flanking a short, long rectangular

Rosewood Atkins 30-Day Shelf Clock

mirrored door opening to an iron & brass patent equalizing lever spring thirty-day movement, labeled on the back of the case, ca. 1855-58, 17 3/4" h. (ILLUS.)...... **3,525**

Shelf or mantel, Birge & Fuller, Bristol, Connecticut, Gothic Revival double-steeple style mahogany veneer case, the pointed upper case w/pointed corner steeple finials above the pointed two-part glazed door, the upper panel showing the painted dial w/Roman numerals & an open escapement, the short lower panel reverse-painted w/a green border surrounding a silver, white & red diamond design, the stepped-out lower case w/two pointed corner steeple finials above a case w/a long low rectangular glazed door reverse-painted w/a blue border around a design w/a large oval in white on grey reverse-painted w/stylized red & white blossoms & leaves, flat base, thirty-hour movement marked "J. Ives Patent Accelerating Lever Spring Movement," ca. 1845, 24 1/4" h. (ILLUS., top next page)............................ **3,290**

Fine Gothic Double-steeple Shelf Clock

Admiral Dewey Commemorative Clock

Shelf or mantel, commemorative-type, the flat upright bronzed-metal case front w/scrolled sides topped by a wreath enclosing a bust portrait of Admiral Dewey, hero of the 1898 Spanish-American War, "Dewey - Manila" cast below the bust & above the round dial w/a brass bezel & Arabic numerals, the lower case cast w/cannon, weapons & an American shield, non-working, ca. 1898, 9 1/2" h. (ILLUS.).. **348**

Ornate Figural Gothic Revival Clock

Early Clock with Lafayette Portrait

Shelf or mantel, Classical-style, mahogany veneer & stenciled case, the arched crestrail w/a gilt-stenciled basket of flowers on black flanked by mahogany corner blocks, the tall case w/half-round turned columns in black w/gilt stenciled designs flanking the tall two-part glazed door, the upper glass panel showing the floral-painted white dial w/Roman numerals, the taller lower panel w/a reverse-painted gilt-stenciled black border around the reverse-painted bust portrait of General Lafayette, probably produced about the time of his death in 1831, missing weights & pendulum, minor damage to case, unmarked, 33" h. (ILLUS.)............... **1,115**

Shelf or mantel, gilt-bronze & gilt-brass, figural Troubadour-style, the metal Gothic Revival upright rectangular base decorated w/the figure of an angel across the apron & Gothic figures at the front corners centered by figural panels & the small metal dial w/Roman numerals, the top mounted by a large figure of an angel musician guarding the arts of the past & leaning upon a square pedestal inscribed "Francois I - Raphael - Leonardo da Vinci," France, second quarter 19th c., 22 1/2" h. (ILLUS.) **1,150**

Shelf or mantel, Knox (Archibald) for Liberty & Co., London, England, pewter & enamel, Art Nouveau style, the upright rectangular pewter case w/the cut-out front face panel cast w/leaves & berries, the large dial w/Arabic numerals enameled w/a mottled purple & green ground & centered by a red dot & gilt scroll design, ca. 1902-05, 8 1/8" h. **17,925**

Sevres Parian Figural Clock

Lovely French Porcelain & Metal Clock

Shelf or mantel, Louis XVI-Style, gilt-metal porcelain-mounted case, a tall upright case topped w/an ornate gilt-metal urn w/a porcelain body painted in dark blue around a reserve of birds & flowers, the arched main case w/cast ribbons & flower finials above sides w/cast corner busts, rosettes & leafy fruiting vines, a large round porcelain dial w/blue outlining white blocks w/Roman numerals centered by a ring of painted florals, a large open porcelain panel below the dial h.p. w/a color scene of peasant lovers resting beneath a large tree, the wide rounded & stepped lower case raised on ornate outswept scroll feet joined by a fruit-and-leaf-cast apron, France, ca. 1890, missing pendulum, 16 1/2" h. (ILLUS.)................ **805**

Shelf or mantel, Parian & gilt-bronze, figural, the oval base w/small gilt-bronze feet & a gilt-bronze band topped by a Parian figure group forming the clock case, a young girl wearing a bonnet leaning against one side & looking into a nest of small birds, a flowering rose vine up the other side, all centering a brass bezel & domed glass door opening to a porcelain dial w/Roman numerals, incised mark of the Sevres factory, France, second half 19th c., 10" h. (ILLUS., top next column) **345**

European Slate & Marble Mantel Clock

Shelf or mantel, polished slate & green marble, the long rectangular slate base w/a serpentine apron banded around the top w/green marble, the top fitted w/a pair of heavy slate scrolls w/small oval marble insets supporting a large cylindrical slate case w/a marble ring front enclosing the dial w/a porcelain chapter ring w/Roman numerals around the open escapement movement, Europe, ca. 1900, 17" h. (ILLUS.)... **288**

Shelf or mantel, Terry (Eli) & Sons, Plymouth, Connecticut, Federal era Pillar & Scroll clock, mahogany veneer case, a broken-scroll pediment centered by a brass urn-form finial & flanked by matching corner finials, the case w/slender colonettes flanking the two-part door, the large upper glazed panel showing the painted dial w/Arabic numerals, the short rectangular lower glass door panel reverse-painted w/a landscape w/river &

Fine Terry Pillar & Scroll Clock

mansion, a thin molded base w/serpentine apron & thin French feet, labeled inside, ca. 1820, 31 1/2" h. (ILLUS.) **4,140**

Seth Thomas Walnut Gingerbread Clock

Shelf or mantel, Thomas (Seth) Clock Co., Plymouth, Connecticut, fancy walnut gingerbread-style case, the very tall scrolled & arched crest mounted at the center w/an arched plaque w/roundel & matching roundels at the corner wings, overall line-incised vines, the arched panel door opening to a white dial w/Roman numerals, the lower door gilt-stenciled w/stylized ferns, blossoms & scrolls, pointed

scroll wings flanking the lower door, on a flaring molded base, late 19th c., 22 3/4" h. (ILLUS.) **207**

Victorian Renaissance Walnut Clock

Shelf or mantel, Victorian Renaissance Revival walnut & burl walnut gingerbread-style, the high upper case topped w/a peaked & pierced crestrail w/blocks above a flaring molded flat cornice over a line-incised frieze band & a tall scroll-cut glazed door opening to a painted metal dial w/Roman numerals & an open escapement, the lower door stenciled in silver w/stylized florals & exposing the fancy brass pendulum set w/a white on black cameo, deep molded base w/incised lines, a center roundel & small burl panels, time-and-strike movement, late quarter 19th c., 21" h. (ILLUS.) **173**

Typical Waterbury Ogee Shelf Clock

Shelf or mantel, Waterbury Clock Co., Waterbury, Connecticut, Classical ogee-case style, mahogany veneer, the upright rectangular case centered by a tall two-part glazed door, the upper panel over the painted dial w/Roman numerals & open escapement, the lower panel undecorated & exposing the works & pendulum & original paper label inside, mid-19th c., 26" h. (ILLUS.)................................... 150

Welch Classical-style Shelf Clock

Shelf or mantel, Welch (E.N.) Manufacturing Co., Bristol, Connecticut, Classical style mahogany veneer case, tall upright form w/a flat peaked crestrail flanked by corner blocks above flat side pilasters flanking the tall two-part glazed door, the upper panel w/gilt-stenciled spandrels around the large white dial w/Roman numerals, the lower glass panel w/a gilt-stenciled design of flowers & twigs framing a central oval reserve showing a scene of ships in a harbor, flat molded base, second-half 19th c., 26 1/2" h. (ILLUS.)............. 259

Shelf or mantel clock, Ansonia Clock Co., Ansonia, Connecticut, black cast-iron "Irving" model case, two full fluted green columns on the front w/applied gilt ornaments, enameled dial w/Roman numerals, eight-day movement, time & strike, ca. 1910, 5 x 11 3/8", 12" h. 595

Ansonia Marble Temple Clock

Shelf or mantel clock, Ansonia Clock Co., Ansonia, Connecticut, black marble temple-style case, thin flat rectangular top above the blocked front w/a central brass bezel around the dial w/Roman numerals, the side panels w/incised scrolls & small inset blocks of tan marble, deep rectangular flat base w/inset tan marble trim, eight-day movement, time & strike, open escapement, ca. 1890, 7 x 17 1/2", 10 1/4" h. (ILLUS.) **400-450**

Shelf or mantel clock, Ansonia Clock Co., Ansonia, Connecticut, ornate porcelain case w/a high scalloped & arched top & wide serpentine sides flaring to scroll feet & a serpentine apron, brass bezel around the large round dial w/Arabic numerals & a visible escapement, front decorated w/transfer-printed color scenes of cherubs & children, time & strike movement, late 19th - early 20th c. **534**

Shelf or mantel clock, Ansonia Clock Co., Ansonia, Connecticut, ornate porcelain "Wyoming" model case, high upright scroll-bordered waisted case decorated w/blue florals around the large brass bezel & dial w/Arabic numerals, time & strike movement, 11 3/4" h. **534**

Simple Ansonia Cottage Clock

Shelf or mantel clock, Ansonia Clock Co., Ansonia, Connecticut, simple dark hardwood case w/veneering removed, upright rectangular case w/a two-pane door, the large upper pane over the large faded dial w/Roman numerals & gilt trim above a narrow rectangular glass panel reverse-painted black w/geometric gilt loops, deep molded base, time & strike, second half 19th c., 4 x 8 1/2", 11 3/4" h. (ILLUS.).. **90**

"Bonapart's Son" Figural Shelf Clock

Shelf or mantel clock, figural "Bonapart's Son" model, high stepped ormolu case w/a figure of a seated boy on the top w/his elbow resting on a draped table holding world map & books (one a "Memorial" of Napoleon, the other titled "Code Napoleon"), the table enclosing the round dial w/patterned gilt bezel & black Roman numerals, all on rectangular stepped base w/panels of scroll, floral & shell decoration, notched design & ribbing, waveform feet & corner decorations, engine-turned time & strike movement, dial w/a stress fracture, ca. 1870, 17" h. (ILLUS.) **1,232**

Shelf or mantel clock, figural, miniature faience model of an ornate grandfather clock w/scrolls around the top round dial section above a tall waisted body on a high scroll-footed base, overall scenic & floral decoration, French eight-day Tiffany-style movement, 12 1/2" h. (chips, lines in case) **309**

Gilbert "Necho" Model Shelf Clock

Shelf or mantel clock, Gilbert (Wm. L.) Clock Co., Winsted, Connecticut, walnut "Necho" model, a pointed scroll-carved pediment above scroll-cut & line-incised cornice above the rounded & reeded glazed door w/ornate silver stenciled drapery design over the large dial w/Roman numerals & a brass pendulum w/applied grape leaves, scroll cutouts at the lower sides above the flaring stepped base, eight-day movement, time, strike & alarm, ca. 1890, 5 x 13 1/4", 20 3/4" h. (ILLUS.) **300-350**

Gilbert Miniature Steeple Clock

Shelf or mantel clock, Gilbert (Wm. L.), Winsted, Connecticut, miniature steeple-type clock, walnut case w/pointed pediment flanked by turned finials above the pointed two-pane glazed door, the upper pane opening to the white metal dial w/Roman numerals & painted spandrels, the lower panel w/a reverse-painted windmill scene, flat base, possibly a salesman's sample, eight-day time & strike movement, mid-19th c., 4 1/2 x 6 1/2", 10 3/4" h. (ILLUS.) **250**

Shelf or mantel clock, Jerome & Darrow, Bristol, Connecticut, tall upright rectangular Classical mahogany veneer case, the serpentine flat crest rail decorated w/a stenciled design flanked by corner blocks, painted half-round columns flank the tall two-pane glazed door, the large upper pane over the painted wood dial w/Arabic numerals, the short lower pane reverse-painted w/a landscape w/building, flat base on carved paw front feet, good label inside, 30-hour wood time & strike movement, ca. 1830-40, 28 1/2" h. **563**

Shelf or mantel clock, Johnson (William S.), New York, New York, double-steeple type, mahogany veneer two-part case, the upper section w/a pointed crest flanked by short turned finials above half-round short columns flanking the two-pane glazed door, the upper pane over the pointed painted metal dial w/Roman numerals & the narrow lower pane etched w/a diamond lattice design, the stepped-out lower case w/turned finials & corner blocks above half-round columns flanking a large rectangular glass door w/a repainted decoration of crossed flags, flat base, good label inside, eight-day brass movement, mid-19th c., 23 1/2" h. **1,013**

Cased German Skeleton Clock

Shelf or mantel clock, Kieninger, Germany, skeleton movement in an upright walnut case w/beveled glass front door & back, open ring steel dial w/Roman numerals, brass movement & bell, eight-day movement, 7 3/4 x 10 7/8" d., 16" h. overall (ILLUS.) **600**

Shelf or mantel clock, Mitchell (George), Bristol, Connecticut, tall upright rectangular Classical mahogany veneer case, the arched serpentine crest rail w/stenciled decor flanked by corner blocks w/knob finials, carved front columns flank the tall two-paned glazed door, the large upper pane over the painted wood dial w/Roman numerals, the narrow lower pane reverse-painted w/a repainted landscape scene, partial label inside, 30-hour wood time & strike movement, ca. 1830-40, 29 1/2" h. **1,913**

Fancy German Music Box Clock

Shelf or mantel clock, music box clock, fruit wood case w/domed top w/ring-turned finial & crosshatch & scroll carving

w/matching corner finials above the stepped flaring cornice, a large brass bezel around the white dial w/Arabic numerals & scrolled brass spandrels flanked by ring-turned finials at each corner, flaring stepped base on small bun feet, eight-day movement, Germany, ca. 1930s, 4 1/4 x 7 1/4", 13" h. (ILLUS.) **250-300**

Fine Early Thomas Two-deck Clock

Shelf or mantel clock, Thomas (Seth) Clock Co., Plymouth, Connecticut, Classical-style two-deck decorated mahogany veneer case, the deep ogee blocked top above large gilt-decorated half-round columns flanking the tall two-pane door, the upper pane over the dial w/Roman numerals, the lower pane decorated w/elaborate reverse-painted gilt decor of a scalloped frame enclosing lattice centered by a colored urn of flowers, the deep lower case w/heavy ogee scrolls flanking a small glazed door reverse-painted w/further gilt stencil decoration centering a diamond & bowl of colored flowers, flat base, dated 1863, eight-day movement, time & strike, original finish, 5 1/8 x 18 1/2", 32 1/2" (ILLUS.) **1,200-1,500**

Fine Quality Chiming Thomas Clock

Shelf or mantel clock, Thomas (Seth) Clock Co., Plymouth, Connecticut, simulated adamantine wood finish on temple-style case, gently arched top w/flat cornice above the blocked case centering a brass-framed glass door over the porcelain dial w/Arabic numerals, deep platform base on tiny brass knob feet, eight-day movement, time & strike w/Sonora chimes, early 20th c., 7 x 15 1/4", 13 1/2" h. (ILLUS.) **700-800**

Fine Seth Thomas Temple Clock

Shelf or mantel clock, Thomas (Seth) Clock Co., Plymouth, Connecticut, temple-style case, beige marbleized wood w/cast-metal scroll feet & lion heads at each end, flat rectangular top w/a stepped cornice over the blocked center w/an ornate brass bezel & dial flanked by stepped-back side panels w/applied gilt-metal scroll cartouches, a deep molded flat base, eight-day movement, time & strike, ca. 1890, 7 x 16 1/2", 10 3/4" h. (ILLUS.).. **250-300**

Shelf or mantel clock, Welch, Spring & Co., Forestville, Connecticut, walnut case, Victorian Renaissance Revival style, peaked pediment w/dentil-cut crest rail centered by a block w/a carved classical bust above a molded cornice & a line-incised frieze above the arched, molded glazed door decorated w/a silver stenciled design of stalks of wheat & small desert & seascape vignettes, rectangular platform base w/flaring sides & line-incised decoration, dial w/Roman numerals, brass pendulum w/inset glass medallion, paper label on the back, eight-day movement, time & strike, ca. 1880, missing top finial, 5 x 13 1/2", 21" h. **300-500**

Swinging arm clock, bronzed white metal, a round plinth base supporting a tall cast-metal figure of a Classical maiden painted in natural colors, one arm to her chin, the other raised to support the swinging clock movement composed of a large gilt-metal ball mounted w/Arabic numerals & enclosing the clock movement & attached to the swinging open bar pendulum w/a heavy ball base drop, late 19th c., 28" h. (ILLUS., top next column) **1,064**

Swinging arm clock, gilded cast spelter figure of a young boy in tattered clothes holding fruit in one arm & holding the round movement & dial aloft w/the other, Junghans, German-type movement, late 19th c., 12" h. (regilded, on replaced wood base).. **394**

Fine Victorian Swinging-Arm Clock

French Brass Pendulum Wall Clock

Wall clock, Bourgis-Chevalier, Billom, France, brass, the top case front composed of a large rectangular stamped brass plate topped by scrolls w/fruits & flowers around the sides & bottom all enclosing a large white enameled dial w/Roman numerals & signed by the maker, a long openwork wire pendulum w/a large brass lyre-topped pendulum bob, 19th c., 13" w., 54 3/4" h. (ILLUS.).............. **805**

Sample Size Waterbury Wall Clock

Wall clock, Waterbury Clock Co., Waterbury, Connecticut, short-drop salesman's
sample, stained softwood, dial w/Arabic
numerals, eight-day movement, time-
only, ca. 1920, 4 3/8 x 8", 12 1/2" h.
(ILLUS.)... **200-300**

Elaborate Oak Hanging Clock

Wall clock, Welch (E.N.) Mfg. Co., Bristol,
Connecticut (attributed), hanging oak
kitchen-style, the high arched crest w/a
carved shell above scrolls & blocked corners above carved scrolls & notch-cut
sides flanking the angled arched door
w/beaded edging & ornate gilt stencil
decoration, dial w/Roman numerals, flat
built-in shelf above a scroll-stamped
apron centered by an inset level above
the pointed scallop-cut drop, eight-day
movement, strike & alarm, old case refinish, late 19th c., 4 1/2 x 14 3/8",
27 3/4" h. (ILLUS.) **350-400**

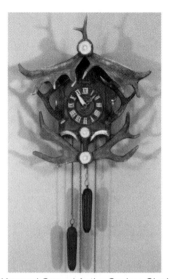

Unusual Carved Antler Cuckoo Clock

Wall cuckoo clock, antler-mounted carved
lindenwood, the small central wooden
case centered w/a chapter ring mounted
w/carved bone Roman numerals & handles, suspending long chains w/long
weights, the clock case enclosed by a
pair of peaked carved & polished antlers
joined by a carved roundel, a smaller pair
of antlers below the case forming the
pendulum counterweight, Schwarzwald
region of Germany, late 19th c., lower
antler counterweight broken & spliced,
one bone hand replaced w/an aluminum
one, 18" w., 21" h. (ILLUS.) **201**

Unusual Early Classical Mirror-Clock

Wall mirror-clock, Classical style, large rectangular frame in gilt & black w/corner blocks w/metal florettes joined by half-round ring- & rod-turned spindles, the deep pine case hinged to open, the top panel of the front reverse-painted w/a brown ground & gold, black & reddish-brown leaves framing a clear round center showing the clock dial w/Roman numerals above the long rectangular mirror, the case holding the brass works w/weight, pendulum & key, dial signed "B. Morrill, Boscawen," New Hampshire, first half 19th c., some edge damage & touch-up, hinges & reverse-painted panel replaced, 18 1/4 x 38 1/4" (ILLUS., previous page) **1,265**

Sessions "Regulator E" Wall Clock

French Mahogany Wall Regulator

German Oak Wall Regulator Clock

Wall regulator clock, oak, a simple arched paneled crestrail above a narrow molded cornice above a case w/a long paneled door, the upper wood panel around a brass bezel & enameled dial w/Roman numerals, the lower door panel composed of geometric beveled glass sections, flat base above a pair of quarter-round brackets & an arched drop backboard, Germany, early 20th c., 33" h. (ILLUS.) **316**

Wall regulator clock, Sessions Clock Co., Bristol, Connecticut, "Regular E" model, pressed oak case, a large wide octagonal top w/molded bands around the brass bezel enclosing the original paper dial w/Roman numerals & outer calendar date band w/Arabic numerals, the pointed drop case w/stamped molding on the glazed door printed w/"Regulator," pendulum w/large brass bob, eight-day time & strike movement, ca. 1915, 16 1/2" w. top, 38" h. (ILLUS., top next column) **850-950**

Wall regulator clock, tall rectangular mahogany case w/a long glazed door w/small carved scrolls flanking the arched top, a wide brass bezel enclosing the porcelain dial w/Roman numerals, a long gridiron brass pendulum w/harp design over the large brass disk bob, eight-day time-only pinwheel movement, France, late 19th - early 20th c., 61" h. (ILLUS.) **2,138**

Vienna Regulator in Light & Dark Walnut

Wall Vienna Regulator clock, fancy carved walnut case, a high crest w/a flat top molding above a scroll-carved & pierced panel fitted w/pairs of small turned spindles flanking half-round spindles centered by a carved classical face, the corner blocks w/urn-form finials, the tall arched glass front showing the white enamel dial w/Roman numerals & large brass pendulum, the case sides w/ring-turned columns resting on blocks on a flat base above turned round corner droops & a curved & blocked central drop w/knob finial drop, Europe, late 19th c., 31" h. (ILLUS.).................................. **259**

Vienna Regulator Clock with Fancy Carvings

Wall Vienna Regulator clock, fancy carved walnut case, the broken scroll pediment centered by a turned finial above a panel w/a carved classical bust portrait above a row of small turned spindles flanked by corner blocks w/small turned urn finials, all atop a flat molded flaring cornice above the glass front showing the enameled dial w/Roman numerals & the large brass pendulum, the sides composed of ornate ring, rod- and disk-turned columns, flat base above turned corner drops & a large tapering central drop panel, Europe, late 19th c., 36" h. (ILLUS.).................................. **259**

Vienna Regulator with Decorative Finials

Wall Vienna Regulator clock, fancy carved walnut case, the squared arch molded cornice fitted w/three turned wood finials above a small carved floral panel above the long arched glass front exposing the white dial w/Roman numerals above the long pendulum, the case sides w/pairs of blocks & short finials at the tops & bottoms above the flat base suspending ring-turned corner drops & a central large drop composed of a thick ring-turned rood above a large acorn-shaped drop finial, Europe, late 19th c., 26" h. (ILLUS.)

.... **316**

CLOTHING

Recent interest in period clothing, uniforms and accessories from the 18th, 19th and through the 20th century compels us to include this category in our compilation. While style and fabric play an important role in the values of older gar-

*ments of previous centuries, designer dresses of
the 1920s and '30s, especially evening gowns, are
enhanced by the original label of a noted coutu-
rier such as Worth or Adrian. Prices vary widely
for these garments, which we list by type, with
infant's and children's apparel so designated.*

Early Striped Child's Dress

Dress, child's, chintz-like fabric in brown
w/stripes of colorful flowers, bordered
w/a three-color flower-type stripe, seven
small mother-of-pearl buttons, small collar & half-sleeves, found in Massachusetts, early, some small holes & stains,
27" h. (ILLUS.) **120**

Man's Engineer-type High-top Boots

Boots, man's engineer-type high-top style,
black leather, laced at instep w/uppers
laced w/metal hooks, dated 1934, pr.
(ILLUS.) **$46**

Black Lady's High-top Shoes

Shoes, lady's high-top style w/lace ties,
black leather, ca. 1900, pr. (ILLUS.) **92**

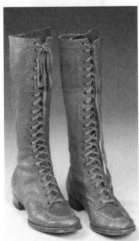

Brown Leather Man's High-top Boots

Boots, man's high-top style w/lace ties,
brown leather, ca. 1935, pr. (ILLUS.) **69**

Bronze-colored Lady's High-top Shoes

Shoes, lady's high-top style w/lace ties, bronze-colored leather, low heals, sharply pointed toes, ca. 1910, pr. (ILLUS.).......... **92**

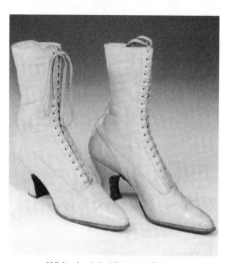

White Lady's High-top Shoes

Shoes, lady's high-top style w/lace ties, soft white leather, sharply pointed toes, ca. 1910, pr. (ILLUS.).. **81**

Tan Leather Lady's High-top Shoes

Shoes, lady's high-top style w/lace ties, tan leather, tapered heals, sharply pointed toes, size 8 1/2 AAA, ca. 1910, some scuffing, pr. (ILLUS.) **92**

COCA-COLA ITEMS

Coca-Cola promotion has been achieved through the issuance of scores of small objects through the years. These, together with trays, signs and other articles bearing the name of this soft drink, are now sought by many collectors. The major reference in this field is Petretti's Coca-Cola Collectibles Price Guide, *11th Edition, by Allan Petretti (Antique Trader Books). An asterisk (*) indicates a piece which has been reproduced.*

Rare Coca-Cola Advertising Handbook

Advertising handbook, for Coca-Cola distributors, stiff covers & wire spiral binding, many colorful pages, ca. 1935-55, excellent condition, 9 1/2 x 12" (ILLUS.).... **$578**

Scarce Coke 50th Anniversary Booklet

Booklet, "50th Anniversary Coca-Cola 1886-1936 - Coca-Cola Bottlers Advertising Price List," w/red Coca-Cola 50th anniversary button logo, 1936, 16 pp., very good condition, 11 x 15" (ILLUS.) **550**

Two Early Coke Celluloid Bookmarks

Bookmark, 1899, celluloid, heart-shaped, beautiful woman w/glass in center, "Drink Coca-Cola - Delicious ... - 5¢ - Refreshing" in border, minute fading & light wear, 2 x 2 1/4" (ILLUS. left with other heart-shaped bookmark) **468**

1915, 1916 & 1917 Coca-Cola Calendars

Bookmark, 1900, celluloid, heart-shaped, beautiful woman w/glass in center, "Drink Coca-Cola - Delicious ... - 5¢ - Refreshing" in border, a couple of shallow crimps, few light surface marks & wear, 2 x 2 1/4" (ILLUS. right with other heart-shaped bookmark) **275**

Bottle, counter display type, 6 oz. size w/caramel coloring & painting, standing in original red cardboard base mounting w/white wording, overall excellent condition, 1950s... **66**

Scarce Aluminum Coke Bottle Carrier

Bottle carrier, aluminum w/textured surface, for a six-pack, rectangular w/end-to-end bail handle & a wire bail handle on the flat cover, "Drink Coca-Cola" in red on the sides, unused condition, ca. 1950s, 11" h. (ILLUS.) **550**

Calendar, 1914, "Betty," color lithographed cardboard, three-quarters length portrait of young woman wearing a pink & white dress & bonnet, rare version w/Betty holding a bottle of Coca-Cola in one hand, acid-free museum mounted, professionally restored, 13 x 32" **9,350**

Calendar, 1915, "Elaine," color lithographed cardboard, full-length portrait of a young woman wearing a pale pink dress & hat seated on a large boulder, holding a glass in one hand & leaning on a closed parasol w/the other, professionally cleaned & restored, 13 x 32" (ILLUS. left

with 1916 & 1917 calendars, top of page) **4,950**

Calendar, 1916, "Girl with Basket of Flowers," color lithographed cardboard, a three-quarters length portrait of a pretty young woman wearing a large hat & standing in front of a large basket of roses & holding a glass of Coca-Cola in one hand, apparently dry-mounted, a number of strong creases & wrinkles, light soiling, w/January page, 13 x 32 1/4" (ILLUS. center with 1915 & 1917 calendars) **688**

Calendar, 1917, "Constance," color lithographed cardboard, full-length portrait of a young woman wearing a white dress seated by a small table holding glass of Coca-Cola in one hand & her closed parasol in the other, bottle on table beside her, palm tree in background, acid-free museum mounted & matted, very light soiling & minor restoration, near excellent, 13 x 31 3/4" (ILLUS. left with 1915 & 1916 calendars)........................... **4,950**

Calendar, 1920, "Golfer Girl," top image only, no pad, young woman wearing frilly pink dress & hat w/large brim & holding a glass, airfield in background, small wrinkle on her chin, few tiny marks & closed tears, 12 x 32"... **1,870**

Calendar, 1922, "Summer Girl," three-quarters length portrait of a beautiful smiling woman w/short dark hair, wearing a pink dress & large hat & holding a glass, a baseball game scene in the background, acid-free museum mounted & framed under glass, three small closed edge tears, March page only, 12 x 32" **770**

Calendar, 1924, "Smiling Girl," three-quarters length portrait of a beautiful smiling woman w/short dark hair, wearing a lacy pink gown & seated holding a glass, an evening garden pool scene in the background, matted & framed, only light soiling, 12 x 24" **1,320**

Sprite Boy Coca-Cola Poster

Poster, color printed paper, long rectangular form, snow drifts w/the head of the Sprite boy & a large bottle of Coca-Cola, reads "Ice Cold - Have a Big King-Size Coke," 1956, few mild stains & light wear, 20 x 36" (ILLUS.) **303**

Poster, color-printed paper, long horizontal rectangular style, right end w/a half-length color portrait of Edgar Bergen & Charlie McCarthy, blue ground w/white wording at the left reading "Coca-Cola brings you Edgar Bergen and Charlie McCarthy - CBS Sunday Evenings," red button logo at center, 1949, matted & framed, light wear, 11 x 23" **248**

Poster, color-printed paper, long, horizontal rectangular style, scene of a young mother seated in a white garden chair & wearing a pale blue dress & sunbonnet, her young daughter wearing a matching outfit standing beside her holding a bottle of Coke, "Hospitality" printed to the left, red button logo at the right end, 1950, matted & framed, only minor wrinkles, 11 x 24" **440**

1950s Coke Santa Sign

Sign, color-printed paper, long, narrow, rectangular banner style, a large half-length of Santa Claus on the right w/two six-packs of Coke on the right below the white wording "Almost everyone appreciates the best...," 1955, matted & framed (ILLUS.) **440**

Rare Canadian Market Hanging Sign

Sign, die-cut cardboard, double-sided hanger-type, round w/a thin gold border

& red background w/the head of the Sprite boy above wording "Drink Coca-Cola - Be Refreshed," for the Canadian market, 1950, near mint, 11" d. (ILLUS.) .. **2,860**

Sign, die-cut cardboard standup floor model, color image of Santa Claus emerging from a stylized rocket ship in white, red & yellow, 1957, strong bend at top point, some bottom edge nicks & bends, light wear, 33" h. **187**

Sign, die-cut cardboard w/easel back, color image of Santa Claus standing in front of a refrigerator & holding a bottle of Coke, his sack of toys on a green chair in front, 1948, a few edge chips, some surface scuffing, 13 1/2" h. **176**

Scarce Foreign Market Coca-Cola Sign

Sign, tin, flat, round form, dark gold background printed in color w/the head of the Sprite boy w/a large bottle of Coke above the red button logo, original string hanger, made for a foreign market, 1940s-50s, only a few paint chips & scratches on border, 12 3/4" d. (ILLUS.) **1,320**

Sign, tin, long, narrow, horizontal form w/narrow raised green border band, white background w/very fine horizontal lines, a long red double fishtail reserve at the left printed in white "Drink Coca-Cola - Sign of Good Taste," a picture of a Coca-Cola bottle beside "Ice Cold" at the right end, 1962, one very shallow dent, slight chipping on border, 18 x 54" (ILLUS. bottom with other long Coca-Cola sign) **275**

Two Long Narrow Coca-Cola Signs

Sign, tin, long, narrow, horizontal form w/narrow raised green border band, white background w/very fine horizontal lines, a long red double fishtail reserve at the left printed in white "Drink Coca-Cola - Enjoy That Refreshing New Feeling," a picture of a Coca-Cola bottle beside "Ice Cold" at the right end, 1962, only slightly ambered, 18 x 54" (ILLUS. top with other long Coca-Cola sign).................................... **303**

Coke Button Sign with the Sprite Boy

Sign, tin, round button-type, white w/a color decal of the Sprite boy looking out from behind a large Coca-Cola bottle, reads "Have a Coke," ca. 1950s, some edge chips, scratches & wear (ILLUS.)................. **385**

Sign, tin, vertical, long, narrow form w/rounded corners & narrow flanged border band, plain white ground w/a large color picture of a Coca-Cola bottle, 1952, only slightly ambered, 18 x 36" (ILLUS. far right with four other Coca-Cola tin signs, bottom of page).................................. **275**

Sign, tin, vertical, long, narrow form w/rounded corners, plain white ground w/a large color decal of a Coca-Cola bottle, 1950s, only minor marks, 16 x 50" (ILLUS. second from right with four other Coca-Cola tin signs, below) **193**

Sign, tin, vertical, long, narrow form w/thin raised green border, white background w/fine horizontal lines, a large red double fishtail-shaped red reserve at top printed in white "Drink Coca-Cola - Enjoy That Refreshing New Feeling," picture of a Coke bottle below, edge wear & chipping, quite a bit of surface wear at top, 1963, 18 x 54" (ILLUS. third from left with four other Coca-Cola tin signs, below)................. **83**

Sign, tin, vertical, long, narrow form w/thin raised green border, white background w/fine horizontal lines, a large red double fishtail-shaped red reserve at top printed in white "Drink Coca-Cola - Sign of Good Taste," picture of a Coke bottle below, light wear, 1963, 18 x 54" (ILLUS. far left with four other Coca-Cola tin signs, bottom of page)... **330**

Sign, tin, vertical, long, narrow form w/thin raised white border, white background w/red wording "things go better with Coke" above a red button logo above a bottle of Coca-Cola, only minor paper marks, 1964, 18 x 54" (ILLUS. second from left with four other tin Coca-Cola signs, bottom of page) **303**

Syrup can, 1 gal. cylindrical form w/a small center spout w/cap, paper label w/red background & round white reserve w/red wording, minor wear & stains, ca. 1940s-50s, 9 1/2" h... **209**

Thermometer, glass & metal, round, red background reading in white "Drink - Coca-Cola - In Bottles," very narrow border band w/gauge numbers, short strong glass scratch, light to medium soiling, 1957, 12" d. (ILLUS. right with other round Coca-Cola thermometer, top next page)... **165**

Selection of Five Coca-Cola Tin Signs

Two Round Coke Thermometers

Thermometer, glass & metal, round, red background reading in white "Drink - Coca-Cola - Sign of Good Taste," very narrow border band w/gauge numbers, only light wear, few very small glass scratches, 1957, 12" d. (ILLUS. left with other round Coca-Cola thermometer) **248**

Thermometer, tin, cigar-shaped vertical oblong form, arched red top printed in white "Drink Coca-Cola in Bottles," oblong white reserve framing the thermometer & printed in red at the bottom "Refresh yourself," 1950s, very fine condition, 30" l. **523**

1941 Coca-Cola Thermometer

Thermometer, tin, shaped oblong form in gold w/two small bottles flanking thermometer scale above "Drink Coca-Cola" in a red rectangle, 1941, excellent condition, 7 x 16" (ILLUS.) **715**

Near-mint 1938 Coke Thermometer

Thermometer, tin, vertical oval form w/a thin gold border band, red background & large Coca-Cola bottle framing the thermometer, complete w/gold hanging string & tassel in original box, 1938, 7 x 16" (ILLUS.)... **1,210**

Larger Version of 1903 Coke Change Tray

Tray, 1903, change, plain gold flanged rim enclosing a band of white & purple mums & "Coca-Cola" at the top above the half-length color portrait of Hilda Clark holding a glass of Coca-Cola in one hand & a closed fan in the other, "Drink - Delicious - and Refreshing" in small letters below her, above average condition, possibly clearcoated, 6" d. (ILLUS.)....................... **2,530**

1910 Hamilton King Girl Tray

Tray, 1910, serving, rectangular, Hamilton King Girl above "Drink Delicious Coca-Cola" in lower right corner & "The Coca-Cola Girl" in left corner, reproduced, few semi-gloss areas on face, minimal crazing & rim nicks, 10 1/2 x 13 1/4" (ILLUS.) **2,200**

Tray, 1914, change, depicts "Betty" in white bonnet w/pink flowers, bow & sash, very mild small check marks, few tiny border nicks, 4 3/8 x 6"... **523**

Tray, 1930, serving, rectangular, red border, center portrait of a seated young woman talking on the telephone, advertising in border band, few tiny scratches, some rim nicks touched up, 10 1/2 x 13 1/4"... **413**

Tray, 1930, serving, rectangular, red border, center portrait of a young woman wearing a white swimsuit & red swim cap, holding a bottle of Coca-Cola while putting on a red, white & black jacket, only a few outer rim nicks, 10 1/2 x 13 1/4" (ILLUS., center next page) **550**

Cavalier Model CS-72-A Vendor

1930 Coke Bathing Girl Tray

1934 "Tarzan & Jane" Serving Tray

Tray, 1933, serving, rectangular, horizontal view of Johnny Weismuller & Maureen O'Sullivan (Hollywood's Tarzan & Jane), average condition w/some chips & nicks, 10 1/2 x 13 1/4" (ILLUS.) **715**

Tray, 1934, serving, rectangular, "Frances Dee," full-length portrait of the young actress seated on a low wall wearing a blue swimsuit & holding a bottle of Coca-Cola, few minor surface marks, some rim chips & nicks, 10 1/2 x 13 1/4" **825**

Tray, 1937, serving, "Running Girl," blonde woman in swimwear running on beach w/a Coca-Cola in each hand and a white cape flowing off her back, American Art

Works, Inc., Coshocton, Ohio, overall excellent condition, 10 1/2 x 13 1/4" **578**

Tray, 1940, serving, rectangular, "Sailor Girl," young woman in a sailor suit reclining on a dock & fishing, holding a bottle of Coca-Cola in one hand, couple of minor surface marks & few rim nicks, 10 1/2 x 13 1/4" **330**

Vending machine, Cavalier Model CS-72-A, upright style w/narrow two-pane door at front left, white & red, ca. 1960, 57" h. (ILLUS., top of previous column) **1,610**

COMPACTS & VANITY CASES

A lady's powder compact is a small portable cosmetic make-up box that contains powder, a mirror and puff. Eventually, the more elaborate compact, the "vanity case," evolved, containing a mirror, puffs and compartments for powder, rouge and/or lipstick. Compacts made prior to the 1960s when women opted for the "au natural" look are considered vintage. These vintage compacts were made in a variety of shapes, sizes, combinations, styles and in every conceivable natural or man-made material. Figural, enamel, premium, commemorative, patriotic, Art Deco and souvenir compacts were designed as a reflection of the times and are very desirable. The vintage compacts that are multipurpose, combined with another accessory—the compact/watch, compact/music box, compact/fan, compact/purse, compact/perfumer, compact/lighter, compact/cane, compact/hatpin—are but a few of the combination compacts that are not only sought after by the compact collector but also appeal to collectors of the secondary accessory.

Today vintage compacts and vanity cases are very desirable collectibles. There are compacts and vanities to suit every taste and purse. The "old" compacts are the "new" collectibles. Compacts have come into their own as collectibles. They are listed as a separate category in price guides, sold in prestigious auction houses, displayed in museums, and several books and many articles on the collectible compact have been written. There is also a newsletter, Powder Puff, written by and for compact collectors. The beauty and intricate workmanship of the vintage compacts make them works of fantasy and art in miniature.

For additional information on the history and values of compacts and vanity cases, readers should consult Vintage and Vogue Ladies' Compacts *by Roselyn Gerson, Collector Books.*

Alligator minaudiere with alligator carrying handles, three-sided, one section opens to reveal a comb, writing slate & pencil, second section for cosmetics (pli for powder) & mirrored cover, third section reveals cigarettes & matches, brass closures on top engraved, one w/a cigarette, one w/an envelope & one w/a pli puff indicating appropriate interior contents **$650**

Bakelite compact, round, dark green marbleized case, cover decorated w/pink

Silvertone Compact/Dress Clip

carved Bakelite roses & painted green leaves, interior w/a beveled mirror & powder compartment, plastic link carrying chain w/finger ring 275

Black celluloid compact, round, cover decorated w/profile of a beautiful Art Deco woman's face, hand-engraved & painted, Antonion of France 200

Black damask vanity bag, embroidered w/gold, green & pink flowers, embroidered carrying handle, one side opens to reveal compact, second side opens to reveal cigarette case, center section w/a mirror & pockets for comb, lipstick tube & perfume tube, Ritz 325

Black silk beaded minaudiere, w/pink tambour embroidered flowers on handle, front & back, gilded interior reveals mirror, comb & compartments for powder, lipstick & perfume, pocket behind mirror, Minois, Weber Creation, Paris, France 450

Black vanity box w/semi-rounded top, handle & brass lock & key closure, interior lid w/full-sized etched mirror, celluloid compact, lipstick container, rouge container, plastic comb & drawstring powder puff holder in sleeves on the lower portion of the vanity box, when this section is lifted there is a compartment for personal necessities 250

Estee Lauder Zodiac Compact

Black enamel compact, oblong, Zodiac design designed by Erte, featuring Sagittarius, the cover w/outside rim enhanced w/rows of clear crystals framing a black star-studded silhouette of a centaur, the figure centered on a blue flowered cloud w/bow & arrow, Estee Lauder (ILLUS.) 90

Black enamel silvertone compact/dress clip, round, black cover centered w/white profile silhouette of woman's face, interior revealing metal mirror and perforated rotating powder well, shown closed and opened (ILLUS., top of page) 150

Wadsworth Compact

Black & white enameled compact, round, the cover decorated w/a woman w/red skirt & blue blouse, "Simplicity Printed Pattern 25 cent" printed on one side of cover, Wadsworth (ILLUS.) 225

Brown leather compact, oval, designed to resemble football, Elgin American 75

Brown suede vanity bag/purse, beautiful vanity centered on top, filigree vanity cover enhanced w/enamel & highlighted w/pearls & red & green stones, vanity cover opens to metal mirror & compartments for powder & rouge, satin-lined interior has shirred pocket & change purse, suede carrying handle, Evans 450

Brushed goldtone compact, round, cover decorated w/polished goldtone stars, black silk carrying wrist cuff, reverse side of wrist cuff has snap-shut mini pocket for money, complete w/black tassel, interior reveals mirror & pocket well 300

Brushed goldtone compact, round, "PEP-SI-COLA" engraved on cover, outer rim of compact decorated w/polished goldtone design, Stratton 95

Brushed goldtone compact, square, the cover w/an actual dime centered on it, Volupte 60

Brushed goldtone compact, stylized heart shape, the cover decorated w/polished goldtone Comedy & Tragedy masks, Elgin American 75

Brushed goldtone compact w/matching lipstick, square, cover of compact decorated w/applied rhinestone poodle, matching rhinestone poodle head decorates lipstick tube, comes complete w/black silk fitted carrying case, by Ciner 325

Coppertone compact, round, w/embossed black enamel cat centered on cover w/finger ring chain 125

Corner Compact Costume Bag, black & silvertone mesh vanity bag w/silver & purple enameled compact on outside corner of frame, lined interior, powder sifter, metal mirror & compartment for rouge in lid of compact, complete w/metal carrying chain, Whiting & Davis 1,000

Enameled "beadlite" mesh vanity bag, white w/black satin underskirt, white enameled cover decorated w/pink flowers, powder & rouge compartments in top cover, interior of bag lined, snake carrying chain, Evans.. 450

Volupte Brooch/Pendant Compact

Enameled brooch/pendant compact, round, cover decorated w/applied blue enamel design enhanced w/crystals, re-

movable pin decorated w/an enlarged version of design on lid, Volupte (ILLUS.) 300

Enameled compact, unique shape, gilded & silvery blue enamel, front cover decorated w/exquisite hand-painted scene, back of case beautifully engraved, interior reveals deeply beveled mirror & powder well, carrying pouch reads "David Webb, Inc. New York".............................. 1,200

Enameled compact/keychain combination, cream colored enamel cover decorated w/goldtone stripes, interior reveals mirror & puff, Pinaud..................................... 45

Enameled Goldtone compact, square, cover w/a colorful enameled picture of Madam DuBarry, outer rim on cover reads "QUITE A GAL WAS MADAM DUBARRY --- WAS SHE A LADY? - WELL NOT VERY," interior mirror & powder compartment, Wadsworth 150

Enameled light blue compact, square, ccover decorated w/goldtone vintage automobiles, interior w/mirror, puff & powder well, Zell... 55

Whiting & Davis Vanity Bag

Enameled mesh vanity bag w/silvertone metal cover, multicolored pink, green & brown embossed enamel design, metal oblong vanity cover opens to reveal compartments for powder, rouge & comb, complete w/carrying chain, "El sah" imprint on attached interior metal tag, Whiting & Davis (ILLUS.) 450

Enameled vanity & matching tango chain lipstick, oval, Art Deco style, green & blue cover, interior reveals beveled mirror, powder & rouge compartments w/puffs 650

Engine-turned Goldtone, "Initial Compact," complete w/original goldtone key needed to set initials, interior reveals framed mirror, powder well & puff, Stratton 150

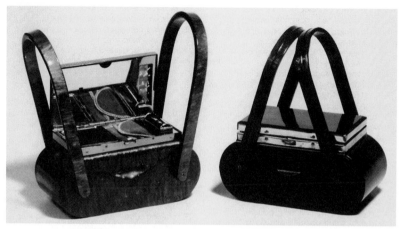

Lucite Vanity Purse & Tortoiseshell -colored Vanity Purse

Goldtone vanity bag, eight-sided, pearls & red stones set on round filigree compact lid & around circumference of multicolored silk bag, metal jeweled tassel & carrying chain, antique **400**

Antique Vanity Bag Compact

Goldtone vanity bag, round, filigree compact set w/blue stones on front of lid, top opening reveals interior bag w/shirred pockets, black silk carrying cord w/metal tassel, antique (ILLUS.).............................. **550**

Green enamel tandem powder/rouge compacts, octagonal, matching lipstick attached to the two compacts by two goldtone chains, enameled lids decorated w/pink roses, unique, the set **850**

Hand-engraved Kyoto mother-of-pearl inlaid compact, cover decorated w/Asian scene, beveled interior mirror, puff & powder well, Schildkraut **100**

Ivory, coral & green composition compact, the cover decorated w/a Bohidsattva in a lotus blossom, interior reveals mirror & powder well, comes w/green carrying cord & tassel **550**

Lucite grey marbleized vanity purse, w/envelope closure & swinging handles, lids are set w/carryall complete w/mirror, powder well, comb in case, lipstick & compartment for cigarettes behind fold-down mirror, Wilardy Original (ILLUS. closed at right with tortoiseshell Lucite purse, top of page)...................... **250**

Lucite tortoiseshell-design vanity purse, w/envelope closure & swinging handles, the lids set w/carryall complete w/mirror, powder well, comb in case, lipstick & compartment for cigarettes behind fold-down mirror, Wilardy Original (ILLUS. open at left with grey marbleized Lucite vanity purse, top of page) **250**

Miniature Goldtone compact, designed to resemble a fan, exterior cover decorated w/yellow, pink, goldtone & silvertone flowers, pearl twist lock, interior reveals mirror & powder well **35**

Miniature Goldtone compact, designed to resemble an armchair, coin decorates cover, chair w/cabriole legs, interior reveals beveled mirror, puff & sifter, Robert Original-signed **550**

Multicolored Dresden mesh vanity bag, "Swinging Compact Costume Bag," light blue enameled frame & link carrying chain, light blue enameled silvertone vanity incorporated on center of exterior frame, compact contains compartment for powder sifter, rouge & metal mirror contained on inside upper lid of compact, lined interior, Whiting & Davis **1,300**

Neck pendant compact w/chain, round gilt & enamel, colorful enamel cover decorated w/Egyptian motifs, interior wire framed mirror, powder well & puff **225**

Playing Card Compact

Orange, black & goldtone mesh vanity bag, the cover w/an amethyst cabochon thumb piece, powder & rouge compartments, mesh carrying chain & tassel, "Delysia" by Whiting & Davis **900**

Pewter colored metal tango-chain vanity bag, eight-sided, cover of compact & outer circumference of bag enhanced w/filigree work set w/green stones, interior w/shirred pockets, silk back & metal tassel & filigree lipstick holder, antique **450**

Playing card compact, oblong, designed to resemble playing card, one side showing Queen of Hearts, reverse side showing King of Hearts, interior containing framed mirror, puff and powder well (ILLUS. of two views, top of page) **175**

Rare Round Cork Compact

Rare round cork compact, goldtone metal decorated w/a blue & orange abstract enamel design (ILLUS.) **150**

Red leather & goldtone fitted clutch vanity purse, red faille-lined interior reveals pockets w/Evans cigarette case, lighter, lipstick case, compact & comb, opposite side has pocket w/red change purse, Evans **175**

Rigid mesh multicolored necessaire, hexagonal, decorated w/pearls & blue stones, carrying chain & tassel, mirror contained in top lid w/powder section attached to bottom part of top lid, tassel attached to interior lipstick tube **350**

Silvertone charm/photograph compact, square, cover decorated w/nine charms in high relief, interior reveals metal mirror that swings open for photograph, powder well, puff & sifter, Evans **225**

Silvertone compact, round, cover designed to resemble shell of a turtle, twist closure, Polly Bergen **60**

Estee Lauder Compact

Polished silvertone compact, round, Art Deco style, the cover decorated w/an enamel design of circular motifs in shades of pink, plum & violet, Estee Lauder (ILLUS.) **125**

Sterling silver mesh tango-chain Dresden vanity bag, light blue enameled cover decorated w/colorful flowers, vanity includes powder & rouge compartments, the lipstick case attached by a blue & black enamel link chain, Foster & Bailey .. **1,500**

Stratton blue cobalt enameled Canadian souvenir compact, round, lid decorated w/colorful maple leaf, interior reveals framed mirror, puff, powder well & sifter **90**

Suede & Brass Vanity Bags

Suede & brass vanity bags, enhanced w/rhinestones on lid & around cinched center, top cover contains compact, silk lined bag & complete w/suede handle, each (ILLUS. left black suede vanity bag shown closed, right brown suede vanity bag shown opened)...................................... **400**

Trifari lip-lock brushed goldtone compact, lid decorated w/applied framed disc of colored stones, pull-out lipstick opens compact, interior reveals signed powder well & mirror **155**

White enameled dresser/vanity, cover decorated w/stylized red lips, blue bottom lid, interior reveals wells for lipstick, powder & rouge cases, Tangee **125**

White marbleized vanity purse, envelope closure, swinging handle w/decorative cut-out openings at either end, when lid is lifted front panel lowers to reveal small carryall & powder compartments, second compartment reveals lipstick tube & mirror, mirror folds down to reveal cigarette compartment, Elgin American **350**

CURRIER & IVES PRINTS

This lithographic firm was founded in 1835 by Nathaniel Currier, with James M. Ives becoming a partner in 1857. Current events of the day were portrayed in the early days, and the prints were hand-colored. Landscapes, vessels, sport and hunting scenes of the West all became popular subjects. The firm was in existence until 1906. All prints listed are hand-colored unless otherwise noted. Numbers at the end of the listings refer to those used in Currier & Ives Prints - An Illustrated Checklist, by Frederick A. Conningham (Crown Publishers).

A Good Chance

A Good Chance, large folio, 1863, framed, 2424, mat stain, subtle toning, minor foxing, repaired tear in corner edge, old tape residue on face edges & back (ILLUS.)
.... **$4,700**

American Forest Scene - Maple Sugaring

American Field Sports: Flush'd

American Field Sports: Flush'd, large folio, 1857, framed, 149, hinged at top, mat stain, small loss on lower corner (ILLUS.) **3,173**

American Forest Scene - Maple Sugaring, large folio, 1856, N. Currier, framed, 157, mat staining, toning, staining on back (ILLUS., bottom previous page)...... **19,975**

American Winter Scenes - Evening

American Winter Scenes - Evening, large folio, 1854, framed, 207, hinged at top, several repaired tears, minor toning (ILLUS.) **3,408**

American Winter Sports - Deer Shooting "On the Shattagee"

American Winter Sports - Deer Shooting "On the Shattagee," large folio, N. Currier, 1855, framed, 209, several repaired tears, some into image, light toning & stains (ILLUS.) **3,055**

American Winter Sports - Trout Fishing "On Chateaugay Lake"

American Winter Sports - Trout Fishing "On Chateaugay Lake," large folio, 1856, N. Currier, framed, 210, light mat stains, minor tears, loss on margin edge (ILLUS.).. **4,994**

Awful Conflagration of the Steamboat LEXINGTON In Long Island Sound on Monday Eve'g Jan'y 13th 1840 by which melancholy occurrence; over 100 PERSONS PERISHED, small folio, undated, N. Currier, framed (minor toning, minor creases at center, three repaired tears)... **3,055**

Camping Out "Some of the Right Sort"

Camping Out "Some of the Right Sort," large folio, 1856, framed, 777, small loss in upper right corner (ILLUS.) **3,408**

Catching a Trout, large folio, after Arthur Tait, 1854, framed, minor foxing & corner staining (ILLUS., top next page) **3,819**

The Celebrated Horse Lexington

Catching a Trout

Celebrated Horse Lexington (The), large folio, 1855, framed, 887, toning, light stains, hinged at top (ILLUS., previous page) **2,233**

Central Park, Winter. The Skating Carnival

Central Park, Winter. The Skating Carnival, small folio, undated, framed, 953, repaired tear in lower margin (ILLUS.) **3,173**

Clipper Ship Dreadnought Off Tuskar Light

Clipper Ship Dreadnought Off Tuskar Light, large folio, 1856, N. Currier, framed, 1144, toning, vertical light brown

stains, scattered black stains in margins, faded inscriptions (ILLUS.) **2,350**

Clipper Ship "Nightingale"

Clipper Ship "Nightingale," large folio, 1854, framed, 1159, scattered light spotty stains & few light vertical streaks (ILLUS.) **2,938**

Clipper Ship "Red Jacket"

Clipper Ship "Red Jacket," large folio, 1855, framed, 1165, hinged at top, toning, light stains, few fox marks (ILLUS.) **4,994**

Popular "Midnight Race on the Mississippi River" Print

Midnight Race on the Mississippi (A), large folio, 1860, 4116, some surface wear, reinforced crease, margin damage w/missing title, framed (ILLUS., top of page) **2,875**

Mill-Dam at "Sleepy Hollow" (The), large folio, undated, framed, 4124, margins cut off, repaired, light toning (ILLUS., next column) **823**

Mink Trapping - Prime, large folio, 1862, framed, 4139, tears in right edge, repaired tear in upper right edge, old tape remaining on back, light mat staining & minor foxing (ILLUS., bottom of page) **15,275**

Minute-Men of the Revolution (The), small folio, 1876, unframed, overall good condition, 4144 .... **460**

The Mill-Dam at "Sleepy Hollow"

Mink Trapping - Prime

DECOYS

Mason Factory Bluewing Teal Drake

Decoys have been used for years to lure flying water fowl into target range. They have been made of carved and turned wood, papier-mâché, canvas and metal. Some are in the category of outstanding folk art and command high prices.

Bluewing Teal drake, carved & painted wood, Mason factory, Challenge grade, original paint w/minor to moderate flaking & wear, several tiny dents & shot marks, branded "DWH" (ILLUS., top of page)..... **$8,250**

Canada goose, John Reeves, Port Rowan, Ontario, Canada, hollow body, branded "MEREDITH," "H.N.T." & "F.B.G." for St. Clair Flats Shooting Company members Howard G. Meredith, Frank B. Gaylord & Harry N. Torey, professional repair to part of bill, last quarter, 19th c. **12,650**

Canada goose, Sam Soper, Barnegat, New Jersey, swimming pose, hollow-carved w/good feather detail, original paint w/good patina, minor wear, repair to crack in neck, early (ILLUS., bottom of page)... **2,200**

Canvasback drake, Charles Bergman, Astoria, Oregon, hollow body w/original paint, tight diagonal crack at neck, one shot mark, first quarter, 20th c. **7,150**

Canvasback drake, Thomas Chambers, Toronto, Ontario, Canada, hollow long body model, branded "GEO. M. HENDRIE" of the St. Clair Flats Shooting Company, original paint, last quarter, 19th c. - first quarter, 20th c. **11,825**

Canvasback drake & hen, unknown maker, St. Clair Flats Shooting Company, lightweight hollow bodies, unusual form, very early dry cracked paint appears to be original, may be only known pair, light shot marks, professional bill repair to hen, last quarter, 19th c., pr. **9,350**

Canvasback hen, Mason Decoy Factory, Detroit, Michigan, Premier grade, original paint, first quarter, 20th c. (moderate wear, thin chip missing from base on neck, small shot scar on top of tail).......... **1,320**

Canvasback hen, Thomas Chambers, Toronto, Ontario, Canada, hollow long body model, branded "GEO. M. HENDRIE" of the St. Clair Flats Shooting Company, dry original paint, first quarter 20th c. **9,075**

Sam Soper Swimming Canada Goose Decoy

Mason Merganser Drake Decoy

Merganser drake, carved & painted wood, Mason factory, Challenge grade, taken down to original paint w/minor wear, numerous dents & shot marks, some old neck filler replaced, first quarter 20th c. (ILLUS., top of page).................................. **3,575**

Merganser hen, attributed to Eugene Cuffee, Shinnecock Reservation, Eastern Long Island, New York, cork & wood, initials "EN" carved on underside, original paint, rare..................................... **880**

Merganser hen, Marcel Dufour, Verdun, Quebec, Canada, swimming position, relief wing carving, original paint **715**

Mergansers, Dodge Decoy Factory, Detroit, Michigan, worn original paint, very rare, ca. 1890 .... **2,640**

Mergansers, Harry V. Shourds, Tuckerton, New Jersey, first quarter, 20th c. (paint & bill restoration to both), pr. **1,100**

Miniature Canada goose, by Elmer Crowell, East Harwich, Massachusetts, on semicircular base, original paint, Crowell's circular stamp w/penciled date of 1920 written on bottom & red & white paper label inscribed "COMMON CANADA GOOSE" (repair to tail)............................. **2,310**

Redhead drake, Charlie Joiner, Chestertown, Maryland, branded w/"ER" on underside, original paint, mid-20th c.............. **413**

Redhead drake, Harry V. Shourds, Tuckerton, New Jersey, carved & painted wood w/original paint & minor wear, slight roughness on bill edge, some tiny dents, last quarter 19th c. (ILLUS., bottom of page).. **1,540**

Redhead drake, Thomas Chambers, Long Point, Ontario, Canada, rare "long bodied" style, original paint, first quarter, 20th c. (crack in breast, shot marks)................ **2,200**

Redhead drake & hen, Tom Schroeder, Detroit, Michigan, hen w/original anchor made by Schroeder, 1938, pr. **8,525**

Redhead hen, Nate Quillen, Rockport, Michigan, hollow body, classic inlet lowhead model, old repaint, last quarter, 19th c. **2,915**

Redheads, maker unknown, St. Clair Flats Shooting Company, Ontario, Canada, hollow bodies w/very thin shells, serrated mandibles, branded "MEREDITH" & "H.N.T." for St. Clair Flats Shooting Company members Howard G. Meredith & Harry N. Torey, last quarter, 19th c., pr. **19,800**

Harry Shourds Redhead Drake Decoy

Extremely Rare Wood Ducks from Ontario

Wood drake & hen, carved & painted wood, glass eyes & highly detailed bill carving, both were used as stick-ups & floaters, each w/painted initials "GRW" on the bottom, original paint w/fine patina & very minor wear, slight roughness on hen's tail & tiny chip under her bill, very msalll chip on top of drake's tail, both lightly hit by short, only five of these are known, Ontario, Canada, ca. 1900, pr. (ILLUS.) **110,558**

DISNEY COLLECTIBLES

Scores of objects ranging from watches to dolls have been created showing Walt Disney's copyrighted animated cartoon characters, and an increasing number of collectors now are seeking these, made primarily by licensed manufacturers.

ALSO SEE Antique Trader Toy Price Guide.

Alice in Wonderland White Rabbit Cel

Alice in Wonderland movie cel, the White Rabbit running, shown in profile, gouache on celluloid, 1951, 3 x 4" (ILLUS.).............. **$239**

Part of Disney Characters Card Set

Disney characters card set, "Walt Disney Cartooning Cards," each w/a color picture of a different Disney character including Dumbo, Lady & the Tramp, Pinocchio & Mickey Mouse, the back of each w/instructions on how to draw the character, 1959, complete set of 18 cards (ILLUS. of part) **278**

Donald Duck parasol, child's, white fabric printed around top w/three different color vignettes of the early long-billed Donald, wooden handle, 1930s, excellent condition, 20" d. open, 19 1/2" l. (ILLUS. of two views, top next page) **276**

Dwarf Dopey movie cel, half-length portrait of Dopey wearing an oversized jacket, applied to a wood veneer background, original descriptive label on the back, 1937, cel 3" w., overall 5 1/2 x 6" (ILLUS., next page) **1,793**

Unusual Early Donald Duck Child's Parasol

Dwarf Dopey Movie Cel

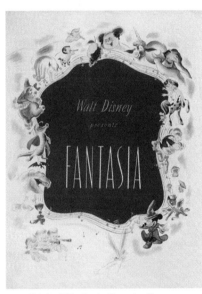

Original Fantasia Premier Program

Fantasia movie premier program, large format souvenir-type printed on the cover w/a large black title panel surrounded by colored sketches of various characters from the movie, virtually mint, 1940, 9 1/2 x 12 1/2" (ILLUS.) **225**

Fantasia pre-production sketch, pastel on paper, a scene of two centaurettes frolicking, in shades of green, yellow & blue, 1940, matted & framed, 7 x 11" (ILLUS., top next page) **1,315**

Mickey Mouse game, "Pin The Tail On 'Mickey'," a large cloth banner printed in red, black & white w/a rear few of Mickey, comes w/original cloth tails & original cardboard box, Marks Bros., Boston, apparently never used, early 1930s, box 9 x 10 1/2", banner 17 x 21", the set (ILLUS., next page) **604**

Movie Cel of Dwarfs Doc & Dopey

Dwarfs Doc & Dopey movie cel, Dopey & Doc looking at diamonds, applied to a wood veneer background, original sticker on the back, minor chipping & some wrinkling on the cel, 1937, cel 4" sq., overall 7 x 9" (ILLUS.)... **3,346**

Fantasia Pre-production Pastel Sketch

1959, 1 1/2 x 3" (ILLUS., bottom of page)
.... **837**

Early "Pin The Tail On 'Mickey'" Game

Mickey Mouse poster, for a color cartoon, a bright yellow background printed w/a large image of Mickey & colorful wording reading "now in Technicolor - Walt Disney's Mickey Mouse - Released thru United Artists," one-sheet, 1935, linen-backed, 27 x 41" (ILLUS., next column).. **14,350**

Sleeping Beauty movie cel, a forest landscape w/a small figure of Briar Rose walking w/her basket, gouache on celluloid applied to an airbrushed background,

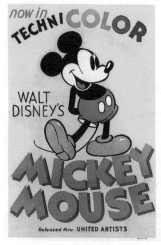

Rare Early Mickey Mouse Cartoon Poster

Small Sleeping Beauty Movie Cel

Original Snow White at the Wishing Well Movie Cel

Snow White & the Seven Dwarfs movie cel, scene of Snow White gazing down into the wishing well w/eight doves perched around the rim, gouache on celluloid applied to an airbrushed background, vintage matte board w/handwritten pencil notation, also marked on the back & w/copyright stickers, 1937, 4 x 5 1/2" (ILLUS.).................................... **4,541**

Autographed Walt Disney Photograph

Walt Disney photograph, black & white image signed by Walt Disney, framed & mounted on an 8 x 10" mat board, photo 7 x 9" (ILLUS.) **3,123**

DOLL FURNITURE & ACCESSORIES

Bed & doll, mahogany low-poster bed w/turned head- and footposts fitted w/turned whalebone finials, fitted w/original tiny bisque head doll, mattress, linens & patchwork quilt, made by Captain David Folger for Lydia N. Folger, Nantucket, Massachusetts, ca. 1850, bed 9 1/2 x 15 1/2", 11 1/2" h., the set (ILLUS., top next page) **$8,365**

Handmade Doll Bedroom Set

Bedroom set: double bed, chest of drawers w/mirror, commode, rocking chair without arms & side chair; each painted red w/gold pinstriping, all made for Catherine Bell Black by her father, late 19th c., includes a 1930s photo of the owner as a grandmother, the set (ILLUS.) **184**

Rare Early Low-poster Bed & Original Doll

Large Set of Delicate Pierce-carved Bedroom Furniture

Bedroom set: high-backed double bed, chest of drawers w/tall mirror, settee, commode, round-topped side table, armchair, rocking chair & side chair; each of delicately pierce-carved hardwood, mid-19th c., bed 13" l., the set (ILLUS.) **224**

Broom, dollhouse-type, green plastic handle, Renwal, 1950s, rare, 5" l. (ILLUS.) **150**

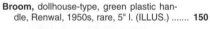

Rare Renwal Dollhouse Broom

Finely Decorated Early Doll-sized Chair

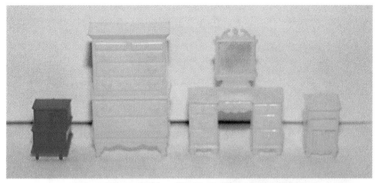

Four Pieces of Marx Plastic Dollhouse Furniture

Chair, painted & decorated wood, Federal "fancy" style, the flat, slightly curved & tapering stiles flanking a flat top stretcher w/a gilt stenciled globe w/crossed arrows flanked by leaves on the original red & black-grained ground, a center stepped stretcher w/gilt-stenciled acanthus leaves above a thin lower stretcher w/a gilt band, the rest of the chair also w/the grained background & highlighted overall w/gilt stenciled leaves & banding, woven rush yellow-painted seat, ca. 1830, minor wear & edge damage to front seatrail, overall 13 3/4" h. (ILLUS., previous page).. **1,840**

Chairs, painted & decorated wood, balloon-back style, scalloped crest on the rounded top above turned spindles, wooden seat, turned legs, black paint w/gold trim & pink roses painted on the crestrail, mid-19th c., 13 1/4" h., pr. (one repainted, both w/some wear, one w/tack holes)....... **1,150**

Chest-on-chest, dollhouse-type, creamy molded plastic, two long drawers in the lower section & five drawers in the upper section, Louis Marx & Co., New York, New York, 1950s (ILLUS. second from left with other pieces of Marx dollhouse furniture, top of page)...................................... **3**

Dulev Brown Plastic Dining Table

Dining table, dollhouse-type, brown molded plastic, by Dulev, 1950s, 4" l., 2" h. (ILLUS.).. **15**

Woven Wicker Doll Carriage

Doll carriage, tightly woven wicker, half-round body & hinged hood in natural wicker w/a printed green diamond design, wire handle, wire-spoked wheels, early 20th c., slight losses to wicker, 27" l., 27" h. (ILLUS.) **115**

Fine Victorian Wooden Doll Carriage

Doll carriage, wood & iron, the shallow wooden body painted black w/red trim & burgundy satin upholstered seat w/a pierced cast-iron seat back, wire upright for the fringed canopy of burgundy satin,

Late 1950s Marx Dollhouse with Fallout Shelter

tall upright wooden push handle, two large wooden rear wheels w/two smaller front wheels, second half 19th c., some minor paint wear, 10 1/2 x 24", 25 1/2" h. (ILLUS., previous page) **891**

Early Hooded Doll-sized Cradle

Doll cradle, painted poplar, hooded-type, the angle-topped hood on the raised ends of the gently canted sideboards w/square nail construction joining them to the canted end boards, raised on long low rockers, old dark finish, mid-19th c., 25" l., 12 1/2" h. (ILLUS.) **345**

Dollhouse, color-printed metal, two-story traditional style w/siding over brick lower half, front bay window, end garage area replaced w/a fallout shelter, back open to show the rooms w/printed wall & floor decoration, Marx Toys, New York, 1959, excellent condition (ILLUS., top of page) **200**

Fine Handmade Victorian Dollhouse

Dollhouse, painted & decorated wood, in the Victorian Queen Anne style, a pedimented shingled roof & turret & paneled sides & back, glazed double-hung working windows, the rear open to reveal a floored interior w/some traces of old wallpaper, late 19th c., America, 20 1/2 x 32", 46" h. (ILLUS.) **3,585**

Renwal "Jolly Twins" Dollhouse & Boxed Furnishings

Dining Room Table & Chairs from a Strom-Becker Furniture Set

Dollhouse & original furnishings, "Jolly Twins" two-story traditional-style lithographed metal seven-room dollhouse w/a red & black roof, includes furnishings in original boxes for the nursery, bedroom, dining room (damaged), living room, bathroom, kitchen & Little Red Schoolhouse, overall good played-with condition, colorful boxes, about 60 pieces of furniture, Renwal, the set (ILLUS., bottom previous page) **604**

Dulev 1950s Brown Dresser

Dresser, dollhouse-type, molded brown plastic, a long rectangular top above a case molded w/drawers & doors & an arched center apron, Dulev, 1950s, 4" l., 2 1/2" h. (ILLUS.) **15**

Dressing table & mirror, dollhouse-type, creamy molded plastic, the square upright mirror w/a broken-scroll pediment above the top over two stacks of drawers flanking a center kneehole opening, Louis Marx & Co., New York, 1950s (ILLUS. second from right with other Marx dollhouse furniture) **3**

Firehouse, color-lithographed paper on wood, Bliss Fire Station #2, two-story Victorian structure w/opening double front doors, a balcony & windows in the upper story, paper overall quite bright & largely intact, possibly missing a dormer above the second story window, one door hinge missing, late 19th c. (ILLUS., top next column).. **403**

Furniture set: dining table, two side chairs, crib, chest of drawers, wardrobe, outside patio table & chairs; fine light hardwood, set No. 144, Strom-Becker Mfg. Co., Mo-line, Illinois, ca. 1954, complete in original box, the set (ILLUS. of the dining set, top of page)... **45**

Bliss Victorian Firehouse

Late Victorian Doll Highchair

Highchair, wood, the wide back w/rounded edges decorated w/a lithographed paper picture of a small baby framed by red & blue gold-trimmed panels, turned back stiles & open arms flanking the plank seat, on tall canted slender square legs w/a footrest & slender rungs, made by Bliss-Whitney Reed, late 19th c., minor wear, 27" h. (ILLUS., previous page) **345**

Renwal Green Plastic Ladder

Ladder, dollhouse-type, green plastic, opens up, five steps & support to hold tiny paint tray, Renwal, 1950s, 4 1/2" h. (ILLUS.).. **45**

Nightstand, dollhouse-type, creamy molded plastic, Louis Marx & Co., New York, 1950s (ILLUS. far right with other Marx dollhouse furniture) **3**

Nightstand, dollhouse-type, red molded plastic, Louis Marx & Co., New York, 1950s (ILLUS. far left with other Marx dollhouse furniture) **3**

Ideal Dollhouse Picnic Table

Picnic table, dollhouse-type, molded red plastic, No. 1-1001, Ideal Toy Company, 1950s, 4 1/2" l. (ILLUS.) **15**

Finely Carved Victorian Sideboard

Sideboard, carved walnut, a back super-structure w/arched crest & serpentine shelf supported on ring-turned posts, the rectangular top w/serpentine sides above a case w/a long curved drawer above a pair of glazed cupboard doors opening to a mirrored back & flanked by turned columns, flat molded base, bottom board cracks, mid-19th c., 7 3/4 x 12 1/2", 17" h. (ILLUS.) **431**

Wall cupboard, step-back style, birch w/old reddish brown alligatored finish, the top section w/a pair of doors w/glass panes above the stepped-out lower section w/a pair of raised-panel doors, a drawer in the center, original turned wood knobs, 19th c., 7 1/4 x 9 7/8", 15" h. (one pane cracked, two pulls missing) **748**

DOLLS

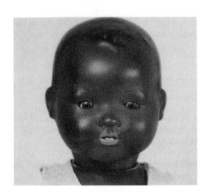

Armand Marseille Black Baby

A.M. (Armand Marseille) bisque socket head black baby, marked "AM Germany 351/6.K.," brown sleep eyes, open mouth w/two teeth, painted molded hair, jointed composition body, wearing replacement clothes, left thumb & right forefinger broken, neck worn, needs restringing, 20" (ILLUS.).. **$661**

Armand Marseille Baby

A.M. bisque socket head baby, marked "A.M. - Germany - 351./4.K," solid dome, blue sleep eyes, softly blushed brows, open mouth w/two lower teeth, lightly molded & painted hair, composition bent-limb baby body, wearing antique baby gown & slip, diaper, new sweater & bonnet, 16" (ILLUS.) **200**

A.M. bisque socket head baby, marked "A.M. - Germany - 351./8.K," solid dome, blue sleep eyes, softly blushed brows, open mouth w/two lower teeth, molded & painted hair, composition baby body, wearing antique long white baby dress, diaper, booties & sweater, 22" (minor repairs on left foot & leg, lower front of torso, left fingers).. **300**

A.M. bisque socket head boy, marked "500 - Germany - A. 0M. - DRGM," solid dome, blue intaglio eyes, single-stroke brows, closed mouth, molded & painted hair, jointed wood & composition body w/straight wrists, wearing blue velvet two-piece suit, lace-trimmed shirt, socks & handmade shoes, 11 1/2" **225**

A.M. bisque socket head girl, marked "H 1894 - A.M. 5/0 DEP," set blue eyes, open mouth w/four upper teeth, original blonde mohair wig, jointed wood & composition body w/straight wrists, wearing regional costume representing Finistere, Brittany, France, a black wool skirt & jacket edged w/black velvet, gold lace trim on skirt, black velvet laced vest, chemisette w/embroidered yoke, white pleated collar edged w/lace, pink silk tablier

A.M. Girl in Brittany Costume

w/bib & trimmed w/lace, muslin underclothes, original black stockings & leather shoes, lace coiffe over pink lace-trimmed silk skull cap, long lace brides & pink silk ribbon trim, 11" h. (ILLUS.) **660**

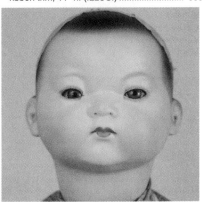

Large Oriental Toddler Doll

A.M. bisque socket head Oriental toddler, marked "Oriental AM 353" on body, dark blue eyes, closed mouth, molded hair, five-piece repainted toddler body, 24" (ILLUS.) **920**

A.M. "googlie" child, marked "322 - A. 11/0 M. - Germany" on back of head, bisque socket head w/blue intaglio "googlie" eyes to the side, single-stroke brows, closed smiling mouth, molded & painted boy's hair, five-piece composition body w/unfinished torso, molded & painted socks & one-strap shoes, wearing one-piece belted romper, minor repair on right upper arm, 6 1/2" (ILLUS., top next page)

.... **375**

Armand Marseille Googlie

Madame Alexander Jane Withers Doll

"Just Me" Doll

A.M. "Just Me," marked "Just Me - Registered - Germany - A. 310/3/0.M." on back of head,bisque socket head w/blue sleep eyes to side, single-stroke brows, painted lashes, closed mouth, blonde mohair wig, five-piece composition body w/bent right arm, wearing factory original organdy dress w/red collar & trim, original underclothing, cotton socks & black leatherette shoes, tip of right little finger missing, 11" (ILLUS.).. **2,600**

Alexander (Madame) Jane Withers, marked on back of head & on original dress tag, all-composition w/brown sleep eyes w/real lashes, closed mouth, original brown mohair wig, five-piece jointed body, wearing print dress w/pink collar &

cuffs, replaced underwear combination, original socks & black oilcloth snap shoes, original black velvet beret, w/extra peach organdy dress, eyes cloudy, ca. 1936, 19" (ILLUS.) **1,210**

Madame Alexander Maggie Walker

Alexander (Madame) Maggie walker, marked "Madame Alexander - All Rights Reserved - New York U.S.A." on dress tag, hard plastic head w/walking mechanism, blue sleep eyes w/real lashes, feathered brows, closed mouth, original wig, five-piece hard plastic body w/walking mechanism, wearing blue & white taffeta dress w/white collar & cuffs, white taffeta slip & panties, original stockings, black center-snap shoes, 17" (ILLUS.) **700**

All-bisque "Our Fairy" Child Doll

All-bisque "Our Fairy" child, marked "222 - 12," green paper label on the torso, stiff neck, side-glancing brown sleep eyes, open-closed smiling mouth w/two painted upper teeth, original blonde mohair wig, jointed arms, legs molded together, overall excellent, Germany, early 20th c., 5" (ILLUS.)... **468**

Alt, Beck & Gottschalck Baby

Alt, Beck & Gottschalck bisque socket head baby, marked "No. 5 - 1322 - 50," blue sleep eyes, two-tone single stroke brows, open mouth w/two upper teeth & molded tongue, antique blonde mohair wig, jointed composition baby body, wearing fine antique baby dress w/lace bodice, tucks & lace inserts on skirt, antique bonnet, new underclothes, left little finger replaced, 18" (ILLUS.)........................ **385**

Alt, Beck & Gottschalck 911 Girl

Alt, Beck & Gottschalck bisque socket head girl, marked "911-8," set brown eyes, open-closed mouth w/white space between lips, pierced ears, original blonde mohair wig, jointed composition body w/straight wrists, separate balls at shoulders, elbows, hips & knees, wearing a faded blue silk dress, white lace-trimmed blouse, slip & pants made of old fabric, antique black socks, black leather side-snap shoes, small chip on upper rim of right eye, 16" (ILLUS.) **825**

American Character Toni Fashion Doll

American Character "Toni" lady, marked "An American Character Doll" on box label, all-vinyl fashion lady w/blue sleep eyes, rooted brown hair, fully jointed including at waist, high heel feet, wearing a rose gown w/double pleated skirt, panties, stockings, black high heel shoes, pearl necklace, rhinestone earrings, in original box w/extra clothing purchased separately, 1950s, 14" (ILLUS.).................. **300**

Bisque Walking Doll

Bisque socket head walking child, marked "DEP - 6" on back of head, blue sleep eyes w/real lashes, painted lower lashes, feathered brows, open mouth w/four upper teeth, pierced ears, antique mohair wig, composition body jointed at shoulders, wrists & hips, key-wind walking mechanism in legs, wearing boy's two-piece suit, shirt, socks & antique shoes, walking mechanism reattached w/wire, minor touchups, 16 1/2" (ILLUS. without clothes) **800**

Bru Girl with Circle Dot Mark

Bru bisque socket head girl, marked "1" above Circle Dot crescent on head, large blue eyes, feathered brows, open mouth w/molded teeth, pierced ears, remnants

of original skin wig under replacement blonde mohair wig, jointed kid body, bisque hands, wearing original shoes marked "1," body repainted, clothes later replacements, 17" (ILLUS. without clothes) **13,513**

Fine Bru Cabinet-sized Doll

Bru Jne. bisque head girl, impressed "2," light blue threaded reset paperweight eyes, molded tongue, antique blonde mohair wig, kid Bru body w/bisque lower arms, jointed at the elbows, paper label at back of torso from a New Jersey doll hospital, wearing a simple white cotton dress, comes w/a newer elaborate dress, some restoration to lower right eyelid, cabinet-sized, 13" (ILLUS.) **9,488**

Bru Bisque Doll with Fancy Costume

Bru Jne. bisque head girl, marked "3/0," amber glass eyes, closed mouth, blonde curly mohair wig, on a proper style kid body w/square shoulder plate, bisque hands, wearing elaborate cotton dress & straw hat, antique brown leather shoes, 14" (ILLUS., previous page) **8,050**

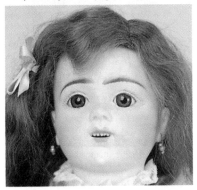

Bru "Walking, Kiss-Throwing" Doll

Bru "Walking, Kiss-Throwing" bisque head girl, marked "Bru Jne R" on head, blue sleep eyes, feathered brows, painted lashes, open mouth w/upper teeth, brown h.h. wig, jointed body, pulling a string attached to her torso raises her right forearm, simulating blowing a kiss, intact working crying mechanism, wearing antique white silk dress & original marked shoes, right hand repainted, 22" (ILLUS.) **2,243**

Buddy Lee Boy in Original Costume

Buddy Lee boy, all-composition w/painted side-glancing eyes, closed smiling mouth, molded & painted hair, composition body jointed at shoulders only, painted black boots, wearing original blue shirt, matching blue paints w/black vinyl belt & matching cap w/black visor, tag on back of pants

reads "Union Made - Lee - Reg. U.S. Pat. Off.," tag on front of cap reads "Union Made - Lee - Fade Proof - Sanforized," very minor damage, 12" (ILLUS.) **578**

Original Bye-Lo Baby Doll

Bye-Lo Baby, marked "Copr. by - Grace S. Putnam - Made in Germany," stamped on front of body "Bye-lo Baby - Pat. Appl'd for - Copy. By - Grace - Storey - Putnam," also blue button w/"Bye-Lo Baby - reg. U.S. Pat. Off. - Patent Applied for - K and K - Copyright 1922 - by Grace Storey," original dress tag reading "Bye-Lo Baby - None Genuine Without Signature - Grace Story Putnam," solid dome bisque flange head, blue sleep eyes, closed mouth, lightly molded & painted hair, cloth body w/celluloid hands, wearing original baby dress & lace-trimmed bonnet, 10" head circumference, 11" (ILLUS.) **358**

Cameo "Margie" Composition Doll

Cameo "Margie," unmarked, composition head w/side-glancing painted blue eyes, open/closed smiling mouth w/four upper teeth, molded & painted hair w/molded band of ribbon, composition torso, segmented wood arms & legs, composition hands, wearing probably original print dress, slip & panties combination, replaced blue ribbon on hair, light wear, couple of flakes on hair, 15" (ILLUS., previous page)... 468

Chase stockinette baby, marked "Chase - Stockinette - Trade Marke" in a face stamped on upper left leg, oil painted head, painted blue eyes w/molded lids, single-stroke brows, painted upper lashes, closed mouth, applied ears, textured oil painted hair, cloth body w/sateen covered torso, oil painted lower arms & lower legs, wearing blue baby romper w/white collar & cuffs, underclothing, cotton socks, white baby shoes, 27" (most of painted lashes worn off, facial paint crazed, hair paint flaking, touchup at joints, general crazing on body) 425

China shoulder head "covered wagon" lady, unmarked, painted blue eyes, single-stroke brows, closed mouth, molded & painted hair w/seven curls, new cloth body w/china lower arms lightly tinted pink, china lower legs w/flat feet, redressed in antique-style dress, antique underclothing, 8 1/4" (replaced right china leg) 325

Brown-eyed China Head Lady

China shoulder head lady, unmarked, painted brown eyes w/red lid line, single stroke brows, closed mouth, molded center-part curly black hair w/exposed ears, cloth body stitch-jointed at hips, no hands or fingers indicated, wearing short gold dress, possibly original underclothing, socks & fine red leather shoes, homemade aged body, 23" (ILLUS.)..................... 468

Curly Top China Should Head Lady

China shoulder head lady, unmarked, molded black curls w/brush strokes at ends of curls on forehead, painted blue eyes, single-stroke brows, closed smiling mouth, cloth body w/kid lower arms, jointed at shoulders, hips & knees, individually stitched fingers, wearing antique green plaid silk taffeta gown, antique underclothing, new leather boots, 1/4" fine scratch on back of shoulder plate near sew hole, replaced body may have some age, 15 1/2" (ILLUS.) 475

China shoulder head lady, unmarked, painted blue eyes w/red accent, single-stroke brows, closed mouth w/accent line between lips, molded & painted black hair w/braided coronet, curly brush strokes around face & on nape of neck, partially exposed ears, cloth body w/leather hands, stitch-jointed at elbows, hips & knees, wearing white blouse made of antique fabric, antique red & white polka dot skirt, underclothing, socks & original homemade brown leather boots, 22" (minor repair on lower back) 1,600

China shoulder head man, marked "4" on both china hands, painted blue eyes w/red accent lines, single-stroke brows, closed mouth w/red accent line between lips, molded & painted wavy hair w/center part & exposed ears, replaced cloth body w/antique china lower arms, new china lower legs, wearing black velvet suit, maroon velvet vest, white shirt, 21" (body & lower legs are new replacements) 200

China shoulder head " Sophia Smith" lady, marked "8" on shoulder plate, painted blue eyes w/lightly molded lids, light red accent line, closed mouth, molded black hair w/thirteen vertical sausage curls & center part, cloth body w/china lower arms, well redressed in two-piece antique-style dress labeled "Made by Hazel Ulseth," underclothing, stockings & shoes, replaced body w/some age, antique china arms, 23" (ILLUS. of three views, top next page)............................... 3,850

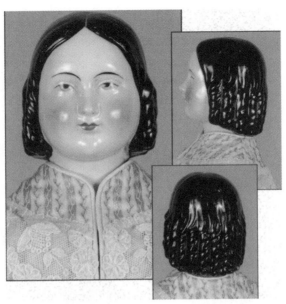

"Sophia Smith" Style China Head Lady

Clement (Pierre) bisque head lady, body stamped "Brevete," reflecting Clement's 1869 patent, dark blue stationary eyes, closed mouth, pierced ears, long curled blonde mohair wig over original cork pate, lightweight patented "blown kid" or embossed leather body, wearing original white undergarments, white cotton blouse, black & white checked silk taffeta dress, leather shoes, France, ca. 1870, 17" (some melting on front of dress, tiny eye chip filled in, top of page) **6,463**

Creche dolls, carved wood w/painted gesso, a standing bearded man w/a pensive expression, fully articulated body painted body down to molded sandals, the young woman w/glass eyes looking downward, fully articulated body in blue, finely detailed hands, possibly representing Mary & Joseph, probably Italy, early 19th c., some inpainting, woman missing wig, 23", pr. (ILLUS.) **2,160**

Pair of Fine Creche Dolls

Dewees Cochran "Cindy" Doll

Dewees Cochran "Cindy" girl, composition head w/painted eyes & mouth, composition body w/jointed shoulders & hips, long blonde hair, wearing a print cotton dress & black shoes w/white socks, cracks to four fingers, minor foxing & chip to left leg, 14 1/2" (ILLUS.)............................ **403**

Door of Hope Female Child Doll

Door of Hope female child, carved wooden head w/finely detailed painted features & black hair, carved & painted arms & legs, wearing original pink silk coat w/pale blue binding & red shoes, China, ca. 1920s, 7 1/2" (ILLUS.) **1,140**

Door of Hope Doll of Older Gentleman

Door of Hope older gentleman, carved & painted finely detailed head w/carved age lines & laugh lines, painted black hair on top w/long black pigtail, cloth body

w/feet but no wooden hands, wearing white pants, white shirt, blue pants, purple velvet leggings, green brocade long robe, black slippers, clothing slightly aged & faded, small hole in right shoe, China, ca. 1920s, 12" (ILLUS.) **935**

French E.D. Bisque Girl

E.D. bisque head girl, marked "E. 9 D.," blue paperweight eyes w/mauve eye shadow, a full, well-defined closed mouth, jointed composition body, light brown h.h. (human hair) wig, wearing a French-style fancy newer dress & lace-trimmed hat, antique baby blue leather shoes, some peppering on bisque, France, 21" (ILLUS.) **1,725**

Effanbee "Lovums" in Box

Effanbee "Lovums," marked "Effanbee - Lovums - © - Pat. No. 1.283.558" on back of shoulder plate, composition shoulder head w/brown sleep eyes w/real lashes, open mouth w/two upper & two lower teeth, molded tongue, molded & painted hair, cloth mama doll body w/non-working crier, composition arms & lower legs, wearing original white organdy baby dress & bonnet, slip, undershirt, socks, leatherette baby shoes w/pompons, pink baby jacket w/embroidered collar, in original box marked "Lovums - Trademark - Reg. - An - Effanbee - Durable - Doll - The Doll With - The Golden Heart - 6022," 25" (ILLUS., previous page)........................ **675**

Effanbee "Patsyette," marked "Effanbee - Patsyette - Doll" on back, composition head w/painted brown eyes, single-stroke brows, closed mouth, molded & painted hair, five-piece composition child body w/bent right arm, wearing original blue & white checked dress w/matching romper, original blue & white socks, white leatherette shoes w/buckles, 9" **205**

Effanbee "Wee Patsy" with Box

Frozen Charlotte, pink tint, blue painted eyes, rosy cheeks, black hair w/fine comb marks pulled behind exposed ears, molded one-piece body w/arms held straight down, bare feet, wearing brown printed cotton dress, Germany, mid-19th c., 4 1/2".. **999**

Effanbee "Skippy" Soldier Doll

Effanbee "Skippy" soldier, composition head w/painted blue side-glancing eyes, painted mouth, molded & painted brown hair, wearing original military uniform & hat, fine crazing to face, minor chipping to paint, 14" (ILLUS.)................................... **345**

Effanbee "Wee Patsy," composition head w/painted features, jointed composition body, all-original w/her "Fairy Princess" cardboard box, minor paint chip on white sock, 5 3/4" (ILLUS., top next column)......... **403**

Fine Gaultier Lady Doll

Gaultier (Francois) bisque socket head lady, marked "F. 3. G.," brown paperweight eyes, feathered brows, closed mouth w/accented lips, pierced ears, brown mohair wig on cork pate, jointed wood & composition body w/straight wrists, separate balls at shoulders, elbows, hips & knees, redressed in an ecru two-piece outfit trimmed w/black braid & pale green, straw bonnet w/feather trim, underclothing, socks & old shoes, 12" (ILLUS.)........................... **3,575**

Jumeau Portrait Doll with Wardrobe

Ideal "Toni," marked "P-91 - Ideal Doll - Made in U.S.A." on head, "Ideal Doll - P-91" on back, hard plastic head w/blue sleep eyes w/real lashes, single-stroke brows, closed mouth, original brunette wig, five-piece hard plastic body, wearing original dress w/pink pique bodice, blue & gold print skirt w/matching drawstring purse, attached white cotton half slip, matching panties, white rayon socks, white leatherette center-snap shoes, new pink hair ribbons, 15" (evidence of tag cut off dress at right rear waist).......................... **250**

Ideal "Toni" in trunk, marked "P-91 - Ideal Doll - Made in U.S.A." on head, "Ideal Doll - P-91" on back, "Genuine Toni Doll - with Nylon wig - Made by Ideal Toy Corporation" on dress tag, hard plastic head w/blue sleep eyes w/real lashes, single-stroke brows, closed mouth, platinum blonde hair, five-piece hard plastic body, wearing original dress w/attached slip, matching panties, original socks & center-snap shoes, contained in red metal trunk w/one vintage dress, newer yellow organdy dress w/panties, new pajamas, robe, play suit & two sweaters, 15" (originality & set of wig undetermined) **355**

Ideal "Toni" walker, marked "90W -Ideal Doll" on head, "Ideal Doll - 90W" on back, "Ideal Toy Corp. - 14" on shoes, "Ideal's New - Toni - Walker Doll" on original box & wrist tag, hard plastic head w/walker mechanism, blue sleep eyes w/real lashes, closed mouth, original nylon wig in original set, five-piece hard plastic walking body jointed at shoulders & hips, wearing original dotted organdy dress, panties, socks & vinyl shoes, w/permanent wave set in "Toni Play Wave" box including Directions, Lotion, Curlers, Shampoo, End Tissues & comb, doll &

set contained in original box, 14 1/2" (box aged, dented & torn) **625**

Jumeau bisque head portrait doll w/wardrobe, indecipherable mark on head, body stamped "Jumeau Medaille d'Or Paris," almond-shaped hand-cut eyes w/blue spiral irises, closed mouth, original skin wig, fully articulated eight-ball composition body, 14", w/wardrobe trunk containing original & added items, most commercially made, including seven dresses & a coat, three hats, a bonnet, undergarments, leg warmers, muff, accessories, dark brown ankle-strap shoes & white leather shoes marked "Jumeau," ca. 1880 (ILLUS., top of page) **28,200**

Tall Jumeau Doll with Open Mouth

Jumeau (E.) bisque socket head girl, marked "1907 - 10" on back of head, shoes marked "9 - Paris [bee] - Depose," blue paperweight eyes, heavy feathered brows, open mouth w/six upper teeth, accented lips, pierced ears, brown h.h. wig, jointed wood & composition body w/jointed wrists, wearing antique white dress w/tucks & lace inserts & trim, underclothing made w/antique fabric, tiny inherent firing line on back neck rim, flake at left earring hole, repainted hands, left thumb broken & reglued, left second finger replaced, shoes worn w/half of right sole missing, bows & buttons replaced, 23" (ILLUS., bottom previous page) **880**

Lovely Tall Portrait Jumeau Doll

Jumeau (E.) bisque socket head portrait girl, marked "7" on back of neck, the blue stamped mark "Jumeau - Medaille d'Or - Paris" on lower back under repaint, head w/fine pale coloring, set blue threaded eyes, two-tone feathered brows, closed mouth w/accented lips & small white space between lips, pierced ears, replaced cork pate w/antique brown h.h. wig, jointed eight-ball composition body w/straight wrists, wearing antique low-waisted dress w/lace trim, wide antique ribbon below waist, new underclothing & socks, antique leather shoes, grey velvet hat, body poorly repainted, clothing fragile, 19" (ILLUS.) **7,425**

Jumeau (Emile) bisque socket head girl, marked "1907 - 10," blue paperweight eyes, feathered brows, open mouth w/accented lips & six upper teeth, pierced ears, antique mohair wig, jointed wood & composition body, redressed in copy of factory Jumeau dress, underclothing, cotton socks, old leather shoes, 23" (hands repainted, repair on left big toe) **1,800**

Jumeau (Emile) bisque socket head girl, marked "Depose - Tete Jumeau - 2" as partial red stamp, red & black artist marks, "Bebe Jumeau - Bte S.G.D.G. Depose" on body, large blue paperweight eyes, heavy feathered brows, closed mouth w/accented lips, pierced ears, h.h. wig, jointed wood & composition body, redressed in new turquoise French-style outfit w/matching bonnet, new underclothing, old socks & shoes, 26" (composition & finish damaged on toes) **2,100**

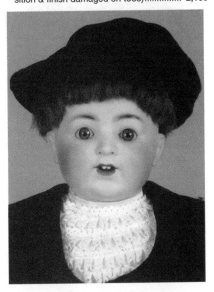

K & K Bisque Shoulder-head Baby

K & K bisque shoulder-head baby, marked "45 - K & K - 58 - Made in Germany," blue sleep eyes, feathered brows, open mouth w/two upper teeth, original short brown mohair wig on original cardboard pate, cloth body w/composition lower arms & legs, wearing maroon velvet suit w/lace-trimmed shirt, matching tam, new socks & shoes, finish repainted, cracked & flaking off arms & legs, right foot repaired, 20 1/2" (ILLUS.) **330**

K [star] R (Kammer & Reinhardt) bisque socket head baby, marked "36 K [star] R - 100," solid dome, painted blue eyes w/molded eyelids, single-stroke brows, open-closed mouth w/shaded lips, molded & brush-stroked hair, composition baby body, wearing long antique pink baby dress w/lace trim, long slip & diaper, 14" **275**

Fine K*R Character Boy

K [star] R (Kammer & Reinhardt) bisque socket head character boy, marked "K*R - Simon & Halbig - 115 - A - 42," blue sleep eyes, feathered brows, closed pouty mouth, antique short brown mohair wig, jointed wood & composition toddler body w/diagonal hip joints, jointed at shoulders, elbows, wrists & knees, wearing fine knit outfit w/maroon sweater & cap w/tassel, white knit pants, black socks & leather sandals, 16" (ILLUS.) **3,520**

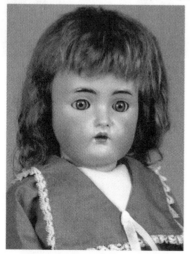

K*R Model 403 Bisque Head Girl

K [star] R (Kammer & Reinhardt) bisque socket head girl, marked "K*R - Simon

& Halbig - 403 - Germany - 43" on back of head & "1918" on rear rim, blue sleep eyes w/missing real lashes, feathered brows, painted upper & lower lashes, open mouth w/four upper teeth, pierced ears, antique brown mohair wig, jointed wood & composition body, redressed in new antique-style sailor dress, antique underclothing, new socks & antique shoes, overall excellent, 16" (ILLUS.).......... **413**

K [star] R (Kammer & Reinhardt) celluloid socket head toddler, marked "K [star] R - 1728/7 - Germany - [turtle mark]," blue sleep eyes w/remnants of real lashes, single-stroke brows, open mouth w/two upper teeth & molded tongue, original mohair wig, five-piece composition toddler body, wearing pale pink dress tagged "Alexander," slip, diaper, new socks & shoes, 17 1/2"................. **315**

Near Mint 1950s Kathe Kruse Girl

Kathe Kruse girl, all-stockinette, molded face w/painted blue eyes & red lips, blonde wig, body w/jointed shoulders & hips, wearing blue sweater w/white collar & pink pleated skirt, white socks & shoes, outfit w/original paper hang tag, signed on left foot "Aug. 22, 1955," near mint, 14 1/2" (ILLUS.) **390**

Kestner (J.D.) bisque character doll set: Model 178 character girl w/ball-jointed composition body in the original box w/side compartments holding two close-mouthed bisque character heads w/a blonde or light brown wig & one open-mouthed glass-eyed Model 174 character head w/long light brown wig, doll body wearing a white long dress & socks w/white & black leather shoes, slight wear on body, the set (ILLUS., top next page)... **12,650**

Rare Kestner Character Doll Set with Four Interchangeable Heads

Kestner (J.D.) bisque shoulder head girl, marked "7," set brown eyes, multi-stroke brows, closed mouth w/accent line between lips, replaced h.h. wig, kid body w/bisque lower arms, pin-jointed at elbows, hips & knees, wearing yellow print dress w/ruffle, antique underclothing, new socks & shoes, 15" **425**

Kestner No. 143 Bisque Head Baby

Kestner (J.D.) bisque socket head baby, marked "C made in - Germany 7 - 143,"

stamped in red on lower back "Germany - 0," brown sleep eyes, feathered brows, open mouth w/accented lips & two upper teeth, light brown mohair wig on cardboard pate, jointed wood & composition Kestner body, wearing old faded green wool two-piece suit, eyelet collar, old socks, replaced shoes w/some age, 13 1/2" (ILLUS.) **660**

Kestner (J.D.) bisque socket head baby, marked "made in - Germany - J.D.K. - 257 - 28" on head, "Germany" stamped in red on back, blue sleep eyes w/real lashes, feathered brows, open mouth w/two upper teeth & spring tongue, dark brown antique mohair wig, five-piece composition Kestner baby body, wearing possibly original lace-trimmed baby dress, slip & panties, 11 1/2" **550**

Kestner (J.D.) bisque socket head baby, marked "F. made in 15 Germany 10 - 247 - J.D.K. - 10," brown sleep eyes, feathered brows, open mouth w/two upper teeth, replaced h.h. wig, composition Kestner baby body, wearing ecru antique baby dress, replaced underclothing, socks & shoes, 13" (body repainted) **600**

Kestner (J.D.) bisque socket head baby, marked "G. made in - Germany 11 - 211 - J.D.K.," blue sleep eyes, feathered brows, open mouth w/two lower teeth, original blond mohair wig over plaster pate, bent-limb composition Kestner baby body, wearing antique baby dress w/embroidery & ribbon trim, slip & diaper, 14" (left little finger replaced) **500**

Kley & Hahn Bisque Head Baby

Kley & Hahn bisque socket head baby, marked "K & H (in banner) - Germany - 572-6," set blue eyes, feathered brows, open mouth w/tongue that falls back in w/a weight, antique short blonde mohair wig, composition baby body, wearing antique white baby dress, underclothing made w/antique fabric, socks & booties, chip & flake at hole on back of head, 14 1/2" (ILLUS.) **248**

Large Kley & Hahn "Walkure" Girl

Kley & Hahn bisque socket head "Walkure" girl, marked "18 - Walkure - Germany," set blue eyes, molded & feathered brows, open mouth w/four upper teeth, pierced ears, replaced synthetic blonde wig, jointed composition body,

wearing old pink child's dress, new underclothing, socks & cloth shoes w/buttoned strap, small flake at left earring hole, repairs at both shoulder sockets, 33" (ILLUS.) **550**

Kling bisque shoulder head lady, marked "152-2" along lower edge of rear shoulder plate, "2" stamped on lower rear of torso, socket head, pale blue paperweight eyes, painted lashes, feathered blonde brows, closed mouth, pierced ears, blonde mohair wig, cloth body stitch jointed at shoulders, hips & knees, leather lower arms w/stitched fingers, wearing antique brown two-piece gown w/ribbon trim, matching hat, antique underclothing, cotton socks & paper shoes, 15 1/2" (small chip at left front sew hole, body aged & soiled, wear on leather arms) **500**

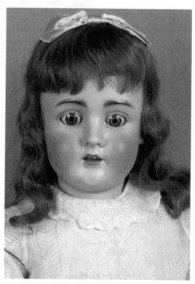

Konig & Wernicke Large Girl Doll

Konig & Wernicke bisque socket head girl, marked "4711 - 105," blue sleep eyes, molded & feathered brows, open mouth w/outlined lips & four upper teeth, replaced red h.h. wig, jointed wood & composition body w/opening in side for crier (most parts missing), wearing antique child's dress w/white net overlay over blue, new underclothing, socks & shoes, right eyeball cracked, minor firing lines over ears, possible old body repaint, 42" (ILLUS.) **1,210**

Kuhnlenz (Gebruder) all-bisque girl, marked "31 - 13" on back of head & arms, bisque socket head w/set blue eyes, closed mouth, brown mohair wig, body jointed at shoulders & hips, molded & painted white ribbed stockings & black one-strap shoes, wearing a plaid taffeta dress, slip made of antique fabric, blue crocheted hat, 5 1/2" (ILLUS., top next page) **303**

Gebruder Kuhnlenz All-bisque Girl

Kuhnlenz (Gebruder) bisque socket head girl, marked "G.K. 38-27" along edge of back of shoulder plate, blue threaded paperweight eyes, feathered brows, painted lashes, closed mouth, pierced ears, old mohair wig, kid body w/cloth torso & top of arms, gussets at elbows, hips & knees, bisque lower arms, wearing antique white dress w/tucks & eyelet, underclothing, straw bonnet decorated w/flowers, possibly original black stockings & red leather high button boots, 18" (left eyeball has crack, light cheek rubs, cloth torso & arms aged & fragile, numerous patches on kid & cloth, especially at gussets).. **425**

Blonde Lenci Girl in Blue Outfit

Lenci pressed felt socket head girl, molded face w/brown side-glancing eyes &

red lips, blonde mohair wig, wearing a light blue felt coat w/dark blue trim & triangular patches around the hem, a matching hat, lightly soiled, few moth holes, 13" (ILLUS.)....................................... **450**

Lenci Spanish Lady

Lenci pressed felt socket head Spanish lady, surprised expression w/wide flirty blue eyes that go from side to side, raised feathered brows, mouth formed in "O," wearing black & red Spanish outfit w/black lace mantilla & large spiral-form dangling earrings, 20" (ILLUS.)................. **1,725**

All-original Lenci Girl with Button Tag

Lenci pressed felt swivel head girl, Lenci silver metal button on underwear, the molded head w/painted brown sideglancing eyes, feathered brows, closed mouth, original curly blonde mohair wig, all-felt body jointed at shoulders & hips, stitched fingers, separate thumb, wearing original blue felt & organdy dress, matching hair bow & shoes, original teddy & slip & original socks, somewhat faded, a few small moth holes, 16" (ILLUS.) **495**

Parian Lady with Tiara

Parian shoulder head lady, unmarked, untinted shoulder head w/painted blue eyes w/red accent lines, single-stroke brows, closed mouth w/accent line between lips, pierced ears, molded & painted cafe au lait hair w/molded blue tiara trimmed in gold, molded braid across top, on lower sides & down middle of back of head, old cloth body w/red leather boots as part of legs, wearing white dotted Swiss & lace dress, antique underclothing, new arms by Emma Clear, three beads on tiara repaired by Charles Buysse, 24" (ILLUS.) **1,900**

American-made Philadelphia Baby

Philadelphia Baby, molded cloth, the head w/molded painted dark eyes, pink open/closed mouth & painted brown hair, cloth body, redressed in blue outfit, overall wear to top half of head w/some touchup on the cheeks, 19th c., 21" h. (ILLUS.) **805**

14" Poupee Peau

Poupee Peau, marked "1" on back of head & on both shoulders, bisque socket head on bisque shoulder plate, pale blue threaded paperweight eyes, multi-stroke brows, painted lashes, closed mouth, pierced ears, mohair wig, kid body w/gussets at elbows, hips & knees, individually stitched fingers, redressed in greyish two-piece outfit trimmed w/lace & accent buttons, underclothing, antique socks, no shoes, small chip below right eye, repairs at gussets, 14" (ILLUS.) **1,000**

Poupee Peau bisque shoulder head black lady, marked "0" on shoulder plate, black face w/painted brown eyes, single-stroke brows, closed mouth, black mohair curls for wig, pink kid body w/arms painted black, wearing colorful outfit of antique fabric, antique underclothing, socks & boots, coral bead necklace, 11" (tiny touchup on tip of nose, black paint on arms worn & kid showing through, small split in seam between legs) **900**

Rohmer (Mme.) bisque swivel-neck Fashion doll, Rohmer name on body, bisque head w/set blue eyes, closed mouth & deep pink cheeks, blonde wig, gusseted kid body w/bisque lower arms & jointed lower legs, wearing lovely antique black gown w/long train, matching hat & black German shoes, repaired finger on left hand, France, late 19th c., 16" (ILLUS., top next page) **3,163**

Fine Mme. Rohmer Fashion Doll

S.F.B.J. Jumeau Mold Girl

**S.F.B.J. (Société Francaise de Fabrica-
tion de Bébé & Jouets) bisque socket
head Jumeau mold girl,** marked
"S.F.B.J. - Paris - 9," blue sleep eyes w/re-
al lashes, feathered brows, open mouth
w/four upper teeth, pierced ears, replaced
brown h.h. wig, jointed wood & composition body, wearing a fragile antique silk
dress w/lace trim, hat, antique underclothing, socks & leather shoes, eyes crossed
& in need of repair, 20" (ILLUS.) **880**

S.F.B.J. Bisque Head Girl

S.F.B.J. bisque socket head girl, marked
"21 - D - S.F.B.J. - 60 - Paris - 3" &
marked "Made in France" on lower edge
of right hip, blue sleep eyes w/real lash-

S.F.B.J. Model 301 Girl

S.F.B.J. bisque socket head girl, marked
"S.F.B.J. - 301 - Paris - 11," also marked
"11 - Paris [bee] - Deposé" on bottom of
Jumeau shoes, blue sleep eyes w/real
lashes, molded & feathered brows, open
mouth w/accented lips & four upper
teeth, pierced ears, original brown h.h.
wig on original cardboard pate, jointed
wood & composition French body, wearing original ecru satin blouse, replaced
silk shirt, original underclothing, original
faded blue socks, ecru satin Jumeau
shoes, faint hairline at front of crown,
hands repainted, 25" (ILLUS.) **495**

Spectacular Bruno Schmidt Wendy Character Doll

es, feathered brows, open mouth w/accented lips & four upper teeth, original brown mohair wig, jointed wood & composition French body, redressed in new peach satin outfit, matching hat, new underclothing, new socks & shoes, some flaking on one leg & arm, 19" (ILLUS.)......... **385**

S.F.B.J. (Société Francaise de Fabrication de Bebes et Jouets) solid dome bisque socket head boy, marked "226 - 8" on head, "78" incised on bottoms of feet, set blue "jewel" eyes, single-stroke brows, open-closed laughing mouth, lightly molded & brush-stroked hair, jointed wood & composition French-type body, redressed in brown velvet two-piece outfit, gold satin shirt, socks, antique French-style shoes, 19 1/2" (replaced soles on shoes, part of sole of right foot missing, hands repainted, flaking on feet touched up, small hole & stain on back of torso) **1,300**

Schmidt (Bruno) bisque socket head character "Wendy," marked "BSW 537 (in heart below) 2033," brown sleep eyes, molded & brushed eyebrows, finely molded closed mouth, antique blonde mohair wig, jointed composition body, wearing old, if not original, pink, blue & green plaid long dress w/wide green collar & cuffs,

pale blue shoes & socks, small professional restoration to one finger on each hand, rare, 23" h. (ILLUS., top of page) **36,225**

Bruno Schmidt Bisque Head Girl

Schmidt (Bruno) bisque socket head girl, marked "BSW (in heart below) Made in Germany," blue sleep eyes, blonde curly wig, open mouth w/teeth, jointed composition body, redressed in a red antique-style dress, body repainted, 31" (ILLUS.) **690**

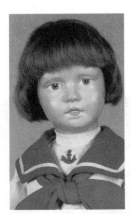

Schoenhut Boy with Replaced Sailor Suit

**Schoenhut wooden socket head charac-
ter boy,** marked "Schoenhut Doll - Pat.
Jan. 17th 1911 - U.S.A. - & Foreign Coun-
tries" on oval label on back, painted brown
intaglio eyes, open/closed smiling mouth
w/four upper teeth, brown h.h. wig, wood-
en body spring-jointed at shoulders, elbows, wrists, hips, knees & ankles, nicely
redressed in white pique Schoenhut-style
sailor suit w/blue collar, cuffs & low belt,
new socks & old replacement shoes,
touch-up on cheeks, 21" (ILLUS., top next
page) **660**

Schoenhut wooden socket head toddler,
marked "H.E. Schoenhut - © - 1913" on
round label on head, "Schoenhut Doll -
Pat. Jan. 14th 1911 - U.S.A." on oval label on back, painted blue eyes, single-
stroke brows, closed mouth, original mohair wig, toddler body spring-jointed at
shoulders, elbows, wrists, hips, knees &
ankles, wearing antique white low-waisted dress, underclothing, old white cotton
socks, white leatherette shoes, 11" **325**

1930s Shirley Temple in Cowgirl Outfit

Shirley Temple doll, all-composition, sleep
eyes cloudy, original blonde wig, jointed
composition body, wearing original cowgirl outfit, missing hat & pin, 1930s, 11"
(ILLUS.).. **1,380**

1957 All Original Shirley Temple Doll

Shirley Temple doll, marked "Ideal Doll -
ST-12," all-vinyl, head w/sleep eyes,
rooted curly hair w/original set & ribbon,
wearing original Scottie dress of white
pique w/red & white striped trim, original
cotton panties, original white socks &
black vinyl shoes, unplayed-with, in original marked box, ca. 1957, 12" (ILLUS.)....... **250**

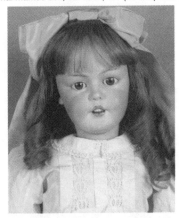

Large Simon & Halbig Character Girl

**Simon & Halbig bisque socket head char-
acter girl,** marked "S & H 1279 - DEP -
Germany - 14 1/2," blue sleep eyes
w/molded & feathered brows, open
mouth w/accented lips & triangle accent
on lower lip & upper teeth, pierced ears,
replaced brown h.h. wig, jointed wood &
composition body, wearing an antique
child's dress & slip, pants made from antique fabric, new socks & shoes, hands
repainted, 32 1/2" (ILLUS.) **2,860**

Well-marked Steiner Figure A Girl

Steiner Figure A bisque socket head girl, marked "J. Steiner - Bte. S.G.D.G. - Paris - Fre A 17," also stamped on left hip "Le Petit Parisien - Bebe J. Steiner - Marque Depose - Medaille d'Or - Paris - 1889," blue paperweight eyes, heavy feathered brows, closed mouth w/accented lips, pierced ears, antique h.h. brown wig on replaced cardboard pate, jointed composition body w/long slender fingers, wearing dress made of antique fabric, new socks & shoes, hairline from front of crown nearly to right eyebrow, small flake at left earring hole, 24" (ILLUS.)............... **3,630**

Pretty Figure A Steiner Girl

Steiner Figure A bisque socket head girl, marked "J. Steiner - Bte. S.G.D.G. - Paris - Fre A7," also stamped on left hip "Le Petit Parisien - Bebe Steiner," lovely blue paperweight eyes, multi-stroke brows,

closed mouth, replaced brown synthetic wig w/replaced pate, jointed composition body w/straight wrists & short stubby fingers, redressed in lavender silk dress w/lace overlay, matching new undergarments, socks & new maroon leather shoes, lower legs are old German replacements, 14" (ILLUS.).......................... **3,080**

Steiner "Gigoteur" Bisque Baby Doll

Steiner "gigoteur" bisque head doll, unmarked, solid dome head w/straight neck, set blue eyes, feathered brows, open mouth w/accented lips & five upper & five lower teeth, pierced ears, antique blonde mohair wig, cloth-covered carton torso w/clockwork mechanism inside, composition arms attached to mechanism, metal upper legs covered w/kid, composition lower legs, wearing antique white dress, antique underclothing & bonnet, new socks & shoes, winding mechanism causes doll to move arms & cry, mechanisms to turn head & move legs not working, 18" (ILLUS.) **1,155**

Swaine & Co. Bisque Head Girl

Swaine & Co. bisque socket head girl, marked "DIP - 1 - Geschutzt - S. & Co. - Germany," squinty brown sleep eyes, closed mouth, original blonde mohair wig, jointed wood & composition body, wearing factory chemise, new pants & slip & new socks & shoes, small hairline at back of crown, replaced old legs don't match, 11" (ILLUS., previous page) **385**

Rare A. Thullier Baby

Thullier (A.) bisque head baby, marked "A4T," amber paperweight eyes, feathered brows, closed mouth, jointed kid body, bisque hands, replaced clothes but original marked shoes & socks, small damage to right knee joint, missing cork pate & wig, right hand missing thumb, 13 1/2" (ILLUS.) **19,550**

Unis France Bisque Head Girl

Unis France bisque socket head girl, marked "Unis - France - 301 - (71 149 on each side) E.® T. 6," blue sleep eyes w/remnants of real lashes, open mouth w/four upper teeth, replaced blonde h.h. wig, jointed wood & composition French body w/jointed wrists, redressed in turquoise French-style dress trimmed w/lace, antique underclothing, new socks & shoes, 17" (ILLUS.) **358**

Near Mint Vogue Ginny in Original Outfit

Vogue "Ginny," marked "Vogue Doll" on back, all-hard plastic, blue sleep eyes w/painted upper lashes, closed mouth, original blonde wig in original set & yellow bow, body w/jointed shoulders & hips, wearing original yellow pique dress w/pastel multi-colored stripes at bottom, multi-colored felt flowers on bodice, matching yellow pique panties & yellow socks & blue leatherette center snap shoes, ca. 1953, near mint, 7 1/2" (ILLUS.) **1,540**

All-Original Near Mint Vogue Ginny

Vogue "Ginny," marked "Vogue Doll" on back, all-hard plastic, blue sleep eyes w/painted upper lashes, closed mouth, original brown wig in braids, body w/jointed shoulders & hips, wearing original blue print dress w/yellow trim & zipper up the back, matching panties, original white socks, blue leatherette snap shoes, blue straw hat w/yellow daisy on top, also original dress & wrist tags, ca. 1953, near mint (ILLUS.).. **1,595**

Vogue Toddles Red Riding Hood Doll

Vogue "Toddles" Little Red Riding Hood, marked "Vogue" on back of head & back, all composition, blue painted side-glancing eyes, red lips, original blonde mohair wig in original set, jointed shoulders & hips, wearing original white dress w/Vogue tag & matching panties, original white rayon socks, red leatherette center snap shoes, red jersey cape w/print lining, light crazing on face & body, 7 1/2" (ILLUS.).. **303**

Walker (Izannah) cloth doll, oil painted brown eyes, mouth, short dark hair w/molded ears showing through, oil painted lower limbs, wearing old white undergarments & soft red print dress, Central Falls, Rhode Island, ca. 1860s, 16 1/2" (wear & crazing to head, separation at left ankle, old restitching on limbs, one Band-Aid-type repair) **6,463**

Wax head lady, reinforced poured wax shoulder head w/blue glass eyes, multi-stroke brows, painted upper & lower lashes, shapely closed mouth, original blonde mohair wig, cloth body w/wax over composition lower arms & legs w/brownish black boots w/pink tassels, stockings w/lace garters, wearing a wonderful original gold silk brocade gown, lace gloves & shawl, flower hair decoration, antique

Lovely Poured Wax Lady in Fancy Gown

underclothing w/three half slips, repairs to shoulder plate & around neck, some fading on face, a few cracks, legs restitched at hips, dress deteriorated, 19th c., 27" (ILLUS.) **440**

Poured Wax Detailed Man Doll

Wax head man, the poured wax shoulder head w/set blue eyes, real hair eyebrows, mustache & goatee inserted into the wax, h.h. inserted into wax for hair, well detailed facial features & ears, on a cloth body w/poured wax lower arms & legs, wearing an original chemise, white shirt w/ "JH" cross-stitched on lower right side of bottom, separate collar, tie made of ribbon, grey vest w/buttons, matching grey jacket & pants, leather high button boots, straw hat, generally excellent condition, 19th c., 19" h. (ILLUS.)................... **1,210**

FARM COLLECTIBLES

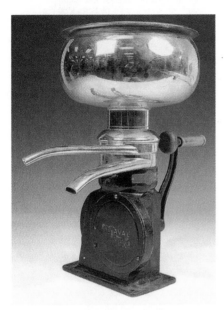

DeLaval Junior #2 Cream Separator

Cream separator, DeLaval Junior #2 table-top model, large squatty bulbous chromed metal bowl top above a pair of projecting arms, all mounted on a black-painted metal base enclosing the mechanism w/a cast-iron crank handle w/wood grip on one side, red-enameled metal tag label, excellent condition, early 20th c., minor paint wear, 22" h. (ILLUS.) **$259**

Early Egg Carrier & Glass Setting Eggs

Egg carrier, wooden, low rectangular box form w/twelve open compartments each fitted w/a milk glass setting egg, printed black advertising on the sides & ends, "Star Egg Carriers and Trays...," flat wire bail carrying handle across center, early 20th c., 6 1/2 x 8 1/2" (ILLUS.) **230**

Complete Hitching Post with Horse Head

Hitching post, cast iron, a figural horse head terminal above a tall reeded column w/two hitching rings, cast lions' face masks around the base, complete w/tall upright for burying in the ground, America, mid-19th c., overall 68" h. (ILLUS.) **1,265**

Swan Head Hitching Post

Hitching post, cast iron, a tall slender reeded column base topped w/the tall looped neck & head of a preening swan, black paint, 19th c., overall 64" h. (ILLUS.) **863**

Unusual Spaniel Hitching Post

Hitching post, cast iron, the terminal in the form of a seated spaniel w/a ring in its mouth, on an octagonal platform atop the tall slightly tapering octagonal post, black paint, late 19th c., overall 57" h. (ILLUS.)... **1,955**

Detailed Cast-bronze Stable Post Finial

Stable post finial, cast bronze, very finely detailed model of a purebred horse w/reins & bit & a model of a saddle cast at the front, later polychroming over a nickled finish, early 20th c., 15" h. (ILLUS.).............. **518**

FIRE FIGHTING COLLECTIBLES

American fire fighting "antiques" are considered those items over 100 years old that were directly related to fire fighting, whereas fire fighting "collectibles" are items less than a century old. Pieces from both eras are very sought-after today.

Foreign-made fire fighting antiques and collectibles have a marketplace of their own and, for the most part, are not as expensive and in demand as similar American pieces.

Early Fire Engine Advertising Litho

Advertising lithography, chromolithography on paper showing the "Warren Engine No. 4 Charlestown, Mass.," produced by

Four Early Leather Fire Buckets

J.H. Buffords, ca. 1850, staining, toning, framed, image 19 3/4 x 27 5/8" (ILLUS., bottom previous page) **$1,645**

Rare Daguerreotype of a Fireman

Daguerreotype of a fireman, sixth-plate, a young gentleman wearing a top hat-style fire hat, holding a mouth trumpet & wearing a crocheted scarf, old tag reading "John in fire man suit when volunteer fire man were in service in 1850," additional typed note w/family history, original seal, slightly tinted, in geometric Union case, rare subject matter, ca. 1850s (ILLUS.) **5,500**

Fire bucket, gently swelled cylindrical form w/padded collar, leather-covered rope handle, painted black ground w/mustard yellow lettering reading "No. 1 Cambridge-Port Society" flanking a red oval w/"Fire" above "E. Kimball 1811," part of handle detached, applied protective varnish, Cambridgeport, Massachusetts, ca. 1811, 14" h. (ILLUS. far right with three other fire buckets) **2,350**

Fire bucket, painted leather, swelled cylindrical form painted in powder blue w/black lettering "M. Shop 21," black collar & leather handle, early 19th c., some wear, 17 3/4" h. (ILLUS. far left with three other fire buckets) **1,116**

Fire buckets, each slightly tapering cylindrical leather, painted black background & red collars, one w/a red heart & No. 28 over white lettering "G.W. Ellery - 1824," the other painted in white w/"No. 2. - Wm. Ellerey 1800," leather-covered rope handles, handles detached, wear, Rhode Island, early 19th c., 10 5/8" & 11 1/4" h., pr. (ILLUS. center with two other fire buckets) **5,875**

Blue Harden's Fire Grenade

Fire grenade, sapphire blue, segmented rounded form w/four panels embossed "Harden's Hand - Fire - Extinguisher - Grenade," ground mouth, footed smooth base, late 19th c., pinhead flake on body, 4 3/4" h. (ILLUS.) **560**

Fire mark, cast iron, oval w/a raised design of clasped hands & the date "1776," used by the Baltimore Equitable Society, ca. 1837, old gold & black paint, 9 3/4 x 10 1/2" (old well done soldered corner restoration).. **834**

Fire mark, cast iron, round, cast w/the image of an early hand pumper wagon above "F.I. Co.," emblem of the Fireman's Insurance Company, Baltimore, Maryland, ca. 1835, hanging ring at the top, 13" d. **690**

Late Victorian Firehouse Bell & Yoke

Firehouse bell, mounted in original double metal yoke, bell marked "2," lower yoke cast "No. 2 Voke 1886," upper yoke cast "No. 2 Upright 1886 - Crystal Metal" & painted grey, clapper present, manufactured by The Hart Hardware Co., Louisville, Kentucky, late 19th c., bell 16" d. (ILLUS.)... **230**

Early Leather Fireman's Belt

Fireman's belt, stitched leather, stitched & raised lettering in red in a white panel on the black belt, reads "Hutting Hose Co.," 19th c., 37" l. (ILLUS.).................................. **115**

Victorian Lithograph of Early Engine

Lithograph, printed in colors, titled "Engine of the Red Jacket Veteran Fireman's Association ... Champion of the New England League, 1894," the early engine in the center flanked by flaming torches, printed for the Brooks Bank Note Company, Boston, 17 1/4 x 22 1/2" (ILLUS.)........ **1,410**

Staffordshire figurine, earthenware, a standing figure of an early fireman in uniform leaning against a water pump w/his fire horn, h.p. in black, red, orange, fleshtones & gilt trim around the hat badge, England, mid-19th c., minor wear to paint on the front, 9 1/4" h. (ILLUS. right with similar Staffordshire fireman figure)............ **575**

Two Similar Staffordshire Firemen

Staffordshire figurine, earthenware, a standing figure of an early fireman in uniform leaning against a water pump w/his fire horn, h.p. in black, red, orange, fleshtones & gilt trim around the hat badge, England, mid-19th c., 9 1/4" h. (ILLUS. left with similar Staffordshire fireman figure) **748**

FIREARMS

Blunderbuss, Noyes flintlock model, brass barrel octagonal to round w/cannon muzzle, a 12 1/2" l. spring-loaded triangular bayonet mounted to the top, top of barrel marked "Warminster" & left flat side w/two English proof marks, well made lock marked "Noyes," reinforced hammer & safety w/roller frizzen w/boat-shaped waterproof pan, mounted in a one-piece walnut stock w/brass furniture consisting of a ramrod guide & nose pipe containing the original brass-tipped rammer w/worm on small end, trigger guard flared wide in middle & engraved w/a long nicely detailed pineapple finial, buttplate w/narrow engraved tang, fine checkered wrist & the barrel secured w/two wedges through the forestock without escutcheons, bayonet w/brazed repair, stock w/stress crack on right side & hairline in front of trigger guard, barrel 13 1/2" l. (ILLUS.) **$3,680**

Early English Blunderbuss

Sharps & Hankins Model 1862 Carbine

Carbine, Burnside 4th Model, .54 cal., straight walnut stock w/carbine butt, barrel w/standard sights, saddle bar & ring on left side of stock, Civil War era, Serial No. 5657, barrel 22" l. (no original finish, refinished wood, missing breechlock guide screw).. **805**

Carbine, Sharps & Hankins Model 1862, .52 cal., walnut stock, Serial No. 6340, 24" l. barrel, ca. 1859, fair condition, pitting & bruises to metal, nicks & separation to stock, overall 39" l. (ILLUS., second from top)... **748**

Carbine, Sharps New Model 1863 Conversion model, .50 cal., silver blade front sight & carbine ladder rear sight, chamber marked "New Model 1863," standard uncheckered wood stock w/a cartouche midway on the left side of buttstock & inspector's initials "AWM" on top of the comb, a sling bar & ring on left side w/a Model 59-style buttplate notched for a patchbox, very fine w/most original bluing, top of original priming mechanism missing, three-groove barrel 22" l. **2,645**

Sharps Model 3B Derringer

Derringer, Sharps Model 3B, .32 cal. rim fire, four barrels, cluster of barrels w/Sharps & Hankins address, Sharps patent markings on right side of frame, button barrel release & the barrels without extractor, smooth rosewood grip panels, barrels w/95 percent glossy bluing, Serial No. 11399, barrels 3 1/2" l. (ILLUS.)................ **1,725**

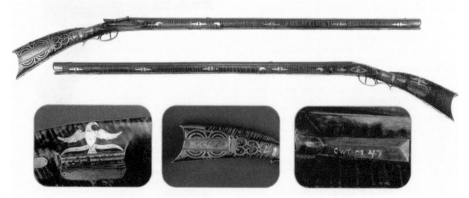

Various Views of a Very Rare Early Kentucky Long Rifle

Tiger Stripe Maple Long Rifle

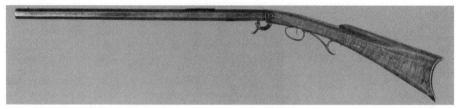

Vermont-made Percussion Long Rifle

Long rifle, Morrison (Samuel) side hammer model, .50 cal., highly decorated w/an octagonal barrel, fine brass front sight & wide fixed rear sight w/lightly engraved decorations, muzzle decorated w/stars & dots, the top flat signed in script "JM" separated by an engraved star, full-length maple stock w/applied striping & brass furniture, a plain nose cap w/two long faceted guides & a long plain nose pipe, also a 6" l. narrow brass wear plate on the bottom of the stock, typical simple trigger guard, brass buttplate w/a faceted top tang & filigree toeplate w/four cut-outs & a ball finial, the roach-back comb w/a long, thin decorative brass plate attached w/iron pins, lockplate screws passing through brass escutcheons, one of which is an elliptical-shaped filigree w/two cut-outs, forestock & buttstock w/22 sterling silver inlays in various designs, some quite elaborate & the most elaborate being a fine spread-winged American eagle w/light engraving mounted on the small cheek piece, unusual brass shield-shaped inlay w/pick slot below, right side of buttstock w/an extremely fancy & delicate four-piece brass filigree patchbox w/a lightly engraved lid, dbl. set triggers, left side of buttstock, between the cheek piece & buttpiece, lightly incised in arabesque designs, the forestock w/an incised line by the ramrod channel, pictured in the book "The Kentucky Rifle" by John G.W. Dillin, overall very fine condition, barrel 40 1/4" l. (ILLUS., bottom previous page)............ **14,375**

Long rifle, Pennsylvania-type, boy's, percussion-style, curly maple stock w/old finish & good figure, brass hardware including engraved patchbox w/half-moon piercings & three matching half-moon inlays on either side, ten nickel silver inlays, early 19th c., octagonal barrel 33" l. (breech plug an old replacement) **1,438**

Long rifle, percussion-type w/tiger stripe maple full stock, left-handed side-action lock set w/multiple brass dome-head tacks, first half 19th c., barrel 36" l. (ILLUS., top of page).................................. **661**

Long rifle, underhammer percussion-type made by Nicanor Kendall, .50 cal., tiger strip maple stock, Windsor, Vermont, ca. 1850, octagonal barrel 23 2/3" l. (ILLUS., above).. **2,875**

Mauser "Black Widow" Luger

Luger, Mauser "Black Widow" model, .9 mm. cal., barrel w/all bluish-black finish & checkered black composition grips w/proper fxo WaA 37 magazine, extremely fine condition, Serial No. 8348, barrel 4" l. (ILLUS.) **1,150**

1937 Model Luger

Luger, S/42 1937 Model, .9mm cal., standard type w/all bluish-black finish w/full checkered wood grips & an aluminum based magazine w/no. 373n, British proofs on various parts, 95 percent original dark finish, right grip severely bruised, Serial No. 2278, barrel 4" l. (ILLUS., second from top)... **978**

Rare Berdan Conversion of Colt Model 1861 Special Musket

Savage Model 1861 Rifle Musket

Musket, Berdan conversion Colt Model 1861 Special model, .58 cal. centerfire, original barrel w/square base front sight/bayonet lug, three bands w/two-blade musket rear sight, mounted in original one-piece walnut stock w/musket buttplate & a small metal tag on the toe w/number "7," converted by cutting away about 3" of rear of barrel & fitting a lifting breechlock, muzzle counterbored about 5/8", w/a small brass & leather tampion w/patent date in 1863, very fine condition, only known example extant, barrel 40" l. (ILLUS., top of page) ... **5,750**

Musket, Savage Model 1861 rifle model, .58 cal., standard Civil War era rifle musket w/long barrel, square base front sight/bayonet lug w/two-leaf, three-position musket rear sight, usual barrel & lock markings dated 1863, walnut stock w/a crisp cartouche, cleaned & stock restored, minor damage on stock, barrel 40" l. (ILLUS., second from top) **2,358**

Colt 1911A1 Military Model Pistol

Pistol, Colt 1911A1 Military Model, .45 cal. ACP, barrel w/fixed sights, short trigger & short wide hammer spur w/long grip safety & arched main spring housing, greyish-green parkerized finish w/full checkered brown plastic grips, Serial No. 744948, most original finish, barrel 5" l. (ILLUS.) **1,380**

Joseph Manton Double-barreled Flintlock Pistol

Pistol, Manton (Joseph) double-barreled flintlock model, .20 cal., barrels mounted in nicely figured one-piece walnut stock w/raised side panels around the lockplate w/a smooth round grip w/knob at the bottom, a decorative nosepipe for the iron-tipped rammer & an urn finial on the plain trigger guard, lock plates & gooseneck hammers w/light engraving & the maker's name & "London" on each side, locks slightly curved w/stepped ends without teats & roller frizzens w/separate pans & platinum flash holes, barrel secured in stock w/two wedges, stock w/crack in front of each lock, fine medium patina, barrels 10 1/8" l. (ILLUS.) **1,380**

Early Model 1816 Flintlock Pistol

English Model 1842 Army Percussion Pistol

Very Rare Early Morrill Elgin Cutlass Pistol

Pistol, Model 1816 flintlock relic model, .54 cal., no visible markings except "US" proof on breech end of barrel, all-iron furniture w/brass upward-tilting pan, severely pitted, wooden grip also eroded, top jaw appears to be replacement, stock w/crack, overall 15 1/2" l. (ILLUS., bottom previous page) **633**

Pistol, Model 1842 EIG Army percussion-type, .65 cal., heavy military type w/round barrel, fixed sights, front action lock, nickeled brass furniture w/captive rammer & a sling loop in the button, lock dated 1867 - Burningham w/a large cartouche on the left flat that is also marked "Woodward & Sons," very fine w/95 percent original bluing, barrel 8" l. (ILLUS., top of page)......... **1,150**

Pistol, Morrill Elgin small-frame cutlass model, .36 cal., authentic w/9 3/8" l. blade w/an integral trigger guard, attached to a small frame box lock side hammer pistol w/a one-piece bag-shaped walnut grip, blade w/etched panels on both sides w/spread-winged early American eagles, left side eagle w/banner in beak reading "Liberty" & 17 stars above & inscription of maker in Amherst, Massachusetts below, right side of blade w/eagle & another inscription & spray of flowers, barrel w/thin half-moon sight w/a fixed rear sight, blade dovetailed into bottom of barrel & held w/a screw, rare, Serial No. 42, barrel 4" l. (ILLUS., second from top)... **11,500**

Allen & Wheelock Belt Model Revolver

Allen & Wheelock Belt Percussion Model Revolver

Colt 1851 Navy Model Revolver in New Case

Revolver, Allen & Wheelock belt model percussion model, 36 cal., side hammer w/4 3/4" l. octagonal barrel w/German silver front sight & two-piece walnut grips, cylinder engraved w/a forest scene w/deer, dogs & birds, good condition, no original finish remains, medium brown patina, broken nipples, Serial Number 301 (ILLUS., bottom previous page) **518**

Revolver, Allen & Wheelock belt percussion model, .36 cal., two-piece walnut grips, side hammer w/octagonal barrel w/German silver front sight, cylinder w/an engraved forest scene w/deer, dogs & birds, no original finish, Serial No. 84, barrel 5 3/4" l. (ILLUS., top of page) **920**

Revolver, Colt 1851 Navy model, .36 cal., standard Navy w/7 1/2" l. octagonal barrel, tiny brass front sight, blue- and case-colored w/one-piece walnut grips, in a modern red-lined, compartmented case containing a ball bullet mold, a modern flask, & a tin of modern caps, very fine condition, Serial No. 143416, the set (ILLUS., second from top) **949**

Revolver, Colt early martially-marked single-action model, .45 cal., very rare Samuel B. Lewis-inspected cavalry Colt, barrel slightly reduced in length, original front sight modified, one-piece walnut grips, barrel nickel-plated, barrel w/slant one-line address w/daggers at each end, small "L" proofs on various parts, original bull's-eye ejector rod head, Serial No. 16293, barrel 7 5/16" l. (ILLUS., below).... **8,338**

Rare Early Colt .45 Revolver Inspected by Samuel B. Lewis

Smith & Wesson No. 2 Army Civil War Revolver

Smith & Wesson Triple-lock Revolver

Revolver, Smith & Wesson No. 2 Army model, .32 cal. rim-fire, keyhole barrel, half-moon front sight, unfluted cylinder w/two-piece rosewood grips, Civil War-era inscription for Union officer from Kentucky, about 25 percent original nickel-plating, dark patina, grips w/chipped toes, Serial No. 8215, barrel 6" l. (ILLUS., top of page) **3,738**

Revolver, Smith & Wesson triple-lock DA model, 44 cal. Russian, blued finish w/half-moon integral front sight, fixed rear sight, diamond-checkered medallion magnum grips, 6 1/2" l. barrel w/half-lug & a third fastener in barrel lug, very good condition, refinished, replacement grips, Serial Number 2022 (ILLUS., second from top) **1,323**

Whitney Navy Percussion Revolver

Revolver, Whitney Navy percussion model, .36 cal., a rare tin- or nickel-plated model, martially mark "Whitney Navy," octagonal barrel w/small pin front sight w/two-piece walnut grips, legible cartouche on left grip, visible inspector marks on some parts, all-matching parts, Serial Number 15421 (ILLUS., bottom previous page) **1,035**

Rifle, Buswell (J.) underhammer percussion model, .45 cal., sporting model, walnut buttstock w/narrow wrist, long top tang & grip fashioned as part of the trigger guard, right side w/a simple two-piece oval patchbox that contained the lollipop peep sight for the top tang & the left side w/a shallow cheek piece, buttplate of crescent-shaped iron, octagonal barrel w/early style front sight w/dainty windage adjustable rear sight, barrel marked on top w/maker's name & "Glens Falls -

N.Y.," iron furniture w/three ramrod guides & a replacement hickory rod, good condition, barrel 29 7/8" l. **575**

Rifle, Hilliard percussion underhammer model, .40 cal., tiger stripe maple stock w/very stylish cheek pieces & a crescent steel buttplate, the right side fitted w/a reverse opening simple two-piece iron patchbox, a small trigger guard/grip w/independent main spring & a shielded nipple, octagonal barrel w/muzzle turned for a false muzzle w/narrow original front sight & the broken base of an open rear sight in the dovetail, attached long target sight at rear of the barrel, left flat side marked "DH Hilliard - Cornish - N.H." & cast steel along w/Serial No. 2434, fine condition, barrel 23 3/8" l. (hammer nose chipped, buttstock missing oval star inlay) **920**

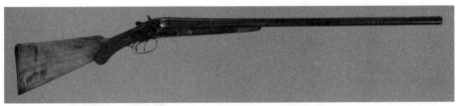

H. & J. King 12 Gauge Percussion Shotgun

Pieper 12 Gauge Double-barrel Shotgun

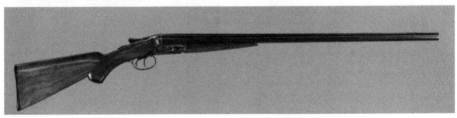

A.H. Fox Sterlingworth Hammerless Double-barrel Shotgun

Shotgun, King (H. & J.) percussion double-barrel 12 gauge model, walnut stock, double hammers & triggers, 19th c., fair condition, 32" l. barrels, overall 48" l. (ILLUS., first, abovr) **288**

Shotgun, Pieper (H.) side by side 12 gauge model, walnut stock, double barrels, triggers & hammers, for black

powder, ca. 1900, barrels 30" l., overall 46 1/4" l. (ILLUS., second) **403**

Shotgun, Sterlingworth (A.H. Fox) 12 gauge hammerless double-barrel model, walnut stock w/checkered grip, Serial No. 120404, field grade, first half 20th c., box locks on 30" l. barrels, overall 48 1/8" l. (ILLUS., third) **1,035**

FIREPLACE & HEARTH ITEMS

Figural George Washington Andirons

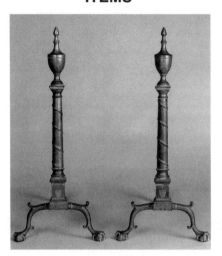

Very Rare American Federal Andirons

Andirons, brass & iron, Federal style, each w/an urn-form finial w/bright-cut & punchwork swag & pendant designs w/beaded borders supported on a tapered column embellished w/spiraling vines, stepped square plinth w/engraved shield & punchwork chevron border, over a shaped skirt w/conforming swag & pendant design, further supported on arched spurred cabriole legs w/claw-and-ball feet, attributed to Daniel King, Philadelphia, 1790-1810, 13 1/4 x 25 1/2", 30 1/2" h. (ILLUS.) **$41,125**

Unusual Cowboy Outlaw Andirons

Andirons, cast iron, figures of cowboy outlaws standing ready to draw their six-shooters, back bar log support, very rusty, 19 1/4" h. (ILLUS.) **1,495**

Unusual Man-in-the-Moon Andirons

Andirons, cast iron, figural, modeled as facing crescent-shaped man-in-the-moon faces w/dramatic features, double-step half-round base, latter 19th c., 9 1/2" w., 14 1/4" h., pr. (ILLUS.) **5,175**

Andirons, cast iron, figure of George Washington standing & leaning on a draped column, a book in one hand & his tricorn hat in the other, on a tall plinth-form base w/drapery & star trim, stepped block feet, 19th c., 9 1/4 x 14 1/4", 21 1/2" h. (ILLUS., top next column) **978**

Ornate Regence-Style French Andirons

Andirons, ormolu, Regence-Style, each composed of a figure of a recumbent sphinx draped w/fleur-de-lis cloth & resting on a large cartouche on a volute-shaped base, France, late 19th c., 14 1/2" w., 19" h., pr. (ILLUS.) **5,975**

Fire back, cast iron, rectangular plaque cast w/a crown over entwined Rs & dated 1758, 16 1/2 x 19 1/2" **330**

Fine English Regency Fireplace Fender

Fire back, cast iron, rectangular plaque cast w/a pair of arches above stylized tulip blossoms above a band cast w/"Staucheuergen" above a pair of tulip & heart devices flanking a reserve w/further initials, 18th c., 18 1/2 x 22 1/2" **385**

Fireplace fender, gilt- and patinated bronze, Regency style, modeled as a stylized long honeysuckle flowerhead-and-scroll bar surmounting a patinated bronze stepped molded base, England, first quarter 19th c., 40 1/2" l., 8 1/2" h. (ILLUS., top of page) **1,840**

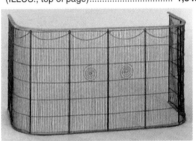

Early American Brass & Wire Fire Screen

Fireplace screen, brass & wire, Federal style, tall U-form screen w/a brass top support band, fine wire banding highlighted w/swags along the top & small central spirals, early 19th c., 34" l. (ILLUS.) **717**

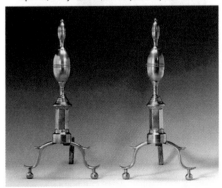

Federal Andirons from a Fireplace Set

Fireplace tool set, brass, Federal style, the ring-turned oval top w/a matching finial, above a hexagonal support on arching spurred cabriole legs on ball feet, togeth-

er w/a matching pair of tongs & a shovel, New York, New York, ca. 1800-20, andirons 21 1/2" h., the set (ILLUS. of andirons only) **2,868**

Flue Cover with Pretty Victorian Girl

Flue cover, lithographed paper in frame, a round colorful bust portrait of a pretty late-Victorian girl wearing a large bonnet w/deep reddish plumes & poppy blossom & tied w/matching sash, thin brass frame w/a pierced hanging mount at the top, minor water stain at bottom, ca. 1900, 14 1/2" d. (ILLUS.) **259**

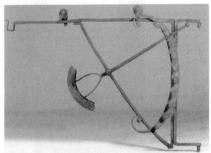

Early Wrought-iron Hearth Crane

Hearth crane, wrought iron, a large L-bracket w/C-form adjusting mechanism & support bar w/adjusting bar arm, Pennsylvania, 18th c., 47 1/2" w., 34" h. (ILLUS.) **2,990**

FOOT AND BEDWARMERS

Bedwarmer, brass, round pan w/hinged cover pierced w/small holes & engraved w/overall florals, on a long turned wood handle, late 18th - early 19th c., overall 43" l. (age split in handle)............................ **$196**

Foot warmer, painted wood & tin, nearly square mortised wood frame w/baluster-turned corner posts, the tin panel sides punched w/diamonds & concentric circles w/worn grey paint, framed w/old reddish brown paint w/red dots & yellow arrows, painted inscription on underside reading "Foot stove for Susan Ann Hankinson before 1840...died feb. 11th 1884...Painted by George W. Roy...NJ. January, 1886," 7 3/4 x 8 1/2", 5 3/4" h........ **358**

FURNITURE

Furniture made in the United States during the 18th and 19th centuries is coveted by collectors. American antique furniture has a European background, primarily English, since the influence of the Continent usually found its way to America by way of England. If the style did not originate in England, it came to America by way of England. For this reason, some American furniture styles carry the name of an English monarch or an English designer. However, we must realize that, until recently, little research has been conducted and even less published on the Spanish and French influences in the area of the California missions and New Orleans.

After the American revolution, cabinetmakers in the United States shunned the prevailing styles in England and chose to bring the French styles of Napoleon's Empire to the United States and we have the uniquely named "American Empire"

(Classical) style of furniture in a country that never had an emperor.

During the Victorian period, quality furniture began to be mass-produced in this country with its rapidly growing population. So much walnut furniture was manufactured, the vast supply of walnut was virtually depleted and it was of necessity that oak furniture became fashionable as the 19th century drew to a close.

For our purposes, the general guidelines for dating will be: Pilgrim Century - 1620-85 William & Mary - 1685-1720 Queen Anne - 1720-50 Chippendale - 1750-85 Federal - 1785-1820 Hepplewhite - 1785-1820 Sheraton - 1800-20 American Empire (Classical) - 1815-40 Victorian - 1840-1900 Early Victorian - 1840-50 Gothic Revival - 1840-90 Rococo (Louis XV) - 1845-70 Renaissance - 1860-85 Louis XVI - 1865-75 Eastlake - 1870-95 Jacobean & Turkish Revival - 1870-95 Aesthetic Movement - 1880-1900 Art Nouveau - 1890-1918 Turn-of-the-Century - 1895-1910 Mission (Arts & Crafts movement) - 1900-15 Art Deco - 1925-40

All furniture included in this listing is American unless otherwise noted.

Bedroom Suites

Art Deco: bedstead, two tall two-door cabinets fitted w/drawers, a pair of nightstands, a side table, a shelving unit & a mirrored vanity table & stool; lacquered & painted creamy white, simple rectangular forms, designed by Jules Bouy for Carlos Salzedo, ca. 1931, cabinets 17 1/2 x 20", 4' 6" h., the set (ILLUS., bottom of page)
.... **$4,780**

White Art Deco Bedroom Suite

Eastlake Half-tester Bed from Suite

Victorian Eastlake substyle: double half-tester bed, a marble-topped chest of drawers w/mirror, a marble-topped washstand w/mirror; walnut & burl walnut, the half-tester on the bed w/a stepped angular cornice w/panels carved w/stylized flowers between corner blocks, flat serpentine brackets supporting it above the high headboard w/a matching carved cornice, the lower flat-topped footboard w/floral-incised arched & burl panels above rectangular panels, the other pieces w/matching crests, white marble tops & arrangements of drawers w/stamped brass pulls w/angular bails, marble on chest w/old repair & cracks, ca. 1880, bed 63 1/2 x 79 1/2", 8' 3" h., 3 pcs. (ILLUS. of bed only) **7,188**

Victorian Renaissance Revival substyle: high-backed double bed & chest of drawers; walnut & burl walnut; each piece w/an extremely ornate crest w/a large urn finial above a broken-arch raised center pediment flanked by turned T-form spindles above a heavy molded arch flanked by large angled side pediments w/fanned ears, the headboard w/a large arched burl center panel flanked by smaller rectangular panels each separated by short heavy turned columns on blocked brackets separating further burl panels, the lower arched footboard w/panels, a roundel & columns matching the headboard, the ornate chest crest above columns & blocks flanking the long rectangular mirror flanked by two side compartments w/square inset marble tops supporting a block & column w/a round disk shelf, each compartment w/a shaped & carved molding over three small drawers, refinished, ca. 1870, bed 68 x 80", 9' h., 2 pcs. (ILLUS., bottom of page) **25,000**

Elaborate Renaissance Suite

Beds

Arts & Crafts Stickley Oak Bed

Arts & Crafts, oak, three-quarters size, the headboard composed of two pairs of vertical slats flanking a wide central slat between rails joined to the tapering square corner posts, the slightly shorter footboard of matching design, mattress slats & original side boards, good original finish, one broken peg, decal label of L. & J.G. Stickley, early 20th c., 50 3/4 x 80", 46" h. (ILLUS.).. **2,300**

Classical Bed with Baluster Finials

Classical low-poster bed, mahogany, the wide arched & scroll-carved headboard flanked by paneled posts topped by leaf-carved baluster-and-ring-turned finials, heavy tapering ring-turned legs, original dark finish, ca. 1830s, 58 x 78", 5' h. (ILLUS.).. **1,000**

Classical Revival Fancy Bed

Fine Classical Mahogany Bed

Early Painted Child's Rope Bed

Country-style child's rope bed, painted, the wide peaked headboard between block-and-rod-turned spots w/large button finials & on baluster-turned lower legs, a matching lower footboard, original side rails, original black paint, mid-19th c., 36 x 68 1/2" (ILLUS.)............................... **460**

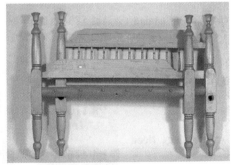

Simple Country-style Maple Rope Bed

Classical tall-poster bed, mahogany, the high paneled headboard w/notched corners flanked by tall slender baluster-and-ring-turned posts w/acanthus leaf carving & baluster-form finials w/knobs, matching foot posts joined by a rail, brass-capped casters, ca. 1835, refinished, 60 x 80", 7' 6" h. (ILLUS.) **7,500**

Classical Revival tall-poster bed, mahogany, the wide headboard w/a broken-scroll crestrail centered by a pointed knob finial & flanked by rope-twist-turned posts w/knob-turned finials, the slightly shorter foot posts joined by a ropetwist-, knob- and ring-turned rail above a wide scroll-ended lower rail, short knob-turned feet, refinished, early 20th c., 58 x 78", 5' h. (ILLUS., top of page) **850**

Country-style low-poster rope bed, three-quarters size, maple, the headboard w/a long arched crestrail above a row of slender turned spindles between the block-, rod- and ring-turned headposts w/flared turned finials, the footboard w/a single arched rail above the end rail between footposts matching the headposts, refinished, mid-19th c., 54" w., 40" h. (ILLUS.) **138**

Danish Modern twin beds, teak, an upright headboard composed of a woven wicker panel, plain rectangular frame on cylindrical legs, Dansk form designed by Hans Wegner & manufactured by Getama, ca. 1960, pr. **1,093**

Nice Federal Maple Canopy Bed

Federal tall-poster canopy bed, red-stained maple, a delicate arched canopy frame raised on baluster-, ring- and urn-turned reeded posts above corner blocks & baluster- and ring-turned legs ending in peg feet, the simple arched headboard between plain turned & tapering head-posts, old surface, minor imperfections,

New England, ca. 1815, 51 x 70", 6' 8" h. (ILLUS.).. **4,994**

Nice Quality Victorian Eastlake Bed

Victorian Eastlake substyle bed, high-back-style frame, walnut & burl walnut, the tall headboard w/a stepped crown-form cornice composed of a low gallery rail between small turned finials projecting above a long narrow floral-carved panel above a grouping of three floral-carved solid panels flanked by bobbin-turned lattice panels between the blocked back styles, a long plain horizontal burl panel above a plain panel in the lower headboard, the low footboard w/a flat crestrail above a narrow floral-carved panel above a long rectangular burl panel, original side rails, ca. 1880, 57 x 74", 6' 7 1/2" h. (ILLUS.)...................................... **546**

Finely Carved Victorian Renaissance Revival Bed

Very Rare Victorian Rococo Half-Tester Bed

Victorian Renaissance Revival substyle bed, walnut & burl walnut, highback-style, the tall headboard w/a large central carved fleur-de-lis form cartouche centered by the relief-carved face of a maiden w/flowing hair, steeply angled crest molding on each side above a very large oval composed of concentric rings w/a large central burl panel, the square side posts w/large urn-form finials & a pendant band of fleur-de-lis down each sides, the low arched footboard w/a curved raised burl band w/central carved sprig above a banded burl oval panel, the curved low corner posts carved w/a fanned shell device above a bold oblong scroll cartouche, shaped siderails w/raised molding trim, attributed to Mitchell & Rammelsberg, ca. 1870s, 80 x 88", 7' 3" h. (ILLUS., bottom previous page) **9,775**

Victorian Rococo bed, walnut & rosewood veneer, the tall headboard w/a tall peaked crest ornately carved w/scrolls, a cartouche & a flower cluster above the large molded oval panel flanked by heavy paneled posts w/urn-form finials, the low arched & scalloped footboard w/an oval panel w/carved scrolls, curved side panels w/further ovals & scroll carving, refinished, ca. 1860, original side rails, 72" w., 8' 2" h. **2,750**

Victorian Rococo half-tester bed, mahogany, the top half-tester frame w/serpentine sides w/a button- and scroll-carved front crest & reeded urn-turned corner finials, the tall arched headboard w/a shell- and rondel-carved crest & scroll-carved stepped crestrails above a rectangular burled panel flanked by heavy tapering tall posts, shaped & scroll-carved siderails & footboard flanked by heavy short columns w/arched raised panels & ring- and knob-turned pointed finials, attributed to Charles Lee, Manchester, Massachusetts, ca. 1860, 74 1/2 x 88 1/2", headboard 113" h. (ILLUS., top of page) **19,550**

Victorian Rococo Revival substyle tall-
poster full-tester bed, carved rosewood, the large tester frame decorated
on each side w/an ornate arched & scroll-
carved crestrail centered by a shell cartouche above a flared cornice band over
a paneled frieze band w/a central roundel, raised on four heavy paneled knob-
and ring-turned posts above heavy paneled legs ending in heavy paneled feet,
the fairly low headboard w/a simple central arched crest above a plain panel, the
paneled side rails centered by a florette &
trimmed on top w/scroll-carved corner
brackets & a central serpentine-carved
crest, America or France, ca. 1850,
84 x 89", 10' h. **13,800**

Benches

Arts & Crafts Oak Hall Bench

Arts & Crafts hall bench, oak, the wide
concave crestrail above three shaped

back splats between slender stiles
w/curved corner ears, sharply tapering flat
open arms above incurved flat supports
forming the front legs, hinged plank seat,
early 20th c., 16 x 40", 41" h. (ILLUS.).......... **633**

Painted Poplar Bucket Bench

Bucket (or water) bench, country-style,
painted poplar, the narrow rectangular top
above a narrow stepped-back enclosed
shelf & chamfered one-board ends w/boot-
jack feet flanking two lower open shelves,
old red wash, 19th c., wear to back corners
of lower shelves, 12 x 43 1/4", 47" h.
(ILLUS.).. **1,093**

Early Pine Stained Bucket Bench

Bucket (or water) bench, country-style, pine w/old red wash & traces of blue paint, a narrow top shelf above one-board sides incurved at the top flanking an upper shelf w/a narrow back brace & front apron above a deeper bottom shelf on a flat apron, old splits w/small notches out of lower front corners, early square nail construction, 13 x 43 1/2", 42" h. (ILLUS., bottom previous page)..... **2,070**

Bucket (or water) bench, painted pine, a narrow rectangular shelf raised atop high incurved tapering side supports flanking a wide rectangular top on a case w/a large two-panel door w/a cast-iron & porcelain latch, gently arched apron, square nail construction, old finely crazed yellow paint graining over a white base coat & evidence of original grey, 19th c., 17 x 38", 43" h. **5,225**

edged in tassels, the knob- and ring-turned legs & stretchers joined by corner blocks on bun feet, Flemish, late 18th c., 18 x 24", 13" h. (ILLUS., below)............... **1,265**

Early Upholstered Flemish Bench

Fancy American Classical Window Bench

Classical window bench, parcel-gilt carved mahogany, the deep upright upholstered S-scroll end arms faced w/carved gilt-trimmed dolphins, a flat molded seatrail raised on ornate gilded scrolled dolphin legs, America, early 19th c., 19 x 50", 32" h. (ILLUS.)....................... **8,625**

European upholstered bench, walnut, the deep rectangular seat upholstered in a figural tapestry w/a floral background &

Louis XVI-Style Painted Bench

Louis XVI-Style bench, polychrome-painted wood, the long oval top w/a separate cushion above a beaded apron & raised on four turned tapering fluted legs headed by leaf clusters & joined by an H-stretcher centered by a turned knob & ending w/incurved end rungs, simple baluster-turned feet, creamy white w/other colors, France, early 20th c., 14 1/2 x 35", 20" h. (ILLUS.) **978**

Nelson Modern-style Slatted Bench

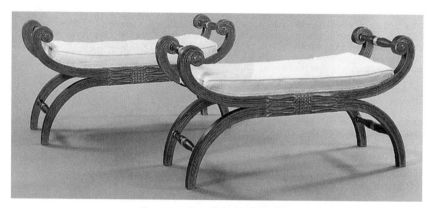

Regency-Style Window Benches

Modern-style bench, hardwood, the long narrow rectangular top divided into two sections composed of closely spaced slats in natural wood, raised on ebonized box-style legs, designed by George Nelson for Herman Miller Furniture Co., 18 1/2 x 48", 14" h. (ILLUS., bottom previouis page)... **633**

Fine Regency Curule Bench

Regency curule bench, carved, rosewood-grained & parcel-gilt wood, flaring U-form outswept upper rails raised on inverted U-form legs ending in giltwood paw feet, seat upholstered in green velvet w/brass tack trim, England, first quarter 19th c., 28 1/4" w., 29" h. (ILLUS.)........................ **4,370**

Regency-Style window benches, ebonized giltwood, long reeded inwardly scrolled top raised & joined at the ends by baluster-turned cross-rails, long upholstered cushion seat on long slender reeded arched legs joined by baluster-turned cross-rails, England, late 19th - early 20th c., 20 x 48 1/2", 26" h. (ILLUS., top of page)... **1,725**

Bookcases

Art Deco "Skyscraper" Bookcase

Art Deco bookcase, mahogany, "Skyscraper" design, two-part construction: the tall upper section composed of a three-stepped section w/various openings to hold books; the lower section w/a rectangular top above an asymmetrical arrangement of two large flat doors & various book shelves, designed by Paul Frankl, ca. 1928, overall 49 1/2" h. (ILLUS., previous page) **7,170**

Large Simple Classical Bookcase

Nice Single-door Arts & Crafts Bookcase

Arts & Crafts bookcase, oak, single-door style, the rectangular top w/a three-quarters gallery w/through-tenons above the single wide 16-pane glazed cupboard door w/rectangular metal pull, through-tenon base board w/low arched end aprons, attributed to L. & J.G. Stickley, refinished, at least one replaced glass pane, early 20th c., 12 x 39", 4' 8 1/2" h. (ILLUS.) **5,175**

Classical bookcase, mahogany & mahogany veneer, the rectangular top w/a stepped cornice above a frieze band w/a thin carved arch band above a pair of tall four-pane glazed cupboard doors each w/a plain bottom panel & completely framed w/thin beaded banding, opening to wooden shelves, deep molded flat base on thin block feet, ca. 1850, 15 x 60", 7' 9" h. (ILLUS., top next column) **6,325**

Early 20th century bookcase, oak, lawyer's stacking-type, five-section, each rectangular section w/a rectangular glass lift-front door, single long drawer w/angled bail pulls at the bottom, label of Globe-Werneke, 34" w., 6' 1" h. **891**

Fine Federal Massachusetts Bookcase

Federal bookcase, mahogany & mahogany veneer, two-part construction: the upper section w/a rectangular top & two-part concave cornice separated by veneered blocks above a narrow flared cornice & frieze band above a pair of tall nine-pane glazed cupboard doors w/Gothic arch top panes & opening to four adjustable wooden shelves; the stepped-out lower section comprising two pairs of drawers w/round florette brass pulls, the corner blocks w/acanthus leaf & fluted carving, raised on ring- & knob-turned reeded legs, old refinish, imperfections, Boston or Salem, Massachusetts, ca. 1815-20, 18 1/2 x 50", overall 7' 3 1/2" h. (ILLUS., bottom previous page) **9,988**

Regency Breakfront Bookcase

Regency breakfront-style bookcase, mahogany, the long rectangular top above a case w/a projecting central section, the central section w/a pair of astragal-glazed doors opening to wooden shelves over a case w/a long deep fold-down secretary drawer over three long graduated drawers, the set-back end sections each w/a single astragal-glazed door over a single drawer & paneled door, narrow flat plinth base, England, second quarter 19th c., 22 x 93 1/2", 7' 7" h. (ILLUS.) **7,763**

Small Golden Oak Bookcase

Victorian Golden Oak bookcase, oak, an arched & scroll-carved three-quarters gallery above a single tall glazed door opening to adjustable shelves, simple serpentine apron & block feet, refinished, ca. 1900, 15 x 24", 5' h. (ILLUS.) **600**

Victorian Golden Oak bookcase, rectangular top w/thin flared cornice above serpentine corner brackets flanking a tall glazed door w/angled carved top corner brackets, opening to three adjustable shelves, glass sides, molded apron on simple cabriole legs, ca. 1900, 30" w. 5' 3" h. **604**

Victorian Gothic Revival bookcase, mahogany & mahogany veneer, two-part construction: the very long rectangular top w/a wide coved cornice topped by a long arched low serpentine crestrail w/turned corner finials all above a beaded frieze band over an arrangement of four tall two-pane glazed doors w/Gothic arch scrolls in the upper half of each, opening to four adjustable wooden shelves; the stepped-out lower section w/a row of four deep drawers w/turned wood knobs, the wide coved flat base w/a thin beaded rim band, probably Southern U.S., ca. 1840, 25 x 96", 7' 7" h. (ILLUS., top next page) **5,750**

Simple Renaissance Revival Bookcase

Victorian Renaissance Revival substyle bookcase, walnut & burl walnut, the rectangular top w/a wide flattened cornice w/rounded front corners above a conforming frieze band above a case w/two tall arched & glazed doors opening to five adjustable wooden shelves, the case w/rounded front corners topped at each side w/bold S-scroll brackets, on a flat molded apron w/a beaded band, ca. 1870, 23 x 65", 6' 11" h. (ILLUS.) **2,760**

Fine Victorian Gothic Revival Large Bookcase

Renaissance-Style Oak Bookcase

Victorian Renaissance-Style bookcase, carved oak, a rectangular top w/a deep flaring carved cornice above a wide frieze band w/ornate scroll carving centered by a cartouche above a molded rail over a pair of tall glazed cupboard doors w/arched panes enclosed w/narrow gadrooned molding & flanked by carved fruiting vines down the sides, a wide flaring mid-molding above a pair of paneled cupboard doors w/square beaded molding enclosing carved scrolled grape clusters flanked by further fruiting vines at the sides, deep flaring carved base molding, original finish, Europe, last quarter 19th c., 22 x 40", 6' 2" h. (ILLUS., left).............. **2,500**

Bureaux Plat

French Empire Revival Bureau Plat

Simple French Directoire Bureau Plat

Directoire bureau plat, brass-mounted fruitwood, the rectangular top overhanging an apron fitted w/two small drawers, raised on square tapering fluted legs, Southern France, early 19th c., 27 1/2" h. (ILLUS.)... **1,380**

Empire Revival bureau plat, gilt bronze-mounted mahogany, the rectangular top inset w/gilt-tooled green leather within a wooden frame above the case w/a pair of small cross-banded drawers flanking a single long drawer, each mounted w/a long pierced scrolling brass, the square tapering legs headed by gilt carved Egyptian masks & palmettes & ending in a gilt paw foot, France, ca. 1900, 30 x 55", 30 1/2" h. (ILLUS., top of page) **1,380**

Louis XVI-Style bureau plat, burlwood & mahogany, the rectangular top w/a large leather inset above a simple apron w/a long diamond panel inlay flanked on each side by pairs of matching smaller drawers, gilt-metal & carved ebonized wood panels atop the square tapering legs ending in brass caps, France, ca. 1900, 32 x 55 1/2", 29 1/2" h. (ILLUS., bottom of page)... **1,725**

Restrained Louis XVI-Style Bureau Plat

Very Fine Louis XVI-Style Bureau Plat

Louis XVI-Style bureau plat, ormolu-mounted kingwood, the rectangular top w/serpentine ormolu edging around an inset leather writing surface, the serpentine apron w/fine banded veneering, two narrow drawers w/an ormolu escutcheon or pull separated by a long pierced scroll mount from the single long central drawer, the reverse apron fitted w/matching faux drawers, raised on simple cabriole legs w/ornate scroll & floral mounts at the knees & ending in leaf & scroll metal sabots, France, late 19th c., 31 1/2 x 56 1/2", 30" h. (ILLUS., above) **5,060**

Cabinets

Early American Apothecary Cabinet

Apothecary cabinet, painted wood, two-part construction: the upper section w/a rectangular top w/a narrow cornice above a row of five large open compartments above an arrangement of 20 small drawers w/tiny brass pulls in five rows; the lower section w/a pair of raised-panel cupboard doors w/a brass keyhole escutcheon, scrolled bracket feet, old black paint, early 19th c., 15 1/2 x 40", 5' 10 1/2" h. (ILLUS.) **7,170**

English Georgian Cellaret Cabinet

Cellaret (wine cabinet), mahogany, a deep square box w/a hinged flat lid opening to a lead-lined interior w/missing dividers, raised on a molded frame raised on knob- and ring-turned legs of later date, the sides of the box mounted w/brass lion masks & ring handles, England, George II period, ca. 1810, 12" w., overall 26 1/4" h. (ILLUS.) **2,185**

Fine Mission-Style China Cabinet

China cabinet, Mission-style (Arts & Crafts movement), oak, the rectangular top projecting above a case w/two long cabinet doors w/a six-pane glazed top section above a long single pane, hammered copper hardware, matching glazed sides, gently arched front & side aprons, Handcraft label of L. & J.G. Stickley, No. 746, cleaned finish, early 20th c., 16 x 44", 5' 2" h. (ILLUS.) **6,900**

China cabinet, Victorian Baroque Revival style, oak, two-part construction: the upper section w/a high scroll-carved crest centered by a cartouche over a flat flaring cornice flanked by projecting blocks w/urn-form finials above a wide scroll-carved frieze band flanked by carved blocks over a pair of tall arch-topped glazed doors opening to shelves & flanked by barley-twist columns; the stepped-out lower section w/a gadrooned edge above a pair of scroll-carved drawers w/cartouche-form pulls over a pair of paneled doors w/raised molding centering boldly carved scenes of game birds, barley-twist columns at the sides above the blocked flaring molded base on small bun feet, mid-19th c., 24 x 53", 7' 9" h. **3,248**

China cabinet, Victorian Classical Revival style, the wide D-form top w/a narrow molded cornice over a thick half-round frieze band finely carved w/scrolling leaf bands & cartouches, the case w/curved glass sides flanking a wide curved glass door, the door & sides separated by ornately carved columns headed by a lion

Finely Carved Classical Revival Cabinet

head above large acanthus leaf scrolls, cartouches & bellflowers, the stepped molded base raised on heavy carved front paw feet & plain block rear feet all raised on casters, ca. 1890s, 23 x 53 1/2", 6' 1 1/4" h. (ILLUS.) **2,990**

Oak Cabinet with Tambour Base

China cabinet, Victorian Golden Oak style, the D-form top w/a deep carved band of stylized leaves over wide central curved glass door flanked by curved glass sides above a conforming lower case w/a tambour-style base w/a curved cabinet door centered by a large round carved medallion, beaded base band on heavy turned & tapering feet, refinished, ca. 1900, 18 x 30", 6' 6" h. (ILLUS., bottom previous page) **1,600**

Dark Golden Oak China Cabinet

China cabinet, Victorian Golden Oak style, the D-form top w/projecting center section above a conforming case w/curved glass sides & a wide curved glass door opening to three adjustable wooden shelves w/a mirror back at the top, a flared stepped base band raised on four squared & gently curved legs ending in acanthus leaf-carved feet, dark original finish, ca. 1900, 14 x 38", 4' 11" h. (ILLUS.)............................ **604**

Large Three-section Oak China Cabinet

China cabinet, Victorian Golden Oak style, the wide case in a step-down form w/a tall long arching scroll-carved back crest composed of a long low arched mirror flanked by carved scrolls & quarter-round end mirrors, the central tall cabinet section w/a rectangular top w/a molded cornice above a large single-pane glazed door w/the glass enclosed by delicate carved scroll molding & opening to four adjustable wooden shelves, the shorter quarter-round end display sections w/curved glass fronts, the D-form base molding raised on four scroll-carved feet, replaced back & mirrors, ca. 1890s, 57" w., 6' h. (ILLUS.).................................. **2,070**

Large Cabinet with Lion Heads

China cabinet, Victorian Golden Oak style, wide D-form top centered by a high serpentine crest boldly carved w/three lion heads above columns flanking the tall curved glass door, wide curved glass sides, mirrored interior back w/four fixed wooden shelves, molded base on heavy paw feet on casters, refinished, ca. 1895, 20 x56", 6' 4" h. (ILLUS.) **3,300**

China cabinet, Victorian Rococo substyle, mahogany & mahogany veneer, two-part construction: the upper section w/an arched pierced scroll-carved crestrail over a deep ogee cornice above a pair of glazed doors w/pierced scroll-carved grillwork at the top, flanked by chamfered front corners w/carved top & bottom drops; the stepped-out lower section w/four long graduated crotch grain-veneered drawers w/ornate scroll-carved center pulls, chamfered front corners w/carved drops, deep scroll-carved apron, polished original finish, ca. 1855-60, 20 x 42", 7' 8" h. (ILLUS., top next page).. **3,000**

Mahogany Rococo China Cabinet

Simple Colonial Revival Curio Cabinet

Curio cabinet, Colonial Revival style, the rectangular top w/a low arched back crest & a thin gadrooned cornice above the tall glazed door divided by three slender mullions, opening to two glass shelves, flat glass sides, narrow molded apron raised on four cabriole legs ending in claw-and-ball feet, early 20th c., 24" w., 4' 5" h. (ILLUS.).................. **374**

Very Elaborate Chinese Curio Cabinet

Curio cabinet, Oriental, carved hardwood, two-part construction: the upper section w/a rectangular top mounted w/a very ornate arched crest pierce-carved w/fine looping scrolls above a superstructure w/an open back composed of two stepped shelving units w/a high central shelf flanked by lower shelves, each shelf w/low pierce-carved galleries & corner brackets, ornate pierce-carved end panels; the lower section w/a pair of cupboard doors w/finely reeded framing enclosing ornate floral-carved panels, pierced loop apron band, dark finish, China, late 19th c., 15 x 39", 6' 10 1/2" h. (ILLUS.)................... **2,760**

Curio cabinet, Rococo style, japanned & gilded wood, two-part construction: the upper section w/a very high broken-scroll arched crest trimmed in gilt, a central shell crest flanked by figural dragons & leafy scrolls, all above a conforming black japanned panel decorated w/a large Oriental landscape w/numerous buildings, the case w/a pair of very large six-pane glazed doors w/narrow mullions opening to two shelves & flanked by three glass panes at each side; the lower section w/a mid-molding over a case w/a pair of long black-japanned drawers w/Oriental landscape scenes above a deep curved & boldly scalloped apron in giltwood carved w/ornate scrolls & a central shell above a border band of fruit carving, raised on four cabriole legs w/shell-carved knees & ending in ball-and-claw feet, Europe, late 18th - early 19th c., some decoration chips, 15 x 55", 7' 7 1/2" h. (ILLUS., top next page)... **6,325**

Ornate Japanned Rococo Curio Cabinet

Dental tool cabinet, paneled mahogany, a rectangular trunk form w/a hinged top & nickeled brass fittings, a front zinc-lined copper compartment fitted w/a copper & brass alcohol burner & steam boiler for sterilizing dental tools, bail end handles, second half 19th c., 7 x 11 3/4", 8" h. (ILLUS., bottom of page) **230**

English Aesthetic Display Cabinet

Display cabinet, Victorian Aesthetic Movement style, ebonized wood, the superstructure w/a central shaped crest over a spindled gallery centered by a plaque featuring an avian scene, w/a beveled mirror below, flanked at each side by a spindled gallery & open shelf, the lower section canted & fitted w/a central drawer over a tri-paneled cupboard door featuring an avian scene, flanked at each side by open shelves, joined to a lower open shelf, raised on turned bulbous feet, incised overall w/gilt-decorated designs on the black ground, England, late 19th c., 16 x 59 1/2", 6' 6 1/2" h. (ILLUS.) **920**

Interesting Mahogany Dental Tool Cabinet

Miniature French Provincial Vitrine

Georgian-Oriental Side Cabinet

Side cabinet on stand, Georgian, the upper green-lacquered Oriental cabinet w/a rectangular top over a pair of large doors w/strap hinges & pierced metal lock plate & decorated overall w/gilt & polychrome figural landscapes & opening to 12 similarly decorated drawers & cupboards, fitted on a Georgian stand w/a rectangular molded top w/a gilt-trimmed acanthus leaf-carved border & raised on six heavy squared S-scroll legs joined by cross-stretchers & resting on heavy bun feet, England, early 19th c., 21 1/2 x 43", overall 5' 6" h. (ILLUS.) **6,900**

Storage cabinet, late Victorian country-style, pine, stepped-back style, the upper section w/a rectangular top w/molded cornice above two stacks of 12 narrow pull-out drawers w/center half-round cut-outs for opening, the stepped-out lower section w/two stacks of seven deeper drawers, each w/an iron curved finger-grip pull, flat molded base, 32 1/2" w., overall 4' 11" h.............................. **489**

Vitrine cabinet, French Provincial, miniature, fruitwood, the arched top above a conforming frieze above the single glazed door opening to a wooden shelves, chamfered front corners & double-paneled sides, an arched serpentine & line-incised front apron & short cabriole front legs, France, mid-19th c., 11 x 23", 37" h. (ILLUS., top next column) **518**

Giltwood Louis XV-Style Vitrine Cabinet

Vitrine cabinet, Louis XV-Style, ormolu-mounted giltwood, the half-round shape w/a flat top over a narrow molded cornice & frieze band centered by a h.p. floral spray, a large curved glass front door w/a wide arched base panel centered by a raised panel of relief-carved birds within an oval framed by ornate leafy scrolls, curved glass sides w/serpentine base molding, the door flanked by flat pilasters headed by molded floral swags & centered by painted florals sprigs, raised on tall slender squared cabriole legs, mirrored interior back, crazing & minor paint loss, France, ca. 1880, 14 3/4 x 33 3/4", 5' 2 3/8" h. (ILLUS., previous page) **1,150**

Large Vernis Martin Vitrine

Vitrine cabinet, Louis XV-Style, the high arched & molded crestrail centered by a pierced scroll crest above the swelled frieze band & conforming bombé case decorated in the Vernis Martin style, the top frieze painted w/a large floral bouquet above a pair of tall curved glass panels over serpentine lower panels painted w/figures of lovers in a landscape, glass side panels above further bowed landscape panels, on cabriole legs w/ormolu mounts, France, late 19th c., 14 1/2 x 39", 6' 2" h. (ILLUS.) **2,070**

Vitrine cabinet, North African exotic style, parquetry decorated walnut, two-part construction: the upper section w/a three-sided front w/deep cornice supported by multiple small shaped brackets above a narrow paneled frieze band inlaid in ivory w/Arabic inscriptions, a tall front door & overall framework ornately inlaid w/thuya, various hardwoods & geometric ivory design, the glazed door w/a pointed Arabic arch opening to two shelves, the glazed sides w/matching arches; the lower stand base w/bands of ornate inlay above a conforming apron raised on four paneled & in-

Unusual Ornate No. African Vitrine

lay-banded legs topped by pierced angular corner brackets, a lower shelf supported on thin bun feet, underside signed in pencil "B. Galver," late 19th c., 15 1/2 x 39 3/8", 6' 4 1/2" h. (ILLUS.) **7,768**

Chairs

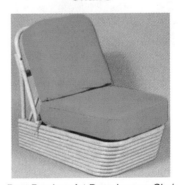

Bent Bamboo Art Deco Lounge Chair

Art Deco lounge chair, bent bamboo, the elongated base platform composed of long curved strips of bamboo w/an adjustable bent bamboo back cushion support, red cushions, ca. 1935-50, 30" h. (ILLUS.) **144**

Rare Ruhlmann French Art Deco Side Chairs

Art Deco side chairs, Cuillernic-style, Macassar ebony, each w/a simple arched barrel-form upholstered back above the over-upholstered seat, square tapering front legs w/brass feet, squared & canted rear legs, designed by Jacques-Emile Ruhlmann, France, ca. 1925, 35" h., pr. (ILLUS., top of page).............................. **35,850**

Carved Arts & Crafts "Morris" Chair

Arts & Crafts "Morris" armchair, carved oak, the adjustable slatted back above a pair of flat shaped arms above five square curved spindles, the flat wide shaped arm supports continuing into large carved claw-and-ball front feet, a deep serpentine front apron, on casters, old finish, minor wear, ca. 1900 (ILLUS.)..... **518**

Arts & Crafts side chair, oak, the tall back w/a wide flat crest above multiple narrow slats continuing down behind the upholstered slip seat, square legs joined by an H-stretcher, designed by Frank Lloyd Wright for the Peter A. Beachy House, Oak Park, Illinois, ca. 1906, 36 1/4" h. (ILLUS., next column) **15,535**

Rare Lloyd-designed Oak Side Chair

Baroque Revival side chair, oak, the very tall back completely pierce-carved w/elaborate designs, the arched crestrail topped by plumes above scrolls & a cartouche over the tall wide splat completely carved w/scrolls, ribbons, shells & banding all between the slender ring-turned reeded stiles, the back raised above the wide over-upholstered seat w/a front drop, the block-and-ring-turned legs joined by box stretchers w/a pierced, arched scroll-carved front stretcher, on knob feet, Europe, second half 19th c., old dark finish, some upholstery damage, overall 49 1/2" h. (ILLUS., top next page) **403**

European Baroque Revival Side Chair

Chippendale commode armchair, walnut, the oxyoke crest ending in carved flaring ears & centering a carved shell above a scrolled vasiform splat flanked by raking back stiles, open shaped arms w/scrolled handholds on incurved supports above the upholstered slip seat, the deep valanced scratchbeaded apron above cabriole front legs ending in carved claw-and-ball feet & raked rear legs, refinished, Pennsylvania, ca. 1760-80, 42" h. (imperfections) **4,113**

Chippendale Cherry Side Chair

Chippendale country-style side chairs, cherry, pierced scroll, diamond & heart back splat w/serpentine crest & shaped ears, square legs w/beaded edges &

cross stretchers, molded seat frame w/two-tone brown or tan upholstery, America, attributed to Massachusetts, one slip seat damaged, a few later pegs & glued splits, seats 17 1/2" h., overall 38 1/2" h., set of 4 (ILLUS. of one w/two-tone brown upholstery) **4,600**

Chippendale Cherry Side Chair

Chippendale side chair, cherry, the oxbow crestrail w/outswept ears above the pierced vasiform splat between the raked stiles, trapezoidal slip seat within a beaded frame above cabriole front legs w/arris knees & ending in raised pad feet, chamfered raked rear legs, refinished, minor imperfections, Connecticut, late 18th c., 38" h. (ILLUS.) **2,115**

One of Two Walnut Chippendale Chairs

Chippendale side chairs, carved walnut, the shaped crestrail above a pierced Gothic-style splat between raked stiles

Simple Chippendale Revival Dining Chairs

above the trapezoidal slip seat w/a molded & valanced frame joining front cabriole legs ending in stockinged trifid feet, outward flaring rear legs, refinished, Pennsylvania, ca. 1870, 39" h., pr. (ILLUS. of one, previous page)........... **3,290**

Classic Chippendale Wing Chair

Chippendale wing chair, mahogany, the high arched upholstered back flanked by canted & rounded upholstered wings above rolled upholstered arms above the cushion seat, raised on square molded Marlborough front legs joined by flat stretchers to the chamfered canted rear legs, refinished, probably New England, late 18th c., 45 1/4" h. (ILLUS.)................. **4,700**

Chippendale Revival dining chairs, walnut, simple ox-yoke crest above solid vasiform splat over a woven rush seat, cabriole front legs ending in claw-and-ball feet, legs joined by turned H-stretcher, two chairs w/shaped open arms, original finish, five side chairs & two armchairs, 42" h., set of 7 (ILLUS., top of page)... **1,750**

One of Two Chippendale-Style Armchairs

Chippendale-Style "lolling" armchairs, mahogany, the tall & wide arched upholstered back flanked by padded open arms w/molded incurved arm supports above the wide over-upholstered seat, molded square front legs joined by an H-stretcher to the rear legs, Hickory Chair Co., 20th c., 40" h., pr. (ILLUS. of one, previous page) **805**

Chippendale-Style Ribbon-back Chair

Chippendale-Style side chairs, mahogany, the back composed of four pierced ribbon rails between the canted reeded styles over the upholstered slip seat, square legs joined by an H-stretcher, old brown finish, America, late 19th - early 20th c., 39" h., set of six (ILLUS. of one) **1,208**

Elaborate Chippendale-Style Chair

Chippendale-Style side chairs, mahogany, the double-arch crestrail w/fancy notch carving & scroll-carved ears above an elaborate pierce-carved splat composed of ribbons & scrolls & flanked by scroll-carved S-form stiles, the wide up-

holstered seat on a scalloped scroll-carved seatrail & boldly carved front cabriole legs ending in scroll feet, England, late 19th c., 35" h., set of 12 (ILLUS. of one) **5,750**

One of 14 Chippendale-Style Chairs

Chippendale-Style side chairs, mahogany, the serpentine pierced crestrail above a delicate & ornately pierced splat above the upholstered seat, square molded front legs w/corner blocks & ending in pad feet, England, late 19th c., 39" h., set of 14 (ILLUS. of one) **4,370**

Very Rare Labeled Classical Armchair

Classical armchair, carved mahogany, the flat rolled crestrail atop backswept serpentine stiles w/carved acanthus leaf trim above the wide upholstered back flanked by padded open arms w/fine C-form scroll-carved arm supports joined to the wide gently curved siderails, a narrow blocked front apron above flute- and ring-turned front legs raised on brass sockets & casters, the serpentine canted rear legs also w/brass casters, remnants of original paper label of William Hancock, Boston, ca. 1820-30, very rare (ILLUS., previous page) **97,990**

One of Two Nice Classical Side Chairs

Classical side chairs, carved mahogany, the flat gently bowed crestrail above a lower pierce-carved rail w/a spread-winged eagle over cornucopia, the molded backswept stiles carved at the top w/acanthus leaf & continuing to form the rails around the caned seat, reeded front seatrail above reeded front sabre legs, outswept rear legs, possibly by Ernest Hagan in the manner of Duncan Phyfe, 31" h., pr. (ILLUS. of one) **2,760**

One of Six Decorated Country Side Chairs

Country-style side chairs, green-painted & decorated, a wide arched crestrail in green decorated in yellow, black, red & dark green w/scrolls & a central rose blossoms above the vase-form bootjack splat w/a rose & yellow banding between the turned canted stiles, the shaped saddle seat raised on simple turned front legs trimmed in yellow & gold bands & joined w/box stretchers to the canted rear legs, first-half 19th c., one back split, 33 1/4" h., set of 6 (ILLUS. of one) **1,035**

Child's Country Rocking Chair

Early American child's country-style rocking chair, ash & hickory, turned elements w/later hickory bark seat by Hunter Maney, North Carolina, two splats, backs w/drawknife marks, old red paint w/minor chips & losses, 21" h. (ILLUS.) **99**

Early Tall Ladder-back Side Chair

Fine Pair of Empire-Style Bergeres

Early American ladder-back side chair, turned maple, very tall turned stiles w/pointed knob finials joining five re- verse-graduated arched slats above the woven rush seat, rod- and ring-turned front legs w/pointed knob feet joined by a baluster- and ring-turned front stretcher, side & rear box stretchers, old surface, Delaware River Valley, late 18th c., 45 1/2" h. (ILLUS., previous page)............ **4,113**

Early American "ladder-back" side chairs, walnut, the back w/three splats between ring- and rod-turned stiles w/pointed knob finials, woven fiber seat, ring- and rod-turned front legs w/double stretchers, old varnish surface, one leg w/wooden peg construction, replaced seats, 35" h., pr. **330**

Empire-Style bergeres (closed-arm arm- chairs), mahogany, the squared back rail around the wide upholstered back & con- tinuing above the closed upholstered arms above the cushion seat, each arm support mounted w/a gilt-bronze classi- cal female term & rosette, a slightly curved front seatrail, square arm sup- ports continuing into the front legs ending in gilt-brass paw caps, France, early 20th c., 37 1/2" h., pr. (ILLUS., top of page) **1,840**

Federal armchair, the tall rectangular uphol- stered back w/a serpentine crest above low rolled upholstered arms & trapezoidal cushion seat, on molded square tapering legs joined by H-stretcher, Massachu- setts, 1790-1810, 40 3/4" h. **4,183**

Federal "Fancy" Side Chairs

Very Rare Pair of Southern Federal Side Chairs

Federal "fancy" side chairs, painted & decorated, a slightly serpentine crestrail stenciled w/gold scrolls above a lower shaped rail w/ornate gilt leaf and roundel stenciling, shaped stiles above the woven rush seat w/ring-turned seatrail, gilt-line decorated front sabre legs joined by a flattened gilt-trimmed front stretcher, rosewood-grained background, probably New York City, first quarter 19th c., 33" h., pr. (ILLUS., bottom of previous page) **920**

decorated w/a gold harp & flowers above a pierced central splat carved & painted as a cluster of ribbon-tied musical instruments, the splat flanked by a slender turned colonnette, the flat back stiles w/gold banding above the woven rush seat within a narrow decorated seatrail, knob- and rod-turned front legs joined by a flattened front stretcher, simple turned box stretchers, one w/rush damage & replaced front stretcher, both slightly loose, some wear, New England, ca. 1800, 35" h., pr. (ILLUS. of one) **3,910**

Delicate Decorated Federal "Fancy" Chair

Federal "fancy" side chairs, red-painted & decorated, the narrow stepped crestrail

Federal-Style Child's Wing Chair

Federal side chairs, inlaid mahogany, the delicate looped heart-shaped back w/molded framing, the central open oval w/central slender splat w/a pierced fan at the top & inlaid fans & a paterae down the front, the back raised on reeded curved uprights above the wide over-upholstered seat w/a serpentine front & raised on squared tapering legs ending in spade feet, the front of each leg w/fine line inlay enclosing bellflower pendants, canted rounded rear legs, refinished, repairs, probably Norfolk, Virginia, ca. 1800, 38 3/4" h., pr. (ILLUS., top of previous page) **27,025**

Federal-Style child's wing chair, mahogany, the high flat-topped upholstered back flanked by shallow wings above the rolled upholstered arms over the upholstered seat, 20th c., faded upholstery, 29" h. (ILLUS., bottom previous page) **604**

English Louis XVI-Style Tub Chair

Louis XVI-Style tub chair, mahogany, the U-form molded bellflower band-carved crestrail above the upholstered back curving down to form the shaped outscrolled closed arms w/incurved leaf-carved arm supports, a cushion seat above the dentil-carved seatrail over baluster- and ring-turned front legs ending in peg feet, England, ca. 1900, 35" h. (ILLUS.) **1,093**

Unique Early Modernist Armchair

Modernist style armchair, ebonized & painted wood, "Billet Chair," the tall flat rectangular back slightly swept back, flanked by rod-form cross supports & stiles w/projecting flat rectangular arms, the rectangular seat canted toward the back panel & supported on front cross rods joined to simple turned rod legs w/rod stretchers, designed by Gerrit Thomas Rietveld, executed by G. van de Groenekan, 1923 or 1924, 33" h. (ILLUS.) **83,650**

Rare Rietveld Plywood Armchair

Modernist style armchair, molded & painted plywood, the wide U-form back supported by wide side uprights w/bent-over tops, braced under the wide inverted U-form seat raised on flat tapering legs, painted white, designed by Gerrit Thomas Rietveld, ca. 1950, 23 5/8" h. (ILLUS.)...... **38,240**

Modernist style side chairs, molded laminated birch, DCW-style, a wide curved back rest supported on a flat upright above the wide dished & rolled seat, on four flat outswept legs, designed by Ray & Charles Eames for Herman Miller, camel-colored finish, unmarked, ca. 1950s, 29" h., pr. (ILLUS., top next page) **460**

Ornate Dragon-carved Chinese Armchair

Pair of Classic Eames Side Chairs

Oriental armchair, carved mahogany, the elaborately carved back composed of two small entwined dragons centered atop the curling tails of large dragons curving around to form the open arms, their heads holding large pearls forming the ends of the arms, the wide flat seat w/a central carved reserve above a deep serpentine seatrail w/ornate floral carving continuing into the cabriole legs w/scroll feet, China, early 20th c., 23" h. (ILLUS., bottom previous page) **460**

Chinese Armchair with Carved Iris

Oriental armchair, carved teakwood, a wide arched crestrail ornately pierce-carved w/iris & leaves above a shaped solid iris-carved splat flanked by iris-carved stiles, the open arms terminating in carved dragon heads on incurved arm supports, the wide seat w/molded border above scroll-carved arms & cabriole front legs w/bat-carved knees & ending in scroll feet, old dark reddish brown finish, China, late 19th - early 20th c., 44" h. (ILLUS.)....................... **546**

Pilgrim Century great chair, turned hardwood, the tall back composed of three slats w/ogee shaping between baluster- and ring-turned stiles topped by large knob finials, open downward slanting arms w/large turned hand grips above baluster- and ring-turned supports continuing to form the front legs joined by double-turned stretchers, old red surface, Norwich or Lebanon, New London County, Connecticut, 1660-1715, 42 1/2" h. (legs ended out)....................................... **3,055**

Extremely Rare Pilgrim Century Chair

Pilgrim Century side chair, red oak & maple, the low rectangular back panel of tack-trimmed leather between the square stiles continuing to form the back legs, the lower leather-upholstered seat raised on block- and knob-turned front legs joined by a block-and-bobbin-turned stretcher, box side & back stretchers, 19th c. leather, imperfections, Essex County, Massachusetts, 1665-95, 36" h. (ILLUS., bottom previous page) **34,075**

Queen Anne country-style armchair, painted, the shaped crest w/rounded corners above a vasiform splat resting on a molded rail & flanked by raked chamfered stiles, molded scrolled arms above block-, vase- and ring-turned supports continuing into the front legs ending in Spanish feet & joined by a bulbous turned front stretcher, square side stretchers, old red paint, woven rush seat, New England, mid-18th c., 39 1/2" h. (imperfections) **4,406**

Country Queen Anne Painted Armchair

Queen Anne country-style armchair, painted wood, the shaped & arched crestrail above a simple vasiform splat raised on a lower rail between the shaped & molded stiles, long shaped open arms w/scrolled grips raised on baluster-turned arm supports above the woven rush seat, the block-and-knob-turned front legs joined by a turned double-knob & disk stretcher, simple box side & rear stretchers, old dark red repaint over earlier black, restorations to front legs, back feet ended out, late 18th c., 44" h. (ILLUS.) **1,783**

Queen Anne side chair, carved walnut, the shaped crestrail centered by a scrolled shell above a raked vasiform splat flanked by shaped stiles, the upholstered compass slip seat in a conforming apron raised on cabriole front legs w/a shell-carved knee &

Rare & Fine Boston Queen Anne Chair

ball-and-claw feet, jointed by swelled stretchers, refinished, restoration, Boston, ca. 1740-60, 39" h. (ILLUS.)......... **29,375**

Queen Anne side chair, cherry, the yoked & spooned crestrail above a vasiform splat flanked by raked stiles, an upholstered seat over a valanced apron & cabriole front legs w/shaped knee returns & ending in pad feet, joined to the rear raking chamfered legs by block-, vase- and ring-turned stretchers, old refinish, probably Massachusetts, mid-18th c., 39" h. (minor imperfections) **1,880**

English Queen Anne Side Chair

Fancy Caned Regency Armchairs

Queen Anne side chair, mahogany, the shaped crest above a solid vasiform splat flanked by shaped stiles above the upholstered balloon slip seat, cabriole front legs w/shell-carved knees ending in pad feet, turned & raked rear legs w/pad feet, two seat returns replaced, old refinishing, England, 18th c., 39 1/2" h. (ILLUS., bottom previous page) **1,610**

Queen Anne-Style side chairs, mahogany, scrolled ox-yoke crestrails above vasiform splats, molded stiles over the upholstered slip seat, front cabriole legs w/pad feet, turned H-stretcher base, probably England, 19th c., several replaced glue blocks, old refinishing, repairs to legs, 40" h., pr. **2,200**

Regency armchairs, painted & decorated, the backswept & knob-turned back stiles flanking a half-round caned panel w/a small polychrome painted tablet above two thin rails, squared open arms raised on incurved arm supports above the wide caned seat, raised on knob-turned slightly curved front legs, overall black paint w/gilt highlights, England, first quarter 19th c., 33 1/2" h., pr. (ILLUS., top of page) **4,140**

Restauration armchairs, mahogany, the tall upholstered back framed by backswept molding above the padded open arms on incurved scroll-carved arm supports, the wide upholstered seat above a plain seatrail raised on heavy S-scroll carved front legs, France, second quarter 19th c., 40 1/4" h., pr. (ILLUS. of one, next column).. **2,300**

Victorian bamboo corner chair, the rectangular openwork back panels composed of bamboo lattice centered by a tightly woven panel, a tightly woven seat above the legs joined by lattice-form stretchers, some wear, late 19th c., 32 1/4" h. (ILLUS., bottom next column) **259**

French Restauration Armchair

Victorian Bamboo Corner Chair

Simple Renaissance Revival Dining Chairs

Hunzinger Patented Rocking Chair

Victorian "patent" rocking chair w/arms, walnut, a tall flaring upholstered back w/top corner knob finials flanked by long angled ring-turned rails mounted w/padded ring-turned angular arms flanking the upholstered seat, ring-turned front stretcher w/two short spindles, patented by George Hunzinger Co., New York, New York, ca. 1870s, original finish, newer upholstery, 32" h. (ILLUS.)...................... **400**

Hunzinger-signed Victorian Patent Chair

Victorian "patent" side chair, walnut, the back composed of ring-turned stiles w/acorn finials joined by a turned crest bar topped by a fancy sunburst finial above the arched tufted upholstered back panel, scrolled half-arms joined to upright rods at the back of the wide upholstered seat, canted front legs joined by a turned cross stretcher below a turned H-stretcher & joined to the canted rear legs w/slender turned stretchers, signed by the George Hunzinger firm, ca. 1880s, old repairs to arms, break in top crest, 34 1/2" h. (ILLUS.) **489**

Victorian Renaissance Revival dining chairs, walnut, arched & scalloped line-incised crestrail w/eared corners above a reeded splat centered by a large roundel, square stiles w/S-scroll skirt-guards flanked by upholstered seats, simple ring-turned front legs joined by double ring-and-rod-turned stretchers, probably originally had caned seats, original finish, ca. 1875, 34" h., set of 6 (ILLUS., top of page)... **600**

Unusual Renaissance Revival Recliner

Victorian Renaissance Revival fixed-back recliner armchair, walnut & burl walnut, the backswept serpentine upholstered back w/molded stiles continuing down to low upholstered arms w/large carved feathered scrolls & rondel sides above scrolled & burl-paneled side seat rails flanking the wide upholstered seat, a turned side column above the widely outswept scrolled & paneled front & rear legs, ca. 1875 (ILLUS.) **489**

Nice Renaissance Revival Side Chair

Victorian Renaissance Revival side chair, walnut & burl walnut, the gently flaring squared back w/a gently arched crestrail w/narrow burl panels centered by a small sunburst crest above carved scrolls & a rondel, shaped corner ear

above the molded stiles & lower rail enclosing the upholstered back panel, concave skirt guards at the sides of the wide spring-cushioned upholstered seat w/a narrow burl-paneled seatrail w/a central carved drop, ring- and rod-turned tapering front legs w/peg feet raised on casters, squared outswept rear legs, ca. 1875 (ILLUS.).. **150-200**

"Rosalie with Grapes" Belter Armchair

Victorian Rococo armchair, carved & laminated rosewood, the tall balloon-form back w/a high arched flower-carved crestrail continuing down to enclose the upholstered back panel, open serpentine arms on incurved arm supports, wide upholstered seat w/a serpentine seatrail carved w/floral scrolls flanked by demicabriole front legs w/flower-carved knees & raised on casters, "Rosalie with Grapes" patt., John H. Belter, New York, New York, ca. 1885, 44" h. (ILLUS.)......... **6,000**

Victorian Rococo armchair, pierced & laminated rosewood, the high balloon back w/a tufted upholstered oblong center panel enclosed by an ornately piercecarved frame topped by a high arched crestrail centered by a scroll-carved crest above a floral cluster, the serpentine sides w/further pierced scrolls, shaped padded open arms on incurved arm supports above the wide shaped upholstered spring seat w/a serpentine molded seatrail centered by a carved cartouche, demi-cabriole front legs on casters, in the "Henry Ford" pattern by J. & J.W. Meeks, New York City, ca. 1855, 48" h. (ILLUS., top next page)... **6,900**

"Henry Ford" Pattern Meeks Chair

Fine Carved Belter Armchair

Victorian Rococo armchair, pierced & laminated rosewood, the tall corseted balloon back w/an upholstered panel framed by an arched crestrail w/an arched grape-and-leaf-carved crest above pierce-carved fruit vines continuing down the sides & flanked by open padded arms on incurved arm supports, wide upholstered spring seat on a serpentine seatrail, a floral-carved reserve flanked by carved leafy scrolls & continu-

ing to the incurved carved cabriole front legs ending in scroll feet on casters, attributed to John H. Belter, New York City, ca. 1855, 47" h. (ILLUS.) **8,625**

Victorian Rococo armchair, rosewood, high balloon-shaped back w/leaf-and-scroll-carved crestrail continuing down to frame the tufted upholstered back flanked by rolled upholstered closed arms w/scrolled, incurved arm supports, scroll-and-medallion-carved serpentine seatrail on scrolled demi-cabriole front legs on casters, ca. 1860, 45" h.................. **448**

One of Two Rococo Armchairs

Victorian Rococo armchairs, carved rosewood, the shaped balloon-back w/an arched crestrail carved w/fanned scrolls & continuing to form the serpentine frame around the tufted upholstered back panels, shaped padded open arms on incurved arm supports over the wide upholstered seat w/a serpentine seatrail centered by a carved cartouche, demi-cabriole front legs ending in scroll feet on casters, refinished, ca. 1860, 36" h., pr. (ILLUS. of one)... **950**

Victorian Rococo side chairs, pierced & laminated rosewood, the tall balloon back centered by an oval upholstered panel enclosed by an ornately pierce-carved frame, the arched crestrail centered by a high arched floral-carved crest & continuing to form the pierced vine- & scroll-carved sides, the rounded upholstered spring seat on a conforming seatrail centered by a carved floral cluster, on demi-cabriole front legs on casters, the "Fountain Elms" pattern, ca. 1855, 38" h., pr. (ILLUS. of one, next page)...................... **15,525**

Simple Victorian Rococo Side Chairs

Belter "Fountain Elms" Side Chair

Victorian Rococo side chairs, walnut, simple balloon back w/molded railing centered by a cartouche-carved crest above the original horsehair-upholstered back panel, curved skirt guards flank the rounded horsehair-upholstered seat w/a serpentine seatrail above simple cabriole front legs, refinished, ca. 1865, 34" h., set of 4 (ILLUS., top of page) **800**

Fancy Carved Belter-style Side Chair

Victorian Rococo substyle side chair, carved laminated rosewood, the ornate back w/an outer frame composed of C-scrolls, an arched top crest of carved roses & flowers & the central long oval upholstered back panel surrounded by finely pierce-carved vines of grapes & acorns, the wide over-upholstered needlework seat w/a serpentine seatrail carved w/a cluster of roses framed by leafy vines, molded cabriole front legs ending in scrolls on casters, canted rear legs, attributed to John Henry Belter, New York, New York, ca. 1855, old break in side carving, 35 1/2" h. (ILLUS.) **1,725**

Windsor "Comb-back" Rocker

Windsor "comb-back" rocking chair w/arms, painted & decorated wood, the small back comb w/a rectangular crest raised on four small spindles above the flat crestrail over seven bamboo-turned spindles flanked by backswept tapering stiles, shaped arms over a turned spindle & arm supports, wide shaped plank seat raised on canted bamboo-turned legs joined by turned box stretchers & mortised into rockers, old dark green paint, restored split where comb meets crest, America, ca. 1830, 38 1/4" h. (ILLUS.) **345**

Windsor "Rabbit Ear" Side Chair

Windsor "rabbit ear" side chairs, hardwood w/reddish brown refinishing, flat slightly curved crestrail over five turned spindles between the curved & tapered

styles, rounded plank seat, bamboo turned legs reinforced underneath w/shims, incised shield-shape seats, glued spindle restorations, one seat w/repaired split, seats 15 3/4" h., overall 32" h., set of 4 (ILLUS. of one) **518**

Fine Sack-back Windsor Highchair

Windsor "sack-back" highchair, painted hardwood, the bowed crestrail over seven turned spindles continuing through a medial rail forming the flat shaped arms raised on a short spindle & a canted baluster- and knob-turned arm support, the wide shaped saddle seat raised on tall canted baluster-, ring- and rod-turned legs joined by a swelled H-stretcher, old black paint, split on one arm, overall 32 1/2" h. (ILLUS.) **8,625**

Writing-arm Windsor with Family History

Windsor "writing-arm" armchair, birch & poplar, the tall back w/a stepped crestrail above squared stiles flanking six tall simple spindles, one shaped arm w/a canted baluster-turned support & two spindles, the other arm mounted w/a wide curved teardrop-shaped writing surface w/old oilcloth covering above a wide shallow drawer, the wide plank seat raised on heavy tapering canted legs joined by a ring-turned front stretcher & plain box stretchers, old documents in drawer give history of the piece, old brown finish, ca. 1770s, Massachusetts, restoration to arm join, glued split on the writing arm, 45" h. (ILLUS., bottom of previous page) **863**

Chests & Chests of Drawers

Arts & Crafts chest of drawers, oak, the rectangular top w/a molded cornice above a pair of cupboard doors w/wide frames enclosing h.p. stylized landscapes in shades of green & yellow, the lower case w/a pair of drawers above two long drawers all w/simple bail pulls, simple bracket feet, paneled ends, from The Byrdcliffe Arts & Crafts Colony, 1904, branded mark & date, 23 3/4 x 57", 5' h. (ILLUS., bottom of page)....................... **273,500**

Blanket chest, Chippendale country-style, pine, the hinged rectangular top opening to a deep well, the front facade composed of two large cross-band panels flanking two small square center raised panels,

Rare Southern Chippendale Blanket Chest

molded base raised on shaped bracket feet, Eastern Shore of Maryland or Virginia, 18th c., 52" l., 36" h. (ILLUS.).............. **14,340**

Blanket chest, Chippendale country-style, walnut, dovetailed construction, the rectangular molded lid w/exterior battens & original iron strap hinges opening to an interior w/lidded till, dovetailed case on a molded base w/original bracket feet w/pointed returns, interior of lid inscribed "Salem, Ohio" & interior of till lid w/"Surplus indigo, Salem (?)," w/indistinct writing on back (possibly maker's name), front & till locks missing, later brass escutcheon, stains, 18 3/4 x 50", 25" h........ **1,430**

Extremely Rare Signed & Dated Arts & Crafts Chest

Southern Walnut Blanket Chest

Blanket chest, inlaid walnut, the rectangular top opening to a dovetailed well, a molded base on shaped bracket feet, line-inlaid panels on the front & sides w/fans within the front panels & graduated inverted flowers below the diamond-shaped inlaid lock escutcheon, Southern United States, refinished, glued restoration on back foot, replaced strap hinges, small pierced repairs, late 18th - early 19th c., 19 1/4 x 42 1/2", 24 1/2" h. (ILLUS.)........... **1,495**

Rare Chippendale Block-front Chest

Chippendale "block-front" chest of drawers, mahogany, the rectangular top w/blocked front & molded edge above a conforming case fitted w/four long graduated drawers, a molded base w/central drop on scrolled bracket feet, appears to retain original brasses, Boston, Massachusetts, 1760-80, 20 x 36", 30 1/2" h. (ILLUS.)... **53,775**

Chippendale chest of drawers, cherry, the rectangular top w/molded edges & a double-blocked front above a conforming case fitted w/four long graduated drawers, a conforming molded base w/a central drop pendant raised on ogee bracket feet w/shaped returns, brass bail pulls & pierced brass keyhole escutcheons, Boston, Massachusetts, or Hartford, Connecticut, 1770-90, 19 1/2 x 36 1/2", 32" h. **23,900**

Chippendale chest of drawers, mahogany, a rectangular top w/molded edges above a conforming case w/four long graduated drawers w/brass bail pulls, on a molded base on ogee bracket feet, Philadelphia, 1770-90, 21 1/2 x 40 3/4", 34 1/2" h. **4,541**

Rare Tiger Maple Chest on Chest

Chippendale chest-on-chest, tiger stripe maple, two-part construction: the upper section w/a rectangular top w/a flaring stepped cornice above a case w/five long thumb-molded graduated drawers w/butterfly brasses & keyhole escutcheons; the lower w/a mid-molding above a case w/four long graduated drawers w/matching brasses, molded base on ogee scroll-cut bracket feet, original brasses, old refinish, southwestern New England, late 18th c., 19 x 37 3/4", overall 6' 3" h. (ILLUS.)... **24,675**

Chippendale Walnut Chest of Drawers

Chippendale "Chinese style" chest of drawers, walnut, four graduated dovetailed drawers w/scribed borders, original brass pulls & inlaid kite escutcheons, vertical backboards w/cut nails, bracket feet, Virginia, last quarter 18th c., old refinishing, replaced feet, added drawer runners, repairs, 20 x 42", 36" h. (ILLUS.) **4,400**

New England Chippendale Tall Chest

Chippendale tall chest of drawers, maple, the rectangular top w/a molded cornice above a case w/a pair of narrow drawers above a stack of six long graduated thumb-molded drawers each w/butterfly brasses & keyhole escutcheons, molded base on scroll-cut bracket feet, brasses appear to be original, old red-stained surface, minor imperfections, probably Massachusetts, last half 18th c., 18 1/2 x 36", 4' 9" h. (ILLUS.)... **8,813**

Classical Bow-front Chest of Drawers

Classical "bow-front" chest of drawers, mahogany & mahogany veneer, a rectangular top w/a gently bowed front flanked by projecting ovolo corners above spiral-turned columns flanking the bowed case of four long graduated drawers w/round brass pulls, a scalloped apron & ring-turned legs w/peg feet, probably Salem, Massachusetts, early 19th c., 20 x 44", 42" h. (ILLUS.)............... **1,955**

Classical Chest with Swiveling Mirror

Classical chest of drawers with mirror, mahogany & mahogany veneer, a long rectangular framed mirror swiveling between tall large S-scroll uprights raised atop a long narrow rectangular framework enclosing six thin drawers all set back on the rectangular top of the main case, the main case w/a long narrow ogee-front drawer projecting over two long graduated lower drawers w/lion mask & ring pulls flanked by heavy side columns, flat apron, raised on heavy carved paw front feet, ca. 1820s, 22 1/2 x 42", overall 5' 6" h. (ILLUS.)........ **1,380**

New England Seven-drawer Chest

Classical country-style chest of drawers, hardwood w/old mustard paint, three setback drawers on the rectangular top, over four dovetailed drawers w/original embossed brass pulls, turned feet, New England, evidence of later red paint, 18 x 39 1/2", 41 1/2" h. (ILLUS.) **1,610**

Inlaid Federal Chest of Drawers

Federal "bow-front" chest of drawers, inlaid mahogany & mahogany veneer, the rectangular top w/a gently bowed front above a conforming case of four long graduated drawers each w/banded inlay panels & original oval brasses w/a running dog design, serpentine apron & tall French feet, old refinishing, early backboards possibly replacements, replaced base & feet, late 18th - early 19th c., 21 1/4 x 38 3/4", 33" h. (ILLUS.) **1,380**

Inlaid Cherry Federal Chest

Federal chest of drawers, inlaid cherry, rectangular top above a case w/a long deep drawer over three long graduated drawers, each w/line border inlay & original oval brasses, serpentine apron above tall bracket feet, band inlay on the top, refinished, glued split, restoration to drawer edges, late 18th - early 19th c., 20 1/2 x 42", 41 1/2" h. (ILLUS.) **1,840**

Federal chest of drawers, walnut, rectangular top above a case w/two over three dovetailed drawers decorated w/string inlay w/canted corners & teardrop inlay at original brass pulls, triple-line inlay on edge of top & at base, base w/original skirt & French feet, vertical backboards, handwrought nails, American South, feet &

Southern Federal Chest of Drawers

glue blocks probable replacements, tripleline inlay possibly not original, stains, separations & scattered small repairs, 20 x 42", 37" h. (ILLUS.) **3,520**

Very Fine Federal Chest with Mirror

Federal chest of drawers with mirror, mahogany w/tiger stripe & bird's-eye maple veneer, a superstructure w/an upright rectangular mirror w/a narrow frame & arched crest swiveling between slender uprights flanked by fancy long C-scroll brackets & set above a narrow compartment w/three small drawers faced in bird's-eye maple & w/round ring pulls, the stepped-out rectangular case top w/ovolo corners above reeded columns flanking the case w/a pair of drawers over two long drawers, all w/bird's-eye maple & round ring pulls, all raised on tapering reeded legs w/a ring-turned top segment, ending in peg feet, attributed to John & Thomas Seymour, Boston, ca. 1820, replaced pulls, old finish, minor imperfections, 20 1/2 x 36", overall 6' h. (ILLUS.)
.... **38,188**

Tall Mission Chest of Drawers with Mirror

Mission-style (Arts & Crafts movement) tall chest of drawers with mirror, the top w/a square-framed mirror swiveling between flat braced uprights atop the rectangular top over a case w/a pair of small drawers above four long graduated drawers all w/turned wood knobs, flat apron & simple tapered front bracket feet, original finish, Quaint metal tag mark of the Stickley Brothers, veneer lifting on bottom, early 20th c., 21 x 36", overall 5' 7 1/2" h. (ILLUS.) **2,185**

Modern style chest of drawers, walnut, rectangular long top above three stacks of drawers w/two narrow drawers over two drawers at the left end, the other stacks composed of three drawers each, short cylindrical legs, Heritage Line designed by Frank Lloyd Wright & manufactured by Henredon, late 1940s - early 1950s, 61" l., 28" h. **1,380**

Flame-grained Country Mule Chest

Mule chest (box chest w/one or more drawers below a storage compartment), country-style, painted & decorated pine & poplar, the rectangular top opening to a deep well above a single long drawer w/old walnut pulls, deeply scalloped apron & short bracket feet, original reddish brown flame graining on a tan ground, top w/later sponge decoration on interior, age splits, New England, first half 19th c., 18 1/4 x 36 3/4", 31 1/2" h. (ILLUS.) **1,265**

Sponge-decorated Mule Chest

Mule chest (box chest w/one or more drawers below a storage compartment), country-style, painted & decorated pine, the thick rectangular top opening to a deep well fitted w/a covered till & small drawer, the lower case w/two long graduated drawers w/original turned wood knobs, decorated overall in original brown over yellow sponging on the front panels w/dark red over brown on the rest of the case, slight loss to height, pad added to one rear foot, first half 19th c., 20 x 37", 37 3/4" h. (ILLUS.) **2,415**

Pilgrim Century chest, carved & painted red oak, the rectangular thumb-molded & cleated top opening to a deep well w/covered till, the lid decorated w/punchwork & carved "MF 1696," the front w/a narrow serrated band above the three-panel front composed of four pairs of black-painted split spindles separating the three large molded diamonds enclosing a cross design composed of four oval buttons, a lower rail above a pair of narrow drawers w/raised rectangular molding & separated by three pairs of short half-round turned spindles, long rounded base molding, flat stile front feet, paneled ends & five-panel back, black & red paint shows some touch-up, wooden pulls appear original, some replacements, South Scituate, Massachusetts area, 21 1/4 x 54 1/2", 34 1/2" h. (ILLUS., top next page) **25,850**

Rare Early Pilgrim Century Dated Chest

English Queen Anne Chest of Drawers

Scarce Early Queen Anne Chest-on-Frame

Queen Anne chest of drawers, walnut & burl walnut veneer, rectangular top w/molded edges above a case w/a row of three drawers over three long graduated drawers w/butterfly brasses & keyhole escutcheons, molded base raised on large bun feet, England, ca. 1720, 38" w., 38" h. (ILLUS.) **2,875**

Queen Anne chest-on-frame, maple, rectangular top w/a flaring molded cornice above a case w/a pair of narrow drawers above four long graduated drawers w/butterfly brasses & keyhole escutcheons, set on a base w/a molded edge above the deeply scalloped apron raised on short cabriole legs ending in pad feet on platforms, brasses appear to be original old refinish, Massachusetts or New Hampshire, mid-18th c., imperfections, 16 3/4 x 35 3/4", 4' 1 1/4" h. (ILLUS., top next column).. **6,463**

Inlaid Queen Anne-Style Chest

Late Italian Renaissance-Style Chest

Queen Anne-Style chest of drawers, inlaid walnut & burl walnut veneer, the rectangular top w/molded edges above a case w/a pair of drawers w/banded inlay above three long graduated drawers w/pairs of rectangular inlay bands, the bottom drawer centered by a starburst inlay, molded base on bun feet, small ring pulls, partially composed of antique elements, England, late 19th - early 20th c., 21 1/2 x 37 1/2", 34" h. (ILLUS., bottom previous page) **1,955**

Renaissance-Style chest, walnut, the long rectangular hinged top w/carved gadrooned edge opening to a deep well, the front formed of a pair of smaller vertical heavily molded panels enclosing two half-round & an oval panel, a large horizontal panel w/matching design across the center front, stepped & molded flat base, Italy, late 19th c., worn finish, 22 x 68", 22 1/2" h. (ILLUS., top of page) . **1,380**

Southern Cherry Sugar Chest

Sugar chest, country-style, cherry, a rectangular hinged top opening to a deep interior, the front w/a diamond-shaped ivory keyhole & two small drawers across the bottom, double-knob turned feet, Kentucky or Tennessee, ca. 1820, 20 x 36", 29" h. (ILLUS.)... **3,738**

Cherry Sugar Chest

Sugar chest, cherry, dovetailed construction, lift top w/breadboard ends, interior w/three compartments, original lock, dovetailed drawer w/original wooden pulls, turned legs, first half 19th c., top w/old separation, old refinishing, chips, light scratches, 40 x 28 x 20" (ILLUS.)...... **8,800**

Nice Victorian Aesthetic Chest with Mirror

Victorian Aesthetic Movement chest of drawers with mirror, inlaid mahogany, the superstructure w/a wide flat cornice band decorated w/festoons of garlands inlaid in mixed metal & mother-of-pearl above simple uprights flanking the large rectangular mirror swiveling above the rectangular top w/molded edges, the case w/a pair of drawers ornately carved & decorated to match the top cornice above two long molded drawers w/simple bail pulls, flat base raised on short stile feet, attributed to Gottlieb Vollmer, Philadelphia, ca. 1880s, 22 x 53", overall 6' 9" h. (ILLUS., bottom previous page) **1,150**

Tall Victorian Eastlake Chest of Drawers

Victorian Eastlake tall chest of drawers, mahogany & burl walnut, a rectangular top w/molded cornice above a case w/a pair of drawers w/fine burl veneer & simple pulls above a stack of five matching long graduated drawers, molded plinth base, paneled ends, ca. 1885, 20 x 43 1/8", 5' 4 1/8" h. (ILLUS.) **863**

Golden Oak Chest of Drawers & Mirror

Victorian Golden Oak chest of drawers w/mirror, a large irregular rectangular

beveled mirror in a conforming frame w/leafy scrolls across the top & swiveling between tall serpentine uprights flanking an arched lower back panel decorated w/fancy carved scrolls all on the rectangular top w/a bowed front above a case w/a pair of matching bowed drawers above two long flat-fronted drawers all w/pierced brass pulls, thin serpentine apron, short legs on new casters, ca. 1900, 44" w., overall 6' 2" h. (ILLUS.) **259**

Walnut Renaissance Revival Chest

Victorian Renaissance Revival chest of drawers, walnut & burl walnut, the rectangular top above a long top drawer w/a pair of raised shaped burl panels w/rectangular plate & ring brass pulls centering a shield-shaped raised burl panel, projecting above two matching long drawers flanked by turned columns above a forth matching long projecting bottom drawer, deep plinth base, ca. 1875, 17 x 40", 41" h. (ILLUS.) **259**

Simple Walnut Renaissance Chest

Victorian Renaissance Revival chest of drawers, walnut, the rectangular top fitted w/a pair of small hanky drawers w/a raised panel front & pairs of small wooden knobs joined by a shaped back crest, the case composed of four long graduated drawers each w/a pair of long narrow raised panels flanking a central rondel, turned wood knobs, shaped bracket feet, ca. 1875, 43" w., 42" h. (ILLUS., bottom previous page) **259**

Fancy Renaissance Revival Tall Chest

Victorian Renaissance Revival chest of drawers with mirror, walnut & burl walnut, the tall superstructure w/a very tall arched crest w/an ornate scroll & cartouche design above curved panels above the tall round mirror swiveling between the side frames mounted w/small candleshelves above two small thin hanky drawers on the rectangular white marble top, the case w/three long graduated drawers w/raised oval banding, round wooden knobs & small carved drop scrolls at the top of the chamfered front corners, deep molded flat base, ca. 1875, 19 x 41", overall 7' 11" (ILLUS.) **748**

Rococo Walnut Serpentine Chest

Victorian Rococo chest of drawers with mirror, walnut & feather-grained walnut veneer, the tall oblong mirror in a shaped frame swiveling below a high arched & pierced scroll-carved crest centered by a cartouche supported on reeded columnar uprights raised on large scroll-carved brackets, the rectangular white marble top w/molded edges & a serpentine front above a conforming case w/three long feather-grained veneered serpentine drawers above the serpentine scroll-cut apron above bun feet on casters, refinished, ca. 1860, 22 x 44", overall 7' 2" h. (ILLUS.) **1,800**

Unusual Signed Victorian Rococo Chest

Victorian Rococo chest of drawers with mirror, rosewood, the tall superstructure w/a broken-scroll crest centered by a shield-form crest above an arched fruit- and scroll-carved frame above the large arched mirror flanked by narrow vertical mirrored panels mounted w/small half-round shelves above two small hanky drawers, the wide rectangular case top w/projecting ovolo corners above projecting columns flanking the case w/a long narrow top drawer w/scroll-carved pulls projecting slightly over the three long lower graduated drawers, plinth base on casters, stenciled label reading "Springmeyer Brothers, late J.H. Belter & Co., 722 Broadway, New York," old worn & dark finish, some mirror deterioration, ca. 1865-67, 27 x 56", 7' 11" h. (ILLUS.) **3,910**

William & Mary "mule" chest (box chest w/one or more drawers below a storage compartment), painted pine, the rectangular one-board top w/molded edges, opening to a deep well w/the front composed of a pair of false drawers over two long false drawers above two long real drawers at the bottom, simple butterfly brasses & escutcheons, flaring molded base, raised on large turned bulb feet, rosehead nail construction, old bluish green paint over earlier red, areas of touch-up, base a replacement, pieced restorations & some replaced moldings, early 18th c., 18 x 36" (ILLUS., below)...... **2,070**

Early William & Mary Mule Chest

Cradles

Low cradle on rockers, walnut, dovetailed construction w/an arched & canted headboard & lower footboard flanked by scroll-carved sides w/heart-shaped rope holes, on deep arched rockers, early 19th c., 24 1/2 x 40 1/2", 22" h. **460**

Early Painted Windsor Cradle

Windsor cradle on rockers, painted wood, an oval bentwood crestrail above twenty-four ring-turned slanted canted side spindles above the oval base, raised on canted baluster-, ring- and rod-turned legs w/inset rockers & jointed by box stretchers, old white paint over earlier colors, early 19th c.,17 1/2 x 39 3/4", 22" h. (ILLUS.)..... **518**

Cupboards

Scarce Early Apothecary Cupboard

Apothecary cupboard, pine, one-piece construction, rose-head nail construction, a narrow rectangular top w/a narrow molding above canted upper section enclosing three long drawers above a midsection composed of an arrangement of twenty-one dovetailed drawers of graduated sizes w/turned wood knobs all above an open bottom shelf on the molded base w/bracket feet, old refinishing, feet & cornice old replacements, 15 1/4 x 38 1/4", 5' 8 3/4" h. (ILLUS.) **2,588**

Early Painted Chimney Cupboard

Chimney cupboard, painted pine, a rectangular top above a tall single door w/one small & two large panels within a raised molded & off-center outer framework, opens to five shelves, light greenish grey exterior, flat base, first half 19th c., 17 x 36 1/2", 7' 7" h. (ILLUS., bottom previous page).. **1,150**

Rare Chippendale Corner Cupboard

Corner cupboard, Chippendale, painted pine, one-piece construction, the flat top over a very high stepped & molded cornice w/blocked ends above a pair of tall eight-pane glazed cupboard doors opening to shelves & flanked by wide reeded pilasters at the sides, a mid-molding above a pair of shorter doors w/pairs of raised panels, molded base w/scroll-cut bracket feet, old blue paint, Eastern Shore of Virginia, ca. 1770-90, 28 x 47 1/2", 7' 2" h. (ILLUS.)... **35,850**

Corner cupboard, Classical style, painted poplar, two-part construction: the upper section w/a stepped molded cornice above a frieze centered by a rosette block flanked by half-round turned acorn knobs above a pair of arched eight-pane glazed cupboard doors opening to two shelves & flanked by half-round ring- and baluster-turned colonnettes w/tall acorn finials; the lower section w/a mid-molding above a row of three drawers over a pair of paneled cupboard doors, molded base on simple bracket feet, lat-

er white paint, restored splits near top, cornice partially replaced, pieced repairs to feet, possibly Ohio, ca. 1850, 25 1/2 x 55", 7' 10" h. (ILLUS., below)..... **2,300**

Painted Poplar Corner Cupboard

Corner cupboard, Federal country-style, cherry, one-piece construction, the flat top w/a coved cornice above a dentil molding over a pair of tall paneled doors above a pair of shorter paneled doors in the lower section, serpentine apron & simple bracket feet, ca. 1840-50, 39" w., 5' 11" h. (some alterations) **1,495**

Ohio Cherry One-piece Corner Cupboard

Corner cupboard, Federal country-style, cherry, the flat top w/a wide molded cornice above an upper case w/a pair of tall paneled cupboard doors opening to five shelves, a mid-molding above a pair of shorter lower paneled doors, serpentine apron & simple bracket feet, cornice & hinges old replacements, one foot ended out, Ohio, mid-19th c., 24 x 49 5/8", 6' 2 1/4" h. (ILLUS., bottom previous page) **2,185**

Federal Country Corner Cupboard

Two-piece Cherry Corner Cupboard

Corner cupboard, Federal country-style, cherry, two-part construction: the top section w/a deep coved cornice above a single large nine-pane glazed cupboard door w/wooden knob opening to two shelves; the lower section w/a mid-molding above a pair of drawers w/wooden knobs over a pair of paneled cupboard doors w/wooden knobs, scalloped apron & short bracket feet, old dark finish, glued split in cornice, small piece of mid-molding missing, first half 19th c., 23 1/2 x 45 3/4", 6' 6 1/2" h. (ILLUS.) **3,738**

Corner cupboard, Federal country-style, hardwood, two-part construction: a cove-molded cornice above a pair of eight-pane glazed doors opening to three shelves & flanked by applied quarter-round bead molding; the base w/a pair of paneled cupboard doors flanked by half-round bobbin- and knob-turned spindles, vertical yellow pine backboards w/hand-wrought nails, original brass hinges, Buncombe County, North Carolina, 19th c., repairs to proper right bottom door, old refinishing, minor scratches, finish flaws & scattered paint drips, 24 x 52", 7' 6" h. (ILLUS., top next column) **7,040**

Federal Inlaid Corner Cupboard

Corner cupboard, Federal country-style, inlaid cherry, the top w/a cove-molded inlaid cornice above a pair of 6-pane glazed doors framed w/rope & tassel inlay, a medial molding above two paneled doors w/canted corner string inlay, original bracket feet, vertical backboards w/original nails, panes reglazed, hinges possibly replaced, 18 1/2 x 49", 6' 2 1/2" h. (ILLUS.) **9,900**

Corner cupboard, Georgian style, mahogany, two-part construction: the upper section w/a scrolled broken-arch pediment over two tall geometrically glazed doors w/through muntins opening to three shelves, the sides w/raised panel decoration, vertical backboard w/original hand-wrought nails; the lower section w/two frame-and-panel doors on a molded base w/original bracket feet & glue blocks, England, late 18th - early 19th c., old refinishing, interior painted white, minor separations, several dents, 22 x 38", 7' 6" h." h. **3,190**

Unusual Hanging Corner Cupboard

shelves above a small one-door cupboard w/a scallop-cut top flanked by canted corners all above a wide demilune scallop-cut drop apron, old salmon paint bordered w/bluish grey striping, possibly New England, early 19th c., 12 1/2 x 17 1/2", 31" h. (ILLUS.) **2,468**

Victorian Mahogany Corner Cupboard

Corner cupboard, Victorian Rococo substyle, carved mahogany, one-piece construction, the arched & molded cornice centered by a rondel above arrow canted front corners w/carved arched scrolls at the top & base corners flanking a pair of tall four-pane glazed doors opening to three painted shelves above a pair of short paneled lower doors, molded base on scroll-carved bracket feet, attributed to the workshop of William McCracken, New Orleans, ca. 1860-70, 28 1/2 x 40", 7' 2" h. (ILLUS.).. **1,265**

Hanging corner cupboard, painted poplar, the ornate top w/scrolled backboards joined by two small quarter-round

Very Rare Chippendale Hanging Cupboard

Hanging cupboard, Chippendale, walnut, a shaped top back crestboard above the rectangular top w/a deep stepped molded cornice above a single door w/double raised panels & H-form iron handles, small metal knob, narrow flat molded base, locking hidden compartment in top, Pennsylvania, 18th c., 17 3/4 w., overall 30" h. (ILLUS.) **14,340**

Painted Poplar Hanging Cupboard

Hanging cupboard, painted pine, the rectangular top w/a deep flaring & stepped cornice above a pair of paneled cupboard doors opening to three shelves, a small brass pull, old green paint, glued split on right door, 19th c., 10 x 33 3/4", 31 1/4" h. (ILLUS.) **1,093**

Hanging cupboard, painted poplar, a rectangular top w/a flaring molded cornice & a small arched back tab w/a hanging hole, the case w/a single large arched panel door w/lock & brass hinges opening wallpaper-lined interior w/a replaced shelf, distressed exterior black paint, square nail construction, late 18th - early 19th c., 8 1/2 x 17 1/2", 20" h. (tin repair above hanging hole)..................................... **605**

Early Tennessee Jackson Press Cupboard

Jelly (a.k.a. Jackson press) cupboard, Classical style, cherry, the low arched back crest above a rectangular top above a pair of drawers w/early pressed glass knobs projecting over a pair of wide paneled cupboard doors flanked by

freestanding columns, a reeded central stile between the doors, double-knob-turned feet, signed under one drawer & dated 1835, Tennessee, 23 x 44", 46" h. (ILLUS.) **4,025**

Painted Pine Jelly Cupboard

Jelly cupboard, painted poplar, the rectangular top w/a narrow cornice above a single large door w/six glass panes above two lower panels, opening to four shelves, molded base on small disk feet, old red paint, interior w/later blue paint, reconstruction, 19th c., 17 x 43 1/2", 5' 5 1/4" h. (ILLUS.) **1,035**

Simple Pine Jelly Cupboard

Jelly cupboard, pine, the rectangular top above a large single two-panel cupboard door opening to three shelves, low scalloped apron & bracket feet, refinished, some reshaping of aprons, latch replaced, first half 19th c., 16 1/2 x 45", 4' h. (ILLUS.)... **805**

Early South Carolina Linen Press

Linen press, country-style, painted pine, rectangular top w/a deep molded cornice above a single tall two-panel door over a single long drawer all flanked by wide side stiles, bracket feet, retains most of the original paint, Laurens County, South Carolina, first half 19th c., some paint wear & nicks, 14 3/4 x 41 3/8", 6' 2 3/8" h. (ILLUS.) **1,265**

Large Rare Federal Linen Press

Linen press, Federal, inlaid walnut, two-part construction: the upper section w/a rectangular top & deep stepped flaring cornice above a pair of tall two-panel doors w/brass H-hinges & hardware; the lower section w/a mid-molding above a case w/a row of two small drawers & one long drawer above a pair of large drawers, molded base on tall shaped French feet, Pennsyl-

vania, 1780-1810, 25 3/4 x 62 3/4" w., 7' 11 3/4" h. (ILLUS.) **19,120**

Fine English Georgian Linen Press

Linen press, George III style, mahogany, two-part construction: the upper section w/a rectangular top w/a narrow molded cornice above a pair of large paneled cupboard doors opening to a shelved interior; the lower section w/a mid-molding over a pair of drawers over three long graduated drawers all w/pierced brass butterfly pulls, flat base on low shaped bracket feet, England, late 18th c., 25 x 56", 6' 8 1/2" h. (ILLUS.) **3,450**

Georgian Mahogany Linen Press

Linen press, Georgian, mahogany, two-part construction: the upper section w/a rectangular top w/a flaring stepped & dentil-carved cornice over a crotch-grain veneer panel over a pair of tall paneled cupboard doors opening to a compartmented interior; the lower section w/a mid-molding over a pair of drawers over two long drawers all w/oval brasses, scalloped apron on tall French feet, England, late 18th c., 21 1/2 x 48", 7' 3" h. (ILLUS., bottom previous page) **2,990**

Early Two-part Pewter Cupboard

Pewter cupboard, country-style, maple & cherry, two-part construction: the upper section w/a flat top & flaring stepped cornice above a tall open compartment w/two tall shelves, the upper shelf w/a molded strip from side to side; the stepped-out lower section w/a row of three drawers above a row of three paneled cupboard doors all w/wood knobs, simple stile square feet, New England, late 18th - early 19th c., restored, 17 1/2 x 58 3/4", 6' 7" h. (ILLUS.) **4,406**

Early Southern Pie Safe

Pie safe, country-style, pine, rectangular top w/molded cornice above a case w/center two-panel cupboard door flanked by compartments missing their original punched tin or screen wire covering, the lower case w/another two-panel central door flanked by plain side panels, square stile legs, old worn finish, Newberry or Kershaw County, South Carolina, mid-19th c., 19 x 53 1/2", 5' 8 1/4" h. (ILLUS.)..................................... **1,115**

Painted Double-door Pie Safe

Pie safe, hardwood w/old brown paint, the rectangular top above two dovetailed drawers above two doors each w/a large four-section tin, each tin section w/diamond-shaped central medallion w/stars, punched-tin side panels, turned feet, horizontal backboards w/cut nails, Cocke County, Tennessee, scrapes, scuffs & losses to painted surface, 18 1/2 x 54 1/4", 42" h. (ILLUS.) **2,750**

Old Painted Pine Pie Safe

Pie safe, painted pine, single-board rectangular top w/old breadboard ends added above a pair of tall two-panel doors inset w/two pierced-tin panels decorated w/flower designs, two matching tins in each side, flat apron on angled bracket feet, old brown paint, backboards replaced, 19th c., 16 1/2 x 42", 4' 1 5/8" h. (ILLUS.)....................................... **748**

Nice Married Step-back Cupboard

Step-back wall cupboard, country-style, walnut & pine, two-piece construction: the upper section w/a rectangular top w/a wide flaring & slightly angled cornice above a pair of tall eight-pane glazed doors opening to three shelves; the stepped-out lower section w/a pair of drawers w/wooden knobs over a pair of paneled cupboard doors, simple bracket base, refinished, a marriage w/replaced top doors, lower right door restored at hinge rail, 19th c., 20 1/2 x 48", 6' 11" h. (ILLUS.).. **1,093**

Step-back Wall Cupboard

Step-back wall cupboard, country-style, yellow pine, two-part construction: the upper section w/a pitched pediment w/open front above two six-pane glazed doors opening to two shelves; the broad stepped platform base w/a long double-panel door decorated w/chip-carved flowers & vines, scalloped skirt & bracket feet, vertical backboards w/cut nails & circular saw marks, probably Piedmont, North Carolina, mid-19th c., refinished, stains, scratches, chip missing from proper left skirt, 31 x 39 1/2", 7' 1 1/2" h. (ILLUS.).. **3,520**

French Provincial Step-back Cupboard

Step-back wall cupboard, French Provincial, fruitwood, two-part construction: the upper section w/a rectangular top w/a molded cornice above a pair of large cupboard doors w/serpentine-sided rectangular panels w/long brass plates flanking the central stile inlaid w/a starburst, all above a high arched & scroll-edged pie shelf; the stepped-out lower section w/a pair of scroll-carved drawers over a pair of long rectangular doors all flanking a central stile inlaid w/a stylized leaf above a bird on a tree design w/an oval reserve at the center of the serpentine molded apron continuing into short scroll feet, France, early 19th c., 22 x 48", 6' 8" h. (ILLUS.).. **3,450**

Step-back wall cupboard, hardwood, the rectangular top w/a flat flaring cornice above a pair of two-panel cupboard doors, the stepped-out lower section w/two drawers above a pair of two-panel cupboard doors, the drawers w/cut nails, the back w/horizontal tongue-and-groove boards w/cut nails, Texas history, later

Texas Step-back Wall Cupboard

cornice, old red paint w/chips, abrasions & dents, 20 x 45 1/2", 7' 4" h. (ILLUS.)...... **2,200**

French Provincial Hutch Cupboard

Step-back wall hutch cupboard, French Provincial style, fruitwood, two-part construction: the upper section w/a rectangular top w/coved cornice above an open compartment w/a row of turned drop balls above a shelf w/a low spindled front rail

above a matching lower shelf; the lower section w/a pair of drawers w/wooden knobs above a pair of paneled cupboard doors, serpentine apron & curved bracket feet, France, mid-19th c., 21 1/2 x 52 1/2", 6' 4" h. (ILLUS.) **1,840**

Tall French Provincial Cupboard

Step-back wall hutch cupboard, Louis XV-Style Provincial type, fruitwood, two-part construction: the upper section w/a deep flaring cornice widely arched at the center above a conforming leafy scroll & lattice-carved frieze band above a tall arched open central compartment w/a shelf over another smaller open compartment w/serpentine scroll-carved framing, a tall paneled cupboard door at each side ornately carved w/shells, scrolls & quatrefoil; the stepped-out lower section w/a row of three scroll-carved drawers w/simple bail pulls over a large central cupboard door w/an arched panel enclosing a large shell carving & flanked by smaller paneled doors w/scroll carving, a serpentine scroll-carved apron on short scroll feet, ca. 1900, 23 1/2 x 62 1/2", 8' 10" h. (ILLUS.).. **2,760**

Wall cupboard, country-style, painted & decorated poplar, the rectangular top w/a deep flaring cornice cut flat at the right side above a single tall three-paneled door opening to one original & two later shelves, molded case, original red flame graining w/an old coat of overvarnish, Sonnenberg Ward, originally built-in, right side unfinished, 19th c., 20 1/2 x 32 1/4", 6' 1 1/4" h. (ILLUS., top next page) **1,150**

Flame-painted Wall Cupboard

Colorful European Wall Cupboard

Wall cupboard, country-style, painted & decorated, two-part construction: the upper case w/a rectangular top & molded cornice above a frieze band decorated w/carved & painted scrolling foliage on a white ground against a mottled dark green ground, a white upper molding above a pair of tall diamond-paneled cupboard doors w/matching floral designs & green trim & background; the lower section a molded platform base w/another long narrow white-decorated panel against the green ground, on square stile

legs, Europe, mid-19th c., stress crack at upper right hinge, 15 x 41 7/8", 5' 6 1/4" h. (ILLUS.) **633**

Country-style Wall Cupboard

Wall cupboard, country-style, walnut, the rectangular top over a pair of small paneled doors above two larger paneled doors, scalloped skirt w/shaped feet, chamfered panels throughout, original brass hinges, white pine vertical backboards w/cut nails, possibly Piedmont, North Carolina, early 19th c., old refinishing, top w/dents, separations & stains, probably missing molding on back of top, minor chips & scratches, 18 x 42", 4' 1/2" h. (ILLUS.) **2,530**

Short Country Wall Cupboard

Wall cupboard, country-style, walnut, unusual hinged lid on top opening to shallow divided interior, single 6-pane door below w/three interior shelves, old finish, one pane of glass newer, lock escutcheon missing, one lower corner w/split, 10 1/4 x 28 1/2", 33 1/2" h. (ILLUS.) **1,093**

European Provincial Pine Cupboard

Wall cupboard, provincial-style, pine, two-part construction: the upper section w/a rectangular top w/a coved cornice over a pair of tall paneled cupboard doors w/a tall panel above a short panel; the lower section w/a mid-molding over a pair of paneled cupboard doors, molded base on bun front feet, paneled sides, lower section w/a Danish label reading "J.L. Harb---, Odense/JLH No. 3," mid-19th c., 25 x 46", 6' 6" h. (ILLUS.).......................... **1,150**

Welsh cupboard, provincial-style, oak, two-part construction: the upper section w/a rectangular top w/a flaring stepped cornice above a scallop-cut frieze over

Nice Oak Welsh Cupboard

two open compartments centered by a small cupboard w/a square paneled door above a lower open shelf all flanked by scallop-cut sides; the projecting lower section w/a row of two long & a short drawer w/pierced batwing pulls above a double arched & scalloped apron raised on three baluster- and ring-turned supports above an open wide bottom shelf, Britain, 19th c., 16 x 53 1/2", approximately 6' h. (ILLUS.) **1,610**

Desks

Art Deco desk & chair, rosewood & chromed metal, the desk w/a white leather

Fine Art Deco Desk & Chair

Rare Louis Majorelle Art Nouveau Desk

top slightly raised in the center above a pair of small drawers, the narrow side sections in rosewood each w/an open compartment above two small drawers above a flared rectangular base, the chair w/a wide gently curved rosewood back above a squared cushion seat, on squared tapering & slightly curved legs, France, ca. 1925, desk 19 x 40 1/4", 28 1/4" h., chair 31 1/4" h., pr. (ILLUS., bottom previoius page) **11,950**

Art Nouveau desk, gilt-bronze mounted mahogany, "Aux Nenuphars" patt., the rectangular top w/raised undulating back corners mounted w/water lilies & pads in gilt-bronze continuing down the forked rear legs & ending in pad leaf feet, the leather-inset top above an apron w/two drawers w/looped vine & bud pulls above the outswept front legs mounted w/gilt-bronze pond lily buds, vines & leaves, designed by Louise Majorelle, France, ca. 1900, 27 1/4 x 48", 32 1/2" h. (ILLUS., top of page) **47,800**

Baroque Revival style, walnut-finished hardwood, the superstructure w/a scroll-carved crest centered by a carved full-figure putto above an arcaded shelf w/three scroll-carved openings above a deep molding & carved platform behind a central slant top finely carved w/frolicking putti above a pull-out working surface projecting above deep curved brackets carved w/full-figure grotesque beasts & backed by

a panel carved w/a grotesque mask, Italy, late 19th c., 31 1/2 x 47", 5' 2" h. (ILLUS., below).. **3,450**

Ornately Carved Italian Desk

Chippendale-Style Library Desk

Very Rare Chippendale Block-front Desk

Chippendale "block-front" kneehole desk, carved mahogany, the rectangular top w/molded edges & round-fronted blocks above a conforming case w/a long central drawer w/the interior fitted w/dividers above a central recessed & paneled door opening to a shelved interior, flanked by three curved block-front drawers all raised on a molded base & serpentine aprons on tall bracket feet, apparently original butterfly brasses, Massachusetts, ca. 1760-80, 18 1/2 x 32 1/2", 30" h. (ILLUS.) **65,725**

Chippendale slant-front desk, bird's-eye maple, birch & pine, dovetailed construction, a narrow top above a hinged slant front opening to an interior w/six dovetailed drawers & three horizontal letter slots w/some alterations at center section, the base w/four dovetailed drawers w/molded edges & old replaced oval brass

Chippendale Slant-front Desk

pulls, finely scalloped bracket base, late 18th - early 19th c., 17 1/4 x 35 1/2", 41 3/4" h. (ILLUS., top next column) **2,070**

Chippendale-Style library desk, steel-mounted mahogany, the rectangular top w/serpentine molded edges centering an inset gilt-tooled leather top, the front apron fitted w/pairs of small serpentine drawers w/gadrooned bottom edges flanking a single long flat central drawer w/an arched kneehole opening, the opposite side w/blind drawers, raised on cabriole legs w/acanthus-carved knees & ending in scroll feet, England, ca. 1900, 37 1/2 x 64", 30 1/2" h. (ILLUS., top of page) **1,840**

Unusual Colonial Revival Desk

Colonial Revival slant-front bombé desk, mahogany veneer, a narrow rectangular top above the wide hinged slant front opening to a fitted interior above a pair of small square pullouts over the wide bombé case fitted w/three long drawers, serpentine apron & short curved legs w/claw-and-ball feet, original finish, ca. 1900, 20 x 42", 40" h. (ILLUS.) **1,800**

Country Schoolmaster's Desk

Country-style schoolmaster's desk, walnut, two-part construction: the upper section w/a rectangular top w/a deep ogee cornice above a tall arrangement of twelve pigeonholes above a drawer on the left centered by larger open compartments & w/a group of tall letter slots over a drawer on the right; the lower section w/a wide fixed slant top writing surface above an apron w/a row of three drawers, raised on heavy ball-, ring- and baluster-turned legs on ball feet, ca. 1850-1880, 50" w., 5' 3" h. (ILLUS.) **748**

Country Italian Slant-front Desk

Country-style slant-front desk, walnut, a small rectangular slant top w/molded edges opening to an interior well above a casinet w/a single door paneled w/a raised diamond-lattice design, plinth base on bun feet, Italy, mid-18th c., 17 x 24", 42" h. (ILLUS.) **1,035**

Country-style slant-top desk, pine & poplar, mortise-and-tenon construction, a narrow rectangular top over the hinged wide slant lid opening to an interior w/eight cubbyholes, tapered square legs, hand-wrought nails, pit-sawn lumber, possibly original dark red/brown finish, America, 19th c., hinges replaced & reset, missing lock, 23 x 31", 36" h. **990**

English Slant-front Davenport Desk

Davenport desk, mahogany, a low brass gallery on the narrow rectangular raised top above the wide hinged leather-lined slant-top writing surface opening to compartments for stationery in the bird's-eye maple interior, one side of the case fitted w/four pigeonholes opposite four dummy drawer fronts w/pairs of turned wood knobs, plinth base w/extended disk feet on casters, stress cracks, new hinges on slant top, England, mid-19th c., 21 x 21", 33 1/2" h. (ILLUS., bottom previous page) **1,093**

Federal Bow-front Slant-front Desk

Federal "bow-front" slant-front desk, inlaid mahogany & cherry, a narrow rectangular top above a wide hinged slant front centered by an inlaid satinwood diamond panel bordered by rosewood crossbanding & stringing opening to an interior fitted w/eight drawers & seven valanced compartments, the lower bowed case w/a stack of four long graduated cockbeaded drawers bordered by crossbanding above a curved inlaid molded base w/a serpentine apron & tall French feet, replaced butterfly brasses, old refinish, minor imperfections, possibly Worcester County, Massachusetts, ca. 1800, 21 x 38 3/4", 44" h. (ILLUS.) **4,406**

George III slant-front desk, inlaid oak, a narrow rectangular top above a hinged slant top w/banded inlay opening to a gilt-tooled leather writing surface & a variety of small drawers & pigeonholes flanking a central banded door, the case w/four long graduated & inlay-banded drawers w/pierced batwing brasses, molded base on ogee bracket feet, England, late 18th c., 22 x 48", 46" h. (ILLUS., below) **1,840**

Oak George III Slant-front Desk

Georgian-Style Slant-front Desk

Georgian-Style slant-front desk, inlaid mahogany, a narrow rectangular top above the hinged slant front opening to two small hand-dovetailed & cockbeaded drawers flanking prospect door w/six cubbyholes, the case w/three long graduated drawers w/oval brasses, molded base on scroll-cut bracket feet, original brass hinges & pulls, full dust panels, England, probably late 19th or early 20th c., 20 1/2 x 36", 41 1/2" h. (ILLUS.) **990**

French Louis XVI-Style Provincial Writing Desk

Louis XVI-Style Provincial writing desk, fruitwood, the rectangular top widely overhanging an apron fitted w/two fluted drawers w/simple bail pulls, raised on knob- and ring-turned legs centered by fluted columns & ending in knob feet, France, late 19th c., 27 1/2 x 57", 29" h. (ILLUS., top of page).................................. **748**

Unsigned Gustav Stickley Desk

Mission-style (Arts & Crafts movement) fall-front desk, oak, the rectangular top w/a low three-quarters gallery w/gently arched sides w/through mortises above a wide hinged fall front opening to a fitted interior, the lower case w/a pair of narrow drawers above three long graduated drawers all w/hammered brass plate & bail pulls, flat front apron & low arched side cut-outs, fine new finish, unmarked Gustav Stickley, Model 729, early 20th c., 15 x 36 1/2", 45" h. (ILLUS.) **3,738**

Nice 1950s Heywood-Wakefield Desk & Chair

Modern-style desk & chair, birch w/wheat finish, the desk w/a rectangular top above a long top drawer over the knee-hole opening flanked by curve-fronted stacks of three drawers each w/a long narrow curved pull, on short block feet, the matching chair w/two horizontal slats in the back above the upholstered slip seat on squared legs, by Heywood-Wakefield, ca. 1955, desk 24 x 50", 30" h., the set (ILLUS.)................................. **661**

Queen Anne slant-front desk, carved & inlaid cherry, a narrow top above a hinged slant front opening to a fitted interior w/a central star-inlaid drawer flanked by serpentine & blocked tiers of small drawers & further flanked by shaped drawers & pigeonholes, the conforming case fitted w/four long graduated drawers over a molded apron above a shaped central drop, on short cabriole legs ending in pad feet, Connecticut, 1750-70, 20 1/4 x 41", 43" h. **33,460**

Golden Oak Rolltop Desk

Victorian Golden Oak rolltop desk, oak, narrow rectangular top above the paneled S-roll top opening to an interior fitted w/numerous pigeonholes & two small drawers, the case w/a single central drawer over the kneehole opening flanked by a stack of three drawers on one side & four drawers on the other, plinth base, ca. 1900-10, 50" (ILLUS.) **805**

Golden Oak Lady's Slant-front Desk

Victorian Golden Oak lady's slant-front writing desk, Colonial Revival style, oak, a narrow serpentine top crestrail w/carved scrolls above a wide rectangular hinged paneled slant front decorated w/stamped brass decorative border bands above an apron w/a single long drawer, raised on tall slender cabriole legs w/stamped brass mounts at the knees & feet, ca. 1900, 44" w., 32" h. (ILLUS.) **259**

Truly Outstanding American Victorian Renaissance Revival Pedestal Desk

Victorian Renaissance Revival substyle pedestal desk, walnut & burl walnut, the rectangular leather-lined top w/a wide molded edge above a long central drawer w/fine burl, gilt incised lines & a cartouche flanked by raised panels, the two side pedestals each w/an ornate projecting top drawer above a pair of ornately carved & gilt-trimmed columns flanking a stack of three burl-paneled drawers, the sides w/finely paneled upper panels above pairs of large burl panels, the reverse composed of matching blind drawer facings, on bold toupie feet, ca. 1875, 33 1/2 x 62", 29" h. (ILLUS., bottom previous page)... **4,888**

Victorian Renaissance Revival substyle plantation-type desk, walnut, two-part construction: the upper section w/an angular cut-out crown-form crest decorated w/a narrow raised band w/central rondel & leaftip ends above a long narrow shelf over a long molded rectangular panel flanked by cut-out ends above another shelf over the wide flat fold-down front opening to a lined writing surface & a large interior fitted w/drawers, cubby holes & letter slots; the lower section w/a molded edge above an apron w/a pair of drawers raised on turned tapering rod-and ring-turned legs, ca. 1875, 39" w., overall 7' 7" h. (ILLUS., below).................... **863**

Renaissance Revival Plantation Desk

Dining Room Suites

Colonial Revival style: dining table, six chairs, a sideboard & a china cabinet; Jacobean design in walnut & burl walnut,

Colonial Revival 1920s Dining Suite in the Jacobean Design

Colonial Revival Dining Suite with Solid Doors

the china cabinet w/a tall arched top above a geometrically glazed door above a long deep drawer w/banded carving & burl, the sideboard w/similar details & a case w/two long center drawers flanked by end doors, all the pieces raised on heavy turned legs w/very large central knobs & small bun feet all joined by H-stretchers, ca. 1920s, the set (ILLUS., bottom previous page) **2,070**

Colonial Revival style: dining table w/two leaves, six chairs, a sideboard, small server & a china cabinet; Jacobean design in walnut & burl walnut, the case pieces w/flat tops over slightly angled fronts, the sideboard & server w/a pair of arched carved central doors w/ring pulls flanked by slightly angled matching doors, the china cabinet w/a large arched carved door above a long carved drawer all flanked by angled side panels, boldly turned knob-, ring- and block-decorated legs on bun feet, the case pieces w/open base shelves w/serpentine fronts, made in Rockford, Illinois, ca. 1920s, table 45 x 66" plus leaves, sideboard 44" l., the set (ILLUS., top of page)............................. **863**

Rare George Nakashima Dining Room Suite

Heywood-Wakefield 1950s Dining Table & Chair from Set

Modern Style: dining table & four "Mira" chairs; walnut, the table w/a square top supported on a simple pedestal on a cross-form foot, each chair w/a wide curved crestrail above seven spindles over a triangular saddle seat, three simple turned & canted legs, by George Nakashima, ca. 1965, table 26 1/4 x 32", 26" h., chairs 27 1/4" h. (ILLUS., bottom previous page) **14,340**

Modern Style: drop-leaf dining table & six dining chairs; birch w/a champagne finish, the table w/a rectangular top flanked by wide D-form drop leaves & raised on a set of three arched pedestal legs, Model M197G by Heywood-Wakefield, together w/Heywood-Wakefield chairs Model M553A w/a curved back crest above a cross-form splat between the canted stiles above the upholstered seat, squared tapering legs, ca. 1950-53, the set (ILLUS. of part, top of page)................... **431**

Dry Sinks

Nice Country American Cherry Dry Sink

Cherry, the hinged rectangular top opening to a well above a pair of paneled cupboard doors w/brass H-hinges & latches, simple bracket feet, sink missing liner & replaced w/plywood panel, mid-19th c., 20 x 36 3/4", 33 3/4" h. (ILLUS.) **690**

Fine Painted Pine Hutch-type Dry Sink

Painted pine, hutch-style, a raised back w/a long narrow shelf raised on shaped brackets above the long well, the case w/a pair of paneled doors opening to a shelf, old mustard green over the original blue, some scrapes, original cast-iron door latch w/porcelain knob, mid-19th c., 18 1/2 x 43", 40 1/2" h. (ILLUS.) **1,495**

Old Painted Pine Maine Dry Sink

Painted pine, the open rectangular top well above a case w/a single raised panel door w/H-hinges & a metal latch, simple delicate bracket feet, old red wash, first half 19th c., from Maine, replaced hardware, 18 x 37", 33" h. (ILLUS.) **900**

Rare Large & Long Hutch-style Dry Sink

Painted walnut, hutch style, the raised back w/a low arched long crestrail above a narrow shelf over the long zinc-lined well w/curved sides, the case fitted w/two large double-paneled doors w/turned wood knobs & a very small drawer at the top corner of one end, simple bracket feet, old brown over mustard yellow paint, wear & chips to base, mid-19th c., 22 x 70 1/4" l., 47" h. (ILLUS.).. **2,875**

Two-door Country Pine Dry Sink

Pine, the open rectangular top w/slightly angled sides above the case w/a pair of paneled cupboard doors opening to a shelf, flat base on low bracket feet & low arch-cut ends, honey brown patina, second half 19th c., 20 1/2 x 46 1/2", 35 1/2" h. (ILLUS.) **575**

Garden & Lawn

Cast iron unless otherwise noted.

Armchairs, "Laurel" patt., each w/a multi-arched crestrail curving to form end arms all above panels of large fanned leaves, half-round pierced matching seat, canted bar rear legs, figural winged griffin front legs, painted white, pattern registered by the English Coalbrookdale Company in 1875 but was also made in the United States, probably American, late 19th - early 20th c., 27" h., pr. (ILLUS., top next page)... **1,093**

Simple Pine Dry Sink

Pine, a serpentine back rail above a rectangular well on one side & a rectangular work top above a single drawer at the other, a single paneled door in the base w/cast-iron latch w/porcelain knob, serpentine apron & bracket feet raised on casters, second half 19th c., 28 1/2" w., 30 1/2" h. (ILLUS.) **345**

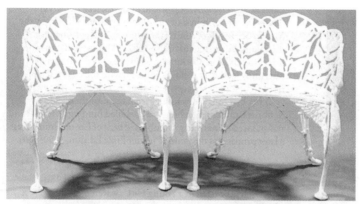

Pair of Laurel Pattern Garden Armchairs

Fine Carved Marble Italian Garden Bench

Bench, carved white marble, the rectangular back w/an arched pediment carved w/griffins flanking an urn, above a fielded panel carved in relief w/scrolling foliage, flanked at the sides by volute-form armrests carved w/a satyr mask & grapevine, on volute supports carved w/acanthus leaves, Italy, last quarter 19th c., 19 3/4 x 51", 45 3/4" h. (ILLUS.) **26,290**

Chaise longue, oak & wrought iron, the adjustable back & long seat tied w/rope webbing & covered w/a pad, half-round & quarter-round oak rod arms flanking the seat, two hard rubber-rimmed wooden spoked wheels at one end, late 19th - early 20th c., 64" l. (ILLUS., next column)
.... **2,629**

Settee, high serpentine long back composed of openwork oak leaves & acorns entwined w/arches, the straight end arms w/alternating ivy & berry & oak leaves & acorns w/figural dog head hand grips, a wooden slat seat above an iron oak leaf

& acorn apron above cabriole legs w/paw feet, painted black, mid-19th c., 32 x 59", 37 1/2" h. (ILLUS. left with matching settee, top next page) **1,265**

Oak & Iron Early Chaise Longue

Two Matching Oak Leaf & Acorn Garden Settees

Settee, high serpentine long back composed of openwork oak leaves & acorns entwined w/arches, the straight end arms w/alternating ivy & berry & oak leaves & acorns w/figural dog head hand grips, a wooden slat seat above an iron oak leaf & acorn apron above cabriole legs w/paw feet, painted black, mid-19th c., 32 x 59", 37 1/2" h. (ILLUS. right with matching settee) **1,495**

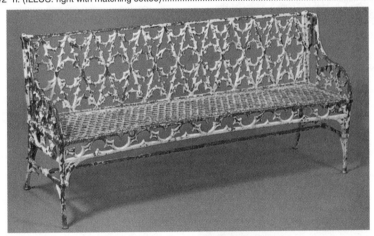

Long Gothic Design Garden Settee

Settee, in the Gothic taste, the long back w/a flat crestrail above a continuous row of Gothic arches & quatrefoils, downswept lacy end arms, grillwork seat w/a narrow Gothic design apron, bar legs, similar to examples by James Yates, Effingham Works, England, second quarter 19th c., white paint w/overall rusting, 19 x 73 1/2", 35" h. (ILLUS., above) **4,370**

Settee, "Laurel" patt., the curved back & side arms composed of arched panels enclosing fanned leafy branches, half-round openwork seat on figural winged griffin front legs, probably American, mid-19th c., old white paint w/some rusting, 31 x 40", 36" h. (ILLUS., next column) **1,265**

Victorian Laurel Pattern Settee

Modern Designer-type Metal Garden Furniture Set

One of Two Oak Leaf & Acorn Settees

Settees, the serpentine crestrail composed of rings of oak leaves & acorns above a matching back, the flat pierced leaf panel arms w/figural dog head hand grips, slatted seat w/a long oak leaf & acorn apron, cabriole legs w/paw feet, painted green, minor rusting, mid-19th c., 21 1/2 x 70 1/2", 34" h., pr. (ILLUS. of one)... **2,415**

Victorian Marble & Iron Garden Table

Table, a rectangular white marble top raised on scrolling lyre-form end legs joined by a pierced leafy scroll stretcher, scroll feet, New York, ca. 1850, 24 x 35 3/4", 28 3/4" h. (ILLUS.) **2,530**

Table & chairs, a round table w/pierced top decorated w/two oval medallions w/raised classical figures above an ornate scrolling apron continuing into four curved cabriole legs, four side chairs each w/an arched tall back w/a bow crest over the wreath-pierced back centered by an oval medallion w/a classical figure, round pierced seat & four scroll-cast cabriole legs ending in hoof feet, painted white w/some rust, second half 19th c., table 24" d., 25" h., the set.......................... **920**

Table & chairs, painted metal, the table w/a round metal meshwork top & curlicue apron raised on a pedestal of tapering & then flaring bar clusters centered by a looped metal ring, each chair w/the tapering back composed of slender bars rolled at the top, armchairs w/matching rolled top arms, round metal mesh seats, simple metal bar chair legs joined by a cross-stretcher, painted white, designed by Mathieu Mategot, ca. 1950, table 39 1/2" d., 29" h., chairs 32" h., the set (ILLUS., top of page).............................. **14,340**

Tete-a-tete, wirework, the S-scroll back composed of slender arched loops of wire above the oblong wire grid seat w/a looped wire apron, S-scroll bar legs joined by an X-stretcher, painted light green, second half 19th c., 21 x 45 1/2", 29" h. (ILLUS., top next page)..................... **633**

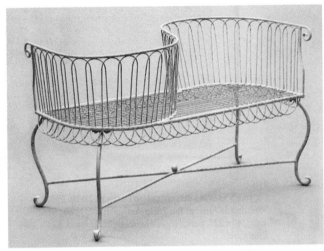

Victorian Serpentine Wirework Tete-a-Tete

Hall Racks & Trees

Victorian Aesthetic Taste Hall Tree

Hall tree, Victorian Aesthetic Movement style, walnut & burl walnut, the tall crenelated pediment & finials above a molded cornice & geometrically pierced frieze, all above an arched beveled mirror flanked by projecting line-incised vertical bars fitted w/turned pegs for hats & coats, the rectangular white marble lower top over a drawer & pierced support flanked by rectangular open supports for umbrellas above the plinth base fitted w/metal drip pans above the blocked feet, ca. 1880, 11 x 36", 7' 7" h. (ILLUS.)............................. **920**

Fine Victorian Bamboo Hall Tree

Hall tree, Victorian bamboo-style, the peaked & arched pediment composed of bamboo rods above a projecting shelf above a pair of lacquered corner panels w/Oriental designs above bamboo rods flanking a tall rectangular mirror, the lower section w/a small stepped-out top above a small drawer over a tall narrow paneled door flanked on each side by racks for umbrellas or walking sticks, ca. 1880s, 12 x 44", 6' 8" h. (ILLUS.).............. **1,495**

Simple Golden Oak Hall Tree

Hall tree, Victorian Golden Oak style, a large upper octagonal section w/wide flat board sides decorated w/a thin center band flanking a large beveled mirror & mounted w/four double metal coat hooks, the lower paneled back above a hinged-top storage compartment flanked by flat shaped open arms w/the supports forming the front legs, ca. 1900, 27" w., 6' 3" h. (ILLUS.) **518**

Scrolling Pierced Oak Hall Tree

Hall tree, Victorian Golden Oak style, oak, the ornate upper section w/a high peaked & scroll-carved center crest & outscrolled carved ears above serpentine pierced sides enclosing a round beveled mirror & above a pierced & scroll-carved splat above a row of slender turned spindles, flat side stiles, mounted w/four ornate cast-brass double coat hooks, shaped open arms on flat S-scroll arm supports above the lift seat over a deep well, flat serpentine front legs & serpentine apron, refinished, ca. 1900, 20 x 30", 7' h. (ILLUS.).. **1,500**

Mirrored Oak Hall Tree with Slats

Hall tree, Victorian Golden Oak style, quarter-sawn oak, a broken-scroll crest rail w/a band of carved scrolls above double flat side stiles flanking a large diamond-form beveled mirror above a tall panel of seven flat slats, flat open arms on square arm supports flanking the wide lift seat, cabriole front legs w/scroll feet, ca. 1900, 17 x 28", 7' h. (ILLUS.)............................... **1,250**

Hall tree, Victorian Renaissance Revival style, walnut & burl walnut, an ornate high crestrail w/a fan-carved peak over a blocked center panel flanked by long pierced scrolls on a molded cornice centered by a large oval burl panel above a long rectangular burl panel above long columnar drops w/pointed drop finials flanking the framework enclosing a tall rectangular mirror above pierced scroll-cut lower brackets w/roundels above a burl panel & rounded side rings above the rectangular white marble top w/rounded corners over a small paneled drawer w/burl panels supported on turned & tapering knob- and rod-turned supports to deep rounded base side panels holding the cast-iron drip pans, fitted w/six iron hooks, ca. 1875 (ILLUS., top next page) **1,950**

High-crested Walnut Hall Tree

Fancy Renaissance Revival Hall Tree

Hall tree, Victorian Renaissance Revival substyle, walnut & burl walnut, the tall back w/a large shell- and scroll-carved crest centered by a large cabochon above & flanked by a pedimented crest w/a molded cornice above a burled & scroll-cut frieze band continuing down the sides w/narrow raised burl panels all mounted w/six long coat pegs & surrounding a large arched mirror w/a raised molded border, shaped raised burl panels below the mirror & above a narrow rectangular white marble top above a single long narrow drawer w/pear-shaped drop pulls supported on slender columnar supports flanked by C-scroll side bars, the oblong platform base w/round cast metal drip pans at the sides & a wide incurved central apron, ca. 1875, 14 x 48", 7' 8" h. (ILLUS.)........................... **1,208**

Simple Victorian Radiating Hall Tree

Hall tree, Victorian Renaissance Revival substyle, walnut, the upper section in a sunburst form w/seven radiating arms each fitted w/a peg & centered by a small round mirror, the tall slender double-vase form support also fitted near the top w/a single peg & below w/a C-form bar for umbrellas w/two slender supports above the rectangular base fitted w/a metal drip pan, ca. 1875, 6' 6" h. (ILLUS.).................... **259**

Love Seats, Sofas & Settees

Chaise longue, Louis XV-Style, carved giltwood, one end w/a caned back w/a gently arched crestrail centered w/shell carving & flanked by scrolling foliage, low curved caned arms w/acanthus leaf grips, on a scroll-carved & molded apron raised on carved cabriole legs ending in scroll feet & joined by U-form stretchers, w/a tapestry cushion, France, late 19th - early 20th c., 30 x 64", 39 1/2" h. .... **2,990'**

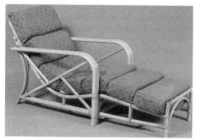

Modernist Style Bamboo Chaise Longue

Chaise longue, Modernist style, a bent
bamboo frame w/long curved back & seatrail flanked by round-fronted arms,
bamboo rod framing, ca. 1940s-50s,
w/upholstered cushion, 64" l. (ILLUS.)......... **144**

Daybed, Louis XV-Style, parcel-giltwood,
each end w/an upright scrolling crestrail
continuing to scrolling stiles & upholstered sides above a scalloped floral and
molded apron continuing to cabriole legs
w/scrolling toes, the scalloped siderails
also upholstered in a rose & white floral &

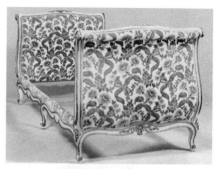

Louis XV Style Upholstered Daybed

ribbon velvet fabric, France, late 19th c.,
36 x 75", 36" h. (ILLUS.) **633**

Daybed, Louis XVI-Style, polychromed
wood, the matching head- and footboard
w/arched crests flanked by small pineapple finials over currently velvet-uphol-
stered panels, joined by molded polychrome rails, France, late 19th c.,
32 x 75", 35" h. (ILLUS., below)............... **2,530**

Louis XVI-Style Polychromed Wood Daybed

Louis XVI-Style Upholstered Beechwood Daybed

Rare Belter Henry Clay Pattern Meridiennes

Daybed, Louis XVI-Style, upholstered beechwood, the matching head- and footboard w/an arched molded crestrail & sides enclosing upholstered panels, the flat seatrails centered by small carved panels, raised on short tapering fluted legs, France, late 19th c., 39 x 78", 38" h. (ILLUS., bottom previous page) **1,610**

Rare Belter Rosewood Meridienne

Meridienne, Victorian Rococo substyle, carved & laminated rosewood, the high arched back w/an ornate floral-carved crest atop undulating rails that taper down to form one arm & a partial back section above the long upholstered seat w/a rounded end & serpentine molded seatrails, raised on demi-cabriole legs, the "Rosalie without Grapes" pattern by John H. Belter, New York City, ca. 1855, 36 1/2" h. (ILLUS.) **3,910**

Meridiennes, Victorian Rococo substyle, carved & laminated rosewood, the high arched upholstered side & back at one end topped by an ornately carved crestrail w/a floral crest above an inverted C-scroll enclosing shell carving, the crestrail composed of C- and S-scrolls continuing down around the tufted back & end arm, long oval upholstered seat w/a molded serpentine seatrail raised on demi-cabriole legs ending in scroll feet on casters, Henry Clay patt., attributed to John Henry Belter, New York, ca. 1855, 26 x 38", 36 1/2" h., pr. (ILLUS., top of page) **11,500**

Fine Quality Classical Philadelphia Recamier

Rare French Art Deco Macassar Ebony Settee

Recamier, Classical style, carved mahogany, the long stepped serpentine backrail carved w/a foliate design & w/a C-scroll above the low upholstered back, one end w/a high S-scroll upholstered arm w/a bolster & a carved reeded & leaf-carved arm support continuing down to the long rounded flat seatrail terminating in a lower outswept S-scroll end arm, raised on ornately carved scrolling figural dolphin front legs, an upholstered cushion seat, possibly by Anthony Quervelle, Philadelphia, ca. 1820-30, 22 x 72", 31" h. (ILLUS., bottom previous page) **4,183**

Settee, Art Deco, upholstered Macassar ebony, the long gently arched wooden crestrail above a tufted back flanked by rolled upholstered arms w/flat heavily grained front supports continuing into simple shaped front legs, the scalloped seatrail connected by four flat front legs, long cushion seat, made by Sue et Mare, France, ca. 1925, 27 x 75", 37 1/2" h. (ILLUS., top of page) **71,700**

Settee, Art Nouveau style, mahogany marquetry, the simple narrow crestrail above a three-section back composed of narrow loop stiles alternating w/tapering serpentine splats decorated w/ornate leafy marquetry designs, shaped molded open arms above the long upholstered seat on a flat seatrail & square tapering legs joined by a high slender H-stretcher, designed by Louise Majorelle, France, ca. 1905, 19 x 42 1/2", 38" h. (ILLUS.) **5,378**

Arts & Crafts Settee with Motto

Settee, Arts & Crafts style, oak, the tall back w/a wide flat crestrail carved w/the motto "Rest Ye And Thankful Be" above a solid back panel flanked by raised side arms w/small arched rests flanking the seat w/a hinged lid over a storage compartment, paneled ends w/stiles forming the legs, early 20th c., 18 x 42", 43" h. (ILLUS.) **949**

Fine Majorelle Art Nouveau Settee

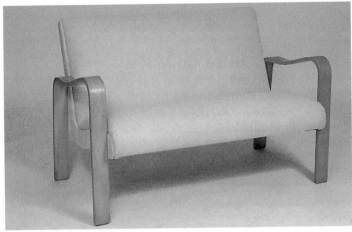

Thonet Laminated Birch Modern Settee

Settee, Modern style, laminated & bent birch, the rectangular upholstered & slightly angled back above the rolled upholstered seat flanked by arched & undulating flat birch one-piece legs & arms, after Alvar Alto, made by Thonet, New York, ca. 1950s, 60" l., 30" h. (ILLUS., top of page) **201**

Queen Anne-Style Winged Settee

Very Ornate Chinese Carved Settee

Settee, Oriental style, carved & stained hardwood, the high arched back elaborately carved & pierced w/entwined large birds & serpents w/two serpents continuing to form the end arms above the pierce-carved seat w/a serpentine seatrail above a pierced bat-carved seatrail raised on five cabriole legs w/scroll feet, China, ca. 1880, minor losses, 26 x 57", 44 1/2" h. (ILLUS.) **2,875**

Settee, Queen Anne-Style, the wide high & gently arched upholstered back flanked by flared wings above rolled arms flanking a two-cushion seat above the upholstered seatrail, raised on simple front cabriole legs w/snake feet, flat canted rear legs, some fabric wear, early 20th c., 51" l. (ILLUS., next colunn) **173**

English Country Pine Settee

Settee, Victorian country-style, pine, the long back w/a bamboo-turned crestrail rod above the two-panel solid back flanked by heavy bamboo-turned back stiles w/bulbous ring-turned finials, the closed side arms w/turned faux bamboo trims flanking the padded seat w/a deep front seatrail trimmed w/half-round bamboo-turned rods, flat front stile armrests & legs, England, late 19th c., 20 x 50", 39" h. (ILLUS.) **1,955**

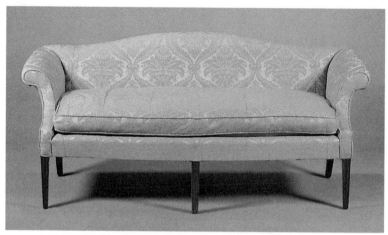

Chippendale-Style Upholstered Camel-back Sofa

Sofa, Chippendale-Style, mahogany, the long serpentine upholstered back flanked by high upholstered scrolled arms above the long cushion seat & upholstered seatrail, raised on six square tapering legs, old repair to one rear leg, restorations & alterations, late 19th c., 73 1/2" l., 33 1/2" h. (ILLUS.) **1,265**

Restrained Classical Mahogany Sofa

Sofa, Classical, carved mahogany & mahogany veneer, the rounded scrolling raised central back crestrail continuing above the shaped upholstered back flanked by incurved upholstered scrolling arms ending in molded terminals & w/bolsters, the half-round straight seatrail ending in blocked ends raised on outswept leaf-carved legs ending in paw feet on casters, some veneer chips, arm joints slightly loose, ca. 1835, 84 1/2" l., 38" h. (ILLUS.) **1,150**

Scroll-armed Classical Sofa

Sofa, Classical, mahogany, the long flat crestrail flanked by leaf-carved scrolls over the upholstered back flanked by high scrolled arms w/leaf-carved supports continuing down to form the flat seatrail, on carved paw feet w/large wing-carved returns, on casters, refinished, new upholstery, ca. 1840s, 24 x 72", 36" h. (ILLUS.) **950**

Early Federal Mahogany Upholstered Sofa

Sofa, Federal, mahogany & mahogany veneer, the long narrow gently arched veneered crestrail above the upholstered back continuing into shaped reeded arm framing above upholstered arms & ending in baluster-turned reeded columns above bird's-eye maple veneer panels flanking the long cushion seat & upholstered seatrail, raised on four ring- and rod-turned tapering reeded front legs w/peg feet, canted squared rear legs, old refinish, feet repairs, Massachusetts or New Hampshire, early 19th c., 32 1/4" h. (ILLUS., top of page) **2,820**

Sofa, Georgian-Style, the high rectangular back composed of four caned panels divided by three wide splats painted in polychrome w/classical figural & floral vignettes & drapery swags, caned arms w/baluster-turned arm supports above the long caned seat, decorated flat seatrail on six square tapering decorated legs on casters, England, early 20th c., 71" l. **3,680**

Sofa, Louis XV-Style Provincial type, fruitwood, the long upholstered back w/a serpentine floral-carved crestrail continuing to form the back frame flanked by padded open arms w/incurved arm supports, the long upholstered seat w/a serpentine three-section floral-carved seatrail raised on four cabriole front legs ending in scroll feet on pegs, France, late 19th c., 25 x 74", 42" h. (ILLUS., bottom of page) **2,760**

Sofa, Louis XVI-Style, rosewood, a gently curved carved crestrail on the long upholstered back, padded open arms on acanthus-carved incurved arm supports, the long upholstered seat w/a bowed seatrail on four tapered & reeded legs, France, late 19th c., front legs w/repair & ending out, proper right front leg rebuilt about 4", minor stains to upholstery, 27 x 43", 72" l. **660**

Louis XV-Style Provincial Fruitwood Sofa

Sofa, Victorian Rococo substyle, mahogany, an unusual ornate back w/an oval balloon panel at one end enclosed by a wide looping pierce-carved frame beside a low arched & boldly pierced leafy scroll-carved central section connecting to the simple high arched molding around a high tufted back section, a rolled closed upholstered arm at one end & an open padded arm at the other, incurved arm supports flanking the long serpentine-fronted seat w/a conforming seatrail centered by a carved flower, on demi-cabriole front legs on casters, refinished, ca. 1855, 24 x 68", 36" h. **2,500**

Double-chairback Rococo Sofa

Sofa, Victorian Rococo substyle, mahogany, double-chair-back style w/tufted upholstery, two high balloon-shaped end sections w/high pierced & scroll-carved crestrails continuing down to the low arched center section w/another high pierced & scroll-carved crest, low upholstered half-arms on incurved arm supports, long serpentine seat w/simple conforming seatrail, on demi-cabriole front legs on casters, old refinish, older upholstery, ca. 1850s, 26 x 62", 40" h. (ILLUS.)... **1,600**

Rococo Sofa with Carved Birds

Sofa, Victorian Rococo substyle, walnut, the long pierce-carved crestrail centered by a pair of facing birds w/nest of eggs & flowering leafy scrolls curving down around the tufted upholstered back, open padded arms w/incurved arm supports, long upholstered seat w/a deep scalloped scroll-carved apron on semi-cabriole

front legs, refinished, ca. 1850s, 31 x 71", 41" h. (ILLUS.) **3,500**

Fine Decorated Country Wagon Seat

Wagon seat, country-style, painted pine, double-back style, each ladder-back back section w/three graduated slats & flanked by a flat shaped open arm on a ring- and baluster-turned front support continuing into the turned front leg, woven rush seat w/front tacked rail, triple turned front & side stretchers, original red paint w/blue medallions on the crestrail & a lady w/parasol, yellow line borders, edge wear, one arm w/glued split, mid-19th c., 16 1/2 x 34 1/2", 34 1/2" h. (ILLUS.) **1,495**

Mirrors

One of Two Chippendale Revival Mirrors

Chippendale Revival style, mahogany & mahogany veneer, the ornate scroll-carved crestrail centered by a gilt Prince of Wales plumes design, the long rectangular mirror within a raised molding, the ornate scroll-carved base rail centered by a pierced gilt shell, glued splits & old restorations w/regilding, late 19th c., 22 1/2 x 43 1/2", pr. (ILLUS. of one, bottom previous page) **2,185**

Chippendale wall mirror, mahogany, the gilded broken swan's-neck crest terminating in carved rosettes & centering an urn finial issuing flowers, the rectangular mirror in a narrow frame w/gilt borders & flanked by pierce-carved gilt floral drops, an ornate scroll-carved base drop w/shaped ears, American or English, 1760-80, 22 1/2 x 49 1/2" **6,573**

Philadelphia Chippendale Wall Mirror

Chippendale wall mirror, mahogany, the high arched & scroll-cut crest above a tall rectangular mirror plate above the arched scroll-cut bottom crest, old surface, minor imperfections, John Elliot Jr., Philadelphia, 1796-1804, 18 1/4 x 38" (ILLUS.) **2,115**

Chippendale-Style Wall Mirror

Chippendale-Style wall mirror, mahogany, the high arched scroll-carved top crest centered by a pierced circle enclosing a gilt carved scroll, the tall rectangular mirror plate framed by a narrow molding & thin gilt liner, the base w/a scroll-carved drop crest, America, early 20th c., 21 x 39" (ILLUS.) **719**

Classical wall mirror, gilt gesso, rectangular w/a split baluster frame joining corner block rosettes & enclosing an upper rectangular molded tablet w/a grape cluster above the rectangular mirror, probably Massachusetts, ca. 1825, 16 1/2 x 36" (some regilding) **353**

Classical wall mirror, painted & decorated wood, rectangular frame w/applied split-balusters headed by corner rosettes, a rectangular reverse-painted landscape scene in the top panel above the rectangular mirror, ca. 1840, 12 x 20 1/2" **940**

Classical-Style Buffet Mirror

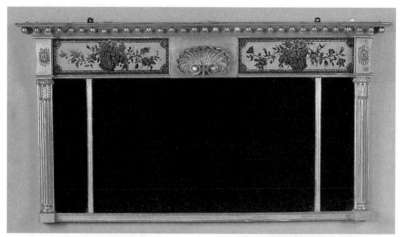

Fine Giltwood & Gesso Federal Overmantel Mirror

Classical-Style buffet mirror, gilt gesso, wide rectangular frame divided into three panels, half-column rails w/florette corner bosses, America, late 19th or early 20th c., traces of original gilding, losses & chips, replaced mirrors, 27 x 64" (ILLUS., bottom previous page) **605**

Federal overmantel mirror, giltwood & gilt gesso, the long narrow molded cornice applied w/a band of small drop balls above a frieze band centered by a large molded gilt shell flanked by églomisé tablet w/gilt on white baskets of flowers above the three-part mirror flanked by top corner blocks over half-round reeded side columns, narrow molded base rail, England or America, early 19th c., restoration, 55 1/2", 29 1/2" h. (ILLUS., top of page) **3,408**

Federal wall mirror, carved giltwood & gesso, a large spread-winged eagle finial on a rectangular molded plinth fitted w/a small églomisé tablet flanked by figural corner urns above the narrow molded & stepped cornice w/applied balls above a larger rectangular églomisé tablet w/ovolo corners & decorated w/a building in a landscape in a central oval against a white ground, above the rectangular mirror flanked by slender reeded columns w/Corinthian capitals on square plinths w/lion heads, restoration, possibly New York City, ca. 1810-15, 24" w., 5' h. (ILLUS., next column) **19,975**

Exceptional Federal Wall Mirror

Ornate Louis XVI-Style Tall Mirror

Louis XVI-Style overmantel mirror, painted & parcel-gilt beechwood, the wide flat rectangular frame carved at the top center w/a large leaf & wreath swag w/ribbons below a coronet, long arrow gilt-lined side panels topped by gilt-carved floral clusters & carved at the bottom w/gilt flower-filled urns, ropetwist inner gilt molding around the mirror, France, ca. 1900, 46" w., 6' 4" h. (ILLUS.) **3,680**

Louis XVI-Style wall mirror, giltwood, the arched crest centered by a shell-and-acanthus cast openwork crest flanked by corner scrolls w/bird finials, the arched mirror surrounded by an annulated slip, mirrored panels & an egg-and-dart-molded frame, France, late 19th c., 60 1/2 x 94" (ILLUS.) **3,450**

Louis XVI-Style Delicate Mirror

Louis XVI-Style wall mirror, giltwood, the large narrow lappet-carved oval frame decorated across the top w/delicate carved floral swags joined at the top center by a finial carved w/images of birds & floral sprigs, France, late 19th c., 41 x 60" (ILLUS.) **2,530**

Ornate Louis XVI-Style Mirror

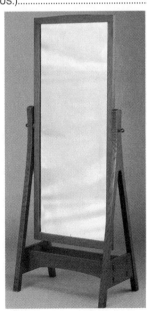

Very Rare Gustav Stickley Cheval Mirror

Roycrofters Mission Oak Wall Mirror

Mission-style (Arts & Crafts movement) cheval mirror, oak, the tall narrow oak frame enclosing the rectangular mirror swiveling between tall wishbone legs joined by wide arched stretchers mortised through the sides & w/iron hardware, fine original finish, large red decal label of Gustav Stickley, Model 914, four small repaired holes on corners, 17 x 28", 5' 9" h. (ILLUS., bottom previous page) **21,850**

Mission-style (Arts & Crafts movement) wall mirror, oak, the wide flat rectangular frame enclosing a long horizontal mirror, two hanging chains at the top, the sides & bottom rail mounted w/six iron coat hooks, unmarked but attributed to the Roycrofters, 30 x 50" (ILLUS., top of page) **2,990**

Napoleon III Mirror with Urn Finial

Napoleon III overmantel mirror, giltwood, the tall narrow rectangular molded frame topped by an urn finial flanked by laurel leaf garlands & oak leaf sprays, France, third quarter 19th c., 46 x 78 3/4" (ILLUS.) **920**

Early French Neoclassical Mirror

Neoclassical wall mirror, rosewood-inlaid hardwood, a wide flat rectangular frame w/each corner inlaid w/delicate rosewood scrolls, later mirror plate, France, first quarter 19th c., 13 3/4 x 17" (ILLUS.) **920**

Neoclassical-Style entryway mirror, gilt & black-painted gesso, the high, widely flaring & stepped cornice w/blocked corners decorated w/a top leaf band over dentil & gadrooned bands, a blocked frieze band in black w/ornate gilt leafy scrolls in the central panel & rosette side blocks, the sides molded in full-relief w/large grotesque male caryatids on tapering bellflower-trimmed pilasters, the wide blocked & stepped-out base w/a black band trimmed w/a molded gilt cartouche & scrolls, late 19th c., very large floorsize **1,750**

English Rococo Giltwood Wall Mirror

Rococo wall mirror, carved giltwood, the ornate undulating & scrolling outer frame topped by a figural spread-winged bird finial, the surface of the asymmetrical mirror overlaid w/interlocked scrolls w/a small lattice panel near the bottom, in the style of Thomas Johnson, England, third quarter 18th c., 31 1/2" w., 5' h. (ILLUS.).. **6,900**

20th Century Italian Wall Mirror

Rococo-Style wall mirrors, giltwood, the wide flat frame composed of slender leaf-

carved giltwood rails enclosing long mirror panels & framing the rectangular mirror plate, Italy, early 20th c., 43 x 57", pr. (ILLUS. of one)... **2,530**

Late Victorian Venetian Mirror

Venetian wall mirror, the tall shield-form mirrored frame composed of panels of floral- and leaf-engraved designs below the tall scroll & cartouche crest w/further engraving, enclosing a conforming unengraved mirror, Italy, ca. 1900, 24 x 47" (ILLUS.)... **805**

Nice Victorian Eastlake Pier Mirror

Victorian Eastlake substyle pier mirror, walnut & burl walnut, the large projecting top cornice w/sawtooth edge above stepped bands & edge blocks decorated w/line-incised details above the tall rectangular mirror w/a gilt liner flanked by narrow reeded stiles w/rondel blocks, the base w/a small projecting central shelf on carved supports against a burled back panel w/additional line-incised decoration, lower shelf missing marble top, ca. 1880, 32" w., 8' 11 1/2" h. (ILLUS., bottom previous page) **690**

Giltwood Victorian Rococo Overmantel Mirror

Victorian Rococo substyle overmantel mirror, carved giltwood, the wide & deep rectangular frame molded & carved overall w/scrolls & leaf bands, second half 19th c., 65" w., 7' 7" h. (ILLUS.) **2,530**

Fine Victorian Overmantel Mirror

Victorian Rococo substyle overmantel mirror, giltwood, the tall arched ropetwist-carved frame topped by a large pierced scroll-carved crest flanked by floral swags, the bottom corners w/large ornate carved scrolls, France, third quarter 19th c., 46" w., 6' 9" h. (ILLUS.)............................. **1,610**

Victorian Rococo Pier Mirror

Victorian Rococo substyle pier mirror, walnut, the tall molded arched frame w/a tall pierce-carved crest of scrolls & fruit trimmed in gold, scroll-carved base corner brackets, original dark finish, ca. 1870, 20 x 48" (ILLUS.) **600**

Victorian Rococo Wall Mirror

Victorian Rococo substyle wall mirrors, gilt gesso, rectangular wide frame w/elaborate scroll decoration & shell, bead & scroll corner work, Europe, 19th c., gilding restored, several chips & losses, replaced mirrors, 47 1/4 x 57 1/2", pr. (ILLUS. of one).. **3,190**

Parlor Suites

Settee from Rare Art Deco Parlor Suite

Art Deco: settee & two armchairs; upholstered giltwood, each w/an arched tufted upholstered back w/a narrow giltwood crestrail continuing down to form the low upholstered arms, deep cushion seat above a curved upholstered seatrail w/a giltwood band, on tapering reeded giltwood feet, designed by Maurice Dufrene, France, ca. 1927, settee, 52 1/2" l., 34 1/2" h., the set (ILLUS. of settee) **23,900**

Empire-Style: sofa, two open-arm armchairs & two side chairs; ormolu-mounted mahogany, each piece w/a rolled crestrail flanked by molded stiles w/ormolu leaf mounts flanking the raised upholstered back panel, squared open arms w/large figural gilt sphinx armrests above the over-upholstered seats, the flat seatrails w/a slender ormolu leaf band mount w/corner rosettes above front legs formed by winged gilt griffins & ending in a gilt paw foot, square canted rear legs, France, late 19th c., sofa 63" l., the set (ILLUS., bottom of page) **26,290**

Louis XVI-Style: settee, two armchairs & two side chairs; giltwood, the settee w/a rectangular upholstered back within a beaded & ribbon-carved narrow frame w/ribbon crest raised above the long rectangular seat flanked by squared padded open arms, narrow beaded seat rail, round tapering stop-fluted legs, matching chairs w/square backs, France, late 19th c., settee 52" l., the set **2,300**

Louis XVI-Style: settee & two armchairs; walnut, the settee w/a long oval upholstered back w/a narrow husk-carved frame raised above the long upholstered seat flanked by padded open arms, husk-carved seat rail raised on round tapering stop-fluted legs, matching armchairs w/oval backs, France, early 20th c., settee 51" l., the set **1,035**

Outstanding Empire-Style Ormolu-mounted Mahogany Parlor Suite

Marked Heywood-Wakefield Set

Modern style: two armchairs & a corner table; bent ashwood w/faux bamboo turnings, each w/a light framework enclosing a square back cushion & seat cushion & supported on a box stretcher base w/U-form front stretchers, the two-tier table w/an incurved upper shelf above the round-cornered top supported on faux bamboo legs joined by curved stretchers & a lower shelf, marked by Heywood-Wakefield, ca. 1955, the set (ILLUS.).. **316**

Rare Signed Pottier Stymus Victorian Parlor Suite

Victorian Renaissance Revival: sofa & armchair; ormolu-mounted ebonized wood, the sofa w/a raised central tufted back section w/a narrow arched crestrail centered by a carved shell crest all flanked by the lower curved upholstered back sections ending in closed arms w/gilt-bronze & metal putto busts & leaves flanking the long tufted upholstered seat on a gently curved seatrail w/gilt incised trim & a central drop, on tapering front legs ending in hoof-style feet, square canted rear legs all on casters, the matching armchair w/the crestrail centered by a round copper-plated panel flanked by a small recumbent gilt-bronze figural putto, worn original tufted upholstery, signed by Pottier Stymus, New York, New York, ca. 1875, sofa 70" l., 36 1/2" h., two pcs. (ILLUS.) **4,600**

Ornate Victorian Rococo Sofa from Large Set

Victorian Rococo: sofa, two armchairs & four side chairs; carved mahogany, the triple-back sofa w/two large round tufted upholstered panels flanking a lower oval tufted upholstered panel, all framed & joined by ornately pierce-carved scrolls & flowers, shaped padded open arms on scrolled arm supports above the long upholstered seat, a serpentine scroll-carved seatrail centered by a C-scroll & blossoms reserve, on S-scroll front legs ending in paw feet on casters, Eastern United States, ca. 1860, sofa 85" l., 50" h., the set (ILLUS. of sofa) **4,140**

Triple-back Rococo Sofa from a Large Suite

Victorian Rococo style: sofa, two armchairs & four side chairs; carved mahogany, the triple-back sofa w/two large vertical oval tufted upholstery back panels flanking a matching horizontal oval panel, each panel w/an arched pierced & floral-carved crest w/scrolling pierced-carved panels between the panels, padded open arms on S-scroll arm supports above the long upholstered seat w/a serpentine seatrail w/undulating molding & a central floral-carved cluster, S-scrolled front legs ending in paw feet, square canted rear legs all on casters, ca. 1860, sofa 85" l., 4' 2" h., the set (ILLUS. of sofa) **4,600**

Nice Signed Heywood-Wakefield Wicker Set

Wicker: loveseat & armchair; each piece w/a wide tightly woven rolled crestrail curving down to form the outswept rolled arms over tightly woven sides, the upper back w/a padded brown leather panel over a tightly woven panel, leather-upholstered seats, deep tightly woven & gently arched aprons, original natural finish, both signed w/a Heywood-Wakefield plaque, early 20th c., loveseat 25 x 41 1/2", 36 1/2" h., 2 pcs. (ILLUS., top of page) **1,380**

Screens

Very Rare Brandt Art Deco Firescreen

Firescreen, Art Deco, wrought iron, a gently arched square bar framework enclosing alternating thick flat vertical bars & pairs of slender bars, all centered by a large openwork oval enclosing a cluster of pine cones & pine bough, slightly arched trestle feet, designed by Edgar Brandt, ca. 1925, 12 1/2 x 35 5/8", 32 7/8" h. (ILLUS.)................................. **33,460**

Fine French Art Nouveau Firescreen

Firescreen, Art Nouveau, "Fougeres" patt., carved giltwood, the upright rectangular molded framework w/gently incurved sides, molded tightly scrolled fern leaves at the top corners & along the bottom edge, trestle base w/curled fern leaf feet, upholstered w/gold & white Art Nouveau floral fabric, designed by Louis Majorelle, France, 1905, 23" w., 40 1/4" h. (ILLUS.)
.... **9,560**

Rare Arts & Crafts Metal & Wood Screen

Folding screen, two-fold, Oriental style, hardwood, lacquer & carved ivory, each rectangular panel w/an arched crest above a panel decorated w/three rondels, the large framed central panel decorated w/inlaid lacquer & ivory & horn scenes of exotic birds & bamboo, lower rectangular pierce-carved foliate panels, simple bracket feet, probably China, ca. 1900, some losses, overall 68" w., 6' 1" h. (ILLUS., next column) **604**

Folding screen, three-fold, Arts & Crafts style, walnut & hammered copper, the wooden framework carved overall w/geometric & block designs, each tall copper panel hammered w/a different motif, the left panel w/buckeye tree leaves, the center panel w/palm leaves & the right panel w/ sycamore leaves, Cincinnati Art, metalwork attributed to Mary Louise McLaughlin, excellent condition, late 19th c., overall 66" w., 6' h. (ILLUS., top of page) **6,900**

Nicely Inlaid Oriental Folding Screen

Early Neoclassical Marquetry Four-fold Screen

Folding screen, four-fold, Neoclassical style, marquetry, each tall panel decorated overall w/delicate inlaid designs including floral swags w/bows, clusters of musical trophies & floral wreaths, the narrow frames w/ropetwist carving, brass hinges, Europe, early 19th c., some cracking & crazing, old touch-up, some gesso loss, open 92" w., 6' 10" h. (ILLUS., top of page) **4,600**

Ornate Pierce-carved Rosewood Screen

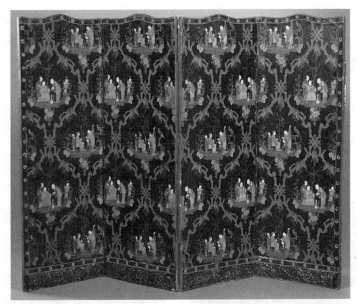

French Restauration Screen

Folding screen, four-fold, Oriental style, pierced & carved rosewood, each panel w/an arched crest pierced w/scrolling grapevines above two smaller & one tall central pierce-carved panel w/various floral & rosette motifs including grapevines & grape clusters, the flat stiles & cross stretchers lightly carved w/additional designs, some damage to one crest & other losses & repairs, ca. 1900, possibly Anglo-Indian, overall 80" w., 6' h. (ILLUS., bottom previous page) **575**

Folding screen, four-fold, Restauration style, painted paper, the four wide panels slightly arched at the top & painted w/an overall Chinoiserie design of figural vignettes enclosed by gilt scrolls, all on a black ground, France, first quarter 19th c., each panel 22 1/2" w., overall 4' 3 3/4" h. (ILLUS., top of page) **1,840**

Pole screen, mahogany & black lacquer, the long rectangular lacquer adjustable screen decorated w/gilt & florals on the black ground, raised on a baluster- and ring-turned slender standard on a triangular platform base on bun feet, England, second half 19th c., 4' 5" h. (ILLUS. left with other lacquered pole screen, next column) **518**

Pole screen, mahogany & black lacquer, the long rectangular lacquer adjustable screen decorated w/gilt & florals & birds on the black ground, raised on a baluster- and ring-turned slender standard on a triangular platform base on bun feet, England, second half 19th c., 4' 5" h. (ILLUS. right with other lacquered pole screen, next column) **518**

Two Victorian Lacquered Pole Screens

Secretaries

Chippendale Secretary-Bookcase in Walnut

Very Fine Chippendale Secretary

Chippendale "oxbow serpentine-front" secretary-bookcase, cherry, two-part construction: the upper section w/a rectangular top over a deep stepped flaring cornice above a pair of serpentine-edged paneled doors opening to adjustable shelves & above two small exterior candle slides; the lower section w/a hinged slant-top opening to an interior w/eight small drawers & ten valanced compartments above a case w/four long graduated drawers all w/a double-arched carved top or front, a conforming molded base on scroll-cut ogee bracket feet, old bail pulls & keyhole escutcheons & old surface, probably Massachusetts, ca. 1780, imperfections, 21 x 41", 7' 1/2" h. (ILLUS.)..................... **17,625**

Chippendale secretary-bookcase, walnut, two-part construction: the top w/molded & dovetailed cornice over two doors w/inlaid kite escutcheon, over two pull-out candle boards, built-up base molding, back w/four chamfered panels; the dovetailed base w/interior w/crotch-figure prospect door w/two dovetailed drawers behind each flanked by four dovetailed drawers, four cubbyholes above w/shaped moldings, fall board above four graduated, dovetailed & lipped drawers, hand-cut nails throughout, vertical pine backboards w/rose-head nails, America, both pieces (marriage) w/old refinishing, two cubbyhole moldings off, lock & hinges on fall board replaced, old replaced ogee bracket feet w/repairs & restorations, several backboards loose, 23 x 42", 7' 4" h. (ILLUS.).......................... **2,420**

Simple Country Pine Secretary-Bookcase

Simple Classical Secretary-Bookcase

Classical secretary-bookcase, mahogany & mahogany veneer, two-part construction: the upper section w/a rectangular top w/a deep ogee cornice above a pair of two four-pane glazed doors opening to wooden shelves above a pair of shallow drawers w/original pressed glass pulls; the lower projecting section w/a hinged fold-out writing surface above a case of three long graduated drawers all w/pairs of original pressed glass pulls, on scroll-cut bracket feet, ca. 1840, 20 x 45", 6' 6" h. (ILLUS.) **1,495**

Country-style secretary-bookcase, pine, two-part construction: the upper section w/a rectangular top w/flared cornice above a pair of tall two-pane glazed cupboard doors opening to wooden shelves above a pair of shallow drawers; the lower section w/a wide hinged slant lid opening to a well & raised on baluster-, ring- and rod-turned legs w/knob feet, natural finish, late 19th c., 43 1/2" w., overall 6' 8" h. (ILLUS., top next column) **518**

Fine French Empire-Style Secretary

Empire-Style secrétaire-à-abattant (fall-front secretary), walnut & ebonized wood, the rectangular white marble top above a case w/a long flat top drawer w/a gilt-metal mount & flanked by gilt-metal wreath mounts projecting above the wide hinged flat fall front opening to an inset leather writing surface & an interior fitted w/a variety of drawers surrounding a mirrored cupboard door, three long drawers below each w/gilt-metal wreath pulls, all flanked by tall free-standing ebonized columns & raised on ebonized paw front feet, France, late 19th c., 19 1/2 x 39", 4' 11 1/2" h. (ILLUS., bottom previous page) **2,990**

Inlaid Mahogany Secretary-Bookcase

Federal secretary-bookcase, inlaid mahogany, two-part construction: shaped cornice w/three brass urn finials above two eight-pane doors w/through muntins, interior w/three drawers & seven cubbyholes; the base w/fold-out writing surface w/black string inlay above three graduated dovetailed & cockbeaded drawers, probably original brass pulls, tapered legs, pit-sawn drawer bottoms w/handwrought nails, old refinishing, drawer runners rebuilt, patches, repairs & separations in veneer, replaced felt writing surface, 22 x 41", 6' 4 1/4" h. (ILLUS.) **3,740**
Federal secretary-bookcase, mahogany, satinwood & mahogany veneers, two-part construction: the top w/broken-arch pediment w/turned ringed oval finials over two glazed 15-pane doors w/through muntins & central octagons, applied half-round quilted-diamond medi-

Federal Mahogany Secretary-Bookcase

al molding, two adjustable shelves; the base w/four dovetailed & cockbeaded drawers w/original wooden pulls & ivory inlaid shield escutcheons, the top drawer w/fall front, six interior dovetailed drawers & eight cubbyholes, reeded pilasters, turned feet, New England, first quarter 19th c., one shelf probably replaced, three broken glass panes, 23 1/2 x 44", 8' 11" h. (ILLUS.) **10,450**
George III "breakfront" secretary-bookcase, mahogany, two-part construction: the upper section w/a long rectangular top w/a narrow cornice continuing across the projecting central case, the central section w/a pair of tall geometrically glazed doors opening to three wooden shelves flanked by a set-back matching single door at each end; the conforming lower section w/the projecting central

George III "Breakfront" Secretary-Bookcase

section fitted w/a long top fold-down drawer opening to reveal an inset tooled leather work surface & fitted interior above a stack of three long graduated drawers w/rectangular brass pulls, the set-back side sections w/a single paneled cupboard door, molded flat base, England, ca. 1800 & later, 21 1/2 x 89", 8' h. (ILLUS.) **6,613**

Nice George III Secretary

George III secretary-bookcase, mahogany, two-part construction: the upper section w/a rectangular top over a stepped cornice above a pair of tall geometrically glazed cupboard doors opening on four wooden shelves; the stepped-out lower section w/mid-molding w/a fold-down top drawer opening to a leather-inset writing surface & various drawers & pigeonholes, all above three long graduated drawers, simple bail pulls, serpentine apron & French feet, England, late 18th c., 22 1/2 x 46 1/4", 8' h. (ILLUS.) **2,760**

Gothic Revival secretary-bookcase, mahogany, two-part construction: the upper section w/a rectangular top w/a pointed pediment crest above the deep ogee cornice above a pair of tall multi-paned glazed cupboard doors w/ornate Gothic motifs in the upper panes & opening to four shelves above a row of three very narrow drawers w/small wooden knobs; the stepped-out lower section w/a flat fall-front opening to an interior composed of pigeonholes & small drawers all trimmed in bird's-eye maple above the writing surface, a pair of paneled doors below outlined in wavy molding w/vertical bands of wavy molding down the front sides, scroll-carved feet, Baltimore, ca. 1830, 23 x 47", 8' 4" h. (ILLUS., top next page)

.... **4,140**

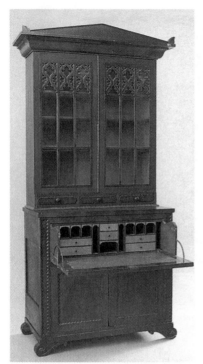

Early American Gothic Revival Secretary

Flat-topped Oak Double Secretary

Victorian Golden Oak secretary-bookcase, quarter-sawn oak, rare double side-by-side-style, the flat rectangular top w/a molded cornice above a case w/tall flat glazed doors at each side, each w/a carved leafy scroll band at the top, the center section w/a pair of short flat glazed doors opening to shelves above a wide hinged fall front w/long ornate scrolled brass hinges & lockplate & decorated w/a

large inverted clover-shaped panel w/clusters of fanned carved leaves, the desk above a stack of three long drawers w/stamped brass pulls, molded base over a narrow curved apron & simple bracket feet, original hardware, refinished, ca. 1900, 20 x 54", 6' h. (ILLUS.) **2,800**

Oak Side-by-Side with Mirrors

Victorian Golden Oak secretary-bookcase, quarter-sawn oak, side-by-side-style, a high flat-topped scrolled crest board behind a long narrow shelf w/down-curved ends raised above the two-part case, the left side w/a tall curved glass door opening to wooden shelves, the right side w/a long rectangular arch-topped beveled mirror at the back & a small vertical rectangular beveled mirror at the side above an open shelf above a narrow drawer over the wide hinged fall front centered by a scroll-stamped cartouche panel, a long ogee-fronted drawer over two flat drawers below the desk, each w/pierced brass pulls, simple apron on ogee bracket feet on casters, refinished, ca. 1890s, 18 x 40", 5' 8" h. (ILLUS.) **1,600**

Victorian Golden Oak secretary-bookcase, quarter-sawn oak, side-by-side-style, the high serpentine crest w/a small scroll-carved center crest & outwardly-scrolled corner ears above long C-form moldings above a wide panel w/a long flaring section of applied scrolls above the two-part case, the left side w/a tall curved & leaded glass door opening to shelves, the right side w/a large rounded beveled glass mirror over a scrolled band

Secretary with Scrolls & Leaded Door

above a narrow shelf atop the flat rectangular fall front w/a large cartouche of carved scrolls, a serpentine long drawer below the desk w/simple bail pulls above a long flat rectangular base door, on ogee front legs w/heavy paw feet, refinished, ca. 1900, 18 x 40", 5' 10" h. (ILLUS.).. **2,500**

Victorian Renaissance Secretary

Victorian Renaissance Revival "barrel-front" secretary-bookcase, walnut & burl walnut, two-part construction: the upper section w/a rectangular top w/a flaring cornice over a narrow burl frieze band above a large single-pane glazed door w/rounded molded upper corners & opening to three shelves; the lower section w/a top molding above a quarter-round mechanical cylinder opening to long shelves & a pull-out writing surface above a long upper drawer w/two raised burl panels projecting above two long lower drawers each w/pairs of raised panels, plinth base, good original finish, interior compartments replaced, ca. 1875, 32" w., 7' 2" h. (ILLUS.).................. **1,265**

Fancy Renaissance Cylinder-front Secretary

Victorian Renaissance Revival "barrel-front" secretary-bookcase, walnut & rosewood, two-part construction: the upper section w/an arched molded cornice w/projecting corners above a wide frieze band w/a thin band of molding above a pair of arched glazed cupboard doors opening to three shelves; the lower section w/a rim molding above the quarter-round mechanical cylinder front opening to reveal an interior of pigeonholes & small drawers trimmed w/bird's-eye maple, the edge molding above a long drawer projecting above a pair of lower cupboard doors each centered by a large rondel, molded plinth base, ca. 1875, carved pediment missing, 24 x 49", 7' 1" h. (ILLUS.) **2,530**

Sideboards

Extraordinary French Art Deco Inlaid Sideboard

Art Deco sideboard, mother-of-pearl & ebony-inlaid rosewood, the rectangular top w/a molded edge above a deep case w/a pair of wide tapering doors in a basketweave design further inlaid across the front w/a black & white bouquet of flowers & small scattered blossoms, rounded front corner stile w/small gilt-bronze inset bands continuing to the tapering legs w/gilt-bronze feet, wide curved apron, tag of Jules & Andre Leleu, France, ca. 1946, 16 x 53 1/4", 34" h. (ILLUS.) **17,925**

Fine "Chicoree" Pattern Art Nouveau Sideboard by Majorelle

Art Nouveau sideboard, carved oak & marquetry, "Chicoree" patt., the wide arched & molded crestrail centered by a large carved blossom above a wide back panel w/a scale design centered by a lower open shelf on leaf-carved corner brackets flanked on each side by an upright glass-door display cabinet w/a single glass shelf all on the long rectangular top overhanging a lower case w/a pair of central drawers over a pair of large paneled doors decorated w/a marquetry floral design, two open shelves at each end w/a serpentine leaf-carved front bracket, stepped & molded plinth base, designed by Louis Majorelle, France, ca. 1905, original label on the back, 23 x 89 1/2", 6' 6 1/8" h. (ILLUS.) **16,730**

Fine Classical Sideboard Attributed to Quervelle

Classical Server with Nice Columns

Classical server, mahogany & mahogany veneer, the high arched & scroll-cut backsplash on the rectangular top above a case w/a long veneered drawer w/round brass pulls overhanging another long drawer over a deep center drawer flanked by deep bottle drawers, spiral-turned freestanding columns at each side, on heavy baluster-turned legs, refinished, replaced pulls, ca. 1830, 22 x 46", 4' h. (ILLUS.) **650**

Classical sideboard, mahogany & mahogany veneer, a drop-well rectangular top w/an upright back composed of a pair of large finely carved cornucopias flanking the marble-topped drop well fitted w/a high central rectangular mirror w/a classical pediment & turned columns, the side sections w/a round-fronted drawer above a tall paneled door flanked by classical free-standing columns, the central section w/two long narrow drawers over a pair of paneled cupboard doors, the

blocked base on leaf-carved trumpet-form front legs, early pressed glass pulls on the drawers, attributed to Anthony Quervelle, Philadelphia, ca. 1835, veneer restorations, 23 1/4 x 67", 4' 11" h. (ILLUS., top of page)................................. **3,163**

Classical sideboard, mahogany & mahogany veneer, a rectangular drop central section w/a concave front flanked by raised end sections w/molded hinged tops, one opening to a zinc-lined cavity for wine, the other opening to a cavity, a central long flush concave drawer beside a smaller flat flush drawer, all above a pair of tall paneled cupboard doors flanking a pair of concave paneled central doors, the front divided by four columns w/leaf-carved capitals, the flat conforming base raised on short round leaf-carved front feet, old surface, attributed to Emmons & Archibald, Boston, ca. 1815, 24 1/2 x 71 3/4", 46 1/2" h. (some veneer loss) **6,463**

Classical Boldly Veneered Sideboard

Quality Classical Sideboard

Classical sideboard, mahogany & mahogany veneer, the rectangular top above pair of long round-fronted drawers w/round brass pulls flanked by carved corner blocks & slightly projecting over two tall turned & tapering freestanding side columns flanking an arrangement of two deep center drawers over two paneled cupboard doors flanked on each side by a stack of three tall narrow drawers all w/round brass pulls, flat apron, short front legs w/acanthus leaf-carved knees over heavy paw feet on casters, refinished, ca. 1830s, 22 x 50", 4' h. (ILLUS., bottom previous page) **1,800**

Classical sideboard, mahogany & mahogany veneer, the top w/a crossbanded gallery w/scrolled-end returns above a projecting section w/a pair of small drawers at each end centered by a long false drawer folding down to a writing surface, the stepped-back lower case w/a row of four paneled cupboard doors separated by four freestanding ring-turned columns on blocks above the four beehive-turned legs, round brass pulls, mid-Atlantic states, ca. 1830, 24 x 71", 4' 2" h. (ILLUS., top of page)
.... **3,910**

Unusual Southern Country Sideboard

Very Fine Federal Serpentine-front Inlaid Sideboard

Country-style sideboard, maple, a low arched back crest flanked by short end blocks w/button-turned finials above the long rectangular top above a narrow zig-zag-carved frieze band above a row of three drawers w/pairs of turned wood pulls over three-section front w/zigzag-carved stiles, the central section w/a drawer above an arched panel door, each side section w/a stack of three drawers w/pairs of turned wood pulls, simple block feet, old dark surface, attrib-uted to Georgia, 19th c., 21 1/2 x 60", 4' 3/4" h. (ILLUS., bottom previous page) **1,725**

Federal serpentine-front sideboard, inlaid mahogany, the rectangular top w/a ser-pentine front above a case w/a conform-ing long central drawer over a double-arched apron & flanked by doors, all w/oval inlaid banding & inlaid border trim & panels, on square tapering legs, round brasses, very minor shrinkage cracks in top & one side panel, Maryland or Virginia, ca. 1810, 22 3/4 x 72 1/2", 41 1/4" h. (ILLUS., top of page) **13,800**

Fine Mahogany Federal Server

Federal server, mahogany, the rectangular top w/a three-quarters gallery w/scrolled ends above a case w/a long deep drawer decorated by a recessed arch, raised on ring- and rod-turned supports joined by a medial shelf w/an incurved front & corner

Federal Mahogany Sideboard with Serpentine Front

Quality George III-Style Mahogany Sideboard

blocks on tapering ring-turned feet, restorations, ca. 1825, 20 x 41 1/2", 38 1/2" h. (ILLUS., previous page) **3,450**

Federal sideboard, mahogany & mahogany veneer, the rectangular top w/a serpentine front above a case w/two small bow-front drawers & a bow-front door on each side flanking the concave center section w/a long drawer over a pair of cupboard doors flanked on each side by a short & deep drawer, arched central apron, raised on four ring-turned tapering & reeded front legs w/peg feet, ca. 1820, old refinish, probably old replacement pulls, 22 x 70", 40" h. (ILLUS., bottom previous page) **2,000**

George III-Style sideboard, mahogany, the rectangular top w/a serpentine front above a conforming case w/two concave drawers flanking a bowed central drawer above an arched opening, on square tapering legs ending in spade feet, England, mid-19th c., 21 x 53", 35" h. (ILLUS., top of page) **4,600**

Louis XV-Style Provincial server, fruitwood, the rectangular top w/rounded corners above a conforming case w/notched front corners flanking a pair of arched paneled cupboard doors w/long brass latch mounts above the molded serpentine apron & short bracket feet, France, first half 19th c., 24 x 48 3/4", 44 3/4" h. (ILLUS.).. **3,450**

Louis XV-Style Provincial Server

Louis XV-Style Provincial Sideboard

L. & J.G. Stickley Mission Oak Sideboard

Louis XV-Style Provincial sideboard, walnut, three-piece construction, the top w/ornate carved pediment above door w/20 beveled panes flanked by two carved side doors; the base w/two drawers above two large bay doors, cabriole legs w/carved scroll feet, panels w/detailed carving throughout, carved & paneled central backboard, France, 24 x 59", 9' h. (ILLUS., bottom previous page) **3,080**

Mission-style (Arts & Crafts movement) server, oak, the back w/a low plate rail above the rectangular top overhanging an apron w/a single long drawer w/squared hammered copper pulls & an arched apron, flanked by through-tenon side stiles, the square legs joined by a lower medial shelf w/an incurved front & a narrow rear rail, original finish, some foot wear, delamination on back panel, branded mark of the Charles Limbert company, early 20th c., 17 1/4 x 40", 40 1/2" h. (ILLUS., next column) **2,185**

Mission-style (Arts & Crafts movement) sideboard, oak, the top w/a wide plate rail above the long rectangular top above a case w/a stack of three central drawers flanked by flat doors all w/copper plate & ring pulls, a long drawer across the bottom, square stile legs, good original finish, branded mark of L. & J.G. Stickley, early 20th c., 20 x 48", 44" h. (ILLUS., top of page) **4,600**

Limbert Mission Oak Server

Provincial sideboard, pine, two-piece construction, the top w/two doors w/scroll & floral carved decoration, two turned supports; the base w/two drawers above two carved doors, France, 20th c., 18 x 51", 7' 4" h. **413**

Aesthetic Movement Sideboard

Victorian Aesthetic Movement sideboard, mahogany, the upper section w/a rectangular top w/a flaring cornice over a gadrooned frieze band projecting over a long rectangular beveled mirror & supported by reeded columnar front supports on a lower shelf projecting above a panel-backed section w/incurved end brackets, all above the rectangular top on the lower case composed of a long drawer above a pair of cupboard doors w/oblong floral-carved panels on one side & a stack of three drawers above a short open compartment w/a serpentine border on the other side, looped hammered brass pulls, molded base on thin bun feet, original dark finish, late 19th - early 20th c., 24 x 77", 6' h. (ILLUS.) **1,610**

Canopied Baroque Oak Sideboard

Victorian Baroque Revival sideboard, oak, the tall canopied superstructure w/a raised rectangular top over a deep coved band carved w/long leafy vines above the flaring cornice over a scroll-carved frieze band & serpentine apron centered by a carved lion mask all supported on tall columns w/large leaf-carved knobs, the tall back centered by a tall rectangular beveled mirror flanked by large scroll-carved panels centered by a carved lion mask & a quarter-round open shelf over a small rectangular beveled mirror, the rectangular top on the case w/a wide egg-and-dart-carved border & scroll-carved frieze band above a case fitted w/a pair of four-panel cupboard doors centered by a diamond flanking two scroll-carved drawers w/lion mask pulls over an open compartment w/scroll-carved side brackets, narrow scroll-carved bands down the sides above the large bulbous bun feet, Europe, ca. 1890, refinished, 24 x 59", 7' 8" h. (ILLUS.) **3,200**

Golden Oak Server with Lions

Victorian Golden Oak server, quarter-sawn oak, a serpentine crestrail supported on seated winged lion brackets above a conforming long beveled mirror over the rectangular top, the case w/a pair of long slightly projecting drawers over a long deeper drawer above a pair of flat cupboard doors centered by a scroll-carved panel, front animal legs ending in paw feet, on wooden casters, refinished, ca. 1900, 22 x 48", 5' h. (ILLUS.) **950**

Victorian Renaissance Revival sideboard, chestnut, walnut & walnut veneer, the tall superstructure topped by a wide peaked scroll-carved crest w/a fan-carved finial above an arched molding above a long arched burl panel flanked by side scrolls & narrow burl panels over a long rectangular shelf w/rounded cor-

Tall Chestnut & Walnut Sideboard

Oak Sideboard with Carving of Game Birds

ners supported on tall blocked brackets w/turned drop finials above a long narrow rectangular mirror & scrolled side brackets, the long rectangular white marble top w/rounded front corners above a conforming case, the case w/a central stack of five small molded drawers flanked at each side w/a burled drawer w/brass ring pulls over large cupboard doors w/a rectangular raised burl panel & notch-carved dark border molding, flat molded base, original finish, 1870s, 22 x 52", 8' h. (ILLUS.) **2,400**

Victorian Renaissance Revival sideboard, oak, the high superstructure topped by a tall arched crest carved w/large scrolls flanking a carved cluster of fruit above a narrow rounded shelf w/a sawtooth-cut narrow apron supported on bold scroll-carved brackets flanking a long narrow raised scroll-carved panel & scrolled side brackets above a matching longer shelf on matching brackets flanking another raised panel w/carving of a cluster of fruit all resting on the long rectangular top w/a deep flared apron w/carved scrolls at the sides & w/two long scroll-carved drawers at the front separated by three blocks w/a lion mask carved in relief, a pair of large paneled cupboard doors below each centered by relief-carved decoration of game birds, three long dividing columns down the front each carved in bold relief w/bands of fruit & leaves, blocks & scroll-carved flat base band, Europe, ca. 1875, refinished, 22 x 50", 7' 8" h. (ILLUS., top next column) **2,800**

Renaissance Sideboard with Burl

Victorian Renaissance Revival sideboard, walnut & burl walnut, the superstructure w/a serpentine crestrail w/a high arched central section w/full-relief carving of a cluster of fruit flanked by small raised burl panels, small turned finials at the corners above a narrow long shelf supported on large scroll brackets above a long narrow raised burl panel above another long narrow shelf supported on scroll brackets above a larger long raised burl panel flanked by scallop-cut quarter-round outside corner brackets over the long rectangular top w/inset white marble, the case w/two long narrow drawers each w/two raised burl panels & black pear-shaped pulls flanked by burl corner blocks above a pair of large cupboard doors each centered by a large square raised burl panel enclosed by carved scrolls, the inner door molding ebonized, blocked raised burl panels at each side of the case above the flat molded base w/an ebonized band, old refinish, ca. 1875, 22 x 54", 7' h. (ILLUS.)... **2,400**

European Renaissance Sideboard

Victorian Renaissance Revival sideboard, walnut & burl walnut w/ebonized trim, the tall superstructure w/a high scroll-carved crestrail w/an arched raised center crest w/a carved cartouche above a carved fruit cluster, a long narrow top shelf raised on four ring-, rod- and knob-turned spindles resting on another shelf supported on matching spindles, both shelves in front of a large rectangular beveled mirror w/an ebonized border, the rectangular ebonized top on a case w/a pair of long narrow burl drawers w/ebonized borders flanked by small reeded blocks, a medial molding above a pair of large paneled doors w/burl & rectangular ebonized molding forming a panel centered by a large cluster of carved fruit, deep molded flat base on turned bun front feet, original finish, Europe, ca. 1875, 20 x 46", 6' 8" h. (ILLUS.)............... **1,600**

Very Ornate Rococo Carved Sideboard

Victorian Rococo sideboard, carved oak, two-part construction: the tall superstructure w/a high arched & boldly scroll-carved crest centered by a figural stag head above a long half-round top shelf raised on columnar front supports & w/a paneled back flanked by openwork side S-scrolls all above a matching lower shelf supported by fancy carved supports featuring hound heads; the lower section w/a rectangular white marble top over a case w/a pair of narrow paneled drawers w/nut-carved pulls above a pair of arch-paneled doors, one centered by a boldly carved cluster of fish, eels & lobsters, the other w/a cluster of game including rabbits & fowl, the canted front corners w/carved top corner drops, deep plinth base, attributed to Alexander Roux, New York, New York, ca. 1860, 23 1/2 x 59", 7' 6" h. (ILLUS.).. **4,600**

Victorian Rococo sideboard, carved rosewood & marquetry, the long white marble top w/a serpentine bowed front above a conforming case w/three front sections, each w/a boldly scrolling leaf-carved band above a wide central bowed door flanked by smaller concave side doors, each door w/panels outlined w/scrolled molding enclosing floral marquetry bouquets, scrolling leaf-carved base bands, the three front sections separated by very large & boldly carved leafy scroll pilasters ending in shell-form feet, ca. 1850s, 23 1/2 x 73", 38" h. (ILLUS., top next page).. **6,900**

Exuberant Carved Rosewood & Marquetry Victorian Rococo Sideboard

New Orleans Rococo Sideboard

Victorian Rococo sideboard, walnut & burl walnut, the superstructure w/a low pierced & scroll-carved back crest on the long narrow top shelf supported on large ornate S-scroll front supports joined by a lower shelf & a solid back, the rectangular white marble top above a case w/a row of three ogee-front drawers above a beaded mold-ing over three cupboard doors w/raised carved rectangular panels separated by vertical beaded moldings, a beaded base molding on the serpentine scroll-carved apron, scroll-carved bracket feet, attributed to the New Orleans warerooms of William McCracken, ca. 1850s, 22 1/4 x 54 1/2", 5' 11" h. (ILLUS.)............. **2,760**

English William IV Mahogany Sideboard

William IV sideboard, mahogany, a tall upright paneled crestboard w/rounded corners above the rectangular top w/slightly projecting ends above a conforming case w/end pedestal sections each w/a drawer over a paneled cupboard door flanking a center drawer over the open center, molded bases, England, second quarter 19th c., 23 1/2 x 78", 4' 2" h. (ILLUS.)....... **1,380**

Stands

Simple Victorian Blanket Stand

Blanket stand, Victorian country-style, mahogany, side turned uprights w/a forked rolled top joined by two bars, three cross bars down the uprights, flared & arched forked feet, second half 19th c., 29 1/2" h. (ILLUS.) **1,434**

Interesting Revolving Book Stand

Book stand, oak & iron, folding & revolving-type, the top w/oak board racks that fold together & adjust above a slender metal rod that goes through two rectangular oak shelves w/pairs of lattice supports, revolving above a base w/four serpentine outswept slender legs on casters, marked by R.M. Lambie, New York, ca.

1900, missing top slat on central shelf section, some scratches, 16 x 16", 43 1/2" h. (ILLUS.) **690**

Cherry Candlestand with Inlaid Top

Candlestand, Chippendale country style, cherry, the top w/shaped sides & oval inlay of mixed hardwoods, on turned pedestal above three saber legs on padded snake feet, probably Massachusetts, late 18th c., 16 1/2 x 16 3/4", 25 1/2" h. (ILLUS.) **2,530**

Interesting Chippendale Candlestand

Candlestand, Chippendale, mahogany, a round white marble top enclosed by a pierced brass low gallery above a ring-turned columnar pedestal over the tripod base w/cabriole legs ending in claw-and-ball feet, New York, New York, ca. 1760-80, 17 3/4" d., 27" h. (ILLUS., previous page) **3,824**

Federal Country-style Candlestand

Candlestand, Federal country style, stained birch, the two-board square top w/a slight warp raised on an urn-turned pedestal on a tripod base w/spider legs, original dark red wash, minor hairlines, late 18th - early 19th c., 18" w., 30 1/4" h. (ILLUS.).. **690**

Candlestand, Federal, mahogany, tilt-top style, the rectangular top w/canted corners, on turned pedestal on a tripod base w/spider legs, accession number on base of pedestal, inscribed under top "From the manor house of Capt. John Overstreet's Woodland Plantation, Princess Anne County, Virginia, 1832," yellow pine plate possible replacement, repaired splits to pedestal, 18 1/8 x 21 3/4", 28 1/2" h. **1,760**

Candlestand, Federal style, inlaid cherry, the small square top w/fan-inlaid corners & cloverleaf line inlay above the urn-turned columnar pedestal on a tripod base w/cabriole legs ending in slipper feet, Connecticut, 1790-1810, 13" w., 26 1/4" h. (ILLUS., top next column) **4,780**

Candlestand, Federal Style tilt-top type, carved mahogany, the oblong shaped top tilting above a pedestal composed of three leaf-carved C-scroll supports resting on a tripartite platform above three leaf-carved outswept C-scroll legs w/scrolled tips & resting on small ball feet, marked w/an embossed label reading "This piece reproduced courtesy of Mr. Henry Ford - Original on display at the Edison Institute - Colonial Mfg. Co., Zeeland, Michigan," old refinishing, res-

torations to one support, ca. 1930, 19 1/8 x 25 3/4", 28 1/2" h. (ILLUS., bottom this column)... **316**

Federal Inlaid Cherry Candlestand

Early Licensed Ford Museum Reproduction

Simple Federal Tilt-top Candlestand

Candlestand, Federal tilt-top style, mahogany, the oval top tilting above a columnar pedestal on a tripod base w/cabriole legs ending in slipper feet, Massachusetts, ca. 1790-1810, 16 x 22 3/4", 27 3/4" h. (ILLUS.) **3,107**

European Provincial Candlestand

Candlestand, primitive provincial-style, hardwood, the square top w/canted corners raised on a pedestal composed of tapering square sections centered by a large turned ball, all raised on a tripod base w/angular canted legs, peg con-

struction, Europe, early 19th c., 12 1/4" d., 31" h. (ILLUS.) **575**

Rare Early American Candlestand

Candlestand, William & Mary country-style, painted maple, the central slender screw pole w/a ring-turned two-arm candleholder above a turned platform over a ring- and ball-turned pedestal on a tripod base w/three widely canted rod- and knob-turned legs, old red paint, New England, 1730-50, 43 1/4" h. (ILLUS.) **3,585**

Ornate Mahogany Canterbury

Canterbury (music stand), Regency style, mahogany, a rectangular top framework w/a pointed finial at each corner & arched cut-out rim handles at the ends above four ornate pierced scroll-cut panels forming four vertical slots above a deep ogee apron w/a hidden drawer on one side, raised on disk-turned legs w/original brass cap casters, England, first-half 19th c., refinished, 16 x 24", 20" h. (ILLUS., bottom previous page) **1,400**

Ornate Rosewood Rococo Canterbury

Canterbury (music stand), Victorian Rococo style, rosewood, a rectangular top frame w/knob-turned corner finials enclosing four ornately pierce-carved vertical panels centered by a lyre design & fitted at the top center w/an arched & pierced handle, bobbin-turned corner posts above an apron w/a single long drawer, bobbin-turned short feet, mid-19th c., 14 x 20", 15 1/2" h. (ILLUS.) **1,150**

Painted Country-style Crock Stand

Crock stand, country style, painted pine & poplar, an arched crest flanked by arched sides on the one-board sides w/arched

base cut-outs, two closed-back shelves, square & round head nail construction, old green paint, backboards w/varnished splits, two feet w/added pads, second half 19th c., 13 1/2 x 37 1/4", 44 1/4" h. (ILLUS.) **403**

Signed Stickley Mission Oak Drink Stand

Drink stand, Mission-style (Arts & Crafts movement), oak, a round copper-covered top overhanging a narrow apron & four gently flaring square legs joined by arched cross stretchers, red Handcraft decal mark of L. & J.G. Stickley, original excellent condition w/some stains in the top, early 20th c., 18" d., 28 1/4" h. (ILLUS.) **7,475**

Marked Limbert Mission Magazine Stand

Magazine stand, Mission-style (Arts & Crafts movement), oak, the rectangular top above arched cornices fitted into legs by through-tenons, fitted w/four lower shelves flanked by side splats, the bottom shelf w/arched aprons & through-tenons at the legs, original finish w/over-coat, branded mark of the Charles Limbert Furniture Co., early 20th c., 12 x 20", 42" h. (ILLUS., bottom previous page)...... **2,185**

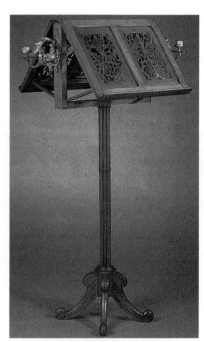

Early French Rosewood Music Stand

Marked Stickley Oak Magazine Stand

Magazine stand, Mission-style (Arts & Crafts movement), oak, the rectangular top w/an arched back crest & downswept low sides above three shelves w/a closed back, the bottom shelf w/a narrow arched apron, worn original finish, "The Work of..." mark of L. & J.G. Stickley, early 20th c., 12 x 22", 44 3/4" h. (ILLUS.)................. **2,415**

Music stand, Louis Philippe style, rosewood, duet style, the top composed of two angled adjustable racks each enclosing a pair of delicately pierce-carved panels & flanked by gilt-bronze scrolling candlearms, adjusting on a clustered columnar pedestal on a tripod base w/outswept C-scroll flat legs w/scrolled toes, France, ca. 1835, 45" h. (ILLUS., top next column)....................................... **1,725**

Ornate Rococo Papier-maché Music Stand

Music stand, Victorian Rococo style, inlaid papier-maché, tilt-top style, the oblong cartouche-form tilt top w/serpentine sides fitted w/a narrow music rack against a black background ornately inlaid w/moth-

Fine French Art Deco Nightstands

er-of-pearl florals & gilt trim, raised on a heavy spiral-turned pedestal on a tripod base w/flattened scroll-carved legs decorated w/fancy gilt scrolls, in the manner of Jennens & Bettridge, England, ca. 1850, 18 x 18", 43" h. (ILLUS., bottom previous page).. **2,300**

Nightstands, Art Deco style, rosewood & sycamore, the rectangular top above flat sides w/curved-out bases, flanking a narrow sycamore top drawer w/ring pull & a lower medial shelf w/sycamore facing, designed by Jean Pascaud, France, ca. 1933, 13 3/4 x 15 1/2", 19 3/4" h., pr. (ILLUS., top of page) **5,975**

Fine American Rococo Nightstands

Nightstands, Victorian Rococo style, carved rosewood, rectangular white marble top above a case w/a narrow frieze drawer above a tall paneled door outlined w/a thin gadrooned band & flanked by canted front corners w/bold upper & lower carved scrolls, plinth base raised on disk feet, ca. 1850s, 16 x 20", 32" h., pr. (ILLUS.).. **7,188**

Parlor stand, Victorian Gothic Revival style, hardwood w/round marble top above three shaped & tapered columns surrounding tapered octagonal central pedestal, finely carved friezes w/grapes, cartouches & grotesque heads, feet w/relief-carved leaves, berries & vines, England, 19th c., base missing three glue blocks & 4" carved piece, 19 1/2 x 19 1/2", 4' h. **1,045**

Queen Anne-Style Nightstands

Nightstands, Queen Anne-Style, mahogany, a square top above a single small door w/raised rectangular panel, raised on delicate tapering legs ending in pad feet, England, early 19th c., 12 1/2" sq., 31 1/2" h., pr. (ILLUS.) **2,530**

Fancy Onyx & Gilt-bronze Plant Stand

Plant stand, late Victorian, onyx & gilt-bronze, composed of two square inset pieces of white onyx in an ornate metal framework w/onyx columns & finials raised on delicate scrolling & outswept gilt-bronze legs w/dolphin feet, ca. 1900, 16" w., 34 1/2" h. (ILLUS.)............................ **978**

Ornately Carved Walnut Plant Stand

Plant stand, Victorian Aesthetic Movement style, carved walnut, the round top w/a wide band of foliate carving above the three-paneled apron carved w/detailed leaves & florals, raised on three square & highly carved legs joined by carved flat stretchers joined by a central post w/a

carved & domed finial, outswept paw-carved feet, Cincinnati Art Club, Ohio, ca. 1880s, 12" d., 29" h. (ILLUS.) **1,725**

Victorian Bamboo Planter with Liner

Plant stand, Victorian, bamboo type, a long narrow rectangular well w/a metal liner supported in a geometric bamboo framework centered on each side w/a square plaque painted w/an Oriental figure, bamboo rod trestle base w/bamboo bracket trim, France, mid-19th c., 11 x 37 1/2" l., 30" h. (ILLUS.) **863**

Simple Renaissance Plant Stand

Plant stand, Victorian Renaissance Revival style, walnut, a round white marble top above a coved apron w/two low arched & scalloped drops, raised on a baluster- and ring-turned pedestal flanked by three scalloped S-scroll legs w/outswept scroll feet, original finish, ca. 1870s, 16" d., 34" h. (ILLUS.) **350**

Plant Stand with Carved Putti

Plant stand, Victorian Rococo style, carved oak, a wide thin round dished top raised on a slender round pedestal carved in full relief w/twining grapevine & two full-figure putti above a round platform issuing four outswept long scroll-carved legs each topped by a carved boar head, Europe, ca. 1870, original finish, 16" d., 26" h. (ILLUS.) **2,000**

Fine Classical Revival Plant Stands

Plant stands, Classical Revival style, mahogany, a square top w/a tapering pointed drop finial at each corner, raised on a heavy tapering columnar pedestal w/a ring of beads above a heavy baluster-turned base section resting on a square platform w/tiny ball feet, original dark finish, late 19th c., 14" w., 40" h., pr. (ILLUS.) **2,800**

Plant stands, Regency-Style, mahogany, circular top above molded frieze, three supports w/scrolled mounts, shaped base, stylized paw feet, England, late 19th c., losses & separations to veneer, finish losses & wear, some legs loose, 42" h., pr. **605**

Portfolio stand, Victorian Aesthetic Movement, carved cherry, frame-&-panel construction w/raised holly & berry borders, sides w/carved cranes, fall front w/recess behind for storage of prints, hinged lip forms stay of easel base, lock & key, late 19th c., leg joints reglued, minor losses & separations, several small repairs, possibly old refinishing, 19 x 33", 4' 2" h., extends to 5' 11" when back is raised........... **1,980**

Fancy Golden Oak Shaving Stand

Shaving stand, Victorian Golden Oak style, quarter-sawn oak, a shaped oval frame enclosing a beveled mirror swiveling between curved uprights over rectangular top above a deep apron w/undulating panels on the front drawer & sides, raised on spiral-turned supports above a rectangular lower shelf w/a low gallery raised on tapering spiral-turned & slightly outswept legs, refinished, ca. 1890s, 14 x 16", 5' 2" h. (ILLUS.) **1,600**

Nice Classical Marble Top Washstand

Washstand, Classical style, mahogany & mahogany veneer, the top w/a high scroll-cut three-quarters gallery over the grey marble rectangular top above an apron w/a round-fronted long drawer w/two early pressed glass knobs above a pair of paneled cupboard doors flanked by reeded stiles, on short ring- and knob-turned feet, Philadelphia, ca. 1830, 19 x 28", 36 1/2" h. (ILLUS.) **2,070**

Country Federal Cut-out Washstand

Washstand, Federal country style, painted pine, the square top w/a three-quarters gallery above a large cut-out round top hole w/a smaller cut-out hole beside it, square supports continuing to form the legs & joined by a medial shelf above a drawer w/two small wooden knobs, origi-

nal dark red paint, first half 19th c., 16 1/2" sq., 31 3/4" h. (ILLUS.) **460**

Federal Country-style Washstand

Washstand, Federal country style, tiger stripe maple, the rectangular top w/a high backboard flanked by downswept sides, raised on ring- and rod-turned supports above a medial shelf above a single narrow drawer w/glass pull, on tall ring-turned legs ending in knob feet, shrinkage across top, break at front of bottom shelf, ca. 1835, 15 1/2 x 19 1/2", 34 1/2" h. (ILLUS.) **460**

English Regency Washstand

Washstand, Regency style, mahogany, a high gallery w/a narrow shelf at the top of the back & tapering serpentine sides over the rectangular top over a deep solid apron, raised on four knob- and rod-turned tapering legs joined by a rectangular shelf w/scroll-cut front corners, on short knob-and-peg feet on original brass cap casters, original finish, England, ca. 1820, 18 x 28", 36" h. (ILLUS., bottom previous page) **650**

Aesthetic Movement Carved Washstand

Washstand, Victorian Aesthetic Movement substyle, carved walnut, the tall superstructure w/an undulating carved crest above a molding & foliate-carved frieze band above a large round beveled mirror w/triangular foliate-carved panels at each corner, raised atop a white marble backsplash & rectangular marble top above a case fitted with two long drawers w/incised decoration & pierced brass pulls w/squared bails, a pair of paneled doors at the bottom, each centered by large round panels, plinth base on casters, ca. 1880, 17 x 36", 6' 2" h. (ILLUS.) **805**

Washstand, Victorian country style, walnut, the rectangular top w/a high arched & scroll-cut backsplash decorated w/two rondels & flanked by outswept open end towel bars, the carved top edge above a single long drawer w/long wooden bar pull raised on bobbin-turned supports joined by a medial shelf w/incurved front above the bobbin-turned feet, ca. 1870-80, 33" w., 29" h. (ILLUS., top next column) **127**

Victorian Country Turned Washstand

Small Country Victorian Washstand

Washstand, Victorian country-style, walnut, the wide serpentine splashback & serpentine front brackets joined at each side by a turned towel bar, the rectangular top over a drawer w/a leaf-carved pull over a paneled cupboard door centered by a roundel, shaped bracket feet, original finish, ca. 1870, 15 x 22", 35" h. (ILLUS.) **400**

Marble-top Renaissance Washstand

Washstand, Victorian Renaissance Revival style, walnut, a low vertical white marble backsplash above the rectangular white marble top over a case w/a long drawer w/raised oval molded & carved pulls above a pair of cupboard doors w/arched molding panels, plinth base on casters, ca. 1875, 16 x 27", 31" h. (ILLUS., bottom previous page) **374**

Renaissance Revival Washstand

Washstand, Victorian Renaissance Revival substyle, rosewood, the rectangular top w/projecting front corners above a conforming case w/a long paneled drawer flanked by beveled front corners w/half-round ring-turned drops above a pair of paneled cupboard doors flanked by beveled front corners w/half-round ring-turned inverted drops, molded base w/rounded front corners raised on disk feet on casters, ca. 1860-70, 19 x 35", 33" h. (ILLUS.) **863**

Classical Three-drawer Stand

Classical three-drawer stand, tiger stripe maple & walnut, the rectangular walnut top & sides w/a tiger stripe facade w/three graduated drawers w/pairs of turned wood pulls, two wide shaped swing-out supports at the back opening to hold a wide walnut drop leaf, raised on

ring- and rod-turned legs w/knob feet, ca. 1840, 18 x 25", 29" h. (ILLUS.) **1,265**

Country-style One-drawer Stand

Federal country-style one-drawer stand, cherry, rectangular one-board top, square posts finely tapered below dovetailed drawer w/shelf above, original brass bail pull, original dark brown surface, top has been reset w/small knot hole, 16 1/4 x 22", 28 3/4" h. (ILLUS.) **1,150**

Cherry Country Federal Stand

Federal country-style one-drawer stand, cherry, the square two-board top above a single dovetailed drawer w/a burl veneered front, raised on slender turned & tapering legs w/knob feet, original wooden pull, early 19th c., 19 3/4" w., 29" h. (ILLUS., bottom previous page) **345**

Fine Early Painted Maine Stand

Federal country-style one-drawer stand, painted pine, the nearly square top overhanging an apron w/a single flush dovetailed drawer, raised on square tapering legs, good old red paint, from Maine, early 19th c., 16 1/2 x 18", 29" h. (ILLUS.) **2,300**

Federal country-style two-drawer stand, walnut, square top above two hand-dovetailed drawers w/hand-planed bottoms, tapered legs, sides & back walnut veneer over pine, probably shop-made early 20th c., some elements possibly earlier, 18" sq., 31" h. **193**

Federal one-drawer stand, cherry & curly maple, nearly square one-board top over an apron w/one curly maple dovetailed drawer w/clear pressed glass knob, raised on ring- and rod-turned slender legs, found in Montgomery County, Pennsylvania, early 19th c., 16 7/8 x 17 1/4", 30 1/4" h. **770**

Stools

Classical organ stool, rosewood, the square upholstered top adjusting above a ring- and rod-turned pedestal w/flaring gadrooned band above the trefoil platform raised on scroll feet, old repair on base, possibly Vose Cabinet Shop, Boston, Massachusetts, ca. 1825, 11" w., 21" h. (ILLUS. left with two other organ stools, bottom of page) **316**

Classical organ stool, rosewood, the squared upholstered seat w/serpentine edges adjusting above the paneled baluster-form heavy pedestal raised on a platform w/four outswept log legs, ca. 1840, 14 1/2" w., 20" h. (ILLUS. right with two other organ stools, bottom of of page)... **259**

Classical stool, mahogany, the deep rectangular top upholstered in floral needlepoint on a wooden frame w/double-scrolled legs centering a boss, ending in scrolled feet, old refinish, Boston, ca. 1825, 14 1/2 x 20 1/2", 15 3/4" h. (minor imperfections) **1,116**

Folk art stool, the seat formed by actual whale vertebrae raised on three canted slender turned & tapering legs, America, 19th c., 24" h. **4,780**

Two Classical & a Victorian Organ Stool

Louis XV-Style Giltwood Stool

Louis XV-Style stools, giltwood, the rectangular top w/rounded corners above a
serpentine apron ornately carved
w/scrolls & shells, on cabriole legs w/leaf-
carved knees & scroll feet joined by a
shaped X-stretcher, France, 19th c.,
17 1/2" h., pr. (ILLUS. of one) **1,610**

Rare Early Modernist Piano Stool

Unmarked Mission Oak Footstool

**Mission-style (Arts & Crafts movement)
footstool,** oak, a rectangular deep leather-covered cushion top above a simple
rectangular framework w/square legs &
box stretchers, worn original finish, few
chips to legs, unmarked L. & J.G. Stickley,
early 20th c., 17 x 38 1/4", 17" h. (ILLUS.)
.... **518**

Modernist piano stool, ebonized wood &
leather, the low back w/a narrow leather
cross strap, turned back stile legs & tall
front legs joined by a leather seat,
w/blue-stained terminals, designed by
Gerrit Thomas Rietveld, ca. 1923,
29 1/2" h. (ILLUS., top next column) **11,353**

Regency Stool with Crossed Legs

Regency stool, mahogany, the square tufted top upholstered in light brown suede,
raised on serpentine crossover end legs
joined by a ring-, baluster- and knob-
turned stretcher, England, second quar-
ter 19th c., 24" sq., 20" h. (ILLUS.) **1,610**

Victorian organ stool, mixed wood, the tall
back w/a wide shaped crestrail raised on
baluster- and ring-turned canted stiles
flanking five matching spindles, above
the round adjustable seat above a round
platform atop four canted tapering knob-
and ring-turned legs ending in metal &
glass claw-and-ball feet & joined by short
turned spindles to a central post, ca.
1900 (ILLUS. center with two Classical
organ stools) **175**

Tables

Rare Modern Lalique Cactus Pattern Center Table

Art Deco center table, clear & frosted glass, "Cactus" patt., the wide round top overhanging the frosted glass base composed of eight gently arched cactus stems issuing from a frosted clear round base, Marc Lalique, 1989, engraved "25-5-1989 No. 15," & "1-82," 64" d., 28 1/2" h. (ILLUS., top of page) **26,290**

French Art Deco Cocktail Table

Art Deco cocktail table, blond mahogany, in the Chinese taste, the round top w/a rounded apron raised on five square legs on blocked feet & small corner blocks, w/an applied metal tag marked "Gouffé," France, ca. 1930, 35" d., 17 1/2" h. (ILLUS.)...................................... **288**

Very Rare Art Deco Side Table

Art Deco side table, ivory-inlaid Macassar ebony, the round top w/a radiating wood grain design edged w/a band of small ivory dots, on three flattened & arched legs, designed by Jacques-Emile Ruhlmann, ca. 1925, France, 19 7/8" d., 25 1/2" h. (ILLUS.) **77,675**

Biedermeier Cherry Center Table

Biedermeier center table, cherry, the nearly square top overhanging an apron fitted w/one long drawer, on simple cabriole legs, good wood figure, Europe, first-half 19th c., 29 1/4 x 30 1/2", 30" h. (ILLUS.)... **1,495**

Chippendale dining table, Santo Domingo mahogany, rectangular top flanked by 18 1/2" w. drop leaves, deep apron w/arched-cut ends, raised on four cabriole legs w/claw-and-ball feet, wrought-iron leaf hinges initiated "W.S.," eastern Pennsylvania or Maryland w/characteristics of examples by John Shaw, 18th c., top closed 17 5/8 x 52", 27 1/2" h. (hinges & top reset, some replaced returns) **6,600**

Chippendale serving table, mahogany, a rectangular colored marble top w/rounded corners & molded edges above a conforming apron w/ornately shaped cyma curves & arches, raised on cabriole legs ending in pad feet, original marble w/repaired break, Boston, Massachusetts, 1740-60, 24 x 47", 32" h....................... **101,575**

Rare Chippendale Tea Table

Chippendale tea table, mahogany, circular dished top w/piecrust border tilting on figured mahogany "birdcage" above the ring- & urn-turned pedestal above tripod base, pad feet, original iron spider, original spindles & plate, batten & latch appear to be original & untouched, probably original surface, Virginia family history, 18th c., stains, losses, cracks, chips & separations, 26 1/8 x 26 3/4", 27 1/4" h. (ILLUS.)... **19,800**

Chippendale tea table, mahogany, the round top w/molded edge tilting on a birdcage platform above a spiral-carved baluster- and ring-turned pedestal on a tripod base w/cabriole legs ending in claw-and-ball feet, refinished, America, 18th c., 23 3/4" d., 28" h.................................... **1,410**

Chippendale-Style Tea Table

Chippendale-Style tea table, lacquered & decorated wood, the scalloped round top decorated w/gilt & gesso Oriental landscape, on a turned tapering pedestal above a tripod base w/cabriole legs w/acanthus leaf-carved knees & ending in ball-and-claw feet, England, third quarter 19th c., 19 1/2" , 28" h. (ILLUS.) **805**

Late Classical Mahogany Card Table

Classical card table, mahogany & mahogany veneer, the rectangular fold-over top w/concave edges above a deep ogee-form apron w/a serrated edge raised on a heavy scroll-carved U-form pedestal atop a rectangular platform w/heavy outswept scroll-cut legs on casters, minor veneer chips, probably New York, ca. 1845, 18 x 34 1/2", 29" h. (ILLUS., bottom previous page) **345**

Fine Marble-topped Classical Table

Classical center table, carved rosewood, the inset white marble rectangular top w/serpentine sides within a conforming deep apron w/a gadrooned border band above foliate & floral clusters centered on each side over a thin beaded bottom edge band, all raised on heavy S-scroll legs w/acanthus leaf carving at the top & joined by an arched cross-stretcher w/a fan-carved crest, in the manner of J. & J.W. Meeks, New York, New York, ca. 1840, 26 x 41", 29 1/2" h. (ILLUS.,) **2,070**

Rare Classical Dressing Table

Classical dressing table, carved mahogany, the superstructure composed of a tall rectangular beveled framed mirror swiveling between large leafy scroll carved uprights w/brass mounts, the rectangular top over an apron w/a single long drawer w/round brass pulls flanked by brass anthemion mounts above reeded & leaf-carved front columns & incurved sides to an incurved lower shelf & back centered by a large brass mount, front corner blocks w/brass rosettes above the fluted disk front legs & simple turned rear legs on brass casters, attributed to Emmons and Archibald, Boston, 1815-25, base 18 x 34", overall 5' 5 1/2" h. (ILLUS.) **15,535**

Fork-based Classical Games Table

Classical games table, mahogany & mahogany veneer, the rectangular fold-over top w/rounded corners above a conforming top over a deep ogee apron, raised on a widely flaring forked scroll-cut support raised on a stepped flaring platform base w/small ogee bracket feet, original finish, ca. 1845, 18 x 36", 30" h. (ILLUS.) **600**

Classical games table, mahogany & mahogany veneer, the rectangular serpentine-edged fold-over top above a conforming veneered apron, raised on a flattened lyre-form pedestal above a deep rectangular coved apron & platform raised on pierced scroll-cut feet, Boston, ca. 1830, original finish, 18 x 36", 30" h. **650**

Classical pier table, rosewood, faux bois, marble & giltwood, the rectangular white marble top above a gilt-stenciled apron featuring a central cluster of shaded fruit & flowers, the white marble corner columns headed by giltwood Ionia capitals, the back supports designed as marble pilasters flanking a rectangular mirror, the concave bottom shelf bordered w/a geometric stenciled design, the gilt heavy front paw feet w/large giltwood heavy cornucopia brackets, New York City, ca. 1830, 20 1/2 x 44 1/2", 37 1/2" h. (ILLUS., top next page) **16,100**

Fine New York Classical Pier Table

Classical Work Table on Carved Base

Classical work table, mahogany & mahogany veneer, rectangular top over a deep case w/two drawers w/brass ring pulls & inlaid brass keyholes, small turned drops at each corner, raised on a bulbous acanthus leaf-carved short pedestal above four outswept leaf-carved legs ending in hairy paw feet, original finish, replaced hardware, ca. 1830, 15 x 20", 28" h. (ILLUS.) **1,250**

Paw-footed Classical Work Table

Classical work table, mahogany & mahogany veneer, the rectangular top above a deep case w/two veneered drawers w/turned wood knobs, raised on a tapering turned & reeded pedestal atop a quadripartite platform w/scroll-carved paw feet on casters, probably Southern United States, ca. 1830, 17 1/4 x 21 1/2", 31 3/4" h. (ILLUS.) **575**

Classical Table with Yarn Drawer

Classical work table, mahogany & mahogany veneer, the rectangular top flanked by rectangular drop leaves w/rounded corners flanking the deep case w/two shallow drawers over a deep yarn drawer supported by a vasiform trestle base w/outswept scroll legs on casters, ca. 1840, closed 19 x 20 3/4", 28 1/2" h. (ILLUS.).................... **805**

Classical Two-drawer Work Table

Classical work table, mahogany & mahogany veneer, thin rectangular top w/rounded front corners above a conforming case w/curved acanthus leaf-carved panels at the front corners flanking two round-fronted drawers w/brass pulls & keyhole escutcheons, raised on a ring-turned & acanthus leaf-carved pedestal above four

flattened outswept legs carved on knees w/acanthus leaves & ending in small paw feet on casters, original finish, ca. 1830, 16 x 22", 30" h. (ILLUS.) **1,200**

Colonial Revival Tray-top Coffee Table

Colonial Revival coffee table, walnut, the oval glass tray lift-off top w/molded edges & end handles above an oval top carved in the center w/a nude figure, raised on four carved cabriole legs ending in scroll & peg feet, ca. 1920s, 27" l., 19" h. (ILLUS.)... **219**

Early Painted Chair-Table

Country-style chair-table, painted pine, the large round four-board top w/a scrubbed top tilting above simple turned arms & a rectangular seat base w/a lift-top compartment on simple turned legs, old red paint on base, late 18th - early 19th c., 49 1/2" d., 29" h. (ILLUS.) **4,485**

Very Early American Tavern Table

Early Southern Heart Pine Work Table

Yellow Pine Country Work Table

Country-style tavern table, chestnut, rectangular board top w/rounded corners overhanging an apron w/a single long drawer w/a turned knob & a scalloped shallow skirt, raised on ring- and block-turned legs joined by molded stretchers above knob feet, separation cracks, old inset damage, America, 17th c., 20 3/4 x 30 3/4", 28 1/2" h. (ILLUS., bottom previous page) **1,955**

Country-style work table, heart pine, the large square plank top overhanging an apron w/a long drawer w/two turned wood knobs on each side, simple tapering octagonal legs, nicks, scuff & separations in top, Southern U.S., ca. 1790, 48" w., 32 1/2" h. (ILLUS., top of page)..... **1,093**

Country-style work table, yellow pine, two-board top w/cut nails, four turned legs w/mortise-and-tenon construction, 19th c., old refinishing, separations, two legs ended out, 30 1/2 x 123", 29 1/2" h. (ILLUS., second from top) **2,200**

Federal card table, inlaid mahogany & flame-birch, the rectangular hinged top w/concave front & shaped rounded corners above a conforming apron inlaid w/an oval flame-birch panel flanked by similar rectangular panels over an inlaid lower edge, on four ring-turned & reeded tapering legs w/slender peg feet, Boston, possibly the shop of John & Thomas Seymour, 1800-10, 17 x 36", 30" h. **14,340**

Early Card Table with Reeded Legs

Federal Two-part Mahogany Dining Table

Federal card table, inlaid mahogany, the rectangular hinged top w/wide rounded corners above a matching top above the conforming apron centered by narrow bands of inlay, tall slender reeded tapering legs topped by a ring-turned section & ending in double-knob feet, top refinished, ca. 1820, 20 x 38", 30" h. (ILLUS., bottom of previoius page) **1,100**

Federal card table, mahogany, the D-shaped fold-over top w/outset front & reeded edges above a conforming apron, raised on four ring-turned & reeded tapering legs w/knob & peg feet, Philadelphia, ca. 1800-15, 18 x 36", 29 1/2" h. **3,107**

Federal Country-style Tea Table

Federal country-style tilt-top tea table, cherry, two-board top w/small wooden pegs & some figure, ring-turned column, cabriole legs w/raised panels at tops & ending in tripod snake feet, decorated w/incised vining down the legs & around the top w/small fans at the corners of top, cleats w/mix of rose head & square cut nails & some later screws, attributed to Connecticut, old refinishing, 26 x 26 1/4", 27" h. (ILLUS.) **2,128**

Federal dining table, mahogany, two-part, each section w/a D-form top above a conforming apron & w/a back drop-leaf supported by a swing-out leg, spiral-turned legs w/knob feet on casters, ca. 1825, open, 45 x 92", 30 1/2" h. (ILLUS., top of page) **1,495**

Federal Pembroke table, curly maple, the rectangular top flanked by two hinged drop leaves w/rounded corners, the apron fitted w/a drawer w/round brass knob at one end, raised on baluster- and ring-turned tapering legs ending in knob feet, New England, 1800-20, open 41 x 26", 28 1/2" h. **3,824**

Nicely Veneered Federal Work Table

Federal work table, bird's-eye maple & oak veneer, the rectangular top flanked by two D-shaped drop leaves above a deep apron w/a narrow & deep veneered & string inlaid drawer on the front & matching faux fronts on the back, raised on four ring- and baluster-turned supports on a trestle-style base w/outscrolled legs joined by block- and baluster-turned end stretchers & long double baluster- and ring-turned cross stretchers, old refinish, Middle Atlantic states, ca. 1815-25, imperfections, 17 1/4 x 18", 28 1/4" h. (ILLUS.) **2,703**

Federal work table, mahogany, a rectangular top above a deep conforming case w/two drawers w/round brass pulls, raised on ring-turned & acanthus leaf-carved legs w/ringed ankles raised on brass casters, stenciled label of George W. Miller (w. 1821-31), New York, New York, 18 x 23 1/2", 30 1/2" h. **5,019**

Federal Three-drawer Work Table

Federal work table, mahogany & mahogany veneer, square top flanked by hinged drop leaves w/rounded corners above a case of three shallow drawers w/round brass pulls, on ring-turned & spiral-carved legs ending in disk-and-peg feet, old finish, ca. 1820s, 16 x 30" open, 30" h. (ILLUS. half open)............................... **600**

Early French Refectory Table

French Provincial refectory table, walnut, the rectangular top above draw leaves fastened w/wrought-iron hasps, the paneled apron inlaid w/the initials "M.S.," "AM.IH," & numbers "1751," heavy baluster- and ring-turned legs headed by marquetry tulips, the flattened stretchers

raised on bun feet, France, mid-18th c., 25 x 66", 31" h. (ILLUS.) **7,188**

George III Mahogany Games Table

George III games table, mahogany, the rectangular fold-over top w/shaped & rounded projecting corners above an apron raised on cabriole legs w/leaf-carved knees & ending in claw-and-ball feet, England, late 18th c., 34" l., 30 1/2" h. (ILLUS.) **2,990**

George III Mahogany Side Table

George III side table, mahogany, the rectangular top flanked by gadroon-edged drop leaves w/rounded corners, the apron w/two drawers at one end & two false drawers at the other, raised on square tapering legs w/spade feet, joined by arched & pierced cross-stretcher, England, late 18th c., 20 x 29", 23 1/2" h. (ILLUS.).. **1,610**

Streamlined Modern Nakashima Walnut Coffee Table

Stickley Mission Oak Dining Table

minum tray above the base w/four wide flat tapering & arched legs, designed by Isamu Noguchi for Herman Miller, ca. 1947, 24 3/4 x 26 1/4", 19 3/4" h. (ILLUS.) **83,650**

Modern-style coffee table, walnut, the long tapering naturalistic board top raised on a canted post at one end & a wide rectangular upright board at the other, joined by a long base stretcher board, inscribed w/the name of the client & designer George Nakashima, 1975, 23 x 62", 15" h. (ILLUS., top of page) **17,925**

Mission-style (Arts & Crafts movement) dining table, oak, extension-type, the round divided top raised on a five-post divided pedestal w/blocked shoe feet, includes four 12" leaves in a storage rack, good original finish, decal label of L. & J.G. Stickley, early 20th c., closed 48" d., 29" h. (ILLUS.) **3,450**

Very Rare Noguchi Modern Chess Table

Modern-style chess table, ebonized plywood, the nearly square top w/serpentine sides in black w/small plastic inserts forming the chess board, raised on a cast alu-

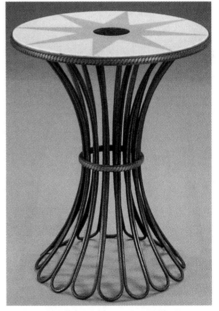

Rare Modern-style Iron & Marble Table

Modern-style side table, iron & marble, the round top in white marble inset w/a pale golden starburst centered by a black dot, a ropetwist metal rim band, raised on a pedestal base composed of waisted iron loops joined at the center by a ropetwist band, Model No. 1483, designed by Gilbert Poillerat, ca. 1953, two paper labels under the top reading "Made in France" & "X169/91," 21 1/2" d., 24 3/4" h. (ILLUS.) **19,120**

Fine Mahogany Queen Anne Dining Table

Country-style Tavern Table

Queen Anne country-style tavern table, maple w/old red paint, pegged construction, single-board oval top, splayed & tapered legs w/pad feet, top slightly warped, age splits, pegged restorations to one leg, minor repairs to pads of two feet, 24 x 29 1/4", 27 1/2" h. (ILLUS.) **6,038**

Queen Anne dining table, mahogany, a long narrow rectangular top flanked by wide rectangular drop leaves, shaped apron, block-and-turned legs ending in pad feet, old refinish, Rhode Island, mid-to-late 18th c., repaired, open 50 3/4 x 51 1/2", 27 1/4" h. (ILLUS. closed, top of page) **3,525**

Queen Anne dining table, mahogany, a rectangular top w/rounded ends flanked by wide half-round drop leaves, rectangular skirt w/cyma curved ends, on cabriole legs ending in pad feet, Massachusetts, 1740-60, open 48 x 48 3/4", 28" h... **5,019**

Queen Anne dining table, maple, a rectangular top flanked by rectangular hinged drop leaves, overhanging the apron w/a shaped skirt & raised on cabriole legs ending in pad feet, New England, 18th c., refinished, open 38 3/4 x 39", 27" h. (imperfections) **1,998**

Early Queen Anne Dressing Table

English Regency Mahogany Console Table

Queen Anne dressing table, walnut, the rectangular top w/molded edges & shaped corners overhanging a case w/a cockbeaded long drawer over a row of three deep drawers, the central one fancarved, the valanced shaped apron continuing into four cabriole legs w/arris knees & ending in raised pad feet, some old brasses, old refinish, probably Massachusetts, ca. 1740-60, imperfections, 20 1/4 x 29 3/4", 29" h. (ILLUS., bottom previous page) **22,325**

Nice Queen Anne Tavern Table

Queen Anne tavern table, figured maple, the oval top overhanging a deeply scalloped apron raised on turned slightly canted legs ending in raised pad feet, New England, 1740-70, 26 1/2 x 35 1/2", 27 1/2" h. (ILLUS.) **7,170**

Regency console table, mahogany, the long rectangular top w/recessed central section on a deep flaring cornice w/a beaded edge, raised on four heavy scrolling front supports ending in large paw feet resting on rectangular plinths, pairs of flat rear supports, England, first quar-

ter 19th c. or later, 27 x 78", 37 1/2" h. (ILLUS., top of page) **4,140**

English Regency Dining Table

Regency dining table, mahogany, extension-type, the oval top above a deep plain apron raised on baluster- and ring-turned legs on peg feet w/brass cap casters, England, second quarter 19th c., 34 x 47", 30" h. (ILLUS.) **431**

English Regency Sofa Table

Regency sofa table, mahogany, the long rectangular top flanked by short half-round drop leaves, the apron w/a pair of long paneled drawers w/knobs, a trestle-form base w/a pair of slender baluster-and ring-turned supports at each end resting on cross stretchers over outswept legs w/brass paw caps on casters, a long slender baluster-turned stretcher from end to end, polished original finish, England, ca. 1820, 22 x 46", 30" h. (ILLUS., bottom previous page) **1,400**

Inlaid Rococo Revival Side Table

Rococo Revival side table, inlaid mahogany, the round top centered by a large inlaid star-shaped dark panel centered by a light circle & bordered by inlaid swags, the molded edge above the deep serpentine apron pierce-carved w/leafy scrolls, raised on four incurved slender square legs ending in paw feet & joined at the center w/a serpentine-sided shelf pierce-carved w/acanthus leaves, original finish, ca. 1920s, 22" d., 30" h. (ILLUS.) **500**

Baroque Dining Table with Masks

Victorian Baroque Revival dining table, carved mahogany, extension-type, the square top w/rounded corners above a deep apron w/carved ropetwist border, raised on six legs composed of blocks, a reeded egg-shaped knob over a large leafy scroll, all joined by angled wide scroll-carved solid panels centered by large carved grotesque faces, original finish, w/six leaves, ca. 1890s, 60" w. closed, 30" h. (ILLUS.) **5,000**

Smaller Fruit-carved Dining Table

Victorian Baroque Revival dining table, oak, extension-type, the round top w/a gadrooned edge over an apron w/a thin knob-carved rim raised on a bulbous rosette-carved column on a heavy post issuing four outswept leafy scroll-carved legs ending in scroll feet carved on top w/clusters of fruit, on casters, original finish, ca. 1890, w/four leaves, 48" d., 30" h. (ILLUS.) **2,000**

European Baroque Dining Table

Victorian Baroque Revival dining table, oak, extension-type, the round top w/loop-carved border above a plain apron, raised on a heavy bulbous line-incised column on four outswept legs each carved at the top w/a figural fox head holding fruit it its mouth, crude paw feet on casters, Europe, late 19th c., w/two leaves, sold refinished, 48" d., 30" h. (ILLUS.) **1,200**

Baroque Table with Columnar Legs

Victorian Baroque Revival dining table, quarter-sawn oak, extension-type, square top w/plain apron raised on six columnar legs w/reeded bun feet, two fixed center legs, outer legs pull out to extend table & are joined by a high arched & scroll-caved panel, w/four leaves, refinished, ca. 1900, 60" w., 30" h. (ILLUS. with leaves on top)
.... **2,800**

Baroque Parlor Table on Columns

Victorian Baroque Revival parlor table, quarter-sawn oak, the round top w/a bead-carved edge raised on four columnar legs resting on large bun feet, the legs joined by a heavy cross stretcher topped by large heavy pierced & scroll-carved brackets, refinished, ca. 1890s, 28" d., 30" h. (ILLUS.) **700**

Victorian Country Pine Dining Table

Victorian country-style dining table, pine, the rectangular top flanked by narrow drop leaves, raised on rod- and ring-turned legs, second half 19th c., 39" l., 28" h. (ILLUS.) **161**

Victorian Eastlake Parlor Table

Victorian Eastlake-style parlor table, walnut, a rectangular pink marble top above a line-incised apron w/stepped brackets

& small turned corner drops, raised on four flat outswept legs joined by wide arched stretchers composed of cross-stretchers & turned knobs joined to a central round post, on casters, ca. 1880, one corner of marble top chipped, 19 1/2 x 27 3/8", 30 1/4" h. (ILLUS.) **200-300**

Unique Inlaid Victorian Table

Victorian novelty side table, inlaid mixed wood, the square top ornately inlaid w/a large central checkerboard surrounded by a wide inlaid band decorated w/fan-inlaid corners & various geometric designs above the shaped apron inlaid w/rectangular panels & diamond & small stars, fitted w/a single drawer w/a black pear-shaped rope pull, large baluster-, ring- and tapering rod-turned legs composed of stacked multicolored woods, original finish, ca. 1890, 26" w., 30" h. (ILLUS.) **750**

Victorian Renaissance Revival dining table, walnut, extension-type, the round top w/molded apron raised on a heavy split pedestal w/scroll-carved projecting legs mounted w/roundels & raised on casters, holds four 12"-wide leaves, ca. 1875, open 45 x 93", 30 1/2" h. (ILLUS. open, top next page) **1,150**

Simple Renaissance Library Table

Fine Renaissance Revival Walnut Dining Table

Victorian Renaissance Revival-style library table, walnut, the rectangular top w/rounded ends inset w/leather, the long side fitted w/two drawers w/turned wood pulls, the rounded ends w/small raised panels, raised on four trumpet-turned & fluted legs joined by an H-stretcher w/incurved ends & centered by a small urn finial, refinished, ca. 1875, 20 x 48", 30" h. (ILLUS., bottom previous page)... **700**

Victorian Renaissance Revival-style parlor center table, mahogany, cartouche-shaped top of lavender, raspberry, ivory & amber marble, four turned, tapered & fluted legs, central urn, end legs w/eagle carving, surface w/extensive burl wood panels & original gilt decoration, cross-stretcher base w/central lidded urn, possibly by John Jelliff, ca. 1860, missing leg bracket for one side, end of bracket off but present, urn lid missing finial, one foot w/old repaired break, one foot w/crack, one drop finial w/damage, 26 x 42", 31" h. **1,870**

Renaissance Revival Marble-topped Table

Victorian Renaissance Revival style parlor center table, rectangular white marble top w/projecting wide corners & molded edges above the reeded apron w/gently arched brackets, raised on four flattened scallop-cut C-form legs joined to a central ring-turned post, on casters, ca. 1875, 24 x 33", 30" h. (ILLUS.) **300-350**

Simple Renaissance Revival Parlor Table

Victorian Renaissance Revival style parlor center table, walnut, an oval white marble top w/molded edges above a simple molded apron w/gently arched brackets, raised on four flat molded serpentine legs joined to an urn- and ring-turned central post w/turned drop finial, ca. 1860-70 (ILLUS.) **374**

Victorian Renaissance Parlor Table

Victorian Renaissance Revival style parlor center table, walnut & burl walnut,

Fine Rosewood Rococo Console Table

the rectangular top w/rounded ends inset w/tan marble with the molded edging above the blocked & paneled apron trimmed w/burl veneer, raised on Greek key-carved trumpet legs blocked at the base & joined by an anthemion-carved X-form stretcher, on casters, ca. 1870, 23 x 39", 29 1/2" h. (ILLUS., previous page) **748**

Victorian Rococo-style console table, rosewood, the rectangular top w/inset white marble enclosed by a narrow gadrooned band above the deep apron w/a pair of large drawers w/bead-molding enclosing panels carved w/long scroll & shell-carved bands, a bead-carved front molding over a long scroll-carved drop, raised on pair of double C-scroll endings on casters joined by a long H-stretcher composed of ornate C-scrolls, New York City, ca. 1850, original finish, 18 x 52", 30" h. (ILLUS., top of page) **2,500**

green felt, the deep apron fitted w/four drawers alternating w/round panels, all centered by a carved cartouche & scrolls, raised on four heavy scroll-carved supports centered by a squatty bulbous finial all resting on a platform issuing four thick outstretched scroll-carved legs, old refinish, ca. 1865, 34" w., 30" h. (ILLUS.) **1,500**

Victorian Rococo-style parlor table, carved rosewood, a white marble "turtle top" above a conforming apron ornately carved w/scrolls, beaded panels & large fruit-carved reserves, raised on bold S-scroll legs on casters joined by a delicate S-scroll cross stretcher centered by a large bulbous spiral-turned urn finial, attributed to Prudent Mallard, New Orleans, Louisiana, 1850s, original finish, 28 x 50", 30" h. **6,500**

Large Walnut Rococo Games Table

Victorian Rococo-style games table, walnut, the octagonal top inset w/replaced

Nice Mahogany "Turtle-top" Table

Victorian Rococo-style parlor table, mahogany, a tan marble "turtle top" above a conforming molded apron w/tall incurved pierced scrolls w/carved bead bands connecting to a small round platform centered by a tall turned finial & raised on long outswept S-scrolls legs on casters, old refinish, ca. 1860, 16 x 24", 30" h. (ILLUS., bottom previoius page) **2,400**

"Turtle-top" Mahogany Parlor Table

Victorian Rococo-style parlor table, mahogany, a white marble "turtle top" above a conforming apron w/large carved oval cartouches centering the long sides, raised on four wide ornately pierce-carved supports joining a central post w/a large squatty urn finial & also raised on slender posts above the cross-form base composed of four long outswept scroll-carved legs joined to a central post & fitted on casters, refinished, ca. 1850s, 18 x 30", 30" h. (ILLUS.) **1,800**

Restrained "Turtle-top" Table

Victorian Rococo-style parlor table, mahogany, a white marble "turtle top" above a conforming molded apron supported by four flat serpentine leg w/carved knobs joined by an arched, pierced & scroll-carved cross stretcher centered by a tall ring-turned finial, on casters, original finish, ca. 1860, 24 x 36", 30" h. (ILLUS.) . **2,000**

Fine Victorian Rococo Dressing Table

Victorian Rococo-style dressing table, carved mahogany, the superstructure w/a large oval mirror in a molded frame topped by an ornately scroll- and foliate carved crest centering a large cabochon, swiveling between tall pierced scroll-carved uprights, the rectangular inset white marble top within a conforming apron w/a fancy scroll-carved front center boss & scroll- and leaf-carved knees on the cabriole legs raised on casters, New Orleans, ca. 1850s, 20 1/2 x 39", overall 6' 6" h. (ILLUS.) **4,313**

Nice Victorian Wicker Side Table

Wicker side table, a rectangular oak top raised on a wide apron composed of wicker spindles & w/corner curlicues, wrapped legs joined by a lower oak shelf w/wicker banding & a low spindle gallery, natural finish, ca. 1890s, 16 x 20", 28" h. (ILLUS.) **863**

Wardrobes & Armoires

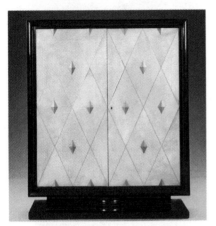

Rare French Art Deco Armoire

Armoire, Art Deco style, lacquered, parchment-veneered & bronze, the rectangular flat top in black continuing to form the square framework enclosing a pair of wide doors w/a diamond lattice design in parchment inset w/bronze diamonds, the interior w/two shelves, on a later long low black platform base, designed by Jean Pascaud, France, ca. 1930, 21 1/4 x 59", 5' 10 3/4" h. (ILLUS.)............................... **11,950**

Simple Classical Mahogany Armoire

Armoire, Classical style, mahogany, the rectangular top w/a wide flattened cornice above a cast w/a pair of tall paneled doors opening to a bank of three drawers, raised on bracket feet, restored original finish, ca. 1840, 22 x 60 1/2", 6' 9 1/2" h. (ILLUS.) **1,840**

French Provincial Walnut Armoire

Armoire, French Provincial, kingwood & carved walnut, the rectangular top w/an arched & molded crestrail centered by a large pierced scroll-carved crest & upright scroll corner finials, the arched frieze band above a pair of arched tall doors w/mirrors framed by raised molding, scroll-carved angled front corners continuing to short front cabriole legs w/scroll feet joined by a deep serpentine leaf scroll-carved apron, France, late 19th c., 20 x 59", 8' 6" h. (ILLUS.)............. **1,840**

Ornately Carved Provincial Armoire

Armoire, Louis XV-Style Provincial type, fruitwood, the rectangular top w/a coved border w/scroll-carved corners & centered by a large upright ornate carved shell crest, above a molded cornice over a two-panel scroll-carved frieze band above a pair of three-panel doors, the scroll-carved top panel over a two-oval center panel above a lower panel w/incurved top, two narrow drawers at the bottom above the serpentine scroll-carved apron & short scrolled legs w/scroll feet, France, 19th c., 26 x 55", 8' 8" h. (ILLUS., bottom previous page) **2,760**

Unique Gothic Revival Armoire

Fine Neoclassical Painted Armoire

Armoire, Neoclassical, polychrome painted wood, the rectangular top w/a molded cornice above a pair of tall doors painted overall w/elaborate scrolling heraldic patterns in shades of grey, white, maroon & gold, the side painted w/trompe l'oeil panels, on a flat plinth base, Italy, late 18th c. or later, 18 x 59", 6' 6" h. (ILLUS.) **8,050**

Armoire, Victorian Gothic Revival style, walnut, the pediment composed of two front & two side Gothic arch panels w/scrolling trim & centering raised scrolling burl panels, three tall fluted columns w/tall tapering ring-turned finials dividing the pair of tall paneled doors each decorated w/raised tracery centered by a small cabochon, raised on heavy compressed ring- and knob-turned feet, Mid-Atlantic states, ca. 1855, 26 x 62", 8' 1" h. (ILLUS., top next column) **4,140**

Armoire, Victorian Rococo style, carved rosewood, the top w/a high arched scroll-carved crestrail w/a large central cabochon above small pierce-carved panels & flanked by pointed knob corner finials, the deep arched & molded cornice above

Victorian Rococo Rosewood Armoire

a pair of tall paneled doors opening to a divided interior containing shelves, a single drawer & a half void, the canted front corners decorated w/scrolled pendants at the top corners, the slightly stepped-out lower section enclosing a pair of paneled drawers w/turned wood knobs above the plinth base, probably New York City, ca. 1855, 22 x 64", 9' 2" h. (ILLUS.) **4,600**

Early Mennonite One-door Kas

Kas (a version of the Netherlands kast or wardrobe), country-style, maple & walnut, a rectangular top w/angled front corners & a low cornice w/a dentil-carved band above a tall single raised four-panel door decorated w/four star & dot inlays & w/the original brass pull, the canted front corners decorated w/double bands of chip-carving & further star inlays, conforming stepped apron on tapering block front feet, opening to interior side liners & four adjustable shelves, attributed to the Sonnenburg Mennonites, hinges replaced, old red wash, 23 x 53", 6' 4 1/4" h. (ILLUS.) **5,175**

Large Nicely Detailed Flemish Kas

Kas (a version of the Netherlands kast or wardrobe), walnut, the rectangular top w/a widely flaring stepped cornice above a dentil-carved frieze band above a narrow molding over the pair of tall cupboard doors each w/tall raised-molding panels above & below a smaller rectangular center panel, wide side stiles w/narrow raised panels, heavy molded base raised on wide blocked pad feed, Flanders, mid-19th c., 27 x 60", 7' 2" h. (ILLUS.)............. **5,750**

English Arts & Crafts Wardrobe

Wardrobe, Arts & Crafts style, oak, a gently arched crestrail w/a squatty heart cutout above a pair of tall doors, one fitted w/a long mirror & long copper strap hinges, the other w/geometric glass panels above three narrow vertical panels decorated w/stamped copper bosses, a long drawer across the base w/stamped copper pulls & a band of three hearts in each side panel, flat base, original finish, unmarked, England, ca. 1900, 17 1/4 x 45 1/2", 6' 6 3/4" h. (ILLUS.)...................................... **2,760**

Wardrobe, country style, cypress, a rectangular top w/a flaring cornice w/stamped acanthus designs above three tall four-paneled doors opening to a blind interior, the separate lower section composed of two long drawers w/metal pulls above a molded plinth base, early 20th c., 29 x 85", 9' h. (ILLUS., top next page)...... **3,163**

Large Three-door Cypress Wardrobe

Early Painted Breakdown Wardrobe

Wardrobe, country style, painted pine, breakdown type, the rectangular top w/a molded cornice above a deep plain frieze band over a pair of tall double-raised panel doors w/a diamond panel in the top half, cast-iron lift-off hinges, flat molded base, old red paint over earlier green, two removable interior shelves & peg racks, originally had feet, tin patches over old holes, attributed to Ohio or Indiana, 19th c., 22 3/4 x 51 1/2", 6' 2 1/2" h. (ILLUS.)... **1,265**

Wardrobe, country-style, oak, rectangular top above a narrow molding over a tall arched door set w/a beveled mirror flanked on each side by a molded arched panel above a tall rectangular panel, a single long drawer at the base w/drop pulls, simple bracket feet, early 20th c., 48" w., 7' h. **374**

Victorian Eastlake Wardrobe

Wardrobe, Victorian Eastlake style, walnut & burl walnut, demountable, the rectangular top w/a wide flaring cornice above a narrow burl frieze band over a pair of tall beveled glass mirrored doors topped by narrow raised burl panels, a slender half-round colonette down the center & flanking the doors, a pair of burl veneered drawers w/stamped brass pulls at the bottom, flat molded base w/wafer feet, original hardware, refinished, ca. 1875, 20 x 52", 7' 4" h. (ILLUS.) **2,400**

Wardrobe, Victorian Renaissance Revival style, walnut & burl walnut, the rectangular top w/a small arched center crest on the widely flaring stepped cornice above a frieze band w/a pair of long narrow raised burl bands flanking a central rondel, all above a pair of tall arched doors fitted w/mirrors below triangular raised panels in the upper corners, the doors flanked by pairs of long raised burl panels & rondels, the base w/a pair of drawers w/large raised burl panels & turned wood knobs above the plinth base on casters, ca. 1875, 20 x 57", 8' 2" h. (ILLUS., top next page) **1,495**

Victorian Renaissance Wardrobe

Massive Renaissance Wardrobe

Wardrobe, Victorian Renaissance Revival style, walnut, demountable, the rectangular top w/a high arched & deeply molded crestrail above an arched panel centered by a carved ring over a pair of tall arch-paneled doors centered by a narrow tall oval panel, flat molded & flaring base, open interior, refinished, ca. 1875, 22 x 60", 7' 10" h. (ILLUS.) **2,400**

Whatnots & Etageres

Rare French Art Nouveau Etagere

Etagere, Art Nouveau style, carved mahogany & marquetry, a high arched back crest w/a marquetry floral band above a top shelf flanked by curved sides above an ornately pierce-carved floral apron curving around the sides of the case & tapering to form a center stile, a large recessed compartment w/original pleated fabric above a lower case composed of a pair of tall tapering cupboard doors w/whiplash marquetry leaves & flowers & opening to a shelf, a flaring & scroll-carved base, designed & signed by Louis Majorelle, ca. 1900, France, 15 x 28 1/2", 5' 5" h. (ILLUS.) **31,070**

Etagere, Art Nouveau style, mahogany, the tall back composed of a large oblong beveled mirror in a narrow frame w/a carved crest above a tall vertical rectangular lower mirror, all supported on an arrangement of two curved long front legs & two shorter straight rear legs w/various sized oblong open shelves down the front, ca. 1910 (ILLUS., top next page)....... **431**

Open Art Nouveau Style Etagere

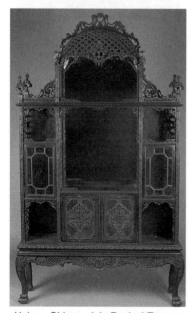

Unique Chippendale Revival Etagere

Etagere, Chippendale Revival style, carved mahogany, the scrolled pediment above a trelliswork half dome fronted by a pierced cartouche, the mirrored back divided by a shelf & over a pair of relief-carved doors, each side w/a shelf surmounted by finials, a glazed center door & two open compartments, on a base w/scroll-carved serpentine apron raised on short cabriole legs w/paw feet, in the manner of Edward and Roberts, London, England, ca. 1900, 13 x 51", 5' 10" h. (ILLUS.) **5,463**

American Classical Etagere

Etagere, Classical style, mahogany, a rectangular base cabinet w/two cockbeaded drawers above bracket feet on casters, the top supporting four open shelves joined by graduated baluster-turned supports, Boston, ca. 1830, 18 x 23", 5' 2" h. (ILLUS.).. **1,725**

English Regency-Style Etagere

Etagere, Regency-Style, mahogany, an arrangement of four open shelves on graduated baluster-turned supports above a bottom shelf over a narrow drawer w/two round brass pulls, on turned peg feet on casters, England, last quarter 19th c., 17 7/8 x 22", 5' 1 3/4" h. (ILLUS., bottom previous page) **2,070**

turned feet, ca. 1850-60, 16 x 35", 6' 1" h. (ILLUS., below) **690**

Ornate Pierce-carved Rococo Etagere

Large Marble-topped Rococo Etagere

Etagere, Victorian Rococo style, rosewood-grained hardwood, the tall superstructure w/a high arched & pierce-carved crest w/an acanthus leaf cartouche over a tall arched mirror flanked on each side by four graduated quarter-round open shelves w/S-scroll supports & pierce-carved back brackets, the mirror above a molded rectangular panel flanked by scroll brackets on a half-round marble-topped base w/serpentine molded edges above a conforming apron w/a central drawer & trimmed w/carved scrolls & raised on four cabriole legs ending in scroll feet, ca. 1850s, 52" w., 7' 6" h. (ILLUS.) **3,450**

Etagere, Victorian Rococo style, walnut, the upper section composed of three graduated & shaped open shelves supported by cut-out & molded serpentine brackets, each shelf w/a pierced back crest & gallery, the lower cabinet w/an oblong top above a conforming case w/a pair of cabinet doors w/pierced fretwork panels, serpentine apron above knob-

Late Victorian Whatnot with Desk

Whatnot, Victorian country style, walnut, two narrow rectangular shaped & graduated open shelves joined by pairs of baluster-turned spindles above a rectangular compartment w/a fall front opening to a small writing surface & interior fitted w/small drawers & pigeonholes, raised on two larger matching open shelves supported on matching spindles & turned feet, ca. 1870-80 (ILLUS.) **250-400**

GLASS

Amberina

Amberina was developed in the late 1880s by the New England Glass Company and a pressed version was made by Hobbs, Brockunier & Company (under license from the former). A similar ware, called Rose Amber, was made by the Mt. Washington Glass Works. Amberina-Rose Amber shades from amber to deep red or fuchsia and cut and plated (lined with creamy white) examples were also made. The Libbey Glass Company briefly revived blown Amberina, using modern shapes, in 1917.

Amberina Label

Basket, tall flaring optic swirled body w/two sides of the rim pulled up & joined by a tall pointed rigaree amber handle, lightly crimped rim, raised on four applied amber petal feet, 11" h. **$230**

Shallow Amberina Bowl

Bowl, 7 3/4" d., 2 1/2" h., wide shallow round form, ridged bottom resembling a snowflake surrounded by diamond quilted designs, fuchsia rim shaded to amber, attributed to the New England Glass Co. (ILLUS.).. **316**

Pitcher, 8" h., bulbous ovoid melon-lobed body tapering to a cylindrical neck w/a pinched spout, Inverted Thumbprint patt., applied clear reeded handle, ground pontil... **604**

Vase, 6 5/8" h., lily-form shape, delicate optic ribbing, swirled fuchsia rim shading to amber, small scratch inside body (ILLUS., top next column) **230**

Amberina Fuchsia Lily Vase

Tall Ruffle-topped Amberina Vase

Vase, 10" h., a squatty compressed base below the tall cylindrical sides w/a widely flaring crimped & ruffled rim, Optic Swirl patt. (ILLUS.)... **300**

Animals

American Glass Boxer Dogs

Americans evidently like to collect glass animals. For the past sixty years, American glass manufacturers have turned out a wide variety of animals to please the buying public. Some were produced for long periods and some were later reproduced by other companies, while others were made for only a short period of time and are rare. We have not included late productions in our listings and have attempted to date the productions where possible. Evelyn Zemel's book, American Glass Animals A to Z, *will be helpful to the novice collector. Another helpful book is* Glass Animals of the Depression Era *by Lee Garmon and Dick Spencer Collector Books, 1993.*

Bird, w/long tail, ruby, Viking Glass, No.
1311 .... **$45**
Boxer dog, lying, clear, American Glass
Co., 4 3/4" h. (ILLUS. left, top of page) **55**
Boxer dog, sitting, clear, American Glass
Co., 4 3/4" h. (ILLUS. right, top of page) **65**
Bulldog, doorstop, black, Westmoreland,
8 1/2" h. **475**
Cat, milk glass, U.S. Glass Co., 11" h. **350**
Cat, light blue, Fostoria Glass Co., 3 1/4" h. **30**
Cat, dark medium blue, No. 1322, 1960s,
Viking Glass Co., 8" h. **45**
Chick, clear, New Martinsville Glass Co.,
1" h. **25**
Chinese pheasant, light blue, Paden City
Glass Co., 13 1/2" l. **195**
Dog, dark medium blue, No. 1323, 1960s,
Viking Glass Co., 8" h. **55**
Donkey, clear, Heisey Glass Co., 5" l.,
6 1/2" h. (ILLUS., next column) **350**
Dove, head down, clear, Duncan & Miller,
11 1/2" l. **165**
Dragon, candleholder, Cathay line, clear
satin, Imperial Glass Co., 6 3/4" h. **185**
Dragon swan, clear, Paden City Glass Co.,
9 3/4" l., 6 1/2" h. **175**
Duck, mama, amber frosted, Fostoria Glass
Co., 4" h. **42**
Duckling, head down, cobalt blue, Fostoria
Glass Co., 1 1/2" h. **24**
Eagle, book end, Cambridge Glass, clear,
6" w., 6" h. **85**

Heisey Glass Co. Donkey

Eagle, book end, clear, Fostoria Glass Co.,
7" h. **125**
Eagle, book end, clear, Fostoria Glass Co.,
7" h. **125**

Cambridge Glass Co. Eagle

Eagle, three-part relish dish, clear, Cambridge Glass Co., 8" w. (ILLUS., bottom previous page) 85
Egret, ruby, Viking Glass Co., 10 to 12" h. 65

Co-Operative Glass Elephant

Elephant, covered dish, black, Co-Operative Flint Glass, 7" h. (ILLUS.) 155
Elephant, covered dish, Co-Operative Flint Glass, black, 4 1/4" h., 7 1/2" l. 195
Elephant w/trunk raised (Baby), clear, Heisey Glass Co., 1944-53, 5" l., 4 1/2" h. 325
Fawn, w/flower floater & sockets for three candles, copen blue, Tiffin Glass Co., ca. late 1940s, 14 1/2" l., fawn 10" h. 350
Fish, book end, clear, Heisey Glass Co., 6 1/2" h. 185
Fish, candleholder, clear, A.H. Heisey & Co., 1941-58, 5" h. 225
Goldfish, horizontal form, Fostoria Glass, clear, 1 1/4" h. 175

Fostoria Glass Co. Goldfish

Goldfish, vertical, clear, Fostoria Glass Co., 4" h. (ILLUS.) 175
Goose, clear frosted, L.E. Smith Glass Co., 4 1/2" h. 27
Goose, wings half up, clear, A.H. Heisey & Co., 1947-55, 5 1/2" l., 5" h. 100
Goose, pale blue, Paden City Glass Co., ca. 1940, 5" h. 125
Horse, Clydesdale, clear, Heisey Glass Co., 7" l. 450
Horse, reclining form, amber, L.E. Smith Glass, 4 3/4" h., 8 1/2" l. 170
Horse head, book ends, clear, A.H. Heisey Co., 1937-55, 6 7/8" h., pr. 375

Horse & rider, book end, clear, K.R. Haley, 6" h. 55
Lion, book end, clear, Cambridge Glass Co., 6" h. 235
Owl, book end, black, Westmoreland Glass Co., 6" h. 250
Papa bear, clear, No. 489, New Martinsville Glass Co., satin finish, 6 1/2" l., 4" h. 250
Pelican, clear, Fostoria Glass Co., 3 3/4" h. 75

Heisey Glass Co. Plug

Plug horse "Oscar," clear, A. H. Heisey & Co., clear, 1941-46, 4" l., 4" h. (ILLUS.) 125
Polar bear on ice, clear, No. 611, Paden City Glass Co., 4 1/2" h. 85
Pouter pigeon, book end, clear, Indiana Glass Co., 5 1/2" h. 28
Pouter pigeon, book ends, clear, Cambridge Glass Co., 4 x 5" base, 6" h., pr. 190
Rabbit, large mama, clear, No. 764, New Martinsville Glass Co., 2 1/2" h. 325
Rabbit, clear, No. 6808, Viking Glass Co., 6 1/2" h. 35
Rabbit (Thumper), clear, Viking Glass Co., 6 1/2" h. 25
Ringneck pheasant, clear, Heisey Glass Co., 1942-53, 12" l., 5" h. 175
Rooster head stopper, clear, A.H. Heisey & Co., 4 1/2" h. 75
Sailfish, blue opalescent, Duncan & Miller, 5" h. 650
Sea gull, flower frog, Cambridge Glass, clear, 10" h. 75

New Martinsville Glass Co. Seal

Seal, large w/ball, clear, New Martinsville Glass Co., 7" h. (ILLUS., bottom previous page).. **58**

Sparrow, clear, A.H. Heisey & Co., 1942-45, 4" l., 2 1/4" h... **125**

Squirrel, clear, No. 674, New Martinsville Glass Co., 4 1/2" h. (no base)....................... **70**

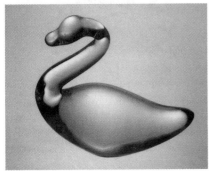

Duncan & Miller Swan

Swan, Pall Mall patt., solid back, clear, Duncan & Miller, 3" l. (ILLUS.).............................. **58**

Swordfish, clear, Duncan & Miller Glass Co., 5" h. **275**

Wolfhound, black, No. 716, Dalzell/Viking Glass Co. reissue of New Martinsville Glass Co., 7" h. **450**

Blown Three Mold

This type of glass was entirely or partially blown in a mold and was popular from about 1820 to 1840. The object was formed and the decoration impressed upon it by blowing the glass into a metal mold, usually of three—but sometimes more—sections hinged together. Mold-blown glass actually dates back to ancient times. Recent research reveals that certain geometric patterns were reproduced in the 1920s; some new pieces, usually sold through museum gift shops, are still available. Collectors are urged to read all recent information available. Reference numbers are from George L. and Helen McKearin's book, American   Glass.

Pieces are clear unless otherwise noted.

Rare Cobalt Blue Blown Three Mold Creamer

Creamer, geometric, bulbous body tapering to a tall cylindrical neck w/a flaring rim

w/pinched spout, applied foot & applied solid handle, cobalt blue, 3 7/8" h., GII-45 (ILLUS.).. **$3,360**

Rare Barrel-shaped Decanter

Decanter w/no stopper, geometric, barrel-shaped w/a tall neck & applied sloping collar mouth, pontil scar, bright yellowish forest green, possibly Keene, New Hampshire, mouth roughness & chipping, pt., GII-7 (ILLUS.)............................. **1,344**

Olive Keene, New Hampshire, Decanter

Decanter w/no stopper, geometric, bulbous ovoid body w/a tapering neck to a sheared mouth, pontil scar, light to medium yellowish olive, Keene Marlboro Street Glassworks, Keene, New Hampshire, ca. 1820-40, pt., GIII-16 (ILLUS.) **672**

Keene, New Hampshire Decanter

Decanter w/no stopper, geometric, ovoid tapering to a tooled lip, pontil scar, yellowish olive green, Keene, New Hampshire, 1820-40, 6 7/8" h., GIII-16 (ILLUS.) **784**

Yellow Whale Oil Sparking Lamp

Sparking lamp, geometric, yellow w/a topaz tone, short cylindrical font w/narrow rings, ground mouth w/tin whale oil burner, smooth base, 2 1/2" h., GI-2 (ILLUS.)..... **336**

Bohemian

Numerous types of glass were made in the once-independent country of Bohemia and fine colored, cut and engraved glass was turned out. Flashed and other inexpensive wares also were made; many of these, including amber- and ruby-shaded glass, were exported to the United States during the 19th and 20th centuries. One favorite pattern in the late 19th and early 20th centuries was Deer & Castle. Another was Deer and Pine Tree.

Bowl, 4 1/4" d., 2 3/4" h., squatty round shaped w/three-crimp rim, salmon pink iridescence decorated overall w/random aubergine threading, Rindskopf factory, ca. 1900 (ILLUS. bottom row, second from left, bottom of page) **$173**
Bowl, 8" d., 4" h., wide flattened squatty body tapering to a crimped rim w/two fold-over loop handles, salmon pink iridescence decorated overall w/random violet threading, Pallme-Konig factory, ca. 1900 (ILLUS. bottom row, far left, bottom of page).. **345**

Bulbous Green Threaded Vase

Vase, 3 3/4" h., footed squatty bulbous body tapering to a sheared & rolled & ruffled wide collar, olive green randomly threaded w/burgundy bands, attributed to Pallme-Konig (ILLUS.) **316**

Squatty Swirled Ruby Bohemian Vase

Group of Bohemian Bowls & Vases

Vase, 5" h., footed squatty bulbous body tapering to a wide crimped rim, swirled ruby & aqua body w/a wide band of pointed gold panels around the neck trimmed w/white enamel, gilded applied loop shoulder handles, gold wear & minor scratches (ILLUS., previous page).............. 633

Vase, 5 1/2" h., squatty bulbous body tapering to a trumpet neck, salmon pink iridescence decorated w/overall random violet threading, Pallme-Konig factory, ca. 1900 (ILLUS. top row, second from right, bottom previous page) 143

Vase, 6 1/2" h., footed wide squatty body tapering to a wide ruffled flaring split-front neck, iridescent purple decorated overall w/random violet threading, Pallme-Konig factory, ca. 1900 (ILLUS. top row, far left, bottom previous page) 316

Vase, 7" h., swelled cylindrical form w/pinched & twisted sides below the bulbous cupped tri-fold rim, iridescent surface drizzled w/latté-textured drops overlaid w/four cobalt blue leaf pods, attributed to Rindskopt 230

Vase, 7" h., footed squatty nearly spherical body tapering to a wide flared split nexk w/one side rolled down, salmon rose iridescence decorated w/overall aubergine random threading, Pallme-Konig factory, ca. 1900 (ILLUS. top row, far right, bottom page 700) 661

Vase, 12" h., footed bulbous body w/pinched sides tapering to a cylindrical neck issuing three long rolled-over handles attaching to the shoulder, salmon rose iridescence decorated overall w/random amethyst threading, some grinding on base, Pallme-Konig factory, ca. 1900 (ILLUS. top row, second from left, bottom of page 700) 633

Vase, 4 1/2" h., spherical body tapering to a flaring ruffled rim, iridescent red decorated overall w/random violet threading, Pallme-Konig factory, ca. 1900, pr. (ILLUS. bottom row, second from right, bottom page 700) 288

Bride's Baskets & Bowls

These berry or fruit bowls were popular late Victorian wedding gifts, hence the name. They were produced in a variety of quality art glasswares and sometimes were fitted in ornate silver plate holders.

Shaded Butterscotch Bride's Bowl

Butterscotch to yellow, widely flaring ruffled & crimped edges w/overall swirled ribbing & V-form ribs at the rim flutes, 9 5/8" d., 3 1/4" h. (ILLUS.) **$92**

Very Small Cased Bride's Basket

Cased bowl, apricot shaded to white interior w/a fancy tri-ruffled & fluted rim, white exterior, fitted in a fancy silver plate frame marked by the Rockford Silver Plate Co., small size, bowl 5 1/2" d., overall 5 1/2" h. (ILLUS.)............................. 161

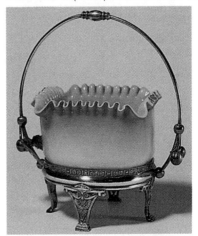

Blue & Pink Bride's Bowl in Frame

Cased bowl, turquoise blue interior & deep shaded pink exterior, wide cylindrical body w/a squared crimped & ruffled rim, fitted in a fancy silver plate frame w/figural cherries applied to the high arched handle, marked by Meriden, two leaves missing on frame, ca. 1890s, bowl 4" h., overall 10 1/2" h. (ILLUS.)............................ 345

Burmese

Burmese is a single-layer glass that shades from pink to pale yellow. It was patented by Frederick S. Shirley and made by the Mt. Washington Glass Co. A license to produce the glass in England was granted to Thomas Webb & Sons, which called its articles Queen's Burmese. Gundersen Burmese was made briefly about the mid-

dle of the 20th century, and the Pairpoint Company is making limited quantities at the present time.

Small Satin Burmese Footed Bowl

Bowl, 3" h., three small yellow peg feet supporting the squatty bulbous body tapering to the widely flaring ruffled rim, satin finish, attributed to Thomas Webb & Sons, minor polishing on feet (ILLUS.)................ **$230**

Decorated Miniature Burmese Bowl

Bowl, 3 1/2" d., 2" h., miniature, waisted cylindrical sides enameled w/yellow & white mums on meandering leafy stems, satin ground, Mt. Washington (ILLUS.)................ **633**

Rare Folded & Enameled Burmese Bowl

Bowl, 6 1/2" w., 2 1/2" h., a diamond-quilted design, round flat base & widely flared sides w/two sides pulled up & pinched in, a pale yellow crimped band around the exterior rim, the exterior & interior finely enameled w/large mums & green leaves, satin finish, Mt. Washington (ILLUS.)........ **2,645**

Caster set: two shakers & a bottle fitted on a silver plate stand; the cylindrical ribbed shakers w/silver plate caps, the matching bottle w/the original facet-cut stopper, the stand w/a round flat base w/a lightly ruffled rim, a tall central wire handle w/a large hoop top fitted below w/three rings to hold the shakers & bottle, frame

marked by Pairpoint, Mt. Washington, overall 7 1/2" h., the set (ILLUS., below) .. **1,093**

Lovely Burmese Caster Set

Decorated Burmese Cracker Jar

Cracker jar w/original silver plate rim, cover & ornate bail handle, barrel-shaped, enameled w/a delicate band of leafy branches & pine cones, attributed to Thomas Webb, 6" h. (ILLUS.).................. **1,020**

Glossy Footed Burmese Creamer

Creamer, footed round-bottomed cylindrical form w/a small pinched rim spout & applied yellow handle, glossy finish, small bubble encased near spout, Mt. Washington, 3 5/8" h. (ILLUS., bottom previous page) **173**

Open Squatty Burmese Sugar Bowl

Sugar bowl, open, delicate applied yellow wishbone feet supporting the widely flaring shallow bulbous body w/a wide low flared rim, raspberry prunt on pontil, satin finish, Mt. Washington, 3 3/8" d., 2 1/2" h. (ILLUS.) **633**

Unusual Burmese Toothpick Holder

Toothpick holder, a squatty bulbous body molded w/delicate flaming scrolls below the flaring lightly crimped rim, delicate enameled florals & fern leaves, Mt. Washington, 2 1/4" h. (ILLUS.) **1,150**

Miniature Webb Burmese Vase

Vase, 3 3/4" h., miniature, a squatty bulbous base below the cylindrical sides below

the flaring ruffled & crimped rim, satin finish, Thomas Webb & Sons (ILLUS.) **403**

Pretty Decorated Webb Burmese Vase

Vase, 6 1/4" h., slender baluster form w/a gently flared flat rim, enameled w/cascading slender branches supporting lavender blue flowers & green leaves, Thomas Webb (ILLUS.) **1,035**

Cambridge

The Cambridge Glass Company was founded in Ohio in 1901. Numerous pieces are now sought, especially those designed by Arthur J. Bennett, including Crown Tuscan. Other productions included crystal animals, "Black Amethyst," "blanc opaque," and other types of colored glass. The firm was finally closed in 1954. It should not be confused with the New England Glass Co., Cambridge, Massachusetts.

NEAR CUT

Cambridge Marks

Etched Rose Point Pattern
Ashtray, oval, No. 3500/131, Crystal, 4 1/2" l. **$72**
Basket, favor-type, No. 3500/79, Crystal, 3" w. **500**
Bell, Crystal.. **175**
Bowl, soup, 8 1/2" d., flat, Crystal.................... **265**
Bowl, 10" d., salad, Pristine blank No. 427, Crystal.. **185**
Bowl, 12" d., footed, No. 3400, Crystal........... **165**
Bowl, 13" d., 12" l., No. 3400/1, flared, Crystal.. **110**
Cake salver, No. 170, scalloped edge, Crystal, 13" d. **295**
Candleholders, No. 3121, w/prisms, Crystal, 7 1/2" h., pr... **235**
Candlestick, single-light, No. 3400, keyhole stem, Crystal, 5 1/4" h.................................... **65**
Candy box, cov., ram's head finial, No. 3500/78, flat, ram's head finial, Crystal, 6" d... **365**
Candy dish, cov., No. 500, three-footed, rose finial, Crystal, 7" d. **390**
Cigarette holder, No. 1066, oval, w/ashtray foot, Crystal... **265**

Etched Rose Point Pieces

Claret, No. 3121, Crystal, 6 1/4" h. **120**
Cocktail icer, No. 187 Pristine blank w/non-etch liner, footed, Crystal, 2 pcs. (ILLUS. w/plate & salt & pepper shakers) **165**

Cambridge Crystal Compote

Compote, 5" h., No. 3500/148, Crystal (ILLUS.) **65**
Compote, blown, one-ball stem, Crystal, 5" h. **90**
Cordial, No. 7966, flared, cone shape, Crystal **175**
Creamer & open sugar, flat, No. 137, Crystal, 6 oz., pr. **295**

Creamer & open sugar bowl, individual, gold-encrusted, Crystal, pr. **75**
Cup & saucer, No. 3400, flat, Crystal **48**
Decanter w/stopper, No. 1372, Crystal, 28 oz., 13 1/4" h. **1,950**
Goblet, No. 3121, water, Crystal, 11 oz., 8 3/4" h. **50**
Ice bucket, Crystal w/chrome handle, scalloped top, 5 3/4" h. **195**
Model of a hat, No. 1703, Crystal, 6" h. **560**
Nappy, cereal, 6" **120**
Oyster cocktail, No. 3121, Crystal **40**
Pitcher, No. 3400, w/ice lip, Crystal, 76 oz. **300**
Pitcher w/ice lip, No. 79, Crystal, 20 oz. **450**
Plate, 9 1/2" d., No. 3400, Crystal (ILLUS. w/cocktail icer & salt & pepper shakers) **60**
Plate, 10 1/2" d., No. 3900, Crystal **190**
Plate, 14" d., torte, large center, #3400/65, Crystal **175**
Relish dish, No. 3400, three-handle, three-part, Crystal, 8" **56**
Relish dish, round, No. 3500/67, five inserts & tray, 12" d. **375**
Salt & pepper shakers, chrome lids, footed, No. 3400/77, Crystal, pr. **65**
Salt & pepper shakers, No. 3400, footed, Crystal, 3 1/2" h., pr. (ILLUS. w/plate & cocktail icer) **75**
Sherbet, low footed, No. 3500, Crystal, 7 oz. **25**
Tumbler, flat, No. 3400, Crystal, 2" h. **140**
Tumbler, No. 3121, footed, Crystal, 7" h. **35**
Tumbler, No. 3400/38, flat, Crystal, 12 oz. **75**
Vase, 6" h., No. 1410, round rose bowl type, Crystal **175**

Vase, 10" h., No. 575, cornucopia, smooth top, Crystal 260

Miscellaneous Patterns

Ashtray, round, Apple Blossom etching, yellow, 6" d. 145

Ashtray, Silhouette line, Royal Blue bowl on clear Nude Lady stem 275

Ashtray/card holder, pressed Caprice patt., footed, Moonlight Blue 22

Basket, etched Chantilly patt., two handles turned up, Crystal, 6" h. 48

Cambridge Crystal Handle Basket

Basket, applied crystal handle, No. 119, amber, 7" w. (ILLUS.) 65

Bitters bottle, etched Elaine patt., No. 1212, Crystal 295

Bonbon, pressed Caprice patt., low, footed, Moonlight Blue, 6" sq. 65

Bouillion w/liner, Decagon line, Dianthus Pink 18

Bowl, almond-type, footed, Decagon line, No. 611, Dianthus Pink 24

Bowl, cereal, Apple Blossom etching, pink 62

Bowl, cream soup, Decagon line, Willow Blue 28

Bowl, 2" d., almond-type, four-footed, pressed Caprice patt., No. 95, Crystal 25

Bowl, 5 3/4" d., flat rim, Decagon line, Dianthus Pink 18

Bowl, 7 1/2" d., footed, Azurite 55

Bowl, 8" l., Seashell patt., oval four-footed, milk glass 45

Bowl, 8 1/2" sq., four-footed, pressed Caprice patt., No. 50, Moonlight Blue 155

Bowl, 10" d., three-part, on silvered metal base, etched Chantilly patt., Crystal............. 185

Bowl, 11" d., etched Apple Blossom patt., low footed, gold-encrusted, Mandarin Gold (light yellow)....................................... 120

Bowl, 11 1/2" d., No. 81 cupped gardenia bowl, footed, low, pressed Caprice patt., Moonlight Blue 130

Bowl, 12" l., oblong, crimped, etched Wildflower patt., No. 3900/160, Crystal................ 95

Bowl, 12" w., four-footed, square, etched Diane patt., Crystal 75

Bowl, 12" w., square, four-footed, flared, etched Wildflower patt., No. 3400/4, gold-encrusted Crystal....................................... 85

Bowl, 13" d., crimped rim, four-footed, Caprice patt., No. 66, Crystal 48

Butter dish, cov., open handles, etched Elaine patt., No. 3400/52, Crystal 219

Butter dish, cov., open handles, etched Wildflower patt., No. 506, Crystal................. 195

Cake plate, etched Daffodil patt., Crystal, 11 1/2" d... 75

Candleholders, two-light, etched Imperial Hunt patt., keyhole stem, Dianthus Pink, 6" h., pr. 155

Cambridge One-Light Candlestick

Candlestick, one-light, No. 627, etched Grape patt., green, 4" h. (ILLUS.) 35

Cambridge Statuesque Line Candlestick

Candlestick, Statuesque Line (nude stem), Crown Tuscan, 9" h. (ILLUS., previous page) 135

Candlestick, three-light, cascading style, pressed Caprice patt., Crystal, 6" h. 55

Candlestick, three-light, etched Wildflower patt., keyhole stem, No. 638, Crystal 85

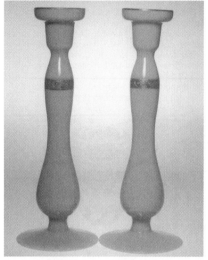

Cambridge Azurite Candlestick/Vases

Candlestick/vases, Azurite w/gold band, 9 1/2" h., pr. (ILLUS.) 125

Candlesticks, one-light, etched Diane patt., w/bobeches & prisms, Martha line blank, Crystal, 6 1/2" h., pr. 350

Candlesticks, one-light, Gadroon (No. 3500) line, molded ram's heads on the socket, Amber, 4 1/2" h., pr. 155

No. 3121 Candlestick

Candlesticks, one-light, No. 3121, w/bobeches & prisms, Crystal, 7 1/2" h., pr. (ILLUS. of one) 145

Candlesticks, one-light, No. 639, ringed stem, Cobalt blue, 4" h., pr. 150

Candlesticks, one-light, pressed Caprice patt., No. 67, Crystal, 2 1/2" h., pr. 40

Candlesticks, three-light, cascading-type, pressed Caprice patt., No. 1338, Mandarin Gold, 6" h., pr. 165

Candlesticks, two-light, etched Wildflower patt., fleur-de-lis stem, No. 3400/647, gold-encrusted Crystal, 6" h., pr. 150

Candlesticks, two-light, pressed Caprice patt., No. 69, w/bobeches & prisms, Moonlight Blue, 7" h., pr. 750

Candy box, cov., etched Wildflower patt., No. 3900/165, Crystal, 7" d. 100

Candy dish, cov., blown Line No. 3121, tall, Crystal, 5 3/8" d. 125

Candy dish, cov., etched Diane patt., Crystal, 7" d. 130

Champagne, etched Apple Blossom patt., No. 3130, Topaz 40

Cheese & cracker dish, Decagon line, Willow Blue 60

Cigarette box, cov., Caprice patt., crystal, 3 1/2 x 4 1/2" 28

Cigarette box, cov., etched Elaine patt., No. 615, Crystal, 3 x 3 1/2" 165

Cigarette holder, etched Diane patt., round w/ashtray foot, Crystal, 4" 168

Claret, pressed Alpine Caprice patt., Moonlight Blue 185

Coaster, pressed Caprice patt., Moonlight Blue, No. 20, 5 1/2" d. 35

Cocktail, blown Caprice patt., No. 300, Crystal, 3 oz. 30

Cocktail, etched Chantilly patt., No. 3625, Crystal 35

Cocktail, high stem, blown, Tally Ho patt., Royal Blue, 3 oz. 39

Cocktail, Mt. Vernon line, footed, Crystal, No. 26, 3 1/2 oz. 10

Cocktail, Statuesque (No. 3011) line, Amethyst bowl, clear Nude Lady stem, 4 1/2 oz., 6 1/2" h. 110

Cocktail icer, No. 3600, footed, etched Diane patt., Crystal 78

Comport, two-handled, Mt. Vernon line, Emerald green, 5 1/2" w. 65

Mt. Vernon Compote

Compote, Mt. Vernon line, w/ball stem, two handles, Crystal, 6" w., 6 1/4" h. (ILLUS., previous page) 32

Compote, open, cheese-type, Decagon line, Willow Blue 30

Compote, open, 7" d., pressed Caprice patt., low, footed, tab handled, Crystal 30

Console bowl, etched Apple Blossom patt., rolled edge, Gold Krystol, 12 1/2" d. 125

Console set: 9" d., ram' s head-handled bowl & pair 9 1/2" h. Doric Column candlesticks; Jade (blue-green opaque), 3 pcs 425

Cordial, etched Chantilly patt., No. 3625, Crystal, 1 oz. 75

Cordial, etched Diane patt., Crystal 85

Cordial, etched Imperial Hunt patt., plain stem, green, 1 oz. 200

Cordial, Line 1341, mushroom-style, Carmen (bright red) 25

Cordial, Mt. Vernon line, footed, Crystal, 1 oz. 22

Cordial, pressed Cambridge Square patt., Crystal, 2 1/8" h 32

Creamer, Decagon line, flat, Dianthus Pink 15

Creamer & open sugar bowl, etched Elaine patt., No. 1402/33, Crystal, pr. 65

Crown Tuscan candy dish, cov., shell-shaped, gold decoration, 6" w. 70

Crown Tuscan compote, 6" d., Nude Lady stem, gold-encrusted 200

Crown Tuscan plate, torte, 14" d. 125

Crown Tuscan vase, 10" h., Seashell patt., pedestal base 120

Cup, handled, Tally Ho patt., Forest Green, 2 1/2 oz. 18

Cup, pressed Caprice patt., No. 17, Crystal 15

Cup & saucer, demitasse, No. 3400 line, Crystal 15

Cup & saucer, etched Wildflower patt., No. 3400, Crystal, pr 35

Cup & saucer, pressed Caprice patt., Mocha 40

Cup & saucer, Tally-Ho line, Royal (cobalt blue) 70

Decanter & stopper, footed, etched Elaine patt., crystal 250

Decanter w/stopper, etched Portia patt., No. 3400/92, Crystal, 32 oz 375

Decanter w/stopper, Emerald body in Farberware metal holder, 8" h. 95

Figural flower holder, Draped Lady, green, 13" h 375

Figure flower holder, Draped Lady, Emerald, 8 1/2" h. 250

Figure flower holder, Two Kids, Crystal, 9 1/4" h. (ILLUS., top next column) 195

Finger bowl & liner, pressed Caprice patt., No. 16, Moonlight Blue 110

Goblet, blown Caprice patt., water, No. 300, Crystal, 5 7/8" h. 30

Goblet, Cambridge Square patt., water, Crystal, 5" h 20

Goblet, Decagon line, water, Willow Blue 32

Goblet, etched Apple Blossom patt., No. 3400, Topaz, 9 oz. 40

Goblet, etched Diane patt., No. 3122, Crystal, 9 oz 35

Two Kids Figure Flower Holder

Goblet, etched Elaine patt., water, No. 3121, Crystal 48

Goblet, etched Portia patt., sherry, No. 7966, Crystal, 2 oz. 50

Goblet, Mt. Vernon line, Crystal, 10 oz. 15

Goblet, pressed Caprice patt., water, No. 200, Crystal, 9 oz. 38

Hurricane lamp, keyhole candle base, w/prisms, etched Chantilly patt., Crystal, 11 1/2" h. 395

Ice bucket, chrome handle, etched Apple Blossom patt., Crystal 120

Ice bucket, etched Candlelight patt., No. 3900, Crystal 135

Ice pail, etched Cleo patt., No. 851, Mandarin Gold 169

Icer w/insert, etched Gloria patt., Crystal, 2 pcs. 75

Martini jug, etched Apple Blossom patt., No. 1408, Crystal, 60 oz. 950

Martini pitcher, etched Diane patt., Crystal, 60 oz. 1,995

Mayonnaise bowl & ladle, etched Portia patt., Pristine blank, Crystal, 2 pcs 55

Mayonnaise set: bowl, underplate & ladle; etched Wildflower patt., No. 3900/129, gold-encrusted Crystal the set 125

Model of a swan, Crown Tuscan, 6" h. 150

Nut bowl, individual, pressed Caprice patt., No. 93, square, tab handles, Moonlight Blue 60

Oil bottle & stopper, Caprice patt., No. 101, Moonlight Blue, 3 oz. 90

Parfait, blown Caprice patt., No. 300, Moonlight Blue, 6 1/2" h. 240

Perfume atomizer, footed, Ivory w/enamel Basket etching 275

Pickle dish, Decagon patt., w/etched Cleo patt., light blue, 9" l. 78

Royal Blue Divided Relish Dish

Pickle dish, etched Apple Blossom patt., No. 3400/59, Topaz, 9" l. 45

Pitcher, cov., No. 955, footed, etched Cleo patt., Amber, 62 oz...................................... 150

Pitcher, Doulton-style w/chrome base, handled, Amber...................................... 48

Pitcher, etched Apple Blossom patt., ball-shaped, Dianthus Pink, 80 oz. 495

Pitcher, etched Diane patt., ball-shaped, Crystal 245

Pitcher, etched Portia patt., ball-shaped, gold-encrusted, Mandarin Gold.................... 300

Pitcher, pressed Caprice patt., ball-shaped, No. 183, Crystal, 80 oz................................ 225

Plate, crescent-shaped salad, etched Chantilly patt., Crystal... 150

Plate, 6 1/2" d., etched Candlelight patt., Crystal 15

Plate, 7" d., etched Cleo patt., Decagon line, Moonlight Blue... 20

Plate, 7 1/2" d., Decagon line, Willow Blue 14

Plate, 8" d., No. 3400 line, Crystal 8

Plate, 8" d., pressed Caprice patt., Crystal 15

Plate, 8 1/4" d., Decagon line, off-center indent, Dianthus Pink...................................... 28

Plate, 8 1/2" d., etched Apple Blossom patt., Dianthus Pink.. 20

Plate, 8 1/2" d., Everglade patt., Crystal 20

Plate, 9 1/2" d., pressed Caprice patt., dinner, Crystal... 60

Plate, 10 1/2" d. dinner, Tally Ho patt., Carmen... 145

Plate, 11", cabaret-type, four-footed, pressed Caprice patt., Moonlight Blue.......... 95

Plate, 11" d., three-footed, pressed Caprice patt., Crystal... 35

Plate, 14" d., three-footed, pressed Caprice patt., Crystal... 40

Platter, 13 1/2" l., etched Apple Blossom patt., rectangular w/tab handles, Mandarin Gold 110

Relish, cov., oblong, five-part, w/dome cover, No. 397, Royal Blue, 12" l. (ILLUS., top of page)... 450

Relish, etched Rosalie patt., oval pickle, green, 9" l.. 45

Cambridge Round Four-part Relish

Relish, No. 3500/62, round four-part, Crystal w/applied dark green handles, 7" d. (ILLUS., bottom previous page) 48

Relish dish, etched Candlelight patt., three-part, three-handled, No. 3400, Crystal, 8" l. 50

Relish dish, etched Elaine patt., No. 3500/152, four-part, Crystal, 11" l. 100

Relish dish, etched Elaine patt., No. 3500/67, Crystal, 12" d., 6 pcs. 195

Relish dish, etched Portia patt., No. 862, four-part w/center handle, Crystal, 8 3/4" d. 120

Relish dish, etched Wildflower patt., No. 3400/88, two-part, Crystal, 8 3/4" 55

Relish dish, Gadroon (No. 3500) line, three-part, handled, Crystal, 6 1/2" l. 20

Relish dish, No. 3400 line, three-part, Emerald, 7" l. 28

Rose bowl & flower frog, pressed Caprice patt., footed, No. 235, Moonlight Blue, 6" d., 2 pcs. 450

Salt & pepper shakers, etched Candlelight patt., flat, Crystal, pr. 135

Salt & pepper shakers, etched Elaine patt., footed, Crystal, 3 1/4" h., pr. (one glass lid) 65

Salt shaker w/original chrome top, No. 3400 line, Cobalt 30

Salt shaker w/original top, etched Wildflower patt., No. 3900/1177, flat, Crystal, 3 1/2" h. 25

Caprice No. 300 Sherbet

Sherbet, blown Caprice patt., low, No. 300, Crystal, 6 oz. (ILLUS.) 18

Sherbet, etched Apple Blossom patt., Mandarin Gold, tall, No. 3130, 6 oz. 35

Sherbet, etched Daffodil patt., tall, Crystal, 6 oz. 20

Sherbet, etched Elaine patt., Crystal, No. 3035, 4 3/4" h. 20

Sherbet, Mt. Vernon line, Crystal, 6 1/2 oz. 10

Sherbet, pressed Caprice patt., No. 2, Moonlight Blue, 4 1/2" h. 45

No. 1713 Smoker Set in Ebony

Smoker set: cov. receptacle w/two ashtrays; No. 1713, dolphin footed receptacle w/clear lid, two rectangular ashtrays fit on top of lid, Ebony, 4 pcs. (ILLUS.) 120

Smoker set, pressed Caprice patt., shell-footed, Moonlight Blue, six pieces in original box, the set 110

Tray, for individual creamer & sugar bowl, pressed Caprice patt., Crystal.................... 20

Tray, wafer-type, etched Cleo patt., Emerald 365

Tumbler, blown Caprice patt., footed, No. 180, Moonlight Blue, 5 oz. 65

Tumbler, blown Caprice patt., footed, No. 184, Dianthus Pink, 12 oz. 50

Tumbler, blown Caprice patt., footed, No. 300, Moonlight Blue, 10 oz. 55

Tumbler, blown Caprice patt., iced tea, No. 300, Crystal, 6 1/8" h. 36

Tumbler, blown Caprice patt., iced tea, No. 310, flat, Crystal, 5 1/4" h. 170

Tumbler, blown Caprice patt., juice, No. 310, flat, Moonlight Blue, 5 oz. 85

Tumbler, blown Caprice patt., No. 300, footed, Crystal, 10 oz. 28

Tumbler, blown Caprice patt., Old Fashioned, No. 310, Moonlight Blue, 7 oz. 165

Tumbler, etched Apple Blossom patt., No. 3130, footed, Mandarin Gold, 12 oz. 40

Tumbler, etched Apple Blossom patt., whiskey, footed, Topaz, 2 oz. 65

Tumbler, etched Diane patt., Crystal, 9 oz. 32

Tumbler, etched Imperial Hunt patt., juice, footed, Dianthus Pink, 5 oz. 40

Tumbler, etched Portia patt., footed, No. 3077, Crystal, 12 oz. 25

Tumbler, etched Portia patt., No. 3400/38, flat, Crystal, 12 oz. 60

Tumbler, juice, flat, etched Gloria patt., green, 5 oz. 45

Tumbler, Panel Optic patt., flat, iced tea, Rubina, 12 oz. 75

Tumbler, pressed Caprice patt., footed, Moonlight Blue, No. 12, 3 oz. 95

Tumbler, pressed Caprice patt., footed, No. 10, Moonlight Blue, 10 oz. 50

Tumbler, wine, footed, Mount Vernon patt., milk glass, 3 oz. 18

Vase, 6" h., etched Apple Blossom patt.,
No. 3400/103, Topaz 150
Vase, 6" h., etched Wildflower patt., footed,
No. 6004, Crystal 75
Vase, bud, 6" h., etched Elaine patt., No.
6004, Crystal 60
Vase, 6 1/2" h., etched Wildflower patt.,
globe-shaped, No. 3400/103, Mandarin
Gold.. 375
Vase, 8 1/2" h., ball-shaped, pressed Ca-
price patt., No. 239, plain top, Amber.......... 195
Vase, 9" h., etched Candlelight patt., key-
hole shape, Crystal 74
Vase, 10" h., bud, etched Candlelight patt.,
Crystal 110
Vase, bud, 10" h., etched Chantilly patt., No.
1528, spherical bottom, Crystal.................... 125
Vase, 11" h., etched Cleo patt., Emerald 200
Vegetable bowl, cov., etched Cleo patt.,
Amber, 9" l. 240
Water set: pitcher & four tumblers; Gyro
Optic line, Amber, the set.............................. 95
Water tray, Decagon line, etched Cleo patt.,
Amber, 13" 90
Wine, blown Caprice patt., No. 301, Crystal,
5 5/8" h.. 35
Wine, etched Chantilly patt., Farberware
stem & base, crystal...................................... 30
Wine, pressed Caprice patt., No. 6, Crystal 38
Wine, pressed Caprice patt., No. 6, Moon-
light Blue, 3 oz. 100

Carnival

*Earlier called Taffeta glass, the Carnival glass
now being collected was introduced early in the
20th century. Its producers gave it an iridescence
that attempted to imitate that of some Tiffany
glass. Collectors will find available books by leading authorities Donald E. Moore, Sherman Hand,
Marion T. Hartung, Rose M. Presznick, and Bill
Edwards.*

April Showers (Fenton)
Vase, 7 1/2" h., purple $80
Vase, 8" h., green... 90
Vase, 8" h., marigold 55
Vase, 11" h., blue 100
Vase, 12" h., vaseline....................................... 250

Basket (Fenton's Open Edge)
Blue 55
Celeste blue 550
Green 95
Marigold 30
Purple 80
Red 325
White, 6".. 275

Basket or Bushel Basket (Northwood)
Aqua opalescent, 4 1/2" d., 4 3/4" h. 350
Blue 175
Green 350
Ice blue, ... 450
Ice green 400
Marigold 100
Purple 160

Butterfly & Fern (Fenton)

Butterfly & Fern Blue Water Pitcher
Pitcher, water, blue (ILLUS.) 425

Captive Rose

Captive Rose Plate
Plate, 9" d., green (ILLUS.) 400

Corn Vase (Northwood)
Green 700
Ice blue 1,700
Ice green 300
Marigold 850
Purple 600
White 200

Daisy & Plume
Compote, green.. 45
Compote, marigold 30
Compote, purple 55
Rose bowl, blue, three-footed 475
Rose bowl, green, stemmed.............................. 50
Rose bowl, green, three-footed........................ 125
Rose bowl, marigold, stemmed 35
Rose bowl, marigold, three-footed 125
Rose bowl, purple, stemmed............................ 50
Rose bowl, purple, three-footed 125

Diamond Lace (Imperial)

Diamond Lace Pitcher

Pitcher, water, purple (ILLUS.) **250**

Fashion (Imperial)
Creamer, marigold **40**
Pitcher, water, marigold **150**
Pitcher, water, purple **1,100**
Punch bowl & base, smoky, 12" d., 2 pcs. .. **3,000**
Punch cup, marigold **15**
Punch cup, smoky **45**
Punch set: 12" d. bowl, base & 6 cups;
    marigold, 8 pcs. **275**
Tumbler, marigold **20**
Tumbler, purple **200**
Tumbler, smoky **100**

Floral & Grape (Dugan or Diamond Glass Co.)

Floral & Grape Pitcher

Pitcher, water, blue (ILLUS.) **225**

Fruits & Flowers (Northwood)
Bonbon, aqua opalescent, stemmed, two-
    handled **650**
Bonbon, blue, stemmed, two-handled **225**
Bonbon, green, stemmed, two-handled **150**
Bonbon, ice blue, stemmed, two-handle **600**
Bonbon, ice green, stemmed, two-handled **650**
Bonbon, marigold, stemmed, two-handled **85**

Bonbon, purple, stemmed, two-handled **100**
Bonbon, white, stemmed, two-handled **400**

Grape & Cable (Northwood)

Grape & Cable Electric Blue Bonbon

Bonbon, two-handled, blue w/electric iri-
    descence (ILLUS.) **180**

Hearts & Flowers (Northwood)

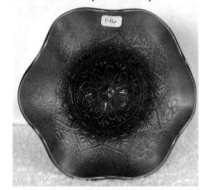

Hearts & Flowers Ruffled Compote

Compote, 6 3/4" h., blue (ILLUS.) **325**

Hearts & Flowers Ruffled Compote

Compote, 6 3/4" h., powder blue opales-
    cent (ILLUS.) **3,250**

Nesting Swan (Millersburg)

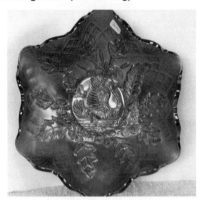

Nesting Swan Ruffled Purple Bowl

Bowl, 9" d., ruffled, purple (ILLUS.) **225**

Peacock & Grape (Fenton)

Peacock & Grape Marigold Plate

Plate, 9" d., collared base, marigold (ILLUS.)
.... **1,750**

Peacock & Urn (Millersburg, Fenton & Northwood)

Bowl, 7 1/2" d., "shotgun," ruffled, green **325**
Bowl, 9" d., ruffled, blue (Fenton) **250**
Bowl, 9" d., ruffled, purple (Fenton) **300**
Bowl, 9" d., ruffled, white **450**
Bowl, 9 1/2" d., berry, purple (Millersburg)....... **450**
Bowl, 10" d., ice cream shape, aqua opal-
  escent (Northwood)............................... **25,000**
Bowl, 10" d., ice cream shape, blue (North-
  wood) **1,100**
Bowl, 10" d., ice cream shape, blue, stip-
  pled (Northwood).................................... **1,400**
Bowl, 10" d., ice cream shape, green
  (Northwood) **3,000**
Bowl, 10" d., ice cream shape, ice blue
  (Northwood) **1,300**
Bowl, 10" d., ice cream shape, ice green
  (Northwood) **1,500**
Bowl, 10" d., ice cream shape, marigold
  (Millersburg) **350**

Peacock Ice Cream Shape Bowl

Bowl, 10" d., ice cream shape, marigold,
  Northwood (ILLUS.) **300**
Bowl, 10" d., ice cream shape, purple **750**
Bowl, 10" d., ruffled, marigold......................... **125**
Bowl, master ice cream, stippled, marigold
  (Northwood) **750**
Bowl, master, blue (Millersburg) **2,500**
Bowl, master, green (Millersburg)................... **650**
Ice cream dish, marigold, small **80**
Ice cream dish, blue, small (Northwood)......... **125**

Small Ice Cream Dish

Ice cream dish, green, small (ILLUS.)............. **220**
Ice cream dish, green, small (Northwood) **650**
Ice cream dish, ice blue, small....................... **275**
Ice cream dish, ice green, small **275**
Ice cream dish, purple, small **85**
Ice cream dish, white, small............................ **175**
Sauce dish, blue (Millersburg)........................ **800**
Sauce dish, green (Millersburg) **250**
Sauce dish, marigold (Millersburg)................. **150**
Sauce dish, purple (Millersburg)..................... **175**

Poppy (Northwood)

Poppy Pickle Dish

Pickle dish, blue (ILLUS., previous page) 225

Rosalind (Millersburg)

Rosalind Bowl

Bowl, 10" d., ruffled, green (ILLUS.) 140

Rustic Vase
Blue, 7" to 12" h. 60
Blue, 16" h. 150
Blue, funeral, 18" h., 5" base 950
Green, 6" h. to 10 1/2" h. 80
Green, 16" h. 250
Marigold, 6" to 10 1/2" h. 40
Marigold, 16" to 21 1/2" h., 5 1/2" base 95
Marigold, funeral, 19" h., marigold 600
Purple, 6" to 10 1/2" h. 70
Purple, 15" h. 150

Star of David & Bows (Northwood)
Bowl, 7" d., dome-footed, green 175
Bowl, 7" d., dome-footed, marigold 100
Bowl, 7" d., dome-footed, purple 125

Star of David (Imperial)
Bowl, ruffled, green 150
Bowl, ruffled, marigold 150
Bowl, ruffled, purple 250

Strawberry (Fenton)
Bonbon, two-handled, amber 65
Bonbon, two-handled, blue 80
Bonbon, two-handled, green 225
Bonbon, two-handled, ice green opalescent 300
Bonbon, two-handled, marigold 30
Bonbon, two-handled, red 800

Strawberry (Northwood)
Bowl, 8" to 9" d., blue, stippled, piecrust rim 900
Bowl, 8" to 9" d., green, ruffled, Basketweave exterior 155
Bowl, 8" to 9" d., marigold, ruffled, Basketweave exterior 75
Bowl, 8" to 9" d., purple, ruffled, Basketweave exterior 140
Bowl, 8" to 9" d., stippled, ruffled, purple 300
Bowl, ice blue, stippled, piecrust rim 7,000
Bowl, 9" d., green, piecrust rim 200
Bowl, 9" d., marigold, piecrust rim 100
Bowl, 9" d., purple, piecrust rim 195
Plate, 9" d., green 250
Plate, 9" d., marigold 150
Plate, 9" d., purple 225
Plate, stippled, ice blue 12,000

Plate, stippled, ice green 15,500

Tree Trunk Vase (Northwood)
Aqua opalescent, 9" to 12" h. 900
Blue, 8" to 10" h. 225
Blue, 13 1/2" h. 900
Green, 10" h. 125

Tree Trunk Vase

Green, 13" h. (ILLUS.) 1,600
Green, 22" h., funeral 3,000
Ice blue, 8" to 10" h. 750
Ice green, 12" h. 450
Ice green, 22" h., funeral 8,500
Marigold, 11" h. 85
Marigold, 12" h. 175
Purple, 8" to 11" h. 100
Purple, 13" h. 350
Purple, 22" h., funeral 2,500
White, 9" h. 325

Central Glass Works

From the 1890s until its closing in 1939, the Central Glass Works of Wheeling, West Virginia, produced colorless and colored handmade glass in all the styles then popular. Decorations from etchings with acid to hand-painted enamels were used.

The popular "Depression" era colors of black, pink, green, light blue, ruby red and others were all produced. Two of its 1920s etchings are still familiar today, one named for the then President of the United States and the other for the Governor of West Virginia - these are the Harding and Morgan patterns.

From high end Art glass to mass-produced plain barware tumblers, Central was a major glass producer throughout the period.

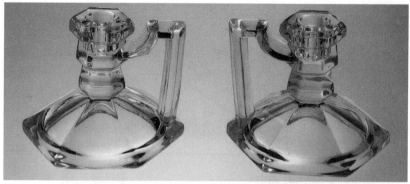

Central Glass Chippendale Toy Candlestick

Bonbon, two-handled, Morgan etching,
  pink, 6" d. **$155**
Bowl, berry, 5" d., Frances patt., pink **20**
Bowl, 7" d., flat soup, Balda etching, Orchid **68**

Frances Pattern Bowl in Amber

Bowl, 9", crimped triangular form, three-
  footed, Frances patt., amber (ILLUS.)............ **65**

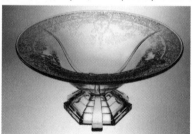

Central Glass Footed Bowl

Green 4" Frances Candlestick

Bowl, 10 1/2" d., footed, No. 2025, pink,
  #61 etching (ILLUS.) **75**
Candleholder, one-light, Frances patt.,
  green, 4" h. (ILLUS., top next column)........... **42**
Candlestick, one-light, Chippendale patt.,
  w/cutting, crystal, 6 1/2" h. (ILLUS., bot-
  tom next column).. **35**
Candlestick, toy, handled, Chippendale
  patt., crystal, 2" h., pr. (ILLUS., top of
  page) **58**
Candlesticks, art glass, cobalt blue & opal,
  15" h., pr.. **475**
Candlesticks, Balda etching, one-light, wa-
  fer stem, amber, 3" h., pr. **95**
Candy dish, cov., No. 500, Harding etching
  on lid, green **125**

*Central Glass Chippendale One-light
Candlestick*

Black Creamer & Sugar on Tray

Celery vase, Frances patt., two-handled, clear, 7 1/2" h. 48

Champagne, hollow stem, Thistle etching, crystal, 5 1/2" h. 95

Champagne, Morgan etching, clear w/green stem & foot, 5 1/2" h. 55

Champagne, Morgan etching, pink, 5 7/8" h. 85

Claret, Thistle etching, crystal, 5 oz. 28

Cocktail, No. 1426, crystal diamond optic bowl, blue stem & foot, 5 1/4" h. 12

Compote, 6 1/2" h., Hester etching, yellow bowl, crystal stem and foot....................... 350

Compote, art glass, green & opal 375

Cordial, tapered, Scott's Morning Glory etching, crystal 45

Cream soup bowl, two-handled, Harding etching, pink.................................... 85

Creamer, fan handle, Hester etching, crystal 68

Creamer & open sugar on handled tray, No. 1450 patt., black, 3 pcs. (ILLUS., top of page) 75

Cup & saucer, Morgan etching, pink, pr. 350

Cup & saucer, No. 1450, square form, Lotus Butterfly etching, yellow, pr. 55

Decanter w/stopper, Morgan etching, flat, pink.. 375

Goblet, Balda etching, water, orchid 65

Goblet, Morgan etching, water, pink 125

Goblet, No. 1426, "Spiral" Line, water, pink 28

Goblet, No. 1426, water, crystal diamond optic bowl, blue stem & foot, 7 1/2" h. (ILLUS. left with cocktail).......................... 16

Goblet, water, w/beaded stem, amber bowl, black foot & stem.................................. 35

Ice tub, Morgan etching, tab handled, green, 7 1/2" d... 375

Ice tub, two-handled, pink, Lotus La Furiste etching, 4" h. 135

Pitcher, cov., Thistle etching, crystal, 80 oz. 250

Pitcher, water, Harding etching, flat, clear w/green handle.................................. 350

Plate, dinner, Harding etching, clear 75

Plate, 6" d., crystal, Thistle etching 15

Plate, 7" d., salad, No. 1450, Hester etching, yellow 35

Plate, 7" sq., No. 1450, Morgan etching, clear w/black enamel center......................... 35

Plate, 8" d., Balda etching, orchid 30

Plate, 8" d., Scott's Morning Glory etching, pink 25

Plate, 8 1/2" sq., No. 1450, Lotus Butterfly etching, yellow 38

Plate, 9 1/2" d., Morgan etching, green........... 125

Teapot, cov., No. 733, Thistle etching No. 310, clear .... 220+

Tray, center-handled, No. 1450, black......... 65

Tumbler, footed, green bowl, black square base, 5 1/2" h................................... 25

Tumbler, Morgan etching, flat, pink, 2" h. 75

Tumbler, water, flat, Thistle etching, crystal, 8 oz. 25

Vanity dresser tray, cov., Morgan etching, green.. 750

Vase, 8 1/2" h., flat w/crimped rim, Frances patt., pink 85

Gold Encrusted Thistle Etching Vase

Vase, 10" h., bud, footed, pink, gold encrusted Thistle etching (ILLUS.)................ 95

Flip-type Vases with Smetak Etching

Vases, 8" h., flip-type, No. 2001, amber, Smetak etching, pr. (ILLUS.)......................... **78**
Wine, large, No. 1448, Wheeling Floral etching, crystal bowl w/black stem & foot, 6 1/2" h. **28**

Crown Milano

This glass, produced by Mt. Washington Glass Company late in the 19th century, is opal glass decorated by painting and enameling. It appears identical to a ware termed Albertine, also made by Mt. Washington.

Printed Crown Milano Mark

Lobed Crown Milano Cracker Jar

Cracker jar w/original silver plate rim, cover & bail handle, the bulbous melon-lobed body in dark peach w/a sienna band around the top, decorated in gold & natural colors w/a design of leaves & berries around the body, the cover decorated w/an embossed crab design, base signed "CM 522," 6 1/2" d., 5 1/4" h. (ILLUS.).................................. **$1,320**

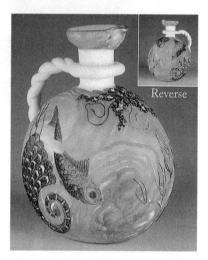

Very Rare Crown Milano Aquatic Ewer

Ewer, nearly spherical body w/a small white cylindrical neck below a blue & gold cupped rim, white ropetwist entwined handle & band from neck to shoulder, the main body w/a shaded & mottled blue ground decorated to represent water & coral w/applied gilt fish, shells & coral, 10" h. (ILLUS.) **9,200**

Cup Plates

Produced in numerous patterns beginning more than 170 years ago, these little plates were designed to hold a cup while the tea or coffee was allowed to cool in a saucer. Cup plates were also made of ceramics. Where numbers are listed below, they refer to numbers assigned to these plates in the book American Glass Cup Plates by Ruth Webb Lee and James H. Rose. Plates are of clear glass unless otherwise noted. A number of cup plates have been reproduced.

L & R-188, round w/40 bull's-eye scallops, starburst in center surrounded by six large bull's-eyes, swirled & stippled panels in outer border, very rare, Midwestern, some light tipping, 3 1/2" d. **$132**
L & R-190, round w/33 even bull's-eye scallops in border, central large scroll-edged cross w/arm tips ending in a small bull's-eye & a large bull's-eye between each arm, Midwestern, very rare, 3 1/16" d......... **523**
L & R-197-C, round w/44-scallop rim, snow-flake center motif surrounded by an inner band of leafy vines, fleur-de-lis alternating w/stippled circles at outer rim, violet blue, very rare, Midwestern, 3 1/4" d. **935**

Two Blue Sailing Ship Cup Plates

L & R-221, round w/plain rope rim, top & bottom, florette in center w/four large swirled arms ending in large bull's-eyes alternating w/stippled panels, very rare, probably Midwestern, near proof, 3 1/2" d. **2,640**

L & R-432, rounded w/nine large scallops alternating w/hearts in the border, blocked cross in the center surrounded by a swirled & stippled inner band, very rare, unknown origin, clear w/some cloudiness, several small rim chips w/rim flaking, 3 1/2" d. **523**

L & R-455, round w/twelve-heart border band around a four-petal & four-diamond center design, possibly Boston & Sandwich Glass Co., bright emerald green, very minor damage, 3 7/8" d. **2,310**

Unique Jenny Lind Blue Cup Plate

L & R-582 Jenny Lind, round w/fifty-six even scallops, electric blue, possibly unique, only minor tipping, 3 3/4" d. (ILLUS.) **1,980**

L & R-610-A, sailing ship, twenty-three bold scallops, Boston & Sandwich Glass Co., brilliant dark blue, chip to reverse rim, light tipping, 3 5/8" d. (ILLUS. left with other sailing ship cup plate, top of page) **88**

L & R-610-B, sailing ship, twenty-three bold scallops, Boston & Sandwich Glass Co., peacock blue, twenty-five flat scallops, partial loss to several scallops, 3 5/8" d. (ILLUS. right with other sailing ship cup plate, top of page) **99**

Custard

"Custard glass," as collectors call it today, came on the American scene in the 1890s, more than a decade after similar colors were made in Europe and England. The Sowerby firm of Gateshead-on-Tyne, England had marketed its patented "Queen's Ivory Ware" quite successfully in the late 1870s and early 1880s.

There were many glass tableware factories operating in Pennsylvania and Ohio in the 1890s and early 1900s, and the competition among them was keen. Each company sought to capture the public's favor with distinctive colors and, often, hand-painted decoration. That is when "Custard glass" appeared on the American scene.

The opaque yellow color of this glass varies from a rich, vivid yellow to a lustrous light yellow. Regardless of intensity, the hue was originally called "ivory" by several glass manufacturers then who also used superlative sounding terms such as "Ivorina Verde" and

"Carnelian." Most Custard glass contains uranium, so it will "glow" under a black light.

The most important producer of Custard glass was certainly Harry Northwood, who first made it at his plants in Indiana, Pennsylvania, in the late 1890s and, later, in his Wheeling, West Virginia, factory. Northwood marked some of his most famous patterns, but much early Custard is unmarked. Other key manufacturers include the Heisey Glass Co., Newark, Ohio; the Jefferson Glass Co., Steubenville, Ohio; the Tarentum Glass Co., Tarentum, Pennsylvania; and the Fenton Art Glass Co., Williamstown, West Virginia.

Custard glass fanciers are particular about condition and generally insist on pristine quality decorations free from fading or wear. Souvenir Custard pieces with events, places and dates on them usually bring the best prices in the areas commemorated on them rather than from the specialist collector. Also, collectors who specialize in pieces such as cruets, syrups or salt and pepper shakers will often pay higher prices for these pieces than would a Custard collector.

Key reference sources include William Heacock's Custard Glass from A to Z, *published in 1976 but not out of print, and the book* Harry Northwood: The Early Years, *available from Glass Press.* Heisey's Custard *is discussed in Shirley Dunbar's* Heisey Glass: The Early Years *(Krause Publications, 2000), and Coudersport's production is well-documented in Tulla Majot's book* Coudersport's Glass 1900-1904 *(Glass Press, 1999). The recently formed Custard Glass Society holds a yearly convention and maintains a web site: www.homestead.com/custardsociety.*

- James Measell.

Grape & Cable Sauce Dish

Sauce dish, flat (ILLUS.) **45-60**

Grape & Cable Tumbler

Tumbler (ILLUS.) **75-85**

INVERTED FAN & FEATHER (Northwood at Indiana, Pa., ca. 1900)

Inverted Fan & Feather Master Berry Bowl

Bowl, master berry (ILLUS.) **200-225**

Northwood

Northwood Script Mark

GRAPE & CABLE, NORTHWOOD GRAPE, OR GRAPE & THUMBPRINT (Northwood at Wheeling, ca. 1913-15)

Grape & Cable Pitcher

Pitcher, water (ILLUS.) **$400-550**

Inverted Fan & Feather Pitcher

Pitcher, water (ILLUS.) **750-800**

PAGODA OR CHRYSANTHEMUM Sprig (Northwood at Indiana, Pa., ca. 1899)

Pagoda Custard Glass Pitcher

Pitcher (ILLUS.) **550-650**

Pagoda Tumbler in Custard Glass

Tumbler (ILLUS.) **80-125**

Cut

Cut glass most eagerly sought by collectors is American glass produced during the so-called "Brilliant Period" from 1880 to about 1915. Pieces listed below are by type of article in alphabetical order.

Hawkes, Hoare, Libbey and Straus Marks

Baskets

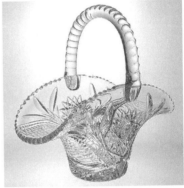

Cut Glass Pairpoint "Cactus" Basket

Pairpoint, "Cactus," 12" h. (ILLUS.) **$1,595**

Bowls

Blackmer Columbia Orange Bowl

Blackmer, orange bowl, Columbia patt., 8 x 11 1/2", 4 1/2" h. (ILLUS.) **775**

Large Clark Mercedes Bowl

Clark, 14" d., Mercedes patt. (ILLUS., bottom previous page) **2,750**

Hawkes "Kohinoor" Bowl

Hawkes, 11 3/4" x 8 1/4" oval, Kohinoor patt., clear (ILLUS.) **2,700**

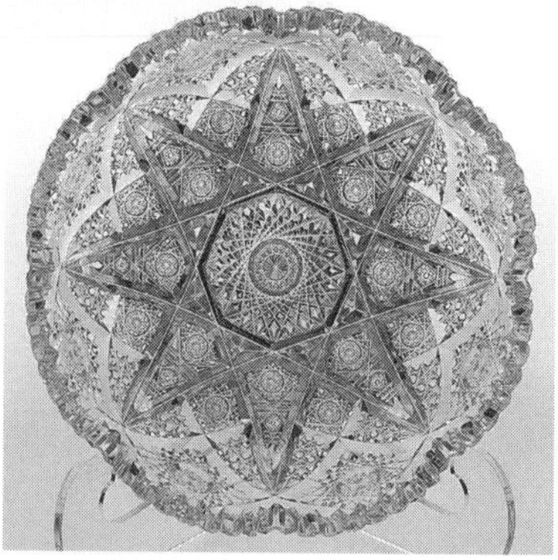

Hawkes Kensington Low Bowl

Hawkes low bowl, 9 3/8" d., Kensington patt. (ILLUS.) **1,275**

Hawkes-signed, round w/scalloped & notched rim, the bottom center w/a small hobstar surrounded by two graduated rows of pointed petals, an outer border of small hobstars, 9" d. **259**

"Carolyn" Napoleon's Hat Fruit Bowl by J. Hoare

Hoare (J.) & Co., Napoleon's hat fruit bowl, Carolyn patt., clear, 9 x 13 1/2", 4" h. (ILLUS.) **1,650**

Bowl by Jewel Cut Glass Co.

Jewel Cut Glass Co., 8" d., 3 1/2" h., Margaret patt. (ILLUS.) **495**

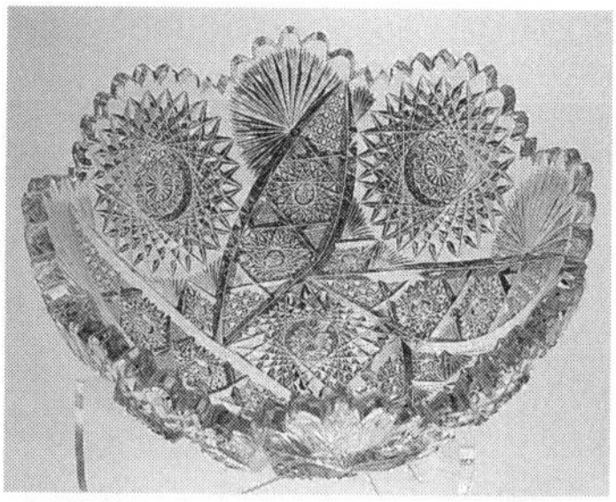

Pitkin & Brooks Cypress Bowl

Pitkin & Brooks, 9" d., 4" h., Cypress patt. (ILLUS.) **395**

Boxes

Extraordinary Cranberry to Clear Box

Dresser, rectangular w/hinged cover w/original metal hardware & key, cranberry cut to clear w/an overall button & rayed button pattern, 4 3/4 x 9 3/4", 5 1/4" h. (ILLUS.) **3,450**

Champagnes, Cordials & Wines

Lovely Flashed & Russian Cut Dorflinger Wines

Wines, Dorflinger Russian Cut hock wines in cranberry cut to clear, facet-cut knob stems w/a controlled bubble, each 4 3/4" h., set of 9 (ILLUS., above) **3,450**

Compotes

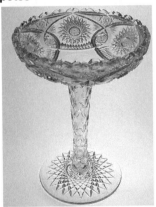

Monroe Tempt Compote

Monroe, Tempt patt., 8 x 11" (ILLUS.) **795**

Decanters

Clark Lakewood Whiskey Decanter

Clark (T.B.) & Co., whiskey decanter, Lakewood patt., 10" h., signed (ILLUS.) **795**

Hawkes Ship's Decanter in Flutes Pattern

Hawkes, ship's decanter, Flutes patt. (ILLUS.) **575**

Libbey Harvard Decanter

Libbey, Harvard patt., 15 1/2" h. (ILLUS.) **975**

Stevens & Williams Amethyst Decanter

Stevens & Williams, baluster shape with teardrop stopper, amethyst with clear decoration, the body with floral and scrolling designs, a band of cross-cut diamonds on the base & the foot with a single band of beads, rare, 9" h. (ILLUS.) **6,500**

Ice Tubs

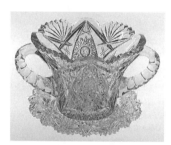

Blackmer Crescent Ice Tub

Blackmer, Crescent patt., handled tub w/underplate, 6" h. (ILLUS.) **1,450**

Miscellaneous

Dorflinger Finger Bowl in American Pattern

Finger bowl, Dorflinger, American patt., 4 3/4" d., 2 1/4" h. (ILLUS.) **145**
Flower center, Pairpoint, Sillsbee patt., 9 1/2" h. (ILLUS., top next column) **1,350**

Pairpoint Sillsbee Flower Center

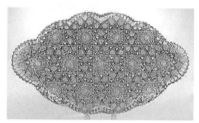

Empire Seneca Ice Cream Tray

Ice cream tray, Empire, Seneca patt., 18" l. (ILLUS.) **1,775**

Straus Imperial Olive Dish

Olive dish, Straus, Imperial patt., 7 1/8" l. (ILLUS.) **195**

Perfumes & Colognes

Dorflinger Belmont Square Cologne Bottle

Dorflinger, Belmont patt., square shape, 9" h. (ILLUS.) **495**

Pitchers & Jugs

Libbey Harvard Jug

Libbey jug, Harvard patt., 8" h. (ILLUS.) **395**

Tankard-type, cylindrical w/a flared base, notched rim & applied notched handle, the sides cut w/a panel of vertical bars around the handle, large diamond-shaped panels alternating w/hobstars & simple cross-hatching around the sides, 8 1/2" h. **184**

Plates

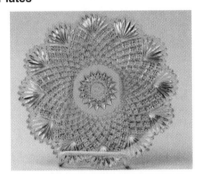

Very Rare Alexandrite-type Cut Plate

8 1/4" d., Alexandrite-type coloring w/strawberry diamond & fan cutting, possibly America, late 19th c. (ILLUS.) **2,013**

Punch bowls

Clark Mercedes Punch Bowl

Clark, Mercedes patt., 14" d., 11 1/2" h., signed (ILLUS.) **4,950**

J. Hoare & Co. Two-piece Punch Bowl

Hoare (J.) & Co., Rookwood patt., two-piece (ILLUS.) **4,450**

Fern Pattern Punch Bowl

Ohio Cut Glass Co., Fern patt., two-piece, 12" h., 12" d. (ILLUS.) **4,250**

Rose Bowls

Clark Baker's Gothic Rose Bowl

Clark, Baker's Gothic patt., 7" (ILLUS.) **650**

Trays

Blackmer Estelle Round Tray

Blackmer, Estelle patt., 14" d. (ILLUS.) **4,450**

Blackmer Princess Round Tray

Blackmer, Princess patt., 12" d. (ILLUS.) **1,750**
Hawkes North Star patt., large round shape w/scalloped & notched rim, a circle of large hobstars centered w/starbursts alternating w/small starbursts, a large starburst in the center surrounded by small cut fans, 15" d. (some minor rim chips, one point damaged)........................ **2,645**

Vases

Sheldon Pattern Chalice Vase

Bergen (J.D.) Co., 12" h., chalice form, Sheldon patt. (ILLUS.) **975**

Clark American Beauty Vase

Clark (T.B.) & Co., 14" h., American Beauty patt., clear (ILLUS.)...................................... **795**

Rare Small Cranberry Cut to Clear Vase

Cranberry cut to clear, 4" h., footed waisted cylindrical body cut w/vertical flutes, applied clear loop side handles, applied flaring silver rim band (ILLUS.) **1,323**

Lovely Cranberry to Clear Chalice Vase

Cranberry cut to clear, 9 1/2" h., chalice-form bowl on a hollow blown lapidary-cut applied stem w/applied cut foot (ILLUS.)
.... **1,955**

Dorflinger "Honesdale" Vase

Dorflinger, 8" h., "Honesdale," sinuous shape w/Art Nouveau-style whiplash design (ILLUS.) **1,475**

Dorflinger Green to Clear Vase

Dorflinger, 12 5/8" h., green cut to clear, tall form with bulbous base and long, thin neck flaring slightly at rim, decorated overall w/engraved floral & leaf designs (ILLUS.) **4,850**

Hawkes Navarre Variation Vase

Hawkes, 14" h., Navarre patt. variation, clear (ILLUS.) **595**

Hawkes-signed, tall waisted cylindrical shape w/a four-lobed rim, cut w/wide panels of hobstars & strawberry diamonds alternating w/narrow panels of zipper bar cutting, 12" h. **196**

J. Hoare 12" Marquise Vase

Hoare (J.) & Co., 12" h., Marquise patt., clear (ILLUS.) **1,250**

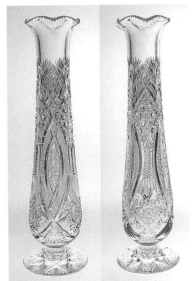

Two Views of 13" Hoare Vase

Hoare (J.) & Co., 13" h., footed, slightly tapering cylindrical body w/fluted flared rim, decorated overall w/crosscut diamonds, fans, strawberry diamonds, stars, sunbursts, hobstar vesicas, clear (ILLUS. of two views) **995**

Maple City Olga Vase

Maple City, 14" h., Olga patt., clear
(ILLUS.).. **695**

Small D'Argental Cameo Vase

Cameo vase, 4 1/8" h., swelled cylindrical
shape w/a wide flat rim, olive green &
mauve decorated w/an upper band of
cameo butterflies & a lower wider band of
cameo daisies, engraved mark, tiny sur-
face bubbles (ILLUS.) **$460**

Tuthill 9" Vase with Ruffled Rim

Tuthill, 9" h., footed form with flaring body &
wide ruffled rim, w/geometric design, a
16-point hobstar decorating the foot,
clear (ILLUS.) **775**

D'Argental

*Glass known by this name is so-called after its
producer, who fashioned fine cameo pieces in St.
Louis, France in the late 19th century and up to
1918.*

D'Argental Mark

Tall Slender D'Argental Cameo Vase

Cameo vase, 13 3/4" h., cushion foot on the
tall slender baluster-form body, a long
stem of flowering blossoms down one
side w/a sailboat on water scene on the
other, signed in cameo (ILLUS.) **1,035**

Daum Nancy

*This fine glass, much of it cameo, was made by
Auguste and Antonin Daum, who founded a fac-*

tory in 1875 in Nancy, France. Most of their cameo and enameled glass was made from the 1890s into the early 20th century.

Daum Nancy Marks

Rare Square Daum Cameo Inkwell

Cameo inkwell, squared form in an overall mottled dark green, orange, yellow & frosted clear, cameo cut w/large oak leaves, some w/applied acorns, an insect or faceted foil-backed cabochon, w/fitted domed cap, incised signature on the side, 4" w., 4" h. (ILLUS.) **$7,500**

leaves down from the rim, signed in cameo (ILLUS.) **900**

Daum Cameo & Enameled Vase

Cameo vase, 6" h., footed tapering cylindrical body w/a cupped top pulled into three points, a mottled orange shading to green ground cameo-cut & enameled w/colorful flowers & field grasses, gilt trim & oblong panels of tiny scrolls around the lower body, signed in gilt (ILLUS.) **5,290**

Rare Very Tall Daum Cameo Vase

Cameo vase, 17 1/2" h., a cushion foot below the very tall cylindrical body, mottled shaded light to dark blue to brown ground, cameo cut & enameled w/brown leaves & stems below white-petaled flowers & buds (ILLUS.) **10,350**

Miniature Daum Nancy Cameo Vase

Cameo vase, 4" h., miniature, ovoid body tapering to a flat mouth, a colored ground cameo-etched & enameled w/rosehips &

Boldly Decorated Daum Art Deco Vase

Vase, 11 1/2" h., footed swelled cylindrical body w/a short widely flaring & flattened rim, Art Deco style in aquamarine cut around the lower half w/bold overlapping pointed designs w/a glossy finish below the rough-textured upper body, etched mark (ILLUS.)... **1,610**

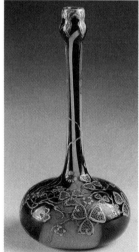

Bottle-form Daum Vase with Trefoils

Vase, 11 3/4" h., bottle-form, a large squatty bulbous base centered by a very tall & slender neck topped by a knopped rim, deep maroon alternating w/light blue panels & bands up the neck, decorated around the base w/enameled trefoils & white blossoms w/a long vine up the neck ending in a white blossom, signed on the bottom (ILLUS.)... **5,290**

de Latte

Andre de Latte of Nancy, France, produced a range of opaque and cameo glass after 1921. His company also produced light fixtures, but his cameo wares are most collectible today.

de Latte Marks

de Latte Cameo Vase with Floral Vines

Cameo vase, 7 1/4" h., squatty bulbous lower body w/a tall tapering neck w/a small flaring rim, mottled colored ground overlaid & cameo cut w/large flowering leafy vines, cameo-signed (ILLUS.)........... **$460**

Signed de Latte Cameo Vase

Cameo vase, 9 1/4" h., footed bulbous ovoid body tapering to a narrow trumpet neck, chocolate brown over a mottled pumpkin orange & cameo cut w/a large side of an Ohio Buckeye bearing spiny husked fruit & large foliage, small surface bubbles, signed in cameo 518

Depression

The phrase "Depression Glass" is used by collectors to denote a specific kind of transparent glass produced primarily as tablewares, in crystal, amber, blue, green, pink, milky-white, etc., during the late 1920s and 1930s when this country was in the midst of a financial depression. Made to sell inexpensively, it was turned out by such producers as Jeannette, Hocking, Westmoreland, Indiana and other glass companies. We compile prices on all the major Depression Glass patterns. Collectors should consult Depression Glass references for information on those patterns and pieces that have been reproduced.

ADAM, Jeanette Glass Co., 1932-34 (Process-etched)

Ashtray, green, 4 1/2" sq. $25
Ashtray, pink, 4 1/2" sq. 28
Bowl, 4 3/4" sq., dessert, green 20
Bowl, dessert, 4 3/4" sq., pink............................ 22
Bowl, cereal, 5 3/4" sq., green 50
Bowl, cereal, 5 3/4" sq., pink............................. 50
Bowl, nappy, 7 3/4" sq., green 28
Bowl, nappy, 7 3/4" sq., pink 28
Bowl, cov., 9" sq., green 85
Bowl, cov., 9" sq., pink...................................... 75
Bowl, 9" sq., green... 42
Bowl, 9" sq., pink 40
Bowl, 10" oval, vegetable, green 40
Bowl, 10" oval, vegetable, pink 35
Butter dish, cov., green 375
Butter dish, cov., pink.. 95
Butter dish, cov., w/Sierra patt., pink 1,600
Cake plate, footed, green, 10" sq. 38
Cake plate, footed, pink, 10" sq. 35
Candlestick, green, 4" h. 60

Pink Adam 4" Candlestick

Candlestick, pink, 4" h. (ILLUS.) 50
Candlesticks, Delphite, 4" h., pr..................... 250

Candlesticks, green, 4" h., pr......................... 120
Candlesticks, pink, 4" h., pr. 100
Candy jar, cov., green 125
Candy jar, cov., pink 98
Coaster, green, 3 1/4" sq................................... 24
Coaster, pink, 3 1/4" sq. 20
Creamer, green.. 24
Creamer, pink 22
Cup & saucer, green 36
Cup & saucer, pink.. 11
Cup & saucer, yellow 165
Lamp, green 275
Lamp, pink 250
Pitcher, 8" h., 32 oz., cone-shaped, clear.......... 35
Pitcher, 8" h., 32 oz., cone-shaped, green 60
Pitcher, 8" h., 32 oz., cone-shaped, pink.......... 48
Pitcher, 32 oz., round base, clear...................... 19
Pitcher, 32 oz., round base, pink 65
Plate, sherbet, 6" sq., green.............................. 12
Plate, sherbet, 6" sq., pink 10
Plate, salad, 7 3/4" sq., green 22
Plate, salad, 7 3/4" sq., pink............................. 20
Plate, dinner, 9" sq., green................................ 35
Plate, dinner, 9" sq., pink 30
Plate, grill, 9" sq., green 28
Plate, grill, 9" sq., pink..................................... 25
Plate, salad, round, pink.................................... 50
Plate, salad, round, yellow 85
Platter, 11 3/4" l., green 38
Platter, 11 3/4" l., pink...................................... 35
Relish dish, two-part, green, 8" sq. 24
Relish dish, two-part, pink, 8" sq...................... 20
Salt & pepper shakers, footed, green, 4" h., pr. 120
Salt & pepper shakers, footed, pink, 4" h., pr. 95
Saucer, green, 6" sq. 8
Saucer, pink, 6" sq.. 7
Saucer, round, pink.. 65
Saucer, round, yellow 75
Sherbet, green, 3" h... 38
Sherbet, pink, 3" h. 32
Sugar bowl, cov., green 75
Sugar bowl, cov., pink....................................... 50
Tumbler, cone-shaped, green, 4 1/2" h., 7 oz. 38
Tumbler, cone-shaped, pink, 4 1/2" h., 7 oz. 38
Tumbler, iced tea, green, 5 1/2" h., 9 oz. 75
Tumbler, iced tea, pink, 5 1/2" h., 9 oz. 80
Vase, 7 1/2" h., green 98
Vase, 7 1/2" h., pink 375

CHERRY BLOSSOM, Jeannette Glass Co., 1930-38 (Process-etched)

Bowl, berry, 4 3/4" d., Delphite 18
Bowl, berry, 4 3/4" d., green 22
Bowl, berry, 4 3/4" d., pink 24
Bowl, cereal, 5 3/4" d., green............................. 48
Bowl, cereal, 5 3/4" d., pink 60
Bowl, soup, 7 3/4" d., green................................ 90
Bowl, soup, 7 3/4" d., pink 95
Bowl, berry, 8 1/2" d., Delphite 50
Bowl, berry, 8 1/2" d., green 50
Bowl, berry, 8 1/2" d., pink 50
Bowl, berry, 8 1/2" d., yellow 300
Bowl, 9" oval vegetable, Delphite 55
Bowl, 9" oval vegetable, green 50
Bowl, 9" oval vegetable, pink 60
Bowl, two-handled, 9" d., Delphite..................... 40
Bowl, two-handled, 9" d., green......................... 70

Bowl, two-handled, 9" d., Jadite...................... 350
Bowl, two-handled, 9" d., pink............................ 52
Bowl, fruit, three-footed, 10 1/2" d., green 95
Bowl, fruit, three-footed, 10 1/2" d., Jadite 350
Bowl, fruit, three-footed, 10 1/2" d., pink.......... 110
Butter dish, cov., green.................................. 115
Butter dish, cov., pink..................................... 95
Cake plate, three-footed, green, 10 1/4" d. 42
Cake plate, three-footed, pink, 10 1/4" d. 38
Coaster, green 18
Coaster, pink... 20
Creamer, Delphite... 24
Creamer, green... 12
Creamer, pink... 4
Cup, green... 24
Cup, pink.. 8
Cup & saucer, Delphite 26
Cup & saucer, green 12
Cup & saucer, pink 30
Junior Set, creamer, Delphite........................... 50
Junior Set, creamer, pink 55
Junior Set, cup & saucer, Delphite 50
Junior Set, cup & saucer, pink.......................... 56
Junior Set, sugar bowl, Delphite....................... 50
Junior Set, sugar bowl, pink 52
Mug, green, 7 oz. 250
Mug, pink, 7 oz. 325
Pitcher, 6 3/4" h., 36 oz., overall patt.,
   green 75
Pitcher, 6 3/4" h., 36 oz., overall patt., Del-
   phite 95
Pitcher, 6 3/4" h., 36 oz., overall patt., Ja-
   dite 300
Pitcher, 6 3/4" h., 36 oz., overall patt., pink 68
Pitcher, 8" h., 36 oz., footed, cone-shaped,
   patt. top, green 60
Pitcher, 8" h., 36 oz., footed, cone-shaped,
   patt. top, pink.. 70
Pitcher, 8" h., 42 oz., patt. top, green 65
Pitcher, 8" h., 42 oz., patt. top, pink................. 75
Plate, sherbet, 6" d., Delphite........................... 12
Plate, sherbet, 6" d., green 10
Plate, sherbet, 6" d., pink 10
Plate, salad, 7" d., green 26
Plate, salad, 7" d., pink 28
Plate, dinner, 9" d., Delphite............................. 24
Plate, dinner, 9" d., green................................. 28
Plate, dinner, 9" d., pink 30
Plate, grill, 9" d., green 35
Plate, grill, 9" d., pink 38
Plate, grill, 10" d., green 125
Platter, 9" oval, pink 975
Platter, 11" oval, Delphite 48
Platter, 11" oval, green 58
Platter, 11" oval, pink 65
Platter, 13" oval, green 95
Platter, 13" oval, pink 95
Platter, 13" oval, divided, green 75
Platter, 13" oval, divided, pink.......................... 75
Salt & pepper shakers, green, pr................. 1,200
Salt & pepper shakers, pink, pr. 1,450
Sandwich tray, handled, Delphite,
   10 1/2" d. 35
Sandwich tray, handled, green, 10 1/2" d. 38
Sandwich tray, handled, pink, 10 1/2" d............ 45
Saucer, Delphite... 5
Saucer, green... 6
Saucer, pink 6
Sherbet, Delphite 20

Sherbet, green.. 26
Sherbet, pink.. 24
Sugar bowl, cov., Delphite 28
Sugar bowl, cov., green 45
Sugar bowl, cov., pink...................................... 55
Sugar bowl, open, Delphite 24
Sugar bowl, open, green 22
Sugar bowl, open, pink..................................... 20
Tumbler, patt. top, green, 3 1/2" h., 4 oz. 28
Tumbler, patt. top, pink, 3 1/2" h., 4 oz............. 24
Tumbler, juice, footed, overall patt., Del-
   phite, 3 3/4" h., 4 oz..................................... 28
Tumbler, juice, footed, overall patt., green,
   3 3/4" h., 4 oz.. 24
Tumbler, juice, footed, overall patt., pink,
   3 3/4" h., 4 oz.. 20
Tumbler, footed, overall patt., Delphite,
   4 1/2" h., 8 oz.. 36
Tumbler, footed, overall patt., green,
   4 1/2" h., 8 oz.. 42
Tumbler, footed, overall patt., pink,
   4 1/2" h., 8 oz.. 40
Tumbler, patt. top, green, 4 1/4" h., 9 oz. 26
Tumbler, patt. top, pink, 4 1/4" h., 9 oz............. 25
Tumbler, footed, overall patt., Delphite,
   4 1/2" h., 9 oz.. 35

Green Cherry Blossom Tumbler

Tumbler, footed, overall patt., green,
   4 1/2" h., 9 oz. (ILLUS.) 42
Tumbler, footed, overall patt., pink,
   4 1/2" h., 9 oz.. 42
Tumbler, patt. top, green, 5" h., 12 oz. 95
Tumbler, patt. top, pink, 5" h., 12 oz............... 110

Junior Set:
Cup, pink.. 50
Saucer, Delphite 5
Saucer, pink 3

COLUMBIA, Federal Glass Company, 1938-42 (Press-mold)
Bowl, cereal, 5" d., clear.................................... 20
Bowl, soup, 8" d., clear..................................... 24
Bowl, salad, 8 1/2" d., clear 20
Bowl, ruffled rim, 10 1/2" d., clear..................... 20
Butter dish, cov., clear...................................... 20
Cup, clear.. 8
Cup & saucer, clear... 10
Cup & saucer, pink 35
Plate, bread & butter, 6" d., clear 4
Plate, bread & butter, 6" d., pink 12

Plate, luncheon, 9 1/2" d., clear 10
Plate, luncheon, 9 1/2" d., pink 30
Plate, chop, 11" d., clear 12
Saucer, clear.. 2
Saucer, pink 10
Snack plate, handled, clear 20
Snack plate, handled, w/cup, clear.................... 28
Tumbler, juice, 2 7/8" h., 4 oz., clear 20
Tumbler, water, clear, 9 oz. 30

DAISY OR NUMBER 620, Indiana Glass Company, 1933-40 (Press-mold)

Bowl, 4 1/2" d., berry, clear.................................. 4
Bowl, berry, 4 1/2" d., amber 8
Bowl, berry, 4 1/2" d., red 8
Bowl, cream soup, 4 1/2" d., amber................... 10
Bowl, cream soup, 4 1/2" d., clear 5
Bowl, cream soup, 4 1/2" d., red....................... 10
Bowl, cereal, 6" d., amber.................................. 25
Bowl, cereal, 6" d., clear 8
Bowl, cereal, 6" d., red....................................... 25
Bowl, berry, 7 3/8" d., amber 12
Bowl, berry, 7 3/8" d., clear.................................. 6
Bowl, berry, 7 3/8" d., red 12
Bowl, berry, 9 3/8" d., amber 25
Bowl, berry, 9 3/8" d., clear................................ 10
Bowl, berry, 9 3/8" d., red 25
Bowl, 10" oval vegetable, amber 14
Bowl, 10" oval vegetable, clear............................ 6
Bowl, 10" oval vegetable, red 14
Creamer, footed, amber.. 8
Creamer, footed, clear 4
Creamer, footed, red... 8
Cup, amber.. 5
Cup, clear 2
Cup & saucer, amber 7
Cup & saucer, clear... 3
Cup & saucer, red 7
Plate, sherbet, 6" d., amber.................................. 3
Plate, sherbet, 6" d., clear 1
Plate, sherbet, 6" d., red....................................... 3
Plate, salad, 7 3/8" d., amber 5
Plate, salad, 7 3/8" d., clear 2
Plate, salad, 7 3/8" d., red 5
Plate, luncheon, 8 3/8" d., amber 6
Plate, luncheon, 8 3/8" d., clear 3
Plate, luncheon, 8 3/8" d., red 6
Plate, dinner, 9 3/8" d., amber.............................. 8
Plate, dinner, 9 3/8" d., clear 4
Plate, dinner, 9 3/8" d., red................................... 8
Plate, grill, 10 3/8" d., amber 6
Plate, grill, 10 3/8" d., clear 3
Plate, grill, 10 3/8" d., red 6
Plate, cake or sandwich, 11 1/2" d., amber 16
Plate, cake or sandwich, 11 1/2" d., clear 8
Plate, cake or sandwich, 11 1/2" d., red 16
Platter, 10 3/4" l., amber.................................... 12
Platter, 10 3/4" l., clear... 6
Platter, 10 3/4" l., red.. 12
Relish dish, three-part, amber, 8 3/8" 20
Relish dish, three-part, clear, 8 3/8" 10
Relish dish, three-part, red, 8 3/8" 20
Saucer, amber... 2
Sherbet, footed, amber 6
Sherbet, footed, clear 3
Sherbet, footed, red 6
Sugar bowl, open, footed, amber 8
Sugar bowl, open, footed, clear............................ 4
Sugar bowl, open, footed, red 8
Tumbler, footed, amber, 9 oz.............................. 14

Tumbler, footed, clear, 9 oz................................. 6
Tumbler, footed, red, 9 oz. 14
Tumbler, footed, amber, 12 oz. 30
Tumbler, footed, clear, 12 oz. 10
Tumbler, footed, red, 12 oz. 30

DIANA, FEDERAL GLASS CO., 1937-41 (Press-mold)

Ashtray, clear, 3 1/2" d. 2
Ashtray, pink, 3 1/2" d. 4
Bowl, 5" d., cereal, pink 8
Bowl, cereal, 5" d., amber.................................. 12
Bowl, cereal, 5" d., clear 4
Bowl, cream soup, 5 1/2" d., amber................... 18
Bowl, cream soup, 5 1/2" d., clear 5
Bowl, cream soup, 5 1/2" d., pink 20
Bowl, salad, 9" d., amber................................... 18
Bowl, salad, 9" d., clear 10
Bowl, salad, 9" d., pink 24
Bowl, scalloped rim, 12" d., amber 20
Bowl, scalloped rim, 12" d., clear....................... 10
Bowl, scalloped rim, 12" d., pink........................ 30
Candy jar, cov., round, amber 45
Candy jar, cov., round, clear............................... 20
Candy jar, cov., round, pink................................ 50
Coaster, amber, 3 1/2" d..................................... 10
Coaster, clear, 3 1/2" d. 2
Coaster, pink, 3 1/2" d. 8
Console bowl, amber, 11" d................................ 24
Console bowl, clear, 11" d. 12
Console bowl, pink, 11" d. 30
Creamer, oval, amber 10
Creamer, oval, clear.. 5
Creamer, oval, pink... 12
Cup, demitasse, clear 8
Cup, demitasse, pink... 35
Cup, amber 10
Cup, clear 3
Cup, pink 20
Cup & saucer, demitasse, clear 12
Cup & saucer, demitasse, pink 45
Cup & saucer, amber 15
Cup & saucer, clear... 5
Cup & saucer, pink.. 28
Junior set, child's plate, 5 1/2" d., clear 2
Junior set, Child's plate, 5 1/2" d., pink............... 4
Plate, bread & butter, 6" d., amber....................... 3
Plate, bread & butter, 6" d., clear 1
Plate, bread & butter, 6" d., pink 4
Plate, dinner, 9 1/2" d., amber 10
Plate, dinner, 9 1/2" d., clear 5
Plate, dinner, 9 1/2" d., pink 18
Plate, sandwich, 11 3/4" d., amber 16
Plate, sandwich, 11 3/4" d., clear......................... 6
Plate, sandwich, 11 3/4" d., pink 24
Platter, 12" oval, amber...................................... 16
Platter, 12" oval, clear... 8
Platter, 12" oval, pink... 30
Salt & pepper shakers, amber, pr. 95
Salt & pepper shakers, clear, pr. 24
Salt & pepper shakers, pink, pr. 85
Saucer, demitasse, pink...................................... 10
Saucer, amber 5
Saucer, clear 2
Sherbet, amber 10
Sherbet, clear 3
Sherbet, pink... 12
Sugar bowl, open, oval, amber 8
Sugar bowl, open, oval, clear................................ 4
Sugar bowl, open, oval, pink.............................. 12

Tumbler, amber, 4 1/8" h., 9 oz. 28
Tumbler, clear, 4 1/8" h., 9 oz. 8
Tumbler, pink, 4 1/8" h., 9 oz. 45

Junior set
Junior set: 6 cups, saucers & plates
  w/round rack; clear, set 120
Junior set: 6 cups, saucers & plates
  w/round rack; pink, set 320

DOGWOOD OR APPLE BLOSSOM OR WILD ROSE, MacBeth-Evans, 1929-32 (Process-etched)
Bowl, cereal, 5 1/2" d., Cremax 6
Bowl, cereal, 5 1/2" d., green 38
Bowl, cereal, 5 1/2" d., Monax 6
Bowl, cereal, 5 1/2" d., pink 30
Bowl, cereal, 5 1/2" d., yellow 60
Bowl, berry, 8 1/2" d., Cremax 35
Bowl, berry, 8 1/2" d., green 120
Bowl, berry, 8 1/2" d., Monax 35
Bowl, berry, 8 1/2" d., pink 65
Bowl, fruit, 10 1/4" d., Cremax 120
Bowl, fruit, 10 1/4" d., green 275
Bowl, fruit, 10 1/4" d., Monax 120
Bowl, fruit, 10 1/4" d., pink 550
Cake plate, heavy solid foot, pink, 11" d. 1,350
Cake plate, heavy solid foot, Cremax, 13" d. 185
Cake plate, heavy solid foot, green, 13" d. 145
Cake plate, heavy solid foot, Monax, 13" d. 185
Cake plate, heavy solid foot, pink, 13" d. 150
Coaster, pink, 3 1/4" d. 500
Creamer, thin, green, 2 1/2" h. 45
Creamer, thin, pink, 2 1/2" h. 24
Creamer, thick, footed, pink, 3 1/4" h. 24
Cup, Cremax 36
Cup, green 24
Cup, Monax 30
Cup, pink 24
Cup & saucer, Cremax 50
Cup & saucer, green 30
Cup & saucer, Monax 50
Cup & saucer, pink 30
Pitcher, 8" h., 80 oz., American Sweetheart
  style, pink 625
Pitcher, 8" h., 80 oz., decorated, green 575
Pitcher, 8" h., 80 oz., decorated, pink 275
Plate, bread & butter, 6" d., Cremax 20
Plate, bread & butter, 6" d., green 10
Plate, bread & butter, 6" d., Monax 20
Plate, bread & butter, 6" d., pink 10
Plate, luncheon, 8" d., clear 5
Plate, luncheon, 8" d., green 10
Plate, luncheon, 8" d., pink 12
Plate, luncheon, 8" d., yellow 60
Plate, dinner, 9 1/4" d., pink 38
Plate, grill, border design, 10 1/2" d., pink 28
Plate, grill, overall patt., 10 1/2" d., pink 30
Plate, grill, overall patt. or border design
  only, 10 1/2" d., green 28
Plate, salver, 12" d., Cremax 18
Plate, salver, 12" d., Monax 18
Plate, salver, 12" d., pink 40
Platter, 12" oval, pink 750
Saucer, green 6
Saucer, pink 6
Sherbet, low foot, green 125
Sherbet, low foot, pink 38
Sugar bowl, open, thin, green, 2 1/2" h. 42
Sugar bowl, open, thin, pink, 2 1/2" h. 24

Sugar bowl, open, thick, footed, pink,
  3 1/4" h. 20
Tumbler, decorated, pink, 3 1/2" h., 5 oz. 350
Tumbler, decorated, green, 4" h., 10 oz. 110
Tumbler, decorated, pink, 4" h., 10 oz. 55
Tumbler, decorated, green, 4 3/4" h., 11 oz. 125
Tumbler, decorated, pink, 4 3/4" h., 11 oz. 60
Tumbler, decorated, green, 5" h., 12 oz. 120
Tumbler, decorated, pink, 5" h., 12 oz. 85
Tumbler, molded band, pink 24

FLORAL OR POINSETTIA, Jeannette Glass Co., 1931-35 (Process-etched)
Bowl, berry, 4" d., Delphite 60
Bowl, berry, 4" d., green 24
Bowl, berry, 4" d., pink 20
Bowl, cream soup, 5 1/2" d., green 800
Bowl, cream soup, 5 1/2" d., pink 750
Bowl, salad, 7 1/2" d., Cremax 85
Bowl, salad, 7 1/2" d., Delphite 65
Bowl, salad, 7 1/2" d., green 35
Bowl, salad, 7 1/2" d., pink 30
Bowl, cov. vegetable, 8" d., Delphite 75
Bowl, cov. vegetable, 8" d., green 65
Bowl, cov. vegetable, 8" d., pink 55
Bowl, 9" oval vegetable, green 28
Bowl, 9" oval vegetable, pink 24
Butter dish, cov., green 100
Butter dish, cov., pink 95
Candlesticks, green, 4" h., pr. 95
Candlesticks, pink, 4" h., pr. 85
Candy jar, cov., green 85
Candy jar, cov., pink 75
Coaster, green, 3 1/4" d. 18
Coaster, pink, 3 1/4" d. 16
Compote, 9" d., green 1,100
Compote, 9" d., pink 950
Creamer, Cremax 65
Creamer, Delphite 85
Creamer, green 18
Creamer, pink 16
Cup, green 16
Cup, pink 14
Cup & saucer, green 24
Cup & saucer, pink 22
Flower frog for vase, green 750
Ice tub, oval, green, 3 1/2" h. 850
Ice tub, oval, pink, 3 1/2" h. 800
Lamp, green 300
Lamp, pink 275
Pitcher, 5 1/2" h., 24 oz., green 575
Pitcher, 8" h., 32 oz., cone-shaped, green 42
Pitcher, 8" h., 32 oz., cone-shaped, pink 38
Pitcher, lemonade, 10 1/4" h., 48 oz., green 275
Pitcher, lemonade, 10 1/4" h., 48 oz., pink 245
Plate, sherbet, 6" d., green 8
Plate, sherbet, 6" d., pink 6
Plate, salad, 8" d., green 15
Plate, salad, 8" d., pink 14
Plate, dinner, 9" d., Delphite 175
Plate, dinner, 9" d., green 24
Plate, dinner, 9" d., pink 20
Plate, grill, 9" d., green 275
Platter, 10 3/4" oval, Delphite 175
Platter, 10 3/4" oval, green 24
Platter, 10 3/4" oval, pink 22
Platter, 11" oval, scalloped edge, pink 125
Powder jar, cov., green 250
Refrigerator dish, cov., green, 5" sq. 75
Refrigerator dish, cov., Jadite, 5" sq. 55

Relish, two-part, oval, green 24
Relish, two-part, oval, pink 22
Rose bowl, three-footed, green 575
Salt & pepper shakers, footed, green,
     4" h., pr. 60
Salt & pepper shakers, footed, pink, 4" h.,
     pr. 50
Salt & pepper shakers, flat, pink, 6" h., pr. 60
Saucer, green 8
Saucer, pink 8
Sherbet, Delphite 75
Sherbet, green 20
Sherbet, pink 18
Sugar bowl, cov., green 38
Sugar bowl, cov., pink 35
Sugar bowl, open, Cremax 65
Sugar bowl, open, Delphite 85
Sugar bowl, open, green 18
Sugar bowl, open, pink 16
Tray, closed handles, green, 6" sq. 24
Tray, closed handles, pink, 6" sq. 20
Tray, dresser, green, 9 1/4" oval 225
Tumbler, footed, green, 3 1/2" h., 3 oz. 175
Tumbler, juice, footed, green, 4" h., 5 oz. 24
Tumbler, juice, footed, pink, 4" h., 5 oz. 20
Tumbler, water, footed, Delphite, 4 3/4" h.,
     7 oz. 200
Tumbler, water, footed, green, 4 3/4" h., 7
     oz. 24
Tumbler, water, footed, pink, 4 3/4" h., 7 oz. 22
Tumbler, green, 4 1/2" h., 9 oz. 195
Tumbler, lemonade, footed, green,
     5 1/4" h., 9 oz. 60
Tumbler, lemonade, footed, pink, 5 1/4" h.,
     9 oz. 50
Vase, 6 7/8" h., octagonal, clear..................... 350
Vase, 6 7/8" h., octagonal, green 550

LORAIN OR BASKET OR NUMBER 615, Indiana Glass Co., 1929-32 (Process-etched)

Bowl, cereal, 6", clear 20
Bowl, cereal, 6", green 45
Bowl, cereal, 6", yellow 65
Bowl, salad, 7 1/4", clear 22
Bowl, salad, 7 1/4", green 48
Bowl, salad, 7 1/4", yellow 70
Bowl, berry, 8", clear 50
Bowl, berry, 8", green 120
Bowl, berry, 8", yellow...................................... 175
Bowl, 9 3/4" oval vegetable, clear..................... 25
Bowl, 9 3/4" oval vegetable, green 60
Bowl, 9 3/4" oval vegetable, yellow................... 65
Creamer, footed, clear 10
Creamer, footed, green 20
Creamer, footed, yellow 30
Cup clear 6
Cup, green.. 14
Cup, yellow 18
Cup & saucer, clear 9
Cup & saucer, green 18
Cup & saucer, yellow... 23
Plate, sherbet, 5 1/2", clear 4
Plate, sherbet, 5 1/2", green............................. 10
Plate, sherbet, 5 1/2", yellow 12
Plate, salad, 7 3/4", clear 5
Plate, salad, 7 3/4", green 12
Plate, salad, 7 3/4", yellow 16
Plate, luncheon, 8 3/8", clear 8
Plate, luncheon, 8 3/8", green 18

Plate, luncheon, 8 3/8", yellow 30
Plate, dinner, 10 1/4", clear............................... 35
Plate, dinner, 10 1/4", green.............................. 75
Plate, dinner, 10 1/4", yellow............................. 85
Platter, 11 1/2", clear 15
Platter, 11 1/2", green.. 35
Platter, 11 1/2", yellow 48
Relish, four-part, clear, 8" 12
Relish, four-part, green, 8"................................. 26
Relish, four-part, yellow, 8"................................ 38
Saucer, green 4
Saucer, yellow.. 5
Sherbet, footed, clear 10
Sherbet, footed, green 24
Sherbet, footed, yellow 32
Sugar bowl, open, footed, clear 10
Sugar bowl, open, footed, green 20
Sugar bowl, open, footed, yellow 30
Tumbler, footed, clear, 4 3/4" h., 9 oz. 10
Tumbler, footed, green, 4 3/4" h., 9 oz. 24
Tumbler, footed, yellow, 4 3/4" h., 9 oz. 32

MADRID, FEDERAL GLASS CO., 1932-39 (Process-etched)

Ashtray, amber, 6" sq...................................... 225
Ashtray, green, 6" sq....................................... 200
Bowl, cream soup, 4 3/4" d., amber.................. 20
Bowl, sauce, 5" d., amber.................................... 8
Bowl, sauce, 5" d., blue 35
Bowl, sauce, 5" d., clear 5
Bowl, sauce, 5" d., green 8
Bowl, sauce, 5" d., pink 10
Bowl, soup, 7" d., amber.................................... 20
Bowl, soup, 7" d., blue 65
Bowl, soup, 7" d., clear 8
Bowl, soup, 7" d., green..................................... 20
Bowl, salad, 8" d., amber................................... 18
Bowl, salad, 8" d., blue 45
Bowl, salad, 8" d., clear 8
Bowl, salad, 8" d., green 16
Bowl, large berry, 9 3/8" d., amber 24
Bowl, large berry, 9 3/8" d., clear 10
Bowl, large berry, 9 3/8" d., pink...................... 20
Bowl, salad, deep, 9 1/2" d., amber.................. 35
Bowl, 10" oval vegetable, amber 24
Bowl, 10" oval vegetable, blue........................... 42
Bowl, 10" oval vegetable, clear.......................... 10
Bowl, 10" oval vegetable, green 24
Bowl, 10" oval vegetable, pink........................... 20
Butter dish, cov., amber.................................... 75
Butter dish, cov., clear...................................... 35
Butter dish, cov., green..................................... 85
Cake plate, amber, 11 1/4" d. 30
Cake plate, clear, 11 1/4" d. 15
Cake plate, pink, 11 1/4" d. 24
Candlesticks, amber, 2 1/4" h., pr.................... 24
Candlesticks, clear, 2 1/4" h., pr...................... 10
Candlesticks, iridescent, 2 1/4" h., pr. 28
Candlesticks, pink, 2 1/4" h., pr........................ 24
Console bowl, flared, amber, 11" d. 24
Console bowl, flared, clear, 11" d. 10
Console bowl, flared, iridescent, 11" d. 28
Console bowl, flared, pink, 11" d. 20
Cookie jar, cov., amber 52
Cookie jar, cov., clear.. 20
Cookie jar, cov., pink 30
Creamer, amber 8
Creamer, blue 30
Creamer, clear 5
Creamer, green... 16

Cup, amber.. 6
Cup, blue.. 15
Cup, clear.. 2
Cup, green... 8
Cup, pink.. 8
Cup & saucer, amber 9
Cup & saucer, blue................................... 25
Cup & saucer, clear.................................... 4
Cup & saucer, green 13
Cup & saucer, pink................................... 13
Gelatin mold, amber, 2 1/8" h. 16
Gravy boat & platter, amber 2,800
Gravy boat platter, amber..................... 1,500
Hot dish coaster, amber, 5" d. 65
Hot dish coaster, clear, 5" d. 25
Hot dish coaster, green, 5" d. 60
Hot dish coaster w/indentation, amber 85
Hot dish coaster w/indentation, clear.......... 35
Hot dish coaster w/indentation, green 75
Jam dish, amber, 7" d................................ 28
Jam dish, blue, 7" d.................................. 38
Jam dish, clear, 7" d................................ 12
Jam dish, green, 7" d............................... 24
Lazy Susan, walnut base w/seven clear hot
    dish coasters...................................... 975
Pitcher, juice, 5 1/2" h., 36 oz., amber.............. 48
Pitcher, 8" h., 60 oz., square, amber 55
Pitcher, 8" h., 60 oz., square, blue.............. 195
Pitcher, 8" h., 60 oz., square, clear.................. 28
Pitcher, 8" h., 60 oz., square, green 148
Pitcher, 8" h., 60 oz., square, pink 45
Pitcher, 8 1/2" h., 80 oz., jug-type, amber 75
Pitcher, 8 1/2" h., 80 oz., jug-type, green 225
Pitcher w/ice lip, 8 1/2" h., 80 oz., amber
    85
Pitcher w/ice lip, 8 1/2" h., 80 oz., green 250
Plate, sherbet, 6" d., amber................................. 6
Plate, sherbet, 6" d., blue 12
Plate, sherbet, 6" d., clear................................. 3
Plate, sherbet, 6" d., green................................ 5
Plate, sherbet, 6" d., pink................................. 5
Plate, salad, 7 1/2" d., amber 12
Plate, salad, 7 1/2" d., blue............................... 24
Plate, salad, 7 1/2" d., clear 5
Plate, salad, 7 1/2" d., green............................. 10
Plate, salad, 7 1/2" d., pink.............................. 10
Plate, luncheon, 8 7/8" d., amber 8
Plate, luncheon, 8 7/8" d., blue 20
Plate, luncheon, 8 7/8" d., clear......................... 4
Plate, luncheon, 8 7/8" d., green 10
Plate, luncheon, 8 7/8" d., pink.......................... 8
Plate, dinner, 10 1/2" d., amber......................... 60
Plate, dinner, 10 1/2" d., blue........................... 85
Plate, dinner, 10 1/2" d., clear........................... 25
Plate, dinner, 10 1/2" d., green........................... 50
Plate, grill, 10 1/2" d., amber 10
Plate, grill, 10 1/2" d., clear 5
Plate, grill, 10 1/2" d., green 16
Platter, 11 1/2" oval, amber 24
Platter, 11 1/2" oval, blue................................. 30
Platter, 11 1/2" oval, clear................................ 10
Platter, 11 1/2" oval, green............................... 20
Platter, 11 1/2" oval, pink................................ 16
Relish plate, amber, 10 1/2" d. 20
Relish plate, clear, 10 1/2" d. 10
Relish plate, green, 10 1/2" d. 18
Relish plate, pink, 10 1/2" d............................. 14
Salt & pepper shakers, flat, amber,
    3 1/2" h., pr.. 48

Salt & pepper shakers, flat, clear,
    3 1/2" h., pr.. 24
Salt & pepper shakers, flat, green,
    3 1/2" h., pr.. 65
Salt & pepper shakers, footed, amber,
    3 1/2" h., pr... 135
Salt & pepper shakers, footed, blue,
    3 1/2" h., pr... 170
Salt & pepper shakers, footed, clear,
    3 1/2" h., pr... 45
Salt & pepper shakers, footed, green,
    3 1/2" h., pr... 145
Saucer, amber 3
Saucer, blue.. 10
Saucer, green 5
Saucer, pink.. 5
Sherbet, amber.. 6
Sherbet, blue 18
Sherbet, clear 3
Sherbet, green 12
Sugar bowl, cov., amber 58
Sugar bowl, cov., blue.................................... 230
Sugar bowl, cov., clear.................................... 25
Sugar bowl, cov., green 81
Sugar bowl, open, amber................................. 8
Sugar bowl, open, blue 30
Sugar bowl, open, clear 5
Sugar bowl, open, green 16
Tumbler, juice, amber, 3 7/8" h., 5 oz.............. 15
Tumbler, juice, blue, 3 7/8" h., 5 oz................ 40
Tumbler, juice, clear, 3 7/8" h., 5 oz.............. 8
Tumbler, juice, green, 3 7/8" h., 5 oz.............. 30
Tumbler, footed, amber, 4" h., 5 oz................. 28
Tumbler, footed, clear, 4" h., 5 oz. 14
Tumbler, footed, green, 4" h., 5 oz. 40
Tumbler, amber, 4 1/2" h., 9 oz. 16
Tumbler, blue, 4 1/2" h., 9 oz. 35
Tumbler, clear, 4 1/2" h., 9 oz. 8
Tumbler, green, 4 1/2" h., 9 oz. 22
Tumbler, pink, 4 1/2" h., 9 oz. 16
Tumbler, footed, amber, 5 1/4" h., 10 oz. 34
Tumbler, footed, clear, 5 1/4" h., 10 oz. 15
Tumbler, footed, green, 5 1/4" h., 10 oz. 48
Tumbler, amber, 5 1/2" h., 12 oz. 24
Tumbler, blue, 5 1/2" h., 12 oz. 45
Tumbler, clear, 5 1/2" h., 12 oz. 10
Tumbler, green, 5 1/2" h., 12 oz. 28

MODERNTONE, Hazel Atlas Glass Co., 1934-42, late 1940s & early 1950s (Press-mold)

Ashtray w/match holder, cobalt blue,
    7 3/4" d.. 175
Ashtray w/match holder, pink, 7 3/4" d. 85
Bowl, cream soup, 4 3/4" d., amethyst 25
Bowl, cream soup, 4 3/4" d., cobalt blue 26
Bowl, cream soup, 4 3/4" d., platonite 8
Bowl, berry, 5" d., amethyst.............................. 28
Bowl, berry, 5" d., cobalt blue 30
Bowl, berry, 5" d., platonite 6
Bowl, cream soup w/ruffled rim, 5" d., ame-
    thyst 50
Bowl, cream soup w/ruffled rim, 5" d., cobalt
    blue 65
Bowl, cream soup w/ruffled rim, 5" d., plato-
    nite 12
Bowl, cereal, 6 1/2" d., amethyst 85
Bowl, cereal, 6 1/2" d., cobalt blue 95
Bowl, cereal, 6 1/2" d., platonite 8
Bowl, soup, 7 1/2" d., amethyst 120

Bowl, soup, 7 1/2" d., cobalt blue.................... 185
Bowl, soup, 7 1/2" d., platonite 18
Bowl, large berry, 8 3/4" d., amethyst 48
Bowl, large berry, 8 3/4" d., cobalt blue 60
Bowl, large berry, 8 3/4" d., platonite 12
Butter dish w/metal lid, cobalt blue............... 120
Cheese dish w/metal lid, cobalt blue, 7" d. 475
Creamer, amethyst... 14
Creamer, cobalt blue.. 16
Creamer, platonite.. 6
Cup, amethyst 14
Cup, cobalt blue 15
Cup, platonite 5
Cup & saucer, amethyst...................................... 18
Cup & saucer, cobalt blue 20
Cup & saucer, platonite.. 7
Custard cup, amethyst 24
Custard cup, cobalt blue 28
Plate, sherbet, 5 7/8" d., amethyst 6
Plate, sherbet, 5 7/8" d., cobalt blue 8
Plate, salad, 6 3/4" d., amethyst......................... 12
Plate, salad, 6 3/4" d., cobalt blue 15
Plate, salad, 6 3/4" d., platonite........................... 5
Plate, luncheon, 7 3/4" d., amethyst................... 10
Plate, luncheon, 7 3/4" d., cobalt blue............... 12
Plate, luncheon, 7 3/4" d., platonite..................... 6
Plate, dinner, 8 7/8" d., amethyst 16
Plate, dinner, 8 7/8" d., cobalt blue 20
Plate, dinner, 8 7/8" d., platonite 8
Plate, sandwich, 10 1/2" d., amethyst 50
Plate, sandwich, 10 1/2" d., cobalt blue 85
Plate, sandwich, 10 1/2" d., platonite 24
Platter, 11" oval, amethyst 45
Platter, 11" oval, cobalt blue 50
Platter, 11" oval, platonite 20
Platter, 12" oval, amethyst 60
Platter, 12" oval, cobalt blue 85
Platter, 12" oval, platonite 24
Salt & pepper shakers, amethyst, pr. 45
Salt & pepper shakers, cobalt blue, pr. 48
Salt & pepper shakers, platonite, pr. 15
Saucer, amethyst.. 4
Saucer, cobalt blue 5
Saucer, platonite 2
Sherbet, amethyst... 12
Sherbet, cobalt blue 12
Sherbet, platonite.. 5
Sugar bowl, open, amethyst............................... 14
Sugar bowl, open, cobalt blue 16
Sugar bowl, open, platonite.................................. 6
Sugar bowl w/metal lid, cobalt blue................. 42
Tumbler, whiskey, clear, 1 1/2 oz. 10
Tumbler, whiskey, cobalt blue, 1 1/2 oz............. 45
Tumbler, whiskey, platonite, 1 1/2 oz. 12
Tumbler, juice, amethyst, 5 oz............................ 45
Tumbler, juice, cobalt blue, 5 oz. 60
Tumbler, juice, platonite, 5 oz............................ 15
Tumbler, water, amethyst, 4" h., 9 oz. 40
Tumbler, water, cobalt blue, 4" h., 9 oz. 45
Tumbler, water, platonite, 4" h., 9 oz. 15
Tumbler, iced tea, amethyst, 12 oz..................... 95
Tumbler, iced tea, cobalt blue, 12 oz.............. 145
Little Hostess Party Set, cup & saucer,
    dark 22
Little Hostess Party Set, cup & saucer,
    pastel.. 15
Little Hostess Party Set, creamer,
    1 3/4" h., dark... 15

Little Hostess Party Set, creamer,
    1 3/4" h., pastel.. 14
Little Hostess Party Set, cup, 1 3/4" h.,
    dark... 14
Little Hostess Party Set, cup, 1 3/4" h.,
    pastel 10
Little Hostess Party Set, sugar bowl,
    1 3/4" h., dark... 15
Little Hostess Party Set, sugar bowl,
    1 3/4" h., pastel.. 14
Little Hostess Party Set, teapot, cov.,
    3 1/2" h., dark... 195
Little Hostess Party Set, teapot, cov.,
    3 1/2" h., pastel.. 145
Little Hostess Party Set, saucer, 3 7/8" d.,
    dark... 8
Little Hostess Party Set, saucer, 3 7/8" d.,
    pastel 5
Little Hostess Party Set, plate, 5 1/4" d.,
    dark... 12
Little Hostess Party Set, plate, 5 1/4" d.,
    pastel 10

NORMANDIE OR BOUQUET & LATTICE, Federal Glass Co., 1933-40 (Process-etched)

Bowl, berry, 5" d., amber 8
Bowl, berry, 5" d., pink....................................... 12
Bowl, berry, 5" d., Sunburst iridescent................ 4
Bowl, cereal, 6 1/2" d., amber............................ 24
Bowl, cereal, 6 1/2" d., pink 36
Bowl, cereal, 6 1/2" d., Sunburst iridescent 12
Bowl, large berry, 8 1/2" d., amber 28
Bowl, large berry, 8 1/2" d., pink....................... 40
Bowl, large berry, 8 1/2" d., Sunburst irides-
    cent 14
Bowl, 10" oval vegetable, amber 24
Bowl, 10" oval vegetable, pink........................... 45
Bowl, 10" oval vegetable, Sunburst irides-
    cent 14
Creamer, footed, amber...................................... 12
Creamer, footed, pink... 16
Creamer, footed, Sunburst iridescent 8
Cup, amber 9
Cup, pink 14
Cup, Sunburst iridescent...................................... 5
Cup & saucer, amber 12
Cup & saucer, pink.. 18
Cup & saucer, Sunburst iridescent...................... 7
Pitcher, 8" h., 80 oz., amber 90
Pitcher, 8" h., 80 oz., clear 45
Pitcher, 8" h., 80 oz., pink................................ 185
Plate, sherbet, 6" d., amber 6
Plate, sherbet, 6" d., pink................................... 10
Plate, sherbet, 6" d., Sunburst iridescent............ 3
Plate, salad, 8" d., amber................................... 18
Plate, salad, 8" d., pink 14
Plate, salad, 8" d., Sunburst iridescent.............. 12
Plate, 9 1/4" d., luncheon, Sunburst irides-
    cent 12
Plate, luncheon, 9 1/4" d., amber....................... 20
Plate, luncheon, 9 1/4" d., pink 16
Plate, dinner, 11" d., amber 45
Plate, dinner, 11" d., pink 120
Plate, dinner, 11" d., Sunburst iridescent.......... 10
Plate, grill, 11" d., amber 18
Plate, grill, 11" d., pink 35
Plate, grill, 11" d., Sunburst iridescent 8
Platter, 11 3/4" oval, amber 32
Platter, 11 3/4" oval, pink.................................. 38

Platter, 11 3/4" oval, Sunburst iridescent........... 14
Salt & pepper shakers, amber, pr.................... 55
Salt & pepper shakers, pink, pr. 95
Saucer, amber.. 3
Saucer, pink 4
Saucer, Sunburst iridescent................................. 2
Sherbet, amber 6
Sherbet, clear.. 3
Sherbet, pink 10
Sherbet, Sunburst iridescent................................ 5
Sugar bowl, cov., amber 98
Sugar bowl, cov., pink 175
Sugar bowl, open, amber 12
Sugar bowl, open, pink 16
Sugar bowl, open, Sunburst iridescent................. 8
Tumbler, juice, amber, 4" h., 5 oz..................... 45
Tumbler, juice, pink, 4" h., 5 oz. 95
Tumbler, water, amber, 4 1/2" h., 9 oz. 35
Tumbler, water, pink, 4 1/2" h., 9 oz. 75
Tumbler, iced tea, amber, 5" h., 12 oz............... 55
Tumbler, iced tea, pink, 5" h., 12 oz. 135

OYSTER & PEARL, Anchor Hocking Glass Corp., 1938-40 (Press-mold)

Bowl, heart-shaped, w/handle, 5 1/4" w., clear 6
Bowl, heart-shaped, w/handle, 5 1/4" w., pink.. 14
Bowl, heart-shaped, w/handle, 5 1/4" w., white w/green... 8
Bowl, heart-shaped, w/handle, 5 1/4" w., white w/pink.. 10
Bowl, w/handle, 5 1/2" d., pink........................... 14
Bowl, w/handle, 5 1/2" d., ruby 20
Bowl, handled, 6 1/2" d., clear 10
Bowl, handled, 6 1/2" d., pink 18
Bowl, handled, 6 1/2" d., ruby 24
Bowl, fruit, 10 1/2" d., clear 12
Bowl, fruit, 10 1/2" d., pink 28
Bowl, fruit, 10 1/2" d., ruby 55
Bowl, fruit, 10 1/2" d., white w/green.................. 16
Bowl, fruit, 10 1/2" d., white w/pink 18
Candleholder, pink, 3 1/2" h. 18
Candleholders, clear, 3 1/2" h., pr. 10
Candleholders, pink, 3 1/2" h., pr...................... 36
Candleholders, ruby, 3 1/2" h., pr. 60
Candleholders, white w/green, 3 1/2" h., pr... 16
Candleholders, white w/pink, 3 1/2" h., pr......... 18
Plate, sandwich, 13 1/2" d., clear 12
Plate, sandwich, 13 1/2" d., pink 20
Plate, sandwich, 13 1/2" d., ruby........................ 55
Relish, divided, clear, 10 1/4" oval..................... 14
Relish, divided, pink, 10 1/4" oval 30

PARROT OR SYLVAN, Federal Glass Co., 1931-32 (Process-etched)

Bowl, berry, 5" sq., amber.................................. 22
Bowl, berry, 5" sq., green................................... 28
Bowl, soup, 7" sq., amber 38
Bowl, soup, 7" sq., green 50
Bowl, large berry, 8" sq., amber......................... 80
Bowl, large berry, 8" sq., green.......................... 98
Bowl, 10" oval vegetable, amber 72
Bowl, 10" oval vegetable, green 68
Butter dish, cov., amber............................... 1,350
Butter dish, cov., green 425
Creamer, footed, amber 60
Creamer, footed, green 55
Cup, amber... 48

Cup, green 45
Cup & saucer, amber 63
Cup & saucer, green 60
Hot plate, green, scalloped edge.................... 950
Hot plate, green, 5" d...................................... 850
Jam dish, amber, 7" sq....................................... 40
Pitcher, 8 1/2" h., 80 oz., green.................... 2,950
Plate, sherbet, 5 3/4" sq., amber........................ 28
Plate, sherbet, 5 3/4" sq., green......................... 38
Plate, salad, 7 1/2" sq., green 40
Plate, dinner, 9" sq., amber................................ 48
Plate, dinner, 9" sq., green................................. 58
Plate, grill, 10 1/2" sq., amber 45
Platter, 11 1/4" oblong, amber............................ 75
Platter, 11 1/4" oblong, green............................. 62
Salt & pepper shakers, green, pr. 295
Saucer, amber 15
Saucer, green 15
Sherbet, footed, cone-shaped, amber 24
Sherbet, footed, cone-shaped, blue................. 245
Sherbet, footed, cone-shaped, green 30
Sherbet, green, 4 1/4" h................................ 1,300
Sugar bowl, cov., amber 550
Sugar bowl, cov., green 275
Sugar bowl, open, amber................................... 60
Sugar bowl, open, green 50
Tumbler, amber, 4 1/4" h., 10 oz..................... 125
Tumbler, green, 4 1/4" h., 10 oz....................... 165
Tumbler, footed, amber, 5 1/2" h., 10 oz. 150
Tumbler, footed, cone-shaped, amber, 5 3/4" h.. 120
Tumbler, footed, cone-shaped, green, 5 3/4" h.. 145

PETALWARE, MacBeth-Evans Glass Co., 1930-40 (Press-mold)

Bowl, cream soup, 4 1/2" d., clear 5
Bowl, cream soup, 4 1/2" d., decorated Cremax or Monax 22
Bowl, cream soup, 4 1/2" d., Florette................. 32
Bowl, cream soup, 4 1/2" d., pink 20
Bowl, cream soup, 4 1/2" d., plain Cremax or Monax 14
Bowl, cream soup, 4 1/2" d., Red Trim Floral.. 40
Bowl, cereal, 5 3/4" d., clear 5
Bowl, cereal, 5 3/4" d., decorated Cremax or Monax 12
Bowl, cereal, 5 3/4" d., Florette......................... 24
Bowl, cereal, 5 3/4" d., pink 16
Bowl, cereal, 5 3/4" d., plain Cremax or Monax 8
Bowl, cereal, 5 3/4" d., Red Trim Floral............. 32
Bowl, soup, 7" d., decorated Cremax or Monax 65
Bowl, soup, 7" d., plain Cremax or Monax........ 45
Bowl, large berry, 9" d., clear............................. 10
Bowl, large berry, 9" d., cobalt blue 60
Bowl, large berry, 9" d., decorated Cremax or Monax 30
Bowl, large berry, 9" d., Florette 45
Bowl, large berry, 9" d., pink............................. 23
Bowl, large berry, 9" d., plain Cremax or Monax 20
Bowl, large berry, 9" d., Red Trim Floral............ 33
Creamer, footed, clear 3
Creamer, footed, cobalt blue.............................. 35
Creamer, footed, decorated Cremax or Monax 12
Creamer, footed, Florette................................... 18

Creamer, footed, pink.. 20
Creamer, footed, plain Cremax or Monax........... 6
Creamer, footed, Red Trim Floral 28
Cup, clear.. 3
Cup, decorated Cremax or Monax 10
Cup, Florette... 15
Cup, pink... 10
Cup, Red Trim Floral 22
Cup & saucer, clear.. 5
Cup & saucer, clear w/platinum trim................... 6
Cup & saucer, decorated Cremax or Monax 14
Cup & saucer, Florette 20
Cup & saucer, pink... 14
Cup & saucer, plain Cremax or Monax 10
Cup & saucer, Red Trim Floral.......................... 24
Lamp shade, Monax, 6" h.................................. 10
Lamp shade, Cremax, 9" h................................ 12
Lamp shade, pink, 10" h.................................... 25
Lamp shade, Monax, 11" h................................ 18
Lamp shade, pink, 12" h.................................... 30
Mustard jar, no metal cover, cobalt blue 10
Mustard jar, w/metal cover, cobalt blue............. 16
Pitcher, 80 oz., clear w/decorated bands........... 25
Plate, 6" d., sherbet, Red Trim Floral 22
Plate, sherbet, 6" d., clear 2
Plate, sherbet, 6" d., decorated Cremax or
   Monax 5
Plate, sherbet, 6" d., Florette............................. 7
Plate, sherbet, 6" d., pink 8
Plate, sherbet, 6" d., plain Cremax or
   Monax 3
Plate, salad, 8" d., clear 3
Plate, salad, 8" d., clear w/platinum trim 4
Plate, salad, 8" d., decorated Cremax or
   Monax 8
Plate, salad, 8" d., Florette 10
Plate, salad, 8" d., pink.................................... 10
Plate, salad, 8" d., plain Cremax or Monax 4
Plate, salad, 8" d., Red Trim Floral 24
Plate, dinner, 9" d., clear 5
Plate, dinner, 9" d., decorated Cremax or
   Monax 20
Plate, dinner, 9" d., Florette.............................. 35
Plate, dinner, 9" d., pink................................... 18
Plate, dinner, 9" d., plain Cremax or Monax....... 12
Plate, salver, 11" d., clear 6
Plate, salver, 11" d., clear w/platinum trim 8
Plate, salver, 11" d., decorated Cremax or
   Monax 14
Plate, salver, 11" d., Florette 20
Plate, salver, 11" d., pink.................................. 15
Plate, salver, 11" d., plain Cremax or Monax 10
Plate, salver, 11" d., Red Trim Floral 28
Plate, salver, 12" d., decorated Cremax or
   Monax 24
Plate, salver, 12" d., Florette 28
Plate, salver, 12" d., plain Cremax or Monax 18
Plate, salver, 12" d., Red Trim Floral 36
Platter, 13" oval, clear...................................... 10
Platter, 13" oval, decorated Cremax or
   Monax 25
Platter, 13" oval, Florette 30
Platter, 13" oval, pink....................................... 25
Platter, 13" oval, plain Cremax or Monax 18
Saucer, clear... 1
Saucer, decorated Cremax or Monax 3
Saucer, Florette... 3
Saucer, pink 4
Saucer, plain Cremax or Monax......................... 2

Sherbet, low foot, clear, 4 1/2" h........................ 4
Sherbet, low foot, cobalt blue, 4 1/2" h. 30
Sherbet, low foot, decorated Cremax or
   Monax, 4 1/2" h... 16
Sherbet, low foot, Florette, 4 1/2" h. 24
Sherbet, low foot, pink, 4 1/2" h. 15
Sherbet, low foot, plain Cremax or Monax,
   4 1/2" h... 24
Sherbet, low foot, Red Trim Floral, 4 1/2" h. 38
Sugar bowl, open, footed, clear 3
Sugar bowl, open, footed, cobalt blue............... 35
Sugar bowl, open, footed, decorated Cre-
   max or Monax 12
Sugar bowl, open, footed, Florette 18
Sugar bowl, open, footed, plain Cremax or
   Monax 6
Sugar bowl, open, footed, Red Trim Floral 28
Sugar bowl, open, pink...................................... 20
Tidbit server, clear 15
Tidbit server, decorated Cremax or Monax 28
Tidbit server, Florette....................................... 32
Tidbit server, pink 28
Tidbit server, plain Cremax or Monax............... 24

PRINCESS, Hocking Glass Co., 1931-35 (Process-etched)

Ashtray, Apricot Yellow, 4 1/2" 110
Ashtray, green, 4 1/2".. 75
Ashtray, pink, 4 1/2" 80
Bowl, berry, 4 1/2", Apricot Yellow.................... 50
Bowl, berry, 4 1/2", green 28
Bowl, berry, 4 1/2", pink.................................... 30
Bowl, berry, 4 1/2", Topaz 50
Bowl, cereal, 5", Apricot Yellow 40
Bowl, cereal, 5", green...................................... 35
Bowl, cereal, 5", pink.. 40
Bowl, cereal, 5", pink frosted 35
Bowl, cereal, 5", Topaz 40
Bowl, salad, 9" octagon, Apricot Yellow 145
Bowl, salad, 9" octagon, green.......................... 50
Bowl, salad, 9" octagon, pink............................ 60
Bowl, salad, 9" octagon, Topaz 145
Bowl, 9 1/2" hat shape, Apricot Yellow............. 150
Bowl, 9 1/2" hat shape, green............................ 55
Bowl, 9 1/2" hat shape, green frosted............... 55
Bowl, 9 1/2" hat shape, pink 65
Bowl, 9 1/2" hat shape, pink frosted 60
Bowl, 9 1/2", hat shape, Topaz......................... 150
Bowl, 10" oval vegetable, Apricot Yellow........... 60
Bowl, 10" oval vegetable, green 40
Bowl, 10" oval vegetable, pink........................... 45
Bowl, 10" oval vegetable, Topaz....................... 60
Butter dish, cov., Apricot Yellow 750
Butter dish, cov., green.................................... 125
Butter dish, cov., pink 145
Butter dish, cov., Topaz................................... 750
Cake stand, green, 10"...................................... 45
Cake stand, pink, 10" 48
Candy jar, cov., green 60
Candy jar, cov., pink... 68
Coaster, Apricot Yellow, 4" 120
Coaster, green, 4"... 75
Coaster, pink, 4" 85
Coaster, Topaz, 4 " 120
Cookie jar, cov., blue....................................... 950
Cookie jar, cov., green 60
Cookie jar, cov., green frosted 50
Cookie jar, cov., pink.. 75
Cookie jar, cov., pink frosted............................ 65
Creamer, oval, Apricot Yellow........................... 18

Creamer, oval, green 14
Creamer, oval, pink 16
Creamer, oval, pink frosted 14
Creamer, oval, Topaz.. 18
Cup, Apricot Yellow 8
Cup, blue.. 145
Cup, green... 13
Cup, pink 15
Cup, Topaz.. 10
Cup & saucer, Apricot Yellow..................... 18
Cup & saucer, blue................................... 200
Cup & saucer, green 23
Cup & saucer, pink 25
Cup & saucer, Topaz................................... 20
Pitcher, 6" h., 37 oz., jug-type, Apricot Yel-
low.. 700
Pitcher, 6" h., 37 oz., jug-type, green 65
Pitcher, 6" h., 37 oz., jug-type, pink 70
Pitcher, 6" h., 37 oz., jug-type, Topaz............. 700
Pitcher, 7 3/8" h., 24 oz., footed, green 575
Pitcher, 7 3/8" h., 24 oz., footed, pink 650
Pitcher, 8" h., 60 oz., jug-type, Apricot Yel-
low.. 120
Pitcher, 8" h., 60 oz., jug-type, green 60
Pitcher, 8" h., 60 oz., jug-type, pink 65
Pitcher, 8" h., 60 oz, jug-type,Topaz............. 120
Plate, sherbet, 5 1/2", Apricot Yellow 8
Plate, sherbet, 5 1/2", blue 175
Plate, sherbet, 5 1/2", green.............................. 10
Plate, sherbet, 5 1/2", pink 10
Plate, sherbet, 5 1/2", Topaz............................. 12
Plate, salad, 8", Apricot Yellow 12
Plate, salad, 8" d., green 14
Plate, salad, 8", pink.. 16
Plate, salad, 8", Topaz 18
Plate, dinner, 9", Apricot Yellow 24
Plate, dinner, 9", green..................................... 28
Plate, dinner, 9", pink 30
Plate, dinner, 9", Topaz.................................... 16
Plate, grill, 9", Apricot Yellow 8
Plate, grill, 9", blue 175
Plate, grill, 9", green... 14
Plate, grill, 9", pink... 16
Plate, grill, 9", Topaz 8
Plate, sandwich, 10 1/4", handled, Apricot
Yellow.. 175
Plate, sandwich, 10 1/4", handled, green.......... 28
Plate, sandwich, 10 1/4", handled, pink 30
Plate, sandwich, 10 1/4", handled, Topaz 175
Plate, grill, 10 1/2", closed handles, Apricot
Yellow.. 12
Plate, grill, 10 1/2", closed handles, green 14
Plate, grill, 10 1/2", closed handles, pink........... 15
Plate, grill, 10 1/2", closed handles, Topaz 10
Platter, 12" oval, closed handles, Apricot
Yellow.. 65
Platter, 12" oval, closed handles, green 28
Platter, 12" oval, closed handles, pink 30
Platter, 12" oval, closed handles, Topaz........... 65
Relish, Apricot Yellow, 7 1/2" 245
Relish, green, 7 1/2" 185
Relish, pink, 7 1/2" 195
Relish, Topaz, 7 1/2".. 245
Relish, divided, Apricot Yellow, 7 1/2" 95
Relish, divided, green, 7 1/2".............................. 26
Relish, divided, pink, 7 1/2".............................. 28
Relish, divided, Topaz, 7 1/2" 95

Salt & pepper (or spice) shakers, green,
5 1/2" h., pr. 50
Salt & pepper shakers, Apricot Yellow,
4 1/2" h., pr. 85
Salt & pepper shakers, green, 4 1/2" h., pr. ... 65
Salt & pepper shakers, pink, 4 1/2" h., pr......... 70
Salt & pepper shakers, Topaz, 4 1/2" h.,
pr... 85
Saucer, green 10
Sherbet, footed, Apricot Yellow 35
Sherbet, footed, green...................................... 25
Sherbet, footed, pink.. 25
Sherbet, footed, Topaz 35
Sugar bowl, cov., Apricot Yellow....................... 36
Sugar bowl, cov., green 29
Sugar bowl, cov., pink 28
Sugar bowl, cov., Topaz.................................... 36
Sugar bowl, open, Apricot Yellow 12
Sugar bowl, open, green.................................... 14
Sugar bowl, open, pink...................................... 16
Sugar bowl, open, pink frosted.......................... 14
Sugar bowl, open, Topaz 18
Tumbler, juice, Apricot Yellow, 3" h., 5 oz. 35
Tumbler, juice, green, 3" h., 5 oz....................... 33
Tumbler, juice, pink, 3" h., 5 oz......................... 35
Tumbler, juice, Topaz, 3" h., 5 oz...................... 35
Tumbler, water, Apricot Yellow, 4" h., 9 oz....... 30
Tumbler, water, green, 4" h., 9 oz...................... 28
Tumbler, water, pink, 4" h., 9 oz........................ 30
Tumbler, water, Topaz, 4" h., 9 oz. 30
Tumbler, square footed, green, 4 3/4" h., 9
oz.. 60
Tumbler, square footed, pink, 4 3/4" h., 9
oz.. 65
Tumbler, footed, Apricot Yellow, 5 1/4" h.,
10 oz.. 28
Tumbler, footed, green, 5 1/4" h., 10 oz. 32
Tumbler, footed, pink, 5 1/4" h. 10 oz............... 35
Tumbler, footed, Topaz, 5 1/4" h., 10 oz. 22
Tumbler, footed, Apricot Yellow, 6 1/2" h.,
12 1/2" oz. 165
Tumbler, footed, green, 6 1/2" h., 12 1/2 oz. 98
Tumbler, footed, pink, 6 1/2" h., 12 1/2 oz....... 110
Tumbler, footed, Topaz, 6 1/2" h., 12 1/2
oz.. 165
Tumbler, iced tea, Apricot Yellow, 5 1/2" h.,
13 oz. 35
Tumbler, iced tea, green, 5 1/4" h., 13 oz. 45
Tumbler, iced tea, pink, 5 1/4" h., 13 oz. 40
Tumbler, iced tea, Topaz, 5 1/4" h., 13 oz. 35
Vase, 8" h., green... 45
Vase, 8" h., green frosted................................. 40
Vase, 8" h., pink 50
Vase, 8" h., pink frosted 45

SHARON OR CABBAGE ROSE, Federal Glass Co., 1935-39 (Chip-mold)

Bowl, berry, 5" d., amber 10
Bowl, berry, 5" d., green 18
Bowl, berry, 5" d., pink...................................... 15
Bowl, cream soup, 5" d., amber........................ 28
Bowl, cream soup, 5" d., green.......................... 58
Bowl, cream soup, 5" d., pink............................ 48
Bowl, cereal, 6" d., amber................................. 24
Bowl, cereal, 6" d., green.................................. 28
Bowl, cereal, 6" d., pink 28
Bowl, soup, 7 1/2" d., amber............................. 52
Bowl, soup, 7 1/2" d., pink 55
Bowl, berry, 8 1/2" d., amber 6
Bowl, berry, 8 1/2" d., green 35

Bowl, berry, 8 1/2" d., pink 35
Bowl, 9 1/2" oval vegetable, amber 20
Bowl, 9 1/2" oval vegetable, green 35
Bowl, 9 1/2" oval vegetable, pink 35
Bowl, fruit, 10 1/2" d., amber............................... 24
Bowl, fruit, 10 1/2" d., green............................... 48
Bowl, fruit, 10 1/2" d., pink................................. 50
Butter dish, cov., amber...................................... 48
Butter dish, cov., green 110
Butter dish, cov., pink... 65
Cake plate, footed, amber, 11 1/2" d. 24
Cake plate, footed, clear, 11 1/2" d.................... 15
Cake plate, footed, green, 11 1/2" d. 65
Cake plate, footed, pink, 11 1/2" d. 45
Candy jar, cov., amber.. 45
Candy jar, cov., green....................................... 165
Candy jar, cov., pink 65
Cheese dish, cov., amber.................................. 195
Cheese dish, cov., pink 1,500
Creamer, amber 14
Creamer, green 24
Creamer, pink.. 20
Cup, amber.. 8
Cup, green 20
Cup & saucer, amber 13
Cup & saucer, green 30
Cup & saucer, pink 25
Jam dish, amber, 7 1/2" d., 1 1/2" h. 45
Jam dish, green, 7 1/2" d., 1 1/2" h. 65
Jam dish, pink, 7 1/2" d., 1 1/2" h. 250
Pitcher, 9" h., 80 oz., amber 140
Pitcher, 9" h., 80 oz., green 475
Pitcher, 9" h., 80 oz., pink 175
Pitcher w/ice lip, 9" h., 80 oz., amber 145
Pitcher w/ice lip, 9" h., 80 oz., green 450
Pitcher w/ice lip, 9" h., 80 oz., pink 195
Plate, bread & butter, 6" d., amber...................... 5
Plate, bread & butter, 6" d., green...................... 10
Plate, bread & butter, 6" d., pink 8
Plate, salad, 7 1/2" d., amber 16
Plate, salad, 7 1/2" d., clear 8
Plate, salad, 7 1/2" d., green 24
Plate, salad, 7 1/2" d., pink................................. 28
Plate, dinner, 9 1/2" d., amber 12
Plate, dinner, 9 1/2" d., green............................. 24
Plate, dinner, 9 1/2" d., pink 24
Platter, 12 1/2" oval, amber 20
Platter, 12 1/2" oval, green 30
Platter, 12 1/2" oval, pink 30
Salt & pepper shakers, amber, pr....................... 35
Salt & pepper shakers, green, pr....................... 70
Salt & pepper shakers, pink, pr. 60
Saucer, amber.. 5
Sherbet, footed, amber 12
Sherbet, footed, green 36
Sherbet, footed, pink.. 18
Sugar bowl, cov., amber..................................... 39
Sugar bowl, cov., green...................................... 64
Sugar bowl, cov., pink 52
Sugar bowl, open, amber 14
Sugar bowl, open, green 24
Sugar bowl, open, pink 20
Tumbler, amber, 4" h., 9 oz. 30
Tumbler, green, 4" h., 9 oz. 75
Tumbler, pink, 4" h., 9 oz. 48
Tumbler, amber, 5 1/4" h., 12 oz. 65
Tumbler, green, 5 1/4" h., 12 oz. 110
Tumbler, pink, 5 1/4" h., 12 oz. 95
Tumbler, footed, amber, 6 1/2" h., 15 oz. 145
Tumbler, footed, clear, 6 1/2" h., 15 oz............. 15
Tumbler, footed, pink, 6 1/2" h., 15 oz. 60

WATERFORD OR WAFFLE, Hocking Glass Co., 1938-44- (Press-mold)

Ashtray, clear, 4" 8
Bowl, berry, 4 3/4" d., clear.................................. 6
Bowl, berry, 4 3/4" d., pink................................. 18
Bowl, cereal, 5 1/4" d., clear.............................. 20
Bowl, cereal, 5 1/4" d., pink............................... 38
Bowl, berry, 8 1/4" d., clear................................ 12
Bowl, berry, 8 1/4" d., pink................................. 28
Butter dish, cov., clear 30
Butter dish, cov., pink 225
Cake plate, handled, clear, 10 1/4" d................ 12
Cake plate, handled, pink, 10 1/4" d................. 30
Coaster, clear, 4" d. 4
Creamer, oval, clear... 5
Creamer, oval, pink.. 14
Creamer, footed, clear (Miss America style) 40
Cup, clear.. 8
Cup, pink 18
Cup & saucer, clear.. 10
Cup & saucer, pink.. 22
Goblet, amber, 5 1/4" h....................................... 25
Goblet, clear, 5 1/4" h. 18
Goblet, clear, 5 1/2" h. (Miss America Style) 35
Goblet, pink, 5 1/2" h. (Miss America style)....... 95
Lamp, clear, 4" h 38
Pitcher, juice, 42 oz., tilt-type, clear................... 28
Pitcher w/ice lip, 80 oz., clear............................ 40
Pitcher w/ice lip, 80 oz., pink.......................... 175
Plate, sherbet, 6" d., clear 3
Plate, sherbet, 6" d., pink 10
Plate, salad, 7 1/2" d., clear 8
Plate, salad, 7 1/2" d., pink 14
Plate, dinner, 9 5/8" d., clear............................. 14
Plate, dinner, 9 5/8" d., pink.............................. 28
Plate, sandwich, 13 3/4" d., clear 14
Plate, sandwich, 13 3/4" d., pink 40
Relish, five-section, clear, 13 3/4" d. 18
Salt & pepper shakers, clear, short, pr............. 12
Salt & pepper shakers, clear, tall, pr. 14
Saucer, clear... 2
Saucer, pink.. 4
Sherbet, footed, clear 5
Sherbet, footed, pink.. 18
Sugar bowl, cov., oval, clear 15
Sugar bowl, cov., oval, pink 65
Sugar bowl, open, footed, clear (Miss America style) 40
Tumbler, footed, pink, 3 1/2" h., 5 oz.............. 110
Tumbler, footed, clear, 5" h., 10 oz. 14
Tumbler, footed, pink, 5" h., 10 oz.................... 28

deVez & Degué

The Saint-Hilaire, Touvier, de Varreaux and Company of Pantin, France used the name de Vez on its cameo glass early in the 20th century. Some of the firm's examples were marked "Degué" after one of its master glassmakers. Officially the company was named "Cristallerie de Pantin."

deVez and Degué Marks

Squatty deVez Cameo Covered Box

Cameo box, cov., wide squatty round form tapering sharply to a flat mouth & fitted cylindrical-sided & slightly domed cover, mottled deep salmon red & yellow & cased & enameled in brown & red w/a meandering leafy vine w/trumpet flowers around a rippled body of water, the cover w/scattered small islands of leafy trees, deVez mark, 4 3/4" d., 3 1/8" h. (ILLUS.) **$1,150**

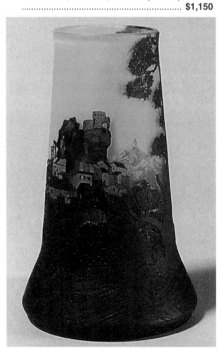

Cameo deVez Vase with Landscape

Cameo vase, 7 1/2" h., flaring base & tapering cylindrical sides cased in cobalt blue & terra cotta & cameo cut w/a continuous scene of a small village below a castle framed by mountains, an aged tree on the back above the cameo deVez signature, against a pale yellow ground (ILLUS.) **920**

Duncan & Miller

Duncan & Miller Glass Company, a successor firm to George A. Duncan & Sons Company, produced a wide range of pressed wares and novelty pieces during the late 19th century and into the early 20th century. During the Depression era and after, they continued making a wide variety of more modern patterns, including mold-blown types, and also introduced a number of etched and engraved patterns. Many colors, including opalescent hues, were produced during this era, and especially popular today are the graceful swan dishes they produced in the Pall Mall and Sylvan patterns.

The numbers after the pattern name indicate the original factory pattern number. The Duncan factory was closed in 1955. Also see ANIMALS.

Ashtray, Caribbean patt. (No. 112), ruby, 3" d. **$45**
Ashtray, Early American Sandwich patt. (No. 41), clear, 3" sq. **10**
Ashtray, etched First Love patt., rectangular, clear, 6 1/2" **28**
Ashtray, leaf-shaped, Lily of the Valley patt., crystal, 3" l. **32**
Ashtray, model of a duck, ruby, 4" **140**
Ashtray, Nautical patt., blue, 3" d. **35**
Basket, Canterbury patt., oval shape, handled, 11 1/2" l. **85**
Basket, etched First Love patt., handled, 10" oval **250**
Basket w/loop handle, Early American Sandwich patt., amber, 6" h. **150**
Bonbon, Early American Sandwich patt., heart-shaped, handled, clear, 5" **25**
Bottle, bitters, Mardi Gras patt., crystal **65**
Bowl, cream soup, Spiral Flutes patt., amber **15**
Bowl, 4" berry, Mardi Gras patt., crystal **18**
Bowl, 4 3/4" d., Puritan patt., pink **12**
Bowl, 5" d., Caribbean patt., fruit, tab handles, blue **32**
Bowl, 6" d., Teardrop patt. (No. 301), handled, clear **15**
Bowl, 6" d., two-part salad dressing-type, Canterbury patt. (No. 115), clear **18**
Bowl, 6 1/4" d., cereal, Plaza patt., amber **9**
Bowl, 7" d., Murano patt. (No. 127), pink opalescent **85**
Bowl, 8" d., Spiral Flutes patt., clear **20**
Bowl, 9", Canterbury patt. (No. 115), oval, clear **30**
Bowl, 9" l., oval vegetable, Plaza patt., green **65**
Bowl, 10" d., Murano patt., milk white **120**
Bowl, 11" d., etched First Love patt., clear **100**
Bowl, 11" d., flared, Canterbury blank, Lily of the Valley cutting, crystal **65**
Bowl, 11 1/2" d., Early American Sandwich patt., flower, crimped rim, clear **75**
Bowl, 6 1/2 x 11 1/2", model of a Viking boat, clear **240**
Bowl, 12" d., Hobnail patt., salad, shallow, clear **35**
Butter, cov., domed, Mardi Gras patt., crystal **85**
Cake salver, Early American Sandwich patt., pedestal foot, clear, 13" d., 5" h. **95**
Candelabrum, three-light, Canterbury patt., w/prisms, clear **225**

Cologne Bottle w/Stopper

Compote with First Love Etching

Spiral Flutes Four-footed Fernery

Goblet, Teardrop patt., clear, 5 3/4" h., 9 oz. 15
Goblet, water, Lily of the Valley pressed
stem, Lily of the Valley cutting on bowl,
crystal... 48
Goblet, water, Plaza patt., crystal opales-
cent 35
Ice bucket, Puritan patt., pink 100
Ivy bowl, Hobnail patt., footed, blue opales-
cent, 6 1/2" d. 75
Lamp shade, Mardi Gras patt., clear 45
Mayonnaise set: bowl, liner plate & ladle;
Lily of the Valley cutting, crystal, the set 55
Mayonnaise set: two-part bowl, liner & two
ladles; Canterbury patt., clear, the set 65
Model of a swan, Pall Mall patt. (No. 122),
milk white w/ruby neck & head, 7" l.............. 425
Model of a swan, Pall Mall patt. (No. 30),
ruby, 7" l. 85
Model of a swan, spread wing-type, yellow
opalescent, 12" w., 11" h.............................. 300
Model of a swan, Sylvan patt., blue opales-
cent, 12" l. 250
Model of a swan, Sylvan patt. (No. 122),
blue opalescent, 7" l. 120
Model of a swan, Sylvan patt., pink opales-
cent, 12" l. 250
Model of a top hat, Canterbury patt., crys-
tal, 3" h. 22
Mustard jar, cov., Caribbean patt., clear 35
Nut dish, two-part, handled, Teardrop patt.,
clear, 6" l. 12

Canterbury Pattern Oil Bottle & Stopper

Oil bottle & stopper, Canterbury patt.,
crystal, 3 oz. (ILLUS.)...................................... 32
Olive dish, two-part, Teardrop patt., clear,
6" l. 15

Pitcher, blown Radiance patt., cobalt blue 250
Pitcher, 8 1/2" h., w/applied amber handle,
Teardrop patt., clear...................................... 140
Pitcher w/ice lip, 8" h., Early American
Sandwich patt., clear, 1/2 gal....................... 170
Plate, 3" d., butter, Mardi Gras patt., crystal 22
Plate, 7" d., Early American Sandwich patt.,
clear... 10
Plate, 7" d., Spiral Flutes patt., amber 5
Plate, 7 1/2" d., Caribbean patt., blue 20
Plate, 8" d., Nautical patt., blue.......................... 45

Pressed Ship Pattern Plate

Plate, 8" d., pressed Ship patt., amber
(ILLUS.).. 18
Plate, 8" d., salad, Early American Sand-
wich patt., clear.. 12
Plate, 8 1/2" d., Canterbury patt., clear 10
Plate, 8 1/2" d., Spiral Flutes patt., green 12
Plate, 8 1/2" d., Spiral Flutes patt., (No. 40),
clear... 6
Plate, 9" d., Canterbury blank, Lily of the
Valley cutting, crystal 38

Early American Sandwich Plate

Plate, 9 1/2" d., Early American Sandwich
patt., crystal (ILLUS.)...................................... 40
Plate, 10 1/2" d., dinner, Puritan patt., clear 25
Plate, 11 1/4" d., dinner, Canterbury patt.,
crystal... 28
Plate, 13" d., Hobnail patt., rolled edge,
clear 35

Punch Set: bowl, stand, 12 cups & ladle;
Mardi Gras patt., crystal, 15 pcs. 295
Punch set: bowl, stand, ladle & 12 cups;
Hobnail patt., clear, 15 pcs. 200
Punch set: punch bowl, 18" d. underplate &
twelve cups; Caribbean patt., clear, cups
clear w/applied ruby red handles, 14 pcs. 265
Relish dish, five-part, Teardrop patt., clear,
12" d. 38
Relish dish, Sylvan patt., milk white w/ruby
handles, 10" l. 180
Relish dish, three-part, Sylvan patt., yellow
opalescent, 10 x 13".. 90
Relish dish, two-part, Caribbean patt., blue,
6" d. 45
Relish dish, two-part, Laguna patt., Smoky
Avocado, 8" l. 24
Relish dish, three-part oval, Canterbury
patt., clear, ca. 1950, 10 1/2" l. 30
Rose bowl, etched Indian Tree patt., 4" d. 130
**Salt & pepper shakers & anchor-handled
tray,** Nautical patt., blue, the set 250
Salt & pepper shakers w/original tops,
Early American Sandwich patt., flat,
clear, 3 3/4" h., pr... 30
Salt & pepper shakers w/original tops,
Mardi Gras patt., clear, pr. 60
Salt & pepper shakers w/original tops,
Teardrop patt., clear, pr.................................. 30
Sherbet, Early American Sandwich patt.,
green.. 25
Sherbet, Teardrop patt., clear, 3 1/2" h.............. 8
Sugar bowl, etched First Love patt., clear........ 25
Toothpick, Mardi Gras patt., crystal 40
Tray, mint-type, Sanibel patt., pink opales-
cent, 7" l. 45
Tumbler, flat, iced tea, Radiance blown
patt., crystal... 15
Tumbler, flat, water, Plaza patt., ruby 18
Tumbler, footed, Caribbean patt., blue,
5 1/2" h. 50
Tumbler, footed, Hobnail patt., clear, 10 oz. 15
Tumbler, high-ball, flat, Teardrop patt.,
clear, 4 3/4" h. 12
Tumbler, iced tea, flat, Early American
Sandwich patt., clear, 5 1/4" h. 18
Tumbler, iced tea, footed, Teardrop patt.,
clear, 5 1/2" h., 14 oz. 16
Tumbler, whiskey, footed, Teardrop patt.,
clear, 3" h. 17
Vase, 2 1/2" h., Chanticleer patt., green
opalescent... 275
Vase, 5" h., cloverleaf-shaped, Canterbury
patt., clear 30

Hobnail Pattern Flared Vase

Vase, 7" h., flared, Hobnail patt., pink opal-
escent (ILLUS.) 125

Vase, 7 1/2" h., Grecian urn-style, milk
glass w/green handles 325
Vase, 8" h., cornucopia-shaped, etched
First Love patt., clear 85

Three Feather Cornucopia Vase

Vase, 8" h., cornucopia-shaped, Three
Feather patt., clear w/cutting (ILLUS.) 55
Vase, 8" h., ruffled rim, Hobnail patt., blue
opalescent... 85
Vase, 9" h., round, Teardrop patt., clear 35
Vase, 10 1/2" h., Venetian patt., (No. 126),
ruby red.. 250
Vase (cigarette holder), 3 1/2" h., Grecian
Urn line (No. 538), clear................................... 15
Vase/flower arranger, 8 1/2" h., Canter-
bury patt., clear 45
Wine, Mardi Gras patt., crystal, 4 1/4" h. 24
Wine, Teardrop patt., clear, 4 3/4" h., 3 oz. 15
Wine, Caribbean patt., clear, 3 oz..................... 25

Durand

*Fine decorative glass similar to that made by
Tiffany and other outstanding glasshouses of its
day was made by the Vineland Flint Glass Works
Co. in Vineland, New Jersey, first headed by Victor Durand Sr. and subsequently by his son, Victor Durand Jr., in the 1920s.*

Blue Iridescent Durand Bowl-Vase

Bowl-vase, bulbous slightly ovoid simple form in striated iridescent blue, signed "Durand - 1995-4," minor scratches, 4" h. (ILLUS., bottom previous page) **$259**

Durand Finger Bowl & Underplate

Finger bowl & underplate, the deep rounded amethyst optic-ribbed bowl w/a flaring rim, matching dished underplate, underplate 6 1/4" d., bowl 2 1/4" h., the set (ILLUS.) **138**

Threaded Gold Durand Table Lamp

Lamp, table model, the baluster-form gold iridescent body wrapped in fine golden threads, fitted w/an ornate cast-metal cap & paneled gilt-metal base w/foliate trim, base marked "M.S. Co. Des. Pat. #0154," w/cloth shade & finial, minor loss to threading, glass body 11 1/4" h., overall 22" h. (ILLUS.) **575**

Pretty Durand Heart & Vine Blue Vase

Vase, 9" h., footed gently swelling tall ovoid body w/a wide flared mouth, blue irides-cent ground decorated w/an overall white heart & vine decoration, gold iridescent foot, signed "Durand 2001-8" (ILLUS.)...... **1,438**

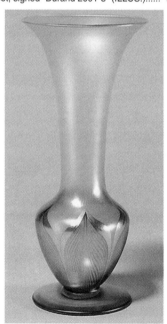

Elegant Pulled-feather Durand Vase

Vase, 9 1/2" h., footed bulbous ovoid lower body tapering to a very tall trumpet neck, iridescent aquamarine ground, decorat-ed around the lower body w/a band of royal blue pulled feathers tipped in silvery

gold, engraved silver script mark, Shape
No. 2022 (ILLUS.) **1,380**

Tall Durand Vase with King Tut Decor

Vase, 12" h., footed tall gently flaring cylindrical body w/a short wide flaring mouth, orange iridescent ground decorated overall w/the blue King Tut swirling decoration, signed, minor pitting on finish (ILLUS.) **2,280**

Durand Vase with Rare King Tut Decor

Vase, 14" h., footed tall gently flaring cylindrical body w/a short wide flaring mouth, green iridescent ground decorated overall w/a rare platinum King Tut swirling

decoration, signed "Durand 2028-19" (ILLUS.) **3,163**

Fenton

Fenton Art Glass Company began producing glass at Williamstown, West Virginia, in January 1907. Organized by Frank L. and John W. Fenton, the company began operations in a newly built glass factory with an experienced master glass craftsman, Jacob Rosenthal, as their factory manager. Fenton has produced a wide variety of collectible glassware through the years, including Carnival. Still in production today, its current productions may be found at finer gift shops across the country.

William Heacock's three-volume set on Fenton, published by Antique Publications, is the standard reference in this field.

Fenton Mark

Barber bottle, Hanging Heart design, custard iridescent **$175**
Basket, Peach Crest, milk white applied handle, 13" d. **195**

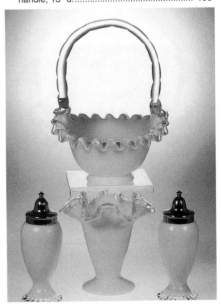

Various Silver Crest Pieces

Basket, Silver Crest w/clear applied handle, 5 1/2" d., 7 3/4" h. (ILLUS. top w/Silver Crest salt & pepper shakers & vase) **38**
Basket, Thumbprint patt., pink, 8 1/2"................ **32**
Basket, wicker handle, Ming etching, green **89**
Basket, Hobnail patt., French Opalescent, 7 1/2" **45**

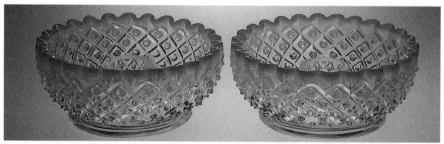

Diamond Lace Candleholders

Beverage set: pitcher & seven tumblers; footed spherical pitcher in canary opalescent Daisy & Fern patt., tapering to a short neck w/widely rolled & crimped rim & pinched spout, applied reeded canary handle, matching tumblers, mid-20th c., pitcher 9 1/4" h., the set **288**

Bonbon, Hobnail patt., double crimped rim, blue opalescent, 6" sq. **38**

Bowl, Apple Blossom Crest, heart-shaped **75**

Bowl, 7" d., cupped, dolphin handles, Rose **48**

Bowl, 9" sq., Block & Star patt., milk glass **15**

Bowl, 9 1/2" d., Hobnail patt., double crimped rim, blue opalescent **70**

Bowl, 10" d., Black Rose patt., crimped rim..... **135**

Bowl, 10" d., deep oval, dolphin handles, No. 1621, black **55**

Bowl, 10" d., salad, Silver Crest....................... **55**

Bowl, 10" d., shallow cupped, Celeste Blue Stretch glass **65**

Bowl, 11" d., three-footed, crimped, Pineapple pattern, light blue (ILLUS.) **75**

Candleholder, two-light, Ming etching, Pineapple patt., crystal, 5" h. **28**

Candleholders, Diamond Lace patt., cupped, blue opalescent, 4" d., 2" h., pr. (ILLUS., top of page)..................................... **65**

Candleholders, one-light, crimped base, No. 7474, milk glass, Violets in Snow decoration, 6" h., pr.. **60**

Candy box, cov., No. 6080, milk glass, Violets in Snow decoration.............................. **135**

Cigarette holder, oval, No. 554, Florentine Green Stretch glass **185**

Coaster, No. 1590, Ming etching, Rose............ **22**

Cookie jar, cov., Big Cookies patt., Jade green, 7" h. **150**

Creamer & open sugar, footed, No. 3, Aquamarine Stretch glass, pr........................ **58**

Cranberry Cruet with Original Stopper

Cruet w/original stopper, Hobnail patt., No. 3863, cranberry (ILLUS.)......................... **95**

Cruet w/stopper, Hobnail, blue opalescent w/clear stopper & applied handle, 6 1/2" h. (ILLUS. left w/Hobnail pieces, top of next page)... **125**

Cruet w/stopper, Hobnail, cranberry opalescent w/clear stopper & applied handle, 6 1/2" h. (ILLUS. right w/other Hobnail pieces, top of next page)............................... **165**

Dolphin-handled Fenton Bowl

Bowl, 10 1/2" d., oval footed, dolphin handles, No. 1608, black (ILLUS.) **145**

Bowl, 11" d., low sides, shallow cupped, Wisteria Stretch glass **120**

Three-footed Pineapple Pattern Fenton Bowl

Fenton Hobnail Pieces

Decanter w/stopper, handled, Hobnail patt., yellow opalescent w/crystal stopper **375**

Epergne, four-piece, crimped bowl w/three horns, Hobnail patt., crystal opalescent, 8" d. **85**

Epergne, three-lily, Diamond Lace patt., white opalescent **200**

Epergne, three-lily, Rose Crest, a wide shallow flaring & crimped base bowl in white w/pink edging tapering up at the center & supporting a tall matching central vase w/crimped & ruffled rim surrounded by three matching Jack-in-the-pulpit shaped vases, ca. 1940s, 12" d., 17" h.. **230**

Flower block, figural, September Morn, ebony **250**

Flower block, figural, September Morn, nymph figure on base, Jade green.............. **225**

Goblet, Hobnail patt., blue opalescent............... **35**

Goblet, water, Georgian patt., ruby................... **16**

Hurricane lamp, Cranberry Spiral Optic shade, milk glass base, 2 pcs. **165**

Hurricane lamps & bases, Black Rose patt., black bases, pr.................................... **650**

Jam & jelly jars, covers & tray, Block & Star patt., milk glass, tray w/metal handle, the set.. **55**

Model of a hat, two sides turned down, Hobnail patt., blue opalescent, 2 3/4" h. **24**

Model of a lady's shoe, Hobnail patt., blue opalescent, 5" l.. **25**

Mustard, cov., Hobnail patt., blue opalescent, crystal paddle, 3 1/2" h.......................... **35**

Nut cup, footed, individual, Topaz Stretch glass... **37**

Nut dish, Cactus patt., flaring bell-form bowl raised on slender stem & round foot, Topaz Opalescent, No. 3428, ca. 1959-60, 5 1/2" h.. **40**

Pitcher, Hobnail patt., Topaz Opalescent, 54 oz. (ILLUS. center w/other Hobnail pieces, top of page) **325**

Pitcher, 9 1/4" h., footed spherical body tapering to a widely rolled & crimped rim w/a pinched spout, cranberry opalescent Daisy & Fern patt., applied clear reeded handle, mid-20th c. **144**

Plate, 8" d., Lincoln Inn patt., salad, green **15**

Plate, 8" d., Ruby Stretch glass **85**

Plate, 11" d., grill, Georgian patt., ruby **27**

Plate, 12" d., Lincoln Inn patt., pink.................... **38**

Punch bowl, one-handled, Hobnail patt., blue opalescent, 10 1/2" d. **550**

Salt & pepper shakers, footed, Lincoln Inn patt., black, pr. **395**

Salt & pepper shakers, Silver Crest w/chrome-plated lids, footed, pr. (ILLUS. left & right w/Silver Crest basket & vase)..... **100**

Toothpick holder, three-footed, Hobnail patt., crystal opalescent, 3" h........................ **27**

Tray, fan-shaped, Hobnail patt., yellow opalescent, 10 1/2" d. **72**

Tangerine Stretch Glass Tray

Tray, lemon, center-handled, Tangerine Stretch glass, 6" d. (ILLUS.) **65**

Royal Blue Lincoln Inn Tumblers & Wine

Tumbler, footed, Lincoln Inn patt., Royal Blue, 12 oz. (ILLUS. far left with other Lincoln Inn tumblers & wine, top of page)........... 50

Tumbler, footed, Lincoln Inn patt., Royal Blue, 4 oz. (ILLUS. far right with other Lincoln Inn tumblers & wine, top of page) 35

Tumbler, footed, Lincoln Inn patt., Royal Blue, 7 oz. (ILLUS. second from left with other Lincoln Inn tumblers & wine, top of page) 45

Tumbler, Hanging Heart, custard iridescent, 10 oz.. 65

Vase, 4" h., Silver Crest, double crimped rim, footed (ILLUS. bottom center w/Silver Crest basket & salt & pepper shakers) 18

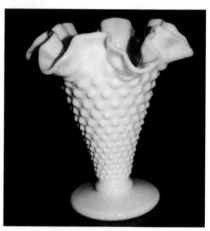

Small Hobnail Vase

Vase, 6" h., Hobnail patt., footed, trumpet-form w/flaring ruffled rim, milk glass (ILLUS.) 15

Vase, 6 3/4" h., Vessel of Gems patt., footed tapering cylindrical body molded w/large berry prunts, from a Verlys mold, reddish orange, No. 8253, 1968 220

Vase, 8" h., double crimp rim, Peach Crest, No. 7258 55

Vase, 8" h., fan-shaped, No. 857, Velva Rose Stretch glass.. 78

Vase, 10" h., Hanging Heart patt., gently tapering cylindrical round body w/trumpet neck, custard w/satin finish, Robert Barber Collection 195

Vase, 14" h., crimped, Vasa Murrhina, Blue Mist 150

Vase, fan-type, dolphin handles, Jade green 55

Wine, Lincoln Inn patt., Royal Blue (ILLUS. second from right with Lincoln Inn tumblers) 35

Blue Overlay Crimped Vase

Vase, 6" h., crimped, Bubble Optic patt., Blue Overlay (ILLUS.) 70

Findlay Onyx & Floradine

In January, 1889, the glass firm of Dalzell, Gilmore & Leighton Co. of Findlay, Ohio began production of these scarce glass lines. Onyx ware was a white-lined glass produced mainly in onyx (creamy yellowish white) but also in bronze and ruby shades sometimes called cinnamon, rose or raspberry. Pieces featured raised flowers and leaves that are silver-colored or, less often, bronze. By contrast the Floradine line was produced in ruby and autumn leaf (gold) with opalescent flowers and leaves. It is not lined.

Creamer, bulbous ovoid body w/an upright ribbed neck, applied handle, creamy white w/silver flowers & leaves, 4 1/2" h. (minute flake on rim) $374
Sugar shaker w/period lid, ivory onyx, 5 1/4" h. 400
Syrup pitcher w/period lid, ivory onyx, 6 3/4" h. 650
Tumbler, ivory onyx 220

Fostoria

Fostoria Glass company, founded in 1887, produced numerous types of fine glassware over the years. Its factory in Moundsville, West Virginia, closed in 1986.

Fostoria Label

Footed Crystal Almond Dish

Almond dish, footed, Alexis patt., crystal (ILLUS.) $15
Almond dish, Oriental etching, clear 25
Ashtray, American patt., clear, 2 7/8" sq. 8
Ashtray, Coin patt., olive green, 5" 15
Ashtray, Coin patt., ruby, 5 1/2" 25
Ashtrays, Spool patt., yellow, set of three nesting ashtrays 32
Banana split dish, American patt., clear, 3 1/2" w., 9" l. 1,200
Bell, American patt., clear 500
Bonbon, American patt., three short feet, blue, 7" d. 175
Bonbon, American patt., three-footed, amber, 7" d. 125
Bonbon, American patt., three-footed, clear 15

Bonbon, American patt., three-footed, red, 7" d. 125
Bonbon, Brocade Oakwood etching, handled, iridescent w/gold trim, Azure blue 65
Bonbon, Century patt., three-footed, clear, 7 1/4" d. 20
Bonbon, Chintz etching, No. 2496/137, three-toed, clear 35
Bonbon, Colony patt., three-footed, clear, 7" d. 16
Bottle w/stopper, ketchup, American patt., crystal 150
Bouillon cup, Fairfax patt., pink 15
Bouillon cup, Versailles etching, footed, blue 65
Bowl, cream soup, American patt., crystal 48
Bowl, Vernon etching, cream soup, No. 2375, Azure 50
Bowl, 4 1/2" d., Colony patt., clear 15
Bowl, 6" d., Fairfax patt., cereal, Rose 26
Bowl, 6 1/4" d., Raleigh patt., Laurel cutting, handled, clear 15
Bowl, 7" d., American patt., cupped, clear 45
Bowl, 7" d., Fairfax patt., lemon, two-handled, Azure 17
Bowl, 8" d., Oriental etching, clear 28
Bowl, 8 1/2" d., Coin patt., footed, frosted ruby 65
Bowl, 9" d., Century patt., lily pond-type, clear 50
Bowl, 9 1/4" oval, Pioneer patt., green 25
Bowl, 10" d., Brocade Oak Leaf etching, scroll handled, Rose 150
Bowl, 10" d., Chintz etching, handled, clear 100
Bowl, 10" d., Romance etching, salad, deep shape, clear 80
Bowl, 10" l., Century patt., oval, two-handled, clear 45
Bowl, 10 1/2" d., American patt., fruit, three-footed, clear 45
Bowl, 10 1/2" d., American patt., three-footed, clear 45
Bowl, 10 1/2" d., Colony patt., high-footed, clear 135
Bowl, 11" d., Century patt., footed, rolled edge, clear 65
Bowl, 11" d., footed console, No. 2333, blue (ILLUS., top next page) 75
Bowl, 11" d., footed oval, Colony patt., crystal 72
Bowl, 11 1/2" oval, American patt., clear 55
Bowl, 12" d., American patt., fruit, footed, clear 200
Bowl, 12" d., Chintz etching, flared rim, clear 95
Bowl, 12" d., Navarre etching, flared rim, clear 85
Bowl, 12" d., Oak Leaf etching, three-footed, pink 110
Bowl, 12" d., Shirley etching, flared rim, clear 75
Bowl, 12 1/2" oval, 2 7/8" h., Flame patt., Navarre etching, clear 100
Bowl, 13" l., Heirloom cutting, oblong, blue 55
Bowl, 14" d., Colony patt., fruit, low, clear 70
Bowl w/underplate, Fairfax patt., cream soup, blue, 2 pcs. 35
Bowl w/underplate, June etching, cream soup, blue, 2 pcs. 95

No. 2333 Blue Bowl

Butter dish, cov., American patt., oblong, clear, 1/4 lb., 3 1/4 x 7 1/2", 2 1/8" h. **35**

Butter dish, cov., Fairfax patt., round, green **100**

Butter dish, cov., Royal etching, round, amber **135**

Cake plate, American patt., three-footed, clear, 12" d. **45**

Cake plate, Baroque patt., Chintz etching, two-handled, clear, 10" d. **85**

Cake plate, Baroque patt., Meadow Rose etching, two-handled, clear, 10" d. **70**

Cake plate, Mayfair patt., two handles, pink **45**

Cake salver, Century patt., footed, clear, 12 1/4" d. **125**

Cake stand, American patt., round, clear, 10" d. (ILLUS., next column) **165**

Cake stand, Coin patt., amber **95**

Cake stand, Coin patt., clear, 10" d. **95**

Candelabra, two-light, Baroque patt., w/bobeches & prisms, clear, pr. **225**

Candleblocks, two-light, Myriad patt., clear, pr. **68**

Candleholders, one-light, Heirloom patt., clear opalescent, 3 1/2" h., pr. (ILLUS., bottom of page) **48**

American Pattern Cake Stand

Candleholders, three-light, Navarre etching, clear, 6" h., pr. **125**

Candlestick, one-light, Baroque patt., Lido etching, clear, 4" h. **32**

Candlestick, one-light, Chintz etching, clear, 5 1/2" h. **30**

Candlestick, one-light, Colony patt., clear, 7" h. **35**

Fostoria Heirloom Candlesticks

Candlesticks with June Etching

Candlestick, one-light, Romance etching,
clear, 5 1/2" h. **45**
Candlestick, three-light, Meadow Rose
patt., clear **65**
Candlestick, two-light, Chintz etching, clear **65**

Fostoria No. 2447 Candlestick

Candlestick, two-light, No. 2447, Wisteria,
5" h. (ILLUS.) **75**
Candlesticks, one-light, Chintz etching, No.
2496/315, clear, 4" h., pr. **50**
Candlesticks, one-light, Colony patt.,
w/eight prisms, clear, 7 1/2" h., pr. **195**
Candlesticks, one-light, No. 2395 1/2, Fern
etching, Ebony, 5" h., pr. (ILLUS. of one,
top next column) **145**
Candlesticks, one-light, No. 2433 "Tripod,"
clear bowl on Ebony base, 3" h., pr. **75**
Candlesticks, one-light, Romance etching,
clear, 5", pr. **90**

Fern Etching Ebony Candleholder

Candlesticks, one-light, Vesper etching,
green, 4" h., pr. **55**
Candlesticks, three-light, Baroque patt.,
Chintz etching, clear, pr. **150**
Candlesticks, three-light, Navarre etching,
clear, 6 3/4" h., pr. **150**
Candlesticks, three-light, No. 2482, June
etching on feet & under center sockets,
Topaz, pr. (ILLUS., top of page) **1,200**
Candlesticks, two-light, Meadow Rose
etching, clear, pr. **95**
Candlesticks, two-light, Romance etching,
No. 6023, clear, pr. **110**

One-light Amber Candlesticks

Fostoria June Etching Cocktail Icer

Jenny Lind Cologne & Tumbler

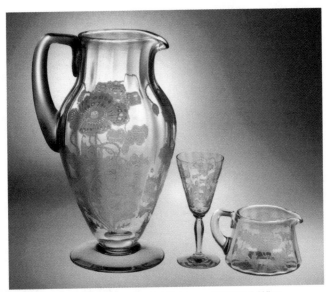

Rogene Etching Crystal Creamer, Pitcher & Wine

Compote, 4 3/8" h., Century patt., clear 25

Compote, 6" d., Spool patt., low shape, Azure blue 35

Compote, cov., 6 1/2 h", Colony patt., clear 40

Compote, 7" d., Vesper etching, low-footed, green 45

Compote, 11" d., Brocade Grape etching, low shape, Orchid 140

Condiment set: two oil bottles w/stoppers, salt & pepper shakers, mustard jar w/cover & spoon, all on cloverleaf-shaped tray; American patt., clear 495

Console bowl, Versailles etching, footed, blue 125

Console set: bowl & pr. of 3 1/2" h. candlesticks; June etching, blue, 3 pcs., the set..... 250

Console set: bowl & pr. of double candlesticks; Chintz etching, clear, the set 125

Console set: No. 2402, angular Art Deco-style bowl & pair of candleholders, Ebony, the set... 85

Cordial, Chintz etching, clear, 1 oz. 80

Cordial, Christiana cutting, clear....................... 50

Cordial, June etching, Topaz, 3 7/8" h. 110

Cordial, Lido etching, clear, 4" h. 50

Cordial, Trojan etching, yellow........................... 95

Cordial, Wheat cutting, clear............................. 40

Creamer, American patt., clear, medium 15

Creamer, Baroque patt., clear, 3 1/3" h., 4 oz. 12

Creamer, Chintz etching, clear........................... 20

Creamer, Fairfax patt., footed, pink.................... 15

Creamer, flat, Rogene etched, crystal (ILLUS. right with Rogene etch pitcher & wine, top of page)... 37

Creamer, individual, Baroque patt., blue............ 35

Creamer, individual, Century patt., clear, 4 oz. 9

Creamer & cov. sugar bowl, American patt., clear, large, pr. 55

Creamer & open sugar, flat, Fairfax patt., green, pr.. 35

Creamer & open sugar bowl, Baroque patt., individual size, blue, pr......................... 70

Creamer & open sugar bowl, Colony patt., clear, pr. 22

Creamer & open sugar bowl, Coronet patt., clear, pr. 15

Creamer & open sugar bowl, Jamestown patt., pink, pr. 65

Creamer & open sugar bowl, Navarre etching, footed, clear, 4 1/4" h., pr. 45

Creamer & open sugar bowl, Rogene etching, flat, clear, pr...................................... 65

Creamer, open sugar bowl & undertray, individual size, Century patt., clear, the set 40

Creamer, open sugar bowl & undertray, Navarre etching, clear, 3 pcs. 65

Cruet w/original stopper, American patt., clear, 7 oz. 45

Cruet w/original stopper, Baroque patt., Topaz, 3 1/2 oz. 295

Cruet w/original stopper, Fairfax patt., pink 195

Cup, Century patt., clear 10

Cup, footed, Colony patt., clear, 6 oz................. 9

Cup & saucer, Baroque patt., clear.................. 20

Cup & saucer, Colony patt., clear 15

Cup & saucer, demitasse, Lafayette patt., green.. 35

Cup & saucer, Fairfax patt., Orchid.................. 16

Cup & saucer, Fairfax patt., pink...................... 15

Cup & saucer, June etching, Azure.................. 50

Cup & saucer, Kashmir etching, blue............... 48

Cup & saucer, Kashmir etching, blue............... 56

Cup & saucer, Vernon etching, demitasse, green.. 30

Regal Blue Decanter & Original Stopper

Decanter & original stopper, No. 2494, Regal Blue (ILLUS.) 155
Decanter w/original stopper, American patt., clear, 24 oz., 9 1/4" h. 100
Decanter w/original stopper, Spool patt., clear 100
Decanter w/stopper, Sunray patt., clear 125
Dinner bell, Chintz etching, clear, w/original label.. 195

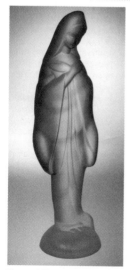

Crystal Figure of Madonna

Figure of Madonna, crystal satin, 10" h. (ILLUS.).. 75
Figure of Madonna & Child, Silver Mist, 13 1/2" h. 500
Finger bowl, American patt., clear, 4 1/2" d. 80
Glove box, cov., American patt., clear............. 600
Goblet, American Lady patt., cobalt blue, 10 oz., 6 1/8" h. 80

Goblet, American patt., clear, 5 1/2" h., 9 oz. 13
Goblet, American patt., hexagonal foot, clear, 10 oz. 18
Goblet, Arcady etching, clear, 9 oz................... 30
Goblet, Buttercup etching, clear, 10 oz............. 25
Goblet, Century patt., clear, 10 1/2 oz., 5 3/4" h. 20
Goblet, Colonial Dame patt., clear, 6 1/2" h. 22
Goblet, Colony patt., clear, 5 1/4" h., 9 oz. 20
Goblet, Corsage etching, clear, 7 3/8" h........... 32
Goblet, Florentine etching, clear bowl w/yellow stem... 35
Goblet, Jamestown patt., blue, 6" h.................. 26
Goblet, Jamestown patt., pink, 6" h.................. 26
Goblet, June etching, Azure, 10 oz.................... 75
Goblet, June etching, clear, 8 1/4" h. 46
Goblet, June etching, Topaz............................. 55
Goblet, Lido etching, clear, 12" h., 12 oz.......... 28
Goblet, Lido etching, clear, 7 1/2" h.................. 28
Goblet, Navarre etching, clear........................... 45
Goblet, Navarre etching, pink, 7 5/8" oz. 85
Goblet, Rogene etching, clear 26
Goblet, Romance etching, clear, 9 oz............... 28

Water Goblet with Shirley Etching

Goblet, Shirley etching, clear (ILLUS.) 30
Goblet, Sunray patt., clear, 5 3/4" h................... 22
Goblet, water, Kashmir etching, blue, 9 oz........ 55
Hair receiver, cov., American patt., clear, 3" sq. 800
Hairpin box, cov., American patt., clear, 1 1/2 x 1 2/4", 3 1/2" l.................................... 850
Ice bowl, Colony patt., footed, clear, 4" h. 250
Ice bucket, Baroque patt., topaz...................... 120
Ice bucket, June etching, pink 175
Ice bucket, Trojan etching, Topaz 118
Ice bucket, Versailles etching, blue................. 145
Ice bucket w/metal tongs, American patt., clear 75

Pitcher w/ice lip, American patt., clear, 1/2 gal. 90
Pitcher w/ice lip, 7 1/8" h., Century patt., clear, 48 oz. 110
Plate, 6" d., Lido etching, bread & butter, clear 8
Plate, 6" d., Trojan etching, bread & butter, pink 10
Plate, 7" d., American patt., salad, clear 12
Plate, 7" d., Baroque patt., salad, clear 8
Plate, 7" d., Mayfair patt., Azure 15
Plate, 7" d., Mayfair patt., salad, green 10
Plate, 7 3/8" d., Kashmir etching, blue 18
Plate, 7 1/2" d., Chintz etching, clear 17
Plate, 7 1/2" d., Chintz etching, salad, clear 18
Plate, 7 1/2" d., June etching, clear 10
Plate, 7 1/2" d., Navarre etching, salad, clear 18
Plate, 7 1/2" d., Versailles etching, blue 20
Plate, 7 1/2" l., Century patt., salad, crescent-shaped, clear 30
Plate, 8" d., Fairfax patt., luncheon, topaz 18
Plate, 8" round, Kashmir etching, yellow 12
Plate, 8 1/4" d., Jamestown patt., blue 25
Plate, 8 1/4" d., Jamestown patt., pink 27
Plate, 8 1/2" d., Meadow Rose etching, luncheon, clear 25
Plate, 8 3/4" d., June etching, Azure 25
Plate, 9" d., Colony patt., dinner, clear 30
Plate, 9" d., Sunray patt., clear 22
Plate, 9 1/2" d., American patt., dinner, clear 24
Plate, 9 1/2" d., Baroque patt., clear 30
Plate, 9 1/2" d., Chintz etching, dinner, clear 70
Plate, 9 1/2" d., Trojan etching, dinner, Topaz 30
Plate, 10" d., Seville etching, dinner, amber 35
Plate, 10 1/4" d., Fairfax patt., dinner, blue 50
Plate, 10 1/4", grill, Fairfax patt., blue 42
Plate, 10 1/2" d., Royal etching, dinner, amber 50
Plate, torte, 13" d., Colony patt., clear 35
Plate, torte, 13 1/2" oval, American patt., clear 100
Plate, torte, 14" d., Baroque patt., Topaz 65
Plate, torte, 14" d. Chintz etching, clear 75
Plate, torte, 14" d., June etching, Azure blue (some wear) 150
Plate, torte, 15" d., Colony patt., clear 60
Plate, torte, 18" d., American patt., clear 175
Plate, torte, 20" d., American patt., clear 195
Platter, 12" l., American patt., clear 65
Platter, 12" oval, Fairfax patt., green 47
Preserve dish, cov., American patt., two-handled, clear, 5 3/4" d., 4 1/4" h. 100
Puff box, cov., American patt., clear, 4 1/2" sq. 1,400
Punch bowl & base, American patt., clear, 14" d. bowl, 2 pcs. 275
Punch set: 18" d. bowl & twelve cups; American patt., clear, 13 pcs. 375
Punch set: punch bowl, base & ten cups; Coin patt., clear, 12 pcs. 950
Relish dish, American patt., boat-shaped, handled, divided, clear, 12" l. 30
Relish dish, American patt., four-part, clear, 10" sq. 190
Relish dish, American patt., four-part, rectangular, clear, 9" l. 45

Relish dish, American patt., three-part, clear, 6 x 9 1/2" 40
Relish dish, Baroque patt., Chintz etching, three-part, clear, 10" 55
Relish dish, Baroque patt., four-part, clear, 10" d. 45
Relish dish, Baroque patt., two-part, blue, 6 1/2" l. 32
Relish dish, Century patt., two-part, clear, 7 3/8" l. 22
Relish dish, Colony patt., three-part, two-handled, clear, 13" 35
Relish dish, Colony patt., two-part, clear, 7 1/4" 20
Relish dish, Fairfax patt., three-part, amber, 11 1/2" l. 25
Relish dish, Holly cutting, two-part, clear, 6 1/2" 20
Relish dish, Lafayette patt., two-part, handled, Topaz, 6 1/2" d. 18
Relish dish, Mayfair patt., four-part, Topaz, 8 1/2" l. 20
Relish dish, Versailles etching, divided, oval, green, 8 1/2" l. 85
Rose bowl, American patt., clear, 3 1/2" d. 20

Baroque Rose Bowl

Rose bowl, Baroque patt., blue (ILLUS.) 100
Rose bowl, Baroque patt., Topaz 60
Rose bowl, Colony patt., footed, clear, 6" 30
Rose bowl, 3 3/4" h., Baroque patt., topaz 75
Salt dip w/spoon, American patt., clear, 2 pcs. 20
Salt & pepper shakers, Century patt., clear, 3 1/4" h., pr. 24
Salt & pepper shakers, Colony patt., clear, 3 5/8" h., pr. 30
Salt & pepper shakers, Coronet patt., footed, clear, pr. 25

Vesper Etched Salt & Pepper Shakers

Salt & Pepper shakers, footed, metal lids, Vesper etching, amber, pr. (ILLUS., bottom previous page) 125

Salt & pepper shakers, Mesa patt., No. 4186, blue, 1960s-70s, pr. 35

Salt & pepper shakers, Navarre etching, clear, 3 1/4" h., pr. 150

Sandwich server w/center handle, Chintz etching, clear, 12" d. 65

Sauce boat & liner, oval, American patt., crystal 57

Sauce boat & underplate, American patt., clear, 2 pcs. 65

Sherbet, American Lady patt., clear, 5 1/2 oz., 4 1/8" h. 18

Sherbet, American Lady patt., cobalt blue, 5 1/2 oz., 4 1/8" h. 60

Sherbet, American patt., footed, handled, clear, 4 1/2 oz. 145

Sherbet, Century patt., clear, 5 1/2 oz., 4 1/4" h. 10

Sherbet, Chintz etching, clear 21

Sherbet, Coin patt., ruby 55

Sherbet, Colony patt., clear, 5 oz. 10

Sherbet, Cynthia cutting, low, clear 18

Sherbet, Florentine etching, low foot, clear, 7 oz. 12

Sherbet, Jamestown patt., amber 9

Sherbet, Jamestown patt., blue, 6 1/2 oz., 4 1/4" h. 17

Sherbet, Jamestown patt., pink 20

Sherbet, Navarre patt., clear, 6 oz. 24

Spooner, American patt., clear, 3 3/4" h. 45

Sugar bowl, cov., American patt., clear, 5 1/4" h. 60

Sugar bowl, Fairfax patt., footed, orchid 24

Sugar bowl, individual, Baroque patt., Topaz 30

Sugar bowl, individual, Century patt., clear, 3 3/8" h. 9

Sugar pail, metal handle, June etching, pink 295

Sundae, American patt., clear, 6 oz., 3 1/8" h. 12

Sweetmeat dish, cov., Baroque patt., clear 175

Toothpick holder, American patt., clear 24

Toothpick holder, Priscilla patt., No. 676, clear 45

Tray, snack, Colony patt., clear, 10 1/2" 40

Tray for creamer & sugar bowl, Colony patt., clear 18

Tumbler, American Lady patt., ice tea, footed, clear, 5 1/2" h., 12 oz. 18

Tumbler, American Lady patt., juice, footed, clear, 5 oz., 4 1/8" h. 14

Tumbler, American patt., footed, clear, 9 oz., 4 3/8" h. 15

Tumbler, American patt., whiskey, clear, 2 oz., 2 1/2" h. 15

Tumbler, Baroque patt., water, clear 16

Tumbler, Century patt., juice, footed, clear, 5 oz. 15

Tumbler, Chintz etching, iced tea, footed, clear, 12 oz. 35

Tumbler, Coin patt., clear, 5 1/2" h. 20

Tumbler, Coin patt., iced tea, ruby, 5 1/2" h. 75

Tumbler, Colony patt., footed, clear, 5 3/4" h., 12 oz. 24

Tumbler, Colony patt., iced tea, footed, clear, 12 oz., 5 1/2" h. 26

Tumbler, Colony patt., juice, clear, 3 5/8" h., 5 oz. 24

Tumbler, Cynthia cutting, water, clear 18

Tumbler, Fairfax patt., footed, blue, 6" h., 12 oz. 25

Tumbler, Holly cutting, iced tea, footed, clear, 12 oz., 6" h. 20

Tumbler, Jamestown patt., iced tea, footed, blue 28

Tumbler, Jamestown patt., juice, footed, blue 21

Tumbler, Jamestown patt., juice, footed, smoke, 5 oz., 4 3/4" h. 10

Tumbler, Jenny Lind patt., milk glass (ILLUS. left w/cologne bottle) 38

Tumbler, June etching, Azure, 9 oz. 50

Tumbler, June etching, footed, clear, 6" h., 12 oz. 35

Tumbler, Lido etching, footed, clear, 9 oz. 20

Tumbler, Line 4020, black foot, clear bowl 15

Tumbler, Midnight Rose etching, Line No. 6009, footed, clear, 12 oz. 24

Tumbler, Navarre etching, water, clear, 10 oz. 24

Tumbler, Priscilla patt., footed, green 25

Tumbler, Rambler etching, iced tea, clear 20

Tumbler, Versailles etching, green, 5 1/4" h., 9 oz. 28

Tumbler, water, footed, Baroque patt., topaz, 9 oz. 27

Three-piece Vanity Box

Vanity box, three-piece, No. 2289, Canary, set (ILLUS.) 275

Vase, Coin patt., clear 65

Vase, 5" h., Navarre etching, No. 4128, clear 150

Vase, 6" h., American patt., bud, cupped-in top, clear 20

Vase, 6" h., American patt., peach 120

Vase, 6" h., Coronet patt., handled, clear 45

Vase, 6 1/2" h., American patt., footed, amber 80

Vase, 6 1/2" h., Baroque patt., clear 90

Vase, 7" h., Colony patt., footed, cupped, clear 60

Vase, 8" h., Coin patt., bud, frosted blue 55

Vase, 8" h., No. 2454, Ebony w/gold-encrusted decoration (ILLUS., top next page) 120

Fostoria No. 2454 Vase

Vase, 8 1/2" h., American patt., bud, flared
rim, clear 38
Vase, 9" h., American patt., w/square foot,
clear 75
Vase, 9" h., footed, Alexis patt., crystal 58
Vase, 10" h., American patt., flared rim,
clear 90
Vase, 10" h., American patt., straight sides,
clear 95
Vase, 10" h., footed, Navarre etching, crys-
tal 220
Vase, 12" h., American patt., straight sides,
clear 150
Vase, 12" h., Colony patt., clear 195
Vase, 18" h., Heirloom patt. No. 5056, blue
opalescent... 175
Water carafe, Carmen patt., ca. 1900, clear 95
Water set: pitcher & six tumblers; Rosby
patt., clear, 7 pcs... 220
Wedding bowl, American patt., clear, small 125
Wedding bowl, cov., American patt., milk
glass, 6 1/2" 125
Wedding bowl, cov., Coin patt., footed,
blue 125
Wedding bowl, cov., Coin patt., frosted,
emerald green 200
Window box w/flower frog cover, Brocade
Oak Leaf etching, green.................................. 295
Wine, American patt., clear, 2 1/2 oz.,
4 3/8" h.. 15
Wine, Chintz etching, clear................................. 48
Wine, Coin patt. clear 30
Wine, Colonial Dame patt., green bowl,
clear foot & stem, 4 3/4" h............................... 36
Wine, Corsage etching, clear, 5 1/2" h. 35
Wine, Jamestown patt., amber, 4 oz., 4
5/16" h. 15
Wine, Jamestown patt., pink, 4 5/16" h., 4
oz. 26
Wine, June etching, pink, 5 3/8" h. 125
Wine, Lido etching, clear, 3 oz. 32
Wine, Navarre etching, clear 60
Wine, Rogene etching, crystal (ILLUS. cen-
ter with Rogene etched creamer & pitch-
er, on page)... 24
Wine, Sunray patt., clear, 4 7/8" h...................... 32

Youth set: mug & bowl; American patt.,
clear, 2 pcs.. 75

Fry

*Numerous types of glass were made by the H.C.
Fry Company of Rochester, Pennsylvania. One of
its art lines was called Foval and was blown in
1926-27. Cheaper was its milky-opalescent oven-
ware (Pearl Oven Ware), made for utilitarian purposes but also now being collected. The company
also made fine cut glass.*

*Collectors of Fry glass will be interested in the
recent publication of a good reference book, The
Collector's Encyclopedia of Fry Glassware, by The
H.C. Fry Glass Society (Collector Books, 1990).*

Beverage set: 10 1/2" h. jug-form pitcher,
6 1/2" h. spherical cov. teapot & six
4 1/2" h. conical tumblers; Foval, each in
a white body decorated around the body
w/a slender silver overlay scroll & vine
design, applied jade green handle on
pitcher & teapot, also teapot spout & feet,
one tumbler w/overlay loss, nicks to tea-
pot cover, the set $2,100
Bowl, 9" d., footed, azure blue 45
Bowl, 14" oval, wavy rim, crystal w/green
threading, controlled bubbles........................... 195
Bowl, 16" d., flared, wavy rim, pink w/pink
threading, controlled bubbles........................... 295
Candlesticks, Jack-in-the-pulpit shape,
light blue w/controlled bubbles & blue
threading, 5" h., pr. 265
Casserole, cov., square, Pearl Oven Ware,
7" w. 65
Champagne, Bubble Girl, etching (not a Fry
etch), pink, 5" h. 30
Compote, 6" d., 3 1/2" h., petal foot, Royal
blue foot & bow w/clear swirl connector....... 225
Compote, 7" d., tall stem w/air bubble, pink
w/controlled bubbles & pink threading 225
Compote, 9 7/8" d., 5 1/4" h., a Delft blue
applied disc foot & compressed knop
stem supporting a pearl white bowl w/a
rippled flaring base below the narrow up-
right rim 550
Creamer, Foval, creamy opalescent body
w/applied green handle................................... 120

Fry Foval Cup & Saucer

Cup & saucer, Foval, cup w/Jade handle,
pr. (ILLUS. w/teapot, previous page) **95**
Cup & saucer, round, azure blue, pr. **18**
Custard cup, Pearl Oven Ware, no handle **10**
Goblet, water, "Cactus Stem," crystal bowl
& foot, green stem **125**

Skyscraper Stem Goblet

Goblet, water, "Skyscraper Stem," crystal
(ILLUS.) **55**

Art Deco Pressed Stem Goblet

Goblet, water, Panel Optic, Art Deco
pressed stem, green, 7 1/2" h. (ILLUS.) **25**
Muffin pan, rectangular, six-part, Pearl
Oven Ware, 9" l. **125**
Percolator top, Pearl Oven Ware **15**
Perfume atomizer, Pearl Art Line w/Jade
base, 7" h. **275**
Pie plate, Pearl Art Line, 5" d. **67**

Footed Amber Pitcher

Pitcher, 10" h., footed, wide panel w/four
bulges, amber (ILLUS.) **85**
Plate, 8 1/2" d., grill, pink **28**
Plate, 8 1/2" d., Pearl Art Line w/Delft blue
applied rim **130**
Plate, 10 1/2" d., grill, cobalt blue **95**
Reamer, ribbed sides, tab handle, amber **395**
Snack plate & cup, plate w/indent for cup,
pink, pr. **60**
Teapot, cov., blown Foval, w/Jade handle &
finial (ILLUS. w/cup & saucer) **395**
Teapot, cov., Foval, pearly opalescent body
w/applied spout, handle & knob finial, ap-
plied sections found in either Jade green
or Delft blue, each version (ILLUS. of
both, top next page) **250-300**
Tumbler, iced tea, handled, Japanese Maid
etching, clear **125**
Tumbler, footed, Bubble Girl etching (not a
Fry etch), pink, 10 oz. **37**
Vase, 6" h., bud, crimped rim, footed,
Anemone etching, clear **75**

Honeysuckle Etching Bud Vase

Vase, 6" h., bud, crimped rim, Honeysuckle
etching, crystal (ILLUS.) **68**

Two Lovely Fry Foval Glass Teapots

Vegetable dish, 9 3/4" d., two-part, Pearl
Oven Ware **47**

Gallé

Gallé glass was made in Nancy, France, by Emile Gallé, a founder of the Nancy School and a leader in the Art Nouveau movement in France. Much of his glass, both enameled and cameo, is decorated with naturalistic motifs. The finest pieces were made in the last two decades of the 19th century and the opening years of the 20th.

Pieces marked with a star preceding the name were made between 1904, the year of Gallé's death, and 1914.

Gallé
Nancy
Déposé

Gallé

* Gallé

Various Gallé Marks

Gallé Cameo Perfume Lamp

Cameo perfume lamp, bulbous nearly
spherical body in frosted clear overlaid

in deep red & cameo cut w/leafy fuch-
sias, signed in cameo & w/paper label,
brass cap marked "Made in France,"
6" h. (ILLUS.) **$2,160**

Huge, Rare Cactus Flower Gallé Vase

Cameo vase, 16" h., 12" d., small foot below the large ovoid body topped by an incurved rim, the ground overlaid w/dark
blue & finely cameo cut w/swirled leafy
stems & large windowpane cactus flowers, signed in cameo, tiny fleabite on rim
(ILLUS.) **31,625**

Gallé Cameo Vase with Red Shrubs

Cameo vase, 11 1/2" h., simple wide ovoid body w/a small round mouth, pink & crimson ground overall cameo cut w/large flowering shrubs, signed in cameo (ILLUS., bottom previous page) **5,175**

Tall Gallé Cameo Vase with Iris

Cameo vase, 13 3/4" h., a flaring foot & disk knop below the tall ovoid body w/a small flaring neck, mottled cream & maroon ground overall w/maroon & cameo cut w/a large iris & leafy stems, signed on the base "Cristallerie E. Gallé - Nancy - Modelé et Déposé," several open bubbles on exterior (ILLUS.) **1,840**

Very Tall & Slender Gallé Cameo Vase

Cameo vase, 15" h., a cushion foot below the ovoid body tapering to a very tall & slender neck w/a flaring rim, frosted ground overlaid & cameo cut w/long leafy vines up & around the sides, minor edge wear on foot (ILLUS.) **2,185**

Tall Slender Gallé Cameo Vase with Lily

Cameo vase, 18 1/4" h., round foot below the very tall & slender ovoid body w/a small flat mouth, salmon shading to cream ground overlaid in dark brown up from the base to dark green & cameo cut w/leaves, stems & lily flower, signed in cameo (ILLUS.) **2,530**

Simple Enameled Gallé Decanter

Decanter w/original triple-bubble stopper, footed squatty bulbous body tapering to a tall cylindrical neck, crystal, lightly optic-ribbed form, the body enameled in blue & white w/a monogram that appears to be a "C," blue & white trim line on foot & rim, signed on the pontil, very light stain

inside the bottom, tiny fleabite on lip,
12" h. (ILLUS.) **1,200**

Exceptional Gallé Sunflower Vase

Vase, 6" h., 8" d., very broad ovoid form
w/a wide short cylindrical neck, the sides
applied w/very large sunflowers, signed
(ILLUS.) **7,475**

Finely Enameled Gallé Vase

Vase, 12" h., enameled "Lion of Lorraine"
decoration, the tall teardrop-form body in
rum amber ornately enameled in gold,
raised on three applied peg feet & w/ap-
plied sharp rigaree up the sides, signed
"E. Gallé - Nancy - Déposé" (ILLUS.) **2,588**

Heisey

*Numerous types of fine glass were made by
A.H. Heisey & Co., Newark, Ohio, from 1895. The
company's trademark, an H enclosed within a
diamond, has become known to most glass collectors. The company's name and molds were
acquired by Imperial Glass Co., Bellaire, Ohio, in
1958, and some pieces have been reissued. The
glass listed below consists of miscellaneous pieces
and types. Also see ANIMALS.*

Heisey Diamond "H" Mark

Moongleam Almond Dish

Almond dish, handled, Octagon patt.,
Moongleam (light green), 3" w. (ILLUS.)...... **$28**
Almond set: six individual footed almonds
& one 6" w. master; Medium Flat Panel,
Flamingo (pink), set (ILLUS., below)............ **175**

Heisey Flat Panel Almond Set

Greek Key Banana Split Dish

Heisey Lodestar Ashtray in Dawn

Ashtray, Lodestar patt., Dawn (light grey),
5" d. (ILLUS.) **98**
Banana split dish, footed, Greek Key patt.,
clear (ILLUS., top of page) **45**
Banana split dish, footed, Yeoman patt.,
Moongleam **37**
Basket, Lariat patt., clear 8 1/2" h. **230**

Heisey Cut Basket No. 466

Basket, No. 466, crystal w/cutting, 8" w.
(ILLUS.)... **325**

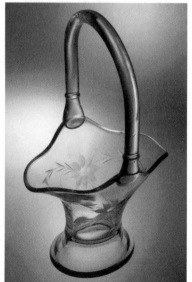

Heisey Basket No. 463 with Cutting

Basket, No. 463, crystal w/cutting, 9" h.
(ILLUS.)... **295**
Bell, Victorian Belle, hollow figure of girl
made into bell, crystal satin, 4" h. **98**
Bowl, 6" d., Empress patt., Sahara (light
yellow)... **35**
Bowl, 8" d., Rococo patt., clear.......................... **85**
Bowl, 8" d., Twist patt., nasturtium type,
Moongleam **109**
Bowl, 9 1/2" d., floral-type, crimped rim, Or-
chid etching, Queen Ann blank, clear **75**
Bowl, 11" d., flared, seahorse feet, Waverly
patt., crystal.. **65**
Bowl, 11" d., floral-type, New Era patt.,
clear **85**

Butter dish, cov., square, Rose etching,
clear 200
Butter dish, cov., 1/4 lb. size, Victorian
patt., crystal.. 75
Cake plate, footed, Rose etching, clear,
15" d.. 325
Cake salver, Plantation patt., clear, 13" d........ 270
Cake stand, Orchid etching, Waverly blank,
clear, 12" d. 200
Candleblocks, one-light, square, Crystolite
patt., crystal, 2" h., pr. 27
Candleholder, single-light, saucer-shaped,
dolphin-footed, Queen Ann patt., No.
1509, clear, 3" h. 45
Candlesticks, one-light, Orchid etching,
clear, 3" h., pr. 75
Candlesticks, two-light, Trident patt., Fla-
mingo, pr. 265

Trident Pattern Candlestick

Candlesticks, two-light, Trident patt., Saha-
ra, pr. (ILLUS. of one) 250
Candlesticks, two-light, w/rectangular
bobeche & prisms, New Era patt., crystal,
pr. 285
Candlesticks, two-light, Lariat patt.
w/Moonglo cutting, clear, pr. 100
Candlesticks, two-light, No. 301, amber
arms, pr. 485
Candlesticks, two-light, Orchid etching, Tri-
dent blank, clear, 5" h., pr. 135
Candlesticks, three-light, Empress patt.,
No. 301, Sahara w/clear bobeches, pr......... 950
Candy dish, cov., tall, Plantation patt.,
clear, 8" h. 175
Candy dish, cov., tall, seahorse finial, Rose
etching, Waverly blank, clear 325
Celery tray, Empress patt., Sahara 45
Celery tray, oval, Coarse Rib patt., clear,
9" l. 18
Celery tray, Rose etching, Waverly blank,
clear, 12" l. 70
Celery vase, Fandango patt., clear................... 85
Champagne, Rose etching, clear 45
Champagne, saucer type, Kohinoor patt.,
clear, 5 1/2 oz... 35
Champagne, saucer type, Minuet etching,
No. 5010, clear, 6 oz. 35
Champagne, saucer-type, Carcassone
patt., clear stem w/Sahara bowl, 6 oz. 40
Champagne, saucer-type, Spanish patt.,
Killarney cutting, clear................................... 42

Champagne, saucer-type, Victorian patt.,
clear 20
Champagne, Spanish patt., cobalt blue
bowl w/clear stem, 5 1/2" oz. 115
Cheese dish, cov., footed, Lariat patt.,
clear, 5" d... 65
Cigarette box, cov., w/small horsehead fin-
ial, Puritan patt., No. 1489, clear................. 125
Claret, New Era patt., clear, 4 oz. 27
Coaster, Plantation patt., clear, 4" d. 50

Heisey Cocktail with Horse Head Stem

Cocktail, figural horse head stem, clear
(ILLUS.).. 365
Cocktail, Gascony patt., Tangerine (deep
orangish red)... 110
Cocktail, high stem, New Era patt., clear,
3 1/2 oz. 25
Cocktail, Orchid etching, clear, 5 5/8" h., 4
oz. 55
Cocktail, Stanhope patt., clear, 3 1/2 oz........... 20
Cocktail shaker, cov., Orchid etching, ster-
ling silver top & base, clear.......................... 295

Cut Rooster-head Cocktail Shaker

Cocktail shaker, rooster head stopper, Barcelona cut, crystal, 14" h. (ILLUS., bottom previous page) 175

Cocktail shaker w/original stopper, Coronation patt., clear........................... 75

Compote, 6 1/2" d., low footed, Rose etching, Waverly blank, clear.............................. 70

Console set: bowl & pair of candle vases w/prisms & inserts; Ipswich patt., clear, bowl 11 1/2" d., 5" h., 3 pcs......................... 600

Cordial, Lariat patt., w/Moonglo cutting, clear... 150

Cordial, Rose etching, clear, 1 oz.................. 200

Cordial, Chintz etching, No. 3389, clear, 1 oz. 120

Cornucopia-vase, Warwick patt., cobalt blue, signed, 5 1/2" h. 295

Cream soup, two-handled, Yeoman patt., Hawthorne (light purple).............................. 29

Creamer, open, dolphin-footed, Empress patt., Flamingo 55

Creamer & open sugar bowl, Crystolite patt., clear, pr. 50

Creamer & open sugar bowl, Danish Princess etching, Queen Ann blank, clear, pr. 120

Creamer & open sugar bowl, footed, Plantation patt., clear, pr. 90

Creamer & open sugar bowl, Petal patt., Moongleam, pr. 110

Cruet w/original stopper, Empress patt., Sahara.. 160

Yeoman Cruet in Moongleam

Cruet w/original stopper, oil-type, Yeoman patt., Moongleam, 2 oz. (ILLUS.) 125

Cruet w/original stopper, Pleat & Panel patt., Flamingo 90

Cruet w/original stopper, Twist patt., Moongleam 175

Crushed fruit jar, cov., Greek Key patt., clear... 500

Cup, Waverly patt., clear.................................... 12

Cup & saucer, after dinner-type, Octagon patt., Flamingo, pr. 32

Cup & saucer, Crystolite patt., clear, pr............. 24

Cup & saucer, Rose etching, clear, pr. 75

Decanter w/sterling stopper, sherry-type, Orchid etching, clear........................... 375

Decanter w/stopper, Old Sandwich patt., cobalt blue, No. 98, 1 pt..................... 625

Domino sugar tray, Narrow Flute patt., Moongleam 160

Epergnette, for candleholder, Waverly patt., crystal, 5" h. 22

Gardenia bowl, Orchid etching, Waverly blank, clear, 13" d. 130

Goblet, Carcassonne patt., clear stem w/Sahara bowl, 11 oz......................... 55

Goblet, Carcassonne patt., Sahara, 9 oz.......... 50

Goblet, Empress patt., Sahara, 9 oz................. 90

Goblet, Impromptu patt., clear 45

Goblet, Ipswich patt., clear, 8 oz..................... 25

Goblet, Lariat patt., Moonglo cutting, clear, 10 oz. 35

Goblet, low stem, Orchid etching, No. 5025, clear, 10 oz. 45

Goblet, Minuet etching, clear............................. 45

Goblet, Old Dominion patt., Alexandrite (lavender) 300

Goblet, Twist patt., Flamingo, 9 oz. 50

Goblet, Old Dominion patt., clear....................... 25

Ice bucket, cov., Empress patt., w/tongs, Alexandrite 325

Ice bucket, Orchid etching, Queen Ann blank, clear.................................... 250

Ice bucket, two-handled, Orchid etching, Waverly blank, clear................................... 280

Ice tub, Puritan patt. (No. 341), clear, 6" d. 120

Lamps, hurricane-type, Plantation patt., clear, 15" h., pr......................... 1,200

Lemon bowl, cov., Ridgeleigh patt., clear, 5 1/2" d.................................. 65

Lemon dish, cov., Tudor patt., clear w/cutting 35

Luncheon set: four cups & plates & dolphin-footed creamer & sugar bowl; Empress patt., Sahara, 10 pcs.......................... 325

Marmalade jar, cov., apple-shaped, Minuet etching, Toujours blank, clear...................... 170

Marmalade jar, cov., Crystolite patt., clear, 6" h.. 50

Puritan Marmalade Jar

Marmalade jar, cov., No. 341 Puritan, crystal, 4" h. (ILLUS.) 85

Salt shaker w/original top, souvenir type, Bead Swag patt., milk white, late 1890s 55

Salt shaker w/original top, Winged Scroll patt., green w/gold trim, late 1890s 110

Sherbet, Lariat patt., blown, crystal, 5 oz.......... 14

Sherbet, low, Rose etching, crystal.................... 35

Sherbet, Orchid etching, No. 5025, crystal, 6 oz. 35

Spooner, Pineapple & Fan patt., emerald green w/gold trim, late 1890s 120

Spooner, Queen Ann patt. (No. 365), crystal 95

Sugar bowl, open, individual, Twist patt., lightning bolt handle, Moongleam, 4 oz.......... 90

Sugar bowl, open, Lariat patt., crystal 20

Sugar bowl, open, Minuet etching, crystal........ 40

Sugar shaker w/metal lid, footed, Yeoman patt., Flamingo 125

Syrup pitcher w/original top, Bead Swag patt., milk white, late 1890s........................ 160

Table set: creamer, cov. sugar bowl, cov. butter dish & spooner; Pineapple & Fan patt., emerald green w/gold trim, 4 pcs. 550

Toothpick holder, Bead Swag patt., milk white w/floral decoration, late 1890s 150

Toothpick holder, Bead Swag patt., ruby-stained, late 1890s 60

Toothpick holder, Fancy Loop patt., emerald green w/gold trim, late 1890s 285

Toothpick holder, Pineapple & Fan patt., emerald green, late 1890s 295

Toothpick holder, Prison Stripe patt., marked, clear 395

Tray, Empress patt., Sahara, 13" d. 60

Tray, center-handled, square, Old Colony etching, Sahara, 12" w. 72

Tumbler, Duquesne patt., Tangerine, 5 1/4" h... 155

Tumbler, flat bottom, Saturn patt., Zircon, 10 oz. 150

Tumbler, iced tea, footed, Rose etching, No. 5072, crystal, 12 oz. 60

Tumbler, iced tea, Minuet etching, No. 2351, crystal, 12 oz. 55

Tumbler, iced tea, Orchid etching, No. 5025, crystal, 9 1/2 oz. 80

Tumbler, juice, footed, Plantation patt., pressed, clear, 5 oz.. 65

Tumbler, juice, footed, Provincial patt., crystal, 5 oz. 18

Tumbler, juice, footed, Rose etching, crystal, 5 oz. 45

Tumbler, juice, footed, Rose etching, No. 5072, crystal, 5 oz. 45

Tumbler, juice, Ipswich patt., Sahara............... 40

Tumbler, Pineapple & Fan patt., clear w/gold trim, late 1890s 35

Tumbler, soda, footed, Twist patt., Marigold (dark yellow), 8 oz. 75

Tumbler, soda, Ipswich patt., crystal, 8 oz......... 20

Tumbler, water, Ipswich patt., Sahara 60

Tumbler, whiskey, Victorian patt., crystal 35

Tumbler, bar-type, Victorian patt., crystal, 2 oz. 38

Tumbler, dolphin-footed, Empress patt., Moongleam, 8 oz.. 195

Tumbler, flat, pressed, Crystolite patt., crystal, 8 oz......... 45

Vase, 4" h., Orchid etching, crystal 165

Vase, 5" h., footed, crimped rim, Lariat patt., crystal... 68

Vase, 7" h., footed, Lariat patt., crystal 45

Vase, 8" h., Empress patt., flared rim, Alexandrite 850

Vase, 8" h., Fancy Loop patt., clear, late 1890s 95

Vase, 8" h., footed, Pleat & Panel patt., Flamingo 85

Vase, 8" h., Pineapple & Fan patt., emerald green w/gold trim, late 1890s........................ 50

Water set: pitcher & four tumblers; Narrow Flute patt., clear, early 20th c., 5 pcs. 200

Wine, Minuet etching, crystal, 2 1/2 oz. 80

Wine, New Era patt., crystal............................... 40

Wine, Spanish patt., cobalt blue..................... 225

Higgins Glass

Fused glass, an "old craft for modern tastes" enjoyed a mid-20th century revival through the work of Chicago-based artists Frances and Michael Higgins of the Higgins Glass Studio. Although known for thousands of years, fusing had, by the 1940s, been abandoned in favor of glassblowing. A meticulous craft, fusing can best be described as the creation of a "glass sandwich." A design is either drawn with colored enamels or pieced with glass segments on a piece of enamel-coated glass. Another piece of enameled glass is placed over this. The "sandwich" is then placed on a mold and heated in a kiln, with the glass "slumping" to the shape of the mold. When complete, the interior design is fused between the outer glass layers. Additional layers are often utilized, accentuating the visual depth. Sensing that fused glass was a marketable commodity, the Higginses opened their studio in 1948 and applied the fusing technique to a wide variety of items: tableware such as bowls, plates, and servers; housewares, ranging from clocks and lamps to ashtrays and candleholders; and purely decorative items, such as mobiles and jewelry. With its arresting mix of geometric and curved lines and bold use of color, Higgins glass transformed the ordinary into decor accent pieces both vibrant and exciting.

Unlike many of their contemporaries, the Higginses received national exposure thanks to an association with Chicago industrial manufacturer Dearborn Glass Company. This collaboration, lasting from 1957 through 1964, resulted in the mass marketing of "higginsware" worldwide. Since nearly every piece carried the lower-case signature "higgins," name recognition was both immediate and enduring.

The Dearborn demand for new Higgins pieces resulted in more than 75 identifiable production patterns with such buyer-enticing names as "Stardust," "Arabesque," and "Barbaric Jewels." Objects created in these patterns included ashtrays of every size (4" "Dinner Dwarfs" to 15" jumbo models), "rondelay" room dividers and an extensive line of tableware. (As evidenced by Dearborn promotional postcards, complete dining tables could literally be set with Higgins glass).

In 1965, the Higginses briefly moved their base of operations to Haeger Potteries before opening their own studio in Riverside, Illinois, where it has been located since 1966. Although Michael Higgins died in 1999 and Frances Higgins in 2004, the Studio today continues under the leadership of longtime artistic associates Louise and Jonathan Wimmer. New pieces celebrate and expand on the traditions and techniques of the past.Higgins pieces created from 1948 until 1957 are engraved on the reverse with the signature "higgins" or the artist's complete name. A raised "dancing man" logo was added in 1951. Pieces created at Dearborn or Haeger (1957-65) bear a gold "higgins" signature on the surface or a signature in the colorway. The marking since 1966 has been an engraved "higgins" on the reverse of an object, with the occasional addition of the artist's name. Pieces produced since the death of Frances Higgins are signed "higgins studio."

Once heralded as "an exclamation point in your decorating scheme," Higgins glass continues, nearly 60 years since its inception, to enchant collectors with its zest and variety.

References on Higgins glass include the Schiffer books Higgins: Poetry in Glass (2005), and Higgins: Adventures in Glass (1997), both by Donald-Brian Johnson and Leslie Pina. Photos for this category are by Dr. Pina.

The Higgins Glass Studio is located at 33 East Quincy Street, Riverside, IL 60546 (708-447-2787), www.higginsglass.com.

Price ranges given are general estimates covering all available patterns produced at Dearborn Glass Company and Haeger Potteries (1957-1965). The low end of the scale applies to the most commonly found patterns (e.g., "Mandarin," "Siamese Purple"), the upper end to those found less frequently (e.g., "Gemspread," "Carousel").

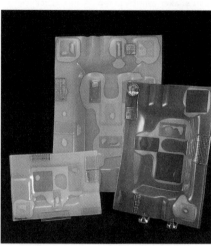

Three Rectangular Higgins Ashtrays

Ashtray, rectangular, Cyclamen Pink patt., 5 x 7" (ILLUS. left with other rectangular ashtrays) **$75-100**

Ashtray, circular, Roulette patt. only in 5 1/2" d. size (ILLUS. of three color variations, bottom of page) **50-75**

Ashtray, geometric, Gemspread patt. only, two sides 5 3/4" **275-325**

Ashtray, circular, various patterns, 7" d., each **100-125**

Three Roulette Pattern Higgins Ashtrays

Butterflies Ashtrays & Cigarette Box

Ashtray, Rogue Freeform Ashtrays Set #1,
Butterflies patt., 7" longest side (ILLUS.
back right with other Butterflies pieces)
.... **150-200**
Ashtray, rectangular, Forget-Me-Not patt.,
7 x 10" (ILLUS. right with other rectangu-
lar ashtrays, previous page)................. **100-175**
Ashtray, geometric, various patterns, two
sides 7 1/4" **125-175**
Ashtray, footed, Birdcages patt., 8" longest
side.. **300-400**

Barbaric Jewels Circular Ashtray

Ashtray, circular, Barbaric Jewels patt.,
8 1/4" to 8 1/2" d. (ILLUS.) **100-150**

Buttercup Ashtray & Plate by Higgins

Ashtray, circular, Buttercup patt., 8 1/4 to
8 1/2" d. (ILLUS. front with Buttercup
plate)... **100-150**
Ashtray, circular, Sunburst patt., 8 1/4" to
8 1/2" d. (ILLUS. left with Sunburst
12 1/4" d. plate, top next page)............ **100-150**
Ashtray, Rogue Freeform Ashtrays Set #2,
Balloons patt., 9" longest side.............. **175-225**
Ashtray, Rogue Freeform Ashtrays Set #1,
Butterflies patt., 9 1/2" longest side
(ILLUS. back left with other Butterflies
pieces, top left of page) **175-250**
Ashtray, rectangular, Variation patt.,
10 x 14" (ILLUS. center with other rect-
angular ashtrays, previous page)......... **150-250**
Ashtray, geometric, Barbaric Jewels patt.
only, two sides 10 1/4" **200-250**
Ashtray, Rogue Freeform Ashtrays Set #2,
Balloons patt., 10 1/2" longest side...... **200-250**
Ashtray, Rogue Freeform Ashtrays Set #1,
Butterflies patt., 12" longest side **250-300**
Ashtray, Rogue Freeform Ashtrays Set #2,
Balloons patt., 15" longest side............ **250-350**
Ashtray-dish, square, Dinner Dwarf patt.,
4" w. **50-95**
Ashtray-dish, square, various patterns,
5" w. **75-100**
Ashtray-dish, square, Barbaric Jewels patt.
only, 6" w. **85-125**
Ashtray-dish, square, various patterns,
7" w. **100-150**
Ashtray-dish, square, various patterns, 9"
to 10" w. **150-250**
Bonbon, various patterns, 6 1/2" h. **225-400**
Bowl, 3 1/2" d., circular, various patterns **50-95**
Bowl, 5 1/4" w., squarish, various patterns
.... **100-150**
Bowl, 6" d., circular, various patterns **100-175**
Bowl, 7" w., squarish, various patterns **125-225**
Bowl, 7" w., squarish w/lip, various patterns
.... **175-300**
Bowl, 7 1/4" to 7 1/2" d., scalloped rim, var-
ious patterns **125-200**

Sunburst Ashtray & Large Plate

Three Color Variations of the Loops Pattern Bowl

Bowl, 8 1/4" d., various patterns (ILLUS. of three Loops patt. variations, above)...... **175-300**
Bowl, 10" w., squarish, various patterns
.... **300-400**

Bowl, 10 3/4" d., circular, various patterns (ILLUS. of Classic Line pattern, top of next page)... **250-300**
Bowl, 11" w., squarish w/lip, various patterns.. **225-400**

Classic Line Pattern Large Bowl

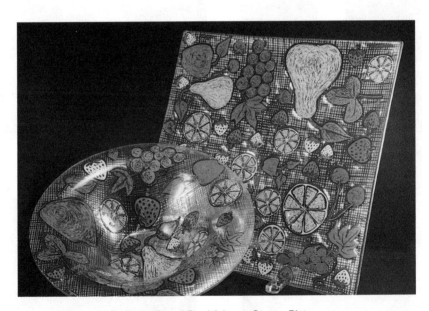

Fruits Round Bowl & Large Square Plate

Bowl, 12 1/4" d., various patterns (ILLUS. of
Fruits pattern, right with large square
Fruits plate) **225-350**
Bowl, 14" w., squarish w/lip, Riviera patt.
(ILLUS., top next page) **400-600**
Bowl, 17" d., circular, various patterns...... **550-750**
Butter dish, cov., various patterns,
3 3/4 x 7 1/2" **95-125**
Cake or jelly stand, circular, various pat-
terns, 10" to 12" d................................ **175-300**

Cakestand, squarish, various patterns,
10" w. **175-300**
Cakestand, squarish, various patterns,
13" w. **200-350**
Candleholders, Petal patt., 2 1/2" h., pr.
.... **100-150**
Candleholders, Petal patt., 4 1/2" h., pr.
.... **150-225**
Candleholders, Colonial patt., 6 1/2" h., pr.
.... **150-250**

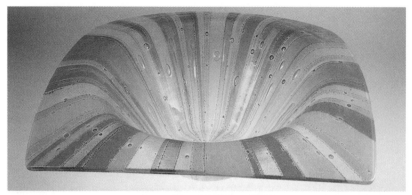

Large Squarish Riviera Bowl

Candleholders, Dinner patt., 8 1/2" h., pr.
.... **250-400**

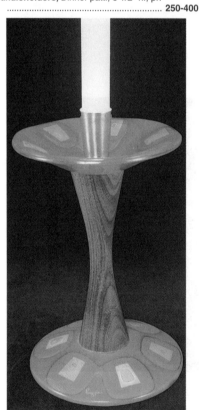

Higgins Mandarin Pattern Candleholder

Candleholders, Mandarin patt., 8 1/2" h.,
pr. (ILLUS. of one)................................ **250-400**
Candy dish, cov., various patterns, 8" d... **350-550**
Cigarette box, cov., rectangular, various
patterns, bases, in order of increasing
value, are of glass, walnut or glass & metal, 4 x 7" (ILLUS. of Butterflies patt., front
with Butterflies ashtrays) **200-300**

Higgins Carnival Pattern Clock

Clock, wall-type, Carnival patt., 11 1/2" sq.
(ILLUS.)... **500-550**
Dipster, various patterns, 12" d. **250-400**

Carousel Pattern Dish & Plate

Two Higgins Stardust Hanging Baskets

Dish, four-sided geometric, various patterns, 10 x 12" longest sides (ILLUS. of Carousel pattern, front with Carousel plate, bottom previous page)................. **150-250**

Epergne, three-tier, circular, various patterns **350-500**

Fruit & nut server, two-tier, circular, various patterns **250-400**

Goblet/vase with lip, various patterns, 7 3/4" d... **150-225**

Hanging baskets, various patterns, 7 1/2" d. (ILLUS. of two Stardust pattern versions, top of page)........................... **200-300**

Plate, 6" d., various patterns **100-150**

Plate, 7 1/4" w., squarish, various patterns **75-125**

Plate, 8 1/4" d., circular, various patterns **125-225**

Plate, 10 1/2" w., squarish, various patterns **100-200**

Plate, 12 1/4" d., circular, various patterns (ILLUS. Buttercup patt., back with Buttercup ashtray) **200-300**

Plate, 12 1/4" d., circular, various patterns (ILLUS. Sunburst patt. right with Sunburst ashtray) **200-300**

Plate, 13 1/2" w., squarish, various patterns **150-250**

Plate, 14" square, various patterns (ILLUS. of Fruits pattern, back with Fruits pattern bowl, two pages previously) **200-300**

Plate, 16 3/4" d., circular, various patterns (ILLUS. of Carousel pattern, with Carousel pattern dish).................................... **400-575**

Posy pocket, various patterns, 5 x 7" **250-400**

Posy pocket, various patterns, 7 x 10" **300-475**

Relish server, circular, various patterns, 15" d. **300-475**

Server, double-sided rectangular form, various patterns, 7 x 14" **150-250**

Server, squarish, two-tier, various patterns **250-400**

Server, circular, three-pocket, various patterns, 9 1/2" d. **150-225**

Server, circular, three-pocket, various patterns, 13 1/2" d. **200-300**

Server, circular, six-pocket, various patterns, 18" d. **400-600**

Trifle dish or "Long John," various patterns, 7 x 10" **400-500**

Imperial

Imperial Glass Company, Bellaire, Ohio was organized in 1901 and was in continuous production, except for very brief periods, until its closing in June 1984. It had been a major producer of Carnival Glass early in the 20th century and also produced other types of glass, including an art glass line called "Free Hand Ware" during the 1920s and its "Jewels" about 1916. The company acquired a number of molds of other earlier factories, including the Cambridge and A.H. Heisey Companies, and reissued numerous items through the years.

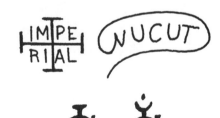

Imperial Marks1-Imperial Nucut Mark2-Early Imperial Cross Mark3. Later Imperial Marks

Candlewick
Ashtray, heart-shaped, No. 400/172, clear, 4 1/2" **$12**

Ruby Candlewick Bowl

Imperial Eagle Ashtray

Ashtray, eagle, No. 1776/1, milk glass, 6 1/2" (ILLUS.) 65
Ashtray set, nested, round, No. 400/450, clear, 3 pcs. 26
Baked apple dish, No. 400/53X, blue, 6 1/2" 85
Basket, No. 400/40/0, clear, 6 1/2" h. 40
Bonbon bowl, heart-shaped, handled, No. 400/40H, clear, 5" 25
Bonbon bowl, heart-shaped, No. 400/174, caramel slag, 6 1/2" 175
Bonbon dish, heart-shaped, No. 51H, clear w/gold trim, 6" w. 36
Bowl, 5" d., cream soup, two-handled, No. 400/50, crystal 48
Bowl, 5" d., fruit, 400/1F, clear 10
Bowl, 5 1/2" d., cream soup, No. 400/50, clear 65

Bowl, 6" d., lily-type, black, wide rounded bowl w/beaded rim, raised on three knob feet, enameled w/a cluster of gold, white & orange Cosmos blossoms & leaves, No. 400/74N **575-600**
Bowl, 6" square, No. 400/232, crystal 135
Bowl, 7" d., two-handled, No. 400/62B, red 250
Bowl, 7" sq., No. 400/233, clear 225
Bowl, 8-8 1/2" d., No. 400/74B, ruby 350
Bowl, 8 1/2" d., No. 400/698, clear w/cutting 55
Bowl, 9" d., four-toed, square crimped, No. 400/74SC, black amethyst 325
Bowl, 9" d., No. 400/74SC, square, crimped bowl, four-toed, ruby (ILLUS., top of page) 325
Bowl, 9-10" d., heart-shaped, No. 400/73H, clear 175
Bowl, 11" l., oval, divided, No. 400/125A, clear 550
Butter dish, cov., oblong, w/beaded top, No. 400/161, clear, 1/4 lb. 45
Butter & jam dish, No. 400/262, three-part, clear, 10 1/2" 193
Cake stand, No. 400/67D, low-footed, clear, 10" d. 75
Calendar, 1947, crystal 275
Canape set, plate No. 400/36 & 3 1/2 oz. tumbler, No. 400/142, clear, 2 pcs. 60
Candleholders, footed urn shape, No. 400/129R, clear, 6" h., pr. 200
Candleholders, mushroom, No. 400/86, clear w/gold beading, pr. 100
Candleholders, No. 400/81, handled, 3 1/2" h., clear, pr. 112
Candleholders w/applied handle, No. 400/90, clear, 5" pr. 100
Candlestick, w/finger-ring, No. 400/81, crystal, 3 1/2" d. 58
Candy box, cov., No. 400/259, clear, 7" d. 130
Candy box, cov., three-part, No. 400/110, clear, 7" d. 160
Candy dish, No. 400/51C, handled, crimped, clear, 6" d. 40
Center bowl, No. 400/131B, oval, flat, clear, 14" 350
Cheese & cracker set, No. 400/88, clear, 10" d., 2 pc. 65

Candlewick Set with Silver Deposit

Candlewick Cigarette Box with Grapes

Cigarette box, cov., rectangular base w/large beads around bottom, flat fitted mirrored copper-colored top w/an applied cluster of clear grapes, No. 40/135 (ILLUS.) **125-150**

Compote, 4 1/2" h., No. 400/63B, no bead stem, clear.. **65**

Compote, 8" d., No. 400/48F, five-bead stem, clear.. **325**

Compote, 8", No. 400/48F, 4-bead stem, clear **85**

Compote, 10" h., fruit, No. 400/103C, clear..... **275**

Cordial, No. 3400, clear, 1 oz. **48**

Cordial decanter, applied handle, No. 400/82, clear etched.................................... **750**

Cream soup bowl w/underplate, two-handled, No. 400/50, clear, 5" d. bowl & 6 3/4" d. underplate, 2 pcs. **75**

Creamer & open sugar bowl, No. 400/18, beaded, domed feet, clear, pr. **325**

Creamer & open sugar bowl, No. 400/30, clear w/silver deposit Lily of the Valley patt., pr. (ILLUS., top of page)................. **75-100**

Creamer & open sugar bowl, pedestal base, beaded feet, No. 400/31, clear, pr........ **75**

Cruet w/original stopper, applied handle, No. 400/279, clear, 6 oz. **85**

Cruet w/original stopper, No. 400/121/0, etched "oil," clear... **85**

Cup & saucer, coffee, No. 400/37, clear, pr. **14**

Decanter w/original stopper, No. 400/163, beaded base, plain stopper, clear, 26 oz. **650**

Decanter w/original stopper, No. 400/18, crystal, 18 oz... **390**

Epergne set, No. 400/196, clear, 2 pc............. **295**

Etched Imperial Candlewick Goblet

Goblet, No. 3400, tall bell-form bowl w/plate-etched scrolling design & an etched gold rim band, knobbed stem (ILLUS.) **75-100**

Goblet, No. 3400, water, black, 7 1/2" h.. .... **295**

Goblet, No. 3400, water, ruby, 7 1/2" h.. .... **150**

Goblet, No. 400/190, water, beaded foot, clear, 10 oz. **25**

Honey dish, No. 400/157, clear, 4 3/4" **119**

Ice tub, No. 400/168, tab-handled, clear, 7" **220**

Icer & liner, No. 400/53, clear........................ **135**

Jar tower, three sections w/cover, No. 400/655, clear **850**

Jelly/ashtray, No. 400/33, clear, 4" d. **14**

Ladle, mayonnaise, No. 400/165, crystal.......... **15**

Mayonnaise bowl & underplate, No. 400/23, blue, 2 pcs. **65**

Mustard jar, spoon & underplate, No. 400/156, clear, 3 pcs..................................... **75**

Candlewick Nappy on Wooden Base

Nappy, No. 400/1F, shallow round bowl raised on a turned wood pedestal base (ILLUS.) **75-100**

Pastry tray, No. 400/68D, center handle, clear, 11 1/2" d. 45

Pitcher, No. 400/18, beaded base, clear, 40 oz. 300

Pitcher, water, No. 400/24, clear, 80 oz. 175

Pitcher, plain, No. 400/424, crystal, 80 oz. 65

Plate, 6" d., bread & butter, No. 400/1D, clear 8

Plate, 6" d., canapé, w/off-center indentation, No. 400/36, clear 20

Plate, 7" d., salad, No. 400/3D, clear 12

Plate, 8" d., luncheon, No. 400/5D, clear 12

Plate, 8 1/2" d., handled, crimped rim, No. 400/62C, clear 30

Plate, 10" d., dinner, No. 400/10D, clear 55

Plate, 10" d., two-handled, No. 400/72D, blue 90

Plate, 10" d., two-handled, No. 400/72D, clear 35

Plate, 12 1/2" d., torte, cupped edge, No. 400/75V, clear 45

Plate, 14" d., two-handled, No. 400/113D, clear 50

Punch bowl & underplate, 13" d. bowl No. 400/20B & 17" d. underplate No. 400/20V, clear, 2 pcs. 250

Punch set: 13" d. punch bowl, 17" d. cupped-edge underplate, 12 cups & ladle; No. 400/20, clear, 15 pcs. 300

Relish dish, five-part, No. 400/209, clear, 13 1/2" d. 70

Relish dish, three-part, No. 400/208, clear, 10" l. 95

Relish dish, No. 400/54, handled, clear, 6 1/2" 20

Relish tray, four-part, No. 400/55, clear, 8 1/2" d. 65

Relish tray, three-part, No. 400/56, clear, 10 1/2" d. 65

Salt dip, No. 400/61, 18 beads, clear, 2" d. 12

Salt & pepper shakers, No. 400/167, amethyst, pr. 125

Salt & pepper shakers, No. 400/96, clear, pr. 24

Salt & pepper shakers w/chrome tops, No. 400/247, straight sides, clear, pr. 45

Sherbet, tall, No. 400/190, clear, 5 oz. 18

Tray, heart-shaped center handle, No. 400/149D, clear, 9" d. 45

Tray, lemon, center-handled, No. 400/221, clear, 5 3/4" 42

Tray, oblong waisted form, No. 400/29, clear, 6 1/2" l. 20

Tumbler, juice, No. 400/19, clear, 5 oz. 12

Tumbler, No. 400/15, footed beaded base, clear, 6 oz. 200

Tumbler, iced tea, footed, No. 400/19, clear, 6" h., 12 oz. 26

Vase, 8" h., fan-shaped, Starlight cut, No. 400/87F, clear 70

Vase, 8" h., flip-type, ruffled rim, No. 400/143C, clear 145

Vase, bud, 7" h., domed foot, No. 400/186, clear 450

Vase, 8" h., fan-shaped, beaded handles, No. 400/87F, clear 45

Vase, 8 1/2" h., No. 400/21, flared rim, clear 413

Vase, 10" h., beaded foot, straight sides, crystal 325

Water set: 80 oz. pitcher No. 400/24 & six 12 oz. tumblers No. 400/19; clear, 7 pcs. 269

Cape Cod

Ashtray, No. 160/134/1, clear, 4" d. 12

Ashtray, rectangular, No. 160/134, crystal, 4" l. 15

Bar bottle, clear 195

Basket, No. 160/73/0, shallow, clear 195

Bowl, 5" w., heart-shaped, No. 160/49H, clear 20

Bowl, 5 1/2" w., cream soup, tab-handled, No. 160/198, clear 40

Bowl, 6 1/2" d., spider, divided, handled, No. 160/187, clear 38

Bowl, 9" d., fruit, footed, No. 160/67F, clear 65

Bowl, 10" d., footed, No. 160/137, crystal 65

Bowl, 10" d., footed, No. 160/137B, clear 70

Bowl, 12" l., oval, crimped rim, No. 131C, clear 180

Butter dish, cov., round, handled, clear 52

Cake plate, square, four-footed, No. 160/220, clear 10" w. 125

Cake stand, round, footed, No. 160/67D, clear 10 1/2" d. 55

Imperial Two-light Candlestick

Candlestick, two-light, No. 160/100, crystal (ILLUS.) 85

Candlestick, single-light, clear, 5" h. 24

Cigarette box, cov., one handle, clear, 4 1/2" 45

Cigarette holder, handled mug-style, No.
  160/200, crystal... 35
Coaster, clear, 3" sq. 25
Comport, 4 1/2" h., square ball stem, clear 22
Compote, 6" h., cov., footed, No. 160/140,
  clear 85
Compote, 7" d., No. 160/48B, clear.................. 55
Cordial, No. 1602, milk white, 1 1/2 oz. 25
Cracker jar, cov., bamboo handle, clear,
  6 1/2" h... 85
Creamer, footed, wafer stem, clear,
  4 1/2" h... 10
Cruet w/original stopper, spherical, No.
  160/119, amber, 4 oz. 35
Cruet w/original stopper, No. 160/70,
  clear, 5 oz... 27
Decanter w/original stopper, shot glass
  top, embossed clear, 8 1/2" h. 175
Decanter w/original stopper, ruby-stained,
  30 oz., 9 3/4" h. 119
Decanter w/original stopper, square-
  shaped, No. 160/212, clear, 24 oz. 80
Egg cup, No. 160/225, clear 35
Egg cup, No. 160/225, crystal.......................... 32
Epergne, plain center, No. 160/196, clear, 2
  pcs.. 250
Goblet, water, No. 160, wafer stem, cobalt
  blue, 9 oz.. 48
Goblet, water, stemmed, No. 1600, clear,
  10 oz. 20
Goblet, water, wafer stem, clear, 8 oz.,
  5 1/2" h.. 10
Goblet, water, No. 1602, Verde green, 9 oz. 12
Horseradish bottle w/stopper, clear, 5 oz. 70
Mayonnaise bowl, handled, spouted, crys-
  tal 48
Mayonnaise bowl, ladle & underplate,
  clear, 3 pcs... 48
Mug, clear, 4 3/4" h. 65
Nut cup/tray, No. 183, three-handled, clear 24
Perfume bottle w/original stopper, round,
  clear 48
Pitcher, 10" h., martini-type, 44 oz., clear........ 240
Pitcher w/ice lip, No. 160/239, clear, 60 oz. 95
Plate, 8" d., No. 160/5D, ruby.......................... 28
Plate, 8 1/2" d., pink 19
Plate, 10" d., dinner, No. 160/10D, clear........... 40
Plate, 13 1/2" d., torte, clear............................ 45
Plate, 16" d., cupped, No. 160/20V, clear 50
Punch cup, clear.. 8
Punch set: punch bowl, underplate &
  twelve cups; clear, 1 gal., 14 pcs. 220
Relish dish, three-part, oval, No. 160/55,
  plain rim, clear, 9 1/2" l................................ 25
Salad serving set: fork & spoon; clear,
  9 1/2" l., the set 35
Salt & pepper mill, amber, pr........................... 55
Salt & pepper shakers, straight-sided,
  clear, 4" h., pr.. 30
Salt & pepper shakers w/original tops,
  Verde green, pr. 40
Sherbet, No. 1600, clear, 6 oz. 12
Sundae, No. 1602, ball stem, clear, 4" h........... 7
Tom & Jerry punch bowl, footed, No.
  160/200, clear 290
Tumbler, flat, clear, 6 1/2" h., 14 oz.................. 22
Tumbler, flat, No. 160, clear, 10 oz................... 10
Tumbler, iced tea, amber, 6" h. 12
Tumbler, iced tea, pink, 6" h. 34
Tumbler, juice, footed, No. 1602, Verde
  green, 6 oz. 15
Tumbler, water, No. 160, clear, 10 oz............... 12
Vase, 11" h., flip-type, crystal 190

Whiskey set w/metal rack, No. 160/260,
  clear bottles w/raised letters "Bourbon,"
  "Rye" & "Scotch," the set............................. 650
Wine, No. 1600, clear, 4 1/2" h. 10

Imperial Crystal Wine Carafe & Stopper

Wine carafe & stopper, footed, handled,
  No. 160/185, crystal (ILLUS.)....................... 220

Free-hand Ware

Blue & White Imperial Free-Hand Vase

Vase, 4 5/8" h., 7 7/8" d., a blue rim wrap on
  a broad & ruffled rim of opal glass decorated w/mottled blue hearts on a trailing
  vine, the interior & exterior flashed orange, polished pontil w/gold foil Imperial
  Free Hand label, ca. 1924 (minor wear) 450

Pair of Draped Imperial Free-Hand Vases

Vase, 6 1/2" h., flat-bottomed wide ovoid body tapering to a trumpet neck, cobalt blue ground decorated overall w/random white threading & heart-shaped leaves (ILLUS., bottom of previous page) **500**

Vase, 6 1/2" h., Mosaic design, deep cobalt blue body shaded & swirled w/opal & lined in iridescent orange **495**

Vase, 7" h., iridescent orange w/dark threading **325**

Vase, 7 3/8" h., 3 1/2" d., cushion footed baluster form w/flared rim, overall white decoration on butterfly blue iridescent ground, ca. 1924 .... **400**

Vase, 8 1/2" h., blue iridescent ground, gold iridescent interior **275**

Vase, 8 1/2" h., cylindrical, iridescent green heart & vine design on a white ground, marigold lining w/some wear **385**

Vase, 8 1/2" h., cylindrical shape, white drape design over mustard ground, orange iridescent interior **325**

Vase, 8 1/2" h., simple cylindrical form, orange iridescent ground decorated w/blue hanging heart design, cased over white, rim possibly ground **575**

Vase, 9 1/2" h., bulbous base w/a wide flared neck, white cased to a cobalt blue exterior, interior of rim flashed in brilliant iridescent orange, polished pontil, early 20th c. **575**

Vase, 9 3/4" h., iridescent orange over opaque white **185**

Vase, 9 3/4 h., iridescent orange over tooled trefoil rim, dark iridescent body decorated w/orange hearts & vines **750**

Vase, 10" h., baluster form w/flaring foot & rim, opaque white heart & vine decoration on a translucent cobalt blue ground **575**

Vase, 10" h., Hanging Vine & Heart, white cased w/orange **450**

Vase, 10" h., iridescent yellow orange exterior, blue interior **250**

Vase, 10 1/2" h., jack-in-the-pulpit-form, wide flared mouth of opaque white w/orange stretch iridescence, raised on an elongated stem w/blue pulled loops, on a blue disk foot w/overall orange & gold iridescence on exterior, polished pontil w/gold foil label, ca. 1925 .... **1,610**

Vase, 10 3/4" h., very slender baluster-form body w/flaring short neck, overall orange iridescence w/a blue pulled drapery design cased on milk glass **750**

Vases, 9 1/8" h., simple baluster-form body w/a trumpet neck, draped chartreuse festoons down the sides against a dark iridescent ground w/bronze, green & purple highlights, citron yellow interior, pr. (ILLUS., top of page) **805**

Kitchenwares

Imperial Milk Glass Hottle

Hottle w/crystal stopper, milk glass (ILLUS., bottom previous page) 16

Measuring pitcher, 2-cup, Custard w/Red Polka Dots patt. 68

Miscellaneous Patterns & Lines

Animal covered dish, lion laying down on lacy-rimmed base, caramel slag, copy of antique original, 6 x 7 1/2" base, 7" h. 150

Animal covered dish, rooster on lacy base, jade green 175

Animal covered dish, rooster on lacy base, purple slag 200

Ashtray, Caramel Slag, No. 1608/1, 7" d. 30

Basket, w/arched overhead handle, Monticello patt., No. 698, clear, 10" h. 55

Bowl, Cathay Line, figural Phoenix, No. 5026, blue satin, marked "Virginia B Evans" in script (ILLUS.) 200-300

Bowl, 5 1/2" d., one-handled, Mt. Vernon patt., crystal 9

Bowl, 8" d., Fancy Colonial patt., two-handled, green 75

Bowl, 8" d., pearl amethyst iridescent stretch glass, Iron Cross mark 145

Bowl, 10 1/2" oval, No. 320, ruby Stretch glass 295

clear satin, marked "Virginia B Evans" in script (ILLUS.) 295

Candlestick, single-light, No. 3130, spiral, green, 3 1/2" h. 24

Candlesticks, single-light, Twisted Optic patt., green, 8" h., pr. 65

Champagne, Fancy Colonial patt., teal, 6 oz. 25

Cordial, Fancy Colonial patt., pink, 1 oz. 45

Creamer & open sugar, Reeded patt., Steigel green, pr. 55

Creamer & sugar bowl, models of owls, red slag, pr. 70

Cup & saucer, Hazen patt., ruby, pr. 29

Flower bowl, Cathay Line, model of a Chinese junk, No. 5010, clear satin, marked "Virginia B Evans" in script (ILLUS., top next page) 225

Paperweight, model of a tiger, Heisey mold, amber & caramel slag 145

Pickle dish, oval, Monticello patt., clear, 6" 14

Pitcher, Mt. Vernon patt., clear, 54 oz. 35

Imperial Pitcher in Reeded Pattern

Pitcher, Reeded patt., No. 701, green w/clear applied handle (ILLUS.) 80

Plate, 8" d., Spun patt., reeded, clear 12

Plate, 8" d., Twisted Optic patt., pink 7

Imperial Cathay Line Candle Servant

Candlestick, single-light, Cathay Line, figural Candle Servant (female), No. 5035,

Imperial Blaise Plate

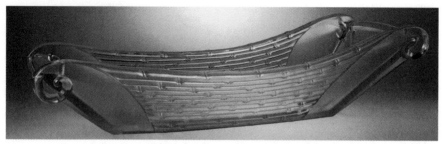

Cathay Linbe Junk Flower Bowl

Plate, 8" w., Blaise patt., pink (ILLUS., bottom previous page) 15
Plate, 8" w., Katy Blue patt., blue opalescent 35
Plate, 10 1/2" sq., Monticello patt., clear 24
Powder jar, cov., Twisted Optic patt., canary 75

Imperial Crystal Punch Bowl

Punch bowl, footed, pressed, No. 292 line, crystal, 10" d. (ILLUS.) 120
Punch set: bowl, base, ladle & twelve punch cups; Mt. Vernon patt., crystal, 15 pcs.. 135
Sherbet, low, footed, Spun patt., cobalt blue 24

Imperial Katy Blue Sugar

Sugar, open, Katy Blue patt., blue opalescent (ILLUS.) 38

Tray, No. 760, "Hazen," center-handled, pink, 10 1/2" d. **48**

Imperial Marine Lamp Tumbler

Tumbler, flat, Marine Lamp patt., ruby w/gold decoration (ILLUS.) 26
Tumbler, Windmill patt., marigold Carnival, unmarked.. 18
Urn, Snake Dance patt., pink, 8 1/2" h. 95
Vase, Hobnail patt., No. 742, flip, amber............ 38
Vase, 8 1/2" h., model of a dancing lady, red slag 120
Vase, Peachblow, cased heat sensitive red over white.. 180
Wine, Old Williamsburg patt., Azalea................. 18

Lalique

Fine glass, which includes numerous extraordinary molded articles, has been made by the glasshouse established by René Lalique early in the 20th century in France. The firm was carried on by his son, Marc, until his death in 1977 and is now headed by Marc's daughter, Marie-Claude.

All Lalique glass is marked, usually on or near the bottom, with either an engraved or molded signature. Unless otherwise noted, we list only those pieces marked "R. Lalique," produced before the death of René Lalique in 1945.

Lalique Marks

Lalique "Suzanne" Lamp

Lalique Perruches Pattern Bowl

Bowl, 9 3/4" d., "Perruches," round w/upright gently curved sides, clear & frosted opalescent molded w/a band of large parakeets, introduced in 1931 .... **$4,800**

Lamp, table model, "Suzanne," frosted opalescent molded in full relief as a nude dancer w/outstretched arms holding lengths of drapery, w/gilt-bronze base & silk shade, molded "R. Lalique," inscribed "France," ca. 1925, 8 7/8" h. (ILLUS.)..... **19,120**

Lalique Formose Pattern Vase

Large Lalique Ondines Bowl

Bowl, 12" d., "Ondines," wide shallow form w/a flat rim, molded in medium relief w/a band of swirling mermaids around the border, clear opalescent, engraved "R. LALIQUE - FRANCE," introduced in 1921 (ILLUS.)... **3,107**

Vase, 6 3/4" h., "Formose," large spherical body on a tiny footring & w/a small, short cylindrical neck, translucent white w/a pale blue tint, molded in medium and low relief w/an overall design of large Japanese goldfish w/long delicate tails & fins, retains traces of original aquamarine patina, molded mark, introduced in 1924 .... **2,040**

Domrémy & Soleils Lalique Vases

Vase, 8 1/4" h., "Domrémy," wide ovoid clear opalescent body tapering to a short wide rolled neck, molded in relief w/large round thistle heads & molded tall thistle stems, white stain, introduced in 1926, engraved signature (ILLUS. right with Soleils vase) **2,151**

Lalique Chardon Pattern Vase

Vase, 8 1/2" h., "Chardon," bulbous ovoid body tapering to a small neck w/flattened flared rim, opalescent molded in relief w/large round seed heads among serrated leaves, blue patina, signed "R. Lalique France" (ILLUS.) **3,120**

Vase, 9 1/2" h., "Soleils," swelled cylindrical form w/a wide short cylindrical neck, molded overall w/large sunbursts, clear & frosted w/a blue patina, introduced in 1936, etched mark "R. Lalique" (ILLUS. left with Domrémy Vase, top of page) **3,585**

Vase, 10" h., "Penthievre," nearly spherical body w/a small flaring neck, blue, inscribed "R. LALIQUE," introduced in 1926 (ILLUS., top next column) **19,120**

Rare Blue Penthievre Lalique Vase

Fine Blue Perruches Lalique Vase

Vase, 10" h., "Perruches," bulbous ovoid body w/a low flat mouth rim, electric blue molded w/fourteen pairs of love birds perched on flowering branches, frosted &

polished to enhance the design, signed "R. Lalique - France," introduced in 1919 (ILLUS., previous page) **11,950**

Very Rare Blue Lalique Vase

Vase, 13 1/4" h., "Lezards et Bluets," ovoid body w/a small cylindrical neck, molded in relief w/lizards & flowers, blue, molded "R. LALIQUE," inscribed "France," introduced in 1913 (ILLUS.) **28,680**

Legras

Cameo and enameled glass somewhat similar to that made by Gallé, Daum Nancy and other factories of the period was made at the Legras works in Saint Denis, France, late in the 19th century and until the outbreak of World War I.

Typical Legras Mark

Miniature Legras Cameo Bowl-Vase

Cameo bowl-vase, miniature, wide squatty bulbous form, a close-up design of deep reddish cameo-cut seaweed & greenish stems against a peach-colored ground, signed, 3 1/8" h. (ILLUS.) **$345**

Small Legras Cameo Vase

Cameo vase, 5" h., flat-based ovoid body tapering to a cylindrical cupped rim, cased in maroon & tan & cameo cut w/nasturtiums on a vine enameled in earth tones against the pinkish tan ground, tiny pin nicks inside rim, small bruise on cupped rim (ILLUS.) **259**

Tall Legras Cameo Vase

Cameo vase, 13 3/8" h., tall slender waisted form w/a flaring rim, cased & cut w/burgundy vines laden w/fruit down the sides against a frosted textured & ribbed clear ground, cameo signature & stamped mark of retailer, Ovington, New York (ILLUS.) **460**

Enameled Legras Vase with Pheasant

Vase, 11 7/8" h., simple swelled cylindrical body w/hexagonal neck, a pale pink ground finely enameled w/a scene of a golden pheasant strutting among tall fern leaves, signed in paint, small bubble on back (ILLUS.) **200-400**

Lustres

Lustres were Victorian glass vase-like decorative objects often hung around the rim with prisms. They were generally sold as matched pairs to be displayed on fireplace mantels. A wide range of colored glasswares were used in producing lustres and pieces were often highlighted with colored enameled decoration.

Cased pink, the cylindrical deep pink top bowl w/a scalloped rim raised on a slender tapering stem w/a knop above the round cushion foot, decorated overall w/pairs of enameled flower blossoms in blue & white w/green leaves, the top suspending long triangle spearpoint clear glass prisms, Bohemia, late 19th c., 14 1/2" h., pr... **$2,530**

One of Two Ornate Cranberry Lustres

Cranberry, flaring foot tapering to a very tall slender body w/a wide rolled rim ending in pointed panels, the exterior ornately decorated w/delicate gold vining florals & gold foot band, the rolled rim enameled in white w/gold trim, suspended w/large tri-

angular facet-cut prisms, Europe, late 19th c., 10" h., pr. (ILLUS. of one) **604**
Emerald green, a wide deep bowl-shaped top w/scalloped rim & heavily painted w/gold leafy scrolls & green & yellow flowerheads, raised on a tapering cylindrical pedestal w/a round cushion foot also decorated overall w/gold scrolls, clear triangular facet-cut prisms suspended from top rim supporting the bowl top, marked "Made in Germany - U.S. Zone," late 1940s - early 1950s, 14" h., pr. (shallow flake on one rim)...................... **431**

McKee

The McKee name has been associated with glass production since 1834, first producing window glass and later bottles. In the 1850s a new factory was established in Pittsburgh, Pennsylvania, for production of flint and pressed glass. The plant was relocated in Jeanette, Pennsylvania, in 1888 and operated there as an independent company almost continuously until 1951, when it sold out to Thatcher Glass Manufacturing Company. Many types of collectible glass were produced by McKee through the years including Depression, Pattern, Milk Glass and a variety of utility kitchenwares. See these categories for additional listings.

Early McKee Mark, ca. 1880

Kitchenwares
Bowl, 9" d., 5" h., flared, Red Ships patt. on white opal.. **$37**
Butter dish, cov., rectangular, Skokie Green... **85**
Coffee canister, square, press-on metal lid, Chalaine Blue.. **785**
Drawer pull, single, Chalaine Blue **28**
Egg beater bowl w/spout, Skokie Green **50**
Egg cup, Chalaine Blue **32**

McKee Skokie Green Flour Shaker

McKee Orange Slag Candleholders

Flour shaker w/original metal lid, Skokie Green (ILLUS., bottom previous page) 75

Flour shaker w/original metal top, Roman Arch style, Chalaine blue 190

Flour shaker w/original metal top, Roman Arch style, French Ivory, 4 1/4" h. 45

Flour shaker w/original metal top, Roman Arch style, Red Polka Dot patt. on French Ivory, 4 1/4" h. 65

Mixing bowl, Skokie Green, 6" d. 37

Mixing bowl, Custard w/Red Polka Dots patt., 9" d. 45

Mixing bowl, Skokie Green, 9" d. 48

Pepper shaker w/original metal top, Roman Arch style, French Ivory, 4 1/4" h. 35

Pie plate, heart-shaped, crystal 22

Reamer, marked "Sunkist," Skokie Green 75

Reamer, embossed "McK" mark, milk glass, 6" d. 38

Refrigerator water dispenser, cov., oblong, Skokie Green, faucet is stuck 260

Salt & pepper shakers, Custard w/Black Polka Dots patt., pr. 72

Skillet, handled, Range-Tec, crystal 17

Sugar shaker w/original metal top, black w/white lettering 35

Rock Crystal Pattern

Bowl, 10 1/2" d., salad, scalloped edge, pink.. 55

Candleholders, orange slag, 5" d., pr. (ILLUS., top of page)..................................... 375

Candleholders, two-light, cobalt blue, pr......... 345

Candy dish, cov., green, 7" d. 85

Celery, oblong, green, 12" l................................ 45

Cordial, crystal, 1 oz. 17

Finger bowl, plain edge, clear, 5" d. 18

Goblet, low footed, amber, 8 oz. 28

Plate, 6" d., scalloped edge, crystal 8

Plate, 10 1/2" d., dinner, large center design, scalloped edge, clear............................. 60

Relish, six-part, clear, 14" l. 65

Relish, two-part, ruby, 11 1/2" l. 90

Spooner, crystal.. 48

Sugar bowl, cov., crystal 55

Miscellaneous Patterns & Pieces

Bowl, 6" d., cereal, Laurel patt., jade green....... 32

Bowl, berry, 9" d., Laurel patt., French Ivory 25

Bulb bowl, 5 1/2" d., three-footed, jade green.. 39

Candlesticks, octagonal, rolled edge, Brocade etching, pink, pr...................................... 65

Candlesticks, one-light, Laurel patt., Poudre Blue, pr. 120

Clock, Tambour-style, blue, 14" l. 675

Creamer & open sugar, Laurel patt., Skokie Green, 4" h., pr. 90

Decanter w/stopper, lifesaver shape, pink 425

Goblet, water, Lenox patt., pink......................... 24

Brocade Etching Mayonnaise Set

Mayonnaise set: footed bowl, ladle & underplate; Brocade etching, pink, 3 pcs. (ILLUS.)... 75

Mug, Bottoms-Up patt., handled, Skokie Green.. 250

Plate, child's, 6" d., Laurel patt., French Ivory 20

Platter, 10 3/4" l., oval, Laurel patt., French Ivory 27

Tom & Jerry set: 11" d. bowl & 8 mugs; sled scene on milk glass, set 85

McKee "Jolly Golfer" Tumbler

Tumbler, "Jolly Golfer," missing cap, green,
4" h. (ILLUS.) 48
Tumbler, Laurel patt., French Ivory, 9 oz. 50
Tumbler, flat, Laurel patt., French Ivory, 12
oz., 5" h. 50
Vase, 8" h., Sarah patt., Skokie Green 95
Whiskey tumbler & base, Bottoms-Up
patt., Seville Yellow, 2 pcs. 350

Morgantown (Old Morgantown)

Morgantown, West Virginia, was the site where
a glass firm named the Morgantown Glass Works
began in the late 19th century, but the company
reorganized in 1903 to become the Economy Tum-
bler Company, a name it retained until 1929. By
the 1920s the firm was producing a wider range
of better quality and colorful glass tablewares; to
reflect this fact, it resumed its earlier name, Mor-
gantown Glass Works, in 1929. Today its many
quality wares of the Depression era are growing
in collector demand.

Bar bottle, Ruby w/silver "Rye" **$225**

Basket, No. 4357 Trindle, crimped, Spanish
Red w/clear twist applied handle, 9" 950
Basket, Clayton, Stiegle Green w/crystal
applied handle, 10" h. 550
Bowl, 10" d., El Mexicano patt., Seaweed
green 200
Bowl, 13" d., Janice patt., No. 4355, Stiegel
Green w/clear applied rim 275

Pineapple Guild Candle/Vase

Candle/vase, Guild, No. 83 Patrician, Pine-
apple (deep yellow), 8" h. (ILLUS.) 36
Candlestick, Guild, No. 9935 Barton, Moss
Green, 3 3/4" h. 15
Candlesticks, Golf Ball Jacobi patt., Span-
ish Red w/crystal stem & foot, 4" h., pr. 295
Candlesticks, 4 3/4", No. 7620 Fontanne,
Fontinelle etching, crystal w/ebony fila-
ment stem, pr. 165
Candy box, cov., Guild, No. 3033 Moon-
scape, Steel Blue 175

Morgantown Champagnes & Cocktails

Champagne, No. 7704 Harmon, Spanish Red bowl, twist stem w/red filament (ILLUS. second from right w/other champagne & two cocktails, bottom previous page) 100

Champagne, No. 7720 Palazzo, clear w/Stiegel Green filament stem (ILLUS. far right w/other champagne & two cocktails, bottom previous page) 90

Champagne, Plantation patt., Spanish Red 45

Champagne, Tinkerbell etching, Azure blue, 5 1/2 oz. 92

Champagnes, Hampton No. 7614, green Palm Optic bowl, crystal stem, set of 4 100

Claret, Old English patt., Stiegel Green, 5 oz. 50

Cocktail, amber, w/Farber chrome holder 15

Cocktail, Carlton etching, platinum Marco decoration, No. 7653, 3 1/2 oz. 35

Cocktail, dark green, w/Farber chrome holder 15

Cocktail, Golf Ball patt., cobalt bowl w/clear golf ball stem 36

Cocktail, No. 7620 Fontanne w/Fontinelle etching, clear w/Ebony filament stem (ILLUS. far left w/other cocktail & two champagnes, bottom previous page) 130

Cocktail, No. 7633 Lexington w/Fairwin etching, clear w/Ritz Blue filament stem (ILLUS. second from left w/other cocktail & two champagnes) 125

Cocktail, Superba etching, Legacy patt., No. 7654-1/2, clear 40

Cocktail, Top Hat, amethyst foot & bowl 68

Compote, 6 1/2" h., No. 7947 Mirimar, clear bowl & foot, Nanking blue stem 95

Cordial, Sunrise Medallion (Dancing Girl) etching, crystal 75

Cordial, No. 7654 1/2 Legacy, crystal w/Moonstone stem, 1 1/2 oz. 95

Cordial, Tinkerbell etching, Azure blue, 1 1/2 oz. 275

Creamer & sugar, footed, No. 7643 Golf Ball patt., Ritz Blue w/crystal stem & foot, pr. 365

Decanter & stopper, El Mexicano patt., Ice color 195

Finger bowl, footed, Virginia etching, Golden Iris 35

Goblet, Golf Ball patt., iced tea, Ritz Blue bowl w/clear golf ball stem, 6 3/4" h. 55

Goblet, Golf Ball patt., water, ruby bowl w/clear golf ball stem 55

Goblet, Majesty patt., Spanish Red 55

Goblet, No. 7634 Tiburon w/Westchester Rose cutting, water, Anna Rose color (ILLUS., top next column) 55

Goblet, Plantation patt., water, No. 8445, cobalt blue 75

Goblet, water, Queen Anne shape, Sunrise Medallion etching, crystal (ILLUS., bottom next column) 72

Hurricane lamp, Guild, No. 9923 Colonial, Peacock Blue, 8 1/2" h., 2 pc. 59

Ivy ball vase, Peacock Optic patt., No. 7643, Meadow Green w/golf ball stem, 4" d. 100

Martini mixer, Guild, 9895 1/2 Hoffman House, Steel Blue, 9" h. 35

Goblet with Westchester Rose Cutting

Queen Anne Crystal Goblet

Muddler, reeded handle, Crystal w/Stiegel Green filament 46

Pitcher, Crinkle patt., juice, amethyst 65

Pitcher, No. 7621 1/2 Corona, footed, Golden Iris, 54 oz. 175

Pitcher, Guild, No. 3000 Festival, amber, 64 oz. 85

Plate, 7 1/2" d., American Beauty etching, Anna Rose pink 17

Plate, 7 1/2" d., Queen Louise silkscreen decoration, crystal **165**
Plate, 8" d., El Mexicano patt., Seaweed color **25**
Sherbet, Golf Ball patt., amethyst bowl w/clear golf ball stem...................................... **30**
Sherbet, Golf Ball patt., low, ruby bowl w/clear golf ball stem...................................... **35**
Sherbet, Golf Ball patt., smoke bowl w/clear golf ball stem.. **30**
Sherbet & underplate, Golf Ball patt., Ritz Blue, Platinum Vernay band, 2 pcs. **95**
Stack jar, four-part, Guild, No. 9949 Christmas Tree, crystal.. **125**
Tumbler, Crinkle patt., juice, amethyst, 6 oz. **10**
Tumbler, Golf Ball patt., juice, footed, ruby bowl w/clear golf ball stem **40**
Tumbler, Golf Ball patt., Stiegel Green w/clear golf ball stem, 12 oz......................... **48**
Tumbler, flat, No. 7619 Arena, Spanish Red, 4" h. **18**
Tumbler, flat, juice, Guild, No. 9844 Swirl, amethyst, 6 oz.. **8**
Tumbler, 19th Hole On-the-Rocks patt., white opaque bowl w/green foot, 11 oz......... **75**
Tumbler, footed, No. 20069 Melon, Alabaster w/Ritz Blue foot, 12 oz. **135**
Vase, 5" h., Guild, No. 1962 Santiago, Gloria Blue **47**

Golf Ball Pattern Vase

Vase, 6 1/2 h"., Golf Ball patt., Kimball, Stiegel Green (ILLUS.).. **75**
Vase, 7" h., flip-type, Snowball El Mexicano patt., Ice color.. **125**
Vase, 10" h., Guild, Freeform, Amberina.......... **110**
Vase, 12 1/2" h., No. 88 Romana, Old Amethyst w/clear twist applied handles (ILLUS., top next column) **1,500**
Vase, 12 1/2" h., No. 88 Romana, Old Amethyst w/crystal applied handles **1,200**
Wine, American Beauty etching, No. 7565, clear, 2 oz.. **45**

No. 88 Romana Handled Vase

Wine, Golf Ball patt., No. 7643, crystal w/clear golf ball stem, 3 oz............................ **30**
Wine, Golf Club patt., ruby bowl w/clear golf ball stem.. **45**

Moser

Ludwig Moser opened his first glass shop in 1857 in Karlsbad, Bohemia (now Karlovy Vary, in the former Czechoslovakia). Here he engraved and decorated fine glasswares especially to appeal to rich visitors to the local health spa. Later other shops were opened in various cities. Throughout the 19th and early 20th century lovely, colorful glasswares, many beautifully enameled, were produced by Moser's shops and reached a wide market in Europe and America. Moser died in 1916 and the firm continued under his sons. They were forced to merge with the Meyer's Nephews glass factory after World War I. The glassworks were sold out of the Moser family in 1933.

Small Cranberry Moser Bowl

Bowl, 2 5/8" h., an oblong cranberry form w/a flaring & pointed-crimp rim, an applied gold-painted clear branch handle at one end, raised on four heavy pointed gilt-trimmed root-form feet, the interior decorated w/a gold vine enameled w/strawberries & florets, minor gilt loss (ILLUS.)... **$374**

Long Finely Engraved Amethyst to Clear Signed Moser Bowl

Moser Decorated Amethyst Bowl

Rare Moser Animor Series Cameo Vase

Large Ornate Moser Chalice

Bowl, 8 3/4" d., 3 5/8" h., wide flat bottom w/shallow rounded sides w/a flat rim, light amethyst w/optic-ribbed design, decorated on the exterior w/gilded sprigs of moss w/enameled florets & three butterflies, the interior w/a brown enameled beetle crawling on a mossy sprig, minimal gold wear (ILLUS.) **345**

Bowl, 15 1/2" l., 5" h., long oblong form w/optic-ribbed sides tapering slightly to a flat rim, amethyst shaded to clear, the sides engraved w/large blossoms & buds, fine acid-etched signature, barely visible bruise on rim (ILLUS., top of page) **805**

Cameo vase, African Safari patt. from the "Animor" series, ovoid body tapering to a ringed neck w/flared rim, a chartreuse textured ground cased in garnet red & cameo cut around the sides w/a pair of reticulated giraffes, a rhinoceros, a grazing water buffalo, all beneath several palm trees & flying birds, upper & lower red rings, all accented w/gold, signed in the gilded grass "Moser Karlsbad" & the artists' initials "R.W." & "LMK" (ILLUS., next column) **5,520**

Chalice, a round flat-topped rainbow diamond-quilted bowl enameled w/delicate gold leafy vines, supported on two gilt squatty knops above the tall flaring clear ringed pedestal stem trimmed in gold, signed, minimal wear, 8 1/8" h. (ILLUS., bottom of previous page) **575**

Moser Egg-shaped Decorative Vase

Vase, 5" h., the ovoid egg-shaped optic-ribbed body w/a five-crimp rim & raised on three gilt peg feet, in pale teal shaded to clear & ornately decorated overall w/gold scrolls & floral vines, minimal wear (ILLUS.) **460**

Very Ornate Moser Fan-shaped Vase

Vase, 6" h., fan-shaped, three applied gilded scroll feet supporting a round ball below the tall flattened & fanned sides, pale teal ornately enameled overall w/vines & stylized flowers attracting butterflies, design continuing on the ball-form base, minuscule rim nicks (ILLUS.) **633**

Moser Vase with Enameled Maiden

Vase, 7 1/2" h., squatty bulbous optic-ribbed base below the cylindrical sides opening to a widely flaring & crimped rim w/up-turned back, amethyst w/an applied clear rim band, decorated in colored enamels on the side w/a portrait of a maiden against a stenciled background, executed in Theodore Rossler's enamel "color cake" technique, late 19th c. (ILLUS.) **196**

Vase, 9 1/2" h., a deep amber swelled cylindrical form w/flaring rim, deeply etched w/repeated design of large Art Deco scrolled leaves below a cluster of tall sword-shaped leaves alternating w/large petaled blossoms, signed "Moser M.M.," ca. 1925 (shallow flake on base) **575**

Tall Moser Vase with Irises

Vase, 12 7/8" h., three clear applied stylized figural salamander feet supporting the flared base tapering to the tall cylindrical optic-ribbed body, deep amethyst shading to clear, enameled w/large yellow & purple irises above tall leafy green stems, trimmed in gold, tiny chips on feet & rim (ILLUS.) **374**

Nash

A. Douglas Nash, a former employee of Louis Comfort Tiffany, purchased Tiffany's Corona Works in December 1928 and began his own operation there. For a brief period Nash produced some outstanding glasswares, but the factory closed in March of 1931 and Nash then became associated with Libbey Glass of Toledo, Ohio. This quality glass is quite scarce.

Tumbler, Chintz patt., a flaring trumpet-form bowl in striped green & amethyst glass applied to a clear knob & round foot, signed on pontil, ca. 1930, 6 1/2" h. **$161**

Deep Red Nash Vase with Silvery Blue

Vase, 4 1/8" h., footed swelled cylindrical body w/a trumpet neck in deep scarlet red w/a silvery blue zipper design accenting ten spiral ribs, attributed to Libbey Nash (ILLUS.) **345**

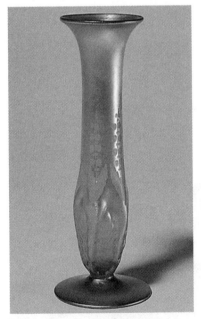

Slender Gold Iridescent Nash Vase

Vase, 8 1/8" h., footed tall very slender cylindrical body w/a flaring mouth, iridescent gold ground engraved w/delicate

lily-of-the-valley blossoms up the sides, engraved mark "Nash - 568 - C-1" (ILLUS.) **690**

New Martinsville

The New Martinsville Glass Mfg. Co. opened in New Martinsville, West Virginia, in 1901 and during its first period of production came out with a number of colored opaque pressed glass patterns. Also developed was an art glass line named "Muranese," which collectors refer to as "New Martinsville Peach Blow." The factory burned in 1907 but reopened later that year and began focusing on production of various clear pressed glass patterns, many of which were then decorated with gold or ruby staining or enameled decoration. After going through receivership in 1937, the factory again changed the focus of its production to more contemporary glass lines and figural animals. The firm was purchased in 1944 by The Viking Glass Company (later Dalzell-Viking).

Basket, four-footed, Janice patt., light blue, 9" h. **$175**
Basket, No. 132 square, crystal, 14" h. **52**
Batter set: cov. batter jug, cov. syrup, handled rectangular tray; amethyst, 5 pcs. **425**
Bitters bottle, No. 38, ruby **85**
Book ends, Clipper Ship patt., No. 499, clear, 5 3/4" h., pr. **80**
Bowl, 6 3/4" d., Moondrops patt., soup, red **90**

Moondrops Bowl in Evergreen

Bowl, 9 1/2" d., Moondrops patt., crimped sides, three feet, Evergreen (ILLUS.) **55**
Bowl, 10" d., crimped, Radiance patt., ruby **60**
Bowl, 10" d., Emerald Glo, salad, star cut **35**
Bowl, 11" oval, Janice patt., No. 4551-2SJ, two swan handles, red **125**

New Martinsville Janice Pattern Bowl

Bowl, 11 1/2" l., oval, Janice patt., blue (ILLUS.) **70**
Butter, cov., oval, Prelude etching, clear, 6 1/2" l. **65**

No. 38 Creamer & Open Sugar

Addie Candlestick with Lions Etching

Candlestick, No. 34 Addie patt. w/Lions etching, pink, 3" h. (ILLUS.) **35**

Candy box, cov., Janice patt., crystal w/cobalt blue swan neck & head, 5 1/2" d. **100**

Casserole, cov., oval, Moondrops patt., dark green **135**

Celery, oblong, Janice patt., crystal, 11" l. **18**

Cigarette holder, saucer foot, No. 149/2, blue, h.p. flowers.. **60**

Cocktail shaker, chrome lid, No. 125, No. 25 Brocade etching, crystal........................... **89**

Condiment set: three jars w/metal lids, spoons & tray; Emerald Glo, star cut, the set **85**

Creamer, Carnation patt. (No. 88 Line), clear w/ruby-stain & gold decoration............ **125**

Creamer & open sugar, low footed, Janice pattern, ruby, pr... **45**

Creamer & open sugar, No. 34 Addie, cobalt blue, pr. **48**

Creamer & open sugar, No. 38, amber, pr. (ILLUS., top of page)..................................... **28**

Creamer & sugar bowl, Moondrops patt. (No. 37 Line), amber, pr. **22**

Creamer & sugar bowl w/tray, Janice patt. (No. 45 Line), individual, light blue, the set **80**

Cup & saucer, No. 35 Fancy Squares patt., unknown etching, crystal cup, black saucer (ILLUS. top right with other Fancy Squares pieces, bottom of page).................. **22**

Decanter & stopper, Moondrops patt., dark green, 8 3/4" h. **78**

Decanter w/fan stopper, No. 24 Ribbon etching, amber **135**

Fancy Squares Pieces

Hand-painted Dresser Set

Dresser set: two perfume bottles w/original stoppers & powder box on rectangular tray; green w/h.p. floral decoration, the set (ILLUS.)... 275

Dresser set: two-footed colognes & stoppers, one flat powder box & lid; green, set 147

Guest set: cov., pitcher & flat tumbler on rectangular tray; blue, 4 pcs....................... 165

Ice tub, tab handles, No. 38, cobalt blue............ 95

Luncheon set: Newport patt., four each 8" plates & cups & saucers, one creamer & sugar, dark green, 14 pcs. 145

Mayonnaise set, three-piece, Radiance patt., light blue, set...................................... 120

Night lamp, miniature, By-the-Sea patt., opaque pink.................................... 425

Pitcher, 9 1/2" h., Oscar patt., flat, ruby............. 95

Plate, 8" w., No. 35 Fancy Squares patt., unknown etching, black (ILLUS. lower right with Fancy Squares cup & saucer) 22

Plate, 8 1/2" d., Moondrops patt., amber............ 12

Plate, 10" w., handled, No. 35 Fancy Squares patt., unknown etching, black (ILLUS. left with Fancy Squares cup & saucer & other plate)..................................... 48

Plate, 13 1/2" d., Newport patt., ruby 58

Platter, 13" oval, Janice patt., blue 95

Punch bowl, 9" d., Janice patt., emerald green.. 135

Punch cup, Radiance patt., cobalt blue............. 18

Salt & pepper shakers, Radiance patt., light blue, pr... 98

Sandwich tray, No. 35 (Fancy Squares), jade green.. 80

Sherbet, footed, No. 34 Addie, jade.................. 17

Sherbet, Moondrops patt., red, 4 1/2" h............. 30

New Martinsville Smoking Set

Smoking set, two ashtrays & cigarette pack holder on rectangular tray, amethyst, the set (ILLUS.).. 175

Syrup jug & lid, amber...................................... 55

Tray, two-handled rectangular, Moondrops patt., cobalt blue, 15" l. 95

Tumbler, Klear-Kut (No. 705 Line), clear w/ruby-stain... 85

Tumbler, Rock Crystal patt. (No. 49 Line), water, overall gold decorated....................... 45

Tumbler, Moondrops patt., whiskey, red, 1 3/4" h.. 22

Tumbler, Moondrops patt., red, 3 1/4" h., 3 oz. 20

Tumbler, flat, No. 36 Oscar, ruby, 9 oz............. 18

Tumbler, footed, No. 34 Addie, ruby, 9 oz........ 16

Black Modernistic Vase

Vase, Modernistic patt. (No. 33 Line), black (ILLUS.)... 100

Vase, 6" h., cornucopia-style, No. 650, crystal 45

Vase, 10" h., crimped top, ruby 135

Vase, 10" h., Meadow Wreath etching, crimped, clear 60

Northwood

Harry Northwood (1860-1919) was born in England, the son of noted glass artist John Northwood. Brought up in the glass business, Harry immigrated to the United States in 1881 and shortly thereafter became manager of the La Belle Glass Company, Bridgeport, Ohio. Here he was responsible for many innovations in colored and blown glass. After leaving La Belle in 1887 he opened The Northwood Glass Company in Martins Ferry, Ohio, in 1888. The company moved to Ellwood City, Pennsylvania, in 1892 and Northwood moved again to take over a glass plant in Indiana, Pennsylvania, in 1896. One of his major lines made at the Indiana, Pennsylvania, plant was Custard glass (which he called "ivory"). It was made in several patterns, and some pieces were marked on the base with "Northwood" in script.

Harry and his family moved back to England in 1899 but returned to the U.S. in 1902 at which time he opened another glass factory, in Wheel-

ing, West Virginia. Here he was able to put his full talents to work; under his guidance the firm manufactured many notable glass lines including opalescent wares, colored and clear pressed tablewares, various novelties and, probably best known of all, Carnival glass. Around 1906 Harry introduced his famous "N"-in-circle trademark, which can be found on the base of many, but not all, pieces made at his factory. The factory closed in 1925.

In this listing we are including only the clear and colored tablewares produced at Northwood factories. Dr. James Measell, Marietta, Ohio

Northwood

Northwood Signature Mark, ca. 1898¶Northwood "N" in Circle Mark, ca. 1906

Leaf Mold Satin Spatter Toothpick Holder

Toothpick holder, Leaf Mold patt., red & white spatter w/mica flecks, satin finish, polished rim w/tiny pin nicks, 1 7/8" h. (ILLUS.) **$127**
Tumbler, Leaf Umbrella patt., cranberry (poorly polished rim) 45
Tumbler, Netted Oak patt., opaque white w/pink, green & goofus decoration 50
Tumbler, Panelled Sprig patt., opaque white w/green, brown & gilt decoration 50
Tumbler, Parian Swirl patt., pink satin cased 70

Paden City

The Paden City Glass Manufacturing Company began operations in Paden City, West Virginia, in 1916, primarily as a supplier of blanks to other companies. All wares were handmade, that is, either hand-pressed or mold-blown. The early products were not particularly noteworthy, but by the early 1930s the quality had improved considerably. The firm continued to turn out high quality glassware in a variety of beautiful colors until financial difficulties necessitated its closing in 1951. Over the years the firm produced, in addition to tablewares, items for hotel and restaurant use, light shades, shaving mugs, perfume bottles and lamps.

Bowl, cream soup, two-handled, Crow's Foot patt., ruby $24
Bowl, 5" d., Gadroon patt., cream soup, #330, red 30
Bowl, 10 1/4" d., Orchid etching, two-handled, red 250
Bowl, 11" d., footed, Mrs. "B" line, yellow 35
Bowl, 11 3/4" d., Black Forest etching, rolled edge, pink 185
Cake plate, Cupid etching, footed, pink, 11 1/4" d. 180
Cake salver, Regina, No. 210 line, clear 40
Cakestand, Cupid etching, pink, 2" h. 175

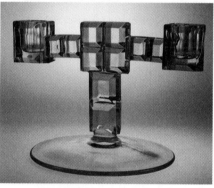

No. 2000 Mystic Candlestick

Candlestick, two-light, No. 2000 Mystic, light blue (ILLUS.) 75
Candlesticks, two-light, Crow's Foot (No. 890) line, round, red, pr................................ 180
Candlesticks, Crows Foot patt., square, Orchid etching, ruby, 5 3/4" h., pr. 200
Candlesticks, Nerva patt., crystal, 6" h., pr. (ILLUS., top next page) 45
Candy dish, cov., flat, Nora Bird etching, green, 7" d. 270
Candy dish, cov., heart-shaped, three-part, No. 555, clear... 50
Cheese & cracker set: 10" d. plate & 5" d. stand; Ardith etching, yellow, the set 145
Cheese plate, Lela Bird etching, green, 10 1/2" d... 95
Cocktail shaker, footed, chrome lid, Party Line patt., green 75
Compote, 6 5/8" d., Crow's Foot (No. 412) line, Orchid etching, yellow 110
Compote, 10" d., Maya patt., light blue 65

Crow's Foot Pattern Creamer

Nerva Pattern Candlesticks

Creamer, Crow's Foot patt., milk glass, w/silver overlay (ILLUS., previous page)........ **65**

Creamer, No. 412 Crow's Foot patt., opal w/silver overlay... **75**

Creamer & open sugar bowl, Black Forest etching, green, pr. **145**

Creamer & open sugar bowl, No. 210, Black Forest etching, black, pr. **145**

Cup, Futura patt., No. 836 line, cobalt blue........ **20**

Cup & saucer, Crow's Foot (No. 412) line, red, pr. **25**

Popeye & Olive Decanter with Stopper

Decanter w/stopper, Popeye & Olive patt., ruby w/silver overlay, crystal shot glass stopper (ILLUS.).. **245**

Goblet, water, low foot, Penny Line patt., pink, 9 oz.. **14**

Gravy boat, flat w/two spouts, Crow's Foot patt., ruby.. **89**

Ice bucket, metal handle, Peacock & Wild Rose etching, pink **250**

Ice tub, tab handle, Cupid etching, pink.......... **325**

Ivy ball, footed, Ardith etching, yellow **78**

Mayonnaise dish, Peacock & Rose etching, pink... **85**

Mayonnaise set: Orchid etching, yellow, 3 pcs. **77**

Plate, 6" d., Party Line patt., pink........................ **5**

Plate, 8" d., Crow's Foot patt., cobalt blue **18**

Plate, 9 1/2" d., Gadroon patt., ruby (ILLUS. left with sherbet, top next page).................... **25**

Plate, 10" sq., Orchid etching, handled, red..... **140**

Plate, 10 1/2" d., Cupid etching, green **130**

Plate, 16" d., beaded edge, Gazebo etching, light blue.. **95**

Salt & pepper shakers, flat, Penny Line patt., ruby, pr... **65**

Paden City Swan-necked Server

Server, swan-necked center handle, Gazebo etching, Line 1504, clear, 10" d. (ILLUS.)... **75**

Sherbet, No. 994 "Popeye & Olive," tall, cobalt blue **28**

Sherbet, Gadroon patt., ruby, 4" h. (ILLUS. right with plate)... **24**

Sugar shaker w/metal lid, Party Line patt., pink **175**

Ruby Gadroon Pattern Plate & Sherbet

Syrup w/metal lid, Party Line patt., green,
8 oz. **65**
Tray, center-handled, Ardith etching, cobalt
blue, 10" sq. **265**
Tray, center-handled, "Mrs. B" (No. 411)
line, Ardith etching, yellow............................. **75**
Tumbler, cone-shaped, footed, Party Line
(No. 191) line, pink, 5 3/4" h.......................... **12**

Pink Party Line Tumbler

Tumbler, footed, Party Line patt., pink, 12
oz. (ILLUS.) **15**
Vase, 7" h., footed fan shape, Party Line
patt., green.. **38**
Vase, 10" h., cupped, Crow's Foot patt., co-
balt blue.. **155**
Vase, 10" h., Lela Bird etching, green **185**
Vase, 10" h., Peacock & Rose etching, pink **245**

Pattern

Though it has never been ascertained whether glass was first pressed in the United States or abroad, the development of the glass pressing machine revolutionized the glass industry in the United States, and this country receives the credit for improving the method to make this process feasible. The first wares pressed were probably small flat plates of the type now referred to as "lacy," the intricacy of the design concealing flaws.

In 1827, both the New England Glass Co., Cambridge, Mass., and Bakewell & Co., Pittsburgh, took out patents for pressing glass furniture knobs; soon other pieces followed. This early pressed glass contained red lead, which made it clear and resonant when tapped (flint.) Made primarily in clear, it is rarer in blue, amethyst, olive green and yellow.

By the 1840s, early simple patterns such as Ashburton, Argus and Excelsior appeared. Ribbed Bellflower seems to have been one of the earliest patterns to have had complete sets. By the 1860s, a wide range of patterns was available.

In 1864, William Leighton of Hobbs, Brockunier & Co., Wheeling, West Virginia, developed a formula for "soda lime" glass that did not require the expensive red lead for clarity. Although "soda lime" glass did not have the brilliance of the earlier flint glass, the formula came into widespread use because glass could be produced cheaply.

An asterisk (*) indicates a piece which has been reproduced.

ADONIS (Pleat & Tuck or Washboard)
Bowl, 8 1/2" d., master berry, blue.................. **$40**
Bowl, 8 1/2" d., master berry, canary yellow **40**
Bowl, 8 1/2" d., master berry, green **40**
Bowl, 8 12/" d., master berry, clear.................... **25**
Cake stand, blue, 9" d. **85**
Cake stand, canary yellow, 9" d. **85**
Cake stand, clear, 9" d. **55**

Cake stand, green, 9" d. 85
Cake stand, 11" d., blue 95
Cake stand, 11" d., canary yellow 95
Cake stand, 11" d., clear 75
Cake stand, 11" d., green 95
Celery, blue 65
Celery, canary yellow 65
Celery, clear 40
Celery, green 65
Compote, open, jelly, blue, 4 1/2" d. 45
Compote, open, jelly, canary yellow,
  4 1/2" d. 45
Compote, open, jelly, clear, 4 1/2" d. 30
Compote, open, jelly, green, 4 1/2" d. 45
Compote, cov., blue, 6" d. 90
Compote, cov., canary yellow, 6" d. 90
Compote, cov., clear, 6" d. 65
Compote, cov., green, 6" d. 90
Compote, cov., blue, 7" d. 100
Compote, cov., canary yellow, 7" d. 100
Compote, cov., clear, 7" d. 85
Compote, cov., green, 7" d. 100
Compote, cov., 8" d., blue 110
Compote, cov., 8" d., canary yellow 110
Compote, cov., 8" d., clear 85
Compote, cov., green, 8" d. 110
Creamer, blue 75
Creamer, canary yellow 75
Creamer, clear 35
Creamer, green 75
Pitcher, milk, blue 100
Pitcher, milk, canary yellow 100
Pitcher, milk, clear 55
Pitcher, milk, green 90
Pitcher, water, blue 120
Pitcher, water, canary yellow 120
Pitcher, water, clear 65
Pitcher, water, green 100
Plate, 10" d., blue 65
Plate, 10" d., clear 35
Plate, 10" d., canary yellow 65
Plate, 10" d., green 65
Relish dish, blue 35
Relish dish, canary yellow 35
Relish dish, clear 24
Relish dish, green 35
Salt shaker w/original top, blue 30
Salt shaker w/original top, canary yellow 30
Salt shaker w/original top, clear 20
Salt shaker w/original top, green 30
Sauce dish, blue 18
Sauce dish, canary yellow 18
Sauce dish, clear 12
Sauce dish, green 18
Spooner, blue 60
Spooner, canary yellow 60
Spooner, clear 35
Spooner, green 60
Sugar bowl, cov., blue 85
Sugar bowl, cov., canary yellow 85
Sugar bowl, cov., clear 45
Sugar bowl, cov., green 85
Syrup pitcher, clear 95
Vase, on silver plate foot, clear, 8 1/2" h. 75

AMBERETTE - see Klondike Pattern

APOLLO
Bowl, 5" d. 15

Bowl, 6" d. 20
Bowl, 7" d. 25
Bowl, 8" d. 30
Bowl, 10 1/2" d., salad 65
Butter dish, cov., flanged rim 80
Butter dish, cov., plain rim 50
Cake stand, 8" d. 65
Cake stand, plain, 9" to 10 1/2" d. 75
Cake stand, 10" d. 90
Celery tray 24
Celery vase 55
Compote, open, 6" d. 45
Compote, cov., 6" d. 65
Compote, cov., 7" d. 75
Compote, cov., 8" d., 8" h. 95
Compote, open, square w/vertical pattern,
  rare 225
Compote, open, 5" d. 35
Compote, open, 7" d. 55
Compote, open, 8" d., 8" h. 70
Creamer, plain 50
Cruet w/original stopper, frosted 110
Cruet w/original stopper, plain 65
Goblet, engraved 45
Goblet, frosted 45
Goblet, plain 35
Lamp, kerosene-type, clear, 7" h. 75
Lamp, kerosene-type, blue, 8" h. 185
Lamp, kerosene-type, clear, 8" h. 85
Lamp, kerosene-type, amber, 9" h. 195
Lamp, kerosene-type, blue, 9" h. 195
Lamp, kerosene-type, canary yellow, 9" h. 195
Lamp, kerosene-type, clear, 9" h. 95
Lamp, kerosene-type, amber, 10" h. 205
Lamp, kerosene-type, blue, 10" h. 205
Lamp, kerosene-type, canary yellow, 10" h. 205
Lamp, kerosene-type, clear, 10" h. 105
Pitcher, milk 55
Pitcher, water, bulbous 75-85
Plate, 9 1/2" sq. 25
Salt dip, master size 35
Salt shaker 35
Sauce dish, flat or footed 20
Spooner 35
Sugar bowl, cov. 65
Sugar shaker w/original top 75
Syrup pitcher w/original top 90
Tray, water, sq. 75

AURORA (Diamond Horseshoe)
Bowl, 7" 20
Bowl, 8" d. 30
Cake stand, 8" d. 75
Cake stand, 9" d. 85
Celery vase 35
Compote, open, 6" d. 90
Compote, open, 7" d. 110
Creamer 35
Decanter w/original stopper, clear 75
Decanter w/original stopper, ruby-stained 150
Goblet 55
Mug, applied handle 40
Pickle dish, horseshoe-shaped 25
Pitcher, milk, tankard, 9 1/2" h. 55
Pitcher, water, tankard, 12" h. 90
Relish, oval, 4 x 7" 25
Salt shaker w/original top 30
Tray, water 45
Tray, wine, clear, 10" d. 30
Tray, wine, ruby-stained, 10" d. 85

Tumbler 30
Wine, clear 35
Wine, ruby-stained 55

BALTIMORE PEAR
Bowl, 7" d., open, flat 60
Bowl, cov., 7" d. 75
Bowl, 8" d., open, flat 70
Bowl, cov., 8" d. 85
*Butter dish, cov. 85
*Cake stand, high pedestal, octagonal,
   9" d. 95
*Celery vase 90
Compote, open, 6" d. 60
Compote, open, 7" d. 70
Compote, open, 8" d. 80
Compote, cov., 7" d., high stand 75
Compote, cov., 8" d., low stand 40
Compote, open, jelly, 5" d. 45
*Creamer 65
*Goblet 45
*Pitcher, milk 65
*Pitcher, water 145
*Plate, 9 1/2" d. 55
*Plate, 10" d. 30
Relish, 4 x 8" l. 38
*Sauce dish, flat 25
*Sauce dish, footed 35
Spooner 50
*Sugar bowl, cov. 75
Tray, water, round, no handles, scarce 95

BANDED PORTLAND (Portland w/Diamond Point Band, Virginia (States series), Portland Maiden Blush (when pink-stained)
Bowl, 6" d., berry 25
Bowl, 7" d., berry 35
Bowl, 8" d., berry 45
Bowl, 9" d., berry 55
Bowl, 9" d., berry, pink-stained 110
Butter dish, cov., clear 65
Butter dish, cov., pink-stained 200
Candlestick, blue-stained, 9" h. 175
Candlestick, clear, 9" h. 135
Candlestick, yellow-stained, 9" h. 175
Carafe, water, clear 110
Carafe, water, pink-stained 350
Celery tray, clear 40
Celery tray, pink-stained 80
Celery vase, clear 55
Celery vase, pink-stained 125
Cologne bottle w/original stopper, clear,
   large size 85
Cologne bottle w/original stopper, clear,
   pink-stained, large size 215
Cologne bottle w/original stopper, clear,
   pink-stained, small size 140
Cologne bottle w/original stopper, clear,
   small size 55
Compote, cov., jelly, 6" d. 55
Compote, open, jelly, 6" d. 30
Compote, cov., high stand, 7" d. 95
Compote, open, 7" d. 40
Compote, cov., high stand, 8" d. 105
Compote, open, scalloped rim, 8 1/4" d.,
   8" h. 50
Compote, open, high stand, 10" d. 75
Creamer, clear 45
Creamer, oval individual size, clear 25

Creamer, oval individual size, pink-stained 40
Creamer, pink-stained 95
Creamer, toy tankard-style, clear 35
Creamer, toy tankard-style, pink-stained 55
Cruet w/original stopper, clear 60
Cruet w/original stopper, large size, pink-
   stained 395
Cruet w/original stopper, regular size,
   pink-stained 185
Dresser jar, cov., clear, 3 1/2" d. 40
Dresser jar, cov., pink-stained, 3 1/2" d. 85
Dresser tray, clear 85
Goblet, clear 45
Goblet, pink-stained 75
Pin tray, oval, clear, souvenir-type 15
Pin tray, oval, pink-stained, souvenir-type 35
Pitcher, water, clear, 9 1/2" h. 95
Pitcher, water, pink-stained, 9 1/2" h. 225
Punch bowl, footed, clear 250
Punch cup, clear 15
Punch cup, pink-stained 35
Relish, olive, clear, 4 x 6 1/2" 20
Relish, olive, clear, 4 x 8 1/2" 25
Relish, olive, pink-stained, 4 x 6 1/2" 35
Relish, olive, pink-stained, 4 x 8 1/2" 40
Ring tree, gold-painted 95
Ring tree, pink-stained 190
Salt shaker w/original top, clear 25
Salt shaker w/original top, pink-stained 50
Sardine dish, cov., rare 110
Sauce dish, boat-shaped, clear, 4 3/4" l. 20
Sauce dish, boat-shaped, pink-stained,
   4 3/4" l. 30
Sauce dish, round or square, clear, 4 1/2" 20
Sauce dish, round or square, pink-stained,
   4 1/2" 30
Spooner, clear 35
Spooner, pink-stained 75
Sugar bowl, cov., clear 55
Sugar bowl, cov., pink-stained 110
Sugar bowl, open, individual size, clear 25
Sugar bowl, open, individual size, pink-
   stained 40
Sugar shaker w/original top, clear 65
Sugar shaker w/original top, pink-stained 200
Syrup pitcher w/original top, clear 90
Syrup pitcher w/original top, pink-stained 350
Toothpick holder, clear 35
Toothpick holder, pink-stained 80
Tumbler, clear 35
Tumbler, pink-stained 70
Vase, 6" h., clear 20
Vase, 6" h., pink-stained 40
Vase, 9" h., clear 35
Vase, 9" h., pink-stained 55
Vase, 10" h., pink-stained 45
Wine, clear 30
Wine, pink-stained 65

INDIANA
Bowl, 8" d. 35
Bowl, 6" d. 20
Butter dish, cov. 75
Celery tray 45
Creamer 40
Cruet w/original stopper 35
Olive dish, round, handled 25
Pitcher, water 75
Relish dish 30
Salt shaker w/original top 30

Sauce dish 24
Spooner 35
Sugar bowl, cov. 45
Tumbler 30

JEWEL & DEWDROP - see Kansas Pattern

KANSAS (Jewel & Dewdrop)

Banana stand, plate w/rolled-up side 65
Banana stand, two rolled-up sides, high
    stand 110
Bowl, cov., 6 1/2" d. 65
Bowl, open, 6 1/2" d. 30
Bowl, cov., 7 1/2" d. 75
Bowl, open, 7 1/2" d. 40
Bowl, cov., 8 1/2" d. 90
Bowl, open, 8 1/2" d. 55
Bread tray, "Our Daily Bread," 10 1/2" oval 70
Butter dish, cov. 110
Cake stand, 8" d. 65
Cake stand, 9" d. 85
Cake stand, 10" d. 115
Cake tray, "Cake Plate," 10 1/2" oval 95
Celery vase 95
Compote, open, 6" d. 45
Compote, open, 9 1/2" d., saucer-shaped,
    low stand 75
Compote, cov., 6" d., high stand 75
Compote, cov., 7" d., high stand 95
Compote, cov., 8" d., high stand 145
Compote, open, jelly, 5" d. 35
Compote, open, 7" d., high stand 65
Compote, open, 7" d., low stand 55
Compote, open, 8" d., low stand 65
Compote, open, 8" d., high stand 75
Creamer 75
Goblet, clear 125

Goblet, grey version 85
Mug, small, 3 1/2" h. 25
Mug, large 65
Pickle dish 35
Pitcher, milk 155
Pitcher, water 85
Relish, 8 1/2" oval 35
Salt shaker w/original top 50
Sauce dish, 4" d. 18
Spooner 75
Sugar bowl, cov. 125
Syrup jug w/original top 225
Toothpick holder 75
Tumbler, water, footed 75
Whiskey tumbler, handled 35
Wine, clear 95

KLONDIKE (Amberette or English Hobnail Cross)

Bowl, 7 1/4" sq., scalloped top, clear w/amber cross (ILLUS. front row, second from
    left with other Klondike pieces, bottom of
    page) 125-175
Bowl, oval, 9 1/4" l., frosted w/amber cross
    (ILLUS. back row, second from right with
    other Klondike pieces, bottom of page) 100-200
Butter dish, cov., frosted w/amber cross
    (ILLUS. front row, second from right with
    other Klondike pieces, bottom of page)
    450-475
Celery vase, frosted w/amber cross (ILLUS.
    top row, far right with other Klondike pieces, bottom of page) 115
Condiment set: tray, cruet, salt & pepper
    shakers & toothpick holder; frosted
    w/amber cross, 4 pcs. (ILLUS. top row,
    second from left with other Klondike pieces, bottom of page) 1,035

Large Grouping of Klondike Pattern Pieces

Square Klondike Water Pitcher

Pitcher, water, square, frosted w/amber cross, 9" h. (ILLUS.) **748**

Pitcher, water, round, tankard type, applied handle, frosted w/amber cross, 10" h. (ILLUS. top row, far left with other Klondike pieces) **1,093**

Punch cups, frosted w/amber cross, set of 5 (ILLUS. bottom row, far right with other Klondike pieces).................................... **400-600**

Vase, 8" h., trumpet-shaped, frosted w/amber cross (ILLUS. bottom row, far left with other Klondike pieces).................................. **259**

PLEAT & TUCK - See Adonis Pattern

U.S. Coin

*Bread tray, frosted dollars & half dollars, 7 x 10" (ILLUS. middle row, second from right with other U.S. Coin pieces, bottom of page).. **748**

Butter dish, cov., frosted dollars & half dollars (ILLUS. front row, far left with other U.S. Coin pieces, bottom of page)............... **518**

Cake stand, frosted dollars, 10" d. (ILLUS. back row, far right with other U.S. Coin pieces, bottom of page) **518**

Celery vase & spooner, frosted quarters on each, the two pieces (ILLUS. center row, third from left with other U.S. Coin pieces, bottom of page) **633**

*Compote, cov., 6" d., high stand, frosted dimes & quarters (ILLUS. back row, far left with other U.S. Coin pieces, bottom of page).. **748**

Compote, cov., 7" d., high stand, frosted dimes & quarters (ILLUS. back row, second from right with other U.S. Coin pieces, bottom of page)..................................... **633**

Compote, cov., 8" d., high stand, frosted quarters & half dollars (ILLUS. back row, second from left with other U.S. Coin pieces, bottom of page) **748**

Compote, open, 8 1/4" d., high stand, straight rim, frosted quarters & dimes (ILLUS. middle row, far right with other U.S. Coin pieces, bottom of page)............. **518**

Lamp, kerosene-type, round font, clear dollars, 11 1/2" h. (ILLUS. back row, third from left with other U.S. Coin pieces, bottom of page).. **978**

Pickle dish, frosted half dollars, very minor flakes, 3 3/4 x 7 1/2" (ILLUS. front row, second from left with other U.S. Coin pieces, bottom of page) **230**

Pitcher, milk, frosted half dollars, 8 1/2" h. (ILLUS. middle row, far left with other pieces of U.S. Coin, bottom of page).......... **978**

Large Grouping of U.S. Coin Pieces

Grouping of Westward Ho Pieces

Sauce dish, flat, plain rim, frosted quarters, 3 3/4" d. (ILLUS. front row, second from right with other pieces of U.S. Coin, bottom previous page) **173**

*Sugar bowl, cov., frosted quarters & half dollars, damage to finial (ILLUS. middle row, second from left with other pieces of U.S. Coin, bottom previous page) **317**

Syrup jug w/original dated pewter top, frosted quarters, minor loss to lid, 7" h. (ILLUS. middle row, third from right with other pieces of U.S. Coin, bottom previous page) **1,035**

*Toothpick holder, frosted dollars (ILLUS. front row, far right with other pieces of U.S. Coin pattern, bottom previous page) **288**

Washboard - see Adonis Pattern

Westward Ho
*Butter dish, cov. (ILLUS. center with other Westward Ho pieces, top of page) **175-200**

*Creamer (ILLUS. far left with other Westward Ho pieces, top of page) **100-125**

*Goblet (ILLUS. far right with other Westward Ho pieces, top of page) **95**

Spooner (ILLUS. second from left with other Westward Ho pieces, top of page) **95-125**

*Sugar bowl, cov. (ILLUS. second from right with other Westward Ho pieces, top of page) **125-150**

Peach Blow

Several types of glass lumped together by collectors as Peach Blow were produced by half a dozen glasshouses. Hobbs, Brockunier & Co., Wheeling, West Virginia, made Peach Blow as a plated ware that shaded from red at the top to yellow at the bottom and is referred to as Wheeling Peach Blow. Mt. Washington Glass Works produced an homogeneous Peach Blow shading from a rose color at the top to pale blue in the lower portion. The New England Glass Works' Peach Blow, called Wild Rose, shaded from rose at the top to white. Gundersen-Pairpoint Co. also reproduced some of the Mt. Washington Peach Blow in the early 1950s and some glass of a somewhat similar type was made by Steuben Glass Works, Thomas Webb & Sons and Stevens & Williams of England. New England Peach Blow is one-layered glass and the English is two-layered.

Another single-layered shaded art glass was produced early in the 20th century by the New Martinsville Glass Mfg. Co. Originally called "Muranese," collectors today refer to it as "New Martinsville Peach Blow."

New England

Raspberry Peach Blow Finger Bowl

Finger bowl, rounded base w/deep cylindrical sides, deep raspberry w/band of white at base, satin finish, 4 1/4" d., 2 5/8" h. (ILLUS.).. **$230**

Wheeling

Scarce Wheeling Peach Blow Claret Jug

Claret jug, tall conical body w/an applied amber rigaree band below the dark cylindrical neck w/a pinched rim spout, applied reeded angled amber handle down the side, 10" h. (ILLUS.) **1,955**

Wheeling Peach Blow Punch Cup

Punch cup, rounded shape w/applied coiled amber handle, satin finish, tiny rim nicks, 2 3/8" h. (ILLUS.) **196**

Small Wheeling Peach Blow Vase

Vase, 4 1/8" h., Wheeling Peach Blow, bulbous ovoid body w/a short cylindrical neck, deep ruby shading to yellow, ca. 1886 (ILLUS.) **500**

Satin Wheeling Peach Blow Bottle Vase

Vase, 8" h., bottle form, footed spherical body w/a tall stick neck, satin finish (ILLUS.) **690**

Peking Glass

This is Chinese glass, some of which has overlay in one to five colors, which has attracted collector interest. Peking Imperial glass is the most valuable.

Bowls, 6 1/4" d., overlay-type, each w/a white ground overlaid in green & carved to depict a continuous Chinese landscape w/scholars, pavilions & flowering plum trees, on carved rosewood stand, 19th c., pr. **$575**

Vase, 7" h., bottle-form, overlay-type, the imperial yellow ground overlaid in bright red & carved w/a continuous design of squirrels & fruiting grapevines above rockwork, a lappet neck rim border, 19th c. **1,955**

Pomona

First produced by the New England Glass Company under a patent received by Joseph Locke in 1885, Pomona has a frosted ground on clear glass decorated with mineral stains, most frequently amber-yellow, sometimes pale blue. Some pieces bore smooth etched floral decorations highlighted with staining. Two types of Pomona were made. The first Locke patent covered a technique whereby the piece was first covered with an acid-resistant coating that was then needle-carved with thousands of minute crisscrossing lines. The piece was then dipped into acid, which cut into the etched lines giving the finished piece a notable "brilliance."

A cheaper method, covered by a second Locke patent on June 15, 1886, was accomplished by rolling the glass piece in particles of acid-resistant material, which were picked up by it. The glass was then etched by acid, which attacked areas not protected by the resistant particles. A favorite design on Pomona was the cornflower.

Pomona Cornflower Decorated Bowl

Bowl, 8" d., 3" h., a petaled round foot below the wide round body w/upright sides & a crimped rim, blue Cornflower decoration, 2nd patent (ILLUS.) **$575**

Miniature Pomona Creamer & Sugar

Creamer & open sugar bowl, miniature, bulbous ovoid body w/a Tiny Thumbprint patt. tapering to a squared flaring neck, applied stained handles, 1st patent, 2" h., pr. (ILLUS.) **978**

Pomona Spooner with Blueberries

Spooner, crimped foot supporting the ovoid body, w/a tapering crimped rim, Blueberry patt., 2nd patent (ILLUS.) **750-1,000**

Royal Flemish

This ware, made by Mt. Washington Glass Co., is characterized by very heavy enameled gold lines dividing the surface into separate areas or sections. The body, with a matte finish, is variously decorated.

Rare Royal Flemish Pitcher

Pitcher, 9 1/2" h., bulbous nearly spherical body w/a small cylindrical neck & wide shallow cupped rim w/a pinched spout, small gilt ropetwist handle from edge of neck to shoulder, the body decorated w/large gilt & pale green baroque scrolls against a segmented ground in shades of tan, ochre, deep gold & brick red all within heavy gold outlining, the shoulder decorated w/a wide band of various armorial shields in shades of royal blue, brick red, gold, black & green, deep brown rim trimmed w/a gold leafy scroll band (ILLUS.) **$2,645**

Royal Flemish Dragon Vase

Vase, 7 1/2" h., broad ovoid body w/a short cylindrical neck, the wide panels around the sides outlined in heavy gold, a large gold winged dragon down one side & a mythological beast head on the over, background panels in shades of amber, tan & peach (ILLUS., previous page) **4,313**

Outstanding Rare Royal Flemish Vase

Vase, 9 3/8" h., bulbous body tapering to a small neck w/a deep cupped rim, applied gold shoulder handles, gold-outlined panels w/stylized flowerheads & leaves in shades of tan, beige, maroon & green, the shoulder w/scrolling dark brown gold-outlined leafy floral vines on a lighter brown ground, the cupped rim w/narrow brown panels outlined in gold (ILLUS.) **5,290**

Satin

Satin glass was a popular decorative glass developed in the late 19th century. Most pieces were composed of two layers of glass with the exterior layer usually in a shaded pastel color. The name derives from the soft matte finish, caused by exposure to acid fumes, which gave the surface a "satiny" feel. Mother-of-pearl satin glass was a specialized variety wherein air trapped between the layers of glass provided subtle surface patterns such as Herringbone and Diamond Quilted. A majority of satin glass was produced in England, Bohemia and America, but collectors should be aware that reproductions have been made for many years.

Pitcher, 6 3/8" h., spherical body w/wide cylindrical neck w/wide arched spout, shaded pink mother-of-pearl Diamond Quilted patt., applied frosted clear handle (ILLUS., top next column) **$259**

Mother-of-Pearl Satin Pink Pitcher

Webb Mother-of-Pearl Sugar Shaker

Sugar shaker w/original top, ovoid body, peach mother-of-pearl Peacock Eye patt., signed by Thomas Webb, minor dents in top, 5 1/4" h. (ILLUS.) **719**

Rare Satin Glass Sugar Shaker

Sugar shaker w/original top, swelled cylindrical form, shaded apricot mother-of-pearl Coin Spot patt., delicate floral enameling, rare, 5 1/2" h. (ILLUS.) **750-1,200**

Vase, 5 1/4" h., 3" d., ovoid body tapering sharply to a tall trumpet neck, shaded deep yellow to pale yellow, decorated overall w/heavy gold leaves & butterflies, attributed to Thomas Webb, England, ca. 1880s, white lining **250-275**

Vase, 7 3/4" h., 3" d., ribbed Cut Velvet satin in deep pink shaded to light pink, white lining **175-200**

Vase, 7 7/8" h., 6" d., squatty melon-lobed base below the trumpet-form heck w/a four-lobed crimped rim, blue mother-of-pearl Raindrop patt., white lining **200-250**

Swirl Mother-of-Pearl Satin Vase

Vase, 8" h., ovoid body tapering to a short ringed tapering neck, shaded dark blue to dark rose mother-of-pearl Swirl patt., attributed to Stevens & Williams, England (ILLUS.)... **900 - 1,200**

Fine Rainbow Mother-of-Pearl Vase

Vase, 8 1/2" h., bulbous base w/tall cylindrical sides & a four-lobed rolled & crimped rim, rainbow mother-of-pearl Diamond Quilted patt., deep colors, Mt. Washington Glass Co. (ILLUS.).................. **1,500 - 2,000**

Vase, 10 1/4" h., 7 1/2" d., Jack-in-the-pulpit style, a squatty bulbous body tapering down to a rounded knob & tapering up to a wide neck w/a crimped, rolled & upturned rim, shaded lavender mother-of-pearl Diamond Quilted patt., raised on three applied frosted clear looped branch legs, late 19th c. (ILLUS., next column) **748**

Fine Diamond Quilted Satin Vase

Steuben

Most of the Steuben glass listed below was made at the Steuben Glass Works, now a division of Corning Glass, between 1903 and about 1933. The factory was organized by T.G. Hawkes, noted glass designer Frederick Carder, and others. Mr. Carder devised many types of glass and revived many old techniques.

Steuben Marks

Acid Cut-Back

Fine Acid Cut-Back Covered Jar

Lovely Tall Gold Aurene Candlesticks

Jar, cov., ovoid body tapering to a short cylindrical neck w/a fitted domed cover w/pointed knob finial, green Jade cut back to Alabaster in the "Chinese" patt., Shape No. 5000, minor in-the-making roughness on rim of cover, 6 3/8" h. (ILLUS., previous page) **$2,530**

Aurene

Lovely Aurene Short Candleholders

Candleholders, a wide round slightly domed foot below the knopped stem w/tiny applied prunts supporting the tall cylindrical candle socket w/a widely rolled rim, bluish gold iridescence, signed, Shape No. 6384, 3 3/4" h., pr. (ILLUS.) **1,265**

Candlesticks, round domed foot supporting the slender ribbed stem entwined w/a slender applied rib leaf, a tapering ribbed bud-form candle socket, brilliant gold iridescence, Shape No. 7613, signed, 11 5/8" h., pr. (ILLUS., top of page) **6,613**

Finger bowl & underplate, the deep rounded bowl w/a six-crimp flaring rim, matching ruffled underplate, overall gold iridescence w/stretcher surface, Shape No. 171, underplate 6 1/4" d., bowl 2 1/2" h., pr. (ILLUS., next column) **500**

Aurene Finger Bowl & Underplate

Lovely Blue Aurene Urn-form Vase

Vase, 5 3/4" h., urn-form shape, a wide round foot supporting the wide bulbous urn-form body w/a wide shoulder centering a wide flaring neck, three applied upright fleur-de-lis ornaments around the edge of the shoulder, deep blue iridescence, signed, Shape No. 6627 (ILLUS.) **2,300**

Cintra

Fine Yellow Cintra Table Lamp

Lamp, table model, a footed swelled cylindrical body w/a short flaring neck, golden yellow acid-cut in the "Sculptured" patt. showing pods of fruit on a meandering leafy vine, mounted on a silvered metal base ring w/a Greek key design & raised on four scroll legs, domed silvered metal top mount, body Shape No. 6375 on base foot bent inward, body 12" h., overall 30 1/2" h. (ILLUS.) **2,415**

Rosaline
Bowl, 10" d., widely flaring flat sides w/rounded shoulders & wide closed rim, unmarked **403**
Cup & saucer, wide shallow saucer & half-round cup w/applied opal handle, unmarked, saucer 4 1/2" d. **345**

Spanish Green
Vase, 8 1/4" h., fan-shaped body attached to a double-knop stem & round foot, marked w/Steuben trademark **230**

Threaded
Vases, 9" h., 6" d., footed colorless inverted bell-form body w/overall controlled bubbles, the flaring rim applied w/random amber threading, unsigned, pr. **316**

Topaz
Vase, 10 1/4" h., flared wide foot tapering to a cylindrical swirled optic ribbed body w/a flared & ruffled rim, signed w/Steuben fleur-de-lis mark **230**

Verre de Soie

Unusual Verre de Soie Steuben Basket

Basket, cylindrical base w/two widely flaring sides pulled up & joined by a high arched applied handle, large deep maroon blossom w/a pair of green leaves applied at each side of the handle base, similar to Shape No. 453, pontil w/original serrated round paper label, one flower petal professionally repaired, a line within the same blossom, 8" h. (ILLUS.) **460**

Set of Twelve Verre de Soie Salt Cellars

Salt cellars, disk foot supporting the deep rounded bowl w/a widely flared rim, Shape No. 3067, unmarked, 1 1/2" h., set of 12 (ILLUS., bottom previous page) **1,380**

Miscellaneous Wares

Fine Steuben Crystal Pegasus Vase

Vase, 7 1/4" h., "Pegasus," crystal, disk foot supporting the tall cylindrical sides w/a rounded base, the side wheel-engraved w/a large design of the mythological animal, by Sidney Waugh, signed, minor surface scratches (ILLUS.)........................ **1,495**

Tiffany

This glassware, covering a wide diversity of types, was produced in glasshouses operated by Louis Comfort Tiffany, America's outstanding glass designer of the Art Nouveau period, from the last quarter of the 19th century until the early 1930s. Tiffany revived early techniques and devised many new ones.

Various Tiffany Marks & Labels

Unusual Tiffany Bottle

Bottle w/original stopper, bulbous squatty body tapering sharply to a slender gently bent neck fitted w/a silver collar & ball stopper, overall green pulled-feather decoration around the body, may have been a Persian sprinkler form damaged & adapted to this shape, signed on base "L.C. Tiffany Favrile 8530N," 8 1/2" h. (ILLUS.) **$1,553**

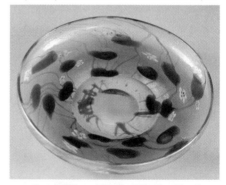

Small Tiffany Millefiori Shallow Bowl

Bowl, 5" d., footed wide flattened shallow form, millefiori-type, large green leaves & vines swirling around w/white & green millefiori flowers scattered, small open bubble on inside, signed on base "L.C.T. R6115" (ILLUS.).. **1,323**

Large Tiffany Cameo-cut Vase

Cameo vase, 10 1/2" h., flaring base tapering to tall cylindrical sides, internally decorated w/areas of rich green shading dark to light, exterior w/wheel-carved large grape vines & clusters against a frosted ground, signed on base "L.C. Tiffany Favrile 6242C," rim slightly reduced (ILLUS.)... **4,083**

Gold Tiffany Candlestick Lamp

Candlestick lamp, the tapering swirled gold iridescent base w/a flaring rim, fitted w/a Bakelite insert supporting the open-topped domed & ruffled gold iridescent shade, both portions signed, unelectrified, overall 15" h. (ILLUS.) **2,520**

Small Iridescent Tiffany Creamer

Creamer, slightly swelled cylindrical shape w/a flat rim & pinched rim spout, applied angled handle, light greenish iridescent tint shading to blue opalescent w/a dark blue iridescent rim & interior, signed on the base, 3 1/4" h. (ILLUS.) **1,035**

Gold Favrile Tiffany Cup & Saucer

Cup & saucer, footed squatty rounded cup w/a flat rim & applied C-form handle, shallow dished matching saucer, gold iridescence intaglio-cut w/grape & leaf band on each piece, cup signed "9776E L.C. Tiffany Favrile," saucer w/just initials, saucer 5 1/2" d., cup 2 1/2" h. (ILLUS.) **1,093**

White Opalescent Tiffany Flower Frog

Flower frog, pinched cylindrical white opalescent center applied w/two bands of clear loops & open loops across the top, signed on base, one loop cracked, 3 5/8" h., 2 1/4" h. (ILLUS., previous page) **200-400**

Gold Favrile Tiffany Salt Dip

Salt dip, witch's cauldron-style, wide squatty lower body w/a very wide flaring rim, tiny applied loop handles, overall gold iridescence, signed "LCT - Favrile X621," 1" h. (ILLUS.) **345**

Tiny Green & Platinum Tiffany Vase

Vase, 2 1/8" h., miniature, round base flaring widely to a squatty rounded shoulder centered by a wide low flared mouth, green iridescent ground w/a scattered Art Nouveau platinum iridescence, signed "LCT - V3785" (ILLUS.) **2,040**

Small Flower-form Tiffany Vase

Vase, 6" h., floraform, wide round foot supporting a slender stem flaring to a tall ovoid body w/a flat rim, gold iridescent ground decorated w/green leaves & vines, signed "L. C. Tiffany - Favrile - 7198D" (ILLUS.) **2,128**

Rare Tiffany Vase with Applied Designs

Vase, 6" h., 5 1/4" d., wide bulbous ovoid body tapering to a wide flat mouth, gold & platinum iridescent ground applied w/pod & tendril designs in a rare blue, an Art Nouveau hooked design around the mouth, signed "LCT R3291" (ILLUS.) **18,400**

Flower-form Pulled-Feather Tiffany Vase

Vase, 9" h., floraform, a domed & ribbed foot supporting the knopped slender stem continuing to the flaring upright ruffled flower-form bowl, the bowl w/a pulled-feather design in shades of iridescent browns, golds & mauves, rum & green stem & foot, signed "LCT M1940" (ILLUS.) **8,625**

Tall Tapering Tiffany Vase

Vase, 10 1/4" h., a wide conical base tapering sharply to a very tall slender & slightly flaring stick neck, overall blue iridescence w/purple & gold highlights, blue pulled feathers around the flaring base, signed "L.C. Tiffany - Favrile - X137 1116 7912K" (ILLUS.) **2,990**

Wall Pocket Vases

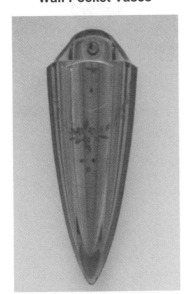

Amber Silver Deposit-decorated Vase

Amber, bullet-shaped w/molded vertical ribbing, decorated w/silver deposit floral swags, Style #1881, Fostoria Glass Co., 8 1/4" l. (ILLUS.) **$90-100**

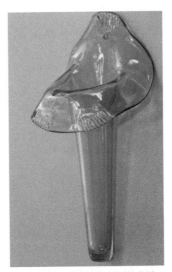

Amber Jack-in-the-Pulpit Wall Vase

Amber, free-blown jack-in-the-pulpit design w/ruffled rim (ILLUS.) **100-125**

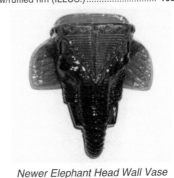

Newer Elephant Head Wall Vase

Amber, model of an elephant head, based on a Victorian glass match holder, new vintage, 4 1/2" l. (ILLUS.) **20-30**

Fine Tiffin Amethyst Wall Pocket Vase

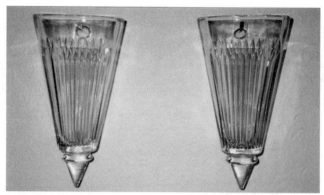

Two Jeannette "Anniversary" Pattern Wall Pocket Vases

Amethyst with satin finish, wide inverted bell-form w/a half-round pointed base drop & arched back w/hanging hole, Tiffin Glass Co. (ILLUS., previous page) **275-300**

Fostoria Black Wall Pocket Vase

Decorated Black Glass Wall Pocket

Black, bullet-shaped w/a three-paneled front, interior molded vertical ribbing, Style #1881, Fostoria Glass Co., 8 1/4" l. (ILLUS.)... **90-100**

Black, V-shaped, molded design of a bird perched among grapevines all painted in shades of red, black & gold, Dugan-Diamond Glass Co., 7 3/4" l. (ILLUS., next column) **65-75**

Canary yellow with satin finish, conical w/a pointed finial at the bottom, Tiffin Glass Co., Style #320 (ILLUS., bottom next column).. **125-150**

Clear, bullet-shaped, fine pointed vertical ribbing & a pointed bottom finial, "Anniversary" patt., Jeannette Glass Co., 6 1/2" l. (ILLUS. left with pink version, top of page).. **12-15**

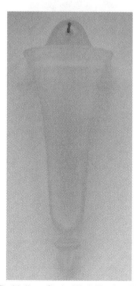

Tiffin Yellow Satin Wall Pocket Vase

Paint-decorated Clear Wall Pocket Vase

Clear, V-shaped, vertical panels, decorated w/a wide pink band around the top & deep pink, yellow & lavender flowers in an orange basket on the front, 6" h. (ILLUS.) **25-35**

Clear Frosted Glass Wall Pocket Vase

Frosted clear, V-shaped, molded vertical ribbing, 6" h. (ILLUS.) **20-25**

Fostoria Silver Deposit-decorated Vase

Green, bullet-shaped w/molded vertical ribbing, decorated w/a swagged silver deposit floral design, Style #1881, Fostoria Glass Co., 8 1/4" l. (ILLUS.) **90-100**

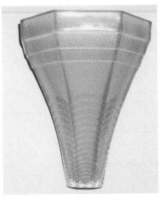

Light Green Paneled & Ribbed Vase

Light green, V-shaped w/a three-panel front w/three graduated bands at the top & fine arched panels up from the base, 6 1/2" h. (ILLUS.) **100-125**

Marigold Carnival Crackle Wall Pocket

Marigold carnival glass, V-shaped, Crackle patt., 5 3/4" l. (ILLUS.) **50-60**

Orange-painted Wall Pocket Vase

Orange-painted, free-blown bullet shape w/black rim trim, 6 1/8" l. (ILLUS.)............. **40-60**

Pink, bullet-shaped, fine pointed vertical ribbing & a pointed bottom finial, "Anniversary" patt., Jeannette Glass Co., 6 1/2" l. (ILLUS. right with clear version) **30-45**

Red, brilliant finish, slender conical form w/pointed end finial, Style No. 320 by Tiffin Glass Co., 3 3/8 x 9 1/8" **150-185**

Wave Crest

Now much sought after, Wave Crest was produced by the C.F. Monroe Co., Meriden, Connecticut, in the late 19th and early 20th centuries from opaque white glass blown into molds.

It was then hand-decorated in enamels and metal trim was often added. Boudoir accessories such as jewel boxes, hair receivers, etc., predominated.

WAVE CREST WARE
Wave Crest Mark

Wave Crest Pansy Mold Box

Box w/hinged lid, Pansy blown-out mold, dark green low flaring box & domed cover molded w/a large pink & amethyst pansy blossom, original metal fittings, signed on base, 4" w., 2 3/8" h. (ILLUS.).................... **$863**

Box w/hinged lid, Helmschmeid Swirl mold, opal decorated w/delicate pink apple blossoms & tiny leafy stems, on ormolu scroll feet, 7 1/2" d............................. **431**

Cracker jar, cov., squared shape in opal w/a border of tiny molded scrolls on each side enclosing a cluster of pink blossoms, silver plate rim, cover & bail handle, cover marked "C.F.M. Co.," 9" h........................ **219**

Cracker jar, cov., squared shape in pale green w/a border of tiny molded scrolls on each side enclosing a cluster of pink blossoms, silver plate rim, cover & bail handle, 9" h. **207**

Dresser box w/hinged cover, round squatty cover w/ornate wide border of molded scrolls enclosing a cluster of large pink daisy-like flowers against a pink blush ground, the low matching base w/matching decoration, unsigned, 7 1/2" d............... **259**

Ferner, Egg Crate mold, decorated w/clusters of pink blossoms on long leafy

stems, gilt metal ropetwist rim, unmarked, 6 1/2" sq... **230**

Rare Large Wave Crest Iris Vase

Vase, 12" h., large ovoid body w/a wide short cylindrical neck decorated around the middle w/a wide serpentine blue band painted w/large white & yellow irises, white top & bottom bands w/gilt trim, mounted in a gilt-metal ring base w/scroll feet & w/a gilt-metal rim band issuing long large open scroll handles down the sides (ILLUS.) **2,300**

Webb

This glass is made by Thomas Webb & Sons of Stourbridge, one of England's most prolific glasshouses. Numerous types of glass, including cameo, have been produced by this firm through the years. The company also produced various types of novelty and "art" glass during the late Victorian period. Also see BURMESE, ROSE BOWLS, and SATIN & MOTHER-OF-PEARL.

Red Webb Cameo Vase with Flowers

Cameo vase, 9 1/2" h., ovoid body tapering to a wide cylindrical neck, deep red overlaid in white & cameo cut around the sides w/leafy flowering vines, a band of pointed leaves around the neck, unsigned (ILLUS.) **$2,530**

Tall Yellow Webb Cameo Vase

Cameo vase, 11" h., the ovoid body tapering to a tall stick neck, frosted yellow ground cased in white & cut w/an overall design of vining morning glory blossoms, a butterfly on the reverse, banner mark on base, interior w/faint silhouetted bubble under design (ILLUS.) **1,265**

Webb Tall Satin Iced Tea Tumbler

Iced tea tumbler, shaded deep rose pink to pale pink cased satin, bubble encased in mid-body, polishing to edge of rim, 5 5/8" h. (ILLUS.) **173**

Westmoreland

Westmoreland Specialty Company was founded in East Liverpool, Ohio, in 1889 and relocated in 1890 to Grapeville, Pennsylvania, where it remained until its closing in 1985.

During its early years Westmoreland specialized in glass food containers and novelties but by the turn of the 20th century it had a large line of milk white items and clear tableware patterns. In 1925 the company name was shortened to The Westmoreland Glass Company. It was during that decade that more colored glasswares entered its lineup. When Victorian-style milk glass again became popular in the 1940s and 1950s, Westmoreland produced extensive amounts in several patterns that closely resemble late 19th century wares. These and the figural animal dishes in milk white and colors are widely collected today, but buyers should not confuse them for the antique originals. Watch for Westmoreland's "WG" mark on some pieces. A majority of our listings are products from the 1940s through the 1970s. Earlier pieces will be indicated.

Early Westmoreland Label & Mark

Animal covered dish, Cat on a lacy base, glass eyes, opaque blue, copied from the Atterbury original **$125**

Animal covered dish, duck, rimmed base, blue opaque glass **75**

Animal covered dish, Hen on Nest, looking left, green slag **65**

Animal covered dish, Hen on nest, red & yellow slag, copied from antique original **135**

Animal covered dish, Rabbit, ruby Carnival **50**

Animal covered dish, Robin on Twig Nest, light blue, copied from antique original by Portieux, France **75**

Ashtray, English Hobnail patt., ruby, 8" sq. **45**

Ashtray, Paneled Grape patt., square, milk white, large **19**

Ashtray, turtle-shaped, Thousand Eye patt., crystal w/ruby stain **12**

Basket, No. 752, ruby-stained ribs w/h.p. floral medallion **52**

Basket, Pansy patt., two handles meet from sides, amber **12**

Basket, Princess Feather patt., crystal, 8" h. **48**

Basket, Wakefield patt., crystal w/ruby stain, 6" h. **75**

Basket, Paneled Grape patt., No. 118, milk white, 8" h. **75**

Three-light Block Candleholder

Bell, No. 1902, green satin w/h.p. white dai-
sy.. **18**

Bowl, 3" sq., cranberry-type, English Hob-
nail patt., crystal **15**

Bowl, 6" d., crimped rim, Paneled Grape
patt., footed, milk white **32**

Bowl, cov., 7" sq., high-footed, Beaded
Grape patt., milk white **42**

Bowl, 8 1/2" d., lipped rim, Paneled Grape
patt., milk white **90**

Bowl, cov., 9" h., square, high-footed,
Beaded Grape patt., milk white..................... **65**

Bowl, 9 1/2" d., 3" h., bell-shaped, Paneled
Grape patt., milk white **120**

Bowl, 12" oval, footed, lipped rim, Paneled
Grape patt., milk white **125**

Bowl/nut dish, 6 1/2" oval, Paneled Grape
patt., No. 49, milk white................................ **25**

Box, cov., figural, Santa in Sleigh, milk
white w/painted decoration............................ **75**

Butter dish, cov., Old Quilt (No. 500) patt.,
milk white, 1/4 lb.. **35**

Cake salver, Paneled Grape patt., skirted
rim, bell-footed, No. 59, milk white, 11" d. **85**

Candelabrum three-light, Paneled Grape
patt., skirted, No. 90, milk white, pr. **410**

Candleholder, three-light block, Paneled
Grape patt., milk glass (ILLUS., top of
page)... **170**

Candleholders, Della Robbia patt., clear
w/ruby staining, low, pr.................................. **50**

Candlestick, single-light, Mission patt., two-
handled, No. 1015, clear, 7" h........................ **35**

Candlestick, single-light, Spiral wrap
around square base, black, 7" h. **32**

Candlesticks, dolphin-form standard w/a
petal-form socket, round scalloped foot,
Blue Moonstone, 1930-31, 9 1/2" h., pr. **358**

Candlesticks, English Hobnail patt., turquoise, 8" h., pr. (ILLUS. right & left
w/pink lamp, top next page) **125**

Candlesticks, Paneled Grape patt., milk
white, 4", pr. **32**

Green Dolphin Stem Candlesticks

Candlesticks, dolphin-form standard w/a
petal-form socket, hexagonal foot, green,
9" h., pr. (ILLUS.) **168**

Candy box, cov., round, flat, Della Robbia
patt., crystal w/ruby stain **120**

Candy dish, cov., Della Robbia patt., No.
DR-17, pastel stained fruit, 7 1/2" h. **95**

Candy dish, cov., Paneled Grape patt.,
three-footed, No. 103, milk white **35**

Candy dish, cov., three-footed, Paneled
Grape patt., milk glass **30**

Candy jar, cov., footed, No. 26, Paneled
Grape patt., milk white, 6 1/2" h.................... **28**

Celery vase, footed, pinched rim, Beaded
Grape patt., milk white, 6 1/2" h. **20**

Champagne, Thousand Eye patt., clear........... **10**

Cheese dish w/domed cover, Old Quilt
patt., milk white, 4 1/2" h. **45**

Chocolate box, cov., round, Paneled
Grape patt., milk white, 6 1/2" d.................... **50**

Cigarette box, cov., English Hobnail patt.,
green, 2 1/2 x 4 1/2"...................................... **38**

Cigarette box, cov., turtle-shaped, Thousand Eye patt., crystal w/ruby stain **35**

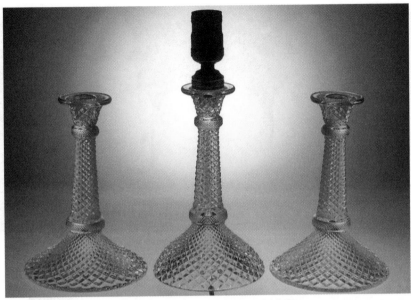

English Hobnail Candlesticks and Lamp

Cocktail, square footed, English Hobnail patt., clear, 3 oz................................. **8**
Compote, cov., square, low footed, 5" h., Old Quilt patt., milk white **26**

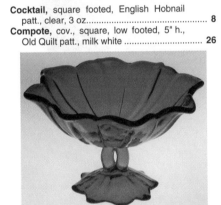

Flamed-colored Lotus Compote

Compote, 5 1/2" d., 3 1/2" h., open stem, Lotus patt., Flame red (ILLUS.)....................... **30**
Compote, cov., 7" h., Paneled Grape patt., milk white **48**
Compote, 8" h., Mother of Pearl Dolphin & Shell line, shell-shaped bowl w/dolphin base, milk white w/mother of pearl finish **85**
Compote, 9 1/4" d., Princess Feather patt., Golden Sunset (ILLUS., next column)............ **68**
Compote, 10" d., 5 1/2" h., open, footed, crimped & ruffled, Waterford patt., No. 32, clear w/ruby stain **128**
Console set: 9 1/2 x 12" oval, footed bowl w/flared rim & two 4" h. candlesticks; Paneled Grape patt., milk white, 3 pcs......... **150**
Cordial, square base, English Hobnail, clear, 3 3/4" h. **15**

Princess Feather Pattern Compote

Cordial, Thousand Eye patt., crystal, 1 oz......... **14**
Creamer & cov. sugar bowl, lacy edge, Paneled Grape patt., milk white, pr............... **70**
Creamer & open sugar bowl, Della Robbia patt., clear w/ruby staining, pr...................... **50**
Creamer & open sugar bowl, footed, English Hobnail patt., milk white, pr. **25**
Creamer & open sugar bowl, Maple Leaf (Bramble) patt., milk white, pr. **22**
Creamer & open sugar bowl, Thousand Eye patt., clear, pr.. **30**
Cruet w/original stopper, Della Robbia patt., milk white **35**
Cruets w/stoppers, English Hobnail patt., milk white, 6 1/2" h., set of 2 .... **50**
Cup & saucer, Beaded Edge patt., milk glass w/h.p. fruit, pr...................................... **17**
Cup & saucer, English Hobnail patt., milk white, pr. **12**

Paneled Grape Milk Glass Dresser Set

Demitasse cup & saucer, English Hobnail patt., pink, pr. **75**

Dresser set: two colognes w/stoppers, cov. round puff box, oval tray w/scalloped edge; Paneled Grape patt., milk glass w/Roses & Bows decoration, the set (ILLUS., top of page) **395**

Egg cup, American Hobnail patt., clear, 4 1/2" h. **15**

Egg cup, model of a chick, milk glass w/red trim **22**

Fairy lamp, two-part, Thousand Eye patt., Brandywine blue.. **35**

Fairy lamp, two-part, Wakefield patt., crystal w/ruby stain **95**

Fruit cocktail w/underplate, Paneled Grape patt., milk white, 3 1/2", 2 pcs. **24**

Goblet, American Hobnail patt., milk white, 6" h. **9**

Goblet, Della Robbia patt., stained ruby, 6" h. **55**

Goblet, Paneled Grape patt., ruby, 6" h. **29**

Goblet, square base, English Hobnail patt., clear, 6" h. **15**

Goblet, water, Della Robbia patt., milk white w/red stain, 8 oz. **35**

Goblet, water, footed, Beaded Grape patt., milk white, 9 oz. **11**

Goblet, water, square footed, English Hobnail patt., green, 8 oz.................................... **34**

Honey, cov., Beaded Grape patt., milk white w/gold grapes, 5" d. **40**

Ivy ball, footed, English Hobnail patt., milk glass, 6 1/2" h. (ILLUS., next column)........... **26**

Jardiniere, cupped, Paneled Grape patt., milk white, 5" h. **25**

Lamp, English Hobnail patt., electric, pink, 8" h. (ILLUS. center w/turquoise candlesticks) **75**

Mayonnaise dish, underplate & ladle, Paneled Grape patt., milk white, 3 1/2" d., 3 pcs. **40**

Mint compote, Waterford patt., footed, crimped rim, No. 34, clear w/ruby stain, 5 1/2" w. **65**

English Hobnail Ivy Ball

Model of owl, on two stacked books, cobalt carnival, 3 1/2" h. **26**

Model of Pouter Pigeon, apricot mist, 2 1/2" h.. **35**

Model of sleigh, milk white w/holly decoration, No. 1872, 9" l. **120**

Napkin ring, Paneled Grape patt., milk glass... **24**

Nappy, round, handled, Paneled Grape patt., milk white, 5" d. **14**

Novelty, model of a top hat, English Hobnail patt., milk white, 3" h. **16**

Pitcher, footed, Paneled Grape patt., crystal w/ruby stain, 1 qt. (ILLUS., top next page).. **145**

Pitcher, 8 1/2" h., Old Quilt patt., ruby Carnival.. **89**

Planter, window-type, Paneled Grape patt., oblong, milk white, 3 x 8 1/2" **35**

Plate, Three Kittens patt., milk white................. **45**

Paneled Grape Pattern Pitcher

Plate, 7" d., Beaded Edge patt., No. 64-2, fruit decoration **15**

Plate, 7 1/4" d., Della Robbia patt., crystal **10**

Plate, 8" d., Princess Feather patt., pink **18**

Plate, 8 1/2" d., English Hobnail patt., milk white.. **10**

Plate, 10 1/2" d., dinner, Beaded Grape patt., milk white **30**

Plate, 10 1/2" d., English Hobnail patt., green... **45**

Plate, 13" d., Lotus patt., pink **65**

Puff box, cov., Paneled Grape patt., milk white, 4 1/2" d. **32**

Punch bowl & base, Princess Feather patt., bell-shaped, purple Carnival, 2 pcs. **450**

Punch cup, Paneled Grape patt., milk white, 2 1/2" h. **19**

Punch set: 5 qt. punch bowl w/pedestal base, 12 cups & ladle; Paneled Grape patt., milk white, 15 pcs.. **600**

Relish, six-part, Thousand Eye patt., crystal, 10" d. **27**

Salt dip, individual, Lotus patt., green................ **24**

Salt & pepper shakers w/original tops, Beaded Grape patt., milk white, pr.............. **20**

Salt & pepper shakers w/original tops, Princess Feather patt., footed, clear, pr. **28**

Sherbet, footed, Beaded Edge patt., milk glass w/red painted beads **10**

Soap tray, tab handles, Paneled Grape patt., milk glass w/Roses & Bows decoration, 5 x 6 3/4" **125**

Tumbler, footed, Beaded Edge patt., milk glass w/h.p. fruit or flowers, 8 oz................... **20**

Tumbler, footed, Beaded Edge patt., milk white... **16**

Tumbler, iced tea, footed, Wakefield patt., crystal w/ruby stain, 12 oz............................. **38**

Tumbler, iced tea, Paneled Grape patt., milk white **25**

Tumbler, iced tea, round base, English Hobnail patt., clear, 6" h. **14**

Tumbler, juice, Paneled Grape patt., milk white... **24**

Tumbler, iced tea, flat, Princess Feather patt., pink, 12 oz... **32**

Vase, bud, American Hobnail patt., lilac opalescent.. **28**

Vase, 7" h., No. 1913, flared shape, three ball feet, green **55**

Vase, 9" h., fan-type, octagonal-shaped foot, Beaded Grape patt., milk white............. **48**

Vase, 12" h., swung-type, English Hobnail patt., milk glass **48**

Vase, 14" h., Paneled Grape patt., milk white.. **40**

Vase, 16" h., swung type, flat, Paneled Grape patt., milk white **48**

Vase/straw jar, 10" h., English Hobnail patt., clear.. **85**

Wine, Della Robbia patt., stained dark colors, 4 3/4" h.. **65**

Wine, Paneled Grape patt., clear, 4" h.............. **18**

GRANITEWARE

This is a name given to metal (customarily iron) kitchenware covered with an enamel coating. Featured at the 1876 Philadelphia Centennial Exposition, it became quite popular for it was lightweight, attractive, and easy to clean. Although it was made in huge quantities and is still produced, it has caught the attention of a younger generation of collectors and prices have steadily risen over the past few years. There continues to be a constant demand for the wide variety of these utilitarian articles turned out earlier in this century and rare forms now command high prices.

Tea set: child's size, cov. teapot, open sugar bowl, creamer & four cups & saucers; Solid Blue, bulbous teapot w/domed cover & C-form handle, cylindrical creamer, late 19th - early 20th c., teapot 3 1/4" h., 13 pcs. **$450**

Tea set: child's size, cov. teapot, four cups, four saucers, creamer & cov. sugar bowl; white w/blue design, teapot 3 1/4" d., 5 1/4" h., the set (ILLUS., top next page)..... **450**

Scarce Chrysolite Tea Steeper

Tea steeper, cov., Chrysolite & White Swirl (dark green & white) patt., cylindrical w/rim spout & black strap side handle, domed cover w/knob finial, late 19th - early 20th c., 4 1/4" d., 5" h. (ILLUS.) **450**

Child's Blue & White Graniteware Tea Set

Blue & White Tea Steeper with Tin Lid

Tea steeper, cov., Blue & White Swirl patt., cylindrical w/rim spout, strap side handle, domed tin cover w/wooden knob finial, 5" d., 5" h. (ILLUS.) **250**

Large Blue & White Swirl Teakettle

Teakettle, cov., Blue & White Swirl patt., wide flat bottom & domed body w/a domed cover w/knob finial, wire bail swing handle w/turned wood grip, serpentine spout, late 19th - early 20th c., 10" d., 7" h. (ILLUS.) **300**

Miniature Solid Blue Teakettle

Teakettle, cov., Solid Blue, miniature, wide flat bottom & domed body w/domed cover & knob finial, serpentine spout, overhead swing strap handle, late 19th - early 20th c., 3" d., 2 1/2" h. (ILLUS.) **400**

Columbian Graniteware Teakettle

Teakettle, cov., Blue & White Swirl patt., wide flat bottom & domed body w/domed cover & knob finial, wire swing bail handle w/turned wood grip, serpentine spout, Columbian Ware, late 19th - early 20th c., 10 1/2" d., 7" h. (ILLUS.) **650**

Cobalt Blue & White Swirl Teakettle

Teakettle, cov., Cobalt Blue & White Swirl patt., wide flat bottom w/high domed body, domed cover w/knob finial, serpentine spout, coiled iron swing bail handle, late 19th - early 20th c., 7 1/4" d., 7 1/4" h. (ILLUS.) **800**

Diamond Ware Blue & White Teapot

Teapot, cov., Blue Diamond Ware (Iris Blue
& White Swirl patt.), bulbous body tapering to a domed cover w/button finial, serpentine spout, C-form handle, late 19th -
early 20th c., 5 1/2" d., 6" h. (ILLUS.)........... **700**

Graniteware Agate Ware Child's Teapot

Teapot, cov., child's, Agate Ware, ovoid
body on disk foot, tapering to domed lid
w/finial, C-form handle, serpentine spout,
decorated w/simple line decoration in
blue, 3 1/2" h. (ILLUS.).................................... **35**
Teapot, cov., Grey Mottled patt., spherical
w/low domed cover & wooden knob finial,
serpentine spout, C-form handle, late 19th
- early 20th c., 3 1/2" d., 5" h. (ILLUS. right
with other miniature Grey Mottled teapot) **200**

Toy White Agate Ware Teapot

Teapot, cov., toy-sized, Agate Ware, overall white, domed cover, strap handle,
long serpentine spout, probably made in
Germany or Austria, ca. 1890, 5" l., 3" h.
(ILLUS.) **75**
Teapot, cov., Willow Ware design, Blue Wil-
low, slightly tapering cylindrical shape
w/shoulder sloping in to short neck, C-form
handle, serpentine spout, slightly domed

lid w/finial, dark blue handle, spout, finial &
rim, early 20th c. (ILLUS., below) **50-75**

Blue Willow Graniteware Teapot

Grey Graniteware Miniature Teapots

Teapot, cov., Grey Mottled patt., spherical
w/low domed cover & wooden knob finial,
straight spout, C-form handle, late 19th -
early 20th c., 3 1/2" d., 5" h. (ILLUS. left
with other miniature Grey Mottled teapot) **200**

Bulbous Solid Blue Teapot

Teapot, cov., Solid Blue, bulbous body
w/hinged domed cover w/button finial,
serpentine spout, C-form strap handle,
late 19th - early 20th c., 4 1/2" d.,
5 1/4" h. (ILLUS.) **80**

Blue Willow Enamel Teapot

Teapot, cov., Willow Ware design, Blue Willow, slightly tapering cylindrical body,
short shoulder sloping to lid w/button finial, C-form handle, serpentine spout, un-
marked, 7" h. (ILLUS.) **75-85**

HALLOWEEN COLLECTIBLES

Although Halloween is an American tradition and holiday, we must credit the Scottish for bringing it to the United States. The earliest symbols of Halloween appeared around the turn of the 20th century. During Victorian times, Halloween parties became popular in the United States. Decorations were seasonal products, such as pumpkins, cornstalks, vegetables, etc. Many early decorations were imported from Germany, only to be followed by increased demand in the United States during World War I, when German imports ceased.

Today Halloween collectibles are second in demand only to Christmas collectibles. Remembering the excitement one felt as a child dressing up in costume, going treat or treating, carving pumpkins, bobbing for apples, etc., the colors of orange and black trigger nostalgia for our youth for many of us.

The variety of Halloween collectibles is immense. Whether it be noisemakers, jack o' lanterns, candy containers, paper or plastic goods, candy molds or costumes, with the availability, the choice is yours.

Remember to buy the best, be it the very old or not so old. Search antiques shops, flea markets and house sales.

Bell-shaped Candy Container

Candy container, glass w/reverse painting, bell shape w/painted orange face & green leaves for hair, riased eyes & nose, deeply sunken painted mouth w/teeth showing, large ring loop on top, gold-tone screw-on closure, ca. 1920, 3 1/2" h. (ILLUS.).. **604**

Luggage-shaped Candy Container

Candy container, paper-covered pressed board, luggage-shaped, yellow jack-o'-lantern face w/strap, ca. 1916, Germany (ILLUS.)... **295**

Black Cat Candy Container

Candy container, flat-bodied black cat sitting atop glass simulated wooden crate w/recessed top embossed "Black Cat for Luck" across front & "Pat." below cat, cat marked "Pat. Apl'd for," gold-colored tin slide-on closure, 1 3/4 x 2 3/4", 4 1/4" h. (ILLUS.)... **$1,265**

Candy container, glass, smiling face jack-o'-lantern w/screw top **286**

Candy container, glass, smiling face jack-o'-lantern w/witch's hat, screw top **275**

Black Cat Candy Container

Candy container, papier-mâché, black cat w/yellow eyes, arched back, ca. 1940-50 (ILLUS.)... **95**

German Candy Container w/Candleholder Head

Candy container, papier-mache & composition, figural cat w/tail sticking straight up, w/wide grinning mouth, big staring eyes & stand-up ears, the head serving as holder for candle & detaching for access to candy container body, Germany, pre-WWII, split at one leg, 5 1/2" h. (ILLUS.)...................... **2,530**

Papier-mache Watermelon Candy Container

Candy container, papier-mache & composition, figural watermelon w/wide grimacing smile, big eyes & triangular nose, Germany, 4 1/2" w. (ILLUS.) **920**

Mad Cat with Jack-O'-Lantern Die-cut

Decoration, die-cut cardboard, mad cat w/jack-o'-lantern, ca. 1950s, 5" h. (ILLUS.) **5-10**

Mean Flying Witch Die-cut Decoration

Decoration, die-cut cardboard, mean flying witch, America, ca. 1940s, 14 1/2" h. (ILLUS.) **10-20**

Owl on Branch Die-cut

Decoration, die-cut cardboard, owl on branch, H.E. Luhrs, ca. 1950s (ILLUS.) **8-12**

Screaming Cat Die-cut Decoration

Decoration, die-cut cardboard, screaming cat w/big orange eyes, USA, ca. 1940s, 21" h. (ILLUS.) **12-20**

Cat on Fence Lantern

Lantern, papier-mâché, black cat w/paper inserts, green eyes, red mouth w/pointed white teeth, on black & orange fence-form base, ca. 1940s-50s, USA, mint condition (ILLUS.) **150**

Black Cat Lantern

Lantern, papier-mâché, heavy, black cat w/yellow eyes, crepe paper accordian neck, ca. 1920s, Germany, if in mint condition (ILLUS.) **400**

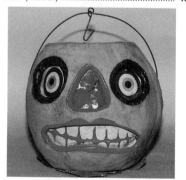

Early German Jack-O'-Lantern

Lantern, papier-mâché, heavy, orange, red & black JOL w/paper inserts at eyes, nose & mouth, ca. 1920, Germany (ILLUS.) **275**
Lantern, papier-mâché w/printed tissue insert, black cat, 6 1/2" h. **490**
Lantern, papier-mâché w/tissue insert, black cat.. **358**

Model of Owl

Model of owl, papier-mâché, black w/yellow eyes (ILLUS.)... **85**

Witch with Fangs Tin Noisemaker

Noisemaker, tin round, lithographed witch w/fangs, w/wooden handle, 4" l. (ILLUS.) . **20-30**

Round Tin Litho Noisemaker

Noisemaker, tin, round, w/green plastic handle, cat in center, US Metal Toy, 3 1/2" h. (ILLUS.) **15-25**

Tin Noisemaker with Wooden Handle

Noisemaker, tin w/wooden handle, circular-shaped, orange w/black & white lithographed scene of a jack-o'-lantern, witch w/broom, cat, demon & bat, ca. 1925 (ILLUS.) **65**

Halloween Scene on Paper Plate

Paper plate, design of cats, jack-o'-lantern & haunted house, ca. 1950s, 9" l. (ILLUS.).... **10-20**

HAWAIIANA

Hawaiiana is a blossoming collectibles arena, one which holds many surprises for the newcomer. For starters, some of the best Hawaiiana was not made in Hawaii, and some of the most valuable pieces are brand new. Tiki mugs comprise one of the most active categories of Hawaiiana collectibles, and many of the priciest mugs are those of recent vintage designed by artists Shag and Munktiki. Hawaiiana covers a broad range of items, from vintage rayon shirts to surfboards to rattan furnishings and original artwork from the likes of Witco, Frank MacIntosh and Frank Oda (Hale Pua). With the current popularity of vintage tropical and tiki lounge decor, this is one collector area that is fun for everyone.

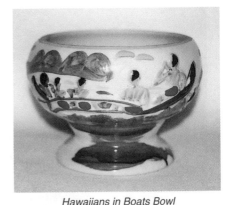

Hawaiians in Boats Bowl

Bowl, Hawaiians in boats, Trader Dick's Restaurant, Reno, 4 x 5 1/2" (ILLUS.) **$8-15**

Ceramic Canister Set from Italy

Canister set, ceramic w/net pattern, Italy, ca. 1950s, 8 1/2" l., the set (ILLUS.) **30-50**

Rattan Chair by Paul Frankl

Chair, rattan, rare 8-banded square "pretzel style" by Paul Frankl, ca. 1940s, 32 x 34" h. (ILLUS.) **500-800**

Printed Bamboo Coasters

Coasters, bamboo, "Aloha!" w/hula girl graphics, printed bamboo, 1960-1970s, set of 4 (ILLUS.).. **12-20**

Plastic Hula Girl Doll

Doll, plastic, hula girl w/grass skirt, lei, sitting, ca. 1950s-1960s, 7" h., (ILLUS.)
.... **30-45**

Figurine, ceramic, brown w/white crackle glaze, hula girl, Treasure Craft, ca. 1950s, 7 1/2" h., (ILLUS., next column) **15-25**

Figurine, plastic, miniature hula girl, "Hawaii" written on base, ca. 1950s, 1 1/2" h. (ILLUS., next column) **10-15**

Ceramic Hula Girl

Miniature Plastic Hula Girl Figurine

Carved Wood Tiki Figure

Figurine, Tiki figure, carved wood, made in Philippines for Margal of California, ca. 1950s, 8" h. (ILLUS.)............................... **20-40**

Bamboo Floor-type Lamp

Lamp, bamboo, floor-type, no shade, ca. 1960s (ILLUS.) **95-150**

Bamboo Magazine Rack

Magazine rack, bamboo, ca. 1950s, 23 1/2" h. (ILLUS.) **15-20**

Menu Cover by Frank MacIntosh

Menu cover, artwork by Frank Macintosh for Master Cruise Lines, 9 x 12" (ILLUS.) **60-75**

Ceramic Cylindrical Shaped Mug

Mug, ceramic, cylindrical shaped w/hula girl relief, Orchids of Hawaii, Japan, 6 3/4" h. (ILLUS.)... **8-12**

Kava Craft/Hawaii Ltd. Ceramic Mug

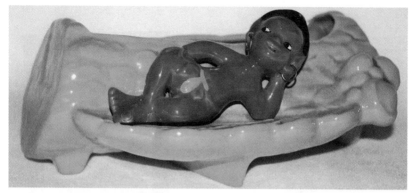

Tropical Native on Log Planter

Mug, ceramic, Hawaiian name translations on back, brown ceramic, Kava Craft/Hawaii Ltd., ca. 1960s (ILLUS.) **5-10**

Tiki Mug with Three Faces

Mug, Tiki mug, three faces, Otagiri, Japan, ca. 1950s-60s, 4" l. (ILLUS.) **20-30**

Figural Hula Girl/Child Music Box

Music box, plastic, figural hula girl/child w/poseable arms, ca. 1960s, 11" h., (ILLUS.) **10-15**

Planter, ceramic, tropical native w/metal earring on log, Gilner, ca. 1940s, 8 3/4" l. (ILLUS., top of page) **20-40**

Palm Tree and Coconut Shakers

Salt and pepper shakers, palm tree w/attached coconut shakers, Treasurecraft, ca. 1950s, 5" h., pr. (ILLUS.) **15-20**

Figural Hula Girls Salt and Pepper Shakers

Salt and pepper shakers, topless hula girls, composition, ca. 1930s, 3" h., pr. (ILLUS.) **30-50**

Orchids with Grey Border Serving Tray

Serving tray, tin, litho w/orchids, grey border, ca. 1940s-1950s, 11 x 18" l., set of 4 (ILLUS. of one)................................... **25-40**

Sheet music, "My Hawaiian Sunshine," early 1900s (ILLUS.) **12-20**

Tropical Leaves behind Wood Shelf

Shelf, wood, tropical leaves behind angular modern shelf, ca. 1940s-1950s, 19 x 20" (ILLUS.)... **50-75**

"My Hawaiian Sunshine" Sheet Music

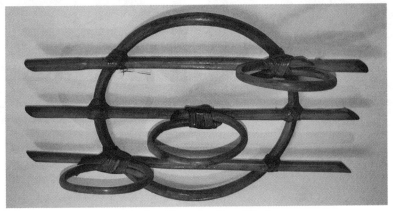

Bamboo Three-ring Towel Rack

Towel rack, bamboo, w/three rings, mounts on wall, ca. 1950s-1960s (ILLUS., previous page) **35-50**

HORSE COLLECTIBLES

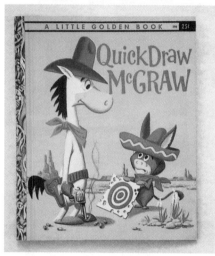

"QuickDraw McGraw" Book

Book, "QuickDraw McGraw," Little Golden Book #398, cover w/color illustration of title character w/sidekick Baba Looey, 1960 (ILLUS.)... **$12-20**

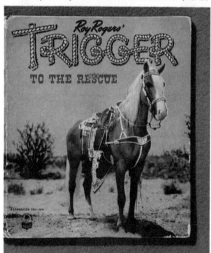

"Roy Rogers' Trigger to the Rescue"

Book, "Roy Rogers' Trigger to the Rescue," cover w/color photo of standing Trigger in ornate saddle & bridle in desert landscape, Cozy Corner, 1950s (ILLUS.) **15-25**

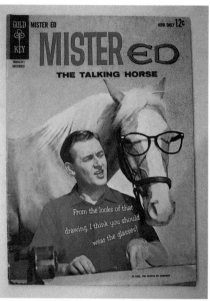

"Mister Ed" Comic Book

Comic book, "Mister Ed The Talking Horse," w/color picture of bespectacled Mister Ed looking over Wilbur's shoulder, Gold Key, 1963 (ILLUS.)............................ **8-20**

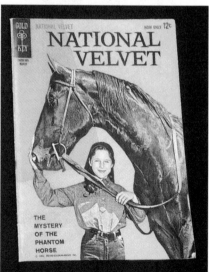

"National Velvet" Comic Book

Comic book, "National Velvet, The Mystery of the Phantom Horse," cover w/color photo of horse & actress from TV series, Gold Key, 1963 (ILLUS.)............................ **5-10**

Porcelain Horse & Rider

Figure group, porcelain, finely detailed
18th c. figure in tricorn hat w/powder horn
mounted on standing horse, on base simulating meadow or forest floor, Nymphen-
burg, early 1900s, 8 1/2" (ILLUS.)......... **200-300**

Art Deco Ceramic Donkeys

Figurine, ceramic, Art Deco-style donkey
foals, red & orange, 1930s, red 3 1/2", orange, 2 3/4", each (ILLUS. of both sizes)... **15-25**

Chinese Ceramic Horse Figurine

Figurine, ceramic, Asian horse painted gold
on blue rectangular base, w/molded sad-
dle & bridle, China, 1970s, 6" (ILLUS.) **15-25**

Ceramic Horse Made in Italy

Figurine, ceramic, Asian-style horse, black
w/white mane, tail, face & four socks,
w/molded saddle & bridle, on white rectangular base, Italy, 1970s, 14 x 16" (ILLUS.).. **50-75**

Norleans Ceramic Horse

Figurine, ceramic, black horse w/white
socks, Norleans, Japan, 4 1/2" (ILLUS.)..... **6-12**
Figurine, ceramic, dappled grey No. 1862
racehorse w/jockey, Beswick, England,
1963-83... **500-700**

Ceramic Donkey Figurine

Figurine, ceramic, donkey w/oversize ears, chartreuse green w/gold accents, Pearl China, 1950s, 5" (ILLUS., previous page)... **18-26**

Ceramic Draft Horse Figurine

Figurine, ceramic, stylized prancing draft horse, aqua blue, 1930s, 2 3/4" (ILLUS.).. **20-30**

Ceramic & Rabbit Fur Horse

Figurine, ceramic, tan & white caricature horse w/rabbit fur mane & tail, 1960s, 4 x 5" (ILLUS.).. **18-24**

Ceramic Bay Horse Figurine

Figurine, ceramic, walking horse, bay w/white stockings, 5 1/2" (ILLUS.) **15-20**

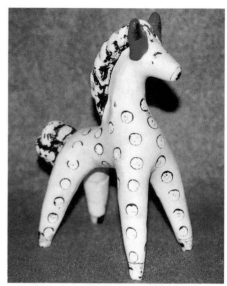

Clay Horse Figurine

Figurine, clay, stylized design of splay-legged white horse w/black circle accents & mane & tail & red ears, 4 1/5" (ILLUS.) . **10-15**

Breyer Dappled Grey Belgian Horse

Figurine, glossy dappled grey Belgian w/dark mane & tail, bald face, Breyer, 1960s (ILLUS.)...................................... **300-500**

Breyer's Misty of Chincoteague

Figurine, Misty of Chincoteague pinto pony, tan & white, Breyer, about 5 1/2" (ILLUS., previous page) **15-25**

Breyer Palomino Figurine

Figurine, Paso Fino Tesoro palomino, Breyer, early 1990s, 9" (ILLUS.) **15-20**

QuickDraw McGraw Hand Puppet

Hand puppet, QuickDraw McGraw, cloth w/vinyl head, blue shirt w/red hat, bib & hands, Knickerbocker, 1962, 10" (ILLUS.) **15-25**

Hartland Plastics Foal

Model of foal, unpainted brown plastic, Hartland Plastics, 1960s (ILLUS.)............... **5-10**

Model of Running Horse

Model of horse, bronzed metal, running pose, 6 1/4" (ILLUS.) **30-40**

Carnival Chalkware Circus Pony

Model of horse, Carnival chalkware circus pony, w/glitter accents, white w/black mane & tail, molded bridle & reins, 1940s-50s, 11" (ILLUS.) **50-75**

Circus Pony on Red & Yellow Base

Model of horse, Carnival chalkware circus pony, white w/black mane & tail & black molded bridle & reins, on yellow & red base, 1950s, 6" (ILLUS.) **25-35**

Stone Carved Running Horse

Model of horse, stone carved on wooden base, running form w/flowing mane & tail, China, 1980s, 3 1/2 x 5" (ILLUS.) **25-35**

Model of horse, unpainted grey plastic, Hartland Plastics, 1960s, 7" **8-15**

Swedish Good Luck Horse

Model of horse, wood, Swedish Good Luck horse, h.p. red/orange, yellow/green, gold & white decoration on black body, Sweden, 1970s, 5 1/4" (ILLUS.)................ **12-20**

Reproduction Cast Iron Pony

Model of pony, cast iron, unpainted black reproduction, 3 1/5" (ILLUS.) **4-8**

Brass Model of Racehorse

Model of racehorse, brass, w/molded saddle & cropped tail, "My Old Kentucky Home" on saddle, 2 1/2" (ILLUS.)............. **25-35**

Roy Rogers & Trigger

Model of Roy Rogers on Trigger, plastic, Trigger w/molded black saddle & bridle, chain reins, Roy in molded blue shirt, yellow neckerchief, white hat, brown chaps, silvered decoration on saddle & chaps, Hartland Plastics issued standing, half rearing & full rearing versions, each (ILLUS. of standing version) **150-250**

Trigger in Half Rearing Pose

Model of Trigger, plastic, half rearing pose, w/black bridle & reins but no saddle, Hartland Plastics (ILLUS., previous page) **25-30**

Horse Push Puppet

Puppet, push-type, wooden, grey horse w/comical expression on cylindrical natural wood base, Europe, 1960s, 2 1/2" (ILLUS.) **20-30**

"Fury" Jigsaw Puzzle

Puzzle, jigsaw type, "Fury," w/picture of black horse & boy at fence, "Jr. Jigsaw Puzzle, not too hard - not too easy" at top, Whitman, late 1950s (ILLUS.) **12-20**

Toy, My Little Pony, Beddy-Bye Eyes, eyes close when ponies are laid down, Hasbro, 1980s **4-8**

Toy, My Little Pony, clothing outfit on card, Hasbro, 1980s **15-35**

Toy, My Little Pony, Dance N Prance Ponies, knob on chest makes tail swirl, Hasbro, 1980s **7-15**

Toy, My Little Pony, first series of six standing ponies, flat feet w/inner circles, Hasbro, 1982, each **20-50**

Toy, My Little Pony, First Tooth Babies, Hasbro, 1980s **5-10**

Toy, My Little Pony, Newborns, tiniest baby ponies, Hasbro, 1980s **5-10**

My Little Pony Plush Toy

Toy, My Little Pony, Plush Hasbro Softies, 1980s (ILLUS.) **8-15**

Toy, My Little Pony, pony w/outfit, loose, Hasbro, 1980s **20-30**

Toy, My Little Pony, Rainbow Curl Ponies, w/curly mane & tail & rainbow stripes, Hasbro, 1980s **5-10**

Toy, My Little Pony, Rainbow Ponies, w/rainbow striped mane & tail, Hasbro, 1980s **5-10**

Toy, My Little Pony, So Soft Ponies, covered w/fuzzy flocking, Hasbro, 1980s **8-15**

Circus Horse Ramp Walker

Toy, Ramp Walker circus horse, plastic, red w/green legs, 1940s-50s, 2 1/2 x 3" (ILLUS.) **18-24**

Relpo Horse Head Vase

Vase, ceramic, two horse heads, tan & white w/black manes, on black base, Relpo, 1940s, 1 x 6" (ILLUS.) **15-25**

INDIAN ART & ARTIFACTS

Beaded Child's Bandolier Bag & Two Beaded Pillows

Items are based on prehistoric stone artifacts of the Northeastern United States. Values are of whole, complete specimens. Breaks would knock prices down. Colorful flint or stone would increase the value as will any item with line designs or effigies involved.

Bandolier bag, Woodlands, child's size, beadwork on fabric featuring on the front two tiny American flags below a bird perched atop a flowering stem flanked by colorful starbursts & flowers on stems on a white ground, a red-beaded border band w/zigzag beading, the wide red strap w/further stylized leaf beading, stroud backing worn & deteriorated, strap 38" l., bag 7 x 9" (ILLUS. left with two beaded pillows, top of page) **$633**

Cradleboard, Great Basin, girl's, oblong, yellow-stained ochre leather, possibly for a small baby, close tied w/the Apache evident in the wooden base loop, traditional Ute wicker frame retained, deep sky blue favored by the Ute w/green, black & pearly white beading in a floral design, missing hood, a few loose beads, one missing row, original lace inside, ca. 1890, 8" w., 21" h. (ILLUS. bottom with Ute girl's cradleboard) **1,150**

Cradleboard, Ute, girl's, wide arched & tapering backboard, yellow ochre staining, arched beaded band across the top w/red & blue designs on a white ground, one of the two loom-beaded ornaments w/initials "M.E.," piece overlapped & sewn shut but is child-sized & should be replaced, flat beaded w/clear, red 'white hearts,' green-edged w/blue & old yellow, the hood & board ornaments beaded w/Ute blue, ruby, yellow & dark blue along w/white, tab rim stained, long leather fringe on back, some bead loss & mi-

nor wear, 19th c., 34 1/4" l. (ILLUS. top with Great Basin cradleboard, below) **4,600**

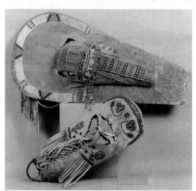

Two Girl's Cradleboards

Cradleboard, Ute, large tapering oblong backboard stained yellow for a girl, a beaded band arching acrosss the top in white & colors featuring rare American flag designs, finger-like rows of beading on the flap covering the laces done on early red & blue strouding w/red 'white hearts,' navy black unstable beads, greasy yellow & green beads, Transmontane style used from 1860-80, red stroud trade cloth beaded in black & white at hood edge, the cross flap at top of the opening geometrically beaded w/later beads such as cut metallic, orangey red 'white hearts' & translucent blue & green, attached to it is an umbilical fetish bead wrapped in white heart reds & blue w/brass bead drops, a weasel claw amulet, a miniature brass shoe sold & a small Victorian key, fringe at the back, replaced laces, perhaps in the 1880s, good provenance, 39" l. (ILLUS., below) **6,900**

Rare Ute Beaded Cradleboard

Fine Toy Chippewa Cradleboard & Cover

Cradleboard & beaded cover, Chippewa, toy-sized, the slightly tapering rectangular wooden back w/a heart cut-out at the top, a lovely curved bow & heart pierced decoration on the backboard, all painted in a muted green, the beaded cover finely decorated w/large pink & blue flowers & green leafy stems again a black velvet background, glued break along backboard, ca. 1860, 6 x 14" (ILLUS.) **1,438**

Apache Moccasins & Child's Cradleboard

Cradleboard & doll, Apache, child's, sunshade hood stained orange, muslin doll w/thread features, the leather cradle & the Western Apache doll mocassins stained w/yellow ochre beaded in rows of blue, white & black beads, noses on the moccasins, one bead earring missing, two bead rows missing, 21 3/4" h., the set (ILLUS. left with Apache moccasins) .. **2,013**

Gauntlets, Plateau, beaded leather, the top finely beaded w/tiny seed beads in many shades to from lance-shaped finger stripes, patriotic flags & shields on the top of the hands & bright stylized floral designs on the cuffs, cloth interior of cotton homespun, work of an Umatilla, Nez Perce or Yakima master craftsman, very early Pendleton Roundup-type wear, worn binding & slight insect damage, patch at right thumb, 19th c., 8 1/2" w., 13 1/2" l., pr. (ILLUS., top next page)........ **1,495**

Fine Early Zuni Pueblo Painted Jar

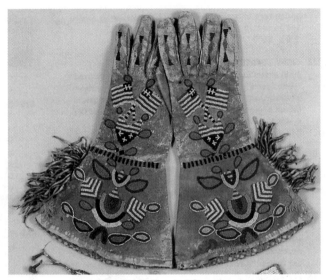

Rare Finely Beaded Gauntlets

Jar, Zuni, pottery, wide bulbous form w/a wide flat rim, painted in red ochre & black on typical white slip w/relief figures of frogs & a swirling stylized floral design, ca. 1880-1900, 7 1/2" d., 6" h. (ILLUS., previous page) **6,900**

Pillow, Iroquois, beaded souvenir-type, rectangular w/serpentine sides, boldly beaded w/two American flags above a spread-winged bird w/a flower above, colored leaf-style border band, the type soldd aaround Niagara Falls, ca. 1890s, 8 1/4 x 10 3/4" (ILLUS. top right with child's bandolier bag & other pillow, page 834) **230**

Pillow, Iroquois, beaded souvenir-type, rectangular w/serpentine sides, boldly beaded w/two angled American flags above a spread-winged bird w/a flower above, colored leaf-style border band, the type soldd aaround Niagara Falls, ca. 1890s, 8 3/4 x 10 3/4" (ILLUS. bottom right with child's bandolier bag & other pillow, page 834) **345**

Rug, Navajo, Ganado or Klagetoch area, central elongated diamond design in hand-carded natural, black & grey wool w/double dye red border design, ca. 1930, stains, wear, 4' 4" x 6' 7" (ILLUS., bottom of page) **1,380**

Early 20th Century Navajo Rug

JEWELRY
Antique (1800-1920)

French Antique Garnet Bar Pin

Bar pin, garnet, diamond & 14k gold, centering a sugarloaf garnet surrounded by rose-cut diamonds, three large garnets at each end & set throughout w/faceted garnets, French hallmarks, missing one stone (ILLUS.) **$1,058**

Bar Pin with Large Center Garnet

Bar pin, garnet, diamond & 15k gold, the center set w/a large garnet surrounded by 18 round diamonds flanked by gold bar ends, one diamond replaced, Victorian (ILLUS.) **413**

Bar pin, ruby & diamond, long narrow form centered by a line of bezel-set oval rubies surrounded by forty-two old European- and full-cut diamonds weighing 2.28 cts., platinum-topped 14k gold mount, letter mark & Austrian guarantee mark, ca. 1910 .... **3,525**

Band Bracelet with Overall Garnets

Bracelet, garnet & silver, gradually tapering band set overall w/prong-set garnets in bands & other patterns, early 20th c., 2 1/2" w. (ILLUS.) **345**

Bracelet, gem- and seed pearl-set 18k gold, oval links in tricolor gold, each collet-set w/various stones including aquamarine, topaz, chrysoberl & garnet surrounded by beads & wirework alternating w/scroll-edged links composed of small beads, centered seed pearls & two half pearls, second half 19th c., 6 3/4" l. (evidence of solder) **1,175**

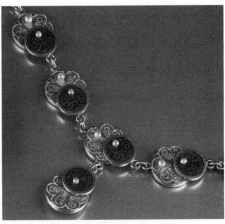

Gold & Enamel Link Bracelet

Bracelet, gold (14k), enamel & seed pearl, composed of circular engraved gold links surmounted by blue enamel circles each set w/a seed pearl, one link is a drop, 7 1/2" l. (ILLUS.) **940**

Fine Victorian Gold Mesh Bracelet

Bracelet, gold (14k) & enamel, slide-type, wide flat adjustable mesh band w/the flat slide enameled w/blue palmettes centered by a pearl on a black-enameled ground, foxtail fringe (ILLUS.) **1,998**

Bracelet, gold (14k) & sapphire, bangle-type, a narrow band w/delicate openwork scrolls set around the sides w/five bezel-set round sapphires, Edwardian era, England, interior circumference 7" d. **382**

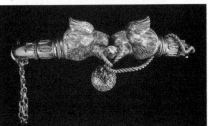

Hinged Victorian Gargoyle Bracelet

Bracelet, gold (14k yellow), circular tubular form w/a section of two facing gargoyle

heads w/a small diamond six-prong setting above a ball drop, hinged to open,
small safety chain, unmarked, Victorian,
2 1/4 x 2 1/2" (ILLUS., previous page) **2,300**

Fine Platinum, Gold Snake Bracelet

Bracelet, platinum, 14k gold & diamond, designed as a coiled snake w/a platinum &
yellow gold mesh body, the head set
w/an old European-cut diamond weighing approx. 1.01 cts., rose-cut eyes offset
by dark patination, stamped "PD,"
11 1/2" l. (ILLUS.)..................................... **7,050**

Gold, Diamond & Sapphire Bangle

Bracelet, sapphire, diamond & 14k gold,
bangle-type, simple hinged gold band bezel-set w/three old European-cut diamonds alternating w/two circular-cut sap-
phires, Edwardian (ILLUS.) **3,525**
Bracelet, sapphire & diamond, narrow oval
links alternating w/five bezel-set cushion-
cut sapphires or five old European-cut diamonds, millegrain accents, ca. 1915,
7 3/4" l. **3,643**
Bracelets, enamel & 14k gold, buckle-form
hinged bangle-type, wide w/overall black
enamel, the gold clasp section w/en-
graved edges, second half 19th c., interi-
or diameter 6", pr. (loss to enamel) **1,175**
Bracelets, gold (14k), turquoise & enamel,
bangle-type, the hinged ring decorated
w/black enamel tracery & engraved accents, the top w/an engraved gold ring
surrounding a cluster of turquoise cabochons, second half 19th c., interior diam-
eter 6", pr. **1,175**
Brooch, amethyst & 14k gold, Arts & Crafts
style, a large oval bezel-set amethyst set
in a rectangular gold frame decorated
w/pierced heart-shaped leaves & berry
clusters, designed & signed by Jose-
phine Hartwell Shaw, early 20th c. **3,408**
Brooch, aquamarine & 14k gold, a large
cartouche form composed of gold openwork engraved scrolls, four aquamarines
set around the sides w/a scrolling wire-

work drop pendant mounted w/another
aquamarine, second half 19th c. **1,528**
Brooch, enamel, diamond & 18k gold, the
purple enameled flowerhead centered by
a prong-set old European-cut diamond,
signed by Tiffany & Co., approximate
weight .75 cts., second half 19th c.
(enamel loss) **2,115**
Brooch, gold (14k) & diamond, two rounded
intertwined engraved gold bands suspending a pair of long tassels, at the center a large round boss w/a textured surface centered by a star enclosing a small
rose-cut diamond, second half 19th c. **294**
Brooch, gold (18k), enamel & pearl, Renaissance Revival style, oval form composed
of small openwork scrolls decorated
w/black & white enamel & set in the center
& around the sides w/seven pearls, a hair
compartment on the back, marked by T.B.
Starr, second half 19th c. **1,645**

Plique-à-Jour & Gold Dragonfly Brooch

Brooch, gold (18k) & plique-à-jour, Art Nouveau-style model of a dragonfly w/a yellow gold body set w/one oval blue sapphire, the shoulder of the wings, mouth,
eyes & body set w/small round dia-
monds, early 20th c. (ILLUS.) **1,725**

Micromosaic Butterfly Brooch

Brooch, micromosaic, a round wide gilt-
metal frame w/wirework & bead accents
centering a round color design of a but-
terfly on a white ground (ILLUS.) **1,293**

Ornate Gold & Amethyst Victorian Earrings

Earrings, amethyst & 14k gold, ornate oblong
gold leaf & coiled wirework frame enclosing
a large collet-set pear-shaped amethyst
w/a smaller amethyst above & below, Vic-
torian, missing tops, pr. (ILLUS.) **1,645**

Ruby, Diamond & Gold Earrings

Earrings, ruby, diamond & gold, a round
openwork gold frame bezel-set w/rubies
surrounded by rose-cut diamonds, one
small ruby missing, ca. 1890, pr. (ILLUS.) **633**

Jabot pin, diamond, pearl & 18k gold, each
fan-shaped end w/pavé-set diamond
melée framing a golden & ivory-toned
cultured pearl, pearl possibly natural, Edwardian, England, early 20th c. **3,878**

French Gold, Pearl & Diamond Locket

Locket, gold, pearl & diamond, oval set
w/an outer band of pearls around a large
stylized flower set w/24 partial-cut diamonds & a central pearl, scrolled top for
hanging ring, French hallmarks, 19th c.
(ILLUS.) **403**

Necklace, diamond, citrine & 14k gold, Art
Nouveau style, a large oblong facet-cut

citrine flanked by large leafy scrolls continuing into the leafy scroll chain accented by collet-set small diamonds, Europe-
an hallmark, ca. 1900, 16" l. **5,288**

Edwardian Diamond & Ruby Necklace

Necklace, diamond & ruby, negligee-style,
two rose-cut diamond flower terminals
framed by calibré-cut rubies suspended
from knife-edge bar links highlighted by
bezel-set full- and rose-cut diamonds,
millegrain accents, completed by a fancy
link chain, platinum & 18k gold mount,
Edwardian, w/original fitted Parisian jew-
eler's box, 20" l. (ILLUS. of part).............. **4,935**

Necklace, garnet, a central long scrolled
mount w/a six-petal blossom at the center set overall w/round & pear-shaped
rose-cut garnets, suspending three
drops, each w/a cluster of three garnets
above a single round garnet suspending
a teardrop garnet, the links in the chain
each set w/a round garnet, gilt-metal
mount, second half 19th c., 16 1/2" l........ **1,116**

Fine Victorian Garnet Necklace

Necklace, garnet, graduated wide form set
overall w/faceted garnets in a graduating
florette design, gilt-metal mount, Victorian, one stone missing, 14 1/2" l. (ILLUS.
of part).. **1,763**

Enamel & Diamond Portrait Pin

Pin, enamel & diamond, a large central round enamel plaque h.p. w/a bust portrait of a costumed lady w/diamonds inset into her headdress & shoulder, within an outer band of 40 rose-cut diamonds, set in 18k yellow gold (ILLUS.) **2,200**

Pin, gold (14k) & coral, a wide gold ring decorated w/applied beads & wirework, centered by a large angelskin coral cabochon, second half 19th c. **176**

Pin, gold (14k), diamond & seed pearl, designed as a sword & scabbard connected by a trace link chain, the handle set w/seed pearls & four prong-set old European-cut diamonds, further seed pearls at the top, Edwardian, ca. 1905 .... **235**

Pin, gold (14k), enamel & diamond, Art Nouveau style, in the shape of a dogwood blossom w/the petals decorated w/black enamel, the center w/an old European-cut diamond weighing .50 cts., American mark, ca. 1900 .... **764**

Pin, gold (18k) & diamond, a tapering silver-topped baton set w/graduated bead-set rose-cut diamonds, entwined w/an engraved yellow gold slender rope tipped by a pearl, French guarantee mark, late 19th c. **323**

Pin, turquoise, diamond & 14k gold, a round narrow mount set w/small old mine-cut diamonds & centered by a large turquoise cabochon, open gallery, second half 19th c... **646**

Ring, diamond, an oblong silver-topped 18k gold mount composed of pairs of openwork scrolls collet-set w/rose-cut diamonds, 19th c., size 3 3/4 .... **499**

Ring, gold (18k), diamond & enamel, mourning-type, the round top centered by a small round compartment for a lock of hair surrounded by a circle w/four black enamel panels alternating w/four old mine-cut diamonds weighing .60 cts., the shank w/champlevé enameled rings, 19th c., size 5 1/4 .... **470**

Ancient Roman Gold & Carnelian Ring

Ring, gold & carnelian, Ancient Roman piece w/a plain hollow gold hoop flat on the interior & rounded on the exterior, expanding at the shoulders, set w/a convex oval carnelian engraved w/a standing draped figure of Fortuna, the goddess holding a cornucopia in one hand & sheaves of wheat & a ship's rudder in the other, ca. 1st century A.D. (ILLUS.).......... **1,035**

Very Fine Ruby & Diamond Ring

Ring, ruby & diamond, a large central cushion-shaped ruby framed by ten old mine-cut diamonds, diamond-set shoulders, platinum-topped 18k gold mount, size 5 (ILLUS.).. **10,575**

Ring, sapphire & 18k bicolor gold, an oval cut sapphire in an oval mount engraved w/delicate flowers & leaves, size 7 1/2 .... **999**

Ring, sapphire & diamond, the round top centered by a large round sapphire surrounded by a ring of ten old European-cut diamonds, 14k gold mount, w/a Bigelow, Kennard Co. box, early 20th c., size 8 1/2 .... **1,058**

Amethyst Dog Head Stickpin

Stickpin, gold (18k), amethyst, diamond & enamel, the top w/an amethyst carved as a spaniel head w/a rose-cut diamond collar & chain, hallmarks of Cabrelli, Paris, France (ILLUS.)... **2,350**

Sets

Brooch & earrings, chalcedony, coral & 14k gold, the round brooch w/an outer ring of milky chalcedony enclosing a ring of engraved gold centered by a coral bead, matching earrings, second half 19th c., the set... **646**

Fine Gold & Garnet Victorian Set

Brooch & earrings, gold (14k) & amethyst, the brooch designed as a ringed knot set w/a spray of amethyst berries, applied wire-twist decoration, a glass compartment on the back, the earrings of similar design, Victorian, the set (ILLUS.) **1,410**

Brooch & earrings, gold (14k) & enamel, the brooch composed of an inverted U-form pin w/incurved sides & topped w/scrolls flanking a button, the sides w/a textured surface trimmed w/black enamel, suspending a long lyre-form drop w/a large central button drop flanked by tiny drop beads, also w/a textured surface & black enamel trim, the earrings matching the lyre-form drop, ca. 1872, the set **2,468**

Pendant-brooch & earrings, amethyst & 14k gold, the earrings w/two graduated gold rings, each set w/a facet-cut amethyst w/delicate wirework scrolls at the bottom suspending a foxtail gold fringe, the brooch w/an engraved center gold ring centering a large amethyst & flanked by smaller rings holding smaller amethysts, delicate wirework scrolls at the top & bottom w/a foxtail gold fringe at the bottom, brooch signed "W. & S.B.," boxed, second half 19th c., the set (earrings w/later screw-backs, evidence of solder) **1,175**

Rare Blossom-form Diamond Slides

Slides, each designed as a Queen Anne's Lace blossom set w/rose-cut diamonds & demantoid garnets, circular-cut ruby blood spot, platinum-topped 18k gold mounts, w/Tiffany box, unsigned, minor losses, pin stems added, Edwardian, England, early 20th c., pr. (ILLUS.) **10,281**

Costume Jewelry

Costume Jewelry refers to jewelry made of inexpensive materials. It was originally designed to accessorize designer's clothing collections, and was meant to be discarded along with the clothing when it went out of style. Women saved this jewelry for its beauty, and today it is a very important collectible. It was inexpensive in its time, and was made in the most up-to-the-minute designs. Today collectors can pay more for certain costume jewelry than for some precious jewelry.

Bar pin, goldplate, carnelian glass, Art Deco Chinese character writing w/center carved carnelian glass flower, 2 3/4" w... **$55-75**

Bar pin, sterling, applied cats & kittens faces, 2 3/4" w., 1/2" h. **65-85**

Bar pin, white metal, three center emerald green square stones, clear rhinestone trim, 2 1/4" w. **55-70**

Belt buckle, silver plate, two-piece Art Nouveau design w/center fleur-de-lis, 3 1/4" w., 1" h. **25-35**

Steel Belt Buckle

Belt buckle, steel made in marcasite style, 3 3/4" w., 1 3/4" h. (ILLUS.)......................... **25-35**
Belt buckle, steel made in marcasites style, two-piece, 1 1/2" h. **25-35**
Bracelet, glass, coral color molded glass flowers & leaves section threaded on elastic, unsigned Czechoslovakian components, 7/8" w...................................... **75-90**
Bracelet, gold filled, "bricks" style w/center rectangular amethyst 3/4 x 1/2" stone, bracelet is 7" l., 5/8" w............................... **65-85**
Bracelet, gold filled, child's size, hinged bangle-type, 1/4" w., initials, Victorian **30-45**
Bracelet, gold filled, cobalt blue stones, 3/4" h., alternating w/gold circles, 7" l., 3/4" w. **90-110**

Goldplate & Glass Bracelet

Bracelet, goldplate, glass, carved oval links in scarab style, each link a different color, 1/2" w. (ILLUS.) **45-60**
Bracelet, vermeil (gold over sterling) flexible links of amber triangular stones, hallmarked, 1/4" w.................................... **85-110**
Bracelet, white metal set w/multicolor agate style glass stones, links style, w/one link hanging as a charm, 6 1/2" l., 3/4" w. (ILLUS., top next column) **45-65**
Dress clip, Bakelite, black, densely carved leaves, vines design, 2" h. **45-70**

White Metal Bracelet

Goldplated Insect Dress Clip

Dress clip, fur-type, goldplated insect motif, green rhinestones eyes, purple center diamond-shaped stone on body, 1 1/2 x 1" (ILLUS.)... **40-55**
Dress clip, plastic yellow iridescent bubbles design, 2" **35-45**

Blue Marquise Dress Clip

Dress clip, rhinestones, all deep blue marquise stones in openwork design, 2" x 2 3/4" (ILLUS., previous page) **55-65**

Round Flower Design Dress Clip

Dress clip, rhinestones, round flower design set w/red, blue, green, amber petals, 1 3/4" d. (ILLUS.) **30-45**

Dress clips, cabochon set, blue, red, green stones in open design, 2 1/4" h., pr. **65-85**

Dress clips, duette, red enamel Art Deco motif, rhinestones trim, 2 3/4" w., signed Coro **90-120**

Dress clips, three rows faux moonstones in inverted pyramid style rows, Art Deco, 1 1/2 x 1 1/2" l., pr. **60-80**

Goldplate Clip-on Earrings

Earrings, goldplate & glass beads, clip-on drop style, three large black glass beads suspended from three chains, 2" l., pr. (ILLUS.) **35-50**

Earrings, pearls, large 3/8" d. ball pearl drop w/smaller pearl on top, 1" h., clip-ons, signed "Richelieu," pr. **40-60**

Earrings, sterling silver, leaf motifs, screw-ons, mint in original box, 1 1/4", pr. **40-55**

Earrings, white metal, round, center black enamel flower w/cultured pearl centers, screw-on type, 5/8" d., pr. **25-35**

Hatpin, goldplate, head of cat, yellow rhinestone eyes, head is 1" w., overall 9" **110-125**

Hatpin, sterling, Art Nouveau head of woman w/long flowing hair, three purple stone accents, head is 1 1/4 x 3/4", overall 7" l. **150-175**

Handpainted Hatpins

Hatpins, plastic, black flat large heads with h.p. multicolor dots, heads 3 3/8" l. x 1" w., overall 7 1/2" h., pr. (ILLUS.) **70-90**

Necklace, beads, crystal, yellow, graduated, ca. 1925, 28" l. **100-125**

Necklace, beads, garnets, graduated sizes, faceted, self bead clasp, 16" l. **125-150**

Necklace, goldplated chain, w/thirteen assorted hanging goldplated charms, some moveable, 30" l. **30-45**

Necklace, goldplated, chains, five strands alternating w/green glass beads, signed "Kramer," adjusts to 16" **55-75**

Necklace, goldplated, library chain style, copy of Medieval design, 31" l. **25-40**

Necklace, plastic, beads, African style ridged large silver beads w/faux carved ivory accent beads, 16 1/2" l. **25-35**

Necklace, rhinestones, Aurora Borealis, individually set 3/8" d. stones, adjusts to 16" **35-50**

Pendant, copper, abstract design on 21" copper chain, signed "Bell," 1 1/2" x 2" **35-50**

Pendant, copper, embossed 1960s Art Nouveau revival motif, woman in profile wearing a headdress over long flowing hair, 1 3/4 x 2 1/4", chain 24" l. **35-50**

Four-swag Chain Pin

Pin, goldplate & large cabochon purple & blue glass stones, four swag chains on bottom, signed "Christian Dior-Germany," dated "1965," 1 1/2 x 2 1/2" (ILLUS.) **75-90**

Christmas Joy Pin

Pin, goldplate, rhinestones, enamel, Christmas motif, word "JOY" w/red enamel on the "J" & "Y," center "O" in form of a wreath w/red rhinestones, green enamel, w/original box, 1 1/2 x 2" (ILLUS.) **15-25**

Pin, goldplate, scarecrow motif w/green stone face, rhinestone trim, hanging chains forming arms & body, signed "Pauline Rader," 2 1/4" h. **55-75**

Christmas Ball Pin

Pin, goldplated, rhinestones, Christmas ball design set w/multicolored large & small

rhinestones, goldplated holly leaves top, 1 1/2" w., 2 1/4" h. (ILLUS.) **25-35**

Letter "E" Pin

Pin, mahogany, letter "E" carved inside center oval, 2 1/2 x 2" (ILLUS.)...................... **25-40**

Butterfly Pin

Pin, mother-of-pearl & goldplate, butterfly motif w/etched mother-of-pearl wings, unsigned, designer quality, 3 1/4" w., 2" h. (ILLUS.) **55-75**

Coach & Horse Pin

Pin, rhinestones, enamel & antiqued white metal, model of a coach w/enameled coachman driving four horses motif, coach & horses set w/blue, green, pink, & clear rhinestones, wheels on coach spin, unsigned, designer quality, 3" w., 1 1/2" h. (ILLUS.) **75-95**

Pin, rhinestones, goldplate, basket of flowers motif w/clear stones, flowers in larger red, blue, purple rhinestones, 1 3/4" h., 2" w. **35-50**

Pin, sterling, figure of Asian man w/yoke across his shoulders, w/two balls attached to yoke, 2 1/2" h., 2 1/4" w............. **60-85**

Pin, sterling, open circle w/two stylized flowers in center overlapping the outer rim of the circle, 1 1/2" d. **55-75**

Pin, vermeil (pink gold over sterling), large flower, curved petals, made in Mexico, unknown hallmark, center 3/4" faux blue topaz, 2 3/4" d. flower **125-150**

Pin/pendant, goldplate, glass, plastic, rhinestones, raised pink glass center w/purple & pink rhinestones, fancy metal folds w/purple plastic centers, ca. 1943-1948, 3" d... **55-75**

Heart Pin/Pendant

Pin/pendant, red enamel stylized heart, made in France, signed "YSL" (Yves St. Laurent), 1 1/2 x 1 1/2" (ILLUS.) **45-65**

Sets

Goldplate Necklace

Necklace & bracelet, goldplate w/rhinestone trim, flexible brickwork design, necklace made like a collar, adjustable length, matching bracelet, both pieces signed "Denbe," necklace adjusts to 14", matching bracelet is 6" l., 1" w., the set (ILLUS. of necklace)............................. **120-145**

Goldplate & Faux Opal Set

Pendant & earrings, goldplate & faux opal center stones, flower motif on chain, center opal stone in clear rhinestone frame, 1/2" d., 16" fine chain, matching screw-on earrings, 12" d., the set (ILLUS.) **50-75**

Rhinestone Trim Pin & Earrings

Pin & earrings, enamel, w/rhinestone trim, curved blue enamel feather motif, matching earrings, signed "Kramer," pin 1 3/4" x 2, mint in original gift box, the set (ILLUS.)... **150-175**

Tan & White Fur Pin & Earrings

Pin & Earrings, goldplate, w/black, tan & white fur, pin w/two fur-set circles on S-shaped design, 3 1/4" w., clip-on earrings 1" d., the set (ILLUS.)....................... **35-50**

Ice Blue Snowflake Pin & Earrings

Pin & earrings, rhinestone, ice blue baguettes, ovals in snowflake motif, pin 2" d., screw-on earrings, 3/4" h., the set (ILLUS., top of page)................................. **65-80**

Pins, sterling, pair of seated tall cats, signed "Beau Sterling," 2 1/2" h., the set **75-95**

Modern (1920-1960)

Bar pin, diamond & platinum, the long narrow filigree mount centered by an old European-cut diamond approximately .75 cts., further set w/fourteen bead & bezel-set old European-cut diamonds, millegrain accents, gold pin, ca. 1930.............. **999**

Art Deco Sapphire Bar Pin

Bar pin, platinum, pink star sapphire & diamond, Art Deco style, the narrow mount bezel-set w/six sapphire cabochons alternating w/sevel full-cut diamonds (ILLUS.) **1,528**

Bracelet, platinum, diamond & carved sapphire & ruby, Art Deco style, composed of sapphire & rubby leaves interspersed w/eight old marquise, 16 old mine-cut & 75 single-cut cuts, completed by interlocking circular single-cut diamond links, approx. 2.28 cts., one diamond & two colored stones missing, 7" l. (ILLUS., bottom of page).. **7,050**

Bracelet, platinum, diamond, emerald & onyx, Art Deco style, composed of three long flexible plaques spaced by pairs of oblong links, set throughout w/318 old European- and single-cut diamonds, approx. 8.40 cts., highlighted by carved emerald leaves & cabochon onyx, millegrain accents & open gallery, a few nicks & abrasions to emeralds, 7" l. (ILLUS., second on bottom of page).......................... **14,100**

Art Deco Diamond & Carved Sapphire & Ruby Bracelet

Rare Art Deco Platinum, Diamond, Emerald & Onyx Bracelet

Art Deco Sapphire & Diamond Bangle

Bracelet, platinum, sapphire & diamond, Art Deco bangle-type, the hinged mount set w/43 calibré-cut sapphires & 173 old European- and single-cut diamonds, approx. 5.55 cts., millegrain accents & engraved sides, probably European hallmark (ILLUS.) **6,463**

Bracelet, platinum, sapphire & diamond, Art Deco style, a long slender form composed of long narrow loop links bead-set w/old European- and single-cut diamonds alternating w/straight links channel-set w/step-cut sapphires, signed by Tiffany & Co., ca. 1930, 7" l. **6,169**

Very Fine Art Deco Bracelet

Bracelet, platinum, sapphire & diamond, Art Deco style, composed of semi-flexible plaques bead-set w/176 old European-cut & 44 single-cut diamonds highlighted by a channel-set French-cut sapphire Greek key motif, approx. 7.70 cts., millegrain accents, 7 1/2" l. (ILLUS.) **15,275**

Gem-set Flowerpot Brooch

Brooch, amethyst, ruby, sapphire, blue spinel, spessarite, garnet, green beryl, diamond & 14k gold, a large faceted oval amethyst flowerpot overflows w/leafy gem-set stems & blossoms, silver-topped gilt & 14k gold mount, ca. 1940 (ILLUS.) .. **1,058**

Brooch, diamond & platinum, Art Deco style, a long open oval frame centered by a large old European-cut diamond weighing 1.29 cts., the outer frame set w/78 French-, baguette- and round-cut diamonds, millegrain accents, signed by Raymond Yard, ca. 1930 .... **5,640**

Brooch, diamond & platinum, Art Deco style, oblong filigree mount w/a rounded central section flanked by pointed end sections, the openwork mount set overall w/navette bead & bezel-set old European-cut diamonds, millegrain accents, gold pin, approximate weight 2.33 cts., ca. 1930.. **1,528**

Brooch, diamond & platinum, Art Deco style, oblong mount w/a rectangular center flanked by fanned end sections joined by ringed side sections, set in the center w/two round diamonds each approximately .69 cts., together w/162 bead & collet-set old European & single-cut diamonds, highlighted by eight straight baguette-cut diamonds, approximate total weight 10.44 cts., ca. 1930 .... **4,700**

Stylized Floral Retro Style Brooch

Brooch, diamond, synthetic rubies & 14k rose gold, Retro style, a swirled styled leafy floral design, the center set w/an old European-cut diamond flanked by 38 small diamonds & synthetic rubies, 14k rose gold mount, mid-20th c. (ILLUS.)......... **275**

Brooch, jade, platinum & diamond, Art Deco style, a long rectangular central plaque of green jade carved w/scrolling openwork vines & gourds, two opposing corners w/two squared & stepped brackets set w/a total of 22 single-cut diamonds, French guarantee stamps & hallmark, ca. 1930..................................... **2,585**

Art Deco Round Diamond Brooch

Brooch, platinum & diamond, Art Deco style, round shape bead-set w/156 old European- and mine-cut diamonds, approx. 7.80 cts., millegrain accents (ILLUS.) **8,813**

Brooch, platinum, emerald & diamond, Art Deco style, designed as two slender overlapping rings bead-set w/old European- and single-cut diamonds & centering a bezel-set large rectangular step-cut emerald, millegrain accents (missing on diamond) **940**

Brooch, platinum, synthetic emerald & diamond, Art Deco style, a central oval ring set w/old European-cut, single-cut & baguette diamonds enclosing a large prong-set emerald-cut synthetic emerald, diamond-set oblong side rings centered by a diamond-set leaftip, gold pin stem, approximate weight 1.52 cts. **1,998**

Dress clip, diamond & 18k gold, Art Deco shield-shape, bead & bezel-set w/old European- and single-cut diamonds, millegrain accents, W.M. Wise & Son, approximate weight .88 cts., ca. 1930.......... **1,880**

One of Two Very Rare Dress Clips

Dress clips, platinum & diamond, Art Deco style, each of palmette form set throughout w/54 old European-cut diamonds, approx. 20.00 cts., further set w/32 French-cut, two baguette & 102 single-cut diamonds, approx. 29.00 cts., 14k white gold findings, ca. 1930 (ILLUS. of one)... **48,175**

Earrings, citrine & 18k yellow gold, each w/a mounting fashioned as leafy cluster centered by a pear-cut citrine, total weight approx. 26.81 cts., Tiffany & Co., ca. 1940 .... **1,380**

Earrings, jade & diamond, Art Deco style, a small square set w/a small oblong piece of green jade & bead-set single-cut diamonds above a diamond-set band suspending a large green jade teardrop, platinum mounts, later silver screw-back findings, pr. (missing one diamond) **1,763**

Earrings, pearl, sapphire & 14k gold, Retro-style, an abstract flower form w/a curved row of pearls up the center flanked by rows of small round sapphires, all enclosed by stylized gold leaves, signed by Tiffany & Company, late 1940s - early 1950s, pr. **441**

Jabot pin, platinum, 18k gold & diamond, Art Deco style, designed as a small arrow bead-set at the flared top & pointed base w/old European- and single-cut diamonds, millegrain accents, signed by Cartier, numbered & w/a French guarantee stamp, ca. 1930 .... **1,293**

Necklace, diamond & platinum, a large slender ring-form w/the thin sides graduating to a wider front section composed of two rows of diamond-set bands flanking a long central looping openwork section, set throughout w/92 transitional-, old European-, baguette- and rectangular step-cut diamonds, weighing 5.20 cts., ca. 1930, 14 3/4" l. **17,625**

Necklace, pearl, platinum & diamond, Art Deco style, composed of 79 ivory pearls graduating in size from 4.30 to 8.81 mm, completed by a box clasp set w/a cushion-cut diamond weighing 1.22 cts. framed by a ring of small calibré-cut rubies, ca. 1930, 23 1/2" l. **3,173**

Art Deco Emerald & Diamond Pendant

Pendant, emerald, diamond & 14k yellow gold, Art Deco style, teardrop-shaped lacy mount mounted in the center w/a large 14 ct. pear-shaped emerald surrounded by round-cut diamonds, 4.5 cts., gold mount (ILLUS.)................................ **10,350**

Art Deco Carved Jade Pendant

Pendant, platinum, jadeite & diamond, Art Deco style, the rectangular green jade plaque pierced & carved w/stylized florals, the openwork bail set w/diamond melée, suspended from a delicate trace link chain, 17" l. (ILLUS.)............ **2,938**

Pendant, sterling silver & enamel, rectangular Art Deco plaque design, divided into four rectangular panels, two corner ones w/small squares diagonally divided & decorated w/coral & black enamel, the other two corner squares set w/faceted black stone panels, probably onyx, gilt chain marked "935," pendant stamped w/initial mark of Theodor Fahrner & "935," Europe, ca. 1930 .... **1,880**

Pin, gold (14k), Retro-style, modeled as bow in pink & yellow gold, signed by Tiffany & Co., late 1940s - early 1950s........... **353**

Rare Cartier Mughal-design Pin

Pin, platinum, diamond & ruby, Art Deco style, Mughal design w/a central leaf-carved ruby framed by old mine- and single-cut diamonds on a diamond-set stem accented w/emerald & ruby cabochons, signed by Cartier (ILLUS.)...................... **11,750**

Ring, diamond & 18k white gold, the rounded top w/two back-to-back curved sections & V-form side panels, centered by a large old European-cut diamond flanked by slightly smaller diamonds, the bands bezel- and bead-set w/smaller diamonds, millegrain accents, ca. 1930, total weight 1.56 cts., size 7 3/4 .... **1,998**

Ring, diamond & platinum, Art Deco style, the filigree navette mount set w/nine old European-cut diamonds, millegrain accents, size 4 1/2 .... **646**

Ring, diamond & platinum, Art Deco style, the oblong top centered by a row of four bezel-set old European-cut diamonds framed by sixteen bezel-set smaller old European-cut diamonds, weighing 1.24 cts., millegrain accents, ca. 1930, size 5 1/2 (w/a ring guard).............................. **1,880**

Ring, diamond & platinum, Art Deco style, the squared top w/rounded corners centered by a large old European-cut diamond weighing 1.14 cts., enclosed by a ring of single-cut diamonds that continue

down the bezel & shank, ca. 1930, size 6 1/4 .... **5,581**

Cartier Diamond & Platinum Ring

Ring, platinum & diamond, Art Deco style, bezel-set w/an old mine-cut diamond approx. 1.00 cts., surrounded by 12 old mine- and European-cut diamonds, approx. 2.34 cts., worn signature of Cartier, ca. 1930s, size 8 3/4 (ILLUS.)...... **8,225**

Ring, platinum, diamond & emerald, Art Deco style, round top composed of an outer ring of eighteen single-cut diamonds around a narrow ring of French-cut emeralds, all enclosing a large old European-cut diamond weighing .8 cts., single-cut diamond-set split shoulders, openwork gallery & engraved shank, size 5, ca. 1930 (two emeralds chipped)......... **3,819**

Ring, platinum, diamond & sapphire, Art Deco style, rounded form centered by a large bezel-set old European-cut diamond flanked by angled lines of bead-set smaller old European-cut diamonds w/two small bands of channel-set sapphires, millegrain accents, ca. 1930, size 4 .... **1,175**

Fine Heart-shaped Diamond Ring

Ring, platinum & diamond solitaire, Art Deco style, bezel-set w/a faceted heart-shaped diamond, approx. 2.25 cts., openwork scrolling gallery bead-set w/old single-cut diamonds, bezel-set marquise-cut diamond shoulders, engraved shank, chip to girdle, size 6 1/4 (ILLUS.) **17,625**

Art Deco Sapphire & Diamond Ring

Ring, platinum, sapphire & diamond, Art Deco style, prong-set w/a large facetedd oval sapphire, the prongs, open gallery & shoulders bead-set w/old European- and single-cut diamond mélée, one mélée missing, size 4 1/2 (ILLUS.).................... **8,225**

KITCHENWARES
Egg Timers

Goebel Baker Egg Timer

Baker, ceramic, Goebel (ILLUS.) **$50**

Black Baby Egg Timer

Black baby, ceramic, sitting w/left arm holding timer (ILLUS.) **95**
Black chef, ceramic, sitting w/arm up holding timer, variety of sizes, Germany **85**

Black Chef with Fish Egg Timer

Black chef, ceramic, standing w/large fish, timer in fish's mouth, Germany, 4 3/4" h. (ILLUS.) **125**

Black Chef w/Frying Pan Egg Timer

Black chef with frying pan, composition, Japan (ILLUS.) **95**

Bo-Peep Egg Timer

Bo-Peep, ceramic, "Bo-Peep" on base, Japan (ILLUS.) **90**
Boy, ceramic, skiing pose, marked "Germany," 3" h. **50**
Chef, ceramic, winking, white w/black shoes & trim, turning figure on its head activates sand, 4" h. **40**
Chef, composition, w/cake, Germany **95**
Chick with cap, ceramic, Josef Originals **40**
Chicken, on nest, green plastic, England, 2 1/2" h. **25**

Goebel Owl Egg Timer

Owl, ceramic, Goebel, Germany (ILLUS.) **65**
Parlor maid with cat, ceramic, Japan **50**
Penguin, chalkware, England, 3 3/4" h. **45**
Rabbit with floppy ears, ceramic, stand-
ing, tan, Germany **75**
Rabbits, ceramic, double-type, various col-
or combinations, Goebel, Germany, 4" h. **65**
Telephone, ceramic, black, Japan **40**
Vegetable person, ceramic, Japan **175**
Veggie man or woman, bisque, Japan,
4 1/2" h., each **175**
Welsh woman, ceramic, Germany,
4 1/2" h. **40**

Windmill with Pigs Egg Timer

Windmill, ceramic, w/pigs on base, Japan,
3 3/4" h. (ILLUS.) **75**

Napkin Dolls

*Until the 1990s, napkin dolls were a rather
obscure collectible, coveted by only a few savvy
individuals who appreciated their charm and*
*beauty. Today, however, these late 1940s and
1950s icons of postwar America are hot commodi-
ties.*

*Ranging from the individualistic pieces made
in ceramics classes to jeweled Japanese models
and the wide variety of wooden examples, these
figures are no longer mistaken as planters or miniature dress forms. Of course, as their popularity
has risen, so have prices, putting smiles on the
faces of collectors who got in on the ground floor
and stretching the pocketbooks of those looking to
start their own collections.*

*Bobbie Zucker Bryson is co-author, with Debo-
rah Gillham and Ellen Bercovici, of the pictorial
price guide* Collectibles For The Kitchen, Bath &
Beyond - Second Edition, *published by Krause
Publications. It covers a broad range of collectibles including napkin dolls, stringholders, pie
birds, figural egg timers, razor blade banks,
whimsical whistle milk cups and laundry sprinkler bottles. Bryson can be contacted via e-mail at
Napkindoll aol.com.*

Ceramic, figure of a genie holding a lantern,
marked "Genie at Your Service," by
Enesco, 8" h. **$100-135**

Newer Napkin Lady Holding Tray

Ceramic, figure of a woman, black hair,
wearing a long white dress w/red bodice
& puffy sleeves, one hand on hip & the
other holding up a blue tray, newer vin-
tage, 9 1/4" h. (ILLUS.) **30**
Ceramic, figure of a woman, blonde hair
pulled back into a bun, pink dress w/a
white collar, holding a white heart,
marked on bottom "Brockmann,"
6 1/2" h. **65-85**

Napkin Doll-Candleholder Tall Lady

Ceramic, figure of a woman, her black hair pulled back into a bun & wearing a wide-brimmed red-trimmed hat forming a candleholder, her hands behind her back & wearing a long white jacket w/pale blue trim over a red bodice, the long white dress w/slits & hem trimmed w/thin red lines, 12 3/4" h. (ILLUS.) **75-95**

Ceramic, figure of a woman on a base, black hair, molded pink lustre apron, one arm holding a toothpick holder bowl on her head, by Marcia of California, 13" h. **125-150**

Green-dressed Lady with Candleholders

Ceramic, figure of a woman, red hair covered w/a green kerchief, wearing a long green dress w/a white blouse w/gold trim, each arm supporting a tall square-based

columnar white candlestick at the side, 10" h. (ILLUS.) **115-135**

Newer Rosie Napkin Doll Lady

Ceramic, figure of a woman, red hair pulled back & parted in the middle w/a pink flower above each ear, wearing a long white dress w/a pink shawl collar, holding a pink rose in front, marked "Rosie," Holland Mold (H-132), newer vintage, 7 1/2" h. (ILLUS.) **25-35**

Napkin Doll with Bowl on Her Head

Ceramic, figure of a woman, short brown hair, long blue dress w/puffy sleeves & h.p. flowers on the front, her arms up holding a wide, low gold-trimmed bowl on her head, marked "Japan," 9 1/4" h. (ILLUS.) **50-65**

Ceramic, figure of woman wearing white dress w/lavender flowers, hands holding large hat on head, iridescent finish, marked "Duncan Enterprises 1980," 6 1/2" h. **40-50**

Women with Fans Napkin Dolls

Ceramic, green figure of woman, fan masks candleholder, jewel-decorated, marked "Kreiss & Co.," 8 3/4" h. (ILLUS. right w/pink woman w/fan)..................................... **65**

Davar Originals Napkin Doll

Ceramic, half doll, figure of milkmaid w/brown braids, wearing red dress w/white apron & polka dots, blue bow, blue & white cap, carrying buckets on yoke across her shoulders, on wire skirt-like base that holds napkins, marked "Davar Originals," 6" h. (ILLUS.) **95-110**

Spanish Lady Napkin Doll

Ceramic, half-doll, figural of Spanish lady w/black hair w/red & white flowers, wearing green dress w/white ruffled sleeves, holding red & white fan in one hand, other raised to her head, on wooden stand w/wires to hold napkins, 9 1/2" h. (ILLUS.).................................. **100-150**

Half-doll Napkin Holder

Ceramic, half-doll, figure of woman w/black hair wearing green off-the-shoulder dress, on wooden stand w/wires to hold napkins, Goebel X97, ca. 1957, 8 1/4" h. (ILLUS.)... **225-250**

Ceramic, model of rooster, red, black & white w/yellow beak, slits in tail for napkins, w/egg-shaped salt & pepper shakers, 5 1/4" h. **35-45**

Ceramic, pink figure of woman, fan masks candleholder, jewel-decorated, marked "Kreiss & Co.," 10 1/2" h. (ILLUS. left w/green woman w/fan) **85**

Ceramic & metal, half-figure of a lady, red hair, wearing a pink & white off-the-shoulder dress, holding streamers to matching pink & white hat, on a brass stand w/wires to hold napkins, 8" h. **135-175**

Ceramic & metal, half-figure of a Mexican lady, wearing a yellow dress w/white, red & blue scarf over her shoulder, one hand holding a matching yellow sombrero w/a red design, on a wooden stand w/wires to hold napkins, original box marked "Napkin Holder No. 405," 9" h. **150-185**

Ceramic & metal, half-figure of a milk maid, light brown hair, wearing a red dress w/white dots, white apron w/blue trim, light blue bow at neck, w/matching blue & white cap, carrying buckets across shoulders, "Davar Originals" sticker, 6" h. **95-110**

Ceramic & metal, half-figure of a milk maid, wearing a red dress w/white apron & polka dots, blue bow & a blue & white cap on her brown braids, carrying buckets across her shoulders, marked "Davar Originals," 6" h. **95-110**

Ceramic & metal, model of a chicken & rooster, white w/gold trim, removable salt & pepper shaker heads, wire in tails to hold napkins, "Lefton" foil label, 4 3/8" h. ... **25-35**

Chalkware, figure of a woman w/hands behind her back, light brown hair, wearing a green dress & matching hat w/candleholders, 13" h. **95-125**

Metal, model of an umbrella, chrome w/metallic red base, fitted w/red & blue napkins, 9" h. **15-35**

Metal, rear view figure of a dancer's legs w/upturned dress, marked "Can Can Serviette Holder," England, 4" h. **95-135**

Sweetie Napkin Doll in Original Box

Plastic, half-figure of a young girl, synthetic black hair & open-close eyes, wearing a

light blue & pink satin dress, plastic base for napkins, in original box marked "Sweetie Napkin Doll," ca. 1959, 11" h. (ILLUS.)... **40-60**

Wood, figure of a woman dressed in yellow, Finland, ca. 1949, 10 1/4" h. **40-50**

Wood, figure of a woman, jointed arms, wearing a pink dress w/blue bodice trimmed in black, a strawberry w/toothpick holes on her head, 8" h...................... **60-75**

Painted Wood Napkin Doll

Wood, figure of woman w/jointed arms wearing dark pink dress w/white flowers & bodice & black hat, marked "Artefatos Catarinenses Ltda., Ave. Argalo, 80-Sao Bento do Sul, Santa Catarina, N-94, Industria, Bruseleira," 6 3/8" h. (ILLUS.) **60-75**

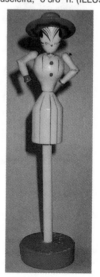

Wooden Napkin Doll Painted Yellow & Red

Wood, figure of woman w/stylized face, standing w/hands on hips, painted yellow w/red buttons, cuffs & hat, on red circular base, 11" h. (ILLUS.) **30-40**

Wood, half-figure of a woman w/yellow braids, red bodice, white Dutch hat, on a yellow & red base, 9 3/4" h. **20-25**

Wood, model of dodo bird, w/slits in rear for napkins, 7" h. **25-35**

Wood, red half-figure, base marked "Napkins," ca. 1952, 11 1/2" h. **35**

Wood & glass, figure of a woman, jointed arms, wearing a green outfit w/white trim, matching picture hat, marked "Servy-Etta - USD Patent No. 159,005," a Woodnote Product, ca. 1951, 11" h. **35-45**

Reamers

Reamers are a European invention dating back to the 18th century. Devised to extract citrus juice as a remedy for scurvy, by the 1920s they became a must in every well-equipped American kitchen. Although one can still purchase inexpensive glass, wood, metal and plastic squeezers in today's kitchen and variety stores, it is the pre-1950s models that are so highly sought after today. Whether it's a primitive wood example from the late 1800s or a whimsical figural piece from post-World War II Japan, the reamer is one of the hottest kitchen collectibles in today's marketplace - Bobbie Zucker Bryson

Ceramic, boat-shaped, pale green w/pink, blue & white flowers, cream reamer cone, handle & inside bowl, Shelley - England, 7" h. **$250**

Ceramic, boat-shaped, white w/gilt line trim, decorated w/rust-colored leaves & navy blue, small loop handle, 3 1/2" h. (ILLUS., top next column) **65-85**

Boat-shaped Ceramic Reamer

Lemon-yellow Boat-shaped Reamer

Ceramic, boat-shaped, yellow w/black trim & white interior & cone, side w/image of anchor & word "Lemon" in black, 3" h. (ILLUS.) **85-115**

Ceramic, clown head in saucer, maroon & white cone hat w/maroon trim, loop handle, Germany, 5" d. **225-275**

Ceramic, model of a rose blossom, pink w/green leaves & brown handle, marked "Erphila - Germany," 1 3/4" h. **200-250**

Ceramic, model of a swan, two-piece, off-white w/pink rose designs & green trim, 4 1/4" h. (ILLUS., bottom of page) **75-85**

Swan-shaped Two-piece Reamer

Orange Czechoslovakian Ceramic Reamer

Ceramic, model of a white elephant w/pink highlights & green feet, marked "Mideramica - Made in Portugal" 2" h. **25-35**

Ceramic, saucer-shaped, light orange exterior w/dimpled finish, white interior & green loop end handle, marked "Czechoslovakia," 3" h. (ILLUS., top of page) **55-65**

Ceramic, saucer-shaped, strainer cap on front, green, table handle w/hanging hole, Japan.. **40-45**

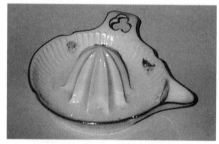

Saucer-style Ceramic Reamer

Ceramic, saucer-style, white w/gold trim, decorated w/images of sewing implements, the handle w/cloverleaf cutout, 5 1/4" d. (ILLUS.) **40-50**

Ceramic, saucer-style, white w/gold trim & designs, petal-style tab handle, Japan, 3" h.. **145-150**

Simple Reamer with Autumn Leaves

Ceramic, simple round shape w/spout, beige w/autumn leaf design on sides & tab handle, gold foil sticker reads "Limited Edition Produced Exclusively by China Specialties," 6" h. (ILLUS.).............. **125-175**

Caricature Woman Reamer

Ceramic, two-piece, caricature of woman w/brown face, crossed eyes & oversize red lips, wearing yellow bandana & gold hoop earrings, yellow & white cone forming hat, marked "Made in Germany," 2 3/4" h. (ILLUS.) **175-200**

Reamer Marked "Frances - Limoges"

Ceramic, two-piece, cylindrical body decorated w/multicolored flowers & gold trim on pale blue ground, spout & cone also pale blue & white w/gold trim, marked "Frances - Limoges," 3 1/2" h. (ILLUS.)
.... **160-185**

Ceramic, two-piece, figural white face w/expressive black eyes, rosy cheeks & red lips, Japan, 4 1/2" h.................................. **75-85**

Reamer with Matching Tumbler

Ceramic, two-piece, model of house, white w/brown roof & handle, blue windows, green grass & cherry trees in front, marked "Made in Japan," 5 1/2" h., w/matching juice tumbler (ILLUS., top of page) **95-125**

Ceramic, two-piece, octagonal bottom, white, marked "Thomas Maddock & Sons, Trenton, NJ," 5" h. **100-125**

Ceramic, two-piece, pale blue w/multi-colored flowers & gold trim, marked on base "Limoges - France," 3 1/2" h. **160-185**

Quimper Pottery Reamer

Petal-form Ceramic Reamer

Ceramic, two-piece, teapot-style, bright orange petal bottom w/bright yellow top, loop handle, marked "Made in Japan," 3 3/4" h. (ILLUS.) **55-65**

Universal Potteries Pitcher Reamer

Ceramic, two-piece, pitcher-style, off-white decorated w/scene of blue & green garden gate & flowerpots on steps, marked "Universal Potteries Oven Proof," 9" h. (ILLUS.) **165-195**

Ceramic, two-piece, round bottom, spring action ceramic core, yellow, marked "Ade-o-Matic Genuine Coorsite Porcelain," 7 1/2" h. **125-150**

Ceramic, two-piece, saucer shape, beige w/red, yellow, blue & tan trim, "Quimper Ivoire Corbell" patt., marked "Henriot Quimper France 1166," 2 3/4" h. (ILLUS., next column)
.... **200-250**

Ceramic Mexican Man Reamer

Floral-decorated Teapot-style Reamer

Ceramic, two-piece, teapot-style, figure of Mexican man wearing bright orange jacket, yellow, orange, green & black serape & black pants, the yellow & orange cone forming his sombrero, one hand on hip forming handle, sitting next to green cactus that forms spout, 5 1/2" h. (ILLUS., previous page) **250-300**

Ceramic, two-piece, teapot-style, maroon w/black stripes, Japan, 3 1/2" h. **40-45**

Ceramic, two-piece, teapot-style, off-white w/rose & blue floral band around the footed base, blue & rose pink trim on the reamer top, marked "Made in Japan," 5 3/4" h. (ILLUS., top of page) **55-65**

Ceramic Reamer with Pebble Finish

Ceramic, two-piece, teapot-style w/clown head cone w/green & white hat, white pebble finish decorated w/maroon & blue flowers & green leaves, dark blue/green trim, 6" h. (ILLUS.) **45-60**

Teapot-style Reamer with Violets

Ceramic, two-piece, teapot-style, paneled bulbous base w/wide rim spout & squared reamer top, white decorated w/light purple violets & green leaves, 4 3/4" h. (ILLUS.) **20-25**

German Reamer with Sailboat Scene

Ceramic, two-piece teapot-style, white w/a blue sailboat scene around the base w/blue trim, marked "Germany" on the base, 3 1/4" h. (ILLUS., previous page) **75-85**

Ceramic, two-piece teapot-style, yellow w/an orange lobster wrapped around the handle & side, Japan, 4 1/4" h. **75-85**

Ceramic, two-piece, the base a model of a purple pansy blossom, decorated w/a yellow & purple pansy, white top w/ruffled rim, 4" h. **75**

Ceramic, two-piece w/bowl-style base w/spring-action cone top, green, marked "Ade-O Matic - Genuine Coorsite Porcelain" on the base, 7 1/2" h. **125-135**

Ceramic, two-piece, white & cobalt blue w/gold trim, ruffled top, 3 1/2" h. **150-160**

Two-handled Reamer with Chicks Scene

Ceramic, two-piece, wide tapering cylindrical base w/angled handles, off-white ground molded in relief w/three small yellow chicks jumping rose, blue & red thin border bands, marked "Japan," 4" h. (ILLUS.) **55-65**

Clear Glass Boat-shaped Reamer

Glass, boat-shaped, clear, w/long spout & tab handle, ridged sides, seed dam, 3 7/8" w. (ILLUS.) **45-60**

Glass, boat-shaped on pedestal base, clear, 3 1/4" h. **50-55**

Pacific Coast Glass Works Reamer

Glass, clear, round shape w/fluted sides, loop handle, marked "Sunkist Oranges Lemons," Pacific Coast Glass Works, 6" d. (ILLUS.) **40-50**

Glass, green/yellow slag, loop handle, fleur-de-lis embossed on side, 6 1/4" d. **425-500**

Glass, round w/square loop handle & large, flat grapefruit reamer cone, opaque black color, McKee Glass Co., 6" d. **1,250-1,350**

Glass, saucer-shaped w/loop handle, transparent green, embossed "Valencia" on the front, 6" d. **190-250**

Glass, saucer-style, blue opaque color, ruffled edge & tab handle, 5" d. **110-120**

Glass, saucer-style, oblong tab handle & Hobnail pattern on bottom, clear, Nickel Plate Glass Co., 4" d. (ILLUS.) **30-40**

Glass, saucer-style, round tab handle & Hobnail pattern on bottom, clear, Nickel Plate Glass Co., 4" d. **30-40**

Glass, saucer-type, blue opaque color, Fenton Art Glass Co., 6 3/8" h. **3,000-3,800**

Pink Glass Jeannette Reamer

Glass, saucer-type, concentric circles forming the base w/a tab side handle, pink, Jeannette Glass Co., 5 7/8" d. (ILLUS.).... **40-50**

Glass, saucer-type, deep orangish Amberina-type color, limited edition by Edna Barnes, marked on the bottom w/a "B" in a circle, 2 1/2" d. (ILLUS. right with pale blue opaque reamer)................................. **15-20**

Glass, saucer-type, molded stars & hearts design, square table handle & seed dam, transparent pink, 4 7/8" d. **50-75**

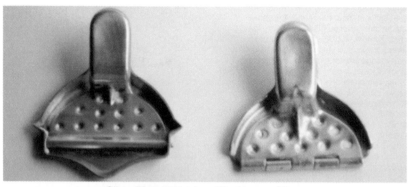

Silver Plate & Stainless Steel Lemon Slices

Silver plate, half-round scoop-style lemon slice w/tab handle, 3" l. (ILLUS. left with stainless steel lemon slice, top of page) **15**

Bernard Rice Silver Plate Reamer

Silver plate, two-piece, simple round shape w/leaf-form tab handle, marked "Apollo EPNS, Made By Bernard Rice's Sons, Inc., 5230," 2 3/4" h. (ILLUS.) **125-235**

Silver plate, two-piece w/leaf-shaped tab handle, marked "Apollo EPNS - Made by Bernard Rice's Sons, Inc. 5230," 2 3/4" h. **125-235**

Stainless steel, half-round scoop-style lemon slice w/tab handle, 3" l. (ILLUS. right with silver plate lemon slice) **8-10**

Stainless steel, model of a bird, 4" l. **8-12**

Sterling silver, saucer-style, marked "Black Starr - Gorham Sterling 909," 4 1/4" d. . **225-275**

Wood, hand-held type w/ribbed reamer cone, ca. 1850, 5 3/4" l. **35-45**

Wood & ceramic, hand-held type w/ceramic bowl & hinged wood top w/reamer cone, 9 1/2" l. **45-55**

String Holders

String holders were standard equipment for general stores, bakeries and homes before the use of paper bags, tape and staples became prevalent. Decorative string holders, mostly chalkware, first became popular during the late 1930s and 1940s. They were mass-produced and sold in five-and-dime stores like Woolworth's and Kresge's. Ceramic string holders became available in the late 1940s through the 1950s. It is much more difficult to find a chalkware string holder in excellent condition, while the sturdier ceramics maintain a higher quality over time.

Apple, ceramic, handmade, 1947 .... **$35-55**
Apple w/face, ceramic, "PY" **135**
Apple with berries, chalkware, common **15-35**

Apple with Worm String Holder

Apple with worm, chalkware, "Willie the Worm," ca. 1948, Miller Studio (ILLUS.) **50**
Art Deco woman, arched eyebrows, blonde bobbed hair **145**
Baby, chalkware, frowning **150**
Bananas, chalkware, ca. 1980s-present **25-50**

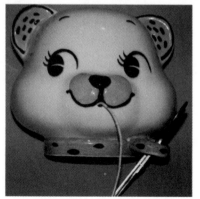

Bear with Scissors In Collar

Bear, w/scissors in collar, ceramic, Japan (ILLUS.).. **40**

Bird, ceramic, green, "Arthur Wood, England," also found in blue & brown................ **25**

"String Swallow" Bird String Holder

Bird, ceramic, in birdhouse, "String Swallow" (ILLUS.) **40**

Bird, chalkware, peeking out of birdhouse....... **175**

Bird & birdhouse, wood & metal...................... **30**

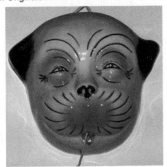

Bird in Birdcage String Holder

Bird in birdcage, chalkware (ILLUS.)................ **95**

Bird on birdhouse, chalkware, cardboard, "Early Bird," bobs up & down when string is pulled, handmade **40**

Bird on branch, ceramic, Royal Copley **55**

Bird on nest, ceramic, countertop-type, Josef Originals **65**

Boy with Tilted Cap

Boy, w/tilted cap, chalkware (ILLUS.) **125**

Brother Jacob and Sister Isabel, chalkware, newer vintage, each **55-60**

Butler, ceramic, black man w/white lips & eyebrows, Japan, hard to find.................... **200+**

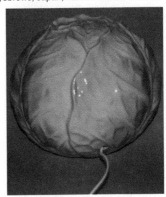

Cabbage String Holder

Cabbage, ceramic, Japan (ILLUS.).................... **65**

Campbell Soup boy, chalkware, face only **250**

Black Cat with Gold Bow

Cat, ceramic, black w/gold bow, handmade (ILLUS.)... **45**

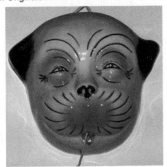

Bonzo Face String Holder

Bonzo face, ceramic, comic character dog, marked "Japan," rare (ILLUS.) **250**

Chef, chalkware, baby face w/chef's hat **150**

Chef with Large Hat

Chef, chalkware, w/large hat facing left (ILLUS.) **95**

Chicken, ceramic, "Quimper of France," found in several patterns, still in production **65-85**

Crock, ceramic, "Kitchen String," by Burleigh Ironstone, Staffordshire, England, w/scissors in top **45**

Scottie String Holder

Dog, ceramic, Scottie, marked "Royal Trico, Japan" (ILLUS.) **95**

Dog, chalkware, Westie, white w/studded color **95**

Dog, wood, "Sandy Twine Holder," body is ball of string **35**

Dog with Black Eye

Dog w/black eye, ceramic, w/scissors holder in collar, right eye only circled in black, England (ILLUS.) **65**

Chalkware Chef String Holder

French chef, chalkware, w/scarf around neck (ILLUS.) **125**

Gourd, chalkware... **95**

Grapes String Holder

Grapes, chalkware, bunch (ILLUS.)................. **135**

Green pepper, ceramic, Lego sticker **50**

Humpty Dumpty String Holder

Humpty Dumpty, ceramic, sitting on wall, white & yellow (ILLUS.) **75**

Indian in Headdress String Holder

Indian w/headdress, chalkware, brightly colored (ILLUS.) **300**
Iron w/flowers, ceramic **75**

Cleminsons House String Holder

Latchstring house, ceramic, California Cleminsons (ILLUS.) **85**
Little Red Riding Hood, chalkware, head wearing hood... **250**
Mammy, bisque, head only **350**

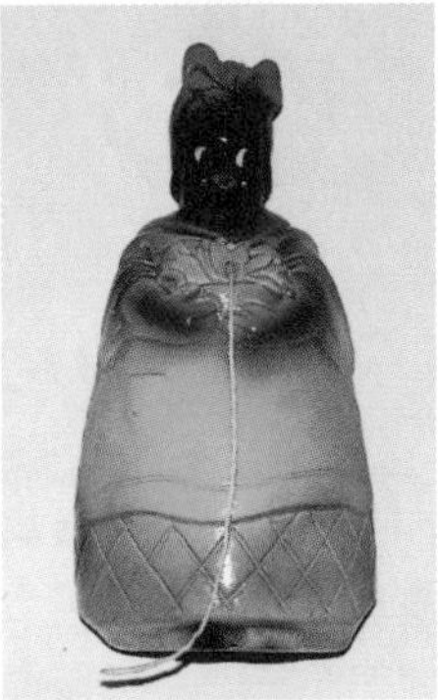

Mammy Holding Flowers

Mammy, chalkware, full-figured, holding flowers, marked "MAPCO" (ILLUS.)............. **175**

Mammy, chalkware, head only, marked "Ty-Me" on neck **250**
Mammy, cloth-faced, "Simone," includes card that reads "I'm smiling Jane, so glad I came to tie your things, with nice white strings," rare... **95**

Coconut Mammy

Mammy, coconut, w/red and blue floral scarf (ILLUS.)... **25**
Mammy, felt, head only, w/plastic rolling eyes **50-75**

Mexican Man with Flowered Hat

Mexican man, chalkware, head only, flower-trimmed hat (ILLUS.) **65**
Mouse, ceramic, England **50**
Owl, Babbacombe Pottery, England **25**

Pancho Villa String Holder

Pancho Villa, chalkware (ILLUS.).................... **195**

LIGHTING DEVICES

Also see Antique Trader Lamps & Lighting Price Guide.

Early Non-Electric Lamps & Lighting

Miniature Lamps

Our listings are generally arranged numerically according to the numbers assigned to the various miniature lamps pictured in the following reference books: Frank R. & Ruth E. Smith's book Miniature Lamps, *now referred to as Smith's Book I (Smith I) and Ruth Smith's sequel,* Miniature Lamps II *(Smith II), and Marjorie Hulsebus' books,* Miniature Victorian Lamps *(Hulsebus I or H-II) and* Miniature Lamps of the Victorian Era *(Hulsebus II or H-II).*

Rare Atterbury Lamp & Match Holder

Amber, finger-type, cylindrical ribbed font w/attached basket w/ring handle for holding matches, matching ribbed shade, Nutmeg burner, Atterbury & Co., ca. 1870s, 3 3/4" h., Smith I, Fig. 53 (ILLUS.) **$700-750**

Very Rare Atterbury Shoe Finger Lamp

Amber, finger-type, model of a lady's shoe w/molded handle, patented by Atterbury & Co. in the late 1860s, Hornet burner, 3 1/2" h., Smith I, Fig. 52 (ILLUS.) **850-900**

Rare Amber Honeycomb Mini Lamp

Amber, squatty bulbous honeycomb-patterned font on applied clear feet, open-topped matching shade, Nutmeg-type burner, 6 1/2" h., Hulsebus I, Fig. 304 (ILLUS.) **700-750**

Amber Hobnail Miniature Lamp

Amber, stem-type, Hobnail patt. font & flaring shade, Nutmeg-type burner, 7" h., Smith I, Fig. 477 (ILLUS.) **425-475**

Amber, stem-type, pedestal base & squatty round font both pressed w/a fish scale design, Nutmeg burner, 5" h., Smith I, Fig. 116 .... **125-135**

Real & Repro Daisy & Cube Mini Lamps

Amber, stem-type, pressed Daisy & Cube patt., original model w/2 3/8" h. shade, Nutmeg burner, 7 7/8" h., Smith I, Fig. 482 (ILLUS. right with L.G. Wright reproduction) **350-400**

Amber, stem-type, reproduction pressed Daisy & Cube patt., w/2 5/8" h. shade, newer burner, produced by L.G. Wright, ca. 1960 (ILLUS. left with authentic version) .... **Not available**

Dark Blue Little Buttercup Finger Lamp

Blue, finger-type, dark waisted font embossed "Little Buttercup," blue applied handle, Acorn burner, 2 3/4" h., Smith I, Fig. 36 (ILLUS.) **115-125**

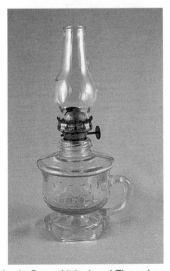

Apple Green Little Jewel Finger Lamp

Apple green, finger-type, footed cylindrical font embossed "Little Jewel," applied handle, Acorn burner, 2 3/4" h., Smith I, Fig. 44 (ILLUS.) **120-135**

Blue Finger Lamp with Molded Handle

Blue, finger-type, foot w/molded ring handle & squatty round font, Acorn burner, 3 1/2" h., Smith I, Fig. 47 (ILLUS.) **200-225**

Blue, stem lamp w/optic ribbed base & ball shade, white enameled decoration, Spar Brenner burner & clear glass chimney, 9" h., Hulsebus II, Fig. 455 (ILLUS., top next page) **400-450**

Blue Stem Lamp with White Trim

Blue Miniature Stem Lamp

Blue, stem lamp w/optic ribs in font, Hornet sized burner, 6" h., Hulsebus I, Fig. 64 (ILLUS.)... **175-200**

Blue Cased Satin Molded Lamp & Shade

Blue cased satin, melon-lobed base & molded pansy design ball shade, Nutmeg-type burner, 7" h., Smith I, Fig. 389 (ILLUS.)... **450-600**

Blue Opaque Lamp with Vine Decor

Blue opaque, footed low cylindrical font embossed w/a vine & leaf design, Nutmeg-type burner, 3" h., Hulsebus II, Fig. 72 (ILLUS.)... **75-85**

Blue Opaque Ribbed Miniature Lamp

Blue opaque, ribbed cushion foot & columnar stem & ribbed swirl chimney shade, collar marked "JKA DRGM," European burner, 7 1/2" h., Hulsebus II, Fig. 92 (ILLUS.)... **225-250**

Improved Little Favorite Finger Lamp

Clear, finger-type, cylindrical font embossed "Improved Little Favorite," applied handle, milk glass chimney, Olmsted-type burner, overall 4" h., Smith I, Fig. 16 (ILLUS.) **150-170**

Clear Finger Lamp with Sun Ray Design

Clear, finger-type, squatty rounded font w/an embossed sun ray design, applied clear handle, Pet Ratchet burner, 2 1/2" h., Smith I, Fig. 42 (ILLUS.) **150-175**

Atterbury Log Cabin Finger Lamp

Clear, finger-type, model of a log cabin w/molded handle, patented by Atterbury & Co. in the late 1860s, Hornet burner, 3 3/4" h., Smith I, Fig. 51 (ILLUS.) **350-375**

Two Squatty Round Miniature Lamps

Clear, squatty rounded font embossed "Little Fire Fly," milk glass chimney, Olmsted-type burner, overall 4 1/2" h., Smith II, Fig. 55 (ILLUS. left with cobalt blue Little Harry's lamp) **125-150**

Clear Stem Lamp with Medallions

Clear, stem-type, embossed medallions on font & base, Acorn burner, 5 1/2" h., Smith I, Fig. 113 (ILLUS.)........................... **85-95**

Clear, stem-type, notched, ribbed & eye patt., called "Famous," Nutmeg burner, 8 3/4" h., Smith I, Fig. 478 .... **1,100-1,200**

Clear & blue opaque, blue opaque pedestal base supporting the squatty clear embossed font, milk glass chimney, Olmsted-type burner, overall 6 7/8" h., Smith I, Fig. 11 right **350-375**

Spanish Lace Lamp with Silver Filigree

Clear opalescent, Spanish Lace patt., ovoid base & bowl-form shade, covered w/delicate silver filigree, Nutmeg burner, 7" h., Smith I, Fig. 473 (ILLUS.) **1,100-1,200**

Cobalt blue, squatty rounded font embossed "Little Harry's Night Lamp," milk glass chimney, Olmsted-type burner, overall 4 1/2" h., Smith I, Fig. 15 (ILLUS. right with Little Fire Fly clear lamp, previous page) **300-350**

Cranberry Little Beauty Mini Lamp

Cranberry, optic ribbed cylindrical & ringed base & conical shade, early ad called it "Little Beauty," 8 1/4" h., Smith I, Fig. 439 (ILLUS.)... **375-400**

Tall Cranberry Miniature Lamp

Cranberry, optic ribbed hexagonal base & conical shade w/flaring rim, Hornet burner, 9" h., Smith I, Fig. 438 (ILLUS.)....... **400-425**

Green Finger Lamp with Wire Handle

Green, finger-type, waisted cylindrical font embossed "Nutmeg," w/wire bail handle, Nutmeg burner, 2 3/4" h., Smith I, Fig. 29 (ILLUS.)... **125-150**

Squatty Painted Milk Glass Lamp

Milk glass, a low disk-form round font tapering to the burner, ball shade, each painted deep maroon w/large shaded green leaves, Nutmeg burner, 7 1/2" h., Smith I, Fig. 312 (ILLUS.).................................... **325-350**

Green Riverside Floral Design Lamp

Green, stem-type, embossed floral design, made by Riverside Glass Works, Acorn burner, 5 1/2" h., Smith I, Fig. 114 (ILLUS.)... **150-165**

Pink-painted Ribbed Miniature Lamp

Milk glass, brass foot supporting the squatty bulbous melon-ribbed font painted pink, w/colored flowers, matching ribbed ball shade & clear glass chimney, Nutmeg burner, 10" h., Smith I, Fig. 303 (ILLUS.)... **400-450**

Rare Figural Owl Miniature Lamp

Milk glass, model of an owl, the base forming the body, the ball shade forming the head, overall green paint, inset eyes on each side, Nutmeg-type burner, clear glass chimney, 7 3/4" h., Smith I, Fig. 497 (ILLUS.).. **1,300-1,400**

Pairpoint Mini Lamp with Dutch Scenes

Milk glass, squatty bulbous font & ball shade embossed w/scrolls & flowers & painted w/blue Dutch scenes, marked under base "Amsterdam," made by Pairpoint Mfg. Co., E.M. Boudoir burner, Junior size 11 3/4" h., Smith I, Fig. 331 (ILLUS.) **500-550**

Tall Miniature Lamp with Mottos

Milk glass, painted blue edge bands, painted w/floral sprigs on base & shade & painted "Tof Godt" on the shade & "God Natt" on base, Spar Brenner burner, clear glass chimney, 8 1/8" h., Hulsebus II, Fig. 284 (ILLUS.).................................... **325-350**

Milk Glass Shell-embossed Lamp

Milk glass, squatty bulbous font embossed w/shell designs trimmed in gold, matching open-topped ball shade, Olmsted-type burner, 4 3/4" h., Smith I, Fig. 24 (ILLUS.) **150-165**

Pink Opaque Lamp with Gilt Florals

Pink opaque, wide squatty rounded base & ball shade both w/fired-on gold floral design, Nutmeg burner, 8 1/2" h., Smith I, Fig. 386 (ILLUS.)............................. **1,100-1,200**

Embossed Red Satin Miniature Lamp

Red satin glass, footed squatty bulbous base & domed open top shade, both w/embossed designs, clear glass chimney, Nutmeg burner, 7 3/4" h., Smith I, Fig. 401 (ILLUS.).................................. **400-450**

Lamps, Miscellaneous

Argand lamps, a central patinated brass urn-form font w/pineapple finial on a cylindrical shaft supporting two straight arms, each ending in a burner w/a tall frosted & cut tulip-form shade, the lower stem on a square foot, metal tag marked "Manufactured by M.N. Hooper & Co., Boston," early 19th c., 16" w., 17" h., pr. **$1,763**

Composite-type Banquet Lamp

Banquet lamp, composite-style, a white metal domed footed base supporting a tall brass stem & embossed brass font w/burner supporting a replaced bulbous frosted & etched clear shade w/ruffled open top, marked "New Juno" burner, electrified, late 19th c., 26" h. (ILLUS.) **288**

Banquet lamp, kerosene-type, a blown squatty bulbous font in green glass w/an oil spot finish & decorated w/random brown threading, on a ringed brass connector to the matching cylindrical glass standard on a stepped square metal base, brass collar & burner marked w/the Star of David & Freya Brenner Patent, glass by Pallme-Konig, Bohemia, ca. 1890, overall 20" h. **1,093**

Banquet lamp, kerosene-type, mold-blown melon-lobed shaded cranberry mother-of-pearl satin glass font holder in the Diamond Quilted patt., raised on a brass stem & pierced cast-brass foot, fitted w/a wide brass collar & burner supporting the tulip-shaped ribbed matching shade w/a ruffled & crimped rim, late 19th c., electrified, overall 16" h. **1,208**

Banquet lamp, three-section, milk glass baluster-form standard molded w/acanthus leaves & painted w/pink roses joined to a bulbous matching font w/inset burner supporting the matching tulip-form shade, on a gilt-iron openwork squared foot, Consolidated Lamp & Glass Co., ca. 1890s, overall 35" h. (ILLUS., top next page).. **1,035**

Cut-overlay table lamp, kerosene-type, a squatty bulbous tapering white cut to clear font w/overall punties, tooled brass stem on a square white marble base, brass fine line collar, 7 1/4" h. (ILLUS. center with two large cut-overlay lamps)...... **231**

Cut-overlay table lamp, kerosene-type, an unusual bulbous swelled & stepped-style font in light green cut to clear w/overall punties, a spiral-twist brass stem & dome on a white marble foot, fine line collar w/a

No. 1 burner & clear chimney, minor edge flakes on some cuts, collar dents, ca. 1870, 9 1/4" h. (ILLUS. right with two other cut-overlay lamps)................ **413**

Tall Consolidated Banquet Lamp

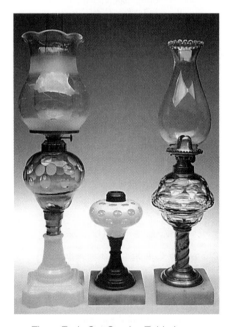

Three Early Cut-Overlay Table Lamps

Cut-overlay table lamp, kerosene-type, the inverted pear-shaped cranberry cut to clear font in a design of clustered circles, joined by a brass connector to a white opaque Baroque variant pattern base, brass collar w/reducer & late HB&H lip burner, Boudoir-style shade ring soldered to burner, a 3 1/4" h. clear engraved & frosted Oregon shade & early lip chimney, ca. 1870, open bubble on side of font, 10 3/4" h. (ILLUS. left with two other cut-overlay lamps)........................ **440**

Finger lamp, clear domed foot below the squatty bulbous Hobbs' blue opalescent Coin Dot - No. 326 Windows patt. font, brass collar w/No. 1 slip burner & clear chimney, applied blue handle, Hobbs, Brockunier & Co., Wheeling, West Virginia, ca. 1880s, minute body crack to left of upper handle attachment, 4 3/4" h. (ILLUS. second from right with other blue Coin Dot lamps, center next page) **413**

Finger lamp, footed, cobalt blue Coolidge Drape - Bellevue patt. w/ornate pressed ring & scroll handle, brass collar w/No. 1 slip burner & early crimp-top chimney, 6" h. (ILLUS. second from right with other Coolidge Drape & Turkey Foot lamps, top next page)... **330**

Finger lamp, kerosene-type, cobalt blue Coolidge Drape - Bellevue patt., tin collar w/No. 0 slip burner & early piecrust chimney, applied blue handle, 3 3/4" h. (ILLUS. second from left with other Coolidge Drape & Turkey Foot lamps, top next page).. **385**

Finger lamp, kerosene-type, squatty bulbous Hobbs' blue opalescent Coin Dot - No. 326 Windows patt., brass collar w/No. 0 slip burner & clear chimney, applied blue handle, Hobbs, Brockunier & Co., Wheeling, West Virginia, ca. 1880s, crack to body beneath handle, 3" h. (ILLUS. far right with other blue Coin Dot lamps, center next page) **143**

Finger lamp, kerosene-type, squatty bulbous Hobbs' blue opalescent Coin Dot - No. 326 Windows patt., brass collar w/No. 0 slip burner & clear chimney, applied blue handle, Hobbs, Brockunier & Co., Wheeling, West Virginia, ca. 1880s, 4 3/4" h. (ILLUS. second from left with other blue Coin Dot lamps, center next page).. **880**

Gone-with-the-Wind table lamp, decorated milk glass, the domed pierced cast-metal foot supporting a bulbous squatty font w/blown-out lion heads alternating w/small Egyptian landscapes all on a deep rusty brown ground, brass collar & font insert supporting the matching ball shade, some damage, 22" h. (ILLUS., bottom left next page) **403**

Gone-with-the-Wind table lamp, milk glass bulbous base & ball shade h.p. w/a dark shaded green ground & clusters of large white mums & small red daisies & green leafy stems, cast-metal scroll-decorated base & brass collar connector, ca. 1890s, electrified, 22" h. (ILLUS., bottom right next page)... **316**

Group of Coolidge Drape & Turkey Foot Kerosene Lamps

Four Hobbs' Coin Dot Kerosene Lamps

Lion Head Gone-with-the-Wind Lamp   *Green Decorated Gone-with-the-Wind Lamp*

Victorian Swirled Cranberry Hall Lamp

Hall lamp, blown spherical deep cranberry
swirled ribbed shade w/a brass base cap
& drop finial, the top w/a brass crown
band w/hanging chains, electrified, 12" h.
(ILLUS.)... **316**

Nice Leaded Glass Hall Lamp

Hall lamp, gas-type, leaded glass & brass,
a tall square form w/each side composed
of clear leaded segments centered by an
amber & red cross design, metal corner
finials & four arched top bars & drop center burner joined to hanging cap, ca.
1890s, electrified, 9" w., 24" h. (ILLUS.) **633**

Hanging parlor lamp, kerosene-type,
frosted & shaded open-topped domed
cranberry shade w/a Diamond Quilted
patt. fitted on an ornate shade ring suspending facet-cut prisms above a very
elaborate brass framework centered on
each side by a red jewel, an ornate
brass cap & drop framing the matching
Diamond Quilted font, ca. 1880s, shade
14" d. (ILLUS., top next column).............. **3,450**

Very Elaborate Hanging Parlor Lamp

Hanging parlor lamp, kerosene-type, the
open-topped domed milk glass shade
decorated w/delicate blossom branches in
pink, yellow & green, pierced shade ring
suspending facet-cut prisms, lower brass
frame supporting the similar but not
matching bulbous font, brass shade
crown, hanging chains & smoke bell, minor warping to shade crown, 34" h.
(ILLUS. right with red floral-decorated
hanging lamp)... **165**

Two Victorian Hanging Parlor Lamps

Hanging parlor lamp, kerosene-type, the
open-topped   domed   milk   glass
shade h.p. w/large deep red & white flowers & green leaves on a tan ground,
pierced brass shade ring suspending facet-cut prisms, looping brass frame supporting the bulbous milk glass font w/dec-
oration matching the shade, complete
w/hanging chains, crown & brass smoke
bell, solder repair within brass font cup,

late 19th c., overall 36" h. (ILLUS. left with white-shaded hanging lamp)................ **440**

Large Victorian Cranberry Parlor Lamps

Parlor table lamps, kerosene-type, mold-blown cranberry glass, each w/a round cushion foot below the large baluster-form ringed body supporting the burner ring & large Diamond Quilted matching tulip-form shades, overall ornate gilt leafy scroll decoration, burner marked "Duplex," some wear & minor flakes, overall 29" h., pr. (ILLUS.) **1,610**

Peg lamp, cranberry optic-ribbed onion-form font enameled w/dainty white flow-ers & a dotted gold center band, original brass fittings & burner, 3 3/8" d., 5 5/8" h. **95**

Fine Early Sinumbra Table Lamp

Sinumbra table lamp, gilt-lacquered bronze, the cut-and-etched clear tulip-form shade resting on a circular shade ring above a tall reeded vasiform standard w/a pair of foliate-cast handles, on a columnar stand joined to a square plinth base, mid-19th c., America or England, electrified, overall 33" h. (ILLUS.) **2,185**

Fine & Ornate Double-arm Victorian Student Lamp

Three Colorful Table Lamps with "Detroit" Style Bases

Student lamp, double style, the ornate brass body w/raised design of lion heads surrounded by scrolled designs, central bulbous ringed font flanked by upturned large arms each supporting a ring & ribbed white-cased pink open-topped shade & clear chimney, drilled & electrified, width shade to shade 24", shades 10" d., overall 18" h. (ILLUS., bottom previous page).................................... **2,300**

Table lamp, kerosene-type, blue domed foot & Leaf & Jewel patterned stem supporting the squatty bulbous Hobbs' blue opalescent Coin Dot - No. 326 Windows patt. font, brass collar w/No. 1 slip burner, Hobbs, Brockunier & Co., Wheeling, West Virginia, ca. 1880s, cracks to brass collar (ILLUS. far left with other blue Coin Dot lamps).................................... **715**

Table lamp, kerosene-type, blue opalescent Coin Spot squatty bulbous font joined by a brass connector to a "Detroit" style pedestal base composed of swirls of reds, yellow & white, a brass collar w/a No. 2 slip burner & clear chimney, screw connector, one foot flake, ca. 1880s, 9 1/4" h. (ILLUS. center with two other Detroit-based table lamps, top of page)....... **605**

Table lamp, kerosene-type, blue Turkey Foot patt., brass collar w/No. 2 slip burner & early crimp-top chimney, 10" h. (ILLUS.

far left with Coolidge Drape & other Turkey Foot lamps) **440**

Adams Temple & Ripley Marriage Lamps

Table lamp, kerosene-type, clear Adams Temple - Applesauce design, round plinth-style base supporting four open columns centered by a glass dome w/apparently original contents, the squatty bulbous patterned font w/brass shoulder & shade ring fitted w/a frosted Oregon shade, No. 2 burner & chimney, rim below columns molded "Patented March 20 1883 July 25 1882," cork on center dome w/paper label reading "Fruit Bowl Patented Nov. 15 1881 July 25 1882," Ripley, Vogeley & Adams Co., overall 13" h. (ILLUS. left with Ripley Marriage lamp) **880**

Table lamp, kerosene-type, clear Ripley Marriage Lamp, the round foot & flattened shaped standard below the brass connector supporting a pair of bulbous fonts centered by a cylindrical match holder over a diamond-shaped panel, brass collars w/No. 0 burners & early chimneys, match holder molded "Patented Sept. 20 1870," base embossed "Patd. Feb 1st 1870 - Ripley & Co.," 13 1/2" h. (ILLUS. right with Adams Temple lamp, bottom previous page) **1,100**

Table lamp, kerosene-type, clear Turkey Foot patt., the font h.p. w/a pale yellowish ground & blue flowers, brass collar w/No. 2 slip burner, some paint wear, 9 3/4" h. (ILLUS. third from left with Coolidge Drape & other Turkey Foot lamps) **154**

Table lamp, kerosene-type, cobalt blue Coolidge Drape - Bellevue patt., brass collar w/No. 1 slip burner & chimney, 8 1/2" h. (ILLUS. far right with other Coolidge Drape & Turkey Foot lamps) **275**

Table lamp, kerosene-type, cranberry opalescent Coin Spot squatty bulbous font joined by a brass connector to a "Detroit" style pedestal base composed of swirls of reds, yellow & white, a brass collar w/a No. 2 slip burner & clear chimney, screw connector, one foot flake, two open bubbles on foot, ca. 1880s (ILLUS. left with two other Detroit-based table lamps) **660**

Table lamp, kerosene-type, squatty bulbous cranberry & white spatter font joined by a brass connector to a "Detroit" style pedestal base composed of swirls of reds, yellow & white, a brass collar w/a No. 2 slip burner & early piecrust chimney, screw connector, minute foot flake, ca. 1880s, 9 1/2" h. (ILLUS. right with two other Detroit-based table lamps) **495**

Ripley Marriage Lamp with Shades

Table lamp, "Ripley Marriage lamp," two bulbous translucent blue fonts flanking a central covered match holder & joined on a tapering flange to a threaded brass connector on an opaque milk glass stepped, square pedestal foot, connector dated "1868," lamp marked "D.C. Ripley, Patent Pending," brass font collars w/kerosene burners & shade rings supporting clear tulip-shaped etched chimney shades, one shade cracked, overall 19 3/4" h. (ILLUS.) **1,265**

Electric Lamps & Lighting

Handel Lamps

The Handel Company of Meriden, Connecticut (1885-1936), began as a glass and lamp shade decorating company. Following World War I it became a major producer of decorative lamps that have become very collectible today.

Floral Leaded Glass Handel Lamp

Table lamp, 16" d. domical leaded glass shade w/large caramel slag honeycomb bands above a wide floral border in shades of pink, white & mottled green, on a bronzed-metal slender lobed base w/embossed Handel mark, ca. 1910, overall 21" h. (ILLUS.) **$1,725**

Table lamp, 18 1/2" w. squared tapering open-topped shade w/each panel etched & enameled w/a Medieval knight & coat-of-arms, raised on a bronzed metal three-light candelabra-style base w/faceted glass stem & saucer base on paw feet, shade signed "Handel 7463," small heat fracture in one shade panel, ca. 1920, overall 26" h. (ILLUS., top next page) **1,495**

Handel Lamp with Four-panel Shade

Handel Leaded Glass Table Lamp

Table lamp, 19 1/2" w. octagonal domical leaded glass shade w/each panel composed of amber slag glass w/a leaded appliqué of cattails in green & brown, on a bronzed-metal slender four-lobed base, original patina, shade & base both signed, overall 25" h. (ILLUS.) **3,105**

Moss Lamps

Moss, "the lamps that spin," were the work of San Francisco's Moss Manufacturing Co. The best-known of these plexiglass creations of the 1940s and '50s are those that incorporate motorized revolving platforms into their design. Figurines by many prominent ceramics firms of the time - among them, Ceramic Arts Studio, Yona, Hedi Schoop, Lefton, and deLee Art - adorn the platforms. The overall styling of each lamp complements the theme and costuming of the figurine utilized.

The choice of plexiglass as the base material for Moss lamps grew out of World War II metal rationing. Company co-owner Thelma Moss served as the guiding force and inspiration for the lamp designs, which were then realized by staff designers Duke Smith and John Disney. Plexiglass proved easy to work with and particularly suitable for the fanciful Moss creations; the striking visual impact was often highlighted by gigantic "spun glass" shades. Moss quickly built on its reputation for novelty with unique and at times bizarre additions to the line: aquarium lamps, fountain lamps, intercom lamps, and even motorized "double shade" lamps with the shades rotating independently in opposite directions.

The final Moss lamps were produced in 1968. Today, these prime examples of mid-20th century whimsy make attention-grabbing focal points in any decor. The lamps also have a dual appeal for those who collect specific figural ceramics of the era.

Moss Lamps of California is an msn.com group site devoted to the lamps. Complete information on Moss Manufacturing and its extraordinary product line is included in Moss Lamps: Lighting the '50s by Donald-Brian Johnson and Leslie Pina (Schiffer Publishing Ltd., 2000). Photos for this category are by Dr. Leslie Pina.

"Siamese Dancer" Clock Lamp

Clock lamp, "Siamese Dancer," No. XT 815, deLee Art male figurine, 2' 11" h. (ILLUS., previous page) **$275-300**

Fish tank lamp, "Fish Tank Bar Lamp," No. 6001, portable bar w/inset lighted aquarium **2,400-2,500**

"Cocktail Girl" Floor Lamp

Floor lamp, "Cocktail Girl," No. 2317, marble pattern plexiglass, Decoramic Kilns figurine, 5' h. (ILLUS.) **600-625**

Floor lamp, "Cocktail Girl," No. X 2404, pink plexiglass, Decoramic Kilns figurine, 5' 1" h. **525-550**

Floor lamp, "Leaning Lena," No. 2293, butterfly Plexiglass, 4' 7" h. **275-300**

Floor lamp, "Male Siamese Dancer," No. 2345, triple finials, 6' h. **475-500**

Floor lamp, "Marilyn," No. 2378, pole-style, Decoramic Kilns figurine in birdcage, 9' h. **750-800**

Floor lamp, "Mr. Mambo," No. 2310, Decoramic Kilns figurine, 28" sq. red fringed shade, 5' h. **600-625**

Floor lamp, No. 2318, birdcage lantern design, 5' 1" h. **525-550**

Floor lamp, No. 2328, triple red pagoda-style shade, 6' 5 1/2" h. **400-425**

Floor lamp, No. 2334, suspended cone-style shade, 5' 8" h. **500-525**

Fountain lamp, "Bali Dancer Fountain Lamp," No. XT 853, figural w/an operating fountain, Yona figurine, 4' 4" h. **1,100-1,200**

Music box lamp, "Harlequinade Boy & Girl," No. T 534, Lefton figurines, 2' 5" h. (ILLUS., top next column) **275-300**

Table lamp, "Bali Dancer," No. T 681, corner table-type, double rectangular shades, Decoramic Kilns figurine, 3'4" h. **300-325**

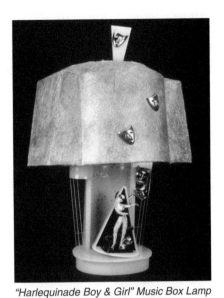

"Harlequinade Boy & Girl" Music Box Lamp

Table lamp, "Bell Girl," No. T 544, corner table-style, triple pod shades, Decoramic Kilns figurine, 2' 10" h. **300-325**

Table lamp, "Black Luster Dancer," No. XT 832, Johanna figurine, 3' h. **125-150**

Table lamp, "Egyptian Woman," No. XT 821, 2' 8" h. **200-225**

Table lamp, "Escort," No. XT 827, torchere shade, Decoramic Kilns figurine **375-400**

"Las Maracas" Table Lamp

Table lamp, "Las Maracas," No. XT837, double pod shades, 3' 8 1/2" h. (ILLUS.) **300-325**

Table lamp, "Male Ballet Dancer," No. XT 840, triple horizontal shades, Decoramic Kilns figurine, 3' 3" h. **225-250**
Table lamp, "Mambo," No. XT 838, double cone shades, Decoramic Kilns figurine, 4' 4 1/2" h. **325-350**

"Phantasy Lady" Table Lamp

Table lamp, "Phantasy Lady," No. XT 807, Hedi Schoop figurine, 2' 5 1/2" h. (ILLUS.) **250-275**
Table lamp, "Poodle Girl," No. XT 806, Hedi Schoop figurine, 2' 11" h. **275-300**

"Prom Girl" Table Lamp

Table lamp, "Prom Girl," No. T 731, Decoramic Kilns figurine, 3' 7 1/2" h. (ILLUS.) **300-325**
Table lamp, "Siamese Dancer," No. XT 815, partner to No. XT 815 clock lamp but no clock, deLee Art female figurine, 2' 11" h. **200-225**

Pairpoint Lamps

Well known as a producer of fine Victorian art glass and silver plate wares between 1907 and 1929, the Pairpoint Corporation of New Bedford, Massachusetts, also produced a wide range of fine quality decorative lamps.

Pairpoint Boudoir Lamp & Shade

Boudoir lamp, 8" w. squared domical reverse-painted "Portsmouth" shade decorated w/purple flowers & green leaves outlined in black, raised on a squared baluster-form bronze base impressed w/red leaves, both shade & base signed, some wear to base, 16" h. (ILLUS.) **$3,163**

Pairpoint Lamp with Florence Shade

Table lamp, 13" d. domical closed-top reverse-painted "Florence" shade decorated w/turquoise blue striped background & red & yellow stylized floral designs, obverse of shade highlighted w/gold trimmings, on a silvered metal rectangular tapering standard on a rectangular foot

w/pierced designs on four sides, base
signed, small spot on rim of shade possibly ground, some wear to base finish,
19 1/2" h. (ILLUS.) **3,163**

Very Rare Puffy Orange Tree Lamp

Table lamp, 14" d. domical "Puffy" reverse-
painted Orange Tree shade, raised on an
unsigned tree trunk base, shade signed,
overall 24" h. (ILLUS.) **51,750**

Puffy Pairpoint with Stratford Shade

Table lamp, 14" d. domical "Puffy" shade in
the "Stratford" shape w/a border of large
roses & hummingbird against a lattice
background in cream & pale blue, on a
signed paneled trumpet-form bronze-
metal base w/round gadrooned foot, No.
D30441, 23" h. (ILLUS.) **4,830**

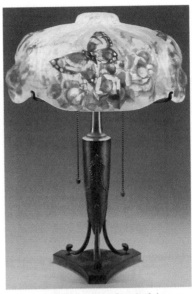

Fine Puffy "Papillon" Shade & Lamp

Table lamp, 15 1/2" d. "Puffy" closed-top
"Papillon" patt. shade, large red, yellow &
black butterflies on red, yellow & pink
roses & green leaves, on a signed tall
slender bronzed-metal urn-form base
w/three scroll legs resting on a tri-corner
foot, No. B3011, 21 1/2" h. (ILLUS.) **13,225**

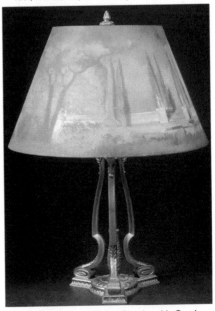

Reverse-painted Seville Shade with Gardens

Table lamp, 16" d. tapering conical reverse-
painted "Seville" shade, decorated w/a
continuous Italian garden scene in

shades of orange, yellow, green, red & blue, raised on a gilt-metal base w/three serpentine legs flanking a central column all on a tripartite foot, No. D3084, minor flake, overall 21" h. (ILLUS.) **3,335**

Tiffany Lamps

Tiffany Kerosene-type Desk Lamp

Desk kerosene-type lamp, 15 3/4" d. domical open-topped greenish yellow damascene shade signed w/initials, raised on bronze spider arms above the dome-topped cylindrical metal font fitted into a bulbous bronze base w/etched band & supported by a ring raised on three legs, oil canister stamped "Tiffany Studios - New York" w/Tiffany Glass & Decorating Co. monogram, ca. 1910 (ILLUS.) **11,353**

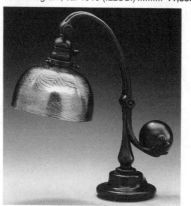

Fine Tiffany Counterbalance Desk Lamp

Desk lamp, counterbalance style, a 14" d. domed blue iridescent damascene shade supported at the end of a high bronze S-scroll counterbalance arm on a slender stem & stepped domed base, shade engraved "L.C.T. Favrile," base stamped "Tiffany Studios - New York 416," ca. 1910, overall 14" h. (ILLUS.) **17,925**

Rare Tiffany Laburnum Floor Lamp

Floor lamp, "Laburnum," a 24 1/4" d. domical leaded glass shade composed of green & brown leafy branches w/touches of purple suspending long clusters of yellow flower clusters w/an uneven rim, domed & pierced "pigtail" finial, on a tall slender reeded standard on a wide low cylindrical base decorated w/tight coils & raised on knob feet, shade w/stamped mark & base w/stamped plate "Tiffany Studios - New York - 7878," overall 6' 6 1/2" h. (ILLUS.) **298,700**

Fine Tiffany Apple Blossom Table Lamp

Table lamp, "Apple Blossom," 25 1/8" d. domical leaded glass shade w/bronze openwork branch design at the top center surrounded by an overall design of mottled green leaves, mottled red buds & white & yellow blossoms, uneven edge, supported on a bronze tree trunk base, shade & base both w/stamped marks, overall 29 3/8" h. (ILLUS., previous page) **136,000**

Tiffany Black-eyed Susan Table Lamp

Table lamp, "Black-eyed Susan," 16" d. domical leaded glass shade decorated w/large yellow & brown daisies w/mottled light green leafy stems against a blocked ground of creamy white to mottled dark green, raised on a slender ribbed standard continuing into a wide disk base w/ribs ending in ribbed leaves, raised on small scroll feet, base stamped "D794 - 8" & Tiffany Glass & Decorating Co. monogram, overall 21 1/2" h. (ILLUS.).... **26,290**

Rare Drophead Dragonfly Tiffany Lamp

Table lamp, "Drophead Dragonfly," 22" d. domical leaded glass shade composed in the upper portion of elongated & oblong mottled dark & light green glass & amber tiles, the border band composed of a band of large green dragonflies w/red eyes, on a gilt-bronze Art Nouveau base w/a pod design on the standard & pierced leaf designs around the rounded base on small tab feet, shade stamped "Tiffany Studios - New York - 1507," base stamped "Tiffany Studios - New York - 397," overall 28 1/2" h. (ILLUS.) **185,500**

Simple Geometric Tiffany Table Lamp

Table lamp, geometric, a 10 1/4" d. domical leaded glass shade composed of radiating bands of rectangular tiles in mottled emerald green & sea green opalescent glass, raised on a bronze three-arm support continuing to a cylindrical standard & circular base cast w/overlapping uneven lappets, shade w/impressed mark, base stamped "Tiffany Studios - New York - 445," two panels cracked, rewired, 17 1/4" h. (ILLUS.) **14,950**

Tiffany Pansy Pattern Table Lamp

Table lamp, "Pansy," 16" d. domical leaded glass shade composed of graduated mottled pale yellowish green to dark green tile ground decorated w/a wide band of colorful pansies in shades of purple, yellow & green, supported on bronze arms above the slender standard w/fine reeding & loops above the wide rounded knobby base on small scroll feet, shade w/stamped tag, base stamped "Tiffany Studios - New York - 23617" & Tiffany Glass & Decorating Co. monogram, 22 1/2" h. (ILLUS.) **50,190**

Lamps, Miscellaneous

1940s Aladdin Alacite Table Lamp

Aladdin table lamp, Alacite glass, the glass base in a footed ovoid form of ivory opaque molded w/long panels separated by a mint green ground & gilt foot bands, the slender neck supporting the original tall tapering cylindrical waxed paper shade in mint green w/deep rose stylized leaves topped by a glass "Precision" Aladdin finial, ca. 1949, 31" h. (ILLUS.) **144**

Art Deco table lamp, glass & chrome, the shade composed of three flat round tired disks of satin amber glass w/chrome banding raised on a slender chrome standard above the ringed flaring chrome foot, ca. 1925, 20 1/2" h. (ILLUS., top next column) **374**

Art Nouveau desk lamp, harp-style, the tall arched harp w/electric socket suspending a bell-shaped signed Quezal shade decorated on the exterior w/a green & gold pulled-feather design on a creamy white ground, iridescent gold interior, harp joined to a ringed flaring base, base unsigned & w/minor finish discoloration, shaded 5 1/2" d., overall 14" h. (ILLUS., next column) **1,080**

Unusual Glass & Chrome Art Deco Lamp

Quezal Shade on Art Nouveau Desk Lamp

Arts & Crafts Lamp with Slag Shade

Arts & Crafts table lamp, 18" d. domical caramel & green slag glass shade composed of alternating radiating graduated caramel slag & mottled green & amber tiles above the flattened drop edge w/uneven rim, raised on a bronzed metal base w/a slender tapering square standard w/stylized bamboo corner above the square pyramidal foot w/a large molded fleur-de-lis on each side, early 20th c., 22" h. (ILLUS., bottom previous page)........ **978**

Arts & Crafts table lamp, a four-sided domical geometrically woven wicker shade raised on a four-sided wicker & wrapped post standard on a flaring woven wicker foot, new linen lining inside the shade, unmarked, first quarter 20th c., 20" w., 31" h. **468**

Bigelow & Kennard Water Lily Lamp

Bigelow & Kennard table lamp, 16 1/2" d. "Water Lily" leaded glass shade, composed of graduated radiating mottled bluish green rectangular tiles & large water lilies & leaves in white, yellow & green, on a bronzed metal base w/a slender standard & domed foot on ball feet, shade & base marked "Bigelow. Kennard & Co. Boston" & "Bigelow Studios," very few hairlines in shade, minor base wire, needs to be rewired, 22 1/2" h. (ILLUS.).............. **8,050**

Bigelow Studios Leaded Boudoir Lamp

Bigelow Studios boudoir lamp, the conical leaded glass shade w/an Art Nouveau design of blossoms around the top & leaves around the bottom edge, raised on a slender bronzed metal standard w/disk base & thin bun feet, based signed "Bigelow Studios," shade unsigned, early 20th c., top vent cap soldered to shade, 14" h. (ILLUS.) **2,040**

Vaseline Glass Engraved Boudoir Lamp

Boudoir lamp, vaseline glass, a conical glass shade w/cylindrical lower sides engraved overall w/daisy-like blossoms & leafy stems, supported on a brass ring suspending facet-cut prisms raised above a matching conical base w/slightly scalloped base rim, ca. 1920s, 14" h. (ILLUS.) **374**

Bradley & Hubbard Leaded Glass Lamp

Bradley & Hubbard table lamp, 20" d. umbrella-form leaded glass shade composed of radiating mottled green rectangular tiles above the wide drop border band w/red grape clusters alternating w/large green leaves, on a bronzed-metal footed inverted trumpet-form base embossed "Bradley & Hubbard" w/triangle mark, ca. 1910, 28" h. (ILLUS., previous page) **2,645**

Fine Tall Slender Daum Nancy Lamp

Daum Nancy table lamp, 12" d. domical etched & enameled shade decorated w/a continuous winter landscape w/large brown & black trees in the foreground of a snowy background in black, mottled brown & pale yellow, raised above a tall slender swelled matching glass base w/a flaring round foot, enameled mark w/the Cross of Lorraine, ca. 1905, overall 25 1/2" h. (ILLUS.) **35,850**

Fine Dirk Van Erp Copper Table Lamp

Dirk Van Erp table lamp, hand-hammered copper, the bulbous ovoid copper base supporting a large conical shade w/a copper frame fitted w/four mica panels above the two original electric sockets, original mica, new patina, Open Box mark, San Francisco, early 20th c., 18" d. shade, overall 18" h. (ILLUS.) **10,925**

Unique Metal & Glass Pheasant Lamp

Novelty lamp, blown glass & metal, a model of a large pheasant w/the openwork metal body internally blown w/amber glass w/foil inclusions, the tail, raised head & legs of finely executed metal, standing on a thin rectangular metal base w/an Art Deco design, all mounted on a rectangular grey marble foot, metal base signed "Chapelle Nancy France," ca. 1930s, overall 20" l., 17" h. (ILLUS.) **7,475**

Carved Alabaster Figural Novelty Lamp

Novelty lamp, carved alabaster, figural, depicting a seated nude woman beside an umbrella-form leafy outcropping, lighted from behind, probably Italian, early 20th c., overall 14" h. (ILLUS.) **604**

Bent-panel Slag Glass Table Lamp

Slag glass table lamp, wide domical eight-paneled shade w/a gilt-metal framework, each panel w/a caramel slag panel above a large mottled & swirled blue, pink & white slag panel overlaid w/a delicate floral metal filigree, raised on a slender gilt-metal urn-form standard w/a serpentine round & ribbed foot, ca. 1910, 24" h. (ILLUS.)............ **805**

Double Student Lamp with Quezal Shades

Student lamp, double style, ornate brass leaf-cast slender standard & arched arms each suspending a socket w/a signed bell-form Quezal shade decorated in a gold & green pulled-feather design on a creamy white ground, the standard raised on a stepped black marble base, early 20th c., overall 18" h. (ILLUS.) **1,080**

Other Lighting Devices

Chandeliers

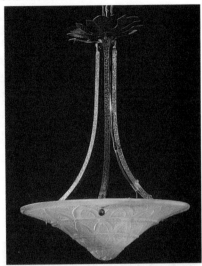

Art Deco Blue Glass & Iron Chandelier

Art Deco, glass & iron, a widely flaring inverted conical molded shade in frosted blue glass w/an arched geometric design, suspended by a hammered wrought-iron frame, ca. 1925, 16" d., 23" h. (ILLUS.) **460**

Unusual Copper Art Deco Chandelier

Art Deco, spun copper, a ringed pointed conical copper center w/four protruding etched pink glass wings, pink etched disk glass top, ca. 1925, 18" d. (ILLUS.) **604**

Art Nouveau, 10-light, bronze & glass, "Chicoree" patt., the long central post w/an upturned leaf ceiling cap above a cluster of scrolling arms w/sockets ending in small blown milky opalescent bell-shaped glass shades above a bottom ball issuing large looping & curling arms suspending four milky opalescent flaring conical ribbed shades, a central rounded matching shade at the center bottom, designed by Louis Majorelle, France, ca. 1905, 37" d., 49" h. (ILLUS., next page)

.... **10,755**

American Fancy Brass Gasolier

Fine Chicoree Art Nouveau Chandelier

Arts & Crafts Bronze & Slag Chandelier

Arts & Crafts, bronze & caramel slag glass, five caramel slag bent panels fit-

ted in an ornate hand-wrought bronze framework w/bold scrolls & cabochons, suspended by large wrought-bronze chain links, unmarked, ca. 1905, 23" d., 34" h. (ILLUS.)... **1,495**

Brass, five-light gasolier style, a reeded rod leading to a stem of pierced ball shape, supporting five scrolling arms w/turned & fluted finial candle sockets, ornate scrolls from the center to the arms decorated w/large blossoms, America, ca. 1890, electrified, 27" d., 39" h. (ILLUS., top of page).. **2,070**

Very Rare Early Eight-arm Gasolier

Very Elaborate Venetian Blown Glass Chandelier

Gilt-brass, Rococo Revival-style gasolier, eight-arm, the large cast arms w/foliate & leaf decor surrounding the central bowl profusely adorned w/rococo mounts & tassels, the fluted shaft w/a large bell canopy w/applied decoration, attributed to Starr, Fellows & Co., New York, New York, ca. 1850, 40" d., overall 58" h. (ILLUS., previous page) **27,600**

Muller Freres Glass & Iron Chandelier

Muller Freres, four-light, a wide bowl-form central shade internally decorated in mottled peach, red, green, blue & amethyst, suspended from wrought-iron bars & fitted around the rim w/three metal sockets each suspending a matching tapering cylindrical glass shade, glass etched "Muller Fres - Luneville," France, early 20th c., 18" d., 29" h. (ILLUS.) **1,840**

Slag Glass Bent-panel Chandelier

Slag glass, bent-panel type, six wide tapering slag panels in mottled blue, tan & white fitted into a cast-metal framework w/bands of floral filigree along the bottom of each panel, ca. 1920, 15" d. (ILLUS.)...... **259**

Venetian blown glass, eight-light, in the 18th c. taste, the faux candles emanating from large scalloped coupes atop upswept clear glass arms, the whole adorned w/arched & twisting leaves, multicolored flowerheads & strawberries, ca. 1900, electrified, 34" d., 34" d. (ILLUS., top of page)... **4,140**

Wood & iron, eight-light, a baluster-turned wooden hub painted white, now grey w/age, issuing eight slender serpentine iron arms ending in tin candle sockets, America, late 18th c., imperfections, 29 1/2" d., 15" h. (ILLUS., top next page) **2,820**

Early American Wood & Iron Chandelier

Lanterns

Unusual Prairie School Lantern

One of Three Beaux Arts Lanterns

Arts & Crafts, leaded glass & bronze, Prairie School style, the rectangular flat bronze top overhanging the four leaded glass panels w/amber Glasgow roses over frosted glass, original patina, a couple of short hairlines in the glass, unmarked, early 20th c., 12" sq., 10 3/4" h. (ILLUS.).. **1,955**

Beaux Arts, patinated metal & glass, outdoor wall-mounted type, each consisting of a downward tapering frame holding curved glass panes surmounted by a curving pierced top, the whole attached to a rectangular backplate w/scroll brackets, early 20th c., 13 1/2 x 14 1/2", 39" h., set of 3 (ILLUS. of one, top next column)

.... **2,990**

Candle lantern, glass & wood, a primitive wooden frame w/one side forming a door, glass sides, domed tin top vent & wire bail handle, 19th c., 11" h. (ILLUS., bottom next column).. **161**

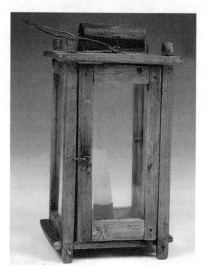

Early Wood & Glass Candle Lantern

Colorful Variety of Old Skater's Lanterns

One of Two Regency-Style Lanterns

Regency-Style, wrought iron & glass, each w/a backplate supporting an arm fixed to a pendant lantern w/a scrolling iron frame w/iron leaves enclosing a cylindrical glass insert, England, late 19th c., electrified, 26 1/2" h., pr. (ILLUS. of one) **1,955**

Skater's lantern, glass & tin, a domed tin font base & burner ring fitted w/a deep cobalt blue baluster-form shade topped by a pierced tin cap w/wire bail handle, usual rust, two scratches, late 19th - early 20th c., 7" h. (ILLUS. third from left with other skater's lanterns, top of page) **518**

Skater's lantern, glass & tin, a domed tin font base & burner ring fitted w/a deep amethyst baluster-form shade topped by a pierced tin cap w/wire bail handle, shade & top marked "Jewel," usual rust, late 19th - early 20th c., 7" h. (ILLUS. second from left with other skater's lanterns, top of page) **834**

Skater's lantern, glass & tin, a domed tin font base & burner ring fitted w/a deep amethyst baluster-form shade topped by a pierced tin cap w/wire bail handle,

shade & top marked "Jewel," usual rust, late 19th - early 20th c., 7" h. (ILLUS. far left with other skater's lanterns, top of page) **1,093**

Skater's lantern, glass & tin, a domed tin font base & burner ring fitted w/a grass green baluster-form shade topped by a pierced tin cap w/wire bail handle, late 19th - early 20th c., 7" h. (ILLUS. second from right with other skater's lanterns, top of page) **546**

Skater's lantern, glass & tin, a domed tin font base & burner ring fitted w/a peacock blue baluster-form shade topped by a pierced tin cap w/wire bail handle, split in tin top, short crack in glass, late 19th - early 20th c., 7" h. (ILLUS. far right with other skater's lanterns, top of page) **173**

Unusual Tiffany Moorish-style Lantern

Tiffany "Moorish" style, leaded glass & bronze, a cylindrical central shade composed of mottled green rectangular panels enclosed by wide arched scroll-pierced bronze fins joined to a top ring w/three hanging chains, a knob drop finial at the base, overall 36 1/2" h. (ILLUS.) **16,730**

Shades

Four Early Cranberry Glass Shades

Cranberry, domed cylindrical Diamond Quilted design w/a flaring crimped rim, 5" d. fitter, w/a No. 2 P&A burner & shade ring, late 19th - early 20th c., 5" h. (ILLUS. far left with other cranberry shades, top of page).................................... **165**

Cranberry, Hobnail patt., rounded top w/wide deeply ruffled flaring rim, 4" fitter, 5 3/4" h. (ILLUS. far right with other cranberry shades, top of page) **88**

Cranberry, Hobnail patt., wide flaring w/pinched-ruffle rim, 5" d. fitter & No. 2/3 Duplex double wick burner w/raised shade ring, 5" h. (ILLUS. second from right with other cranberry shades, top of page)... **132**

Cranberry opalescent, Hobnail patt., round w/deeply ruffled flaring sides, 4" fitter, 4 1/4" h. (ILLUS. second from left with other cranberry shades, top of page)........... **121**

Early Fostoria Blown Shade

Fostoria, slender trumpet form, opal exterior decorated w/an iridescent gold zipper over green pulled decoration, 7 1/4" h. (ILLUS.)... **431**

Hurricane shade, clear blown etched & cut glass, tall baluster form w/overall diamond lattice cut design highlighted w/four-petal designs & punties, folded bottom rim, first half 19th c., 22" h. (ILLUS., top next column) **1,315**

Scarce Early Blown Hurricane Shade

Blue Pulled-feather Quezal Shade

Quezal-signed, tall ovoid form w/flaring scalloped rim, opal ground decorated w/gold-tipped blue pulled-feather decoration, gold iridescent interior, two fitter flakes, 6" h. (ILLUS.).................................... **431**

Two Pairs of Quezal Art Glass Shades

Quezal-signed, tall trumpet form w/a gold iridescent ground decorated around the lower half w/a white & gold dragged loops design, 5 3/4" d., 6 1/2" h., pr. (ILLUS. left with other pair of Quezal shades, top of page) **834**

Quezal-signed, trumpet form w/wide disk-form top below the fitter, gold iridescent ground decorated w/green-tipped white pulled-feather design & overall random green threading, slight loss, 5 1/2" h., pr. (ILLUS. at right with other pair of Quezal shades, top of page) **316**

Bent-panel Slag Glass & Enamel Shade

Slag glass, 17 1/2" w. octagonal bent-panel style, the eight curved & tapering caramel slag glass panels in an enameled metal frame w/metal overlay leaf & flower brackets at the base of each panel, enameled in green, yellow & orange, ca. 1920 (ILLUS.)... **288**

Three Gold & Green Steuben Shades

Steuben-signed, lightly ribbed trumpet form, opal ground decorated around the base w/green-tipped gold pulled-feather decoration, 5 1/4" h., set of 3 (ILLUS.)......... **690**

Steuben-signed, ringed base w/trumpet-form body w/a closed rim, opal ground decorated w/long gold-tipped blue pulled-feather decoration, gold iridescent interior, small chip to one fitter rim, 5 1/4" h., set of 6 (ILLUS., below) **2,875**

Set of Six Steuben Blue Pulled-feather Shades

Set of Three Steuben Pulled-feather Shades

Steuben-signed, trumpet-shaped form w/ringed base & flaring ruffled rim, gold iridescent ground decorated w/turquoise pulled-feather design around the rim, 6" h., set of 3 (ILLUS.) **1,093**

Rodney Kent Condiment Server

MARBLES

Glass, sulfide, girl sitting in chair, 1 9/16" d. (bubble around figure, minor surface dings) **$259**

Glass, sulfide, light amber, standing sheep dog, 1 1/4" d. **748**

Glass, sulfide, sitting frog, 1 13/16" d. (bubble around figure, slight surface wear) **201**

Glass, sulfide, standing bear, 1 5/16" d. (slight surface wear) **144**

Glass, sulfide, standing chicken, 1 13/16" d. **115**

Glass, sulfide, standing cow, 1 11/16" d. (bubble around cow, surface abrasions) **144**

Glass, sulfide, standing dog w/curly tail, 1 3/4" d. **115**

Glass, sulfide, standing sheep, 2 3/16" d. (bubble around sheep, surface wear) **173**

METALS

Aluminum

Coasters, hammered, spiral design, Everlast, set of 6 .... **$16**

Coasters, polished, beaded edge, in caddy w/double looped handle, Buenilum, set of 8 .... **25**

Condiment server, hammered, revolving-type, cruets & covered jars in apple design, twisted center handle, Continental **45**

Condiment server: oval handled tray & two cov. glass containers; the hammered tray w/an arched & pierced central handle w/a ribbon & flower design, lids on containers w/spoon slots & bud finials, Rodney Kent, the set (ILLUS., top of page) **50**

Crumber set: tray & brush; hammered, looped handles, Buenilum, the set **35-40**

Crumber set: tray & scraper; hand-forged, tray w/angular handle, both w/fruit designs, Everlast **27-35**

Crumber set: tray & scraper; long tray w/serpentine edges, half-round scraper w/flat end handle, rose decoration, Everlast, 2 pcs. **27-35**

Small Fish-shaped Dish

Dish, rounded flattened model of a fish, old circular Everlast mark, small (ILLUS.) **25-40**

Jewelry, brooch, hammered, pine design, Wendell August, 1 1/2 x 2" **45**

Jewelry, cuff bracelet, hammered, flowers & leaves, unmarked **25**

Pencil sharpener, cast, in the form of a milk bottle, 5/8 x 1 1/4" **40**

Silent butler, round, hammered, bird on twig decoration, N.S. Co., 6" d. **12-15**

Silent butler, round, hammered, floral bouquet w/roses decoration, Canterbury Arts, 6" d. **20**

Silent butler, round, hammered, rose decoration, Everlast, 6" d. **12**

Tray, hammered, loop handles, apple blossoms decoration, fluted sides, Federal Silver Co., 11 1/2 x 15 1/2" **20**

Tray, hammered, handled, gold anodized, chessmen decoration, Arthur Armour, 10 x 16" **45-55**

Tray, hammered, handled, bird & flowers decoration, N.S. Co., 11 x 16" **27**

Tray, double handles curved to side w/flower decoration, hammered frame w/berry stems, American Limoges plate insert, Wrought Farberware, 16 1/2" d **35-45**

Tray, machine-embossed, handles, hunt scene, crimped edges, Beautyline Designed Aluminum, 11 1/2 x 16 1/2" **10**

Tray, hammered, bar handles, hunt scene, Keystone, 13 x 17" **35-45**

Tray, hammered, handled, oak leaf & acorn decoration, Continental #520, 17 1/2" l. **30**

Tray, flat handles w/flowers, simulated hammer marks, machine-embossed roses, World, 14 x 20".. **15-18**

Tray, hammered, handled, Bali Bamboo patt., Everlast, 14 1/2 x 20 1/2" **45**

Tray, hammered, tab handles, saguaro cactus decoration, Wendell August, 13 1/4 x 21" **150-175**

Tray, hammered, grooved bar handles, hunt scene, Arthur Armour, 14 1/2 x 21 1/2" **150-195**

Wastebasket, hammered, oval, dogwood & butterfly decoration, Arthur Armour.............. **115**

Wastebasket, hammered, oval, floral bouquet decoration, Canterbury Arts **150-195**

Brass

Decorative Victorian Brass Fire Shield

Fire shield, flattened arch form w/ornate relief decoration, a floral band across the top above two panels featuring gamebirds in wooded setting, floral swags at the bottom above the heavy arched feet, Victorian, late 19th c., 30 1/2" w., 34" h. (ILLUS.)... **1,495**

Pierced Brass & Iron Kettle Stand

Kettle stand, D-form cast brass top w/ornate pierced scroll & floral medallions around the skirt, raised on three wrought-iron cabriole legs ending in large penny feet, a decorative rosette missing on front, 19th c., 10 1/2 x 13", 13 1/2" h. (ILLUS.).............. **460**

Kettle Stand with Cabriole Legs

Kettle stand, the rectangular top w/a slightly bowed front above a conforming scroll-cut front apron w/front cabriole legs, iron rod back legs, a cast brass handle flanking the top, 19th c., 11 3/4 x 18 3/4", 12" h. (ILLUS.) **201**

Large Indian Brass Palace Jar

Palace jar, wide bulbous body w/a wide shoulder tapering to a short flaring neck, overall delicate chased designs of various deities within a scrolled field, India, early 20th c., 17" d., 16" h. (ILLUS.) **414**

Russian Imperial Era Samovar

Samovar, a square base on knob feet supporting a two-part pierced pedestal below the large nearly spherical body w/large scroll & bar handles & a large spigot, a gadrooned top band w/large inserted top w/wooden knob handles flanking the tall ringed chimney, Imperial era, Russia, marked, 15" h. (ILLUS.) **374**

Samovar, Tray & Bowl Set

Samovar, tray & bowl, the samovar w/a footed square base & vented pedestal supporting the wide urn-form body w/scroll-and-bar side handles & a large spigot w/a fancy scroll handle, the ringed flaring top fitted w/a stepped & ringed top w/wooden knob handles flanking the flaring vented chimney, w/a shallow widely flaring bowl for under the spigot, both on a conforming shaped undertray, marked, Russia, ca. 1890, overall 18 1/2" h., the set (ILLUS.) **546**

Small Marked Brass Teakettle

Teakettle, cov., deep cylindrical sides w/domed top w/low domed cover & knob finial, long angled spout, overhead strap bail swing handle, marked "Toronto Fletcher Co. Ltd.," early 20th c., 6" l., 3 3/8" h. (ILLUS.) **30**

Early 19th Century Brass Teakettle

Teakettle, cov., flat-bottomed bulbous body w/a short cylindrical neck, angled snake spout, upright shape strap swing bail handle, ringed domed cover w/knob finial, early 19th c., 9 1/2" h. (ILLUS.) **604**

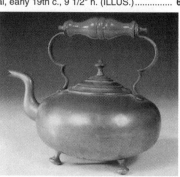

Brass Teakettle with Glass Handle

Teakettle, cov., wide squatty bulbous body raised on four small knob feet, serpentine spout, fixed upright scrolls in handle joined by a baluster-form blue opaline glass hand grip, probably Europe, late 19th c., 10" l. (ILLUS.) **51**

Bronze

Very Rare French Art Deco Ashtray

Ashtray, Art Deco style, a deep rounded bowl supported on stylized half-figures of cats w/two front legs, a wide flattened rim

Wide Shallow Japanese Jardiniere

w/an overall scale design fitted w/four figural butterfly cigarette rests, bronze liner,
designed by Armand-Albert Rateau,
France, ca. 1925, 4 1/8" h. (ILLUS.) **107,550**

Bronze Gothic-style Footed Casket

Casket, Gothic-style, upright rectangular
chapel form w/Gothic arch window sides
above a flaring band & slim scroll band,
canted corners w/columns at each corner
& open block feet, peaked roof-form
hinged cover opening to reveal a padded
velvet-lined interior, probably France,
19th c., 6 x 8 1/2", 7 1/4" h. (ILLUS.)............ **978**

Censer, a wide flat-bottomed squatty bulbous bowl-form cast in relief w/figures of
people, birds & animals in a landscape,
each side mounted w/a figural lotus blossom handle, the domed & floral-cast cover w/pierced oblong openings, China,
early 19th c., 12" d., 9 1/2" h. (one handle
loose) **748**

Jardiniere, a wide shallow lobed & incurved
bowl form raised on dragon-form legs,
dark patina, Japan, late 19th c., 15" d.
(ILLUS., top of page)................................. **1,434**

Columbian Exposition Medallion

Medallion, commemorative, round w/raised
rim, "World's Columbian Exposition -
1892-93" in banner across front & decorated w/embossed images of a spread-
winged eagle, Christopher Columbus,
George Washington & the signing of the
Declaration of Independence, 2 1/4" d.
(ILLUS.)... **125**

U.S.S. Enterprise Medallion

Medallion, commemorative, silver finish,
embossed w/image of U.S.S. Enterprise
aircraft carrier surrounded by "U.S.S. Enterprise - World's Largest Ship - First Nu-
clear Powered Aircraft Carrier," com-
memorates its launching on Sept. 14,
1960 at Newport News, Va., 2 1/2" d.
(ILLUS.)... **45**

Bronze Medallion with Bust

Medallion, round w/relief-cast bust of a
Classical goddess, 5 3/4" d. (ILLUS.) **350**

Mirror with Unusual Figural Bronze Frame

Mirror, the upright three-sided metal frame
designed to resemble a stage w/a figure
wearing a fancy costume standing at the
left side holding back the high curtain that
forms the top cross bar, enclosing a rectangular mirror, late 19th - early 20th c.,
10 3/4" h. (ILLUS.) **184**

Fine Japanese Meiji Era Bronze Vase

Vase, footed baluster form w/a tall flaring lotus blossom neck mounted w/a pair of flying birds & w/a pair of figural foo lion handles suspending ribbon-draped rings,
each side of the body w/an incised cartouche decorated w/relief-cast birds &
blossoms, Japan, Meiji Era, late 19th c.,
9 3/4" d., 19 3/4" h. (ILLUS.) **1,495**

Very Rare French Art Nouveau Vases

Vases, Art Nouveau style, gilded figural
type, "Reves" ("Dreams"), a bulbous
lobed inverted blossom-form lower body
mounted on one w/a semi-nude female &
on the other w/a semi-nude male, tall
slightly flaring & lightly ribbed neck w/a
ruffled rim, the sides in low relief w/fig-
ures in landscapes, copper liners, based
on a model by Francois Raoul Larche,
France, ca. 1900, 21 1/4" h., pr. (ILLUS.)
.... **1,795**

Copper

Unusual Tall Lobed Copper Bowl-Vase

Bowl-vase, Arts & Crafts style, hand-hammered, a small round footring below the
very deep widely flaring & lobed sides,
die-stamped mark of Marie Zimmer-
mann, clean patina, few minor dents to
body & bends to rim, 6 3/4" d., 10 3/4" h.
(ILLUS.) **500**

Two Gustav Stickley Copper Bowls

Bowls, Arts & Crafts style, hand-hammered, wide squatty bulbous body w/low riveted buttress feet & a rolled rim, unmarked Gustav Stickley, some cleaning to patina, early 20th c., 6" d., pr. (ILLUS., top of page) **748**

Large Old Copper Candy Kettle

Candy kettle, a large half-round form w/a heavy rolled rim & heavy riveted iron loop rim handles, early 20th c., 20" d. (ILLUS.) **259**

Early Floral-inlaid Copper Chargers

Chargers, round shallow dished form, hammered exterior, the interior inlaid overall w/small flowerheads, soldered silver rim, early 19th century or earlier, 11 1/2" d., pr. (ILLUS.) **127**

Unusual Early Copper Covered Kettle

Kettle, a deep cylindrical form w/a slightly rounded bottom, the slightly domed hinged cover pierced w/overall decorative holes, iron side rim handle for holding wooden extension, early 19th c., 19" l. (ILLUS.).. **104**

Early French Copper Lavabo Set

Lavabo, the half-round wall-hanging font w/a domed gadrooned cover w/urn finial, the paneled flaring sides above the bulbous lobed base w/a brass spigot, the separate round bowl also lobed & fitted w/two small loop hanging handles, France, early 19th c., bowl 13" d., overall 24" h., the set (ILLUS.) **150**

Ornate Copper Log Holder with Lions & Eagle

Log holder, tall U-form sides decorated w/a repousse high-relief design w/large rampant lions flanking a fierce looking spread-winged eagle w/a shield on its breast below a cast lion mask w/ring handle, broad riveted border band, raised on six paw feet, possibly England, late 19th c., 27 1/8" l., 14 1/2" h. (ILLUS.)................... **690**

Two Early Copper Teakettles

Teakettle, cov., bulbous ovoid body w/a flat bottom, wide short cylindrical neck w/a fitted domed cover w/brass knob finial, angled snake-form spout, overhead swing strap bail handle, possibly European, early 19th c., 10 liter size, body 11 1/2" h., w/handle 15 1/2" h. (ILLUS. left with smaller teakettle)......................... **1,150**

Teakettle, cov., flat-bottomed dovetailed body w/a wide base & tapering sides to a short cylindrical neck w/a fitted low domed cover w/baluster-form finial, angular snake spout, overhead brass strap swing bail handle, stamped number "6," American-made, 19th c., overall 13" l. (ILLUS., next column) **1,208**

Teakettle, cov., flat-bottomed spherical body w/an overall hand-hammered design, flat dished cover w/knob finial, serpentine spout, fixed uprights joined by a

turned black wood grip forming the handle, mark of the Gorham Mfg. Co., Providence, Rhode Island, date code for 1883, 7 1/2" h. (ILLUS. left with other Gorham teakettles, top next page)..................... **200-400**

American Dovetailed Copper Teakettle

Tall Oval Copper Teakettle

Teakettle, cov., oval cylindrical body w/deep sides below the wide angled shoulder, ringed domed cover w/mushroom finial, angular snake spout, fixed tall brass curved supports joined by a bar handle, tin-lined, 19th c., 11" h. (ILLUS.)
.... **201**

Three Gorham Victorian Teakettles

Revere Ware Copper Teakettle

Teakettle, cov., Revere Ware, domed beehive body w/applied black Bakelite handle and bird whistle spout, marked on
bottom "Revere Solid Copper - Rome,
N.Y.," 7 1/4 x 7 1/2" (ILLUS.) **100**

Teakettle, cov., wide flat bottom & slightly
tapering cylindrical sides w/a wide rounded shoulder centering a short neck w/a
fitted domed cover w/knob finial, angular
snake-form spout, tall fixed brass
scrolled uprights joined by a copper bar
forming handle, early 19th c., 11" d.,
12 1/4" h. (ILLUS. right with 10 liter tea-
kettle) **805**

Teakettle on stand, cov., flat-bottomed
spherical hand-hammered body applied
w/polished silver designs of flowering
stalks, butterflies & storks in the Japa-
nesque taste, flat dished cover w/knob
finial, serpentine spout, fixed uprights
joined by a turned black wood handle,
mark of Gorham Mfg. Co., Providence,

Rhode Island, date code for 1883,
7 1/2" h. (ILLUS. right with other Gorham
teakettles) **2,350**

Teakettle on stand, cov., kettle w/wide
squatty bulbous hand-hammered body
applied w/dark silver figures of butterflies,
birds & flowering branches in the Japa-
nesque taste, a short neck w/a fitted
domed & ribbed cover w/button finial,
serpentine spout, fixed short copper
scrolls joined by a high arched wooden
handle, raised on a stand w/forked uprights above a platform w/a burner &
raised on four canted legs, mark of
Gorham Mfg. Co., Providence, Rhode Island, date code for 1883, 11" h. (ILLUS.
center with other Gorham teakettles, top
of page) **1,293**

Teakettles, cov., wide slightly flaring cylindrical body w/wide rounded shoulder
centering a flat mouth, ringed domed
cover w/acorn finial, angled spout, fixed
overhead brass handles w/cylindrical
copper grip, Scotland, ca. 1900, graduated sizes 11" h., 13" h. & 14" h., the set
(ILLUS., top next page) **403**

Copper Teapot on Iron Legs

Three Graduated Scottish Copper Teakettles

Teapot, cov., bulbous nearly spherical body w/an angled shoulder to a short cylindrical neck w/a fitted domed cover w/scroll finial, tapering cylindrical side handle fitted w/a baluster-turned black wood handle w/pointed terminal, body raised on three straight riveted wrought-iron legs, probably Europe, 19th c., wear, spout pressed in, 8" h. (ILLUS.) **125**

Early Roycrofters Copper Vase

Vase, Arts & Crafts style, hand-hammered, wide squatty bulbous body centered by a gently flaring cylindrical neck, original patina, Orb & Cross mark of the Roycrofters, East Aurora, New York, early 20th c., 6 1/2" d., 4 1/4" h. (ILLUS.) **690**

Iron

Fireplace roaster, hand-wrought, a long flat tapering handle ending in a heart-shaped loop, the round rotating roasting rack divided into four quadrants, each w/three tight scrolls, raised on arched feet, America, late 18th c., overall 28" l., rack 12" d., 3 1/2" h. **1,150**

Ornate Cast-iron European Room Heater

Heater, cast, room-type model, an upright rectangular form w/a pierced elaborate floral design & pierced arched doors & side panels, supported on leaf-form feet, w/original fitting, converted to gas, Europe, ca. 1890, 17 1/2 x 25", 35" h. (ILLUS.) **330**

Fine Gothic Revival Iron Jardinieres

Jardinieres, cast, Gothic Revival style, rectangular w/the openwork sides cast as Gothic arches above a band of brass crosses, the square corner posts topped by tall turned finials w/brass tops & w/pointed brass finials around the top rim, tin liner, Europe, 19th c., 27 1/2 x 44", 33" h., pr. (ILLUS., top of page) **3,220**

Late Victorian Floor Safe on Wheels

Safe, cast, floor model, upright rectangular form w/rounded corners, on four heavy wheels, the door decorated w/a small rectangular color landscape scene above "Alpine Lock and Safe Co. Cincin., Ohio," locked w/no combination, drilled later, ca. 1900, 23 1/2" h. (ILLUS.) **92**

Stove plate, cast, flat rectangular form w/a relief Peaceable Kingdom theme w/a man in the center playing a violin, original polychrome paint, probably made at the Reading foundry, Lancaster County, Pennsylvania, some wear, late 18th - early 19th c., 17 1/4" w., 13" h. **2,300**

Vases, hand-wrought, the patinated tall trumpet flower-form bowls raised on a leaf cluster above a scrolling iron stem, copper liners, early 20th c., 14 1/2" d., 24" h., set of 4 (ILLUS., bottom of page).................... **1,725**

Wafer iron, cast, traditional scissor-form w/a pair of hinged round disks on long handles ending in a loop catch, one disk intaglio-cast w/a spread-winged American eagle & shield w/a banner in its beak reading "E Pluribus Unum," Pennsylvania, ca. 1800, overall 29 1/4" l. **1,610**

Wafer iron, hand-wrought, hinged scissor-form w/long slender handles ending in a pair of rectangular plates each incised w/a rectangular zigzag border enclosing

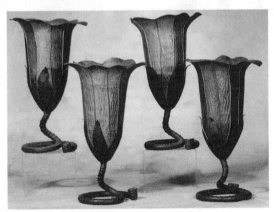

Unusual Flower-form Iron Vases

a monogram "E.R.D." & heart on one & initials "I.D." & a heart on the other, dated 1763, Pennsylvania, overall 32 1/2" l. **978**

Early American Wrought Wall Sconce

Wall sconce, hand-wrought, a shaped top hanging plate above top scrolls behind a projecting candle socket & drip tray, the lower backplate composed of straight & undulated bars w/a heart & scrolls highlight, the bottom cross bar supporting two candle sockets & drip trays, America, early 19th c., 6 x 11", 22" h. (ILLUS.) **633**

Figural Putto Cast-iron Wall Sconces

Wall sconces, cast, figural, a round wall plate issuing a serpentine arm supporting a figural winged putto holding an urn-form candle socket atop its head, France, late 19th c., white paint w/overall rusting, 24" h., pr. (ILLUS.) **748**

Wall sconces, hand-wrought, three long upturned S-shaped arms supporting a socket & fitted into a wrought-iron wall mount, America or England, early 19th c., 15 1/8" w., 15" h., pr. **2,115**

Whale branding iron, hand-wrought, the end stamped "Stmr. Wanderer," America, 19th c., 30" l. **1,195**

Letter "W" Windmill Weight

Windmill weight, cast, modeled as a large letter "W" w/side support bar, by Althouse-Wheeler Co., early 20th c., 17" l. (ILLUS.) **287**

Pewter

Beakers, tall cylindrical form w/flaring rim, touch marks of Boardman & Hart, New York, ca. 1840s, polished w/some battering, 5 1/4" h., pr. (ILLUS. of one, bottom row, second from right at back, top next page) **345**

Candlesticks, domed foot w/slender ringed standard & cylindrical candle socket w/flattened rim, touch mark of Freeman Porter, Maine, 1835-1860s, polished w/minor wear, one w/soldered repair, 6 1/8" h., pr. (ILLUS. top row, second from left, top next page) **546**

Cups, gently flaring cylindrical form, one w/a C-scroll handle, one by Samuel Hamlin Sr. or Jr., Providence, Rhode Island, & Rufus Dunham, Westbrook, Maine, one polished w/minor damage, 3 1/8" & 3 1/2" h., the two (ILLUS. bottom row, second from right at bottom, top next page) **1,265**

Tall Early Boardman Covered Flagon

Large Variety of Early American Pewter

English Art Nouveau Pewter Pieces

Flagon, cov., flaring ringed base tapering to a tall slightly tapering cylindrical body w/a hinged stepped domed cover w/urn-form finial & scrolled thumbrest, short enclosed rim spout, long S-scroll handle, Thomas D. & Sherman Boardman, Hartford, Connecticut, ca. 1815-20, 3 qt., 14" h. (ILLUS., previous page) **3,819**

Frame, Art Nouveau style, flattened rectangular form w/a gently arched top, cast around the sides w/berried ivy-like vines, Archibold Knox for Liberty & Co., England, ca. 1900-05, 6 x 7 5/8" (ILLUS. right with Art Nouveau inkwell & vase, second from top) **5,019**

Inkwell, Art Nouveau style, a shallow square tray base set at each corner w/a blue enamel cabochon, the central tall cylindrical well w/flattened overhanging cover centered by a blue enameled square plaque, w/glass insert, designed by Archibald Knox for Liberty & Co., England, ca. 1902-05, stamped "5 - Tudric - 0141," 6" sq., 3 1/4" h. (ILLUS. center with other English Art Nouveau pieces, second from top) **3,585**

Ladle, deep round bowl w/a long tapering & arched handle w/rounded end, Daniel Curtiss, Albany, New York, 1822-40, scratched initials "AE," repair to juncture of handle & bowl, 13 1/4" l. (ILLUS. top row, far right, second from top) **144**

Lamp, whale-oil type, a bulbous lozenge-shape font w/a double whale oil burner, swelled standard on a ringed domed foot, polished, J.B. Woodbury, eastern Massachusetts or Rhode Island, ca. 1820-35, 8 1/4" h. (ILLUS. top row, far left)................. **489**

Pitcher, tall foot below the squatty bulbous body below tall flaring sides, wide arched rim spout & C-scroll handle, Roswell Gleason, Dorchester, Massachusetts, 1822-71, polished, minor denting, 9 1/2" h. (ILLUS. bottom row, third from left)........................ **748**

Plate, round w/flanged rim, Parks Boyd, Philadelphia, 1795-1819, polished, light scratches & minor dents, 8" d. (ILLUS. bottom row, far right).................................... **345**

Plate, round w/flanged rim, David Melville, Newport, Rhode Island, 1755-1793, polished, light wear & pitting, 8 1/4" d. (ILLUS. bottom row, far left)........................ **345**

Plates, round w/flanged rim, Robert Palethorpe, Philadelphia, ca. 1817-22, polished, one w/light knife scratches, other w/pitting & light battering, 8 3/8" d., pr. (ILLUS. of one, top row, third from left)........ **489**

Porringer, round shallow bowl w/openwork tab handle pierced w/stylized florals w/circular eagle & anchor touch mark of Samuel Hamlin Jr., Providence, Rhode Island, 1801-56, engraved monogram "LAH" & date "1820," 5 3/8" d. (ILLUS. far left with other porringers) **1,528**

Porringer, round shallow bowl w/openwork tab handle pierced w/crescents & hearts, attributed to Richard Lee or Richard Lee Jr., Springfield, Vermont, 1788-1820, 3 1/4" d. (ILLUS. center with other porringers, bottom of page).................... **588**

Porringer, round shallow bowl w/openwork tab handle pierced w/stylized florals w/circular lion touch mark of Gershom Jones, Providence, Rhode Island, 1774-1809, minor wear, 4 1/4" d. (ILLUS. second from right with other porringers, bottom of page)... **2,350**

Porringer, round shallow bowl w/openwork tab handle pierced w/stylized florals w/circular eagle & anchor touch mark of Samuel Hamlin Jr., Providence, Rhode Island, 1801-56, 4 1/2" d. (ILLUS. second from left with other porringers, bottom of page)... **1,058**

Syrup pitchers, cov., flared base & tall cylindrical sides below the hinged domed cover w/disk finial, high rim spout & long ornate C-scroll handle, Sellew & Co., Cincinnati, Ohio, 1830-60, both polished, one out of shape, 7 1/2" h., pr. (ILLUS. of one, bottom row, second from left, bottom of page).. **259**

Tea set: cov. teapot, cov. sugar, creamer, waste bowl & four handleless cups; miniature, the serving pieces footed w/bulbous bodies & flaring rims w/domed covers & C-scroll handles, attributed to W. Tufts, Boston, ca. 1875, partially cleaned, teapot 4" h., the set (ILLUS. of part, top row second from right, bottom of page)... **259**

Rare Early American Pewter Teapot

Teapot, cov., pear-shaped body w/a hinged domed cover w/turned metal finial, serpentine spout, ornate C-scroll wooden handle, "Lovebird" touch mark, Pennsylvania, ca. 1800, 7" h. (ILLUS.) **8,963**

Vase, Art Nouveau style, three slender open arched buttress supports center a bullet-shaped vase decorated around the center w/raised stylized floral vines w/inset blue enamel heart-shaped blossoms, designed by Archibald Knox for Liberty & Co., England, ca. 1902-05, stamped "English Pewter 0226," 7 1/2" h. (ILLUS. left with other English Art Nouveau pieces).... **4,183**

Grouping of Early American Pewter Porringers

Sheffield Plate

One of Two Sheffield Chambersticks

Chambersticks, shallow dished round base w/gadrooned border, a curved side finger handle w/conical snuffer, the open-centered center shaft w/an urn-form candle socket w/a swirled gadrooned flattened rim, by Matthew Bolton, England, ca. 1785, some copper bleeding through, missing wick trimmers, 7" w., 4 1/4" h., pr. (ILLUS. of one).. **500**

English Sheffield Entree Dish

Entree dish, cov., rectangular base w/rounded corners raised on large ball feet, large looped acanthus leaf & cornucopia handles at each end, fitted w/a liner w/an elaborate gadrooned flanged rim, the conforming domed cover w/a gadrooned band around the top centered by the upright gadrooned loop handle, I. & I. Waterhouse, Sheffield, England, ca. 1835, 10 x 14 1/2", 8 1/2" h. (ILLUS.) **489**

Hot water urn, neoclassical urn form, the square base on ball feet & decorated w/a delicate swag border band, the tapering pedestal supporting the tall urn-form body w/another delicate swag band around the top, projecting base spigot w/fanned ebony handle, upright incurved scrolled leaf shoulder handles flanking the very tall slender waisted cover w/a tiered finial, large area of wear above the spigot, England, ca. 1790, 10 1/2" d., 22" h. (ILLUS., top next column) **863**

Tall Early English Sheffield Hot Water Urn

Regency Era Sheffield Mirror Plateau

Mirror plateau, the round concave table frame w/an ovolo base border band & a top cast shell & acanthus leaf rim band enclosing the mirror, Creswick mark on hinged mounts, Regency Era, England, ca. 1825, 17 3/4" d., 2 1/4" h. (ILLUS.)... **1,035**

Tankard, cov., tapering cylindrical body w/a molded base band & raised medial band, hinged domed cover w/thumbrest & S-scroll handle, inset turned wood base, England, ca. 1780, 8 1/2" h......................... **518**

Neoclassical Early Sheffield Tea Caddy

Tea caddy, cov., Neoclassical style, tall oval & slightly flaring sides inlaid & chased w/silver bands & a crest, the concave curved shoulder around the domed cover w/knob finial, lock on the front, George III Era, England, ca. 1770, unmarked, 6 1/4" h. (ILLUS., previous page) **546**

Early Sheffield Plate Tea Urn

Tea urn, cov., tall urn-form body raised on a slender pedestal above a round domed & ringed base, low domed cover w/an urn-form finial, long arched loop strap side handles, extended spigot near the bottom w/a decorative scroll handle, unmarked, England, ca. 1800, some small dents, 18" h. (ILLUS.) **431**

Silver

American (Sterling & Coin)

Oval Pierced Towle Silver Basket

Basket, shallow oblong form w/a serpentine scroll-trimmed rim, the sides pierced overall w/delicate scrolls around the oval bottom panel engraved w/a script monogram, Towle Silversmiths, Newburyport, Massachusetts, early 20th c., 9 x 12", 2 3/4" h. (ILLUS.) **431**

Berry server, large oblong gilded bowl w/thin enameled scrolls at the top of the bowl & around the oblong handle, Gorham Mfg. Co., Providence, Rhode Island, ca. 1900, 9" l. (ILLUS., top next column) **50-100**

Bowl, silver & mixed metal, three round tapering peg feet supporting a wide shallow bowl w/hand-hammered surface & curved sides applied w/a cluster of silver

Large Enameled Gorham Berry Server

leaves & copper berries on one side, an applied flying bird on another side, as well as a copper applied beetle, two butterflies & a cherry blossom spray, mark of Gorham Mfg. Co., Providence, Rhode Island, 1883, 8 3/8" d. **5,975**

Ornate Frank Smith Silver Bowl

Bowl, the lobed circular bowl w/a wide undulating rim decorated in high relief w/scrolls & foliage, bowl center w/an engraved script monogram, Frank W. Smith Silver Co., Gardner, Massachusetts, early 20th c., 11 7/8" d., 2" h. (ILLUS.) **316**

American Silver Brandy Warmer

Brandy warmer, squatty bulbous bowl tapering to a flaring double-spout rim, baluster-turned wooded side handle, F.B.

Rogers Silver Co., Taunton, Massachusetts, ca. 1900, 4 3/4 x 9 3/4", 3 1/4" h. (ILLUS.) **100-150**

Cake basket, coin, an oval low pedestal foot w/an engraved gadrooned border supporting a long, shallow oval basket w/a scalloped border & embossed inside w/flowering branches & two rocaille cartouches w/an engraved monogram, large slender ringed swing bail handle, mark of Grosjean & Woodward for Tiffany & Co., New York, New York, ca. 1854-65, 11 1/4" l. **2,868**

Cann (mug), coin, a baluster-form body on a molded round foot, a leaf-capped scroll handle, mark of Samuel Tingley, New York, New York, ca. 1765, 4 1/8" h. **2,629**

Cann (mug), coin, a baluster-form body on a molded round foot, a leaf-capped scroll handle, mark of John Brevoort, New York, New York, ca. 1750, 5 1/4" h. **3,585**

Centerpiece bowl, shallow round hand-hammered form w/very wide lightly ribbed flower-form flaring sides, mark of William Waldo Dodge, Asheville, North Carolina, 1935, 14" d. **2,868**

Very Rare Ornate Tiffany Coffeepot

Coffeepot, cov., Aesthetic Movement style, tall slender waisted shape w/a hand-hammered ground, tall slender spout & C-form long handle w/ivory insulators, the sides wrapped w/chased & applied dandelion flowers, buds & leaves, the low domed hinged cover w/chased curly dandelion stem & ball finial, mark of Tiffany & Co., New York, New York, 1881-91, 7 1/4" h. (ILLUS.) **19,120**

Coffeepot, cov., coin, the tall baluster-form body on a round foot, the scroll spout w/a baluster drop, the later silver scroll handle w/ivory insulators, foliate join at the top & diamond join at the bottom, the hinged domed cover w/an urn finial, each

side engraved w/a round reserve w/a foliate monogram, mark of Thomas Underhill & John Vernon, New York, New York, ca. 1790, 13 1/4" h. **20,315**

Creamer, coin, bulbous tapering body w/a long arched spout & scalloped rim, raised on three shaped hoof feet, a double-scroll handle, mark of Benjamin Burt, Boston, ca. 1765, 3 1/2" h. **3,824**

Fruit bowl, coin, a round & domed foot w/a beaded border supporting a deep widely flaring bowl w/a beaded rim band, mark of Gerardus Boyce, New York, New York, ca. 1825, 9 3/8" d., 6" h. **3,346**

Loving cup, a round disk foot supporting a smooth trumpet-form body inlaid w/copper-bordered panels, three large angled rounded loop handles, Tiffany & Co., New York, New York, 1909-47, 7 1/4" h. **2,271**

Fine Gorham Floral-chased Pitcher

Pitcher, Art Nouveau style, footed bulbous baluster-form body w/a wide flared rim w/high arched spout, ornate floral-cast C-scroll handle, the body chased around the top & base w/sprays of intertwining flowers & leaves, engraved foliate monogram on the side, Gorham Mfg. Co., Providence, Rhode Island, 1903, 9 1/2" h. (ILLUS.) **5,378**

Pitcher, silver & mixed metal, jug-form, the baluster-form hand-hammered silver body applied w/silver & copper bamboo, a butterfly & a dragonfly above a base band of stylized Chinese fretwork, the handle w/foliate terminals, mark of Tiffany & Co., New York, New York, ca. 1880, 7" h. **5,378**

Porringer, coin, a round wide shallow dish w/incurved sides, a pierced scroll keyhole handle, mark on handle of Samuel Burt, Boston, ca. 1750, overall 8" l. **2,629**

Punch bowl, coin, a domed round foot supporting a deep round bowl, the body & foot embossed w/flowering vines, two figural cast horse head handles at the rim of the bowl, the bowl w/a cast classical bust medallion on one side & a name-inscribed cartouche on the other, maker's mark "P" on base w/"New Orleans," ca. 1860, overall 13" w. **5,975**

American Classical Coin Silver Tea Set

Early Tiffany Sterling Silver Tea Set

Federal Era American Classical Tea Set

Tea set: cov. teapot, cov. sugar bowl & creamer; coin, Classical boat-shaped style, round stepped pedestal base supporting bulbous oblong lower body below a wide curved shoulder band w/leafy vine motif below the curved & rounded shoulder & domed hinged cover w/pineapple finial, high arched fancy C-scroll handles, tall serpentine spout on teapot, each piece w/engraved monogram on the side, mark of Peter Chitry, New York, New York, ca. 1830, teapot 9 3/4" h., the set (ILLUS. of teapot & sugar bowl, top previous page) **1,195**

Tea set: cov. teapot, cov. sugar bowl & creamer; Neoclassical style, each piece w/a tall ovoid body raised on three long scroll legs ending in paw feet, domed cover & arched C-scroll handles, narrow shoulder & cover bands of classical designs, each leg headed by a Bacchanalian mask, mark of Tiffany & Co., New York, New York, ca. 1860-64, teapot 9 1/2" h., the set (ILLUS., second from top previous page) **2,760**

Tea set: cov. teapot, cov. sugar bowl, creamer & waste bowl; coin, Classical style, each piece of rectangular shape w/a partly fluted body on a conforming base, the finial, rim & base w/a band of embossed shells, a medial body w/bright-cut scrolled floral & foliate designs, acorn designs above the fluting, angular handles, the teapot w/ivory handle insulators, each piece marked by William Thomson, New York, New York, 1815-34, teapot 7 3/4" l., 4 1/2" h., the set (minor imperfections).. **39,950**

Tea set: cov. teapot, cov. sugar urn & creamer; coin, Classical style, the oval teapot w/flat sides & a concave shoulder band w/a hinged tapering domed cover w/urn finial, tall helmet-shaped creamer & sugar urn w/tall waisted cover w/urn finial, both on a square foot, each w/bright-cut floral swags centering a cartouche w/drapery mantling, monogram in the cartouche, beaded borders, straight spout on teapot & C-scroll black wood handle, mark of William G. Forbes, New York, New York, ca. 1790, teapot 12 1/2" l., the set (ILLUS., bottom of previous page).. **13,145**

Tea tray, coin, rectangular w/rounded corners on four ball feet, a narrow gadrooned border & arched leaf & shell-clad end loop handles, the center engraved w/a monogram, mark on handle of William B. Heyer, New York, New York, ca. 1815, overall 25 1/2" l. **5,378**

Teakettle on stand, cov., Classical deep oblong body w/wide band of fluting around the lower half, the wide tapering shoulder fitted w/a hinged domed & reeded cover w/button finial, a fixed arched overhead handle w/ivory insulators, serpentine spout, raised on slender curved upright supports above an oval base centered by a burner, tiny bun feet on base, the pot inscribed on the side "EEH 1899," Whiting Mfg. Co., New York, New York, Pattern No. 5800, ca. 1900, 8 1/2" w., overall 11 1/4" h. (ILLUS. right w/Reed & Barton silver plate teakettle on stand).......... **690**

American Coin Silver Teakettle

Teakettle on stand, cov., coin, the bulbous fluted body w/a ring-banded short neck & hinged domed cover w/flower finial, scroll-trimmed serpentine spout, arched scroll swing handle, raised on a burner base w/four ornate scroll legs ending in shell feet & joined by serpentine straps centered by the burner ring, engraved inscription w/later date, mark of Ball, Tompkins & Black, New York City, ca. 1839-51, no burner, overall 15" h., the set (ILLUS.)... **1,150**

Very Rare Early Philadelphia Silver Teapot

Teapot, cov., coin, Classical style, a round ringed & domed foot tapering to a short pedestal below the round-bottomed cylindrical body decorated w/a wide band of guilloche enclosing stars & accented w/acanthus leaves on a linework ground, the wide rounded shoulder tapering to a short cylindrical neck w/a hinged domed cover w/a spherical finial, a squared serpentine spout topped w/a patera roundel, a tall upright squared flute-carved fruitwood handle, mark of Chaudron's & Rasch, Philadelphia, ca. 1812, 9" h. **1,058**

Teapot, cov., coin, inverted pear-shaped body on a disk foot, domed hinged cover w/pointed finial, serpentine spout w/cast leafy scrolls, C-scroll wooden handle w/scrolled silver terminal & leaf-clad joins, the shoulder engraved w/diaperwork, rocaille scrolls & flowering vines, the edge of the cover engraved w/a scallop band, base engraved w/block initials "H" over "IM," also w/mark of maker John Bayly, Philadelphia, ca. 1765, overall 9 1/4" l. (ILLUS., top of page) **71,700**

Federal Era American Teapot

Rare Colonial Rhode Island Teapot

Teapot, cov., coin, oval upright body w/a flat shoulder centered by a hinged domed cover w/pineapple finial, straight angled spout, C-scroll wooden handle w/silver joins, the sides engraved w/a drapery cartouche enclosing a monogram, mark on base of Daniel Van Voorhis, New York, New York, ca. 1790, 7 1/8" h. (ILLUS., bottom previous page) **4,780**

Teapot, cov., coin, wide bulbous inverted pear-shaped body on a domed foot, domed hinged cover w/a pinecone finial, serpentine spout w/cast shell & scroll decoration, black wooden C-scroll handle w/scroll-decorated joins, the body engraved w/a rococo cartouche enclosing monogram "HPG," the shoulder engraved w/a strapwork bird & mask border, base w/mark of Samuel Casey, South Kingstown, Rhode Island, ca. 1760, overall 10" l. (ILLUS., top of page) **47,800**

Early South Carolina Silver Tray

Tray, coin, round w/a foliate-decorated rim band, the center engraved w/a coat-of-arms, raised on four small cartouche-form feet, marked by John Mood, Charleston, South Carolina, ca. 1825, small dent on side of rim, minor body warping, 9" d., 1 1/4" h. (ILLUS.) **3,450**

Tray, coin, round w/three tab feet, a border w/a reeded rim, mark of Garret Eoff, New York, New York, ca. 1810, 7 1/8" d. **1,315**

Tray, oval, a stylized trefoil border against a matte ground, the center engraved w/a wide band of flowers in the Islamic taste centering a round reserve engraved w/a crest & monogram, mark of Gorham Mfg. Co., Providence, Rhode Island, 1874, 24 1/2" l. **4,183**

Vase, four small figural frog feet supporting a wide squatty bulbous lower body chased w/swirled waves, frogs & lily pads, centered by a tall trumpet neck decorated around the top w/pierced leaves & applied figural cattails, mark of George W. Shiebler & Co., New York, New York, ca. 1895, 8 3/8" h. **5,975**

Vase, round slightly domed foot supporting a tall slender trumpet-form body, etched w/repeating small classical shields & tall feathered crests suspending stylized leafy swags, mark of Tiffany & Co., New York, New York, early 20th c., 20" h. **6,573**

Waste bowl, coin, deep round bowl on a round pedestal foot, the bowl engraved w/wrigglework band, a reeded border band on the neck & foot, one side engraved w/a monogram, mark of William G. Forbes, New York, New York, ca. 1790, 7" d. **1,439**

English & Other

Early English Pierced Silver Basket

Basket, oval footring w/pierced diamond & star designs below the deep flaring basket pierced overall w/delicate cross, dot & chevron design, serpentine narrow gadrooned rim band, twisted arched swing handle, mark of William Vincent, London, England, 1773-74, 8 3/4" l. (ILLUS.) **863**

Early Swedish Silver & Parcel-gilt Beaker

Beaker, parcel-gilt, a narrow flared gadrooned foot below the tall flaring cylindrical body w/the upper rim engraved w/a band of rocaille & flowers against a matted ground, a gilt molded rim, marked under foot by Johan Andersson Starin, Stockholm, Sweden, 1753, 7 5/8" h. (ILLUS.)..................................... **2,390**

Ornate Japanese Cigarette Box

Cigarette box, cov., rectangular w/hinged cover, the sides decorated w/répoussé flying birds above turbulent seas, the cover decorated w/bold répoussé chrysanthemums & leaves, opening to a cedar-lined interior, raised on narrow bracket feet, Japanese Export, ca. 1900, 3 1/2 x 6 1/2", 3" h. (ILLUS.) **1,955**

Small Russian Silver Cup

Cup, flared base & cylindrical sides w/high arched loop handle, the body engraved w/Art Nouveau flowers, gold-washed interior, Russian touch marks, 19th c., 3 1/2" h. (ILLUS.) **345**

Tall Elaborate English Silver Ewer

Ewer, cov., tall slender baluster form, a small round flaring foot, the body inset w/four oval plaques decorated w/cast figures representing the Four Seasons, surrounded by large chased flowers & scrolls, the slender neck w/cast scrolls continuing around the high arched spout, hinged domed cover w/flower finial, the ornate C-scroll leaf-clad handle w/ivory insulators, marked by Thomas, James & Nathaniel Creswick, London, England, 1852, 14 1/4" h. (ILLUS.) **2,629**

Very Rare Hoffmann-designed Austrian Silver Tea Set

Soup tureen, cov., Rococo style, the deep undulating oval base raised on four large pierced rocaille feet, the body répoussé & chased w/floral garlands & centering two vacant rocaille cartouches, large leafy scroll end handles, the high domed & stepped cover w/conforming decoration & a cast bird on branch figural finial, mark of Gottfried Bartermann, Augsburg, Germany, 1751-53, also later French control marks, overall 15 1/2" l. (ILLUS., top of previous page) **28,680**

Spanish Colonial Silver Stirrups

Stirrups, foot-shaped flat sole w/the pointed toe guard elaborately chased & répoussé w/leafy scrolls & flowers, Spanish Colonial, probably Peru, stamped "925," 9" l., pr. (ILLUS.).. **633**

English Mid-18th Century Sugar Bowl

Sugar bowl, cov., silver-gilt, inverted pear-shaped body raised on a round domed foot, chased w/rococo floral garlands & centering a vacant cartouche, the domed cover w/matching decoration & a figural spread-winged bird finial, mark of Samuel Taylor, London, England, 1746, 5 3/8" h. (ILLUS.) **1,673**

Tankard, cov., baluster form w/round foot & medial body band, hinged stepped domed cover, a heavy scroll handle w/baluster drop & openwork thumbpiece, initial mark probably of John King, London, England, 1770, 8 3/4" h. (ILLUS., top next page).. **2,629**

18th Century English Silver Tankard

Tea set: cov. teapot, cov. sugar bowl, cov. creamer, waste bowl, tongs & oval tray; each piece w/a squatty bulbous boldly lobed shape w/ivory handles & ivory lobed finials, designed by Josef Hoffmann & produced by The Wiener Werkstatte, Austria, ca. 1920s, tray 20 1/2" l., teapot 7 3/4" h., the set (ILLUS., top previous page) **71,700**

Fine Mexican Silver Tea Set

Tea set: cov. teapot, cov. sugar bowl & creamer; each footed piece w/a squatty melon-lobed body, lobed domed covers w/figural flower finials, ornate C-scroll handles, one piece marked "F. Guzman - Mexico," .900 quality, 20th c., the set (ILLUS.) **1,150**

Rare Wiener Werkstatte Tea Set Designed by Hoffmann

Tea set: cov. teapot, cov. sugar bowl, creamer, teakettle on stand & oval tray; the serving pieces w/upright flat oval bodies w/hinged tapering covers w/brass ball finials, cylindrical rosewood side handles, the kettle on a conforming burner stand w/pierced side holes, designed by Josef Hoffmann, manufactured by The Wiener Werkstatte, tray w/original Wiener Werkstatte lace doily, Austria, ca. 1923, tray 14 1/4" l., teakettle & stand 9 1/2" h., the set (ILLUS.) **53,775**

English George II Silver Kettle on Stand

Simple Elegant George III Tea Urn

Tea urn, cov., George III era, tall Classical urn-form body w/a tall slender tapering cover w/acorn finial, beaded shoulder band, long arched reeded side handles, a projecting spigot near the base w/a dark ivory handle, raised on a slender flaring pedestal on a square foot, interior fitted w/a heating column, cover engraved w/a crest, the body engraved w/a coat-of-arms, mark of John Wakelin & William Tayler, London, England, 1784, overall 20 1/2" h. **4,780**

Teakettle on stand, cov., George II era, spherical body w/a flat hinged cover w/wooden knop finial, serpentine spout, overhead swing bail handle w/shaped uprights joined by a baluster-turned black wood grip, the body finely engraved w/a border of brickwork, scrolls, putti & foliate as well as a coat-of-arms, on a round stand raised on three leafy scroll legs w/wooden knob feet joined by shaped braces centered by a deep burner, marks of Peze Pilleau, London, England, 1731, burner dating from 1956, overall 22 1/2" h. (ILLUS., top next column) **3,824**

Teakettle on stand, cov., George II era, wide inverted pear-shaped body chased overall w/ornate flowers, scrolls & quilted shells, the hinged domed cover w/ivory bud finial, overhead bail swing handle w/scrolled supports joined by a wrapped hand grip, on a stand w/ornate openwork leafy scroll & flower apron raised on three

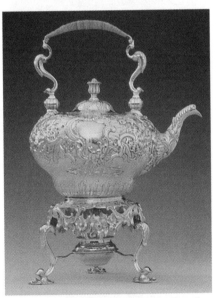

Early Scottish Silver Teakettle & Stand

leafy scroll legs joined by braces centering a burner, the body also engraved w/a coat-of-arms, mark of James Welsh, Edinburgh, Scotland, 1755, overall 15" h. (ILLUS.) **10,158**

Early English Provincial Silver Teapot

Early 18th Century English Teapot

Teapot, cov., George I era, footed spherical body w/small hinged cover w/knop finial, angled faceted straight spout, C-scroll wooden handle, body engraved w/a crest, base engraved w/initials "E.R.," mark of Seth Lofthouse, London, England, 1720, overall 8 1/4" l. (ILLUS.) **4,183**

Teapot, cov., George II era, footed spherical body w/a small flat detachable cover w/reeded border & wooden disk finial, curved spout w/stylized petal join, C-scroll wooden handle, marked "RP," English provincial maker, ca. 1740, overall 8 5/8" l. (ILLUS., top of page) **3,760**

Paul Storr English Silver Teapot

Teapot, cov., George III era, footed wide inverted pear-shaped body w/domed hinged cover w/pointed knob finial, ribbed serpentine spout, C-scroll handle, the body swirl-fluted & decorated w/repoussé & chased rococo floral & scroll designs w/a vacant cartouche, mark of Paul Storr, London, England, 1814, 6 7/8" h. (ILLUS.) **1,610**

George III Classical Silver Teapot

Teapot, cov., George III era, oval upright body w/flat shoulder & hinged flat cover w/wooden disk finial, angled straight spout, wooden C-scroll handle, the body engraved around the base & shoulder w/a floral & foliate band, the body engraved w/a coat-of-arms, mark on base of Richard Gardner, London, England, 1774, overall 9" l. (ILLUS.) **3,585**

Scarce Early English Miniature Teapot

Teapot, cov., miniature, waisted cylindrical body w/flared shoulder & short neck w/fitted domed cover w/knop finial, flat C-scroll handle & angled straight spout, chased w/C-scroll & floral decoration, mark on base of James Goodwin, London, England, 1727, two solder marks on base, 4" h. (ILLUS.) **518**

Silver Plate (Hollowware)

Cute Silver Plate Ash Receiver

Ash receiver, figural, a small figure of a chick & wishbone beside a round dished base centered by a stem centered by a fan-shaped cigar trimmer below the tall cup-shaped top match holder w/a hammered dot design, mark of the Derby Silver Co., ca. 1880s, 4 1/2" h. (ILLUS.) **127**

English Silver Plate Biscuit Box

Biscuit box, upright hinged shell shape w/engraved scrolls, an arched scrolling top border w/center ring handle, raised on a trestle-style base w/outswept scrolled legs, England, early 20th c., 6 x 81 2/", 10" h. (ILLUS.) **225**

Unusual Silver Plate Breakfast Set

Breakfast server set, a footed diamond-shaped base w/engraved edge supporting a ring-engraved footed salt cup & matching shaker flanking the central tall arched handle enclosing a napkin ring w/an ornate pierced finial & resting atop a tiny seated boy & applied leaf, mark of the Meriden Britannia Co., ca. 1880s, overall 7" h. (ILLUS.) **403**

Unusual Breakfast Set on Shell Tray

Breakfast server set, a shell-shaped tray on ball feet centered by a tall loop handle w/a napkin holder & a side bracket to support a ruffle-rimmed butter pat above a pair of attached small tapering waste cups flanking the bulbous salt & pepper shakers, all decorated w/floral engraving, impressed mark of the Aurora Silver Plate Mfg. Co., tray 6 3/4" d., overall 7 1/2" h., the set (ILLUS.) **633**

Fine English Silver Plate Hot Water Urn

Hot water urn, Neoclassical style, the large ovoid body w/reeded band & concave top w/a domed cover & vasiform finial, the sides w/ringed lion-mask handles, raised on four flat reeded columnar legs ending in paw feet connected by a concave square base centered by a bowl-shaped burner, the whole w/four flattened bun feet, plain downturned spout w/pineapple spigot, England, ca. 1890, 10 1/2" d., overall 20 1/2" h. (ILLUS.) **863**

Fine Pairpoint Jewelry Casket

Jewelry casket, oblong form, the arched top w/two hinged covers flanked by arched sides w/a pierced design of flowers & leaves & raised on four leaf-sprig feet, a slender arched handle from side to side, mark of the Pairpoint Mfg. Co., portions of base reinforced & some leaves missing, 1890s, 6 1/2" l., 9" h. (ILLUS.) **633**

Salt cellar, in the form of a dolphin carrying a shell on its back, rimmed base w/design depicting ocean waves, handle in the form of a ribbed leaf, 2 x 2 3/4 x 4 1/2" (ILLUS., top next column) **275**

Figural Silver Plate Salt Cellar

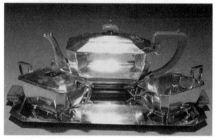

English Art Deco Silver Plate Tea Set

Tea set: cov. teapot, cov. sugar, creamer & rectangular tray; Art Deco style, each piece w/a squatty slightly flaring rectangular body & wide tapering shoulder, low domed cover w/reddish amber rectangular Bakelite finials, teapot w/angled Bakelite handle, tray w/cut corners & matching Bakelite squared end handles, England, ca. 1925, tray 15" l., the set (ILLUS.) **196**

American Silver Plate & Sterling Silver Teakettles on Stands

Teakettle on stand, cov., footed paneled bulbous body w/a wide conforming shoulder centering a short rolled neck, hinged pointed & domed cover w/pointed finial, a fixed reeded loop overhead handle, scroll-trimmed serpentine spout, raised on open serpentine side supports on a paneled round base centered by a burner, mark of Reed & Barton, late 19th - early 20th c., overall 13" h. (ILLUS. left with Whiting sterling teakettle on stand, bottom previous page) **230**

Fine English Silver Plate Kettle & Stand

Teakettle on stand, cov., Victorian, Orientalist taste, the decagonally paneled body tapering to a short neck w/thin pierced gallery & hinged domed & stepped cover w/spherical finial, a pointed Arabesque arch fixed overhead handle, serpentine spout, the panels engraved as arches enclosing ornate quatrefoils above a chain band, raised on a platform base w/a wide top & thin gallery around a narrower pierced & paneled pedestal enclosing the burner, the wide dished & paneled base w/short columns forming the feet, by Elkington & Company, Birmingham, England, 1854, overall 10 1/2" w., overall 8 1/2" h. (ILLUS.) **1,150**

Teapot, cov., round flat base below the wide rounded lower body w/a gadrooned medial band below the tall tapering sides w/a flaring rim, hinged domed cover w/knob finial, tall slender serpentine spout, C-scroll handle, trademark w/a lion on either side of a shield above "Silverplated - Est. 1905," early 20th c., 9 1/4" w., 9 3/4" h. (ILLUS., top next column) **65**

Early 20th Century Silver Plated Teapot

Attractive Silver Plate Teapot

Teapot, cov., round foot below the wide squatty bulbous body tapering to a short flared neck w/a domed hinged cover, leafy scroll-trimmed spout & C-scroll handle, marked on bottom "Silver on Copper [crown] S [shield]," probably England, late 19th - early 20th c., 8" h. (ILLUS.)......... **100**

Early 20th Century English Silver Plate Teapot with Dated Inscription

Teapot, cov., squatty bulbous boat-shaped body w/widely flaring flanged rim & hinged stepped, domed cover w/wooden disk finial, ribbed serpentine spout, pointed angular handle, the sides w/an ornate engraved floral cartouche enclosing a gift inscription dated 1911, marks for an English silver plate firm, 11 1/2" l., 5 3/8" h. (ILLUS.)... **85**

Nice English Silver Plate Warming Platter

Warming platter, oval frame raised on scroll feet, the scroll-cast side fitted w/a small filling hole, ornate scrolled end handles, fitted w/a well-and-tree insert, base marked "D & S," England, early 20th c., 17 1/2 x 24", 3 1/2" h. (ILLUS., top of page) 575

Spelter

Bill Drite Figural Paperweight

Paperweight, figural advertising-type, standing bearded gnome smoking a pipe & holding a toolbox, marked on front of the square base "Bill Drite with Insulite," "Bill Drite" also on the sides of base, copper finish, 2 1/2" sq., 4" h. (ILLUS.) $85

Black Uncle Sam Pencil Sharpener

Pencil sharpener, caricature of black man wearing Uncle Sam-type top hat & bow tie, original black, red, white & blue paint, made in Occupied Japan, 1/2 x 1 1/8 x 2" (ILLUS.).. 165

Pistol Pencil Sharpener

Pencil sharpener, in the form of a pistol w/hinged tin top & original green paint, made in Germany, 1/2 x 1 3/4 x 2 5/8" (ILLUS.)... 75

Greyhound Bus Salt & Pepper Shakers

Salt & pepper shakers, model of Greyhound bus, original rubber wheels, silver paint w/blue trim & cork stoppers, Japan, 2 3/4" l., pr. (ILLUS.) 79

Spelter Souvenir Shakers

Salt & pepper shakers, square tapering form, cast w/scenes & souvenir markings for Ft. Snelling, Minnesota, scroll trim, early 20th c., 2 3/8" h., pr. (ILLUS.) **20**

Spelter Sewing Case

Sewing case, rectangular, w/hinged lid, top w/rectangular miniature framed photo of the Mohawk Trail set in oval garland & bow border, 2 x 2 1/2" (ILLUS.) **75**

Steel

Cast-steel Schuco Limousine with Box

Toy, cast, keywind, red limousine w/original box, marked "Varianto-Limo 3041" & "Made in U.S. Zone Germany," Schuco, 1 1/2 x 1 1/2", 4 1/4" l. (ILLUS.) **250**

Steel Pan American World Toy Plane

Toy airplane, friction, in the style of Pan American World plane, wings detach, painted red, green & tan, made in Japan, 11 1/2" l. (ILLUS.) **395**

Toy Airplane with Plastic Propellers

Toy airplane, in the style of Pan American plane, w/plastic propellers & retractable wheels, blue & white, marked "Made in Western Germany," 11 1/4" l. (ILLUS.) **195**

Steel Toy Hansom Cab

Toy hansom cab, figure of horse pulling blue hansom cab w/driver perched at rear, painted image of a man in bowler hat inside, possibly German, 12 3/4" l. (ILLUS.) **450**

Tin & Tole

Nice Early Tin Chamberstick

Chamberstick, tin, the conical base tapering to a tall cylindrical socket fitted w/a flat drip pan issuing a flattened S-scroll strap handle attached to the center of the base, minor dents, 19th c., 5 1/2" h. (ILLUS.) **230**

Outstanding Early Tole Coffeepot

Coffeepot, cov., tole, tall tapering cylindrical body w/a long domed hinged cover, long angled straight spout & C-form strap handle, original red ground w/ornate stylized floral designs in yellow, green & unusual black & white, yellow flourishes on the cover, some wear, America, first half 19th c., 8" h. (ILLUS., top of page).................. **5,463**

Document box, cov., tole, rectangular w/domed hinged cover w/brass bail handle, original yellow, red & black paint w/fruit, foliage & flourishes, tin hasp, some wear, first half 19th c., 4 3/4 x 8 3/4", 5 1/4" h............................... **1,121**

Document box, cov., tole, rectangular w/domed hinged cover w/brass ring handle & damaged tin hasp, original painted decoration of red & orange scrolls w/yellow fans, dark, almost black, japanned ground, finely alligatored finish, cover wear, first half 19th c., 4 x 8", 4 1/8" h.......... **661**

Document box, cov., tole, rectangular w/domed hinged cover w/wire ring handle & tin hasp, original painted decoration of red & white roses w/green & yellow foliage on three sides & yellow decoration on the cover, japanned ground, wear, mainly on cover, damage to hasp, first half 19th c., 4 3/4 x 9 3/4", 6 1/4" h. **805**

Document box, cov., tole, rectangular w/hinged domed cover w/wire loop handle, original painting w/black ground decorated on the front w/a yellow band trimmed w/large red berries & green leaves, overall yellow swags & petal devices, artist-initials "d/c" on a white band, minor wear, America, 19th c., 4 3/4 x 8 3/4", 5 1/2" h. (ILLUS., below).... **1,495**

Black-decorated Tole Document Box

Document box, cov., tole, rectangular w/rare flat hinged cover w/wire ring handle & tin hasp, original polychrome floral design including red & yellow tulips & unusual blue flowers on a black ground, some wear, attributed to Stevens Plains, Maine, first half 19th c., 5 x 9", 5" h. **575**

Match safe, tole, original japanned ground & paint w/a tulip on a white band on the front & swags on the cut-out & crimped crest, wear, 19th c., 7 1/2" h. **575**

English Victorian Floral-decorated Tray

Rare Early American Tole Teapot

Teapot, cov., tole, tall oval body w/a slightly domed top fitted w/a hinged strap cover, straight angled spout, C-form strap handle, black ground, decorated on the sides w/a large deep red circle painted w/white leaf sprigs, the circle beneath an arched wreath of red & orange blossoms & shaded green leaves, probably Pennsylvania, ca. 1830, 6" h. (ILLUS.) **5,019**

Fine Victorian Tole Tray with Landscape

Tray, tole, rectangular w/rounded corners, the black ground decorated w/delicate gold leafy scrolls around the sides, the center painted w/a large romantic landscape w/a lake w/bridges & a boat & build-

ing & trees on the left shore, England, late 19th c., 22 3/4 x 28 3/4" (ILLUS.) **1,150**

Tray, tole, rectangular w/rounded corners, the black ground decorated w/delicate gold leafy scrolls around the sides, the center painted w/a large colorful bouquet of flowers topped by a perched exotic bird, England, third quarter 19th c., on a later stand, 22 x 30" (ILLUS., top of page) **1,265**

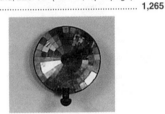

One of Two Early Mirrored Sconces

Wall sconces, tin, a round pan back reflector inset w/radiating mirror segments, a projecting tin & wood candle socket, a few mirror segments missing, one portion of one socket replaced, America, early 19th c., 9 1/2" d., 11 1/8" h., pr. (ILLUS. of one) **3,055**

MID-CENTURY MODERN DESIGN

An area of increasing interest to collectors today is Mid-Century Modern Design. This broad field includes all sorts of objects first introduced immediately after World War II and continuing into the 1960s. Baby Boomers in particular recall with nostalgia the furniture, dishes, decorative accent pieces, appliances and kitchenwares that featured the hot new shapes, colors and materials widely sold in postwar America.

Some Mid-Century objects were the work of famous designers and can be expensive. However, there is still a plethora of everyday affordable wares that can provide a nostalgic touch to any home.

Long Wooden Clock with Tile Inlay

Fiberglass Eames Chair for Herman Miller

Chair, molded fiberglass, intricate steel rod base, designed by the Eames for Herman Miller, ca. 1949 (ILLUS.) **$300-500**

Clock, wall-type, a long narrow rectangular board inset at one end w/a row of three colorful tiles by Harris Strong, stylized clock dial at the opposite end, ca. 1950s, 11 x 43" (ILLUS., top of page) **300-450**

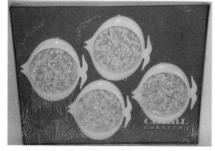

1950s Coral Coasters Boxed Set

Coaster set, "Coral Coasters," plastic rounded fish shapes w/colorful interior, in original box, 1950s (ILLUS.) **20-30**

Turquoise Blue Covered Cooking Pot

Cooking pot, cov., deep round turquoise blue metal sides w/black plastic handles, domed black cover w/abstract white line design, 1950s, 10 1/2" d. (ILLUS.) **20-25**

Modernistic Decanter & Tumblers Set

Decanter set: very tall, slender decanter w/ringed sides & four matching tumblers; the decanter & two tumblers w/blue mottled tops above woodgrained lower halves & two tumblers in mottled green over woodgrain, by Jaru of California, 1950s-60s, decanter 18" h., the set (ILLUS.) **40-50**

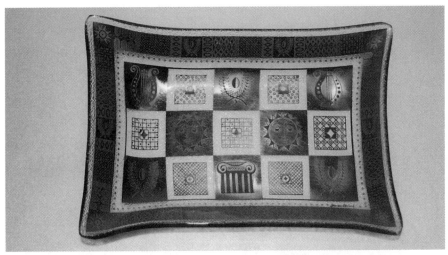

Briard-designed Modernist Long Dish

Dish, glass w/printed gold & white blocked
mosaic decoration, designed by Georges
Briard, 1950s, 5 1/4 x 7 3/4" (ILLUS.) **8-12**

Monterey Jade Ceramic Dish

Dish, square ceramic form w/a drippy abstract design in shades of blue & green,
Monterey Jade, ca. 1950s-60s, 5 1/2" w.
(ILLUS.) **15-25**
Figure group, ceramic, tall stylized brown-
glazed entwined heads of lovers, unsigned, 1960s, 12" h. (ILLUS., next col-
umn) **18-28**

Tall Stylized Ceramic Heads Figure

Unusual String & Metal Ceiling Lamp

Lamp, ceiling-type, a string art covered block suspended by metal tongs, ca. 1960s (ILLUS.) **175-300**

Unusual Modernist 1950s Table Lamp

Lamp, table model, an angular black boomerang-style foot issuing three upright

curved metal bands supporting the original textured waxed paper shade, by Majestic, ca. 1950s, overall 28" h. (ILLUS.) **150-200**

Unusual Metal Mesh Table Lamp

Lamp, table model, metal, rectangular white mesh base supporting a copper-colored conical frame enclosing the conical paper shade decorated w/stars, the other end fitted w/an upright rectangular photo frame, 1950s, 8 x 9 1/2" (ILLUS.) **30-50**

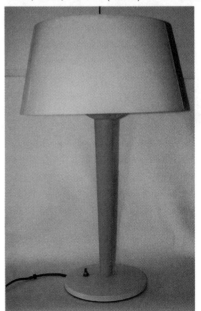

Simple Modernist Table Lamp

Lamp, table model, round white plastic foot & slender orange plastic shaft, original wide cylindrical plastic shade, made by Lightolier, 1960s-70s, 22" h. (ILLUS.) **25-50**

Model of a Ceramic Stylized Gazelle

Peter Max Limited Edition Lithograph

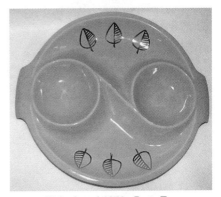

Pink-glazed 1950s Party Tray

Dyed Turquoise Alpaca Fur Pillow

Lithograph, Peter Max limited edition, signed & numbered, matted & framed, 1973, 8 x 8" (ILLUS.).............................. **300-500**

Model of gazelle, ceramic, recumbent stylized animal w/long arching horns, aqua w/white horns & tail, 1950s, 12" l., 10" h. (ILLUS., top of page)................................ **25-35**

Party tray, ceramic, round w/two round indentations & tab side handles, pink glaze w/stylized gold leaf trim, by Miramar of California, 1950s, 13" d. (ILLUS., next column) **10-15**

Pillow, squared form in dyed turquoise blue alpaca fur, 15 x 15" (ILLUS., last next column)... **20-35**

Italian Pottery Yellow Ringed Plate

Plate, pottery, glazed w/concentric circles in shades of yellow, Italy, ca. 1960s, 12" d. (ILLUS.)... **20-25**

Brass Plate with Mosaic Tile

Plate, round thin brass base decorated in the center w/a raised round mosaic design w/butterflies, 1960s, 11 1/2" d. (ILLUS.)..... **30-35**

Glidden Plate with Clown Design

Plate, squared art pottery style, decorated w/a large stylized clown, Glidden, ca. 1935 (ILLUS.)... **25-40**
Poster, "Transistors - Philips," dark yellow ground w/colorful stylized figures of a man & woman on a motor scooter, she holding up a transistor radio, France, 1950s (ILLUS., top next page)............. **250-300**

Round Plastic Panasonic Radio

Radio, plastic spherical shape w/a round dial on one side, w/hanging chain, Pana-pet 70, Panasonic, 4 1/2" d. (ILLUS.) **25-35**

Mod-style Recipe Box

Recipe box, cov., rectangular lithographed tin, covered w/a red, pink & lavender geo-metric design, 1960s, 3 1/2 x 5" (ILLUS.) ... **8-15**

Space Age Record Album Cover

Large 1960s Philips Transistor Radio Poster

Record album cover, "Fantastica - Music From Outer Space by Russ Garcia," Liberty, ca. 1950s (ILLUS., previous page) **35-50**

Franciscan Starburst Pattern Saucer

Saucer, ceramic, Starburst patt., Franciscan, 1950s (ILLUS.)................................... **4-7**

Tile with Stylized Flower Design

Tile, ceramics, an abstract flower design in red, pink & maroon, Fred Roberts Co., Japan, 1950s-60s, 6" sq. (ILLUS.).............. **8-15**

Briard-designed Mosaic Glass Tray

7UP Trash Can with Psychedelic Art

Trash can, tall cylindrical metal design, for 7UP, psychedelic-head design, reads "Give Un to Others," Kim Whitesides artwork, ca. 1969, 15" h. (ILLUS.)............. **40-70**

Tray, long rectangular form in mosaic stained glass in shades of gold, orange, deep red & green, Georges Briard design, 1950s, 16 3/4" l. (ILLUS., bottom previous page) **45-60**

MILITARIA & WARTIME MEMORABILIA

Civil War (1861-65)

Ambrotype, sixth-plate, portrait of three Union soldiers, two seated & one stand-ing, wearing four-button sack coats w/for-age caps, attached pencil note, housed in leatherette case w/split hinge (some emulsion flaking)....................................... **$220**

Canteen, polychrome & gilt-painted tin, flattened round shape, one side painted w/a Civil War battle scene depicting several Union soldiers, one carrying an American flag, an officer on horseback, two injured Union soldiers & two injured Confederate soldiers, the reverse in black w/a gilt banner inscribed "G.A. Hanson - Co. H 51st Reg. Mass Vol. 1" above a later inscription "1861-1865 - G.A.R. 1884 - L.M. Thomson. Pt.," gilt border & spout, 8 5/8" d. (dents, small scattered paint losses)........... **499**

Carte de visite, photo of Lieutenant Colonel Martin Tschudy, 69th Pennsylvania Infantry, killed at the battle of Gettysburg, shown seated w/his knees up, unknown photographer... **1,760**

Carte de visite, photograph of Colonel Joshua Blackwood Howell (1806-64) of the 85th Pennsylvania Infantry, named a brigadier general after his death in 1864, half-length portrait....................................... **275**

Confederate States note, $800 note printed in black & white w/top center vignette, issued in Richmond, Virginia, May 19, 1863, redeemable after July 1, 1868, glued to substrate, some bleeding, foxing & creases, framed, 9 1/4 x 13 1/2" (ILLUS., bottom of page) **104**

Photograph, large albumen print of General Meade & his staff in front of a log cabin, inscribed in pencil on the back "At Hd Qtrs 1st Brig House March 1864," unknown photographer, image 7 1/4 x 9 1/2", mounted on larger board (minor foxing on board)............................ **3,025**

Framed Confederate States $800 Note

Rare Civil War Recruitment Poster

Poster, recruitment-type, printed in black & white, the top w/a large patriotic vignette w/slogan banners & figures w/the American flag, recruiting Volunteers for Company B of Col. E.M. Gregory's Regiment, 22 x 30" (ILLUS.) **3,850**

Civil War Era Revolver & Holster

Revolver & holster, Union Arms Co. single-action pocket model, by Bacon Manufacturing Co., Serial No. 3002, five-shot, fluted cylinder, walnut grips, barrel 4 3/34" l., w/vintage leather holster, ca. 1860, the set (ILLUS.) **460**

Good Tintype of Civil War Soldier

Tintype of a Union soldier, 1/6th plate, seated infantry man wearing his jacket, his infantry overcoat & Hardee hat placed on the table beside him, good strong image, cased (ILLUS.) **431**

Union Soldier with Sword & Pistol

Tintype of a Union soldier, 1/6th plate, seated Union soldier holding a M1860 sword & wearing a belt w/eagle plate & sword knot form which hangs a holstered pistol, cased (ILLUS.) **460**

Spanish-American War (1898)

Spanish-American War Canteen

Canteen, flated round form, used by a soldier, one side h.p. w/a scene of the wreckage of the Battleship Maine, the other side w/a scene of Manilla Bay, original leather strap & cork stopper (ILLUS.) **431**

World War I (1914-1918)

Imperial German World War I Helmet

German helmet, Imperial Prussian EM "pickel haube" style, eagle front plate & spike, missing chinstrap (ILLUS.)................. **316**

World War II (1939-1945)

World War II Era German Luger

German Luger, 1942 BYF model, P.08 cal., Nazi markings, Serial No. 490, good condition (ILLUS.) **575**

Unusual World War II Novelty Pin

Novelty pinback button, a 7/8" d. celluloid button in white w/read wording "Let's All Pull Together," w/a string suspending a cardboard color cut-out of a hanging Hitler, unusual (ILLUS.) **1,099**

MOVIE MEMORABILIA
Also see: ADVERTISING ITEMS; CAT COL-
LECTIBLES; DOLLS; HORSE COLLECTIBLES
and POP CULTURE MEMORABILIA.

Costumes

Judy Garland "Harvey Girls" Costume

Jacket & skirt, "The Harvey Girls," MGM,
1946, two-piece period costume worn by
Judy Garland throughout the first part of
the musical, made of light blue wool, the
top a fitted jacket w/a white applique design on the lapel & lace around the collar,
Judy Garland & MGM labels inside, the
floor-length skirt w/matching decoration
& also labeled, now faded & discolored
w/age (ILLUS.) **$25,095**

Jumpsuit, "Speedway," MGM, 1968, off-
white cotton suit worn by Elvis Presley
portraying Steve Grayson in the musical
also starring Nancy Sinatra, light blue
stripes down arms & legs, name "Steve"
stitched on chest, included a reprinted
color image of Presley wearing the outfit
(ILLUS.) **16,730**

Tailcoat from "Citizen Kane"

Tailcoat, "Citizen Kane," RKO, 1941, worn
by Orson Welles as he portrayed Charles
Foster Kane, made of navy blue wool w/a
cut-away front, peaked lapels, a large "K"
embroidered on either cuff, Western Costume Company label w/Welles name &
size written on it (ILLUS.) **9,560**

Elvis Presley Jumpsuit from "Speedway"

Gold Warm-up Suit from "Goldmember"

Warm-up suit, "Austin Powers in Gold-member," New Line Cinema, 2002, mustard yellow velour suit worn by Mike Meyers portraying Goldmember, w/letter of authenticity & reprinted color image of Myers in the costume (ILLUS., previous page) **717**

Lobby Cards

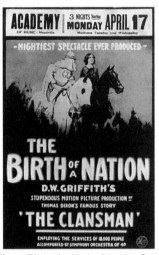

Rare "Birth of a Nation" Lobby Card

"Birth of a Nation (The)," D.W. Griffith, 1915, window-type, lithographed paper, the lower half w/a black ground printed in white outlined in red, the top section w/a green ground w/a scene of a woman & Klansman on horseback, 14 x 22" (ILLUS.) **3,107**

"Bringing Up Baby" Lobby Card

"Bringing Up Baby," RKO, 1938, starring Katharine Hepburn & Cary Grant, a yellow & white ground w/a sketched color scene of the characters in the center above black & white bust photos of the stars, black & red wording, 14 x 22" (ILLUS.).................. **2,868**

"Cat on a Hot Tin Roof" Lobby Card

"Cat on a Hot Tin Roof," MGM, 1958, insert-type, starring Elizabeth Taylor, Paul Newman & Burl Ives, tall orange & yellow background w/a large color photo of Taylor seated on the edge of a bed, color bust photos of the other leads below, paper-backed, 14 x 36" (ILLUS.) **1,076**

1940s "Kismet" Insert Lobby Card

"Kismet," MGM, 1944, insert-type, starring Ronald Colman & Marlene Dietrich, yellow ground w/a large full-length color photo of Dietrich in costume above a bust photo of Colman & black & white scenes, 14 x 36" (ILLUS., previous page) **239**

Rare "Public Enemy" Lobby Card

"Public Enemy (The)," Warner Bros., 1931, window-type, starring James Cagney & Jean Harlow, a large top colored circle w/portraits of the stars w/the wording & sketched figures below, 14 x 22" (ILLUS.) **10,158**

Early "Robin Hood" Window Lobby Card

"Robin Hood," United Artists, 1922, window-type, starring Douglas Fairbanks, full color lithographed scene of Robin

Hood perched in a leafy tree ready to shoot an arrow, 14 x 22" (ILLUS.)............. **1,673**

"Vertigo" Insert Lobby Card

"Vertigo," Paramount, 1958, insert-type, starring James Stewart & Kim Novak, the top half in dark orange w/black type & a white spiraling design w/a falling man, the lower section w/an orange-tinted black & white photo and Stewart & Novak kissing, 14 x 36" (ILLUS.) **1,076**

Posters

"Attack of the 50 Ft. Woman" Poster

"Attack of the 50 Ft. Woman," Allied Artists, 1958, color image of a huge woman picking up cars, yellow background w/large red & black lettering, one-sheet, 27 x 41" (ILLUS., previous page) **4,183**

style-B, one-sheet, linen-backed, 27 x 41" (ILLUS.) **5,019**

Bette Davis "Dark Victory" Poster

Scarce "Beau Geste" Poster

"Beau Geste," Paramount, 1939, starring Gary Cooper, large yellow title at the top against a dark shaded orange ground w/a large bust portrait of the star below,

"Dark Victory," Warner Bros., 1939, starring Bette Davis w/a color bust portrait of the star in the upper half above a black box w/white wording, one-sheet, linen-backed, 27 x 41" (ILLUS.) **5,975**

Re-release of Classic "Dracula" Poster

"Dracula," Universal, re-release of 1930s classic starring Bela Lugosi, red background w/a color scene of Dracula choking one of his victims, scattered skulls & black & yellow promotional wording, paper-backed, half-sheet, 22 x 28" (ILLUS.) **3,107**

Classic "Sunset Boulevard" Poster

"Sunset Boulevard," Paramount, 1950, starring Gloria Swanson, William Holden & Erich von Stroheim, a wide vertical red stripe w/a head portrait of Gloria Swanson glaring down at Holden & his girlfriend, a twisted strip of black film holding

the title in yellow, one-sheet, linen-backed, 27 x 41" (ILLUS.)........................ **5,975**

"The Blue Dahlia" Poster

"The Blue Dahlia," Paramount, 1946, starring Alan Ladd, Veronica Lake & William Bendix, color portraits of the various stars against a black ground, title & wording across the bottom, one-sheet, linen-backed, 27 x 41" (ILLUS.)........................ **3,824**

"The Graduate" Poster

"The Graduate," Embassy, 1967, starring Dustin Hoffman, Anne Bancroft & Katharine Ross, black ground w/classic color circle showing Hoffman looking on as Bancroft puts on a stocking, British quad size, linen-backed, 30 x 40" (ILLUS.) **598**

"You Only Live Twice" James Bond Poster

Three-sheet "Manchurian Candidate" Poster

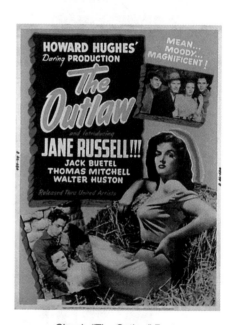

Classic "The Outlaw" Poster

"The Manchurian Candidate," United Artists, 1962, starring Frank Sinatra, Laurence Harvey, Janet Leigh & Angela Lansbury, black, blue & red bands across the top w/portraits of the stars above the white lower half w/red & black wording, three-sheet, linen-backed, 41 x 81" (ILLUS.) **598**

"The Outlaw," Howard Hughes, 1946, starring Jane Russell, upper portion w/a pink ground & maroon panel w/white & pink wording, classic black & white pose of Russell & other black & white scenes from the movie, style B, unfolded, framed, 30 x 40" (ILLUS.) **1,554**

Greta Garbo-signed Check

"They Died With Their Boots On" Poster

"They Died With Their Boots On," Warner Bros., 1941, starring Errol Flynn & Olivia de Havilland, red & black ground w/color portraits of the stars, white, yellow & black wording, one-sheet, linen-backed, 27 x 41" (ILLUS.)...................................... **1,673**

"You Only Live Twice," United Artists, 1967, starring Sean Connery, large color action scene to the upper right, red wording & portrait of Bond to the right, style A subway-type, linen-backed, 45 x 60" (ILLUS., top of previous page)...... **538**

Miscellaneous

Check, signed by Greta Garbo, handwritten in purple felt-tip pen and dated June 25, 1980, made out to a doctor for $200, 2 1/2 x 6" (ILLUS., top of page).................... **956**

Walter Plunkett Costume Sketch

Design sketch, watercolor & pencil on board, sketch by designer Walter Plunkett showing Vivien Leigh as Scarlett O'Hara wearing a red dress, produced during the pre-production phases of "Gone With The Wind," 1939, 16 x 19" (ILLUS.)... **8,963**

Fur stole, once owned by Marilyn Monroe, white fox fur w/a triple-pleated ivory silk lining & a label reading "Teitelbaum Furs - Beverly Hills," apparently the one she wore to the premieres of "How to Marry a Millionaire" & "The Seven Year Itch" (ILLUS., top next page)......................... **17,925**

Marilyn Monroe White Fox Stole

Early Harlow Photo Inscribed to C. Gable

Photograph, vintage black & white print of Jean Harlow attired in a fitted dress, inscribed in black fountain pen to Clark Gable w/a mysterious phrase, "E's (sic) in the part - Cabini - Just - Jean," in original 1930s wood & mirrored frame, mirror portion w/some staining, 11 x 14" (ILLUS.).. **14,350**

Early Marilyn Monroe Magazine Cover

Magazine, "Laff," January 1947 issue w/color photo of "Norma Jean Daugherty" (sic), later Marilyn Monroe, inscribed in black fountain pen to her hairdresser, "To Sylvia, Thanks a million - for everything - Your (sic) really wonderful - Love Always, - Norma Jeane," Sylvia Barnhart was the Hollywood hairdresser who first bleached Norma Jeane's hair golden blonde, 10 x 13" (ILLUS.)...................................... **3,107**

Rare Childhood Photo of Marilyn Monroe

Photograph, vintage sepia photograph of a nine-year-old Norma Jeane (aka Marilyn Monroe), finely hand-tinted in shades of yellow, light blue & pink, shot in Hollywood, in original metal frame, once owned by one set of foster parents who took care of Norman Jeane, 1935, 2 1/2 x 3 1/2" (ILLUS.) **31,070**

Early French Sofa Used in "Gone With The Wind"

Prop, 18th c. French sofa upholstered in teal blue velvet, from "Gone With The Wind," MGM, 1939, used in the scene of the napping young women at the barbecue outing, w/letter of authenticity from Katherine G. Rinneg dated 1940, 32" h., 72" l. (ILLUS., top of page)........................ **3,107**

Prop, scaled down hull of the Titanic used in scenes of the movie "Titanic," 20th Century Fox, 1953, starring Barbara Stanwyck, Clifton Webb & Robert Wagner, made in two separate sections & painted teal blue, ship name stenciled on stern, one side w/a large gash where the iceberg hit, 36" l., 21" h. (ILLUS.) **598**

"On The Waterfront" Prop Handgun

Prop, heavy prop metal handgun painted black, used in "On The Waterfront," Columbia, 1954, some paint wear (ILLUS.)... **5,019**

"Gold Diggers of 1933" Standee Sign

Standee sign, "Gold Diggers of 1933," painted plywood, tall cut-out of a lovely young Ginger Rogers in a scanty costume, black lower section w/wording in gold & red, Warner Bros., 1933, 26" w., 5' 9" h. (ILLUS.) **2,390**

Model Hull from 1953 "Titanic"

OFFICE EQUIPMENT

National Cash Register & Oak Base

Cash register, National Cash Register Model 333, nickel-plated brass under later gold paint, early 20th c., 17 1/2" w. (ILLUS. on top of oak floor-style case) **$259**

National Cash Register Model 91

Cash register, National Cash Register Model 91, ornate embossed bronze leaf-leaf case, original natural finish w/dark patina, early 20th c., 23" w. (ILLUS.) 345

Cash register base, oak, National Cash Register model w/a rectangular top above a case w/six narrow drawers each w/a brass letter & small brass knob, a deep drawer at the bottom flanked by serpentine corners continuing to flared feet w/brass caps, one drawer letter missing, early 20th c.,

27" w., 45" h. (ILLUS. with the National Cash Register Model 333) 661

Victorian Plunger Seal Stamp

Corporate seal stamp, cast iron, plunge-type, tall upright scroll handle supported by an arched upright figural lion head & ending in a die-cut logo stamp, stamp marked "Brooklyn Majestic Theatre of New York," painted black w/gold trim, ca. 1885 (ILLUS.) 205

Pencil lead sharpener, wood, a long thin wood platform centered by a thin rectangular metal sheet flanked by upright knobs joined by a wooden rod fitted w/a thin band of metal saw teeth, a round wooden disk w/a pencil opening moves along the toothed rod & rotates, early 20th c., overall 10 1/4" l................................ 172

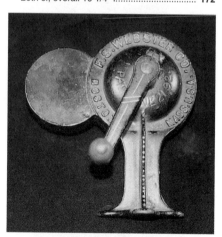

Rare Victorian Pencil Sharpener

Pencil sharpener, cast iron, rotary type, upright style w/round disk-form top on flattened pedestal w/screw holes at the base, large side crank handle w/wooden grip, embossed "The Webster Pencil Sharpener - Patent June 21, '92 - F.S. Webster Co. New York, Boston, Chicago," 98 percent original japanning, rare (ILLUS.)... 375

PAPERWEIGHTS

Baccarat, Clichy & Gillinder Paperweights

Baccarat "Garland" weight, round clear glass set w/a "C" shape composed of blue millefiori canes set upon an upset white muslin ground, surrounded by a garland of blue & white cane flowers in red, green & white, dated cane for 1848, 2 3/4" d. (ILLUS. left with Clichy & Gillinder paperweights) **$1,315**

A Baccarat Rose & Two St. Louis Paperweights

Baccarat "Thousand Petalled Rose" weight, the flower composed of numerous shaded red recessed petals growing from a green stalk, issuing six leaves & five further leaves around the flower, star-cut base, mid-19th c., 2 7/8" d. (ILLUS. left with two St. Louis weights).. **3,346**

E.T. Hurley Figural Turtle Paperweight

Bronze, model of a turtle, by E.T. Hurley, molded "ETH/0?6," fine original patina, early 20th c., 4 1/4 x 6 1/2" (ILLUS.) **1,840**

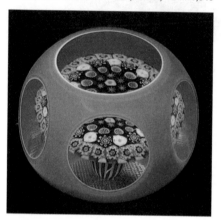

Fine Clichy Double-overlay Paperweight

Clichy "Faceted Double-overlay Concentric Mushroom" weight, the tuft composed of four rows of assorted millefiori canes in shades of blue & salmon pink & salmon pink & white, alternating w/seven white & green roses w/purple & white flowers & pink, white, claret & yellow, around a central white millefiori cane, set in a basket of elongated alternating cobalt blue & white staves, overlaid in opaque white & turquoise & cut on the top & five sides w/printies, grid-cut base, mid-19th c., 2 7/8" d. (ILLUS.) **3,824**

Clichy "Patterned Millefiori" weight, clear set w/an eight-petalled flower composed of clusters of millefiori canes in shades of white, pink, green, turquoise & red surrounding a central white & yellow cane within two rows of blue & white & green & white millefiori canes, set on a translucent red ground, mid-19th c., 3 1/8" d. (ILLUS. center with Baccarat Garland & Gillinder mushroom weight) **1,195**

Gillinder "Faceted Mushroom" weight, clear set w/numerous rows of elongated crimped canes in shades of turquoise, pale green & white, w/a central pale green crimped hollow floret, a basket of elongated hollow white cogwheel canes, America, mid-19th c., 2 5/8" d. (ILLUS.)
.... **2,868**

Metal "Dreadnought" Anchor Weight

Nickel-plated cast metal, model of a working ship's anchor, Taylor's Patent "Dreadnought" weight, early 20th c., unusual, 4 x 7" (ILLUS.) **94**

St. Louis "Fuchsia" weight, clear set w/a cobalt blue & rich pink blossom issuing a deep pink stamen, growing from a translucent purple stalk w/two similarly colored buds & four green leaves, set on a swirling white latticinio ground, mid-19th c., 3 1/4" d. (ILLUS. center with Baccarat Rose & St. Louis Strawberry weights) **1,554**

Colorful St. Louis Marbrie Weight

St. Louis "Marbrie" weight, clear set w/four bright loops in red, green & white w/a central cobalt blue & white composite pastry-mold & edelweiss cane, mid-19th c., 3 1/8" d. (ILLUS.) **2,868**

St. Louis "Strawberry in Three Stages of Growth" weight, the flower composed of five white ribbed petals w/a yellow center, growing from a long green stalk flanked by two ripe fruits & four green leaves, set on a swirling white latticinio ground, mid-19th c., 2 1/2" d. (ILLUS. right with Baccarat Rose & St. Louis Fuchsia weights) **896**

Stankard (Paul) Morning Glory weight, a bee on hive in center of two blue morning glories, three orange berries & two yellow flowers on a sandy ground, root figure & word canes "Moist" & "Fertile" beneath, signed "Paul J Stankard V32 '97," 3 1/4" d. **2,875**

Tiffany Bronze & Glass Paperweight

Tiffany Studios, bronze & glass, an Art Nouveau wavy design on bronze & glass, signed "Tiffany Studios - New York" w/Tiffany Glass & Decorating Co. logo, numbered "21565," 3 7/8" w. (ILLUS.) **3,120**

Trabucco (Victor) Magnum Pansy weight, purple pansy blossom & bud w/leafy stem on white lace cushion, signed "Trabucco 1998," 3 1/2" d. **633**

PERFUME, SCENT & COLOGNE BOTTLES

Decorative accessories from milady's boudoir have always been highly collectible, and in recent years there has been an especially strong surge of interest in perfume bottles. Our listings also include related containers such as pocket bottles and vials, tabletop containers & atomizers. Most readily available are examples from the 19th through the mid-20th century, but earlier examples do surface occasionally. The myriad varieties have now been documented in several recent reference books, which should further popularize this collecting specialty.

Rare Amethyst Mold-Blown Cologne

Amethyst glass, cologne, mold-blown ovoid body tapering to a tall neck w/flattened rim, sixteen ribs swirled to the left, tubular pontil scar, probably Pittsburgh region, ca. 1820-60, 6" h. (ILLUS.) **$1,904**

Tall Canary Yellow Toilet Water Bottle

Canary yellow glass, toilet water, pattern-molded cylindrical body w/a tall slender neck w/molded mouth, eight vertical ribs swirled to the right on the neck, probably Pittsburgh district, ca. 1840-70, ring-ground pontil scar, 12 1/4" h. (ILLUS.)......... **840**

Rare Mold-blown Blue Cologne Bottle

Sapphire blue glass, cologne, mold-blown flattened corseted shape w/palmette scrolled acanthus w/crosshatching, inward rolled mouth, pontil scar, America, ca. 1840-60, 5 3/4" h. (ILLUS.) ... **2,128**

PLANT WATERERS

Here's a collectible as popular and useful today as it was 50+ years ago. Plant waterers are the clever invention that allows stored water to seeps through a porous "stem" to the plant. Most are designed to supply water for up to seven days, keeping plants watered while the homeowner is away. Both decorative and functional, these often whimsical objects really have an identity prob-

lem. They're often confused, priced and sold as the expensive collectible pie birds. Now that the dish-sitting baby feeders have become so popular, plant waterers are also being incorrectly classified in this group. For the most part, plant waterers are still affordable but, as their popularity rises, it's only a matter of time before market prices start to climb.

Ceramic, bird, dark blue w/removable head, 4 1/2" h. **$25-35**

Shawnee Pottery Bird Plant Waterer

Ceramic, bird, off-white breast & yellow back w/pink & green highlights, impressed "USA," Shawnee Pottery, 6" h. (ILLUS.) **35-45**

Plump Bird Plant Waterer

Ceramic, bird, plump perched bird in white w/gold & black wings, tail & head w/small yellow beak, 5" h. (ILLUS.) **25-35**

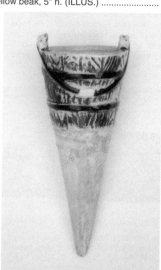

Bucket-shaped Plant Waterer

Ceramic, bucket, brown w/black bands & bail handle, 4" h. (ILLUS.) **6-8**
Ceramic, butterfly, yellow & decorated w/pink flowers, 4 1/2" h. **8-12**
Ceramic, deer, white, two legs showing, 9" h. **18-25**
Ceramic, Dutch girl, dressed in yellow, 5 1/4" h. **8-12**
Ceramic, frog sitting on lily pad, Neal the Frog, made for Sears, 5 1/2" h. **25-35**

Stylized Frog Plant Waterer

Ceramic, frog, stylized animal w/legs spread to the sides, dark green glaze, 5" h. (ILLUS.) **12-15**

Ceramic, lady/nymph in a bent pose, green glaze, marked "INARCO," 5 1/2" h. **12-18**

Ceramic Alligator Plant Waterer

Ceramic, model of alligator, green w/black trim & eye, 4 1/4" h. (ILLUS.) **10-12**

Ceramic, model of bird w/open mouth, green & blue speckled, 3 1/2" h. **6-8**

Ceramic Bird Plant Waterer

Ceramic, model of bird w/wings raised, blue, yellow & black, brown beak & legs, 6" h. (ILLUS.) **20-25**

Ceramic, model of bird, white w/yellow beak, removable head, 5 1/8" h. **15-18**

Ceramic, model of commode, white, 6 1/2" h. **6-8**

Ceramic Commode Plant Waterer

Ceramic, model of commode, yellow w/red speckles, 6 1/4" h. (ILLUS.) **6-8**

Ceramic Duck Plant Waterer

Ceramic, model of duck, white w/yellow highlights, brown face w/black eyes & gold beak, 4" h. (ILLUS.) **8-12**

Ceramic, model of elephant, red, 4 1/2" h. ... **10-15**

Ceramic, model of fish, green, Shawnee, marked "USA," 5" h. **50-75**

Light Brown Owl Plant Waterer

Ceramic, model of owl, light brown w/darker
highlights, molded feathers, 3 5/8" h.
(ILLUS.)... **6-8**

Ceramic Quail Plant Waterer

Ceramic, model of quail, white w/yellow &
black trim, 6" h. (ILLUS.)........................... **15-20**
Ceramic, model of rose, yellow, 5 1/4" h. **15-20**
Ceramic, model of snail, light brown w/black
eyes, 4 1/4" h. **8-15**

Pink Poodle Plant Waterer

Ceramic, model of poodle, sitting up on hind
legs as if begging, all pink, 9" h. (ILLUS.)
.... **40-55**

Ceramic Squirrel Plant Waterer

Ceramic, model of squirrel, sitting & holding
nut in front paws, light brown w/darker
trim, 4 1/4" h. (ILLUS.) **6-8**
Ceramic, model of squirrel w/detachable
head, brown, 4 1/2" h. **25-35**

Black & Yellow Turtle Plant Waterer

Ceramic, turtle, legs extended, head forward, black body w/yellow neck & head w/a black eye, 3" h. (ILLUS.) **8-12**

Long-necked Turtle Plant Waterer

Ceramic, turtle w/head raised, dark green glaze, 5" h. (ILLUS.) **12-15**
Ceramic, water pump & bucket, light brown, 6" h. **12-15**

Brown & Yellow Watering Can Plant Waterer

Ceramic, watering can, mottled brown & yellow sides & spout w/black handle & trim, 5" h. (ILLUS.) **8-12**
Plastic, bird, chubby yellow body, 4" h. **8-12**
Plastic, bluebird, 4" h. **8-12**
Plastic, dog, white, 4" h. **5-8**
Plastic, elephant, pink, 4" h. **5-8**

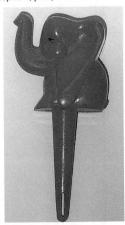

Red Plastic Elephant Plant Waterer

Plastic, elephant, red, 4" h. (ILLUS.) **8-12**
Plastic, wishing well, aqua w/a pebbled side & bar across the top, 4" h. **8-15**
Plastic, wishing well, red, 4" h. **8-12**

POLITICAL & CAMPAIGN ITEMS

Campaign Items

1896 William McKinley Bust Cane

Cane, 1896 presidential campaign of William McKinley, a figural metal bust handle w/gilt finish, marked w/his name around the base, on a wooden shaft, top 3 1/8" h., overall 35 1/2" l. (ILLUS. of top) **$403**

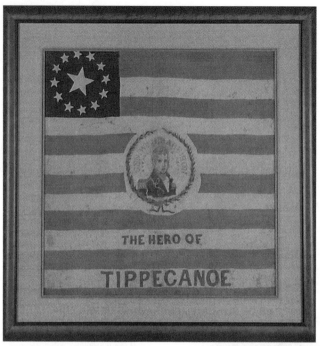

Very Rare 1840 William Henry Harrison Campaign Flag

1976 Jimmy Carter Campaign Cane

Cane, 1976 presidential campaign of Jimmy Carter, the molded metal handle in the shape of a large peanut w/the raised name of the candidate, painted in light & dark brown, on a brown-finished hardwood shaft, overall 33" l. (ILLUS.)................ **196**

Flag, 1840 campaign of William Henry Harrison, printed silk, a square-shaped American flag w/a circle of white stars on blue in the upper left, the wide red & white stripes centered w/a sepia-colored wreath enclosing the name & bust of the candidate, the slogan "The Hero of Tippecanoe" in white stripes below, archivally framed, extremely rare, some very fine professional restoration to a few small holes, 27 x 28" (ILLUS., top of page).. **10,189**

Unusual 1872 Grant-Wilson Glass Goblet

Goblet, 1872 campaign of Ulysses S. Grant, clear pressed glass w/an oval bust portrait medallion on each side, one of Grant & the other of his running mate, Wilson (ILLUS.)... **159**

Famous "Dewey Defeats Truman" Paper

Newspaper, 1948 Harry Truman campaign, famous "Chicago Daily Tribune" error edition headlined "Dewey Defeats Truman," complete edition, near-mint condition, 16 1/2 x 23 1/2" (ILLUS.) **892**

1924 Coolidge Phonograph Record

Phonograph record & sleeve, 1924 Calvin Coolidge campaign, the gold-colored recording centered by a black & white portrait of Coolidge & titled "A Campaign Talk - 1924 - President Calvin Coolidge," near mint, the set (ILLUS.) **168**

1896 McKinley-Hobert Jugate Pin

Pin, 1896 McKinley & Hobart campaign, jugate type, stamped brass w/a spread-winged eagle above two oval openings w/a cardboard photo of McKinley & his running mate, Hobart, a shield & crossed flags at the bottom, fine condition, 1 1/4 x 1 1/4" (ILLUS.) **271**

Rare Cox 1920 Anti-Prohibition Button

Pinback button, 1920 campaign of James M. Cox, slogan type, blue ground printed in white "Cox and Cocktails," referring to his anti-Prohibition stance, very rare, 7/8" d. (ILLUS.) **1,006**

Scarce 1940 Wilkie-McNary Jugate Button

Pinback button, 1940 Wilkie-McNary campaign, jugate type, blue printed bust photos of the candidates surrounded by American flag banners, scarce, 7/8" d. (ILLUS.) **443**

Pinback button, 1960 John F. Kennedy campaign, large round size centered by a blue portrait of Kennedy w/red & blue border bands printed in white "America Needs Kennedy," pristine, 4" d. (ILLUS. left with Kennedy & Johnson slogan pin, top next page) **665**

Pinback button, 1960 Kennedy-Johnson campaign, slogan type, a dark green ground printed in white "Greene Country - Kennedy and Johnson - Team For The 60's," very limited issue, fine condition, 3" d. (ILLUS. right with Kennedy portrait button, top next page) **754**

Rare Kennedy Portrait Button & Kennedy-Johnson Slogan Button

Rare Early Andrew Jackson Plate

Plate, 1828 campaign of Andrew Jackson, china w/a center printed w/black & white bust portrait of Andrew Jackson framed by the wording "General Jackson - The Hero of New Orleans," narrow & white pink lustre band trim, near mint, very rare, 6 1/4" d. (ILLUS., to the left) **2,271**

Political box, 1876 campaign of Samuel J. Tilden & Thos. A. Hendricks, mechanical type, heavy brass, the top w/two oval openings for images protected by a thin sheet of mica, the windable paper scroll advancing to show side-by-side portraits of every president from George Washington to Ulysses Grant, in working order, only known example, 1 7/8 x 3 1/8", 1/2" h. (ILLUS., bottom of page) **2,444**

Very Rare Tilden-Hendrix 1876 Mechanical Campaign Box

Unusual Hayes-Wheeler-Garfield 1876 Campaign Streamers

Unusual 1932 Hoover Campaign Poster

Poster, 1932 campaign of Herbert Hoover, printed in black & white, artwork by Christy w/the large upper portrait showing the figure of Victory holding a wreath aloft & standing on the back of a large eagle, reading "the Dawn of Victory - Stand By Our President - Re-Elect Herbert Hoover," one small edge tear at bottom, unusual, 22 1/2 x 32" (ILLUS.) **944**

Poster, 1960 campaign of John F. Kennedy & Lyndon Johnson, jugate type, cardboard w/a dark blue ground printed w/black & white photo of the candidate and white & red wording reading "Go Forward with John F. Kennedy & Lyndon B. Johnson - For Progress and Security - Vote Democratic," very minor color retouching, some minor creasing, 22 x 28" (ILLUS., top next column) **622**

Scarce Kennedy-Johnson Color Poster

Streamers, 1876 campaign of Rutherford B. Hayes, three red, white & blue ribbons, one stenciled w/the name of the presidential candidate, Hayes, the second w/the name of his running mate, Wheeler, and the third "Garfield," for James Garfield (later president), then running for Congress, brown cord connecting them, each ribbon 2 x 14" (ILLUS., top of page) **190**

Scarce 1860 Lincoln-Hamlin Tintypes

Tintype buttons, 1860 presidential campaign of Abraham Lincoln & Hannibal Hamlin, a round brass two-sided frame w/the stamped name of the candidate enclosing a small tintype of that candidate, excellent condition, small (ILLUS. of both sides) **685**

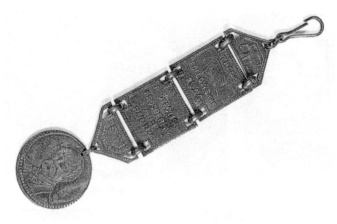

Roosevelt-Fairbanks Watch Fob

1904 Parker-Davis Toothpick Holder

Toothpick holder, 1904 campaign of Alton Parker & Henry Davis, milky opalescent pressed glass in the Ring & Beads patt., printed in black w/oval portraits of the candidates surrounded by American flags, a flying eagle, American shield & their names, 2 3/8" h. (ILLUS.)..................... **818**

Watch fob, 1904 campaign of Theodore Roosevelt & Charles Fairbanks, brass, composed of triangular top & bottom links connecting two square links, all stamped w/slogans, a round portrait medal suspended at the bottom, 5 1/2" l. (ILLUS., top of page).. **69**

Non-Campaign

Badge, tin shell-type pinback badge printed w/a sepia bust profile portrait of President Grover Cleveland, possibly a souvenir of his 1893 inauguration, worn gilt border band, 1 1/2 x 2" (ILLUS., top next column).. **84**

Grover Cleveland Souvenir Badge

Banner, painted & appliqued fabric, first displayed at the Great Central Sanitary Fair in Philadelphia in June 1864, the month Abraham Lincoln visited the Fair, a dark blue ground w/deep red border band, large gold wording across the top reading "Proclamation of Emancipation" above a large oval portrait of Lincoln flanked by anti-slavery medals & above an American eagle & shield, the lower half w/a large ribbon printed in gold "By The President of the United States of America" over another ribbon flanking the U.S. Capitol dome & reading "June 1864," fringe along the bottom & hanging ribbons at the top, extremely rare & unique, 68 x 69" (ILLUS., top next page)........... **123,258**

Extraordinary Lincoln Emancipation Proclamation Banner

Figural Franklin Roosevelt Cane

Cane, figural, the handle formed as a brass bust of President Franklin Roosevelt, his name at the front & also marked "Century of Progress," sold at the Chicago Century of Progress world's fair in 1933, on a black wooden shaft, top 2 3/4" h., overall 36" l. (ILLUS.).. **403**

Impeachment ticket, black-printed orange paper, large section reading "U.S. Senate - Impeachment of the President - Admit The Bearer - Gallery - April 2, 1868," for the impeachment trial of President Andrew Johnson, complete w/stub, minor spotting (ILLUS., top next page) **1,903**

Roosevelt Ship of State Novelty Lamp

Lamp, table model, bronzed metal & glass, figural, the base w/the figure of President Franklin Roosevelt dressed as a slicker-clad sailor at the helm of the Ship of State, across the front base stamped "FDR - The Man of the Hour," original closed bulbous pink shaded to blue glass Art Deco style shade, w/original cord & plug, early 1930s, 16 1/2" h. (ILLUS.).......... **716**

Andrew Johnson Impeachment Trial Ticket

Unusual Early George Washington Memorial Textile

Memorial textile, brown printed on tan cloth, a memorial for George Washington, depicting a large arched portico w/Washington standing on a pedestal in the center, a fort & harbor in the background & a memorial urn, flags & other patriotic emblems below him, tall obelisks flanking the portico, long memorial quote across the top, signed at the bottom "Printed & Published at Glasgow - C.G. 1819," small tears & holes, minor staining, pinned to card backing, in early 20th c. frame, image 19 1/4 x 24 3/4" (ILLUS.).................. **2,645**

Breath Mint Tin with Lincoln Portrait

Mint tin container, round small brass box sold to hold breath mints, the top stamped w/a bust portrait of Abraham Lincoln below his arched name, meant to hold cachou & cardamom pills for the breath, a similar example known showing President James Buchanan, ca. 1860s, 1 1/2" d. (ILLUS.) **1,332**

Photograph, albumen print of Abraham Lincoln at Antietam w/military officers including General McClellan in front of a tent after the battle, above the photo in red ink "The key to this picture was given by Brig. Genl O.B. Willcox of the Soldier's Home," image 7 1/4 x 9", mounted on board **5,225**

1893 Cleveland Inaugural Souvenir Pin

Pin, gilt brass, a souvenir of the 1893 inauguration of Grover Cleveland, top pin bar reading "Souvenir," shield-shaped pendant stamped w/profiles of President & Mrs. Cleveland & "Courage - Consistency," 1 1/4 x 1 1/2" (ILLUS.) **130**

Spanish-American War Souvenir Plate

Plate, porcelain, Spanish-American War commemorative, a dark blue border band, the center printed in color w/American flags & the Statue of Liberty along w/a small oval portrait of President McKinley & other American military leaders, banner reading "A Souvenir of the Cuban War 1898," 12" d. (ILLUS.) **299**

Early Theodore Roosevelt Sheet Music

Sheet music, a rebus-style title for "Roosevelt" subtitled "His Second Term," pink ground w/large green rose & banner, black & white oval photo of Theodore Roosevelt, verses celebrating his 1904 re-election, 1905, 10 1/2 x 13" (ILLUS.)....... **152**

POP CULTURE COLLECTIBLES

The collecting of pop culture memorabilia is not a new phenomenon; fans have been collecting music-related items since the emergence of rock and roll in the 1950s. But it was not until the coming of age of the postwar generation that the collecting of popular culture memorabilia became a recognized movement. The most sought-after items are from the 1960s, when music, art, and society were at their most experimental. This time period is dominated by artists such as The Beatles, The Rolling Stones and Bob Dylan, to name a few. From the 1950s, Elvis Presley is the most popular. Here we offer a cross-section of popular culture collectibles ranging from the 1950s to the present day.

Beatles autographs, blue fountain pen on paper, on a piece of Oberoi Intercontinental letterhead signed by all four band members while they were in India, 1967, 5 1/2 x 7" (ILLUS., top next page).......... **$3,107**

Beatles Autographs on Letterhead

Guitar Signed by Beatles Band Members

Beatles guitar, Hofner bass guitar w/a violin-shaped body in a sunburst finish & a later-replaced mahogany neck signed by John Lennon, Paul McCartney & George Harrison as well as Chet Atkins, Jim Reeves, Chubby Checker, Cliff Richard & Joe Frasier, each signature later carved into the wood, guitar ca. 1959, signed in 1964, overall 41" l. (ILLUS.)..................... **7,170**

Beatles Cards from Rare Topps Set

Beatles gum card set, Topps Gum, test issue that was very unsuccessful, includes 52 of the 55 oversized "Beatle Plaks" cards, very rare, 1964, the group (ILLUS. of part)... **991**

Infamous Beatles "Butcher Cover"

Beatles record album, "The Beatles Yesterday And Today," infamous "Butcher Cover" showing the four w/pieces of raw meat & doll parts, pulled from the market, first state, Capitol Records, partially sealed, 1966, 12 1/2" sq. (ILLUS.)............ **4,780**

John Lennon Pocket Watch

John Lennon pocket watch, Howard white-gold men's watch owned by Lennon, dial polished w/applied gold-tone Arabic numerals, octagonal case w/a floral design, hands in blued steel, suspended from a fancy line white metal chain (ILLUS.).. **31,070**

John Lennon "Rock 'N Roll" Album

John Lennon record album, "Rock 'N Roll," features covers of classic rock tunes released on the Apple label in 1975, signed by Lennon in blue ballpoint ink on the right side, 12 1/2" sq. (ILLUS.)
.... **3,585**

Paul & Linda McCartney magazine, "Manchete," Brazilian magazine, April 1990, signed in black felt-tip pen by the couple, 9 x 12" (ILLUS., top next column)
.... **478**

Magazine Signed by the McCartneys

Andy Warhol book, "Andy Warhol's Index," first edition copy of a cult book that documented The Factory's social whirl during the 1965-66 period, containing black & white photos of Factory regulars, interviews, pop-ups, fold-out pages, & a Velvet Underground 45 rpm "flexi" record w/an image of Lou Reed on it, signed on the flyleaf in black felt-tip "to Jerry - Andy Warhol," record signed "to Denny - Andy Warhol," 1967, some 70 pp. (ILLUS. open, top next page)................................ **1,554**

Aretha Franklin RIAA Gold Record

Aretha Franklin RIAA Gold Record, for her album "Lady Soul," marked the sale of one million dollars worth of this Atlantic Records long-playing record album, matted & framed, 16 x 21" (ILLUS.) **837**

Scarce Copy of Signed "Andy Warhol's Index" Book

Early Bob Dylan Hand-written Lyrics

Hirschfeld Caricature of Elvis

Bob Dylan lyrics, hand-written in black ballpoint pen on a piece of paper, reading "I'll know your song - well before you start - singing - And it's a Hard - Rain's a gon- na- Fall! - Bob Dylan - '63," 1963, 5 1/2 x 8" (ILLUS.)...................................... **3,346**

Elvis Presley caricature, done by well known artist Al Hirschfeld, Number 147 out of an edition of 150, large 15 x 20" (ILLUS.).. **1,021**

Eric Clapton Signed Fender Guitar

Rare Elvis-worn Brown Studded Vest

Signed Fleetwood Mac Album Jacket

Menu with Signed Sinatra Sketch

Elvis Presley vest, brown polyester & tan suede adorned w/numerous gold-colored studs, worn by Elvis, interior label reads "JC Costume Co. - Hollywood, California," w/1992 letter of authenticity that indicates this was worn as everyday wear by Elvis (ILLUS.) **23,900**

Eric Clapton guitar, blue Fender Stratocaster electric guitar, signed in gold ink by the musician (ILLUS., top of page)....... **2,390**

Fleetwood Mac album, the album "Fleetwood Mac" printed in black & white, the jacket signed by all members of the band in blue or black felt-tip ink, also w/two black & white glamour photos of Stevie Nicks, 12 1/2" sq. (ILLUS., next column) **299**

Frank Sinatra signed menu & sketch, a printed paper Jilly's menu in red, white & black, centered by a quickly rendered Sinatra self-portrait & signed "John - Frank Sinatra," done in blue felt-tip ink, noted in lower left-hand corner in orange by a different hand "Tuesday night 5/9/72," 10 x 12" (ILLUS.) **1,195**

Keith Richards-signed Fender Telecaster Electric Guitar

Jim Morrison-endorsed Check

Rolling Stones Signed Concert Program

Jim Morrison check, written to Morrison on November 6, 1970 in the amount of $100, endorsed by him on the back in blue ballpoint pen, 3 1/2 x 8 1/2" (ILLUS.) **1,434**

Keith Richards guitar, amber-colored Fender Telecaster electric guitar, signed in black felt-tip ink "YCAGWYW - '97 - Keith Richards," meaning "You Can't Always Get What You Want," w/color snapshot of Richards w/this guitar (ILLUS., top of page) **2,868**

Rolling Stones concert program, printed in black & white, signed on one page by all members of the band in blue fountain pen, together w/the program cover signed by all members of The Ronettes, who were on the same bill, 1964, 7 x 9 1/2" (ILLUS., top next column) **1,793**

The Who drumhead, round Remo brand drumhead signed in blue felt-tip by Pete Townsend, Roger Daltry & John Entwistle, who added a drawing of a spider, 14" d. (ILLUS., bottom next column) **657**

The Who-signed Drumhead

PURSES & BAGS

Black leather, supple black calfskin handbag w/goldtone hardware, detachable shoulder strap, leather interior w/three pockets, w/original felt protection insert & box, signed "Kelly" model by Hermes, 20th c. **$2,350**

Blue leather, large handbag w/silvertone hardware, two shoulder straps, leather interior w/four pockets, signed "Kelly" model by Hermes, 20th c. **1,763**

Brown leather, rigid pebbled leather handbag w/goldtone hardware, detachable shoulder strap, leather interior w/three pockets, w/original felt protection insert & box, signed "Kelly" model by Hermes, 20th c. **4,818**

Gold mesh, yellow gold (14k), the squared serpentine gold hinged frame gypsy-set w/eleven old mine- and European-cut diamonds, approximate weight 3 cts., as well as gypsy-set oval sapphires & round rubies, trace link chain mesh, Russian hallmarks, late 19th c. **6,169**

Needlework, folding type, opens to reveal two double pockets, w/flame stitch design w/"Simon Pinder April 23, 1772" worked into the borders, green, yellow, pink & amethyst woolen yarns, lined in green linen w/twill tape binding, 8 x 8" open **2,644**

Petit point pocketbook, early petit point worked double-pocketbook, w/flame stitch panel divider, pale green ground decorated on one side w/birds, stars, a bowl of fruit & "John Joseph Heriges" on an orange panel, the other w/trees, stars & possibly an altar or memorial w/flames, the flap w/apple tree & two nesting birds, in orange, blue, red, greens, brown, yellow & white, the interior lined w/grey cloth & divided into two sections of pockets made from cloth-covered paper, green ribbon tie, minor wear w/old blue cloth patches on the underside of the flap, old ribbon tie is damaged, 4 x 6 1/4" closed **2,090**

Red alligator, rigid handbag w/goldtone hardware, H-shaped magnetic closure, shoulder strap, leather interior w/two pockets, signed "Constance" model by Hermes, 20th c. **3,525**

Whiting & Davis

One of the most successful marketing campaigns of the early 20th century was conducted by the Whiting & Davis Company to promote its line of mesh handbags. Prior to the 1909 invention of the automatic mesh-making machine, mesh was hand-linked, a process both lengthy and costly. With automation, bags could be produced quickly and economically. Whiting & Davis capitalized on this by promoting its product as both an affordable fashion accessory and as a desirable "special occasion" gift. Early film favorites including Joan Crawford appeared in Whiting & Davis ads, and such fashion arbiters as Paul Poiret and Elsa Schiaparelli contributed exclusive designs to the line.

Many Whiting & Davis decorative patterns are reflective of the firm's 1920s and 1930s heyday, featuring Art Deco-influenced geometrics and arresting color combinations. Scenic and figural depictions were also popular, with subjects ranging from modernistic skylines and moonlit beaches to exotic birds, dancing couples, and even movie stars. Over the years, variations on the traditional Whiting & Davis bag have included compact bags, gate-top bags, miniature coin purses, and children's purses. Although other mesh manufacturers emerged, including Evans, Napier, and Miller Brothers, Whiting & Davis remained the industry leader. The company's most resilient competitor, Mandalian Mfg. Co., specialized in bags with a Middle Eastern flavor, often heavily trimmed with metal fringe and drops. Whiting & Davis acquired Mandalian in the 1940s, soon incorporating the company's techniques and stylings into it own designs.

In the late 1940s and 1950s, Whiting & Davis moved into "solids" - mesh bags all in one color, often gold. In the 1980s and '90s, the company also briefly expanded beyond mesh bags to the manufacture of other mesh accessories: vests, gowns, belts, headbands, and even jewelry. Among the designers whose work has appeared under the Whiting & Davis logo are Anna Sui, Richard Tyler, and Anthony Ferrara. Today, the company name and tradition continue in bags designed by Inge Hendromartono for Inge Christopher.

Complete information on the Whiting & Davis Co. is included in Whiting & Davis Purses: The Perfect Mesh by Leslie Pina and Donald-Brian Johnson. (Schiffer Publishing Ltd., 2002). Photos for this category are by Dr. Pina.

Beadlite mesh (armor mesh with the appearance of a beaded bag), Egyptian motif in orange, black & gold.............. **$225-275**

Blue enameled compact bag, fine enameled ring mesh, "Renaissance Filigree" fringe, 1920s **550-650**

Bubble mesh wallet, 1990s **30-40**

"Chain mail" ring mesh shoulder bag, Leo Narducci design **300-400**

Charlie Chaplin Bag

Charlie Chaplin bag, 1976 "Star Series" (ILLUS., bottom previous page) **1,300-1,500**
Clark Gable bag, 1976 "Star Series" .. **2,000-2,200**
Compact bag, tri-color "Sunset" ring mesh **1,300-1,500**
"Deylsia" vanity bag **700-900**
"Dresden mesh" bag, domed frame, double-tier ring mesh fringe **225-275**

Fine Ring Mesh Bag

"Dresden mesh" bag, fine ring mesh, pull-bead clasp (ILLUS.) **300-350**
Evening clutch bag, gold mesh, 1990s **25-45**
Fine silver ring mesh, Venetian fringe, silver cord strap **325-375**

Fountain Design Bag

Fountain design on gold mesh, blue metal drops at base (ILLUS.) **350-400**
"Gate Top" bag, expansion opening, gold mesh, 1940s **100-125**

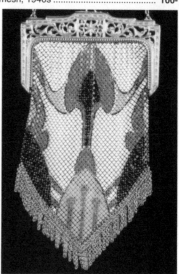

Gold Metal Frame & Fringe

Grey tones on white mesh, gold metal frame & fringe (ILLUS.) **325-375**
"Libby" compact bag, 1996, W & D "120th Anniversary Heritage Collection" **350-450**
Lighthouse design, in shades of green mesh **350-400**
Mandalian Mfg. dome-shaped bag, "Lustro-Pearl" sheen, red teardrops at base **375-425**
Mandalian Mfg. "Gloria Bag," bracelet frame.. **325-375**

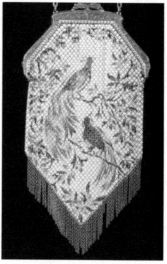

Mandalian "Peacocks" Bag

Mandalian Mfg. "Peacocks" bag, (ILLUS.) **300-350**

RADIO & TELEVISION MEMORABILIA

Not long after the dawning of the radio age in the 1920s, new programs were being aired for the entertainment of the national listening audience. Many of these programs issued premiums and advertising promotional pieces that are highly collectible today.

With the arrival of the TV age in the late 1940s, the tradition of promotional items continued. In addition to advertising materials, many toys and novelty items have been produced that tie in to popular shows.

Below we list alphabetically a wide range of items relating to classic radio and television. Some of the characters originated in the comics or on the radio and then found new and wider exposure through television. We include them here because they are best known to today's collectors because of television exposure. ALSO SEE: Cat Collectibles, Horse Collectibles and Western Character Collectibles.

Clarabell Clown Marionnette & Box

Clarabell Clown marionette, composition head w/painted features, hinged lower jaw w/string controls, original clothing, unplayed-with condition in original colorful box marked "A Howdy Doody Marionette - Clarabell Marionette," 15" h. (ILLUS. of marionette & box) **370**

Flub-A-Dub Marionette & Box

Flub-A-Dub marionette, composition head w/sleep eyes & real lashes, hinged lower jaw & sleep eyes controlled by strings, original clothing, unplayed-with condition w/original box, box reading "A Howdy Doody Marionette - Flub-A-Dub Marionette," 11 1/2" h. (ILLUS. of marionette & box) **330**

Howdy Doody marionette, plastic head, hands & boots, airbrushed head w/moving jaw & sleep eyes, boots marked "H.D.," Pelham, 16" h. **173**

Early Charlie McCarthy Doll

Charlie McCarthy doll, composition shoulder-head, marked on shoulder plate "Edgar Bergen," the head w/painted brown eyes, hinged lower jaw that opens & closes by pulling string in back, metal monocle on right eye, molded & painted auburn hair, cloth body w/composition lower arms & feet molded as white shoes, wearing original white flannel suit w/matching cap, dark blue shirt, yellow print bow tie, original button printed "Edgar Bergen's Charlie McCarthy - An Effanbee Play-Product," 1930s, light crazing, clothing lightly aged, 20" h. (ILLUS.) **$550**

Howdy Doody-Lookalike Windup Toy

Howdy Doody-lookalike windup toy, celluloid hand-painted jointed figure flips around bar on A-frame stand, in original box w/color graphics of swinging figure & labeled "Jackie the Farmer Boy on Trapez," very rare, "My Friend" Trademark Japan, 1950s, some splits to celluloid, box w/soft corners & splits, 5" h. figure, 9 1/2" h. overall (ILLUS.) **1,320**

Early Howdy Doody Marionette & Box

Howdy Doody marionette, composition head w/painted features, hinged lower jaw controlled by string, original clothing, unplayed-with condition in original box, marked "Howdy Doody - ©Bob Smith -

Marionette - manufactured by Peter Puppet Playthings, Inc. - Made in U.S.A.," 16" h. (ILLUS. of marionette & box) **240**

Indian Princess Marionette from Howdy Doody

Indian Princess marionette, character from Howdy Doody show w/black braided wool hair & animated eyes, wearing hand-painted fringed suede costume & moccasins, constructed by Rufus & Margo Rose, ca. 1959 (ILLUS.) **10,297**

Liberace Costume from Batman TV Show

Liberace costume, worn on an episode of "Batman" (1966) when he played the dual roll of Chandell & his evil twin brother, Harry, on the episode titled "The Devil's Fingers," the fancy ensemble consisting of a belted smoking jacket in black silk w/elaborate gold-thread embroidery & the Liberace trademark signature w/piano logo stitched on the inside lining, matching black pants, white elastic suspenders, a video cassette of the episode included, the group (ILLUS.) **3,585**

1970s The Shadow Coloring Book

Shadow (The) coloring book, cover w/dark gold background w/wording in white, black & purple, a large figure of The Shadow in black, red & white, Saalfield Publishing Co., 1974, 8 1/4 x 11" (ILLUS.)....................................... **25**

Timmy Shirt from Lassie TV Series

Timmy Martin shirt, red & white checkered long-sleeved child's shirt worn by Jon Provost as Timmy Martin on the Lassie series, repaired rip & some wear, 1954-1974 (ILLUS.)... **1,076**

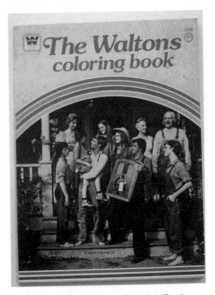

1975 The Waltons Coloring Book

Waltons (The) coloring book, the cover w/a large color group photo of the cast below an arch of colored bands & a top panel in dark yellow w/red lettering, Whitman Publishing, Racine, Wisconsin, 1975, 8 x 10 3/4" (ILLUS.).............................. **20**

RADIOS & ACCESSORIES

Airlite Instand Novelty Radio

Airlite, Instand novelty radio, thin Bakelite, 1930s (ILLUS.) **$250**
Emerson, Model 868, Magic Wand antenna, portable, 1950s 50

FADA Catalin Radio

FADA, Model 1000, Catalin, mid-1940s (ILLUS.) **1,250**

RCA Oversized Tabletop Radio

RCA, Model 66X1, Bakelite, oversized tabletop, ca. 1946 (ILLUS.) 45
Silvertone, Model 3001, plastic, 1954 35
Silvertone, plastic, table model, green, lattice work on front speaker panel, 1955 50

RAGGEDY ANN & ANDY COLLECTIBLES

Say the names Raggedy Ann and Andy and visions of red yarn hair, floppy striped legs, and friendly smiling faces come to mind. Without a doubt, they are the most famous rag dolls of all time. Books that feature the famous duo and dolls number high in this collectible field. Other Raggedy Ann and Andy items have always been out there, but not in the numbers that appeared in the early 1970s when there was a newfound interest in these lovable characters.

Book, "Raggedy Andy Goes Sailing," 1943, McLoughlin, the "Westfield Classics" series **$40**
Book, "Raggedy Andy Stories," 1920, Volland 150
Book, "Raggedy Andy's Treasure Hunt," 1973, Tell-a-Tale 5
Book, "Raggedy Ann and Andy and the Nice Fat Policeman," 1942, illustrations by Worth Gruelle 40
Book, "Raggedy Ann and the Cookie Snatcher," 1972, Little Golden Book 8
Book, "Raggedy Ann and the Left-Handed Safety Pin," 1935, Whitman 45
Book, "Raggedy Ann's Lucky Pennies," 1932, Donohue 55
Book, "Raggedy Ann's Lucky Pennies," dust jacket, 1932, Volland 210

"Raggedy Ann's Sunny Songs"

Book, "Raggedy Ann's Sunny Songs," 1930, Miller Music (ILLUS.) 70

Raggedy Ann Colorforms Toy

Magic Pebble Game

Colorforms, Raggedy Ann Dress-Up Kit,
    1967 .... **15**
Doll, camel w/wrinkled knees, Knickerbock-
    er **150-175**
Game, Magic Pebble, Milton Bradley, 1941
    (ILLUS., top of page) **90**
Game, Raggedy Ann, Milton Bradley, 1954 .... **45**

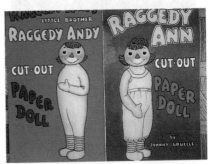

Raggedy Ann & Andy Paper Dolls

Paper dolls, Raggedy Ann & Andy, Whit-
    man, 1935 (ILLUS.) **75-150**

Beloved Belindy Greeting Card

Greeting card, Beloved Belindy card/book-
    let, Hallmark, 1974 (ILLUS.) **25**
Music box, ceramic, revolving, 1950s **40**
Ornament, Christmas, satin ball, Hallmark,
    1975 .... **50**
Paper doll, Raggedy Ann cut-out dolls
    w/dresses, Milton Bradley, 1941 .... **55**
Paper dolls, Raggedy Ann & Andy, Flip a
    Page, Change An Outfit, Whitman, 1967 .. **12-20**
Paper dolls, Raggedy Ann & Andy, Fun
    Fashions, Whitman, 1974 .... **9-15**

Raggedy Ann & Andy Paper Dolls

Paper dolls, Raggedy Ann & Andy, Whitman, 1966 (ILLUS., previous page) **15-25**
Paper plates, Bobbs Merrill, 1974 .... **5**
Party favor, Ann or Andy, Merry Miniature, Hallmark, 1974, ea. **110**

Raggedy Ann & Andy Pattern

Pattern, Ann & Andy, McCalls, 1970 (ILLUS.).. **10**

Raggedy Ann & Andy Plaques

Plaques, ceramic, Ann & Andy, 1970s, pr. (ILLUS.).. **50**

Raggedy Ann Purse

Purse, vinyl, shaped like Raggedy Ann, zippered at top, 1971 (ILLUS.) **23**
Puzzle, Raggedy Ann, frame-tray, Milton Bradley, 1944, boxed set of three **70**
Quilt, single bed, 1970s **37**
Tea set, tin, mint in box, 1940s **100**
Thimble, pewter, Ann or Andy, each **12**

RIBBON DOLLS

For centuries a lady was judged by her talent with a needle and thread. In the 1920s and 1930s, women and young girls put this practical education to good use by creating ribbon dolls or ribbon lady pictures. Many of the handcrafted examples originated from a kit which provided assembly instructions, the necessary materials, background fabric and, in some cases, even the frame and glass. Others were completely homemade and the paper doll itself was either cut from a magazine or hand-drawn. Recently uncovered information reveals that these pretty pieces were also commercially produced as decorative wall art.

While the majority of these pictures are of women, occasionally a male model, either singly or paired with his female counterpart, will surface on the market. Women dressed in Colonial-style attire seem to be the most prevalent, with some wearing more unusual costumes in a variety of unique poses. Although it appears that ribbon dolls fell out of favor by the 1950s, they're back in vogue once again, coveted by collectors who appreciate their vintage form and historical significance.

Boy, w/blond hair, wearing a straw hat, redchecked overalls & green shirt, brown shoes, holding purple & yellow ribbon flowers, pink & yellow ribbon flowers at his feet, 5 x 7" **$50-60**
Boy & girl, the girl in a red dress & hat w/lace & multi-colored ribbon flower trim, a green bow at her neck, the boy in grey trousers & mauve shirt w/lace collar, holding a multi-colored ribbon bouquet w/ribbon streamers, 3 1/2" h. **95-125**

Early Fancy Bride Ribbon Doll

Bride, blonde paper hair, wearing an off-white satin ribbon dress w/lace streamers at the waist, lace pantaloons, holding a white floral bouquet, w/a trailing fine net veil, framed, 6 3/4 x 8 1/2" (ILLUS., previous page)... **60-75**

Bride, wearing an off-white ribbon dress & veil, holding a bouquet w/ribbon streamers, headpiece & veil trimmed w/pearls, 9 x 11"... **115-135**

Bride, wearing lilac-colored dress w/pink ribbon streamers, high-topped veil & velvet flowers in hair, carrying multicolored bouquet, 9 x 11"....................................... **65-85**

1950s Dol-Lee Dolls Ribbon Doll Lady

Colonial lady, wearing a wide tiered & ruffled lace-trimmed dress w/lace pantaloons & matching bonnet, holding a lace-encircled colorful rose bouquet, by Dol-Lee Dolls, ca. 1951, framed, 9 1/2 x 11 1/2" (ILLUS.).............................. **40-55**

Colonial Lady with Red Boa

Colonial lady, white-haired, in peach dress w/mesh overlay & green ribbon trim,

holding red boa feather, 6 3/4" w x 8 3/4" h. (ILLUS.)................................. **35-50**

Colonial man, white hair, wearing a pink satin waistcoat & green kneebreeches, lace collar & cuffs, 8 1/2 x 11"................... **60-75**

Colonial woman, blonde, wearing a dark & light pink ribbon ruffled dress, sitting in a chair & working on a spinning wheel, 8 1/4" h... **75-85**

Colonial Woman Holding Feather

Colonial woman, pink satin ribbon dress decorated w/black & red appliques, holding large white feather, 10 1/2" w x 12 1/2" h. (ILLUS.)............................. **40-50**

Colonial woman, transparent yellow shell-like dress trimmed in marcasite beads & ribbon flowers, no hair, 9" h. **30-40**

Couple, a man on bended knee gazing up at a woman wearing a pink petal dress decorated w/black marquisette beading, a full moon & trees in the background, titled "The Proposal" in a panel below, framed, 9 x 11".. **50-60**

Dancing lady, wearing a green dress trimmed in beige lace & adorned w/pink rosebuds, pink & yellow roses at waist & one shoulder, holding her flaring skirt, marked "Copyright 1935 by T.B. & Co. Chicago," 11 x 13"................................... **95-125**

Dutch girl, wearing a beige dress w/large bow in back, a white apron & cap w/lace trim, wooden clogs, carrying a red & yellow bouquet of flowers, 9 1/2 x 10" **50-60**

Faceless girl, wearing a pale green dress w/large matching hat that hides her profile, trimmed w/white lace & white ribbon streamers at the waist, holding a pink & white rose ribbon bouquet, 8 1/2 x 11"...... **50-60**

Faceless girl, wearing an orange dress & large-brimmed matching hat w/green ribbon trim, carrying a lace-encircled bouquet w/red ribbon flowers & green streamers, 9 x 11"................................... **50-60**

Faceless lady, brown hair w/curling locks, wearing a yellow paper dress w/black ribbon sash adorned w/pink flowers, a large-brimmed hat w/black band, yellow & pink flowers, holding in one hand a small pink & yellow rosebud bouquet encircled w/lace, yellow, pink & red rosebuds on the background, 10 1/2 x 12 3/4" **50-60**

Female clown, wearing an orange & brown ribbon tutu, conical hat w/pink ponpoms, her arms extended & standing on toes in ballet slippers, 7 3/4 x 9 3/4" **75-85**

Harlequin-style male, in a dancing pose w/one leg lifted, wearing a burnt orange & brown ribbon costume w/a ruffled collar & mask, framed, 7 3/4 x 9 3/4" (ILLUS.)....... **75-85**

Lady in Pale Blue Lace-Layered Dress

Lady, blonde hair, pale blue & lace layered dress w/large blue bow & streamers at waist, w/matching cap & bouquet & lace pantaloons, 8 3/4" w. x 10 3/4" h. (ILLUS.) **35-40**

Girl Wearing Pink Ribbon Dress

Girl, faceless, wearing pink ribbon dress & pink flapper-style hat trimmed in pastel colored roses, holding pastel ribbon bouquet surrounded by lace, 8 3/4" w. x 10 3/4" h. (ILLUS.)................... **35-45**

Girl, w/real long brown hair, pink & blue dress w/matching bonnet, 7 3/4" h. **50-60**

Dancing Harlequin Man Ribbon Doll

Little Girl with Colonial Bonnet

Little girl, dressed in rose & ivory ribbon outfit w/matching large colonial-style bonnet & rose ribbon shoes, holding small ribbon rose bouquet, mounted on vintage handkerchief, 12" w. 13 1/2" h. (ILLUS.)... **40-50**

Man in Morning Suit Ribbon Doll

Man, standing wearing a satin morning suit w/a yellow stripe down the pant leg, holding a cane in one hand, his other arm behind him holding his top hat, framed, 5 x 7" (ILLUS.).. **75-95**

1951 Dol-Lee Dolls Pattern & Envelope

Pattern, paper, in original illustrated envelope for the "Colonial Doll" model doll, illustrates the doll carrying a lace umbrella & wearing a wide ruffled ribbon dress, by Dol-Lee Dolls, ca. 1951 (ILLUS.) **15-20**

1920s Complete Pattern & Envelope

Pattern, paper, in original illustrated envelope for the "Elvira" model doll, includes
ribbon, black cloth background, glass & a
10 x 12" frame, ca. 1929, the set (ILLUS.,
bottom previous page) **75-95**

Pattern, paper w/design for a lady w/red
hair in a Colonial-style set, standing on
tiptoe w/toes peeking out from hoop skirt,
holding a circle for a bouquet, includes instructions, all packed in a cellophane envelope w/a sticker reading "Salem Chem-
ical Mfg. Co." **8-12**

Pin-up Girl Feathered Ribbon Doll

Pin-up girl, blonde hair, wearing a short
dark blue feather dress, silver apron &
headpiece, light blue feathers fanning out
behind her head, against a black background & in a vintage oval frame,
10 1/2 x 13 1/2" (ILLUS.)............................ **60-80**

Set: boy & girl; the girl in red ribbon dress &
hat w/lace & multicolored ribbon flower
trim & green bow at neck, the boy in grey
trousers & mauve shirt w/lace collar,
holding multicolored ribbon flower bouquet w/ribbon streamers, each 3 1/2" h.
.... **95-125**

Southern Belle, in pale pink satin w/black
velvet & ivory lace trim, wearing matching
bonnet decorated w/white feathers & carrying coordinating parasol, 12 1/2"
w x 16" h. (ILLUS., top next column)......... **60-75**

Spanish dancer, black-haired woman
wearing a dress of silver-trimmed white
ribbon w/a matching ribbon sash, beige
lace petticoat, yellow beads over one
shoulder, holding a large lace fan behind
her head, her other hand on her hip,
9 x 11" **110-150**

Woman, black hair, wearing a red dress &
matching hat, her arms extended,
9 1/2 x 11" **65-75**

Woman, blonde hair, black ribbon dress
w/white ribbon petticoat, flaring skirt re-
veals legs, 9 1/4" h. **75-100**

Southern Belle Carrying Parasol

Woman, blonde hair, wearing a peach
feather skirt & waving a matching feather
fan, topless w/pasties tassels, 10 x 15" .. **85-100**

Ribbon Doll with Lacy Outfit

Woman, blonde in gold ribbon dress w/lace
overlay, pale pink & green ribbon streamers around waist, matching hat, holding
lace encircled bouquet, 11" w. x 13" h.,
(ILLUS.).. **45-65**

Woman with Garland in Her Hair

Woman in Pink Dress & Bonnet Standing Among Flowers

Woman, brown hair, ribbon roses garland on her head, wearing pink layered ribbon dress w/lace pantalettes & matching lace around her waist, shoulders & bouquet, 9" w. x 11" h. (ILLUS., bottom previous page) **45-55**

Woman, brunette hair, wearing a rose-colored layered ribbon dress, large pale pink bow at waist, pale pink streamer around her neck w/a trailing matching hat adorned w/multi-colored flowers, on a black background decorated w/three-dimensional colored flowers & leaves, in a tray frame, 11 x 15 1/2" (ILLUS., top of page) **85-95**

Woman, front-view, her hair in red banana curls, wearing a beige lace dress, pink pillbox hat w/a black veil, purple ribbon sash, streamers & flower buds on the dress, 5 x 7 1/2" **55-65**

Woman, full-face pose, white hair, wearing a pink ruffled dress w/pink & green lace trim at the hem, a black velvet sash w/pink & green flowers, pink lace at shoulders w/green lace & net shawl, 11 x 13" **85-100**

Woman, full-skirted woman in ivory lace dress, trimmed in pink satin ribbon, w/large pink satin bow in back, carrying pastel rose ribbon bouquet, wearing matching pink satin cap, trimmed in ivory lace & pastel rose ribbons, 9" w. x 11" h. (ILLUS., next column) **45-65**

Woman, her hair in red sausage curls, wearing a white satin ribbon dress & hat, black velvet streamers at waist, lace trim around pink ribbon bouquet, lace trim on head, wearing high heals, 8 1/2 x 10 1/2" **50-60**

Woman, in bright orange dress trimmed in lace w/complimenting orange & yellow large brimmed hat, 8 3/4" w. 10 3/4" h. (ILLUS., bottom next column) **30-40**

Woman Carrying Ribbon Bouquet

Woman in Bright Orange Dress

Young Woman With Lampshade Hat

Young woman, pink satin dress w/black satin bow & streamers at waist, trimmed in ecru lace w/matching pantaloons & shoes, w/coordinating "lampshade hat," 9" w. x 11" h. (ILLUS.) **45-55**

RUGS - HOOKED & OTHER

Hooked

Cherries & leaves, long rectangular form, a central row of large red cherries & green leaves against a mottled brown ground, large angled leaves in each corner, late 19th c., 25 1/2 x 37 3/4" (three areas of patched reinforcements on reverse) **$823**

Long Dining Table Setting Hooked Rug

Dining table setting, long narrow rectangular form, depicting a folky design of a din-

ing room table top set w/plates, cups & saucers, a platter, water pitcher & teapot, in shades of maroon, dark blue, yellow & brown on a tan ground w/maroon end sections, olive green burlap backing, late 19th - early 20th c., 36 x 88" (ILLUS.) **2,990**

Floral vines & grapes, round, a center pink & red floral bouquet surrounded by a meandering vine w/pink & red flowers, green leaves & purple grape clusters against a light tan ground, green wool felt binding, woven tan cotton backing, 19th c., 42" d. . **1,293**

Long Flowers & Scrolls Hooked Rug

Florals, long rectangular form w/a central design of large red & dark gold flowers w/green leaves surrounded by black leafy scrolls outlined in red, smaller white, blue & red flowers at the ends, on a shaded tan ground, stabilized w/a burlap backing, late 19th c., small area of fabric loss, 33 1/2 x 66" (ILLUS.) **470**

Geometric, long cotton & wool runner w/a central design of a band of large colorful diamonds framed w/a border of colored stepped pyramidal blocks, dark brown ground, late 19th - early 20th c., 35 3/4 x 77 3/4" (ILLUS., top next page) **1,434**

Washington on Horseback Hooked Rug

Long Hooked Geometric Runner

George Washington on horseback, a large colorful central design of Washington in uniform on a white stallion, a banner below reading "Father of His Country," flanked by dark maroon stage curtains, dark tan background, late 19th - early 20th c., 35 x 48" (ILLUS.) **2,185**

Unusual Rug with Two Squirrels

Squirrels, two large facing seated brown squirrels on a black band against a grey background, narrow black border, small section of one squirrel missing material, 36" sq. (ILLUS.) **900**

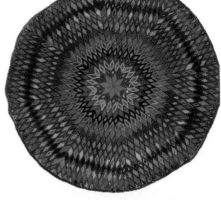

Fine Large Round Starburst Rug

Starburst, large circular form composed of radiating bands of multicolored diamond-shaped segments & a central red eight-point star, applied wool braided edge, possibly Shaker, 19th c., some wear, 79" d. (ILLUS.) **5,875**

Rare Maine Village Scene Hooked Rug

Village landscape, long rectangular form, worked in a variety of solid & mottled wool & cotton threads depicting the town of East Machias, Maine, hooked by Catherine Walker, White House Station, New Jersey, 35 1/2 x 65" (ILLUS.) **5,378**

SCIENTIFIC INSTRUMENTS
Barometers
Stick-type

Simmons & Company Barometer

American, Simmons & Company, long narrow rectangular case w/ripple or piecrust
border, Fenton, New York, 19th c.
(ILLUS.).. **$950**

Admiral Fitzroy Polytechnic Barometer

English, Admiral Fitzroy-type, marked on
upper dial "Royal Polytechnic Barometer," top-of-the-line model, one of 12
types (ILLUS.)... **3,800**

Adie Rosewood Barometer

English, Adie, rosewood case w/stepped
cornice, double vernier (ILLUS.) **3,500**

Mason of Dublin Stick Barometer

English, bow-front case w/beveled glass, double vernier, Mason of Dublin (ILLUS.) **3,800-4,000**

Cremonini-Wolverhampton Model

English, Cremonini-Wolverhampton, dark oak case w/angled pediment centered by an urn finial above freestanding columns flanking the central thermometer over the lower case w/a large round dial (ILLUS.) .. **1,800**

Fortin or Kew-type Barometer

English, Fortin or Kew or laboratory-type, long wooden board w/milk glass inset at top (ILLUS.) **1,000**

Wheel-type

French, wheel-type, boulle-work tortoiseshell inlay, a shaped case decorated w/scrolling floral brass inlay, F. Lesage, Paris, France, 19th c., 11" w., 28" h. (some chips to shell, some loose or missing brass) **748**

SCOUTING MEMORABILIA

Boy Scouts

Early Boy Scout Bicycle Bell

Bicycle bell, round nickel-plated handlebar-mounted style, the top w/an embossed bust of a Boy Scout & the words "Be Prepared," some minor pitting, early 20th c., 2 1/2" d. (ILLUS.) **$120**

Early Boy Scout Story Book

Book, "The Boy Scouts at the Panama-Pacific Exposition," by Lieut. Howard Payson, 1915, hard covers, good condition (ILLUS.).. **10**

Boxed Set of Early Boy Scout Figures

Figure set, group of 42 die-cut Boy Scout figures on wooden bases, in original colorful box w/large scene of a Boy Scout camp on the front, McLoughlin Brothers, Set 5855, early 20th c., the set (ILLUS., previous page) **127**

Girl Scouts

Early Girl Scout Lunch Pail

Lunch pail, printed steel, rectangular w/rounded corners & twin strap swing bail handles, dark brown ground printed in tan w/scenes of girls involved in activities including swimming, tennis & basketball as well as two girls in Scout uniforms, ca. 1930s, 5 1/4 x 7 1/4", 4" h. (ILLUS.)... **89**

SCRIMSHAW

Scrimshaw is a folk art byproduct of the 19th century American whaling industry. Intricately carved and engraved pieces of whalebone, whale's teeth and walrus tusks were produced by whalers during their spare time at sea. In recent years numerous fine grade hard plastic reproductions have appeared on the market, so the novice collector must use caution to distinguish these from the rare originals.

Box, cov., whalebone & mahogany, the oval flat mahogany lid w/a whalebone rim above a conforming bone box w/swing bail handle, the sides decorated w/a whaling scene, encloses a whaling scene pocket mirror, America, early 20th c., box 6 x 8", w/handle 10" h. **$2,032**

Corset busk, long narrow flat form w/rounded ends, decorated w/two ships flying the American flag, a sailor, a wreath w/inscription & an American eagle w/shield & banner inscribed "Don't Give Up the Ship," America, 19th c., 12 1/2" l. **4,183**

Ditty box, cov., rectangular w/flat sliding lid, composed of six pieces of panbone, the top engraved w/a three-masted ship under full sail & flying an American flag, the four sides engraved w/spouting whales &

whaling scenes, America, late 19th c., 5 1/4" l., 2 3/4" h....................................... **3,824**

Pie crimper, a flattened handle intricately pierced w/small diamonds & heart designs, a fan-carved round wheel, America, 19th c., 7 1/2" l. **956**

Whale teeth, one engraved & trimmed in polychrome w/a portrait of a standing man wearing a cape, the other w/a half-length portrait of a woman in fancy Victorian dress holding a fan, probably American, second half 19th c., each 4 1/2" l., pr.. **1,793**

Whale tooth, engraved & highlighted in polychrome w/a three-masted ship w/detailed rigging & an American flag on one side, a figure of a woman in fancy dress on the other side, America, 19th c., 8" l. (small chip on tip, base cracks)................ **7,768**

Whale tooth, engraved & trimmed in polychrome on one side w/a scene of a young girl wearing a hat & placing spectacles on her dog, the other side w/a three-quarters length portrait of a young Victorian woman in fancy dress, America, mid-19th c., 6 1/4" l... **5,736**

Whale tooth, engraved & trimmed in polychrome w/a standing figure of a young sailor w/a blue jacket, his arms folded in front, probably American, 19th c., 6 1/8" l... **3,346**

Whale tooth, etched on both sides w/large bust portraits of lovely Victorian ladies in fancy dress, the tip carved into the form of a whale or porpoise head w/red tongue, America, 19th c., 6 1/4" l. **1,673**

Whale tooth, etched on one side w/a bust portrait of George Washington & on the other w/a woman in fancy dress wearing a red hat & belt, America, 19th c., 7" l. **5,378**

Whale tooth, one side etched w/a large spread-winged eagle clutching branches & arrows in its talons & a banner in its beak reading "E Pluribus Unum," the back engraved w/a three-masted sailing ship in calm waters, America, 19th c., 6" l... **3,107**

SEWING ADJUNCTS

For years, sewing tools have been very popular collectibles. With so many shapes, sizes and forms to hunt for, collectors have enjoyed the wide variety available. Many originated in England and Europe, but collectors can easily find American antique sewing tools also. Reproductions have been made of pincushions, thimbles, thimble holders and several other kinds of sewing items, so new collectors need to determine they are paying for genuine vintage tools when buying. A good book - now out-of-print - is "An Illustrated History of Needlework Tools" by Gay Ann Rogers. Other good sewing tool reference books are available and not hard to find through your favorite bookseller or on-line - all are invaluable to a collector interested in building a collection.

Victorian White Metal Chatelaine

Chatelaine, white metal, four-section w/thimble basket, tape measure, scissors holder & pin disc, France, late 19th c. (ILLUS.) **$695**

Crochet hook, bone end with long wood handle, England, 19th c. **55**

Crochet hook, bone with turned design, American, late 19th c. **10**

Crochet hook, set of four, Susan Bates, American, 1930s **25**

Darner, blue glass, American, early 20th c. **50**

Darner, large ebonized wood egg form w/repousse sterling handle, America, ca. 1900 .... **65**

Darner, large egg form, checkerboard style, maple, cherry, walnut, marked "Germany," ca. 1900 .... **75**

Darner, rare Peach Blow Glass, 19th c. **195**

Darner, wood w/marbleized paint, America, 1920s **30**

Emery, double strawberries with beaded seeds, ca. 1920s **65**

Emery, double-ended vegetable ivory, ornately carved, 1870s **95**

Emery, make-do, large velvet strawberry form on glass base with multiple hanging smaller strawberries, America, 19th c. **950**

Emery, pedestal style with waxer base, vegetable ivory, simple style, 1880s **135**

Emery, tomato form in orange fabric w/plaid design, Japan, 1950s **20**

Hemming gauge, sterling, Art Nouveau florals, America, unmarked, ca. 1900 .... **160**

Knitting needle case, Mauchline Ware, w/Shakespeare's home in black transfer, Scottish, 1870s... **165**

Knitting needle point guards, sterling, simple style, England, 19th c. **255**

Knitting needles, red, white & blue plastic, America, WWII era, uncommon **30**

Knitting needles, steel, very fine, America, ca. 1900 .... **15**

Nanny's pin, brass with goldstone, England, 19th c. **185**

Needle book, beaded floral design with interior flannel leaves, England, late 19th c. **85**

Needle book, Mauchline Ware, w/English port scene in black transfer, Scottish, 1870s **145**

Needle book, picture under glass of church, English, 1870s-80s **175**

Needle case, Avery, brass, figural wheelbarrow, English, 19th c. **595**

Needle case, blue mitralleuse cylinder, English, 1890s... **65**

Needle case, bone w/Stanhope, umbrella form, English, 19th c. **165**

Needle case, bone w/steel inlaid design, English, 19th c. **110**

Needle case, celluloid, American, 1930s........... **40**

Needle case, ivory, The Fisherwoman, 19th c., rare **650**

Needle case, rolling pin form, made of wood, early 20th c.. **55**

Needle case, sterling, Art Nouveau florals, American, 1890s.. **175**

Needle case, vegetable ivory, ornately carved, 19th c. **95**

Needlework kit, Shaker, leather sewing roll, large, w/sewing tools, ca. 1900 .... **210**

Pin disc, linen fabric with handstitched floral design, 19th c., 2" d. **55**

Pin roll, Shaker, leather, 3" x 5", ca. 1900 .... **175**

Figural Bisque Pincushion

Pincushion, bisque, model of a rabbit pulling a cart, cloth pincushion in the cart, ca. 1900 (ILLUS.).. **120**

Ceramic Pincushion Dog

Pincushion, ceramic dog with cushion in back, Japan, 1950s (ILLUS.) **25**

Pincushion, handmade folk art cat of fabric
with painted details, American, 1920s 95
Pincushion, large heart shape, crocheted
exterior over satin, American, 1930s 15

Blue Glass Base Pincushion

Pincushion, made-do, blue glass base, red
& tan sections of fabric, late 1800s
(ILLUS.) 245
Pincushion, vegetable ivory, carved pedes-
tal form with original velvet top, 1880s 155
Scissors, ornate floral sterling w/matching
sheath, English, ca. 1850 250
Scissors, sterling, Art Deco design, Ameri-
can, 1930s 65
Scissors, sterling, in fitted case w/matching
thimble, Charles Horner, English, 19th c 195
Scissors, sterling, small, floral, unmarked,
American, 1880s 55
Sewing basket, bentwood, four-fingered
oval, Shaker, w/handle, also pincushion,
thimbleholder, 1920s 695
Sewing bird clamp, brass w/pincushion,
American, 19th c. 265
Sewing bird clamp, simple steel form,
American, 19th c. 195
Sewing box, bentwood, three fingered-lap,
Shaker, oval, w/handle, includes pin-
cushion, interior silk linen, marked "Sab-
bathday Lake," 20th c 485
Sewing box, burl walnut w/cut steel decora-
tion on top, fitted interior w/complete im-
plements, Palais Royale ca. 1820 3,500

Brass Egg-shaped Sewing Kit

Sewing kit, brass, egg-shaped, engraved
scrolling decoration, w/thread, needle
holder & thimble, heavy, England, ca.
1900 (ILLUS.) 48
Sewing kit, French enamel on sterling,
glass top thimble, early 20th c 250

Sewing kit, ivory, fitted style w/gilt scissors
& matching thimble, French, 1820s 725
Sewing ruler, Mauchline Fernware,
w/marking pencil stored inside, Scottish,
1870s 165
Sewing trade card, Domestic Sewing Ma-
chines, horse, "Rochester," early 1900s 20
Sewing trade card, Domestic Sewing Machines, woman at treadle machine, ca.
1900 18
Sewing trade card, J & P Coats Six Cord
thread, 2 comical women w/greyhound
and pug, 19th c. 22
Sewing trade card, Singer, woman seated
at treadle machine, early 1900s 15
Sewing trade card, Standard Rotary Shuttle Sewing Machine, word puzzle
style, ca. 1890s 20
Spool rack, whalebone, ivory & hardwood,
the central ivory finial above two rotating
tiers of whalebone & lignum vitae spools
& spool holders, on a turned lignum vitae
base w/ivory ball feet, America, 19th c.,
9 1/4" h 837
Stiletto, lathe turned bone, 3" long, 19th c. 12
Stiletto, ornate gilt on sterling design,
French, 19th c. 95
Tambour hook, turned ivory handle w/four
different steel points, English, 19th c. 150
Tape measure, celluloid fish, 1930s, Japan 135
Tape measure, celluloid sitting dog, 1930s,
unmarked 125
Tape measure, metal & celluloid clock, Ger-
many, 1920s 185
Tape measure, spring-loaded disc-style
w/Niagara Falls scene, American, 1920s 45

Vegetable Ivory Tape Measure

Tape measure, vegetable ivory, barrel form
w/original silk tape, English, 1860s
(ILLUS.) 110

Tape Measure with Cat's Face

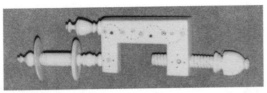

Ivory Winding Clamp

Tape measure, white metal, round, an embossed cat's face featuring green rhinestone eyes, marked "Germany," ca. 1900 (ILLUS., previous page) 110

Barrel-shaped Tape Measure

Tape measure, wooden, model of a barrel, manual-wind, English, 1860s (ILLUS.)......... 175

Tatting shuttle, carved horn w/inlaid mother of pearl, ca. 1900 95

Tatting shuttle, copper w/etched design, unusual, ca. 1900.. 85

Tatting shuttle, pink celluloid, American, 1930s 25

Tatting shuttle, Tartanware, Scottish, 1870s 350

Thimble, gold, Louis XV-style scrolled rim, Simons, American, 1920s 195

Thimble, Jasperware by Wedgwood, pink, English, 1980s.. 95

Thimble, sterling, Colombian Exposition souvenir, 1893.. 575

Thimble, sterling over steel, Charles Horner, in original velvet thimble box, English, 19th c. 95

Thimble, sterling, palmate design on band, unmarked, American, 1920s 45

Thimble, sterling, Simons Bros., "A Stitch in Times Saves Nine," American, unmarked 495

Thimble, sterling w/rings on band, amber glass top, unmarked, American, early 20th c. 110

Thimble, sterling w/steel top, early 1800s, American, unmarked.................................... 125

Thimble box, Mauchline Ware, Scottish, 1870s 185

Thimble holder, acorn-form, 18k gold, American, 19th c. 250

Thimble holder, cylinder shape, Tartanware plaid, Scottish, 19th c. 245

Thimble holder, egg-shaped Mauchline Ware, Scottish, 1870s................................. 225

Thimble holder, vegetable ivory acorn form w/matching thimble, 19th c. 195

Thimble holder, velvet shoe-form, English, 19th c. 135

Thread box, Mauchline Ware, florals w/transfer of Scottish village, 19th c. 195

Thread reel for multiple spools, Shaker, walnut, 6" tall w/top pincushion, 1880s 450

Thread stand, carved Black Forest bear, Austrian or German, 1890-1930s................ 295

Thread winder, bone, pillow-shaped, English, 1840s.. 40

Thread winder, bone, snowflake-style, English, 1850s.. 55

Thread winders, celluloid, set of six in multiple colors, American, 1920s........................ 45

Winding clamp, carved ivory, spool top w/netting knob, Asia, ca. 1840 (ILLUS., top of page).. 365

SHAKER ITEMS

The Shakers, a religious sect founded by Ann Lee, first settled in this country at Watervliet, New York, near Albany, in 1774. By 1880 there were nine settlements in America. Workmanship in Shaker crafts is an extension of their religious beliefs and features plain and simple designs reflecting a chaste elegance that is now much in demand though relatively few early items are common.

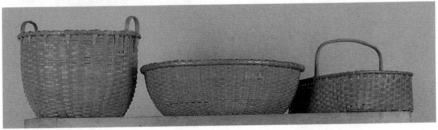

Row of Three Early Shaker Baskets

Basket, woven splint, round w/a flat bottom & wrapped single-lashed rim, probably New Hampshire or Maine, 19th c., 25 5/8" d., 8 1/4" h. (ILLUS. center with two other Shaker baskets, bottom previous page) **$705**

Basket, woven splint, low rectangular form w/slightly canted sides, single lashing on rim & arched upright bentwood handle, probably New Hampshire or Maine, 19th c., some wear, 13 1/4 x 21 1/2", 12 1/4" h. (ILLUS. left with two other Shaker baskets, bottom previous page)....... **235**

Basket, woven splint, deep round sides w/a domed base, bentwood rim handles, double lashing around the rim, vertical spokes alternately cut-out & turned down on the exterior, minor breaks & losses, 19th c., 19 3/8" d., 15 5/8" h. (ILLUS. right with two other Shaker baskets, bottom previous page) **118**

Rare Painted Shaker Bucket

Bucket, three belted wooden staves down the sides w/two raised tabs holding the bentwood handles, original wooden pegs remain through the handle, old dry green exterior paint & white on the interior, black initials stenciled on the base, attributed to the Enfield, New Hampshire, Community, 11 3/4" h. (ILLUS.) **7,188**

Early Shaker Painted Butter Churn

Butter churn, pine stave construction w/iron hoops, wooden cover & pine dasher w/maple handle, painted blue, Alfred, Maine, 19th c., imperfections, overall 46" h. (ILLUS.) **353**

Mt. Lebanon Shaker Lowback Chair

Chair, lowback style, original black finish w/gold stenciled label, tapered legs & rear posts w/small domed finials, old replaced tape seat w/minor warp to one foot, Mt. Lebanon Community, overall 28" h. (ILLUS.) **604**

Early Pine Shaker Steps

Steps, stained pine, three risers on one-board shaped sides w/angled flat rear legs, flat stretchers & an X-form back brace, old dark surface, probably Enfield, Connecticut, 1830-50, 18 3/8 x 22 1/4", 30 1/4" h. (ILLUS.) **3,819**

Large Cherry Shaker Trestle Table

Stack of Bentwood Shaker Boxes

Storage box, cov., oval bentwood, old natural finish w/two-finger lapped construction & copper tacks, illegible writing on lid in brown ink, rare size, 3 3/4" l. (ILLUS. top of stack of Shaker storage boxes).......... **633**

Storage box, cov., oval bentwood, old natural finish w/two-finger lapped construction & copper tacks, 6" l. (ILLUS. second from top of stack of Shaker storage boxes).. **460**

Storage box, cov., oval bentwood, old natural finish w/thin coat of varnish, three-finger lapped construction & copper tacks, 9" l. (ILLUS. third from top of stack of Shaker storage boxes)............................. **403**

Storage box, cov., oval bentwood, old golden brown finish, three-finger lapped con-

struction & copper tacks, slight loss to lower edge on side of cover, 11" l. (ILLUS. fourth from top of stack of Shaker storage boxes).. **690**

Storage box, cov., oval bentwood, old natural finish, four-finger lapped construction & copper tacks, 13 1/2" l. (ILLUS. bottom of stack of Shaker storage boxes)
.... **1,093**

Table, trestle type, cherry, the large rectangular two-board top supported by through-tenoned vertical members ending in arched feet w/pointed toes, restored, Harvard or Shirley, Massachusetts, Community, ca. 1830, 30 1/2 x 72", 28 1/2" h. (ILLUS., top of page) **4,406**

SIGNS & SIGNBOARDS

Willys-Overland Whippet Sign

Automobile, "Whippet Automobile," tin, red w/embossed gold letters reading "Dollar for Dollar Value - Whippet - Product of - Willys-Overland Company," by M.C.A. Sign Company, Massillon, Ohio, wood frame, ca. 1920s, 15 x 25" (ILLUS.).... **$200-275**

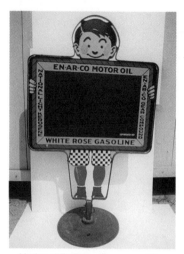

National Refining Company Sign

Automotive, "National Refining Co.," two-sided lithographed tin, curb-type on signed iron base, figure of boy wearing black & white checked knee pants & red stockings holding rectangular black sign w/red border & yellow border w/black letters reading "En-Ar-Co Motor Oil - En-Ar-Co Gear Compound - White Rose Gasoline - National Light Kerosene," litho by Mathews Ind. Inc., Detroit, Michigan, ca. 1917, 27 3/4 x 45" (ILLUS.).............. **3000-4500**

Anheuser-Busch Malt Nutrine Sign

Baby formula, "Malt Nutrine," rectangular, self-framed tin w/cardboard back, depicts a stork carrying in its beak two bottles tied together & flying over a man w/a raised whip in a carriage pulled by a racing white horse, titled "A Hurry Call," frame marked "Malt Nutrine," Anheuser-Busch Brewing Company, St. Louis, Missouri, ca. 1915, 7 1/2 x 12 1/2" (ILLUS.)........................ **250-350**

Baby formula, "Malt Nutrine," rectangular, self-framed tin w/cardboard back, scene of a doctor dressed in black carrying his bag & an umbrella up the lane towards a house in the distance, his shadow cast in the form of a stork, titled "Coming Events...," Anheuser-Busch Brewing Company, St. Louis, Missouri, ca. 1915, 7 1/2 x 12 1/2" (ILLUS., top next column)
.... **250-350**

Malt Nutrine Sign "Coming Events... "

Pabst Blue Ribbon Beer Sign, Ca. 1938

Beer, "Pabst Blue Ribbon Beer," rectangular cardboard, scene of African-American in waiter's uniform, one hand holding a tray of bottles & glasses, reads "Quality - Yes - Suh-h," ca. 1938, Pabst Brewing Company, Milwaukee, Wisconsin, 24 x 34" (ILLUS.) **450-600**

Pabst Blue Ribbon Beer Sign, Ca. 1933

Beer, "Pabst Blue Ribbon Beer," rectangular cardboard, smiling elderly gentleman pouring beer from a bottle into a glass, reads "Pabst Blue Ribbon - The Beer of Quality," ca. 1933, Pabst Brewing Company, Milwaukee, Wisconsin, 20 x 25 1/2" (ILLUS., bottom previous page) **300-379**

Framed Pabst Blue Ribbon Beer Sign

Beer, "Pabst Blue Ribbon Beer," rectangular color lithograph scene of two bottles w/blue ribbons tied around the necks, a filled glass & a plate of oysters, signed wood frame, ca. 1920s, Pabst Brewing Company, Milwaukee, Wisconsin, 22 x 25 1/2" (ILLUS.)............................. **300-450**

Ziegler's Beer Sign

Beer, "Ziegler's Beer," rectangular tin w/cardboard back, black w/bottle on right, white & white outlined w/red lettering reading "Drink Ziegler's Beer - Beaver Dam, Wisconsin," ca. 1920s, 8 1/4 x 11 1/2" (ILLUS.)......................... **200-275**

Cook's Beer & Ale Sign

Beer & ale, "Cook's Beer and Ale," tin, oval blue center w/hand holding a bottle of beer & a bottle of ale, self-framed brown border marked at the top "Cook's Goldblume" & at the bottom "Beer and Ale," F.W. Cook Company, Evansville, Indiana, ca. 1920, 14 x 17 1/2" (ILLUS.) **225-300**

Packard Cable Sign

Cable, "Packard Cable," rectangular paper, lake scene of young girl dressed in red sitting on post w/attached cable marked "Tie To Packard Cable," wood frame, ca. 1900, 18 1/2 x 25 1/2" (ILLUS.) **400-600**

Wrigley's P.K. Gum Trolley Sign

Chewing gum, "Wrigley's P.K. Gum," rectangular cardboard, trolley-type, black background w/hand open & holding three packages of gum, yellow, white & black lettering reading "Wrigley's P.K. New Handy Pack - 3 Packs 5¢ - Sugar Coated Chewing Sweet Peppermint Flavor," wood frame, ca. 1928, 11 3/4 x 22" (ILLUS.) **650-750**

Hoffmanettes Cigars Sign

Cigars, "Hoffmanettes Cigars," rectangular cardboard, scene of two men leaning out of a window to see a man standing below & smoking a cigarette, reads "'It's up to you' - Smoke - Hoffmanettes 5¢ Cigar - The Hilson Co. Makers - New York," wood frame, ca. 1900, 15 1/2 x 21 1/2" (ILLUS.) **450-650**

Cigars, "La Venga Cigars," rectangular, reverse-painting on glass, black w/logo in center flanked by embossed brass scrolls, "La Venga" above & "Havana Cigars - Celestino Vega & Co. Tampa, Fla." below, wood frame, ca. 1910, 20 1/2 x 26 1/2" (ILLUS., top next column) **400-600**

La Venga Cigars Sign

Optimo Cigars Sign

Cigars, "Optimo Cigars," rectangular tin w/center oval depicting bust of man w/mustache & wearing hat, tie & coat w/colorful tropical scene in background, reads "Optimo - Mild - Aromatic - Sweet," wood frame, ca. 1910, 23 x 27" (ILLUS.) **550-700**

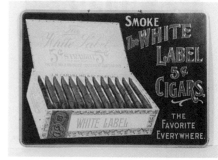

White Label Cigars Sign, Ca. 1900

Cigars, "White Label Cigars," rectangular tin, black w/lithographed image of white box containing cigars on the left, right side marked in yellow "Smoke - The Favorite Everywhere," green embossed letters outlined in yellow reading "The White Label 5¢ Cigars," litho by Sentenne & Green, New York, ca. 1900, 9 1/2 x 14" (ILLUS.) **250-325**

Framed Chase & Sanborn Coffee Sign

Coffee, "Chase & Sanborn Coffee," rectangular paper, scene of four older men sitting around an old round heating stove, dog lying nearby, the shopkeeper in the background, titled "An Old Fashioned New England Grocery" & "Compliments of Chase & Sanborn," signed mat & wood frame, Chase & Sanborn, Boston, Massachusetts, ca. 1897, 22 1/2 x 24 1/2" (ILLUS.)........................ **600-750**

De Laval Cream Separators Sign

Cream separator, "DeLaval Cream Separator," lithographed tin on wood, rectangular, center oval reserve depicting milk maid & cow flanked by four colorful farm scene vignettes featuring the separator, red background w/yellow letters reading "De Laval Cream Separators - Save $10 to $15 Per Cow Every Year of Use - 1,750,000 in Use" & marked below center image "The De Laval Separator Company" w/several locations listed at bottom, ornate gold Victorian-style frame w/"DeLaval" tag on bot-

tom edge, ca. 1910, 29 1/2 x 40 1/2" (ILLUS.)... **4,000-5,000**

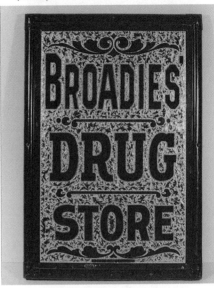

Broadies' Drug Store Sign

Drugstore, "Broadies' Drug Store," rectangular, reverse-painting on glass, gold leaf on glue chip glass, scroll decoration, copper frame, ca. 1890, 17 1/2 x 25 1/2" (ILLUS.) **1,000-1,400**

Paper Sign Advertising Farm Machinery

Farm machinery, paper, rectangular, chromolithograph of woman holding scythe & bundle of wheat amid circular insets showing scenes of farm machinery harvesting wheat, "Adriance Buckeye Harvesting Machinery" at top, "Adriance, Platt & Co. - Poughkeepsie, New York USA" at bottom, ca. 1890s, 20 x 26" (ILLUS. in old original frame) **1,323**

E.D. Pinaud's Hair Dressing Sign

Hair dressing, "E.D. Pinaud's Eau de Quinine," rectangular tin, bottle in center flanked by embossed florals, w/"Use Only The Genuine - E.D. Pinaud's" above & "Eau de Quinine - An Ideal Hairdressing" below, wood frame, ca. 1900, 17 1/2 x 23" (ILLUS.)............................ **250-350**

Van Camp Hardware Flange Sign

Hardware, "Van Camp Hardware," round die-cut tin, flange-type, blue & white w/center image of windmill under large red letters reading "Van Camp - Trade Mark" & white letters around border reading "Highest Grade - Van Camp Hardware & Iron Co. Indianapolis, Ind." & blue letters on flange reading "Goods Bearing This Trade-Mark Are Of The Highest Quality," litho by New York Metal Sign Works, New York, ca. 1890, 13 1/2 x 18" (ILLUS.)... **650-750**

Hose supporters, "Foster Hose Supporters," rectangular, porcelain over cardboard, image of corset & hose supporters & woman wearing red skirt & green blouse, reads "The Foster Hose Supporters - 'The Name is on the buckles,'" litho by F.F. Pulver Co., Rochester, New York, ca. 1890, 9 x 17" (ILLUS., top next column) **900-1,200**

Foster Hose Supporters Sign

City of New York Insurance Co. Sign

Insurance, "City of New York Insurance Company," rectangular, reverse-painted glass w/"City of New York - Insurance Company - Fire" above & below oval sepia scene of New York City flanked by embossed brass scrolls, wood frame, ca. 1920s, 21 1/2 x 30" (ILLUS.)................. **500-650**

Traders Insurance Company Sign

Insurance, "Traders Insurance Company," rectangular tin, lithograph by Charles Shonk, black w/gold lettering reading "The Traders Insurance Co. Chicago," wood frame, ca. 1910, 17 x 23" (ILLUS.)
.... **325-425**

Houbigant Perfume Sign

Perfume, "Houbigant Parfums," rectangular, paper on cardboard, scene of young woman standing at an open window & holding & smelling blossoms on vine beside the window shutter, mat marked "Parfums Houbigant - Paris," ornate frame, ca. 1920s, 16 1/2 x 20 1/2" (ILLUS.) **300-400**

Chicago & Alton Railroad Sign

Railroad, "Chicago & Alton Railroad," rectangular, paper & cardboard w/hand-colored photographs, the center showing an engine & freight car w/"Chicago & Alton R.R. - 'The Only Way,'" in white letters below & w/a photograph on the left of a passenger car interior & on the right an interior photograph of the dining car, wood frame, ca. 1910, 15 x 39" (ILLUS.) **635-775**

Grand Trunk Pacific Railway Photo

Railroad, "Grand Trunk Pacific Railway," duo-tone photograph titled "Moose Lake British Columbia," signed mat & frame, ca. 1900, 28 1/2 x 35" (ILLUS.) **650-750**

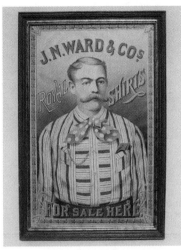

J.N. Ward & Co. Shirt Sign

Shirts, "J.N. Ward & Co. Shirts," rectangular, lithographed paper on cardboard, depicts man wearing blue & white striped shirt, blue & white polka dot tie, red & white letters read "J.N. Ward & Cos. Royal Shirts - For Sale Here," wood frame, litho by J.W. Frank & Sons, Peoria, Illinois, ca. 1880, 14 x 21" (ILLUS.) **500-750**

Red Goose Embossed Celluloid Sign

Shoes, "Red Goose Shoes," embossed die-cut w/molded celluloid goose body, easel-back, marked "Red Goose Shoes," flanked by running schoolgirl & schoolboy w/books, marked at the bottom "They're Half the Fun of Having Feet," ca. 1910, Friedman-Shelby Shoes, 11 x 13 1/2" (ILLUS.) **900-1,300**

Cherry Blush Sign

Soft drink, "Cherry Blush," rectangular tin w/cardboard back, black w/bunch of cherries & leaves & "Cherry Blush" in white outlined in red in center, red lettering above w/"Drink" & green lettering at bottom reading "Cherries Only Rival," ca. 1900, 6 1/4 x 9" (ILLUS.)...................... **750-900**

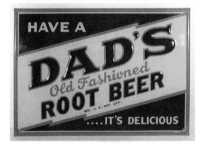

Dad's Root Beer Sign

Soft drink, "Dad's Root Beer," rectangular tin, black & yellow w/embossed lettering in black outlined in red, "Have A Dad's Old Fashioned Root Beer ....It's Delicious," ca. 1950s, 19 x 27" (ILLUS.)....................... **250-375**

Green Spot Orange-Ade Sign

Soft drink, "Green Spot Orange-Ade," rectangular cardboard, young woman remov-

ing a bottle from ice-filled cooler, reads "Thirsty?," cooler marked "Ice Cold - Green Spot - Orange-Ade 5¢," ca. 1920s, 23 x 33" (ILLUS.) **150-250**

Hires Root Beer Sign

Soft drink, "Hires Root Beer," rectangular tin, flange-type, green w/yellow & black lettering reading "Hires - Made with Roots - Barks - Herbs - So Refreshing," ca. 1940s, 12 x 14" (ILLUS.) **225-300**

Nehi Sign

Soft drink, "Nehi," rectangular cardboard w/easel back, outdoor scene of two boys running, reads "Hey Gang! Mom's Treating Us to Nehi - in Your Favorite Flavor," ca. 1930, 26 x 39" (ILLUS.) **550-750**

Orange-Julep Paper Sign

Soft drink, "Orange-Julep," rectangular paper, black w/yellow lettering outlined in red, "Drink - In Bottles - At Fountains -

How's Orange-Julep - The Perfection of Orange Drinks," wood frame, ca. 1915, 12 x 30 1/2" (ILLUS.)............................. **200-250**

International Stock Food Co. Sign

Stock food, "International Stock Food Company," rectangular paper, scene of pacer horse "Dan Patch" & jockey, information on horse at lower left, marked at bottom "Dan Patch 1:55 - Owned by International Stock Food Co., Minneapolis, Minn.," wood frame, ca. 1910, 20 x 27 1/2" (ILLUS.)........................... **300-450**

Garland Stoves Sign

Stove, "Garland Stoves," square tin, curved corner-type, porcelain on tin, white w/black logo printed "Garland Stoves and Ranges" w/banner at bottom marked "'The World's Best,'" B.S. Co., State St., Chicago, Illinois, 24 x 24" (ILLUS.) **1,500-2,100**

Stove, "Peninsular," rectangular tin, curved corner-type, porcelain on tin, black w/white image of double eagle heads & wings over shield shape formed w/bars & chain links reading "'Peninsular' - Furnaces - Stoves and Ranges" w/"Warrant-

ed - The Best" on banner at the bottom, made by B.S. Co., State St., Chicago, Illinois, ca. 1890, 18 x 24" (ILLUS.) **1,500-2,100**

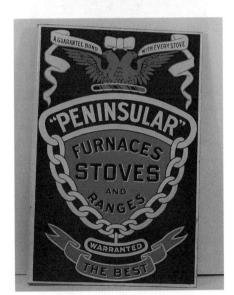

Peninsular Stoves Sign

Peninsular Stoves Flange-type Sign

Stove, "'Peninsular Stoves,'" rectangular, flange-type, porcelain on tin, black, white & red, marked on ribbon at top "A Guarantee Bond - With Every Stove" & "'Peninsular' - Furnaces - Stoves and Ranges" w/"Warranted - The Best," ca. 1890, 15 1/2 x 23 1/2" (ILLUS.) **2,000-2,750**

Solona White Port Wine Sign

M. Hommel Wines Sign

Oshkosh Work Clothes Sign

Wine, "M. Hommel Wines," rectangular, lithograph w/center scene of vineyard below medals & bunches of grapes flanked by wine bottles, top marked "M. Hommel - Highest Awards Over All American Champagnes - At World's Columbian Exposition - 1893," the bottom marked "Sandusky, Ohio - U.S.A.," wood frame, litho by Wittemann Litho Co., New York, ca. 1910, 28 x 34 1/2" (ILLUS.)
.... **300-450**

Wine, "Solona White Port Wine," rectangular paper, scene of woman in green dress w/her arm on the shoulder of a dark-haired man in dark suit, white shirt & bow tie, the couple seated at a table trimmed w/pink flowers, two glasses & wine bottle, wood frame, ca. 1900, 16 x 18" (ILLUS., top of page) **250-375**

Work clothing, "OshKosh Work Clothes," tin, red & yellow w/embossed white & yellow letters reading "OshKosh B'gosh - Union Made - Work Clothes," ca. 1930s, 9 1/4 x 13 1/2" (ILLUS., top next column)
.... **175-250**

SPICE CABINETS & BOXES

Cabinet, oak, six dovetailed drawers w/brass ring pulls, three over two over one, raised molding around base & top, the door w/brass hinges & escutcheon w/incised border detail, turned feet, 8 1/4 x 13", 12" h. (replaced feet & lock escutcheon, internal lock missing) **$1,210**

Cabinet, painted pine, small upright rectangular case w/two vertical stacks of four small drawers each, dark bluish green paint, large brown-stained turned wood knob on each drawer, America, mid-19th c., 5 1/4 x 8 1/4", 12 1/4" h. (paint wear)... **4,313**

Chest, walnut w/pine secondary wood, molded base w/step-down cornice at top, square nail construction, eleven drawers retain original turned pulls & situated four over three, 9 1/2 x 20 1/4", 13 3/4" h. (edge chips, two screw added in top) **1,980**

Spice box, cov., pine, three tiers w/nine drawers w/turned wooden knobs, natural finish, America, 19th c., 9 1/8 x 17 3/4", 10 1/8" h.. **881**

Spice box, pine, six-drawers w/turned wooden knobs, old surface, America, 19th c., 7 1/2 x 15", 13" h. (wear)................ **940**

Spice box, wood, round shape w/lapped construction containing eight small cylindrical cov. wood containers w/stenciled spice label on each lid, America, 19th c., 9" d., 3 3/8" h.. **235**

SPORTS MEMORABILIA
Also see BASEBALL MEMORABILIA

Basketball

Basketball, all-rubber, vintage Draper-Maynard model ball w/original cardboard box, includes two unopened printed envelopes w/inflating needles, ca. 1930s, the group (ILLUS., bottom of page)................. **$163**

Michael Jordan-signed Wilson Basketball

Basketball, Wilson Jet model issued by Upper Deck, signed by Michael Jordan in black marker (ILLUS.).................................. **805**

Signed UNC Replica Jordan Jersey

Jersey, replica of University of North Carolina #23 Michael Jordan jersey, blue & white, Nike size 46, produced by Upper Deck, autographed by Jordan in black marker, w/letter of authenticity, mint condition (ILLUS.).. **725**

Early Draper-Maynard Basketball & Box

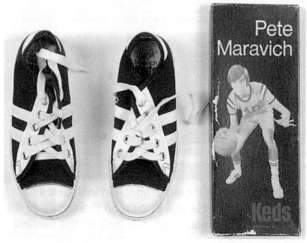

Pete Maravich Youth Sneakers

Sneakers, "Pete Maravich - Keds," youth size 13 pair in black & white, w/original box w/black & white image of Maravich on the lid, minor wear to box, 1970s (ILLUS., top of page).................................... **144**

Boxing

1951 Tops Boxing Ringside Cards

Boxing cards, Topps Ringside collection, color-printed paper, 1951, mounted in plastic sleeves, collection of 27 cards, the set (ILLUS. of part)...................................... **805**

Novelty Figural Joe Louis Clock

Clock, figural, cast bronzed-metal, a half-length figural of Joe Louis above a wreath enclosing the clock dial w/Roman numerals & sweep seconds hand, original label on the back for the Oxford Metal Spinning Co., minor stress crack in the metal, original card, plug & works, not running, 1930s, 12 1/2" h. (ILLUS.) **668**

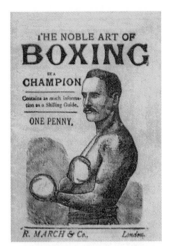

Early Boxing Guide Pamphlet

Pamphlet, "The Noble Art of Boxing - By a Champion," printed paper w/a dark yellow cover printed in black & w/a half-length portrait of a period boxer, providing the guidelines for the Queensbury Rules, published in London, 1860s, single staple missing, pages loose, 30 pp. (ILLUS.)... **127**

Poster for Movie of Louis-Conn Fight

Poster, "Now Showing - Extra! - Exclusive Fight Pictures - Joe Louis vs. Bill Conn - Return World's Heavyweight Championship Battle ... Better than a Ringside

Seat..." colorfully hand silk-screened poster in red, white, blue & tan, RKO Pictures, copyright 1946, overall excellent condition, 40 x 60" (ILLUS.)...................... **1,624**

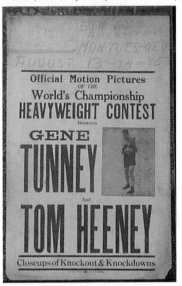

Poster for Early Championship Fight

Poster, "Official Motion Pictures of the World's Championship Heavyweight Contest between Gene Tunney and Tom Heeney - Closeups of Knockouts & Knockdowns," white cardboard printed in black, top portion w/pencil notations on a local showing, includes photo of Tunney, light surface soiling, bottom right corner missing, 1920s, 14 x 22" (ILLUS.) **213**

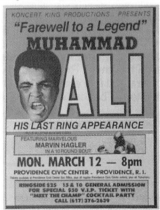

Poster for Ali's Last Ring Appearance

Poster, rectangular cardboard printed in orange, yellow & black, reading "'Farewell to a Legend' - Muhammad Ali - His Last Ring Appearance ... Mon. March 12 - 8 pm...," black & white head photo of Ali, excellent condition, 12 1/2 x 22" (ILLUS.) **403**

Original Liston-Clay Fight Program

Program, "World Heavyweight Championship - 15 Rounds - Sonny Liston vs Cassius Clay - Miami Beach Convention Hall - Tuesday, February 25, 1964 - $1.00 - Dundee-MacDonald Enterprises, Inc.," printed in red, white & blue, 12 pp., single vertical fold, triangular corner piece missing on back cover, 9 x 12" (ILLUS.) **731**

Football

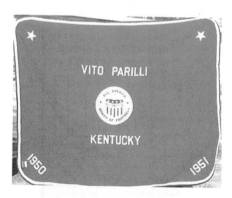

Early Vito Parilli Stadium Blanket

Blanket, stadium type, award model in red w/white lettering for All-American Vito Parilli, Kentucky, 1950-1951, large size, 58 x 66" (ILLUS.).. **796**

Unopened 1961 Fleer Card Set

Card set, 1961 Fleer football unopened pack, near mint in plastic mount (ILLUS.) **207**

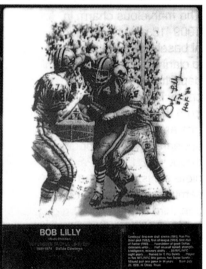

Original Bob Lilly Hall-of-Fame Display

Display, special backlit acrylic & Plexiglas piece honoring Bob Lilly, originally in the Pro Football Hall of Fame, large image of Lilly in action above a black band w/biographical information, signed near the image in bold blue Sharpie "Bob Lilly - #74 - HOF '80," w/letter of authenticity, 24 x 32" (ILLUS.) **1,903**

Early Radio Sports Baseball/Football Game

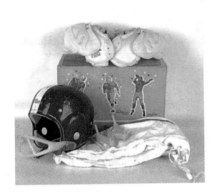

Set of Child-sized Football Equipment

Super Bowl MVP-signed Outfit

Football equipment, child-sized set, includes pants, helmet, shoulder pads & two kicking tees, in original color cardboard box w/portraits & facsimile signature of players Paul Hornung, Y.A. Tittle, John Brodie & Hugh McElhenny, the group (ILLUS.)... **104**

Game, Radio Sports Inc. - Baseball/Football Game, one side providing a baseball game board, the reverse w/a football field, both games endorsed by Graham McNamee, football game licensed by Knute Rockne, board framed in oak w/wooden easel props, playing surfaces in heavy cardboard, w/twelve-page instruction booklet & original box w/some damage, ca. 1931, box 18 x 25" (ILLUS., top of page)... **252**

Jacket & helmet, Super Bowl Most-Valuable-Player limited edition leather jacket & helmet, each piece autographed by numerous Super Bowl Most-Valuable-Player winners including Joe Namath, Joe Montana, Troy Aikman, Jerry Rise, Steve Young & many others, w/letter of authenticity, the set (ILLUS., top next column) **1,938**

Knute Rockne Football Paperweight

Paperweight, bronzed metal, a model of a football w/the oval dished interior centered by a bust portrait of Knute Rockne, ca. 1930, 2 x 3" (ILLUS.) **159**

Rare Early Football Pillow Case

Pillow case, cloth printed in full color, the center w/a large scene of early football players in action, a red border decorated w/flowering vines, ca. 1900, minor area of fading, 21 x 22" (ILLUS.)...................... **1,525**

Unusual Early Football Poster

Poster, "Football - Wisconsin vs. Chicago - at Camp Randall - Madison - Oct. 21...," rectangular cardboard printed in green, red, black & brown, a large cover image of a player running w/the ball, from 1904, three fine tack holes in margins, diagonal crack at lower right corner, matted & framed, image 9 1/2 x 14" (ILLUS.) **447**

Poster, "National League Football ... Portsmouth Spartans vs. Green Bay Packers ... City Stadium - Green Bay - Sunday - November 2 ...," rectangular paper printed in black, ca. 1930, some minor imperfections, 18 x 24" (ILLUS., top next page) **731**

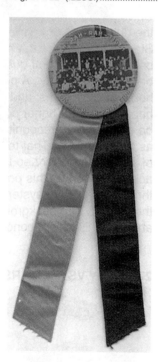

Rare Early Princeton Pinback & Ribbons

Pinback button, round celluloid w/a sepia-toned photograph of the 1901 Princeton football team, suspending 5" l. orange & black silk ribbons representing the school colors, button printed around the edge w/the cheer "Rah-Rah-Rah-Tiger - Sis-Boom-Ah - Princeton," by Whitehead & Hoag, minute holes in ribbons, near mint (ILLUS.)... **511**

Special Super Bowl XXX Signed Poster

Poster, "Super Bowl XXX," very colorful desert landscape w/title & silver football at the top, under the management of the National Sports Autograph Network

Rare Early Green Bay Packers vs. Portsmouth Spartans Poster

twenty-two members of the Super Bowl XXX victors, Dallas Cowboys, autographed the image, image replicates the original game program cover, w/letter of authenticity, 23 x 25" (ILLUS.) **411**

Super Bowl XVIII Replica Trophy

Trophy, Super Bowl XVIII replica, produced by Upper Deck, autographed by Marcus

Allen, letter of authenticity, 1984, 18" h. (ILLUS.).. **1,730**

1931 Notre Dame Football Yearbook

Yearbook, "Official Football Review - University Notre Dame - 1931 - Rockne Memorial Edition," black cover printed in silver in an Art Deco design that includes a portrait of Rockne, extensive coverage & photos of the 1931 team & tributes to Rockne, few light & subtle cover creases, 111 pp., 8 1/2 x 11" (ILLUS.) **117**

STATUARY - BRONZE, MARBLE & OTHER

Bronzes and other statuary are increasingly popular with today's collectors. Particularly appealing are works by "Les Animaliers," the 19th-century French school of sculptors who

turned to animals for their subject matter. These, together with figures in the Art Deco and Art Nouveau taste, are common in a wide price range.

Bronze

Dalou Figure of Seated Worker

Dalou, Aime Jules, "Moissonneur Affutânt sa Faux," a seated metalworker hammering on a sheet of metal, brown patina, signed "Sasse Freres ed. Paris - Dalou," 5 x 6", 5 1/2" h. (ILLUS.) **$1,380**

Leduc Bronze of Centaur & Nude

Leduc, Arthur Jacques, "Nessus et Dejanire," gilt-bronze group of a centaur w/a nude female riding on his back, rectangular base on a red marble plinth, France, late 19th c., 9 x 32", 30" h. (ILLUS.).......... **5,175**

Modern Bronze of Mare & Her Colt

Ghiglieri, Lorenzo E., "First Jump," model of a mare & her colt making its first jump, patinated, on a conforming wood base, signed at base & dated "1999 - 25/135," limited edition, 10 1/4 x 28", 22" h. (ILLUS.) **5,750**

Mene Equestrian Figure of Arab

Mene, Pierre-Jules, "Fauconnier Arabe," equestrian group of an Arab w/a falcon, oblong naturalistic base w/Mene name inscribed, France, ca. 1890, 30 1/2" h. (ILLUS.)...................................... **7,170**

Art Deco Nude & Fawn Bronze

Traverse, Pierre, Art Deco style group of a nude female walking w/a leaping fawn at her side, rectangular base on a black marble plinth, signed in the maquette & w/the mark of the La Stele Foundry, France, ca. 1925, 11 1/2" l., 16 1/8" h. (ILLUS., top of page)................................. **7,765**

Figure of a nude youth seated examining one foot, titled "The Spinario," after the Antique, probably made in Florence, late 19th c., 24 1/2" h. (ILLUS.) **1,725**

Marble

Marble Figure of a Youth after the Antique

Fine Lapini Marble of a Young Girl

Lapini, Cesare, figure of a young girl seated on a chair w/her legs crossed, sewing, squared base inscribed at the front "Vouloir C'est Pouvoir," signed & dated, Florence, Italy, 1888, on a green marble pedestal, figure 27 1/2" h. (ILLUS.)......... **29,875**

Bust of Alexandra, Princess of Wales

Noble, Matthew, bust of "Alexandra, Princess of Wales," signed & dated London, 1867, on a socle base w/some damage, 11 1/2 x 19 1/2", 29 3/4" h. (ILLUS.) **5,175**

Other

Victorian Alabaster Figure of a Maiden

Alabaster, figure of a standing young maiden wearing a peasant costume & holding a lute, square marble base, some losses, 19th c., 19" h. (ILLUS.) **259**

Rare Cupid Figure by A. Piazza

Piazza, A., figure of Cupid perched on rockwork, after a design by Bouguereau, Carrara, Italy, atop an ormolu-mounted onyx pedestal, ca. 1890, figure 27 3/4" h., pedestal 42" h. (ILLUS.) **15,535**

Modern Alabaster Figure of a Cockatoo

Alabaster, model of a cockatoo w/ebony-stained features & glass eyes, on a black plinth base, ca. 1970-80, overall 32" h. (ILLUS.) **920**

STEINS

Leroux Terra Cotta Nude Female Figure

Terra cotta, figure of a nude female reclining in a chair, by Etienne F. Leroux, impressed name & date of 1867, France, end of one finger missing, 9 1/2 x 20", 31" h. (ILLUS.) **2,990**

Wright Figures of Nakoma & Nakomis

Terra cotta, stylized figures of Native Americans "Nakoma" & "Nakomis," by Frank Lloyd Wright, ca. 1929, impressed Wright monogram, she 12 1/4" h., he 18" h., pr. (ILLUS.).. **5,975**

Colorful 19th Century Faience Stein

Faience, cylindrical, h.p. around the sides w/oblong deep rose panels each w/a colorful flower, a background of small blue stars & small colored blossoms, Erfurt, domed pewter cover w/ball thumbrest, cover hinge a replacement, ca. 1870, 1 L, 11" h. (ILLUS.) **$817**

Pretty Pink Cut-Overlay Stein

Glass, blown cut-overlay, clear cased in white to pink & cut w/long panels & small printies, white glass-inlaid pewter cover, .3 L, 5 3/4" h. (ILLUS.) **483**

Deep Ruby Panel-cut Glass Stein

Glass, blown deep ruby, panel-cut sides decorated w/scrolling gold enamel, matching glass-inlaid pewter cover, factory impression on handle at strap attachment, Germany, ca. 1850, .5 L (ILLUS.)...... **500**

Three Colorful Hauber & Reuther Steins

Hauber & Reuther, pottery, etched color decoration of a trumpeter on horseback, ringed & domed pewter cover, .5 L (ILLUS. center with two other Hauber & Reuther steins, previous page) **247**

Hauber & Reuther, pottery, etched color decoration of men bowling, high ringed & pointed dome cover, No. 175, .5 L (ILLUS. left with two other Hauber & Reuther steins, top of page) **277**

Hauber & Reuther, pottery, etched colorful design of people rowing in a boat, peaked & domed pewter cover, No. 446, .5 L (ILLUS. right with two other Hauber & Reuther steins, top of page) **261**

Meissen porcelain, cylindrical w/a hinged porcelain cover, the front w/a large four-lobed reserve painted in full color w/an elaborate battle scene w/men on horseback, the cobalt blue background completely covered w/ornate gold leafy scrolls, blue Crossed Swords mark, 19th c., .25 L, 5 1/4" h. (ILLUS.) **4,649**

Bismarck & Comic Scene Mettlachs

Mettlach, No. 1794, etched portrait of Otto von Bismarck, inlaid cover, .5 L (ILLUS. left with Mettlach No. 2880 stein) **506**

Mettlach, No. 2176-1055, painted-under-glaze (PUG) w/a colorful festive scene, signed by artist H. Schlitt, domed pewter cover, 2.1 L (ILLUS. center with two other tall Mettlach steins, top next page) **524**

Mettlach, No. 2261-1012, PUG, a colorful scene of Germans meeting Romans, artist H. Schlitt, domed pewter cover, 2.25 L (ILLUS. left with two other tall Mettlach steins, top next page) **564**

Lovely Meissen Porcelain Stein

Three Tall Colorful Mettlach Steins

Two Mettlach Steins with Pointed Covers

Mettlach, No. 2382, etched color design of an armored knight in a tavern, titled "The Thirsty Rider," pointed roof-style pottery cover, hairline repair in rear, 1 L (ILLUS. left with Mettlach No. 2580, top of page)...... **544**

Mettlach, No. 2430, etched color scene of a Cavalier seated on the edge of a tavern table, inlaid cover, 3 L (ILLUS. right with two other tall Mettlach steins, top of page) **1,208**

Mettlach, No. 2580, etched scene of a knight & village people, DeKannenburg, pointed pottery roof-style cover, 1 L (ILLUS. right with Mettlach No. 2382 stein) **1,032**

Mettlach, No. 2880, etched scene of men pouring water down a sleeping man's

shirt, artist F. Quidenus, inlaid cover, 1 L (ILLUS. right with No. 1794 Bismarck stein) **357**

Large Mettlach Faience Stein

Mettlach, No. 5102, faience, footed tall baluster-form body w/a flaring neck, domed hinged pewter cover w/ball thumbrest, h.p. w/shades of dark blue w/a portrait of a man in Renaissance

Three Old European Pewter Steins

dress holding a goblet, blue scalloped band trim, .5 L (ILLUS.).............................. **1,265**

Pewter, footed bulbous body w/a low domed hinged cover, the front cast in relief w/a horned devil head, pewter cover, marked "Riceszinn 559," Germany, 19th c., .5 L (ILLUS. right with two other pewter steins, previous page)........................... **193**

Pewter, round domed foot & cylindrical plain sides w/a flattened domed cover, cover etched w/"FWF 1827," touch marks under cover, minor dents & scratches, Europe, 1 L (ILLUS. left with two other pewter steins, top of page) **190**

Pewter, three ringed ball feet supporting the cylindrical body w/cartouches above each foot & a large engraved crest on the front, stepped & domed cover, pewter lid w/coin in center, marked "F. Samesson Stockholm Hvit Metall," Sweden, 19th c., 1 L (ILLUS. center with two other pewter steins, top of page)...................................... **144**

Regimental, pottery, tall ringed cylindrical body w/a flaring base, the wide center band painted w/a soldier on horseback above a small bust portrait, four side scenes & roster, domed pewter cover w/eagle thumblift, marked "2 Comp. Hannov. Train Batl. Nr. 10 Hannover 1909-11," dent to finial, .5 L, 13 1/2" h. (ILLUS. right with other Regimental stein, top of page).. **725**

Regimental, pottery, tall ringed cylindrical body w/a flaring base, the wide center band decorated w/German sailors & naval symbols, two side scenes & roster,

marked "S.M.S. Rheiland 1908-11," domed pewter cover w/figural eagle thumblift w/inset Stanhope, 1 L, 14 1/2" h. (ILLUS. left with other Regimental stein, below)................................. **1,328**

Two German Regimental Steins

TEXTILES

American Flags

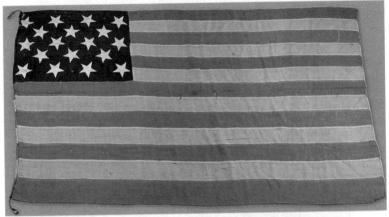

Very Rare Early 18-Star Hand-sewn American Flag

Eighteen-star, commemorating Louisiana statehood on April 30, 1812, hand-sewn w/thirteen stripes & eighteen double-appliqué cotton-muslin stars on a three-piece wool bunting canton, canton & stripes rolled at hoist end to form a hand-sewn pocket w/a period hemp rope, reverse side of first star inscribed in pencil "Caroline Whiting - 2nd Division," w/a notarized letter of provenance, ca. 1812-16, 5' 1" x 8' 4" (ILLUS., top of page) **$25,875**

Small 19th Century 13-Star Flag

Thirteen-star, small hand-stitched version w/the stars arranged in a circle on the blue canton, old ink inscription "Made by Sara M. Wilson - Great-grand daughter of Betsy Ross," wear, losses, mounted under glass, 19th c., 5 5/8 x 10 3/8" (ILLUS.) **1,763**

Thirty-five star, hand-sewn in wool gauze w/cotton stars appliqued on one side, cut-out & overcast on the reverse, the twill hoist w/sewn eyes, ink inscribed "Eustis," the other side stenciled "Boston R.M. YALE," scattered fabric losses, ca. 1863, 40 x 65" (ILLUS. top with twenty-six star flag) **2,468**

Early 26-star and 35-star American Flags

Twenty-six star, hand-sewn in wool gauze w/cotton double-applique stars, the cotton hoist w/three overcast buttonholes, Michigan admitted to the Union in 1837, ca. 1837, small fabric losses, repair, 40 x 70" (ILLUS. bottom with 35-star flag) **5,875**

Coverlets

Jacquard, double-weave, two-piece, Biederwand-type, in navy blue, tomato red, gold & natural, a central design of rose medallions, the borders w/grapes, birds & roses, eagle corner blocks w/"Knox

Group of Four Colorful Jacquard Coverlets

County, Ohio - 1845," 72 x 84" (ILLUS. top right with three other colorful coverlets) **$920**

Jacquard, double-weave, two-piece, Biederwand-type, in navy blue, tomato red, gold & natural, the center w/circular medallions w/a bird & foliage swag border, border drops w/"BB," corner blocks woven "W. in Mt. Vernon - Know County - Ohio - by Jacob and Michael Ardner - 1853," minor wear, fringe loss, 76 x 86" (ILLUS. upper left with three other colorful coverlets, top of page) **1,495**

Jacquard, double-weave, two-piece, Biederwand-type, in red, green, navy blue & natural, the center w/floral medallions surrounded by rose & bird borders, corner block woven w/"Winesberg - Holmes County - Ohio - 1844 - Christian Nusser," fringe loss, some edge damage, 74 x 82" (ILLUS. bottom left with three other colorful coverlets) **978**

Jacquard, double-weave, two-piece, in dark blue & natural, an interior design w/a central star & floral medallions, side borders of birds, undulating grapevines & pine trees, lower border w/eagles & willow trees over the name "DEWITT," corner blocks w/a flower in a vase flanked by "SA" over "C" over "N.Y. 1841," toning, 82 x 86" (ILLUS. center right with large group of quilts & other coverlet) **499**

Jacquard, double-weave, two-piece, in dark blue & natural, an interior design of six large floral medallions on a polka-dot-ted background, border designs of Independence Hall flanked by eagles w/overhead stars & eagles w/Masonic compass & square & columns, corner blocks woven "Phebe Hulse Oct. 14 1824," minor toning & stains, attributed to James Alexander, Orange County, New York, 79 x 94" (ILLUS. center left w/large grouping of quilts & other coverlet) **3,408**

Coverlet with Interesting Inscription

Jacquard, double-weave, two-piece, in navy blue & natural, the center w/floral medallions bordered by buildings & American eagles flanked by Masonic columns, monkeys & small human figures, corner blocks woven "Agriculture & Manufactures are the Foundations of our Independence," attributed to Duchess County, New York, unknown maker, some stains & edge damage, 78 x 82" (ILLUS.) **863**

Jacquard, double-weave, two-piece, in shades of blue, red & natural, a geometric Optical patt. w/a pine tree border, some wear & a repair, mid-19th c., 70 x 80" **518**

Jacquard, single-weave, one-piece, in navy blue, salmon red, gold & natural, the center w/large urns of flowers & grapes & nesting birds, a Christian & Heathen buildings border, unsigned, wear, some damage, 74 x 84" (ILLUS. bottom right with three other colorful coverlets) **201**

1848 Ohio Jacquard Coverlet

Jacquard, single-weave, two-piece, in red, green, navy blue & natural, the center w/rose & star medallions w/eagle borders w/letters "EA" along the bottom, corner blocks woven "J.P. Heifner - Hayesville - Ohio - 1848," wear & fringe loss, 65 x 73" (ILLUS.) **633**

Linens & Needlework

Commemorative fabric, blue printed on white w/vignettes of General Lafayette arriving at Independence Hall, his arrival in New York Harbor & a central vignette of a bust portrait of Lafayette, commemorating his visit to the United States, printed by Germantown Print Works, Pennsylvania, ca. 1820s, 14 x 14 1/2" (some toning & evidence of previous glue on edges) **1,320**

Indian Silk Floral Embroidered Panel

Embroidered panel, silk on silk, an oval black ground finely embroidered w/a circle of colorful flowers & leaves, India, mid-19th c., 14 x 28" (ILLUS.)..................... **173**

Early Printed Patriotic Textile

Patriotic textile, square of off-white cloth printed in black w/a large spread-winged American eagle across the top holding a ribbon w/"E Pluribus Unum," below are three columns each w/a different poem, titled "Union-Liberty," "Life Without Freedom" & "Liberty," the reverse w/images of early American patriots, New England Chemical Print Company, mid-19th c., framed, 10 1/4 x 10 1/2" (ILLUS.) **441**

Fine Embroidered & Crocheted Show Towel

Show towel, embroidered & crocheted on homespun, the embroidery in pale gold silk thread featuring tulips & two peacocks on either side of an urn of flowers, also bands of white geometric designs

Appliqued Table Runner with Various Colorful Animals

w/additional openwork, crocheted designs include a double-headed eagle w/a heart & horses & two roosters flanking two soldiers that appear to be Hessians, end w/tied fringe, blue stitched initials "IHD" in the middle, probably early 19th c., 13 x 48" (ILLUS. of part, previous page).. **690**

Table runner, appliqued, hand-stitched w/various fabrics including chintz, a large flower at the center flanked by hearts, chickens, horses, leaves & an elephant, 19th c., areas of bleeding on the cream ground, 25 1/2 x 42 1/2" (ILLUS., top of page)... **230**

Needlework Pictures

Lady in landscape, silk threads on silk, the pensive young woman seated beneath a tree w/her dog at her side & distant mountains in the background, painted face, hands & background, surrounded by a black & gilt églomisé mat w/oval opening, rectangular gilt gesso frame, probably American, late 18th - early 19th c. **382**

Landscape with academy building, silk embroidery w/the building in gold thread w/the front door open & a horse & carriage approaching, rolling hills & fields in the foreground, painted background w/rolling hills & trees below a wide blue sky w/a single white cloud, monogrammed in lower left "EM," worked by Elizabeth Motter, Sr., St. Joseph's Academy, Emmitsburg, Maryland, retains original giltwood frame & original glass inscribed "View of Saint Joseph's Near Emmitsburg - E. Motter 1825," 17 x 23 3/4" (ILLUS., bottom of page)
.... **50,190**

Very Rare American Needlework Academy Landscape

English Embroidered Landscape Scene

Landscape with lady, embroidered silk, a shepherdess in 18th c. costume seated overlooking a stream w/a cottage & trees in the background, watercolored silk sky & details, w/original gold-banded black liner in a modern frame, England, ca. 1810, image 16 x 18 3/4" (ILLUS.).............. **633**

Early Mixed Media Memorial Picture

Memorial scene, depicting a woman holding a book beside a monument inscribed "Werter," mixed media w/cut-out wool felt monument, figure & background, watercolor on paper head & hands, wool & silk threads, oval format in giltwood frame, early 19th c., scene 12 3/4" d. (ILLUS.) **1,175**

Needlework Old Testament Story

Old Testament story, brightly colored wool cross-stitch on a linen ground, the scene w/three angels announcing to Abraham that he & his wife, Sarah, in their old age, would soon conceive & have a son, embellished w/various animals including rabbits, a squirrel, birds & a dog, America or England, 18th c., framed, 16 7/8 x 18" (ILLUS.).. **3,290**

Quilts

Amish Double Nine-Patch Quilt

Amish Double Nine-Patch patt., in shades of purple, red, grey & blue w/large corner blocks, Lancaster County, rayon & crepe wool, Pennsylvania, ca. 1930-40, 83 1/2" sq. (ILLUS.).. **403**

Modern Amish-made Quilt

Amish Triple Irish Chain patt., in dark brown highlighted by bright blue, red & purple, cotton, Holmes County, Ohio, ca. 1981, 82" sq. (ILLUS.) **259**

Appliqued Blackberry & Vine patt., sixteen white blocks each w/a vine in aqua & pendant blackberries, each block separated by an aqua grid also forming the border, white cotton backing w/intricate quilting, minor stain, 82 x 86" (ILLUS. upper right with grouping of other quilts & two coverlets, top next page).................. **3,995**

Grouping of Various Quilts & Two Jacquard Coverlets

Appliqued Floral Sprigs & Blossoms patt., sixteen white blocks separated by a diagonal red grid, each w/the floral design in solid red, yellow, blue & green, accented w/wool yarn & cotton embroidered buds & leaves, quilted white backing, New England, late 19th c., losses & fading, 80 1/2 x 90" (ILLUS. center with grouping of other quilts and two coverlets, top of page) **1,410**

Appliqued Blue Oak Leaf Quilt

Appliqued Oak Leaf patt., sixteen blocks w/a white ground decorated w/a four-leaf cross-form cluster w/square & cross at the center of each, hand-stitched, 68 x 76" (ILLUS.) **259**

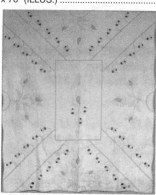

Appliqued Tulips & Vines Quilt

Appliqued Tulips & Vines patt., the sides w/large angled panels appliqued w/pale pink tulips on pale green leafy stems, border bands of small blue blossoms, light yellow bordering & central rectangle w/another tulip & blue blossoms, probably 20th c., faded & stained, 76 x 88" (ILLUS.) **150**

Appliqued Vining Floral Quilt

Appliqued Vining Floral patt., the white ground hand-stitched w/a large arched central cluster of vining blue, yellow & red flowers & berries on leafy green vines, matching designs in each corner, scalloped border, 72 x 88" (ILLUS.) **219**

Ornate Appliqued Baltimore-style Quilt

Baltimore-style quilt, appliqued in the center w/a large flower-filled basket framed w/a large leafy floral wreath within a narrow rectangular border, a boldly scalloped outer border w/green scallops each enclosing colorful floral swags, monogrammed near center, finely stitched w/eleven stitches per square inch, probably Baltimore, Maryland, ca. 1830 (ILLUS.) **2,588**

Crib quilt, crazy quilt-style, rectangular, composed of a wide variety of random blocks in various materials, many finely embroidered w/roses, flowers, fans & other designs, a narrow border band of green four-leaf clusters, four corner blocks embroidered "To Edna - From Grandma - Dec. 25 - 1882," scattered losses, 35 x 52" (ILLUS., top next column) **2,070**

Crib-sized Crazy Quilt

Pieced Basket patt., rows of sixteen baskets composed of white & yellow triangles on a white ground w/double yellow borders, white cotton backing quilted w/feather medallions, diamond & undulating feather border, possibly made by a Mennonite, ca. 1900 (ILLUS. top left with grouping of other quilts & two Jacquard coverlets) **1,528**

Four Varied Pieced Quilts

Pieced Basket patt., rows of small pale green baskets on a white diamond quilted ground, green border band, some stains, 76 x 80" (ILLUS. bottom left with three other pieced quilts) **316**

Pieced Drunkard's Path patt., blue dotted fabric on a white ground, hand-sewn w/small stitches, wavy line & scallops background quilting, stapled tag reads

"Grace," some edge damage, small tear & light stains, 76 x 85" (ILLUS. upper left with three other pieced quilts) **201**

Pieced Ocean Waves patt., large crosses composed of small red & white triangles on a white ground w/hand-sewn diamond quilting, few light stains, 68 x 84" (ILLUS. top right with three other pieced quilts) **316**

Pieced Robbing Peter to Pay Paul patt., bold red & black design, hand-stitched w/machine-sewn edging, the backing in burgundy w/white dotting, 70 x 81" (ILLUS. bottom right with three other pieced quilts) **575**

Pieced Stars & Blocks patt., composed of 42 blocks of eight-point stars set on the diagonal in a variety of printed fabrics separated by floral-printed blocks in red, yellow & black, triangle block border & edged in same floral design, natural woven cotton backing, chevron & concentric diamond quilting stitches, ca. 1870, minor stains, 80 x 90" (ILLUS. bottom center with various other quilts and two Jacquard coverlets) **1,763**

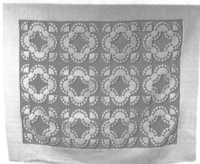

Red & White Tennessee Trail Quilt

Pieced Tennessee Trail or Rattlesnake patt., composed of twelve large white & red lobed designs alternating w/smaller red & white crosses in squares, early 20th c., 70 x 86" (ILLUS.) **460**

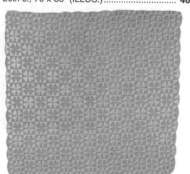

Fancy Whirligig Pieced Quilt

Pieced Whirligig or Winding Ways patt., overall design of small crosses alternating in red on fawn or fawn on red, scalloped border, early 20th c., 78 x 85" (ILLUS.) **460**

Samplers

Mid-Victorian Sampler

Alphabet & numerals above a floral bouquet, a diamond lattice border & signed at the bottom "L. Palmire 1864," color fading, staining to foundation (ILLUS.)......... **345**

Rare Colonial American Sampler

Alphabets & geometric designs, long narrow rectangle w/rows of alphabets across

Fine Signed Sampler with an Ornate House, Trees & Flowering Urns Design

the top, a long section w/stylized diamond designs & flowers worked in gold, green, blue & black silk threads on a linen ground, scattered various initials & dated 1746, w/a paper label inscribed "Worked by Sarah Riddell," possibly Virginia, 1746, 10 x 19" (ILLUS.)............................ **10,158**

Sampler with Willow Trees & Vine Border

Alphabets, pious verse & landscape, finely stitched in shades of ivory, gold, green & some red silk thread on a linen ground, a large center rectangular border around the alphabets & pious verse w/the inscription "Mary B. Nath - Aged 11 Years - July 1825," all above a pair of arching willow trees, one over a memorial monument, & flanking a basket filled w/a large spray of flowers, an undulating strawberry vine border up the sides & across the top, ma-

hogany veneer frame, attributed to coastal Maine, 18 3/4 x 19 1/2" (ILLUS.)............... **6,038**

Alphabets, pious verse & landscape, silk threads on a linen ground, a central rectangular panel of alphabets above a pious verse & inscribed by Lucy Parham, born in 1811 & wrought in her 11th year, the lower border w/a landscape showing a two-story home flanked by leafy trees & small animals, each lower corner w/a large urn issuing leafy flowering vines up each side w/a flower-filled basket at the top center, by Lucy Parham, Tyngsboro, Massachusetts, 1822, toning, scattered stains, framed, 17 x 18" (ILLUS., top of page).. **27,025**

Fine Early Family Tree Sampler

Family tree, all stitched in silk including the gold background, a large slender tree w/leafy branches, inscribed w/various family members, Samuel & Grace Barnes, married October 22, 1774 at the bottom, the branches w/apples & the names of their eight children, the last being born in 1794, included are records of Samuel & Grace & her family line, stains, the greens w/bleeding, in mahogany flame veneer frame, 15 x 17" (ILLUS.) **2,990**

Sampler with Building, Verse & Trees

Pious verse, building, trees & flowers, linen w/silk thread in pretty colors & tiny stitches, a bold tri-colored strawberry border around a thin rectangle enclosing designs, a three-story brick house flanked by trees at the top above a row of potted flowers over a long pious verse above tall flowering trees & a pair of deer flanking the inscription "Emily Pattinson - Aged eleven years - 1825," molded frame, two small stitched repairs, one w/a well-done reweave, 14 3/4 x 17" (ILLUS.) **1,610**

Tapestries

Early German Tapestry Cushion Cover

North German, cushion cover woven w/a central scene of peasant figures bathing, a king in a tower looking on & a village in the background, a wide border w/large stylized flowers in vases, late 16th - early 17th c., in a giltwood frame, 22 3/4 x 23 3/4 (ILLUS.) **2,390**

Novelty Card Table Top Tapestry

Novelty-type, tightly woven, almost carpetweight, represents the top of a card table w/colorful hands of cards & poker chips around the border flanked by narrow gold zigzag pattern bands, ca. 1920s (ILLUS.) **743**

French Restauration Era Tapestry

Restauration era, a rectangular panel depicting a rustic couple by a barn populated by a cat & cow, France, first quarter 19th c., now laid-down on masonite & in a plain slat frame w/half-round brass facade edge, 42" h. (ILLUS.) **863**

THEOREMS

During the 19th century, a popular pastime for some ladies was theorem painting, or stencil painting. Paint was allowed to penetrate through hollow-cut patterns placed on paper or cotton velvet. Still life compositions, such as bowls of fruit or vases of flowers, were the favorite themes, but landscapes and religious scenes found favor among amateur artists who were limited in their ability and unable to do freehand painting. Today these colorful pictures, with their charming arrangements, are highly regarded by collectors.

Basket of fruit, on paper, blue & green grapes w/red cherries, green & brown pears, green grape leaves w/small blue & burgundy flowers, in 19th-c. molded frame w/old gold paint, 19 1/2 x 23 1/4" in frame (light staining from separations in original back boards) **$1,430**

Distlefinks on bowl of fruit, watercolor on velvet by "Bill Rank" (20th-c. folk artist), two long-tailed blue & yellow distlefinks perched on bowl of fruit that includes grapes, strawberries & heart-shaped plums, in contemporary red w/black sponged frame, 16 3/4 x 18 1/2" **275**

Flowers in a basket, watercolor on velvet, high rounded arrangement including large roses & other flowers, unsigned, second quarter 19th c., framed, 22 x 24 1/2" (imperfections) **546**

Rosebush, watercolor stencil on card paper, unsigned, framed, 21 1/4 x 26 3/4" (minor scattered foxing, laid down) **2,703**

TOBACCIANA

Although the smoking of cigarettes, cigars & pipes is controversial today, the artifacts of smoking related items - pipes, cigar & tobacco humidors, and cigar & cigarette lighters - and, of course, the huge range of advertising materials are much sought after. Unusual examples, especially fine Victorian pieces, can bring high prices. Here we list a cross section of Tobacciana pieces.

Also see: CANS & CONTAINERS and Antique Trader Advertising Price Guide.

Advertising Items

Cigar cutter, cast iron, model of a standing pig on a raised platform base embossed "Krank Havana Cigars," original black paint, ca. 1900, 7" l. **$431**

Tobacco cutter, cast iron & wood, advertising, store counter-type, the long hinged iron blade w/long rounded wood handle, mounted on a long narrow wood board, iron embossed "Smoke McApins Puff - Chew Chocolate Cream Plug," late 19th c., overall 12 1/2" l. **172**

Tobacco package, "Plow Boy Chewing and Smoking," color-lithographed paper w/scene of a plow boy, unopened w/contents, early 20th c., 4 1/2" h. (ILLUS., top next column) **46**

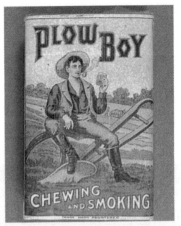

Early Plow Boy Paper Tobacco Package

Early Red Man Paper Tobacco Package

Tobacco package, "Red Man - Made From Good Cigar Leaf," paper printed in green, red & white, unopened w/contents, early 20th c., 5" h. (ILLUS.) **40**

Ashtrays

Unusual Griffin-form Ashtray

Bronzed cast iron, silent-butler style, modeled as a griffin-like creature w/the curled tail attached to the hinged shell-form cover, copper liner, late 19th - early 20th c., 11" l. (ILLUS., previous page) **374**

Porcelain, figural ashtray-matchholder, an oblong shallow dish mounted w/a large seated pink pig printed on the back "Scratch My Back," a seated piglet beside it printed w/"Me Too," a barrel-shaped match holder beside large pig, Germany, early 20th c., 4" l......................... **138**

Cans & Containers

Polar Bear Tobacco Store Counter Tin

Tobacco store tin, "Polar Bear Tobacco," countertop rectangular container w/a hinged slant top, blue ground w/white wording, the sides showing a rearing polar bear w/a package, the lower front w/an image of the package, front w/overall staining & wear, late 19th - early 20th c., 14 x 18", 14" h. (ILLUS.)........................... **316**

Tobacco store tin, "Sweet Cuba Chewing Tobacco," countertop rectangular container w/a hinged slant top, dark yellow ground printed overall w/advertising in red & black, good condition, late 19th - early 20th c., 14 x 18", 12" h. (ILLUS., bottom of page) **431**

Bagdad Short Cut Tobacco Pocket Tin

Tobacco tin, "Bagdad Short Cut Pipe Smoking," pocket-type, blue ground w/white wording & color center portrait of a Turkish man wearing a fez, some wear, 3 1/4" w., 3 3/4" h. (ILLUS.) **230**

Dixie Queen Plug Cut Tobacco Tin

Sweet Cuba Chewing Tobacco Store Tin

Tobacco tin, "Dixie Queen Plug Cut," large cylinder w/fitted flat cover, yellow ground printed in orange & black w/a central portrait of a pretty Victorian lady, some rust & scratches, late 19th - early 20th c., 5" d., 6 1/2" h. (ILLUS., previous page) **144**

Cigar & Cigarette Cases & Holders

Alligator Skin & Silver Cigar Case

Cigar case, alligator skin & silver, two-piece model that slides open, the base section w/an ornate scroll & lappet sterling silver band by the Gorham Mfg. Co., ca. 1930s, 4 1/2 x 5 1/2" (ILLUS.) **303**

Japanese Gilt-metal Cigarette Case

Cigarette case, gilt-metal, flattened rectangular form, one side decorated w/a landscape of a Japanese building & figures, the other side w/birds in a landscape, Japan, first quarter 20th c., 2 1/2 x 3 1/2" (ILLUS.) **230**

Cigarette case, silver & cloisonné enamel, flattened rectangular form w/rounded corners, the cover w/an overall ornate scrolling design in blues, red & white w/a central panel of flowered angled bars in blue & white, by Nikolai Zverev, Moscow, Russia, 1898-1914, 3" l. (ILLUS., top of column) **460**

Cigarette case, silver, flattened rectangular shape, the hinged cover decorated w/niello-work depicting the Shatt-al River, Basra, Iraq, signed by an unknown maker, Iraq, ca. 1910, 3 1/4 x 3 3/4" (ILLUS. center with two other Iraqi silver cigarette cases, next column) **173**

Cigarette case, silver, flattened rectangular shape, the hinged cover decorated w/niello-work, one side depicting a Mid-eastern city scape, the other side in-

Fine Russian Enamel Cigarette Case

Three Iraqi Silver Cigarette Cases

scribed "Florence Taylor," Iraq, ca. 1910, 2 1/2 x 3 1/2" (ILLUS. bottom with two other Iraqi silver cigarette cases, above) **201**

Cigarette case, silver, flattened rectangular shape, the hinged cover decorated w/niello-work depicting the Shatt-al River, Basra, Iraq, the other side depicting a scene of camels & figures in the desert, signed by an unknown maker, Iraq, ca. 1910, 2 1/4 x 3" (ILLUS. top with two other Iraqi silver cigarette cases, above) **230**

Russian Art Nouveau Silver Case

Cigarette case, silver, thin rectangular shape, decorated in the Art Nouveau taste w/an undulating ribbon design centering a small stone, a small button latch w/stone, marked w/84 standard, Moscow, Russia, ca. 1890, 2 1/4 x 3" (ILLUS.) **259**

Cigarette case, sterling silver, Art Nouveau style, flattened rectangular shape stamped w/a design of a maiden w/long hair seated on a rock above the ocean, Unger Brothers mark, ca. 1900, 3" l. **92**

Matchsafes & Holders

Molded Terra Cotta Match Box

Match box, cov., terra cotta, rectangular w/embossed woodland scenes around the sides, the flat cover centered by a reclining dog, dark brown finish, Europe, late 19th - early 20th c., 3 1/2" l. (ILLUS.) **57**

Match holder, cast iron, advertising wall-mounted type, a half-round vase-form container surrounded by openwork scrolls pointed at the top & bottom, narrow strike bars at each side, container embossed "Wilson Bros. Grinding Mills," ca. 1900, 6 1/4" h. **80**

Match holder, cast iron, hanging-type, advertising "Michigan Stove Co.'s Stoves - Art The Best," a pointed serpentine top plate w/hanging hole & stamped wording above a half-round projecting holder, a narrow tray base for used matches, late 19th c., 7" h. **172**

Match holder, cast iron, table model, advertising "Acorn Ranges," acorn-shaped container suspended between scrolled uprights above a domed star-shaped base, late 19th - early 20th c., 4 3/4" h. **69**

Match holder, stoneware pottery, advertising-type, sharply tapering cylindrical form w/a dark blue base band below a

stamped shield & American eagle trimmed in blue w/"American Brew. Co. - Rochester, N.Y.," early 20th c., 3" h. **149**

Match holder-dispenser, cast iron, a rectangular box-form base w/an open slot in top, a hinged model of a woodpecker w/a pin-tipped bill perched on the rim at one end, ca. 1900, 4 1/2" l. **57**

Victorian Cast-Iron Holder-Dispenser

Match holder-dispenser, cast iron, upright container w/scroll-cast hinged rounded front lid above the word "Matches," dispensing slot & tray at bottom front, late 19th c., 5" h. (ILLUS.) **138**

Match holder-dispenser, cast iron, wall-mounted type, a pointed top backplate w/a hanging hole above a rectangular projecting compartment w/an angled hinged cover, an opening in the lid & box, flat curved bottom backplate, embossed "C. Parker - Pat.," late 19th c., 5 1/2" h. **80**

Tobacco Jars & Humidors

Comical English Pottery Tobacco Jar

Pottery, cylindrical w/flaring base & stepped domed cover w/pointed finial, the sides transfer-printed in bright colors w/a comical golfing scene, marked "A.G.R. & Company Ltd. - England - Ducal," early 20th c., 7" h. (ILLUS.) **472**

Two German Figural Terra Cotta Jars

Terra cotta, figural jar, modeled as a man in German attire seated on a tree stump base, No. 2765, Germany, late 19th - early 20th c., 11 1/2" h. (ILLUS. left with boy on nut jar) **604**

Terra cotta, figural jar, modeled as a small German boy seated atop a large walnut, marked "JM8488," Germany, late 19th - early 20th c., 9" h. (ILLUS. right with figural man on stump jar) **380**

Comical German Pig Waiter Jar

Terra cotta, figural jar, modeled as a standing pig waiter wearing a green polka dot shirt, red bow tie & green pants, marked "JM3515," Germany, late 19th - early 20th c., 8 1/4" h. (ILLUS.).............................. **776**

Wood, carved presentation-type humidor, carved walnut in the form of a knotty tree stump wrapped in leafy vine w/a rabbit below, the flat inset cover carved w/a wooden branch handle, inscribed on the side "Vive Le Vin Lamour et le Tabac 1871," ("Long Live Wine, Love and Tobacco"), probably French, 7" w., 6 1/2" h. (ILLUS., top next column) **316**

Finely Carved Walnut Tobacco Humidor

Rare Ornately Carved Tobacco Box

Wood, figural box, the squared tall base carved at each corner w/buttress-style scrolls & blocks, each side panel carved & painted w/a different scene including a house & palm trees, a stag in water, a boy w/dog & fighting animals, the large cover carved as domed rockwork supporting a large carved model of a lion, Spanish cedar wood, tail of lion reattached, late 19th c., 7 x 8", 13" h. (ILLUS.) **4,313**

TOYS

Early Cast-iron Fire Engine Pumper

Fire engine pumper, cast iron, early steam model w/original red paint & gold trim, spoked iron wheels, early 20th c., 6" l. (ILLUS.).. **345**

Bradley's Toy Village Play Blocks

Blocks, lithographed paper on wood, "Bradley's Toy Village," colorful original box cover showing a Victorian mother & her children w/the blocks, played-with condition, box 8 1/2 x 11 1/2", the set (ILLUS.) **69**

Hubley Fire Water Cannon Truck

Fire water cannon truck, cast metal, long red body mounted in the back w/a silver water cannon & search light, a silver wooden globe on the hood, black rubber tires, Hubley, ca. 1930s, 7 1/2" l. **125**

G-Man Kilgore Cap Gun

Cap gun, nickel-plated cast iron, Luger-style, cast w/"G-Man" on the side, Kilgore, ca. 1935, 6" h. (ILLUS.) **81**

Machine Gun-type Cap Gun

Cap gun, nickel-plated cast iron, machine gun style w/"Ra-Ta-Ta-Tat" cast below the short barrel, Kilgore, ca. 1938, crank missing, 5 1/8" l. (ILLUS.) **69**

Rare Ben Butler Mechanical Figure

Mechanical figure, Ben Butler Zouave figure, the famous Civil War general dressed as a Zouave in a blue jacket & red pantaloons, windup key at side & wooden rollers under his shoes, head & hands w/original paint, Ives, ca. 1870s, non-working (ILLUS.) **2,755**

Airfix Corythosaurus Kit

Model kit, Corythosaurus, Airfix, plastic kit, Britain - France, 1979 (ILLUS.) **30-40**

Aurora Cougar Kit

Model kit, cougar, 1/8 scale, Aurora, 1962 (ILLUS.) **25-65**
Model kit, Davey the Way-out Cyclist, Hawk, Weird-ohs, designed by Bill Campbell, 1963 .... **40-90**
Model kit, Dead Elvis, "Tiny Terrors," zombie in Elvis jumpsuit, Mad Lab, resin kit sculpted by Michael Parks, 1990s-present **15-30**
Model kit, Dempsey vs Firpo, Great Moments in Sport series, 1/14 scale, Aurora, 1965 (ILLUS. top next column) **45-110**

Aurora Dempsey vs Firpo Kit

Model kit, Digger the Way-out Dragster, Hawk, Weird-ohs, designed by Bill Campbell, 1963 .... **40 -90**
Model kit, Dimetrodon, 1/13 scale, Monogram (re-issues from Aurora's Prehistoric Scenes line), 1979 & 1987 .... **15-25**
Model kit, Dimetrodon, Pyro reissue, 8 1/4" l., Lindberg, plastic kit, 1979 .... **10-18**

Revell Drag Nut Kit

Model kit, Drag Nut, Revell, plastic kit, Custom Monsters Series, designed by Ed "Big Daddy" Roth, 1963 (ILLUS.) **45-150**
Model kit, Endsville Eddy, Hawk, Weird-ohs, designed by Bill Campbell, 1963 .... **30-75**
Model kit, Evel Knievel's Sky Cycle, Addar, plastic kit, 1974 .... **30-75**

Revell Knight Rider Chopper Trike Kit

Model kit, Evil Iron, Knight Rider Chopper Trike, Revell, plastic kit, 1976, 14" l. (ILLUS.) **15-40**

Mad Lab Famous Monsters Cover Card

Model kit, Famous Monsters cover card, Curse of the Werewolf, painted by Joe Fex, Mad Lab, resin kit sculpted by Michael Parks, 1990s-present, 4 1/2" h. (ILLUS.).................................... **10-25**

Model kit, Fat Max, Lindberg, plastic kit, Lindy Loonys, "The Hep Model in the 'Square' Box," 1965.................................... **35-80**

Model kit, Fink-Eliminator, Revell, plastic kit, Custom Monsters Series, designed by Ed "Big Daddy" Roth, 1965 .... **50-200**

Model kit, Flying Reptile, No. 734, 1/13 scale, orange, Aurora, 1971..................... **50-75**

Model kit, Forgotten Prisoner of Castel-Mare (The), Frightening Lightning, glow version, Aurora, 1969........................... **150-350**

Prisoner of Castel-Mare, Glow Version

Model kit, Forgotten Prisoner of Castel-Mare (The), glow version, Aurora, 1972 (ILLUS.).. **100-300**

Model kit, Forgotten Prisoner of Castel-Mare (The), painted by Evan Stuart, Aurora, 1966 (ILLUS.,) **150-400**

Model kit, Francis the Foul, Hawk, Weird-ohs, designed by Bill Campbell, 1963 .... **30-75**

Forgotten Prisoner of Castel-Mare Kit

Model kit, Frantic Banana Punishing the Skins, Hawk, Frantics, designed by Reuben Klamer, 1965.................................... **40-80**

Hawk Freddy Flameout Kit

Model kit, Freddy Flameout, Hawk, Weird-ohs, designed by Bill Campbell, 1963 (ILLUS.).. **30-75**

Model kit, Giant Bird, No. 739, 1/13 scale, blue-silver, Aurora, 1971.......................... **40-50**

Pinhead Cenobite Kit

Model kit, Pinhead Cenobite, from Hellraiser, w/altar of souls, 1/4 scale, Screamin' Productions, large vinyl kit, 1993 (ILLUS.)

.... **75-100**

Aurora Tar Pit Kit

Model kit, Tar Pit, No. 735, 1/13 scale, orange, Aurora, 1971 (ILLUS.) **40-50**

Aurora Three-Horned Dinosaur Kit

Model kit, Three-Horned Dinosaur (Triceratops), No. 741, 1/13 scale, silver, Aurora, 1971 (ILLUS.) **70-85**
Model kit, Tingo the Noodle Stroodle, Revell, plastic kit, Dr. Seuss Series, 1958... **100-250**

Titanic Kit

Model kit, Titanic, 1/570 scale, Revell, plastic kit, 1976, 18 1/2" l. (ILLUS.) **400-475**
Model kit, Totally Fab, Hawk, Frantics, designed by Reuben Klamer, 1965 (ILLUS., top next column) **40-80**
Model kit, Triceratops, Monogram (re-issues from Aurora's Prehistoric Scenes line), 1987 .... **30-40**
Model kit, Triceratops with Velociraptor diorama, plastic kit, Tamiya, Japan, 1994.... **35-45**

Hawk Totally Fab Kit

Model kit, Tyrannosaurus, Pyro reissue, Lindberg, plastic kit, 1979 .... **10-18**

Nice Victorian Wooden Noah's Ark

Noah's Ark, carved & painted pine, the large ark w/removable roof, comes w/a plaster figure of Noah & 28 assorted polychromed animals, minor wear, some edge damage to the animals, 19th c., ark 18 1/4" l., 9" h., the set (ILLUS.) **891**

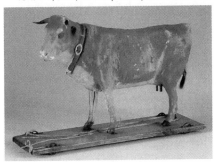

Cow on Platform Pull-Toy

Pull-toy, cow on wheeled wooden platform, leather-covered body w/inset glass eyes & realistic horns, will moo when the head is pushed to the right, thin rectangular wood platform on tiny metal wheels, original leather collar, early 20th c., 13" l. (ILLUS.)
.... **489**

Child-sized Muzzle-loader Rifle

Fine Early Horse Pull-Toy

Pull-toy, horse on narrow platform w/small metal wheels, carved wood body w/original bridle & saddle, painted brown, by Converse, late 19th c., 16" l., 20" h. (ILLUS.) **748**

Rifle, child-sized muzzle-loader, tiger stripe maple stock, metal fittings & original ramrod, repaired crack in stock (ILLUS., top of page) **150**

Rocking horse on platform, carved wood horse w/original heavily dappled black & white decoration, oil cloth saddle w/worn gold velvet saddle blanket & cast-iron stirrups, raised on an arched rocking mechanism above the red-painted wooden base w/white scrolled stenciling, slits in saddle & portions of flaps are missing, touch-up to paint, some leather trappings replaced, 19th c., 14 1/2 x 39 1/2", 33" h. (ILLUS. bottom with smaller white rocking horse, top next column) **1,093**

Rocking horse on platform, carved wood white horse w/black smoke decoration, a brown oil cloth-covered saddle w/painted decoration on the saddle blanket, glass eyes, mounted on a large arched metal rocking bar above a red-painted wooden platform base w/white stenciling & line detail, minor areas of wear, 12 3/4 x 32", 30 1/2" h. (ILLUS. top with larger dappled rocking horse, top next column) **460**

Two Victorian Rocking Horse Toys

Early Rocking Horse on Platform

Rocking horse on platform, the standing horse covered in brown mohair w/an oilcloth bridle & small saddle, mounted on a flat rectangular board w/scalloped edges & small cast-iron wheels, removable from the yellow-painted rocker platform, mane missing, mohair worn, 19th c., base 15 1/4 x 39", 29 1/2" h. (ILLUS.) **437**

Rare Victorian Child's Sled

Sled, child-sized, painted & decorated wood, the long narrow shaped rectangular platform painted red w/yellow lettering "Gen. Sheridan 1866 F.W.P.," yellow outline & dark red scroll-decoration, iron-trimmed runners, minor paint wear, second half 19th c., 14 3/4 x 55 1/2", 5 1/2" h. (ILLUS., top of page) **3,819**

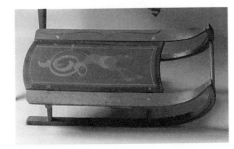

Nicely Painted Small Child's Sled

Sled, child-sized, painted & decorated wood, the rectangular platform w/a center panel painted w/a running brown horse w/yellow scrolling on a darker brown ground w/black borders, red-painted black-trimmed outer frame, on wooden runners, some wear, 19th c., 27 1/2" l. (ILLUS.)... **1,610**

Bucks Junior #4 Kitchen Range

Stove, cast iron, kitchen range, black w/nickel-plated upright warming shelf, top & doors w/scrolling designs, marked on oven door "Bucks Stove & Ranges - Bucks Junior #4," on cabriole legs, missing one door & three surface lids, late 19th - early 20th c., 12 x 16", 22" h. (ILLUS.).................... **200-400**

Early Tintograph Stencil Set in Box

Stencil set, "Tintograph Stencil Outfit No. 1257 - Soldiers & Sailors," colorful original box w/battle scene on the cover, Baumgarten & Co., patented June 15, 1915, complete w/16 stencils, the set (ILLUS.) **58**

"Little Eva" Child-sized Toy Stove

Stove, cast-iron laundry-style model, low rectangular body w/tin chimney, removable burners & interior grates, pair of front doors over front base shelf, raised on three cabriole legs, marked "Little Eva," ca. 1900, 9 x 18", 14" h. (ILLUS.)....... **431**

Britains Danish Army Life Guards Set

French Foreign Legion Britains Set

German Infantry Set by Britains

Toy soldiers, Britains Danish Army Life Guards, each in full dress in red & blue, in original box, first half 20th c., each 3" h., the set (ILLUS., top of page)............... **285**

Toy soldiers, Britains French Foreign Legion set, six marching soldiers & one on horseback, in original box, first half 20th, each 3" h., the set (ILLUS., second from top of page)... **285**

Toy soldiers, Britains German Infantry set, seven marching soldiers & one standing officer, in original box, first half 20th c., each 3" h., the set (ILLUS., third from the top)... **285**

Group of Cast-Iron Toy Soldiers

Toy soldiers, cast iron, group of marching soldiers w/four carrying rifles & one hold-

ing a flag, ca. 1930s, each 2 1/4" h., each (ILLUS.)... **10**

Toy soldiers, Ducal, Set No. 176, Regimental Band of the Black Watch, 1905, marching in review order w/full instrumentation & drum major, original box, set of 12 (a few chips).. **170**

Toy soldiers, Greenwood & Ball & Graham Farish, British Military Units, comprised of officers of the Cameron Highlanders, 16th Lancers, Royal Horse Artillery, Argyll & Sutherland Highlanders, Greenwood & Ball; two boxed figures of the Garter King of Arms, 1953 Coronation, Royal Artillery officer, 1835, Graham Farish, set of 6 .... **475**

Toy soldiers, Hill and Company Boer War set, seven soldiers each in a different pose, John Hill & Company, England, in original box w/colorful cover printed w/action scenes, first half 20th c., each 3" h., the set (ILLUS., top next page).................... **190**

Train car, boxcar, O-gauge, New Hampshire, wooden side, yellow, green & multicolor, Lionel No. 7609, 1975-76.................. **55**

Train car, boxcar, O-gauge, Virginia, wooden side, orange, blue & multicolor, Lionel No. 7610, rare, 1975-76............................... **180**

Hill and Company Boer War Soldier Set

Lionel No. 2363 Engine

Train car, boxcar, O-gauge, yellow w/green roof, black frame, Ives No. 1514, 1931-32 ...... **40**

Train car, boxcar, S-gauge, Seaboard, operating, brown, American Flyer No. 970, 1956-57 .... **75**

Train car, burro crane, O-gauge, yellow & black, Lionel No. 3360, 1956-57 .... **275**

Train car, cable car, O-gauge, black, wood reel w/rope, Marx No. 556, 1954.................... **40**

Train car, caboose, "Eagle Eye Caboose," red w/yellow roof & blue frame, Marx Joy Line No. 356, very rare, 1926-28 .... **75**

Train car, refrigerator car, O-gauge, ivory & blue, Lionel No. 814R, rare, 1929-42........... **210**

Train car, searchlight car, olive drab, large single light, Marx No. 561, 1937-42 .... **35**

Train car, stock car, O-gauge, orange w/white lettering, operating horse car, Lionel No. 3656, 1950-55.................................. **75**

Train car, stock car, O-gauge, Southern, brown w/white lettering, Lionel No. 7309, 1985 .... **20**

Train car, tender, "Koal Kar," yellow & blue, Marx Joy Line No. 351, very rare, 1927-33 .... **100**

Train car, "Tie Jector" car, red & white, Lionel No. 55, 1957-61 .... **225**

Train locomotive, diesel AB units, "Santa Fe," grey, red & yellow, Marx No. 1095, 1952 .... **105**

Train locomotive, engine, O-gauge, F-3, Illinois Central AB units, brown & orange w/"Illinois Central" in black lettering, Lionel No. 2363, rare, 1955-56 (ILLUS., second from top of page)................................ **1,550**

Lionel No. 50 Train Engine

Train locomotive, engine, pressed metal body w/iron frame, standard gauge, 0-4-0, electric, round cab, dark green & maroon, "New York Central Lines" on side, Lionel No. 50, 1924 (ILLUS.) **240**

Lionel No. 646 Steam Engine

Lionel No. 671 Steam Engine & Tender

Lionel No. 60 Train Trolley Engine

Train locomotive, steam engine, 4-6-4, Hudson, black w/"Lionel Lines" in white lettering, Lionel No. 646, 1954-58 (ILLUS., bottom previous page) **245**

Train locomotive, steam engine & tender, 6-8-6, Turbine, black w/"Lionel Lines" in white lettering, Lionel No. 671, 1946-49 (ILLUS., top of page).................................... **300**

Train locomotive, trolley, O-gauge, red & yellow, "Lionelville Rapid Transit" in blue lettering on side, Lionel No. 60, 1955-58 (ILLUS., second from top of page).............. **105**

Train set, stamped metal, electronic battery-powered, long rectangular stamped base printed in full color w/printed roadway, town & country scenes, airport & attached dimensional buildings, comes w/six cars, by Woodhaven Metal Stamping Company, Brooklyn, New York, ca. 1950s, w/original box, base 11 x 27 1/2" (ILLUS., bottom of page)............................ **250**

Stamped Metal Train Set by Woodhaven Metal Stamping Company

Windup Tin Fire Pumper Truck

Windup tin fire pumper truck, red body
w/open cab & boiler in the back, black
rubber tires, made in Japan, ca. 1950s,
7" l. (ILLUS.).................................. **125**

Early Man Pushing Cart Windup Toy

Hopping Kangaroo Windup Toy

Windup tin kangaroo, brown animal w/joey
in pouch, hoops when wound w/key,
marked "Germany - Made in U.S. Zone,"
4" l., 4 1/2" h. (ILLUS.) **275**

Windup tin man pushing cart, figure of
man wearing a straw hat, red checked
shirt, yellow pants & black boots pushes
black & yellow cart w/two large yellow
wheels, marked "Wood's Mechanical
Toys," made by Gerard Model Works, Gerard, Pennsylvania, ca. 1930s, 6 1/4" l.,
5 3/4" h. (ILLUS., top next column) **450**

Rare Monkey on Tricycle Windup Toy

Windup tin monkey on tricycle, monkey
wearing red pants, blue jacket & red fez
pedals tricycle when wound, marked "Ar-
nold - Made in Germany U.S. Zone,"
1950s, near mint, 3 1/2" h. (ILLUS.) **450**

Windup tin native standing on alligator,
alligator opens & closes its mouth, rider
tilts back & forth, J. Chein & Co., ca.
1930s, 14 3/4" l. (ILLUS., bottom of
page).. **175-250**

Native on Alligator Windup Tin Toy

Marx Windup "Old Jalopy"

Windup tin "Old Jalopy," crazy car mechanism, black Model T-type auto covered w/colorful silly slogans, Marx, ca. 1930s, 7" l. (ILLUS.).. **350**

Near Mint Windup Lehmann Sedan

Windup tin sedan, closed sedar w/dark green body & silver metal wheels, narrow white band along side reads "U.S.A. 2 Dec. 1913 25 Jan. 1927," Lehmann, Germany, 1920s, near mint, 5 3/4" l. (ILLUS.)
.... **950**

Educational & Scientific

Advertisements, cardboard stand-up style, large rectangles printed in full color, displayed at the A.C. Gilbert Hall of Science, Times Square, New York City, promoting Gilbert Erector Sets, magic sets, American Flyer trains & other toys displayed at the Hall of Science, each sign several feet tall & wide, fine condition, ca. 1920s-30s, very rare, pr. (ILLUS., top next page)
.... **1,000+**

Book, "A Golden Learn-About Book - Jets and Rockets," published by Golden Press, Racine, Wisconsin, color & black & white illustrations, 48 pages w/48 accompanying color stamps, 1961, 8 1/4 x 10 3/4" (ILLUS., top next column) **25**

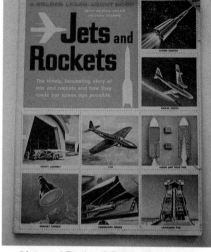

"Jets and Rockets" Golden Press Book

"Gilbert Fun With Chemistry" Booklet

Booklet, "Gilbert Fun With Chemistry," published by A.C. Gilbert, New Haven, Connecticut, color cover of two boys doing experiments surrounded by various science scenes, paperback, additional promotion for other Gilbert sets, 1956, 5 1/2 x 8" (ILLUS.) **25**

Two Rare Early A.C. Gilbert Display Signs

Gilbert Physics Instruction Booklet

Booklet, "Gilbert Physics Instruction Book," published by A.C. Gilbert, New Haven, Connecticut, color cover of a boy & girl observing a light experiment, additional advertising for Gilbert scientific sets, paperback, 1959, 5 x 7" (ILLUS.) **25**

One of the Science Service Series Booklets

Booklets, Science Service Series, published by Nelson Doubleday, Inc., sold through a science book club, various topics, published 1956-1959, each 64-66 pp., 5 1/2 x 8 1/4", each (ILLUS. of one).......... **7**

1959 Lionel Color Catalog

Catalog, Lionel products, printed in full color, shows many chemistry sets & other items, 1959, shown open (ILLUS.)..**45**

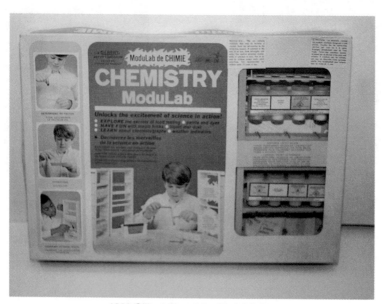

1960 Gilbert Chemistry Modulab Set

Chemistry set, "Chemistry ModuLab," produced by the A.C. Gilbert Chemistry Co., complete set in original box, made for the Canadian market, ca. 1960, box 15 1/2 x 22", the set (ILLUS.)....................................**30**

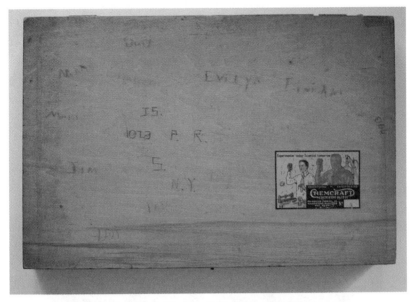

Early Chemcraft Chemistry Set

Chemistry set, wide low rectangular wooden box w/a small rectangular color label in one corner for Chemcraft, made by the Porter Chemical Company, Hagerstown, Maryland, 1930, 8 3/4 x 13 1/4" (ILLUS., top of page) **175**

American Logs Construction Set

Construction set, "American Logs," colorful box cover showing a pioneer chopping a log w/log cabin in background, a competitor of Lincoln Logs, ca. 1950s, complete starter set in box (ILLUS.) **35**

Construction set, "The Vogue Steel Constructional Set #3," battered red cardboard box w/a large colorful label showing the toys in action, manufactured by Vogue Playthings, Melton-Mowbray, England, this set produces a tipper truck & crane, w/instructions, ca. 1920s, set w/battered box (ILLUS., top next page) **40**

Construction set, "Tinkertoy," colorful cardboard tube container w/pry-off metal lid, images of various pieces to construct & pictures of children using the set, ca. 1960s, two sets made for the Canadian market shown, each (ILLUS. of two, middle next page) **20-25**

Crystal radio set, "Remco Radiocraft Easy to Assemble Kit - Crystal Radio," complete set in original colorful box, Remco, 1960, box 11 3/4 x 17", the set (ILLUS., last on next page) **60**

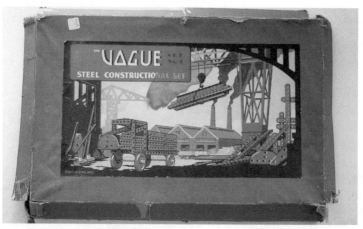

English Vogue Steel Construction Set

Two 1960s Tinkertoy Sets

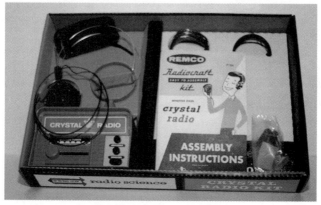

1960 Remco Crystal Radio Set

Early Meccano Instruction Booklet

Instruction booklet, "Meccano - Instructions for No. 3 Outfit," paperback cover in
dark blue, black & white, a scene of a boy
working w/the mechanical kit, ca. 1930s,
7 1/2 x 12 1/4" (ILLUS., top of page) **50**
Instruction sheet, "Big Tinkertoy - For Little
Hands," colorful paper sheet, ca. 1970s
(ILLUS., next column) **10**
Kaleidoscope, "Kaleidoscope - Corning
Glass Center - Corning, N.Y.," cardboard
tube in shaded colors of red, yellow,
green & blue, Stevens Manufacturing, St.
Louis, Missouri, ca. 1960, 9" l. (ILLUS.,
bottom of page) **25**

Big Tinkertoy Instruction Sheet

Corning Glass Center Kaleidoscope

Steven Kaleidoscope Toy

Kaleidoscope, "Steven Kaleidoscope - Millions of Designs," cardboard silvered paper-covered tube trimmed in red, green & blue, Stevens Manufacturing, St. Louis, Missouri, ca. 1949, 9" l. (ILLUS.) **50**

1933 Gilbert Erector Set Magazine Ad

Magazine advertisement, "A.C. Gilbert Erector Sets," Popular Science, December 1933, full-page ad printed in red, white & black, top half showing a boy working a large Erector Set truck & crane, promotes the new Erector No. 7 set (ILLUS.)... **20**

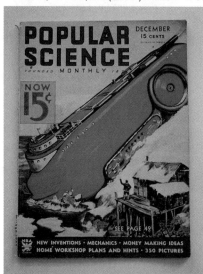

1933 Copy of "Popular Science"

Magazine, "Popular Science," December 1933, colorful cover image of a giant red tractor-ship, contents include many ads for A.C. Gilbert Erector sets, trains, Chemcraft chemistry set, Aero Monorail Construction sets & other period advertisements, paperback, 350 pp. (ILLUS.)......... **30**

1933 Stanlo Construction Toy Ad

Magazine advertisement, "Stanlo - The New Metal Construction Toy in Brilliant Colors," Popular Science, December 1933, black & white ad showing parents looking on as their children play w/the set, produced by Stanley Tools, New Britain, Connecticut (ILLUS.)............................... **20**

1933 Chemcraft Magazine Ad

Magazine advertisement, "The Secrets of Chemistry made easy for Everyone...Chemcraft - The Chemical Outfit," December 1933, black & white photos of various chemistry kits offered by Chemcraft, a branch of The Porter Chemical Company of Hagerstown, Maryland, later purchased by the Lionel Train Company (ILLUS.).. **15**

1955 Tinkertoy Magazine Ad

Magazine advertisement, Tinkertoy full-page ad printed in black & white, Decem-

ber 1955 Saturday Evening Post, larger upper photo of many children playing w/the sets, advertising below (ILLUS.).......... **10**

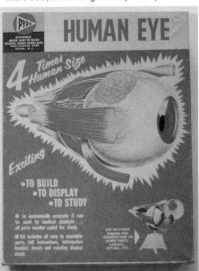

Pyro Human Eye Model Kit

Model kit, "Pyro - Human Eye," one of a series of plastic kits, this one showing how to assemble a model of the human eye, by Pyro Plastics, Pyro Park, New Jersey, 1950s, complete set in original colorful box, box 9 1/2 x 12" (ILLUS.)...................... **100**

German Toy Steam Engine & Box

Steam engine, cast-metal model of a working engine, w/plain cardboard box w/image of item on the front, unknown German maker, 1948 (ILLUS.)........................... **250**

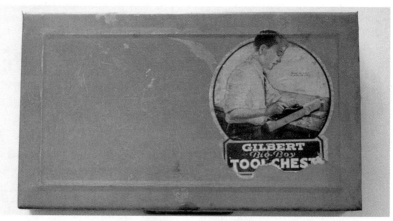

Early Gilbert Big Boy Tool Chest

Buildmaster Tool Set

Tool chest, "Gilbert Big Boy Tool Chest," long low red metal box w/color decal label showing a boy using the tools, contains hammer, screwdriver, ruler, small plane, other tools & instructions, ca. 1920s, the set as shown (ILLUS., top of page) **150**

Tool set, child-sized, "Buildmaster Tool Set," long rectangular metal woodgrained box w/wire bail handle decorated w/a colored scene of boys building a dog house, produced by PAX for the Canadian market, includes eleven pieces, ca. 1950s (ILLUS., second from top) **80**

TRAYS - SERVING & CHANGE

Change, "Antikamnia Tablets," rectangular, metal, red & gold, image of woman sitting in chair, lettering near her reads "Feeling is a Sense - Feeling Pain is Nonsense - No Matter When or Where - Antikamnia Tablets - Two Every Three Hours," border marked "Insomnia and Nervousness - Pain, Fever, La Grippe," Antikamnia Chemical Company, St. Louis, Missouri, souvenir of 1904 St. Louis World's Fair, by American Can Co., New York & Chicago, Illinois, 3 1/4 x 4 3/4" (ILLUS., below) **125-175**

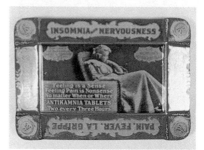

Antikamnia Tablets Change Tray

Carnation Chewing Gum Change Tray

Change, "Carnation Chewing Gum," round, metal, yellow & green w/pink carnations & white package in center, red letters reading "Dorne's Carnation Chewing Gum" w/black letters at bottom reading "Chew Dorne's Carnation Gum" & "Taste The Smell" in red letters in the top & bottom border, ca. 1900, 4 1/4" d. (ILLUS.) **300-375**

City & Suburban Homes Change Tray

Change, "City and Suburban Homes Co.," round, metal w/scalloped rim, image of three white horseheads in center, border reads "City and Suburban Homes Co., Ltd. - Real Estate - Loans - Renting Agents - Fire Insurance - 35 and 37 State St., Detroit," litho by H.D. Beach Co., Coshocton, Ohio, ca. 1910, 4 1/4" d. (ILLUS.) **125-175**

DeLaval Separators Change Tray

Change, "DeLaval Cream Separators," round, metal, scene of woman in long red dress & white apron at separator, young child near doorway, gold lettering on border reads "DeLaval Cream Separators - The World's Standard," ca. 1906, 4 1/4" d. (ILLUS.) **325-400**

Fraternal Life Insurance Change Tray

Change, "Fraternal Life & Accident Insurance Company," rectangular, metal, center scene of large building, scalloped & ruffled blue border reading at the top "Fraternal Life and Accident Insurance - Reserve Deposited with the State of Iowa" & at the bottom "Home of the Brotherhood of American Yeomen, Des Moines, Iowa," ca. 1920, 3 1/4 x 5" (ILLUS.) **75-125**

Frost Wire Fence Co. Change Tray

Change, "Frost Wire Fence Co.," round, metal w/scalloped rim, lithographed metal, center w/three white horseheads, the border marked "Compliments of The Frost Wire Fence Co. - Cleveland, O.," litho by H.D. Beach Co., Coshocton, Ohio, ca. 1910, 4 1/4" d. (ILLUS.) **150-200**

Change, "Globe-Wernicke Bookcases," round, lithographed metal, scene of woman seated on a rug & holding a book near a man standing before a bookcase, the border reading "Globe-Wernicke - Sectional Bookcases - The Orleans Furniture & Undertaking Co. - Licensed Embalmers - Orleans, Ind.," litho by Charles Shonk Co., Chicago, Illinois, ca. 1915, 4 1/2" d. **150-200**

Miller High Life Beer Change Tray

Change, "Miller High Life Beer," rectangular, metal, center blue w/stars & Miller girl sitting on crescent moon holding glass, marked "Miller - High Life - The Champagne of Bottle Beer," goldtone border, ca. 1960s, 4 1/2 x 6 1/2" (ILLUS.) **50-75**

Monticello Whiskey Change Tray

Change, "Monticello Whiskey," oval, lithographed metal, fox hunt scene w/large building in background, gold border marked "Monticello - It's All Whiskey," litho by Charles Shonk Co., Chicago, Illinois, ca. 1915, 4 3/8 x 6 1/8" (ILLUS.) **225-275**

National Cigar Stands Change Tray

Change, "National Cigar Stands Co.," round, metal, center w/young girl wearing red sleeveless one-shouldered gown, holding daisies & w/a wreath of daisies in her dark upswept hair, the border designed w/various cigar band seals, marked at the top "Our Brands" & at the bottom "National Cigar Stands Co.," ca. 1910, 6" d. (ILLUS.) **100-150**

Quick Meal Ranges Change Tray

Change, "Quick Meal Ranges," oval, lithographed metal, scene of young chicks near an empty shell, red border reading "'Quick Meal' Ranges - Made in St. Louis, Mo.," litho by Ohio Art Company, Bryan, Ohio, ca. 1900, 3 1/4 x 4 1/4" (ILLUS.) **150-200**

Robert Burns Cigars Change Tray

Change, "Robert Burns Cigars," metal, round, bust portrait of man in center, border w/"Robert Burns - Cigars," ca. 1910, 4" d. (ILLUS.) **100-150**

Rock Island Buggy Co. Change Tray

Change, "Rock Island Buggy Co.," metal, rectangular, ornate scrolled, pleated & scalloped border centering scene of buildings & trees, marked in upper left corner "Compliments of Rock Island Buggy Co., Rock Island, ILL," souvenir of St. Louis World's Fair, ca. 1904, 3 1/4 x 5" (ILLUS.).. **125-175**

Rockford Watch Co. Change Tray

Change, "Rockford Watches," lithographed metal, rectangular, white, green & pink geometric design border centering an outdoor scene of a young woman in a long green gown sitting on a bench before a tree, at the top "Rockford High Grade Watches" & "For Sale at Dan S. Jones - Independence, IA," litho by H.D. Beach Co., Coshocton, Ohio, ca. 1900, 3 1/4 x 5" (ILLUS.)................................ **150-200**

Sears, Roebuck and Co. Change Tray

Change, "Sears, Roebuck and Co.," oval, metal, scene of factory w/waist-length image of woman holding scales on right, marked at top "Sears, Roebuck and Co. - Chicago" & at the bottom "Originators of the Guarantee that Stands the Test in the Scales of Justice," ca. 1920, 4 3/8 x 6" (ILLUS.).. **125-175**

Sen-Sen Aluminum Change Tray

Change, "Sen-Sen Chewing Gum," rectangular, aluminum w/scalloped rim, center w/embossed ribbon-tied package marked "Sen-Sen - 5¢," ca. 1910, 3 1/4 x 4 1/4" (ILLUS.) **75-125**

Stollwerck Chocolate & Cocoa Tray

Change, "Stollwerck Chocolate & Cocoa," round, lithographed metal, gold & red, marked "Stollwerck" in center w/"Gold Brand" above & "Chocolate & Cocoa" below, scrolled border, litho by Kaufmann & Strauss Co., New York, ca. 1910, 5" d. (ILLUS.).. **100-150**

WATCHES

Lady's Elgin Hunting Case Watch

Lady's hunting case watch, Elgin, delicately engraved gold-filled Dueber case, keywind mechanism, late 19th c., 1 3/4" d. (ILLUS.) **$173**

Fine French Art Deco Pendant Watch

Lady's pendant watch, Art Deco style, the round silvertone engine-turned dial w/Arabic numerals, a jeweled damascene nickel movement, platinum matte polished hunting case bow-set w/rose-cut diamonds & sapphires w/a cabochon sapphire in the center, w/a 14k white gold & sapphire bar pin, case interior inscribed "Paris," ca. 1920s (ILLUS.)........................ **2,115**

Howard 14k Gold Hunting Case Watch

Man's hunting case watch, E. Howard Watch Co., seventeen jewel movement, 14k yellow gold case w/central shield on engine-turned ground, case marked "Keystone," ca. 1903 (ILLUS.) **805**

Fine Man's Gold Hunting Case Watch

Man's hunting case watch, Elgin, lever-set movement, in a finely engraved 14k gold case applied w/an elk head, w/original Elgin mahogany case, late 19th c., w/short watch chain (ILLUS.).................................... **460**

Very Fine 14k Gold Illinois Watch

Man's hunting case watch, Illinois, lever-set movement, finely engraved 14k yellow gold case, slight case wear, minor hairlines in dial, ca. 1880 (ILLUS.)............ **1,035**

E. Howard Open-face Man's Watch

Man's open-face watch, E. Howard Watch Co., open-faced w/marked dial w/Arabic numerals, small seconds dial, seventeen jewel movement, 14k yellow gold case marked "KW.C.C.O.," minor hairline in dial, tiny fleck at numeral 4, ca. 1900 (ILLUS., previous page) **403**

WEDDING MEMORABILIA

Once considered valuable only to the persons who owned them, wedding cake toppers have become increasingly sought after collectibles. Sugar confections in European bakeries in the early 1800s started the true "icing on the cake" idea. By the late 1800s, American bakeries were copying from their European counterparts, using marzipan, gum paste, wood, plaster of Paris and even crystal beads. Porcelain, celluloid, composition, saltware, plastic and china would all be used over the years in the construction of ever more sophisticated toppers.

The majority have no identifying marks with which to accurately date them, although a few produced in the 1940s bear dates and manufacturers' names. Toppers are mostly dated by materials used, clothing styles of bride and groom, and other characteristics such as age-related patina.

Related memorabilia is a wonderful enhancement to a wedding topper collection. Included would be announcement cards for bridal showers and weddings, favors, old marriage licenses, bridal books and an assortment of unique handcrafted and commercially produced items.

Old wedding mementos, especially cake toppers, are very fragile and irreplaceable. Handle them with care. Prices reflect items in good to fine condition with no serious flaws or missing parts.

Cake Toppers

1900-1920

Gum paste, figure of bride & groom in oblong gazebo w/two round columns supporting lattice roof, two doves perched on roof, lilies of the valley flanking columns, pedestal w/stepped base & intricate raised carvings, 7" h..................................... **$125**

Gum paste, figures of bride & groom on round platform w/filigreed pedestal, the groom in black tuxedo, the bride wearing long dress w/vertical draped trim, a single white sunflower-like bloom behind them, 7" h... **100**

Plaster of Paris, bride & groom, the bride wearing dress w/diagonal draped design & net veil, the groom w/handlebar moustache & center-parted hair, standing on round platform before "Good Luck" horseshoe & flowers, on intricate pierce-decorated base, 8" h. (ILLUS., top next column) **125**

Cake Topper with Horseshoe

1920s

Bisque, Kewpie bride & groom dressed in crepe paper & ribbon fabric, standing under triple arch of wax buds, 6" h. **150**

Cake Topper with Silvered Glass Bell

Gum paste, bride & groom, the bride wearing gown w/handkerchief hemline & flowered headpiece, the groom in black tuxedo, studded bib front & white gloves, standing under arch of white flowers & leaves centered by silvered glass bell, on pierced-design pedestal base, 8" h. (ILLUS.) **125**

1930s

Bisque, figures of bride & groom under heart-shaped bower of large leaves, on satin-over-cardboard base & pedestal w/satin ruffle trim, 7" h................................... **50**

Bisque, single-mold bride & groom under double arch of lilies of the valley w/two silver metal bells overhead, on gum paste base, 7" h. **50**

Celluloid, Kewpie-like figures dressed in crepe paper, standing under arch w/crepe paper bell & two lilies of the valley sprigs, on round green crepe-paper-covered base, 4 1/2" h. **50**

Chalkware, figures of bride & groom on base & pedestal w/concealed music box, decorated w/flowers & center bow, a filigreed bell reading "Marriage" in raised gold letters, 12" h. **150**

Crepe Paper Bride & Groom Cake Topper

Crepe paper, figures of bride & groom w/oversized heads w/stylized decorated facial features, stick-like bodies, the bride w/oversized bouquet, the groom w/oversized shiny black top hat, the figures framed inside heart-shaped arbor of lilies of the valley & leaves, on round ruffled crepe paper pedestal base, 8 1/2" h. (ILLUS.)...................................... **100**

1940s

Chalkware, single-mold World War II-era bride & groom, the groom in white sailor uniform, 3 1/2" h.. **75**

Chalkware, World War II-era Army officer in khaki dress uniform & bride stand together under arch trimmed w/white flowers red, white & blue ribbon, 6" h. (ILLUS., top next column).. **100**

Saltware, figures of World War II-era bride & groom, the groom wearing green & khaki military uniform, the couple flanked by white flower spikes & two 48-star American flags, 5" h. **100**

Chalkware Soldier & Bride Cake Topper

1950s

Chalkware, bride & groom w/bride's head on groom's shoulder, under double heart-shaped arch of lilies of the valley, on ribbon-trimmed base & pedestal , 8" h.............. **40**

1950s Chalkware Cake Topper

Chalkware, figures of bride & groom stand together under arch of white flowers w/green centers, the bride's gown & swirled pedestal in white pearlized paint, 6 1/2" h. (ILLUS.) **45**

Plastic, model of women's high-heeled white shoe w/two white doves on round base, the shoe filled w/white satin padding holding two faux wedding rings held to padding by white satin ribbons, 4" h. **35**

1960s

Bisque, figures of military couple, the green wearing Navy dress uniform in blue, 4" h. **75**

Chalkware & plastic, figures of bride & groom, the groom in dark blue Air Force uniform, the couple framed by heart-shaped lace bower, 7" h. **75**

Plastic, bride & groom, the bride wearing satin & lace overskirt covering pedestal base, under half arch of flowers & leaves, 7" h. **25**

Plastic, figures of bride & groom, the bride w/blond mohair hair, on filigree base, 5" h. **30**

Plastic, figures of bride & groom under heart-shaped lace arch on filigree base, 4 1/2" h. **15**

1970s
Plastic, figures of bride & groom, the bride in satin overskirt, the groom w/long side-burns & wearing white dinner jacket, on pedestal of hearts & swags, 5" h. **15**

Plastic, figures of bride & groom under half arch of lilies of the valley, on pedestal base of filigree hearts on bell-shaped feet, 7" h. **25**

1980s
Bisque, figures of bride & groom kissing, sitting beneath archway w/plastic bell, 6" h. **25**

Miscellaneous

1900-1920
Bride's book, beige cover w/inside pen-and-ink drawings, w/entry pages for wedding day occurrences, guest list, etc., "copyright 1900 - Rev Salem D. Towne, Williamstown, Mass," 1902, 5 x 9" **5**

Postcard, engagement, full color illustration of engaged couple encircled by diamond engagement ring, copyright Roth & Langley, 1910.. **2**

1920s
Magazine, Dennison Party Magazine, May/June issue, cover w/picture of bride, inside features including how-to's for bridal/wedding decorations & food menus, 1927 .... **20**

Streamers from bridal bouquet, silk, four white ribbons tied w/love knots & faux lilies of the valley, 24" l. **20**

1930s
Fabric, ultra sheer, off-white piece from bridal bouquet, 15" w. x 12' l. **10**

Favor for wedding, chenille bride & groom figures, silken coard for hanging, 4" h. **10**

Telegram, Western Union congratulatory wedding message w/color wedding graphics & envelope....................................... **20**

1940s

Spun Cotton Wedding Decoration

Decoration, spun cotton, hand-crafted bride & groom w/painted faces & crepe paper hair, nested in foil-wrapped silver-colored ring on ruffled cellophane base, 6" h. (ILLUS.) **30**

1940s Wedding Favor

Favor for wedding, crepe paper basket holding pipe cleaner bride & groom, flower-decorated handle, 4" h. (ILLUS.) **5**

Wedding-related cards, bridal shower announcement, wedding announcement & gift card, all from same wedding, w/envelopes, set of 3.. **9**

1950s
Container, ceramic, front decorated w/figures of bride, groom, ring bearer & flower girl, glazed finish, used to hold floral arrangement, greeting cards, dinner napkins, etc., 5" l., 4 1/2" h. **15**

Church-shaped Wedding Favor

Favor for wedding, plastic, church w/arched windows & steeple, the front doors opening to reveal pull-out tray decorated w/figures of bride & groom for holding nuts/candy, 4" h. (ILLUS.) **5**

Salt & pepper, ceramic, all white bridal couple, glazed decoration, the groom wearing top hat & standing w/hands behind back, the bride carrying bouquet, bottom stamped "Hollywood," 3 1/2" h., pr................. **10**

WESTERN CHARACTER COLLECTIBLES

Since the closing of the Western frontier in the late 19th century, the myth of the American cowboy has loomed large in popular fiction. With the growth of the motion picture industry early in this century, cowboy heroes became a mainstay of the entertainment industry. By the 1920s major Western heroes were a big draw at the box office, this popularity continuing with the dawning of the TV age in the 1950s. We list here a variety of collectibles relating to all American Western personalities popular this century. ALSO SEE: Horse Collectibles.

Two Views of Buffalo Bill's Wild West Booklet

Buffalo Bill booklet, color-printed paper, "Buffalo Bill's - Wild West," includes 11 full-color illustrations of the show, stamp on last page inscribed "Original Pictures - Buffalo Bill's Wild-West - Cy. 1891," light soiling, 5 x 7" (ILLUS. of two views)............ **461**

Buffalo Bill mug, china, figural, designed as a bust of Buffalo Bill w/a figural buffalo handle, bronze-colored paint finish, early 20th c., 5 3/4" w., 4 3/4" h. (ILLUS. of two views, bottom of page)................................. **152**

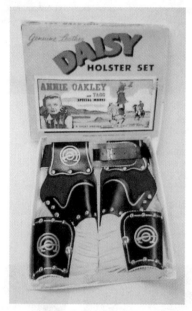

Annie Oakley Holster Set

Annie Oakley holster set, "Annie Oakley Daisy Holster Set," genuine black leather, no pistols included in the set, based on the TV show, ca. 1954-56, near mint in original box (ILLUS.).............................. **$700**

Early Buffalo Bill Glass Paperweight

Buffalo Bill paperweight, oblong flattened thick clear glass w/an early black & white photo of Buffalo Bill applied to the bottom, made by the Abrams Paperweight Company, Pittsburgh, patent dated November 29, 1892, 2 1/2 x 4" (ILLUS.) **230**

Early Buffalo Bill Painted China Mug

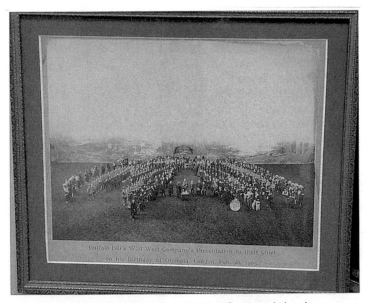

Photo of Buffalo Bill & the Wild West Company in London

Buffalo Bill photograph, large sepia-toned image of the complete Wild West cast in London, titled across the bottom "Buffalo Bill's West West Company's Presentation to their Chief on his Birthday at Olympia, London, February 26, 1903," blindstamp of James E. Hunt, London, England, minor wear along top right corner of images, matted & framed, 9 1/2 x 11 1/2" (ILLUS., top of page) **575**

Early Western Show Program

Buffalo Bill program, printed single-sheet paper, for "Niblo's Garden - Scouts of the Prairie," which included Buffalo Bill Cody, Texas Jack, Ned Buntline & 25 Indian warriors, 1873, 8 1/2 x 11" (ILLUS.) **1,188**
Davy Crockett bow ties, uncut strip of three suede bow ties on the original cardboard backing, non-Disney item, mid-

1950s, mint, overall 8 x 15" (ILLUS., top next page) **159**

Early Gene Autry Cap Gun

Gene Autry cap gun, nickel-plated cast-iron pistol w/red plastic grips, Autry name raised above trigger, by Kenton Hardware, ca. 1940, one grip damaged, 8 3/8" l. (ILLUS.) **81**

Early Lone Ranger Cap Gun

Lone Ranger cap gun, cast-iron pistol w/ivory-colored plastic grips, Lone Ranger name stamped above grips, by Kilgore, ca. 1938, 8 1/2" l. (ILLUS.) **104**

Original Mounted Strip of Davy Crockett Bow Ties

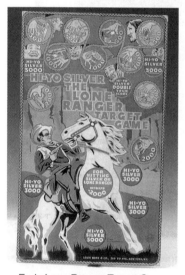

Early Lone Ranger Target Game

Lone Ranger target game, large color-lithographed tin target featuring a large image of the Lone Ranger & Silver below various rope-enclosed circle targets w/various point values, by Louis Marx, ca. 1938, 16 x 27" (ILLUS.)............... **127**

Tom Mix photograph, sepia-toned bust portrait of Mix w/one hand at the brim of his hat, inscribed "Best luck - To my friend Fred Warrell - Tom Mix," Warrell being the assistant manager of the Sells-

Early Signed Tom Mix Photo

Floto Circus where Mix was a star, w/clippings & biographical information on Warrell, 8 x 10" (ILLUS.)..................................... **338**

WOOD SCULPTURES

American eagle, a large carved & gilded pine spread-winged bird carved in the half-round, grasping the American shield in its talons above a large cluster of arrows & a laurel wreath, America, late 19th c., 20 1/4" w., 41" h. **$10,158**

Carved Pine Angel Head & Wings

Angel, one-piece pine plank naively carved w/the face of an angel w/a cheerful expression & outstretched wings w/radiating layered feathers, traces of original polychrome paint, light weathering w/greyish patina, possibly Pennsylvania, 19th c., 41" w., 9" h. (ILLUS., bottom previous page).. **863**

Half-sized Cigar Store Indian Chief

Cigar store Indian Chief, carved & painted, half-sized figure standing & holding a pipe close to his chest, wearing moccasins & a red robe, a feathered headdress & long black hair around his gold face, the natural-colored base carved w/a bundle of cigars & a rock, small hole at front of chest possibly to hold a flag, paint appears original, back w/some nails & loop hardware probably for affixing the figure, metal plaque on the back reading "Bought of H.H. Robertson - National Stockyards, IL," 42 1/2" h. (ILLUS.) **5,750**

Unusual Carved Coconut Creature

Coconut creature, the original oblong nut shell ornately pierce-carved w/entwining

costumed figures leaping over crowned lions, couples dancing, a man riding a bull & various other figures & animals, one end carved as the face of an anthropomorphic creature w/a gaping mouth, Europe, early 19th c., 3 1/2" d., 6" l. (ILLUS.)...................... **690**

Rare Wilhelm Schimmel Carved Eagle

Eagle, carved & painted, folk art bird w/original bright yellow body trimmed in black, red & green, carved by Wilhelm Schimmel (1817-1890), Cumberland County, Pennsylvania, edge damage to tail, 8" h. (ILLUS.).. **6,325**

Fine Public Works Carved Nude

Figure of a nude woman, finely carved in the full round, standing carrying a water jug on her shoulder, titled "The Water

WPA Project Carved Walnut Crouching Panther

Carrier," base w/brass plaque engraved "Public Works of Art Project," ca. 1940, 35" h. (ILLUS.) **5,175**

Spanish Carved Figure of St. Anthony

Figure of St. Anthony of Padua, carved & painted, carved in the full round, long brown robe & flesh-colored hands & head set w/glass eyes, scattered losses, Spain, 18th c., 24" h. (ILLUS.) **1,840**

Panther, carved walnut, long stylized model of a crouching panther, mounted on a pine base, a WPA School project, inscribed "J.S. Iowa City 1933," 20" l. (ILLUS., top of page) **288**

WOODENWARES

Slightly Oblong Carved Burl Bowl

Bowl, carved burl, slightly oblong rounded form w/an integral rim handle w/finger ring hole, 19th c., 9 1/2" l. (ILLUS.) **$632**

Fine Carved Burl Bowl

Large & Well-turned Burl Walnut Bowl

Shaker-carved Black Walnut Long Bowl

Bowl, carved burl, wide well-rounded form w/tight small mottled grain, rich patina, 19th c., 14" d. (ILLUS., previous page) **1,207**

Bowl, turned walnut burl, round w/a small flat bottom w/wide rounded sides & a thick molded rim, 19th c., 18 1/2" d. (ILLUS., top of page) **1,673**

Bowl, carved black walnut, rectangular trencher style, gently curved base, carved end handholds, Shaker-made, Enfield, Connecticut, 19th c., age crack, 15 5/8 x 28 1/2", 6" h. (ILLUS., second from top) **441**

white on the side "C.R. Tartar," illegible lettering on handle, cover w/mark of "N. & J. Howe & Co. Fitzwilliam, N.Y.," 19th c., wear, bands loose, loss on handle peg, 13" d., 16" h. (ILLUS.) **353**

Early Painted Stave Bucket

Bucket, cov., slightly tapering cylindrical form w/stave construction wrapped by three lapped bands, red-painted ground w/flat fitted black cover & black bands, red bentwood swing handle, painted in

Old Oak Stave Butter Churn

Butter churn, lid & dasher, oak, stave construction w/five riveted steel bands, carved bottom, broom-handled dasher, 19th c., 19 1/2" h. (ILLUS.) **288**

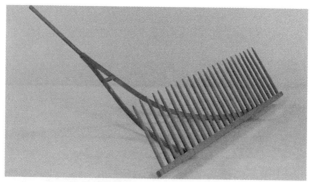

Early Wooden Hay Rake

Early Oak & Iron Flax Hatchel

Flax hatchel, oak & wrought iron, the thick rectangular plank top w/rectangular top handle incised w/a band of hearts & rosettes above the row of long iron comb teeth, early 19th c., 2 3/4" thick, 23" l. (ILLUS.) **173**

Hay rake, the curved forked handle ending in a long thin crossbar fitted w/numerous long pointed teeth, 19th c., 73" w., 67" l. (ILLUS., top of page)................................. **1,195**

Early Pease-type Turned Wood Jar

Jar, cov., turned wood, squatty bulbous body w/incised rings tapering to a domed cover w/large button handle, varnish finish, attributed to Pease of Ohio, splits reinforced w/glue & a pegged hole in bottom, 19th c., 7" h. (ILLUS.)........................... **259**

Mortar & pestle, carved & painted birch, mortar w/a wide band around the base w/an ovoid body, old red paint, good patina, split, overall 8 1/4" h. **230**

Pipe box, painted, hanging-type, the backboard w/a high arched & shaped crest centered by a hanging hole above the open box w/a scalloped rim, a small drawer at the bottom w/a brass knob, old white paint, America, early 19th c., 4 x 6", 17 1/2" h. (paint wear)................................. **705**

Rare Early Painted Hanging Pipe Box

Pipe box, painted walnut, hanging-type, the tall box w/an arched backboard w/small hanging hole above scallop-stepped sides & concave-topped front board, a small drawer in the bottom w/original small brass pull, molded base, old dry red paint, drawer bottom damaged, minor chip on one scallop, New England, late 18th - early 19th c., 5 3/8 x 6 3/4", 20" h. (ILLUS.)... **8,338**

Rare Early Spoon Rack & Spoons

Spoon rack-wall box, cherry & pine, the tall wide backboard w/an angle-carved crest centered by an arched tab w/a hanging hole, two rows of spoon racks holding twelve spoons above a slant-lidded rectangular box at the bottom, together w/eight pewter spoons & one other spoon, New England, 18th c., 6 x 12", 25" h. (ILLUS..) **1,898**

WRITING ACCESSORIES

Inkstands & Inkwells

Tiffany Zodiac Pattern Bronze Inkstand

Bronze stand, Zodiac patt., rectangular box w/pen trays on each side flanking the paneled tapering well w/domed cap & original well insert, green, red & brown patina, stamped mark "Tiffany Studios - New York - 1073," some damage to original well insert, 9 3/4 x 10 1/2" (ILLUS.) **$2,070**

Bronzed cast-metal stand, figural, an ornate scroll-cast domed base on six scroll legs topped by the model of a seated greyhound chained to a fence post, flanked at the lower ends by the original squatty bulbous glass inkwells w/scroll-cast covers, late 19th c., 12" l. (ILLUS., bottom of page) **805**

Unusual Winged Griffin Inkstand

Bronzed cast-metal stand, figural, the thick oblong base w/a cast zigzag border design mounted by the model of a seated winged griffin, the high curved wings supporting two coiled snake pen rests joined by a rod, a large square cut crystal well w/original metal cover in front, verdigris patina, embossed mark, "N. Muller - N.Y. #611," ca. 1900, 6" h. (ILLUS.) **575**

Whimsical Toad Stool & Gnomes Well

Enameled bronze well, figural, designed as a whimsical large toad stool w/a hinged cover flanked by two small seated gnomes, blown glass ink cup, worn original polychrome enamel, Austria, late 19th c., unmarked, 4 1/2" l. (ILLUS.)............ **518**

Bronzed Metal Inkstand with Model of a Seated Greyhound

French Rococo-style Gilt-Bronze Inkstand

Gilt-bronze stand, Rococo-style, the rectangular base w/small dolphin feet supporting incurved sides cast w/long scrolls & grotesque masks, the top w/a low raised gadrooned edge, the high arched & pierced backplate centered by a lion mask framed by scrolls & small pineapple corner finials, the top inset w/two inkwells w/domed ringed covers w/small pineapple finials, France, late 19th c., 14" l. (ILLUS.) **460**

Redware pottery well, short cylindrical disk-form w/a large center hole surrounded by three small holes, pumpkin orange alkaline glaze, early 19th c., 3 1/4" d., 1 3/4" h. (extensive chipping at center hole) **88**

Unusual Arts & Crafts Plated Inkwell

Silver plate well, Arts & Crafts style, a thin rectangular base plate supporting four slender squared legs w/riveted curved feet supporting a rectangular box frame w/a pierced design on the front, the wide flat overhanging cover centered by a large Ruskin cabochon, stamped initials, mark of Duchess Sutherland Cripples Guild, England, late 19th - early 20th c., 3 3/4 x 5 1/4", 5" h. (ILLUS.) **805**

Silver stand, sterling silver, a rectangular form on four scroll bracket feet, the body w/a pen tray, the back fitted w/a pierced gallery for two glass inkwells w/silver covers, a central rectangular hinged box w/a gadrooned cover for stamps, marks of Gorham Mfg. Co., Providence, Rhode Island, 1890, 7 3/4" l. **1,673**

Sterling silver stand, shaped rectangular scroll-trimmed tray raised on four pierced floral feet & w/floral end handles, the long sides w/pen troughs, the top w/two rounded detachable clear cut-glass ink-

Early Rockingham Ware Inkwell

Rockingham ware stand, waisted octagonal form w/flatted top w/large central hole surrounded by four small holes, overall mottled streaky brown glaze, possibly Bennington, Vermont, ca. 1850, 3" w., 2" h. (ILLUS.) **198**

Two Silver Figural Punch Inkwells & a William IV Inkstand

wells w/silver neck mounts & covers, the center w/an urn-form compartment topped by a detachable chamberstick & conical snuffer, marked by Charles Reily & George Storer, London, England, William IV era, 1834, 10 1/2" l. (ILLUS. center with two figural Punch inkwells, top of page) **1,554**

Sterling silver well, figural, formed as a figure of Punch, standing on a simulated wooden base, the hat removes to reveal the well compartment, mark of Charles & George Fox, London, England, 1846, 7" h. (ILLUS. left with other Punch inkwell & William IV inkstand) **2,868**

Sterling silver well, figural, formed as a figure of Punch, standing on a simulated wooden base, the hat removes to reveal the well compartment, mark of Charles & George Fox, London, England, 1844, 6" h. (ILLUS. right with other Punch inkwell & William IV inkstand) **2,868**

Lap Desks & Writing Boxes

Inlaid & veneered mixed woods, handcrafted rectangular form, the flat hinged top inlaid in the center w/a large spreadwinged American eagle & flag, each corner inlaid w/floral sprigs, the widge-form cover opening to a slanted felt-lined writing surface & small compartments, the sides inset w/hand-cut round brass recessed swivel handles, the lower portion w/a hidden compartment, America, Civil

Rare Patriotic Civil War Lap Desk

War era, ca. 1860-65, made for a Field Officer, 11 x 22", 8" h. (ILLUS.) **2,760**

Mahogany, rectangular w/brass banding, a flat hinged cover opening to fitted interiors on a felt writing surface, the case fitted w/a side drawer, resting on a molded mahogany stand w/Marlborough legs of later date, England, ca. 1830, 10 1/2 x 19 3/4", overall 19" h. (ILLUS. left with rosewood writing box, top of page) **748**

Rosewood, rectangular w/brass banding & cartouche-form keyhole escutcheon, the hinged top opening to a slanted writing surface & a fitted interior, resting on a later mahogany stand w/Marlborough legs, Regency period, England, ca. 1825, 10 x 19 1/2", overall 23" h. (ILLUS. right with mahogany writing box, top of page) **920**

Two Early English Writing Boxes on Stands

INDEX

Rare #1 Ponytail Barbie with Box, $9,000

Barber Bottle with White Mill Scene - $364

Bluhill Coffee Lunch Pail 5 lb. Can, $330

Very Large Doulton Turker Platter, $1,200.

Original Snoopy Cartoon Drawing, $1,673

Roy Rogers & Trigger, $150-250

Fine Clichy Double-overlay Paperweight,
$3,824

Magazine Signed by the McCartneys, $1,554

Long Dining Table Setting Hooked Rug, $2,990

Unusual Griffin-form Ashtray, $374.

Fine French Art Deco Pendant Watch, $2,115.

Rockford Watch Co. Change Tray, $150-200.